CONNECT FEATURES

Interactive Applications

Interactive Applications offer a variety of automatically graded exercises that require students to **apply** key concepts. Whether the assignment includes a *click and drag*, *video case*, or *decision generator*, these applications provide instant feedback and progress tracking for students and detailed results for the instructor.

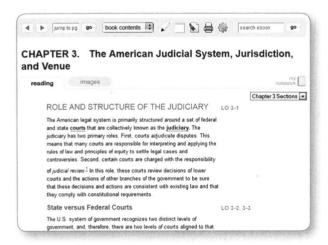

eBook

Connect Plus includes an eBook that allows you to share your notes with your students. Your students can insert and review their own notes, highlight the text, and search for specific information. Using an eBook with Connect Plus gives your students a complete digital solution that allows them to access their materials from any computer.

Tegrity

Make your classes available anytime, anywhere. With simple, one-click recording, students can search for a word or phrase and be taken to the exact place in your lecture that they need to review.

EASY TO USE

Learning Management System Integration

McGraw-Hill Campus is a one-stop teaching and learning experience available to use with any learning management system. McGraw-Hill Campus provides single sign-on to faculty and students for all McGraw-Hill material and technology from within the school website. McGraw-Hill Campus also allows instructors instant access to all supplements and teaching materials for all McGraw-Hill products.

Blackboard users also benefit from McGraw-Hill's industry-leading integration, providing single sign-on to access all Connect assignments and automatic feeding of assignment results to the Blackboard grade book.

POWERFUL REPORTING

Connect generates comprehensive reports and graphs that provide instructors with an instant view of the performance of individual students, a specific section, or multiple sections. Since all content is mapped to learning objectives, Connect reporting is ideal for accreditation or other administrative documentation.

SECOND EDITION

THE LEGAL ENVIRONMENT OF BUSINESS

A MANAGERIAL APPROACH: Theory to Practice

Sean P. Melvin
Elizabethtown College

Michael A. Katz
Delaware State University

Mc
Graw
Hill
Education

THE LEGAL ENVIRONMENT OF BUSINESS: A MANAGERIAL APPROACH: THEORY TO PRACTICE, SECOND EDITION

Published by McGraw-Hill Education, 2 Penn Plaza, New York, NY 10121. Copyright © 2015 by McGraw-Hill Education. All rights reserved. Printed in the United States of America. Previous edition © 2011. No part of this publication may be reproduced or distributed in any form or by any means, or stored in a database or retrieval system, without the prior written consent of McGraw-Hill Education, including, but not limited to, in any network or other electronic storage or transmission, or broadcast for distance learning.

Some ancillaries, including electronic and print components, may not be available to customers outside the United States.

This book is printed on acid-free paper.

1 2 3 4 5 6 7 8 9 0 DOW/DOW 1 0 9 8 7 6 5 4

ISBN 978-0-07-802380-4
MHID 0-07-802380-7

Senior Vice President, Products & Markets: *Kurt L. Strand*
Vice President, Content Production & Technology Services: *Kimberly Meriwether David*
Managing Director: *Tim Vertovec*
Executive Director of Development: *Ann Torbert*
Development Editor II: *Rebecca Mann*
Director of Digital Content: *Patricia Plumb*
Digital Development Editor: *Julie Hankins*
Senior Marketing Manager: *Michelle Nolte*
Content Project Managers: *Marianne L. Musni* and *Joseph A. McCarthy*
Senior Buyer: *Carol A. Bielski*
Design: *Lisa King*
Cover Image: ©*Phillip Jones/Getty Images*
Senior Content Licensing Specialist: *Jeremy Cheshareck*
Typeface: *10/12 Times LT Std.*
Compositor: *Laserwords Private Limited*
Printer: *R. R. Donnelley*

All credits appearing on page or at the end of the book are considered to be an extension of the copyright page.

Library of Congress Cataloging-in-Publication Data

Melvin, Sean P.
  The legal environment of business : a managerial approach : theory to practice / Sean P. Melvin, Elizabethtown College; Michael A. Katz, Delaware State University.—Second Edition.
    pages cm
  Includes index.
  ISBN 978-0-07-802380-4 (alk. paper)—ISBN 0-07-802380-7 (alk. paper)
  1. Businesspeople—United States—Textbooks. 2. Commercial law—United States—Textbooks.
I. Katz, Michael A. II. Title.
KF390.B84M45 2015
346.7307—dc23
                                                                            2013017703

The Internet addresses listed in the text were accurate at the time of publication. The inclusion of a website does not indicate an endorsement by the authors or McGraw-Hill Education, and McGraw-Hill Education does not guarantee the accuracy of the information presented at these sites.

www.mhhe.com

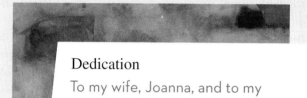

Dedication

To my wife, Joanna, and to my children, Sean and Ally.

S.P.M.

To my parents, my children, and their families, who have always directly and indirectly provided inspiration and support, and in particular to my grandson Isaac, who reminds me every day that working to ensure a safe and secure future is our primary obligation.

M.A.K.

To our students: past, present, and future.

The Authors

Sean P. Melvin is an associate professor of business law at Elizabethtown College (Pennsylvania), where he served as department chair for eight years, won the Delta Mu Delta Outstanding Teacher of the Year award, and received several Faculty Merit awards for teaching and scholarship. Prior to his appointment at Elizabethtown, he was an assistant professor of business at West Chester University of Pennsylvania, where he taught in both the undergraduate and MBA programs. Before his academic career, Professor Melvin was a corporate lawyer in a large Philadelphia-based law firm and went on to become vice president and general counsel at a publicly traded technology company.

Professor Melvin is the author of five books (including three textbooks), has contributed scholarly and professional articles and case studies to dozens of publications, and is a member of the Academy of Legal Studies in Business (ALSB). In 2011, his article "Case Study of a Coffee War" was selected as Best International Case Study at the annual ALSB conference.

Michael A. Katz is a professor of business law at Delaware State University, where he has taught since 1990 and is currently serving as department chair. Prior to his appointment at Delaware State, he maintained general civil law practices as an associate in a 16-member firm and as a solo practitioner. He managed the mortgage origination department at Delaware Trust, the second-largest bank in Delaware at that time. Professor Katz began his teaching career at Goldey Beacom College, where he taught for eight years before moving into banking and the practice of law. He is the author of a dozen scholarly and professional peer-reviewed publications and over a dozen textbook supplements. Professor Katz is a member of the Academy of Legal Studies in Business, for which he was the director of the Academy's Student Research Paper Competition for eight years. He is a past president of both the Midwest Academy of Legal Studies in Business and the Mid-Atlantic Academy of Legal Studies in Business.

Think of this textbook as a road map that guides you through the twists and turns of the laws that impact business entities, owners, and managers. This road map will help you understand ways in which business owners and managers can add value to their companies by using legal insight for business planning and for limiting liability. We have tailored the text, examples, cases, and teaching features to the needs of business students by providing concise explanations of law (theory) and then supplying the tools necessary for students to apply their knowledge in the business environment (practice).

MASTERING THE MATERIAL

The first step in mastering the material is to recognize that you must *internalize* the concepts presented in your courses. This requires more than a casual reading of assignments. For many years, we have asked students who earned an "A" in our courses to write a few sentences of advice to future students on how to internalize the material and achieve a top grade in the course. We offer you some of their collective wisdom:

- At the beginning of the course, match the syllabus with the textbook. Note the areas that the instructor is focused on by comparing the amount of coverage between topics. For example, if it appears from the syllabus that you will be spending several classes on constitutional law, that is an area that will undoubtedly be assessed (through an examination, project, etc.) and requires more intense study and review.

- The day before a class, study the assignment as follows: (1) read the major and minor headings in the textbook to get a general sense of what the material covers; (2) go back and read the text carefully, using a highlighter and pencil to mark important text and make notes in the margins; and (3) review the concept summaries, flowcharts, and self-checks to be sure you understand the material, and put question marks next to any concept you do not understand.

- The day of your class, if possible, take 15 minutes before your class to review the highlighted text, margin notes, and concept summaries.

- During class, be sure that your text is open and that your notes are tied to any assignments in the text. For example, suppose your instructor takes time to go over the concept of jurisdiction in some detail during class, draws a flowchart on the board, and goes over the self-check answers. This is a clear sign that jurisdiction will be assessed in some form (most commonly through an examination or quiz). In your notes on jurisdiction, indicate that the concept is important (and requires more intense study) and cross-reference it with page numbers in your textbook.

- As soon as possible after class (ideally, immediately after class but no later than that same evening), take 15 minutes to write out 10 note cards. First, write out five of the most important concepts covered in class that day. Second, write out five terms (words or short phrases) that were used by the instructor during class. This will give you a convenient and portable resource for reviewing.

Finally, we offer you the same advice for success in your course that we have offered our own students for more than a decade: The secret is that there is no secret. No methodology, advice, or review cards substitute for sustained and diligent study of the material.

A NOTE TO THE INSTRUCTOR

The instructor's materials are based on a turnkey approach that provides a comprehensive set of course materials along with the textbook. These materials have been developed with an eye toward minimizing instructor preparation time while still allowing the instructor to tailor the course in a way that meets the unique needs of instructors and students alike. In addition to the traditional supplementary materials package that includes an Instructor's Manual (written by the authors), test bank, and PowerPoint slides, the instructor's version of the textbook package is also integrated with a robust package of online content including McGraw-Hill's unique interactive exercises via *Connect,* quizzes, links to streaming videos, case updates, sample text-specific syllabi with alternatives for a variety of classroom circumstances, multiple formats, teaching notes, sample questions, and assignment sheets tied to the simulation materials and the Capstone case studies.

Contact Information   We invite you to contact us with any comments, suggestions, or updates. A special link to our e-mail address is located on this textbook's website www.mhhe.com/melvinleb2e.

Sean P. Melvin
Michael A. Katz

Beginning-of-Chapter Features

Each chapter begins with *Learning Objectives* and a short overview that provides students with a map of the chapter. The *Learning Objectives* are a point-by-point checklist of the skills and learning goals that gives students a convenient study guide for previewing and reviewing material in the chapter.

learning **objectives**

After studying this chapter, students who have mastered the material will be able to:

3-1 Explain the role of the judiciary in the context of the American legal system.

3-2 Distinguish between the roles of federal courts and state courts.

3-3 Identify the responsibilities of trial courts versus appellate courts.

3-4 Articulate how the law develops via adjudication of cases.

3-5 Differentiate between subject matter jurisdiction and personal jurisdiction.

3-6 Explain original jurisdiction and how courts may have concurrent jurisdiction.

CASE 3.1 Estate of Weingeroff v. Pilatus Aircraft, 566 F.3d 94 (3d Cir. 2009)

FACT SUMMARY The legal representative of the estate of Weingeroff (Weingeroff), a passenger on a turboprop plane who was killed when the plane crashed near State College, Pennsylvania, brought a negligence and product liability lawsuit against Pilatus Air (Pilatus), the manufacturer of the plane. The plane crashed when approaching a small airport in Pennsylvania on a planned stop en route between Florida and Rhode Island. Weingeroff sued Pilatus in a federal district court situated in the Eastern District of Pennsylvania. Pilatus, a Swiss company, asked the court to dismiss the case for lack of personal jurisdiction. Pilatus claimed that it had no offices, no agents, no commercial transactions with Pennsylvania residents, and no physical presence in the state that constitutes purposeful availment. Weingeroff pointed to evidence that (1) Pilatus had conducted a nationwide marketing campaign in the United States to sell its planes, including in Pennsylvania, and (2) Pilatus had purchased over $1 million in products, services, and equipment from Pennsylvania suppliers. The trial court ruled in favor of Pilatus and dismissed the suit for lack of personal jurisdiction.

SYNOPSIS OF DECISION AND OPINION The Court of Appeals for the Third Circuit upheld the trial court's decision in favor of Pilatus. The court pointed out that Pilatus had not sold any aircraft to purchasers in Pennsylvania or shipped anything directly to persons or entities in Pennsylvania. Moreover, Pilatus had not advertised or marketed its products in Pennsylvania and did not design the plane for the Pennsylvania market.

suppliers in Pennsylvania, this amount represented less than 1 percent of Pilatus's total annual purchases for an approximately five-year period.

WORDS OF THE COURT: Purposeful Availment "We acknowledge that there is a certain reasonableness to an argument that a manufacturer should be subject to suit in a jurisdiction in which its plane crashes if the suit charges that a manufacturing defect caused the crash. Yet it is clear that the critical finding that the defendant purposefully availed itself of the privilege of conducting activities within the forum [state] requires contacts that amount to a deliberate reaching into the forum state to target its citizens. Pilatus's efforts to exploit a national market necessarily included Pennsylvania as a target, but those efforts simply do not constitute the type of deliberate contacts within Pennsylvania that could amount to purposeful availment of the privilege of conducting activities in that state. Rather, any connection of Pilatus to Pennsylvania merely was a derivative benefit of its successful attempt to exploit the United States as a national market."

Case Questions

1. What facts could you change that may sway the court's judgment in analyzing personal jurisdiction over Pilatus in this case?

2. Does this decision mean that Weingeroff is without any legal recourse against Pilatus unless the case is brought in Swiss courts?

Cases

The textbook uses a *hybrid* format to report case law rather than including lengthy excerpts from judicial opinions. Students are provided with (1) a summary of the facts, (2) a decision and opinion synopsis, (3) short excerpts from the actual opinion, called "Words of the Court," that helps students understand a key point in the case, and (4) several case questions to facilitate discussion. Students will find this format useful for understanding legal cases in a business context.

Business Ethics Perspective

The coverage of business ethics reflects its increasingly important place in the business world. In addition to Chapter 5, "Business, Societal, and Ethical Contexts of Law," the textbook features logically placed boxes with discussion questions intended to help students understand ethical decision making in contemporary contexts. *Business Ethics Perspective* boxes cover a wide variety of topics, including an examination of the practices of AIG, Countrywide Mortgage, and others involved in the financial crisis that began in 2008.

 BUSINESS ETHICS PERSPECTIVE

Ethical Issues Involved in Abusive Litigation

While commercial litigation typically involves two parties attempting to resolve a legitimate dispute in good faith, the costs, burdens, and uncontrollable risks of litigation render it subject to potential abuse. Although federal and state courts have strict procedural rules intended to curb abusive litigation, it is sometimes difficult to enforce those rules because of the inherent vagueness in defining what constitutes "abusive." Abusive litigation may be defined as *vexatious* litigation or abuse of the litigation *process*.

Vexatious litigation may be defined as lawsuits that are filed for reasons other than legitimate damages being suffered by the plaintiff. These illegitimate reasons include using a lawsuit to harass, annoy, intimidate, or cause the opposite party to expend unnecessary costs. Consider the case of *Alston v. Advanced Brands and Importing Company* where a group of parents formed a consumer activist group and filed a lawsuit against manufacturers of alcoholic beverages. The suit alleged that the manufacturers' advertising contributed to the illegal purchase of alcohol by minors. The parent group conceded that there was no evidence that their own minor children had actually purchased alcoholic beverages, so the suit was dismissed for lack of standing.[8]

1. Once the company was threatened with a lawsuit, what ethical obligation did the management of Advance Brands have to its stockholders?[9] Should the management have settled the case for a small sum to avoid legal costs even if they were convinced the suit had no merit?

2. Does Advance have an ethical obligation to the community and public? Would that duty include fighting vexatious litigation to prevent future abuses of the legal system?

3. Does management's ethical duty to stockholders to settle this case for minimal costs override any ethical duty owed to the community?

4. Are there any circumstances under which a business could ethically use litigation as a legitimate business strategy?

Abuse of the litigation process occurs when, after the lawsuit is filed, one party engages in a course of conduct that is contrary to the good faith requirements underlying all litigation. Destroying documents, refusing to hand over evidence during discovery, stalling, and making overly broad discovery requests can all be categorized as abuse of the process.

5. Suppose you were a manager who was ordered by your senior manager to shred certain documents. Do you have an ethical obli-

LEGAL/ETHICAL REFLECTION *and* DISCUSSION — NEW!

The UCC sets out different rules regarding contract formation when a sales contract involves two nonmerchants, a merchant and a nonmerchant, or two merchants.

1. Two nonmerchants may strike a $1,000 deal for the sale of a used television, while two merchants may contract to buy 1,000 new televisions for $1 million. Why are the rules of contract formation stricter for the two nonmerchants than they are for the two merchants?

2. Are different rules necessary? Why or why not?

3. Would UCC gap fillers work for nonmerchant contracts? Why or why not?

4. If company A sends a purchase order to company B and company B returns an acknowledgment of the order with additional or modified terms, courts may determine that those additional or modified terms become part of the final contract. Is it ethical to force company A to adhere to the additional or modified terms without an express agreement to them by company A? Is company B acting unethically by adding or modifying the terms of company A's purchase order?

Legal/Ethical Reflection and Discussion

This new feature is strategically placed in parts of the text where the instructor may wish to have students reflect on the ethical dimension of a legal problem. It starts with a short, narrative and ends with a series of questions that fundamentally ask students: What would *you* do?

Self-Checks

Self-Check exercises offer students an opportunity to reinforce and apply the material being studied in the textbook. Students use black-letter law and cases to answer short hypothetical questions on a specific topic. *Self-Checks* appear in the textbook after important legal concepts and are always keyed to problems faced by business managers and owners. Answers to the *Self-Checks* are provided at the end of the chapter.

✓ Self-Check   Source of Constitutional Authority

What is the constitutional source of authority for each of the following laws?

1. A federal statute that makes it more difficult for businesses to qualify for protection under bankruptcy laws.

2. An increase in the federal corporate income tax.

3. A federal statute that adds criminal penalties for patent infringement.

4. A federal statute creating an agency to regulate ground shipping between states.

5. A federal statute that requires that 25 percent of federal government construction contracts be awarded to companies that are women- or minority-owned enterprises.

Answers to this Self-Check are provided at the end of the chapter.

SOLUTIONS FOR MANAGERS   LO 4-8

Online Dispute Resolution

PROBLEM *In situations involving small amounts of money, is there a way for a business to resolve such relatively minor disputes in a cost-effective manner?*

A business may be engaged in hundreds of relatively low-cost transactions per year with various out-of-state vendors such as suppliers, shipping companies, office supply stores, contractors, and the like. When disputes arise, a business may be at a distinct disadvantage and bargaining position because the amount in controversy is too low to justify even the least expensive form of alternative dispute resolution. However, over an extended period of time these small losses add up to unnecessary liabilities, leaving managers with a difficult choice when faced with a dispute over a relatively low amount of money with an out-of-state vendor: (1), Invest in a dispute resolution method despite the fact that the costs may very well exceed the

then sends both parties a fair price based on their initial demands.

Another form of ODR is geared more toward complex transactions—for example, the Square Trade website proposes prewritten resolutions and you have received a damaged shipment of goods. The site might offer a standard menu of solutions such as (1) replacement with an undamaged good, (2) return for a full refund, or (3) keep the merchandise with a partial refund. The parties may also fill in their own solution, but the site's guided approach helps the parties focus on a resolution to the dispute.

If direct negotiation fails to resolve the issue, Square Trade users can request a mediator for a $20 fee per participant plus a percentage fee if the dispute exceeds $1,000. At OnlineResolution.com, mediation fees range between $15 and $25. For disputes of more than $500, each participant pays $50 to $150 per hour, based on the value under dispute.

Solutions for Managers

In keeping with the text's managerial focus, *Solutions for Managers* provides practical answers for legal problems faced by managers and business owners. *Solutions for Managers* is structured in a problem and solution format that allows students to understand how a particular section's legal concepts may be used to solve real-world business problems.

Concept Summaries and Flowcharts

To help students with *reinforcing* and *reviewing* the application of the law in a business context, each major section within each chapter features a summary of the section. When a legal procedure is involved, flowcharts are used to summarize the process.

CONCEPT SUMMARY Jurisdiction

	Federal Trial Courts	State Trial Courts
Personal Jurisdiction	1. Residents and business entities located in the state where the federal trial court sits; or 2. Nonresidents with *minimum* contacts with the state in which the federal trial court sits; or 3. Nonresidents owning property in the state in which the federal trial court sits; or 4. Voluntary	1. Residents and business entities located in the state; or 2. Nonresidents owning property in the state; or 3. Nonresidents with *minimum* contacts with the state according to state long-arm statutes; or 4. Voluntary
Subject Matter Jurisdiction	1. Federal question; or 2. U.S. is a party; or 3. Diversity of citizenship *and* amount in controversy is more than $75,000 (amount required only in diversity cases)	State law matters (statutes, common law, state constitutional issues)

THEORY TO PRACTICE

Santiago Information Systems (Santiago) is a business based in Baltimore, Maryland, that purchases old computers, refurbishes them with new software and hardware parts, and sells them in bulk for about half the price of a new PC. For the past three years, Santiago shipped approximately 40 percent of its inventory to the same client. The client was the Wilmington, Delaware, school system (Wilmington) and the school paid approximately $80,000 to Santiago for the computers per year. Santiago would also visit each school to be sure that the computers were installed correctly and that the school district was satisfied with the order. Santiago has a website that gives contact information for the company, but the site is not interactive because users can transact business only by sending Santiago e-mail via the website.

Recently, Wilmington discovered that large shipments of Santiago's products were defective, and it has been unable to come to a resolution with Santiago over the matter.

1. If Wilmington wishes to sue Santiago, what court(s) would have jurisdiction over this matter?
2. What would be the best venue and why?
3. If a Delaware court decides that it does not have jurisdiction, how may that affect Wilmington's decision on whether or not to file a lawsuit?

Assume that one of Santiago's suppliers, Parts R Us (Parts) is headquartered in Union, New Jersey, and has been shipping Santiago parts for approximately four years in a row. Last year Parts sold approximately $7,000 in hardware to Santiago. In the past 10 years,

End-of-Chapter Features

Each chapter ends with several features crafted to help students review and connect the different sections of the chapter by applying the material learned in the text in a practical way.

Theory to Practice: Each chapter features a hypothetical legal problem faced by a manager that is related to specific material in that chapter. The hypothetical problem is followed by questions that connect the problem to several different sections in the chapter.

Manager's Challenge: This feature allows students to engage in writing or a group work assignment that sets forth a manager's task relating to the material in the chapter. Some challenges are designed for teams, others for individuals.

Key Terms: Key terms for students are boldfaced in the text and listed as a group at the end of the chapter with a definition and reference to the page number in the chapter where the term was first mentioned.

Case Summaries: Several brief case summaries are included, with a heading for each that indicates its general topic reference to the chapter and with questions about the case summary. These cases are intended to reinforce students' knowledge of how laws apply in different fact circumstances.

parties are and (2) the subject matter of the dispute. **Venue** is a determination of the most appropriate court *location* for litigating a dispute.

Jurisdiction and Business Strategy

The increasing integration of advanced technology in product and service delivery has made jurisdiction and venue an important part of business planning for business managers and owners. As with all legal decisions that business owners and managers make, jurisdiction must be considered in a cost-benefit context. For example, consider a dispute between two hypothetical companies, Ultimate Widget Corporation (UWC) and Knock Off Stores Inc. (Knock Off). Suppose UWC, a New York company, is considering suing Knock Off, a California company, over a trademark dispute. UWC management should consider the costs involved in pursuing the suit in a business context. In considering their strategy, UWC's management must consider (1) the total amount of the possible recovery from Knock Off; (2) the actual benefits UWC will reap from the prevention of Knock Off's use of the trademark; and (3) any alternate dispute resolution methods available. If Knock Off is a small company and not likely to dilute the trademark in any of UWC's markets, it may not be worth the costs of litigation to sue UWC in its home state. Pursuing the infringement action would involve UWC's expense of traveling to California, hiring local counsel in California, and losing productive hours of managers and other witnesses who would be required to travel to testify and be deposed for the case. However, if a New York court could possibly have jurisdiction over the dispute, that fact will change the dynamics of the cost-benefit analysis because the expenses of the suit would be markedly lower.

Legal Speak ›))
Jurisdiction An English word derived through the combination of two Latin words: *juris* ("of law" or "of right") and *dictio* ("speaking"). Thus, the combination of the words refers to a specific court's right to *speak the law* or render a decision in a legal dispute.

KEY POINT
The cost-benefit analysis involving jurisdictional restrictions may affect the managerial decision-making process when a company or individual contemplates filing a lawsuit. Litigating disputes in out-of-state courts increases the costs of litigation.

Overview of Jurisdiction

LO 3-6

The origins of federal jurisdiction law are found in the U.S. Constitution, specifically, the Due Process Clause of the Fifth and the Fourteenth Amendments. In essence, the Constitution prohibits the deprivation of a property interest (usually money damages) without a legal process being applied. While origins of jurisdiction lie in the Constitution, appellate courts and legislatures have shaped the framework and rules used by modern courts to analyze jurisdiction questions.

Two-Part Analysis Jurisdiction requires a two-part analysis: A court must have both (1) subject matter jurisdiction and (2) personal jurisdiction (also known as in personam

Other Textbook Features

Key Points briefly reinforce an important concept; *Web Checks* provide websites related to the material in the textbook; *Legal Implications in Cyberspace* apply traditional legal concepts in the context of the Internet; *Legal Speak* presents instant definitions of important legal terms in the margins of the text.

Business Law Simulation Exercises for Managers

The textbook features three business law simulation exercises. In a simulation exercise, students are provided with facts, law, and cases related to a hypothetical business dispute and are assigned to analyze the material, understand the legal and ethical issues presented, and then work toward a resolution. The simulations are also excellent for review and reinforcement because the materials involve cases directly related to one or more topics covered in a particular unit of the textbook.

BUSINESS LAW SIMULATION EXERCISE 1

Restrictive Covenants in Contracts: Neurology Associates, LLP v. Elizabeth Blackwell, M.D.

✓ **learning objectives**

After studying this simulation, students who have mastered the material will be able to:

1. Explain the legal doctrines that govern the use of restrictive covenants.
2. Interpret and apply the rules set forth in current case law.
3. Articulate a cogent argument for each party/side in the dispute.
4. Negotiate a tenable solution as an alternative to a judicial forum.

Chapters 6 through 9 provided you with a variety of legal doctrines and rules governing contract formation and performance and then illustrated how these doctrines and rules apply in the corporate sector context. This simulation is designed to help you understand how the various topics covered in the contract law chapters connect. By focusing on a simulated legal dispute, you will replicate a real-world experience by applying legal doctrines and using analytical and critical-thinking skills. This simulation is a sequential

The simulation is structured in three parts:
- Part 1 is a hypothetical fact pattern describing events leading up to a legal dispute in the hypothetical U.S. state of Longville.
- Part 2 is a set of two hypothetical case summaries from Longville appellate courts that provide a brief set of facts, several legal points, and short excerpts from the opinion itself. While these cases are hypothetical, they are based on actual cases from appellate courts in various

Flexercises

New to this edition: Each Flexercise is a case presented in a way that is scalable (may be used as an individual, team, or full-class exercise) and adaptable (suitable for a writing exercise, discussion, or mock situation). The flexibility allows the professor to vary class assignments and keep students engaged, and it provides a wide range of student-learning assessment opportunities and measures.

UNIT ONE FLEXERCISE

NEW!

The plaintiffs, husband and wife, attended a Halloween party dressed as Little Bo Peep (wife) and a sheep (husband). The wife made her husband's costume from long underwear covered with glued-on cotton batting. The husband was covered with cotton batting from head to toe, excluding his face and hands. During the party the husband attempted to smoke a cigarette, and the flame from his lighter ignited the cotton. The husband admitted that he knew that cotton batting burned but emphasized that he did not know "how it burned." His wife also admitted that she knew that cotton could burn, "[but] not burn that fast." She knew her husband smoked and used a cigarette lighter. The husband suffered burns on one-third of his body, and he underwent several surgeries as a consequence of the fire.

The plaintiffs sued the cotton manufacturer for failing to warn that cotton could ignite so easily and that the flames of the burning cotton would spread so quickly. The jury awarded the husband $550,000 and his wife $70,000 in damages. The defendants motioned for a judgment *non obstante veredicto* (JNOV). (A JNOV asks a judge to disregard the jury's verdict and award the judgment to the moving party.)

ENGAGEMENT QUESTIONS

1. Should a judge have the right to overrule a jury? Why have juries if a single person can overrule the entire jury?
2. Is it feasible for companies to put warning labels on their products listing every possible hazard? When should warning labels be required, if ever?
3. The husband regularly smoked and ignored warnings on cigarette packages. Do you think a warning label on the cotton batting would have deterred him from smoking that night?
4. The wife made the costume so if there had been a warning label on the cotton, the husband most likely wouldn't have been aware of it. Would this change anyone's liability?

CAPSTONE CASE STUDY 1
Coffee Wars: Starbucks v. Charbucks[1]

Overview and Objectives

Two years after opening their family-owned coffee bean roastery, Jim and Annie Clark had become accustomed to long workweeks and bootstrap financing. By 1997, their Black Bear Micro Roastery was finally growing, and the Clarks were hopeful that their new specialty blend, Charbucks, would give their uniquely dark-roasted coffee bean a catchy name to remember. Soon after launching the new blend, Annie Clark received a phone call from an insistent in-house lawyer at coffee giant Starbucks that threatened the very existence of the Clarks' company. Starbucks claimed that the Charbucks name and label infringed on its trademark, and it demanded that the Clarks cease the use of the name Charbucks and that any existing products with that name be removed from supermarket shelves. But the Clarks insisted that they had been careful to design the label with Black Bear Micro Roastery logos and that the name was tied to the dark-roasting process and not to anything related to the name Starbucks. Despite their beliefs that no infringement had taken place, the Clarks entered into settlement negotiations to avoid the legal costs associated with defending a trademark lawsuit. After the settlement negotiations failed, Starbucks sued Black Bear Micro

THE BLACK BEAR MICRO ROASTERY

Jim and Annie Clark were native New Englanders who shared a passion for coffee and an entrepreneurial spirit. After three years of research, they launched Black Bear Micro Roastery in 1995 with a mission of creating a unique methodology for roasting gourmet coffee beans through use of advanced technology and the "traditional Yankee work ethic." The company was situated in the lakes region of New Hampshire and targeted connoisseur coffee drinkers, primarily in the New England area, who appreciated the micro-roastery approach of producing small, high-quality batches of coffee beans. The beans were sold via mail order, from the Black Bear website, and through New England specialty stores and supermarkets. Eventually, Black Bear also sold its products through its own retail outlet and café in Portsmouth, New Hampshire.

True to their belief in the micro-roastery concept and their entrepreneurial courage, the Clarks invested their life savings in the company. In order to start the business, the couple sold many of their assets and refinanced the mortgage on their home for extra cash. They enlisted their teenage daughters as their labor force and committed to seven-day workweeks. The family business was the centerpiece of their family's livelihood.

As with many start-ups, business for Black Bear

Capstone Case Studies

Capstone case studies center on the dilemmas of actual corporations that were faced with a corporate crisis involving legal and ethical issues. They are intended to help students connect several different legal and ethical concepts in a single case study. First, students reread concept summaries from specific chapters to reinforce their knowledge of specific legal issues. Second, students study a narrative of facts of the case, dynamics of the marketplace, and important trends of the time. Discussion questions are grouped by topical subject matter such as negligence, products liability, administrative agency regulation, criminal law, and so forth. Ethical decision-making questions are integrated into each case. The *Capstone Case Study* feature also provides a short exercise designed for use as a writing assignment, small group work, or class discussion.

▇▇SMARTBOOK™

Fueled by LearnSmart—the most widely used and intelligent adaptive learning resource—SmartBook is the first and only adaptive reading experience available today.

Distinguishing what a student knows from what they don't, and honing in on concepts they are most likely to forget, SmartBook personalizes content for each student in a continuously adapting reading experience. Reading is no longer a passive and linear

experience, but an engaging and dynamic one where students are more likely to master and retain important concepts, coming to class better prepared. Valuable reports provide instructors insight as to how students are progressing through textbook content, and are useful for shaping in-class time or assessment. As a result of the adaptive reading experience found in SmartBook, students are more likely to retain knowledge, stay in class, and get better grades.

This revolutionary technology is available only from McGraw-Hill Education and for hundreds of course areas as part of the LearnSmart Advantage series.

How Does SmartBook Work?

Each SmartBook contains four components: Preview, Read, Practice, and Recharge. Starting with an initial preview of each chapter and key learning objectives, students read the material and are guided to topics that need the most practice based on their responses to a continuously adapting diagnostic. Read and practice continue until SmartBook directs students to recharge important material they are most likely to forget to ensure concept mastery and retention.

■LEARNSMART®

LearnSmart is one of the most effective and successful adaptive learning resources available on the market today. More than 2 million students have answered more than 1.3 billion questions in LearnSmart since 2009, making it the most widely used and intelligent adaptive study tool that's proven to strengthen memory recall, keep students in class, and boost grades. Students using LearnSmart are 13% more likely to pass their classes and 35% less likely to dropout.

Distinguishing what students know from what they don't, and honing in on concepts they are most likely to forget, LearnSmart continuously adapts to each student's needs by building an individual learning path so students study smarter and retain more knowledge. Turnkey reports provide valuable insight to instructors, so precious class time can be spent on higher-level concepts and discussion.

This revolutionary learning resource is available only from McGraw-Hill Education, and because LearnSmart is available for most course areas, instructors can recommend it to students in almost every class they teach.

| BUSINESS LAW

MCGRAW-HILL CONNECT BUSINESS LAW

Get *Connect Business Law*. Get Results.

McGraw-Hill *Connect Business Law* is an online assignment and assessment system that gives students the means to better connect with their coursework, with their instructors, and with the important concepts that they will need to know for success now and in the future. With *Connect Business Law*, instructors can deliver assignments, quizzes, and tests easily online. *Connect Business Law* helps students master critical conceptual material in the course. By using *Connect Business Law* to master concepts, students are more prepared to apply those concepts to higher level discussions and topics in the Business Law course. *Connect Business Law* offers you the features described below.

- Chapter quizzes for the 26 chapters, consisting of 15–25 multiple-choice questions, testing students' overall comprehension of concepts presented in the chapter.
- At least 2 specially crafted interactive applications for each of the 26 chapters that drill students in the use and application of the concepts and tools of strategic analysis.
- The majority of the Connect exercises are automatically graded, thereby simplifying the task of evaluating each class member's performance and monitoring the learning outcomes.

> As a student I need to interact with course material in order to retain it, and Connect offers a perfect platform for this kind of learning. Rather than just reading through textbooks, Connect has given me the tools to feel engaged in the learning process.
>
> —Jennah Epstein Kraus, Student, Bunker Hill Community College

Interactive Applications

Interactive Applications offer a variety of automatically graded exercises that require student to apply key concepts. Whether the assignment includes a click & drag, video case, or decision generator, these applications provide instant feedback and progress tracking for students and detailed results for the instructor.

Click and Drag Interactive Applications—These fun and interactive click and drag exercises motivate students to apply concepts within the context of a scenario or case allowing them to think about legal issues.

Comprehension Case Interactive Applications—These cases generate deeper understanding of the core concepts by applying chapter concepts in an open-ended question format. They are the most difficult Interactive Applications in Connect and are the only exercises that are manually graded.

Decision Generator Interactive Applications—These exercises ask students to apply critical thinking skills and allow students to see the interdependencies of their decisions in a mini case scenario.

Video Case Interactive Applications—These case study videos include pop-up questions that appear as the video plays to test concept and/or terminology comprehension.

Student Library

The *Connect Business Law* Student Library gives students access to additional resources such as recorded lectures, online practice materials, an eBook, and more.

MCGRAW-HILL *CONNECT BUSINESS LAW* FEATURES

Connect Business Law offers a number of powerful tools and features to make managing assignments easier, so faculty can spend more time teaching.

Simple Assignment Management and Smart Grading

With *Connect Business Law*, creating assignments is easier than ever, so instructors can spend more time teaching and less time managing.

- Create and deliver assignments easily with selectable interactive applications, quizzes and Test Bank items.
- Go paperless with the eBook and online submission and grading of student assignments.
- Have assignments scored automatically, giving students immediate feedback on their work and side-by-side comparisons with correct answers.
- Access and review each response; manually change grades or leave comments for students to review.
- Reinforce classroom concepts with practice tests and instant quizzes.

Student Reporting

Connect Business Law keeps instructors informed about how each student, section, and class is performing, allowing for more productive use of lecture and office hours. The progress-tracking function enables you to:

- View scored work immediately and track individual or group performance with assignment and grade reports.
- Access an instant view of student or class performance relative to learning objectives.
- Collect data and generate reports required by many accreditation organizations, such as AACSB.

Instructor Library

The *Connect Business Law* Instructor Library is a repository for additional resources to improve student engagement in and out of class. You can select and use any asset that enhances your lecture. The *Connect Business Law* Instructor Library includes access to the eBook version of the text, videos, slide presentations, Instructor's Manual, and Test Bank. The *Connect Business Law* Instructor Library also allows you to upload your own files.

MCGRAW-HILL *CONNECT PLUS BUSINESS LAW*

McGraw-Hill reinvents the textbook learning experience for the modern student with *Connect Plus Business Law.* A seamless integration of an eBook and *Connect Business Law, Connect Plus Business Law* provides all of the *Connect Business Law* features plus the following:

- An integrated eBook, allowing for anytime, anywhere access to the textbook.
- Media-rich capabilities like highlighting and sharing notes.
- Dynamic links between the problems or questions you assign to your students and the location in the eBook where that concept is covered.
- A powerful search function to pinpoint key concepts for review.

In short, *Connect Plus Business Law* offers students powerful tools and features that optimize their time and energy, enabling them to focus on learning.

For more information about *Connect Plus Business Law,* go to **www.mcgrawhillconnect.com,** or contact your local McGraw-Hill sales representative.

Tegrity Campus: Lectures 24/7

Tegrity Campus is a service that makes class time available 24/7 by automatically capturing every lecture. With a simple one-click start-and-stop process, you capture all computer screens and corresponding audio in a format that is easily searchable, frame by frame. Students can replay any part of any class with easy-to-use browser-based viewing on a PC, Mac, iPod, or other mobile device.

Educators know that the more students can see, hear, and experience class resources, the better they learn. In fact, studies prove it. Tegrity Campus's unique search feature helps students efficiently find what they need, when they need it, across an entire semester of class recordings. Help turn your students' study time into learning moments immediately supported by your lecture. With Tegrity Campus, you also increase intent listening and class participation by easing students' concerns about note-taking. Tegrity Campus will make it more likely you will see students' faces, not the tops of their heads.

To learn more about Tegrity, watch a 2-minute Flash demo at **http://tegritycampus.mhhe.com.**

MCGRAW-HILL CAMPUS

McGraw-Hill Campus™ is a new one-stop teaching and learning experience available to users of any learning management system. This institutional service allows faculty and students to enjoy single sign-on (SSO) access to all McGraw-Hill Higher Education materials, including the award-winning McGraw-Hill *Connect* platform, directly from within the institution's website. McGraw-Hill Campus provides faculty with instant access to teaching materials (e.g., eTextbooks, Test Banks, PowerPoint slides, animations, and learning objects), allowing them to browse, search, and use any ancillary content in our vast library. Students enjoy SSO access to a variety of free products (e.g., quizzes, flash cards, and presentations) and subscription-based products (e.g., McGraw-Hill *Connect*). With McGraw-Hill Campus, faculty and students will never need to create another account to access McGraw-Hill products and services.

CUSTOM PUBLISHING THROUGH CREATE

McGraw-Hill Create™ is a, self-service website that allows instructors to create custom course materials by drawing upon McGraw-Hill's comprehensive, cross-disciplinary content. Instructors can add their own content quickly and easily and tap into other rights-secured third party sources as well, then arrange the content in a way that makes the most sense for their course. Instructors can even personalize their book with the course name and information and choose the best format for their students—color print, black-and-white print, or an eBook.

Through Create, instructors can

- Select and arrange the content in a way that makes the most sense for their course.
- Combine material from different sources and even upload their own content.
- Choose the best format for their students—print or eBook.
- Edit and update their course materials as often as they'd like.

Begin creating now at **www.mcgrawhillcreate.com.**

COURSESMART

Learn Smart. Choose Smart.
CourseSmart is a way for faculty to find and review eTextbooks. It's also a great option for students who are interested in accessing their course materials digitally and saving money.

CourseSmart offers thousands of the most commonly adopted textbooks across hundreds of courses from a wide variety of higher education publishers. It is the only place for faculty to review and compare the full text of a textbook online, providing immediate access without the environmental impact of requesting a print exam copy.

With the CourseSmart eTextbook, students can save up to 45 percent off the cost of a print book, reduce their impact on the environment, and access powerful web tools for learning. CourseSmart is an online eTextbook, which means users access and view their textbook online when connected to the Internet. Students can also print sections of the book for maximum portability. CourseSmart eTextbooks are available in one standard online reader with full text search, notes and highlighting, and e-mail tools for sharing notes between classmates. For more information on CourseSmart, go to **www.coursesmart.com.**

Instructor's Manual

The Instructor's Manual, developed by one of the authors, Sean P. Melvin, is designed to be an effective course management tool and an integral part of the turnkey approach used throughout the supplementary material package. The features and format are intended to give instructors maximum flexibility to determine and produce high-quality course content. The IM also has a special "Day One" section addressing important fundamental course decisions for instructors who are new to the course.

Test Bank

The test-bank allows instructors to custom design, save, and generate tests. The test bank includes multiple-choice, true-false, fill-in-the-blank, and essay questions for every chapter in the text. To help instructors meet the requirements of AACSB, each question is tagged with the corresponding chapter learning objective and applicable AACSB categories.

EZ Test Online

McGraw-Hill's flexible and easy-to-use electronic testing program allows instructors to create tests from book-specific items. It accommodates a wide range of question types, and instructors may add their own questions. Multiple versions of a test can be created, and any test can be exported for use with online course management systems. EZ Test Online allows you to administer EZ Test–created exams and quizzes online.

Assurance of Learning Ready

Many educational institutions today are focused on the notion of *assurance of learning,* an important element of some accreditation standards. *The Legal Environment of Business* is designed specifically to support your assurance of learning initiatives with a simple, yet powerful solution.

Each test bank question for *The Legal Environment of Business* maps to a specific chapter learning objective listed in the text. You can use our test bank software, EZ Test and EZ Test Online, or *Connect Business Law* to easily query for learning objectives that directly relate to the learning objectives for your course. You can then use the reporting features of EZ Test to aggregate student results in similar fashion, making the collection and presentation of assurance of learning data simple and easy.

AACSB Statement

The McGraw-Hill Companies is a proud corporate member of AACSB International. Understanding the importance and value of AACSB accreditation, *The Legal Environment of Business* recognizes the curricula guidelines detailed in the AACSB standards for business accreditation by connecting selected questions in the text and the test bank to the six general knowledge and skill guidelines in the AACSB standards.

The statements contained in *The Legal Environment of Business* are provided only as a guide for the users of this textbook. The AACSB leaves content coverage and assessment within the purview of individual schools, the mission of the school, and the faculty. While *The Legal Environment of Business* and the teaching package make no claim of any specific AACSB qualification or evaluation, we have within the text and the test bank of *The Legal Environment of Business* labeled selected questions according to the six general knowledge and skills areas.

PowerPoint Presentation

Each chapter has a PowerPoint Presentation that offers additional support by providing detailed teaching notes, particularly for more complex topics.

Online Learning Center, www.mhhe.com/melvinleb2e

The Online Learning Center includes study materials for students. Use the site to access the chapter review quizzes, key term review, legal resources, additional cases for discussion, online access to the Uniform Commercial Code and U.S. Constitution, and news updates, and other resources.

MCGRAW-HILL CUSTOMER CARE CONTACT INFORMATION

At McGraw-Hill, we understand that getting the most from new technology can be challenging. That's why our services don't stop after you purchase our products. You can e-mail our Product Specialists 24 hours a day to get product-training online. Or you can search our knowledge bank of Frequently Asked Questions on our support website. For Customer Support, call **800-331-5094** or visit **www.mhhe.com/support.** One of our Technical Support Analysts will be able to assist you in a timely fashion.

acknowledgments

We owe a great deal of gratitude to our entire team at McGraw-Hill. Although many team members worked diligently with us in developing and strengthening this book, our Managing Director, Tim Vertovec, our Development Editor, Rebecca Mann, and our Content Project Manager, Marianne Musni, are owed special thanks for their insight in navigating the waters of publication. Sean J. Melvin is owed thanks for his case research contribution.

Throughout the development of the first and second editions of this book, we have been privileged to have the candid and valuable advice of our reviewers and focus group. These reviewers provided us with priceless suggestions, feedback, and constructive criticism. The depth and sincerity of their reviews indicate that they are a devoted group of teacher-scholars. The content of the book was greatly enhanced because of their efforts.

Hakim Adjoua
Columbus State Community College

Wayne Anderson
Missouri State University

Linda Axelrod
Metropolitan State University

David Berkowitz
Chapman University

Perry Binder
Georgia State University

Andrea Boggio
Bryant University

Eli Bortman
Babson College

Michael Bryant
Bryant University

Gretchen Carroll
Owens Community College

Anita Cava
University of Miami

Robert Cherry
Appalachian State University

Tracy Cole
Arkansas Tech University

Angelo Corpora
Palomar College

Rebecca Davis
University of Kentucky-Lexington

Glenn Doolittle
Santa Ana College

Craig Ehrlich
Babson College

Teressa Elliott
Northern Kentucky University

Tim Fogarty
Case Western Reserve University

John Geary
Appalachian State University

Wendy Gelman
Florida International University–Miami

John Gergacz
University of Kansas

Jeane Gohl-Noice
Parkland College

Marc Hall
Auburn University–Montgomery

Eloise Hassell
University of North Carolina–Greensboro

Diane Hathaway
University of Cincinnati

Arlene Hibschweiler
State University of New York–Buffalo

Frederick Jones
Kennesaw State University

Susan Kendall
Arapahoe Community College

Cheryl Kirschner
Babson College

Stan Leasure
Missouri State University

Colleen Less
Johnson and Wales University

Christine Lewis
Auburn University–Montgomery

Mark Lewis
Arkansas State University

Janice Loutzenhiser
California State University–San Bernardino

Nancy Mansfield
Georgia State University

Ernest Mayo
Johnson & Wales University

Martha Novy-Broderick
University of Maine

Les Nunn
University of Southern Indiana

Tom Parrish
Liberty University

Steven Popejoy
University of Central Missouri

Brenda Rice
Ozarks Technical Community College

Alan Roline
University of Minnesota–Duluth

Julie Shadoan
Western Kentucky University

Steven Schamber
St. Louis Community College

Randy Skalberg
University of Minnesota–Duluth

Cheryl Staley
Lake Land College

Kurt Stanberry
University of Houston–Downtown

Connie Strain
Arapahoe Community College

Frank Sullivan
University of Nevada–Las Vagas

Greg Swan
Chandler-Gilbert Community College

Keith Swim
Texas A&M University

Mary Torma
Lorain County Community College

Michael Vasilou
DeVry University–Chicago

Glen Vogel
Hofstra University

Ronald Washburn
Bryant University

Mark Whitaker
Hampton University

Susan Willey
Georgia State University

LeVon Wilson
Georgia Southern University

John Wrieden
Florida International University–Miami

changes to this edition

The authors are committed to ongoing improvement of this textbook through the generous feedback, suggestions, and guidance from over 100 business law professors and reviewers. The second edition of ***The Legal Environment of Business: A Managerial Approach*** features the following:

- *Award winning capstone case:* **Charbucks v. Starbucks**
- *Flexercises:* Scalable and flexible exercises with blind case fact patterns/questions and templates for exercises, assessment, or class discussion.
- *Legal/Ethical Discussion points:* Encourages critical thinking about a particular topic of law and/or ethics of a legal solution.
- *Expanded coverage of contracts* by splitting Chapter 6, "Overview and Formation of Contracts," into two separate chapters Chapter 6 "Overview and Language of Contracts" and Chapter 7 "Contract Formation."
- *New and/or expanded coverage* of the following topics:
    - Affordable Care Act
    - Wall Street Reform Act
    - Regulation of Financial Markets
    - TARP Program
    - Antitrust law and Professional Sports
    - Trademark Dilution
- *Over 40 new cases added* including cutting edge cases such as: *Arizona v. U.S.* (Immigration); *U.S. v. Alvarez* (Stolen Valor Act); *Brown v. Entertainment Merchants Association* (Violent Video Games); *U.S. v. Bhagat* (Insider trading).
- Increased use of popular features including Key Points, Concept Summaries, Legal Speak.

Chapter 1

- Updated Learning Objectives
- Updated Introduction to Law section
- New example added to Purpose of Law section
- Updated Legal Decisions in a Business Environment section
- Updated Table 1.1
- Expanded Role of Counsel section
- Expanded Sources and Levels of American Law
- Expanded Constitutional Law section
- New Case 1.1 added
- Expanded Statutory Law section
- New Case 1.2 added
- New content added to Statutory Scheme and Legislative History section
- Content reworded and expanded in Common Law section
- Law versus Equity and Important Equitable Maxims subheadings moved to later in the chapter
- Expanded Uniform Model Laws section
- Updated Concept Summary for Sources of Law
- Expanded Criminal Law versus Civil Law section
- Expanded Substantive Law versus Procedural Law section
- Expanded Law versus Equity section
- Equitable Maxims content revised with new examples in the Law versus Equity section
- Three new Case Summaries added
- Key Terms added

Chapter 2

- Learning Objectives revised
- Expanded Nature of the Constitution section
- Separation of Powers subsection moved to subheading Article III—Judicial Powers
- Key Point added
- Expanded Amendments section
- Expanded Article I—Congressional Powers
- Expanded Article II—Executive Powers
- Expanded Article III—Judicial Powers
- New Key Point added
- New Case 2.2
- Updated Rational Basis section
- New Case 2.3
- New example added to Constitutional Restrictions on State Regulation of Commerce section
- New Case 2.4
- New Legal/Ethical Reflection and Discussion added
- Expanded Tax and Spend Power section
- Expanded Concept Summary for Structure and Nature of the Constitution: Federal Powers
- Expanded First Amendment section
- New Case 2.5
- Expanded Other Amendments section
- Expanded Fourteenth Amendment section
- Expanded Equal Protection section
- Updated Concept Summary for Constitutional Protections
- Case Summary 2.1 replaced
- Two new Case Summaries added
- Key Terms added

Chapter 3

- Updated State versus Federal Courts section
- Expanded State Trial Courts section
- Expanded State Appellate Courts section
- Updated U.S. District Courts section
- Table 3.1 data updated
- Figure 3.2
- Expanded How the Law Develops section
- Expanded Subject Matter Jurisdiction:
- Expanded In-State Defendants
- Expanded Out-of-State Defendants section
- Expanded Venue section
- New Case Summary

Chapter 4

- New Key Point added to Prelawsuit: Demand and Prelitigation Settlement Negotiations section
- Updated Statutes of Limitations with new Key Point added
- Expanded Answer section
- Expanded Depositions section
- Expanded Interrogatories section
- New Legal Speak added
- New Legal/Ethical Reflection and Discussion feature added
- Expanded Requests for Production section
- New Case 4.1
- Updated Self-Check
- Updated Trial section
- Updated Jury Selection and Opening section
- New Legal Speak added to Deliberations and Verdict section
- Expanded Posttrial Motions and Appeals section
- Expanded Concept Summary Stages of Litigation
- Expanded Expertise section
- Expanded Formal ADR section
- New Case 4.3
- Expanded Federal Arbitration Act section
- Expanded Mediation section

- Expanded Hybrid Forms of ADR section
- Two new Case Summaries added
- Key Terms added

Chapter 5

- Updated Learning Objective
- Expanded Business Ethics Defined section
- Expanded Primary and Secondary Stakeholders section
- Expanded Principles-Based Approach section
- New Self-Check added
- New Concept Summary added
- Expanded Values Management and Challenges to Business Ethics section
- Expanded Strategic Advantages of Values Management section
- New Case 5.1
- New Legal/Ethical Reflection and Discussion feature added
- Expanded Common Traits of Effective Ethical Programs in Business section
- New Case 5.2
- New Concept Summary added to Corporate Social Responsibility section
- New Key Terms added
- Two new Case Summaries added

Chapter 6

- Chapter 6 was split into two chapters.
- Learning Objectives
- Expanded Elements of a Contract section
- New Concept Summary added
- Categories of Contracts section
- New Key Point added
- Expanded Bilateral or Unilateral section
- Expanded Express, Implied or Quasi-Contracts section
- New Case 6.1
- Expanded Valid, Void, Voidable, or Unenforceable section
- New Legal Speak
- New Case 6.2
- New subheadings in Categories of Contracts section

- New Case 6.3
- Two new Self-Checks
- New Concept Summary added
- New Theory to Practice added
- New Manager's Challenge added
- All new Case Summaries
- Key Terms added

Chapter 7

- This is a chapter split from first edition's Chapter 6
- Learning Objectives
- New introduction
- Agreement Part 1: Offer section
- Advertisements as an Offer section
- Updated example in Option Contract section
- Expanded Death, Incapacity, or Destruction section
- Concept Summary title changed from Agreement to Mutual Assent and content added
- Expanded Silence as an Acceptance section
- Expanded Indefinite Terms section
- Expanded Consideration section
- Expanded Amount and Type of Consideration section
- New Legal/Ethical Reflection and Discussion feature added following Preexisting Duty Rule
- Expanded Bargained-for Exchange section
- Expanded Past Consideration section
- New Case 7.4
- Expanded Minors section
- New Key Point added
- Expanded Mental Incompetents section
- Expanded Concept Summary for Contract Formation
- Expanded Fraudulent Misrepresentation section
- New Self-Check, Fraud and Misrepresentation, added
- New Case 7.5
- Expanded Statute of Frauds section
- Expanded Enforceability of Contracts under the Statute of Frauds section
- Two new case Summaries added
- Answers added for new Self-Check content

Chapter 8

- Updated Learning Objectives
- Expanded Categories of Conditions section
- Update Substantial Performance section
- Expanded Mutual Consent section
- Expanded Impossibility section
- Expanded Impracticability section
- Expanded Concept Summary for Performance and Discharge
- Expanded Anticipatory Repudiation section
- New content added to Remedies section
- New Case 8.2
- Expanded Clean Hands and Tender of Performance section
- New Case 8.3
- New Key Terms added
- Two new Case Summaries added

Chapter 9

- Updated Learning Objectives
- Expanded Introduction to Article 2 of the UCC section
- Expanded UCC Coverage and Definitions section
- Expanded Merchant Transactions section
- Legal Speak added to Consideration section
- Expanded Risk of Loss section
- Expanded Goods Picked Up by the Buyer section
- Expanded Cure section
- New Case 9.3
- Updated Concept Summary for Performance of Sales Contracts
- Expanded Goods in Hands of Seller section
- Expanded Cover section
- Updated Concept Summary for Contracts for International Sales of Goods
- New Key Terms added
- Two new Case Summaries added

Chapter 10

- New Learning Objective Added
- Updated Categories of Torts section

- Updated Defamation section
- Updated Qualified Privilege section
- Expanded Fraudulent Misrepresentation section
- False Imprisonment section
- Updated Table 9.1
- Key Point added
- Expanded Intentional Torts section
- Expanded No General Duty to Act section
- Expanded *Res Ipsa Loquitur* section
- Expanded Closest-in-Proximity section
- Expanded Actual Damages section
- Expanded Defenses to Negligence Claims section
- Expanded Abnormally Dangerous Activities section
- Expanded Warranty section
- New Case 10.5
- Expanded Assumption of the Risk section
- New Legal/Ethical Reflection and Discussion feature added
- New Concept Summary added
- New Key Terms added
- Two new Case Summaries added

Chapter 11

- Updated Learning Objectives
- Updated Introduction
- Expanded Independent Contractor section
- New Case 11.1
- New Case 11.4
- New Case Summary added

Chapter 12

- Updated Introduction
- 40-Hour Workweek section
- Expanded Exempt Employees section
- Expanded Self-Check for Exempt versus Covered (Nonexempt) Employees
- Expanded Child Labor Laws section
- Expanded Health Care section
- Expanded Sudden Job Loss section
- Expanded Defenses to Workers' Compensation Claims section

- Expanded FMLA Scope and Coverage section
- Expanded Monitoring of E-Mail and Internet Usage section
- Expanded Telephone and Voice Mail section
- Expanded Americans with Disabilities Act Considerations section
- New Case 12.4
- Updated Labor Unions and Collective Bargaining section
- New Key Point added to Labor Management Relations Act section
- Expanded Random Efforts section
- Legal/Ethical Reflection and Discussion added to Strikes and Other Work Stoppages section
- Expanded Self-Check for Unfair Labor Practices
- New Key Terms added
- Two new Case Summaries added

Chapter 13

- Updated Introduction
- Expanded Definition, Source of Law, and Statutory Origins section
- Expanded Equal Employment Opportunity Commission (EEOC) section
- Expanded Disparate Treatment section
- Expanded Sexual Harassment section
- Expanded Age Discrimination in Employment Act section
- Expanded Substantially Younger Requirement section
- Expanded Reasonable Accommodations section
- Expanded Lilly Ledbetter Fair Pay Act of 2009 section
- Expanded Bona Fide Occupational Qualification section
- New Case 13.4
- Key Point added to Employee Misconduct section
- Expanded Affirmative Action Programs section
- Expanded Legality section
- New Key Terms added
- Two new Case Summaries added

Chapter 14

- Updated Learning Objectives
- New Case 14.1
- New Case 14.2
- Expanded Franchises section
- New Case Summary added

Chapter 15

- Updated chapter title
- Updated Learning Objectives
- Introduction Updated
- Expanded Liability section under Limited Liability Partnerships
- New Case 15.2
- Expanded Other Business Arrangements section
- Updated Theory to Practice section
- Updated Manager's Challenge section
- New Key Terms added
- Two new Case Summaries added

Chapter 16

- Updated Learning Objectives
- Expanded Preincorporation Activity: Liability of Promoters section
- New Case 16.1
- Expanded Piercing the Corporate Veil section
- New Case 16.4
- Expanded Taxation section
- Added new Case Summary

Chapter 17

- Updated Learning Objectives
- Expanded The Securities Act of 1933 section
- New Case 17.2
- Expanded Insider Trading section
- New Case 17.3
- Updated Dodd-Frank Act coverage
- Updated Troubled Assets Relief Program section

Chapter 18

- Learning Objectives
- Expanded Rulemaking section
- New Key Point in Executive Branch section

- Expanded Freedom of Information Act section
- New Case 18.4
- New Case Summary added

Chapter 19

- Updated Learning Objectives
- Expanded Citizen Suits section
- New Case 19.1
- Expanded *Deepwater Horizon* Oil Spill section
- New Case 19.2
- New Case Summary added

Chapter 20

- Updated Learning Objectives
- Expanded Vertical Restraints section
- Added new section on criminal penalties.
- Expanded Professional Sports section
- New Case 20.2
- Added new section on Curt Flood Act
- Added new section on FTC Act and Google investigation
- Price Discrimination section
- New Case Summary added

Chapter 21

- Updated Learning Objectives
- Expanded Secured Transactions section
- Expanded Debtor's Options section
- New Case 21.2
- New Case Summary added

Chapter 22

- Updated Learning Objectives
- Updated Introduction
- Warranties section
- New Case 22.2
- Added new section on bureau enforcement

- Updated Theory to Practice section
- New Case Summary added

Chapter 23

- Updated Learning Objectives
- Expanded Foreign Corrupt Practices Act section
- New Case 23.2
- New Case 23.4
- New Case Summary added

Chapter 24

- Updated Learning Objectives
- New Case 24.1
- New Case 24.3
- New Case Summary added

Chapter 25

- Updated Learning Objectives
- Introduction Updated
- Added new sections on definitions and trade dress
- Expanded Trademarks as a Business Assets section
- Updated content in Source of Law section
- Expanded Secondary Meaning section
- Added new section: Policing the Mark
- Expanded Trademark Application section
- New Case 25.3
- Expanded Patents section

Chapter 26

- Learning Objectives
- Expanded U.N. Convention on Contracts for the International Sale of Goods section
- New Case 26.3
- New Case Summary added

brief table of contents

table of contents

\ UNIT THREE
Regulation in the Workplace

\ UNIT FOUR
Business Entities, Securities Regulation, and Corporate Governance

CHAPTER 17   Regulation of Securities, Corporate Governance, and Financial Markets   474

Fundamentals of the Legal Environment of Business

1 CHAPTER

Legal Foundations

learning objectives

After studying this chapter, students who have mastered the material will be able to:

1-1 Understand the broad definition and origins of law.

1-2 List and explain the purposes of law.

1-3 Explain the importance and benefits of legal awareness for business owners and managers in creating strategy and adding value to a company.

1-4 Articulate the role of counsel in legal decision making in a business context.

1-5 Recognize, explain, and give examples of sources of American law.

1-6 Understand the legal doctrine of stare decisis.

1-7 Classify the law into several broad categories.

1-8 Differentiate between the concepts of law and equity.

1-9 Identify and apply important equitable maxims.

ndertaking the study of law may seem over-whelming. Legal doctrines and rules can be complex and difficult to navigate. Yet the law impacts many facets of our daily life both at home and at work. This textbook is designed to make studying the law more *manageable* by examining legal issues that are most commonly encountered in the business environment. In fact, studies have shown that business owners and managers who have a high level of legal insight create *value* for their business and recognize legal challenges as business planning opportunities. This legal awareness may be gained only by understanding important legal doctrines and processes. Applying this knowledge allows managers to limit risk and incorporate the law into their business strategies. This chapter introduces students to the foundations of the law and explains why the application of legal doctrines is an important part of the business environment. Specifically, in this chapter students will learn:

- How legal issues impact business planning and strategy.
- The foundations, definitions, and scope of various primary and secondary sources of law.
- Categories of law.

INTRODUCTION TO LAW LO 1-1

What Is Law?

The term **law** has been defined in a variety of ways throughout recorded history. A generally accepted generic definition of the law is a *body of rules of action or conduct prescribed by controlling authority and having legal binding force.*[1] When studying law in any context, it is important to think of the law in broad terms. While many equate the law with stacks of neatly bound volumes of codes in a library, this is only one component of a much larger body of law. Law may be set down in a written code as prescribed by an elected legislative body, but also takes the form of judicial decisions and actions of government agencies. While there are many sources of American law, the common characteristic of the current state of law is that it creates *duties, obligations,* and *rights* that reflect accepted views of a given society. Much of the origins of the law dealt with issues related to ownership of property, but modern legal doctrines have evolved into a relatively complex system of principles and protections. Most importantly, the law also provides a mechanism to resolve disputes arising from those duties and rights and allows parties to enforce promises in a court of law. Law is often classified by subject matter so that one refers to certain rules regarding agreements as *contract law* or certain laws that regulate certain rights of employees as *employment law*.

Jurisprudence

Jurisprudence, roughly defined as the science and philosophy of law, defines several schools of

[1] *Black's Law Dictionary.*

thought that are used to describe various approaches to the appropriate function of law and how legal doctrines should be developed and applied. Most schools of jurisprudential thought center on how legal rights are recognized. *Natural law* proponents argue that a system of moral values, which are inherent in humankind, form the basis for all law and those certain principles are of a *higher* authority than national laws (laws defined by a governing body).[2] *Positivists* believe in a specific set of agreed-upon laws that are enforced *uniformly* and strictly unless the law is changed expressly via the government. They reject the natural law notion of a higher authority that surpasses national law. *Legal realism* began to take shape in the United States after World War I and is based on the concept that law is a *social institution* that should be used to promote fairness by taking into account social and economic realities when arriving at legal conclusions. Perhaps the most dramatic example of the legal realism school of thought in practice was the U.S. Supreme Court's formal recognition during the civil rights era of its role in achieving equality for all Americans by interpreting the Constitution as protecting certain rights that courts had previously never recognized.

LO 1-2   Purposes of Law

Although the most visible function of the law on a day-to-day basis is to provide for some system of order that defines crimes and levies punishment for violation of the crimes, there are many other purposes of recognizing a uniform system of laws. The origins of recorded law were initially a collection of rules of powerful tribal chieftains intended to perpetuate domination and power of their authority with little consideration for rights of individuals. However, over the better part of three millennia, the purpose of law evolved substantially into ensuring consistency and fairness. In the United States, lawmakers have increasingly embraced legal mechanisms, such as antidiscrimination laws, to help promote equality and justice in society and especially in education and in the workplace. The law also sets out a system for resolving disputes by providing a basis for deciding the legal interests and rights of the parties. For purposes of studying the impact of law on business, it is important to recognize that the law also serves as an important catalyst for commerce by promoting *good faith dealing* among merchants and consumers and giving some degree of *reliability* that can be considered in business planning and commercial transactions.

For example, assume Clothing Manufacturing Corporation (CMC) orders 100 bales of wool from Woolpack, Inc., in anticipation of a large order for winter clothing from retail outlets. The laws that govern the various transactions that arise from the CMC-Woolpack agreement set a standard of good faith and provide both parties the confidence necessary to set the business process in motion (e.g., financial, operations, marketing). Moreover, the merchants may rely on the courts if either party needs to recoup any losses resulting from the other party's unlawful actions.

Language of the Law

In order to maximize the value of interaction between business owners/managers and attorneys, a basic understanding of legal terminology is useful. Students studying business law face the task of learning legal syntax at the same time as they learn how to apply the legal doctrines in a business context. This is analogous to learning a complicated subject matter in a foreign language, yet it is manageable with careful study. Legal terms are sometimes referred to as *jargon* or *legalese,* but having a working knowledge of some common legal terminology is an important step to mastering the material. Although much of the language of the law has Latin roots, the terminology is primarily a combination of Latin, early and

connect
| BUSINESS LAW

Visit Connect for links to several useful online law dictionaries.

---

[2]Aristotle was perhaps the most famous advocate of the natural law theory.

modern English, and French. The vocabulary of American law is drawn from the various cultures and events that shaped American history. To facilitate your understanding of legal expression, important legal terms are highlighted throughout the text, summarized at the end of each chapter, and also featured alphabetically in the glossary. The authoritative source for legal terms is ***Black's Law Dictionary,*** first published in 1891. There are also several websites that provide definitions and examples for legal terms.

LEGAL DECISIONS IN A BUSINESS ENVIRONMENT: THEORY TO PRACTICE

LO 1-3

While an in-depth understanding of the various areas of law is a vast undertaking requiring years of intensive study, the primary objective of this textbook is to cover a variety of legal topics that are most commonly encountered in the business environment. However, developing legal insight by understanding the fundamentals of legal theory and how they may impact business is only a first step in learning how legal decisions should be made in a business context. The second step involves learning to *apply* legal theories in practice and recognizing that having legal awareness may present opportunities for proactive business planning, empowering business owners and managers to limit liability, gain a competitive edge, and add value to the business. Relying exclusively on attorneys to drive the legal decision-making process in the context of business both is expensive and involves the significant risk that a decision will be made without sufficient knowledge of business operations, objectives, and current economic realities. Instead, studies and research indicate that when managers work *cooperatively* with their attorney, the results contribute to better strategic business decisions that add value to the business. For example,

> **KEY** POINT
> Learning to apply legal awareness in practice involves recognizing opportunities for proactive business planning, limiting liability, gaining a competitive edge, and adding value to the business.

Management teams with legal insight add value to their company by limiting liability and identifying opportunities.

recognizing that having a code of conduct for employees and creating a standardized procedure for hiring new employees are issues that a good manager should view as essential, attorneys regularly play a part in ensuring compliance with applicable federal, state, and local laws. Later in this chapter, we will discuss a mechanism that business owners and managers may use to spot legal issues, apply an appropriate analysis, decide on alternative solutions, and plan a legal and ethical course of action that limits liability and maximizes business opportunities.

LO 1-4 ## Legal Insight and Business Strategy

To understand the way various areas of the law impact business and the importance of having legal insight in a business context, let's examine a typical business planning process. Suppose that the management team at Indiana Printing Company (IPC) is planning to expand its existing business into new markets. The team considers several options and will have to have a sufficient understanding of the legal risks and business opportunities associated with each option. Table 1.1 sets out possible options for IPC's expansion and some of the potential legal impacts for each option.

The list of legal issues in Table 1.1 is meant to be illustrative and not exhaustive. Indeed, issues regarding negligence, criminal law, administrative law, bankruptcy, consumer protection, agency, and many others may present themselves before, during, or after the transaction is complete.

Role of Counsel

Although this textbook emphasizes understanding legal issues in the context of business decision making, this is not to suggest that an attorney's role in this process is diminished—-quite the opposite. The content, features, and exercises contained in this textbook emphasize that working closely with a business attorney results in business opportunities, reduced costs, and limitation of risk and liability. Attorneys, particularly in a business context, may also be referred to as **counsel.** Business owners and managers work with counsel in one of two formats. For larger companies or companies that have extraordinary regulatory burdens (such as complying with securities or patent laws), counsel may very well be a part of the executive or midlevel management team. These attorneys are referred to as *in-house counsel* and usually have the title "general counsel" at the executive management level (e.g., vice president and general counsel). Depending on the size and complexity of the company, the general counsel may also supervise one or more attorneys, usually with the title "associate counsel." Additionally, the general counsel may also serve as a corporate officer of the company, called the secretary, who is responsible for record keeping and complying with notice and voting requirements for the board of directors.[3] The general counsel is also responsible for selecting and supervising lawyers from outside law firms when a particular field of expertise is needed, such as a trial lawyer (also called a *litigator*).

The majority of companies, however, rely on attorneys employed by *law firms* for their legal needs. These attorneys devote a significant amount of their professional time to advising businesses on issues such as formation, governance, labor and employment laws, regulatory agency compliance, legal transactions (such as an acquisition), intellectual property (such as trademarks or patents), and other legal issues important to business operations. These attorneys (known as *business lawyers* or *corporate lawyers*) rarely if ever appear in court or perform other tasks that are associated with lawyers in the minds of the general public. Indeed, the law has become increasingly complex and specialized. Therefore, it is not unusual that more than one attorney's advice is needed when facing a significant

Legal **Speak** ›))
Retainer Fee Some law firms handle certain legal matters on a retainer-fee basis. Although the practice is becoming increasingly rare, a retainer fee is an advanced payment by a client that ensures the availability of an attorney to handle general legal matters. If a business owner or manager has legal questions or requires representation, the attorney's charges are deducted from the retainer fee. While costs exceeding the retainer are due from the client, any unused retainer-fee balance is either rolled over into the next billing cycle or forfeited according to the initial fee agreement.

---

[3]The legal structure of corporations and other business entities is discussed in detail in Unit Three.

TABLE 1.1 Expansion Options and Potential Legal Impacts

Option	Area of Law	Potential Legal Impact
Expansion through acquisition of another company. One common way to expand is to purchase an existing business entity through an acquisition of assets or of stock.	■ Contracts	■ Governs negotiations and agreements for the acquisition.
	■ Property/environmental	■ If the acquisition involves any land purchase, real estate law (such as zoning) and environmental law.
	■ Employment and labor	■ The hiring of new employees by IPC (even former employees of the target company) or the layoff of IPC or target-company employees must be done in conformance with state and federal employment and labor laws.
	■ Tax	■ The transaction may create tax liability under local, state, and/or federal laws.
	■ Antitrust	■ If the acquisition results in IPC's gaining too much market share, federal antitrust laws must be considered and preacquisition approvals may be needed from the government.
Expansion through introducing and aggressively marketing a new product line. Expanding through marketing of a new product line generally involves raising sufficient capital to properly develop, manufacture, and go to market.	■ Securities law	■ Any solicitation by IPC to sell shares of its business to the public is highly regulated by securities laws.
	■ Intellectual property	■ In order to maintain its competitive edge, IPC will need to put measures in place to help guarantee protection of ideas and processes by trade secret law; the final design may be protected by patent law.
	■ Administrative law	■ Federal regulatory agencies have guidelines for advertising and labeling of products.
Expansion through aggressive integration of a highly interactive website and e-marketing campaigns including international markets. In light of the growth in e-commerce, some companies find this to be the most cost-efficient method of expansion.	■ Jurisdiction	■ Website expansion may result in IPC's being subject to the jurisdiction of more out-of-state courts than did the previous business model.
	■ International law	■ IPC may be subject to international agreements and treaties regarding sales and intellectual property.

legal issue such as an employment discrimination lawsuit or when obtaining financing for a corporation from the general public through the sale of stock. Law firms vary greatly in size, from those that have one or just a few lawyers in a local or regional practice to firms that have hundreds of lawyers spread throughout the globe. In a business context, law firms bill clients based on an hourly rate that is tied to an individual lawyer's experience, her reputation in the field, and the market being served (with large cities that are the center of business operations having higher rates).

What advice might Adams seek from an attorney in the following situations?

1. Adams sells custom-designed T-shirts from his basement apartment. The business begins to turn a profit.

2. Adams wants to expand his T-shirt business by renting a kiosk in a local mall and hiring Baker.

3. Adams wants to obtain trademark protection for his products.

4. Baker offers Adams $50,000 to purchase the T-shirt business's name and assets.

Answers to this Self-Check are provided at the end of the chapter.

LO 1-5   SOURCES AND LEVELS OF AMERICAN LAW

American law is composed of a unique blend from various sources based on U.S. historical roots. Fundamentally, much of American law is derived from English legal doctrines that came with the English settlers of the colonies. In the West and Southwest, land once controlled by Mexico, there are strong Spanish influences, while in Louisiana, once French territory, French civil law roots are evident. Modern law in the United States regulating businesses and individuals is generally a combination of **constitutional law, statutory law, common law,** and **administrative** (regulatory) **law** at the federal, state, and local levels. These sources of law are known as *primary sources* of law and may sometimes work in conjunction with one another or independently. For example, law related to the protection of trade secrets[4] is composed from a variety of sources of law. Perhaps the most famous and profitable example of a trade secret is the recipe and process for making Coca-Cola. While most states have specific trade secret statutes that give legal recourse to a party who has suffered a loss as a result of the unlawful use of trade secrets, some do not. Does this mean that the company that owns the Coca-Cola recipe has no legal recourse against someone who steals its trade secret in those states where no *specific statutes* exist? The answer is no because even absent a specific statute, the law still provides the damaged party some recourse against the violator. This recourse is provided court case history (called *common law,* discussed later) that provides guidance to the trial courts deciding trade secret disputes. Even in states that *do* have statutes related to trade secret protection, there is case law that helps courts apply the statute consistently.

Constitutional Law

Legal **Speak** ›))
Enumerated Powers Article I, Section 8, of the U.S. Constitution names 17 specific powers granted to the federal government. These are known as *enumerated powers.*

Constitutional law is the foundation for all other law in the United States and is the supreme law of the land. It functions in tandem with other sources of law in three broad areas: (1) establishing a *structure* for federal and state governments (including qualifications of certain offices and positions), setting rules for amending the constitution, and granting specific *enumerated powers* to the different branches of government; (2) establishing the concept of *federalism,* allowing the federal and state governments shared powers; and (3) establishing individual *civil rights* and providing *procedural protections* for U.S. citizens from wrongful government actions.

Constitutional law is different from other sources of law primarily in terms of *permanence* and *preemption.* In terms of permanence, a constitution is thought to reflect the basic principles of a particular society and should be amended only in extraordinary cases and only when a majority of its constituents agree over a certain period of time. Preemption in

---

[4]Trade secret law, which is covered in detail in Chapter 25, "Intellectual Property," is the legal protection of certain confidential business information.

this context means that constitutional law is supreme over all other sources of law such as federal and state statutes, treaties, and common law. The Constitution further grants federal law supremacy over conflicting state law.

Constitutional law exists at both the federal and state levels because each state has its own constitution that is the highest source of law within the state's borders (so long as it is not inconsistent with federal law). States tend to amend their constitutions more frequently than is the case with the U.S. Constitution. Constitutional issues that impact businesses include Congress's powers to regulate interstate commerce; creation of legal protections for intellectual property (such as patents and copyrights); protection of certain forms of commercial speech from unwarranted government regulation; limitations on a state's authority to tax products and services in commerce; and powers of the executive, legislative, and judicial branches to regulate business activity.

In Case 1.1, the U.S. Supreme Court resolves a conflict between federal and state law by applying constitutional preemption. Preemption and other aspects of constitutional law are discussed in detail in Chapter 2, "Business and the Constitution."

Statutory Law

Statutes are written laws that are passed by the federal or a state legislature and are either approved or rejected by the executive branch. The U.S. Congress is the exclusive legislative body for the passage of federal law. When Congress is drafting a federal statute, but has not yet passed it or had the executive's concurrence, it is known as a *bill*. On the *federal level,* the president is the executive and may sign a bill into law (thereby adopting it as a statute), or the president may veto (reject) the bill subject to the Congress's right to override the veto and make the bill into a statute with a two-thirds majority vote.

At the *state level,* the state legislature (called by different names in different states, such as the *General Assembly*) passes statutes that regulate such areas as motor vehicle laws, business corporation and partnership laws, and other traditional state matters. The governor (as executive) has authority to sign a state bill into law or to exercise other rights as laid out in the state constitution. Written laws at the *local* level are called **ordinances** (sometimes referred to as *local regulations*). Ordinances generally regulate issues such as zoning (regulating where certain businesses, such as factories, may be located) or impose health and safety regulations on local merchants such as restaurants.

Visit Connect to see an example of (1) a federal statute (Employment Discrimination), (2) a state statute (Pennsylvania Business Corporation Law), and (3) a local zoning ordinance.

KEY POINT

Clear and unambiguous language does not mean that everyone who reads the statute will understand it perfectly. For example, the Internal Revenue Code is a federal statute that to the average person may be extremely confusing; however, it makes sense to a person with a background in accounting.

Interpreting Statutes When interpreting statutes, courts initially apply the **plain meaning rule.** This means that if the words in the statute have clear and widely understood meanings, the court applies the statute in accordance with the rule. However, more complex statutes require further analysis, and courts look to two sources for guidance. The structure of the statute itself generally provides some indication of how the legislature intended it to be applied. The structure of the statute and the format of its mandates in a law are referred as its **statutory scheme.** When interpreting statutes, courts also look to the records kept by the legislature, including the debates, committee and conference reports, and legislative findings of fact. These records are known as the statute's **legislative history** and may provide some indication of the intent of the legislative body that passed the statute. For example, in Chapter 2, "Business and the Constitution," we discuss the U.S.

FACT SUMMARY In 2010, the State of Arizona passed the Support Our Law Enforcement and Safe Neighborhoods Act to address problems that the legislature contended were being created by the large number of unlawful immigrants living and working within the state's borders. Among other provisions, the law created state immigration offenses and expanded the authority of local police to enforce immigration laws by requiring that individuals who were lawfully detained by the police (e.g., a traffic stop) verify their citizenship. The law also provided criminal penalties for unauthorized aliens who sought or engaged in work within Arizona. The U.S. Department of Justice filed suit against Arizona seeking to invalidate the law on the basis that federal immigration statutes precluded individual states from enacting their own immigration laws. Arizona argued that weak and uneven enforcement of federal immigration laws necessitated state regulation and that the state law did not conflict with the federal law. The U.S. court of appeals ruled in favor of the United States, and the state of Arizona appealed to the U.S. Supreme Court.

SYNOPSIS OF DECISION AND OPINION The U.S. Supreme Court struck down the Arizona statute as unconstitutional. The Court ruled that the Arizona statute conflicted with the existing federal law and therefore the state statute is preempted and constitutionally unenforceable. The Court reasoned that (1) immigration is a matter within the purview of the federal government and (2) when the federal government creates rules and sanctions with a clear intent to preclude state action, courts will not enforce any state action that conflicts with established federal mandates.

WORDS OF THE COURT: Preemption of a State Statute "Federalism, central to the constitutional design, adopts the principle that both the National and State Governments have elements of sovereignty the other is bound to respect. The Supremacy Clause provides a clear rule that federal law 'shall be the supreme Law of the Land; and the Judges in every State shall be bound thereby, any Thing in the Constitution or Laws of any State to the Contrary notwithstanding.' Art. VI, cl. 2. Under this principle, Congress has the power to preempt state law. . . . State law must also give way to federal law in at least two other circumstances. First, States are precluded from regulating conduct in a field that Congress has determined must be regulated by its exclusive governance. Intent can be inferred from a framework of regulation 'so pervasive . . . that Congress left no room for the States to supplement it' or where a federal interest is so dominant that the federal system will be assumed to preclude enforcement of state laws on the same subject. Second, state laws are preempted when they conflict with federal law, including when they stand 'as an obstacle to the accomplishment and execution of the full purposes and objectives of Congress.'"

Case Questions

1. If a federal law or policy is perceived as weak or ineffective, should a state have the right to legislate in that area without federal intervention?

2. Arizona's law affected Arizona alone and was designed to help Arizona citizens regarding, among other issues, increased employment and reduction of crime. At what point should the federal government have the right to challenge such a state law?

3. Since a challenge based on preemption was known to be an issue from the onset of this statute's consideration, how might Arizona have better approached the solutions to its illegal immigration problem?

Supreme Court's ruling on the constitutionality of the Patient Protection and Affordable Care Act (commonly referred to as "Obamacare").[5] The act includes an individual mandate requiring individuals to be covered by health insurance by a certain date or face a penalty. The court analyzed the application of the mandate from multiple points of view and, using the act's statutory scheme and legislative history, it validated the individual mandate's constitutionality based on its application as a tax rather than as a penalty.

---

[5]26 U.S.C. § 5000A.

Finding Statutory Law The official publication of federal statutory law is the United States Code (U.S.C.), which arranges all existing federal laws in a system organized by title and divided into chapters and sections. The legal community uses a special format, known as a **citation,** to express where a statutory law can be found. You'll note citations in the footnotes of each chapter of this text that identify a specific reference for the statutes being covered in the chapter. For example, later in this textbook, students will study a federal law called the Fair Labor Standards Act (also known, in part, as the "minimum wage" law) in detail. The citation for the law (listed in the footnote) is 29 U.S.C. § 201. This indicates that in order to find the Fair Labor Standards Act, we need to consult Title 29 of the United States Code and turn to section (abbreviated § in singular or §§ in plural) 201 for the first chapter of the statute. Although attorneys and judges often use specialized software and legal research services to find and understand statutes, an increasing amount of information about statutory resources and statutes themselves is available online for free. Note also that Appendix to Chapter 1 ("A Business Student's Guide to Understanding Cases and Finding the Law") provides information on using the Internet to find and apply statutory law.

State statutes have the same fundamental format and purpose as the U.S.C., but the actual term used to refer to state statutes varies from state to state. *Codes* or *consolidated statutes* are two common terms.

Commercial services also sell print and online versions of federal and state statutes in a unique format

The U.S. Congress is the exclusive legislative body for the passage of federal law.

that includes annotations and short comments used to interpret the statutes correctly. Attorneys use these commercial services in performing legal research important to properly counseling their clients on the law.

Common Law

Common law is essentially law made by the courts. Although lawmaking is primarily the responsibility of state and federal legislatures, courts must fill in the gaps when a controversy arises that is not covered under existing law. Consider, for example, the impact of the Internet on the development of law. Settled laws related to contracts, jurisdiction, trespass, obscenity, and many other areas had to be reconsidered in light of the widespread use of the Internet. Courts had to fill in the gaps to apply existing law to Internet use until the legislature could respond with statutory law aimed at resolving cyber-related disputes.

The U.S. system of common law is deep-seated in British common law that developed over several centuries, beginning around 1066 when the Norman kings established uniform methods for resolving (mostly land) disputes in England. The largest industrialized nations using the common law in some form include the United States, the United Kingdom, Canada, Australia, and generally the former colonies of Britain. Other countries, such as Japan and France, use a *civil law* system that requires courts to adhere to a strict interpretation of a legislatively established code or regulation. While the general notion of precedent is recognized

Henry II established English common law courts, called "King's Bench" courts, around 1178.

by civil law, its role is substantially reduced in a civil law system. The power of courts to establish law in matters not specifically addressed by the code is very limited in civil law countries. Legal systems and sources of law of foreign countries are covered in Chapter 26, "International Law and Global Commerce."

Stare Decisis and Precedent   LO 1-6

The common law also includes the application of past judicial decisions to contemporary cases. The **doctrine of stare decisis,** one of the most important concepts in American law, is the principle that similar cases with similar facts and issues should have the same judicial outcome. This allows individuals and businesses to have some degree of confidence that the law will remain reasonably constant from year to year and court to court.

The notion of applying the law of previous cases to current cases with substantially similar circumstances is called **precedent.** Precedent is created when an appellate court renders a decision, known as the *holding* of the case, absent a controlling statute. Should a similar fact situation later occur, all *lower courts,* such as trial courts, are bound to follow the appellate court's decision as long as no new statutory law has been enacted. This provides an element of predictability for lawyers and litigants when they are contemplating legal and business decisions and actions.

When state law is examined, there is nothing common about the common law. Precedent established in one state's court will have no bearing on the courts of other states. A state court facing a case of first impression might look to precedent created in other states for insight; however, nothing requires their adherence to the foreign states' decisions. Note that the court system and how appellate courts form precedent is covered in detail in Chapter 3, "The American Judicial System, Jurisdiction, and Venue."

Stare Decisis and Business

To understand the importance of stare decisis in the business environment, consider the opportunities for business planning that may benefit the company by understanding the legal impact of a certain course of action. Suppose that Jackson is a manager in charge of managing the acquisition of certain assets from another company. One important aspect of such a transaction is how the acquisition will be *taxed.* If Jackson's company enters into an agreement with Main Street Industries (MSI) to acquire certain assets from MSI, how will the transaction be treated by the Internal Revenue Service (IRS)?[6] This, of course, is a very important fact in determining the price of the transaction and planning for allocation of the tax burden between buyer and seller. How can the parties structure the transaction to be sure that the taxation represents the parties' intent? Ultimately, because stare decisis is a deeply rooted concept that applies to all laws, Jackson need only learn how the IRS has treated similar transactions in the past and how courts have ruled on the IRS's interpretation and actions in applying the law. If a certain transaction has been taxed in a certain way

[6]The IRS is the federal government's tax agency.

in the past, the doctrine of stare decisis dictates that if Jackson structures her transaction in a similar fashion, her transaction will be taxed in the same way. With sufficient legal certainty about the taxation impact, the parties may now proceed with negotiations and structure a mutually acceptable agreement. However, strict adherence to precedent and the doctrine of stare decisis has a significant drawback: It doesn't allow for evolving societal standards of behavior or expectations. On a case-by-case basis, courts sometimes justify departing from precedent on the basis that technological or societal changes render a particular precedent unworkable. In Landmark Case 1.2, a state appellate court considered the question of when to abandon standing precedent.

Administrative Law

While statutory law stems from the authority of the legislature and common law is derived from the courts, administrative law is the source of law that authorizes the exercise of authority by *executive branch* agencies and *independent* government agencies. Members of the House and Senate can't be experts on all things and can't be expected to research the details of all matters before Congress. For efficiency, Congress creates administrative agencies to focus on particular areas, much like a large company creates departments and committees to streamline decision making. Federal administrative law is largely authorized by statutes and the Constitution, and rules for applying the law are articulated and carried out by *administrative agencies.* Pursuant to congressional mandates, these agencies are empowered to administer the details of federal statutes and have broad powers to impose regulations, make policy, and enforce the law in their designated area of jurisdiction. State legislatures also are empowered to create administrative agencies to address state matters. For example, the U.S. Environmental Protection Agency (EPA) is charged with drafting regulations that carry out the broad mandates set by Congress in the Clean Air Act (among many others) to reduce air pollution. The EPA sets regulations and imposes restrictions on some industries to help accomplish that goal. The EPA is also empowered to enforce those regulations. Courts are highly deferential to agency decisions involving how and when an agency enforces a regulation. Detailed coverage of this source of law and administrative agencies is featured in Chapter 18, "Administrative Law."

Some of the specific types of laws that impact business owners and managers and are covered in this textbook are featured in Table 1.2.

TABLE 1.2 Laws That Impact Business

Type of Law	Source(s)	Level(s)
Negligence (tort)	Statutory and common law	Primarily state
Employment discrimination	Primarily statutory and administrative	Primarily state and federal, some local
Copyright	Statutory and administrative	Federal
Contracts for sale of goods	Statutory	State
Contracts for services	Primarily common law	State
Bankruptcy	Statutory and administrative	Federal
Securities law (selling company stock to the public)	Statutory and administrative	Federal and state
Zoning ordinances	Statutory	Local
Taxes	Statutory and administrative	Federal, state, and local

FACT SUMMARY   Flagiello, a patient at Pennsylvania Hospital, sued the hospital, claiming it was negligent in maintaining certain conditions on hospital property that resulted in her injuring her ankle. The ankle injury was unrelated to the original reason for Flagiello's admission to the hospital. A Pennsylvania state trial court dismissed the lawsuit without trial because established state common law clearly exempted charitable institutions, such as the Pennsylvania Hospital, from any liability related to their negligence (a concept called the *charitable immunity doctrine*). Flagiello appealed on the basis that (1) she was a paying patient and (2) the charitable immunity doctrine was outdated given the fact that most charity hospitals now received funding from state and local governments.

SYNOPSIS OF DECISION AND OPINION   The Pennsylvania Supreme Court ruled in favor of Flagiello. Although the court acknowledged the important role of stare decisis, it also pointed out that the doctrine is not intended to apply when societal norms dictate otherwise. In this case, the court noted that other states had abandoned the charitable immunity doctrine as no longer necessary and that public benefit and fairness demanded that injured parties who are entitled to recover for their losses be allowed to pursue a negligence action against a charitable institution.

WORDS OF THE COURT: Limits of Stare Decisis   "Stare decisis channels the law. It erects lighthouses and [flies] the signals of safety. The ships of jurisprudence must follow that well-defined channel which, over the years, has been proved to be secure and trustworthy. But it would not comport with wisdom to insist that, should shoals rise in a heretofore safe course and rocks emerge to encumber the passage, the ship should nonetheless pursue the original course, merely because it presented no hazard in the past. The principle of stare decisis does not demand that we follow precedents which shipwreck justice.

"Stare decisis is not an iron mold into which every utterance by a court, regardless of circumstances, parties, economic barometer and sociological climate, must be poured, and, where, like wet concrete, it must acquire an unyielding rigidity which nothing later can change."

Case Questions

1. If Flagiello had been a burglar who was breaking into the medical supply cabinet instead of a patient when she injured her ankle, would the court have been willing to abandon the charitable immunity doctrine? Why or why not?

2. Does this case mean that stare decisis may be discarded whenever a judge perceives that following precedent will "shipwreck justice"?

Legal Speak‹))
Case of First Impression A case with issues that have never been litigated before in the court hearing it.

Primary sources of law are applied consistent with a hierarchy in which one source may trump another source if the two sources conflict. This is preemption. For example, think about where you're seated at this moment. What law applies to you? You're subject to the U.S. Constitution, U.S. treaties, federal statutory and administrative law, and federal common law. You're also in a state, so state constitutional, statutory, administrative, and common law apply to you. County, city, township, and other local laws might also apply. There is certainly a potential for conflict. Figure 1.1 illustrates the hierarchy of primary sources of federal and state law.

LO 1-5   ## SECONDARY SOURCES OF LAW

When interpreting statutory law or applying judicially created law, courts also look to **secondary sources** of law. In the business context, the most important secondary sources of law are (1) the *Restatements of the Law,* a collection of uniform legal principles focused in a particular area of traditional state law, and (2) various sets of **model state statutes** drafted by legal experts as a model for state legislatures to adopt in their individual jurisdictions. The purpose behind these secondary sources of law is to increase the level of uniformity and fairness across courts in all 50 states. The secondary sources of law also feature commentary and examples to help guide courts in applying the law. However, secondary sources of law have *no independent authority* or legally binding

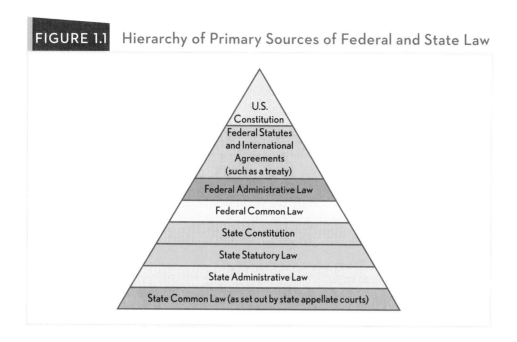

FIGURE 1.1 Hierarchy of Primary Sources of Federal and State Law

U.S. Constitution

Federal Statutes and International Agreements (such as a treaty)

Federal Administrative Law

Federal Common Law

State Constitution

State Statutory Law

State Administrative Law

State Common Law (as set out by state appellate courts)

effect. State legislatures and courts are free to adopt all, adopt part of, or reject secondary sources of law.

Uniform Model Laws

In 1892, the National Conference of Commissioners on Uniform State Laws (NCCUSL) was formed by the American Bar Association for the purpose of establishing uniform standards in areas of the law where national interests would be achieved through use of uniform laws. Imagine that a business in Delaware purchases goods from a seller in New York. While these goods are being shipped by truck on an independent trucking company, they are destroyed in an accident in New Jersey. Which state's law applies? Without a uniform set of laws, businesses would be required to know and apply the law in all 50 states and would be overwhelmed by excessive litigation. Uniform laws solve many of such problems.

The primary focus of the model laws was commerce, and the NCCUSL drafted the Uniform Commercial Code (UCC), which has been adopted in some form by every state except Louisiana. The UCC provides a comprehensive set of rules and principles intended to increase reliability and predictability in business transactions. Although this textbook refers to several different sections of the UCC, extensive coverage is given to Article 2 of the UCC, which governs contracts for the sale of goods. The NCCUSL also created several uniform codes related to the formation and structure of business entities, such as the Uniform Partnership Act and the Model Business Corporation Act. The NCCUSL will from time to time revise these model acts, and the new model laws are referred to, for example, as the *Revised* Uniform Partnership Act.

Restatements of the Law

In the 1920s, the American Law Institute (ALI) was formed to reduce the undue complexity and growing uncertainty of judicial decisions by systematically publishing a *statement* of common law legal principles and rules in a given area of the law, such as torts. The ALI is composed of law professors, judges, and lawyers, and they developed the *Restatements of the Law* in various legal categories. Explanatory notes and applicable examples accompany the Restatements. Restatements are continuously revised, and when the ALI publishes a revision, the new version is referred to by the name and edition; thus, the second edition of the contracts Restatements is called *Restatements (Second) of Contracts.* The areas covered by the Restatements that are included in this textbook are contracts, property, agency, torts, and foreign relations law.

CONCEPT SUMMARY Sources of Law

Primary:

- Primary sources of law include constitutional law, statutory law, administrative law, and common law at both the federal and state levels.
- Constitutions have two primary functions: (1) to prescribe the basic structure and powers of a particular government body and (2) to protect certain rights of individuals and businesses from government encroachment.
- Statutory law is created by a legislative body and approved or disapproved by the executive branch.
- When interpreting statutes, courts often look to two sources for guidance: (1) the structure of the statute itself, called the *statutory scheme,* and (2) the records of the legislative history behind the statute.
- The official publication of federal statutory law is the United States Code (U.S.C.).
- Common law is law made by appellate courts and is based on the fundamentals of previous cases that had similar facts.
- Appellate courts create precedent, and under the doctrine of stare decisis, lower courts apply the precedent to new cases with similar facts.
- Precedent created in a state applies only in that state and has no binding authority in any other state.
- Administrative law is the source of law that regulates the exercise of authority by administrative agencies.
- Pursuant to congressional mandates, administrative agencies are empowered to administer the details of federal statutes and have broad powers to impose regulations, make policy, and enforce the law in their designated area of jurisdiction.

Secondary:

- Secondary sources of law include the *Restatements of the Law* and sets of model statutes such as the Uniform Commercial Code (UCC).
- Secondary sources have no independent authority, nor are they legally binding.
- The *Restatements of the Law* are collections of uniform legal principles in a specific area of law that are designed to reduce the complexity of judicial decisions.
- Model statutes are drafted by legal experts, in hopes that they will be used or adopted by state legislatures so as to provide uniformity in laws between the states.

 Self-Check Sources of Law

What is/are the source(s) and level(s) of law that govern the following business transactions?

1. American Hardware Supply enters into an agreement with a retail home improvement chain to supply the chain with certain inventory.
2. Whitney wishes to apply for a patent for a device he invented.
3. Marshall is considering raising money for his business by selling stock in the company.

4. Bio-Tech Inc. ran out of cash and cannot pay its debts as they come due. Management seeks protection from creditors.

5. Barnum wishes to bring his famous horse show into town and plans to stage it in a residential area of the city.

Answers to this Self-Check are provided at the end of the chapter.

CATEGORIES OF LAW

LO 1-7

Because the body of American law is so vast and diverse, it is sometimes helpful to break down the law into broad categories based on classifications related to a particular legal function or a right afforded by law. It is important to note that these classifications are not mutually exclusive. One particular act or transaction may be classified in more than one legal category. For example, suppose that a party to a contract breaks her promise to the other party (an act known as a *breach of contract*). The remedy for the breach may depend on the legal classification of contracts as *civil law.* At the same time, one party may have rights classified as *substantive law,* which are derived from a source of *statutory law.*

Criminal Law versus Civil Law

Laws, primarily statutes, are either *criminal* or *civil* in nature. **Civil laws** are designed to compensate parties (including businesses) for losses as a result of another's conduct. These losses are known as **damages. Criminal laws** are a protection of society, and the violation of criminal laws results in penalties to the violator such as fines or imprisonment. Criminal fines are paid to the government and do not reimburse the victim. Remember that these categories are not mutually exclusive. For instance, a driver who is intoxicated and injures a pedestrian in an accident has committed both a criminal act (driving while intoxicated), for which he can be prosecuted by authorities, and a civil wrong (negligence), for which the driver can be sued by the injured party to recover for any losses suffered as a result of the injury (medical bills, etc.). Criminal law as it relates to business will be discussed in Chapter 23, "Criminal Law and Procedure in Business."

Substantive Law versus Procedural Law

Substantive laws provide individuals with rights and create certain duties. **Procedural laws** provide a structure and set out rules for pursuing substantive rights. For example, while state common law may provide an individual who has suffered losses due to the negligence of another the right to obtain restitution from the wrongdoer (substantive law), a state statute will prescribe the procedure for using legal means to actually collect the restitution (procedural law). This includes rules that govern court procedures such as how and when to file a lawsuit as well as the process for obtaining the restitution once a court has given the injured party a certain money award. Procedural law also sets out the steps the government must take if it needs to infringe on substantive rights. For example, if the police believe that a business owner is committing a nonviolent crime such as embezzlement or fraud, they may not simply barge into the owner's office without notice to search for and seize evidence. The Fourth Amendment to the U.S. Constitution protects citizens against unreasonable searches and seizures, a substantive right of privacy. The Fourth Amendment also specifies the procedural steps that must be taken to override the substantive rights in question in order to obtain a search warrant. These steps require that the police convince a judge or magistrate, through evidence of probable cause, that a crime is being committed and evidence necessary to prove that crime is in the owner's possession.

LO 1-8 Law versus Equity

Most modern American courts are combined courts of law and equity. However, we still use the terms *law* and *equity* when describing the appropriate *measure of judicial action* intended to compensate an injured party in a civil lawsuit. These measures are known as **remedies.**

Remedies at law generally take the form of *money damages:* A court orders the wrong-doer to pay another party a certain sum of money to compensate for any losses suffered as a result of the wrongdoer's conduct. However, in some cases, a party will not necessarily be fully or even partially compensated through money damages. In such a case, a court may award **equitable relief** instead of (or in addition to) a remedy at law. Most commonly, equitable relief can include an *injunction* or *restraining order* (a judicial order requiring a party to either perform or cease a certain activity) and *specific performance* (an order requiring a party to carry out her obligations as specified in a contract). Specific performance is available only if the goods contracted for are rare or one of a kind. To understand this concept in a business context, suppose that Maxwell enters into a valid written agreement with Book Barn to purchase a first edition of *The Old Man and the Sea,* autographed by Ernest Hemingway, for $25,000. Maxwell leaves the store to obtain a certified check from his bank. When he returns one hour later, the owner of Book Barn refuses to sell him the book because he had received a phone call from another buyer offering $30,000. In this case, Maxwell may file a lawsuit for Book Barn's failure to live up to the agreement (known as *breach of contract,* discussed in Chapter 8, "Contract Performance: Conditions, Breach, and Remedies"), but he has not suffered an out-of-pocket loss because he never had the opportunity to present Book Barn with the check. However, Maxwell could seek a *remedy at equity* from a court, where he would request an injunction to prevent Book Barn from selling the book to another buyer until the court can hear the case. If Maxwell wins the case, he may seek an order of *specific performance* whereby the court orders Book Barn to transfer ownership of the book to Maxwell in exchange for the $25,000 price as specified in the agreement between the parties. Maxwell would likely be awarded these equitable remedies because the legal remedies available to him are not adequate to address his injury.

> **KEY** POINT
>
> When a remedy at law is inadequate, an injured party may also obtain a remedy at equity. When a remedy at law is fully sufficient to bring justice, equitable remedies are not permitted.

LO 1-9

The term *equity* is also used in the context of common law rules that guide courts in deciding cases and controversies before them. These equity rules are called **equitable maxims** and are intended to be broad statements of rules that are based on notions of fairness and justice in applying the law. The most commonly applied maxims are "Equity aids the vigilant," "substance over form," and the "clean hands doctrine." These doctrines are frequently applied in suits seeking both legal and equitable damages.

- *Equity aids the vigilant:* Perhaps the most universal of the maxims is the notion that the law favors those who exercise *vigilance* in pursuing their claims and disfavors those who rest on their legal rights by failing to act to protect their rights in a reasonable period of time. If company A develops new technology, obtains a patent, and soon sees company B infringing on its patent by using that same technology, company A would be successful in obtaining an injunction stopping company B. If, instead, company A waits for company B to go into worldwide production and establish extensive retail partnerships and then sues for injunctive relief years later, the courts would be reluctant to assess punishment and could possibly void the patent protection entirely. A statute of limitations, discussed in Chapter 4, "Resolving Disputes: Litigation and Alternative Dispute Resolution Options," is a formal application of this doctrine.

- *Substance over form:* When applying the law, courts look to the intent of parties involved and adhere to a standard of good faith and fair play instead of applying the letter of the law in a way that would violate fundamental principles of fairness and consistency. In 1992, 8,000 workers sued Microsoft, claiming that they were not being paid benefits owed. Microsoft had hired them through temporary staffing firms and classified them as temporary workers, ineligible for full company benefits. The court determined that these workers, many of whom were employed for more than a year, worked the same hours and performed the same functions as the company's permanent workers. Even though Microsoft had these workers sign agreements stating that they were not regular employees of Microsoft, the court found that despite the label and classification, they were indeed permanent workers entitled to benefits. Microsoft eventually agreed to pay $97 million to settle the claims.[7]

■ *Clean hands doctrine:* Commentators sometimes describe loopholes in the law as responsible for creating injustice and protecting wrongdoers. However, more often than not, courts are not inclined to decide disputes based on technicalities that benefited a party who acted dishonestly. Courts are guided in their decisions not only by the letter of the law but also on the basis that one seeking the aid of a court must come to the court with clean hands that are unstained by bad faith, misrepresentations, or deceit. In Case 1.3, a state appellate court applies the clean hands doctrine.

Public Law versus Private Law

Public laws are those derived from some government entity. Examples include statutes (legislature/executive) and administrative regulations (state or federal administrative agencies). **Private laws** are recognized as binding between two parties even though no specific statute or regulation provides for the rights of the parties. The most common example is a contract for services. For example, suppose Claude hires Pablo to paint a portrait of Claude's wife. After it is complete, Claude thinks Pablo's painting is too abstract and refuses to pay for it. Although no specific public law exists that regulates this relationship, the agreement is still legally binding and the rules of the transaction are governed by the common law of contracts.

CASE 1.3   Kauffman-Harmon v. Kauffman, 36 P.3d 408 (Sup. Ct. Mont. 2001)

FACT SUMMARY Kauffman created a corporation to hold certain assets in a manner intended to minimize tax liability. After creation of the corporation, a judgment was entered against Kauffman as a result of a lawsuit against him. In order to avoid paying the judgment, Kauffman transferred all of his stock into his spouse's name. His spouse eventually transferred ownership of the stock to several Kauffman children. Several years later, a dispute developed between the children concerning the stock, and Kauffman intervened by filing a claim with the trial court requesting that all stock be transferred back to him on the basis that he was the rightful owner of the stock and that the transfer was nothing more than a temporary trust. The children contended that Kauffman is not the equitable owner of the stock and is not entitled to relief due to the clean hands doctrine.

SYNOPSIS OF DECISION AND OPINION The Supreme Court of Montana ruled in favor of the Kauffman children, holding that Kauffman was not entitled to relief. Because Kauffman's transfer perpetrated an exchange of stock only to avoid paying the judgment legally entered against him, the transaction was a bad-faith action that bordered on a fraudulent transaction. The court reasoned that the rightful owner of the stock was the Kauffman children and that Kauffman's claims were barred by the clean hands doctrine. The court concluded that recognizing his claim would result in a gross wrong being done to the children and the shareholders of the corporation.

WORDS OF THE COURT: Clean Hands Doctrine "The doctrine of clean hands provides that parties must not expect relief in equity, unless they come into court

(*continued*)

---

[7]*Vizcaino v. Microsoft,* 120 F.3d 1006 (9th Cir. 1997), *cert. denied,* 118 S. Ct. 899 (1998).

with clean hands. . . . Thus, no one can take advantage of his own wrong. . . . Court[s] will not aid a party whose claim had its inception in the party's wrongdoing whether the victim of the wrongdoing is the other party or a third party."

Case Questions

1. Would the court's ruling be the same if the children had also participated in the transactions and were accused of wrongdoing? Why or why not?

2. Given the court's reasoning, would the result of this case be the same if the transfer of stock was for a legitimate purpose and the only wrongdoing Kauffman had committed involved a third party in an unrelated matter? Why or why not?

SOLUTIONS FOR MANAGERS

Legal Decisions in Business: An Analytical Model

PROBLEM *Legal decision making by managers is reactionary, uneven, and sometimes uninformed.*

SOLUTION *Use a systematic analytical model designed to identify legal issues, and understand those issues as business planning opportunities that enable the management team to add value to the company.*

Understanding the theories and applications of law in a business context is important to meeting legal challenges, but incorporating this knowledge via the use of an analytical model helps to convert legal challenges into astute business planning and potential opportunities. This model may be used for any legal challenge, but a fundamental understanding of applicable legal doctrines and applications is necessary to take full advantage of its use. Keep this model in mind while you are studying the material in this textbook. You'll find that it will become more valuable as your knowledge of substantive law increases. When confronted with a legal challenge, managers with a high level of legal awareness should follow a seven step model: *Identify → Assess → Analyze → Examine Alternatives → Compare* with business mission, objectives, and ethical considerations → *Implement,* monitor, and revise → *Review* for business planning opportunities.

Step 1: *Identify potential legal issues.* One of the objectives of this textbook is to provide students with essential legal doctrines and examples of how the law impacts business operations and planning.

Legal awareness is the primary tool for identifying legal issues and responding appropriately. Businesses should be both proactive and reactive in identifying potential legal issues. Proactive measures include having apparatus in place that limits liability exposures (such as standardized hiring and promotion procedures), while reactive measures require that business owners and managers follow a legally sound course of action once they become aware of a potential legal issue.

Step 2: *Assess the imminence and level of any legal challenge and decide whether to confer with counsel.* While legally adept managers have the ultimate goal of understanding legal challenges as potential planning opportunities, the primary consideration when confronted with a legal challenge is to assess how much potential liability may be involved and to understand the posture of the parties. For example, if a manager of a wholesaling company receives a complaint from a customer about the quality of goods purchased, that is a legal challenge (essentially an allegation of breaking a contract) with potential for litigation in the future, but the level and immediacy of the threat is low. The matter may be worked out amicably, ethically, and legally without counsel. If, during negotiations, the customer begins to indicate that he will be pursuing legal alternatives, the threat level has increased and counsel should be consulted immediately. Although there is no need for counsel to intervene at this point, she should be briefed on the matter in the event that the customer takes more formal action. On the other hand, if a company manager receives a complaint from an employee about being sexually harassed by her co-workers, the *potential* threat is high and it is an imminent threat because the business's liability will continue to accrue rapidly unless immediate action is taken. The costs of this type of legal challenge may be very high, and alternatives become more limited. Thus, counsel should be consulted immediately.

Step 3: *Analyze the legal implications of the legal challenge using the* worst-case scenario *and include an estimate of costs including legal fees and court costs, a losing judgment, and potential draws on human resources required to meet the challenge.* Using the worst-case scenario gives a manager context, which is helpful to understanding the potential liability faced because of the legal challenge. For example, if a customer is threatening to sue his supplier for breach of contract based on a $50,000 loss that he suffered, the worst-case scenario for the *supplier* is that the case goes to trial and the customer wins the judgment. Thus, the expenditure is $50,000 plus legal fees (which vary greatly from case to case and from attorney to attorney, but one could reasonably expect the legal fees and costs to be $25,000 to $100,000 based on the complexity of the case), plus the time and expenses that will be required for officers and employees to participate in the pretrial and trial process. An appeal will be even more costly. The scenario essentially sets the baseline for what a certain course of action could cost the company.

Step 4: *Evaluate alternatives by developing a list of various approaches that could be used to meet the legal challenge. While considering advantages and disadvantages of alternatives, estimate the costs and potential return on expenditures made to meet the legal challenge.* Once a baseline potential for costs has been set, a variety of approaches should be considered. However, it is important that each approach also be subjected to a *cost-benefit analysis* (e.g., what will it cost to invest in this approach, and what benefit will the business reap through the investment?). For example, suppose that TechCo enters into a contract with Big Insurance Company (BIC) to provide installation and maintenance of BIC's computer network based on "industry standards."

After the installation, BIC is unhappy with the work and threatens to sue TechCo on the basis that its work was below industry standards and therefore violates the terms of their agreement. BIC demands that TechCo rewire its entire office (which will cost TechCo $60,000) or it will file a lawsuit. When examining alternatives, TechCo managers will almost certainly consider aggressive litigation as one approach. TechCo could simply refuse to act any further, wait for the lawsuit to be filed, and then hire a law firm that promises to be hard-nosed and refuses to concede even the smallest point or to entertain any settlement offers. If indeed TechCo is within its legal rights to refuse BIC's demand, it will emerge from the trial victorious. However, the cost-benefit analysis is more problematic. Even if TechCo wins, the legal fees[8] for pretrial activities, trial work, and a possible appeal may very well end up being close to or even exceed the amount in dispute. Add the costs of human resources necessary to support this alternative and the possible damage to TechCo's reputation in the market that is inherent in litigation, and this approach begins to look less attractive. The following table lists alternatives along with sample costs, risks, and benefits to meet TechCo's legal challenge.

Step 5: *Compare the alternatives with the business's mission, objectives, and ethical codes of conduct. Which alternatives are consistent with ethical decision-making standards and any statement of corporate social responsibility?[9] May any of the alternatives be turned into a business opportunity?* Once various strategies have been tested in terms of cost-benefit and risks, an equally important comparison should be done in the context of the company's mission, objectives, and ethical codes of conduct. If the company has developed certain statements concerning ethics and/or corporate social responsibility,

[8]Note that in the American legal system, the general rule regarding legal fees is that each side bears its own legal fees and costs of litigation. However, some exceptions exist to this general rule, such as when a statute specifically provides that a successful litigant may recover attorneys' fees from the losing party (e.g., employment discrimination statutes).

[9]Business ethics and corporate social responsibility are discussed in detail in Chapter 5, "Business, Societal, and Ethical Contexts of Law."

(continued)

what alternative is most consistent with those statements? In the TechCo–BIC case discussed earlier, suppose that TechCo's internal policies provided that "TechCo believes that each client must be 100 percent satisfied with our services, or we will work at our own expense until the client is fully satisfied." While TechCo has no legal duty to comply with that internal standard, doesn't this maxim help TechCo's management in selecting an approach to legal challenges by its clients? Also, perhaps this dispute can be turned into an opportunity whereby BIC will potentially spread the word in the business community that TechCo is highly committed to customer service rather than to fighting its clients in a courtroom. Even if TechCo does not make a profit on the BIC agreement, isn't the long-term view more compelling?

Step 6: *Implement the chosen alternative and adjust the solution based on your monitoring of the costs, values, and opportunities. Be ready to revise and seek more opportunities as more information about the*

challenge becomes available. Once a course of action has been determined, the model then shifts toward implementation and monitoring. As more information becomes available or as costs rise unexpectedly, it may be necessary to adjust the alternatives to accommodate the new information. For example, assume that in the TechCo–BIC case, the parties agreed on private arbitration.[10] Just before the arbitration, a TechCo internal investigation concludes that one of its installers incorrectly wired a small segment of the BIC network but that the entire network was not corrupted. At this point, given TechCo's business values, its potential for liability, and the costs of arbitration, TechCo may now be willing to enter into a settlement agreement with BIC rather than risk a loss at arbitration. On the other hand, if BIC continues to demand

[10]Private arbitration is a nonjudicial method for resolving legal disputes. Its costs tend to be much lower than litigation. Arbitration is discussed in detail in Chapter 4, "Resolving Disputes: Litigation and Alternative Dispute Resolution Options."

Alternative	Costs/Risk/Impact	Benefit to the Corporation
Aggressive litigation	**Costs:** *Monetary*—high *Human resources*—high **Risks:** (1) Uncertainty about outcome; (2) irreparable client relations; (3) long-term distractions (3–8 yrs); and (4) potential damage to reputation in the marketplace.	Winning the lawsuit will settle the matter (subject to appeal).
Alternative dispute resolution such as arbitration or mediation.	**Costs:** *Monetary*—medium *Human resources*—medium to high **Risks:** (1) Damage to client relations; (2) potential failure to obtain a satisfactory outcome.	Dispute is settled without costly litigation or (usually) uncertainty of appeal. Potential to repair client relations or reputation in the business community.
Amend existing contract to provide for limited additional services by TechCo that will satisfy the parties (e.g., TechCo will be willing to re-network any computer system exhibiting impaired functionality according to industry standards to a maximum of $30,000).	**Costs:** *Monetary*—low *Human resources*—medium **Risks:** Potential that BIC may still not be satisfied and a lawsuit will still be filed.	Potential to repair client relations and/or increase reputation in the business community as a company that is highly committed to quality and customer service.

a total rewiring costing $60,000, TechCo may opt to take its chances at arbitration.

Step 7: *During monitoring and after the legal challenge has been met, evaluate how the challenge could have been prevented or handled better. Devise a system or process that will help to limit future legal challenges.* While it is natural for managers to move onto other pressing matters after having met a legal challenge, a significant business opportunity may be lost in failing to analyze the dispute with the benefit of hindsight. For example, after resolving the BIC dispute, TechCo could confer with its counsel on possible revisions to future installment contracts that would clarify which installation standards apply instead of using the term "industry" standards. There may also be an opportunity to revise future contracts to ensure that any lawsuit filed as a result of a dispute related to the agreement takes place close to TechCo's headquarters. Adding such language (known as a *forum selection clause*) will help contain TechCo's costs in the event of litigation or arbitration. Other opportunities may include designing a quality control system for future installation, rethinking the company's risk in that particular market segment, and identifying business planning opportunities unique to TechCo's industry and practices.

KEY TERMS

Law p. 3 A body of rules of action or conduct prescribed by controlling authority and having legal binding force.

Jurisprudence p. 3 The science and philosophy of law that defines various approaches to the appropriate function of law and how legal doctrines should be developed and applied.

Black's Law Dictionary p. 5 The leading legal dictionary.

Counsel p. 6 Another term for *attorney*.

Constitutional law p. 8 The body of law interpreting state and federal constitutions.

Statutory law p. 8 The body of law created by the legislature and approved by the executive branch of state and federal government.

Common law p. 8 Law that has not been passed by the legislature but rather is made by the courts and is based on the fundamentals of previous cases with similar facts.

Administrative law p. 8 Refers to both the law made by administrative agencies and the laws and regulations that govern the creation, organization, and operation of administrative agencies.

Ordinances p. 9 Local statutes passed by local legislatures.

Plain meaning rule p. 9 The principle that if the words in a statute have clear and widely understood meanings, the court applies the statute; used as the initial guideline in statutory interpretation to determine how a rule should be applied.

Statutory scheme p. 9 The structure of a statute and the format of its mandates.

Legislative history p. 9 The records kept by the legislature, including the debates, committee and conference reports, and legislative findings of fact used when creating a law, which can be used to show the legislature's intent.

Citation p. 11 The special format used by the legal community to express where a statute or case law can be found.

Doctrine of stare decisis p. 12 The principle that similar cases with similar facts under similar circumstances should have similar outcomes.

Precedent p. 12 Applying the law made in previous appellate court opinions to current cases with similar facts; binding on the trial courts.

Secondary sources p. 14 Sources of law that have no independent authority or legally binding effect but can be used to illustrate a point or clarify a legal issue.

Restatements of the Law p. 14 A collection of uniform legal principles focused in a particular area of the law, which contains statements of common law legal principles and rules in a given area of law.

Model state statutes p. 14 Statutes drafted by legal experts to be used as a model for state legislatures to adopt in their individual jurisdictions in order to increase the level of uniformity and fairness across courts in all states.

Civil laws p. 17 Laws designed to compensate parties for money lost as a result of another's conduct.

Damages p. 17 Money lost as a result of another's conduct.

Criminal laws p. 17 Laws designed to protect society that result in penalties to the violator such as fines or imprisonment.

Substantive laws p. 17 Laws that provide individuals with rights and create certain duties.

Procedural laws p. 17 Laws that provide a structure and set out rules for pursuing substantive rights.

Remedies p. 18 Judicial actions, which can be monetary or equitable, taken by courts that are intended to compensate an injured party in a civil lawsuit.

Equitable relief p. 18 A type of remedy, including injunctions and restraining orders, that is designed to compensate a party when money alone will not do by instead forcing the other party to do (or not do) something.

Equitable maxims p. 18 Common law rules that guide courts in deciding cases and controversies and are intended to be broad statements of rules based on notions of fairness and justice.

Public laws p. 19 Laws derived from a government entity.

Private laws p. 19 Laws recognized as binding between two parties even though no specific statute or regulation provides for the rights of the parties.

THEORY TO PRACTICE

Galaxy Inc. is a supplier of greeting cards, small gifts, tokens, and games appropriate for special occasions such as holidays and birthdays. Galaxy distributes its products primarily through large supermarket and drugstore chains. Increasingly, Galaxy has lost revenue due to supermarkets that prefer to enter into the supplier market by manufacturing these products in a foreign country at a steep discount (instead of buying Galaxy's products) and selling them in their stores at a higher profit. In response to this, Galaxy's management team begins to roll out a new business model whereby Galaxy will begin to retail its own products through newly created Galaxy retail stores. Jackson is a senior manager charged with overseeing the expansion efforts.

1. Suppose that Jackson intends to lease (rent) these new spaces for the Galaxy stores and hire new employees to staff them. What areas of the law may impact Jackson's planning process?

2. What options does Jackson have for legal advice to guide his efforts? What is the role that counsel might play in these transactions?

3. What sources and levels of law would Jackson need to have a fundamental knowledge of to help him protect his company from liability and meet any legal challenges? Give specific examples.

4. Assume that Jackson also plans to acquire the assets of a smaller retail company in order to carry out this expansion. Jackson is concerned about the potential tax impact that may be triggered by the transaction. How can Jackson plan with certainty for a particular type of tax treatment? What legal doctrine allows him to rely on the law in the planning process?

5. Assume that Jackson enters into a contract with Holmes for Holmes to act as store manager in one location. After two weeks, Jackson fires Holmes for incompetence. Holmes believes that Jackson fired him in violation of an antidiscrimination law, but he keeps forgetting to file the appropriate paperwork and eight months pass by. Finally, Holmes gets around to filing a complaint. What equitable maxim would apply to Holmes's complaint? Does this maxim favor Holmes or Jackson?

Midlevel managers are frequently involved with vendors, competitors, customers, and employees on a daily basis, and this makes them invaluable tools for spotting and meeting legal challenges in the early stages. Suppose that in the Theory to Practice problem, Jackson, a senior manager, receives an e-mail from a competing company:

> "Galaxy: You have stolen our trademark. We have the trademark rights for the Hobgoblin Necklace and you don't have our permission to use it. Yet, on a recent visit to one of your stores, you have Hobgoblin Necklaces for sale. Cease and desist or we will turn this matter over to our attorney.
>
> Signed,
> Necklace Emporium

Assume that you are a midlevel manager and that Jackson hands you the e-mail and informs you that, to his knowledge, Galaxy followed all proper legal procedures for the trademark. Using the analytical model presented in Solutions for Managers on page 20, compose a two- to three-page memorandum addressed to Jackson that gives guidance on handling this legal challenge. A sample answer may be found on this textbook's website at www.mhhe.com/melvinleb2e.

CASE SUMMARY 1.1 :: Sokoloff v. Harriman Estate Development Corp., 754 N.E.2d 184 (N.Y. 2001)

EQUITY AND FAIRNESS

Sokoloff purchased land in the Village of Sands Point and, in anticipation of building a home, hired Harriman to provide preconstruction services, including the creation of architectural and landscaping plans. Sokoloff paid Harriman a $10,000 retainer fee and a total of $55,000 for creating and filing the architectural plans with the village. However, when it came time to build the home, Harriman estimated the cost to be over $1.8 million. Sokoloff, finding this amount to be exorbitant, decided to get quotes from other builders, based on the plans he had Harriman design. However, Harriman said that the plans could not be used to construct the home unless he was the builder.

CASE QUESTIONS

1. Can Harriman withhold the plans from Sokoloff?
2. What legal theories or maxims would a court consider in deciding this case?
3. How should the court rule and why?

CASE SUMMARY 1.2 :: Jones v. R. R. Donnelley & Sons Co., 541 U.S. 369 (2004)

STATUTE OF LIMITATIONS

The U.S. Congress enacted a statute providing for a four-year statute of limitations for any cause of action arising out of an act of Congress enacted after 1990. Jones, an African-American employee of R. R. Donnelley & Sons Co. (Donnelley), was denied a transfer to one of Donnelley's other plants when his plant closed. Moreover, while an employee for Donnelley, Jones was subject to a hostile work environment and various acts of discrimination. Jones, an Illinois citizen, wishes to sue Donnelley for violating federal antidiscrimination statutes. It has been three years since Jones worked for Donnelley, and Illinois has a two-year statute of limitations.

CASE QUESTIONS

1. Which statute of limitation governs and why?
2. Will Jones be able to sue Donnelley?

CLEAN HANDS DOCTRINE

Case Credit Corp. (Case) finances the sale of farm equipment to farmers. Day bought farm equipment financed by Case, yet Day never actually signed the sales contract. Instead, an employee of Case forged Day's signature on the sales contract with higher prices in an effort to pocket the difference for himself. Case was aware of the forgery, but did not make any effort to stop him or inform Day. When Day could not pay the loans back, Case filed suit to recover the farm equipment or compel payment.

CASE QUESTIONS

1. If the court applies the clean hands doctrine, will Case be able to recover the farm equipment because Day is unable to make the payments? Why or why not?
2. Are Case's hands clean? Why or why not?

EQUITABLE RELIEF

Monfort, the nation's fifth largest beef packer, is concerned about a merger of the nation's second largest packer, Cargill, with the nation's third largest packer. Monfort believes that the merger will give Cargill almost 21 percent of the market, leaving Monfort with only 5 percent. Monfort believes this merger may result in a violation of federal antitrust laws and wishes to file suit to prevent it.

CASE QUESTION

1. If Monfort files suit and the merger is deemed to violate antitrust laws, what type of remedy will Monfort want to receive and why?

INTERPRETING STATUTES

More than decade before a federal law set a minimum wage for workers, the State of Oklahoma passed a statute that established a minimum wage for workers performing services for the state government. The law based the minimum wage on "the current rate of per diem wages in the locality where the work is to be performe." The state's commissioner of labor charged General Construction with violating the minimum wage law. The commissioner alleged that various workers were being underpaid. General Construction argued that the statute was too vague to be enforceable.

CASE QUESTIONS

1. Is the language "current rate of wages" certain enough to be enforceable? Why or why not?
2. Is there any other ambiguous or vague language in the statute? How could the statute be reworded in order to overcome any notion of vagueness?

PRECEDENT

This case arises from an assessment of a civil penalty against two landowners for violations of the Sedimentation Pollution Control Act of 1973, the North Carolina Department of Natural Resources and Community Development (NRCD). While enlarging one of the subdivisions on the property, between October and December 1983, the owners disturbed approximately 2½ acres of land by grading, cutting, and filling, in order to construct a street to provide access to residential lots. Owners were assessed civil penalties for violations of the act. The trial court concluded that although the assessment was "not effected [sic] by error of law," the authority conferred by the statute allowed the secretary of NRCD to assess civil penalties in his "absolute discretion," and thus the statute constituted a legislative grant of judicial power prohibited by the North Carolina Constitution. A divided panel[11] of the North Carolina Court of Appeals upheld

the trial court's judgment. In doing so, the panel disregarded another panel of the North Carolina Court of Appeals that had, in a previous case with the same issues, found that the NRCD has discretion to assess fines based on its discretion due to guidelines and limitations that exist in the act in question. The North Carolina Supreme Court heard the appeal.

CASE QUESTIONS

1. How is precedent created, and how is it applied in future cases?
2. When two separate panels of the same court hear different cases with similar issues, must the second panel follow the decision made by the first?
3. If precedent has been set by a state appellate panel, who has the power to overrule that precedent?

[11]Often, appellate court justices do not all sit on cases together. For efficiency, smaller groups, frequently called *panels*, may hear and decide cases.

 Self-Check **ANSWERS**

Role of Counsel

1. Laws related to start-up (incorporation), sales of goods (commercial law), ordinances such as zoning (basement location), and taxation of transactions and income.
2. *For business operations*: laws related to lease of a kiosk, credit transactions, local licensing.
   For employees: labor laws (minimum wage, overtime), employment discrimination.
3. How to qualify for trademark protection, the process of registration, enforcement of the mark.
4. Asset purchases, contracts, taxes, trademarks.

Sources of Law

1. A contract issue governed by statutory (UCC) law at the state level.
2. A patent issue governed by statutory law at the federal level.
3. A securities issue governed by statutory and administrative law at the federal and state levels.
4. A bankruptcy issue governed by statutory and administrative law at the federal level.
5. A zoning issue governed by statutory law at the local level.

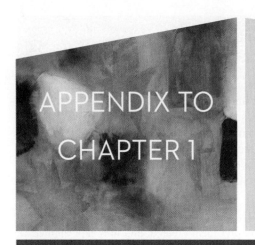

APPENDIX TO CHAPTER 1

A Business Student's Guide to Understanding Cases and Finding the Law

This textbook emphasizes ways in which business owners and managers can add value to their companies by using legal insight for business planning and limiting risk. Using a basic system for understanding court case opinions improves one's ability to grasp the impact of the law on business. Because much of the law is composed of cases and statutes, learning the fundamentals of how and where to find the law allows business owners and managers to work more effectively with counsel and empowers them to become better decision makers by using legal considerations as a part of their strategic planning.

Understanding Case Law: The SUR System

All of the legal cases in this textbook are reported in a unique format designed especially for business students. For each case, students are provided with a summary of the case facts and a synopsis of the court's decision and opinion. Students then read an actual excerpt from the case in the *words of the court* that is directly related to the legal point being covered in the text. All procedural language and parts of the opinion that are unrelated to the legal point have been edited out. This allows the reader to focus on one or two key points of law in the case. However, case law from other sources is likely to be a complete word-for-word reporting without any trustworthy explanation or summary. Understanding cases by reading the full text can be challenging even for attorneys. The *SUR system* provides business students with a systematic method for analyzing cases that will help draw

out essential information without getting bogged down in legal details.

SUR stands for *scan, understand, review.* Although this system is helpful for reading any complex or dense text, it is specifically tailored for reading legal cases. Not only will this method help students fully understand the cases contained in this text, but it is also useful for comprehending full-length cases found in other sources. Figures 1A.1, 1A.2, and 1A.3 illustrate how the SUR system is applied.

Scan the Case

Read the *headings* and *first two sentences* of each section of the case to the end of the opinion. Then read the *last three* sentences of the case. While scanning, use a pencil or highlighter to note names of the parties, the court that decided the case, and the final decision of the court.

Understand the Case

After scanning, begin to read (and reread when necessary) the case from the beginning. Use a pencil to circle important facts and legal terms. At this stage, many students find it useful to draw flowcharts and other summaries in order to understand a chain of facts more clearly. Look up legal terms using the online law dictionary listed in Table 1A.1 later in this appendix. Do your best to skip procedural language such as the standards of review for an appellate court or issues related to pretrial discovery or motions. While reading the fact summary in the beginning of the case, keep the following question in mind:

After the *Scan* stage, the text would appear as follows:

CASE 1.3 Kauffman-Harmon v. Kauffman, 36 P. 3d 408 (Sup. Ct. Mont. 2001)

FACT SUMMARY: Kauffman created a corporation to hold certain assets in a manner intended to minimize tax liability. After creation of the corporation, a judgment was entered against Kauffman as a result of a lawsuit against him. In order to avoid paying the judgment, Kauffman transferred all of his stock into his spouse's name. His spouse eventually transferred ownership of the stock to several Kauffman children. Several years later, a dispute developed between the children concerning the stock, and Kauffman intervened by filing a claim with the trial court requesting that all stock be transferred back to him on the basis that he was the rightful owner of the stock and that the transfer was nothing more than a temporary trust. The children contended that Kauffman is not the equitable owner of the stock and is not entitled to relief due to the clean hands doctrine.

SYNOPSIS OF DECISION AND OPINION: The Supreme Court of Montana ruled in favor of the Kauffman children, holding that Kauffman was not entitled to relief. Because Kauffman's transfer was in perpetrating an exchange of stock only to avoid paying the judgment legally entered against him, the transaction was a bad-faith action that bordered on a fraudulent transaction. The court reasoned that the rightful owner of the stock was the Kauffman children and that Kauffman's claims were barred by the clean hands doctrine. The court concluded that recognizing his claim would result in a gross wrong being done to the children and the shareholders of the corporation.

WORDS OF THE COURT: Clean Hands Doctrine
"The doctrine of clean hands provides that parties must not expect relief in equity, unless they come into court with clean hands. ... Thus, no one can take advantage of his own wrong. ... Court[s] will not aid a party whose claim had its inception in the party's wrongdoing whether the victim of the wrongdoing is the other party or a third party."

ISSUE: What legal *issues* are being created by the party's actions? That is, what legal *question* will the court have to answer?

Once you begin reading the court's ruling, continue to mark potentially important phrases, paying special attention to the court's statement of the current law. Look for wording such as "the statute provides for" or "the only relief available under the statute" to alert you to important language. As you read and mark the text, keep in mind the following questions and jot down any related thoughts:

RULE: What law *generally* applies to this situation, and are there any exceptions? What statute, common law, or other legal doctrine is applicable in this situation? What precedent exists? Courts often start the legal analysis section of their opinions by stating what the law is or by quoting from the statute at issue.

FIGURE 1A.2

After the *Understand* stage, the text would look like this:

CASE 1.3 Kauffman-Harmon v. Kauffman, 36 P. 3d 408 (Sup. Ct. Mont. 2001)

FACT SUMMARY: Kauffman created a corporation to hold certain assets in a manner intended to minimize tax liability. After creation of the corporation, a judgment was entered against Kauffman as a result of a lawsuit against him. In order to avoid paying the judgment, Kauffman transferred all of his stock into his spouse's name. His spouse eventually transferred ownership of the stock to several Kauffman children. Several years later, a dispute developed between the children concerning the stock, and Kauffman intervened by filing a claim with the trial court requesting that all stock be transferred back to him on the basis that he was the rightful owner of the stock and that the transfer was nothing more than a temporary trust. The children contended that Kauffman is not the equitable owner of the stock and is not entitled to relief due to the clean hands doctrine. *(Stock transferred)* *(Issue—"clean hands")*

SYNOPSIS OF DECISION AND OPINION: The Supreme Court of Montana ruled in favor of the Kauffman children, holding that Kauffman was not entitled to relief. Because Kauffman's transfer was in perpetrating an exchange of stock only to avoid paying the judgment legally entered against him, the transaction was a bad-faith action that bordered on a fraudulent transaction. The court reasoned that the rightful owner of the stock was the Kauffman children and that Kauffman's claims were barred by the clean hands doctrine. The court concluded that recognizing his claim would result in a gross wrong being done to the children and the shareholders of the corporation. *(Conclusion)* *(Analysis—"bad-faith action")*

WORDS OF THE COURT: CLEAN HANDS DOCTRINE "The doctrine of clean hands provides that parties must not expect relief in equity, unless they come into court with clean hands.... Thus, no one can take advantage of his own wrong.... Court[s] will not aid a party whose claim had its inception in the party's wrongdoing whether the victim of the wrongdoing is the other party or a third party." *(Rule—doctrine of clean hands)*

This case stands for the proposition that a court will not aid a party who comes with unclean hands. The doctrine of unclean hands prohibits Kauffman from recovering because of his role in the stock transaction.

ANALYSIS: How does the court apply the law to this set of facts? Are there any other factors that the court is considering when applying the law? Are there any legal exceptions or privileges that apply to these facts? Was it necessary to deviate from precedent?

CONCLUSION: What was the court's answer to the question posed in the issue phases of this analysis?

Review the case

Use a highlighter (some students may find it helpful to use a different color for reviewing than the color used for scanning) to go over the case one more time. Read the case at a reading speed that is halfway between scanning and comprehensive reading. Highlight sparingly, marking only what you find to be most important. Many students find it helpful to sketch

FIGURE 1A.3

After the *Review* stage, the text would look like this:

CASE 1.3 Kauffman-Harmon v. Kauffman, 36 P. 3d 408
(Sup. Ct. Mont. 2001)

FACT SUMMARY: Kauffman created a corporation to hold certain assets in a manner intended to minimize tax liability. After creation of the corporation, a judgment was entered against Kauffman as a result of a lawsuit against him. In order to avoid paying the judgment, Kauffman transferred all of his stock into his spouse's name. His spouse eventually transferred ownership of the stock to several Kauffman children. Several years later, a dispute developed between the children concerning the stock, and Kauffman intervened by filing a claim with the trial court requesting that all stock be transferred back to him on the basis that he was the rightful owner of the stock and that the transfer was nothing more than a temporary trust. The children contended that Kauffman is not the equitable owner of the stock and is not entitled to relief due to the clean hands doctrine.

(margin note) Stock transferred

(margin note) Issue—"clean hands"

(margin note) Conclusion {

SYNOPSIS OF DECISION AND OPINION: The Supreme Court of Montana ruled in favor of the Kauffman children, holding that Kauffman was not entitled to relief. Because Kauffman's transfer was in perpetrating an exchange of stock only to avoid paying the judgment legally entered against him, the transaction was a bad-faith action that bordered on a fraudulent transaction. The court reasoned that the rightful owner of the stock was the Kauffman children and that Kauffman's claims were barred by the clean hands doctrine. The court concluded that recognizing his claim would result in a gross wrong being done to the children and the shareholders of the corporation.

(margin note) Analysis—"bad-faith action" {

WORDS OF THE COURT: CLEAN HANDS DOCTRINE
"The doctrine of clean hands provides that parties must not expect relief in equity, unless they come into court with clean hands.... Thus, no one can take advantage of his own wrong.... Court[s] will not aid a party whose claim had its inception in the party's wrongdoing whether the victim of the wrongdoing is the other party or a third party."

(margin note) Rule—doctrine of clean hands

This case stands for the proposition that a court will not aid a party who comes with unclean hands. The doctrine of unclean hands prohibits Kauffman from recovering because of his role in the stock transaction.

out a flowchart or summary of the entire case. After reviewing the case, spot and note the answers to the issue, rule, analysis, and conclusion questions. Then put away the materials, and consider a final question: *What is the fundamental premise of this case?* Write out the answer in two or three sentences, and include it with the case notes for future use. Difficulty in answering that question may be remedied by going back to the *understand* step and refining the issue, rule, and analysis. Remember that you may not look at the case again for several weeks or months until preparing for an exam. The SUR system increases learning intensity and provides a document ready for use when you are studying the material later.

For an example of the SUR system applied to a full-length case, go to this textbook's website at www.mhhe.com/melvinleb2e.

TABLE 1A.1 Reliable Sources for Legal Research on the Internet

Website Name	Source	Description	URL*
Free and low cost legal research	Georgetown University Law Center—Law Library	One of the very best tools for free and low-cost online research. The website provides an excellent overview, links to different types of free materials, and provides direct links to federal and state statutes and cases. It also summarizes the features and costs of less expensive databases.	www.ll.georgetown.edu/guides/freelowcost.cfm
Free Internet legal sources	University of Washington School of Law	Comprehensive offerings and an easy-to-use layout for finding the law. The site also provides an excellent brochure (in pdf) called "How to Research a Legal Problem: A Guide for Non-Lawyers."	http://lib.law.washington.edu/research/research.html#states
All Law: The Internet's premier law portal	Commercial website (primarily generates revenue through advertising)	Very simple layout and direct links that make this website efficient for locating federal or state statutes and cases.	www.alllaw.com/law/
Free legal advice	Commercial website (primarily generates revenue through advertising)	Comprehensive topical information arranged by legal topic (also contains advice related to insurance). However, the site is not useful for finding cases or specific statutes.	www.freeadvice.com/all_topics.php
Online law dictionary	Commercial website (primarily generates revenue through advertising)	Comprehensive law dictionary with search engine.	http://dictionary.law.com

*All Internet research websites may be accessed through this textbook's website at www.mhhe.com/melvinleb2e.

Finding the Law

The Internet has been the single most important force in providing unprecedented public access to the law. Cases, statutes, and topics on legal information are accessible online and largely free of charge. In addition to Internet services, several commercial services (such as LexisNexis and Westlaw) provide special versions of case law that are enhanced with summaries, explanations, and a system that ties cases together based on legal topics. Table 1A.1, above, provides examples of reliable Internet sources for legal research. Table 1A.2 illustrates a four-step method that provides a systematic process for finding the law through either an Internet-based or a commercial service.

Step 1	Identify precise legal question(s) and try to determine what source of law governs the issue(s).	Questions: 1. Is CHC required to permit Adams to take time off for jury duty in a state court? 2. If yes, is CHC obligated to pay Adams for the time he spends on jury duty? Sources: Look in the statutes of the state where CHC employs Adams.
Step 2	Strategize based on resources.	Use Georgetown's website 1. Table of contents: Click on *Statutes and Codes: State Codes*. 2. Choose *State Research Guides* and then *Pennsylvania resources*. 3. Under "Electronic versions" choose *Free Web*, and use the free search engine for the Pennsylvania code. 4. Use the search engine to find a statute by entering "Jury Duty and Employer." 5. Click on the first result, and read the statute. Does it help resolve the question(s)?
Step 3	Find an application.	On the same web page (Pennsylvania resources) click on *Cases and Courts* to use the search engine for any cases involving employers/employees and time off for jury duty.
Step 4	Consult with counsel.	Provide Adams with time off for jury duty, but without pay. Hire a temporary worker for the warehouse (not permitted to discipline or terminate Adams). Icahn checks his plan with his counsel before implementing.

Step 1: Identify a Precise Legal Question

The first step in finding the law is to clearly identify a legal question to answer. Using your knowledge of the levels and sources of law covered in Chapter 1, "Legal Foundations," try to determine whether the question is best answered by a statute or a case. For example, suppose that Adams is an employee of Coats and Hats Co. (CHC), a business with 45 employees. One morning he informs his manager, Icahn, that he has been subpoenaed for jury duty in a state court and will need the next day off with pay. Because the company is performing a crucial inventory count that week, Adams is needed in the warehouse or, alternatively, a replacement will need to be hired. Icahn wants to know

if CHC is legally obligated to permit Adams to take the time off necessary to serve on jury duty. If so, is the company legally responsible for paying Adams while he is on jury duty? Because the issue is related to employer obligations to employees when called for jury duty to a state court, Icahn would likely find guidance in a *state statute*.

Step 2: Strategize Based on Resources

Once you have determined the basic legal question and potential source of law, the strategy for tracking down the answer is necessarily based on resources. If commercial research services are available to you, it may be advantageous to use them in order to get the maximum amount of information in the least amount of time. However, such services are typically very expensive and, therefore, are usually limited to law firms, large companies, and academic institutions. Government, municipal, college, and law school libraries have federal and state statutes in book form. However, finding specific information on the law in books or through commercial services may be difficult without extensive training in legal research. Most legal research by nonlawyers is accomplished through the Internet. Pick the appropriate legal website for your research (see Table 1A.1 for the best websites for finding the law). Depending on which site you choose, try to find a general explanation of the topic. Alternatively, use the legal website's search engine to narrow your search in finding the source. In the CHC-Adams hypothetical, discussed earlier, Icahn may wish to use a website that gives a general explanation on rights of employees, but certain issues he seeks may be too narrow for a general explanation. In this case, Icahn will be best off simply using the website's search engine to find the statute in the state in which CHC employs Adams. For example, if CHC was located in Pennsylvania, Icahn would go to the Georgetown Law Center website and follow these steps: (1) Select *Statutes and Codes/State Codes* from the table of contents on the left side to get to Pennsylvania resources, and (2) find the free electronic version of the statutes, and use the search engine to find any relevant statute. Use of the words "jury duty" may be too general, so narrowing it down with modifiers such as "jury duty and employer," helps to hone in on the answer.

A Word of Caution About Internet Sources

While the Internet has made the law more accessible to the public, it has also created an environment where information goes unchecked and unverified. The best sources for legal research are typically the sites maintained by law school libraries. For more general legal information, websites should be evaluated based on sponsorship (who maintains the website?), authority (are the authors of the information identified, and are they attorneys?), and longevity (how long has the website been in existence?). The websites listed in Table 1A.1 are authoritative, have special features designed for nonattorneys, and are time-tested.

Step 3: Find an Application

Once you have located a statute, learn how the statute was applied in a case. Use the website's search engine, which enables you to find cases by entering the name or citation of the statute. Through the search results, you can read how courts have applied the statute and learn whether any exceptions exist. For example, in the CHC-Adams case, Ichan would use the Georgetown Law Center website to find a case by selecting *Cases and Courts* from the Pennsylvania resources menu and entering terms in the search engine. This will allow him to read how courts have interpreted the statute, if necessary, and help him to understand how it applies to CHC.

Step 4: Consult with Counsel

It is dangerous to make any decision based on legal research by a nonattorney. Once a business owner or manager has a grasp of the issues, she should contact her counsel and discuss the issue and potential consequences of any decisions. The ability to find and understand the law in a business environment should be considered an *enhancement* to helping add value to a company through use of the law in business planning. It is not a substitute for working closely with an attorney. For example, in the CHC-Adams case, based on his research, Icahn is prepared to provide Adams with time off for jury duty (as required by statute) but does not intend to pay him. He will need to hire a temporary worker for the warehouse because he is not permitted to terminate Adams for missing work due to jury duty. However, before implementing his plan, he would consult with his counsel and make any adjustments necessary.

2
CHAPTER

Business and the Constitution

learning **objectives**

After studying this chapter, students who have mastered the material will be able to:

2-1 Explain the federal system in the context of the U.S. Constitution.

2-2 Describe the purpose and structure of the Constitution.

2-3 List the major provisions of the first three articles of the Constitution and explain the underlying assumptions of coequal branches of government.

2-4 Identify the powers of Congress that impact individuals and businesses.

2-5 Recognize the role of judicial review in interpreting the Constitution.

2-6 Recognize the three standards of constitutional review and their application.

2-7 Understand the various applications and limits of congressional power under the Commerce Clause.

2-8 Describe Constitutional restrictions on state regulation of commerce in the business environment.

2-9 Explain how the tax and spend powers impact business.

2-10 List the major protections in the Constitution's Bill of Rights and explain how they apply in the business environment.

2-11 Identify limits imposed on government overreaching by virtue of the Due Process Clause and Equal Protection Clause.

2-12 Explain the right of privacy that has been recognized by the U.S. Supreme Court and Congress.

The U.S. Constitution is the oldest national ruling document in currently continuous use in the world. Officially ratified in 1788, its longevity may be attributed to its flexibility, which allows contemporary interpretation, and its facility to be changed through amendment when necessary. Business managers and owners should be aware of the impact of constitutional law and protections of individuals and business entities across a broad spectrum of sectors. A fundamental knowledge of constitutional law is an important step in understanding the source and application of federal statutory law as well as the power and limits of government agencies that enforce regulations. In this chapter students will learn:

- The structure of the U.S. Constitution and its role in the American legal system.
- The specific powers granted to the three branches of government in the Constitution.
- The protections afforded by the Constitution in the Bill of Rights and the Fourteenth Amendment.

STRUCTURE AND NATURE OF THE CONSTITUTION: FEDERAL POWERS LO 2-1

The United States uses a **federal system** in which a national government coexists with the government of each state. An important concept underlying the

federal system is that the Constitution acts to limit the federal government's powers to regulate individuals and businesses. States are thought of as having more inherent powers to protect the general welfare of their citizenry with only general constitutional authorization.[1] In contrast, the federal government's power to regulate must be *specifically* granted by the U.S. Constitution. For example, the Constitution grants Congress the explicit power to regulate interstate and foreign commerce and to control the issuance of patents and copyrights.

LO 2-2, 2-3   From a broad perspective, the Constitution may be thought of as having three general functions: (1) establishing a *structure* for the federal government (including qualifications for certain government offices) and rules for amending the Constitution; (2) granting specific *powers* for the different branches of government; and (3) providing *procedural protections* for U.S. citizens from wrongful government actions.

Structure of the Constitution

The U.S. Constitution is composed of a **preamble,** seven **articles,** and 27 **amendments.** The first three articles establish a three-part system of government with three coequal branches: the **legislative branch,** the **executive branch,** and the

---

[1]This inherent power of the state to protect its citizenry's health, safety, and general welfare is also referred to as the state's "police powers."

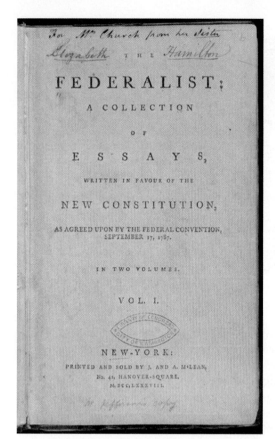

The *Federalist Papers,* written in 1789 by Alexander Hamilton and John Jay as an advocacy publication for ratification of the Constitution, is still cited in modern cases when courts interpret the Constitution.

judicial branch. The underlying rationale for this structure is that each of the branches exercises its respective powers to ensure that one branch does not exceed its authority under the Constitution. This is commonly called the *checks and balances system.*

Specifically, the Constitution begins with a preamble stating the Constitution's broad objectives (e.g., justice, liberty, tranquility, common defense). The articles then set out structure, powers, and procedures. From a business perspective, it is important to note that Congress's powers to directly and exclusively regulate *bankruptcy, patents,* and *copyrights* are set out in Article I. Table 2.1 is a brief synopsis of the provisions in each article.

Amendments

The Constitution has been *amended* (added to or changed) on several occasions since its ratification. These amendments are an important part of the Constitution's function as a protection of the citizenry from unlawful or repressive acts of the government. The first 10 amendments, called the **Bill of Rights,** were added in 1791. The Bill of Rights preserves the rights of the individual U.S. citizens, and in some cases U.S.-based businesses, from unlawful acts of government officials. The Bill of Rights also establishes and protects citizens' rights regarding freedom of speech, religion and assembly as well as protecting against random searches and seizures and other matters. In all, there have been 27 amendments to the Constitution. The applicability of the Bill of Rights in the specific context of business is discussed in detail later in this chapter.

OVERVIEW OF FEDERAL POWERS

Powers granted to the three branches of government in the Constitution are known as **enumerated powers** and are typically *limited in scope.* This means that each act of federal legislation or regulation must come from within one of the very specific, enumerated powers.

Article I—Congressional Powers

The primary authorization of constitutional powers is given to Congress in Article I.[2] Although Congress has enumerated powers in 18 different clauses, the powers that generally impact business owners and managers are (1) the power to *regulate commerce* (**Commerce Clause**); (2) the power to tax citizens and businesses and the spending of government funds (tax and spend provisions); (3) the power to regulate *bankruptcy, patents, and copyrights;* and (4) a *general implied power* to make all laws necessary for carrying out its enumerated powers (**Necessary and Proper Clause**).

Article II—Executive Powers

The president is the chief executive of the United States. Presidential powers that affect business include the powers to (1) carry out laws made by Congress; (2) act as the

> **KEY** POINT
>
> Although the Constitution grants explicit power to the federal government in certain matters, Congress may delegate various powers to state governments. For example, state governments have the right to define exempt-property standards in bankruptcy matters.

LO 2-4

---

[2]§ 8.

TABLE 2.1 Overview of Articles in the U.S. Constitution

Article I	Establishes the legislative branch (a Congress composed of the House of Representatives and the Senate); sets qualifications for members; grants congressional powers (lawmaking).
Article II	Establishes the executive branch (president); sets qualifications for the presidency; grants executive powers (enforcement of laws).
Article III	Establishes the judicial branch with a federal system of courts, including a Supreme Court; grants certain judicial powers.
Article IV	Establishes the relationship between the states and the federal government; describes how to admit new states to the Union.
Article V	Describes the process for amending the Constitution.
Article VI	Establishes the Constitution and federal law as the supreme law of the United States over any conflicting state law; authorizes the national debt (Congress may borrow money); requires that public officials must take an oath to support the Constitution.
Article VII	Lists the requirements for ratification of the Constitution.

commander in chief of the armed forces; (3) enter into treaties (subject to Senate approval) and carry out foreign policy; and (4) appoint federal officers and judges (also subject to Senate approval).

Executive orders have the force of law and are typically issued by the president as a method to carry out executive functions of government. Although there is no constitutional provision that explicitly permits executive orders, Congress may delegate some degree of discretionary power to the president to carry out a federal statute. In cases where there is no congressional delegation, courts have upheld the president's power to issue executive orders based on the general grant of constitutional power to the executive branch for carrying out federal laws. Executive orders may have an impact on business since they touch on areas such as employment discrimination and labor laws. One well-known example is President Lyndon B. Johnson's executive order[3] that prohibited discrimination in employment practices of government contractors and required them to take affirmative action to employ workers without regard to race, color, religion, sex, or national origin.

> **KEY** POINT
>
> The president not only appoints federal officers (with Senate approval) but has the power, in many cases, to unilaterally dismiss those same federal officers.

Article III—Judicial Powers

LO 2-5

The federal judiciary adjudicates (decides) cases and controversies that fall within its authority. In addition to providing for the creation of federal courts, the Constitution also establishes boundaries of **jurisdiction.** Jurisdiction is the legal authority for a court to decide a specific case. Both the U.S. Constitution and individual state constitutions contain language that establishes jurisdiction for certain matters to be heard by certain courts. The concept of jurisdiction is discussed in detail in Chapter 3, "The American Judicial System, Jurisdiction, and Venue."

One of the central concepts in federal constitutional law, **judicial review,** is the notion that federal courts have the right to invalidate state or federal laws that are inconsistent with the U.S. Constitution in some way. The U.S. Supreme Court is the ultimate judge of

---

[3]Executive Order 11246.

federal constitutional law. This authority, possibly the most important judicial power, was not enumerated in the Constitution but was established by the Court in the landmark case of *Marbury v. Madison* in 1803. In *Marbury,* the Court explicitly ruled that (1) the Constitution was superior to federal and state statutes, and (2) when there is a conflict between the Constitution and state or federal law, the Court has the authority to strike down the law as unconstitutional. The Court based these conclusions on the judiciary branch's enumerated powers found in Article III, § 2, which includes authority of matters arising under the Constitution or "laws of the United States."[4] *Marbury,* although decided over 200 years ago, is still considered valid precedent, and federal courts regularly cite the case as a source of authority for the power to invalidate a law that is in conflict with the Constitution. Over the better part of two centuries, the Court further defined its judicial review authority, including the power of federal courts to review state court decisions to the extent that the decisions involve federal law or federal constitutional issues.

In Case 2.1, the U.S. Supreme Court exercises its judicial review power to strike down a federal statute as unconstitutional.

Separation of Powers

The Constitution's enumerated powers are part of an overall scheme that acts to resolve conflicts among the three branches and acts to ensure that no one branch exceeds its constitutional authority. These checks and balances act as a **separation of powers,** ensuring that no one branch becomes overly dominant over the other two.

> **KEY** POINT
> Federal legislation or regulation must be authorized by a specific, enumerated power in the Constitution.

Table 2.2 lists some of the various powers that each branch has that act as a check on the other branches.

LO 2-6 ## Applying the Constitution: Standards of Review

The U.S. Supreme Court has established three standards of review for applying constitutional law. These standards appear in a broad range of constitutional law cases, and the Court has fashioned these standards for use by lower courts in applying the provisions of the Constitution as uniformly as possible. When reviewing a government action for constitutional soundness (such as passage or enforcement of a federal or state law), the Court classifies the action into one of three categories of scrutiny: (1) the **rational basis** category, (2) **intermediate-level scrutiny,** or (3) **strict scrutiny.**

TABLE 2.2 Example of Constitutional Checks and Balances

Branch	Power	Power Checked
Executive	Veto	Congress's lawmaking authority
Legislative	Override veto with supermajority	President's veto authority
Legislative	Impeachment and removal	President and federal judiciary's general powers
Judicial	Invalidate a law as unconstitutional	Congress's authority to make laws; the president's authority to enforce laws

---

[4]Because of its sweeping importance, *Marbury* has been subject to intense analysis, justification, and criticism. Some critics argue that the Supreme Court, in essence, gave the power of judicial review to itself. Most of the criticism of the *Marbury* opinion is derived from the fact that the Constitution does not expressly authorize the courts to invalidate congressional statutes and that such a power is not contemplated in any preratification debates or in advocacy publications such as the *Federalist Papers.*

FACT SUMMARY   The Stolen Valor Act of 2005 made it a federal crime to make false claims related to receiving military decoration or honors. The penalty for false claims about the Congressional Medal of Honor was enhanced to include up to one year in prison. The law was passed largely in response to media stories about various public officials who had exaggerated or lied about their military record during their campaign or while in office. Alvarez was an individual who served as a member of a municipal water district board in Claremont, California. During one public meeting of the board, Alvarez introduced himself and included facts about his past, including that he had served as a marine, been wounded, and received the Congressional Medal of Honor. None of these representations were true. Alvarez was charged with violating the Stolen Valor Act and pleaded guilty, but he reserved the right to challenge the constitutionality of the law based on the First Amendment upon appeal. The U.S. Court of Appeals for the Ninth Circuit struck the statute down as an unconstitutional infringement of free speech under the First Amendment. The government appealed to the U.S. Supreme Court, arguing that because Alvarez's statements were false, he was not entitled to First Amendment protection.

SYNOPSIS OF DECISION AND OPINION   The U.S. Supreme Court ruled in favor of Alvarez and upheld the lower court's decision that the statute violated the First Amendment. The Court ruled that its previous decisions made clear that content-based restrictions on speech were presumed to be invalid and that it was the government's responsibility to demonstrate a compelling interest. The Court rejected the government's argument that false speech is not protected, and it pointed out several instances in which it had previously ruled that falsity alone does not make a statement automatically outside the protection of the First Amendment. The Court acknowledged that the government's interest in protecting the integrity of the Medal of Honor was beyond question. However, the Court's decision to strike the law down as unconstitutional was rooted in the failure of the government to provide evidence of direct link between the statute and the injury to be prevented in protecting the government interest.

WORDS OF THE COURT: Judicial Review/ Compelling Government Interests "The First Amendment requires that the Government's chosen restriction on the speech at issue be 'actually necessary' to achieve its interest. There must be a direct causal link between the restriction imposed and the injury to be prevented. The link between the Government's interest in protecting the integrity of the military honors system and the Act's restriction on the false claims of liars like respondent has not been shown. . . . It must be acknowledged that when a pretender claims the Medal to be his own, the lie might harm the Government by demeaning the high purpose of the award, diminishing the honor it confirms, and creating the appearance that the Medal is awarded more often than is true. Furthermore, the lie may offend the true holders of the Medal. . . . Yet these interests do not satisfy the Government's heavy burden when it seeks to regulate protected speech. The Government points to no evidence to support its claim that the public's general perception of military awards is diluted by false claims such as those made by Alvarez."

Case Questions

1. The dissenting justices argued that allowing First Amendment protection for statements that are lies was a dangerous and unwise path. They also concluded that the link between the statute and the government's interest was more than enough to satisfy any constitutional scrutiny. Are the dissenting arguments compelling? Why or why not?

2. Could Congress have crafted a different law that would have achieved its intended result but survived a constitutional challenge? How?

3. At what point do falsehoods become so serious as to warrant a restriction of the speaker's First Amendment freedom of speech rights?

Rational Basis   Government actions that are in this category are subject to the *least* amount of scrutiny. In order for the court to uphold the action, the government need only show that its action advanced a *legitimate* government objective (such as public welfare, health, or safety) and the action was minimally related to the government's objective. Government actions that fall into this category include those that do not involve any fundamental constitutional rights. Fundamental rights are generally limited to voting, access to criminal appeals, and interstate travel. Therefore, almost every economic- and tax-related law is reviewed using this undemanding threshold, and ultimately the law is found to be constitutional. For example, suppose that, in response to pressure by consumer advocacy groups to regulate Internet access, pricing, and service, Congress passes a law requiring all Internet service providers (ISPs) to be directly regulated by a new federal administrative agency. The law imposes a tax on the ISPs to fund the agency. Mega-Search is an ISP subject to the law and files suit contending the law is an unconstitutional exercise of congressional powers. Because the regulation is purely economic, a court will likely rule against MegaSearch and uphold the law as constitutional using the rational basis category so long as the government provides evidence that the law advanced some legitimate government objective (such as consumer protection). If a state raises its toll fees for a state highway and cites rising maintenance costs, a similar presumption of legality will apply.

Intermediate-Level Scrutiny   Some actions are categorized as subject to intermediate-level scrutiny. Courts will uphold government actions as constitutional so long as the government can prove that its action advanced an *important* government objective (a higher level than the "legitimate" criterion used in the rational basis test) and that the action is *substantially related* (a higher level than "minimally") to the government's objective. A relatively small number of cases fall into this category. For example, courts have used this category in cases involving government action related to regulating time, place, and manner of a political demonstration that is protected under the First Amendment. For example, suppose in the MegaSearch case discussed earlier that the management at MegaSearch organizes a protest against the law and applies for permits to stage demonstrations opposing the law in several cities across the country. One city, Silicone Village, rejects the permit application because MegaSearch's proposed demonstration would block a high-volume traffic area and endanger both pedestrians and drivers. The village also points out that a public park located in the village would be a more appropriate venue. If MegaSearch sues the village for denying the company its First Amendment right to protest, a court would likely find the village's actions permissible under the intermediate-level scrutiny standard because the government's denial of the permit is substantially related to an important government objective (protection of drivers and pedestrians).

Strict Scrutiny   When the government action is related to a fundamental right or is based on a "suspect" classification (i.e., race, national origin, or alienage), courts apply a *strict scrutiny* standard when deciding whether to uphold the government action. Courts will uphold the law only if (1) the government's objective is *compelling,* (2) the means chosen by the government to advance that objective is necessary to achieve that compelling end, and (3) no *less restrictive alternatives* exist. In the strict scrutiny category, the government has the burden of persuasion. As a practical matter, when courts classify government actions as belonging in the strict scrutiny category, they are signaling that the government action is likely to be ruled unconstitutional. For example, suppose that in the MegaSearch case discussed earlier the government passes a law that imposes a higher level of tax on ISPs that cater to Latino users by basing the tax assessment on the number of searches conducted using words and phrases in Spanish. Such a law would be a clear

FACT SUMMARY In 2005, the state of California passed a law that banned the sale or rental of violent video games to anyone under age 18 and required warning labels beyond the existing Entertainment Software Ratings Board's voluntary rating system. The law covered games in which players had the options of killing, maiming, dismembering, or sexually assaulting characters that represent human beings. Entertainment Merchants Association, an association of companies that create and sell or rent video games, brought suit against the state of California seeking to have the law declared unconstitutional. The federal trial court concluded that the statute violated the First Amendment and prevented enforcement of the law. On appeal, the federal appellate court affirmed the decision of the trial court. California appealed to the U.S. Supreme Court.

SYNOPSIS OF DECISION AND OPINION The U.S. Supreme Court ruled in favor of Entertainment Arts and struck down the law as unconstitutional. The Court held that video games are considered speech, similar to plays and movies, and are therefore protected by the First Amendment despite the fact that some people find the video games offensive. Because the law restricted speech, the Court applied a strict scrutiny analysis to the statute and found that (1) California failed to meet its burden of proving a compelling government interest through the use of expert testimony and (2) the law was both too broad (i.e., it covered minors whose parents believed violent video games were harmless) and too narrow (i.e., it did not cover other forms of violent expression such as novels). Finally, the Court distinguished violence from obscenity by ruling that violent speech in this context was protected under the First Amendment.

WORDS OF THE COURT: Due Process and Freedom of Speech "Because the Act imposes a restriction on the content of protected speech, it is invalid unless California can demonstrate that it passes strict scrutiny— that is, unless it is justified by a compelling government interest and is narrowly drawn to serve that interest. The State must specifically identify an 'actual problem' in need of solving, and the curtailment of free speech must be actually necessary to the solution. . . . That is a demanding standard. 'It is rare that a regulation restricting speech because of its content will ever be permissible.' California cannot meet that standard. At the outset, it acknowledges that it cannot show a direct causal link between violent video games and harm to minors. [. . .] The State's evidence is not compelling. California relies primarily on the research of Dr. Craig Anderson and a few other research psychologists whose studies purport to show a connection between exposure to violent video games and harmful effects on children. These studies have been rejected by every court to consider them, and with good reason: They do not prove that violent video games *cause* minors to *act* aggressively (which would at least be a beginning). Instead, '[n]early all of the research is based on correlation, not evidence of causation, and most of the studies suffer from significant, admitted flaws in methodology.' They show at best some correlation between exposure to violent entertainment and minuscule real-world effects, such as children's feeling more aggressive or making louder noises in the few minutes after playing a violent game than after playing a nonviolent game. [. . .] Our cases have been clear that the obscenity exception to the First Amendment does not cover whatever a legislature shocking, but only depictions of 'sexual conduct.'"

Case Questions

1. Why did the state of California have to meet a strict scrutiny standard for this statute to be constitutional?

2. If the expert testimony had been conclusive and scientifically proven, should the court's decision be different? Why or why not?

3. Should a state be legislating regarding this type of conduct, or should such conduct be solely a private issue to be decided on and enforced by parents or guardians?

example of the government's use of a suspect classification (national origin) and would clearly be struck down under a strict scrutiny analysis.

In Case 2.2, the U.S. Supreme Court examines the constitutionality of a California statute regarding a limitation of First Amendment freedom of speech and applies the strict scrutiny standard.

The Supremacy Clause and Preemption

Because our federal system of government contemplates the coexistence of federal law with the various laws of the states, there is sometimes a conflict between federal law and state law. Article VI of the U.S. Constitution provides that valid federal laws (those made pursuant to Congress's constitutional authority and that are constitutionally sound) are always *supreme* to any conflicting state law. This is known as the **Supremacy Clause,** and it invalidates any state law that is in direct conflict with federal law. The power granted by the supremacy clause to override a state law is called **preemption.** In order for preemption to occur, the federal law must be directly in conflict with the state law to the point where the two laws cannot coexist. For example, in *Geier v. American Honda Motor Company,*[5] the U.S. Supreme Court held that a federal regulation giving auto manufacturers the choice between airbags or alternative methods of passenger safety restraints preempted a claim by an injured party against an auto manufacturer under a state common law doctrine based on failing to install airbags. The Court ruled that, because the injured party's case depended upon a claim that auto manufacturers had a legal duty to install airbags and the violation of that duty resulted in the injury, the state common law could not coexist with federal law that specifically allowed auto manufacturers to opt not to install airbags in favor of another type of restraint system.

LO 2-7 COMMERCE POWERS

Congress's broadest power is derived from the Commerce Clause, whereby Congress is given the power to "regulate Commerce among the several states."[6] Under the modern trend, federal courts have been largely deferential to legislative decisions under Congress's commerce powers. Despite some limits placed by the U.S. Supreme Court in the relatively recent past, Congress still exercises very broad powers to pass laws when the activity being regulated affects interstate commerce in any way.

Application of Commerce Powers

Congress exercises its commerce powers in various forms. However, the direct and broad power to regulate all persons and products related to the flow of interstate commerce is the fundamental source of its authority.

Interstate versus Intrastate Commercial Activity   Congress has the express constitutional authority to regulate (1) channels of interstate commerce such as railways and highways, (2) the instrumentalities of interstate commerce such as vehicles used in shipping, and (3) the articles moving in interstate commerce. Even for commercial activity that is purely *intrastate* (taking place within one state's borders), Congress has the power to regulate the activity so long as it has a *substantial economic effect* on interstate commerce. For example, Illinois passed a statute requiring that commercial trucks driving through that state be equipped with a particular style of contoured mudguard. The state provided evidence that the contoured mudguard would provide additional safety for motorists in inclement weather. No other state had such a requirement, and, in fact, the contoured mudguard was illegal in two states. Trucks would have to stop at the border of Illinois and install the guards, which had to be welded on. This meant that some trucks would have to be unloaded and reloaded during the welding process. In the landmark case of *Bibb v. Navajo Freight Lines,* 359 U.S. 520 (1959), the U.S. Supreme Court found that although the law applied to trucks only while in Illinois, the additional burdens of lost time and costs of installation substantially affected interstate commerce. This substantial effect outweighed the minimal additional safety provided by the mudguard's use. In the dynamics

---

[5]529 U.S. 861 (2000).

[6]Article I, § 8.

of the modern-day commercial world, a large amount of seemingly intrastate activity has some degree of economic effect on interstate commerce.

The U.S. Supreme Court has even deferred to congressional regulation of a product that is cultivated for noncommercial purposes solely in one state as sufficiently related to *interstate* commerce. In *Gonzalez v. Raich*,[7] the Court ruled that Congress had the power to criminalize the possession of marijuana even if it was both noncommercially cultivated and consumed under medical prescription in the same state. The case involved a challenge by two California residents to the enforcement by federal officials of the federal Controlled Substances Act after California passed a state law via voter ballot proposition to exempt anyone involved in the cultivating, prescribing, and consuming of marijuana for medical purposes from prosecution. The plaintiffs were each arrested by federal officials for possession of marijuana that had been grown at home. Each had a prescription from a licensed physician. In refusing to invalidate the Controlled Substances Act, the Court noted that Congress could have rationally believed that the noncommercially grown marijuana would be drawn into the *interstate market* and, therefore, the banning of the substance was sufficiently related to interstate commercial activity. *Gonzalez v. Raich* is featured in Case 2.3.

The Commerce Clause and Civil Rights Legislation

A key use of the federal commerce power has been in the area of civil rights legislation. Indeed, the Supreme Court's level of deference for use of congressional commerce powers reached its peak during and directly after the civil rights era. In the 1964 Civil Rights Act, Congress used

President Johnson, seen here with Dr. Martin Luther King, Jr., signed the Civil Rights Act in 1964.

---

[7]545 U.S. 1 (2005).

its commerce power to ban discrimination in places of public accommodation such as restaurants and hotels. In two important civil rights cases decided by the U.S. Supreme Court, the Court ruled that the Civil Rights Act was a permissible application of Congress's commerce powers. In *Heart of Atlanta Motel v. U.S.,*[8] the Court made clear that a federal ban on racial discrimination was a constitutionally permitted use of congressional commerce powers because the hotel was open to *interstate* travelers. Additionally, the Court deferred to a congressional finding of fact that racial discrimination in accommodations discouraged travel by limiting a substantial portion of the black community's ability to find suitable lodging. In a companion case,[9] *Katzenbach v. McClung,*[10] the Court held that a local restaurant that was located far from any interstate highway, and had no appreciable business from interstate travelers, was nevertheless subject to the reach of the federal statute because the restaurant purchased *some* food and paper supplies from out-of-state vendors. Since these purchases were of items that had moved in commerce, Congress could properly exercise its power to regulate a restaurant whose business interests were primarily local.

Noncommercial Activity   In 1995, the U.S. Supreme Court signaled that some limits on Congress's commerce power still exist. In cases where the activity is purely *noncommercial* (such as when Congress passes a criminal statute that is seemingly unrelated to commerce), the Court has used increased levels of scrutiny to be sure that the activity that Congress seeks to regulate has a sufficient nexus (connection) to some legitimate economic interest. In *U.S. v. Lopez,*[11] the Court invalidated a federal statute on the basis that it was beyond Congress's commerce powers. In *Lopez,* the Court struck down the Gun-Free School Zones Act of 1990, which made it a federal crime to possess a gun within a certain distance from a school. The Court rejected the government's argument that gun possession in schools affected economic productivity (by making it more difficult for students to obtain an education) and thus was within the purview of congressional commerce power. The Court held that such a broad interpretation of the commerce power would mean that congressional power was virtually unlimited and that such an expansive authority was directly contrary to the express limits imposed by the Constitution. The Court reasoned that the banning of firearms in local schools was a government police power and, therefore, more appropriately handled by the state government. Five years later, in *U.S. v. Morrison,* the Court invalidated another statute on the same grounds. In that case, the Court struck down the Violence Against Women Act, which gave victims of gender-motivated violence the right to sue their attacker for money damages in a federal court. In light of the *Lopez* decision, Congress made exhaustive findings of fact that detailed the cumulative economic effect of gender-motivated crimes. Nonetheless, the Court held that the congressional findings were too broad to justify use of the commerce power and that virtually any local crime could become a federal offense under a similar justification. As a general rule, the further that Congress strays from regulating commercial activity, the more likely the Court will be to give the law intense constitutional scrutiny.

> **KEY** POINT
>
> Congress's broadest powers are derived from the Commerce Clause. Courts are highly deferential to congressional action in areas that affect interstate commerce.

---

[8]379 U.S. 241 (1964).

[9]Two cases with similar issues are often argued together. The Court publishes both opinions at the same time.

[10]379 U.S. 294 (1964).

[11]514 U.S. 549 (1995).

Constitutional Restrictions on State Regulation of Commerce

The U.S. Supreme Court has ruled that the mere existence of congressional commerce powers restricts the states from *discriminating* against or *unduly burdening* interstate commerce. States often wish to regulate commerce that crosses into their state borders. States are free to regulate commerce so long as (1) it does not impose a discriminatory law (such as a tax) on out-of-state businesses and (2) the state law is a *legitimate* effort to regulate health, safety, and welfare. For example, suppose that in order to protect its own economic interests, the Texas state legislature imposes an inspection requirement and fee on all non-Texas-bred beef sold within Texas. The state legislature justifies this process and fee on the basis that the law is protecting its citizens from diseased beef. A court would likely strike down the law because it discriminates against out-of-state ranchers and its explanation could be seen as a pretext (not the actual reason) since the law presumes that in-state beef is safe. Moreover, the inspection fee and the inspection process could be viewed as unreasonably burdening interstate commerce.

Visit Connect for additional information and case summaries related to constitutional limitations on a state's imposing a tax on out-of-state vendors (including Internet vendors).

In Case 2.3, the U.S. Supreme Court considers whether a state law legalizing purely local cultivation, processing, and use of marijuana burdens interstate commerce.

CASE 2.3 Gonzalez v. Raich, 545 U.S. 1 (2005)

FACT SUMMARY In 1996, California voters approved a proposition legalizing the use of marijuana for medical purposes. The California legislature then adopted the Compassionate Use Act of 1996 to ensure that its residents had access to marijuana for medical use as an alternative to conventional methods. The law created an exemption from criminal prosecution for physicians, patients, and primary caregivers who possess or grow marijuana for medical use with the approval and recommendation of a physician. Raich and Monson were patients diagnosed with a variety of medical conditions that were not alleviated through traditional methods and medications. As a result, physicians in each case prescribed marijuana. Raich's physician testified that marijuana had been the only effective method to alleviate her symptoms and that discontinuing medical marijuana treatments would cause Raich excruciating pain and could very well prove fatal. In 2002, U.S. drug agents arrived at Monson's home and confiscated and destroyed her marijuana plants pursuant to a federal law called the Controlled Substances Act (CSA). Raich and Monson brought suit seeking to prevent federal law enforcement officials from enforcing the CSA in medical marijuana cases. They argued that enforcement of the CSA violated the Commerce Clause because the medical marijuana was cultivated and possessed within state borders and did not enter the stream of commerce. The trial court ruled in favor of the government, but the appellate court reversed the decision and ruled that the intrastate, noncommercial cultivation and possession of marijuana was not intended to enter interstate commerce. The government appealed to the U.S. Supreme Court.

SYNOPSIS OF DECISION AND OPINION The U.S. Supreme Court ruled in favor of the government and held that the CSA was a valid exercise of congressional powers derived from the Commerce Clause. In analyzing the question of purely intrastate production and use of marijuana, the Court pointed out that Congress need only supply a rational basis for believing that locally cultivated marijuana would end up in interstate commerce. The Court held that congressional

(continued)

concerns about distinguishing between marijuana cultivated locally and marijuana grown elsewhere and the concerns about medicinal marijuana's contribution to illicit drug channels were rational and therefore constitutional.

WORDS OF THE COURT: Commerce Clause "The question before us, however, is not whether it is wise to enforce the statute in these circumstances; rather, it is whether Congress' power to regulate interstate markets for medicinal substances encompasses the portions of those markets that are supplied with drugs produced and consumed locally. Well-settled law controls our answer. . . . In assessing the scope of Congress' authority under the Commerce Clause, we stress that the task before us is a modest one. We need not determine whether respondents' activities, taken in the aggregate, substantially affect interstate commerce in fact, but only whether a 'rational basis' exists for so concluding. [Citations omitted] Given the enforcement difficulties that attend distinguishing between marijuana cultivated locally and marijuana grown elsewhere, [citation omitted] and concerns about diversion into illicit channels, we have no difficulty concluding that Congress had a rational basis for believing that failure to regulate the intrastate manufacture and possession of marijuana would leave a gaping hole in the CSA. Thus . . . , when it enacted comprehensive legislation to regulate the interstate market in a fungible commodity, Congress was acting well within its authority to 'make all Laws which shall be necessary and proper' to 'regulate commerce . . . among the several States.' [Citation omitted] That the regulation ensnares some purely intrastate activity is of no moment. As we have done many times before, we refuse to excise individual components of that larger scheme. . . . The congressional judgment that an exemption for such a significant segment of the total market would undermine the orderly enforcement of the entire regulatory scheme is entitled to a strong presumption of validity. Indeed, that judgment is not only rational, but 'visible to the naked eye.'"

Case Questions

1. The CSA expressly prohibits the cultivation, processing, distribution, and use of marijuana, declaring it unfit for any legal use. Since a market for marijuana legally cannot exist, why is this a Commerce Clause case? Do you agree or disagree with the Court that locally grown and locally consumed crops can have an impact on interstate commerce?

2. The California law gave licensed physicians the duty and authority to prescribe medical marijuana. Should a court have the right or power to substitute its judgment for the judgment of a trained professional?

3. California enacted this law to provide relief to certain California citizens deemed to need it. Citizens of other states were excluded from all provisions of this statute. Should the federal government have the right to determine that a federal law preempts a state law designed and intended to affect only the state's residents?

LEGAL/ETHICAL REFLECTION *and* DISCUSSION

In *Gonzalez v. Raich*, Justice Stevens, in the majority decision, wrote, "[O]ur cases have taught us that there are some unscrupulous physicians who overprescribe when it is sufficiently profitable to do so." He also wrote, "The likelihood that all such production (of marijuana) will promptly terminate when patients recover or will precisely match the patients' medical needs during their convalescence seems remote."

Should such speculation and assumption be part of a court's decision-making process?

TAX AND SPEND POWER[12]

Congress has a far-reaching power to tax the citizenry and to spend the federal government's money in any way that promotes the common defense and general welfare. The power to tax is an independent source of federal authority. That is, Congress may tax activities or property that it might not be authorized to regulate directly under any of the enumerated regulatory powers. The power to spend is linked to the power to tax in that the money may be raised by taxation and then spent on the general welfare of the United States. The U.S. Supreme Court has been highly deferential to Congress in terms of what constitutes general welfare and under what circumstances Congress may exercise its authority to tax its citizenry and its decision-making power on how to allocate government money.

In *Federation of Independent Business v. Sebelius,*[13] the U.S. Supreme Court ruled on the constitutionality of the Patient Protection and Affordable Care Act[14] (commonly referred to as "Obamacare"). The most controversial section of the act was the individual mandate. The individual mandate requires that most citizens be covered by minimum essential health care by 2014. Those not covered by 2014 will be required to pay up to $695, to be collected along with their annual federal income taxes. The court rejected the position of the law's supporters that the government may impose this mandate and fee based on commerce powers, ruling that the government may not use its commerce power to compel citizens to act as the government would have them act and that the government may not regulate what citizens legally choose to do or not do. However, the payment required for noncompliance was upheld as a constitutionally permissible tax. Even though the payment for noncoverage was called a "penalty" in the text of the act, because it was not punishment for an unlawful act or omission, the Court deemed it a permissible exercise of the government's taxing powers. The Court reasoned that no one is being forced to obtain insurance and no criminal sanctions are imposed for not buying insurance. Citizens are free to choose not to buy insurance and could opt to pay the tax instead. This tax goes into the general treasury as do other federal taxes.

The expectation was that a large percentage of workers would have health insurance coverage since the Act requires businesses with 50 or more employees to provide insurance to their employees or face a fine. In July 2013, however, Senior Obama adviser Valerie Jarrett announced that the business mandate would be postponed until 2015, even though the individual mandate will still be implemented in 2014, as originally passed.

Necessary and Proper Clause

Congress may also place *conditions* on the use of federal money in order to achieve some public policy objective. Congress generally cites the Necessary and Proper Clause as authorization to set conditions on the spending. This ability to set conditions on the use of federal money has been a somewhat controversial method of congressional regulation because it falls outside the areas of *traditional* regulation. However, the U.S. Supreme Court has upheld federal spending conditions that are tied to individual states' passing certain laws that carry out a congressionally set ambition. State legislatures have objected to

---

[12]Article I, § 8. "The Congress shall have the Power To lay and collect Taxes, Duties, Imposts and Excises . . . to pay the Debts and provide for the common Defence and general Welfare of the United States. . . ."

[13]567 U.S. 1, 132 S. Ct. 2566 (2012).

[14]26 U.S.C. § 5000A.

this type of regulation, characterizing it as a backdoor method for imposing laws on states that are outside Congress's enumerated powers.

In *South Dakota v. Dole*,[15] the Court deferred to Congress's right to attach certain spending conditions related to the legal drinking age (a state law issue)[16] on federal funds distributed to the states for use in repairing and building highways. Unless a state passed a law to raise the legal drinking age to 21 by a certain date, it would lose a certain percentage of its allotted highway funding from the federal government. South Dakota and other states challenged the law as an unconstitutional intrusion by Congress into state affairs and an overreaching use of its spending power to regulate. The Court sided with Congress and ruled that the drinking-age condition is constitutionally permissible under Congress's spending authority so long as the condition itself is not a violation of individual constitutional rights. This case signaled an important victory for Congress, which now regularly uses spending conditions as a form of regulation for individuals and businesses.

✓ **Self-Check**   Source of Constitutional Authority

What is the constitutional source of authority for each of the following laws?

1. A federal statute that makes it more difficult for businesses to qualify for protection under bankruptcy laws.

2. An increase in the federal corporate income tax.

3. A federal statute that adds criminal penalties for patent infringement.

4. A federal statute creating an agency to regulate ground shipping between states.

5. A federal statute that requires that 25 percent of federal government construction contracts be awarded to companies that are women- or minority-owned enterprises.

Answers to this Self-Check are provided at the end of the chapter.

CONCEPT SUMMARY Structure and Nature of the Constitution: Federal Powers

■ Under the federal system used by the United States, the federal government has only limited powers to regulate individuals and businesses.

■ These powers are specifically enumerated in the Constitution and are limited in scope.

■ The limited powers of the legislative branch, which are specifically enumerated in the Constitution, include (1) the power to regulate commerce; (2) the power to tax and spend; (3) the power to regulate bankruptcy, patents, and copyrights; and (4) a general implied authority to make all laws necessary for carrying out its enumerated powers.

■ The president is granted the power to (1) carry out laws made by Congress; (2) be the commander in chief of the armed forces; (3) enter into a treaty and carry out foreign policy; and (4) appoint federal officers and judges.

■ The judiciary is authorized to decide cases and controversies falling within federal jurisdiction.

■ Congress's broadest power is derived from the Commerce Clause.

■ Under the Commerce Clause, Congress has the authority to regulate (1) channels of interstate commerce such as railways and highways; (2) the instrumentalities of interstate commerce such as vehicles used in shipping; (3) the articles moving in interstate

---

[15]483 U.S. 203 (1987).

[16]At that time, 19 states permitted consumption of some or all alcoholic beverages before the age of 21.

- commerce; and (4) any activity that has substantial economic effect on interstate commerce, including activities that are not commercial in nature.
- The U.S. Constitution is composed of a preamble, seven articles, and 27 amendments, the first 10 of which are called the Bill of Rights.
- The first three articles of the Constitution establish a three-part system of government with three coequal branches: the legislative branch, the executive branch, and the judicial branch.
- This structure is designed so that each of the branches exercises its respective powers to ensure that one branch does not exceed its authority under the Constitution (referred to as a separation of powers or checks and balances).
- Under the Supremacy Clause, federal laws preempt (override) any conflicting state laws.
- Congress has the power to tax the citizenry and to spend the federal government's money in any way that promotes the common defense and general welfare.
- Under the Necessary and Proper Clause, Congress may also place conditions on the use of federal money in order to achieve some public policy objective.

CONSTITUTIONAL PROTECTIONS

LO 2-10

In addition to the Constitution prescribing the structure of government and granting the government certain powers, it also provides protection for the citizenry and businesses from unlawful or repressive acts by the government. These protections are contained primarily in the Bill of Rights (the first 10 amendments) and in other amendments, such as the Fourteenth Amendment, that guarantee the right of **due process.** From a business perspective, however, it is important to note that corporations and other business entities do *not* always receive the same level of constitutional protections as individuals.

The Bill of Rights and Business

The Bill of Rights contains many of the rights common in the American vernacular. Among them are freedom of speech, the press, religion, and expression (First Amendment); freedom from government-conducted searches without cause or warrant (Fourth Amendment); rights against self-incrimination and to a speedy jury trial by our peers (Fifth and Sixth Amendments); and freedom from cruel and unusual punishments (Eighth Amendment). While each amendment carries it own significance in a historical and public policy context, the coverage in this textbook is primarily concerned with the Bill of Rights provisions that relate directly to business and management issues.

First Amendment

The First Amendment contains the important introductory phrase "Congress shall make no law" and then articulates several specific protections against government encroachment in the areas of religion, press, speech, assembly, and petition of grievances. The introductory phrase demonstrates that the framers intended the Constitution to function as a *limit* on federal government actions. It was not until the passage of the Fourteenth Amendment that these limitations were constitutionally extended to state government actions. Although certain First Amendment rights for individuals do not extend to business owners, courts have increasingly broadened protections for business owners in the area of free speech. Defamation, a tort discussed in Chapter 10, "Torts and Products Liability," is another limitation on freedom of speech pertinent to business. The right of employees to criticize their employers and the right of employers to disclose negative information on employment references are issues currently being litigated and defined.

Limits on Free Speech   Although the U.S. Supreme Court has given broad protections to speech that involves political expression, the First Amendment is by no means absolute. Justice Oliver Wendell Holmes famously wrote that the First Amendment was not without limits by giving the example that the Constitution did not protect someone who falsely yells "fire" in a crowded theater. Courts have ruled that the government may place reasonable restrictions related to time and place of political expression in cases, for example, where public safety may be threatened.

Commercial Speech   The most common form of commercial speech (ways in which business entities communicate with the public) is *advertising* through print, television, radio, and web-based sources. Traditionally, advertising had little or no First Amendment protection, but the Supreme Court has gradually increased the constitutional protections related to advertising. In *Virginia State Board of Pharmacy v. Virginia Citizens Consumer Council,*[17] the Supreme Court held that purely commercial speech (speech with no political implications whatsoever) was entitled to partial First Amendment protection so long as the speech was truthful and concerned a lawful activity. In the *Virginia* case, the Court struck down Virginia state laws that prohibited a pharmacist from advertising prices for prescription drugs. The Court rejected the state's contention that it has a substantial interest in ensuring that cut-rate prices that may be created by competition among pharmacies don't result in substandard service. Given that the information banned by the statute was limiting the free flow of information to consumers, the Court held that such regulation violated the First Amendment.

Four years after the *Virginia* case, the Court expanded the analytical framework for deciding whether certain regulations were constitutional in *Central Hudson Gas v. Public Service Commission.*[18] The *Central Hudson* case created a framework for a four-part test that subjects government restrictions on commercial speech to a form of intermediate-level scrutiny:

- *Part One:* So long as the commercial speech concerns lawful activities and is not misleading, the speech qualifies for protection under the First Amendment. If the speech is entitled to protection, then the government's regulation must pass the final three parts of the *Central Hudson* test in order for the restriction to be constitutionally sound.
- *Part Two:* A *substantial government interest* in regulating the speech must exist.
- *Part Three:* The government must demonstrate that the restriction *directly advances* the claimed government interest.
- *Part Four:* The government's restriction must be *not more extensive* than necessary (not too broad) to achieve the government's asserted interest.

In Case 2.4, a federal appellate court applies the *Central Hudson* framework to a regulation compelling speech by the tobacco industry.

Advertising and Obscenity Regulation   Sometimes commercial speech runs afoul of government's attempt to ban or regulate materials it deems obscene. However, obscenity regulation of commercial speech is subject to the same scrutiny as any other government regulation of commercial speech. For example, a federal appellate court has ruled that a state agency's decision to effectively prohibit a corporation's use of a certain label on its beer products, which the agency deemed offensive, violated the business owner's right under commercial speech protections. In that case, *Bad Frog Brewery, Inc. v. N.Y. State Liquor Authority,*[19] the U.S. Court of Appeals for the Second Circuit held that labels on the company's beer products, which depicted a frog with his unwebbed "fingers" extended in a manner evocative of a well-known human gesture of insult, were protected commercial speech under the First Amendment. The court ruled that when the New York State Liquor

---

[17]425 U.S. 748 (1976).

[18]447 U.S. 557 (1980).

[19]134 F.3d 87 (2nd Cir. 1998).

FACT SUMMARY The Family Smoking Prevention and Tobacco Control Act, passed in 2009, directed the secretary of the U.S. Department of Health and Human Services to issue regulations requiring that all cigarette packages manufactured or sold in the United States bear one of nine new textual warnings, as well as "color graphics depicting the negative health consequences of smoking." The Food and Drug Administration (FDA) initiated a rulemaking proceeding through which it selected the nine images that would accompany the statutorily prescribed warnings. Among those proposed by the FDA were images of a man exhaling cigarette smoke through a tracheotomy hole in his throat and a pair of diseased lungs next to a pair of healthy lungs. R.J. Reynolds and four other tobacco companies (RJR) challenged the rule, arguing that it would infringe on their commercial speech rights under the First Amendment. The trial court ruled in favor of RJR and the FDA appealed.

SYNOPSIS OF DECISION AND OPINION The U.S. Court of Appeals for the District of Columbia upheld the trial court's decision in favor of RJR. The court applied the *Central Hudson* test and ruled that the FDA had failed to supply any evidence that the rule, which restricted commercial speech, directly advanced a substantial government interest. The court ruled that the labels were not purely factual because they did not convey any warning information or offer any information about the impact of smoking. Rather, the images were intended to generate emotional responses. Therefore, the FDA could not meet its

burden under the *Central Hudson* test with respect to how the graphic warnings directly advanced the government's interest.

WORDS OF THE COURT: Applying the *Central Hudson* Test "Under *Central Hudson,* the government must first show that its asserted interest is 'substantial.' If so, the Court must determine 'whether the regulation directly advances the governmental interest asserted, and whether it is not more extensive than is necessary to serve that interest.' . . . FDA has not provided a shred of evidence—much less the 'substantial evidence' required . . . showing that the graphic warnings will 'directly advance' its interest in reducing the number of Americans who smoke. FDA makes much of the 'international consensus' surrounding the effectiveness of large graphic warnings, but offers no evidence showing that such warnings have *directly caused* a material decrease in smoking rates in any of the countries that now require them."

Case Questions

1. Commercial speech is generally analyzed under intermediate scrutiny rather than under strict scrutiny. Do you think it is appropriate to treat advertising differently than other forms of speech? Why or why not?

2. What did the FDA need to prove in order to prevail in this case?

3. Should compelled speech be analyzed or treated differently than prohibited speech? Why or why not?

Authority denied Bad Frog's application to use the labels in New York on the basis that the labels were offensive, the state agency failed to show that its ruling achieved the agency's asserted interest of protecting children from vulgarity. Because the labels were not misleading and did not concern an unlawful activity, the labels were a protected form of commercial speech and any government regulation must conform with the requirements set out in the *Central Hudson* case. Ruling in favor of Bad Frog, the court remarked that a state must demonstrate that its commercial speech limitation is part of a substantial effort to advance a valid state interest, "not merely the removal of a few grains of offensive sand from the beach of vulgarity."

Visit Connect to see the Bad Frog label.

Political Speech by Corporations Another form of commercial speech, broadly speaking, occurs when corporations and other business entities fund political speech or engage in corporate advocacy of a particular candidate or political issue. May the government regulate such commercial speech under the same standards as the *Central Hudson* case? Generally, the answer depends of the specific form and content of the speech—but typically political speech by corporations is fully protected by the First Amendment.

In *First National Bank of Boston v. Bellotti,*[20] the Supreme Court created a new level of First Amendment protection for corporations engaged in *politically* oriented speech when it struck down a Massachusetts state statute that prohibited corporations from using corporate assets to fund expenditures related to "influencing or affecting the vote on any question submitted to the voters" (known as a *ballot proposition*).[21] In *Bellotti,* the Court held that that while some constitutional rights are not afforded to corporations, freedom of corporate political speech is fully protected. As such, any attempt to regulate politically oriented speech by corporations is subject to *strict scrutiny.* The Court also held that a corporation's freedom of speech is not limited to matters materially affecting its business. Rather, a business has a constitutionally protected right to communicate about any political matter that is consistent with the goal of the First Amendment: societal interest in the free flow of information and debate. For the first time, the Court recognized that speech that otherwise would be within the protection of the First Amendment does not lose protection simply because its source is a corporation.

Political Spending and Corporations In a 2010 case that attracted significant media attention, the U.S. Supreme Court ruled that the government may not ban all political spending by corporations in *candidate elections.* In *Citizens United v. Federal Election Commission,*[22] the Court held that the provisions of the Bipartisan Campaign Reform Act of 2002 (commonly referred to as the "McCain-Feingold Act"), which prohibited corporations and labor unions from using general funds to sponsor "electioneering communications," were unconstitutional. It is important to note that the ruling did not involve a challenge to limits imposed by the law on campaign contributions or to the prohibition of corporate contributions to a candidate. These limits remain intact. Rather, the Supreme Court's ruling applies only to *independent expenditures* on speech. Independent expenditures involve speech (such as advertisements) engaged in by an organization on its own behalf, and not with coordination with any candidate.

> **KEY** POINT
>
> Commercial speech in the form of advertising has partial First Amendment protection (subject to intermediate-level scrutiny) under *Central Hudson.* Corporate *political* speech has full First Amendment protection (subject to strict scrutiny) under *Bellotti* and *Citizens United.*

The case originated when Citizens United, a conservative nonprofit corporation, produced a 90-minute documentary called *Hillary: The Movie* which criticized then-Senator Hillary Clinton and questioned her fitness for office. The group planned to release it during the 2008 Democratic presidential primaries. Fearful that uncertainties in the law would result in enforcement action by the government upon release of the movie, Citizens United filed suit against the Federal Elections Commission (FEC) in federal court, challenging the act. After the group lost that case, Citizens United scrapped its plans to release the movie but continued to appeal the trial court's decision. The U.S. Supreme Court ruled in favor of Citizens United, striking down the provisions of the law that banned Citizens United from releasing the movie. Justice Anthony Kennedy wrote the majority opinion:

> When the government seeks to use its full power, including criminal law, to command where a person may get his or her information or what distrusted source he or she may not hear, it uses censorship to control thought. This is unlawful. The First Amendment confirms the freedom to think for ourselves.

---

[20]435 U.S. 765 (1978).

[21]Also known in certain states as a *referendum* or *ballot initiative.*

[22]558 U.S. 50 (2010).

Other Amendments

In addition to the First Amendment, certain other protections afforded by the Constitution may be important to business owners and managers. The **Fourth Amendment** protects individual citizens' rights to be secure in their "persons, houses, papers and effects." The U.S. Supreme Court has systematically applied a *reasonableness test* to define the limits of when the government may search without a warrant based on probable cause that criminal activity is afoot. From a business perspective, it is important to understand that the law recognizes two basic types of searches. First, when the government wishes to obtain a warrant to search particular premises while investigating a *criminal offense,* it must demonstrate that it has sufficient information, called *probable cause,* that justifies the issuance of a search warrant by a court.[23] Second, the government also investigates noncriminal *administrative violation*s. The standard for the issuance of a warrant for a search in an administrative violation investigation is lower than that for investigating a criminal offense. Administrative warrants may be used by government regulatory agencies (such as the Environmental Protection Agency) to gain access to worksites for compliance inspections. Remember that these protections are in regard to intrusions by federal and state governments. Protections regarding workplace privacy intrusion by private employers are discussed later in this chapter. Administrative agencies and administrative warrants are discussed in detail in Chapter 18, "Administrative Law."

The **Fifth Amendment** provides that no person "shall be compelled in any criminal case to be a witness against himself." Simply put, this amendment guarantees individuals the right to remain silent both during the investigation and during any subsequent judicial proceedings. Although it is clear that this amendment does not apply to corporate *entities* when the government is seeking certain business records, individual corporate officers and employees are entitled to Fifth Amendment protection when facing a criminal investigation by the police or, more commonly in a business context, an administrative agency investigation of a possible criminal offense (e.g., the Internal Revenue Service investigating tax fraud). This right is a central and fundamental part of the Supreme Court's famous decision in *Miranda v. Arizona.*[24] The *Miranda* case set out specific procedures to be used by the government when interrogating possible suspects of criminal wrongdoings. The *Miranda* case is covered in detail in Chapter 23, "Criminal Law and Procedure in Business."

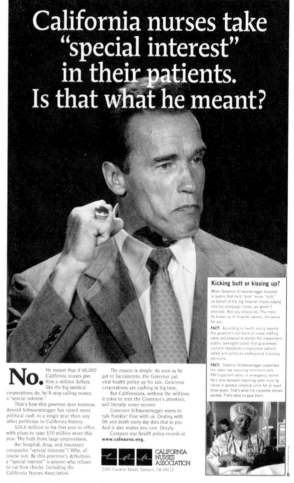

Political speech by corporations, such as the nonprofit California Nurses Association's advertising campaign opposing Governor Arnold Schwarzenegger, is protected under the First Amendment.

---

[23]Criminal offenses and probable cause are discussed in detail in Chapter 23, "Criminal Law and Procedure in Business."

[24]384 U.S. 436 (1966).

DUE PROCESS PROTECTIONS

In addition to protection afforded by the Bill of Rights, the law provides protections to individuals and businesses from government overreaching through constitutional guarantees contained in the **Due Process Clause** of the Fifth and Fourteenth Amendments. These clauses protect individuals from being deprived of "life, liberty, or property" without due process of law. Fundamentally, due process rights require the government to provide some type of *hearing* and *procedure* whenever the government has taken some action that deprives an individual or business of some liberty or property interest.

Fourteenth Amendment

Perhaps the most important role of the Fourteenth Amendment is that it makes the Bill of Rights applicable to the states. Note, for example, that the First Amendment begins with the explicit restriction that "Congress shall make no law . . ." Originally, the framers intended the Bill of Rights to be a protection against certain acts of the *federal* government, and therefore states were not bound by the Bill of Rights. However, in the post-Civil War reconstruction period (mid-1860s), the Fourteenth Amendment was passed, which effectively expanded the protections under the Bill of Rights to include restrictions and actions by *state governments*.

The Due Process Clause has two primary functions. First, it imposes certain *procedural* requirements on federal and state governments when they impair life, liberty, or property. The U.S. Supreme Court has held that procedural due process requires the government to give appropriate notice, a neutral hearing, and an opportunity to present evidence before any government action may be taken that would affect the life, liberty, or property of an individual. The Due Process Clause also limits the *substantive* power of the states to regulate certain areas related to individual liberty. These substantive due process rights require that laws passed by the government be published for public inspection and be specific enough that a reasonable person would understand how the law applies. Laws that are vague or overly broad are unconstitutional under the substantive due process doctrine.

Note how the court examined the due process issue regarding minors' free speech in Case 2.2, *Brown v. Entertainment Merchants Association* discussed earlier in this chapter.

Equal Protection
The Equal Protection Clause is the part of the Fourteenth Amendment that prohibits the government from denying citizens equal protection of the laws.[25] Fundamentally, the clause guarantees that the government will treat people who are similarly situated equally. Recall from our discussion earlier in this chapter that courts use a variety of levels of review when applying constitutional law. This is especially important in equal protection cases, where courts apply one of the three categories of review that are classified by their level of scrutiny (strict, intermediate-level, or rational basis).

Equal protection does not mean that everyone must be treated exactly the same. Constitutionally permissive *categories* may be created, and the categories may be treated differently; however, those within each category must be treated the same. For example, suppose that you attend a state college or university. Do all of the students pay the same base tuition rate? Most likely the answer is no. In-state residents generally pay a lower fee than do out-of-state students because this can be justified by the fact that in-state students (or their parents) pay taxes that help support the school while out-of-state students' tax revenue stays in their home states. This is permissible. A state college or university cannot, however, decide to charge different rates based on the students' different home states (one rate for Delaware, a second for California, a third for Iowa, etc.). Note that charging different rates based on race, religion, or national origin would not be constitutionally valid regardless of a student's state of residence.

---

[25] Although the direct text of the clause applies to state governments, the federal government is also bound by the same rules of equal protection via the Fifth Amendment.

When a government action (such as passing a statute or enforcing a law or regulation) is based on a suspect classification, or if the action impairs a fundamental right, the *strict scrutiny* standard is applied. Courts have held that any government action based on race, national origin, or alienage is automatically considered a *suspect* classification. Courts have held that government actions related to the right to vote, to have access to the courts, and to migrate from state to state are subject to strict scrutiny standards as well.

Note also that *semi-suspect* (also called *quasi-suspect*) classifications trigger *intermediate-level* scrutiny. Courts have used this standard of review when government actions were based on gender or illegitimacy. Recall from earlier in this chapter that economic or tax regulations are judged under the rational basis category.

Legal Speak ›))
Punitive Damages
Money awarded in addition to actual damages of an injured party that is intended to punish the wrongdoer and deter unlawful conduct in the future.

CONCEPT SUMMARY Constitutional Protections

- The Bill of Rights contains protection for citizens from unlawful or repressive acts by the government.

- Corporations and other business entities do not always receive the same level of constitutional protections as individuals.

- Traditionally, advertising had little or no First Amendment protection, but the Supreme Court has gradually increased the constitutional protections related to advertising, allowing purely commercial speech to have partial First Amendment protection so long as it is truthful. Commercial political speech has full First Amendment protection.

- The Due Process Clause of the Fifth and Fourteenth Amendments protects individuals from being deprived of "life, liberty, or property" without due process of law.

- The Fourteenth Amendment makes the Bill of Rights applicable to the states.

- The Due Process Clause serves two purposes. First, it imposes procedural requirements on federal and state governments. Second, it limits the substantive power of the states to regulate certain areas affecting individual liberties.

- The right to equal protection does not necessarily mean that everyone must be treated exactly the same.

PRIVACY

LO 2-12

Although not explicitly mentioned in the Constitution, privacy rights play a central role in constitutional law. The U.S. Supreme Court struggled with the notions of individual rights of privacy during the early 1900s, but the Court did not formally recognize the right to privacy until 1965 in the landmark case of *Griswold v. Connecticut.*[26] The case involved a challenge to a Connecticut statute that criminalized (1) the use of contraceptives and (2) aiding or counseling others in their use. Griswold and others were convicted under the statute for counseling married couples in the use of contraceptives at a local Planned Parenthood office.[27] The U.S. Supreme Court struck down the statute as unconstitutional. The Court held that the right of privacy was implied by language in the First, Third, Fourth, Fifth, and Ninth Amendments, which created a constitutionally protected zone of privacy. The right of privacy recognized in *Griswold* was extended to abortion rights in *Roe v. Wade,*[28] one of the most famous U.S. Supreme Court decisions in

---

[26]381 U.S. 479 (1965).

[27]Note that no users of contraceptives, married or single, were ever charged with violating the statute.

[28]410 U.S. 113 (1973).

American history. The *Roe* Court struck down a state statute, which banned all abortions under any circumstances, as unconstitutional. The Court recognized that a woman's right to privacy is fundamental under the Fourteenth Amendment. Thus, the government has only a limited right to regulate, and could not completely outlaw, abortion procedures and providers. Although the existence of a constitutional right of privacy has generated intense and emotional debate, the U.S. Supreme Court has reaffirmed the central tenets of the privacy rights recognized in *Griswold* and *Roe* over several decades and it has become settled law.

Federal Statutes

In addition to privacy rights afforded by the Constitution, Congress has legislated specific privacy rights such as the Health Insurance Portability and Accountability Act (HIPAA),[29] which regulates health care providers, plans, and plan administrators in gathering, storing, and disclosing medical information about individuals. The law requires that specific policies and record-keeping practices be used in order to ensure the privacy of any medical information, such as diagnoses, tests, medications, and so forth. Congress has also sought to ensure certain privacy protections by mandating that government agencies allow only appropriate public and media access to agency records and reports under the Freedom of Information Act.

One of the more controversial federal statutes that deals with modern privacy issues is the Uniting and Strengthening America by Providing Appropriate Tools Required to Intercept and Obstruct Terrorism Act (called the *USA Patriot Act*). The USA Patriot Act was passed immediately after the terrorist attacks of September 11, 2001, and provides increased authority for government officials to surreptitiously access and/or monitor individual and corporate financial records, e-mail, telephone conversations, and Internet activity when investigating possible terrorism-related activity. Although the law does create an infrastructure that is designed to prevent government overreaching and protect individual privacy (e.g., the government must provide evidence that the investigation is related to terrorism and not being used for investigating other matters), critics have derided the law as lacking appropriate safeguards to prevent invasion of privacy.

Workplace Privacy

Most privacy rights afforded by the U.S. Constitution do not extend to the workplace. Nonetheless, privacy rights have become increasingly important to business owners and managers as Congress and state legislatures seek to clarify workplace privacy rights by statute in areas such as employee drug testing, searches of employee areas (such as lockers or desks) by employers, and electronic monitoring of e-mail and Internet usage. Statutes that regulate the workplace are covered in detail in Chapter 12, "Employment Relationships and Labor Law."

---

[29]29 U.S.C. § 1181.

Federal system p. 37   System in which a national government coexists with the government of each state.

Preamble p. 37   The introductory part of the Constitution that states its broad objectives.

Articles p. 37   The main provisions of the Constitution that set out the government's structure, power, and procedures.

Amendments p. 37   Changes made to the Constitution since its ratification.

Legislative branch p. 37   Established under Article I of the Constitution and consists of the House of Representatives and the Senate.

Executive branch p. 37   Established under Article II of the Constitution and consists of the president and vice president.

Judicial branch p. 38   Established under Article III of the Constitution and consists of the Supreme Court and other federal courts.

Bill of Rights p. 38   The first 10 amendments to the Constitution that preserve the rights of the people from unlawful acts of government officials, establish and protect freedom of speech and religion, and so on.

Enumerated powers p. 38   Those powers that are explicitly granted to the three branches of government in the Constitution.

Commerce Clause p. 38   The constitutional clause giving Congress the exclusive power to regulate foreign commerce, interstate commerce, and commerce with the Indian Tribes.

Necessary and Proper Clause p. 38   The constitutional clause giving Congress the general implied authority to make laws necessary to carry out its other enumerated powers.

Executive order p. 39   An order made by the president which carries the full force of law. They are issued to enforce or interpret federal statutes and treaties.

Jurisdiction p. 39   The legal authority that a court must have before it can hear a case.

Judicial review p. 39   The power of the judiciary to declare a legislative or executive act unconstitutional.

Separation of powers p. 40   The system of checks and balances created by the Constitution whereby the three branches have unique powers that allow them to resolve conflicts among themselves, thus ensuring no one branch exceeds its constitutional authority.

Rational basis p. 40   The lowest level of scrutiny applied by courts deciding constitutional issues through judicial review; upheld if the government shows that the law has a reasonable connection to achieving a legitimate and constitutional objective.

Intermediate-level scrutiny p. 40   The middle level of scrutiny applied by courts deciding constitutional issues through judicial review; upheld if the government shows that a regulation involves an important government objective that is furthered by substantially related means.

Strict scrutiny p. 40   The most stringent standard of scrutiny applied by courts deciding constitutional issues through judicial review when the government action is related to a fundamental right or is based on a suspect classification; upheld if the government shows a compelling need that justifies the law being enacted and no less restrictive alternatives exist.

Supremacy Clause p. 44   The constitutional clause that makes clear that federal law is always supreme to any state law that is in direct conflict.

Preemption p. 44   The concept that primary sources of law are applied consistent with a hierarchy and that a law higher in the hierarchy will overrule and make void a conflicting law lower in the hierarchy. Federal law preempts conflicting state law. State law preempts conflicting city and county law.

Due process p. 51   The principle that the government must respect all of the legal rights that are owed to a person according to the law.

Fourth Amendment p. 55   Protects individual citizens' rights to be secure in their "persons, houses, papers and effects."

Fifth Amendment p. 55   Provides that no person "shall be compelled in any criminal case to be a witness against himself," guaranteeing individuals the right to remain silent both during the investigation and during any subsequent judicial proceedings.

Due Process Clause p. 56   The constitutional clause protecting individuals from being deprived of "life, liberty, or property" without due process of law.

Quick Courier Services (Quick) is a company with 25 employees located in the hypothetical state of Longville. Quick provides services to businesses that require documents or packages to be delivered on a same-day basis. While most of the deliveries are made by car or van, Quick also employs several bicycle couriers to accommodate customers in large cities.

1. After a rash of bicycle courier accidents in several cities, Congress passed a federal statute that banned bicycle couriers. The statute is intended to protect the safety of the public at large. Congress justifies the statute on the basis that couriers are inherently involved in commercial activity. What enumerated power is Congress using as the basis of its authority to pass this statute? If Quick challenges the constitutionality of the statute, what would be its probable legal theory?

2. Suppose that, instead of an outright ban on bicycle couriers, Congress passed a law that banned any companies that used bicycle couriers from receiving any money from federal grant programs or federal contracts. How does that impact your analysis relating to congressional authority?

3. Assume that Quick also does business in the adjoining state of Holmestown. Holmestown's state legislature passes a state law that imposes a registration requirement on all couriers that are headquartered outside Holmestown's state borders. The registration requirement includes an annual fee that is not required of in-state couriers. Has Holmestown infringed on Congress's constitutional authority? What is the standard used by courts to analyze such a law?

4. Assume further that the Occupational Safety and Health Administration (OSHA), a government agency, issues a fine to Quick without giving the company's officers adequate notice to provide evidence that no violation occurred. How would the Due Process Clause protect Quick from OSHA's actions?

5. If OSHA wishes to search Quick's premises for evidence of an administrative violation, what amendment(s) would govern the process? If the purpose of the search was investigation of a criminal conspiracy involving Quick's officers, how would that change your answer?

Assume you are a manager at Quick (in the Theory to Practice problem) and you receive an e-mail from your senior manager:

Quick is considering paying for full-page advertisements, in local newspapers, that encourage people to vote for certain Holmestown politicians based on their opposition to the out-of-state courier registration law [in the Theory to Practice example above]. However, I recently read about the Holmestown legislature considering a law that bans such advertisements if funded by a corporation.

Before I contact our counsel, I would like a two- to three-page background memorandum addressing the question: May Holmestown ban the advertisement on the basis that it is funded by corporate money and not by individual voters or political committees? Why or why not? Is there any important case law to support your answer to this question?

A sample answer may be found on this textbook's website at www.mhhe.com/melvinleb2e.

PREEMPTION

Cipollone brought suit against Liggett for violation of several New Jersey consumer protection statutes, alleging that Liggett (and other cigarette manufacturers) was liable for his mother's death because the company engaged in false advertising, fraudulently misrepresenting the hazards of smoking, and conspiracy to deprive the public of medical and scientific information about smoking. Liggett urged the court to dismiss the state law claims, contending that the claims related to the manufacturer's advertising and promotional activities were preempted by two federal laws:

(1) the Federal Cigarette Labeling and Advertising Act of 1965 and (2) the Public Health Cigarette Smoking Act of 1969.

CASE QUESTIONS

1. What must be shown for the federal laws cited to preempt New Jersey state law?
2. Why would Congress want to preempt state law regarding the advertising and promotion of tobacco products? Do you agree with its decision to do so? Why or why not?

COMMERCIAL SPEECH

During a labor dispute, a local labor union engaged in a protest of what it claimed were unfair labor practices of a local business. As part of this protest, the union displayed a 10-foot inflatable rat-shaped balloon on a public sidewalk in front of a business involved in the dispute. A municipal ordinance banned all public displays of "balloon or inflated" signs except in cases of a grand opening. The union challenged the ordinance as an unconstitutional ban on commercial speech.

CASE QUESTIONS

1. Is the ordinance constitutionally sound?
2. What level of scrutiny will a court apply to the ordinance?

COMMERCE CLAUSE

In 2002, Congress passed the Body Armor Act that made it illegal for anyone who has been convicted of a violent felony to possess body armor. Alderman was convicted of violating the statute and challenged the law's constitutionality during appeal. Alderman contended that Congress had exceeded its authority because the law was not sufficiently related to interstate commerce.

CASE QUESTIONS

1. Is the law constitutionally sound?
2. If Alderman purchased the body armor in the state where it was manufactured, how does that affect "interstate" commerce?

NECESSARY AND PROPER CLAUSE

In an effort to increase Internet access for the public, Congress passed a law creating the E-Rate program (providing for discounted Internet rates) and the Library Services and Technology Act (LSTA), which provides financial grants to libraries. At the same time, Congress also passed the Children's Internet Protection Act (CIPA). CIPA conditions the receipt of federal funds under the E-Rate program and LSTA on libraries' purchasing and installing expensive software that blocks obscene or pornographic material. A group of libraries and citizens filed suit, claiming that connecting LSTA grant funds to CIPA compliance is unconstitutional.

CASE QUESTIONS

1. Is the condition requiring the purchase and installation of blocking software, in order to qualify for discounts and grants, constitutional?
2. Is the First Amendment at issue? Explain your answer.

DUE PROCESS AND PUNITIVE DAMAGES

Campbell was involved in an accident. State Farm, Campbell's insurer, investigated and concluded that Campbell had acted negligently, yet it refused to settle a case brought by the injured parties for the $50,000 policy limit. Prior to trial, State Farm told Campbell (1) that he did not have liability in the case and (2) that their mutual interests were closely aligned, so hiring his own counsel was an unnecessary expense. Based on State Farm's assurances, Campbell did not consult an attorney. At trial, a jury found against both Campbell and State Farm. They awarded the plaintiffs $185,849, far more than the amount offered during pretrial settlement discussions. State Farm refused to pay any amount beyond the $50,000 policy limit, and its general counsel advised Campbell to sell his house to cover the excess award owed to the plaintiffs. Campbell sued State Farm for bad faith, fraud, and intentional infliction of emotional distress. The jury found for Campbell, awarding him $2.6 million in compensatory damages, to compensate him for losses, and $145 million in punitive damages. Consistent with a state statute limiting certain damage awards, the trial court reduced the awards to $1 million in compensatory damages and $25 million in punitive damages. An appellate court reinstated the original $145 million punitive-damage award on the basis that the state's punitive-damage statute allowed larger damage awards if the defendant acted in a particularly reprehensible manner. State Farm appealed.

CASE QUESTIONS

1. State Farm's appeal of the punitive-damage award argued that such a disproportionately large punitive-damage award to a violation of the Due Process Clause. Do you agree or disagree?
2. How can one determine what constitutes an excessive award of damages that violates a defendant's due process compared to one that does not violate the Due Process Clause? Is this distinction clear?

APPLYING THE *CENTRAL HUDSON* TEST

The Village of Glendale, Ohio, passed an ordinance that prohibited parking a vehicle on a public road for the purposes of displaying it for sale. Pagan, a resident of Glendale, parked his car on a public street and posted a "For Sale" sign on the vehicle. A Glendale police officer warned Pagan to take the sign or face a citation for violating the ordinance. Pagan filed suit against the Village of Glendale and Fruchey, Glendale's chief of police (collectively, "Glendale"), claiming that the ordinance was an unconstitutional infringement of his First Amendment commercial speech rights. Glendale contended that its ordinance satisfied the requirements under *Central Hudson* because the government has a substantial regulatory interest in traffic and pedestrian safety. No data or research was presented at trial, but the chief of police testified as to his opinion. After the trial court dismissed Pagan's claim, the U.S. Circuit Court of Appeals reversed in favor of Pagan because there was not a sufficient connection between Glendale's asserted interest (traffic safety) and government regulation (Part Three of the *Central Hudson* test).

CASE QUESTIONS

1. Could the ordinance itself be modified to meet the third part of the *Central Hudson* test?
2. What types of data do you suppose the court wanted from Glendale to support the village's claim that the ordinance advanced its traffic safety interest? Why didn't the court give more weight to the police chief's opinion?

PREEMPTION

Williamson was a passenger in a Mazda minivan who was killed in an automobile accident. Williamson's estate sued Mazda under state tort law, alleging that the company's decision to install lap belts instead of lap-and-shoulder belts contributed to his death. Mazda argued that a federal law, the National Traffic and Motor Vehicle Safety Act of 1966, specifically permitted manufacturers to choose between the two types of belts and that Williamson's claim was preempted by federal law. Williamson contended that the federal statute contained a clause that made clear that compliance with federal safety standards does not exempt the manufacturer from liability under state tort law.

CASE QUESTIONS

1. Who prevails and why?
2. If the federal law had mandated specific standards rather than give manufacturers a choice, how would that impact your analysis?

 Self-Check **ANSWERS**

Source of Constitutional Authority

1. Article 1, § 8: Congress's power to regulate bankruptcy laws.

2. Article 1, § 8: Tax and spend powers

3. Article 1, § 8: Careful! This answer appears to be Congress's power to grant and regulate patents. But the fact that Congress is passing a criminal law would be outside the scope of the narrow patent power. Rather, this law is best thought of as Congress's authority to legislate under the Necessary and Proper Clause because the law was directly ancillary to the enumerated power (patents).

4. Article 1, § 8: Congress's power to regulate interstate commerce.

5. Tax and spending power.

3

CHAPTER

The American Judicial System, Jurisdiction, and Venue

learning **objectives**

After studying this chapter, students who have mastered the material will be able to:

3-1 Explain the role of the judiciary in the context of the American legal system.

3-2 Distinguish between the roles of federal courts and state courts.

3-3 Identify the responsibilities of trial courts versus appellate courts.

3-4 Articulate how the law develops via adjudication of cases.

3-5 Differentiate between subject matter jurisdiction and personal jurisdiction.

3-6 Explain original jurisdiction and how courts may have concurrent jurisdiction.

3-7 Recognize the types of controversies over which federal courts have subject matter jurisdiction and those in which diversity jurisdiction applies.

3-8 Explain the role of long-arm statutes in determining personal jurisdiction.

3-9 Apply the minimum contacts test in both a traditional and *cyber* setting and describe the importance of the *Zippo* sliding scale.

3-10 Articulate the special problems posed by different international jurisdiction standards.

The primary role of the courts is to settle legal disputes. Court decisions often shape or create doctrines that impact business planning and policy. Business owners and managers must have a fundamental knowledge of the structure and function of the court system because they encounter lawsuits as they plan and manage their business operations. In this chapter students will learn:

- The role and structure of the American judicial system.
- The function and authority of state and federal courts.
- How the law develops through court decisions.

Not all courts have the authority to hear all cases. In order for a court to render a binding decision, a court must have authority over both the dispute and the parties in each case that it hears. Specifically, students will learn:

- The circumstances in which a court has the authority to hear a certain case.
- The appropriate location to resolve disputes.

ROLE AND STRUCTURE OF THE JUDICIARY LO 3-1

The American legal system is primarily structured around a set of federal and state **courts** that are collectively known as the **judiciary.** The

judiciary has two primary roles. First, courts *adjudicate* disputes. This means that many courts are responsible for interpreting and applying the rules of law and principles of equity to settle legal cases and controversies. Second, certain courts are charged with the responsibility of *judicial review.*[1] In this role, these courts review decisions of lower courts and the actions of other branches of the government to be sure that these decisions and actions are consistent with existing law and that they comply with constitutional requirements.

State versus Federal Courts LO 3-2, 3-3

The U.S. system of government recognizes two distinct levels of government, and, therefore, there are two levels of courts aligned to that structure. The first level, **state courts,** adjudicates matters dealing primarily with cases arising from state statutory, state common, or state constitutional law. In some cases, state courts also apply federal

---

[1]Recall from Chapter 2, "Business and the Constitution," that the U.S. Supreme Court, in the landmark case of *Marbury v. Madison*, 2 L.Ed. 60 (1803), established the concept of judicial review, now a stalwart power of the federal judiciary.

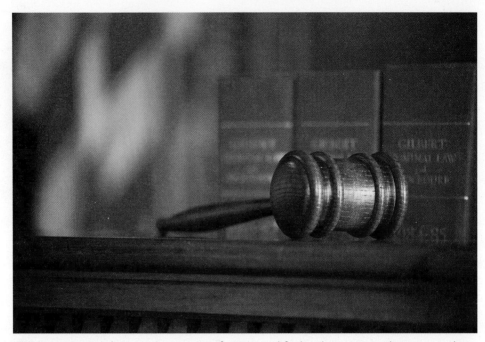

The American judiciary is a system of state and federal courts working in tandem.

constitutional provisions. **Federal courts** are concerned primarily with national laws, federal constitutional issues, and other cases that are outside the purview of state courts.

It is important to note that not all courts have the *authority* to hear all cases. In order for a court, whether state or federal, to hear a case, the court must have legal authority, called *jurisdiction,* over the dispute and parties in the case. Proper venue must also be established. The concepts of jurisdiction and venue are discussed in detail later in this chapter.

State Courts   The majority of court cases filed in the United States are filed in state courts. All states have two types of courts: **state trial courts** and **state appellate courts.**

State Trial Courts   When one party alleges a violation of some legal right or standard, the aggrieved party, called the **plaintiff,** may bring a lawsuit against the alleged violator, called the **defendant,** in a trial court. Trial courts are where cases are originally brought and heard. They are structured to adjudicate matters through an established procedure in which both parties present evidence, question witnesses, and articulate legal arguments about the case.[2]

The names of the courts vary widely from state to state. However, all state trial courts have either *general authority* to hear a case or *limited authority* to hear a particular type of case. Courts of general authority are organized into geographic districts (often divided by county or a set of contiguous counties)[3] and hear many types of cases, including breach of contract, employment discrimination, personal injury, criminal cases, property disputes, and so forth. Courts of limited authority are often confined to a particular type of dispute such as family law matters (e.g., divorce or adoption cases) or probate courts (which deal with issues related to wills and trusts). Some states, notably Delaware, have courts devoted solely to issues relating to equity and commercial law matters. Delaware calls these forums *chancery courts.* It is important to remember that state trial court decisions are binding *only* on the parties involved in the dispute. Trial court decisions do not set precedent for future disputes or parties. Only appellate-level courts set precedent.

---

[2]Note that the role of trial courts is examined in the context of a civil lawsuit, known as *litigation,* in the next chapter.

[3]In the United States, 48 states are divided into counties. Louisiana is divided into parishes, and Alaska is divided into boroughs.

For minor matters and cases with a dollar value that is relatively low, typically less than $10,000 depending on the state, states provide local courts known alternatively as municipal courts, small-claims courts, justice-of-the-peace courts, or district justices. Such courts provide local access to a court for the purpose of resolving relatively simple disputes on an expedited basis. These courts are sometimes referred to as *inferior* trial courts because states provide an automatic appeal for the losing party, usually to the state trial court, for decisions from local judges. This appeal actually takes the form of a new trial, or **trial de novo.**

Trial courts are often divided into those that hear civil matters in which one party seeks redress for a wrong committed by another party (such as a lawsuit for breach of contract) and those that hear criminal matters in which a party accused of a crime (such as theft) is put on trial.

State Appellate Courts   After a trial court has rendered a decision, the losing party must decide whether to file an appeal in the appellate court. Appellate courts are primarily concerned with reviewing the decisions of trial courts. Most states also have an intermediate appellate court, which is where the first appeal is filed. In some states, appeals to any appellate-level courts are *discretionary*. That is, the party requesting the appeal (known as the *petitioning* party or the *appellant*) files a document with the court petitioning for an appeal. Based on a variety of factors, the appellate court then decides whether to allow the appeal to be heard by the court. In other states, the losing party has an automatic right of appeal to the intermediate-level court but only a discretionary appeal to the highest court. If the appellate court denies an appeal, the trial court ruling is *binding* on the parties in that case.[4] If the court grants an appeal, the appellate judges engage in the process of determining whether the trial was conducted in accordance with the legal rules and doctrines of that state. Appellate courts assess the lower court's decision by (1) reviewing lower court transcripts and rulings, (2) reading *briefs*, which are documents written by attorneys for each side articulating legal reasons why their side should prevail, and (3) sometimes allowing the attorneys to engage in *oral argument*, which requires the attorneys for the parties to appear in front of the appellate panel of judges to participate in an oral question and answer session on the legal issues in the case. The court focuses on such issues as the rulings of the trial judges, the admission of evidence, jury selection, and other factors that may have been a factor in the original trial's outcome. Note that appellate courts, except in some rare cases, do *not* consider new evidence in their review. Using these methods, appellate courts determine whether an error was made at the trial level. In cases where the error is substantial enough, a court may reverse the decision of the trial court and **remand** the case back to the trial court.

In certain matters, some state courts may have both original jurisdiction (discussed later in this chapter) and appellate jurisdiction. For example, in the state of Delaware, the Court of Common Pleas and the Superior Court are both general trial courts. The Superior Court is also the state's intermediate appellate court, hearing appeals from the Court of Common Pleas and the state's family and probate courts.

The major distinction between state trial courts and state appellate courts is that appellate court decisions set *precedent* that is binding on all lower courts.[5] Because one of the primary purposes of the law is to provide some degree of reliability and uniformity in adjudicating cases, trial courts are required to follow the rulings of appellate courts. In states where there is an intermediate level of appellate court, the highest court is often

Legal **Speak** ›))
Trial de Novo
A form of appeal in which the appeals court conducts the new trial as if the original trial had never occurred.

Legal **Speak** ›))
Remand To send a case back to the lower court from which it came for further action consistent with the opinion and instructions of the higher court.

---

[4]In extraordinary cases, a petitioning party sometimes has the right to appeal to a higher court if the intermediate appellate court denies the appeal.

[5]Recall from Chapter 1, "Legal Foundations," that the concept of *precedent* springs from the doctrine of stare decisis.

(although not always) called the *state supreme court.*[6] A state supreme court's decision is final and binding on *all* courts situated in that state (including federal courts located in that state) so long as the decision does *not* involve a federal constitutional issue.

States vary as to how state trial court judges are selected. Some states elect all trial and appellate judges as part of their general elections, while others use an appointment process whereby the governor appoints a judge but the appointment is subject to review and rejection by the state legislature (typically the state senate). Some states use a hybrid method whereby local judges are elected and appellate court judges go through an appointment process.

Federal Courts   The federal government also operates a system of courts. The principal trial courts are the **U.S. district courts.** Federal appellate courts are called the **U.S. courts of appeal.** Because these courts are divided into circuits, federal appellate courts are frequently referred to as *circuit courts of appeal.* Finally, the **U.S. Supreme Court,** the ultimate arbiter of federal law, not only reviews decisions of the federal courts but also reviews decisions of state courts that involve some issue of federal law, such as applying a provision of the U.S. Constitution.

U.S. District Courts   District courts serve the same primary trial function as state trial courts but address issues involving federal matters such as federal statutes, regulations, or constitutional issues. There are 94 districts, with at least one federal district court in every state and one for the District of Columbia. U.S. district courts also may decide certain matters involving *state law* when the parties are from different states and meet other jurisdictional requirements. These federal trial courts hear a variety of matters and render decisions that are binding only on the parties involved in the dispute. Some federal courts are specialized for certain areas of law. They include the Bankruptcy Court, the Tax Court, and the Court of International Trade.

U.S. Courts of Appeal   The 13 U.S. courts of appeal, each of which reviews the decisions of federal district courts in the state or several states within its circuit, are the intermediate appellate courts in the federal system. Two exceptions are the Court of Appeals for the District of Columbia, which decides cases originating in Washington, D.C., and the Federal Circuit Court of Appeals, which decides a variety of exclusively federal issues such as patent, copyright, and trademark cases or cases where the United States is named as a defendant. The Federal Circuit is said to have national jurisdiction since its authority is not confined to one particular circuit. Just as with state appellate courts, federal circuit courts of appeal set precedent and their decisions are binding on all the states in that circuit. All appeals to the federal circuit courts of appeal are discretionary.

The circuits are divided geographically. Figure 3.1 illustrates how circuits are broken down.

U.S. Supreme Court   The ultimate arbiters of federal law are the nine justices of the U.S. Supreme Court (the "Court"). The U.S. Constitution does not specify a size for the Supreme Court. Originally established at six members, one chief justice and five associate justices, the Court has ranged from a low of five members to a high of ten members. It has remained at nine members since 1869. Although the Court has both original[7] and appellate jurisdiction, the primary role of the Court is to finalize a legal decision on any given case.

---

[6]For example, in the state of New York, the state's highest court is the New York Court of Appeals. The New York Supreme Court has two divisions, the trial division, which is the state's general trial court, and the appellate division, which is the state's intermediary appellate court.

[7]The Court's original jurisdiction is limited to cases involving ambassadors and selected other public officials and those cases where the disputing parties are two states.

FIGURE 3.1   Map of the U.S. Circuits

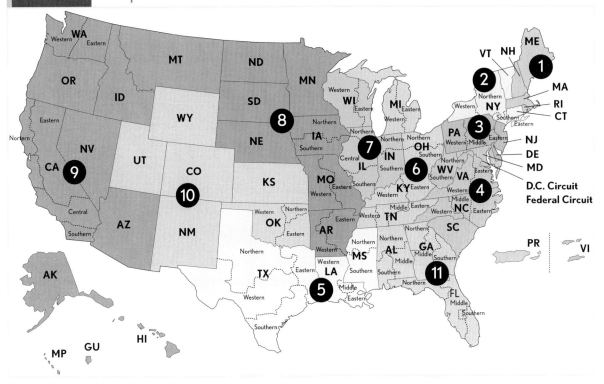

Source: www.uscourts.gov/courtlinks.

In addition to the Court's authority to decide any appeal from the U.S. circuit courts of appeal, the Court may also exercise its appellate authority over state courts when a federal issue is involved. Finally, the Court has the final authority on matters of interpretation of all federal law and the U.S. Constitution.

While the Court is known to most of the citizenry as the court that decides highly publicized and politically charged constitutional issues, more often cases are decided by the Court when conflicting opinions among the appellate courts are issued (referred to by the Court as a *conflict among the circuits*) and relatively complex commercial matters such as cases involving patents, antitrust regulation, or securities laws. Of course, the Court's review is discretionary, and, in fact, the odds of getting a case to the Court are very low. Typically, the Court grants only about 1 percent of the requests it receives to hear a case. An aggrieved party may petition the Court for an appeal using a petition for writ of certiorari that explains the basis for the appeal. Upon review, if four of the nine justices vote to hear the case, the parties in the case are then permitted to pursue the appeal. Table 3.1 sets out the rate of requests versus cases that are actually heard in recent years.

All federal judges are selected via the appointment process. The president nominates candidates for federal trial and appellate courts. The nominees are subject to the review of the Senate. The Senate may either confirm or reject the judicial nominee. If the nominee is rejected, the president nominates candidates until one is confirmed. Once confirmed, the nominee is sworn in as a federal judge and may be removed from office only by impeachment.

Legal Speak ›))
Writ of Certiorari
A discretionary order issued by the Supreme Court (and federal appellate courts) granting a request to argue an appeal. A party filing for an appeal must file a petition for writ of certiorari.

connect
|BUSINESS LAW

Visit Connect for a multimedia reference to the Supreme Court and a virtual tour of the Court's building.

The Supreme Court of the United States, pictured here on the opening day of the October 2010 term, is the ultimate arbiter of federal law.

TABLE 3.1   Supreme Court Case Acceptance Rate

Term	Number of Petitions (requests) for a Writ of Certiorari	Number Granted	Acceptance Rate
2009	7,685	66	Approx. .85%
2010	7,868	90	Approx. 1.14%
2011	8,131	77	Approx. .95%

Source: Clerk's Office, United States Supreme Court.

LO 3-4   # HOW THE LAW DEVELOPS

It can be a somewhat daunting task to figure out how a case works its way through the court system and the role that precedent plays in how the law develops. Fundamentally, state trial courts rule on certain points of state law and render a decision. That decision is binding on the parties, but on no one else. If an appellate court affirms or reverses the findings of the trial court, then from that point on, the appellate court's ruling on that point of law is applied to all future cases. Remember also that federal trial courts within a certain state may rule on *state law* issues in some cases where the federal court has jurisdiction. Figure 3.2 sets out the structure of state and federal courts.

Consider the following case to illustrate how law develops. Assume that in the hypothetical U.S. state of Longville, no precedent exists for the following issue of state law:

FIGURE 3.2 Understanding State and Federal Courts

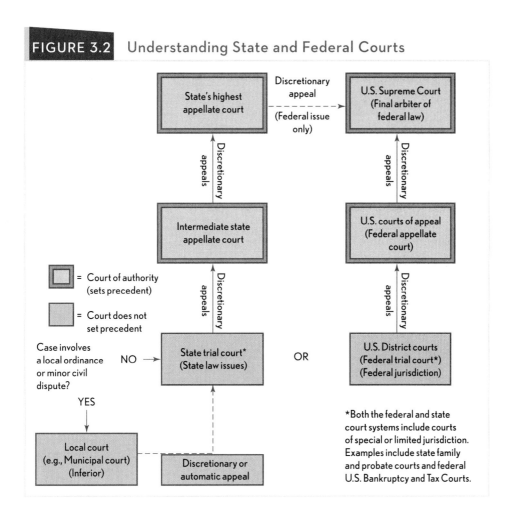

Issue: Does an e-mail constitute a signed writing sufficient to satisfy the Longville state statute that requires certain contracts to be in writing? Further assume that two separate controversies have occurred simultaneously and two separate cases, each with different litigants, have been filed.

Case Number	Court	Date	Ruling on Issue	Effect on Parties and Future Cases
Case 1	Longville state trial court	Jan. 10	*E-mail is sufficient.*	Binding only on parties in Case 1.
Case 2	Federal district court (federal trial) located in Longville Federal jurisdiction has been established	Jan. 15	*E-mail not sufficient.*	Binding only on the parties in this case (Case 2). No effect on the parties in Case 1.

(continued)

Case Number	Court	Date	Ruling on Issue	Effect on Parties and Future Cases
Case 3	Longville state appellate court	Feb. 1	*E-mail is sufficient.*	Binding on all Longville state and federal trial courts in Longville. Case 1 decision is upheld, and its ruling is now applied in Longville state trial courts/federal trial courts in Longville from Feb. 1 onward.
Case 4	Federal court of appeals that includes Longville in its circuit	March 1	Must follow Longville state appellate court's precedent set in Case 3 because it's an issue of state law: *E-mail is sufficient.*	If there are no federal issues, the court applies Longville state law as interpreted by Longville state appellate courts in Case 3. The court's decision is binding only on Longville, not on other states in the circuit.
Case 5	State supreme court of Longville	June 1	Denies appeal from losing party in Longville appellate court decision (Case 3).	Law as decided by the appellate court in Case 3 is settled and binding on all Longville courts. Precedent is undisturbed.

CONCEPT SUMMARY Role and Structure of the Judiciary

- The roles of the judiciary are to (1) apply rules of law and principles of equity equally to settle cases and controversies and (2) review the decisions of trial courts and the actions of the other branches of government to ensure they comply with existing legal and constitutional requirements.
- State courts generally handle matters dealing with state statutory, state common, and state constitutional law. The majority of cases filed in the United States are filed in state courts.
- There are two types of state courts: trial courts, where parties present their cases and evidence; and appellate courts, which review the decisions of lower courts.
- Only appellate courts set precedent. The decisions of trial courts are binding only on the parties in the particular matter before the court.
- Federal trial courts are called U.S. district courts. Federal appellate courts are called U.S. courts of appeal and are often referred to as circuit courts of appeal.
- Courts with general authority hear a wide variety of cases. Courts with limited authority hear specific types of cases such as family law matters.
- The ultimate arbiter of federal law is the U.S. Supreme Court. It has both original and appellate jurisdiction.

LO 3-5 JURISDICTION AND VENUE

As noted earlier, it is important to understand that not all courts have the authority to hear all cases. The law sets out certain rules that govern which courts may decide certain cases. **Jurisdiction** is a court's authority to decide a particular case based on (1) who the parties are and (2) the subject matter of the dispute. **Venue** is a determination of the most appropriate court *location* for litigating a dispute.

Jurisdiction and Business Strategy

The increasing integration of advanced technology in product and service delivery has made jurisdiction and venue an important part of business planning for business managers and owners. As with all legal decisions that business owners and managers make, jurisdiction must be considered in a cost-benefit context. For example, consider a dispute between two hypothetical companies, Ultimate Widget Corporation (UWC) and Knock Off Stores Inc. (Knock Off). Suppose UWC, a New York company, is considering suing Knock Off, a California company, over a trademark dispute. UWC management should consider the costs involved in pursuing the suit in a business context. In considering their strategy, UWC's management must consider (1) the total amount of the possible recovery from Knock Off; (2) the actual benefits UWC will reap from the prevention of Knock Off's use of the trademark; and (3) any alternate dispute resolution methods available. If Knock Off is a small company and not likely to dilute the trademark in any of UWC's markets, it may not be worth the costs of litigation to sue UWC in its home state. Pursuing the infringement action would involve UWC's expense of traveling to California, hiring local counsel in California, and losing productive hours of managers and other witnesses who would be required to travel to testify and be deposed for the case. However, if a New York court could possibly have jurisdiction over the dispute, that fact will change the dynamics of the cost-benefit analysis because the expenses of the suit would be markedly lower.

Legal Speak ›))
Jurisdiction An English word derived through the combination of two Latin words: *juris* ("of law" or "of right") and *dictio* ("speaking"). Thus, the combination of the words refers to a specific court's right to *speak the law* or render a decision in a legal dispute.

> **KEY** POINT
>
> The cost-benefit analysis involving jurisdictional restrictions may affect the managerial decision-making process when a company or individual contemplates filing a lawsuit. Litigating disputes in out-of-state courts increases the costs of litigation.

Overview of Jurisdiction

LO 3-6

The origins of federal jurisdiction law are found in the U.S. Constitution, specifically, the Due Process Clause of the Fifth and the Fourteenth Amendments. In essence, the Constitution prohibits the deprivation of a property interest (usually money damages) without a legal process being applied. While origins of jurisdiction lie in the Constitution, appellate courts and legislatures have shaped the framework and rules used by modern courts to analyze jurisdiction questions.

Two-Part Analysis   Jurisdiction requires a two-part analysis: A court must have both (1) **subject matter jurisdiction** and (2) **personal jurisdiction** (also known as *in personam jurisdiction*). Subject matter jurisdiction is the court's authority over the *dispute* between the parties, while personal jurisdiction is the court's authority over the *parties* involved in the dispute. For example, suppose that Baker is employed by Auto Parts Company (APC) to drive a delivery vehicle. One morning, Baker is on a delivery and due to his lack of care (called *negligence*),[8] hits Cain, a pedestrian who is crossing the street in a designated public crosswalk located directly in front of the hotel where she was staying. Cain is severely injured, and she considers filing a lawsuit against Baker to reimburse her for losses she suffered as a result of the incident. However, Cain discovers that Baker is without assets and, in the state where the incident took place, the law provides that APC is responsible for Baker's actions. Consequently, Cain decides to pursue a lawsuit against APC.

Initially, Cain must decide in *which* court to file the lawsuit. She probably will have some choice, but it will be a limited one. This is true because the court selected must have jurisdiction over the case of this type of dispute (a negligence case) and over the

---

[8]The legal term for such a lack of care is *negligence*. Negligence is discussed extensively in Chapter 10, "Torts and Products Liability."

defendant (APC). Cain will likely bring this suit in a *state* trial court because the jurisdiction of federal courts is limited in this type of case. Be sure to remember the basic facts of the APC-Cain hypothetical as it will be used throughout this section to illustrate various aspects of jurisdiction and venue.

Subject Matter Jurisdiction: Authority over the Dispute

Recall from the discussion at the beginning of this chapter that state and federal statutes define which courts have *general* jurisdiction and which have *limited* jurisdiction. State statutes give state trial courts subject matter jurisdiction on virtually all matters involving a state statute, state common law, or a state constitutional issue.

Federal district courts are limited by the Constitution and by federal statutes as to what types of cases they have authority to hear. In order for a federal court to have subject matter jurisdiction in a case, the issue must generally involve a **federal question** (e.g., some issue arising from the U.S. Constitution, a federal statute or regulation, or federal common law). Federal courts also have *exclusive* jurisdiction over all cases in which the United States is a **party** in the litigation. For example, a business that sues the Internal Revenue Service for a federal tax refund must pursue the matter in federal court since it involves the United States as a party named in the lawsuit.

Even if there is no federal question and the United States is not a party to the litigation, federal courts may have subject matter jurisdiction over cases involving parties from *two different states* (or one party from outside the United States), a situation known as **diversity of citizenship.** An additional requirement in diversity of citizenship cases (only) is that the amount in controversy must be more than $75,000. For example, if a dispute arises in which a business in New York sues a business in California for breach of contract for $80,000, the parties are said to be *diverse* and a federal court sitting in New York or California would have subject matter jurisdiction in the case. Note that the amount-in-controversy requirement applies *only* when a court has jurisdiction via the diversity-of-citizenship requirement. In a diversity case, a federal court will be applying *state law* because the dispute is likely to involve issues governed by state statutes or common law.

Recall the Cain-APC hypothetical from the beginning of this section. Assume that Cain was a resident of Massachusetts who was visiting Texas, where APC is headquartered, when the incident occurred. Cain would likely prefer to file the lawsuit in her home state so that she doesn't have to spend time and resources in traveling to Texas several times for pretrial and trial tasks. Assuming that Cain's injuries were sufficiently severe to warrant damages exceeding $75,000, Cain may consider filing suit in the federal district court in Massachusetts. That court has subject matter jurisdiction because the parties are diverse and the amount in controversy has been satisfied. However, that is only the first part of the jurisdiction analysis. Once it has been determined that the federal district court in Massachusetts has subject matter jurisdiction, Cain must also clear another substantial jurisdictional requirement: *personal jurisdiction.*

LO 3-7 **Original versus Concurrent Jurisdiction** Courts that are authorized to initially hear a case are said to have **original jurisdiction.** However, it is important to note that more than one court may have jurisdiction over the same case. This is called **concurrent jurisdiction.** State courts may have concurrent jurisdiction with other state courts or federal courts. For example, suppose that Longville Ventures Co. alleges that one of its out-of-state vendors has breached a contract that has caused it $100,000 in damages. Longville Ventures will have a choice of several forums for bringing a lawsuit against the vendor. Table 3.2 sets out the various courts that may have concurrent jurisdiction in the case.

TABLE 3.2

Court	Requirements	Subject Matter Jurisdiction in Longville Ventures Case?
Local court	Any case claiming *up to* $10,000 in damages	No
Longville state trial court	Any case in excess of $10,000 in damages	Yes
Longville appellate court	Appeals from Longville State Court	No
Federal trial court situated in Longville	More than $75,000 in damages; diversity of citizenship	Yes

Choice of Forum   Choosing a forum (court location) to litigate a dispute when courts have concurrent jurisdiction is an important strategic choice. A party filing a lawsuit must take into account several factors:

Costs   This factor includes travel costs, filing fees, and legal fees for local counsel (necessary for out-of-state lawsuits).

Judges   The expertise and experience of the judge varies greatly based on the court. Local judges are typically not suited for complex business cases. State and federal judges have earned law degrees and typically had significant legal experience prior to becoming a judge.

Juries   Juries may vary in diversity depending on the location and choice of the forum.

Appeals   In many cases, the losing party in a local court case is entitled to an automatic appeal. Appeals from other courts are typically discretionary.

Time   The amount of time that it takes to actually get to trial varies, depending on the court and the backlog of cases in the court. Local inferior courts often hear cases within a few weeks, while state trial courts and federal courts may take several months if not years to come to trial.

 Self-Check   Subject Matter Jurisdiction

Does a federal district court located in New Jersey have *subject matter* jurisdiction?

1. A New Jersey businessperson sues her in-state business partner for breach of contract that resulted in $40,000 in losses.

2. The U.S. Environmental Protection Agency sues a New Jersey corporation for cleanup costs under a federal statute that regulates local waste disposal.

3. A Pennsylvania resident sues a New Jersey corporation for an injury caused by the corporation's product resulting in $90,000 of unpaid medical bills.

(continued)

Legal **Speak** ›))
Litigant The
generic term used
to describe a party
to a lawsuit.

4. A New Jersey corporation is sued by a New Jersey resident under the federal employment discrimination statutes.

5. A New Jersey resident sues the U.S. government in an appeal from the ruling of the U.S. Copyright Office.

Answers to this Self-Check are provided at the end of the chapter.

Jurisdiction over Property   Courts may also exercise jurisdiction in a lawsuit based on property located within their jurisdictional boundaries. **In rem[9] jurisdiction** typically allows a court the authority to determine title to an object or real estate. **Quasi in rem jurisdiction** occurs when a court uses its in rem jurisdiction to compel a litigant to appear in court by attaching property that belongs to the litigant. This allows a court to obtain jurisdiction even if that court would normally have no personal jurisdiction over that party. For example, suppose that Molony, a resident of Florida, injures Trostle, a resident of Pennsylvania, during Trostle's vacation in Key West. If Trostle wishes to sue Molony in Pennsylvania, normally a Pennsylvania court would not have personal jurisdiction over Molony because he does not live there and the injury did not occur there. However, suppose that Molony owns a bed-and-breakfast in Pennsylvania. In that case, the Pennsylvania court could use its quasi in rem jurisdiction to compel Molony to appear in court and answer the negligence allegations, or Molony may face the seizure of his bed-and-breakfast to reimburse Trostle for any damages suffered as a result of Molony's negligence.

Personal Jurisdiction

Personal jurisdiction, called **in personam jurisdiction,** is a court's authority over the *parties* in a legal dispute. In this context, a party may be either an individual or a business entity such as a corporation. Since 1877, in the landmark case *Pennoyer v. Neff,*[10] the U.S. Supreme Court has articulated a framework for the exercise of personal jurisdiction by lower courts with the objective of providing *fairness* to the parties and complying with federal constitutional requirements related to due process. Of course, courts have modified this framework as necessary based on the realities of industrial and technological advances in society. This framework is used to determine jurisdiction over the defendant by both the state's courts *and* federal district courts within that state. Typically, a jurisdiction analysis focuses on the *conditions* of the controversy and *actions* of the defendant.

In-State Defendants   Personal jurisdiction is obtained by the courts when the business or individual is served with the complaint, initiating the lawsuit. The service of the complaint puts the business or individual on notice of being sued. Complaints will be discussed in detail in Chapter 4, "Resolving Disputes: Litigation and Alternative Dispute Resolution Options."

LO 3-8, 3-9   Out-of-State Defendants   Courts use a two-prong test to determine whether it has personal jurisdiction over a party who does not live in the state in which the court is located. First, the court's jurisdiction must be authorized by a **state long-arm statute** that grants the court specific authorization over the defendant due to the defendant's conduct or other circumstances. As the name implies, long-arm statutes are intended to allow a court to "reach" into another state and exercise jurisdiction over a nonresident defendant. Typically, long-arm statutes[11] provide for jurisdiction if an out-of-state defendant

---

[9]Latin for "against the matter (thing)" (Collins, *Latin 1e*).

[10]95 U.S. 714 (1877).

[11]Many states base their long-arm statute on a model act called the Uniform Interstate and International Procedure Act.

(1) transacts business within the state's borders, or (2) commits a negligent act in that state that results in a loss to another party, or (3) owns property in the state. The second prong requires a court to ensure that exercising jurisdiction over an out-of-state defendant meets the constitutional requirements of *fairness* and *due process*. This means that courts must consider the plight of the defendant who has been forced to defend a lawsuit in another state by taking into account the burden on the defendant. Courts examine two questions in this analysis: First, does the defendant have some level of **minimum contacts**[12] with the state, such as regularly shipping products to that state? If a defendant has continuous and systematic contact with a particular state, this will be sufficient to satisfy the minimum-contacts requirement. Second, has the defendant *purposefully availed* herself by some affirmative directed to that specific state? Whether a company has purposely availed itself in a state was defined by the U.S. Supreme Court in *Asahi Metal Indus. Co., Ltd. v. Superior Court of California,* as when a company performs "some act by which [the company] purposefully avails itself of the privilege of conducting activities within the forum State, thus invoking the benefits and protections of its laws."[13]

In Case 3.1, an appellate court applies the purposeful-availment standard in determining the contacts of an out-of-state vendor.

Injurious Effect

Another important consideration that courts explore in a personal jurisdiction analysis is whether it was reasonably *foreseeable* that the defendant's actions would have an *injurious effect* on a resident of the court's state. This question is usually applied in the context of a dispute involving some *intentional* act by the defendant that results in an injury to an individual or business entity resident in the court's state. For example, in *Calder v. Jones,*[14] the Supreme Court ruled that a California court had jurisdiction over a Florida corporation in a defamation case filed by an actress against a tabloid newspaper. Despite the fact that the defendant had no physical presence or other traditional minimum contacts with California, the Court reasoned that jurisdiction was proper because the defendant knew, or should have known, that the defamation would have an injurious effect on the actress in California, where she lived and worked. This became known as the *effects test* and is now an important part of a personal jurisdiction analysis. Note, however, that courts apply the effects test narrowly and, thus far, only to cases involving intentional injurious acts (such as defamation).[15]

In Case 3.2, a federal court uses an injurious effect analysis in a defamation case filed by a famous athlete.

Physical Presence

The physical presence of an out-of-state party in a particular state is generally an automatic basis for jurisdiction over the defendant by both that state's courts *and* federal trial courts within that state. In a business context, physical presence may include having an office, agent, or personnel (such as a sales team) located within the court's jurisdiction.

In *Ritz Camera Centers, Inc. v. Wentling Camera Shops, Inc., et al.,*[16] a federal court in Maryland dismissed a claim by a Maryland-based camera shop business (Ritz) that sued a California-based camera shop business for breach of contract. The court rejected Ritz's

Legal Speak ›))
Defamation
Discussed in detail in Chapter 10, "Torts and Products Liability," defamation is an intentional act of making an untrue public statement about a party that caused some loss to be suffered by the defamed party.

---

[12]*International Shoe v. Washington,* 326 U.S. 310 (1945).

[13]480 U.S. 102 (1987).

[14]465 U.S. 783 (1984).

[15]The Court also applied the test used to justify jurisdiction in *Keeton v. Hustler Magazine,* 465 U.S. 770 (1984). The case involved a libel claim filed by Keeton in federal district court in New Hampshire. Keeton chose New Hampshire believing it to be a forum favorable to her case. Hustler's only contact with the state was the circulation of copies of its magazine in New Hampshire. The Supreme Court held that a "regular circulation of magazines in the forum State is sufficient to support an assertion of jurisdiction in this case because of the potential for the injurious effect to be felt in New Hampshire."

[16]982 F. Supp. 350 (1997).

FACT SUMMARY   The legal representative of the estate of Weingeroff (Weingeroff), a passenger on a turboprop plane who was killed when the plane crashed near State College, Pennsylvania, brought a negligence and product liability lawsuit against Pilatus Air (Pilatus), the manufacturer of the plane. The plane crashed when approaching a small airport in Pennsylvania on a planned stop en route between Florida and Rhode Island. Weingeroff sued Pilatus in a federal district court situated in the Eastern District of Pennsylvania. Pilatus, a Swiss company, asked the court to dismiss the case for lack of personal jurisdiction. Pilatus claimed that it had no offices, no agents, no commercial transactions with Pennsylvania residents, and no physical presence in the state that constitutes purposeful availment. Weingeroff pointed to evidence that (1) Pilatus had conducted a nationwide marketing campaign in the United States to sell its planes, including in Pennsylvania, and (2) Pilatus had purchased over $1 million in products, services, and equipment from Pennsylvania suppliers. The trial court ruled in favor of Pilatus and dismissed the suit for lack of personal jurisdiction.

SYNOPSIS OF DECISION AND OPINION   The Court of Appeals for the Third Circuit upheld the trial court's decision in favor of Pilatus. The court pointed out that Pilatus had not sold any aircraft to purchasers in Pennsylvania or shipped anything directly to persons or entities in Pennsylvania. Moreover, Pilatus had not advertised or marketed its products in Pennsylvania and did not design the plane for the Pennsylvania market specifically, although it did target the U.S. market generally by designing the plane to ensure its compliance with FAA requirements. Although Pilatus purchased $1,030,139 in products, equipment, and services from

suppliers in Pennsylvania, this amount represented less than 1 percent of Pilatus's total annual purchases for an approximately five-year period.

WORDS OF THE COURT: Purposeful Availment
"We acknowledge that there is a certain reasonableness to an argument that a manufacturer should be subject to suit in a jurisdiction in which its plane crashes if the suit charges that a manufacturing defect caused the crash. Yet it is clear that the critical finding that the defendant purposefully availed itself of the privilege of conducting activities within the forum [state] requires contacts that amount to a deliberate reaching into the forum state to target its citizens. Pilatus's efforts to exploit a national market necessarily included Pennsylvania as a target, but those efforts simply do not constitute the type of deliberate contacts within Pennsylvania that could amount to purposeful availment of the privilege of conducting activities in that state. Rather, any connection of Pilatus to Pennsylvania merely was a derivative benefit of its successful attempt to exploit the United States as a national market."

Case Questions

1. What facts could you change that may sway the court's judgment in analyzing personal jurisdiction over Pilatus in this case?

2. Does this decision mean that Weingeroff is without any legal recourse against Pilatus unless the case is brought in Swiss courts?

3. Suppose the plane had crashed and injured a pedestrian on the ground. Given the court's reasoning, would the victim be able to bring a case against Pilatus in a Pennsylvania (state or federal) court?

---

argument that the Maryland court had jurisdiction in the case because of a series of negotiations that had taken place via telephone, fax, and mail between the parties in Maryland and California. The court ruled that "due process requires that a defendant's contacts with the forum state be tantamount to physical presence there."

Many states have also passed specific statutes that give state courts personal jurisdiction over out-of-state residents who operate motor vehicles within the state for the narrow purposes of allowing a victim of an auto accident to pursue a claim against an out-of-state driver.

Voluntary   A court has personal jurisdiction if the parties agree to litigate in a specific court. Voluntary personal jurisdiction applies when a nonresident party agrees to the jurisdiction of a particular court in a certain state. This voluntary jurisdiction is often done

FIGURE 3.3 Sample Forum Selection Clause

"In the event of any dispute that arises from the performance, breach or any obligations under this contract, the parties agree and expressly consent to litigate any such disputes in the State Court of Common Pleas, located in Philadelphia, Pennsylvania, as the exclusive venue and both parties hereby voluntarily submit to their exclusive jurisdiction over the matter."

through a *forum selection clause* written in a contract between the parties. A forum selection clause is a contractual agreement that obligates the parties to litigate any dispute arising out of the contract in a particular court named in the clause. Essentially, the parties are agreeing to a forum *ahead of time* so that if any litigation involving that particular contract is instituted, both parties are obligated to litigate the dispute in a predetermined court.

In *Carnival Cruise Lines v. Shute*,[17] the U.S. Supreme Court upheld a federal court's ruling that dismissed a personal injury claim by a resident of the state of Washington who had been a passenger on a Carnival Cruise Lines ship and had fallen during a guided tour of the ship. The Court ruled that the passenger ticket was a contract between the passenger and Carnival Cruise Lines and that the ticket contained a forum selection clause whereby the parties agreed to litigate any disputes in Miami, Florida (where Carnival's headquarters was located).

Figure 3.3 is a sample of a typical forum selection clause in a contract.

Recall our Cain versus APC hypothetical. Suppose that Cain files her lawsuit in a federal district court in Massachusetts. In addition to establishing subject matter jurisdiction, she must also meet the court's standards for personal jurisdiction over APC. In this case, given the fact that the incident took place in Texas, it may be difficult for Cain to demonstrate APC's connection with Massachusetts unless APC owns property, maintains an office, regularly sent personnel to Massachusetts, or has some other regular and systematic connection with the state. In its jurisdiction analysis of the Cain versus APC matter, a federal court would first look to the Massachusetts long-arm statute and then to the constitutional requirements of due process and fairness, including APC's level of minimum contacts and purposeful availment in Massachusetts.

CASE 3.2 Clemens v. McNamee, 615 F.3d 374 (5th Cir. 2010)

FACT SUMMARY In the summer of 2007, federal agents contacted Brian McNamee in connection with an investigation of the illegal manufacture and sale of performance-enhancing drugs. McNamee had been an athletic trainer who had worked for both the Toronto Blue Jays and New York Yankees baseball teams. After authorities convinced McNamee that they had sufficient evidence to convict him for injecting athletes with anabolic steroids, McNamee agreed to cooperate with investigators in exchange for immunity from prosecution. During an interview with investigators, McNamee admitted that he had administered the drugs to star pitcher Roger Clemens in both Toronto and New York. McNamee repeated this allegation to Major League Baseball investigators and to a reporter during an interview with *Sports Illustrated*. In 2008, Clemens, a resident of Texas, filed suit against McNamee for defamation in Texas. The trial court dismissed the suit due to lack of personal jurisdiction because the focal point of McNamee's statements was not in Texas. Clemens appealed.

(continued)

[17]499 U.S. 585 (1991).

SYNOPSIS OF DECISION AND OPINION The Court of Appeals for the Fifth Circuit upheld the trial court's ruling in favor of McNamee and dismissed Clemens's complaint. The court rejected Clemens's contention that jurisdiction was proper in a Texas court because he suffered harm from the defamation in Texas. The court analyzed McNamee's contacts with the state of Texas within the context of the alleged defamation claim and concluded that McNamee did not have sufficient minimum contacts as required by the long-arm statute and due process. The court held that to support personal jurisdiction in a defamation claim, the forum must be the "focal point" of the story. Although the court acknowledged that the defamation may cause distress and damage to Clemens's reputation in Texas, it concluded that the alleged defamatory statement was inadequately directed to Texas to satisfy the minimum-contacts requirement.

WORDS OF THE COURT: Minimal Contacts and Injurious Effect "In support of jurisdiction, Clemens points to the harm he suffered in Texas and to McNamee's knowledge of the likelihood of such damage in the forum. Yet under [previous case law], Clemens has not made a prima facie showing that McNamee made statements in which Texas was the focal point: the statements did not concern activity in Texas; nor were they made in Texas or directed to Texas residents any more than residents of any state. As such, the district court did not err in dismissing Clemens' suit for lack of personal jurisdiction over McNamee."

Case Questions

1. What is the practical implication of this decision? Does it mean that Clemens cannot bring suit for defamation in any court?
2. If McNamee had claimed that he injected Clemens with the drugs while in Texas, would that change the court's analysis? How?

CONCEPT SUMMARY Jurisdiction

	Federal Trial Courts	State Trial Courts
Personal Jurisdiction	1. Residents and business entities located in the state where the federal trial court sits; or 2. Nonresidents with *minimum contacts* with the state in which the federal trial court sits; or 3. Nonresidents owning property in the state in which the federal trial court sits; or 4. Voluntary	1. Residents and business entities located in the state; or 2. Nonresidents owning property in the state; or 3. Nonresidents with *minimum contacts* with the state according to state long-arm statutes; or 4. Voluntary
Subject Matter Jurisdiction	1. Federal question; or 2. U.S. is a party; or 3. Diversity of citizenship *and* amount in controversy is more than $75,000 (amount required only in diversity cases)	State law matters (statutes, common law, state constitutional issues)

Venue

While jurisdiction requires an analysis of whether a court has authority over a particular case, venue is the legal concept that defines the most appropriate *location* for the trial. Two or more courts will sometimes have jurisdiction over the very same matter, but it would be more appropriate from a fairness perspective to hear the case in a particular location. Many states have venue rules to determine where a case may be heard. Typically, state statutes provide that venue in a civil case is where the defendant resides or is headquartered, while in a criminal case the venue is ordinarily where the crime is committed. While changes in venue for civil cases are rare, in high-profile criminal cases a defense attorney will ask for a *change of venue* to help select a jury from outside the area where the crime was committed, under the theory that the out-of-area jury will be more impartial and less influenced by the media.

To understand how venue may be important in a business context, suppose two Florida-based companies are involved in a breach of contract dispute and Beta sues Alpha. The transaction involved an order that took place over a website based in Florida, and the order was shipped from Alpha's warehouse in Georgia to Beta's branch office in South Carolina. Although a number of state and federal courts may have jurisdiction over a dispute in this case given the contacts, a Florida court may decide that Florida is the best *venue* for the dispute to be litigated because both parties have their principal office located there and assumedly it is the most convenient forum for the parties. It is likely that the witnesses and records are in Florida as well. Note, however, that a state court cannot unilaterally declare that venue exists in *another* jurisdiction. Courts apply venue statutes to determine whether or not *their* court is the most appropriate venue.

LEGAL IMPLICATIONS *in* CYBERSPACE

Minimum Contacts over the Internet

The technology boom of the 1990s brought new challenges for courts grappling with the concept of minimum contacts in cyberspace. For example, suppose that Copperfield is the principal owner of an advertising firm headquartered in New London, Connecticut. Hoping to attract new clients and generate new leads, Copperfield develops a website that features tips on running an effective marketing campaign and is free to all Internet users so long as they fill out a brief form with the user's contact information. Does that subject Copperfield to the jurisdiction of all 50 states simply because users from across the country could access the website? Because courts have held that advertising in a particular state may be a factor in determining whether minimum contacts exist, couldn't a *website* be the basis for those contacts as well? How does that square with the purposeful availment standard? Suppose that Copperfield starts a subscription-based service and charges users to access the site? What if Copperfield made downloads available for users for a fee—would that change your analysis? Is there any way that Copperfield can limit a court's authority over his firm's minimum contacts? Although the Supreme Court has yet to directly rule on minimum contacts in the context of cyberspace, the law developed thus far gives business owners and managers a relatively clear framework in answering the questions posed in the Copperfield hypothetical.

The *Zippo* Standard

In 1997, a federal district court in Pennsylvania generated the first comprehensive scheme for

(continued)

testing a minimum-contacts analysis of personal jurisdiction based on one party's use of the Internet in its business. Named after the parties in the case, this analytical model became known as the **Zippo standard.** Recall from the earlier discussion in this chapter that federal district courts are trial courts and thus do not set precedent. However, since the case was decided, at least six federal circuit courts of appeal have adopted the *Zippo* standard as the legal framework to be used by trial courts in determining personal jurisdiction when one party is asserting minimum contacts based on a certain level of Internet activity by the defendant.

The *Zippo* standard was established in *Zippo Manufacturing Company v. Zippo Dot Com, Inc.*[18] As one may imagine from its name, the case centers on a trademark infringement dispute between Zippo Manufacturing Company, the famous lighter manufacturing company, and Zippo Dot Com (ZDC), an Internet news subscription service.[19] When Zippo sued ZDC, ZDC asked the court to dismiss the case, claiming a federal court in Pennsylvania did not have personal jurisdiction over ZDC because the company had no offices, agents, or property in Pennsylvania. Zippo argued that ZDC's sale of approximately 3,000 subscription-based memberships to residents of Pennsylvania satisfied both the state's long-arm statute and the constitutional fairness and due process requirements of minimum contacts.

In developing a framework for deciding the case, the court adopted a *continuum,* also called a *sliding scale,* approach for measuring the number of minimum contacts based on the interactivity of a website owner vis-à-vis the user. The court focused this test on the *level* and *nature* of interactivity between source and user that an individual or business transacted over the Internet. The court explained the continuum by using an illustration of three points along the scale: passive, interactive, and integral to the business model.

Passive On one far end of the continuum, a party's passive website that provides information that could be accessed by any Internet user cannot be the *sole basis* for personal jurisdiction. The court analogized this type of website to a billboard advertisement and reasoned that such websites could not meet the purposeful availment standard and, thus, could not satisfy the minimum contacts requirement.

Interactive The middle of the continuum applies when a website provides users with some interactive function whereby users may exchange information, purchase products, download or upload material via the website, or engage in other uses that involve user activity beyond merely viewing the content of the website. For cases that fall into this category, the court would be required to examine the interactivity more closely on a case-by-case basis with a focus on the level of interactivity and commercial nature of the website. For example, was the level of interactivity simply a product order form that could be downloaded, filled out, and faxed to the vendor? If so, the case may fall on the passive side of the scale and no minimum contacts exist. On the other hand, if the interactivity involved credit card purchases from a significant number of users in one particular state via the website or some subscription-based service provided by the website's owner, the case may fall on the active side of the scale, indicating that minimum contacts exist to the extent necessary for personal jurisdiction over the website's owner.

Integral to Business Model The other far end of the scale is a business whose website is an *integral part* of a business model and is used to accomplish commercial transactions with residents in the state of the court's jurisdiction. For example, Internet vendors such as Amazon.com or NetFlix.com regularly transact business with residents of all 50 states (and beyond), and their business model depends almost exclusively on consumers interacting with their websites, including doing financial transactions. In this case, the minimum-contacts and purposeful availment standards are met, and personal jurisdiction is appropriate.

Ultimately, the court ruled that since ZDC contracted with 3,000 residents and seven Internet access providers all located in Pennsylvania, the purposeful availment standard was met, minimum

[18]952 F. Supp. 1119 (W.D. Pa. 1997).
[19]ZDC is now defunct.

contacts existed, and thus the federal court in Pennsylvania had personal jurisdiction over the case.

Figure 3.4 is an illustration of the *Zippo* sliding scale used by many courts to analyze minimum contacts via the Internet.

Adoption of the *Zippo* Standard

Soon after *Zippo* was decided, several other courts began to use the same type of analytical framework. In *Cybersell, Inc. v. Cybersell, Inc.,*[20] a trademark infringement dispute between businesses located in two different states, the Ninth Circuit Court of Appeals used a *Zippo*-like analysis in concluding that the defendant's website, which did little more than advertise the defendant's business services, was essentially passive and did not meet the requisite level of interactivity required to constitute minimum contacts.

In Case 3.3, the Fifth Circuit Court of Appeals became the first federal *appellate* court to expressly adopt the *Zippo* standard and also provided a useful application of the standard when the defendant had a website that involved some degree of interactivity.

[20]130 F.3d 414 (9th Cir. 1997).

FIGURE 3.4   *Zippo* Sliding-Scale Test

Passive/Billboard	Interactive	Integral to Business Model
◄------------------------------------]		[------------------------------------►
No personal jurisdiction	Case by case	Minimum contacts established

Courts in many jurisdictions have adopted the *Zippo* standard when determining personal jurisdiction based on Internet activity.

Self-Check   *Zippo* Standard

Would the court have personal jurisdiction under the *Zippo* standard?

1. Scanner Corp., a Maryland-based corporation with its principal place of business in Baltimore, creates and markets copyrighted photos of models that are used as background material on product packaging and picture frames. AP Picture Co. (AP) wrongfully appropriated hundreds of Scanner's photos and published them on its website, where members could pay to download them. AP received advertisement fees based on the amount of consumer traffic generated by the website. Scanner files suit in a Maryland court against AP and AP's Internet service provider, Megabites, a Georgia corporation with its principal place of business in Atlanta. Does the court have jurisdiction over Megabites?

2. Kristin, a resident of Hawaii, maintains a not-for-profit website from her home that offers information and opinions on commercial household movers. While the website does not charge for its usage, it does accept donations. Last summer, Kristin posted various derogatory and unflattering comments about Moving-U Inc. (MU), a New York corporation, one of which was in response to a user's question. Kristin asserted that MU was operating without the requisite legal authorization and insurance. If MU wishes to sue Kristin in a federal court in New York, does the court have personal jurisdiction?

3. Natural Foods Inc. (Natural) is a Nevada-based firm that sells organic beef. Although it originally did business exclusively in Nevada through a small retail stand, Natural eventually created a website whereby customers throughout the United States could order beef to be shipped from Natural's ranch in Nevada to any city in the United States. When ordering, customers provided their billing and shipping addresses as well as credit card information and could sign up to receive newsletters. Johanna, a resident of Florida, ordered beef via Natural's website and became sick after eating the product. Johanna sues Natural in a federal district court in Florida under a variety of theories. Does Natural have sufficient contact for the Florida court to have personal jurisdiction over the company?

4. Big Bank Securities Inc. (BBS) is a Delaware corporation, with its principal place of business in New York. BBS trades various securities for its own benefit and for its clients. Cheyenne Securities Investors Inc. (CSI) is a Wyoming corporation providing portfolio management for various clients. A trader for CSI contacted BBS through an instant-messaging program used by investors. CSI offered to sell $15 million in bonds to BBS in response to an earlier inquiry. BBS agreed to buy the bonds and set a price and time for delivery of the bond instruments. The entire transaction was completed via the instant-messaging system. The next day CSI reneged on the sale, claiming it believed BBS had insider information. CSI has no offices or agents in New York. Would New York state courts have personal jurisdiction over a BBS versus CSI lawsuit for breach of contract?

Answers to this Self-Check are provided at the end of the chapter.

E-MAIL AND MINIMUM CONTACTS

In a 2002 case, a federal trial court ruled that e-mail communications between parties who had an ongoing business relationship with a party in the forum state had *sufficient* minimum contacts with the state to justify an exercise of jurisdiction.[21] In reaching its decision,

---

[21]*Johnson v. King Media Inc.,* 2002 U.S. Dist. LEXIS 12311. Although several other trial courts have subsequently adopted the reasoning in this case, this particular point of law is still developing in the appellate courts.

FACT SUMMARY Mink, a Texas resident, had experience and expertise in the retail furniture business. He developed a computer program called the Opportunity Tracking Computer System (OTCS) that was designed to analyze information regarding retail furniture sales to pinpoint potential new leads for use in the furniture industry. Mink submitted an application for a patent for OTCS. While the patent application was pending, Stark approached Mink to gauge interest in the possibility of marketing the OTCS software bundled with Stark's existing software through the use of Stark's marketing company called AAAA Development (AAAA). Although Mink declined the offer to market the software together, he later approached Stark to discuss the possibility of AAAA marketing OTCS as a separate product. During the discussions, Stark allegedly shared Mink's ideas and information on the OTCS with Stark's AAAA business partner. AAAA was a Vermont corporation.

Eventually, Mink filed suit in a federal district court in Texas against AAAA Development and its principals, alleging that they conspired to copy Mink's patent-pending OTCS system for their own financial gain. None of the defendants owned property or had any other contact in Texas. In the course of its business, AAAA maintained a website advertising its software products on the Internet. The site was available to all users, including residents of Texas, and Mink argued that the website alone was sufficient contact to warrant jurisdiction in Texas. The federal district court in Texas dismissed the case for lack of personal jurisdiction, and Mink appealed.

SYNOPSIS OF DECISION AND OPINION The Fifth Circuit Court of Appeals ruled in favor of AAAA, holding that the federal district court in Texas did *not* have personal jurisdiction over AAAA by virtue of the website alone. In expressly adopting the *Zippo* standard, the court reasoned that although the website did have some level of interactivity, it was not sufficient to satisfy the minimum-contacts requirement. Further, the court ruled that the district court could not exercise personal jurisdiction over AAAA simply because its website is *accessible* by Texas residents. Courts addressing the issue of whether personal jurisdiction can be constitutionally exercised over a defendant look to the *nature* and *quality* of commercial activity that an entity conducts over the Internet. The court also pointed out that it was not reasonably foreseeable, or particularly fair, that AAAA would be subject to personal jurisdiction in Texas.

WORDS OF THE COURT: *Zippo* Standard "We find that the reasoning of *Zippo* is persuasive and adopt it in this Circuit. . . . Applying these principles to this case, we conclude that AAAA's website is insufficient to subject it to personal jurisdiction. Essentially, AAAA maintains a website that posts information about its products and services. While the website provides users with a printable mail-in order form, AAAA's toll-free telephone number, a mailing address and an electronic mail (e-mail) address, orders are not taken through AAAA's website. This does not classify the website as anything more than passive advertisement [and] is not grounds for the exercise of personal jurisdiction.

"There was no evidence that AAAA conducted business over the Internet by engaging in business transactions with forum residents or by entering into contracts over the Internet.

"We note that AAAA's website provides an e-mail address that permits consumers to interact with the company. There is no evidence, however, that the website allows AAAA to do anything but reply to e-mail initiated by website visitors. In addition, AAAA's website lacks other forms of interactivity cited by courts as factors to consider in determining questions of personal jurisdiction. For example, AAAA's website does not allow consumers to order or purchase products and services on-line.

"[T]he presence of an electronic mail access, a printable order form, and a toll-free phone number on a website, without more, is insufficient to establish personal jurisdiction. Absent a defendant doing business over the Internet or sufficient interactivity with residents of the forum state, we cannot conclude that personal jurisdiction is appropriate."

Case Questions

1. Where did AAAA's website fall on the sliding scale of the *Zippo* standard?

2. As a practical matter, what happens to Mink's case now? May he refile it in another court?

Legal Speak >))
Principal The term used to denote a person with an ownership interest in a business venture.

the court took note that it has become the general rule in modern commercial relationships for parties to communicate by electronic means rather than face-to-face. Jurisdiction in this case was justified by an ongoing relationship that included regular interstate communications by e-mail in the forum state.

The court ruled that the defendant's having a physical presence or agents in the forum state was not necessary when continuous communications were conducted between the parties using electronic and nonelectronic means and the out-of-state party engaged in ongoing business transactions with parties located in the forum state. Compare this ruling to the court's decision in *Ritz Camera v. Wentling,* discussed earlier, in which there was no ongoing relationship but instead discussions regarding only a single transaction.

INTERNATIONAL JURISDICTION FOR INTERNET TRANSACTIONS[22]

LO 3-10

The advances in technology and logistical efficiency make the prospect for engaging in international trade more opportune than ever. While international commerce presents a substantial opportunity for a business's product or service to be advertised and sold to hundreds of millions of potential consumers worldwide, there are attendant legal risks that business owners and managers need to understand. Even with the rapid movement toward global harmonization of laws and regulations, individual countries still have their own political challenges, culture, and identity that impact the way a country applies its laws and legal systems. For example, suppose that Snow Sports Equipment (SSE) decides to expand its business to the European markets. The owners of SSE set up an export chain where by the equipment is sold via a website with computers and servers located in an office in Boulder, Colorado, and then shipped from leased warehouse space in Prague, Czech Republic, to a retail store in Geneva, Switzerland. Who has jurisdiction over any disputes involving the product? Must a U.S. court apply European Union law? Swiss law? Czech law? Can a European consumer sue SSE in Europe under Swiss law or European law? (Note that the Czech Republic is an EU member state, but Switzerland is not.) This uncertainty and the inherent difficulty in determining which nation's law to apply in an Internet transaction creates challenges for business owners and managers. Some degree of cost-benefit analysis is necessary to measure the risks of international trade versus the return on investment.

Country of Origin Standard

The United States, Canada, and the European Union governments have generally agreed to apply the law of the country in which the defendant's servers are *located.* This so-called **country of origin principle** allows courts an easy rule of thumb to determine choice of law. Yet some countries have adopted a *country of reception* approach that increases the risk to a business because, in theory, one would need to have a fundamental knowledge of the laws of each individual country in order to reduce risk of noncompliance.

Other Theories of Jurisdiction in Electronic Commerce

Consider a decision by Australia's highest court issued in December 2002. The court ruled that American-based publisher Dow Jones could be sued in Australia for defamation based on an article that appeared on its website, even though Dow Jones has no presence in Australia and its website and infrastructure (such as the mainframe servers) are located in New Jersey. The plaintiff in the case, Joseph Gutnick, a wealthy Australian businessman,

---

[22]Note that commercial jurisdiction in the general context of international law is discussed in detail in Chapter 26 "International Law and Global Commerce."

likely chose the forum because of its convenience and Australia's relatively pro-plaintiff defamation laws. Dow Jones contended that the case should take place in the United States because that is where the article was uploaded to its computer servers in New Jersey and that is the closest location to where the article was published. The Australian court ruled against Dow Jones, reasoning that the article is actually published where and when the article appeared on the user's computer screen.

CONCEPT SUMMARY Minimum Contacts on the Internet

- The *Zippo* standard is a sliding-scale approach for measuring the amount of minimum contacts a party has based on the interactivity of a website.
- Under the *Zippo* standard, passive websites that provide information that can be accessed by any Internet user alone do not provide a basis for personal jurisdiction. On the other hand, websites that are integral to the business model and used consistently for transactions constitute minimum contacts.
- Websites used with some degree of interactivity are evaluated on a case-by-case basis, with those simply exchanging information generally not being grounds for jurisdiction but those involving subscription services and other purposeful contact may provide the basis for minimum contacts and purposeful availment.
- E-mail communication between parties with ongoing business relationships has been found to be sufficient minimum contact by a limited number of courts.
- In international web transactions, generally the courts in the location of the website's servers will have jurisdiction over any disputes arising out of the use of the website. This is known as the country of origin approach.

KEY TERMS

Court p. 65 A judicial tribunal duly constituted for the hearing and determination of cases.

Judiciary p. 65 A collection of federal and state courts existing primarily to adjudicate disputes and charged with the responsibility of judicial review.

State courts p. 65 Courts that adjudicate matters dealing primarily with cases arising from state statutory, state common, or state constitutional law.

Federal courts p. 66 Courts that adjudicate matters dealing primarily with national laws, federal constitutional issues, and other cases that are outside the purview of state courts.

State trial courts p. 66 The first courts at the state level before which the facts of a case are decided.

State appellate courts p. 66 State-level courts of precedent, concerned primarily with reviewing the decisions of trial courts.

Plaintiff p. 66 The party initiating a lawsuit who believes the conduct of another party has caused the plaintiff to suffer damages.

Defendant p. 66 The party alleged by the plaintiff to have caused the plaintiff to suffer damages.

Trial de novo p. 67 A completely new trial.

Remand p. 67 To send a case back to the lower court from which it came for further action consistent with the opinion and instructions of the higher court.

U.S. district courts p. 68 Federal courts that serve the same primary trial function as state trial courts but address issues involving federal matters.

U.S. courts of appeal p. 68 The intermediate appellate courts in the federal system, frequently referred to as *circuit courts of appeal;* consist of 13 courts, each of which reviews the decisions of federal district courts in the state or several states within its circuit.

U.S. Supreme Court p. 68   The ultimate arbiter of federal law that not only reviews decisions of the federal courts but also reviews decisions of state courts that involve some issue of federal law.

Jurisdiction p. 72   The legal authority that a court must have before it can hear a case.

Venue p. 73   A determination of the most appropriate court location for litigating a dispute.

Subject matter jurisdiction p. 73   The court's authority over the dispute between the parties.

Personal jurisdiction p. 73   The court's authority over the parties involved in the dispute.

Federal question p. 74   Some issue arising from the Constitution, a federal statute or regulation, or federal common law.

Party p. 74   A person or entity making or responding to a claim in a court.

Diversity of citizenship p. 74   Situation in which opposing parties in a lawsuit are citizens of different states or one party is a citizen of a foreign country; the case is placed under federal court jurisdiction if the amount in controversy exceeds $75,000.

Original jurisdiction p. 74   Jurisdiction that enables a court to be the first court to hear the case. The case must be filed first in this court.

Concurrent jurisdiction p. 74   Situation in which two different courts each have subject matter jurisdiction to hear a case.

In rem jurisdiction p. 76   Jurisdiction over real or personal property when the property itself is the principal subject of the lawsuit.

Quasi in rem jurisdiction p. 76   Jurisdiction over real or personal property when the lawsuit has to do with personal liabilities not directly associated with the property.

In personam jurisdiction p. 76   Another term for *personal jurisdiction.*

State long-arm statutes p. 76   State statutes intended to allow a court to reach into another state and exercise jurisdiction over a nonresident defendant due to the defendant's conduct or other circumstances.

Minimum contacts p. 77   A defendant's activities within or affecting the state in which a lawsuit is brought that are considered legally sufficient to support jurisdiction in that state's courts.

Zippo standard p. 82   The legal framework used by trial courts in determining personal jurisdiction when one party is asserting minimum contacts based on a certain level of Internet activity by the defendant.

Country of origin principle p. 86   General agreement between the United States, Canada, and the European Union governments to apply the law of the country in which the defendant's servers are located.

THEORY TO PRACTICE

Santiago Information Systems (Santiago) is a business based in Baltimore, Maryland, that purchases old computers, refurbishes them with new software and hardware parts, and sells them in bulk for about half the price of a new PC. For the past three years, Santiago shipped approximately 40 percent of its inventory to the same client. The client was the Wilmington, Delaware, school system (Wilmington) and the school paid approximately $80,000 to Santiago for the computers per year. Santiago would also visit each school to be sure that the computers were installed correctly and that the school district was satisfied with the order. Santiago has a website that gives contact information for the company, but the site is not interactive because users can transact business only by sending Santiago e-mail via the website.

Recently, Wilmington discovered that large shipments of Santiago's products were defective, and it has been unable to come to a resolution with Santiago over the matter.

1. If Wilmington wishes to sue Santiago, what court(s) would have jurisdiction over this matter?
2. What would be the best venue and why?
3. If a Delaware court decides that it does not have jurisdiction, how may that affect Wilmington's decision on whether or not to file a lawsuit?

Assume that one of Santiago's suppliers, Parts R Us (Parts) is headquartered in Union, New Jersey, and has been shipping Santiago parts for approximately four years in a row. Last year Parts sold approximately $7,000 in hardware to Santiago. In the past 10 years,

Parts R Us shipped to businesses in Maryland, New York, New Jersey, and Connecticut. Parts also e-mailed advertisements to potential leads in each of the 50 states. Wilmington determines that Parts provided the defective parts used in the Wilmington computer order.

4. If Wilmington decides to file suit against Parts in Delaware, would a Delaware court have personal jurisdiction over Parts? Why or why not?

5. If Parts had a website at which customers could order products, pay for them via credit card, and have parts delivered via a delivery service to any U.S. city, how would that affect your jurisdiction analysis?

6. If the only contact that Parts had with Delaware was via its website, what standard would the trial court apply to determine jurisdiction?

MANAGER'S CHALLENGE

Managers are frequently involved in various aspects of business planning and have to be alert to current trends that affect their industry as well as be alert to potential liability during the planning process. Assume that you are a midlevel manager at Santiago Information Systems (from the Theory to Practice problem). After settling with Wilmington in an out-of-court agreement, Santiago embarks on an expansion plan, and you receive the following e-mail from your senior manager:

> We are planning a very aggressive marketing campaign and extending our reach beyond institutions such as Wilmington by targeting individual

consumers as well. This will include revamping and expanding the functionality of the website to include online ordering and the use of e-mail advertisements to selected consumer groups. Write a two- to three-page memorandum advising me of any potential liability associated with the website in terms of out-of-state clients, and make recommendations on how to limit any liability from the marketing plan related to revamping the website and using mass e-mail advertisements to selected consumers. Be sure to include any cost-benefit issues that may be applicable.

A sample answer may be found on this textbook's website at www.mhhe.com/melvinleb2e.

CASE SUMMARY 3.1 :: Bickford v. Onslow Memorial Hospital Foundation, 855 A.2d 1150 (Me. 2004)

PERSONAL JURISDICTION

Bickford, a resident of Maine, received hospital bills over a period of several months from Onslow Memorial Hospital, which had treated a relative of Bickford's ex-wife. Although Onslow eventually acknowledged that Bickford was not legally responsible for the bills, Onslow continued to pursue the debt through collection and reported the debt as delinquent to Bickford's

credit agencies. Bickford filed suit against Onslow in a Maine state court, alleging a violation of several consumer protection laws. Onslow is located in North Carolina and does not own property or have any agents in Maine.

CASE QUESTION

1. Does the Maine court have jurisdiction over Onslow?

JURISDICTION: FORUM SELECTION CLAUSE

Zapata, a Texas corporation, hired Unterweser, a German corporation, to provide a tugboat for pulling Zapata's oil rig. Unterweser prepared a contract, and Zapata signed the contract after having made several changes. The contract contained a forum selection clause requiring any disputes be litigated in an International Commercial Court in London. Zapata had not altered that part of the contract. Unterweser's tugboat departed from Louisiana pulling Zapata's oil rig, but while the tugboat and rig were in international waters off the Gulf of Mexico, a storm arose that resulted in severe damage to the oil rig. Zapata instructed Unterweser to tow the rig to the nearest port, in Tampa, Florida. Zapata then filed a lawsuit in the federal district court in Tampa for $3.5 million against Unterweser.

CASE QUESTIONS

1. Does the court in Tampa have jurisdiction? Why or why not?
2. Will the forum selection clause be enforced? Why or why not?

PURPOSEFUL AVAILMENT

Colelli & Associates (Colelli) is a firm with its principal place of business in Ohio. Colelli was engaged in the manufacture and sale of a specialized oil well solvent, which it sold to several oil producers based in Ohio. Sixty percent of the oil produced by the Ohio producers was shipped to refineries in Pennsylvania, including a refinery owned and operated by Pennzoil Products Company (Pennzoil). Pennzoil, a corporation based in Nevada with refineries around the world, sued Colelli in a federal district court located in Pennsylvania on a product liability claim, contending that Colelli's solvent had damaged its Pennsylvania refinery. Colelli contested the court's jurisdiction because the company had no *direct* contact with Pennsylvania business owners and had no other contacts within Pennsylvania. Pennzoil argued that Colelli knew that its product was being used by Pennsylvania companies and had gained a substantial benefit by virtue of its product being used by Pennsylvania oil refineries such as Pennzoil's.

CASE QUESTION

1. Has Colelli purposefully availed itself to Pennsylvania to warrant personal jurisdiction?

MINIMUM CONTACTS

The Robinsons, residents of New York, purchased a new Audi car from Seaway, a car dealership in New York. Seaway obtained this car from World-Wide Volkswagen, a New York corporation that is a regional distributor for Audi serving the New York, New Jersey, and Connecticut markets. While driving the car through Oklahoma, the Robinsons were severely injured in a car accident. The Robinsons brought a product liability lawsuit against both Seaway and World-Wide Volkswagen in a federal trial court in Oklahoma. World-Wide contended that the Oklahoma court did not have personal jurisdiction because World-Wide had no property, presence, or agents in Oklahoma.

CASE QUESTIONS

1. Who prevails and why?
2. Are the minimum-contacts requirements being met? Why or why not?
3. Since the car is inherently mobile, does that mean that jurisdiction is appropriate in any state where the car has traveled?

MINIMUM CONTACTS VIA THE WEB AND THE *ZIPPO* STANDARD

Toys "R" Us is a Delaware corporation headquartered in New Jersey that owns and operates retail stores worldwide. In 1999, it acquired Imaginarium Toy Centers, including the rights to various trademarks held by Imaginarium. Step Two, a corporation based in Spain, owns franchised toy stores operating under the Imaginarium name in several Spanish cities but does not maintain any offices or stores outside Spain. Each corporation registered multiple e-mail addresses under the Imaginarium name. Step Two's sites were interactive and allowed users to purchase toys online, but the company would ship only within Spain. If a user signed up for Step Two's electronic newsletter, the user was prompted to enter personal information and was provided with a drop-down menu of various Spanish provinces where users were located. This menu did not accommodate mailing addresses within the United States, and Step Two maintains that it has never made a sale in the United States. Toys "R" Us claimed that it had evidence that a resident of New Jersey made two purchases via the website, but it conceded that these purchases were delivered to a Toys "R" Us employee in Spain, who then forwarded the items to the purchaser in New Jersey. Toys "R" Us filed a trademark infringement suit in federal district court in New Jersey.

CASE QUESTIONS

1. Does the federal court in New Jersey have subject matter jurisdiction over this case?
2. Has Step Two purposefully availed itself in New Jersey, thus having the requisite minimum contacts? Why or why not?
3. Analyze this case under both the *Zippo* and *Asahi* frameworks. Describe the analysis and potential outcome under each. Which one is the correct test to use and why?

JURISDICTION: IN REM/QUASI IN REM

In December 2000, Office Depot obtained a judgment against Zuccarini under the Anticybersquatting Consumer Protection Act of 1999 (ACPA) arising out of Zuccarini's registration of the domain name "offic-depot.com." Office Depot was unable to collect on the judgment and eventually assigned the judgment to DSH. DSH registered the judgment in the district court for the Northern District of California. DSH subsequently learned that Zuccarini owned more than 248 domain names registered with VeriSign, of which more than 190 were .com domain names. Targeting the .com domain names, DSH sought to levy against and sell some of those names owned by Zuccarini. The district court appointed a receiver to take control of and auction off some of Zuccarini's domain names in order to satisfy the judgment. DSH never claimed that the district court in the Northern District of California had *in personam* jurisdiction over Zuccarini but instead argued that the court had jurisdiction over Zuccarini's intangible property that is located, for purposes of attachment, in the Northern District. Zuccarini appealed, contending that the Northern District of California is not a proper place to levy against his domain names and that the appointment of the receiver was therefore improper. The ACPA provides that . . . jurisdiction over domain names shall be "in the judicial district in which the domain name registrar, domain name registry, or other domain name authority that registered or assigned the domain name is located. . . . "

CASE QUESTIONS

1. Does in rem and quasi in rem jurisdiction encompass ownership of domain names? Why or why not?
2. Is the court exercising in rem or quasi in rem jurisdiction in this case?
3. Why can the court obtain jurisdiction allowing the seizure and sale of domain names without first obtaining personal jurisdiction over the defendant, Zuccarini?

JURISDICTION THROUGH WEBSITE

Tempur-Pedic brought suit against Go Satellite in a federal court in Texas, alleging that Go Satellite infringed on Tempur-Pedic's registered trademark. The suit alleged that Go Satellite operated two websites that sold Tempur-Pedic brand mattresses without being an authorized dealer for Tempur-Pedic. Go Satellite asked the court to dismiss the claim because the Texas court had no personal jurisdiction over the company since it was based in Kentucky, did not own property in Texas, and had no sales force in Texas. Tempur-Pedic countered that Go Satellite's website was highly interactive, including the ability for consumers to purchase and pay online and to have a virtual chat with a customer service representative, and had, in fact, sold and shipped mattresses to consumers in Texas.

CASE QUESTION

1. What standard should the court apply to determine whether the website constitutes sufficient contacts to warrant jurisdiction?
2. Does the court have personal jurisdiction over Go Satellite? Why or why not?
3. Name some examples of "interactivity" that a court may consider when analyzing personal jurisdiction through a website?

 Self-Check **ANSWERS**

Subject Matter Jurisdiction

1. No. No diversity or federal question.
2. Yes. U.S. government agency is a party to the litigation.
3. Yes. Diversity of citizenship with amount exceeding $75,000.
4. Yes. Federal issue involving a federal statute.
5. Yes. U.S. is a party to the litigation and federal statute at issue.

Zippo Standard

1. No. The court cannot exercise personal jurisdiction over Megabites. The company's conduct is strictly passive and, thus, not sufficient for an exercise of jurisdiction. See generally *ALS Scan, Inc. v. Digital Serv. Consultants, Inc.*, 293 F.3d 707 (4th Cir. 2002).
2. No. Regardless of the acceptance of donations or response to user questions, New York courts would not have jurisdiction for defamatory comments made outside New York. The website in question here can be accessed by anyone in the world, and there is no evidence that Kristin was availing herself of the opportunity to directly conduct business in New York. See generally *Best Van Lines, Inc. v. Walker*, 490 F.3d 239 (2d Cir. 2007).

3. Yes. Considering the interactivity of its website and the fact that consumers can purchase products from it, courts in Florida could exercise jurisdiction over Natural Foods Inc.

4. Yes. A New York court would have jurisdiction because CSI was clearly attempting to do business in New York with BBS through the instant-messaging system. CSI had knowingly contacted BBS in order to initiate the transaction, which culminated in the sale of $15 million in bonds; thus, CSI had entered into New York to conduct business. See generally *Deutsche Bank Sec., Inc. v. Montana Bd. of Invs.*, 850 N.E.2d 1140 (N.Y. 2006).

4 CHAPTER

Resolving Disputes: Litigation and Alternative Dispute Resolution Options

learning objectives

After studying this chapter, students who have mastered the material will be able to:

4-1 Identify the ways in which dispute resolution is used in business planning.

4-2 Explain the meaning and purpose of civil litigation as a method of resolving disputes.

4-3 Name the stages of litigation and identify the characteristics of each stage.

4-4 Articulate the concept of standing.

4-5 List the methods of alternative dispute resolution (ADR) and potential advantages of using ADR.

4-6 Distinguish between arbitration and mediation and explain both processes.

4-7 Apply the legal standards under which an arbitration clause may be held invalid.

4-8 Explain how online dispute resolution can be used to solve small-claim disputes.

4-9 Provide an example of a hybrid form of alternative dispute resolution.

Litigation and dispute resolution are an important part of business planning and strategy. It is inevitable that businesses will occasionally, or even frequently, need to resolve disputes with a customer, another business, or even a local, state, or federal government. Whether those disputes can be resolved without litigation will significantly affect the company's bottom line. It is therefore imperative that managers understand their options and the advantages and disadvantages of alternative dispute resolution (ADR) and litigation. In this chapter students will learn:

- The role of dispute resolution in business planning.
- The process of using civil litigation to resolve disputes.
- Methods of alternative dispute resolution.

DISPUTE RESOLUTION AND BUSINESS PLANNING   LO 4-1

In a business context, dispute resolution is not simply a matter to be delegated to attorneys. While legal counsel is a primary and important source of information and advice, the decisions regarding how to resolve a dispute are decisions for business managers and owners. Dispute resolution can be a crucial part of business planning and strategy that requires a thoughtful cost-benefit analysis. Business managers and owners have an ever-increasing number of options to resolve disputes within and outside the legal system, and each comes with its attendant advantages and disadvantages.

To illustrate how dispute resolution may be used in business planning, suppose that Classic Retail Outlets (CRO) enters into a contract with Sign Designs Company (SignCo). The contract calls for SignCo to design, manufacture, and install signage for several CRO locations. The parties agreed on certain specifications and a payment of 50 percent at the time of signing the contract and 50 percent at the time of delivery. SignCo delivered a prototype of the new sign, but CRO management was unhappy with the design and claimed SignCo had not followed the specifications in the contract. SignCo agreed to work on a new prototype but delayed the process for several months. Finally, SignCo submitted a new prototype, but CRO again rejected the prototype, citing additional flaws in its design. In addition, so much time had passed that CRO had to go through the expense of installing temporary signs.

In this hypothetical, a legal dispute is brewing between CRO and SignCo. Yet the fact remains that at least two business problems still exist: (1) Despite the fact that 50 percent of the contract price has been paid to SignCo, CRO still needs a sign and has now expended more money than anticipated due to the temporary signs; and (2) SignCo has devoted significant time and some materials to the project and may believe that CRO is being unreasonable in its expectations. Business owners and managers have a host of options for resolving such disputes. Therefore, CRO should consider the alternatives presented in Table 4.1 to resolve the dispute in the context of a cost-benefit analysis and business planning.

TABLE 4.1 Dispute Resolution Options for Classic Retail Outlets vs. SignCo

Action	Potential Benefit(s)	Potential Costs	Threats
Lawsuit	Court-ordered resolution to have the deposit refunded and have SignCo pay additional damages to compensate for the temporary signage.	Significant expenditures: legal fees; hard costs (such as travel and fees for experts); human resource costs when time must be devoted to litigation procedures; appellate costs.	1. Loss at trial or loss upon appeal. 2. Legal fees may be higher than the final judgment amount awarded. 3. Possible countersuit by SignCo. 4. Permanent damage to business relationship. 5. Potential for bad publicity.
Nonjudicial dispute resolution Arbitration, mediation, or hybrid form.	Enforceable resolution to have the deposit refunded and have SignCo pay additional damages to compensate for the temporary signage.	Moderate range in legal fees, arbitration/mediation fees; limited human resource expenditures; no chance of appellate fees (if binding).	1. Loss at arbitration that is not appealable (if binding). 2. Win in arbitration, but still have to go to trial (if nonbinding). 3. Potential damage to business relationship.
Informal settlement Cancel the contract, agree not to sue each other, and agree to a figure that (1) compensates CRO for the temporary signage and (2) allows a percentage of the total fee to compensate SignCo for time invested in the project.	1. Parties agree not to sue each other. 2. Potential exists to preserve the business relationship. 3. Time and talent are not used to prepare for dispute resolution methods.	Low range of legal fees; moderate human resource investment; no threat of litigation by SignCo.	Settlement negotiations may drag on, and CRO must find a new vendor.
Revise contract, continue relationship Make contract expectations clearer, and revise payments that compensate both parties for the loss.	Transaction is completed (perhaps even at a profit), and business relationship is preserved.	Low range of legal fees; moderate human resources.	Potential litigation by SignCo and potential for the new contract to generate yet another dispute.

CIVIL LITIGATION

LO 4-2

Civil litigation is the term used to describe a dispute resolution process in which the parties and their counsel argue their views of a civil (noncriminal) controversy in a court of law. While the term *litigation* is sometimes used as synonymous with the word *trial*, the scope of litigation is much broader and includes *pretrial* events as well. There are many varieties of business litigation, including contract disputes and lawsuits related to employment, negligence, collection actions, and bankruptcy. The odds of a business organization becoming involved in litigation have increased precipitously in recent years. From 1980 to 2005, the number of civil cases filed in federal courts more than doubled. The American Bar Association reported that the total number of civil cases filed in state and federal courts now exceeds 20 million cases annually.

STAGES OF LITIGATION

LO 4-3

Litigation is most easily understood when broken down into stages. However, it is important to note that the timing of these stages may sometimes overlap.

Prelawsuit: Demand and Prelitigation Settlement Negotiations

LO 4-4

When a dispute arises between two parties, one party will typically make an informal demand of the other party in which the principals (or their attorneys) lay out the basics of the dispute and demand a certain action. This usually leads to informal discussions directly between the parties without third-party involvement. In some states it is necessary to make a formal demand before filing suit. The demand is often followed by an informal prelitigation settlement discussion involving the parties and their lawyers. If the issues are relatively simple, this can be a cost-effective method for resolving a dispute fairly. However, if the legal issues are more complex or the parties are antagonistic toward each other, the prelitigation discussion will simply act as notice that a party intends to file a lawsuit if an agreement cannot be reached.

> **KEY POINT**
>
> Negotiation is often considered a form of ADR (discussed later in this chapter), since successful negotiations avoid the filing of a formal lawsuit.

Standing   In order for one party to maintain a lawsuit against another party, she must have **standing** to sue. This means that the party asserting the claim (1) must have suffered an *injury in fact;* (2) suffered harm that is *direct, concrete,* and *individualized;* and (3) articulates what *legal redress* exists to compensate for the injury. In a business context, most lawsuits involve economic interests, and, therefore, most parties in commercial litigation have no trouble meeting the requirements for standing. However, businesses and industries can sometimes be the target of consumer advocacy organizations and other groups that use litigation to advance their group's policy objectives.

Statutes of Limitations   Even if standing can be established, the plaintiff must file the lawsuit within a certain time limit or the case could be barred forever. This time limit is called the **statute of limitations.** In most cases, the moment that an injury occurs, the statute of limitations begins to run and the lawsuit must be filed before the time limit expires. For example, suppose a patron is injured after she slips on a puddle of spilled cappuccino at an EspressoCo coffee shop on July 1, 2013. If EspressoCo is located in a jurisdiction where the statute of limitations is set at two years, the patron must file any lawsuit related to the incident no later than July 1, 2015. It may be helpful to think of the statute of limitations as an hourglass with, in this scenario, exactly two years' worth of sand in it. The hourglass is turned when the patron is injured, and any lawsuit related to the injury must be filed before the last grain of sand falls.

The parties may attempt to resolve a dispute through informal negotiations in order to avoid litigation.

Legal **Speak** ›))
Plaintiff The party who initiates a lawsuit by filing a complaint with the clerk of the court against the defendant(s), demanding damages, performance, and/or court determination of rights.

Defendant The party sued in a civil lawsuit or the party charged with a crime in a criminal prosecution. In some types of cases (such as divorce), a defendant may be called a *respondent*.

Note that the lengths of statutes of limitations vary from state to state and also vary by the cause of action alleged. For example, breach of contract statutes run from as short as 3 years to as long as 15 years. Even within a state, some statutes differentiate between written and oral contracts and have different filing limitations on each.

Pleadings Stage

Complaint and Summons
If informal attempts at resolution fail, formal action begins when the plaintiff initiates a lawsuit by filing a **complaint** with the local clerk of courts.[1] This sets the pleadings stage in motion, with both sides filing documents that set out the facts of the case, theories of liability, and any available defenses. At the same time, the plaintiff is typically required to arrange for serving the defendant with a **summons** along with a copy of the plaintiff's complaint. The summons is formal notification to the defendant that she has been named in the lawsuit and informs her that an answer must be filed within a certain period of time. In some cases, the summons and complaint may be served by certified mail to the defendant. In other cases, a deputy sheriff or process server must deliver the documents in person. Statutes and court rules impose time limits on the *litigants* (the adverse parties involved in litigation) requiring pleadings to be initiated within a set time frame. Failing to adhere to the timelines may result in the loss of any legal rights or defenses. The complaint sets out the plaintiff's version of the facts of the case, the damages that have been suffered, and why the plaintiff believes that the defendant is legally responsible for those damages. Court procedures prescribe how the complaint should be served upon the defendant to ensure timely notice of the claims asserted by the plaintiff. Figure 4.1 sets out a sample complaint for the hypothetical *CRO v. SignCo* dispute.

---

[1]Although *clerk of courts* is a common title for the official designated to receive civil complaints, the actual title varies widely among the states.

Daniel J. Webster, Esquire
ID# 70665
1120 Liberty Place
Philadelphia, Pennsylvania 19124
Attorney for Plaintiffs

In the Pennsylvania Court of Common Pleas
Philadelphia County

CLASSIC RETAIL OUTLETS, INC.   :
           Plaintiff,   :

                      :

         v.   :   **Complaint**

                      :   Civil Docket 13-2100

SIGN DESIGNS COMPANY   :
           Defendant,   :

                      :

_____ :

In this complaint, the plaintiff alleges as follows:

1. Plaintiff and defendant are both Pennsylvania business entities headquartered in Philadelphia, Pennsylvania.
2. Jurisdiction over the subject matter is proper under the Pennsylvania Code.
3. On July 1, 2012, plaintiff contracted with defendant for services related to the design and installation of exterior signage for several of plaintiff's retail outlet sites. The contract specified the appearance and features of the signs.
4. The contract called for plaintiff to pay $25,000 at the execution of the contract and $25,000 at the completion of defendant's services.
5. Plaintiff fulfilled its obligation under the contract by paying $25,000 to defendant on July 1, 2012.
6. On July 30, 2012, Troy Machir, a principal in the plaintiff company, met with Matthew Diller, a principal in the defendant company, to review a preliminary version of the designs that defendant had completed.
7. During that meeting, Machir expressed his dissatisfaction with the work done and pointed out several errors where defendant had failed to follow the specifications detailed in the original contract.
8. As a result of that meeting, Diller promised to begin the design process anew and adhere more closely to the specifications of the contract.
9. Over the next two months, Machir attempted to obtain another preliminary design from defendant by contacting Diller and others at the defendant company via telephone and e-mail.
10. Diller, nor anyone else at the defendant company, responded to these calls or e-mails.
11. On October 1, 2012, Machir met with Diller once again, and Diller presented a revised version of the design.
12. At that meeting, Machir expressed continued dissatisfaction with the design and again pointed out that the design was not consistent with the specifications in the contract.
13. In addition, Machir pointed out several instances where the problems identified at their July meeting were not remedied. Diller again promised to fix the problems.
14. On October 15, 2012, Diller informed Machir that the defendant company could not follow the specifications in the contract at the price agreed to and that an additional fee of $20,000 would be necessary to complete the work.
15. Because of the delay caused by the defendant, plaintiff has had to expend $20,000 to erect temporary signage at its retail outlet sites.
16. The failure of Defendant Company to design a sign according to the specifications of the contract is a failure to perform its obligations under their agreement and constitutes a breach of contract.

    WHEREFORE, plaintiffs request judgment in the amount of $25,000 as refund of the deposit, plus $20,000 for the necessary temporary signage, plus statutory interest, and any other damages the court deems appropriate.

Dated: 1st day of October, 2013.

By:_____

Daniel J. Webster, Esquire
Attorney for the Plaintiff

Oliver W. Holmes, Esquire

ID# 40016

One Alpha Drive

Elizabethtown, Pennsylvania 17022

Attorney for Defendants

In the Pennsylvania Court of Common Pleas

of

Philadelphia County

CLASSIC RETAIL OUTLETS, INC.

       Plaintiff,   :

                :

       v.   :   <u>Answer</u>

                :   Civil Docket 13-2100

SIGN DESIGNS COMPANY

       Defendant,   :

                :

—————————————— :

In this answer, the defendant responds to plaintiff's complaint as follows:

1. Admitted.
2. Admitted.
3. Admitted.
4. Admitted.
5. Admitted.
6. Defendant has insufficient information to admit or deny.
7. Defendant has insufficient information to admit or deny.
8. Defendant has insufficient information to admit or deny.
9. Defendant has insufficient information to admit or deny.
10. Denied. Diller contacted Plaintiff Company several times during this period.
11. Defendant has insufficient information to admit or deny.
12. Defendant has insufficient information to admit or deny.
13. Defendant has insufficient information to admit or deny.
14. Defendant has insufficient information to admit or deny.
15. Defendant has insufficient information to admit or deny.
16. Paragraph 16 is a conclusion of law to which no answer is required.

Defendant also denies any and all parts of the plaintiff's complaint not specifically mentioned in this Answer.

Dated: 20th day of October, 2013.

By:_____

Oliver W. Holmes, Esquire

Attorney for the Defendant

Answer Once the defendant is served with the complaint, she must provide a formal **answer** within a prescribed time frame (normally within 20 days). The answer responds to each paragraph of the complaint. Often, the answer is simply a device for the parties to understand what issues they agree on and what issues will be in dispute at trial. Figure 4.2 shows an answer to CRO's complaint. Note how the numbered paragraphs correspond to those in the complaint and how the responses are very limited and general. The defendant is required only to state her position regarding each paragraph, with no need to provide a specific defense at this stage. If the defendant does not answer on time, she is said to *default* and generally will automatically lose the case without the benefit of trial. This is known as a *default judgment.*

Counterclaim   If the defendant believes that the plaintiff has caused her damages arising out of the *very same* set of facts as articulated in the complaint, the defendant files both an answer and a **counterclaim** (in some states, this is called a *countersuit*). The counterclaim is similar to a complaint in that the defendant's allegations and theory of liability against the plaintiff are set out in the pleading. The plaintiff must now answer the counterclaim allegations by the defendant within a prescribed time period.

Cross-Claim   The defendant can also file a **cross-claim** to bring in a third party to the litigation. A cross-claim is filed when the defendant believes that a third party is either partially or fully liable for the damages that the plaintiff has suffered and, therefore, should be involved as an indispensable party in the trial.

Motions

From the time that the pleadings are filed, through discovery and trial, and even after the trial, parties to the litigation may file **motions.** A motion is a document filed by one party that requests court action in a matter pertaining to the litigation. Some of the more common motions are described in Table 4.2.

Discovery Stage

Once the initial pleadings are filed, most lawsuits move into the **discovery** stage, in which the parties attempt to collect more evidence for trial. While it may make television shows and movies more interesting, surprise evidence may not be introduced at an actual trial. Discovery is the legal process for the orderly exchange of evidence. Each side has the right to know and examine the evidence that the other side has, including evidence that is both *inculpatory* and *exculpatory.*

Everything relevant to the dispute is discoverable. Unless the information is protected by a legal privilege, such as certain conversations between attorney and client, it must be produced in discovery if the information is relevant or could be useful in any way for resolving the dispute.

Methods of Discovery   The rules for exchanging information during discovery are set out in court procedures (called the *Rules of Civil Procedure*) and accomplished primarily by four methods: depositions, interrogatories, requests for production, and request for admissions.

Depositions   **Depositions** are oral questions asked of either a party or a witness in the case. A deposition can be taken at a courthouse but is more commonly taken in the setting of a conference room at a law firm. Although there is a court reporter present to create a written record and the witnesses are under oath, no judge is present. Depositions may be taken from any person with relevant information pertaining to the case. This includes the opposing party as well as any witnesses. If the witness is in possession of pertinent evidence, a subpoena *duces tecum* may be served on the witness to bring the evidence to the deposition.

Interrogatories   **Interrogatories** are written questions submitted to the opposing party that must be answered in writing within a time limitation determined by statute. Only

Legal Speak ›))
Inculpatory Evidence Evidence that tends to prove a criminal offense or civil wrong.

Exculpatory Evidence Evidence that tends to prove innocence or nonliability.

Legal Speak ›))
Subpoena A court order compelling a person to testify and/or produce evidence in her possession.

TABLE 4.2 Motions Used during Litigation

Stage of Litigation	Motion	Request
Pretrial	To Dismiss	To dismiss a case because of a procedural defect such as a court's lack of jurisdiction, failure of the plaintiff to state a valid claim, a plaintiff's lack of standing, or the running of the statute of limitations
Pretrial	For Summary Judgment	To enter judgment in the requesting party's favor without a trial because no issues of fact are presented in the case or the answer shows that there is no actual dispute and, thus, no jury trial is needed. The requesting party believes that it wins as a matter of law
Pretrial	To Compel Discovery	To issue a court order demanding that a party comply with a lawful discovery request
Trial	To Dismiss for Mistrial	To stop the trial in progress and dismiss it because of some extraordinary circumstance resulting in prejudice against one side or the other (rare in civil litigation)
Trial	For a Directed Verdict	To stop the trial and dismiss because the opposing party (usually the plaintiff) has not met its burden of proof
Posttrial	For Judgment as a Matter of Law*	To reverse the verdict of the jury because no reasonable jury could have heard the evidence presented at trial and rendered such a verdict

*Also called by some state courts a judgment *non obstante veredicto* (notwithstanding the verdict).

parties to the litigation are required to answer interrogatories. For example, suppose that a professor throws a piece of chalk at a student, hitting her in the eye and causing serious injury. Every student in the room may be required to answer questions at a deposition; however, only the professor and the injured student may be compelled to answer interrogatories. Generally, interrogatories involve questions on points which the litigant does not

LEGAL/ETHICAL REFLECTION *and* DISCUSSION

If a person is a witness to an accident or has pertinent evidence relating to a lawsuit, she may be required by the court to participate in a deposition and may be compelled to testify at trial. This means that the person may need to take off from work, arrange for child care, or be otherwise inconvenienced. Witnesses, other than hired experts, at trial and deposed parties do not get paid for their participation, and they are considered in contempt of court if they do not show up when ordered and may be penalized.

1. Should an injured party be able to compel a witness to testify at trial or participate in a deposition?
2. If a witness can prove a monetary hardship, should she be paid for her participation? Is this practical?
3. Interrogatories are required only of the parties to the lawsuit. Why is it impractical to require interrogatories for witnesses?
4. Would justice be affected if witness participation regarding trial testimony and depositions were voluntary?

have readily available knowledge. The litigant may have to review files, memorandums, transcripts, and so forth in order to properly answer the questions.

Requests for Production These requests are aimed at producing specific items to help one party discover some important fact in the case. **Requests for production** are usually very wide in scope so that a request would cover all documents, memorandums, reports, notes, calendars, videotape, audiotape, e-mail, computer hard drives, and so on. In a complex securities or banking fraud case or one in which many documents are involved, it is not uncommon for the parties to send a truckload of boxes containing materials that were requested by the other side.

> **KEY** POINT
> Unless protected by a legal privilege, all information relative to the case is subject to methods of discovery.

Along with providing an exchange of information and the elimination of surprise at trial, interrogatories and depositions also serve a valuable purpose during the trial. If a witness gives testimony that differs from facts previously stated in her deposition, the deposition may be used to discredit the witness and attack her testimony. Should a witness claim to have forgotten a fact or circumstance (remember that discovery takes place soon after the pleadings are filed while the actual trial may be conducted months or years later), her deposition may be introduced to refresh the witness's memory.

The rules governing civil trials allow parties to obtain discovery regarding any matter, except if it is privileged, that is relevant to the claim or defense of any party.[2] Relevant information need not be admissible at trial if the discovery appears to be reasonably calculated to lead to the discovery of admissible evidence.[3] State rules for civil trials generally adopt the federal rules very closely.

State and federal rules determine when discovery may commence. Usually these rules prohibit discovery for a specific number of days after the pleadings have been filed or require that a pretrial conference has been held before discovery begins. Expedited discovery, subject to court approval, may be requested. It permits discovery to commence sooner than normally permitted under court rules.

In Case 4.1, a federal district court decides whether to permit expedited discovery of the identities of anonymous authors of online postings.

Discovery does have some important limits however. An attorney's work product, including information gathered in preparation for trial, is not discoverable unless the information can no longer be acquired or cannot be obtained without undue hardship. If an attorney has interviewed a witness who has since died, then that interview would be subject to discovery. If an attorney has interviewed a witness who has since moved to, or returned to, another country, then that interview is also discoverable.

One key issue for business owners and managers that can arise in the context of litigation involving one or more business entities is when discovery includes an attempt by the opposing party to obtain legally protected business information (known as *trade secrets*[4]). In Case 4.2, a state appellate court considers a request by an injured party for access to information about a tire company's trade secret: the process for making its products.

Request for Admissions While the first attempt to narrow the issues in dispute is through the defendant's answer, a **request for admissions** furthers the objective of determining what facts are in dispute (and, thus, must be proved at trial) and which facts both parties accept as true. For example, one party may request that the other party admit the existence and date of a certain contract. If the other party refuses to admit those facts, witnesses must be called at trial to prove the existence and date of the contract.

---

[2]Federal Rules of Civil Procedure 26 (b)(1).

[3]*Turner v. Summit Treestands, LLC,* 2011 U.S. Dist. LEXIS 139146 (2011).

[4]Trade secrets are covered extensively in Chapter 25, "Intellectual Property."

FACT SUMMARY   After 20/20 Financial Consulting discovered allegedly defamatory statements about itself posted on various websites and blogs by anonymous authors, the firm conducted an unsuccessful preliminary investigation to discover the names of the authors from the operators of the websites and blogs. Subsequently, 20/20 filed suit naming five unknown authors as "John Doe" defendants and sought a court order to conduct expedited discovery in an attempt to establish the true identities of the authors. The rules that govern federal court procedures allow expedited discovery if the information obtained will make trial more efficient.

SYNOPSIS OF DECISION AND OPINION   The U.S. district court in Colorado found in favor of 20/20 and granted its request for expedited discovery. The court ruled that since the plaintiff had exhausted reasonable attempts to identify the defendants through nonjudicial means, 20/20 was entitled to use the tools of discovery in order to help it locate the anonymous authors of the alleged defamation. Since the court found that discovery would be the only practical way to ascertain the identities of the defendants, it ruled that 20/20 should be given the opportunity to pursue its claim against the defendants in an efficient manner.

WORDS OF THE COURT: Expedited Discovery Appropriate   "The court finds that good cause exists to permit Plaintiff to conduct expedited discovery to discover the identities of Defendants. Indeed, this case is largely analogous to [a previous case] where the court permitted expedited discovery to identify defendants allegedly engaged in copyright infringement by downloading and distributing the plaintiffs' recordings using an online media distribution system. There the court found that the plaintiffs had set forth good cause for expedited discovery because the '[d]efendants must be identified before this suit can progress further.' Much like [the defendants in that case], Defendants here have engaged in anonymous online behavior, which will likely remain anonymous unless Plaintiff is able to ascertain their identities. And thus far, Plaintiff has been unsuccessful in its attempts to ascertain Defendants' identities through informal, pre-lawsuit investigation. Because it appears likely that Plaintiff will continue to be thwarted in its attempts to identify Defendants without the benefit of formal discovery mechanisms, the court finds that Plaintiff should be permitted to conduct expedited discovery."

Case Questions

1. Why will formal discovery be more effective than merely requesting the information informally?

2. From the standpoint of the operators of the blogs and bulletin boards, how does the formal discovery process provide them with real and intangible protection?

FACT SUMMARY   Mayberry filed a product liability action against Bridgestone—and three of its subsidiaries (Bridgestone)—alleging that tire tread separation caused a car accident that killed her son. During pretrial discovery, Mayberry sought the formula for the steel belt skim stock[5] on the tire in question. Bridgestone objected to the request and moved for a court order to prevent disclosure of all trade secrets used to produce the tires, including the skim stock formula. The trial court directed the companies to disclose the formula for the steel belt skim stock on the tire in question, and Bridgestone appealed.

SYNOPSIS OF DECISION AND OPINION   The Indiana Supreme Court ruled in favor of Bridgestone. The court found that Mayberry had not demonstrated the necessity of disclosing the formula and that the record demonstrated that the skim stock formula is a trade secret. Bridgestone demonstrated that the skim stock formula qualified as a trade secret because (1) it frequently took several years to arrive at the detailed

[5]Skim stock is a specially formulated rubber component designed to provide adhesion between the rubber and steel cord and between the belts and surrounding components in a radial tire.

formula for a new rubber compound; (2) the steel belt skim stock formula represented one of the tire companies' most valuable assets and most closely guarded secrets; and (3) access to the formula was very narrowly limited. The court reasoned that although Mayberry successfully demonstrated the general relevance of the skim stock formula, she failed to show that it was necessary to the presentation of her case. An inspection of the failed tire's appearance was a more than adequate substitute for examining the skim stock formula.

WORDS OF THE COURT: Protecting Trade Secrets from Misappropriation during Discovery "For over a quarter century, courts have consistently applied a three-part balancing test when a party seeks an order protecting trade secrets from discovery.... First, the party opposing discovery must show that the information sought is a 'trade secret or other confidential research, development, or commercial information' and that disclosure would be harmful. Then the burden shifts to the party seeking discovery to show that the information is relevant and necessary to bring the matter to trial. If both parties satisfy their burden, the court must weigh the potential harm of disclosure against the need for the information in reaching a decision."

Case Questions

1. If Bridgestone's formula for the tire were already known to its competitors, would Bridgestone have been able to protect it from discovery? Why or why not?
2. Under what circumstances would potential harm of disclosure outweigh the need for the information in a trial using the three-part test?

 Self-Check Methods of Discovery

A delivery van for Read-a-Book Company is involved in a traffic accident with a car driven by Cuthbert. In her negligence suit against Read-a-Book, Cuthbert claimed that she sustained a back injury in the accident and was now unable to work at full capacity in her job. The driver of the delivery van countered that he was driving safely and that it was Cuthbert who caused the accident. What discovery technique(s) could be used to obtain the following evidence?

1. Statements from the passenger who was in Aimee's car at the time of the accident.
2. Copies of doctors' reports prepared by the physicians who treated her alleged injuries.
3. Copies of the hospital report showing Aimee's blood alcohol level when she was treated.
4. An agreement regarding the weather conditions at the time of the accident.
5. A written statement from Aimee in which she presents her version of the accident.
6. A written statement of Aimee's job description and responsibilities.
7. An oral statement of Aimee's ability to perform her job responsibilities after the accident, along with company videotapes of Aimee at her job after the accident.

Answers to this Self-Check are provided at the end of the chapter.

Pretrial Conference

Several weeks before a trial, the parties will typically attend a **pretrial conference** with the judge. The conference is generally held between the attorneys for the parties and the judge in the case, and no court reporter is present. The purpose of the conference is to accomplish two primary objectives. The primary reason is to encourage *settlement.* A judge can often give a neutral face-value view of the case and facilitate some negotiations between the two sides or eliminate any obstacles that have blocked negotiations, such as one party's refusal to discuss settlement. Second, the court will resolve any outstanding motions, confirm that discovery is proceeding smoothly, and dispose of any procedural issues that arose during the pleadings or discovery stages.

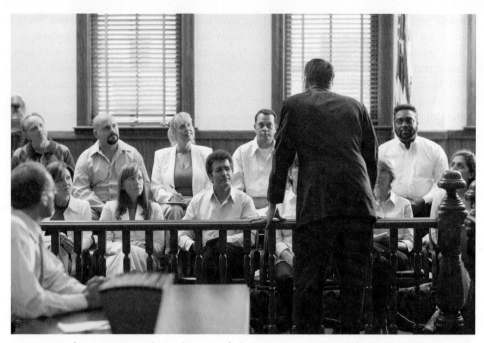

Attorneys first present their theory of the case to the jury during opening statements.

Trial

If the case cannot be settled, the parties will eventually go to **trial.** Think of a trial as being like a novel. The opening statements are the prologue, laying the groundwork for what is to come; the testimony and submission of evidence is the body of the novel or story; and the closing arguments and the charging of the jury are the epilogue, summarizing what has happened and tying up loose ends.

The trial generally takes place in front of a judge as the *finder of law* and with a jury as a *finder of fact.* As the finder of law, the judge determines such important rulings as what evidence will be admitted, what witnesses may testify, what the jury will hear and not hear, and even what legal arguments the attorneys may present to the jury. The jury, as the finder of fact, determines whose version of the facts is more believable by examining the evidence and listening to the testimony of witnesses. In some cases, the judge will act as both the finder of fact and the finder of law at the same time. This is known as a **bench trial.**

Jury Selection and Opening

The actual trial begins with **jury selection.** This is the process of asking potential jurors questions to reveal any prejudices that may affect their judgment of the facts. The questioning process is known as *voir dire.*[6] For a criminal trial, voir dire can be extensive and last for days or even weeks depending on the case. However, in civil litigation the voir dire process is not as extensive, and the jury will usually be seated (selected) in relatively short order. After the jury is selected, the attorneys present their theories of the case and what they hope to prove to the jury in **opening statements.**

Testimony and Submission of Evidence

After the opening statement, the plaintiff's attorney asks questions, known as **direct examination,** of the witnesses on the plaintiff's list. After the plaintiff's attorney finishes questioning a witness, the defendant's attorney may

Legal Speak ›))
Preponderance of the Evidence
A standard used to decide a civil case whereby the jury is to favor one party when the evidence is of greater weight and more convincing than the evidence that is offered in opposition to it (i.e., more likely than not). It is a substantially lower standard of proof than that used in a criminal case.[7]

---

[6]Pronounced "vwar deer," this is a permutation of a Latin word and a French word meaning "to speak the truth."

[7]The standard used in a criminal case is "beyond a reasonable doubt," and is discussed in detail in Chapter 23, "Criminal Law and Procedure in Business."

conduct **cross-examination** of that witness. The cross-examination is composed of questions limited to issues that were brought out on direct examination. The same process is repeated for the defendant's witnesses. Each side also uses its witnesses to introduce relevant evidence. Witnesses may be called upon to authenticate documents, to verify physical evidence, or to provide expert testimony accompanied by charts or graphs shown to the jury.

Closing Arguments and Charging the Jury   Once the testimony is completed and the evidence has been submitted to the jury, each attorneys sums up the case and tries to convince the jury that their version of the case is more compelling. This is known as a **closing argument.** The judge then proceeds with the **charging of the jury,** by giving them instructions on how to work through the process of coming to a factual decision in the case. The judge will also inform the jury that the standard of proof in a civil case is a **preponderance of the evidence.**

Deliberations and Verdict   After receiving the charge, jurors move to a private room and engage in **deliberations.** Although the jury is permitted to send questions to the judge or make other requests (such as a request to reexamine evidence), the jurors are alone in their deliberations and the jury returns a decision, known as the **verdict.** If, however, the jury cannot agree on a verdict, this is known as a **hung jury** and the litigants must start the process all over again with a new jury. Rules in state courts for civil litigation frequently do not require a unanimous verdict, so hung juries are rare in a commercial dispute.

Posttrial Motions and Appeals   As discussed earlier in this section, there may be posttrial motions in which the losing party tries to convince the original judge that the verdict was flawed. Finally, the losing party may appeal to a higher court. Appellate courts engage in judicial review to decide whether any errors were committed during the trial, and they also have the power to *reverse* or *modify* the decisions of trial courts. Appeals are not automatic in most civil trials. They are granted only when prejudicial error can be shown that has affected the trial's outcome.

CONCEPT SUMMARY   Stages of Litigation

Prelawsuit: Demand and Prelitigation Settlement Negotiations
 Standing
 Statute of Limitations
 Jurisdiction (discussed in Chapter 3)
Pleadings Stage
 Complaint and Summons
 Answer
 Counterclaim
 Cross-Claim
Motions
Discovery Stage
 Methods of Discovery
Pretrial Conference
Trial
 Jury Selection and Opening
 Testimony and Submission of Evidence
 Closing Arguments and Charging the Jury
 Deliberations and Verdict
 Posttrial Motions and Appeals
 Collecting the Judgment

Legal Speak ›))
Challenges

A *challenge for cause* may be asserted if a prospective juror demonstrates an obvious bias or circumstance that shows that she may not be able to fairly judge the evidence. A person's prior business relationships with a litigant may likely result in that person's disqualification based on a challenge for cause. *Peremptory challenges* are used by attorneys to shape a jury in a manner they believe most beneficial to their client. No reason must be given for a prospective juror's disqualification; however, race and sex may not be used as a basis for a peremptory challenge. This is now commonly called a *Batson challenge*, from *Batson v. Kentucky*, 476 U.S. 79 (1986).

Ethical Issues Involved in Abusive Litigation

While commercial litigation typically involves two parties attempting to resolve a legitimate dispute in good faith, the costs, burdens, and uncontrollable risks of litigation render it subject to potential abuse. Although federal and state courts have strict procedural rules intended to curb abusive litigation, it is sometimes difficult to enforce those rules because of the inherent vagueness in defining what constitutes "abusive." Abusive litigation may be defined as *vexatious* litigation or abuse of the litigation *process*.

Vexatious litigation may be defined as lawsuits that are filed for reasons other than legitimate damages being suffered by the plaintiff. These illegitimate reasons include using a lawsuit to harass, annoy, intimidate, or cause the opposite party to expend unnecessary costs. Consider the case of *Alston v. Advanced Brands and Importing Company* where a group of parents formed a consumer activist group and filed a lawsuit against manufacturers of alcoholic beverages. The suit alleged that the manufacturers' advertising contributed to the illegal purchase of alcohol by minors. The parent group conceded that there was no evidence that their own minor children had actually purchased alcoholic beverages, so the suit was dismissed for lack of standing.[8]

In the next chapter, the topics of business ethics and corporate social responsibility are covered in detail. For the moment, one need simply understand that a working definition of business ethics is a *consciousness* or awareness of what is right or wrong in the workplace and a commitment to taking responsibility for an ethical course of action given its impact on the business and its constituents. Given that definition, consider the following ethical dilemmas in the *Alston* case:

1. Once the company was threatened with a lawsuit, what ethical obligation did the management of Advance Brands have to its stockholders?[9] Should the management have settled the case for a small sum to avoid legal costs even if they were convinced the suit had no merit?

2. Does Advance have an ethical obligation to the community and public? Would that duty include fighting vexatious litigation to prevent future abuses of the legal system?

3. Does management's ethical duty to stockholders to settle this case for minimal costs override any ethical duty owed to the community?

4. Are there any circumstances under which a business could ethically use litigation as a legitimate business strategy?

Abuse of the litigation process occurs when, after the lawsuit is filed, one party engages in a course of conduct that is contrary to the good faith requirements underlying all litigation. Destroying documents, refusing to hand over evidence during discovery, stalling, and making overly broad discovery requests can all be categorized as abuse of the process.

5. Suppose you were a manager who was ordered by your senior manager to shred certain documents. Do you have an ethical obligation to find out if those documents may be relevant to threatened or pending litigation?

6. Assume that in Question 5 above, you had knowledge that litigation was pending and that the document may be relevant to the case. How does that affect your analysis?

[8]494 F.3d 562 (6th Cir. 2007).
[9]A stockholder (also called *shareholder*) has a legal ownership interest in the company based on the amount of stock owned.

Collecting the Judgment Although the prevailing party may have received a court judgment stating what she is entitled to recover from the defendant, collecting judgments may sometimes be difficult, especially if the defendant's assets are tied up in nonliquid forms, such as real estate, or are exempt from claims of creditors through a bankruptcy filing. However, the law does afford the prevailing party some tools to collect the judgment. For example, some states allow a judgment to be collected through the garnishment of wages, whereby the defendant's employer is ordered by the court to pay part of the defendant's wages directly to the holder of the judgment. The holder of a judgment also becomes a creditor (typically called a *judgment creditor*) and has the right to pursue the defendant's assets to satisfy the debt owed. Rights and regulation of creditors and debtors are discussed in detail in Chapter 21, "Creditors' Rights and Bankruptcy."

ALTERNATIVE DISPUTE RESOLUTION

LO 4-5

Alternative dispute resolution (ADR) is the process (usually conducted in a private setting) by which disputes involving individuals or businesses are resolved outside of the federal or state court system through the help of third parties. According to the American Arbitration Association, an increasing number of businesses and individuals have turned to ADR and use of certain forms of alternative dispute resolution methods has increased between 20 and 31 percent each year for the past five years.

Recall the Classic Retail Outlets (CRO) hypothetical dispute with SignCo at the beginning of this chapter. In that example, several forms of informal and formal dispute resolution offered benefits to CRO and SignCo. If CRO decides to file a lawsuit, the company's management has committed to significant expenditure in terms of legal fees and expenses of litigation. Equally as important, CRO assumes several risks, including (1) it may lose at trial and (2) even if CRO prevails, it will pay more in overall costs than it was awarded or could collect from SignCo. Moreover, any litigation process will result in a dissolution of the business relationship between CRO and SignCo. Aside from those costs, time is wasted that could be spent on more productive activities such as securing new business or executing existing business. Some of the potential advantages of ADR over litigation are:

- *Costs:* ADR could potentially cost a fraction of the normal legal costs. Depending on the location of the trial, trial attorneys may charge anywhere between $200 per hour (in smaller markets) to as much as $1,000 per hour in, for example, New York City. Although some of the more mundane work in litigation may be done by nonlawyer professionals (such as legal assistants or paralegals) at lower rates, the legal fees accumulate quickly once a lawsuit is commenced and accelerate once discovery begins.

- *Preserving the business relationship:* Litigation is, by its nature, adversarial. Allegations and defenses may turn antagonistic and result in termination of any business relationship. ADR, particularly informal ADR (discussed next), is focused on preserving the business relationship as part of the dispute resolution process. Business owners and managers work carefully to build alliances among vendors, suppliers, retailers, advertisers, and many other businesses that add value. ADR can help preserve alliances and avoid unnecessary antagonism over a dispute.

- *Time:* The time spent in ADR is a small percentage of the normal two- to three-year (or more) period normally associated with discovery, a civil jury trial, and possible appeal.

- *Expertise:* In some cases the parties may choose their own party to help resolve the dispute, and this party may be an expert in the industry in question. When a case is before a jury, there is an uncontrollable risk that the jury may have a difficult time grasping the details of a complex case. Even a highly competent judge conducting a bench trial may not have the background to fully understand the technical details and terminology involved in certain industry disputes. For example, knowing how to generally use a computer is very different from understanding the complexities of programming computer codes.

- *Privacy:* ADR may be held in private with no public record required. This ensures that any confidential business information is not at risk of accidental disclosure in the public eye (including competitors) of the court system. The privacy factor is also helpful in avoiding any unwanted publicity in the matter.

Informal ADR

Informal ADR often involves the parties negotiating face-to-face or through intermediaries to arrive at a mutually agreeable solution without the use of a formal process. It can take the form of (1) a *settlement agreement* whereby one party agrees to a payment in exchange for the other party's promise not to sue or (2) an agreement to cancel a contract or to revise an existing contract to better reflect the parties' obligations and needs.

Formal ADR

The most common formal ADR techniques are *arbitration, mediation, expert evaluation,* and some hybrid of those methods. A growing trend is that state or federal courts will require mediation and/or nonbinding arbitration prior to allowing certain civil lawsuits to go to trial. Typically, in a business context, ADR is invoked either via *contract* (including a union contract) or by mutual agreement. In a contractual arrangement, the parties have entered into a contract that contains a clause requiring the parties to submit any disputes to a specific alternative dispute resolution process (usually arbitration or mediation). These ADR clauses are commonly contained in contracts relating to employment, sale of goods, brokerage agreements (such as a stockbroker or online trading account), financing, and licenses to use software. For example, many employment contracts require that employees with job-related grievances enter into binding arbitration and prohibited them from filing a lawsuit against the employer. Should a work-related problem arise, employees often are surprised by such clauses, which they overlooked when signing the contract. If the terms of how the arbitration is implemented are fair, courts will enforce the arbitration clause.

When the agreement is by contract, sometimes the parties argue that the clause is not valid because it is too burdensome on one of the parties. In Case 4.3, a federal appellate court examines the enforceability of a clause in an employment contract requiring arbitration of any dispute arising from the employment relationship.

LO 4-6 ## Arbitration

One of the most common forms of ADR is **arbitration.** During arbitration, an individual *arbitrator* (or group of arbitrators) conducts a hearing between the parties in the dispute. The hearing is similar to a court setting but is less formal. Parties seeking arbitration typically apply for an arbitrator through an ADR agency. The largest provider in the United States is the American Arbitration Association (AAA). The AAA receives the application and first appoints a *tribunal administrator,* who coordinates the case and prepares the parties by informing them of procedures and rules of arbitration. Next, an arbitrator who is mutually agreed upon by the parties is appointed to the case. The arbitrator functions much like a judge would in a standard trial and in some states even has the power of subpoena (the ability to demand certain documents or witnesses). For arbitration cases, although an attorney is not required, parties in a business dispute often opt to be represented by counsel. An arbitration hearing resembles a trial in that there are opening statements, both parties present limited evidence and call a predetermined number of witnesses, each party has the right of cross-examination, and both parties make closing arguments. Unless already mandated in a contract, at the beginning of the arbitration both parties agree to either binding or nonbinding arbitration. If binding, the arbitrator's decision is final unless both parties agree to have the case reopened.

Legally Mandated Arbitration
When the parties agree to arbitrate, this is known as a *private* arbitration. Additionally, most states and the federal judiciary have a requirement (either by statute or a court-imposed procedure) that certain civil lawsuits go through an arbitration hearing before the case proceeds to trial. In this type of arbitration, the arbitrators are typically attorneys from the court's jurisdiction who are fulfilling a duty to serve on an arbitration panel imposed by the professional rules that govern attorneys. Although the arbitration is nonbinding (the losing party has the right of automatic appeal to the trial court), the idea is to encourage the parties to settle before trial. The key advantage of legally mandated arbitration is that each side is able to present the case to a neutral party and the arbitrator's decision can be used as a starting point for settlement negotiations.

FACT SUMMARY   Phillips began working as a bartender at a Hooters restaurant in South Carolina in 1989. Five years later, Hooters initiated an alternative dispute resolution program among its employees. As part of that program, the company conditioned eligibility for raises, transfers, and promotions upon an employee's signing an agreement to arbitrate employment-related disputes including, among other issues, discrimination or sexual harassment claims. The agreement provided for binding arbitration in accordance with a standard set of rules that were created and administered by Hooters. In 1994 and again in 1995, Phillips signed the agreement but did not obtain a copy of the rules. In 1996, Phillips quit her job and refused to arbitrate based on the unfairness of the Hooters arbitration rules. Among the provisions she found to be unfair were:

- The requirement that arbitrators be selected exclusively from a list provided by Hooters.
- Hooters' rights to expand the scope of the arbitration, to move for summary dismissal, and to record the proceeding without any similar rights for the employee.
- Hooters' unilateral authority to bring an arbitration award to court in order to vacate or modify the award if the company could show that the panel had exceeded its authority.

After Phillips notified them that she intended to file suit for sexual harassment and employment discrimination, Hooters filed suit to compel arbitration. The district court ruled in favor of Phillips and held that the arbitration clause was unenforceable and void because it was not a true meeting of the minds required for an enforceable agreement between the parties and that the clause was void as a matter of public policy. Hooters appealed.

SYNOPSIS OF DECISION AND OPINION   The U.S. court of appeals found for Phillips, saying that the Hooters rules, when taken as a whole, were so

unfairly one-sided that their only possible purpose was to undermine the neutrality of the proceeding. Recognizing that arbitration agreements in contracts may be enforceable when fair, the court refused to compel arbitration under the terms of the Hooters agreement. When a valid agreement to arbitrate exists between the parties and covers the matter in dispute, the Federal Arbitration Act requires courts to enforce the agreement. However, the rules created by Hooters were so biased that they create a question as to fundamental fairness, and the court held that the arbitration clause was invalid.

WORDS OF THE COURT: Fairness Requirement "If by odd chance the unfairness of these rules were not apparent on their face, leading arbitration experts have decried their one-sidedness.[10] . . . We hold that the promulgation of so many biased rules—especially the scheme whereby one party to the proceeding so controls the arbitral panel—breaches the contract entered into by the parties. The parties agreed to submit their claims to arbitration—a system whereby disputes are fairly resolved by an impartial third party. Hooters by contract took on the obligation of establishing such a system. By creating a sham system unworthy even of the name of arbitration, Hooters completely failed in performing its contractual duty."

Case Questions

1. Why do you think that Hooters of America, Inc., chose to include a mandatory arbitration clause in its employment contracts?

2. Had Phillips been provided a copy of the rules, but signed the employment contract anyway, would that change your analysis? Why or why not?

[10]The court then quoted senior officials from the American Arbitration Association, the National Academy of Arbitrators, and the International Society of Professionals in Dispute Resolution, who each condemned the terms of the arbitration clause.

Federal Arbitration Act   The Federal Arbitration Act[11] (FAA) is a statute in which   LO 4-7 Congress endorsed the use of arbitration as the preferred dispute resolution method in matters governed by federal law. Congress took this action because of incidents in which state and federal courts invalidated arbitration clauses or overturned arbitration awards. Courts would

[11]U.S.C. §§ 1–15.

An arbitration panel is a common form of alternative dispute resolution.

usually base their decision on the notion that an individual could not effectively pursue her legal rights in an arbitration forum. This hostile view of arbitration caused Congress to pass the FAA in order to make clear that arbitration was preferred over litigation as a method of dispute resolution so long as the parties agreed to an arbitration clause. Specifically, the FAA requires that "a written provision of . . . a contract evidencing a transaction involving commerce to settle by arbitration a controversy thereafter arising out of such a contract . . . shall be valid, irrevocable, and enforceable, save upon such grounds as exists at law . . . for the revocation of any contract."[12] However, it is also important to note that the FAA provides four grounds when courts may *set aside* the award of an arbitrator: (1) the arbitration involved some degree of corruption or fraud, (2) the arbitrator exhibited inappropriate bias, (3) the arbitrator committed some gross procedural error (such as refusing to hear relevant evidence) that prejudiced the rights of one party, and (4) the arbitrator exceeded her explicit powers or failed to use them to make an appropriate final award. Note that some states have passed similar pro-arbitration statutes that define additional rights and responsibilities of the parties.

Although the FAA does not spell out any specific procedure or format for the arbitration, it does provide a means for enforcing both arbitration agreements and the decisions of arbitrators through use of federal courts. In *Gilmer v. Interstate/Johnson Lane Corporation*,[13] the Supreme Court held that the FAA applied to arbitration clauses contained in employment contracts even when an employee brought suit against an employer for violating federal antidiscrimination laws. In the 2009 case of *14 Penn Plaza LLC v. Pyett*,[14] the U.S. Supreme Court decided that unions may agree to mandatory arbitration provisions in collective bargaining agreements when negotiating with the employer, saying that such an inclusion will not act as an unconscionable or severable waiver of a union member's rights.

---

[12]U.S.C. § 2.

[13]500 U.S. 20 (1991).

[14]129 S. Ct. 1456 (2009).

In Case 4.4, the U.S. Supreme Court applied the FAA in the context of a class action arbitration.

Mediation

Another common form of ADR is **mediation.** Mediation is becoming increasingly common as a cost-efficient form of dispute resolution primarily because mediation is relatively informal and does not require as much time or preparation as arbitration. A mediator is typically appointed in much the same manner as an arbitrator, and, in fact, the American Arbitration Association provides mediation services as well. A mediator is often, but not required to be, an attorney who is specially trained in negotiations and dispute resolution and is paid a set hourly rate or fixed fee for a certain period of time (usually per day). The mediator's task is to facilitate discussion, listening to each party's grievances and arguments and ensuring communication between the parties. The mediator defuses some of the antagonism between the two parties and focuses the parties

> **KEY** POINT
>
> The primary difference between arbitration and other methods of ADR is that it provides the parties with a decision on who prevails in the dispute and any monetary award.

CASE 4.4 American Express v. Italian Colors Restaurant, 133 S.Ct. 2304 (2013)

FACT SUMMARY   American Express (Amex) entered into agreements with Italian Colors Restaurant and other merchants (Merchants) that accept American Express credit cards. The agreement contains an arbitration clause which requires that all disputes between Amex and Merchants be resolved through arbitration and prohibits any claim from being arbitrated on a class action basis. Nonetheless, Merchants filed a class action against Amex alleging violation of federal antitrust statutes. Amex moved to compel individual arbitration, but Merchants argued that the clause was invalid because the cost of expert analysis necessary to prove their antitrust allegations would greatly exceed the maximum recovery for an individual merchant plaintiff. The trial court ruled in favor of Amex, but a federal court of appeals reversed the trial court's ruling and held that the clause was unenforceable because of the prohibitive cost structure. Amex appealed to the U.S. Supreme Court.

SYNOPSIS OF DECISION AND OPINION   The U.S. Supreme Court ruled in favor of Amex. The Court held that the Federal Arbitration Act (FAA) does not permit courts to invalidate a contractual waiver of legal rights based solely on the grounds that a plaintiff's dispute resolution costs exceed any potential amounts to be recovered. The Court concluded that the FAA reflects the overarching principle that arbitration is a matter of contract and that courts had a responsibility to rigorously enforce arbitration agreements according to their terms. The arbitration clause in the Amex-Merchants agreements must be enforced by courts unless the FAA's mandate has been overridden by a contrary congressional command.

WORDS OF THE COURT: Congressional Intent   "No contrary congressional command requires us to reject the waiver of class arbitration here. Respondents argue that requiring them to litigate their claims individually—as they contracted to do—would contravene the policies of the antitrust laws. But the antitrust laws do not guarantee an affordable procedural path to the vindication of every claim. Congress has taken some measures to facilitate the litigation of antitrust claims—for example, it enacted a multiplied-damages remedy. In enacting such measures, Congress has told us that it is willing to go, in certain respects, beyond the normal limits of law in advancing its goals of deterring and remedying unlawful trade practice. But to say that Congress must have intended whatever departures from those normal limits advance antitrust goals is simply irrational."

Case Questions
1. If the costs of experts exceed the potential recovery amount, doesn't that frustrate the purpose of having antitrust laws in the first place?
2. Was the waiver of class arbitration by the merchants voluntary? Why or why not?

Online Dispute Resolution

PROBLEM *In situations involving small amounts of money, is there a way for a business to resolve such relatively minor disputes in a cost-effective manner?*

A business may be engaged in hundreds of relatively low-cost transactions per year with various out-of-state vendors such as suppliers, shipping companies, office supply stores, contractors, and the like. When disputes arise, a business may be at a distinct disadvantage and bargaining position because the amount in controversy is too low to justify even the least expensive form of alternative dispute resolution. However, over an extended period of time these small losses add up to unnecessary liabilities, leaving managers with a difficult choice when faced with a dispute over a relatively low amount of money with an out-of-state vendor: (1), Invest in a dispute resolution method despite the fact that the costs may very well exceed the benefits in that particular dispute; or (2) allow the losses to accumulate and potentially seek favorable tax treatment for writing off bad debt.

SOLUTION *Attempt to use online dispute resolution (ODR).*

Businesses are now capable of making small purchases from vendors across the globe and can do so quickly and conveniently. This renders traditional forms of ADR impractical, given the reluctance to pay for an arbitrator or attorney and the fact that traveling to another location to settle a dispute often returns a sum less than the costs of travel. ODR has all of the advantages of traditional forms of ADR: The parties in question can avoid the expense and publicity of trial, plus an agreement is usually reached much faster.

Online technology is ideal for low-cost transactional disputes such as a party seeking a refund for a defective product. Often these types of issues can be resolved using the technology alone. For example, blind-bidding sites like ClickandSettle.com and Cybersettle.com offer an automated service whereby parties individually enter the price they're willing to pay or receive. The software evaluates the numbers submitted and then sends both parties a fair price based on their initial demands.

Another form of ODR is geared more toward complex transactions—for example, the Square Trade website proposes prewritten resolutions and you have received a damaged shipment of goods. The site might offer a standard menu of solutions such as (1) replacement with an undamaged good, (2) return for a full refund, or (3) keep the merchandise with a partial refund. The parties may also fill in their own solution, but the site's guided approach helps the parties focus on a resolution to the dispute.

If direct negotiation fails to resolve the issue, Square Trade users can request a mediator for a $20 fee per participant plus a percentage fee if the dispute exceeds $1,000. At OnlineResolution.com, mediation fees range between $15 and $25. For disputes of more than $500, each participant pays $50 to $150 per hour, based on the value under dispute.

Option 1: Online Mediation. Online mediation is a logical first step to settling disputes. Like traditional forms of mediation, online mediation is generally nonbinding. Parties present their positions to a mediator who considers their arguments and attempts to negotiate a settlement. An advantage to online mediation is that dialogue is carried out via e-mail, so participants can submit responses at their convenience and can think out their replies rather than engage in what may be an antagonistic live hearing.

Option 2: Online Arbitration. Online arbitration is similar to traditional arbitration except that all communications take place using the Internet. The arbitrator convenes the arbitration via a live webcast and issues a decision based on the evidence presented. In an online setting, all communications, including the presentation of evidence, are supplied in electronic form: text, image, audio, or video. Participants in online arbitration agree in advance that they will abide by the arbitrator's decision and that the award may be enforced by an appropriate court. Following completion of the online arbitration, each participant typically completes a brief evaluation of the arbitrator and the process.

on working toward a solution. Note, however, that in mediation no decision is rendered and if the parties do not reach an agreement, they must attempt to resolve their dispute using another method.

Mediation is sometimes required by statute or court procedure before a dispute can be brought to trial. As with legally mandated arbitration, the goal of required mediation is to allow the parties the opportunity to settle the case. Because much of the antagonism that surrounds a legal dispute is dissipated by the mediator's efforts, the process can help parties to see the dispute in a more even-tempered fashion. The ultimate goal is to work toward a mutually satisfactory resolution.

Expert Evaluation

For parties involved in a business dispute where the issues are somewhat complex and are related to the intricacies of a certain industry or profession, **expert evaluation** (neutral fact-finding) by an independent expert who recommends a settlement is an attractive alternative. The **expert evaluator** reviews documents and evidence provided by each party that give a full description of the events and circumstances leading to the claim and the resulting loss. The evaluator follows up with questions and will sometimes take statements from witnesses if necessary. Drawing on her range of experience and expertise in the industry, the evaluator gives her opinion on the merits and value of the claim and recommends a settlement amount. The goal of this process is to facilitate a negotiated settlement without the expense and time of a trial or other methods of ADR.

Other Forms of ADR   LO 4-9

In some cases, parties to a dispute want to have the opportunity to settle the case through mediation also, but also want some degree of certainty in the event that mediation fails. In those circumstances, parties may use a hybrid of mediation and arbitration. In this hybrid form, sometimes known as **med-arb,** both parties first submit to mediation for a set period of time (perhaps two business days). If the mediation fails, the process then moves to binding arbitration. The goal is to reach an agreement with the least amount of formality possible. The hope is that the dispute can be settled during mediation, but since both parties are determined to conclude the matter, arbitration is available as an automatic fallback method should mediation fail.

Summary jury trials are used primarily in federal courts but have occasionally been used by state courts when there are complex issues to be litigated. An abbreviated half- to full-day trial is conducted before a jury, usually after discovery has been completed. Time limits may be set regarding each facet of the summary trial. No live expert testimony is presented, and the attorneys primarily conduct the proceeding through oral argument. Typically, no record is kept. A sitting or retired judge conducts the trial and issues a nonbinding advisory opinion.

Businesses may also use an ADR method called a **minitrial.** Here, a condensed version of the case is presented to the top management from both sides. A neutral party, often an expert in the subject matter of the dispute, conducts the trial. The primary purpose of the minitrial is to allow the management from both sides to see and hear the facts and arguments, hopefully enabling them to engage in more fruitful negotiations and thus avoid litigation. The neutral party does not ordinarily render a decision but may be requested by the parties to provide her expert opinion as to the likelihood of the outcome should the matter proceed to trial.

CONCEPT SUMMARY Alternative Dispute Resolution (ADR)

- The primary advantages of ADR are reductions in costs and time, the preservation of business relationships, having the services of an expert neutral party, and privacy.
- ADR usually arises as a result of a contract between two parties that have agreed ahead of time to resolve any disputes using a certain ADR method, such as arbitration.
- The primary methods of ADR are arbitration, mediation, expert evaluation, and some hybrid of those three methods. Other less common forms of ADR are also available.
- In arbitration, the parties submit their dispute to one or more arbitrators and present evidence and limited witness testimony, and then a decision is made.
- Mediation is the attempt by a trained third party to bring the parties to an agreement on the dispute by proposing possible solutions.
- The primary difference between arbitration and other methods of ADR is that arbitration provides the parties with a decision.
- Online dispute resolution is an attractive alternative for resolving disputes when the amount in controversy is relatively low.

KEY TERMS

Civil litigation p. 97   A dispute resolution process in which the parties and their counsel argue their views of a civil controversy in a court of law.

Standing p. 97   Requirement that, to maintain a lawsuit against another party, the party asserting the claim must have suffered an injury in fact and the harm must be direct, concrete, and individualized.

Statute of limitations p. 97   A time frame, which begins when injury occurs, within which a lawsuit must be filed or the lawsuit will be barred.

Complaint p. 98   The first formal document filed with the local clerk of courts when the plaintiff initiates a lawsuit claiming legal rights against another.

Summons p. 98   Formal notification to the defendant that she has been named in the lawsuit and that her answer must be filed within a certain period of time.

Answer p. 100   Defendant's formal response to each paragraph of the complaint.

Counterclaim p. 101   A claim filed by a defendant who believes that the plaintiff has caused her damages arising out of the very same set of facts as articulated in the complaint.

Cross-claim p. 101   A claim filed by a defendant who believes that a third party is either partially or fully liable for the damages that the plaintiff has suffered and, therefore, should be involved as an indispensable party in the trial.

Motion p. 101   A request made by either party that asks the court to issue a certain order (such as a motion for summary judgment). Motions may be made before, during, and after the trial.

Discovery p. 101   Process for the orderly exchange of information and evidence between the parties involved in litigation (or in some cases arbitration) prior to trial.

Deposition p. 101   Method of discovery in which a witness gives sworn testimony to provide evidence prior to trial.

Interrogatory p. 101   Method of discovery in which one party submits written questions to the opposing party to gather evidence prior to trial.

Requests for production p. 103   Requests aimed at producing specific items to help one party discover some important fact in the case.

Request for admissions p. 103   A set of statements sent from one litigant to an adversary for the purpose of determining what facts are in dispute and which facts both parties accept as true.

Pretrial conference p. 105   A meeting between the attorneys for the parties and the judge in the case several weeks prior to trial, with the objectives of encouraging settlement and resolving any outstanding motions or procedural issues that arose during the pleadings or discovery stage.

Trial p. 106   Stage of litigation that occurs when the case cannot be settled, generally taking place in front of a judge as the finder of law and with a jury as a finder of fact.

Bench trial p. 106   Trial without a jury, in which the judge is both the finder of law and the finder of fact.

Jury selection p. 106   The process of asking potential jurors questions to reveal any prejudices that may affect their judgment of the facts.

Opening statements p. 106   Attorneys' presentations of their theories of the case and what they hope to prove to the jury; made at the onset of the trial.

Direct examination p. 106   The first questioning of a witness during a trial, in which the witness is questioned by the attorney for the party presenting the witness.

Cross-examination p. 107   The opportunity for an attorney to ask questions in court, limited to issues brought out on direct examination, of a witness who has testified for the opposing party.

Closing arguments p. 107   Attorneys' summations of the case, during which each attorney tries to convince the jury to decide the case in her party's favor; occurs after testimony is completed and evidence has been submitted.

Charging of the jury p. 107   Instructions given from the judge to the jury explaining how to work through the process of coming to a factual decision in the case.

Preponderance of the evidence p. 107   A standard used to decide a civil case whereby the jury is to favor one party when the evidence is of greater weight and more convincing than the evidence that is offered in opposition to it.

Deliberations p. 107   The process in which jurors discuss, in private, the testimony and evidence presented at trial and vote to reach their verdict.

Verdict p. 107   The final decision of a jury in a case.

Hung jury p. 107   A jury that cannot come to a consensus decision on which party should prevail in a case.

Arbitration p. 110   Method of alternatives dispute resolution in which the parties present their sides of the dispute to one or more neutral parties who then render a decision; often involves a set of rules designed to move from dispute to decision quickly.

Mediation p. 113   Method of alternative dispute resolution in which a mediator attempts to settle a dispute by learning the facts of the matter and then negotiating a settlement between the two adverse parties.

Expert evaluation p. 115   Method of alternative dispute resolution in which an independent expert acts as the neutral fact-finder; particularly useful for parties involved in a business dispute where the issues are somewhat complex and related to the intricacies of a certain industry or profession.

Expert evaluator p. 115   The neutral fact-finder in expert evaluation who reviews documents and evidence provided by each party and draws on her range of experience and expertise in the industry to offer an opinion on the merits and value of the claim and recommend a settlement amount.

Med-arb p. 115   Method of alternative dispute resolution whereby the parties begin with mediation and, if mediation fails in a fixed time period, the parties agree to submit to arbitration.

Summary jury trial p. 115   An abbreviated trial conducted before a jury and a sitting or retired judge at which attorneys present oral argument without witness testimony and the decision is nonbinding.

Minitrial p. 115   A condensed version of the case is presented to the top management from both sides, with an expert neutral party conducting the trial, allowing them to see and hear facts and arguments so more meaningful negotiations can take place.

Medical Instruments Inc. (MII) required a larger warehouse for its facilities. MII located a 10,000-square-foot building in New Hampshire and signed a lease with Commercial Properties (CP) for one year with a right to renew for five one-year terms upon 60 days' notice. After the first renewal, CP sent back a new lease with substantially the same terms, except that the new lease had a mandatory arbitration clause that required any tenant to go through arbitration in CP's home state of California. MII signed the lease without objection. One month after taking occupancy, MII complained that a leak in the warehouse roof was allowing water to drip into a corner of the warehouse and that MII had to move its hardware equipment out of the warehouse to protect it from water damage. CP did not fix the leak until one month later, and MII suffered losses because its hardware was partially destroyed by the leak and it had additional out-of-pocket losses related to expenses of having the equipment moved to another location.

1. If MII sues CP in a state trial court for the losses it incurred, what would CP's likely defense be?

2. Discuss the significance of the fact that the original lease did not have an arbitration clause but the new one did. Also, is it significant that the place of arbitration would require MII to travel to California? Do these facts give a court any reason to invalidate the arbitration clause?

3. What cases that you studied in this chapter help to support your arguments in Question 2.

4. Assume that *no* arbitration clause existed in the new lease. What would be MII's options to pursue damages if CP refused to compensate MII for the losses it incurred?

5. Assume that MII files a lawsuit against CP. As part of its case, MII wishes to show that CP had notice of the leak and failed to fix it for one month. What methods of discovery would be useful to obtain this information from CP?

6. Suppose that CP refused to turn over all phone records and repair request forms to MII based on the fact that the information is confidential and cannot be disclosed in litigation. What standard will a court use to judge whether the information is a trade secret and therefore not subject to disclosure? What case supports your answer?

Managers are sometimes the first line of opportunity in resolving a dispute before it turns into litigation. Assume that you are an MII manager in charge of the property in New Hampshire described in Theory to Practice, above. Write a two- to three-page memorandum to your senior manager that describes the relative advantages of ADR over litigation in the MII-CP dispute. Using Table 4.1, make suggestions on how this particular dispute may be resolved.

A sample answer may be found on this textbook's website at www.mhhe.com/melvinleb2e.

CASE SUMMARY 4.1 :: Doctor's Assocs. Inc. v. Casarotto, 517 U.S. 681 (1996)

ARBITRATION PROVISION IN CONTRACT

Doctor's Associates Inc. (DAI), the national franchisor for Subway sandwich shops, entered into a franchise contract with Casarotto to open a Subway shop in Great Falls, Montana. Although the franchise was not in Casarotto's preferred location, he agreed to open the shop in a less desirable location based on a verbal agreement that if his preferred location became available, he would have the exclusive rights to that location. Subsequently the location became available, but DAI awarded it to another franchisee. Casarotto claimed his business was irreparably harmed, and as a result he withheld his franchise fee from DAI. The contract executed between Casarotto and DAI did not indicate on the first page that the contract was subject to arbitration. However, page 9 of the agreement contained an arbitration clause mandating the use of American Arbitration Association rules and requiring that the hearing be held in Bridgeport, Connecticut, the cost of which to be born equally by both parties. Casarotto filed suit in a Montana court against DAI for breach of contract. DAI moved to have the case dismissed and moved to arbitration.

CASE QUESTIONS

1. Is the arbitration provision enforceable? Why or why not?
2. Suppose Montana state law required that an arbitration provision be underlined in the text of the contract and also noted on the first page of the contract. In such instances, would the arbitration provision still be enforceable? Why or why not?

CASE SUMMARY 4.2 :: Infinite Energy, Inc. v. Thai Heng Chang, 2008 WL 4098329 (N.D. Fla. 2008)

REQUEST FOR PRODUCTION

Chang was terminated from his employment at Infinite Energy, Inc., for allegedly leaking confidential information to competitors. Litigation ensued, and during discovery Infinite requested access to all of Chang's e-mail accounts. Although Chang turned over e-mails from his work account, he refused to turn over e-mails from his private account with Yahoo! Infinite claimed that the e-mails were essential to its case, and Chang contended that the e-mails were confidential and unrelated to his employment and, therefore, not within the scope of discovery.

CASE QUESTIONS

1. Who prevails and why?
2. Is this information necessary for Infinite's case? Why or why not?

CASE SUMMARY 4.3 :: Exxon Shipping Corporation v. Exxon Seaman's Union, 11 F.3d 1189 (3d Cir. 1993)

ARBITRATION CLAUSES AND PUBLIC POLICY

After the *Exxon Valdez* disaster, Exxon implemented a strict policy of testing its employees who served on tankers for drug and alcohol use and allowed a manager to immediately discharge any employee who was intoxicated while on duty aboard a ship. Fris was an employee who boarded a ship while intoxicated and was discharged when his manager determined that he was unfit for work. However, Fris's union contract allowed him to appeal the discharge through an arbitration procedure. The arbitration panel ordered Fris reinstated, and Exxon filed suit in a federal court to have the arbitration set aside on the basis that the arbitration order violated public policy and subjected Exxon to liability in the event Fris may act negligently while intoxicated. The union argued that the court should give deference to the arbitration system articulated in the union contract.

CASE QUESTION

1. Who prevails and why?

ADR IN CONSUMER CONTRACTS

Leroy purchased a used car from AutoNation, a used-car dealer chain. All buyers entered into a purchase agreement, and those who financed their vehicles through AutoNation also signed a retail installment contract. The purchase agreement included an arbitration agreement, but the retail installment contract did not. Leroy alleged that he and all other customers who signed installment contracts were overcharged as a result of a computer error committed by AutoNation.

He filed a motion in a trial court to have his lawsuit certified as a class action. Although AutoNation argued that the arbitration clause in the purchase agreement controlled the case, the trial court certified the class action, ruling that because the installment contract had no arbitration agreement, the plaintiffs were free to pursue their remedy in court.

CASE QUESTION

1. Did the trial court rule correctly? Explain.

ENFORCEABILITY OF ARBITRATION CLAUSE

Brower purchased a computer from Gateway 2000 through a retail outlet. The computer box contained appropriate manuals and a document titled "Standard Terms and Conditions Agreement," which provided that the terms and conditions in the agreement would become binding if the consumer retained the computer for 30 days. Brower retained the product for more than 30 days. The Gateway agreement contained an arbitration clause mandating that any disputes arising out of the purchase be arbitrated before the International Chamber of Commerce (ICC). The ICC is situated in Europe, and its procedures require arbitration parties to pay an advance fee of $4,000, of which $2,000 is non-refundable regardless of which party prevails. Brower filed suit against Gateway, alleging breach of warranty. Gateway sought to have the suit dismissed from the court and to compel ICC arbitration in accordance with the terms of the Gateway agreement. Brower argued that the arbitration clause was un enforceable because, among other reasons, the ICC rules were too burdensome on the parties and prevented them from protecting their rights.

CASE QUESTIONS

1. Were the ICC rules too burdensome on the parties, preventing them from protecting their rights?
2. How would you rewrite Gateway's clause to be sure that it would be judged reasonable by the New York court?
3. In this case, Brower was the named plaintiff in a potential class action against Gateway. What are the practical implications of Gateway's loss in this case? If Gateway had prevailed, would that change the cost-benefit analysis involved in deciding whether to settle the case?

INTERROGATORIES AND PRIVILEGED INFORMATION

On February 7, 1943, the tug *J.M. Taylor* sank while engaged in helping to tow a car float of the Baltimore & Ohio Railroad across the Delaware River at Philadelphia, and the incident resulted in the death of five crew members. Anticipating litigation, the owners of the tug hired a law firm that conducted interviews with survivors and other witnesses and also obtained statements from representatives of the estates of two of the deceased crew members. One claimant brought suit against the tug owner and, during discovery, sent the following interrogatory: "State whether any statements of the members of the crews of the Tugs *J.M. Taylor* and *Philadelphia*—another tug helping to tow the car float—or of any other vessel were taken in connection with the towing of the car float and the sinking of the Tug *John M. Taylor.* Attach hereto exact copies of all such statements if in writing, and if oral, set forth in detail the exact provisions of any such oral statements or reports." The law firm claimed that the information requested was privileged.

CASE QUESTIONS

1. Should the information gathered by The law firm be made available, or is an attorney's work product privileged and not subject to discovery?

2. If an attorney's work product is declared privileged in corporate-versus-individual cases, does this give a corporate defendant a tremendous advantage in a suit by an individual plaintiff because the corporate defendant could create a veil of secrecy over all the pertinent facts it can collect after the claim arises by merely asserting that such facts were gathered by its large staff of attorneys and claim agents?

3. In its decision, the U.S. Supreme Court said, "Historically, a lawyer is an officer of the court and is bound to work for the advancement of justice while faithfully protecting the rightful interests of his clients. In performing his various duties, however, it is essential that a lawyer work with a certain degree of privacy, free from unnecessary intrusion by opposing parties and their counsel." Do you agree or disagree with this position? Why or why not?

 Self-Check **ANSWERS**

Methods of Discovery

1. A deposition.

2. Request in an interrogatory or a separate motion for the production of documents.

3. Request in an interrogatory or a separate motion for the production of documents.

4. An admission.

5. An interrogatory.

6. Request in an interrogatory or a separate motion for the production of documents.

7. A subpoena *duces tecum* served on Aimee's employer for any video to be produced at the employer's deposition.

---

5 CHAPTER

Business, Societal, and Ethical Contexts of Law

learning **objectives**

After studying this chapter, students who have mastered the material will be able to:

5-1 Articulate a working definition of business ethics.

5-2 Differentiate between primary and secondary stakeholders.

5-3 Categorize alternate approaches to ethical decision making based on different theories of moral philosophy.

5-4 Identify the challenges to business ethics management and articulate a response to each challenge.

5-5 Define values management and articulate several reasons why values management is important in business operations.

5-6 Articulate the differences between the moral minimum and maximizing profit theories of corporate ethics.

5-7 List the common traits of an ethical organization.

5-8 Demonstrate an understanding of how to develop a code of ethics and conduct.

5-9 Employ an ethical decision-making paradigm used by managers for resolving ethical dilemmas.

5-10 Give examples of ethical lapses by using historical case studies of businesses facing ethical dilemmas.

5-11 Articulate the various views on corporate social responsibility and defend a particular view.

Although the law provides one set of guideposts for business operations, a concurrent set of guideposts—business ethics and principles of corporate social responsibility—is equally important to business owners and managers. While some critics argue that business ethics is a recent phenomenon meant simply to fill popular and management literature, one need not look too far back in economic history to discover instances of breaches in ethical behavior (whether legal or not) that have resulted in direct harm to business owners, investors, employees, customers, and wider constituencies such as the community.[1] In this chapter, students will learn:

- The definition of business ethics, systems of ethical reasoning, and goals of values management.

- The importance of ethical decision making in the business environment.

- Fundamentals of corporate social responsibility.

WHAT IS ETHICS?

Ethics addresses how one should act, in a given situation, as defined by society. It comprises the systematic set of rules used to define decision making and choice of action when one is confronted with a moral dilemma.

---

[1]Business ethics actually has an ancient history, including commentary by Cicero in *On Duties*.

People face ethical dilemmas frequently, both in their personal life and at work, whether they are top management or newly hired entry-level workers.

BUSINESS ETHICS DEFINED
LO 5-1

A useful working definition of **business ethics** is a *consciousness* of what is right or wrong in the workplace and a commitment to taking responsibility for an ethical course of action in business operations given its impact on its owners, investors, employees, customers, and the community at large (collectively known as *stakeholders*).

Attention to business ethics is critical during times of fundamental change such as the financial crisis that began in late 2008. In such volatile times, unethical and/or illegal practices are often highlighted as the media and public become aware of the internal strife within preeminent companies that led to their near or total collapse. Some of the practices that had been considered acceptable in various areas of the financial services and corporate sectors are now deemed dubious and even immoral. Practices that were once sanctioned as ethical, such as corporate jets and corporate sponsorship of stadiums and events, are now subject to close scrutiny by boards and shareholders.

Consequently, companies that fail to be committed to managing business ethics as part of their business model have no clear moral compass to guide leaders through complex dilemmas about what is right or wrong. Attention to ethics in the workplace sensitizes business owners and managers in terms of how they should act. Perhaps most important, attention to ethics in the workplace helps ensure that when leaders and managers are struggling in times of crises and confusion, they retain a strong moral compass. Attention to business ethics provides numerous other business and community benefits as well. Although many issues are now defined by statute, such as corporate financial reporting, control of environmental impacts, and various forms of discrimination, interpreting these statutes and regulating internal corporate compliance remain ongoing issues. Therefore, ethics is an essential tool for managers in preventing legal liability for the company.

LO 5-2 Primary and Secondary Stakeholders

Business ethics embraces a broader constituency than just a business's owners and managers. In their planning and operations, many business entities have replaced the word *stockholder* with *stakeholder*. **Stakeholder** is an expansive term that includes a business entity's owners, investors, employees, customers, suppliers, and the wider community. In planning and decision making, many companies now consider both *primary stakeholders* and *secondary stakeholders*. Although various commentators have given a wide variety of definitions for stakeholders, primary stakeholders are generally those who will feel a direct impact based on the decision. Secondary stakeholders are those who do not have any direct connection to the business but may suffer some adverse consequences in an indirect way. For example, during President Obama's first term in office, the Whirlpool Corporation, maker of Maytag and KitchenAid appliances, received $19 million in government stimulus funds intended to create jobs. Nevertheless, in 2010, Whirlpool announced that it was going to close its long-standing American plants in Fort Smith, Arkansas, and in Evansville, Indiana, resulting in approximately 2,100 jobs lost. This was only a part of a decision to cut 5,000 jobs in North America and Europe. Whirlpool shifted manufacturing from those two plants to facilities in Mexico, where workers earn approximately $4 per hour. The primary stakeholders affected certainly include the fired workers and their families. Suppliers to the plants are also directly impacted, as are the cities of Fort Smith and Evansville, which no longer receive tax revenues from Whirlpool. Secondary stakeholders include the area businesses that are not patronized by the former employees, as well as their suppliers and other customers. Remember that a worker who lost her job likely won't be buying pizza from the local restaurant. The restaurant may need to adjust prices to compensate for lost business, thus affecting its customers. The restaurant may also need to lay off workers should business drop substantially. The mayor of Evansville stated that although the city stood to lose 1,000 jobs, he estimated that 10,000 people could be impacted by the plant closure. Primary and secondary stakeholders are an important part of the social responsibility of a corporation, which is discussed in more detail later in this chapter.

Ethical Culture in Which Managers Operate

Managerial misconduct includes illegal, unethical, or questionable practices of individual managers or organizations. There has been a great deal written about managerial misconduct, yet certain attitudes and myths about creating an ethical culture in the workplace still remain. Inevitably, some managers believe that business ethics is merely a matter of preaching the basics of what is right and wrong. More often though, business ethics is a matter of dealing with dilemmas that have no clear indication of what is right or wrong. That is, ethical decision making often involves resolution of moral mazes. Managers are frequently faced with such mazes when dealing with potential conflicts of interest, wrongful use of resources, or mismanagement of assets, contracts, and agreements.

Certain moral philosophies may influence moral judgments such as one's assessment of whether a given situation is viewed as ethical or unethical. This assessment, in turn, then dictates one's reaction and subsequent behavior when confronted with an ethical dilemma. **Morals** are generally accepted *standards* of right and wrong in a given society. These standards may be based on the law and/or religious and personal belief systems. The term **ethics** refers to having a *conscious system* in use for deciding moral dilemmas, and how society dictates one ought to act. Individual approaches to thinking ethically may be based on several broad sources of ethical standards that stem from certain historical theories of morality. Although a close examination of moral philosophy is outside the scope of this textbook, it is important to understand two major approaches and how they apply in a business context.

Principles-Based Approach   Ethical decisions that are made according to a set of established principles or standards such as religious tenets or codes—for example, the Koran (Islamic canonical law) or the Old Testament (Judeo-Christian tradition)—employ a principles-based approach. These religious-based principles are the source of individual decision making and are not subject to exceptions, but are tempered by other religious principles such as mercy and justice.

In addition to religious-based principles, some philosophers and ethicists also use the notion that humans have certain *inherent* moral rights that spring from their ability to reason and choose freely what they do with their lives. The work of famed Prussian-born philosopher Immanuel Kant (1724–1804) that addresses a form of principles-based ethics, which he called *duty-based* ethics in his famous essay *Critique of Practical Reason,* is based on an inherent notion that humans act in accordance with and from a sense of duty to human dignity. Kant theorized that rights imply *duties* and that the duty to respect others' rights was paramount in acting morally.

The notion of *categorical imperatives* is a central theme in Kant's work. This school of thought is centered on the belief that ethical dilemmas must be resolved through a categorical imperative test whereby individuals make ethical decisions with an eye toward the potential consequences that would occur if everyone in society acted the same way. In other words, when considering how to prevent people from acting in a certain way, the question posed is, "What if everybody took that same action?" This question is sometimes called a *universalization* test. If one can consistently act in accordance with the notion that society benefits from everyone acting in that same way, then the action is moral. Kant further believed that one's actions should be based on a moral law that is unconditional and absolute. One should act because it is right, without ulterior motive. People should not lie simply because it is bad to lie, not because telling the truth makes one more popular.

Consequences-Based Approach   This approach emphasizes that the ethical course of action is the one that provides the most good (happiness) for the greatest number of people and has the least harmful consequences for the majority of the community. The approach stems from the **utilitarian** stream of moral philosophy[2] and method for evaluating ethical dilemmas. Under this model, an action is ethically sound if it produces positive results for the most people. Simply put, the course of action that results in the most benefits for the most individuals is the most ethical. If the action impacts the majority of community members in a negative way, it is inherently unethical. Critics of utilitarianism argue that it amounts to using a mathematical formula to decide how decisions impact individuals. Business owners and managers who employ a consequences-based approach seek to produce the greatest balance of good over harm for all who are affected, including owners, employees, customers, investors, and the community at large.

---

[2]The founder of utilitarianism is the famous 18th-century philosopher Jeremy Bentham.

Self-Check Principles-Based Approach or Consequences-Based Approach

For each of the following, choose whether the action or decision best reflects the principles-based or the consequences-based approach.

1. A new corporate vacation policy is implemented that bars all employees of the corporation, at every level, from carrying over unused days into a following year.

2. A new code of conduct and code of ethics are written and disseminated to the entire corporate workforce requiring mandatory compliance by all employees.

3. A company introduces a new approved drug that cures 80 percent of those who take it, has no negative or positive effect on 10 percent of those who take it, and has a negative effect on 10 percent of those who take it.

4. Believing that a corporation has a duty to be a good corporate citizen, a corporation urges its employees to donate to a United Way fund drive emphasized by the corporation. (The United Way is national charity that collects funds and disburses them to numerous local, state, and national organizations encompassing everything from medical research to child protective services to local bicycle trail maintenance.)

Answers to this Self-Check are provided at the end of the chapter.

CONCEPT SUMMARY Moral Philosophy and Ethical Decision Making

- Ethics addresses how one should act, in a given situation, as defined by society. It comprises the systematic set of rules used to define decision making and choice of action when one is confronted with a moral dilemma.

- Morals are generally accepted *standards* of right and wrong in a given society. These standards may be based on the law and/or religious and personal belief systems.

- Business ethics consists of recognizing right or wrong in the workplace and taking responsibility for an ethical course of action in business operations.

- Business ethics requires that primary and secondary stakeholders be identified and considered when companies are making business decisions.

- In a principles-based approach to ethical decision making, decisions are made according to a set of established principles or standards such as religious tenets or codes.

- A consequences-based approach to ethical decision making emphasizes that the ethical course of action is the one that provides the most good (happiness) for the greatest number of people.

Business ethics is concerned chiefly with ethics and morality that will help the company grapple with moral issues confronting the business. For example, suppose that a manager is charged with cutting personnel costs by 10 percent. The two logical choices are option 1, reduce the workforce by 10 percent, or option 2, reduce the wages for the entire workforce by 10 percent.

A principles-based approach may result in the conclusion that option 2 is most ethical because, although all of the employees will suffer some pay cut, no employees will have the severe impact of losing a job. If the manager concludes that the categorical imperative is that everyone keep his or her job, but with a slight reduction in pay, then option 2 is most consistent with an ethical moral decision. A consequences-based approach (utilitarianism) may conclude that option 1 is most ethical because, while 10 percent of the employees would lose their jobs, the majority would neither lose their jobs nor have their pay cut back. The utilitarian-based standard requires that the majority good be placed ahead of the individual good when one is faced with a moral dilemma.

VALUES MANAGEMENT AND CHALLENGES TO BUSINESS ETHICS

LO 5-4

Business ethics in the workplace context emphasizes prioritizing moral values for the organization and ensuring behaviors are aligned with those values. This is known as **values management.** Yet despite evidence that embracing business ethics promotes profitability and contributes to sound public policy, a resistance to values management programs exists in some business cultures. Some of the resistance arises from challenges based on general confusion about the notion of ethics. Other challenges arise from narrow or simplistic views of ethical dilemmas. A very simplistic approach to consider when deciding whether a manager or a company is acting in an ethical manner is to apply a "broadcast news test." Ask yourself, "How would I feel if the business decision was announced to the public on the local and national news?" In today's media environment, very little goes unnoticed or unreported, so it might be even more appropriate to ask how one would feel if a video of a major decision went viral. Table 5.1 lists common challenges and appropriate responses to business ethics and values management.

STRATEGIC ADVANTAGES OF VALUES MANAGEMENT

LO 5-5, 5-6

Managing ethics in the workplace involves identifying and prioritizing values to guide behaviors in the organization and establishing associated policies and procedures to ensure those behaviors are conducted. Values management is also crucial in other management practices such as management of a diverse workforce, total quality management, and strategic planning.

This means that values management has strategic importance on par with other types of managerial systems. There are both business and public policy benefits to values management. Managing values in the workplace legitimizes managerial actions, strengthens the coherence and balance of the organization's culture, improves trust in relationships between individuals and groups, supports greater consistency in standards and qualities of products, and cultivates greater sensitivity to the impact of the enterprise's values and messages. Indeed, companies that have embraced a values management system often report that it has strategic advantages.

Ethics and law, while coexistent, are not synonymous. Acts can be legal without being ethical, and, arguably, some ethical acts can be illegal. How can something be legal but unethical? When a pharmaceutical company markets a new drug, they often inflate the price, in part because they have no competition due to patents they hold on the drug. It is only after the company's patent expires that other companies can begin producing and selling generic versions, usually at a dramatically lower price. Unfortunately, until the generic drugs appear, many people who might be benefited by the drug cannot afford it and must use other, sometimes less effective, alternatives. As owners of the patent, the pharmaceutical companies are acting legally. Nevertheless, some people are harmed by the drug company's pricing policies. Assuming it is profitable and stable, the pharmaceutical company could adopt a moral minimum approach by lowering their profit margin, which would do good for a greater number of people—or it could maximize profits by maintaining high prices, which would deny relief to a part of society that it otherwise could help.

TABLE 5.1 Challenges and Realities in Business Ethics

Challenge	Reality
Business ethics cannot be taught. It is religion and not management.	Altering people's values isn't the objective of an organizational ethics program. Managing values and *conflict* among them is the primary objective.
Business ethics is unnecessary because it asserts the obvious: Act ethically.	The value of a code of ethics to an organization is its priority and focus with respect to certain ethical values in the company. Dishonesty takes a variety of forms. If an organization is confronting varying degrees of dishonesty (including more common examples such as office supply theft) or deceit in the workplace, a priority on honesty is very timely—and honesty should be listed in that organization's code of ethics.
Complying with the law is an organization's sole guide for ethical conduct.	While the law may operate as a baseline for ethical decision making, unethical acts may operate within the limits of the law (e.g., withholding information from superiors, casting revenue in favorable terms with a dubious basis for the projection, spreading rumors). Illegal conduct sometimes has its genesis in unethical behavior that has gone unnoticed.
Ethics can't be managed.	Management inherently incorporates a value system. Strategic priorities (maximizing profit, expanding market share, cutting costs, etc.) can be very strong influences on ethical decision making. Workplace regulations and rules directly influence behaviors in a manner that improves the general good and/or minimizes potential harm to stakeholders.
Business ethics is a philosophical debate that has little to do with the day-to-day realities of running an organization.	Business ethics is a management discipline with a programmatic approach that includes several practical tools. Ethics management programs have practical applications in other areas of management as well.

Businesses are confronted with such predicaments frequently. To avoid fines and lawsuits, companies must ensure that complying with the law remains a priority. To maintain goodwill, attract customers and top-quality employees, and avoid adverse publicity, companies must also monitor their ethical conduct. The principles-based and consequences-based approaches discussed earlier in this chapter, certainly guide managers when they are making business decisions. In addition, viewed from a macro perspective, businesses follow either a **moral minimum** or **maximizing profits** ethical philosophy. The moral minimum theory encourages a business to "do no harm" or, alternatively, "do the least possible harm." As long as the business remains profitable, the company strives to act as ethically as possible, even at the expense of some additional profits. A company that follows a maximizing profits theory strives to make as much money as possible, as long as no laws are broken. For example, suppose that a company is building a factory in a city, and it knows that the factory will produce exhaust fumes in large quantities. The Environmental Protection Agency (EPA) has established air quality standards that the company must adhere to. After extensive research, the company finds that it can spend $5 million to purchase and install

A manager for WidgetCo is approached by a foreign vendor who offers to sell widgets at a substantial discount from what his company is currently paying. When determining WidgetCo's course of action, consider both the moral minimum and maximizing profits approach.

- Would it or should it matter that the widgets offered are not made in the USA?

- Would it or should it matter that the foreign company, in business for 10 years, is not subject to the quality control regulations that the current USA supplier is regulated under?

- Would it or should it matter whether faulty or substandard widgets could adversely affect the company's final product?

- What if faulty or substandard widgets could make the company's final product dangerous to users or to the environment?

equipment that will allow it to meet the EPA required standards exactly. This approach will reduce the pollution to a level that will not affect most of the city's citizens, but a small percentage of those with lung or breathing problems could experience increased discomfort. Through its research, the company also learns that for $8 million it can install equipment that will far exceed the minimum standards. This will provide the cleanest and healthiest environment for the entire city, creating no impact on the city's air quality. Either choice results in a legal decision by the company. If the company chooses a moral minimum approach, it will spend the $8 million to do no harm, while a maximizing profits approach will save the company $3 million but put some people at risk.

In some cases, one must literally break the law to challenge a "bad" law. For example, in 1955, Rosa Parks, a black woman, boarded a bus in Montgomery, Alabama, and sat in the front, or "whites only," section and was arrested. Her arrest allowed her to challenge the segregationist practices prevalent in the South and led to wide-ranging changes in civil rights laws. One can argue that she acted ethically in breaking the law to bring light to unethical policies. Martin Luther King, Jr., similarly acted in an arguably ethical manner by conducting nonviolent sit-ins and marches throughout the South, intentionally violating laws to effect changes in unethical policies.

In Case 5.1, a corporation received substantial benefits from the city it was located in and then made a decision that was detrimental to its employees and the citizens of the city.

Cultivation of Strong Teamwork and Productivity

Values management may help align employee behaviors with the top-priority ethical values preferred by organization's top-level management. Sometimes an organization finds surprising disparity between its preferred values and the values actually reflected by behaviors in the workplace. Ongoing attention and dialogue regarding values in the workplace build openness, integrity, and community, which are critical ingredients of strong teams in the workplace. Employees who feel strong alignment between their values and those of the organization tend to react with strong motivation and performance.

Clarity in Business Operations

Setting ethical standards gives an organization's employees context for executing business operations. This gives more clarity to strategic planning by identifying preferred values and ensuring organizational behaviors are aligned with those values. This effort includes

FACT SUMMARY General Motors Corporation (GMC) operated two plants in Ypsilanti Township, Michigan (Ypsilanti). From 1975 to 1988, GMC took advantage of 11 tax abatements (lowering or eliminating taxes owed on real estate) provided for in a Michigan state statute to encourage business owners to create and maintain jobs in the state. As part of the tax abatement application process, GMC would consistently represent that its plants offered local residents nearly 13,000 jobs. Anxious to retain those jobs, public officials agreed to the tax abatements. In 1991, GMC announced that it was consolidating its operations and that one of the Ypsilanti plants would be closed. More than 4,000 jobs were lost. Ypsilanti sued GMC for, among other claims, allegedly breaching its promise and misrepresentation. The lower court ruled in favor of Ypsilanti finding that GMC's promises were binding and that allowing GMC to close the plant would result in unfairness and an extreme burden on Ypsilanti residents.

SYNOPSIS OF DECISION AND OPINION The Michigan Court of Appeals reversed the lower court and found for GMC. The court found that the promises of long-term relationships and the expectation of continued operations based on receipt of the tax abatements were unfounded and not binding on GMC.

WORDS OF THE COURT: Corporate Promises "First, the mere fact that a corporation solicits a tax abatement and persuades a municipality with assurances of jobs cannot be evidence of a promise. The very purpose of tax abatement legislation is to induce companies to locate and to continue business enterprises in the municipality. . . . The fact that a manufacturer uses hyperbole and puffery in seeking an advantage or concession does not necessarily create a promise. For example, statements such as 'We're partners' and 'We look forward to growing together' were found not to constitute a promise to keep a collective bargaining agreement in force for the foreseeable future so as to create by [a binding promise resulting in] a continuing duty of the employer to honor an expired agreement. . . . It has never been held that an abatement carries a promise of continued employment."

Case Questions

1. What, if anything, could Ypsilanti Township have done to ensure that GMC remained at the plant for an extended period of time?

2. When the plant closed, almost 20 percent of Ypsilanti's population became unemployed. Who were the primary and secondary stakeholders affected?

3. General Motors was found to have the legal right to close the plant. Was its action ethical? Why or why not?

4. From a maximizing profit or moral minimum perspective, how would you describe General Motors actions?

---

identifying the values, developing written policies and procedures to align behaviors with preferred values, and then training all personnel about the policies and procedures. These standards can be the framework for performance, reliability, measurement, and feedback. Business ethicists promote the notion that management techniques are highly useful for managing strategic values, for example, expanding market share, reducing costs, and so forth. A comprehensive values management program may also be used in managing diversity (considering different values and perspectives among stakeholders).

Strong Public Image

Devoting consistent and serious attention to values management also allows a business organization to portray a strong positive image to the public. People see such organizations as valuing people more than profit and as striving to operate with the utmost integrity. Aligning behavior with values is critical to effective marketing and public relations programs.

Ongoing attention and dialogue on values management help to cultivate teamwork and stimulate productivity.

Staying the Ethical Course in Turbulent Times

The financial crisis that began in 2008 is the most recent example of turbulent times in the corporate and financial sectors. Strong leadership in values management is critical during times of fundamental change. Continuing attention to ethics in the workplace sensitizes leaders and staff to how they want to act in a consistent manner.

> **KEY** POINT
> Values management should have strategic parity with other management priorities.

COMMON TRAITS OF EFFECTIVE ETHICAL PROGRAMS IN BUSINESS

LO 5-7, 5-8

Typically, ethics programs convey corporate values, often using codes and policies to guide decisions and behavior, and can include extensive training and evaluation depending on the organizational structure. At a very minimum, ethics programs provide guidance in ethical dilemmas. Business ethicists have various views on how an ideal ethical organization operates, but there are certain common traits:

■ Management has articulated a clear vision of integrity throughout the organization.

■ Reward systems are aligned with the vision of integrity.

■ Responsibility is seen as individual rather than collective in that individuals are willing to assume personal responsibility for actions of the organization.

■ Policies and practices of the organization are aligned with the vision.

■ The vision of integrity is well integrated into the decision-making process so that any significant management decision has ethical value dimensions.

Developing Codes of Ethics and Conduct

PROBLEM *While many organizations have a set of informal values and standards to which they adhere, effectiveness can be limited if the values are not articulated in a fixed medium or if the code is a management directive rather than a product of the entire organization. Informal value systems may be too vague and not helpful in a practical context.*

SOLUTION *Develop a code of ethics and conduct for your organization.*

Such codes should be developed in cooperation with (and not exclusively by) the human resource manager and legal counsel. Codes are insufficient if intended *only* to ensure that policies are legal. The entire organization must see the ethics program being driven by top management and carried out by management and the workforce.

Depending on the organization, a code of ethics and code of conduct may be in the same writing. They are examined here separately.

For a code of ethics, consider the following guidelines:

- Review any values needed to adhere to relevant laws and regulations.

- Review which values produce the top three or four traits of a highly ethical and successful product or service in each area. For example, the chief financial officer may identify objectivity and accuracy as important values. Identify which values produce behaviors that exhibit these traits.

- Identify values needed to address current issues in your workplace. Consider which of these issues is ethical in nature, for example, issues in regard to respect, fairness, and honesty.

- Consider any top ethical values that might be important to primary and secondary stakeholders (expectations of employees, clients/customers, suppliers, lenders, members of the local community).

Examples of ethical values may include:

- *Trustworthiness*: honesty, integrity, promise keeping, loyalty.

- *Respect*: autonomy, privacy, dignity, courtesy, tolerance, acceptance.

- *Responsibility*: accountability, pursuit of excellence.

- *Caring*: compassion, consideration, giving, sharing, kindness.

- *Justice and fairness*: procedural fairness, impartiality, consistency, equity, equality, due process.

- *Civic virtue and citizenship*: law abiding, community service, protection of the environment.

Codes of conduct specify actions in the workplace, and *codes of ethics* are general guides to decisions about those actions. An effective code of conduct contains examples of appropriate behavior. Examples of topics typically addressed by codes of conduct include preferred style of dress, avoiding illegal drugs, following instructions of superiors, being reliable and prompt, maintaining confidentiality, not accepting personal gifts from third parties as a result of a company role or action, avoiding conflict of interest, complying with laws and regulations, not using the organization's property for personal use, conducting business without discrimination, and reporting illegal or questionable activity. Managers should also think beyond these traditional legalistic expectations. It is important to identify what's ethically sensitive in your particular organization as well. Codes of conduct should be integrated into the various areas of the organization, including personnel matters such as job descriptions and performance appraisal forms, management-by-objectives expectations, standard forms, checklists, budget report format, and other relevant control instruments to ensure conformance with the code of conduct.

As with any management practice, the most important outcome is behavior that is consistent with the organization's value system. The best ethical values and intentions are relatively meaningless unless they generate fair and just behaviors in the workplace. All levels of employees in a company need to react to business situations in a fair and consistent manner. Complaints and lawsuits frequently arise when employees, job applicants, or customers are treated, or are perceived as being treated, differently. One of the primary benefits of a code of ethics and/or code of conduct is that it provides employees with rules and ideals that they can universally follow. When a company is dealing with a diverse population of employees, common sense is not always common and the concept of right and wrong is not always easily agreed to. Written codes provide a central source of inspiration and guidance to ensure uniform conduct. That's why practices that generate lists of ethical values, or codes of ethics, must also generate policies, procedures, and training that translate those values into appropriate behaviors.

LEGAL/ETHICAL REFLECTION *and* DISCUSSION

In 2011, the Pennsylvania State University community was stunned by multiple charges of child molestation committed by former assistant football coach Jerry Sandusky between 1994 and 2009. Sandusky had used Penn State's facilities, with permission, for a children's charity organization with which he was affiliated. Soon after the initial charges were filed, allegations of perjury and failure to report the situation were brought against Penn State management. Joe Paterno, the legendary head football coach, was found to have been aware of the situation. Penn State's athletic program motto is "Success with Honor." The football program had never been charged with a severe NCAA rules violation, and the program enjoyed a high graduation rate. A subsequent investigation showed that Mr. Paterno did in fact report the incidents to his superiors but had not taken any independent action. As a result of intense media coverage, a former university vice president and the former athletic director were implicated in a cover-up along with the university president, Graham Spanier. Spanier and Paterno were fired. On June 22, 2012, Jerry Sandusky was convicted of 45 of 48 counts of sexual assault involving 10 boys. Sandusky's appeal is pending. Several of Sandusky's victims have filed civil suits against Penn State for damages. Their cases are pending, and the university announced that it will seek to settle the cases before trial.

Severe sanctions were levied against the university by the NCAA, including (1) a fine of approximately $60 million, (2) exclusion from postseason bowl games for four years, and (3) a reduction in football scholarships. Additionally, the football program

was stripped of all wins from 1998 through 2011, and the entire athletic program was put on probation for five years.

Aside from paying the fine, Penn State has had to pay millions of dollars in investigation costs and has expended considerable amounts of money and man-hours in an attempt to rebuild its image.

1. Mr. Paterno said that he fulfilled his responsibility by reporting what he knew to the university management. Could he have done more? Should he have done more? What specific steps should he have taken?

2. Who are the primary and secondary stakeholders involved in this dilemma?

3. Once the administration became aware of the Sandusky allegations, what specific actions should have been taken?

4. Is it fair for the current Penn State students to be affected by incidents that they had nothing to do with and that happened before many of them entered the university?

5. Did Mr. Paterno and the university management demonstrate a commitment to their stated expectation, "Success with Honor"?

6. Was the cover-up intended to preserve the university's reputation? Is that a justification for the university's failure to act? Are there ever any circumstances in which a cover-up is ethical? Can anything justify the university's failure to act?

For an update on the Penn State case, see this textbook's website at www.mhhe.com/melvinleb2e.

ETHICAL DECISION MAKING: A MANAGER'S PARADIGM

Legal Speak ›))

Vicarious Liability Liability imposed on one person due to the actions of another person; liability imposed upon a company due to the actions of an employee.

Legal Speak ›))

Affirmative Defense An affirmative defense exists when the defendant can introduce evidence that can nullify a plaintiff's claim, even when the plaintiff's evidence supporting her claim is true; if an affirmative defense is proven, the defendant will have no liability for damages.

It is not uncommon for business ethics to be portrayed as a matter of resolving conflicts in which one option appears to be the clear choice. Case studies that present situations where an employee is faced with whether or not to lie, steal, cheat, abuse another, break terms of a contract, and so on are too simplistic. Ethical dilemmas faced by managers are often complex, with no clear ethical choice. The use of a paradigm in the following flowchart (see Figure 5.1) can help business owners and managers apply ethical decision making more consistently.

FIGURE 5.1 Ethical Decision Making

1. Define the dilemma →
How and when did the dilemma occur?
What were the underlying reasons for the conflict?

2. Identify impact →
Which primary and secondary stakeholders will be affected?
How will these stakeholders be affected?

3. Apply standards →
What is the legal impact of the dilemma?
What values and ethical principles has the organization set out for guidance?
What are the consequences of action or inaction?

4. Develop choices and discuss impact with various constituencies →
Which choice results in the most benefit to stakeholders?
Will any of the choices result in harm to stakeholders?
What are the level and severity of the harms?
Which choice upholds the values of the organization?

5. Implement, evaluate, and monitor →
How can this decision be implemented with greatest attention to all stakeholders?
Under what circumstances are you willing to make an exception to your decision?
How could this company avoid this dilemma in the future?

ETHICAL DECISION-MAKING CASE STUDIES

Business ethics cannot be studied in a vacuum. The principles and theories that are discussed in this chapter are useful only if they can be understood in a business context. Study the following two well-known cases in some detail, and apply the concepts that have been covered thus far. Use the ethical decision-making flowchart in Figure 5.1 to assess and discuss the ethical challenges presented in the cases. Several questions for discussion are included at the end of each case study. The first case involves a company that touted a strong values statement but engaged in illegal and unethical conduct that caused direct harm to stakeholders. The second case involves a legally permissible transaction that poses several ethicaldile mmas.

The Enron Scandal

Of the high-profile corporate scandals that erupted at major public companies[3] in 2000 and 2001, Enron is perhaps the most notorious. The systematic looting of a corporation by its

---

[3]A publicly held company is one whose stock is bought and sold in public markets. Regulation of public companies and markets is discussed in detail in Chapter 17, "Regulation of Securities, Corporate Governance, and Financial Markets."

Enron, once a hundred-billion-dollar company, collapsed under the weight of ethical lapses by its management team, who ignored their company's own values management policies.

executives and the massive fraud and subsequent cover-ups that culminated in a public crash made Enron the symbol of corporate greed and arrogance. After the company's meteoric rise to the top, Enron's shareholders lost about $62 billion of value over a period of about two years. Employees, believing in Enron's vision and leadership, filled their retirement portfolios with Enron stock only to have their savings wiped out when the company sank into bankruptcy.

Enron's Business Model   Enron Corporation was a multinational conglomerate[4] with a core business of energy trading. When Congress deregulated the energy markets in the mid-1990s, Enron positioned itself to be a market share leader in the practice of acting as a sort of **energy bank** by purchasing energy from one source at a discount rate and selling it to markets where demand was greatest for energy. This business model depended on Enron's, contracting to buy gas with producers of natural gas while also contracting to sell the gas with regional natural gas suppliers (companies supplying natural gas to the general public). Enron would capture the profits between the price at which it acquired the gas and the price at which it had promised to sell the gas. Enron's executives devised this plan using the model of a bank earning the spread between what it pays depositors and what it collects from borrowers paying interest on a loan.

Rise to the Top   Although the company initially struggled, by the 1990s Enron was in position to benefit from the energy deregulation efforts in Congress. Enron hired Washington's top lobbyists and spread heavy campaign cash to both political parties in a successful effort to pass the California Deregulation Act. Virtually overnight Enron's business model became highly profitable. Its first-quarter revenues went from $12 billon in 2000 to $84 billion in 2001. Employees, many of whom held the rising stock as part of their retirement savings, became fiercely loyal to the company. Using its profits and talented employee

---

[4]A conglomerate is a business entity that has a variety of industries that operate under a common corporate structure.

pool, Enron began to add on additional business ventures that complemented its energy trading business, such as operating power plants. While some of these ventures were successful in terms of revenue, they also provided a convenient hiding place to disguise losses incurred by other Enron entities. Enron continued its growth at a rapid pace by expanding its business holdings into emerging (and risky) technology companies, including major holdings in the new technology of fiber optics.

Wall Street commentators, politicians, and investors alike all acclaimed Enron as the most innovative company since Microsoft. Analysts rated Enron's stock risk as "staggeringly low" and called it the last great technology stock in the new economy. The stock soared, and Enron's executive management's compensation shot up into the tens of millions of dollars based on stock options in the company. Members of the top-level management team all received generous bonus compensation packages that were tied to the performance of Enron's stock. Enron's board of directors, who were in charge of oversight of the company, were equally exuberant because their compensation also included generous stock options and expensive perks.

Key Enron Players   The founder and first CEO of Enron was Kenneth Lay. Observers described Lay as an affable man from humble beginnings who was seen to be the epitome of the American dream. All through Enron's history, Lay was Enron's public face, and Wall Street investors hailed him as one of the greatest innovators of all time. But the real mastermind of Enron was its Harvard Business School–educated former McKinsey consultant, Jeffrey Skilling. Skilling, Enron's chief operating officer, was the architect of Enron's energy trading business model. Andrew Fastow, Enron's young chief financial officer, was a Skilling protégé who oversaw Enron's transactions and was known to browbeat anyone who questioned Enron's accounting or business practices. Rick Causey, Enron's chief accounting officer, deviated from established accounting standards and then pressured auditors to sign off on dubious financial statements that were presented to the board and shareholders.

Vision and Values   Enron's meteoric rise was even more impressive because, according to Lay, Enron was a prime example of a company that could be profitable and ethical. He proclaimed himself the keeper of the company's vision and values, which he defined as "respect, just treating other people the way we want to be treated, we're sincere, we mean what we say, we say what we do." Enron's code of business ethics articulated a philosophy of honesty and transparency. Lay also embraced the concept of community stakeholders and Enron's responsibility to groups beyond its shareholders, including its neighbors and employees.

Visit Connect to see a complete version of Enron's actual code of ethics.

The Fall   So what went wrong? As Enron's stock price climbed, a sort of fervor developed in Enron's executive office suite. The entire company focused its efforts on showing revenue streams, keeping its stock price high, and pushing it even higher. The only way to continue this trend was to keep Wall Street investors enthusiastic about the company and to downplay any bad news. However, as the overall economy began to slow and the technology bubble deflated, Enron's boils began to show. Enron had kept its operations afloat through the use of credit that was now in short supply. By March 2001, the financial news media began to scrutinize Enron's financial transactions, its use of offshore partnerships, its questionable accounting practices, and self-dealing by Fastow. Enron's board issued flat denials and pointed out that all of the company's financial transactions and business operations had been endorsed as proper by Arthur Andersen, one of the world's leading accounting firms.

Yet the media continued its investigative reporting of the company, and investors became increasingly skeptical about Enron's numbers. The stock continued to drop as Enron's various entities ran out of cash to cover expenses. Over the next few months, Enron suffered a barrage of embarrassing publicity that implied that its executives had looted the company to support an opulent lifestyle while the company was suffering billions in losses. Government investigators began several probes into the company's dealings and discovered that Skilling, Fastow, and others had fraudulently hidden Enron's losses from the investor community in an effort to manipulate the stock. Questions were also raised about why Andersen auditors had signed off on the fraud. Amid the allegations, Skilling resigned his position. As Enron's lenders pressured the company to pay back loans, and with Enron's stock in free fall with no end in sight, the company finally filed for bankruptcy on December 2, 2001. It was, at the time, the largest bankruptcy in the history of the United States.[5] Loyal employees and stockholders who had ridden Enron's rising stock as a primary retirement vehicle were wiped out. Nearly 5,000 employees lost their jobs, and the American public was outraged. Enron and its executives, brokers, lenders, auditors, and attorneys were all now the subject of a massive fraud investigation by the Securities and Exchange Commission and the Federal Bureau of Investigation. Congress issued subpoenas to Enron's executives, calling them to Capitol Hill to explain their conduct, but the only one who testified was Skilling. All of the others had followed their counsel's advice to invoke their constitutional right not to testify. Skilling was combative in his testimony, stating that he "absolutely unequivocally thought the company was in good shape" when he resigned.

Arthur Andersen   Enron's long-time auditing firm, Arthur Andersen, was one of the largest and most prestigious professional service firms in the world. After revelations about Enron's fraud surfaced, Andersen became the object of great scrutiny as well. How could the venerable firm, founded in 1913 by an accounting professor who built its reputation on honesty and integrity, have missed the fraud? Because it was inconceivable that such a massive fraudulent cover-up of billions in losses could escape auditing detection, there was only one explanation: Andersen had turned a blind eye and gone along with it. Enron was a very profitable client for the firm, netting nearly $100 million in fees annually at a time when Andersen was seeing its share of the overall auditing market drop. David Duncan, Andersen's lead auditor in charge of Enron, became one of Andersen's top-paid employees primarily due to the massive fees he was collecting from Enron. Duncan, though, became more of an Enron advocate within Andersen rather than an auditor. Any time top-level managers at Andersen questioned the propriety of a transaction or financial report, it was Duncan who argued Enron's case to convince the others in the firm that the structures, although aggressive and pushing the envelope, were perfectly legal. When one senior Andersen manager objected to certain Enron accounting practices, Enron's chief accounting officer demanded that he be removed from the auditing team. Enron kept Andersen in tow by threatening to leave the firm and take its substantial fees to Andersen competitors.

Aftermath   After an intensive investigation, federal prosecutors brought charges of wire fraud, securities fraud, conspiracy, insider trading, falsifying financial reports and tax returns, and obstruction of justice against Skilling, Fastow, Lay, and a host of other Enron executives. In all, 34 people either pled guilty or were convicted on charges stemming from the Enron scandal. Skilling is currently serving a 24-year prison sentence. Fastow was sentenced to 6 years in prison. Kenneth Lay was convicted of fraud but died of a heart attack before he could be sentenced. Other Enron-related defendants received sentences ranging from probation to 5 years' incarceration.

---

[5]The 2008 bankruptcy of investment banking firm Lehman Brothers eclipsed Enron as the largest bankruptcy in U.S. history (in terms of total debt owed).

FACT SUMMARY   As Enron Corporation's financial difficulties became public, Andersen, Enron's auditor, instructed its employees to destroy documents pursuant to its established document retention policy. Andersen was indicted under a federal statute that makes it a crime to "knowingly . . . corruptly persuad[e] another person . . . with intent to . . . cause" that person to "withhold" documents from, or "alter" documents for use in an "official proceeding." The jury returned a guilty verdict, and the Fifth Circuit Court of Appeals affirmed, holding that the district court's jury instructions properly conveyed the meaning of "corruptly persuades" and that the jury need not find any consciousness of wrongdoing in order to convict.

SYNOPSIS OF DECISION AND OPINION   In a unanimous decision by the Supreme Court, Andersen's conviction was overturned. The Court reasoned that the instructions allowed the jury to convict Andersen without proving that the firm knew it had broken the law or that there had been a link to any official proceeding that prohibited the destruction of documents.

The Court specifically held that the jury's instructions—which stated that even if Andersen honestly and sincerely believed its conduct was lawful, the jury could still convict the firm—was a serious error. The statute under which Andersen was charged used the language "knowingly . . . corruptly persuade." Andersen managers did instruct their employees to delete Enron-related files, but those actions were within the firm's document retention policy. If the document retention policy was constructed to keep certain information private, even from the government, Andersen was not corruptly persuading its employees to keep the information private.

WORDS OF THE COURT: Improper Jury Instruction   "The jury instructions failed to convey properly the elements of a 'corrup[t] persuas[ion]' conviction. . . . The jury instructions failed to convey the requisite consciousness of wrongdoing. Indeed, it is striking how little culpability the instructions required. For example, the jury was told that, even if petitioner honestly and sincerely believed its conduct was lawful, the jury could convict. The instructions also diluted the meaning of 'corruptly' such that it covered innocent conduct."

The public outcry over the scandal and waning public confidence in the oversight of financial frauds in the market led Congress to pass several laws to improve the quality of financial disclosure by public corporations. Most famously, Congress passed the Sarbanes-Oxley Act, which dramatically increased the responsibilities of people in charge of running the finances of public companies, including officers, directors, and outsiders such as attorneys and accountants.[6] The law imposes criminal penalties of up to 20 years' imprisonment for willful violations.

The government also indicted the entire firm of Arthur Andersen on charges of obstruction of justice. The charges stemmed from the government's allegations that Andersen insiders, led by Duncan, engaged in a pattern of cover-up by ordering massive shredding of documents once the firm suspected that the Securities and Exchange Commission would investigate Enron. In June 2002, the firm was convicted of the obstruction charges, sentenced to pay a $500,000 fine, and was banned from performing audits for publicly traded companies. It was, in essence, a death sentence, as the firm's clients and key employees defected to competitors. The firm that had once employed 28,000 people around the globe was nearly defunct.

---

[6]The Sarbanes-Oxley Act is discussed in detail in Chapter 17, "Regulation of Securities, Corporate Governance, and Financial Markets."

However, in a stunning reversal that could aptly be described as too little too late, the U.S. Supreme Court reversed Andersen's conviction in 2005 and ordered a retrial. The decision is featured in Case 5.2. Shortly after the Court's decision, the government announced that it would not retry the case.

Enron Scandal: Questions for Discussion

1. Consider Kenneth Lay's statements about Enron's values and visions. Is it possible to reconcile these statements with Enron's business practices? What were the factors that corrupted these values? Is it possible that Lay actually believed that these values were being followed by the company but had been duped by Skilling and Fastow? What steps could Lay have taken to be sure that Enron's business practices were consistent with the values?

2. Lay also instituted a bonus structure based on Enron's revenues and stock price instead of actual profitability. Are such bonuses inherently corrupting?

3. During an interview with *The New York Times* just 10 months after Enron's bankruptcy, Skilling argued that every transaction and report was scrutinized and approved by Enron's auditors and attorneys. In essence, he claimed that so long as Enron had met the technical aspects of the existing law, the company had no further obligations. What's the difference between technical compliance with the law and ethical obligations to stakeholders? Is it ethical to exploit gray areas of the law (areas that are not clearly defined) in the name of profit? What should be the drivers behind decision making at this level?

4. Given the complexity of the transactions and the assurances of auditors, what steps could the board of directors have taken to be sure these transactions were not only legal, but consistent with the company's stated ethical values?

5. Recall Andersen's decision to remove an auditor who refused to go along with Enron's schemes. What pressures was Andersen facing when Enron demanded the removal? Andersen had every legal right to remove the auditor, but by doing so, ignored the firm's own system of ethics. What should Andersen have done when faced with Enron's demands?

6. Consider the government's actions in this case. When the Supreme Court reversed Andersen's conviction, famed defense lawyer Daniel Petrocelli, who had represented Skilling, gave a press statement that lambasted the Justice Department for conducting witch hunts and attempting to criminalize innocent conduct. Defense attorneys argued that the government consistently used scare tactics, pushed the limits of the law, and had indicted Andersen in order to use criminal charges as leverage to garner government witnesses who would testify against the Enron defendants. Did the government act ethically in this case? Were its actions justified, or did they have more to do with politics than justice? Was it good public policy to destroy the world's largest professional service firm for the actions of a handful of employees? Why do you think the government chose not to retry the case?

AIG Bonusgate: Legal, Managerial, and Ethical Perspectives

When *The New York Times* reported that insurance giant American International Group (AIG) had distributed $165 million in performance bonuses to some of its executives, it lit a public and political firestorm. AIG was in the center of the financial crisis of 2008 that culminated in massive government bailouts for financial institutions and others who were considered too important to the financial infrastructure to be allowed to fail. Just months before the bonuses were distributed, AIG had received $173 billion in taxpayer money in exchange for an 80 percent stake in AIG for the U.S. government.

Political Reaction   After the news of the bonuses broke, President Obama immediately denounced the bonuses and castigated AIG for using funds from one of the federal government's original bailout packages in November 2008. He promised the outraged American populace that the government would pursue all "legal means to prevent the bonuses from being paid." Yet, the White House subsequently revealed that Treasury Secretary Geitner had knowledge of the bonuses and did not move to stop them from being paid because they were contractual obligations between a private company and an employee.

Congress reacted to the increasing public outrage by holding press conferences and subpoenaing witnesses for hearings on the bonuses. Representative Barney Frank called a special press conference to express his outrage at the bonuses and announced his plan to introduce a law to *tax* the entire amount of the bonuses retroactively to effectively place the bonus money in the U.S. Treasury. The attorney general of New York (where AIG is headquartered) launched an immediate investigation into the bonuses. During a congressional hearing, Edward Libby, the CEO appointed to revitalize the sagging company, called on AIG executives to return a portion of their bonuses. The public's anger continued to rise. A poll conducted by Gartner Group showed that 8 out of 10 Americans thought that distributing and taking the bonuses was immoral. AIG was forced to hire security for the bonus recipients because of death threats. Pickets were organized in front of AIG's headquarters in New York City.

Mounting Pressures   Initially, most AIG bonus recipients were reluctant to consider the idea of returning their bonuses. These were highly skilled employees who negotiated specific performance goals and agreed to bonus compensation based on their individual goals. Those individual goals, they argued, were met despite the collapse of AIG. Moreover, such bonuses were crucial to retaining the top talent that was necessary to AIG's emerging from insolvency. Yet, as the N.Y. attorney general continued to pressure bonus recipients with the threat of investigation, and Congress threatened to tax 100 percent of the bonus amounts, many recipients returned all or a portion of their bonus money, totaling nearly $50 million.

Cooler Heads   As the weeks passed and network commentators moved on to other pressing issues, the rage dampened down. Despite the rush through the House of Representatives, the more cautious Senate halted the bonus taxation bill. The Obama administration, apparently after a change of heart, urged Congress not to pass any special taxation on bonuses, arguing that such action may make private investors, a key part of the economic recovery plan, reluctant to engage in the investment community. Although congressional leaders continued to hold hearings on what the media had dubbed "bonusgate," no official action was taken either by Congress or the Obama administration. Nevertheless, bonusgate took its toll on AIG. Several key executives defected, and AIG leaders were left picking up the pieces. Even AIG employees who had not received the bonus were scorned and demoralized.

AIG Bonusgate: Questions for Discussion

1. Consider President Obama's initial promise to use any means necessary to recoup the bonus money. It was clear that these recipients were contractually entitled to the bonuses. We'll learn later in this textbook that some contracts can be voided because they are inconsistent with public policy or the public good. It is a very high bar to reach, but courts have recognized this argument as valid. Could the AIG bonuses be

categorized as bad public policy? Does paying the bonuses result in harm to the public in a tangible or intangible way? How? Could it be argued that these bonuses actually benefited the public?

2. Who are the primary and secondary stakeholders in the AIG decision to pay the bonuses?

3. If there was no legal basis for voiding the bonus contract, what ethical dilemmas are posed by accepting the bonuses? If you agreed to give the bonus back, how would that square with utilitarian notions of ethical conduct? If you decided to keep the bonus, would that mean that you followed a principles-based philosophy?

4. Much of AIG's executive management argued that the bonuses were a commonly used method of incentive and that the recipients were high achievers who were necessary to retain if AIG was to avoid insolvency even with the bailout money. Do you believe that bonuses should be banned if the company received government money? Is it ethical to pay out bonuses even when the company, overall, performs poorly?

5. Consider Congress's movement to tax the bonuses retroactively. Setting aside the possibility that the tax may be unconstitutional, is it ethical for the government to attempt to interfere in a private contract between an individual and her employer? Was this a political reaction to an ethical dilemma? Is it good public policy?

6. In general, is it ethical for a country's government to own 80 percent (a controlling stake) of a private business enterprise?

CORPORATE SOCIAL RESPONSIBILITY

LO 5-11

While business ethics may be thought of as an application of ethics to the corporate sector and may be useful as a paradigm for determining responsibility in business dealings, corporate social responsibility (CSR) involves a broader-based identification of important business and social issues and a critique of business organizations and practices. The

Corporate social responsibility includes the notion of recognizing the importance of good corporate citizenship and partnering with the community.

fundamental notion underlying CSR is that *conscience* resides not just in individuals but also in a corporation. Thus, business organizations committed to CSR aim to achieve commercial success in ways that honor ethical values and respect people, communities, and the natural environment in a sustainable manner while recognizing the interests of stakeholders. Stakeholders include investors, customers, employees, business partners, local communities, the environment, and society at large. CSR involves corporate citizenship, which is the adoption by a business of a strategic focus for fulfilling the economic, legal, ethical, and philanthropic social responsibilities expected of it by its stakeholders. There are essentially three schools of thought that define CSR in practice.

The Narrow View: Invisible Hand

In his classic condemnation of the corporate social responsibility movement, Nobel Prize–winning economist Milton Friedman proposed that the only responsibility a business has is to maximize shareholder wealth (the maximizing profits theory). Indeed, an implicit perspective underwriting much of the free enterprise persuasion is that businesses are amoral, and as Friedman would suggest, managers who pursue social initiatives with corporate funds are violating their fiduciary duties to the owners of the corporation. While individuals are free to act morally and behave in a socially responsible manner on their own time and with their own resources, managers are responsible solely to the shareholders to make as much profit as legally possible. As for society's well-being, the argument goes, Adam Smith's invisible hand will provide. According to Smith's invisible hand theory, a deliberate amorality in corporate decision making is encouraged in the name of a new morality: The common good is best served when each of us and our economic institutions pursue not the common good or moral purpose, but rather a competitive advantage.[7] Hence, what is good for business is good for America because the market's efficiencies provide an invisible hand that guides morality and responsibility. Corporations acting unethically would inevitable suffer.

The Moderate View: Government's Hand

Advocates of a more moderate view argue that the government provides the exclusive view of corporate responsibility. The government is seen as the most valuable source of setting guidelines because it represents the moral views of the general public. Under this view, corporations have the responsibility to pursue objectives that are rational, legal, and purely economic. The regulatory hands of the law and the political process, rather than Smith's invisible hand, provide the basis for ethical decision making. Neither the invisible hand view nor the government's hand view trusts corporate leaders with any stewardship over noneconomic values.

The Broad View: Management's Hand

An underlying tenet of the broadest view of CSR is that corporations have a social responsibility and that profitability is secondary (the moral minimum theory). Indeed, in the broadest terms, some business ethicists argue that corporations are allowed to exist only because they can serve some public good. It is not necessary to justify the need for a greater corporate role in social responsibility. Thus, these ethicists often invoke a set of

---

[7]While the overwhelming majority of scholars and commentators use Smith's invisible hand metaphor in the same context as it is used in this textbook, there are some persuasive articles that argue that Smith did not intend the invisible hand metaphor to be a significant part of his economic theories. To read an excellent discussion on the controversy, see Professor Gavin Kennedy's article in *Economic Journal Watch* titled "Adam Smith and the Invisible Hand: From Metaphor to Myth." A link to the article may be found on this textbook's website at www.mhhe.com/melvinleb2e.

societal expectations with the idea that corporations conduct their business on such terms. Their starting point is socially defined goals rather than business objectives.

Within the broad view, the majority is not willing to buy into such a radical notion that business prosperity should be an afterthought. Instead, they argue that CSR is in the public's interest and a company's self-interest *and* that a company does well by employing socially responsible principles in its business operations. In this way, CSR may be thought of as a form of enlightened self-interest because the long-term prosperity of a firm depends not on short-term profits but on societal well being.

An integral part of the broad CSR perspective is the focus on what some ethicists call the *triple bottom line.* Essentially, the triple bottom line emphasizes not only the conventional creation of economic value (profits), but also a company's creation (or destruction) of environmental and social value. This naturally places a great deal more pressure on managers to perform, as it is not uncommon that these three sets of bottom-line issues conflict. It is not enough, then, for managers to aggressively pursue a social agenda; they must also not lose sight of financial and environmental performance. Yet, this may be difficult to do in practice. It is easy for managers to underestimate the linkage between enterprise sustainability and the creation of shareholder value. Rather than looking at the three bottom lines as offsetting, it is more preferable to view them as possessing a cumulative strategic value to a company.

In Landmark Case 5.3, a state appellate court decides a product liability issue in the context of a dangerous design flaw. But this dangerous flaw was known to management and was ignored because the costs of repair were thought to be significantly more than the costs of compensating injured victims. It is a case frequently cited by CSR advocates as an example of the failing of the invisible hand and government's hand approaches.

LANDMARK CASE 5.3   Grimshaw v. Ford Motor Company, 119 Cal. App. 3d 757 (1981)

FACT SUMMARY   In an effort to add a more fuel-efficient car to its offerings, Ford designed the Pinto. During design, Ford engineers became concerned that the placement of the gas tank was unsafe and subject to puncturing and rupturing at low-impact speeds. Crash tests confirmed the dangerous design flaw, and engineers recommended halting production until a solution to the product was developed. However, Ford's management overruled the engineers and pushed the Pinto into the manufacturing phase. There was evidence that Ford considered the alternatives too expensive and decided that the proposed fix would have a higher overall cost than the risk of liability from lawsuits as a result of injuries to its customers. Grimshaw purchased a Pinto and was injured when the gas tank erupted in a low-speed crash. The jury found Ford liable for Grimshaw's injuries and awarded him $125 million. The trial court reduced the award to $3.5 million pursuant to a California state statute.

SYNOPSIS OF DECISION AND OPINION   The California appellate court upheld the jury's verdict and the $3.5 million award. The court pointed out that the dangerous design flaw carried with it the severe risk of injury and that the evidence showed that Ford would have had to spend only $15.30 per car to have made the Pinto safer.

WORDS OF THE COURT: Corporate Malice   "[T]here was substantial evidence that Ford's management decided to proceed with the production of the Pinto with knowledge of test results revealing design defects which rendered the fuel tank extremely vulnerable on rear impact at low speeds and endangered the safety and lives of the occupants. Such conduct constitutes corporate malice."

Case Questions

1. Which view of CSR do you believe Ford's managers were aligned to when making the Pinto decision?

2. Suppose that the changes would have caused Ford to expend $1,000 per car rather than $15.80. Would that have changed the outcome of the case? Could it be argued that, given the fact that Ford's sales plummeted after this lawsuit was filed, Smith's invisible hand actually worked here?

CONCEPT SUMMARY Values Management, Corporate Challenges, and Corporate Social Responsibility

- Companies that practice a moral minimum ethical philosophy strive to act as ethically as possible as long as they remain profitable. These companies are said to follow a management's-hand philosophy regarding corporate social responsibility.

- Companies that practice a maximizing profits ethical philosophy strive to maximize profits, viewing ethics and corporate social responsibility as secondary to increasing shareholder wealth. These companies are said to follow an invisible hand philosophy regarding corporate social responsibility.

- Companies that follow a government's hand philosophy regarding corporate social responsibility look primarily to statutes and regulation for guidance in their decision-making process.

- Values management consists of prioritizing moral values for the organization and ensuring behaviors are aligned with those values.

- Managing values in the workplace legitimizes managerial actions, strengthens the coherence and balance of the organization's culture, improves trust in relationships between individuals and groups, supports greater consistency in standards and qualities of products, and cultivates greater sensitivity to the impact of the enterprise's values and messages.

- Values management may help to align employee behaviors with the top-priority ethical values favored by the organization's top-level management. Behavior in the workplace often conflicts with preferred ethical values, so management must be vigilant.

- Developing written policies and procedures to align behaviors with preferred values, and then training all personnel about the policies and procedures, is essential.

KEY TERMS

Business ethics p. 123 Recognizing right and wrong business behavior and acting responsibly to the business's stakeholders.

Stakeholder p. 124 Any individual or entity affected by a business's operations; includes the business's owners, investors, employees, customers, suppliers, and the wider community.

Morals p. 125 Generally accepted standards of right and wrong in a given society.

Ethics p. 125 A conscious system used for deciding moral dilemmas.

Utilitarian p. 125 Model of moral philosophy which holds that an action is ethically sound if it produces positive results for the most.

Values management p. 127 Managerial system that emphasizes prioritizing moral values for the

organization and ensuring that behaviors are aligned with those values.

Moral minimum p. 128 A corporate ethical philosophy in which a company strives to act as ethically as possible as long as a reasonable profit is made. Ethics and corporate social responsibility are priorities.

Maximizing profits p. 128 A corporate ethical philosophy in which a company strives to make as much money as possible with an emphasis on not breaking the law. Ethics and corporate social responsibility are often secondary concerns.

Energy bank p. 135 Business model adopted by Enron Corporation, after deregulation of the energy markets, in which Enron purchased energy from one source at a discount rate and sold it to markets where demand was greatest for energy.

Java Road (Java) is a corporation that retails high-quality coffee products through coffee carts in conveniently placed locations such as malls and office complexes. Java owns 10 such carts and employs a workforce of 40 to maintain business operations. The owner, Miguel, founded the company 10 years ago with the idea that a high-quality coffee product could be sold at a profit because his overhead was limited to the product, employee compensation, and the cart. Although he has always stressed honesty with his employees, he never developed a written code of ethics.

1. Suppose that Jacob, an employee who works at one of the most profitable carts, has one or two cups of free coffee a day. He bases his justification for doing so on the fact that the cart is so profitable that no one will notice. Given the lack of a written code of ethics or conduct, is it okay for Jacob to drink a free cup of coffee from the cart?

2. Suppose that one customer consistently buys coffee from Jacob and leaves a small tip. In an effort to increase the size of the tip, Jacob gives the customer a free coffee every Friday. Is it ethical for Jacob to do this? Is it ethical for the customer to take the free coffee?

3. What theories of moral philosophy helped your decision making in answering Questions 1 and 2?

4. Suppose that Miguel's general manager suggests that he develop a code of ethics for Java Road. Miguel bristles at the idea and replies that business ethics "cannot be managed—people are either ethical or not." What responses could the general manager use to persuade Miguel to employ a values management system?

5. Assume that Miguel finds a vendor that will sell him coffee beans at a discounted price. However, Miguel reads an article about the fact that the vendor uses child labor in Asia to produce the product. The vendor argues that the beans are high quality and that its practice of employing child labor is perfectly legal in Asia. Which view of CSR would result in Miguel's refusing to buy the beans? What is the vendor's view of CSR?

Assume that you are Miguel's general manager in the Theory to Practice problem. In groups (or individually) draft a two- to three-page code of ethics and/or code of conduct that would be appropriate for Java Road. Use the Solutions for Managers feature in this chapter for guidance.

A sample answer may be found on this textbook's website at www.mhhe.com/melvinleb2e.

CASE SUMMARY 5.1 :: Goswami v. American Collections Enterprise, Inc., 377 F.3d 488 (5th Cir. 2004)

ETHICS IN DEBT COLLECTION

American Collections Enterprise, Inc. (ACEI), is a debt collection company that contracted with Capital One bank to provide debt collection services. Under the terms of the collection agreement, Capital One assigned delinquent accounts to ACEI for collection, and ACEI collected these debts on a contingent fee basis. Under the collection agreement, Capital One gave ACEI the authority to settle any of its accounts at a discount according to a set formula. Goswami owed approximately $900 on her Capital One credit card and failed to pay. Capital One referred that debt to ACEI for collection on March 20, 2001, and ACEI pursued Goswami's delinquent account. The debt collection letter offered to settle the outstanding balance due with a 30 percent discount off the balance owed and stated that no other offers would be forthcoming. Unbeknownst to Goswami, ACEI actually had authority to settle for up to a 50 percent discount according to ACEI's agreement with Capital One. The Fair Debt Collection Act prohibits misleading statements by debt collectors.

CASE QUESTIONS

1. Is the letter misleading?

2. Is it ethical to tell a partial truth as ACEI did here?

3. Do private debt collection agencies serve any public policy functions?

PROFESSIONAL ETHICS

Greenen was a certified public accountant (CPA) licensed by the state of Washington. During the course of her employment as a CPA, Greenen violated a workplace rule by failing to inform her employer's health care plan administrator that she and her spouse had divorced. The effect of her failing to disclose the divorce was that Greenen's ex-husband continued to receive health care benefits that Greenen's employer afforded to its employees' spouses even though he was no longer eligible under the rules of the plan. After her employer discovered the discrepancy, Greenen was charged by the State Board of Accountancy with a breach of the CPA's ethical code

for professional misrepresentation. Greenen countered that the CPA ethical code governed accounting-related transactions and practices only and that she should not be subject to sanction for failing to disclose her divorce.

CASE QUESTIONS

1. Should ethical codes apply to employees outside their scope of employment?
2. If Greenen were accused of a violent crime, would she have been charged by the State Board of Accountancy for an ethical violation?
3. What is the purpose of having mandatory ethical codes for professionals such as CPAs?

CORPORATE SOCIAL RESPONSIBILITY

In 2007, Countrywide was the largest provider of home mortgage loans in the world. Countrywide specialized in so-called subprime mortgage loans that allowed homebuyers with relatively low credit scores the opportunity to qualify for a mortgage by paying a higher interest rate along with a monthly premium to insure the loan in case of a default. One of Countrywide's mortgages featured "teaser rates" that made initial payments artificially low. Nearly 50 percent of Countrywide's customers ended up defaulting within one year of when the teaser rate adjusted upward. Several customers filed complaints with regulatory authorities contending that Countrywide never disclosed

that the payments would increase so dramatically and applicants relied on Countrywide's judgment that they could afford the loan.

CASE QUESTIONS

1. Does Countrywide have an ethical obligation to refuse making risky loans to consumers?
2. Is there an ethical obligation for Countrywide to verify the income of its applicants?
3. What ethical duty does an applicant have when applying for a loan?
4. Could Countrywide's program to offer mortgages to those who otherwise could not buy a home be construed as being socially responsible? Why or why not?

ETHICS

A group of parties injured by the crash of the oil tanker *Exxon Valdez*'s in 1989 brought suit against Exxon charging, among other things, that Exxon was

negligent for allowing the oil tanker to be captained by an employee who had a known history of alcohol abuse. The captain was, in fact, intoxicated at the time of the crash that spilled 11 million gallons of crude oil in Prince William Sound, Alaska. Commercial fisheries were temporarily disabled and permanently damaged as a result of the spill. The jury awarded $5 billion in punitive damages against Exxon. Exxon appealed the judgment on the basis that the damages were grossly excessive. The appellate court upheld the jury's finding, but reduced the punitive damage award by 50 percent.

CASE QUESTIONS

1. What are the ethics of punitive damages awards?
2. Is it ethical to try to bankrupt a company by means of a lawsuit?
3. Should courts be able to reduce punitive damage awards?
4. Is $5 billion excessive against a company as large as Exxon?

CASE SUMMARY 5.5 :: Dodge v. Ford Motor Co., 204 Mich. 459, 170 N.W. 668 (1919)

STAKEHOLDERS' INTERESTS AND CORPORATE SOCIAL RESPONSIBILITY

Henry Ford, majority shareholder of the Ford Motor Company, announced that rather than pay a special dividend to the company's shareholders, he was going to reinvest the accumulated earnings, expanding the company. He stated, "My ambition is to employ still more men, to spread the benefits of this industrial system to the greatest possible number, to help them build up their lives and their homes. To do this we are putting the greatest share of our profits back in the business." He further indicated that he wished to lower the price of the Model T car to make it more accessible to the public. Two minority shareholders, John and Horace Dodge, sued to require payment of the dividend. The Michigan Supreme Court upheld the management's right to make decisions for the benefit of the company (the business judgment rule, discussed in Chapter 16, "Corporations"); however, the court said

that "the corporation is a business, not a charity," finding for the Dodges because Henry Ford's decision was to benefit the public instead of shareholders.

CASE QUESTIONS

1. Should a corporation act solely to maximize shareholder wealth? Should a corporation balance corporate social responsibility with shareholder interests?
2. Were the Dodge brothers primary or secondary stakeholders? Explain.
3. Which moral philosophy approach describes Henry Ford's stated actions? Explain.
4. Although not an issue at trial, the Dodge brothers used the money received to build their own company, Dodge Brothers Company (Dodge Motors), which was later sold to, and became a part of, Chrysler Motors. Many speculate that Henry Ford was actually trying to slow down the formation of the Dodge brothers' new company. If Henry Ford's alleged motive was true, was he acting in an ethical manner?

 Self-Check **ANSWERS**

Principles-Based Approach or Consequences-Based Approach

1. Principles-based approach.
2. Principles-based approach.
3. Consequences-based approach.
4. Principles-based approach.

The plaintiffs, husband and wife, attended a Halloween party dressed as Little Bo Peep (wife) and a sheep (husband). The wife made her husband's costume from long underwear covered with glued-on cotton batting. The husband was covered with cotton batting from head to toe, excluding his face and hands. During the party the husband attempted to smoke a cigarette, and the flame from his lighter ignited the cotton. The husband admitted that he knew that cotton batting burned but emphasized that he did not know "how it burned." His wife also admitted that she knew that cotton could burn, "[but] not burn that fast." She knew her husband smoked and used a cigarette lighter. The husband suffered burns on one-third of his body, and he underwent several surgeries as a consequence of the fire.

The plaintiffs sued the cotton manufacturer for failing to warn that cotton could ignite so easily and that the flames of the burning cotton would spread so quickly. The jury awarded the husband $550,000 and his wife $70,000 in damages. The defendants motioned for a judgment *non obstante veredicto* (JNOV). (A JNOV asks a judge to disregard the jury's verdict and award the judgment to the moving party.)

ENGAGEMENT QUESTIONS

1. Should a judge have the right to overrule a jury? Why have juries if a single person can overrule the entire jury?

2. Is it feasible for companies to put warning labels on their products listing every possible hazard? When should warning labels be required, if ever?

3. The husband regularly smoked and ignored warnings on cigarette packages. Do you think a warning label on the cotton batting would have deterred him from smoking that night?

4. The wife made the costume so if there had been a warning label on the cotton, the husband most likely wouldn't have been aware of it. Would this change anyone's liability?

Law and Commerce

6
CHAPTER

Overview and Language of Contracts

learning objectives

After studying this chapter, students who have mastered the material will be able to:

6-1 Recognize the difference between enforceable contracts and mere agreements.

6-2 Articulate the purpose of contracts and their importance to business.

6-3 Name the required elements of a valid contract.

6-4 Apply the correct source of law to individual contracts.

6-5 Identify and articulate the categories that contracts may be described under.

6-6 Apply the seven categories of contracts and be able to describe individual contracts in seven ways.

The law of contracts is one of the most common and important areas of the law that business owners and managers deal with on a day-to-day basis. Everyone working in a business environment will, in one form or another, deal with contracts throughout his career. Employment contracts, leases, and agreements of sale for assets or land or merchandise are just a few examples of contracts commonly used in business transactions. The simple act of purchasing office supplies from a local merchant is a form of agreement governed by contract law.

Formation and legal enforcement of agreements have been recognized since ancient times. As early as 1780 BC, contracts were being enforced by the Babylonians by virtue of the authority of the Code of Hammurabi. During much of the rule of the Roman Empire, the Justinian Code included the rule *pacta sunt servanda* ("Agreements shall be kept").

Today, contract law is either created by statute or derived from the common law. Many legal scholars, notably Dean Roscoe Pound, have written extensively on the importance of society recognizing legally enforceable promises and providing remedies for those who suffered losses. Consider the consequences of failing to provide for legal enforceability of a promise and its impact on the very fabric of civilized societies.

Since business owners and managers are often involved in day-to-day oversight of various agreements and transactions, understanding contract law reduces risk by limiting liability through the recognition of potential legal issues, crafting an appropriate response, and implementing a system to ensure compliance. Contract law is also essential to structuring business transactions in strategic ways to achieve business objectives without excessive risk.

In this chapter, students will learn:

■ Definitions and categories of various contracts.

■ How the categories of contracts are interpreted and applied.

■ The sources of law that apply to contemporary contracts.

DEFINITION OF A CONTRACT   LO 6-1, 6-2

A contract is more than an agreement between two or more parties. Contracts are *enforceable* agreements between the parties. One generally accepted definition of a contract is a *promise or a set of promises enforceable by law.*[1] Put another way, a contract is simply an **agreement** that a court of

---

[1]For exact wording of the definition, see *Restatement (Second) of Contracts*, § 2.

law will recognize and enforce. Contract law also defines certain circumstances that excuse one or both parties from performing their obligation or enforcing the agreement's promise.

To take a simple example, suppose that Baker hires Downing to paint her apartment. The two agree on price, timing, and paint color. Downing begins to paint the apartment, and while on his lunch break, a pipe breaks and floods the apartment and he is unable to complete the work. Several contract issues are at work in this scenario. First, a court must determine whether Baker and Downing have met all of the elements of a contract (formation). If so, is Downing excused from finishing the job (performance)? Finally, is either party entitled to recover any money from the other (breach and damages)?

Contracts are prevalent in business transactions that range from the sale of a cup of coffee at a diner to the acquisition of the stock of a multinational corporation. Contracts are used to carry out business operations in manufacturing, buying, or selling products and services.

LO 6-3 ELEMENTS OF A CONTRACT

The necessary elements of a contract are simply stated but can be detailed in their interpretation and application:

- *Mutual assent:* There must be an offer and agreement between the parties.
  - Do the parties intend to enter into a contract? Does each party understand what his rights and obligations are?
- *Capacity to contract:* The parties must be of proper age and mental competence.
  - Has each party reached the legal age of consent? Has either party been declared incompetent?
- *Consideration:* There must be a bargained-for exchange of goods and/or services.
  - Have the parties exchanged goods and/or services that were agreed to? Is what has been exchanged recognized under the law as *valuable* consideration?
- *Legal purpose:* The reason and outcome of the contact must be legal.
  - Does the contract itself violate the law? Will the outcome of the contract accomplish a legal purpose?

This is a brief overview of what constitutes a contract. Chapter 7, "Contract Formation," examines each required element in detail.

LO 6-4 SOURCES OF CONTRACT LAW

In general, contracts for *services* (e.g., legal, accounting, or engineering) or *real estate* (such as an agreement of sale for an office building or a lease for a commercial retail space) are governed by **state common law.** Contracts for *goods* or products (defined as items that are movable at the time of identification in the contract) are governed by **state statutory law** based on the Uniform Commercial Code (UCC).[2] The UCC also covers transactions related to leasing of equipment. Note that the UCC provisions for sales and leases are covered extensively in Chapter 9, "Contracts for the Sale of Goods."

Some contracts involve terms for both goods *and* services. These are known as **hybrid contracts.** In a hybrid contract, the source of law is established by determining the *predominant thrust* of the contract subject matter. If the contract is predominantly for services,

---

[2]Recall from Chapter 1, "Legal Foundations," that the UCC is a "model" statute drafted by the National Conference of Commissioners of Uniform State Laws (NCCUSL). Each state legislature makes its own decisions about whether to adopt the UCC in total, in part, or not at all. Louisiana is the only state to have rejected the UCC in its entirety.

The Uniform Electronic Transactions Act (UETA) is best thought of as a procedural model law that applies to transactions as long as the parties to a contract agree to use electronic commerce for the transaction. This means that the UETA does not create substantive rights or protections (such as providing consumers with a right to sue) but rather gives legal recognition to certain electronic media. Whether the parties agreed to conduct a transaction by electronic means is determined from the context and surrounding circumstances, including the parties' conduct. The UETA essentially elevates electronic signatures and records to the same legal status as that accorded to traditional signatures and paper records, memorandums, notices, and so forth. The law covers both e-commerce sale-of-goods transactions and the use of electronic communication alongside paper contracts.

The UETA gives formal legal recognition of electronic records, signatures, and contracts by providing that (1) a record or signature may not be denied legal effect or enforceability solely because it is in electronic form; (2) a contract may not be denied legal effect or enforceability solely because an electronic record was used in its information; (3) if a law requires a record to be in writing, an electronic record satisfies the law; and (4) if a law requires a signature, an electronic signature satisfies the law. Currently, 47 states have adopted the UETA in some form.

and the goods are incidental, then the contract is governed by the common law. If, on the other hand, goods are the main feature of the contract, and the services come incidentally, then the contract is governed by statutory law. For example, Huxley is a manager charged with the task of hiring a portrait artist to paint the portrait of the founder of the company to be displayed in the lobby. Huxley hires Pablo, and Pablo paints the portrait. This is a hybrid contract because it involves services (of the artist) and goods (Huxley gets the canvas, paint, etc., at the conclusion of the services). However, in this case the goods are *incidental* to the services; thus, it is primarily a contract for services and is governed by the common law. In determining the source of law governing a hybrid contract, courts will examine (1) *allocation of price* in the contract (value of goods versus value of services) and (2) *uniqueness* of the services (Did they require special talent, such as that of the portrait artist above?). The more unique the service, the more likely it is that the contract is covered by the common law.

 Self-Check Source of Law

Which source of law governs each contract?

1. A contract for the sale of an office building from Abel to NewCo.

2. A contract providing for installation of networking cable in an office facility where the materials are $5,000 and the labor is $20,000.

3. A consulting contract between a management consulting firm and a software development company.

4. The sale of several completed sculptures from an artist to a retail art dealer for a total of $10,000.

5. A contract between the owner of a building and a painting company to paint the building's lobby over a holiday weekend for $5,000. The owner agrees to supply all of the paint.

Answers to this Self-Check are provided at the end of the chapter.

- A contract is an *enforceable agreement* that obligates the parties to perform, as compared to a mere agreement with no enforceability.
- An enforceable contract has four necessary elements: mutual assent, capacity to contract, consideration, and legal purpose.
- Contracts for services or real estate are governed by state common law, while contracts for goods are governed by state statutory law based on the Uniform Commercial Code.
- Contracts for a combination of goods and services are governed by the source that applies to the most predominant part of the contract.

LO 6-5, 6-6

Categories of Contracts

Because the subject of contracts is so vast, it is useful to categorize the different types of contracts in order to understand various forms of promises and agreements. This is *not* to say that these categories are mutually exclusive. In fact, all contracts may be classified up to seven ways.

Written versus Oral Contracts

While the word *contract* is often used to describe a written document, many contracts are not in writing and yet are enforceable. Any agreement, oral or written, may result in a binding contract so long as it meets certain requirements. Some contracts, however, are *required* to be in writing in order to be enforceable. These contracts are defined by the statute of frauds, which is covered in Chapter 7, "Contract Formation."

Bilateral versus Unilateral Contracts

A **bilateral contract** involves two promises and two performances. Most contracts are bilateral contracts. To take a simple example, suppose Ginny says to Harry: "I offer to pay you $5,000 for your delivery van." Harry responds, "I accept." On the following day, Ginny shows up with a check for $5,000. Harry signs over title to the delivery van to Ginny. Ginny's promise was to pay $5,000 for the delivery van. Harry's promise was to sell the delivery van for $5,000. Ginny's performance was to pay Harry via check for $5,000. Harry's performance was to turn over title of the delivery van to Ginny.

A **unilateral contract** involves one promise, followed by one performance, which then triggers a *second* performance from the offeror (the party making the offer). A second promise is not made, and the contract only becomes enforceable if the action specified in the original promise is performed. Perhaps the best example of a unilateral contract occurs when the offer is in the form of a reward. For example, if Jonah places several reward posters in his neighborhood and offers to pay $500 to anyone who finds his missing dog, this is an example of a unilateral offer. Jonah has made one promise, but there has been no second promise made by any of the neighbors. Therefore, the only way that a neighbor may accept the offer made by Jonah is to *perform* by finding the dog and delivering him to Jonah as specified in the promise (via the reward posters). Once a neighbor has performed, Jonah is now obligated to perform his promise (to pay a $500 reward). Of course, if no one performs, Jonah may not sue his neighbors for recovery because no return promise was ever made.

> **KEY** POINT
>
> The category of a contract will directly impact the parties' rights and obligations. Courts will look first for explicit language in the contract but will examine the parties' intent when such language is missing or ambiguous.

FACT SUMMARY   Chattler applied for a U.S. passport and requested an expedited processing procedure outlined in the application materials. The expedited processing option was included as part of the application's instructions, which stated that expedited requests would be processed by a government passport agency in three business days in exchange for a fee of $60. Chattler paid the expedited fee and filed her application on June 11, 2007. After three months, the passport had still not arrived, and Chattler applied, in person, for a second time. Chattler received her passport in time to fulfill her travel plans, and the government did not dispute that her first expedited request was not processed in the three-day time period. Rather than requesting a refund of the fee, Chattler initiated legal action for, among other allegations, breach of contract. Chattler asserted that the expedited process was a valid offer that she accepted by paying the $60 fee. The trial court held for the government, and Chattler appealed.

SYNOPSIS OF DECISION AND OPINION   The U.S. court of appeals ruled in favor of the government. The court reasoned that no express contract was formed by the timing provision in the passport application. The court cited precedent that maintained that obligations created by statute are not contracts in the usual sense due to the lack of a bilateral exchange. The court also held that the statutes' language—stating that the expedited process "will," rather than *must*—does not explicitly create an underlying obligation.

WORDS OF THE COURT: Mutual Intent   "An express contract with the government requires proof of 'mutual intent to contract, including an offer, an acceptance, and consideration. A contract with the United States also requires that the Government representative who entered or ratified the agreement had actual authority to bind the United States.'. . . Where rights and obligations are prescribed by statute and regulations rather than determined through the mechanics of a bilateral exchange, there is no contract in the usual sense of that word. . . . The word 'will' is often used in this definitional way, without creating an underlying obligation. We also note the use of the passive voice, i.e., 'will be processed,' makes it less likely that the government intended to be bound."

Case Questions

1. Is the precedent that statutory obligations do not truly create contracts sound as the federal government continues to grow and promulgate more and more regulations?

2. Had the government substituted more proactive words for the words "will be processed," could the court have come to a different decision?

3. Chattler could have accepted the government's offer to drop the suit, write a letter requesting a refund, and be done with the matter. What would have been lost had she withdrawn her suit?

Express versus Implied versus Quasi-Contracts   An **express contract** is created when the parties have knowingly and intentionally agreed on the promises and performances. An **implied contract** is one in which the agreement is reached by the parties' *actions* rather than their words. For example, when you order food at a restaurant, the server, after taking your order, does not ask if you promise to pay for the food at the end of the meal. Your act of ordering food and consuming it will create an obligation to pay. The contract was formed as an implied contract *in fact*. In Case 6.1, the court must determine whether an express or implied contract exists between a citizen and the federal government.

In some cases where no express or implied contract exists, a party may still be able to recover losses based on a **quasi-contract.** The law permits quasi-contracts to be enforceable when one party suffers losses as a result of another party's unjust enrichment. This theory of contract is based on an implied-in-law recovery, whereby one party does not actually request a certain service but still benefits from the services rendered. Suppose that an unconscious patient is brought into a hospital, the hospital administers aid, and the patient survives. The hospital will be able to bill the patient for the reasonable costs of its services even though the patient never asked for or agreed to the hospital's assistance. If the patient was able to avoid payment, then he would be receiving a benefit that he did not earn or deserve. This is unjust enrichment. The law will impose a contract based on the benefit the patient received.

For example, suppose that Jon is at home when a commercial paint truck stops at his house and a painter starts painting the exterior by mistake because the job order had the wrong address. Jon sees the mistake being made but says nothing. When the job is completed, does Jon have to pay for the work completed? Yes, because he has acted in a way that brought him a benefit that he did not earn or deserve at the expense of another. This too is unjust enrichment. Jon had the opportunity to mitigate damages and failed to do so. A quasi-contract will be enforced.

Recovery under a quasi-contract theory is also possible when an express contract is unenforceable for some legal reason but one of the parties has gained a benefit. For example, Contractor is hired to install a new floor in ManufactureCo's warehouse. Contractor rips out the old floor, pours the concrete, and waits overnight for the concrete to dry. Before Contractor can install the new floor, a fire destroys the warehouse. Although the contract is now unenforceable due to impossibility (discussed in the next chapter), Contractor may still recover for services of demolition to the old floor since this work directly benefited ManufactureCo. Quasi-contracts are frequently referred to as being *implied in law*.

In Case 6.2, the court must determine whether unjust enrichment has occurred in order to support a quasi-contract.

Valid, Void, Voidable, or Unenforceable Contracts

When a contract has the necessary elements, it is said to be a **valid contract.** A **void contract** is an agreement that lacks one or more of the basic required elements of a contract or that has not been formed in conformance with the law from the *outset* of the agreement and, thus, cannot be enforced by either party. For example, a contract for the sale of an illegal narcotic is void as prohibited by statute and is against public policy despite the fact that two parties may have agreed to the sale. This contract lacks the element of legal purpose. In another example, if a person were to enter into a contract with a person who has been adjudged insane or incompetent, that contract would be void because one party lacked the capacity to contract.

Even when two parties have formed a seemingly valid contract, sometimes the agreement may still *not* be fully enforceable. A **voidable contract** is one that one party may, at its option, either disaffirm or enforce. For example, suppose that Ally, a minor,[3] purchases a used car from a local car dealer. Because the law allows minors (and guardians) the right to cancel a contract up until the time that the minor turns 18, Ally may choose to disaffirm the transaction and return the car or to enforce it by keeping the car until she turns 18. When a party chooses to legally disaffirm a contract that was voidable, this is known as *avoiding* the contract. An **unenforceable contract,** on the other hand, is one that meets the elements required by law for an otherwise binding agreement but is subject to a legal defense, such as the statutory requirement that certain contracts be in writing in order to be enforceable. For example, if two adults enter into an oral agreement involving the sale of a car with a price of $499, that agreement will be valid. If, however, the price is $500, that agreement is required to be in writing to be enforceable under the statute of frauds.

Legal Speak ›))
Mitigate Damages The duty to make reasonable attempts to minimize or avoid injury. Also referred to as *mitigation*.

Legal Speak ›))
Due Diligence Most often used in business or real estate transactions, due diligence is an investigation period provided to one party for the purposes of examining the suitability of a transaction prior to finalizing it.

---

[3]In the context of contract law, almost all states define a minor as one who has not yet reached his 18th birthday.

FACT SUMMARY Georgia Malone & Company (MaloneCo) was a real estate brokerage firm that entered into a confidentiality agreement with CenterRock Realty, LLC, related to CenterRock's potential purchase of a group of buildings in midtown Manhattan. Rieder was the managing member of CenterRock. The agreement required CenterRock to treat all information provided to it by MaloneCo (e.g., financial projections, property conditions) as confidential and to pay MaloneCo a commission fee in the event that CenterRock purchased the property. After considering the confidential information provided by MaloneCo, CenterRock entered into a contract for the sale of the property. Part of the agreement allowed CenterRock to terminate the transaction during its due diligence (inspection) period. On the last day of the due diligence period, CenterRock terminated the transaction. Ultimately, the property was sold to another party through Rosewood Realty Group, one of MaloneCo's competitors, and MaloneCo received no commission.

MaloneCo brought suit against CenterRock, its principals, and others, alleging that CenterRock's principals had sold the confidential information, provided to them by MaloneCo, to Rosewood for $150,000 and that the information had been used by Rosewood in selling the property to its own client. The trial court dismissed some allegations in MaloneCo's complaint and upheld others. The parties appealed.

SYNOPSIS OF DECISION AND OPINION The New York appellate court found in favor of MaloneCo. The court ruled that CenterRock's principals induced MaloneCo into performing valuable functions with reasonable assurances of a contract but instead used MaloneCo's work product for personal gain. The court held that an unjust-enrichment claim is intended to prevent one party from unjustly profiting at the expense of another party. In this case, the confidential information provided to CenterRock's principals was part of a sales transaction that ultimately cheated MaloneCo out of its commission.

WORDS OF THE COURT: Unjust Enrichment "Unjust enrichment is a quasi contract theory of recovery, and is an obligation imposed by equity to prevent injustice, in the absence of an actual agreement between the parties concerned. The plaintiff must show that the other party was enriched, at plaintiff's expense, and that 'it is against equity and good conscience to permit [the other party] to retain what is sought to be recovered.'

"Further . . . a claim will not be supported unless there is a connection or relationship between the parties that could have caused reliance or inducement on the plaintiff's part. . . . Prior cases from this Court and the other Departments have held that an unjust enrichment claim can only be sustained if the services were performed at the defendant's behest. MaloneCo contends that [the principals affirmed their] interest in completing the transaction and assured MaloneCo that it would receive its commission, even if the deal was not completed. Based on these assurances, MaloneCo continued to collect and provide [the principals] and CenterRock with the confidential information. Thus, MaloneCo has sufficiently pleaded that there was direct contact and a relationship with [the principals] that could have caused reliance or inducement."

Case Questions

1. Was MaloneCo justified in relying on the principals' assurances that CenterRock was continuing to pursue the original contract?

2. The court requires a connection or relationship for a quasi-contract claim. How close a connection or relationship must be shown?

3. The court described a quasi-contract as "an obligation imposed by equity to prevent injustice." Explain how equity applies to quasi-contracts.

Issues such as legality, capacity, the statute of frauds, and public policy are discussed in Chapter 7, "Contract Formation."

Figure 6.1 shows how to determine whether a contract is valid, void, voidable or unenforceable.

Formal versus Informal Contracts   A **formal contract** is one that meets one or more specific requirements of construction. Most contracts, while they require evidence that the elements are met, do not require a specific format or ceremony. One could write

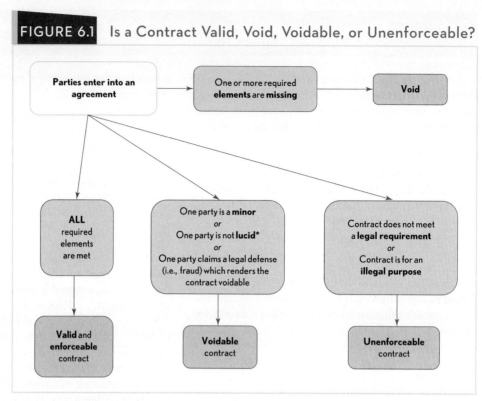

FIGURE 6.1   Is a Contract Valid, Void, Voidable, or Unenforceable?

Parties enter into an agreement

One or more required **elements** are **missing** → **Void**

ALL required elements are met → **Valid** and **enforceable** contract

One party is a **minor**
or
One party is not **lucid***
or
One party claims a legal defense (i.e., fraud) which renders the contract voidable
→ **Voidable** contract

Contract does not meet a **legal requirement**
or
Contract is for an **illegal purpose**
→ **Unenforceable** contract

*Lucid means sane and clear thinking. A party who is otherwise mentally competent may be deemed 'not lucid' when temporarily unable to think clearly due to severe stress, depression, pain, or some other cause. This is discussed in detail in Chapter 7, "Contract Formation."

a contract on a piece of scrap paper, and the courts will enforce it. There are, however, instances in which statutory law requires that a contract be formal. Negotiable instruments are formal contracts. For example, checks that businesses and individuals write when transacting business, while they need not be on specific bank-produced forms, do have to meet specific written content requirements to be valid. A second and more obvious example of a formal contract is a contract under seal. In early England and in the early years of America, when a written contract was formed, hot wax would be applied to the document and a seal would be applied to the wax, leaving a distinct imprint. This formality made the contract legitimate. Over the years the use of wax became obsolete, and the need for a seal diminished. By statute, however, certain contracts continue to require a seal to be enforceable under state laws. Most of these requirements pertain to real estate–related documents such as deeds and mortgages. The modern seal simply consists of the word *seal*[4] preprinted in the contract at the signature lines. Most people probably don't even notice the seal.

If a contract is not required to be under seal by statute or required to possess a certain form or language, it will be considered an **informal contract,** regardless of its size or importance.

Executed versus Executory Contracts   An **executed contract** is a contract that is completed. When one party has completed all of her obligations under a contract, her

---

[4]On some contracts, the letters *L.S.* or the Latin words *locus sigilli* will appear. *Locus sigilli,* or its abbreviation *L.S.,* translates to "the place of the seal" and indicated where the wax was to be applied. Modern courts accept *locus sigilli* or *L.S.* as an acceptable seal when printed on a contract's signature line.

obligations are said to be executed. An **executory contract** is one that is not yet completed. When one party still has duties to perform under a contract, we describe those duties as being executory. Suppose that Malcom agrees to sell his bicycle to Jon for $2,000. Malcom will deliver the bike to Jon and will be paid $1,000 on delivery and $1,000 after 30 days. At delivery and payment of the first $1,000, we would describe Malcom's obligations as executed, Jon's obligations as executory, and the contract as executory. Thirty days later, when the second $1,000 is paid, both Malcom's and Jon's obligations are considered executed and the contract is executed.

Entire versus Divisible Contracts   An **entire contract** is one in which each component of the contract is dependent on every other component. Failure to perform one part usually voids the contract. This requirement is frequently contained in specific language in the contract. This interdependence of contract obligations could also void a contract with no specific contract language. For example, suppose that Computer Place orders custom-sized nuts and bolts needed for parts assembly but the hardware manufacturer only delivers the bolts. Assume that the hardware industry will manufacture custom nuts and bolts only in matched amounts. Those bolts are useless to Computer Place because the nuts are not readily available and bolts are useless without the corresponding nuts. Computer Place will be able to refuse the bolts and have no obligation under the contract. Here the nuts and bolts are dependent on each other. A **divisible contract** is one that can be broken up into independent parts, each part able to stand alone. Suppose that Aimee orders some clothing from an online catalog. She orders three pairs of jeans, three T-shirts, and three pairs of boots. If the jeans and T-shirts are delivered correctly but only one pair of boots arrives, she is still able to use the jeans and boots. The contract will not be voided but will simply be adjusted in price for the missing items. Here each item is independent of every other item and can stand alone. But what if Aimee orderes a three-piece suit for work. If only the vest and skirt of the suit are delivered, these items are not usable *as a suit* without the jacket because a business suit requires all of its components. The order of the suit is considered an entire contract, and she may void the suit delivery entirely.

Divisible contracts are often referred to as *severable contracts* in many states. Frequently, a contract may include a severability clause saying that if one part of the contract becomes illegal or impossible to perform, the remaining contract components remain in effect. This clearly shows that the intent of the contracting parties is the creation of a divisible contract. Case 6.3 involves the interpretation of a severability clause and a determination of whether a contract is to be interpreted as entire or divisible.

 Self-Check   Categories of Contracts 1

Choose the category that applies to each contract.

1. Paul buys a snack from the Student Union Sandwich Shop. (Express/Implied/Quasi)

2. Amanda is going out of town until Sunday and tells Mike that if he mows her lawn, she'll pay him $50. (Offer of a bilateral contract/Offer of a unilateral contract)

3. Amanda is going out of town until Sunday and tells Mike that if he mows her lawn, she'll pay him $50. Mike mows her lawn on Saturday. (Executed/Executory)

4. ColdCo enters into a contract to purchase 800 commercial air-conditioning units at $13,000 each from a manufacturer. (Formal/Informal)

5. Beth's Produce Mart orders five bushels of apples, five bushels of peaches, five bunches of bananas, and five bushels of oranges from Todd's Fruit Farm. (Entire/Divisible)

Answers to this Self-Check are provided at the end of the chapter.

FACT SUMMARY Advanced Technology Services (ATS), Inc., sells a document software imaging program called OptiDoc. Waldron and Heath were employees at ATS who signed an agreement with three components: a noncompetition covenant, a nonsolicitation agreement, and a nondisclosure agreement. The agreement also contained a severability clause. Waldron and Heath resigned from ATS and soon launched their own company, which sold DocUnity, a direct competitor to OptiDoc. ATS brought a lawsuit against Waldron and Heath and sought to enforce their ATS agreement. Waldron and Heath moved to dismiss the suit, arguing that the noncompetition agreement was too broad and therefore unenforceable. Waldron and Heath also contended that because the noncompetition covenant was unenforceable, the entire agreement was unenforceable as well because the contract's term "Specified Activities" required reference to the other two agreement components.

SYNOPSIS OF DECISION AND OPINION The U.S. district court held for ATS. The court ruled that although the noncompetition covenant was unenforceable, the severability clause was enforceable based on the intent of the parties. The illegality of the noncompetition clause did not diminish the value or effectiveness of the remaining agreements.

WORDS OF THE COURT: Divisible Contracts and Severability "The Non-Solicitation and Non-Disclosure agreements can stand on their own as separate agreements; because the parties did not take the time to redefine the term "Specified Activities" each time does not mean that the parties did not intend to give any effect to the severability provision to which they explicitly agreed. When determining whether a contract is severable or not, the Court must consider the intention of the parties. The Court believes that the contract's plain language makes clear that the parties intended to create a severable contract."

Case Questions

1. Even if the contract did not contain a specific severability clause, could the court still have found the contract divisible, leaving the remaining legal agreements in place?

2. How could ATS have worded the agreements so that the question of severability would not have been an issue?

3. If the court had determined that the parties' intent in this contract was that it be entire and not divisible, what would the decision have been? Explain.

 Self-Check   Categories of Contracts 2

Identify each of the categories that describe the following contract.

Professor Blackstone decides to purchase a new bicycle. After choosing a bike costing $3,800 with the advice and assistance of the shop owner, the shop spends an hour making adjustments and fitting the bike to Blackstone's specifications. Blackstone pays cash and receives a receipt. Professor Blackstone rides the bike out of the shop to go home.

Answers to this Self-Check are provided at the end of the chapter.

CONCEPT SUMMARY Categories and Types of Contracts

■ All contract can be described in seven ways.

■ Contracts will be *written* or *oral*. Oral contracts, while harder to prove, are valid and legal unless required to be in writing by statute.

■ Contracts will be *bilateral* when formed by an exchange of promises or *unilateral* when a promise requires acceptance by a required performance.

- Contracts are *express* when the parties knowingly and intentionally come to an agreement. *Implied* contracts arise from the party's conduct, and *quasi*-contracts are imposed by the law in the absence of an express or implied agreement in order to remedy a party's losses due to another party's unjust enrichment at its expense.

- Contracts will be *valid*—a fully enforceable contract; *void*—a contract missing a required element, so the courts do not consider it a contract; *voidable,* a seemingly valid contract that one party has the right to declare void; or *unenforceable,* a contract that does not meet a statutory requirement of construction.

- Contracts will be *formal,* requiring a seal or some specific elements, or *informal,* having no requirements other than the four basic elements of the contract. Whether a contract is formal or informal does not refer to the size or importance of the contract.

- Contracts are either *executed,* meaning completed, or *executory,* meaning still ongoing. These terms may refer to the contract or the individual party's performance regarding the contract.

- Contracts may be *entire,* meaning that the whole contract depends upon the completion of each part of the contract, or *divisible,* meaning that some parts of the contract could drop out or not be performed but this will not affect the rest of the contract. Divisible contracts are also referred to as *severable* contracts.

KEY TERMS

Agreement p. 151   Any meeting of the minds resulting in mutual assent to do or refrain from doing something.

State common law p. 152   The governing body of law of contracts for services or real estate.

State statutory law p. 152   The body of law governing contracts for goods or products; based on the Uniform Commercial Code.

Hybrid contract p. 152   A contract that involves terms for both goods and services; the source of law is established by determining the predominant thrust of the subject matter.

Bilateral contract p. 154   A contract involving two promises and two performances.

Unilateral contract p. 154   A contract involving one promise followed by one performance, which then triggers a second performance from the offeror.

Express contract p. 155   A contract that is created when the parties have knowingly and intentionally agreed on the promises and performances.

Implied contract p. 155   A contract in which the agreement is reached by the parties' actions rather than their words.

Quasi-contract p. 155   A classification that permits a contract to be enforceable in cases where no express or implied contract exists and one party suffers losses as a result of another party's unjust enrichment.

Valid contract p. 156   A contract that has the necessary elements and, thus, can be enforceable.

Void contract p. 156   A contract that lacks one or more of the basic required elements of a contract or that has not been formed in conformance with the law from the outset of the agreement and, thus, cannot be enforced by either party.

Voidable contract p. 156   A contract that one party may, at its option, either disaffirm or enforce.

Unenforceable contract p. 156   A contract that meets the elements required by law for an otherwise binding agreement but is subject to a legal defense.

Formal contract p. 157   A contract that meets one or more specific requirements of construction.

Informal contract p. 158   A contract that is not required to be under seal by statute or to possess a certain form or language.

Executed contract p. 158   A contract that is completed.

Executory contract p. 159   A contract that is not yet completed.

Entire contract p. 159   A contract in which each component of the contract is dependent on every other component.

Divisible contract p. 159   A contract that can be broken up into independent parts, each part able to stand alone.

TractorCo manufactures tractors for consumer and industrial use. Its consumer lines consist of small, lower-horsepower units used by homeowners and small businesses, and its industrial line features large, powerful tractors designed for farm and ranch use. TractorCo's least expensive tractor retails for $999, and its most expensive tractor can cost as much as $50,000. Single commercial-line tractors may be purchased for cash, meaning that the purchaser must arrange its own financing. TractorCo sells the industrial-line tractors only to commercial retailers for resale. Multiunit sales of three or more industrial-line tractors may be made on credit with payment due within 90 days of delivery.

1. When an individual sale is made to a homeowner, when would the contract be considered fully executed? When a sale to a retailer involves credit, when is the contract fully executed?
2. With regard to both the consumer and industrial lines, would the contracts be considered bilateral or unilateral?
3. FarmMart is negotiating a purchase of 20 top-of-the-line industrial tractors for a total price of $1 million. Would the contract be required to be formal and under seal?
4. With regard to both the consumer and industrial lines, would the contracts be considered express, implied, or quasi?

TractorCo's sales manager is negotiating the contract with FarmMart and has called you regarding a request that FarmMart has made. FarmMart would like to add the following language to the contract:

Sale and delivery of the twenty tractors shall be made in five monthly installments of four tractors per month with delivery and acceptance on the first day of the month for five consecutive months beginning on [a date to be determined]. Each installment shall be considered exclusive of the other installments. Should, at any time during this contract, sales drop such that FarmMart has in stock six or more tractors unsold, FarmMart retains the right to cancel future deliveries without penalty.

Draft a memorandum to the vice president of sales outlining the various issues and ramifications that inclusion of the requested language would create, if any. A sample answer may be found on this textbook's website at www.mhhe.com/melvinleb2e.

UNILATERAL CONTRACT

Chambers worked for Travelers as a managing director. Questions arose regarding her management style and effectiveness, and she was fired. Among her claims against Travelers, she claimed that she was due a bonus earned. In February 2007, Travelers provided Chambers a Total Compensation Summary for the year that included a bonus of $30,000. The summary clearly stated that bonuses were at the discretion of Travelers. In September 2007, her boss provided Chambers a written performance review, giving her positive ratings in every performance category. The next month, in response to employee complaints, a climate survey was administered to the employees whom she supervised that came back extremely negative. She was also found to have irregularities in various expense reports, and in January 2008, she was terminated. Chambers alleges that Travelers' failure to pay a $30,000 bonus for her work during 2007 breaching a unilateral employment contract that she accepted by her performance.

CASE QUESTIONS

1. Had Chambers performed her job well, the climate survey come back positive, and no irregularities occurred in her expense reports but she was still terminated due to cutbacks, could she have compelled Travelers to pay her the bonus?
2. Was Travelers' bonus statement in the compensation summary a unilateral offer that could be accepted by performance?

VOID CONTRACT

Rochon Corporation lost the municipal general-contract bidding contest to construct the Lofts at Farmer's Market for the city of St. Paul to Shaw-Lundquist Associates. When the city opened the sealed bids, Shaw-Lundquist appeared to be the clear winner. But Shaw-Lundquist discovered that it had bid $619,200 lower than it had intended due to a clerical error. Bidding instructions included the following: "A bid may not be modified, withdrawn, or canceled by the Bidder for a period of sixty (60) days following the time and date designated for the receipt of bids, and each Bidder so agrees in submitting a bid." Nevertheless, the city allowed Shaw-Lundquist to change its bid, raising it to cover not only the $619,200 error but adding $89,211 more. Still, Shaw-Lundquist's raised bid was lower than Rochon's bid, and the city awarded Shaw-Lundquist the contract for $8,041,411. State common law long held

that a contract entered into in violation of competitive bidding laws is void. The state supreme court had previously stated that a competitive bidding contract is void even "without any showing of actual fraud or an intent to commit fraud, if a procedure has been followed which emasculates the safeguards of competitive bidding."

CASE QUESTIONS

1. The city claimed that it benefited the public by allowing the bid change because it resulted in monetary savings for the city. Does this explanation justify the city's disregard of established precedent? Can the court of appeals disregard established state precedent?
2. Shaw-Lundquist was able to prove that its original bid was wrong due to a legitimate clerical error. Should this have mattered?
3. Why is it good policy to not permit amendments of bids in competitive bidding situations?

IMPLIED CONTRACTS

Forest Park formulated a concept for a television show called *Housecall,* in which a doctor, after being expelled from the medical community for treating patients who could not pay, moved to Malibu, California, and became a "concierge" doctor for the rich and famous. Forest Park created a written series treatment for the idea, including character biographies, themes, and story lines. It mailed this written material to Alex Sepiol, who worked for USA Network. A meeting was then held at which Forest Park explained its concept. It was common practice in the industry for writers and creators to pitch creative ideas to prospective purchasers with the object of selling those ideas for compensation. Sepiol admitted that before hearing the idea for *Housecall,* he had never heard of "concierge" doctors, or doctors who make house calls for wealthy patients, and "thought it was a fascinating

concept for a television show." The parties communicated for a week, and then no further contact occurred. A little less than four years later, USA Network produced and aired a television show called *Royal Pains,* in which a doctor, after being expelled from the medical community for treating patients who could not pay, became a concierge doctor for the rich and famous in the Hamptons, an extremely affluent community on Long Island in New York. Forest Park had no prior knowledge of *Royal Pains,* did not consent to its production, and received no compensation from USA Network for the use of its idea for the show. Forest Park sued, claiming breach of contract.

CASE QUESTIONS

1. Who wins and why?
2. What allows Forest Park to argue that this is an implied contract?

UNENFORCEABLE CONTRACTS

Mary Kay Morrow was hired by Hallmark in 1982. At the start of 2002, while Morrow was working as an

associate product manager, Hallmark adopted, effective January 5, 2002, a policy applicable to its employees called the Hallmark Dispute Resolution Program.

This policy provided that if an employee continued to work for Hallmark after the policy became effective, the employee would thereby be deemed to have agreed to submit to the company's procedures for resolving claims against the company, which included binding arbitration in lieu of litigation. Hallmark reserved the right to unilaterally make changes and retained the right to select the arbitrator. Morrow received a copy of the policy, and she continued working for Hallmark through and after the effective date of January 5, 2002. On April 8, 2003, Hallmark terminated Morrow's employment. Morrow claims that Hallmark discriminated against her because of her age and retaliated against her for complaining about Hallmark policies. Hallmark's position is that Morrow was terminated for poor work performance after failed attempts to improve her performance through coaching and a performance improvement plan. Hallmark seeks to enforce the binding arbitration provision, and Morrow contends that arbitration should not be compelled in this case.

CASE QUESTIONS

1. Employment agreements for binding arbitration are valid only if agreed to. Should Morrow's continued employment be considered an agreement to the Hallmark Dispute Resolution Program terms?
2. Should the binding arbitration provision of the Hallmark Dispute Resolution Program be found enforceable or unenforceable? Why or why not?

CASE SUMMARY 6.5 :: Matrix Realty Group, Inc. v. Food Management Group and Bronx Donut Bakery, Inc., Summary Order (2d Cir. 2011)

DIVISIBLE CONTRACTS

Matrix Realty Group, Inc., appealed a decision of the Southern District Court of New York that affirmed an order of the Bankruptcy Court for the Southern District of New York, which found Matrix liable to Food Management Group, LLC, et al. and Bronx Donut Bakery, Inc. (debtors), for breach of contract and awarded damages in the amount of $9,196,114.11. Matrix had contracted with the debtors to purchase several assets, primarily Dunkin' Donuts franchises and franchise agreements. Each asset was separately listed and separately priced. After the contract was agreed to, but before performance was to occur, Matrix sent a letter to the debtors informing them that it would not perform under the contract and asking for a return of its deposit. Matrix made a similar statement to the bankruptcy court. The debtors showed that they were ready, willing, and able to perform the bulk of the contract.

CASE QUESTIONS

1. Should the U.S. court of appeals affirm or reverse the district court's decision?
2. Was the contract entire or divisible? Explain.

CASE SUMMARY 6.6 :: Stevens & Wilkinson of South Carolina, Inc., et al. v. City of Columbia et al., 721 S.E.2d 455, 396 S.C. 338 (2011)

EXISTENCE OF A CONTRACT

The city of Columbia entered into a memorandum of understanding (MOU) with members of a development team in preparation for the construction of a hotel near the Columbia Metropolitan Convention Center. When the city gave the project to another team approximately one year later, some members of the original development team filed suit against the city for breach of the MOU and other causes of action. The city claimed that the MOU was a framework for anticipated future contracts but not a contract itself. The plaintiffs, the development team, claimed that the MOU was a contract that the city breached. The city based its theory on the premise that the parties would be bound in the future by the written agreements contemplated by the MOU, not by the MOU itself. The MOU supported this theory, as it referred to numerous agreements that were to be negotiated after the parties signed the MOU. The plaintiff's theory was that the parties chose to use the classic contract language "in consideration of the foregoing and the mutual promises contained herein, and other valuable consideration the sufficiency and receipt of which are hereby acknowledged, the parties agree as follows." The MOU also contained provisions excluding liability for certain actions. For example, the MOU stated, "[I]f the City determines that it is not feasible to proceed with the Hotel project it shall have no liability under this MOU." The exclusion of liability under one circumstance is some evidence that the parties intended there to be liability under the MOU in other circumstances. Additionally, one plaintiff corporation submitted affidavits from three of its employees stating they intended the MOU to be a contract and "never would have agreed to put in the effort necessary to develop the Hotel if [they] did not consider the MOU to form a contract."

CASE QUESTION

1. Is the MOU a contract? Why or why not?

 Self-Check **ANSWERS**

Source of Law

1. Common law (real estate).
2. Hybrid contract governed by common law based on (1) price allocation weighted to services and (2) uniqueness of services.
3. Common law (services).
4. Statutory law (sale of goods).
5. Common law (services) because no goods were sold (owner supplied the paint).

Categories of Contracts 1

1. Implied.
2. Offer of a unilateral contract.
3. The contract is executory on Saturday. (Mike's duties are executed on Saturday, but the contract itself is executory until he is paid.)
4. Informal. (It is unlikely that there are any statutory requirements in any states that mandate that a contract between two private businesses be under seal.)
5. Divisible.

Categories of Contracts 2

1. The contract is express due to the specific agreement between Professor Blackstone and the shop owner.
2. The contract is executed because all parties have completed their contractual obligations.
3. The contract is bilateral because it was arrived at through an exchange of promises.
4. The contract is entire because the bike would have likely been unusable if missing most parts.
5. The contract is written as evidenced by the receipt. (We will see in the next chapter that the contract needed to be in writing because it is a sales contract for over $500.)
6. The contract is informal because there are no requirements that the sale of a bicycle be under seal.
7. The contract is valid as there are no legal restrictions that prohibit the sale of the bike, the parties are of legal age and mental capacity (a reasonable assumption for this exercise), there was mutual agreement to purchase the bike, and there was a bargained-for exchange.

7
CHAPTER

Contract Formation

n Chapter 6, "Overview and Language of Contracts," we saw that contracts are more than mere agreements. From the beginning of any business negotiation with an intent to form a contractual relationship, the parties must understand the steps and procedural requirements necessary to ultimately result in an enforceable and legally binding contract. Failure to do so can expose a company to financial and legal liability.

In this chapter, students will learn:

- The legal requirements for forming an enforceable contract.
- Circumstances that can negatively affect contract formation.
- The writing requirements that apply to certain contracts.
- Use of contracts to reduce legal risk.

OVERVIEW OF A CONTRACT TRANSACTION

Before learning the individual components required to form a contract and the rules that govern the parties, it is helpful to consider a typical contract transaction from a macro perspective. First, a contract is formed when two or more parties agree to a particular set of terms. One party typically agrees to provide services, real estate, or goods in exchange for something of value (usually money). An agreement is recognized as legally binding so long as it meets certain *formation* requirements. Second, after the formation requirements are met, the contract is governed by laws that set out requirements for *enforceability* of the agreement. Finally, assuming that the contract was properly formed and is legally enforceable, the law sets out rules and consequences related to how the parties fulfill their obligations to one another. This is known as *performance* (or nonperformance) of the agreement. Table 7.1 provides an overview of the contract transaction.

For example, suppose that Ahab agrees to provide ship repair services to White Whale Industries. Using e-mail exchanges, the parties negotiate a monthly fee and specify that Ahab is to repair and maintain White Whale's fleet of ships as necessary for two years. At this point, a contract is likely to have been *formed,* assuming that all of the necessary elements for mutual assent were met. However, suppose that one month into the agreement Ahab notifies White Whale that he has a better-paying opportunity in another city and

TABLE 7.1	Overview of a Contract Transaction		
Formation	**Enforceability**	**Performance**
Parties reach mutual agreement on terms. All formation elements are met.	Contract meets legal requirements to enforce terms.	Governs parties performing (or not performing) the terms of the agreement and provides compensation if one party fails to perform.

cannot perform the services in the agreement as planned. White Whale counters that the e-mail exchanges were sufficient to meet the legal requirements. The resolution of this issue depends on the *enforceability* of the contract. Alternatively, assume that the parties had a written contract. White Whale notifies Ahab that it will be reducing the monthly fee for the remainder of the agreement by 30 percent. Could Ahab sue White Whale immediately? Does White Whale have any defense? What can Ahab expect to recover to compensate for losses? These are issues of *performance*. Formation and enforceability are covered in this chapter. Performance is covered in Chapter 8, "Contract Performance: Conditions, Breach, and Remedies."

 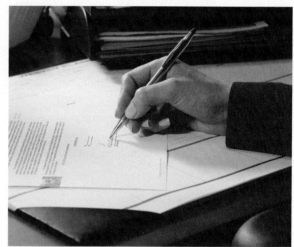

Understanding contract law helps business owners limit their company's liability and manage risk.

LO 7-1, 7-2 ## CONTRACT FORMATION

In Chapter 6, "Overview and Language of Contracts," we saw that contracts consist of four distinct elements. These elements—mutual assent, consideration, capacity, and legality—are each required in order to form a valid contract. Moreover, for the contract to be *enforceable,* the agreement must also be the product of **genuine assent,** and, in some cases, certain terms must be in *writing* as required by the **statute of frauds.**

Mutual Assent

Legal Speak ›))
Assent A conscious approval or confirmation of facts. In contract law, assent is the knowing, voluntary, and mutual approval of the terms of a contract by each party.

The broad underlying requirement that must be met to form an enforceable contract is the notion of **mutual assent** (often referred to simply as *assent, agreement,* or *offer and acceptance*). Mutual assent means that for a contract to be valid, the parties must reach an agreement using a combination of **offer** and **acceptance.** In most cases, the *offeror* must make a valid offer to the *offeree,* who in turn must accept the offer in order for the parties to be bound by the agreement's terms. This true meeting of the minds with the intent to be bound by their agreement, called the *subjective standard,* will result in an express contract. A meeting of the minds may also be inferred from the conduct of the parties, resulting in an implied contract or quasi-contract. This objective standard requires only that each party's acts or words lead the other party to reasonably believe that an agreement has been reached. When the Baltimore & Ohio Railroad Company sued the United States to recover compensation for constructing temporary barracks for the use of U.S. troops under an agreement never expressly entered into by an authorized government agent, the U.S. Supreme Court said, "[A contract may be] founded upon a meeting of minds, which, although not embodied in an express contract, is inferred, as a fact, from conduct of the parties showing, in the light of the surrounding circumstances, their tacit understanding."[1]

Mutual Assent Part 1: Offer

An offer is a promise or commitment to do (or refrain from doing) a specified activity such as selling a good at a certain price or offering to provide services at a given rate. An offer also is the expression of a willingness to enter into a contract by the offeror's promising an offeree that she will perform certain obligations in exchange for the offeree's counterpromise to perform. To take a simple example, suppose that Lewis offers to sell Williams a rare book for $1,000. In this case, Lewis is the *offeror* and is promising to perform through a transfer of ownership rights to the book so long as Williams, as the *offeree,* counter promises to perform by paying $1,000.

> **KEY** POINT
>
> The elements of a contract are (1) mutual assent (offer and acceptance), (2) consideration, (3) capacity, and (4) legality/public policy. To be enforceable, a contract must be a product of genuine assent, not be voidable, and be in writing (in certain cases).

Offers must meet three criteria to be valid. They must be *clear, serious,* and *communicated.* Clear means that the language of the offer must be such that the offeree knows what is being offered. For example, if Peter says to Amy, "I'll sell you my car for $5,000," that sounds pretty clear and straightforward. But what if Peter owns two cars, a 2008 Ford Mustang and a 2004 Dodge Caravan? The subjective view would hold that if Peter is thinking Caravan while Amy is thinking Mustang, the offer would fail because it was not specific enough for Amy, the offeree, to understand exactly what was being offered. The objective view, supported by the *Restatement (Second) of Contracts*[2] and currently the most prevalent view, allows the courts to examine extrinsic evidence to determine what the offeror and offeree intended.

Seriousness of an offer requires that the offeror have an **objective intent** to contract when making the offer. Generally, the offeror must have a *serious intention* to become bound by the offer, and the terms of the offer must be *reasonably certain.* Courts look to the *language* of the offer and *actions* (extrinsic evidence) of the offeror to determine

---

[1] *Baltimore & Ohio Railroad Company v. United States,* 261 U.S. 592 (1923), which cites a long line of supporting cases.

[2] § 17, Comment c.

Legal Speak »))
Extrinsic Evidence
Evidence that is not contained directly within a contract but will explain the meaning or intent of the parties. Extrinsic evidence is usually admissible to explain ambiguities in a contract.

how a reasonable person would interpret that language. Does the language indicate a *serious intent to form* a contract? Or perhaps the language indicates intent to negotiate rather than agree. Or is the language so innocuous that a reasonable person would conclude that there was no intent at all (for example, an offer made in jest)? Note that it does not matter what the offeror *actually* intended. Rather, the objective test is what a reasonable person would ordinarily believe the language and conduct (collectively referred to as *manifestations* of intent) mean in those circumstances. Otherwise, the offer is considered simply an offer to discuss or negotiate the terms of an agreement. For example, an e-mail from the owner of a computer retail store to a computer hardware wholesaler may contain the following language: "I am interested in purchasing 10 new personal computers. Please contact me about the price and delivery terms regarding the computers." This message does not express an immediate objective intention to contract. Rather, a reasonable person would look at this language as an invitation to negotiate.

Under modern case law, the importance of the parties' intention, or lack of intention, to form a contract depends largely upon the context of the agreement. When an agreement is in the context of a business transaction, there is a strong presumption that the parties intended the agreement to be legally enforceable.

In Landmark Case 7.1, one of the most famous in American contract law, a state supreme court considers the circumstances of a transaction and language of the parties in determining whether an offer involved a serious intent to contract.

Finally, offers must be *communicated,* or they may not be accepted. While this sounds obvious, consider the following example: Tina's dog has run away. She places reward posters throughout the neighborhood and places an ad in the local newspaper. Ted, her good friend, sees Tina's dog wandering and takes the dog back to Tina's house without ever seeing a poster or the newspaper advertisement. After he leaves her home, he then sees a reward poster. If he returns and demands the reward, Tina will not be obligated to pay because no contract had been formed. There had been no express agreement, and no implied contract was created, because Ted did not act based on the offer he knew nothing about. Later in this chapter we will see that Ted's claim would also fail because it is based on past consideration.

> ## KEY POINT
> The objective test for intent to form a contract is: Given the language and circumstances of the offer, would a reasonable person in the position of the offeree conclude that the offer was an objective manifestation of serious intent to contract?

Advertisements as an Offer   Most advertisements appearing in the mass media, in store windows, or in display cases are *not* offers. Rather, the law recognizes mass advertisements as an invitation for the consumer to make an offer to the seller to purchase the goods at a specified price. Frequently, these advertisements do not constitute an offer because they do not contain a specific commitment to sell. For example, Big Time Appliances runs an advertisement in a local paper that misprinted the ad as "46-inch plasma screen TV for $10" instead of "$1,000." Ernest shows up at Big Time Appliance with a $10 bill and excitedly hands over the bill to a cashier, saying "I accept your offer to sell me this television for $10." Big Time Appliance is not obligated to perform (i.e., sell the television for $10).[3] The law recognizes Ernest's actions not as an acceptance of Big Time's offer but rather as an offer by Ernest to buy the television—which Big Time may accept or reject. Even a price tag on a product in the store is an invitation for the customer to make an offer and not an offer to sell at that price by the business.

---

[3] *Restatement (Second) of Contracts,* § 26, Comment b. Also note that this example is a contracts analysis. In the case of advertising, certain state consumer laws may apply to protect buyers against merchants acting in bad faith by using advertising as a "bait-and-switch" method (discussed in Chapter 22, "Consumer Protection Law").

FACT SUMMARY   Lucy was a farmer who knew Zehmer for a period of 15 to 20 years. At one point during their relationship, Lucy offered to buy Zehmer's farm for $20,000, but Zehmer rejected the offer outright. Seven years later, Lucy met Zehmer at a restaurant and had a conversation over a period of hours while the two drank whiskey together. During this conversation, Lucy again offered to purchase Zehmer's farm. According to the testimony at trial, the following exchange of words took place:

Lucy:	I bet you wouldn't take $50,000 for that farm.
Zehmer:	You haven't got $50,000 cash.
Lucy:	I can get it.
Zehmer:	But you haven't got $50,000 cash to pay me tonight.

Eventually, Lucy persuaded Zehmer to put in writing that he would sell Lucy the farm for $50,000. Zehmer handwrote the following on the back of the pad: "I agree to sell the Ferguson Place [Zehmer's farm property] to W. O. Lucy for $50,000 cash." The parties then modified this writing several times and discussed terms over a period of 30 to 40 minutes. At the end of the evening, each party had signed the modified document that agreed to a sale of Zehmer's farm to Lucy for $50,000. The next day, Lucy believed that the contract was valid and proceeded to act accordingly by seeking financing for the purchase and checking title. However, Zehmer notified Lucy that he would not transfer title since no contract was formed. Rather, Zehmer had understood the whole transaction as a joke. At trial Zehmer testified that he "was high as a Georgia pine" while modifying and discussing the contract and that he was just "needling" Lucy because he believed Lucy could never come up with the money. Zehmer claimed that before he left the restaurant that night, he told Lucy that it was all a big joke, that the negotiations were just the "liquor talking." Zehmer claimed that he had not actually intended to sell the property, thus the contract lacked serious intent and was void.

SYNOPSIS OF DECISION AND OPINION   The court ruled that Zehmer was bound by the contract even if he had no *actual* (subjective) intent to sell the farm and may have been joking. The court used the objective standard in determining that a reasonable person would have construed Zehmer's actions and words as a serious intent to contract. The court held that evidence from the trial indicated that Zehmer took the transaction seriously, and that Lucy was not unreasonable in believing that a contract was formed under the circumstances. The court made clear that actual mental intent is not required for formation of a contract.

WORDS OF THE COURT: Manifestation of Intent to Contract   "The appearance of a contract; the fact that it was under discussion for forty minutes or more before it was signed; Lucy's objection to the first draft; . . . the discussion of what was to be included in the sale . . . are facts which furnish persuasive evidence that the execution of the contract was a serious business transaction rather than a casual, jesting matter as the defendant now contends.

"An agreement or mutual assent is of course essential to a valid contract but the law imputes to a person an intention corresponding to the reasonable meaning of his words and acts. If his words and acts, judged by a reasonable standard, manifest an intention to agree, it is immaterial what may be the real but unexpressed state of his mind."

Case Questions

1. What factors does the court focus on when deciding whether Lucy's understanding of the contract formation was reasonable?

2. What facts could you change in this case that would result in the court determining that no contract existed?

The primary exception to this rule occurs when the advertisement is *specific* enough to constitute a unilateral contract. Advertisements that offer to sell a particular number of certain products at a certain price may constitute an offer. In the previous example, if the advertisement offered 46-inch plasma televisions for $10 to the first 50 buyers on Friday, then the advertisement would be specific enough to constitute a valid offer requiring Big Time Appliance to sell as promised. Or if the advertisement invites the other party to accept in a *particular manner,* courts will treat this type of advertisement as a valid offer for a unilateral contract. For example, Anti-Flu Inc. sells a herbal inhaler device that it claims will work to prevent the flu as effectively as any flu shot vaccine. The company advertises, "We will pay $1,000 to anyone who uses the Anti-Flu herbal inhaler for two consecutive weeks and still contracts the flu." Pauline uses the device for two weeks (thereby accepting Anti-Flu's offer) and contracts the flu one day later. Anti-Flu would be obligated to perform its promise by paying the $1,000 sum because Anti-Flu's advertisement invited any party to accept the company's offer in a particular manner (by using the device).[4]

In Case 7.2, an appellate court considers whether a claim made by a famous company created an offer through a television advertisement.

Mutual Assent Part 2: Acceptance

A valid offer creates the power of *acceptance* for the offeree. An acceptance is the offeree's expression of agreement to the terms of the offer. An offeree typically communicates the acceptance in writing or orally but, in some cases, may accept via some action or conduct (as in a unilateral contract). So long as the offer is still in force (has not yet been terminated) the offeree may accept the terms of the offer, thereby forming an agreement. Only the party or parties to whom the offer is intended has the power of acceptance and may accept. Suppose that during class, a professor says to a particular student, "I'll sell you my briefcase for $100." Only that student may accept, and no other student present in class has the power of acceptance. If instead the professor says, "I'll sell my briefcase for $100 to the first student in this class who accepts," then the power of acceptance is extended to the entire class, but not to the professor's students in other classes. In order for agreement to exist though, the offer has to be *properly* accepted by the offeree.[5] Note that the offeror is considered the "master" of the offer and, therefore, has the power to terminate, modify its terms, or prescribe the method of acceptance of the offer *up and until the offer has been accepted* by the offeree. Once the offer has been terminated, the offeree has lost the power to accept and form an agreement.

Events Terminating the Power of Acceptance: Action of the Parties versus
LO 7-3 **Operation of Law**   An offer may be terminated by action of the parties in one of three ways: (1) **revocation,** where the offeror revokes (withdraws) the offer prior to acceptance; (2) **rejection,** where the offeree rejects the offer; and (3) **counteroffer,** where the offeree rejects the original offer and proposes a new offer with different terms. Offers may also be terminated by **operation of law.**

Revocation   When the offeror decides to revoke (withdraw) the offer by expressly communicating the revocation to the offeree prior to acceptance, the offer is terminated by revocation. Revocation is consummated through an express repudiation of the offer (e.g., "I revoke my offer of May 1 to paint your office building for $1,000") or by some *inconsistent act* that would give reasonable notice from the offeror to the offeree that the offer no longer existed. For example, on Monday, Owner offers WidgetCo the nonexclusive opportunity to purchase a parcel of land for $100,000 with a deadline of Friday for responding. On Wednesday, WidgetCo learns that Owner has entered into a contract with

---

[4]Based on the landmark case *Carlill v. Carbolic Smoke Ball Co.,* 1 Q.B. 256 (1893).
[5]*Restatement (Second) of Contracts,* §§ 29, 50, 54.

FACT SUMMARY Pepsi ran an advertisement on national television promoting its Pepsi Points program whereby consumers could obtain points by purchasing Pepsi products and then redeem the points for certain apparel and other items. An alternate way to accumulate points was to purchase them for a certain dollar figure. The Pepsi advertisement opened with the morning routine of a high school student. The commercial was based on a *Top Gun* movie theme and depicted the student wearing apparel such as a leather bomber jacket, a Pepsi T-shirt, and aviator sunglasses. For each item, the advertisement would flash the corresponding number of Pepsi points required to obtain the item. For example, when showing the actor with the aviator sunglasses, the advertisement featured the subtitle "Shades 175 Pepsi Points." The advertisement then showed a view of the cover of a Pepsi Stuff Catalog with a narration of "Introducing the new Pepsi Stuff Catalog" and the subtitle "See details on specially marked packages." Finally, the advertisement shows the student arriving at his high school in a Harrier Fighter Jet to the amazement of his friends and teachers. The student hops out of the jet and says, "Sure beats the bus." At this point, the subtitle flashes "Harrier Jet 7,000,000 Pepsi points."

Leonard filled out the Pepsi Stuff order form (located in the catalog produced by Pepsi), but since there was no mention of the Harrier Jet, Leonard simply wrote in the item on the order form and sent the order to Pepsi with a check for $700,000, the amount necessary to purchase the requisite points as stated in the advertisement. Pepsi refused to transfer title on the basis that no contract existed. The trial court ruled in favor of Pepsi. Leonard appealed, among other reasons, on the basis that the Pepsi advertisement was specific enough to constitute a valid offer of a unilateral contract through its advertisement.

SYNOPSIS OF DECISION AND OPINION The court ruled against Leonard. While acknowledging that certain advertisements could be an offer if the promise is clear, definite, and explicit, such was not the case here. The advertisement was not sufficiently definite because it reserved the details of the offer to a separate writing (the catalog).[6]

WORDS OF THE COURT: Requirements for Advertisements as a Unilateral Offer "In the present case, the Harrier Jet commercial did not direct that anyone who appeared at Pepsi headquarters with 7,000,000 Pepsi Points on the Fourth of July would receive the Harrier Jet. Instead, the commercial urged consumers to accumulate Pepsi Points and refer to the catalog to determine how they could receive their Pepsi Points. The commercial sought a reciprocal promise, expressed through the acceptance of, and in compliance with, the terms of the Order Form. . . . [T]he catalog contains no mention of the Harrier Jet."

Case Questions

1. What facts would support Leonard's primary argument as to why this commercial was a unilateral offer to contract?

2. If the wording on the catalog order form had allowed a consumer to write in the item (rather than check a box next to the item), would that change the outcome of this case?

3. Should a reasonable person seeing the television commercial reasonably believe that Pepsi would sell a $23 million Harrier Jet for only $700,000?

To see video of the actual Pepsi advertisement, go to this textbook's website at www.mhhe.com/melvinleb2e.

---

[6]The court also rejected Leonard's other primary argument that the advertisement constituted an objective intent by Pepsi to sell a $23 million Harrier Jet for $700,000. The court ruled, "In light of the obvious absurdity of the commercial, the court rejects plaintiff's argument that the commercial was not clearly in jest."

ServiceCo for the land. On Thursday, WidgetCo calls Owner with an acceptance. No contract exists between Owner and WidgetCo because Owner's inconsistent acts were sufficient to give WidgetCo notice of the transaction.[7]

---

[7]Based on *Restatement (Second) of Contracts,* § 42, Illustration 1.

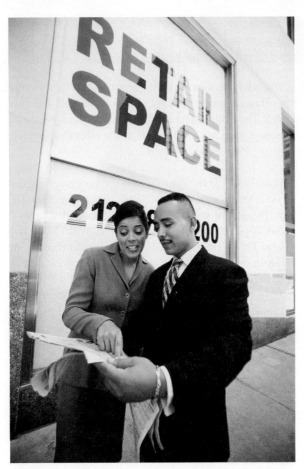

Option contracts are sometimes used to provide flexibility in commercial real estate transactions.

One important issue with revocation is the timing of the revocation. Most states follow the rule that revocation is effective only *upon receipt* by the offeree or the offeree's agent.[8] For example, on Monday, Adams sends, via same-day courier, a letter of revocation to Bell's office. Bell's administrative assistant receives the revocation on that same day, but Bell is traveling in Japan and never actually sees the letter. On Wednesday, from his hotel room in Tokyo, Bell calls Adams and accepts Adams's initial offer. No contract exists because the revocation would be deemed effective upon receipt by Bell's administrative assistant. At that point, even though Bell had no *actual* knowledge of the revocation by Adams, the offer is revoked and Bell may no longer accept the offer.

Note that some offers are **irrevocable:** (1) offers in the form of an option contract; (2) offers that the offeree partly performed or detrimentally relied on; and (3) so-called firm offers by a merchant under the UCC (firm offers under the UCC are discussed in Chapter 9, "Contracts for the Sale of Goods").

Option Contracts   One way to make an offer irrevocable is for the offeror to grant the offeree an *option* to enter a contract. Typically, the offeror agrees to hold an offer open (not enter into a contract with another party) for a certain period of time in exchange for something of value (known as *consideration,* discussed later in this chapter). In the example discussed above, WidgetCo could have protected itself and enforced the "till Friday" deadline by entering into an *option* with Owner. If WidgetCo had paid Owner $1,000 to keep the offer to purchase the land open until Friday, Owner would now be obligated to keep the offer open and not entertain offers by third parties. However, if, at the end of Friday, WidgetCo hadn't communicated an acceptance of the offer to sell, Owner would keep the $1,000 and now be permitted to sell the property to another party.

Partial Performance and Detrimental Reliance   There are certain offers whereby the offeree may, prior to actual formation of the contract, take some action that *relies* on the offer; for example, the offeree begins to perform based on a unilateral offer. Recall that a unilateral offer is one in which the offer makes clear that acceptance can occur only through performance and not through a promise. This is known as *partial performance* and can render an offer temporarily irrevocable. For example, Burns offers Realtor a commission of 10 percent of the sales price if Realtor can find a buyer for the Burns Building for $500,000. Realtor spends funds to research and obtain potential buyer contact information and locates Walters, who is willing to accept the $500,000 offer to sell from Burns. Before any transaction takes place, Burns revokes his offer to Realtor and refuses to sell the property to Walters. Burns's revocation is *not effective.* Burns's promise to pay for a particular performance (a unilateral contract) was rendered irrevocable once Realtor

---

[8]Note that a few states, notably California, do not follow the "receipt" rule, opting instead to make revocation effective upon dispatch of the revocation notice.

performed by finding a buyer for the building.[9] Also, an offer may be rendered irrevocable if the offeree makes preparations prior to acceptance based on a reasonable reliance on the offer. This is known as **detrimental reliance.** For example, SubCo is a subcontractor for GeneralCo. GeneralCo relies on SubCo's bid in preparing to make an offer to renovate a commercial office complex. After GeneralCo is awarded the renovation contract, SubCo notifies GeneralCo that its bid was too low due to the poor business forecasting of one of SubCo's partners. Because it is no longer interested in the job, SubCo attempts to revoke its offer/bid. In this case, SubCo is *still required to perform* even at a loss. GeneralCo reasonably relied on SubCo's bid and would suffer a significant detriment based on this reliance. SubCo's offer became irrevocable once GeneralCo exercised reasonable reliance on the offer.[10]

Rejection and Counteroffer An offer is also terminated once the offeree either rejects the offer outright or makes a counteroffer by rejecting the original offer and making a new offer. Under the common law,[11] the offeree's response operates as an acceptance only if it is the *precise mirror image* of the offer. If the response conflicts with the original offer even slightly, the original offer is terminated and the new offer is substituted. This principle is called the **mirror image rule**. Once the offeree has rejected the offer or made a counteroffer, her power of acceptance is terminated. For example, apply the mirror image rule to the following conversation:

Franz: I will pay you $1,000 to paint the interior of our office building.

Josef: I've seen your office; it is going to cost you more than that.

Franz: How much more?

Josef: I'll do it for $2,000.

Franz: Ah, yes. Well, let's split it down the middle. I'll pay you $1,500.

Josef: OK. I agree to do it for $1,500, but you must also supply the paint, brushes, ladder, tarps, cleaner, and other equipment I need.

Does a contract exist between Josef and Franz? Carefully examine the language of the parties. Josef made an outright rejection of Franz's first offer to paint the office for $1,000. Then Josef made an offer to paint the office for $2,000. Franz then rejected the offer via *counteroffer* and now has made a new offer for Josef to accept or reject his offer to pay $1,500 for the services. Although Josef starts out his response with "OK," he adds additional terms (Franz must supply the paint, etc.). Therefore, Josef has rejected the offer because his acceptance was *not the mirror image* of Franz's offer. Despite the "OK" language, the law treats Josef's response as a counteroffer (and therefore a rejection). Franz's offer is now terminated, and *no* contract exists at this point. Of course, Franz is now free to accept or reject Josef's counteroffer.

> **KEY POINT**
>
> The mirror image rule, which applies to common law contracts (not UCC contracts), requires that any acceptance by the offeree must be the mirror image of the original offer. Any deviation from the original offer results in a rejection and counteroffer.

Termination by Operation of Law An offer may also be terminated by certain happenings or events covered by operation of law. Generally, these include (1) lapse of

---

[9]Based on *Restatement (Second) of Contracts,* § 45, Illustration 5.

[10]Based on *Restatement (Second) of Contracts,* § 87(2), Illustration 6 [*Drennan v. Star Paving,* 51 Cal. 2d 409 (1958)].

[11]Note that the UCC rules are different regarding counteroffers. The UCC rules for counteroffers are discussed in Chapter 9, "Contracts for the Sale of Goods."

time, (2) death or incapacity of the offeror or offeree, (3) destruction of the subject matter of the contract before acceptance, and (4) supervening illegality.

Lapse of Time   Following the "offeror is the master of his offer" rule, the offeror will frequently attach some time limit on the offeree's power of acceptance. Once the time limit has expired, the offer is considered to have terminated via **lapse of time.** If, however, the offeror has not set a time limit, the offer will still expire after a *reasonable time.* Courts determine the "reasonable time period" for an acceptance by analyzing the circumstances that existed when the offer and attempted acceptance were made. When the offer involves a speculative transaction in which the subject matter is subject to sharp fluctuations in value, a reasonable time period will be considerably shorter. For example, Milton sends Dryden an e-mail: "I offer to sell you my private stock in Local Oil Company for $500 per share." Dryden waits one week, and the price of oil skyrockets in the week, making stock in Local Oil rise to $700 per share. He responds to Milton's e-mail: "I accept your offer of last week." In this case, Dryden would likely not be obligated to perform because the subject matter of the offer was so speculative that it dictated a short time period for expiration. On the other hand, if Milton wishes to sell Dryden a used lawn mower for $100, the weeklong time period may still be a reasonable time in which to accept the offer.

Death, Incapacity, Destruction, or Supervening Illegality   In the event that the offeror or the offeree either dies or becomes incapacitated before acceptance, the offer automatically terminates. Similarly, if the subject matter of the contract is destroyed before acceptance, the offer is considered terminated by operation of law. A supervening illegality occurs when changes in the law make a previously legal offer illegal. Suppose that on Monday Ben is walking past a gun shop and sees a sale sign on an AK-47 automatic assault rifle. When he asks the shopkeeper about the gun, he is assured that ownership of such a weapon is legal in the state and that the sale price is good until Saturday. On Wednesday, the state legislature passes a statute making the sale, ownership, and possession of the AK-47 a crime in the state. The gun shop's offer will immediately terminate due to the change in the law. Death, incapacity, destruction, and supervening illegality are all examples of what many courts refer to as *impossibility.*

LO 7-4   When Acceptance Is Effective: The Mailbox Rule   The **mailbox rule** governs common law contracts and is a rule that determines when a contract is considered to be deemed accepted by the offeree, thus depriving the offeror of the right to revoke the offer. In essence, the mailbox rule provides that the acceptance of an offer is generally effective upon dispatch of the acceptance when sent in a commercially reasonable manner. (e.g., when the offeree places the acceptance in the mailbox, sends it by overnight mail, or faxes it) and not when the acceptance is received by the offeror. The time of acceptance depends on whether the offeror specified a method of acceptance or not. Figure 7.1 provides a flowchart that clarifies the rules governing when acceptance is effective.

 Self-Check   Mailbox Rule

For each transaction, does a contract exist? If yes, why, and what is the date of the contract. If no, why not?

PROBLEM 1

Day 1: Conley sent a fax to Raleigh's office: "We offer to provide you with widget-covering services for $1,000 per month for six months starting January 1."

Day 2: Raleigh sends a letter via U.S. mail to Conley: "I accept your offer of Day 1."

(continued)

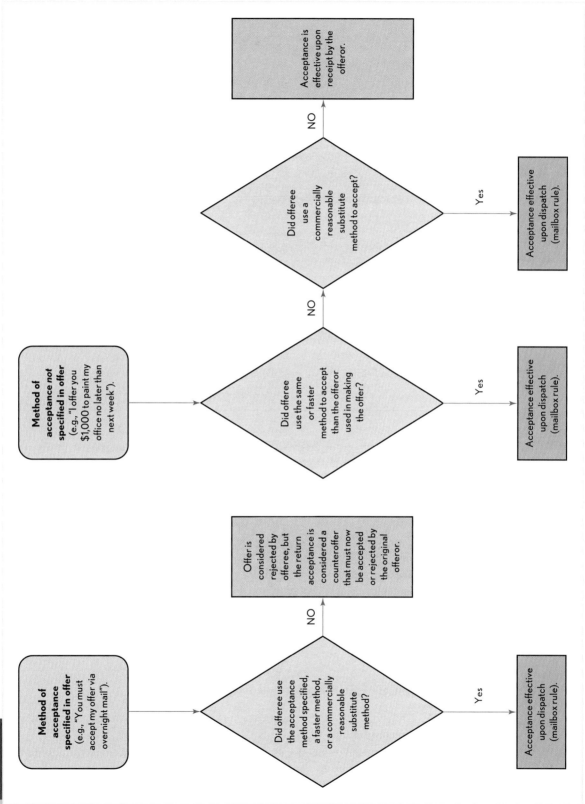

FIGURE 7.1 When Is Acceptance Effective?

Method of acceptance specified in offer (e.g., "You must accept my offer via overnight mail").

Did offeree use the acceptance method specified, a faster method, or a commercially reasonable substitute method?

Yes → Acceptance effective upon dispatch (mailbox rule).

NO → Offer is considered rejected by offeree, but the return acceptance is considered a counteroffer that must now be accepted or rejected by the original offeror.

Method of acceptance not specified in offer (e.g., "I offer you $1,000 to paint my office no later than next week").

Did offeree use the same or faster method to accept than the offeror used in making the offer?

Yes → Acceptance effective upon dispatch (mailbox rule).

NO → Did offeree use a commercially reasonable substitute method to accept?

Yes → Acceptance effective upon dispatch (mailbox rule).

NO → Acceptance is effective upon receipt by the offeror.

CHAPTER SEVEN | Contract Formation   177

Day 3: Conley telephones Raleigh and tells him: "I revoke my widget-covering offer of Day 1." Upon hearing this, Raleigh states, "Too late, I already put my acceptance in the mailbox!"

Day 4: Conley receives Raleigh's letter of acceptance on Thursday.

PROBLEM 2

Day 1: BookCo's manager e-mails an offer to sell a rare first edition of *For Whom the Bell Tolls,* signed by Hemingway, for $50,000 to Rare Book Retailer (RBR).

Day 2: RBR receives the offer, prints out the e-mail, writes "ACCEPTED, 1 Hemingway Book for $50,000. RBR Manager," and faxes BookCo the acceptance.

Day 3 (9:00 a.m.): BookCo's receptionist receives RBR's fax.

Day 3 (12:00 p.m.): BookCo's manager calls RBR to revoke her offer.

Day 3 (1:30 p.m.): The RBR acceptance fax is delivered to BookCo's manager.

PROBLEM 3

Day 1: On Monday, McGlyn mails an offer to Timothy.

Day 2: On Tuesday, McGlyn changes her mind and mails a revocation of the offer to Timothy.

Day 3: On Wednesday, while the revocation is in the mail, Timothy receives McGlyn's offer and immediately mails his acceptance.

Day 4: On Thursday, while the acceptance is in the mail, Timothy receives the revocation.

Day 5: On Friday, McGlyn receives Timothy's acceptance.

Answers to this Self-Check are provided at the end of the chapter.

Silence as an Acceptance Under most circumstances, acceptance cannot be imposed or inferred from an offeree's silence after receiving an offer. Therefore, courts will not enforce a contract in which the offer states that failure to respond will be considered an acceptance of the offer. An exception occurs if the parties had previously agreed that silence acts as an acceptance. For example, restaurants often have delivery agreements with food suppliers to accept deliveries daily. Suppose Mackey's, a restaurant, enters into an agreement with a bakery to supply 10 dozen hamburger and hot dog buns each morning at 7 a.m. The agreement may contain a provision stating that if the bakery does not receive a cancellation of the delivery by 4 p.m., the next morning's delivery will be made and accepted. Mackey's failure to cancel by 4 p.m. on Tuesday, therefore, represents an acceptance of delivery on Wednesday, and so on.

If an offer indicating a unilateral contract is made, performing the required task constitutes acceptance whether the offeree voices her acceptance or not.

CONCEPT SUMMARY Mutual Assent

- The formation of a contract requires mutual assent whereby the parties reach an agreement.
- An agreement results from the offeror's making a valid offer and the offeree's accepting the terms of the offer and agreeing to be bound by its terms. This meeting of the minds may come from a true understanding (subjective intent) or may be inferred through extrinsic evidence (objective intent).

- Advertisements are generally not considered an offer. Rather, they are an invitation for the consumer to make an offer to a seller of goods or services.

- For an offer to be valid, the parties must reach agreement on all of the essential terms of the agreement. An offer that is too vague or indefinite cannot be the basis for an agreement.

- Most offers may be terminated either by the actions of the parties or by operation of law. However, certain offers are considered irrevocable.

- The time acceptance becomes effective is governed by the mailbox rule.

Insufficient Agreement

In some cases the parties may actually have satisfied the elements of offer and acceptance, but the agreement still lacks *mutual assent* and the agreement is insufficient to constitute a properly formed contract. Some common circumstances where parties lack mutual assent are in cases when the agreement's terms are too indefinite or when one or both parties are mistaken about an important term.

Indefinite Terms   For an offer to be valid, the parties must reach mutual assent on all of the *essential terms* of the agreement. Even though two parties who are negotiating with each other may have an objective intent to contract, there is no valid contract if the terms are too vague to be performed. Typically, these terms must either be expressly agreed upon or capable of being reasonably inferred. These essential terms are (1) parties to the contract, (2) subject matter of the contract, (3) time for performance or delivery, and (4) price or other consideration to be exchanged.

Note, however, that courts have become increasingly tolerant of uncertainty in terms before allowing a contract to be voided for indefiniteness. The *Restatement* test requires a court to examine the terms of the agreement to determine whether "they provide a basis for determining the existence of a breach and for giving an appropriate remedy."[12] Thus, even though an agreement does not contain all of the required terms, courts have held that missing terms may be supplied by the court when the term may be implied as "reasonable" or by the course of past dealing. So long as the agreement is definite enough to allow the court to determine whether one party failed to fulfill the obligations of the agreement, and to award some kind of reasonable damages to the wronged party, the contract is not void for indefiniteness. Suppose that LeisureTeesCo has been ordering 50 dozen baby-blue T-shirts from ShirtCo for the past 13 years. Each April an order is placed for baby-blue T-shirts, and each May ShirtCo delivers 600 baby-blue T-shirts to LeisureTeesCo. A new manager has put in this year's order and lists the color on the contract simply as blue. If ShirtCo delivers 600 navy blue tees and LeisureTeesCo rejects them, the court will likely find for LeisureTeesCo and require ShirtCo to provide baby-blue tees. Because the word *blue* is ambiguous, the court will look to the past dealing of the companies and see that, despite the indefiniteness and seeming confusion, the extrinsic evidence mandates an interpretation of baby blue.

Agreements to Agree   In certain circumstances in the business environment, the parties enter into an agreement with an essential term unfilled, intending to agree upon the term in the future. Although historically courts were reluctant to enforce such agreements, the modern trend is to allow such agreements to be enforced with the court supplying the missing term according to industry standards and market values. So long as the court determines that the parties themselves intended to make a binding contract, the agreement is enforceable and a court may supply the missing term. For example, suppose that Ernest offers to purchase

---

[12] *Restatement (Second) of Contracts,* § 33(2).

an office building from Whitehead for $100,000 in 30 days. At the time of the agreement, Ernest is unsure of the method that he will use to pay the purchase price, so the parties leave that term unfilled. On the day of the purchase, Ernest pays Whitehead $10 in cash and signs a promissory note for $99,990. Whitehead refuses to complete the transaction and demands a check or cash for the full $100,000. In this case, a court would likely hold that (1) the agreement to agree on the payment terms was enforceable because it is clear the parties intended to enter into a contractual relationship and (2) the court can supply the missing term with a degree of reasonableness based on the pattern of past practices and/or industry standards (e.g., requiring that Ernest obtain a mortgage or pay in cash for the property).

Mistake   Over the course of a business life cycle, it is inevitable that a manager involved in a contract will make a **mistake** (or contract with a mistaken party). The law recognizes certain mistakes and provides a remedy intended to make the parties whole again. One famous legal commentator wrote that "mistake is one of the most difficult [doctrines] in the law, because so many men make so many mistakes, of so many different kinds, with so many varying effects."[13]

Generally, a mistake is defined in contract law as a *belief that is not in accord with the facts*.[14] It is important to note that not *all* erroneous beliefs are classified as a mistake. A mistake is an erroneous belief about an *existing* fact, not an erroneous belief as to what will happen in the future. Erroneous beliefs about the future are covered by doctrines of impossibility and impracticability, which are discussed in the next chapter. Mistakes are classified as either *mutual* (both parties) or *unilateral* (one party).

A **mutual mistake,** in which both parties hold an erroneous belief, may be the basis for *canceling* a contract (also called *avoiding* the contract). For the adversely affected party to cancel the contract, the mistake must concern a *basic assumption* on which the contract was made.

Other examples of mutual mistakes include mistakes as to the existence of the subject matter (e.g., parties agree to the sale of goods, but the goods were already destroyed by fire at the time of the contract) and quality of the subject matter (e.g., parties agreed to sale of a rare first-edition book that turns out to be a second edition and not nearly as valuable). Courts will *not* generally consider market conditions (such as the fair market value of a piece of real estate) or financial ability (such as relying on one party's representation that she can receive adequate credit to purchase the real estate) as a mistake that allows a contract to be avoided.

Landmark Case 7.3, known as the *Peerless* ship case, is a historically famous analysis of the mutual mistake doctrine. It is still cited by modern courts as a framework for deciding whether the parties attached materially different meanings to the terms of a contract.

In a **unilateral mistake,** only one party has an erroneous belief about a basic assumption in the terms of the agreement. Courts are much less willing to allow a mistaken party to cancel a contract for a unilateral mistake than they are in the case of a mutual mistake. In fact, the general rule is that a unilateral mistake is not a valid reason to avoid a contract. However, if the nonmistaken party had reason to *know* of the mistake or his actions *caused* the mistake, a court will allow the mistaken party to avoid the contract. For example, General Contractor solicits bids from Cement Inc. in order to calculate a bid for a new construction project. Cement Inc. sends a letter offer with a clerical error that promises to provide $20,000 worth of cement for $2,000. General Contractor sends an e-mail accepting the $2,000 bid. A court would likely allow Cement Inc. to cancel the cement contract based on unilateral mistake.[15] Note that courts are much less willing to allow a party to cancel a contract if the unilateral mistake is essentially an error in business judgment rather than a clerical error.

---

[13]*Corbin on Contracts,* Section 103.

[14]*Restatement (Second) of Contracts,* § 151.

[15]Based on *Restatement (Second) of Contracts,* § 154, Illustration 6.

FACT SUMMARY   Wichelhaus contracted to purchase a shipment of expensive cotton from Raffles. The contract required the goods to arrive in England aboard the *Peerless,* a freighter ship from Bombay. Wichelhaus had intended that the contract require the goods to be shipped on the *Peerless* from Bombay in *October.* Raffles believed that the cotton was to be shipped on a different freighter (also called *Peerless*) that left from Bombay in *December.* When the goods arrived in December, Wichelhaus refused to accept them, contending that he had already purchased the cotton from the *Peerless* ship that arrived in October. Raffles sued to recover the damages suffered due to Wichelhaus's refusal to accept delivery of the cotton aboard the December *Peerless* ship.

SYNOPSIS OF DECISION AND OPINION   The court ruled in favor of Wichelhaus on the basis that each party believed the ship *Peerless* to be a different ship. The court determined that the misunderstanding resulted in a lack of mutual assent because the parties attached materially different meanings to an essential term of the contract. Therefore, the parties were discharged from any obligations.

WORDS OF THE COURT: Mistake by Ambiguity   "There is nothing on the face of the contract to show that any particular ship called the *Peerless* was meant; but the moment it appears that two ships called *Peerless* were about to sail from Bombay there is a latent ambiguity . . . showing that the defendant meant one *Peerless,* and the plaintiff another. That being so, there was no consensus . . . and therefore no binding contract."

Case Questions

1. If there were some evidence that one party was unreasonable in his understanding of what *Peerless* meant, would that affect the mistake analysis?

2. What made this mistake one that qualifies as an essential term that required "consensus"?

Consideration

For a binding contract to exist, not only must there be agreement (i.e., offer and acceptance) but the agreement must be supported by **consideration.** Consideration is defined as the mutual exchange of benefits and detriments. In plain terms, this means that each party receives something of value from the other and each party gives up something of value, called *legal detriment,* to the other. This results in a bargained-for exchange. The benefits and detriments may take the form of (1) money, (2) goods, (3) services, or (4) the giving up of a legal right. When someone goes to a store to purchase a sweater, the exchange of goods (the sweater) and cash paid is the contract consideration. When a homeowner hires someone to mow her lawn, the exchange of the cash paid and the service rendered (mowing the lawn) is the contract consideration. Suppose that a neighbor's teen throws a ball through your front window. You and your neighbor agree that if he pays for the cost of replacement, you'll promise not to sue him. Your promise is called **forbearance** and is valuable consideration. However, giving something up does not always create legal forbearance. What is forfeited must be a legal right. For example, suppose that nervous parents tell their 19-year-old daughter, a freshman college student leaving home for the first time, that if she refrains from drinking alcohol for the entire year, they will give her $1,000. Even if she does forgo alcohol for the year, since a 19-year-old is not legally allowed to drink alcohol, she has not given up a legal right and thus has not provided valuable consideration.

Figure 7.2 illustrates a simple exchange of consideration in a contract between a buyer and a car dealer. As Figure 7.2 shows, a detriment does not have to be bad or injurious to be valuable consideration. When the dealer gives up ownership or possessory rights to the car, it is giving up something of value.

Legal Speak ›))
Forbearance The giving up of a right that you *legally* possess. This can be used as consideration in a contract.

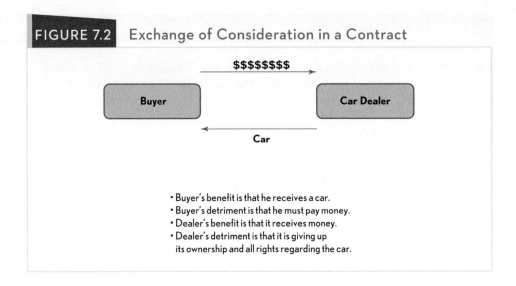

FIGURE 7.2 Exchange of Consideration in a Contract

$$$$$$$$

Buyer → Car Dealer

Car

- Buyer's benefit is that he receives a car.
- Buyer's detriment is that he must pay money.
- Dealer's benefit is that it receives money.
- Dealer's detriment is that it is giving up its ownership and all rights regarding the car.

Legal Detriment Proper consideration requires that the parties suffer some type of detriment that the law recognizes as adequate. This is satisfied if the party promises to perform something that the party is not legally obligated to do (such as promising to sell your car for $5,000) or refrain from doing something that party had a right to do (such as waiving your rights to pursue a lawsuit when you have been injured). In one famous decision from 1891, an appellate court in New York held that one party's promise to abstain from the then-legal practices of drinking, smoking, and gambling until age 21, in exchange for a promise by his uncle to pay him $5,000[16] was sufficient legal detriment for both parties and thus was an enforceable contract.[17] The nephew had given up a legal right that was sufficient to satisfy the legal detriment required (forbearance).

Amount and Type of Consideration Consideration exchanged does not need to be of equal value. Ordinarily, in deciding the validity of consideration, courts will not look to the *amount* or *type* of consideration or the relative bargaining power of the parties (except in the rare case of a contract so burdensome on one party as to indicate unconscionability, discussed later). So long as some bargained-for exchange is contemplated, the contract will be deemed enforceable. For example, Sheila purchases a pair of designer shoes for $1,300. When her husband finds out, he is irate and demands that she return them. When she goes to the showroom to do so, the store will not accept them because she has worn them outside, walking on a sidewalk. If she files a lawsuit claiming that the value she paid was in excess of the cost of the shoes, the court won't care about the cost of the leather or the company's manufacturing costs; it will simply want to know whether Sheila voluntarily entered into the contract and understood that she was paying $1,300 for a pair of shoes.

Contracts may be based on **nominal consideration** (i.e., consideration that is stated in a written contract even though it is not actually exchanged). Most courts have held that the consideration requirement is still met even if the nominal amount is never actually paid so long as the amount is truly nominal (such as $1). In *Bennett v. American Electric Power Services Corp.,*[18] a state appellate court ruled against an employee who had signed an employment agreement that assigned all of his rights for any invention made in the scope

---

[16]Using the consumer price index rate to calculate the time value of money, this sum would be approximately $104,000 in today's dollars.

[17]*Hammer v. Sidway,* 124 N.Y. 538 (1891).

[18]2001 WL 1136150 (Ohio Ct. App. 2001).

of employment to his employer "in consideration of the sum of One Dollar" even though the actual dollar was never paid. The court reasoned that the offer of employment to the employee in the contract was a sufficient bargained-for exchange.[19]

Preexisting Duty Rule

If a party does or promises to do what she is already legally obligated to do, the law generally does *not* recognize this as a legal detriment and, thus, the contract is unenforceable. The classic example is that a police officer cannot collect the reward for arresting a fugitive because the officer had a **preexisting duty** to find and arrest fugitives. More often, however, the preexisting duty rule applies in circumstances where one party claims he wishes to modify an existing contract because of unforeseen difficulties in performing his obligations. For example, Helsel contracts with Mullen to renovate Helsel's office building. During the renovation, Mullen discovers the costs of renovation will be more than he anticipated. Mullen threatens to walk off the job unless Helsel agrees to pay an amount higher than stated in the contract. Because Helsel's choices would be limited to either agreeing or hiring a new contractor and then suing Mullen, he consents to the price increase. Most courts would *not* enforce Helsel's promise to pay the additional amount because Mullen already had a preexisting contractual duty to perform for the original price.

The modern trend in the law recognizes a number of exceptions to the preexisting duty rule.[20] For example, if a party who promises to do what she is already bound to do assumes additional duties, her undertaking of these duties is considered sufficient legal detriment.[21] Also, courts may allow an exception in a case where certain circumstances were not reasonably *anticipated* by either party when the original contract was formed. For example, Waste Disposal Company (WDC) contracts with ManufactureCo to collect garbage from ManufacturerCo's warehouse for one year. Six months into the agreement, WDC requests an additional $5,000 per month to provide this service because the ManfactureCo warehouse is now unexpectedly producing some hazardous material waste that must be removed by specifically designed equipment. The parties then execute a modification to the contract, agreeing to the increase. One month later, ManufactureCo changes managers, and the new manager refuses to pay the additional sum, citing the preexisting duty rule. In this case, most courts would *enforce* the modification as an exception to the preexisting duty rule.[22]

Bargained-for Exchange

Even if a legal detriment is suffered by one party, that alone does not satisfy the consideration requirement. The **bargained-for exchange** aspect of consideration primarily distinguishes contracts from **illusory promises.** Some promises do not support a bargained-for exchange and will not support contractual consideration. Such promises are called *illusory promises.* Examples of illusory promises are (1) deathbed promises, in which you make a promise to a friend or loved one just prior to her death to comfort her; (2) promises of a gift, in which a promise is made but no reciprocal promise is exchanged; (3) promises of love and friendship; and (4) promises that by their terms are not binding. For example, a manager announces to his employees that each may have three personal days in December if he can get it approved by senior management. This is an illusory promise because neither the manager nor the company is bound by his

---

[19]In its opinion, the court wrote, "Although ancient, the best authorities on the issue hold that nonpayment of such nominal consideration will not constitute breach, at least in instances where the actual value of the subject of the contract does not, in fact, correspond to the nominal consideration."

[20]In fact, some states (such as New York) have repudiated the preexisting duty rule altogether and allow a good faith modification made in writing to be enforceable.

[21]*Restatement (Second) of Contracts,* § 73.

[22]Based on *Angel v. Murray,* 332 A.2d 630 (R.I. 1974).

statement. Since gift promises are not enforceable and contract promises are, it is important to understand the precise difference. A performance or return promise is "bargained for" only if it was exchanged for another promise.

Past Consideration   Another type of consideration that is not considered to meet the bargained-for exchange requirement is a promise made in return for a detriment previously made by the promisee. This is known as **past consideration,** and it is not sufficient to meet the consideration requirement. Suppose that O'Connor has been working at her job for 40 years and is retiring. Her boss approaches her a week before her last scheduled day and tells her that because she has been such a faithful and effective employee for the last 40 years, on Friday, her last day, there will be a party and she will be presented with a gold watch. She gratefully thanks him and accepts the offer of a party and watch. On Thursday she is disappointed when informed that there will be no party and she will not receive a gold watch. Although the party and watch contract has both offer and acceptance, it is *unenforceable* because it lacks consideration. O'Connor's contention that her 40 years of dedicated service was sufficient consideration is false because it is past consideration, performed prior to the current agreement. Thus, the offer of a party and watch is an offer of a gift and is not enforceable as a contract. If, however, the company's employment manual, in force since she started work, states that employees receive a gold watch after 25 years of employment, she would be entitled to the watch because she acted based on a promise made before she began performing.

> **KEY** POINT
>
> Consideration must be performed or exchanged after the mutual assent. Any agreements made after the consideration is performed or exchanged will not support a valid contract.

Promissory Estoppel   If one party justifiably relies on the promise of another to her detriment, under certain circumstances the relying party may recover costs of the reliance from the promisor even though the original promise agreement lacked consideration. Under the theory of **promissory estoppel,** a relying party may recover damages if (1) the promisor makes a promise that is *reasonable;* (2) the promisee *actually* relied on the promise (the promise must have induced the act) and suffered an injury; (3) the promisee's reliance was *reasonably foreseeable* to the promisor (what an objectively reasonable person would have foreseen under the same circumstances); and (4) principles of *equity and justice* (did each party act in good faith and fair dealing?) are served by providing compensation to the reliant party.

One particularly important domain of promissory estoppel for managers is promises of employment. Most commonly, this arises in a situation where an employer has made a promise of employment to an at-will[23] employee candidate and then revokes the promise before the employee's start date (or soon thereafter). Typically, the employee would have left her previous position and potentially incurred moving expenses. In those cases, courts have held that the revocation of the employment-at-will promise before any consideration was exchanged triggers the doctrine of promissory estoppel, whereby the innocent party is entitled to damages. In promissory estoppel cases, courts frequently award damages equal to the out-of-pocket costs plus what the employee lost in quitting her job and declining employment elsewhere.[24] For example, suppose that Donatello is given a written offer of employment to go to work for Renaissance Architect Firm (RAF) for an annual salary of $50,000 to begin in 30 days. Donatello gives his current employer notice of his resignation

---

[23]At-will employees are those who may be fired with or without cause because they are not covered by a contract or any other promises of continued employment. Employees at-will are discussed in detail in Chapter 11, "Agency."

[24]Note that generally courts do *not* measure damages by looking at what the employee would have earned from the defendant in a certain time period.

and then moves his home 100 miles in order to be closer to RAF's headquarters. The day before Donatello shows up for work, RAF informs him that due to financial difficulties it can no longer honor its offer of employment. When Donatello attempts to regain his old employment, he is told that his position was filled and there is no chance of rehiring him. Donatello cannot prevail on a breach of contract claim because no consideration was actually ever exchanged and, therefore, the promise is not supported by consideration and not enforceable as a contract. However, a court would likely award Donatello damages based on promissory estoppel. RAF may be liable for damages related to Donatello's actions in reliance on RAF's promise, such as the moving expenses and compensation in connection with Donatello's resignation from his previous employer.[25]

Capacity

LO 7-6

In addition to having to meet the requirements for agreement and consideration, contracts will be enforced by the courts only if each party had the legal **capacity** to enter into a contract. Certain classes of persons have only limited power to contract: **minors** and those with **mental incapacity.** These parties may seek to *avoid* (cancel) the contract immediately, or they may enforce the contract with the option of avoiding it at any time up until the time they regain capacity. Once the party has regained capacity, the contract becomes binding on both parties.

> **KEY** POINT
>
> A minor's age is often referred to as both a sword and a shield. The minor may force the adult to complete a contract (the sword), but the adult may not force the minor to complete the contract if the minor chooses to disaffirm (the shield).

Minors Until a person reaches her majority age, any contract that she may enter into is *voidable* at the minor's option. Minors (referred to as *infants* in legal terminology) are defined by most states as those who are younger than 18. For example, Junior is 17 and enters into an agreement to purchase a pickup truck from Roscoe's Dealership. Junior later changes his mind and decides not to go through with the transaction. Roscoe may not enforce the agreement against Junior. However, Junior may still enforce the contract against Roscoe if he so desires.[26]

LEGAL/ETHICAL REFLECTION *and* DISCUSSION

Isaac is about to graduate from college. He is the first college graduate in the family, and his parents are extremely proud. They tell him that they are buying him a brand-new car as a graduation gift.

1. If the parents don't buy him the promised car, has Isaac performed consideration that could force them to do so? Explain.

2. What if Isaac, the day before graduation, sells his old car in anticipation of the car he expects to get? At graduation his parents tell him that they have changed their mind. Does Isaac have any legal rights?

3. Does it matter what kind of car the parents promised to give to Isaac? Why or why not?

4. Does it matter that the car is a gift?

---

[25]Based on *Grouse v. Group Health Plan, Inc.,* 306 N.W.2d 114 (Minn. 1981).

[26]In cases where the minor misrepresents her age, courts differ in their treatment of the transactions. In some cases, courts place a greater burden of restitution for any misrepresentations. In other cases, courts have allowed either party to avoid the contract. A minority of states allow the nonminor party to be sued for the tort of misrepresentation.

A minor may avoid a contract even before she reaches the age of majority.[27] It is important to remember that a contract made by a minor is not *automatically* void. Rather, the minor either avoids the contract or may enforce the contract. While a minor may avoid a contract up until the age of majority, the minor may also *ratify* the contract upon reaching the age of 18. Note that a minor is assumed to have ratified the contract upon reaching the age of 18 if she fails to *disaffirm* (avoid) the contract in a reasonable time period.[28] In the case where the minor has disaffirmed and avoided the contract, the other party may be entitled to an economic adjustment if the minor received some economic benefit from the contract. Generally, this means that the minor will have to return any goods or make restitution for any damages that affected the value of the good or service. In the example discussed above, suppose that Junior goes through with the truck purchase and avoids the contract on his 18th birthday. Roscoe is entitled to claim the truck back and may be entitled to compensation for the loss of the truck's market value from the previous year.

Virtually all jurisdictions recognize an *exception* to the minor-capacity rule for necessities such as food, clothing, and shelter. Thus, a 16-year-old customer at a restaurant may not disaffirm a contract to purchase french fries when presented with the bill. Another exception applies to contracts that minors enter into on behalf of their own business. When Steve Jobs and Steve Wosniak started Apple Computers, they were in their teens. Any parts or equipment they purchased and any contracts they entered into *for the business* were not treated as voidable.

Mental Incompetents   Like minors, mental incompetents are treated as having limited capacity to contract. This category covers not just obvious cases (such as mental retardation or dementia) but also temporary incompetence such as people who are highly intoxicated, people severely depressed, or people under severe or traumatic pressure. The question is whether the person was **lucid** at the time he entered into the contract. Although there is no universally accepted definition, courts have held that a party who is lucid is one who is not suffering from delusion or confusion.

In general, a person lacks capacity because of mental illness or defect if either (1) she is *unable to understand* the nature and consequences of the contract or (2) she is *unable to act in a reasonable manner* in relation to the transaction and the other party has *reason to know* of her condition.[29] For example, Oliver has Alzheimer's disease and enters into a contract with Wendell to sell 100 widgets for $1 per widget (the widget's fair market value). Oliver may avoid the contract even though the contract terms were fair and Wendell had no notice of Oliver's condition. This is true because Oliver has met the "unable to understand" criteria. Intoxication, whether it be through drugs or alcohol, can also affect capacity. Suppose that Oliver and Wendell were at a bar drinking heavily. Wendell writes on a cocktail napkin: "Because you bought me so many pints of beer, I will sell you 100 widgets for only five cents per widget." The next day Wendell sobers up and realizes what he did. Wendell may avoid the contract because he was so intoxicated that he was unable to act in a reasonable manner *and* because Oliver had *reason to know* of Wendell's condition. On the other hand, if Oliver and Wendell were drinking but neither was obviously impaired, their intoxication would likely have no effect on the validity of

---

[27]Michigan is the only state with an exception to this rule.

[28]There is no definitive test for determining what is a "reasonable time" because the time period may be case-specific depending on individual industry standards and practices.

[29]*Restatement (Second) of Contracts*, § 15(2).

the contract. Remember that in *Lucy v. Zehmer* (Landmark Case 7.1, earlier in this chapter) even though the parties had been drinking, the contract to sell Zehmer's farm was upheld.

In most states contracts made by an incompetent are *voidable,* not void. If the incompetent party regains her mental capacity, or has a guardian appointed, she may ratify the contract. Note that the other party does *not* have the power to avoid the contract. However, many states classify a contract as *void per se* (not valid from the outset) if one party has been legally declared to be incompetent prior to entering into the contract.

Legal **Speak** ›))
Lucid Being able to think clearly and rationally.

Legality

For a contract to be enforceable, it must meet the requirement of **legality;** that is, both the subject matter and performance of the contract must be legal. Depending on the state, some contracts are specifically barred by statute (e.g., a contract related to illegal gambling such as betting on sports events[30] or a contract for the sale of goods that is banned by a trade embargo), while other contracts are illegal because the terms violate some **public policy** objective (such as an overly broad restriction on employment possibilities, known as a *restrictive covenant*). As a general rule, an illegal contract is *void automatically,* and neither party may enforce it against the other. This is true even when only one party's performance is illegal. For example, if Holmes promises to paint Cardozo's home in exchange for Cardozo's promise to smuggle 500 Cuban cigars into the United States in violation of federal law, then neither Holmes nor Cardozo may enforce the contract.

CONCEPT SUMMARY Contract Formation

Mutual Assent	Consideration	Capacity	Legality
The terms must be sufficiently definite, and there must be no mistake (belief by one or both parties not in accord with the facts). The offer must represent a serious, objective intent to contract; proper acceptance of the offer must occur prior to termination by the parties or operation of law.	There must be the possibility of legal detriment to the promisee and a bargained-for exchange on the part of the promisor.	If one of the parties is a minor, the contract is voidable by the minor or the minor's guardian. If one of the parties is mentally incapacitated and the other party had reason to know of the incapacity, the contact may be avoided.	The subject matter of the contract and transaction must be legal.

---

[30]Many states do allow "small games of chance" such as church-sponsored bingo or an office football pool.

Enforcing Contracts with Covenants Not to Compete

PROBLEM *How do you protect the company's interests from employees who depart the company in order to directly compete with their ex-employer?*

One type of special contract that managers are increasingly encountering at a variety of levels in the corporate sector is the **covenant not to compete** (also called a *restrictive covenant*). In such contracts, one party agrees not to compete with another party for a specified period of time. Courts have historically subjected these contracts to close judicial scrutiny. This is not to say that covenants not to compete are unenforceable; rather, courts use a "reasonableness" approach in determining the extent to which the covenant is enforceable. Even if a court finds that the terms of the covenant were unreasonable, most courts will opt to enforce the covenant to the extent required to protect the legitimate interests of the business. For example, Jordan signs a noncompete agreement with Robert, her employer, whereby Jordan agrees not to contact any of Robert's clients anywhere in the United States for two years after she has left Robert's company. After Jordan quits and starts her own firm, Robert finds out that Jordan has been contacting Robert's clients. Robert sues to enforce the covenant. If a court finds the covenant to be too broad, the covenant may be pared back by the court to, say, one year and a more limited geographic region. This is an alternative to striking down the covenant completely.[31]

SOLUTION *Be sure that your company's restrictive covenant agreements are narrowly tailored: keeping the following requirements and standards in mind:*

- **Source:** Covenants not to compete most often arise out of either (1) the sale of a business, whereby the buyer is purchasing business assets, goodwill, and promises by the seller's principals not to compete with the buyer, or (2) part of an employment contract.

- **Sale of a business:** In the context of a sale of a business, courts are willing to enforce such covenants, but are often focused on the geographic area involved. If the covenant restriction is substantially broader than the area in which the buyer and seller are currently doing business, courts are unwilling to enforce such an overly broad restriction.

- **Employment agreements:** Covenants that are part of an employment contract (or an employment relationship) are subjected to a higher degree of scrutiny. Courts will generally permit the employment covenant to stand so long as it is designed to cover a recognized legitimate interest of the employer. Courts recognize an employer's interest in guarding *trade secrets* from being disclosed or used by an ex-employee.[32] Employers also have a legitimate interest in ensuring that former employees do not act in a way that could *damage relationships* with their existing customers. Therefore, courts have permitted contracts that prevent ex-employees from soliciting (or even contacting) customers of the ex-employer for a certain period of time. However, these types of covenants must be *reasonable* in duration, subject-matter scope, and geographic scope. Although these standards vary from industry to industry, some general guidance regarding reasonableness is helpful.

- **Duration:** The higher the position of the employee, the longer the employer can restrict the employee. A sales staffer who quit after only one year would likely not be bound any more than one or two years. The CEO of a corporation may be bound in the range of five years or more. In any case, the duration must be no greater than is required for the protection of the employer while still considering the potential for undue hardship on the employee.

[31]Based on *Restatement (Second) of Contracts,* § 184(2), Comment b, Illustration 2.

[32]Generally, a trade secret is a process, a system, or data (e.g., customer lists, formulas) that give a company a competitive edge over another. Trade secrets are covered in depth in Chapter 25, "Intellectual Property."

- *Scope of subject matter:* The restriction must be directly tied to the employee's work responsibilities. For example, if Foley works 10 years as an insurance agent for Garvey's Insurance Agency, the restrictive covenant may cover only a competing interest of insurance sales. Thus, if Foley quits Garvey Insurance, starts a career as a golf instructor, and contacts customers he met while employed by Garvey, a court would not enforce a covenant to prevent this contact because any such restriction is too broad in terms of the scope of the subject matter.
- *Geographic scope:* Employers must limit the geographic area in which the employer conducts business, *and* the geographic region must not impose an undue hardship on the employee. While some companies may legitimately claim that they do business in all 50 states, courts are still reluctant to allow a restriction to be effective countrywide because that would require ex-employees to move abroad in order to comply with the covenant. On the other hand, a small manufacturing company in Philadelphia may wish to restrict its ex-engineering employees from competing within a radius of several miles of the city. This would likely be seen as a protection of legitimate business interests without an undue burden to the employee.

ENFORCEABILITY

LO 7-7

Once it is determined that the parties have properly formed a contract, the analysis turns to **enforceability.** A contract is of little use if it is not enforceable in a court of law, and business owners and managers can reduce risk and unnecessarily exposing their company to liability by ensuring that contracts are not only properly formed but legally enforceable. Even if the elements of a contract are met, the contract must still (1) be the product of genuine assent and (2) be in writing under certain circumstances.

Legal Speak ›))
Goodwill Intangible assets that represent value to the business, such as its reputation for quality and/or service.

Genuineness of Assent

Recall from the discussion in the previous section of this chapter that an agreement must reflect mutual assent (sufficiently definite terms, lack of mistake, etc.) in order to legally form a contract. For a contract to be enforceable, the contract must *also* be the result of *genuine assent.* This means that for a contract to be valid and enforceable, the law requires the parties to have given genuine assent on the terms of the contract. A lack of genuine assent occurs in cases of (1) misrepresentation and fraudulent misrepresentation, (2) duress, (3) undue influence, and (4) unconscionability.

> **KEY** POINT
> Contracts that include restrictive covenants must protect a legitimate business interest of an employer and be reasonable in terms of scope and duration.

Misrepresentation   When one party to an agreement makes a promise or representation about a material fact that is not true, the other party may avoid the contract on the basis of **misrepresentation.** This is true even if the misrepresenting party doesn't actually know that the promise or representation was false. Consequently, the defense is sometimes called *innocent misrepresentation,* which distinguishes it from *fraudulent misrepresentation* (discussed later). For one party to avoid the contract on the basis of misrepresentation, she must prove (1) the misrepresented fact was *material* (i.e., it concerns a basic assumption in the agreement, or the false representation somehow changed the value of the contract); (2) she *justifiably relied* on the misstatement when forming an agreement (such as determining the price to be paid for a commercial office building); and (3) the misrepresentation was one of *fact* and not just someone's opinion or mere puffing (e.g., "This building's roof is only five years old" is a verifiable fact, whereas "The roof is in great shape" is puffing).

Sometimes it is difficult to distinguish between fact and opinion. In one famous case, a dance student sued her dancing school on the basis of misrepresentations by her instructor who had frequently assured her that she had "excellent potential" for dance so long as she kept purchasing pricey lessons from the dancing school. Eventually, the student sought another teacher who informed her that she had minimal dance aptitude and could barely detect a musical beat. The dance school argued that the advice was merely opinion and, therefore, could not be the basis for a misrepresentation claim. Nonetheless, the court ruled in favor of the student and reasoned that because the dancing school had "superior knowledge" on the subject, its it had a duty to act in good faith in its contract transactions.[33]

Fraudulent Misrepresentation   When one party has engaged in conduct that meets the standards for misrepresentation but that party has actual *knowledge* that the representation is not true, this is known as **fraudulent misrepresentation** (sometimes referred to simply as *fraud*). That is, misrepresentation plus knowledge (also known as *guilty knowledge*[34]) equals fraudulent misrepresentation. The primary difference between misrepresentation and fraudulent misrepresentation, from a manager's perspective, is the relief available to the innocent party. In both cases, the innocent party may *avoid* the contract and be released from any obligations. In cases of misrepresentation, the innocent party has only limited relief in terms of money damages because recovery in many states is limited to any actual out-of-pocket damages. In cases of fraudulent misrepresentation, most states classify the contract as void and the innocent party is generally entitled to recover money damages for any losses incurred plus more for speculative damages such as loss of future profits. Some states go as far as allowing an award of **treble damages,** which are three times the actual damages.

> **KEY** POINT
>
> The elements of misrepresentation (materiality, justifiable reliance, and fact) *plus* the element of actual knowledge of the misrepresented fact is considered fraudulent misrepresentation, and the innocent party may be entitled to additional recovery.

To better understand the difference between innocent misrepresentation and fraudulent misrepresentation, suppose Marshall negotiated to purchase Nino's office building. During the negotiations, Marshall asked Nino if the building had any radon[35] in the underground storage basements. Nino replied that he has owned the building for 10 years and there was no radon. Marshall then agreed to buy the property for $100,000, but before the closing date he found out that radon is present in the basements and it will cost $15,000 for a radon evacuation system to be installed. In this case, the radon was a material fact (changes the value of the contract by $15,000), Marshall relied on that fact in calculating the price, and Nino's representation was of a fact that turned out to be false. Marshall may, therefore, avoid the contract based on *innocent misrepresentation*.

However, suppose that after Marshall cancels the contract, Nino finds another party to buy the building (New Buyer). When New Buyer asks Nino about the radon, Nino gets nervous about the sale falling through, so he lies, saying "as far as I know" there is no radon. New Buyer may avoid the contract on the basis of fraudulent misrepresentation because Nino's statement fits the requirements for misrepresentation but in this case he had knowledge that his statements was false. Thus, New Buyer would also be entitled to additional money damages from Nino for any losses that New Buyer suffered as a result of the *fraudulent misrepresentation*.

---

[33] *Vokes v. Arthur Murray, Inc.,* 212 So. 2d 906 (Fla. Dist. Ct. App. 1968).

[34] The legal term for this type of guilty knowledge is *scienter.*

[35] Radon is an invisible, naturally occurring gas that the EPA has determined to be a risk factor for cancer.

FACT SUMMARY   Jane and Francesco Secchi negotiated a lease for space for purposes of opening the Italian Cowboy restaurant. The negotiations took place through the property manager, Powell, who gave the Secchis various assurances that the leased space was practically new, was in perfect condition, and had no defects. Based on these representations, the Secchis entered into a lease agreement with Prudential (the landlord) for the space and commenced renovations. During this initial period, the Secchis learned that the previous tenant in the space had complained to Powell about a noxious odor that made the space unfit for use. When confronted with the information, Powell denied that the previous tenant had complained and gave further assurances to the Secchis that there had never been a problem with the property. Eventually the odor became sufficiently offensive that the Secchis employed a variety of plumbers and workers to eliminate it, but these attempts were unsuccessful and their restaurant customer base dwindled.

After they confirmed that the former tenant had, in fact, complained about the odor directly to Powell, the Secchis terminated the lease and sued their landlord and property manager for fraudulent misrepresentation. Prudential argued that Powell's representations were puffery and cannot be the basis for a material misrepresentation. The trial court ruled in favor of the Secchis, but the court of appeals reversed.

SYNOPSIS OF DECISION AND OPINION   The Texas Supreme Court found in favor of the Secchis based on fraud. The fact that Powell had been on the premises and had experienced the odor problems firsthand showed that her statements were made with an intention to hide the truth. The court also ruled that the statements were beyond mere puffery and were in fact material to the contract.

WORDS OF THE COURT: Material Fact   "Initially, it defies common sense and any plausible meaning of the word 'problem' to infer from the first two representations that in Prudential's 'opinion,' the sewer gas odor was not a problem for [the previous tenant]. A foul odor is obviously problematic to a restaurant. Testimony indicated that Powell herself personally experienced the odor and described it as 'almost unbearable' and 'ungodly.' According to its regional manager, [the previous tenant] had even indicated to Powell that it was late in making rent payments because of the odor. In light of the circumstances, we conclude that the statements concealing the odor 'problem' are more properly statements of fact, not pure expressions of opinion. . . . We conclude that as a matter of law, Powell's representations were actionable, and legally sufficient evidence existed to demonstrate that they were known to be false when made."

Case Questions

1. Why did the court determine that the statements made by Powell were material?

2. Should the Secchis have contacted the prior tenant to verify Powell's statements?

3. If the Secchis had contacted the prior tenant and found out that a prior problem existed, would that have affected the outcome of this case? Why or why not?

4. Since the court found that fraud existed, what remedies and damages are the Secchis entitled to?

In Case 7.4, a court analyzes a fraudulent misrepresentation claim in the context of promises made by a landlord to a lessee regarding the condition of a building being rented for use as a restaurant.

Concealment of Material Fact   Although many fraudulent misrepresentations stem from affirmative promises (such as the age of a roof), sometimes a fraudulent misrepresentation occurs when one party *conceals* a material fact. While parties do *not* have a general duty to disclose all information to each other, courts have allowed the use of misrepresentation in cases where a party has asserted a half-truth that led to an overall misrepresentation, where one party takes affirmative action to conceal truth from the other, and where one party fails to correct a past statement that the other party subsequently discovers is untrue.

Self-Check Fraud and Misrepresentation

For each transaction, does either fraud or misrepresentation exist?

1. Brittany buys a horse from Tex. She buys the horse because Tex told her that the horse "ran like the wind." In fact, the horse can't run more than 50 yards without stopping to rest.

2. Hawkins is interested in buying Joan's home. He asks her if the roof leaks, and she truthfully answers that she's lived in the home for 13 years and the roof has never leaked. Three days later, it rains and the roof leaks. Hawkins returns a week later, Joan says nothing, and Hawkins purchases the home.

3. Paul bought a used car from John. John had turned back the odometer and had changed public records to hide the fact that the car had been in three accidents. One year later, Paul sold the car to George. George bought the car because it had low mileage and public records showed no accidents.

4. Tony is selling his golf clubs. After Mel comes to look at them, he agrees to buy them and leaves for the bank to get cash. When he returns, he pays Tony and puts the golf clubs in his car. Tony and Mel shake hands, and Tony says, "You got a really good deal—these clubs once belonged to Tiger Woods." A week later, Mel discovered that Tiger Woods never owned or used the clubs.

5. Flo is selling her car. The car has an oil leak, so there is oil evident to anyone who looks at the engine. Just before Tom comes over to look at the car, Flo has the engine steam-cleaned. When Tom looks at the engine, it is spotless and he does not ask if it leaked oil.

6. Lisa needs a new battery for her car. The salesperson tells her that the Try-Hard battery is the best battery that money can buy. She always likes things that are the best, so she buys the battery. A week later she discovers that the Try-Hard battery is inferior and is not very well regarded by those who know car batteries.

Answers to this Self-Check are provided at the end of the chapter.

Duress   If one party to a contract uses any form of unfair coercion to induce another party to enter into or modify a contract, the coerced party may avoid the contract on the basis of **duress.** Generally, the law recognizes three categories of duress: (1) violence or threats of a violent act;[36] (2) economic threats such as wrongful termination or threats to breach a contract; and (3) threats of extortion or other threats where by the other party has no meaningful choice. One important point to consider is that if one party threatens another with a certain act, whether he would ordinarily have the legal right to perform that act is *irrelevant.* This becomes a central principle in a case where some economic duress is at issue. For example, Bloom works for Joyce as an employee at-will (that is, either party may terminate the employment with or without cause).[37] Joyce threatens Bloom that he will be fired unless he agrees to sell his stock to Joyce for $5 per share.

---

[36]Note that duress is one of the few areas of contract law based on the subjective belief of one of the parties in the agreement. That is, regardless of the form and content of the threats, if the coerced party shows that he was, for example, unusually timid or in an unusually vulnerable state of mind, he may use the duress defense even if an ordinarily reasonable person would not have been intimidated by such threats. *See, generally,* J. D. Calamari, J. M. Perillo, and H. H. Bender, *Cases and Problems on Contracts,* 4th ed. (St. Paul, MN: West/Thomson, 2004), p. 309.

[37]Employment-at-will is discussed in detail in Chapter 12, "Employment Relationships and Labor Law."

Bloom has no choice, so he sells the stock. A court will allow Bloom to avoid the contract based on this threat even though Joyce had a legitimate right to fire Bloom with or without just cause.

Undue Influence   The defense of **undue influence** gives legal relief to a party who was induced to enter into a contract through the improper pressure of a trusted relationship. Undue influence allows the influenced party to avoid a contract when the court determines that the terms of the contract are *unfair* and the parties had some type of relationship that involved a *fiduciary duty* or some duty to *care* for the influenced party. For example, Edna is a caregiver for June, a wealthy widow who is confined to a wheelchair. Edna informs June that she can no longer be her caregiver unless June signs a contract to assign to Edna $50,000 worth of Microsoft stock. June cannot imagine the thought of being alone or finding another caregiver, so she goes ahead with the contract. In this case, a court would likely allow June to avoid the contract based on the undue influence that Edna had asserted over her.

Unconscionability   When an agreement is reached between two parties that have met the required elements and are not subject to the defenses discussed previously, the contract may still potentially be avoided on the grounds that one party suffered a grossly unfair burden that shocks the objective conscience. Recall from our discussion of consideration that courts will generally not be inclined to weigh the amount and type of consideration to determine whether the exchange is objectively fair. While this doctrine remains true, the defense of **unconscionability** gives the court the tools to refuse to enforce a contract where the consideration is grossly unequal. For example, in *Waters v. Min Ltd.,*[38] an appellate court allowed one party to avoid a contract in which she signed over an annuity insurance contract with an immediate value in excess of $150,000 in exchange for a check for $50,000. The fully annuitized value of the contract would have been over $530,000. The court ruled that although there was a written contract that met the elements required under the law, the disparity of value in the exchange along with other circumstances such as drug dependency and lack of legal advice was "too hard of a bargain for a court [to enforce]." While courts apply this defense *very* narrowly, it remains a viable defense when one party was induced to enter the contract through oppressive terms and no bargaining was possible. Thus, high-pressure sales tactics that mislead illiterate consumers may be one case in which a court would likely allow a party to avoid the contract.[39] Courts have also been suspicious of standardized preprinted contracts, known as *adhesion contracts,* because there is an assumption that the nondrafter has not genuinely bargained for the terms of the agreement. For example, in *Henningsen v. Bloomfield Motors, Inc.,*[40] an appellate court held that a disclaimer of a warranty that was buried in small print in a preprinted agreement to purchase a used car was *void* because the drafter had "gross inequity of bargaining position" and that an ordinary person would not be able to fully comprehend what legal rights he was giving up. Therefore, the court held that enforcement of the disclaimer was against public policy. In some cases, courts have held that arbitration clauses contained in contracts are unconscionable.[41] The enforceability of arbitration clauses in contracts is discussed in detail in Chapter 4, "Resolving Disputes: Litigation and Alternative Dispute Resolution Options."

---

[38]587 N.E.2d 231 (Mass. 1992).

[39]In the landmark case *Frostifresh Corp. v. Reynoso,* 274 N.Y.S.2d 757 (1966), the court held that a contract in which one party sold a freezer to another party who spoke very little English was unconscionable because of unethical sales practices, an oppressive credit installment agreement, and little benefit to the buyer.

[40]161 A.2d 69 (N.J. 1960).

[41]*Brower v. Gateway 2000, Inc.,* 246 A.D.2d 246 (N.Y. App. Div. 1998).

LO 7-8 Statute of Frauds

The statute of frauds is the law governing which contracts must be *in writing* in order to be enforceable. As its title suggests, the statute's purpose is to prevent fraud by requiring that certain contracts have written evidence of their existence and terms in order to be enforceable. This is not to say, however, that the statute requires all contracts to be in writing. Nor does it require that the contract writing be in a prescribed format. Courts have even held that an agreement on a brown piece of wrapping paper written in crayon between an art buyer and an artist was acceptable as an enforceable writing because it contained a signature, noted the quantity, and was supported by circumstances that indicated a contract with the artist for the sale of paintings.[42] The one element that is uniformly required is a signature of the party against whom enforcement of the contract is sought.

The statute of frauds primarily applies to five types of contracts:[43]

- Contracts that involve the sale of interest in land.
- Contracts that cannot be (i.e., are *not able* to be, by its terms) performed in *under one year.*
- Contracts to pay the *debt of another* (e.g., a loan surety).
- Contracts made in consideration of *marriage* (e.g., prenuptial agreement).
- Contracts for the *sale of goods for $500 or more* and lease transactions for goods amounting to $1,000 or more (UCC contracts).

✔ Self-Check Statute of Frauds

Which of the following contracts would need to be in writing to be enforceable?

1. A contract whereby the president of NewCo gives a personal guarantee (i.e., uses personal assets as collateral) for a $150,000 revolving line of credit loan to NewCo from First National Bank.
2. An agreement of sale for a piece of real estate for a corporation to build a new warehouse for $500,000.
3. A contract for consulting services for $10,000 over the next 90 days.
4. A two-year advertising contract between a retail store and a local newspaper.
5. Phillip purchases a small piece of land for $499.

Answers to this Self-Check are provided at the end of the chapter.

E-Mail and the Statute of Frauds   One question that continues to work its way through various state courts is to what extent e-mail transmissions can be used to satisfy the statute of frauds. In Case 7.5, a New York appellate court uses an "intent to authenticate" standard to determine whether an e-mail satisfies the statute of frauds.

Interpretation Rules for Written Contracts   In adjudicating disputes concerning the contents of a contract, courts use interpretation rules to guide their analysis. Before signing a written agreement, the parties typically engage in preliminary negotiations that involve discussions and perhaps documents, such as letters or memos, which are intended to help the parties come to an agreement. The **parol evidence rule** provides that any writing intended by the parties to be the *final* expression of their agreement may not

---

[42] *Rosenfeld v. Basquit,* 78 F.3d 184 (2d Cir. 1996).

[43] A sixth application (involving executors) exists, but it does not have any implications for business owners or managers.

FACT SUMMARY In a transaction to sell Stevens's public relations firm to Publicis, the parties entered into two agreements. The first was a stock purchase agreement transferring all of Stevens's stock to Publicis for a certain price. The second was an employment agreement whereby Stevens would be employed by Publicis as the CEO of a newly formed subsidiary entity, Publicis-Dialog Public Relations (PDPR), created by virtue of the stock acquisition. The employment agreement required that any modification to the agreement had to be in writing signed by both parties. The agreement defined Stevens's duties as the "customary duties of a Chief Executive Officer." When PDPR failed to reach certain financial targets, Publicis removed Stevens as CEO. Subsequently, an executive from Publicis and Stevens had an e-mail exchange regarding a new role for Stevens at PDPR whereby Stevens would now be cultivating new clients. The e-mail exchanges contained unambiguous terms of acceptance by Stevens to the modification to his terms of employment. Additionally, each e-mail transmission bore the typed name of the sender at the foot of the message. Eventually, Stevens and Publicis had a breach of contract dispute, and Stevens claimed that the modification was not effective because it failed to meet the requirements of the statute of frauds because the e-mails did not constitute a "writing" and did not contain any signatures.

SYNOPSIS OF DECISION AND OPINION The appellate court held in favor of Publicis and ruled that the series of e-mails amounted to signed writings that could be used to modify the employment agreement and met the statute of frauds requirement. The court focused on the fact that the e-mails contained a name at the end of each message that signaled the author's intent to validate its contents.

WORDS OF THE COURT: Satisfying the Statute of Frauds "The e-mails from Stevens constitute 'signed writings' within the meaning of the statute of frauds, since Stevens name at the end of his e-mail signified his intent to authenticate the contents. Similarly, Bloom's (the Publicis executive) name at the end of his e-mail constituted 'signed writing' and satisfied the requirement of the employment agreement that any modification be signed by all the parties."

Case Questions

1. If the parties did not wish to allow e-mail to serve as an appropriate method to modify the contract, what wording could have been used in Stevens's employment agreement?

2. Could the principle that the court articulates apply in a negotiation via e-mail for the sale of goods? That is, if two parties are negotiating a price via e-mail and there is language of agreement by the parties, does that alone satisfy the statute of frauds even if no actual written contract with the parties' signatures exists?

---

be *contradicted* by any oral or written agreements made prior to the writing. Note that the parol evidence rule does not bar admission of the preliminary documents when they are being used to determine the meaning that the parties intended concerning a particular term in the contract. For example, suppose that Mike is negotiating the purchase of a car from Joe's dealership and Joe's promises a 30-day 100 percent warranty on parts and labor. If Mike signs the final contract and the warranty has been left out, Mike cannot introduce evidence of the oral negotiations. If the 30-day warranty is mentioned but the specifics (100 percent warranty on parts and labor) are omitted, Mike will be permitted to provide evidence, if he can, to explain the intent of the parties and terms of the warranty.

Sometimes contracts contain **ambiguous terms.** In such cases, these terms are construed by the court *against the interest* of the side that drafted the agreement. Courts may also *supply* a reasonable term in a situation where the contract is silent and has **omitted terms.**

Enforceability of Contracts under the Statute of Frauds Using the statute of frauds as a defense to a contract can make that contract unenforceable, regardless of whether all of the elements and other requirements are met in the contract. This applies to executory contracts, but does not apply once a contract is executed. Suppose that Maria orally agrees to buy a car from Richard for $600. He will come to her home in two hours to deliver the title and keys, and she will then pay him. When he doesn't arrive at her house, she phones him and he says that he changed his mind and will not sell the car. Maria has no recourse because the violation of the statute of frauds (a sales contract over $500) renders the contract unenforceable. Suppose, however, that Richard does show up and the title, keys, and money are exchanged. The next day Maria phones Richard and says that she changed her mind and wants to rescind the contract because it violated the statute of frauds. She cannot because the contract is now executed and the defense is lost.

KEY TERMS

Genuine assent p. 168   The knowing, voluntary, and mutual approval of the terms of a contract by each party; required for a contract to be enforceable.

Statute of frauds p. 168   The law governing which contracts must be in writing in order to be enforceable.

Mutual assent p. 169   For the formation of a valid contract, the broad underlying requirement that the parties must reach an agreement using a combination of offer and acceptance and that the assent must be genuine.

Offer p. 169   A promise or commitment to do (or refrain from doing) a specified activity. In contract law, the expression of a willingness to enter into a contract by the offeror's promising an offeree that she will perform certain obligations in exchange for the offeree's counterpromise to perform.

Acceptance p. 169   The offeree's expression of agreement to the terms of the offer. The power of acceptance is created by a valid offer.

Objective intent p. 169   For an offer to have legal effect, the requirement that, generally, the offeror must have a serious intention to become bound by the offer and that the terms of the offer must be reasonably certain.

Revocation p. 172   An action terminating an offer whereby the offeror decides to withdraw the offer by expressly communicating the revocation to the offeree prior to acceptance.

Rejection p. 172   An action terminating an offer whereby the offeree rejects the offer outright prior to acceptance.

Counteroffer p. 172   An action terminating an offer whereby the offeree rejects the original offer and proposes a new offer with different terms.

Operation of law p. 172   Termination of an offer by the occurrence of certain happenings or events, which

generally include lapse of time, death or incapacity of the offeror or offeree, destruction of the subject matter of the contract prior to acceptance, and supervening illegality.

Irrevocable offers p. 174   Offers that cannot be withdrawn by the offeror; include offers in the form of an option contract, offers that the offeree partly performed or detrimentally relied on, and firm offers by a merchant under the Uniform Commercial Code.

Detrimental reliance p. 175   Situation in which the offeree acts, based on a reasonable promise made by the offeror, and would be injured if the offeror's promise is not enforced.

Mirror image rule p. 175   Principle stating that the offeree's response operates as an acceptance only if it is the precise mirror image of the offer.

Lapse of time p. 176   An event covered under operation of law in which a contract may be terminated once either the offeror's expressed time limit has expired or a reasonable time has passed.

Mailbox rule p. 176   Principle stating that the acceptance of an offer is effective upon dispatch of the acceptance via a commercially reasonable means and not when the acceptance is received by the offeree; governs common law contracts.

Mistake p. 180   In contract law, an erroneous belief that is not in accord with the existing facts.

Mutual mistake p. 180   An erroneous belief held by both parties that concerns a basic assumption on which a contract was made.

Unilateral mistake p. 180   An erroneous belief held by only one party about a basic assumption in the terms of an agreement.

Consideration p. 181   The mutual exchange of benefits and detriments; for the formation of a valid contract, the requirement that each party receives something of value (the benefit) from the other and that each party gives up something of value (the legal detriment) to the other, resulting in a bargained-for exchange.

Forbearance p. 181 The giving up of a legal right as consideration in a contract.

Nominal consideration p. 182 Consideration that is stated in a written contract even though it is not actually exchanged.

Preexisting duty p. 183 A duty that one is already legally obligated to perform and, thus, that is generally not recognized as a legal detriment.

Bargained-for exchange p. 183 The aspect of consideration that differentiates contracts from illusory promises by holding that a performance or return promise is bargained for only if it was exchanged for another promise.

Illusory promise p. 183 A promise that courts will not enforce because the offeror is not truly bound by his vague promise or because a party cannot be bound by his promise due to the lack of a bargained-for exchange. Promises of gifts and deathbed promises are two examples.

Past consideration p. 184 A promise made in return for a detriment previously made by the promisee; does not meet the bargained-for exchange requirement.

Promissory estoppel p. 184 Theory allowing for the recovery of damages by the relying party if the promisee actually relied on the promise and the promisee's reliance was reasonably foreseeable to the promisor.

Capacity p. 185 For the formation of a valid contract, the requirement that both parties have the power to contract. Certain classes of persons have only limited powers to contract, including minors and those with mental incapacity.

Minors p. 185 Category of individuals who have limited capacity to enter into a contract; includes those younger than the majority age of 18. Until a person reaches her majority age, any contract that she may enter into is voidable at the minor's option.

Mental incapacity p. 185 Category of individuals who have limited capacity to enter into a contract; includes anyone who is unable to understand the nature and consequences of the contract and anyone who is unable to act in a reasonable manner in relation to the transaction when the other party has reason to know of his condition.

Lucid p. 186 Sane and thinking clearly.

Legality p. 187 For the formation of a valid contract, the requirement that both the subject matter and performance of the contract must be legal.

Public policy p. 187 Part of the legality requirement for a valid contract; necessitates that the terms be consistent with public policy objectives.

Covenant not to compete p. 188 Type of contract in which one party agrees not to compete with another party for a specified period of time.

Enforceability p. 189 The ability of a properly formed contract to be enforceable in a court of law; determined by examining whether the contract is a product of genuine assent and is in writing (under certain circumstances).

Misrepresentation p. 189 Situation in which one party to an agreement makes a promise or representation about a material fact that is not true; basis for avoiding a contract.

Fraudulent misrepresentation p. 190 Situation in which one party has engaged in conduct that meets the standards for misrepresentation and that party has actual knowledge that the representation is not true; basis for avoiding a contract.

Treble Damages p. 190 Triple damages; often awarded in fraud cases.

Duress p. 192 The use of any form of unfair coercion by one party to induce another party to enter into or modify a contract; basis for avoiding a contract.

Undue influence p. 193 A defense that gives legal relief to a party who was induced to enter into a contract through the improper pressure of a trusted relationship.

Unconscionability p. 193 A defense that may allow a party to potentially avoid a contract on the grounds that she suffered a grossly unfair burden that shocks the objective conscience.

Parol evidence rule p. 194 Interpretation rule stating that any writing intended by the parties to be the final expression of their agreement may not be contradicted by any oral or written agreements made prior to the writing.

Ambiguous terms p. 195 Contract terms that are vague and indefinite. In contract law, these terms are construed by the court against the interest of the side that drafted the agreement.

Omitted terms p. 195 Contract terms that are left out or absent. In contract law, courts may supply a reasonable term in a situation where the contract is silent.

Big Time Toymaker (BTT) develops, manufactures, and distributes board games and other toys to the United States, Mexico, and Canada. Chou is the inventor of a new strategy game he named *Strat.* BTT was interested in distributing Strat and entered into an agreement with Chou whereby BTT paid him $25,000 in exchange for *exclusive negotiation* rights for a 90-day period. The exclusive negotiation agreement stipulated that no *distribution* contract existed unless it was in writing. Just three days before the expiration of the 90-day period, the parties reached an oral distribution agreement at a meeting. Chou offered to draft the contract that would memorialize their agreement. Before Chou drafted the agreement, a BTT manager sent Chou an e-mail with the subject line "Strat Deal" that repeated the key terms of the distribution agreement, including price, time frames, and obligations of both parties. Although the e-mail never used the word *contract,* it stated that all of the terms had been agreed upon. Chou believed that this e-mail was meant to replace the earlier notion that he should draft a contract, and one month passed. BTT then sent Chou a fax requesting that he send a draft for a distribution agreement contract. Despite the fact that Chou did so immediately after receiving the BTT fax, several more months passed without response from BTT. BTT had a change in management and informed Chou that it was not interested in distributing Strat.

1. At what point, if ever, did the parties have a contract?

2. What facts may weigh in favor of or against Chou in terms of the parties' objective intent to contract?

3. Does the fact that the parties were communicating by e-mail have any impact on your analysis in Questions 1 and 2?

4. What role does the statute of frauds play in this contract?

5. Could BTT avoid this contract under the doctrine of mistake? Explain. Would either party have any other defenses that would allow the contract to be avoided?

6. Assuming, *arguendo,* that this e-mail does constitute an agreement, what consideration supports this agreement?

Managers are frequently on the front lines when ambiguous preliminary agreements are involved and must have a relatively sophisticated knowledge of what constitutes a contract and what rules govern contracts. In the Theory to Practice problem, the BTT manager has done a very poor job protecting BTT from potential liability due to the ambiguity in the e-mails and his actions. Draft an e-mail that a BTT manager could send to Chou after their first meeting that outlines some preliminary working terms. However, your objective is to draft the e-mail in a way that no reasonable person would believe it to be an offer; rather, the e-mail should be thought of as a preliminary attempt to settle terms after a negotiation meeting. For instance, would the subject line be the same as the one the BTT manager used ("Strat Deal")? Also, focus on language in your e-mail that clearly outlines what the parties must do next in order to enter into a formal agreement, and include time frames. A sample answer may be found on this textbook's website at www.mhhe.com/melvinleb2e.

MUTUAL ASSENT/ACCEPTANCE

Lexmark is a manufacturer and distributor of ink cartridges for computer printers. It introduced a rebate plan called Return Program Cartridges whereby a consumer could receive a "prebate" (i.e., a discount upon purchase) on ink cartridges. This price discount was given in exchange for an agreement by the consumer not to tamper with the cartridge. The consumer simply had to agree to return the empty cartridge to Lexmark. The agreement was printed on the ink cartridge box, and Lexmark claimed that by opening the box the consumer agreed to the terms of the Return Program Cartridges program. A consumer group challenged Lexmark's program, contending, among other things, that Lexmark could not enforce an agreement on the box because the consumer had never formally accepted the terms of Lexmark's offer.

CASE QUESTION

1. Can one party be deemed to accept an offer simply by opening a product box even if there is no evidence that the party *actually* read the terms?

CASE SUMMARY 7.2 :: Biomedical Systems Corp. v. GE Marquette Medical Systems, Inc., 287 F.3d 707 (8th Cir. 2002)

LEGALITY

GE Marquette Medical Systems (GE) contracted with Biomedical Systems Corp. to manufacture a new medical instrument based on technology owned by Biomedical. The contract required GE to obtain clearance from the Food and Drug Administration (the federal regulatory agency that covers such medical devices) within 90 days in order to move ahead on the project. After this contract was signed, GE determined that obtaining this clearance was not a prudent path to reach its ultimate objective of having the product approved for selling to the public. Rather than seek the clearance required by the Biomedical contract, GE decided to pursue a different strategy with the FDA

that took several years to complete. When Biomedical sued GE for breach of contract, GE defended on the basis that the clearance provision in the contract was a violation of FDA procedure and, thus, the term was illegal and the contract was void.

CASE QUESTIONS

1. Can a party make a unilateral judgment as to illegality on a term of the contract when there is no affirmative finding from a regulatory authority?
2. If GE had gone ahead with the clearance process and the FDA had told GE that it was not the proper procedure, would the contract be void for illegality?

CASE SUMMARY 7.3 :: Reed's Photo Mart, Inc. v. Monarch, 475 S.W.2d 356 (Tex. Civ. App. 1971)

MISTAKE

Reed owned a small photography store and purchased his price label products from Monarch. Over a period of years, Reed ordered no more than 4,000 labels at a time from Monarch. While preparing a new order form for labels, Reed was interrupted by a customer and wrote "4MM" on the order form instead of "4M." In the industry, *4M* means 4,000 labels, while *4MM* means 4 million labels. Reed sent the mistaken order to Monarch. Despite the course of past dealings and

the fact that the maximum order that Monarch had ever received from a single customer was 1 million labels, Monarch proceeded to produce and deliver 4 million labels to Reed. Reed refused delivery and defended on the basis of mistake.

CASE QUESTIONS

1. Who prevails and why?
2. Is this a unilateral or mutual mistake? What's the difference?

CASE SUMMARY 7.4 :: MediaNews Group v. McCarthey, 494 F.3d 1254 (10th Cir. 2007)

STATUTE OF FRAUDS

McCarthey sold controlling stock interests of his newspaper publishing company to TCI in 1997. During that sale transaction (which involved a

detailed contract covering all aspects of the sale), McCarthey allegedly articulated a "side agreement" with TCI that provided McCarthey with the right to repurchase the stock from TCI on the five-year anniversary of the sale (in 2002). The side agreement was never memorialized. Before the five-year anniversary, TCI sold its interest in the newspaper to MediaNews. When McCarthey sued for breach of the oral agreement, TCI asserted that the statute of frauds barred his claim.

CASE QUESTIONS

1. Is the oral agreement enforceable? Why or why not?
2. Could the parol evidence rule apply here?

CASE SUMMARY 7.5 :: Harley-Davidson Motor Co. v. PowerSports, Inc., 319 F.3d 973 (7th Cir. 2003)

FRAUD

PowerSports applied for a franchise license from Harley-Davidson (Harley) to sell Harley products in Seminole County, Florida. During Harley's interview of PowerSports, officers of PowerSports made certain representations and promises about PowerSports' business practices and procedures. This was an important part of the negotiations because Harley had strict standards of quality and customer service with which all of its dealers had to comply. Based on these representations, Harley granted the franchise license, and PowerSports became an authorized dealer. Just days after it signed the franchise agreement, Harley became aware that PowerSports had taken significant steps toward plans to take the company public (sell company stock on the public market). This was inconsistent with Harley's requirements and conditions for owning a franchise. Harley alleged that the representations made by PowerSports were false, and it sued PowerSports for fraudulent misrepresentation, demanding a rescission of the contract plus additional damages.

CASE QUESTIONS

1. Were PowerSports misrepresentations "material"? Why or why not?
2. Suppose PowerSports went public two years after the awarding of the franchise agreement. Could Harley still sue for recession? How about 10 years?

CASE SUMMARY 7.6 :: Tafel v. Lion Antique Investments & Consulting Services (Dist. Ct. N.D. Ga. 2011)

UNENFORCEABILITY

Tafel Racing Team, Inc. (Tafel Racing), and Lion Antique Investments & Consulting Services, Inc. (Lion), entered into an agreement to purchase two Ferrari race cars. Pursuant to the agreement, Lion agreed to loan the race cars to Tafel Racing for use in the 2008 American Le Mans Series. Tafel Racing was obligated to purchase or sell the race cars 90 days after the conclusion of the 2008 American Le Mans Series. The plaintiff, James Tafel, Jr. (Tafel), is the former CEO of Tafel Racing. East Coast Jewelry (East Coast) agreed to purchase one of the Ferrari race cars for $700,000. Vladislav Yampolsky is a partial owner of East Coast. Although East Coast paid Tafel Racing $700,000, Tafel Racing did not deliver the car or refund East Coast's money. Tafel Racing filed a Voluntary Petition for Bankruptcy and listed Yampolsky as one of Tafel Racing's creditors holding unsecured nonpriority claims in the amount of $600,000. Tafel Racing also identified Tafel as a codebtor for each of Tafel Racing's creditors. At Yampolsky's request, Tafel executed a nonnegotiable promissory note in the principal amount of $600,000, plus $22,454.14 in interest, payable to Yampolsky. Tafel also executed a Deed to Secure Debt granting Yampolsky a security interest in Tafel's residence in Georgia, The note states that it was "executed and delivered . . . in consideration of advances by Yampolsky to Tafel." Tafel, however, made no payments on the note. Yampolsky assigned his rights and interest in the note to Lion. Tafel claims that the note is invalid and unenforceable. (*Hint*: Be sure to make a distinction between *Tafel Racing* and *Tafel*.)

CASE QUESTIONS

1. What defense can Tafel assert that would make the note unenforceable?
2. What must the note contain to make the note enforceable? Give an example.

Self-Check **ANSWERS**

Mailbox Rule

PROBLEM 1
No contract. Conley still had the power to revoke the offer on day 3 because Raleigh used a slower method (U.S. mail) to accept than Conley used to make the offer (fax). Therefore, Raleigh's acceptance could take effect only upon receipt of the acceptance by Conley. Because Conley did not receive the acceptance until day 4, his revocation of day 3 is effective and no contract exists.

PROBLEM 2
Contract exists on day 2 upon dispatch (mailbox rule) because RBR used a reasonable method to accept (using fax to accept an e-mail offer is reasonable because both methods are similar in that they are relatively instantaneous when sending). When the offeror actually received the acceptance is irrelevant.

PROBLEM 3
Contract exists on day 3 upon dispatch (mailbox rule) because Timothy used the same method to accept that was used to convey the offer. It is irrelevant that the revocation was already in the mail and equally irrelevant that the acceptance was received by McGlynn after Timothy had received the revocation.

Fraud and Misrepresentation

1. No fraud or misrepresentation exists. This was sales talk (puffing), so Brittany has no course of action.

2. This is a fraud. Even though Joan initially told the truth, the facts changed and her nondisclosure makes her liable for fraud.

3. John has committed a fraud against Paul by changing the mileage and accident records, two material facts in car negotiations. Paul committed a misrepresentation when he sold the car to George because, even though he had no knowledge of the true facts and did not intentionally conceal anything, the mileage and accident records were nevertheless false representations of material facts.

4. Tony's statement came after the contract had been executed, so Mel did not rely on Tony's statement when making the deal. (If the statement had been made during negotiations and Mel was a huge Tiger Woods fan, it could be argued that the statement was an intentional falsehood of a material fact and therefore a fraud.)

5. Flo is guilty of fraud because she has concealed a material fact, that the engine leaked oil.

6. No fraud or misrepresentation exists. This was sales talk (puffing), so Lisa has no course of action.

Statute of Frauds

1. Writing required. Promise to pay the debt of another.

2. Writing required. Real estate/land.

3. Careful! No writing required. Despite the high fee, the services can be performed in less than one year; thus, the contract is not subject to statute of frauds requirements.

4. Writing required. A two-year contract for services that cannot be performed in less than one year.

5. Writing required. Even though the price is below $500, it is for the purchase of an interest in land.

8
CHAPTER

Contract Performance: Conditions, Breach, and Remedies

learning **objectives**

After studying this chapter, students who have mastered the material will be able to:

8-1 Define what a condition is used for in a contract and distinguish conditions precedent from conditions subsequent.

8-2 Apply the doctrines related to good faith performance, discharge of a contract, and substantial performance.

8-3 Identify the ethical dilemmas that a manager faces in the context of good faith performance.

8-4 Articulate circumstances that give rise to events of discharge via mutual consent and operation of law.

8-5 Recognize events that result in breach of contract and explain anticipatory repudiation.

8-6 Identify the appropriate remedy available to nonbreaching parties.

8-7 Explain the responsibilities of an injured party to mitigate damages, comply with the clean hands doctrine, and tender performance.

8-8 Describe the rights of third parties in a contract assignment, delegation, or as a third-party beneficiary.

Once it has been determined that a valid and enforceable contract exists, the inquiry then necessarily focuses on whether contract obligations were faithfully met through performance by the parties. Most contracts are fully performed by the parties as contemplated, but what happens if contractual commitments are not met? This chapter continues the survey of contract law with attention to rules that govern discharge, performance, and consequences of nonperformance. Rights and obligations regarding assignment and delegation of contracts will also be examined, as will the rights of third-party beneficiaries. In this chapter, students will learn:

■ How conditions are used in a contract to allocate risk between parties.

■ Requirements to meet the standards of good faith performance and substantial performance.

■ Events that discharge a party from having to perform.

■ The consequences of failing to perform as promised, known as a *breach of contract,* and the options of the damaged party after a breach.

■ The rights and obligations of the parties when a contract is assigned or delegated.

■ The rights of third-party beneficiaries to contracts.

NATURE AND EFFECT OF CONDITIONS   LO 8-1

Parties to an agreement sometimes wish to allocate or adjust a particular risk associated with performing a contract. This risk allocation is typically accomplished by attaching some event, known as a **condition,** that must occur before a particular performance obligation is triggered. Ordinarily, the parties express such conditions using language such as "on the condition that" or "provided that" or "unless." For example, suppose that Graham hires Frost as a sales representative. The parties agree to a base salary and other basic employment terms. In addition, Graham offers to pay Frost a $1,000 bonus *provided that* Frost secures 10 new accounts during his first 30 days as an employee. Frost was able to secure only nine new accounts in that time period. Graham has no duty to perform (pay Frost $1,000) because his duty to pay was conditional on the achievement of the 10 new accounts requirement. Because Frost did not meet the condition set in the agreement, Graham is discharged from his obligation to pay the bonus.

Categories of Conditions

A condition is categorized as either a *condition precedent* (event that must occur *before* performance under a contract is due, as in the

Graham-Frost example discussed earlier), or a *condition subsequent* (event that occurs after the performance under the contract and discharges the parties' obligations). Assume that Robert interviews with a trucking company for a position as a driver. The requirement that his employment and start date are conditional upon his producing proof that he possesses a valid commercial driver's license is a condition precedent. The requirement that his continued employment is contingent on retaining his commercial driver's license is a condition subsequent.

Typical condition precedents in a business context include the delivery, inspection, and approval of merchandise prior to payment being due and the securing of financing prior to the closing of a real estate transaction. Condition subsequents include passing the bar exam or CPA exam, or meeting some other licensing requirement, within one year of beginning employment with a company or the ability to secure a zoning permit for a particular business use within 60 days of the date of the contract.

Frequently, a condition subsequent is found in insurance contracts. For example, NewCo enters into a fire insurance contract with Big Carrier Inc. that provides:

> No lawsuit for recovery under this contract shall be valid unless the lawsuit is commenced within 12 months of the fire.

A fire destroys NewCo's office, and the company files an immediate claim; however, Big Carrier refuses to pay based on an exclusion in the policy. NewCo takes no further action until 14 months after the fire and then files a lawsuit to recover damages under the policy. A court will dismiss NewCo's claim because Big Carrier is discharged from its obligation to pay (or even to litigate the dispute) by virtue of the time-period condition in the policy.[1]

The parties may also agree to *concurrent conditions* whereby each party is required to render performance simultaneously. If Abel contracts with Baker to paint Abel's portrait, the parties may agree that Abel will pay the full price of the contract at the same time as Baker delivers the portrait painting to him. If Baker fails to perform, Abel is no longer obligated to meet his obligation and he may seek legal redress for any losses suffered as a result.

Modern contract law does not recognize any substantive difference between these categories of conditions.[2] In fact, today most courts do not make any distinction between them. Rather, the law defines a condition as "an event, not certain to occur, which must occur, . . . before the performance under a contract becomes due."[3] Generally, courts do enforce a

---

CONCEPT SUMMARY Conditions

- A condition is an event that triggers a particular performance in order to allocate the risk that some part of a contract may not be completed.
- Conditions are normally signaled by phrases such as "only if," "unless," or "provided that."
- A condition is categorized as a condition precedent (*before* performance is due), a condition subsequent (*after* performance of one party), or a concurrent condition (simultaneous performance).

---

[1]Based on *Abolin v. Farmers American Mutual Life Insurance,* 100 Pa. Super. 433 (1931).

[2]Note, however, that the two differ *procedurally* with respect to who bears the burden of proof.

[3]*Restatement (Second) of Contracts,* § 230.

strict compliance standard for conditions. In *Luttinger v. Rosen*,[4] an appellate court ruled that a condition—namely, that a real estate buyer be able to obtain financing at a certain rate before going through with the purchase—must be strictly applied.

GOOD FAITH PERFORMANCE AND DISCHARGE

LO 8-2, 8-3

If the promises to perform in an agreement are not conditional, the duty to perform is absolute. Most commonly, the parties agree on terms and the parties perform the contractual obligations in **good faith** in order to complete the contract. This completion is known as **discharge,** because both parties have now "discharged" their obligation to the other by performing the agreed-upon duties. Performance may also be accomplished by delivering products to an agreed-upon location (such as a warehouse). This is known as *tendering goods* (discussed in detail in Chapter 9, "Contracts for the Sale of Goods"). The law also imposes an affirmative duty of good faith in performing obligations. In every contract, the parties

BUSINESS ETHICS PERSPECTIVE

Good Faith and the Nuclear Condition Option

Note that while the law imposes a good faith requirement on all contracting parties, as a practical matter the law may also protect those who are ostensibly acting in good faith but may have unethical motives. In some contracts, the parties agree to a conditional clause sometimes known as a *nuclear condition,* that is, a clause where by one party may cancel the contract completely if a condition is not met to that party's subjective satisfaction. Consider this case: The president of WidgetCo assigns Manager to purchase a piece of real estate. Manager enters into a contract with Owner for the sale of a piece of commercial real estate. Manager insists that the contract contain an "acceptable financing" clause as follows: "As a specific condition precedent to WidgetCo's obligation to close, the parties agree that WidgetCo must obtain financing for the transaction on terms and conditions acceptable to WidgetCo in WidgetCo's sole discretion."

After entering into the agreement with Owner, the president notifies Manager that WidgetCo is no longer interested in the property and that Manager is to use all "legal means" necessary to break the contract with Owner. Assume that Manager

also learns that WidgetCo is able to obtain financing on extremely favorable terms according to industry standards.

1. Given that the contract requires that any financing terms must be acceptable to WidgetCo, what are Manager's legal obligations to go through with the transaction? Does this differ from Manager's ethical obligations?

2. Is it possible for Manager to comply with the good faith requirement and still avoid the contract with Owner?

3. Recall the discussion on ethics decision-making models in Chapter 5, "Business, Societal, and Ethical Contexts of Law." How could these models help guide Manager's course of action?

4. Assume that the president orders Manager to lie on the loan application, thereby ensuring that any financial institution would reject the loan application. Note that lying on a loan application to a bank is a crime. What are Manager's options at that point?

5. Is this a case where using the nuclear option is simply a good, hard-nosed business practice? Are there any circumstances you could articulate under which Manager has no legal obligation but does have an ethical obligation to Owner?

---

[4]316 A.2d 757 (Conn. 1972). The contract in question was conditional upon the buyer obtaining a mortgage at a rate not to exceed 8.5 percent. The only lending institutions in the area that would lend to the buyer charged 8.75 percent. Even after the seller offered to subsidize the loan so that the effective rate was 8.5 percent for the buyer, the court held that the buyer's duty to perform was discharged by failure of a condition.

have the duty of good faith and fair dealing in performance and enforcement.[5] Although the good faith requirement is ordinarily met by the parties' simply performing their obligations completely—a situation known as *perfect performance*—the law recognizes that there are some cases in which one party does *not* perform completely yet has still acted in good faith and is entitled to enforce the remaining obligations in the contract against the other party.

Substantial Performance

Legal **Speak** ›))
Material Something is material to a contract when it is important to the contract. The things material to a contract are necessary and generally indispensable to the contract.

In some situations, the parties agree to terms of a contract and pursue good faith performance, but one party cannot give perfect performance. The law recognizes a party's good faith effort to *substantially perform* her obligations by allowing the **substantial performance** to satisfy the requirements of the agreement and trigger the other party's obligation to perform. In order to prevail in a substantial performance case, the party trying to enforce the contract must show that she acted in good faith and that any deviation from the required performance was not **material.** In this context, material means some deviation from the contract that resulted in a substantial change in value of the contract or that changes a fundamental basis of the agreement. Suppose that a retailer has contracted to purchase 500 pairs of jeans and 500 T-shirts from a clothing manufacturer. Despite a good faith effort, only the jeans and 400 T-shirts can be delivered. Since the delivered jeans and T-shirts can be sold without the missing 100 T-shirts, the missing T-shirts will not be material to the overall contract and the contract will be considered substantially performed.

Note that although the doctrine of substantial performance allows a party to meet her obligations in a contract through less-than-perfect performance, the innocent party is still entitled to collect *damages* to compensate for the imperfect performance. Generally, courts allow the substantially performing party to be paid the full amount of the contract price (or other performance due) *less* any costs suffered. Therefore, in the example discussed above, the clothing manufacturer will be paid only for the jeans and 400 T-shirts. Landmark Case 8.1, known as the *Reading Pipe* case, has been used for decades as a guidepost for applying the doctrine of substantial performance.

 Self-Check   Substantial Performance

Which of the following constitute substantial performance?

1. Wholesaler contracts with Delicatessen to deliver 50 cases of bottled beverages each week in exchange for a $3,000 monthly payment. Due to heavy holiday volume, the December shipment contains only 45 cases.

2. The Yellow Pages agrees to publish a half-page advertisement for Local Dry Cleaner in exchange for $2,000. The advertisement is published, but one digit in the telephone number is incorrect.

3. A vegetable cannery contracts with Farmer to buy 54 units of "fancy-grade" spinach, defined as "dark green in color, firm in texture, and with a leaf/stem ratio of less than 15 percent stem." Farmer delivers spinach with a leaf/stem ratio of 25 percent stem.

4. Widower contracts with Artist to paint a portrait of his late wife. The portrait is done on time and professionally, but the likeness, while resembling her, does not look exactly like the woman.

5. Book publisher agrees to sell and deliver certain named textbooks to a college bookstore with delivery on July 1, eight weeks before classes are to begin. Delivery occurs on July 5.

Answers to this Self-Check are provided at the end of the chapter.

---

[5]*Restatement (Second) of Contracts*, § 205.

FACT SUMMARY Kent contracted with Jacob and Youngs ('JY') for the construction of Kent's vacation home in upstate New York. The contract required JY to use "standard pipe of Reading manufacture." During the construction, one of the JY subcontractors mistakenly used some pipe made by other manufacturers. Just before the construction was complete, Kent's architect discovered the mistake and directed JY to remove the non-Reading pipe. However, the pipe was already sealed off and encased within the walls, and, thus, costly demolition would have been necessary to repair the mistake. JY claimed that the substitute pipe was the same in terms of quality, appearance, market value, and cost as the Reading pipe. Thus, JY completed construction but refused to fix the pipe mistake. Kent refused to pay the remaining balance on the contract, and JY sued to recover the amount due.

SYNOPSIS OF DECISION AND OPINION The court ruled in favor of JY under the doctrine of substantial performance. In its opinion, the court focused on practical application to obtain fairness rather than a strict application of performance requirements and pointed out that trivial and innocent omissions may not always be a breach of a condition. Although there are limits to the substantial performance doctrine, in this case the omission of the Reading pipe was not the result of fraud or willfulness. Moreover, there was no evidence of substantial change in the value of the contract.

WORDS OF THE COURT: Applying Substantial Performance "Where the line is to be drawn between important and trivial cannot be settled by formula. . . . Nowhere will change be tolerated, however, if it is so dominant or pervasive as in any real or substantial measure to frustrate the purpose of the contract. . . . We must weigh the purpose to be served, the desire to be gratified, and the excuse for the deviation by the letter, and the cruelty of enforced adherence."

Case Questions

1. A dissenting opinion in this case pointed out that JY's failing to use the correct pipe was grossly negligent and, thus, JY should bear the costs of reinstalling the Reading pipe. Does that strike you as convincing? Why or why not?

2. If Kent had a vested interest in the use of Reading pipe (suppose Kent was the heir to the Reading pipe fortune), what condition could he have inserted in the agreement that ensured the use of Reading brand pipe?

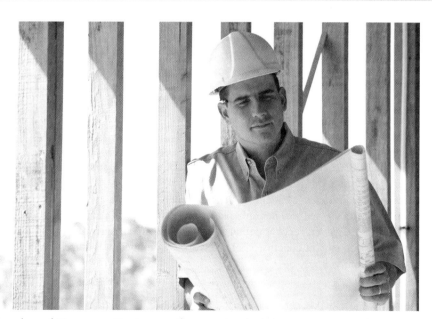

In the *Jacob and Youngs v. Kent* case, the court ruled that a contractor's substitution of non-Reading-brand pipe during construction of a home constituted substantial performance.

OTHER EVENTS OF DISCHARGE

As discussed earlier in this chapter, the most common way for the parties' obligations under a contract to be discharged is by good faith performance. However, there are other circumstances under which the parties may be discharged from obligations. Parties may be discharged via **mutual consent** or **operation of law.**

Mutual Consent

If neither party has fully performed, the parties may agree to cancel the contract. This cancellation is known as a **rescission,** and each party gives up rights under the contract in exchange for the release by the other party from performing their obligations. For example, Earl hires Peter to paint his office lobby for $1,000. The fee was to be paid in a lump sum upon Peter completing the entire lobby. After beginning work and painting one wall, Peter realizes that he vastly underestimated the time and supplies to make the job profitable and he now has another customer across town where he could make a profit. So long as Peter offers to rescind the contract and Earl accepts, the contract is cancelled and Peter no longer has to perform. At the same time, despite the fact that Earl's lobby was partially painted, Earl does not have to pay any sums due under the original contract.[6] It is important to note that rescission occurs only if both parties agree to rescind. A unilateral rescission, by only one party, is not permitted.

In some cases, the parties to a contract agree to accept performance that is different from the originally promised performance. Under the doctrine of **accord and satisfaction,** one party agrees to render a *substitute performance* in the future (known as *accord*), and the other party promises to accept that substitute performance in discharge of the existing performance obligation. Once the substitute performance has been rendered, this acts as a satisfaction of the obligation. Note that discharge of the obligation occurs only when the terms of the accord are actually performed. If the accord performance is *not* rendered, the other party has the option to recover damages either under the original contract or under the accord contact. For example, in the Earl and Peter painting contract example discussed above, suppose that Peter finished the job but that Earl did not have the $1,000 fee to pay Peter in one lump sum. Therefore, Earl offers to pay Peter $1,100 in 60 days. Peter accepts. The new agreement on payment terms is an *accord*. Once Earl has paid the $1,100 in 60 days, his accord has been *satisfied* and Peter will not be able to sue for any damages that he may have suffered as a result of Earl's failing to pay as originally agreed in the contract.[7]

The parties to a contract may also discharge their obligations by replacing the original contract with a **substitute agreement,** also known as a **modification.** The substitute agreement is generally used to compromise when two parties have a dispute as to performance of the contract and wish to amend its terms. The substituted agreement, unlike the accord agreement discussed previously, *immediately* discharges any obligations under the original contract. In the Earl and Peter painting contract discussed above, suppose that Earl and Peter enter into a substitute agreement whereby Earl agrees to pay $1,100 in 60 days so long as Peter agrees to extinguish the $1,000 debt immediately. If Earl does not perform (by paying), then Peter now has only one option: to recover for damages under the *substitute agreement*. He cannot recover damages under the original agreement. Earl's obligation to pay the $1,000 sum at conclusion of the work was immediately discharged by the substitute agreement.

---

[6]Based on *Restatement (Second) of Contracts,* § 283, Illustration 1.

[7]Since an accord does not discharge the previous contractual duty as soon as the accord is made, if Earl does not perform the accord agreement, Peter may recover damages from Earl under either the original contract obligation ($1,000 lump sum due upon completion) or under the accord agreement ($1,100 in 60 days from completion).

When the parties agree to substitute a third party for one of the original parties to the contract, the agreement may be discharged through **novation.** Essentially, a novation is a kind of substitute agreement that involves a substitute third *party* rather than a substitute promise. A novation revokes and *discharges* all of the replaced party's obligations under the old contract. For example, in the Earl and Peter painting contract discussed earlier, suppose that Peter starts work and the next day receives an offer from another customer for a major painting job. Peter proposes to Earl that Pablo (another painter who Peter knows does excellent work) complete the painting work under the original contract. If Earl then agrees

SOLUTIONS FOR MANAGERS

Understanding Check Deposits as Accord and Satisfaction

PROBLEM *In some cases, a business depositing the check of a customer may be an accord and satisfaction without the depositing business fully realizing the impact of depositing the check.*

Managers must have a fundamental understanding of this concept and businesses should have mechanisms in place to avoid an accidental accord and satisfaction claim. For example, General Contractor Inc. (GCI) contracts with Windows R Us (WRU) to install specially designed windows in a new office building, constructed by GCI, for a total of $100,000 to be paid after services are completed. After WRU installs the windows, GCI notifies the contractor that it is dissatisfied with the installation work. WRU claims that the windows were installed to industry standards and demands payment. GCI then sends a check for $50,000 (half of what is owed to WRU under the contract) to WRU's office. The check contains the endorsement "Payment in Full for Installation Services at the Office Center Site."

SOLUTION *Consider WRU's options and the consequences of each option.*

- *Deposit the check as is.* In most states, this option would result in an accord and satisfaction. When GCI sent the check with a restrictive endorsement, in effect it offered to render a substitute performance in the future (pay $50,000 instead of $100,000) as an accord agreement. Most courts view depositing a check as an affirmative acceptance of that accord offer; thus, when the check has cleared the bank's processing, it is considered

a satisfaction of the accord agreement. WRU cannot sue for damages.

- *Write "Under Protest" under the check and deposit it.* In most states, this option would result in an accord and satisfaction. Just as in the previous example, when GCI sends the check with a restrictive endorsement, in effect it has offered to render a substitute performance in the future (pay $50,000 instead of $100,000) as an accord agreement. Most courts view depositing a check as an affirmative acceptance of an accord offer regardless of any attempt by the receiving party to unilaterally alter the check. Thus, writing the words "in protest" ordinarily has no effect. When the check has cleared the bank's process, it is considered a satisfaction of the accord agreement and WRU cannot sue for damages.

- *Strike out the "payment in full" language with a black marker, and then deposit the check.* Same result as above. Unilateral attempts by the offeree to alter the substitute-offer check will not bar GCI's discharge through accord and satisfaction.

- *Return the check to GCI with a letter stating that the offer is rejected and demanding full payment.* This is the only method that will fully protect WRU from accepting the accord via satisfaction. By returning the check with an affirmative statement that the substitute accord is rejected, WRU has made clear that no satisfaction could occur and may then sue for damages if appropriate.

to allow Peter to substitute Pablo for the performance of the lobby-painting duties articulated in the original Earl-Peter contract, then a novation has occurred and Peter is now discharged from his obligation to perform the Earl-Peter contract. Earl is bound only by the new novation terms with Pablo.

Operation of Law

Contract obligations may also be discharged through *operation of law.* Despite the fact that the parties have fulfilled the requirements to form a valid contract, the law provides a discharge under certain circumstances where fairness demands it.

In some cases, after the parties have formed a contract, unexpected events occur that affect the probability of one party's ability to perform. In such cases, the law allows the parties to be excused from performance under the contract. Courts analyze these special circumstances according to three separate doctrines: **impossibility, impracticability,** and **frustration of purpose.**

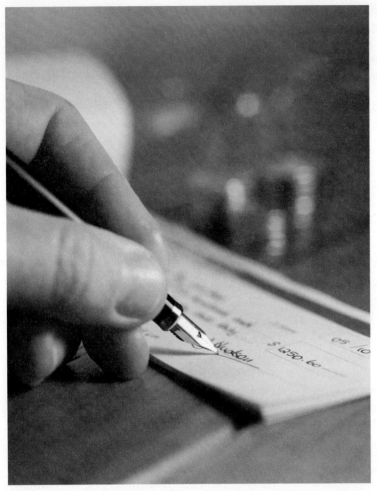

In some cases, depositing a payment check from a customer may be an event of discharge via accord and satisfaction.

Impossibility After the parties have entered an agreement, the contemplated performance of the obligations may become impossible and, therefore, may be subject to discharge. When encountering a situation in which one party is claiming impossibility, it is important for managers to understand that the impossibility must be *objective* (a reasonable person would consider the obligation impossible to perform) rather than subjective (one party decides unilaterally that performance is impossible) in order for the obligation to be discharged.[8] This can sometimes be a tricky distinction, and the modern trend of courts is against allowing impossibility as a defense unless it fits into one of four intervening events:

1. *Destruction* of the subject matter: A promises to sell B 1,000 widgets to be delivered on Tuesday. On Monday, a fire destroys the widgets. A is discharged from her obligation to provide the widgets.

2. *Death or incapacitation* of one of the parties to the contract:[9] A promises to paint B's portrait. Prior to the sitting date for the portrait, A becomes incapacitated. A is discharged from his obligation to paint the portrait.

---

[8]The Restatements, § 261, Comment c, distinguishes between the two standards by giving an example of objective impossibility ("the thing cannot be done") versus subjective impossibility ("I cannot do it").

[9]Note that unless a contract for services calls for *unique personal* services, it cannot be discharged via impossibility. The law contemplates that nonunique personal services should simply be delegated to another appropriate substitute party.

3. The *means of performance* contemplated in the contract cannot be performed: W, a wholesaler, agrees to sell R, a retailer, 5,000 widgets. Prior to the W-R contract, W contracted with M, a manufacturer, to supply him with 10,000 widgets. M halts production and cannot produce the widgets for W. W may be discharged from performance (unless the parties agreed otherwise about risk allocation).

4. Performance of the obligation has *become illegal* subsequent to the contract but prior to performance: Importer promises to buy 1,000 cigars from Producer, a manufacturer in the Dominican Republic. Subsequent to the agreement, but before Producer ships the cigars, Congress passes a federal statute imposing a complete trade embargo on the Dominican Republic. Importer and Producer are discharged from performance based on impossibility.

Legal **Speak** ›))

Supervening Illegality

A supervening illegality occurs when the performance of a contract becomes illegal subsequent to the contract formation but prior to performance.

Sometimes performance is *temporarily impossible* for one or both parties. The illness of a party who is to perform unique personal services may prevent her from performing on a timeline contemplated by the parties. However, in most cases, an illness will not prevent the performance forever. The doctrine of impossibility operates to *suspend* (not discharge) the obligation to perform until the impossibility ceases. Note that an exception to this general rule occurs when, after the temporary impossibility ends, the performance is considerably more burdensome than it would have been if the parties had performed on time (i.e., the lapse of time affected the parties' abilities to perform). Courts then will allow the obligation of the burdened party to be discharged.

Impracticability   There are certain agreements under which, although performance is not objectively impossible (as defined above), performance becomes extremely burdensome due to some unforeseen circumstance occurring between the time of agreement and the time of performance. If the burden is both *unforeseeable and extreme,* courts may allow the burdened parties' obligations to be discharged before performance. Suppose that Ace Pools contracts with Homeowner to install an in-ground pool on her property. Ace is a small company but is profitable because they can complete two pools a week during the spring, summer, and fall seasons. They have installed numerous pools in the neighborhood without any complications. Prior to signing the contract, Ace did a preliminary test dig and found no impediments to excavation. Once they begin actual excavation, they discover that 80% of Homeowner's property is solid rock beginning three feet below the surface. In order to successfully install the pool, explosives must be used, requiring a series of permits and the hiring of demolition experts. This will triple the contract cost and tie up Ace Pools for 30 days at the job site. If Homeowner does not want to pay the additional cost and Ace does not want to lose business being at one site for 30 days, Homeowner and Ace may mutually agree to rescind the contract ending both of their obligations under the contract. But what if Homeowner decided that he wanted the pool installed despite the increased time and cost. Can Ace be required to complete the contract? Ace will be able to claim that the impracticality of losing approximately eight jobs in order to complete this single job is too burdensome and will harm the company. Ace's past experience in the neighborhood and its preliminary experimental dig will be evidence that the burden caused by the rock was both unforeseen and extreme, excusing Ace from performance due to impracticality.

KEY POINT

For a contract to be discharged under impracticability, the burden must be *unforeseeable* and be *extreme* in terms of cost burden.

Frustration of Purpose   In some cases, events may occur that destroy a party's *purpose* in entering into the contract even though performance of the contract itself is not objectively impossible. When one party's purpose is completely or almost completely frustrated by such supervening events, courts will discharge her from performance.[10] Frustration of purpose may be used to discharge an obligation if, after the parties enter into an agreement, (1) a party's *principal purpose* is substantially frustrated without her fault; (2) some event occurred, when the *nonoccurrence* of the event was a central assumption of both parties when entering into the contract; and (3) the parties have not otherwise agreed on who bears the risk of such an occurrence. Just as with impracticability, frustration requires the burdened party to show that the event was unforeseeable and extreme. For example, Padraig contracts with White Hall Inn to rent a room that faces Main Street for a period of two days. Padraig's intent is to have a balcony view of the street to see the St. Patrick's Day parade. One week before the parade is scheduled, White Hall sends Padraig a confirmation of the agreement:

> Confirmed: Balcony Room at White Hall Inn (Guaranteed view of Main Street) for Padraig. $200 per night (St. Patrick's Day Parade Special). Two days. $100 deposit due in 5 days—Balance due upon checkout.

Padraig signs the letter and sends it back with a $100 bill. Much to Padraig's dismay, the St. Patrick's Day Committee cancels the parade due to a last-minute regulatory problem in obtaining a permit. Padraig cancels his reservation. If Padraig sues for his $100 to be refunded (contending that his obligation has been discharged by virtue of frustration of purpose) and White Hall countersues for the $300 balance owed (contending that Padraig could still use the room even if there was no parade), who would prevail? It is likely that Padraig would prevail because the letter sent by White Hall *acknowledges* that the primary purpose of the contract was to have the balcony view of the parade. Assuming a court finds that the parade cancellation was reasonably unforeseeable, was not the fault of Padraig, and was a basic assumption of the agreement, Padraig would prevail due to frustration of purpose.[11]

Consider, alternatively, that the parties had agreed on risk allocation through the use of language in the letter such as "In the event that the St. Patrick's Day parade does not take place for any reason, the parties agree that Padraig will pay only 50 percent of the full price for the room whether he uses the room or not. Such amount shall be due on the checkout date." In that event, a court will very likely consider the parties to have bargained away any notion of frustration (or impossibility for that matter) as an event of discharge and, thus, enforce the agreed-upon terms.

The parties may also be discharged through operation of law when (1) a contract is **unilaterally altered** by a party (the other party is discharged from performing); (2) a contract is subject to relief of the **Bankruptcy** Code (debtor is entitled to complete discharge from any contract once the bankruptcy filing has been approved by a court); (3) expiration of the **statute of limitations** (also known as the *statute of repose* in certain states) where state law imposes a time limit on enforcement of contract obligations.

CONCEPT SUMMARY Performance and Discharge

- If two parties to a contract complete their performances in a manner that is faithful to the mutual goals of the contract, and in good faith, perfect performance has occurred and it will result in a discharge for both parties.
- If a party substantially performs only essential duties of the contract, a court will enforce the agreement though the party remains liable for anything left undone.

---

[10]*Restatement (Second) of Contracts,* § 265.

[11]Based on the landmark case *Krell v. Henry,* 2 K.B. 740 (1903). This is commonly known as the *coronation case* because it involved room reservations to view a parade in connection with the coronation of the king of England. When the king fell ill, Henry refused to use the premises or make payment. When the landlord Krell sued, the court ruled in favor of Henry and the doctrine of frustration of purpose had its modern-day launch.

- A party may be discharged from the original terms of the contract by a mutual consent to rescission, a substitute performance, or a modification to the original agreement.

- A party may be discharged from the original terms of the contract by the operation of law if the contract has become impossible (no one can do it) or impracticable (I can't do it) or if its purpose has been frustrated (why would I want to do it now?).

BREACH OF CONTRACT AND ANTICIPATORY REPUDIATION

LO 8-5

When a party to an agreement owes a duty to perform and fails to fulfill her obligation, she is said to have **breached** the contract. In cases where the breach is material (i.e., relates to a fundamental term of the contract or has an effect on the value of the contract), it is called a *total* breach and the nonbreaching party will be entitled to either suspend performance or be discharged from his obligations completely. The party that suffered the breach is also entitled to sue the breaching party in an attempt to recover *money damages.* Money damage awards are one of the ways in which the law provides a method to compensate the nonbreaching party for losses suffered. These methods are known as **remedies.** Remedies are discussed later in this chapter.

There are some cases where the breach is not material, sometimes referred to as a *partial* breach.[12] In such cases, the nonbreaching party may not be relieved from performing; however, the nonbreaching party may still recover damages related to the breach from the breaching party. Recall the *Jacob and Youngs v. Kent (Reading Pipe)* case earlier in the chapter. In that case the court decided that because the deviation from expected performance was not material, it was only a partial breach. Because the breach was partial, the court awarded the nonbreaching party damages equal to the difference in price between the Reading-brand pipe and the pipe actually used.

Anticipatory Repudiation

After the parties have entered into an agreement but before performance has occurred, it sometimes becomes apparent that one party does not intend to perform as agreed. This may be apparent through the party's words or conduct. Under certain circumstances, the law provides an avenue of recovery for the nonbreaching party even *before* the nonperforming party actually breaches the contract or even before the performance is due. For example, on December 15, Manager enters into an agreement with Consultant to provide operation-consulting services for a period of six months to commence January 2. On December 20, Manager is told to cut costs, so Manager contacts Consultant in an e-mail: "Dear Consultant: We don't require your services. Sorry. —Manager." At this point, Manager has not technically breached the contract because performance is not due until January 2. However, Consultant would still be entitled to sue immediately for damages (or other remedies if appropriate) under the doctrine of **anticipatory repudiation,** without waiting for the actual breach to occur on January 2.

When one party uses unequivocal language (such as in the Manager-Consultant contract in the preceding paragraph) to repudiate, there is no question that the other may file suit immediately. Any threatened breach must be a material, or a total, breach (discussed earlier) for the nonbreaching party to exercise its right to claim an anticipatory repudiation. In Case 8.2, a federal appeals court applied the anticipatory repudiation doctrine.

Legal Speak »))
Anticipatory Breach An *anticipatory repudiation* is also commonly referred to an an *anticipatory breach.* The two terms are synonymous.

---

[12]*Corbin on Contracts,* § 1374 (1963).

FACT SUMMARY DiFolco and MSNBC entered into a two-year employment agreement for DiFolco to work as a television commentator covering the entertainment industry. MSNBC had the right to terminate the agreement after the first year by giving DiFolco 60 days advance notice. DiFolco's first eight months of employment were tumultuous, and she had several disputes with her supervisors over her assignments and working conditions. Through a series of e-mails, DiFolco complained to her supervisors about being forced off the air through MSNBC's change in schedule and coverage. One of these e-mails indicated that she wished to have a meeting to discuss her exit from the shows and to give MSNBC ample time to replace her. In that same e-mail, though, DiFolco also wrote that she wanted to be part of the MSNBC team "for a long time to come." Nonetheless, MSNBC took these e-mails to mean that DiFolco intended to repudiate her contract and sent her a proposed separation agreement claiming that she had resigned. DiFolco filed a breach of contract action against MSNBC. The trial court dismissed DiFolco's claim and ruled that the e-mail constituted DiFolco's anticipatory repudiation of her contract with MSNBC.

SYNOPSIS OF DECISION AND OPINION The Court of Appeals for the Second Circuit reversed the trial court and ruled in favor of DiFolco on the issue of anticipatory repudiation. The court held that repudiation occurs only when there is a definite and final communication of the intention to forgo performance. In this case, the court analyzed several e-mail exchanges and concluded that DiFolco did not manifest a clear and unequivocal repudiation. The e-mails were ambiguous in terms of what DiFolco's future plans may have been and included DiFolco's statement that she did not resign and was merely speculating about future time frames. Any assumptions by MSNBC that she resigned or intended to resign before completing her contract were not justified. Therefore, the court reinstated DiFolco's breach of contract claim.

WORDS OF THE COURT: Repudiation "In any event, we do not agree with the District Court that '[p]laintiff's 8/23 e-mail is . . . unambiguous in expressing [DiFolco's] intention to leave' as a matter of law. There are at least factual issues as to whether DiFolco had made a final and definite communication of an intent to forgo performance or had indicated her refusal to perform in a clear and unqualified way such as to justify a conclusion that she had repudiated her contract."

Case Questions

1. Suggest language that a court might find as expressing an unambiguous intent to repudiate in this case.

2. If you received an e-mail from an employee that concerned her "exit," would you believe she was quitting? Is the situation with DiFolco any different?

However, in cases where the language is more ambiguous or when conduct is the basis for determining the repudiation, the analysis is more complex. Modern courts have held that repudiation occurs in one of three ways:

- A *statement* by one party of her intent not to perform. Note that the statement must be such that a reasonable person would have believed that the promisor is *quite unlikely* to perform. Vague doubts about the statements are insufficient.[13]

- An *action* by the promisor that rendered her performance impossible. For example, A agrees to sell an office building to B with conveyance in 30 days. Several days later B learns that A subsequently sold and conveyed the building to C. B may sue immediately for A's breach and need not wait the full 30-day period in the contract.

- Knowledge by the parties that one party may be *unable* to perform despite both parties' best efforts.

---

[13]Note that under a UCC sales contract, a potentially aggrieved party may ask for "assurances" of performance even for doubts. A right to assurances is covered in Chapter 9, "Contracts for the Sale of Goods."

Enforcing rights under anticipatory repudiation can be crucial to some businesses, particularly if the business depends on products needed as components in its own manufacturing process. Suppose that a doll manufacturer has contracted with a company to produce and deliver 100,000 plastic eyes to be installed on its product. Delivery is scheduled for September 1, which will allow the doll company to install the eyes and ship the finished dolls to retailers in time for the holiday sales season, the company's primary source of profit. On August 1, the doll company discovers that the eye manufacturer has sold its entire stock of plastic eyes to another doll company for a higher profit and will not be able to complete its contract. By claiming an anticipatory repudiation, the doll company will not have to wait until September 1 before the actual breach occurs. It will be able to find another company to supply the needed plastic eyes, salvaging its top selling season. If the second company sells the plastic eyes at a higher price than the first, the doll company will be able to sue the original manufacturer for the difference.

CONCEPT SUMMARY Breach of Contract

- Total breach occurs when one party fails to perform its duties under the contract; partial breach is a failure to perform that is not substantial enough to discharge the nonbreaching party.
- Repudiation occurs by a statement that, reasonably interpreted, communicates nonperformance; an action making performance impossible; or knowledge by the parties that one party will be unable to perform.
- The doctrine of anticipatory repudiation allows a nonbreaching party to suspend performance and recover damages before performance is due if the other party has made an unequivocal statement or action suggesting that performance will not occur.

REMEDIES

LO 8-6

The law provides certain relief for aggrieved parties that suffer losses as a result of another party's breach of contract. These relief mechanisms are collectively referred to as *remedies*. Recall the distinction discussed in Chapter 1, "Legal Foundations," between *remedies at law* and *remedies in equity*. For most contracts, the remedy at law will be **money damages** awarded by the court to the nonbreaching party. This is simply a legal mechanism for compelling the breaching party to compensate the innocent party for losses related to the

MSNBC became embroiled in a contract dispute with a reporter in which the doctrine of repudiation was at issue.

breach. In a contract claim, money damages are primarily limited to (1) *compensatory* (also called *direct* or *actual*) damages, (2) *consequential damages,* (3) *restitution,* and (4) *liquidated damages.*[14]

Compensatory Damages

Compensatory damages cover a broad spectrum of losses for recovery of *actual damages* suffered by the nonbreaching party. These damages are an attempt to put the nonbreaching party in the same position she would have been in if the other party had performed as agreed. This includes such sums as out-of-pocket damages and even potential profits that would have been earned if performance had occurred. For example, BigCo hires LowPrice to prepare BigCo's tax returns and financial statements in time for BigCo's shareholders meeting on March 1 for a fee of $5,000. On February 15, the principal of LowPrice notifies BigCo that she cannot prepare the returns because she decided to switch careers and shut down the tax practice. BigCo must then hire HighPrice to prepare the documents. Because of the short timeline, HighPrice charged a fee of $12,000. BigCo is entitled to recover the difference between the price actually paid ($12,000) and the price that would have been paid if LowPrice had performed ($5,000) as originally agreed. Thus, BigCo is entitled to $7,000 as compensatory damages (plus any additional out-of-pocket costs related to locating and hiring a new accounting firm).

Consider, again, the doll-eye example earlier in this chapter. If the original contract was for 10 cents per eye for a total contract cost of $10,000 and the second firm charged 15 cents per eye, the doll company would have suffered $5,000 in compensatory damages. What if the doll company, after a good faith effort, could not find replacement eyes and couldn't sell its product? Could the breaching plastic-eye manufacturer have reasonably foreseen that without eyes, the dolls couldn't be sold? Such a conclusion seems likely. If the profits lost amounted to $40 per doll and the doll company couldn't sell the 50,000 dolls it had orders for, then the consequential damages could add up to $2 million.

Consequential Damages

Consequential damages compensate the nonbreaching party for *foreseeable indirect* losses not covered by compensatory damages. An aggrieved party is entitled to recover consequential damages if the damages are caused by unique and foreseeable circumstances beyond the contract itself. In order to recover consequential damages, the damages must flow from the breach (i.e., the damages were a consequence of the breach). For example, in the BigCo-LowPrice case discussed above, suppose that LowPrice had breached on the day before the tax returns were due and that BigCo needed the tax returns as documentation for a bank loan on that day. Because the tax returns were not ready until one month after the due date, the bank charged BankCo a delay fee and then raised the interest rate on the loan. These costs to BankCo are related to the unique circumstances (tax returns needed on a certain date) and are foreseeable (assuming LowPrice had reason to know of the bank loan).

The rules that limit damages for which a nonbreaching party may recover were set out in *Hadley v. Baxendale,*[15] a landmark case on consequential damages that has been followed almost universally by U.S. courts. The case involved Hadley, a 19th-century mill owner, who was forced to cease operations due to a broken crankshaft. The mill owner sent the shaft out for repairs by hiring Baxendale to deliver the shaft to a repair shop in another city. Baxendale had no reason to know that the mill was shut down, and, in fact, it

---

[14]Two other forms of civil damages recognized as a remedy at law are punitive damages (intended to deter conduct and/or punish a wrongdoer) and nominal damages (a breach exists, but no actual damages were suffered). However, these forms of damages are rare in contract cases.

[15]156 Eng. Rep. 145 (1854).

was common practice in the industry for mill owners to have a backup shaft for just such an occasion. Baxendale delayed delivery of the shaft, and this resulted in additional days of shutdown for the mill and, thus, lost profits for Hadley. Hadley sued Baxendale for the lost profits as consequential damages. The court ruled in favor of Baxendale because Hadley had not shown that a reasonable person could have *foreseen* Hadley's ongoing damages. Because Hadley had not actually communicated the unique circumstances, Baxendale was not liable for the damages related to the delay.

Restitution

Restitution is a remedy designed to prevent *unjust enrichment* of one party in an agreement. In the event that one party is in the process of performing the contract and the other party commits a material breach, the nonbreaching party is entitled to rescind (cancel) the contract and receive fair market value for any services rendered. For example, BuildCo contracts with WidgetCo to build a new warehouse for WidgetCo's inventory. One-third through the construction, WidgetCo fails to make its payments on time and, therefore, materially breaches the contract. BuildCo rescinds the contract and, in a lawsuit against WidgetCo, BuildCo may recover restitution equal to the fair market value of the work performed.

Liquidated Damages

Liquidated damages are damages that the parties agree to ahead of time. In some cases it may be very difficult to determine actual damages, so parties may agree at the time of the contract that a breach would result in a fixed damage amount. Liquidated damage provisions are commonly used in license agreements (such as a software user's license), whereby the parties agree, for example, that a breaching party will pay $10,000 in the event of a breach caused by one party making unauthorized copies of the software. In order for such provisions to be enforceable, courts have held that liquidated damage clauses must be directly related to the breach and be a reasonable estimate of the actual damages incurred (i.e., damages cannot be excessive so as to penalize the breaching party).

EQUITABLE REMEDIES

Although the usual remedy for a breach of contract is money damages, there are some instances when money damages are insufficient to compensate the nonbreaching party or when one party was unjustly enriched at the other party's expense. In these cases, a court may grant **equitable relief**. This relief comes primarily in the form of (1) *specific performance,* (2) *injunctive relief,* or (3) *reformation.*

Specific Performance

Specific performance is an equitable remedy whereby a court orders the breaching party to render the promised performance by ordering the party to take a specific action. This remedy is available only when the subject matter of the contract is sufficiently *unique* so that money damages are inadequate.[16] Therefore, specific performance is rarely available in a sale of goods case unless the goods are rare (such as a coin collection) or distinctive (such as a sculpture) so the buyer cannot reasonably be expected to locate the goods anywhere else.

One of the most common circumstances in which specific performance is awarded is real estate contracts. Most courts consider each parcel of land to be sufficiently unique to

---

[16]*Restatement (Second) of Contracts,* § 359.

trigger specific performance as a remedy. For example, Andrews agrees to sell Baker an office building in 30 days. At the closing where conveyance of the title is to take place, Andrews breaches the agreement by refusing to sell the building. In this case, Baker cannot be completely compensated for the breach because Baker chose that building for its location, convenience, accessibility, appearance, and other important factors. Baker contracted for a unique parcel of real estate and is entitled to the benefit of the agreement for the same parcel. The court will require Andrews to *perform as promised* by conveying the property to Baker. If, however, Andrews has already sold the property to a good faith buyer, then Baker may be awarded only money damages as a remedy.

Specific performance is also an appropriate remedy in a narrow category of personal-service contracts in which the parties agree that a *specific individual* will perform the services and the individual possesses a *unique quality* or expertise central to the contract. For example, if Marcel contracts with Constantine to paint Marcel's office lobby in whitewash and Constantine breaches, a court would not consider specific performance as an option because the work is not specialized enough. On the other hand, if the Marcel-Constantine contract requires that Constantine paint a special mural on the wall, that would be sufficiently unique to qualify for specific performance.

Injunctive Relief

A court order to refrain from performing a particular act is known as **injunctive relief.**[17] In the Andrews-Baker office building contract, suppose that Andrews promises to sell the building to Baker in 30 days. Baker learns that Andrews is intending to breach the contract and sell the building to Dominguez for a higher price. In this case, both money damages and specific performance are inadequate because Baker still wants the building instead of compensation for the breach. Baker will ask the court to issue an injunction that would prevent the sale of the building to Dominguez as an equitable remedy consistent with the notion of putting the aggrieved party in the same position as he would have been if the other party had performed as agreed.

Reformation

When the parties have imperfectly expressed their agreement and this imperfection results in a dispute, a court may change the contract by rewriting it to conform to the parties' actual intentions. This contract modification is called **reformation.** For example, suppose that in the Andrews-Baker building contract discussed above, Andrews' real estate broker accidentally the decimal in the price, making it $10,000 instead of the parties' agreed-upon price of $100,000. At the closing, Baker gives Andrews the check for $10,000 and refuses to pay any more, citing the price in the contract. So long as there was a sufficient basis for believing the parties intended the price to be $100,000, a court may simply reform the contract. Andrews may then show that Baker breached the contract and request specific performance as an additional remedy.

LO 8-7   AVOIDANCE AND MITIGATION OF DAMAGES

The law imposes an obligation on the parties in a contract to take appropriate steps to avoid incurring damages and losses. So long as a party can avoid the damages with reasonable effort, without undue risk or expense, she may be barred from recovery through a lawsuit. The rule preventing recovery for reasonably avoidable damages is often called the *duty to*

---

[17]The concept of injunctive relief is covered in more detail in Chapter 4, "Resolving Disputes: Litigation and Alternative Dispute Resolution Options."

mitigate.[18] For example, Leonardo contracts with NewCo to design a new office building for NewCo. Midway through the design planning process, NewCo changed its management, notified Leonardo that it believes that the design contract is invalid, and ordered him to stop work. Despite this, Leonardo continues the design process, submits the final work product to NewCo, and demands payment in full. In this case, it is likely that a court will not allow Leonardo to recover for any damages occurring after the NewCo stop order. Once Leonardo learned of NewCo's claim, he had an obligation to avoid the further damages incurred by his failure to stop the work even if NewCo's stop order breached the contract.

Managers may encounter a mitigation of damages issue when dealing with employees who claim that their employer breached an employment contract. If an employee has been wrongfully terminated, for example, that employee has a duty to seek new employment (of similar type and rank) if available in order to avoid damages resulting from the alleged breach by the employer.

In Case 8.3, following a breach of a lease regarding commercial property, the court examines whether a landlord has the duty to mitigate damages.

Clean Hands and Tender of Performance

Along with the duty to mitigate damages, a party suing another for breach of contract must do so with **"clean hands."** *Clean hands* (an equitable maxim discussed in Chapter 1, "Legal Foundations"), as applied to contract enforcement, requires that the party show that it had no fault in the breaching of the contract and that it was ready, willing, and able to perform its required obligations under the contract. This readiness to perform is called **tender of performance.** Suppose that company A has agreed to sell a property and attached building to company B. On the day of settlement, representatives of company A arrive with all paperwork and keys necessary to transfer ownership of the property, but no one from company B shows up. When company A sues for breach of contract, it will be able to show that it was without fault and had tendered performance. If, however, neither party showed up at settlement, company A would not be successful in a breach of contract action because it failed to meet its clean hands burden.

CONCEPT SUMMARY Damages

- For a breach of contract, courts will award monetary damages to the nonbreaching party to remedy the loss suffered by nonperformance.
- Monetary damages can be (1) *compensatory*—direct losses from nonperformance; (2) *consequential*—indirect but foreseeable losses from nonperformance; (3) *restitution*—losses equal to the amount that the breaching party has been unjustly enriched by the nonbreaching party; or (4) *liquidated*—losses of a predetermined value according to the contract.
- Equitable relief is given when the monetary damages are insufficient; it takes the form of (1) injunctive relief, (2) specific performance, or (3) reformation.
- The duty to mitigate is the nonbreaching party's obligation to avoid excessive or unnecessary damages through reasonable efforts or else be barred from recovery for those avoidable costs of nonperformance.

---

[18]*Restatement (Second) of Contracts,* § 350.

CASE 8.3 Austin Hill Country Realty, Inc., d/b/a Re/Max Austin Hill Country
Realtors et al. v. Palisades Plaza, Inc., d/b/a The Palisades,
948 S.W.2d 293 (TX 1997)

FACT SUMMARY Palisades Plaza entered into a five-year commercial lease agreement with Austin Hill Country Realty for office space. The lease called for Palisades to improve and configure the space according to Austin Hill's specifications prior to beginning the lease. Toward the end of the improvements, Palisades began to receive conflicting instructions on finalizing the space and requested that one of Austin Hill's principals be designated to give instructions. Ultimately, the parties could not come to an agreement, and Austin Hill never took occupancy of the leased space. Palisades notified Austin Hill that it considered the contract repudiated and sued Austin Hill for breach of contract. At the same time, Palisades advertised the office space in a local newspaper, but it did not advertise in a widely circulated commercial-property trade paper that it had used in the past. Austin Hill argued that Palisades had not attempted to mitigate its damages and was not entitled to the full judgment for breach of the lease. The trial court and appellate court held for Palisades, ruling that there was no common law duty requiring landlords to mitigate in Texas. Austin Hill appealed to the Texas Supreme Court.

SYNOPSIS OF DECISION AND OPINION The Texas Supreme Court reversed the lower courts and ruled in favor of Austin Hill. While acknowledging that existing Texas law did not require landlords to mitigate damages, the court referred to recent decisions in other jurisdictions and adopted a duty-to-mitigate rule for landlords in Texas. The court distinguished between lawsuits based on a breach of contract and claims based on property rights and concluded that contract-based claims, such as the Palisades–Austin Hill dispute, require the landlord to mitigate damages.

WORDS OF THE COURT: Mitigation of Damages "In discerning the policy implications of a rule requiring landlords to mitigate damages, we are informed by the rules of other jurisdictions. Forty-two states and the District of Columbia have recognized that a landlord has a duty to mitigate damages in at least some situations: when there is a breach of a residential lease, a commercial lease, or both. [A] promise to pay in a lease is essentially the same as a promise to pay in any other contract, and a breach of that promise does not necessarily end the landlord's ongoing duties. Because of the contractual elements of the modern lease agreement, these courts have imposed upon the landlord the contractual duty to mitigate damages upon the tenant's breach. The overwhelming trend among jurisdictions in the United States has thus been toward requiring a landlord to mitigate damages when a tenant abandons the property in breach of the lease agreement. Those courts adopting a mitigation requirement have emphasized the contractual elements of a lease agreement, the public policy favoring productive use of property, and the practicalities of the modern landlord-tenant arrangement as supporting such a duty. We are persuaded by the reasoning of those courts that recognize that landlords must mitigate damages upon a tenant's abandonment and failure to pay rent."

Case Questions

1. Do you agree that innocent parties who are injured due to breach of contract should have a duty to mitigate damages? Defend you position.

2. Why wasn't the advertising done by Palisades sufficient to be considered mitigating damages?

CONTRACTS INVOLVING RIGHTS OF A THIRD PARTY

LO 8-8

In some cases, a party to an existing contract wishes to substitute another party in her place. Because the contract involves more than two parties, the law recognizes a special set of rules to govern such a substitution. One party may wish to do this by transferring to a third party her own rights in the contract (a transfer known as an *assignment*), or by appointing another to perform her duties (a transfer known as a *delegation*). Another form of contract that involves rights of a third party occurs when a person who is not a party to the contract at the time of formation becomes a *third-party beneficiary* because the parties to the contract intended to confer a benefit on that person.

Assignment

An **assignment** is a transfer of current rights (not future rights) under a contract by one party in a contract to a third party. The party making the assignment is known as the *assignor*, and the third party receiving the rights is the *assignee*. Once a valid assignment occurs, the assignor's rights under the contract are extinguished and the rights may then be exercised only by the assignee. The assignee then has the right to demand performance from the other party and to legally enforce the obligations. For example, Abel contracts to sell Baker 10,000 gallons of gasoline at $3 per gallon for Baker's fleet of delivery vehicles. Cain's research reveals that the price of gasoline may jump as high as $10 per gallon over the next year, so Cain contracts to pay Baker $70,000 for an assignment of Baker's rights under the Abel-Baker contract. Baker's rights (the assignor) are now extinguished, and Abel is compelled to perform his obligations by providing the gasoline to Cain (the assignee) at $3 per gallon. If Abel refuses to perform, Cain (but not Baker) may enforce the contract against Abel.

Generally, all rights in a contract are assignable at the sole discretion of the assigning party. Mutual consent is not required. However, in some instances, an assignment would be unfair to the nonassigning party. Therefore, some rights are not assignable:[19]

- Assignment is not permitted when the parties have included an *antiassignment clause,* using such language as "No rights under this contract may be assigned."

- Assignments are invalid when the assignment *materially alters the duty* of the other party by increasing a *burden or risk.* For example, an insurance contract that insures risk of one building against a flood may not be assigned to another building owner who owns a property in a flood plain. The obligor's (insurance company's) risk for the premium paid is materially altered. Thus, this assignment is prohibited.

- Some states have added additional assignment prohibition statutes related to general *public policy* matters (e.g., states that prohibit assignment of alimony payments before they become due).[20]

Delegation

Parties to a contract may also substitute another party to perform any *duties* owed under the agreement. A **delegation** is a transfer of current duties owed by one party under a contract to a third party. The party making the delegation is known as the *delegator*, and the third party receiving the rights is the *delegatee*. One major difference between assignment and delegation is that when a party delegates duty, the delegator remains liable for the obligation. Thus, if the delegatee fails to perform, the delegator must either perform or suffer liability for the breach of contract.

---

[19]*Restatement (Second) of Contracts,* § 322.

[20]J. D. Calamari, J. M. Perillo, and H. H. Bender, *Cases and Problems on Contracts,* 4th ed. (St. Paul, MN: West/Thomson, 2004), pp. 683–84.

Although duties may generally be delegated without mutual consent of the parties, in some circumstances duties are nondelegable:

- When the duties involve *special personal skills,* such as those of an attorney, physician, portrait artist, or actor.
- When a contract contains an *antidelegation clause.*
- When the delegatee is a *competitor* of the obligee (the nondelegating party).[21]

Third-Party Beneficiaries   In an assignment or delegation, the third party's rights occur *after* the formation of the contract. However, sometimes a party may form a contract to benefit not herself, but a third person. In this case, that person, called the **third-party beneficiary,** becomes a party to the contract and certain rights arise to protect the third party. The key to understanding whether these rights arise or not is to examine whether the parties *intended to confer a benefit* on the third party. Such a third party is known as the **intended beneficiaries** and has rights to enforce the contract as appropriate. For example, Ernest borrows money from Scott to pay his living expenses while Ernest writes a novel. When Ernest is negotiating a contract for the novel with Scribner's Publishing, Ernest asks that 50 percent of the royalties be paid to Scott in payment of the debt Ernest owes him. Because Scott is an intended beneficiary of this contract, he may sue Scribner's if it fails to perform by not paying the royalties as agreed.

By contrast, third parties who are not contemplated as beneficiaries by the original contracting parties are known as **incidental beneficiaries.** Incidental beneficiaries may not sue to enforce contractual rights. For example, Perkins owns a retail bookstore in the Main Street Mall (MSM). MSM contracts with Big Buy Appliances for the space next to the Perkins bookstore. Perkins is ecstatic upon learning of this because Big Buy is a major retail chain with high customer drawing power. After the lease is signed, Big Buy backs out. Although Perkins did benefit from the MSM–Big Buy contract, he cannot sue any of the parties in that contract because he is an incidental beneficiary.[22]

CONCEPT SUMMARY Third-Party Rights

- Assignment is the unilateral shifting of rights under a contract from one party to a third party and is permitted only in the absence of an antiassignment clause, material change to the burden, or legal prohibition.
- Delegation is the transfer of contractual duties to a third party when the original party still remains liable for nonperformance, and it is permitted except in cases of special personal skills, a nondelegation clause, or a delegatee who is a competitor of the non-delegating party.
- A third party who benefits from a contractual promise between two other parties may seek damages only if she is an intended beneficiary as opposed to an incidental beneficiary.

---

[21]See *Sally Beauty Company v. Nexxus Products Co.,* 801 F.2d 1001 (7th Cir. 1986).
[22]Based on *Restatement (Second) of Contracts,* § 302, Illustration 16.

FACT SUMMARY Logan-Baldwin and other owners (collectively Logan-Baldwin) contracted with L.S.M. General Contractors (LSM) to renovate a historic residence. LSM subcontracted to Henry Isaacs Home Remodeling (Isaacs) to perform roofing work as part of the renovations. Isaacs then contracted with Brewster to install a new roof on the residence. Soon after the roof was completed, it showed signs of leaking and it became clear that the roof was not installed correctly. LSM and Isaacs attempted to fix the problems, but they were unsuccessful and subsequently abandoned the project. Logan-Baldwin hired other contractors to fix the problems and sued LSM, Isaacs, and Brewster for breach of contract. Isaacs defended that it did not directly contract with Logan-Baldwin and therefore could not be sued for breach of contract. Logan-Baldwin argued that they had contract rights over Isaacs because they were an intended third-party beneficiary. The trial court ruled in favor of Isaacs, and Logan-Baldwin appealed.

SYNOPSIS OF DECISION AND OPINION The N.Y. Supreme Court Appellate Division reversed the trial court and held for Logan-Baldwin. The court reasoned that a nonbreaching party is entitled to damages as long as the underlying contract is entered into for the benefit of a third party. In this case, because Logan-Baldwin, as the owners of the house, were logically the intended beneficiary of the home renovations, they have rights as a third-party beneficiary. Since they were the intended third-party beneficiary, the court ruled that Logan-Baldwin had the right to maintain a breach of contract claim against Isaacs.

WORDS OF THE COURT: Third-Party Beneficiaries "Parties such as the plaintiffs herein who are 'asserting third-party beneficiary rights under a contract must establish (1) the existence of a valid and binding contract between other parties, (2) that the contract was intended for [their] benefit and (3) that the benefit to [them] is sufficiently immediate, rather than incidental, to indicate the assumption by the contracting parties of a duty to compensate [them] if the benefit is lost.' . . . Indeed, '[i]t is almost inconceivable that those who render their services in connection with a major construction project would not contemplate that the performance of their contractual obligations would ultimately benefit the owner. . . . It is obviously inferable that they knew, or should have known, that someone owned the [property], and that such person or entity was to be the ultimate beneficiary of their services.' . . . To the extent that the [trial] court interpreted our decision in . . . as holding that an express contractual provision was required [for an intended beneficiary to exist], the court erred. An express contractual provision concerning third-party beneficiaries 'is but an alternative factor upon which a court might base a finding that a certain party is, in fact, a third-party beneficiary.'"

Case Questions

1. Does an intended beneficiary have to be named in a contract to have rights to enforce the contract? Explain.

2. Suppose that the plaintiff's historical residence was typically open to the public for tours on weekends. Philip, a history buff, plans a trip to tour the home, but upon his arrival he finds it closed because the shoddy roofing work made the premises unsafe for the public. Does Philip have a cause of action against any of the defendants? Why or why not?

In Case 8.4, the court must determine whether a homeowner is an intended or incidental beneficiary of a contract between a general contractor hired by the homeowner and a subcontractor hired by the general contractor

Condition p. 203   An event that must occur before a contract obligation is triggered.

Good faith p. 205   In contract law, the duty to honestly adhere to the contract's common purpose. Under this obligation neither party can do anything to prevent the other party from enjoying the "fruits of the contract." Instead, both must try to make the deal work as written.

Discharge p. 205   In contract law, the removal of all legal obligations under the agreement.

Substantial performance p. 206   Performance of the essential terms of the contract such that performance can be considered complete less damages for anything still unperformed.

Material p. 206   Something that is important to the contract by being necessary and generally indispensable to the contract.

Mutual consent p. 208   Circumstance under which contracting parties may be discharged from their obligation although neither party has fully performed because they agree to cancel the contract.

Operation of law p. 208   Circumstance under which contract obligations may be discharged because fairness demands it through the doctrines of impossibility, impracticability, and frustration of purpose.

Rescission p. 208   Cancellation of a contract that occurs when both parties agree to discharge each other from all duties under the contract and end the agreement, no matter what has been done or left undone.

Accord and satisfaction p. 208   A doctrine that allows one party to create an agreement, or accord, with the other party to accept a substitute performance in order to satisfy the original performance; the completion of the new duty discharges the old one.

Substitute agreement (modification) p. 208   An agreement that replaces the original contract when the two parties agree to different duties, The new duties then replace and dissolve the obligations of the original contract.

Novation p. 209   A type of substitute agreement in which the duties of the contract remain the same but a new, third party assumes the duties of an original party, discharging the original party from further obligations. (*Note*: Many courts use novation for new parties and new terms or substitute agreements.)

Impossibility p. 210   Doctrine that excuses performance when an essential part of the contract has become impossible because a crucial, irreplaceable thing has been destroyed; a crucial person has died; a crucial means of performance no longer exists; or a crucial action has become illegal.

Impracticability p. 210   Doctrine that excuses performance when an extreme circumstance occurs or reveals itself that destroys the value of the performance to the party and that circumstance was not the fault of either party and was not reasonably foreseeable.

Frustration of purpose p. 210   Doctrine that excuses a party from performance if, before a breach, a state of things that was the basis for forming the contract no longer exists, by no fault of either party.

Unilaterally altered p. 212   Term pertaining to a contract in which one party changes a term of the offer or acceptance after the contract was made and without the consent of the other party, who is then discharged from performing.

Bankruptcy p. 212   A procedure by which a debtor's assets are reorganized and liquidated by a court order to pay off creditors and free the debtor from obligations under existing contracts.

Statute of limitations p. 212   State law that places a time limit on the enforcement of certain contracts in order to ensure diligent enforcement.

Breach p. 213   Condition that exists when one party has failed to perform her obligation under the contract. If the breach is material, the nonbreaching party is excused from his performance and can recover monetary damages.

Remedies p. 213   The relief mechanisms by which courts compensate a nonbreaching party for the losses that result from the other party's breach of contract.

Anticipatory repudiation p. 213   Doctrine under which, when one party makes clear that he has no intention to perform as agreed, the nonbreaching party is entitled to recover damages in anticipation of the breach rather than waiting until performance is due. Also called *anticipatory breach*.

Money damages p. 215   Sums levied on the breaching party and awarded to the nonbreaching party to remedy a loss from breach of contract.

Compensatory damages p. 216   Damages that are meant to make the injured party whole again. In contract law, they are an attempt to place the nonbreaching party in the position he would have been in had the contract been executed as agreed. Also called *direct* or *actual damages*.

Consequential damages p. 216   Damages that repay the injured party for any foreseeable but indirect losses that flow from the breach of contract.

Restitution p. 217   A remedy that restores to the plaintiff the value of the performance that he has already rendered to the breaching party and by which the breaching party has been unjustly enriched.

Liquidated damages p. 217   Reasonable estimates of the actual damages that will result if the contract is breached that are agreed to by the parties ahead of time.

Equitable relief p. 217   Relief granted in the form of either specific performance ("do it") or an injunction ("stop doing it") when monetary damages are insufficient due to the unique or irreversible consequence of the breach.

Specific performance p. 217   An equitable remedy whereby a court orders the breaching party to render the promised performance by ordering the party to take a specific action.

Injunctive relief p. 218   A court order to refrain from performing a particular act.

Reformation p. 218   Contract modification in which the court rewrites the contract to conform to the parties' actual intentions when the parties have imperfectly expressed their agreement and the imperfection results in a dispute.

Clean hands p. 219   An equitable doctrine whereby a party seeking to enforce a breach of contract against the opposing party must prove that he has no fault in causing the breach. Clean hands are shown by proving that you are prepared to tender performance.

Tender of performance p. 219   An offer or attempt to perform what is required under a contract.

Assignment p. 221   The transfer of one party's current rights under a contract to a third party, thereby extinguishing original party's rights.

Delegation p. 221   The transfer of one party's current duties under a contract to a third party to perform, with the original party remaining liable for any breach.

Third-party beneficiary p. 222   Someone who, while not a party to a contract, stands to benefit from the existence of the contract. (See **Incidental beneficiary** and **Intended beneficiary** in this Key Terms list.)

Intended beneficiary p. 222   Someone who, while not a party to the contract, stands to benefit from the contract because the contracting parties intended that he receive a benefit. He has enforceable rights under the contract.

Incidental beneficiary p. 222   Someone who, while not a party to the contract, stands to benefit from the contract simply because she may be in the right place at the right time. The contract was not entered into to benefit her specifically and she has no enforceable rights under the contract.

THEORY TO PRACTICE

After a 30-year career as a shipping logistics executive, Ishmael retired and began to offer his services as a logistics consultant. Ishmael entered into a consulting contract with the general manager at ExportCo to provide logistical advice to the company for 12 months. The parties agreed in the contract that Export will pay Ishmael $5,000 per month on the last day of each month. Ishmael promised to devote "100 percent of his professional time" to Export for a period of at least eight consecutive weeks.

1. After one week on the worksite, Ishmael finds that he is devoting more time than he initially believed was necessary to Export, so he attempts to convince Export to pay him $6,000 per month for his consulting services. Export does not agree to any change, so Ishmael begins to cut down his hours so that he is spending only 80 percent of his professional time at Export. If Export sues Ishmael for breach of contract, are there any circumstances under which Ishmael may use the doctrine of substantial performance to complete his performance obligation? Why or why not?

2. Two months after the Ishmael-Export contract, Export loses a large client. The company sends Ishmael a letter explaining that the financial emergency has caused it to consider rescinding Ishmael's contract under the theory that Export was discharged from the remaining months of the contract based on the doctrine of impracticability. Will a court support Export's theory?

3. In Question 2, if a manager from Export notifies Ishmael on March 1 that the company does not intend to pay him for the month of March, must Ishmael wait to sue Export until the date performance is actually due (recall that he is paid his fee on the last day of each month)? What doctrine may help Ishmael recover compensation without incurring further damages by waiting until performance is due?

4. What type of remedies would be most appropriate for Ishmael if a court were to find that Export breached the contract as in Question 2? Would specific performance be appropriate? Why or why not?

5. Suppose that Ishmael meets with another potential client and the needs of the client are such that Ishmael's immediate services are required so he cannot complete the work for Export. Because there is no antiassignment clause in the contract, he assigns the contract to his brother, who is also familiar with importing logistics. Export objects. Must Ishmael perform, or must Export accept Ishmael's brother? What legal doctrines apply?

MANAGER'S CHALLENGE

Although at the beginning of a contract the parties may have a certain understanding, managers are sometimes in a position where a change in the agreement becomes necessary. Clearly in the Theory to Practice problem, the parties need to retool their agreement to reflect (1) Ishmael's concern that the assignment is more work than originally anticipated, (2) Export's weakened financial position, and (3) Ishmael's desire to substitute his brother to complete the assignment. Draft a memorandum to your senior manager outlining specific options and consequences for altering these agreements through rescission, accord and satisfaction, substitute agreement, and/or novation. A sample answer may be found on this textbook's website at www.mhhe.com/melvinleb2e.

CASE SUMMARY 8.1 :: Dalton v. Educational Testing Service, 87 N.Y.2d 384 (N.Y. 1995)

GOOD FAITH AND SPECIFIC PERFORMANCE

Dalton took the SAT exam in May 1991. He retook the exam in November 1992 and scored 410 points higher. The Educational Testing Service (ETS), which administers the exam, has a policy of flagging score differentials greater than 350 points. After analyzing handwriting on the two tests, ETS concluded that someone else may have taken the exam for Dalton. Before the exam, Dalton signed a contract with ETS stating that if he was flagged for cheating, he had five options: Cancel the score, have a third party review it, go to an arbitrator, retake the test, or send in information relevant to whether or not he had cheated. Dalton sent in information showing that he had mononucleosis during the first test and that he had taken a prep course, and he provided affidavits from people who saw him at the test site. Testimony from the ETS showed that officials were convinced that the handwriting issue meant that Dalton had only the option to retake the test and, thus, they failed to consider the information he sent to them unless it dealt directly with the handwriting analysis.

Dalton sued for specific performance to have the scores reported as official by ETS. He argued that by giving him the contractual option of sending in information relevant to the cheating accusation, the ETS had a good faith obligation under the contract to examine and fully consider what he had sent in.

CASE QUESTIONS

1. Who prevails and why?
2. Why is specific performance an option here as a remedy?

REMEDIES

The Steak 'n Shake restaurant chain entered a contract with Pepsi to replace King Cola with Pepsi in all its stores. Several issues surrounding the contract's execution strained the agreement, and Steak 'n Shake canceled the contract and refused to perform. Pepsi sued, and in court Steak 'n Shake insisted that Pepsi had no "legally cognizable" damages because all potential profits were purely speculative. Pepsi argued that it stood to gain from the contract and should be compensated for the breach even though damages could not be calculated exactly. The damages could be equal to what it reasonably stood to gain from the contract if not for Steak 'n Shake's breach.

CASE QUESTIONS

1. Will a court award damages to Pepsi even though the company admitted the damages could not be calculated exactly?
2. What other types of damages or relief could Pepsi seek?

IMPOSSIBILITY

Sechrest Plywood Company contracted with Forest Furniture Company to sell it plywood bottoms for drawers that Forest would manufacture. After the contract, Forest's warehouse, where it intended to make the drawers, was completely destroyed by a fire. Forest asserted that the contract was void for impossibility. Sechrest argued that while the fire prevented Forest from manufacturing drawers, it did not prevent Forest from purchasing the plywood bottoms it had contracted with Sechrest for and, therefore, the doctrine of impossibility does not apply.

CASE QUESTIONS

1. What are the standards for being discharged through impossibility?
2. Do they apply here? Why or why not?

ASSIGNMENT TO A THIRD PARTY

The city of San Francisco contracted with a builder to do several tasks associated with roadwork and refurbishment. The contractor assigned the work to another contractor. The city sought breach of contract for, among other things, inappropriate assignment in that the service was of a personal nature, which under common law cannot be unilaterally assigned to a third party. The contractor argued that the roadwork in the contract was not of a personal nature and thus could lawfully be assigned by the original contractor to the third-party contractor.

CASE QUESTIONS

1. Who prevails and why?
2. Is the task specialized?

TENDER OF PERFORMANCE

William Lien-Shie Huang, Shiang Lan Huang, Jane S. Huang, and May Huang entered into a real estate contract with Kuo Feng Ko to purchase the Walnut property. Prior to settlement, the Huangs received documents from the escrow company, including a preliminary title report, that indicated the title to the Walnut property was in question and that there was a lawsuit pending against Ko. Ko assured the Huangs that the lawsuit and property title would not be a problem. The Huangs made two deposits to the escrow company as required by the purchase agreement, totaling $26,640.

On the date of the scheduled settlement, the Huangs arrived prepared to close on their purchase. Ko also attended the settlement but was unable to deliver title to the property sufficient to satisfy the contract.

CASE QUESTIONS

1. Did the Huangs tender performance on the contract? Why or why not?
2. Did Ko tender performance on the contract? Why or why not?
3. Did a breach of contract occur? Explain.

THIRD-PARTY BENEFICIARIES

Plotkin approached Amagansett in an effort to purchase 2,986 pieces of lumber for use as trim around 130 windows and sliding doors in connection with the construction of Plotkin's house. In response, Amagansett purchased exactly 2,986 pieces of lumber from Keiver, a manufacturer and supplier, and then delivered the lumber to the plaintiff the very next day. The construction manager noticed black marks in the wood, and Amagansett acknowledged that there was a problem but dismissed it. One year later, Plotkin's grandson Max, who was living in the newly constructed home, was diagnosed with cancer. After an investigation to determine whether a toxic mold problem existed that caused Max's condition, it was concluded that the wood sold to Plotkin contained a wood-decaying fungus called "brown rot" that caused a toxic mold problem to occur. Plotkin sued both Amagansett and Keiver for breach of contract and other causes and included Max as a plaintiff, claiming him to be a beneficiary of the contracts between Amagansett, Keiver, and Plotkin.

CASE QUESTIONS

1. Is Max an intended or incidental beneficiary of the contracts to purchase the wood? What must be shown for Max to be classified under either category?
2. Does it matter that Max was never named in any contracts?
3. How does the timing of the requests and purchases affect whether Max and others are intended or incidental beneficiaries of the contracts?

Self-Check **ANSWERS**

Substantial Performance

1. Wholesaler has substantially performed, but Delicatessen is entitled to a reduction in price.

2. No substantial performance. The most important term in the contract (the phone number) was not met by Yellow Pages, and the value of the contract to Dry Cleaner is now zero. Based on *Georges v. Pacific Tel. & Tel. Co.*, 184 F. Supp. 571 (D.C. Or. 1960).

3. No substantial performance. The industry standard is such that a 15 percent leaf/stem ratio is substantially more valuable than the 25 percent leaf/stem ratio. See *Del Monte Corp. v. Martin*, 574 S.W.2d 597 (Tex. Civ. App. 1978).

4. Substantial performance or perfect performance, depending on whether the portrait objectively meets the criteria for a professional painting of that type.

5. Publisher has substantially performed because the delay likely causes no harm to the bookstore with so much time before classes begin.

9 CHAPTER

Contracts for the Sale of Goods

learning objectives

After studying this chapter, students who have mastered the material will be able to:

9-1 Articulate the fundamental purpose and role of the UCC in commercial transactions and explain why it is important to business owners and managers.

9-2 Identify which contracts are governed by UCC Article 2.

9-3 Discuss the requirements for agreement in a sale of goods contract and identify what terms the UCC provides in a sales agreement with open or missing terms.

9-4 Classify which contracts must be in writing and understand what the writing must contain to be enforceable under the statute of frauds.

9-5 Express how risk of loss is allocated among the parties in a sales contract and identify steps managers take to limit risks and ensure performance.

9-6 Recognize and apply the UCC rights and obligations of buyers and sellers and the consequences of breaching a contract.

9-7 Identify appropriate remedies and damages available to buyers and sellers.

9-8 Explain the risks of sales transactions with foreign companies and know how to mitigate that risk by understanding international commercial laws.

This chapter continues the coverage in Chapters 6, 7, and 8 of the challenges that managers face in the formation and performance of contracts, but it focuses on the role of Article 2 of the Uniform Commercial Code (UCC).[1] Article 2 sets out the rules that govern contracts involving the sale of goods. Because UCC transactions typically include shipping, risk of loss, inspection, cure, and other issues unique to goods, it is important for business owners and managers to understand how UCC rules are applied. In this chapter, students will learn:

- The scope of Article 2 coverage.
- Formation of agreements for the sale of goods recognized under the UCC and how it differs from the common law.
- Legal rules regarding passing of ownership and allocation of risk for goods in a commercial transaction.
- UCC provisions governing the obligations of the parties in a sales agreement as well as UCC protections for innocent parties on occasions when the other party violates the agreement.
- How sellers can mitigate or eliminate damages when they initially fail to perform properly.
- The international commercial law principles governing sale of goods contracts with a company in a foreign nation.

INTRODUCTION TO ARTICLE 2 OF THE UCC LO 9-1, 9-2

Recall from the previous chapters that contracts for the *sale of goods* are governed by statutory law in the form of the Uniform Commercial Code (UCC, or sometimes referred to simply as the *Code*). The UCC is a model statute published by the National Conference of Commissioners of Uniform State Laws (NCCUSL).[2] Every state except Louisiana has adopted all (or substantially all) of Article 2 of the UCC. In 2003, the NCCUSL came out with a revised Code, but the revisions were substantial and have met opposition in state legislatures to the point where no state adopted the revised Code.[3] As a result of the opposition by the states, in May 2011, the American Law Institute voted to withdraw the 2003 amendments.

---

[1]Note that the UCC also contains other articles pertaining to different aspects of commercial law. For example, Article 2A covers the *leasing* of goods. Leasing of goods is discussed in Chapter 24 "Personal Property, Real Property, and Land Use Law." This chapter focuses exclusively on Article 2: Sales of Goods.

[2]The NCCUSL and other similar organizations are discussed in more detail in Chapter 1, "Legal Foundations."

[3]Only Kansas, Nevada, and Oklahoma considered adopting the 2003 amendments. The Kansas and Nevada bills never came to a vote, and Oklahoma voted to adopt only a revised definition of goods that excluded information.

UCC Coverage and Definitions

Legal Speak ›))

Goods Tangible personal property that is movable at the time of identification to a contract of sale. Future goods—especially manufactured goods, the unborn young of animals, growing crops, and identified things attached to realty—are included. Money and information are not considered goods under the UCC.

The UCC applies only to **sales contracts** that are agreements for the *sale of goods*. The UCC defines **goods**[4] as properly that is (1) tangible (i.e., has a physical existence, as does a laptop computer) and (2) movable from place to place. Therefore, real estate contracts or employment contracts are *not* covered by the UCC. While many sales contracts involve the sale of goods to a consumer, Article 2 also contains special provisions that apply only in transactions between *merchants*. A **merchant** is one that is *regularly engaged* in the sale of a particular good. The UCC imputes a certain level of knowledge and awareness to merchants and allows their transactions to proceed in an expedited manner without the necessity for safeguards intended for average consumers. For example, suppose that Caesar's Equipment Co. sells a lawn tractor to Sanjay for $600. This sales agreement is subject to Article 2, but because Sanjay is not a merchant, certain UCC requirements exist primarily to protect Sanjay's interests in the sale. However, if Caesar's is a wholesaler and Sanjay is the owner of a retail store, this is a *merchant* transaction and triggers special business standards that are intended to allow the parties to transact business unimpeded by any consumer protections.

Recall from Chapter 6, "Overview and Language of Contracts," that it is important to distinguish between contracts governed by the UCC and those governed by the common law and to understand how to determine the source of law for hybrid contracts. This is critical knowledge for business owners and managers because the parties' rights and obligations under the common law differ from those under the UCC.

Function of the UCC

The underlying policy of the UCC is to promote commercial efficiency by providing standardized procedures that merchants and consumers may rely upon. The provisions of the UCC were drafted with the goal of promoting the *completion* of a business transaction. Article 2 is intended to modify some of the stricter common law requirements and facilitate business transactions by providing merchants and consumers with a standard set of rules for the sale of goods.

In the context of sales contracts, the UCC should be thought of primarily as a *gap filler* in cases where the parties have not agreed otherwise. Typically, two parties will enter into a sales contract after negotiating certain terms. Terms of such a sales contract, assuming that they do not conflict with a UCC prohibition, are fully enforceable. The UCC principally comes into play when the parties to a sales transaction have *not* expressly agreed on certain terms. For example, suppose that on Monday, Hadley and Martha enter into an agreement for the sale of 1,000 Brand-A watches at $1 per Brand-A watch to be delivered to Martha's warehouse on Friday. However, the parties do not bother to negotiate any terms other than price and delivery date. Suppose that Hadley runs out of Brand-A watches and ships 1,000 Brand-B watches. Must Martha accept the watches? What are her options under the law? Suppose that the watches are damaged in transit before they are delivered to Martha's warehouse. What are the parties' rights and responsibilities regarding the sale? Who will bear the risk of the loss? Because the parties have not specifically agreed on this contingency, they must turn to the UCC for the answers regarding those missing terms.

> **KEY POINT**
> Article 2 of the UCC acts to fill in only missing or open terms (when the parties have not expressly agreed otherwise) in a contract for the sale of goods between merchants.

---

[4]UCC § 2-103.

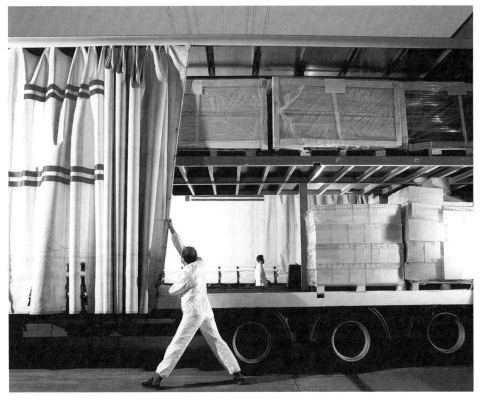

Contracts for the sale of goods are covered under Article 2 of the Uniform Commercial Code.

AGREEMENT IN A SALES CONTRACT: OFFER

LO 9.3

Recall that the UCC generally aims to *promote* a sales transaction to be completed rather than shelter a party who doesn't complete the transaction. The formation elements for a sales contract, for example, are easier to meet and do not require the level of intent required for common law contracts. Article 2 lowers the bar for formation by allowing an enforceable contract to arise "in any manner sufficient to show agreement" between the parties.[5] Therefore, the UCC allows a contract to be enforced based on a larger picture that consists of (1) past commercial conduct, (2) correspondence or verbal exchanges between the parties, and (3) industry standards and norms. In fact, the parties need not even have a definite time of formation, so long as the conduct of the parties indicates some basis for a reasonable person to believe a sales contract *exists*. For example, Wholesaler delivers 1,000 digital music players to Retailer on the 15th of each month. Over a period of six months, Wholesaler has delivered the players on or about the 15th of the month and Retailer has sent Wholesaler a check within 10 days. Assume that in the digital music player industry, payment is generally made within 10 days after delivery. In month seven, Wholesaler delivers the product on the 15th, but Retailer never pays. Most courts would hold that the seventh month was an enforceable contract even if Retailer did not subjectively *intend* to have the music player contract linger into seven months. Under the UCC, the larger picture was that the parties' *conduct* indicated that they had an ongoing series of contracts with certain terms. Retailer must exercise some conduct that would indicate that the contract was at an end (a simple e-mail would suffice) before the delivery date in the seventh month in order for the contract to be considered at an end.

---

[5]UCC § 2-204(1).

Offers with Open Terms

Sometimes merchants wish to engage in a sales transaction, but the parties overlook or are unsure about some key element of the contract, such as quantity, delivery, payment terms, or even price of the goods. The missing provisions, known as **open terms,** are entirely acceptable under the UCC so long as there is evidence that the parties *intended* to enter into a contract and the other terms are sufficiently articulated to provide a basis for some appropriate *remedy* in case of breach. This is where the UCC provides gap filling. The UCC provides a variety of answers based on what terms are missing.

Quantity   While quantity is generally a *required* term necessary to create an enforceable contract, two important exceptions exist to this general rule. First, quantity *may* be an open term if the buyer agrees to purchase *all* of the goods that a seller produces (known as an **output contract**). In this case, the seller has given up the right to sell the goods elsewhere. Second, when the buyer agrees to purchase all or up to an agreed amount of what the buyer needs for a given period (known as a **requirements contract**), a court will generally enforce that agreement despite the missing quantity. For example, suppose that Builder wishes to purchase small pine trees from Grower for use at one of Builder's commercial office complex sites. If Builder agrees to purchase all of the pine trees grown by Grower over the period of one growing season, this is an output contract. If, on the other hand, Builder agrees with Grower to purchase all of the trees that are needed for this site only, the parties have agreed to a requirements contract. In both cases, an enforceable contract exists despite the missing quantity.[6]

Other Open Terms   When a sales contract is missing other terms and the parties have not had an established course of past conduct, the UCC provides the gap fillers as follows:[7]

- *Delivery:* Buyer takes delivery at the *seller's* place of business (i.e., seller is not responsible for delivery). If no time of delivery is specified, the UCC provides for a reasonable time under the circumstances.
- *Payment:* Payment is due at the time and place where the seller is to make delivery and may be made in any commercially reasonable form (such as a business check).
- *Price:* The UCC requires the court to determine a reasonable price at the time of delivery. This is based on industry customs and market value.

Firm Offers by Merchants

Recall from Chapter 7, "Contract Formation," that the *offeror* has the right to revoke or modify an offer at any time prior to acceptance by the *offeree* (i.e., "offeror is the master of the offer"). There are certain exceptions to that principle under the common law, such as an option contract. The UCC creates its own brand of irrevocable offer known as a **merchant's firm offer** that applies only to transactions in which the offeror is a *merchant.* A firm offer is created when a merchant offers to buy or sell goods with an explicit promise, in writing, that the offer will be held open for a certain time period. In general, the UCC provides that the offer can be irrevocable for a maximum period of three months. This obligation is binding on the offeror even though the offeree has paid no consideration. Note that if the offeree has paid consideration tied to the offer, this constitutes an option contract and not a firm offer.

---

[6]UCC § 2-306(1).

[7]Delivery: UCC § 2-308(a); payment: UCC § 2-310; price: UCC § 2-305(1).

AGREEMENT IN SALES CONTRACTS: ACCEPTANCE

Article 2 provides its own rules for accepting an offer in a sales contract that are not as rigid as the common law rules. If the offeror does not clearly provide for a method of acceptance, the UCC allows the offeree to accept the offer in any "reasonable manner."[8] One important difference between acceptance standards in the UCC and the common law is that acceptance may still be effective even if the acceptance does *not* match the offer exactly (recall the common law mirror image rule from Chapter 7, "Contract Formation"). Not only does the UCC recognize that a contract may in some cases be created in which the acceptance does not match the offer, but it also fills in gaps to create certainty for the parties to the transaction.

Battle of the Forms

As a practical matter, businesses frequently use preprinted forms to initiate or respond to an offer to sell a good. These forms usually have some blanks for the particular negotiated terms unique to the transaction. Normally, the offer takes the form of a **purchase order** from the buyer that contains preprinted clauses (which typically favor the buyer) and blanks that a purchase manager fills in with terms such as shipment date, product information, quantity, and so forth. The seller's firm will then typically issue an **acknowledgment form,** which also has preprinted provisions (typically favoring the seller) and also has blanks to accommodate the specifics of that transaction.[9] The UCC provides guidelines on how to resolve a dispute when the terms in these forms conflict. This dilemma is known as the **battle of the forms**.

In a battle of the forms case, the UCC provides that (1) a document may constitute acceptance even though it states terms that are additional to or different from those offered by the offeror and (2) in certain transactions the additional terms proposed in the acceptance may become part of the contract.

Nonmerchant Transactions   If one of the parties in a sales contract is *not* a merchant, the contract is formed as *originally* offered. That is, the contract is considered accepted, but the additional terms are *not* part of the contract.

Merchant Transactions   If both parties are merchants, the rules are more complicated. Between merchants, in a sales contract acceptance with additional terms, the additional terms *automatically* become part of the enforceable contract unless (1) the offeror has expressly and clearly limited acceptance to the original terms through language such as "The terms of this Purchase Order may not be altered or changed and any alteration of the original terms are expressly rejected" (this is common language on a purchase order); or (2) the additional term was a *material* change that diverges significantly from those contained in the offer (i.e., one that changed the value of the contract or affected the parties' obligation to perform in a significant way);[10] or (3) the offeror raises an objection to the additional terms within a reasonable time period according to industry standards.

In some cases, one merchant proposes a certain term in the offering document (e.g., purchase order), but the other merchant's acceptance (e.g., acknowledgment) states a term that is *different* from the offer. In such a case, the majority of states use the **knockout rule.** Under this rule, the conflicting clauses knock each other out and neither clause becomes part of the contract. Instead, the parties look to the UCC's gap-filler provisions to supply the term.

---

[8]UCC § 2-206.

[9]UCC § 2-207.

[10]For example, some courts have held that the insertion of an arbitration clause materially alters an offer. See *Dorton v. Collins & Aikman Corp.,* 453 F.2d 1161 (6th Cir. 1972).

Does a sales contract exist? If so, what are the terms of the contract?

1. Boston Hardware Co. agrees to buy all the snow shovels it needs from New England Shovel Co. In past years this has been around 5,000 shovels per year. The mild winter in 2009 caused Boston Hardware to need only 250 shovels, leaving New England Shovel Co. with over 4,000 unpurchased shovels.

2. New York High School agrees to purchase 200 desks for $100 each from Big Apple School Supply Inc. The desks are to be ready for September 1, 2008, but there are no delivery terms in the contract.

3. A patient has a dentist install porcelain overlays meant to improve the appearance of her teeth. This was not an emergency or even a necessary procedure. The installation of the overlays was incidental to the purchase of the overlays.

4. L.A. Outfitters offers to sell West Coast Burrito Co. 1,100 uniforms by sending them a letter with price, quantity, and delivery terms and an offer to keep the offer open for seven months. Six months later, West Coast Burrito responds with a standard acknowledgment and acceptance form. The standard form includes an agreement to arbitrate.

5. Chicago Toy Depot Inc. sends a purchase order to Midwest Dolls Inc. for 10,000 "Fancy Nancy" dolls by November 1, 2010, in time for the holiday season. Midwest Dolls returns an acknowledgment letter guaranteeing the dolls for January 1, 2011.

Answers to this Self-Check are provided at the end of the chapter.

Consideration

Legal Speak ·))
Sales Contract A sales contract under the UCC is a transfer of title (ownership) to goods for consideration.

Recall from the coverage in Chapter 7, "Contract Formation," that most contracts must be supported by consideration. Remember also that most cases involving a nongoods agreement (i.e., those governed by the common law) cannot be *modified* without some additional consideration. While the UCC follows a similar rule that consideration must support sales contracts, a major difference is that the UCC allows contracts to be modified even *without* any additional consideration. The UCC recognizes that market conditions are not static and that the parties may have good faith reasons for modifying a contract without having some additional burden to continue its enforceability. For example, suppose that Wargrave sells 2,000 golf balls to Owen on credit. Owen agrees to pay Wargrave $1,000 plus 6 percent interest on the principal still owed per month for a period of 24 months. After two months, Owen's cash flow is impaired by an unexpected downturn in Owen's business. Owen and Wargrave agree to modify the contract so that it will allow Owen to pay a smaller monthly payment ($500 per month) but at the same interest rate until the balance is paid off in full. Later, Wargrave runs into his own cash flow problems and demands that Owen honor the original Wargrave-Owen credit contract terms. Despite the fact that no additional consideration was given for the modification, the *modified* Wargrave-Owen contract is fully enforceable and the original contract is canceled.

LO 9-4 ## STATUTE OF FRAUDS

The statute of frauds is a legal requirement that certain contracts be in writing in order to be enforceable. The UCC contains a specific section detailing the writing requirements for sales transactions. Any sales contract for goods with a total value of *$500 or more* must be in writing.[11]

---

[11]UCC § 2-201(1).

While common law contracts require several *specific* terms of a contract to be in the writing, the UCC has a much more liberal rule concerning what must be in the writing. The UCC's statute of frauds provisions are satisfied so long as the writing contains (1) quantity, (2) the signature of the party against whom enforcement is sought, and (3) language that would allow a reasonable person to conclude that the parties intended to form a contract. All other terms and conditions may be proved via testimony concerning oral agreements, past practices, and industry standards. In *Rosenfeld v. Basquiat,* a federal appellate court held that a brown piece of wrapping paper that had quantity, price, a deposit amount, the name of the goods, and the signature of both parties in crayon was more than sufficient to satisfy the UCC's statute of frauds.[12]

The statute of frauds section of the UCC also provides a relatively lenient rule for sales contracts between two merchants. A merchant who receives a signed **confirmation memorandum** from the other merchant will be bound by the memorandum just as if she had signed it, unless she promptly objects. Thus, if Abel telephones Cain to order 1,000 golf balls and then Cain sends a written confirmation of the agreement with the correct quantity and price, Abel will be bound by the contract and the statute of frauds is satisfied.

It is important to note that the UCC recognizes electronic records and signatures in a sales transaction as valid. This means that the hard copies of documents with original signatures are not always necessary. Although the UCC does not require electronic transactions, it makes clear that a sales contract cannot be held unenforceable simply because it is in electronic form.[13]

CONCEPT SUMMARY Formation under the UCC

- In order to encourage the formation and execution of sales contracts, the UCC offers more lenient rules regarding offer, acceptance, consideration, breach, and the statute of frauds.
- An agreement is still valid despite the fact that delivery, pricing, or payment terms are left *open;* the UCC provides standards to fill the gaps left by the missing terms.
- A written offer by a merchant includes an implied promise to keep the offer open for a stated or unstated amount of time even absent consideration for the option.
- When two merchants submit standardized offer and acceptance forms with conflicting terms, the UCC will still consider the contract accepted unless (1) the offer stated explicitly the terms of acceptance, (2) the conflicting terms substantially change the duties of the contract or its value to one party, or (3) the new terms were rejected in a timely manner by the offeror.
- A sales contract can be modified without additional consideration.
- The UCC statute of frauds requires that contracts for sales of goods valued at more than $500 be written but requires only that the document contain (1) quantity, (2) the signature of the party against whom enforcement is sought and, (3) language that reasonably shows the parties intended to form a contract.

---

[12]*Rosenfeld v. Basquiat,* 78 F.3d 84 (2d Cir. 1996). The case involved the famous artist Basquiat who sold several paintings to Rosenfeld, an art dealer. Rosenfeld requested a receipt for a deposit, and Basquiat, who one could justly call eccentric, found a brown piece of wrapping paper and, with crayon in hand, wrote the names of the paintings, the amount paid, and the names of the parties and then signed the paper. Basquiat died soon after the sale of the paintings but before the art dealer could take delivery. Basquiat's estate refused to honor the contract on the basis that the writing was not a formal enough contract because it never specified delivery terms. Rosenfeld sued and won, with the court holding that delivery terms were not required to satisfy the statute of frauds under UCC Article 2.

[13]UCC § 2-211.

The UCC sets out different rules regarding contract formation when a sales contract involves two nonmerchants, a merchant and a nonmerchant, or two merchants.

1. Two nonmerchants may strike a $1,000 deal for the sale of a used television, while two merchants may contract to buy 1,000 new televisions for $1 million. Why are the rules of contract formation stricter for the two nonmerchants than they are for the two merchants?

2. Are different rules necessary? Why or why not?

3. Would UCC gap fillers work for nonmerchant contracts? Why or why not?

4. If company A sends a purchase order to company B and company B returns an acknowledgment of the order with additional or modified terms, courts may determine that those additional or modified terms become part of the final contract. Is it ethical to force company A to adhere to the additional or modified terms without an express agreement to them by company A? Is company B acting unethically by adding or modifying the terms of company A's purchase order?

LO 9-5   # TITLE AND ALLOCATION OF RISK

Business owners and managers must have a working knowledge of the UCC provisions regarding title and risk allocation because these rules play an important part in determining commercial risks at various stages of a business transaction. Once an agreement has been made between the parties, there is likely to be a lapse of time before the buyer actually comes into physical possession of the goods. For example, ManufactureCo agrees to sell a new printing press to CopyCo for $100,000 to be delivered within 30 calendar days. During the delivery process, the press is damaged in a trucking accident. Or suppose that the press is delivered to a port to be picked up by CopyCo, but a warehouse fire destroys the press before the buyer picked it up. Who bears the burden of the loss? In both cases, CopyCo still needs a press, while ManufacturerCo made good faith efforts to deliver the merchandise as agreed upon. The UCC provides answers to these types of questions in its provisions governing **risk of loss**.[14] Of course, as with other provisions of the UCC, the risk of loss rules apply *only* when the parties have not specifically agreed to risk allocation. If the buyer and seller negotiate and agree to provisions relating to the risk of loss and/or the time that the ownership of goods actually passes, the UCC provisions are not applicable.

Title

Title is the legal term for the right of ownership in a good. Thus, the UCC refers to *passing of title* to indicate the point in time when actual ownership of the good is transferred from seller to buyer. A party holds title to a good when (1) the good is actually in *existence* in tangible form and (2) the good is *identified* to the contract.[15] Identification takes place when the seller has marked or designated the good in some fashion (such as by serial number or lot designation). Once the requirements for title have been met, the UCC provides that title passes to the buyer at the time and place that the seller *completes performance* by making a physical delivery of the goods.

---

[14]UCC § 2-401.
[15]UCC § 2-401(1).

Risk of Loss

The UCC provides a delineation as to when the title actually passes between the seller and the buyer, and it allocates *risk of loss* based on whether the agreement is categorized as either a **shipment contract** or a **destination contract**.

- *Shipment contracts* require the seller to use a carrier (such as a delivery company) to deliver the goods. As a general rule, all contracts for goods are considered shipment contracts *unless* the parties have agreed otherwise. Thus, the seller needs only to deliver the goods to the "hands" of the carrier to achieve complete performance. Once the seller has accomplished this, title is deemed to have passed to the buyer.[16] Normally, the *risk of loss* is allocated to the seller until such time as the seller has delivered the goods to the carrier. If the goods are destroyed after that point, the loss is ordinarily borne by the buyer. Note that the buyer may have recourse against the *carrier* but not against the seller. For example, Schubert agrees to sell Beatrice a specially designed grand piano for $50,000. Beatrice instructs Schubert to deliver the piano from his factory via a specific carrier, Piano Delivery Services (PDS), within 10 business days. On day 1, Schubert delivers the piano to PDS in good condition. On day 2, the PDS truck catches on fire and the piano is destroyed. The title and risk of loss passed to Beatrice at the point when Schubert delivered the good (piano) to the carrier (PDS), and Beatrice has no course of action against Schubert but may have a claim against the carrier (PDS).

- *Destination contracts* require the seller to deliver the goods to a *specified* destination. Typically, the destination is the buyer's place of business or home, but it can also be to a third party that the buyer designates. The UCC provides that complete performance occurs when the goods have been **tendered** at the specified destination. Tendering is the legal term for delivery of the *conforming* goods (i.e., the seller delivered what the buyer actually ordered) to the destination that allows the buyer to take delivery.[17] Normally, so long as the goods were properly tendered as agreed, the risk of loss is allocated to the buyer at the time of tender. For example, in the Schubert-Beatrice contract discussed above, suppose that the parties specifically designate their agreement as a *destination contract* and that Schubert must deliver the piano to Beatrice's studio in New York City. Schubert selects his own carrier, Cheapo Trucks, and the truck catches on fire in transit. In this case, the loss must be borne by the seller (Schubert) because the piano had not yet arrived at its New York City destination.[18]

Contracts involving shipping generally include the term *FOB* ("free on board"). In the United States, the **FOB point** generally requires the shipper to get the goods to the named location and put the goods in possession of the common carrier. It is at the named FOB point that title and risk of loss pass from seller to buyer. Once the goods are in the hands of the common carrier, the seller's responsibility ends and the buyer's responsibility begins. Therefore, a contract that says "FOB Buyers Warehouse, Miami, FL," will require the seller to get the goods to the designated location in Miami. If the seller is in San Francisco, it is therefore responsible for the goods until they have crossed the entire country. If the contract read "FOB seller's manufacturing plant, San Francisco, CA," the buyer would take possession in San Francisco and be responsible for the goods from that point on. When FOB is used in international contracts, it applies only to shipping via freighter ship. This is discussed later in this chapter.

Case 9.1 provides an example of a risk of loss analysis.

---

[16]UCC § 2-401(1)(a).

[17]UCC § 2-503(2)(b).

[18]Note that, depending on the circumstances, Schubert may recover his losses from Cheapo.

FACT SUMMARY Jamison purchased a set of encyclopedias from Encyclopedia Britannica for $1,652.08 plus a $95 shipping charge. Jamison paid a $100 deposit, and the remainder was to be paid in 30 monthly installments of $57. Encyclopedia Britannica assigned the contract to Merchants Acceptance to complete the delivery and receive payment. The contract contained shipping instructions and specified Jamison's home address as the place of delivery. Jamison never received the encyclopedias because they were shipped via United Parcel Service (UPS) to her post office box but never to her home. Jamison refused to pay the installments and canceled the purchase. Merchants brought suit for nonpayment; Jamison counterclaimed for her $100 deposit to be returned.

SYNOPSIS OF DECISION AND OPINION The court ruled in favor of Jamison, reasoning that the contract's terms included delivery and specified a place for delivery and, therefore, title to the books could be transferred to Jamison only when they arrived at her home. Because nothing was tendered by Merchants at Jamison's home address, she could properly cancel the contract and owes nothing.

WORDS OF THE COURT: Risk of Loss "Merchants urges that the contract in the present case was a 'shipping' contract, as opposed to a 'destination' contract; thus, warranting a finding that Merchants fulfilled its obligation to Jamison once it delivered the encyclopedias to UPS. However, since the delivery term in the Contract was specified as Jamison's street address, we find that it is unnecessary to delve into the case law describing the differences between 'shipping' versus 'destination' contracts. . . . The risk of loss, therefore, remained with Merchants until the books were 'duly so tendered as to enable [Jamison] to take delivery.'"

Case Questions

1. Why would the law require Merchants to have title to something that was in Jamison's own post office box?

2. Why did the court find it unnecessary to "delve into" the differences between shipment and destination contracts?

Goods Picked Up by the Buyer

In some cases, the goods are not to be delivered by the seller but rather to be picked up by the buyer. In that case, the risk of loss generally depends on whether or not the seller was a *merchant*. Recall from our earlier discussion that a merchant is one who is regularly engaged in the sale of a particular good. If the seller is a merchant, the risk of loss to goods held by the seller passes to the buyer only when the buyer takes physical possession of the goods. If the seller is not a merchant, the risk of loss to goods held by the seller passes to the buyer on tender of the goods.[19] For example, suppose that on Monday, Gates agrees to purchase 20 computers from CompCo, a computer retail outlet. Gates tells CompCo that he will pick up the computers on Friday. CompCo marks each of the 20 computers with a tag "Sold to Gates." However, Gates cannot make it to CompCo's warehouse on Friday. On Saturday, a thief steals all 20 computers. In this case, CompCo bears the loss because CompCo is a merchant and Gates had not yet taken physical possession of the goods. On the other hand, let's suppose Gates agrees to buy 20 used computers from Local College (a nonmerchant) on Monday. Gates tells Local College he will pick them up on Friday. On Thursday, Local College tenders the goods by calling Gates and notifying him that they are ready to be picked up in the lobby of the college's Alpha Hall on Friday any time between the hours of 8 a.m. and 5 p.m. Gates fails to show up on Friday. During the weekend, a

---

[19]UCC § 2-509(3).

thief breaks into the building and steals the computers. In this case, Gates bears the burden of the loss because Local College is not a merchant under the UCC and Local College tendered the computers by giving Gates proper notice about the times pickup could occur and the location of the goods.

 Self-Check   Risk of Loss

Who bears the risk of loss?

1. Marshall Clothing entered a shipment contract with Chase Department Stores to send Chase 3,000 black robes via Mercury Shipping Co. The robes were irreparably damaged in Mercury's warehouse by moths.

2. Taney's Treats purchased 450 gallons of ice cream from Harlan Dairy Co. The contract states that payment is due upon receipt of the ice cream at Taney's store. All 450 gallons melt in transit on a broken truck owned by Hermes Food Delivery Service.

3. Holmes Hats enters a destination contract to deliver 1,000 top hats to Cardozo Men's Stores. The courier delivers 1,000 bowler hats to Cardozo. Before Cardozo can return the incorrect hats, a flood ruins the entire delivery.

4. Smooth Lager is a brewery located in Montana. It enters into a contract to brew 500 kegs of its beer for shipment to a distributor in Alabama. The contract says "FOB Distributor's Warehouse, Mobile, AL." Smooth Lager delivers the 500 kegs to the common carrier, but the kegs are destroyed when the truck carrying the beer has an accident while driving through Nebraska.

5. White purchases a car from Brennan Motors. The contract states specifically that title is not transferred prior to the title document being signed by both parties. The clerk is out sick, so the title papers cannot be produced that day. White drives the car home with the contract signed only by him and crashes the car.

Answers to this Self-Check are provided at the end of the chapter.

CONCEPT SUMMARY   Title and Allocation of Risk

- Any risk allocation provision in the UCC does not control if the contract specifically lays out terms for risk allocation or title transfer.
- Neither the seller nor the buyer can hold title to goods until the goods are in physical existence and have been identified.
- The risk of loss is borne by the party who has title to the goods.
- Tender of goods occurs when the seller produces conforming goods and provides adequate notice of their delivery to the buyer.
- In a shipping contract title is transferred from seller to buyer when the goods are given to the courier, while in a destination contract title passes when the goods are tendered to the buyer.

PERFORMANCE OF SALES CONTRACTS

LO 9-6

Once the parties to a sales contract have agreed on its terms, the law imposes certain other duties and obligations in performing the contract. In addition to the express terms by the parties, the UCC imposes a requirement of *good faith* and spells out the standards for place, time, and acceptance of delivery. Additionally, courts may also look to the customary standards in the particular industry and the course of past dealing between the parties in interpreting the parties' duties and obligations. Of course, the parties may always expressly agree to unique delivery, risk allocation, or payment terms. But if the terms are not expressed, the UCC helps to fill any gaps and the parties are bound by the UCC terms.

Obligations of All Parties

The UCC has a *good faith* provision (similar to the duty of good faith in a common law contract) that imposes a duty of good faith and commercial reasonableness as the bedrock of any sales contract.[20] Good faith is defined in the UCC as "honesty in fact in the conduct or transaction concerned."[21] Additionally, merchants also have the duty to act in a *commercially reasonable* manner. Generally, this means that merchants (merchants only) must observe industry standards and practices that may be unique to a particular industry or field. In Case 9.2, a state supreme court gives an example of a UCC good faith analysis.

CASE 9.2 Sons of Thunder, Inc. v. Borden, Inc., 148 N.J. 396 (1997)

FACT SUMMARY Borden was a company that made clam chowder using clams purchased from commercial fishing boats. Borden had been buying clams from four boats run by a highly competent captain, Capt. Donald DeMusz. The boats would deliver whole clams, which then had to be shucked (deshelled) on land, causing increased costs of processing and shell disposal. To avoid these costs, Borden sought a "Shuck-at-Sea" project wherein all shucking could be done by adding extra equipment onto the boat. None of the four boats was large enough to sustain this project, so DeMusz offered to buy two larger ones if Borden promised to buy a minimum amount of clams from the boats.

Based on Borden's promise to purchase the clams, DeMusz took out loans and bought the *Jessica Lori* and the *Sons of Thunder,* which were equipped with Shuck-at-Sea technology. Soon thereafter, Borden came under new management, which concluded that the Shuck-at-Sea project was not profitable and notified DeMusz that Borden did not intend to honor the old contract. Borden began to buy only a fraction of its clams from DeMusz's boats, and this significantly reduced the revenue produced by the boats. At the same time, Borden increased its clam buying from DeMusz's competitors. With diminished revenue from the clam boats, DeMusz could not pay off the loans and had to sell the boats at a loss. DeMusz and other owners of the *Sons of Thunder* brought suit for breach of good faith obligation under the UCC.

SYNOPSIS OF DECISION AND OPINION The New Jersey court ruled in favor of *Sons of Thunder,* reasoning that Borden urged DeMusz to buy the boats and promised to buy the clams it needed from the *Sons of Thunder.* Instead, Borden's new management expressed that the company had no intention of honoring the contract. In bad faith, knowing that without Borden's clam purchases the *Sons of Thunder* would suffer financially to the point of insolvency, Borden simply reduced its clam buying dramatically.

WORDS OF THE COURT: Honesty in Fact Requirement "Borden knew that *Sons of Thunder* depended on the income from its contract with Borden to pay back the loan. Yet, Borden continuously breached that contract by never buying the required amount of clams from the *Sons of Thunder.* Furthermore, after [management changed, Borden] told DeMusz that [it] would not honor the contract with *Sons of Thunder.* . . . Accepting those facts and the reasonable inferences therefrom offered as true, we determine that the jury had sufficient evidence to find that Borden was not 'honest in fact' as required by the UCC."

Case Questions

1. How should the new management have acted when it saw that its predecessor had entered a bad contract?

2. What would have been a proper remedy for *Sons of Thunder?*

---

[20] UCC § 1-203.

[21] UCC § 1-201(19).

Seller's Obligations and Rights

Fundamentally, the seller's primary obligation is to transfer and deliver conforming goods to the buyer. *Conforming goods* simply means that the goods must conform exactly to the agreed-upon description of the goods. Under the doctrine referred to as **tender of delivery,** the UCC obligates the seller to have or tender the goods, give the buyer appropriate notice of the tender, and take any actions necessary to allow the buyer to take delivery.[22] Absent any specific agreement between the parties to the contrary, the UCC uses a general *reasonableness requirement* to govern the delivery process. That is, the goods must be delivered at a reasonable hour, in a reasonable manner, and in one shipment. In the case of goods that are to be picked up, the goods must be made available at a reasonable time to allow the buyer to take possession.

Perfect Tender   Under the UCC, the seller's obligation actually goes beyond just delivering conforming goods. The seller must tender the goods in a manner that matches the contract terms in every respect. This is known as the **perfect tender rule**.[23] If the seller fails to achieve perfect tender, the buyer has three options: (1) Reject the entire shipment of goods within a reasonable time, (2) accept the shipment of goods as is, or (3) accept any number of commercial units and reject the rest of the goods in a reasonable time (e.g., accepting 100 nonconforming computer chips from a delivery of 500 nonconforming computer chips).

Although the perfect tender rule may sound oppressive, the UCC also gives the seller certain rights intended to promote the completion of the original contract.

Cure   If the seller has delivered goods and the buyer rejects them under the perfect tender rule, the seller has the right to repair or replace the rejected goods *so long as the time period for performance has not expired.* Once the time contemplated for performance has expired, the seller's right to **cure** also expires. If, however, the time for the seller's performance has not expired, the seller may cure by (1) giving notice of her intent to cure and (2) tendering conforming goods in replacement of the rejected goods.[24] For example, on April 1, Lewis contracts with Clarke to provide Clarke with 100 Type-A compasses at $10 per unit to be delivered no later than May 1. Lewis delivers 100 Type-B compasses on April 15, and Clarke rejects the goods as nonconforming. At this point, Lewis has the option to cure because the date for performance is still two weeks away. So, if Lewis notifies Clarke that he intends to cure and then ships 100 Type-A compasses to Clarke on April 30, he has completed performance consistent with the UCC requirements and, assuming the new shipment of goods conforms, Clarke must accept the goods.

In some instances, the right to cure may exist even *after* the time period for performance has come due. The UCC provides that if the seller reasonably believes that the nonconforming goods would be acceptable to the buyer (perhaps because the seller shipped a more expensive product or because of a course of past dealing between buyer and seller) with or without a money allowance, then the seller gets additional time to cure after the time under the contract has passed. The seller must seasonably notify the buyer of her intent to cure.[25]

In the Lewis-Clarke contract discussed above, suppose that Lewis discovered that the Type-A compasses were out of stock, so he instead shipped Clarke Type-A1A compasses (a more expensive and newer model) on the last day for performance. If Lewis rejects the goods, most courts would allow Clarke, so long as he has given Lewis seasonable notice, to cure even though the time period for performance has passed. This is because Clarke was

Legal Speak »)
Seasonable Notice Notification to the other party within either an agreed-upon time or a reasonable amount of time given the nature and goals of the contract.

---

[22]UCC § 2-503(1).

[23]UCC § 2-601.

[24]UCC § 2-508 (1) and (2).

[25]UCC § 2-508 (2).

Performance Assurances

PROBLEM *In ongoing relationships with vendors, there may be a time when a manager becomes wary about a provider's ability to sell or a buyer's ability to continue making regular payments.*

Perhaps this skepticism is based on conduct of certain parties or on conversations with the vendor. What legal methods will help reduce the risk that the company won't be left fighting other creditors in bankruptcy or suffer any further losses? For example, two companies enter into an agreement for the sale of electronic components. Whiteside agrees to purchase 50 lots of components per month, from January through June, from Greenside and to pay Greenside $7,500 per lot *within 10 days* after the lots are delivered. On January 2, Greenside tenders a conforming delivery, and Whiteside pays by check on January 6. In February, Greenside delivers a second lot, but Whiteside fails to make the payment as agreed. As the end of February approaches with Whiteside's monthly invoice still unpaid, Greenside's manager faces a dilemma. While she wishes to preserve the potentially lucrative contractual relation with Whiteside, she is also responsible for protecting Greenside's interests and inventory.

SOLUTION *Greenside's manager should seek assurances about the past-due and future payments.*

The UCC provides both parties the right to demand **assurances** from each other concerning performance. The Code provides that when one party has *reasonable grounds* to believe that the other will not perform, she has the right to demand that the other party give her written assurance that performance will take place as agreed.[26] If that party does not provide adequate assurance of performance within 30 days, the demanding party may then suspend performance until she receives the requested assurance. In the Whiteside-Greenside contract, suppose that one week prior to the date when the March delivery is scheduled, Greenside requests that Whiteside provide her with *written assurances* that (1) Whiteside will pay the amount due immediately and (2) Whiteside will continue to pay Greenside within the 10-day period as stated in the original contract. If Whiteside ignores the request or does not provide the requested assurances, Greenside then has the right to suspend her performance and has no duty to deliver another lot until she receives assurances from Whiteside. By using this UCC protection, Greenside's manager minimizes losses without breaching the original agreement. She preserved the contractual relationship until such time as the payment problems may be worked out to Greenside's satisfaction and delivery may then resume and continue in accordance with the original contract. If, however, conditions are sufficient to allow Greenside to reasonably believe that Whiteside intends to *renege* on his obligations in the contract, Greenside may cancel the contract and pursue legal remedies (such as a lawsuit to recover money damages) under the UCC provisions governing *anticipatory repudiation* (discussed in the next section).

[26]UCC § 2-609 (1)

---

reasonable in his assumption that a newer and more expensive model would be an acceptable substitute for the ordered model.[27]

In Case 9.3, a federal appeals court examines a seller's right to cure when a good faith delivery of nonconforming goods has been made.

Commercial Impracticability   Recall from the previous chapter that the common law excuses performance when a contract becomes **commercially impracticable.** The UCC applies a commercial impracticability rule when a delay in delivery or nondelivery

---

[27]Based on *Bartus v. Riccardi*, 284 N.Y.S.2d 222 (1967).

FACT SUMMARY   Car Transportation (buyer) purchased a Blue Bird luxury motor coach from Blue Bird's authorized dealer, Bleakly (seller), for $650,000. Although neither the buyer nor the seller performed any predelivery inspection, the seller provided assurances to the buyer that the coach was new and in working condition. On the day of the purchase, however, the buyer's principal drove the coach from the seller's lot and began to notice certain defects with the coach's electrical system. The next day, the buyer returned the coach to the seller for repairs, and the seller's service technicians repaired several electrical problems to the buyer's satisfaction. The buyer retook possession of the coach and placed it into service for the buyer's business on January 5.

Over the next two months, the coach had additional electrical system defects and several other mechanical problems. Instead of returning the coach to the seller once again, the buyer opted to return the coach to the manufacturer for repairs. On February 18, the manufacturer returned the coach to the buyer, but the electrical problems were still not fully resolved. On March 22, the buyer notified the seller that it was revoking the acceptance of the coach due to the mechanical problems. Eventually, the buyer sued the seller, asserting, among other claims, revocation of the buyer's acceptance. The seller argued that it had not been given the opportunity to cure as required by Georgia's commercial law statutes. The trial court found in favor of the seller, and the buyer appealed.

SYNOPSIS OF DECISION AND OPINION   The U.S. Court of Appeals for the 11th Circuit affirmed the trial court's ruling in favor of the seller. The court held that the UCC's opportunity to cure required the buyer to provide the seller with a reasonable time in which to attempt to make repairs. What constitutes the reasonable time in which to cure depends on the nature, purpose, and circumstances of the particular case. The court held that the seller was entitled to notice of the additional problems occurring after delivery and an opportunity to repair them at some time during the three months prior to the buyer's revocation.

WORDS OF THE COURT: Inadequate Opportunity to Cure   "[T]he Buyer gave the Seller one opportunity to cure after the defect in the electrical system first became apparent. After these initial repairs, the Buyer did not inform the Seller when the Coach continued to have additional problems; rather, it returned the Coach to the manufacturer for repairs. Nearly three months after acceptance, after the manufacturer also had made one failed attempt to correct the defect, the Buyer informed the Seller that it was revoking its acceptance of the Coach. Based upon this undisputed evidence, we agree with the district court that, as a matter of law, the Buyer provided the Seller with an insufficient opportunity to cure. Providing only one opportunity to repair— before the extent of the defect was truly apparent—is not reasonable, especially where the product in question is as complicated as a motor coach."

Case Questions

1. Shouldn't the buyer's attempts to have the coach fixed by the manufacturer be considered an attempt to cure under the UCC? Why or why not?

2. How much time is "reasonable" to allow the seller to fix the electrical problems? Isn't the buyer suffering additional damages from not having the coach in service?

has been made impracticable by the occurrence of an unanticipated event so long as the event directly affected a basic assumption of the contract. Commercial impractability is a *narrow doctrine*. For example, in *Maple Farms, Inc. v. City School District of Elmira*, a state appellate court in New York ruled that an unexpected increase in prices was *not* sufficient to meet the standard of commercial impracticability for a supplier to be excused from performance because a reasonable businessperson should have been aware that the general inflation at the time (early 1970s) may affect the price of the contract.[28]

---

[28]352 N.Y.S.2d 784. The case involved a supplier of milk who agreed to supply a school district with a certain quantity of milk for the school year 1973–74 at a price set in June 1973. By December, the price of raw milk increased by 23 percent, and the supplier would lose over $7,000 if it continued providing milk at the June price.

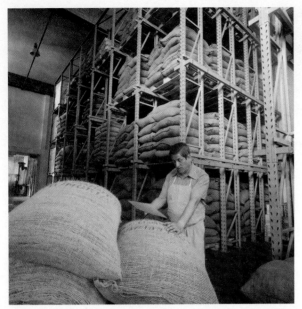

Buyers have a reasonable time to inspect the goods to be sure that they conform to the contract.

Buyer's Rights and Obligations

The buyer's primary obligation is triggered when the seller tenders delivery. Once the buyer has accepted the goods, the buyer must pay for them in accordance with the contract. Payments may come in a variety of forms, and frequently the parties have negotiated and agreed on the details of payments (cash versus credit, terms of payment, etc.). In the absence of agreement, the UCC provides that the buyer must make full payment at the time and place that she has received the goods.[29] When the parties have agreed on credit for payment, the amount owed is paid out over a period of time at a certain rate of interest. Typically, the interest would begin accruing 30 days after shipment.[30]

Buyer's Right of Inspection: Acceptance or Rejection

Unless the parties agree otherwise, the buyer has a reasonable time period to inspect the goods to be sure they conform to the contract. After inspection, the buyer may (1) communicate to the seller that she has accepted the goods; (2) do nothing, and thus be presumed to have accepted the goods unless she gives prompt notice of a rejection (or partial rejection); or (3) notify the seller that she is rejecting the goods[31] (or part of the goods). If the buyer properly rejects the goods, the buyer

---

 Self-Check   Buyer's Rights and Obligations

Does the grocer have an obligation to pay? Why or why not?

1. Grocer orders 100 Grade-A eggs from Farmer per month at market price for a period of three years. Farmer delivered Grade-A eggs every month for one year, but Grocer then began rejecting the eggs, claiming that the market price for eggs was too high and the egg contract was commercially impracticable.

2. Grocer receives 40 bushels of corn rather than the tomatoes he ordered, but he signs a receipt for the corn anyway. The next day Grocer changes his mind and sends back the rejected corn.

3. Grocer orders 50 gallons of whole milk from Dairy to be delivered December 23. On December 20 he receives 60 gallons of skim milk. He rejects the order but does not inform Dairy of his rejection. On January 2, Dairy demands full payment.

4. Two days before Thanksgiving, Grocer orders 100 turkeys, but the delivery the next morning is of 200 chickens. Afraid of losing all his customers the day before Thanksgiving, Grocer accepts 100 chickens and notifies the seller that he is rejecting part of the delivery.

Answers to this Self-Check are provided at the end of the chapter.

---

[29]UCC § 2-310(a).

[30]UCC § 2-310(d) provides that the credit period begins on date of shipment from the seller—not on date of receipt.

[31]Recall the good faith requirement of the UCC. Note that the parties do not have an absolute right to reject the goods. The buyer must have a good faith and lawfully recognized reason to reject (such as when the seller has shipped nonconforming goods). UCC § 2-601 and § 2-602 allow for a rejection of goods on reasonable grounds only.

may also cancel the balance of the contract and pursue any appropriate legal remedies against the seller (breach and remedies for sales contracts are discussed in the next section). The buyer has an obligation to affirmatively notify the seller of the rejection in a timely manner so that the seller still has some opportunity to cure or a reasonable amount of time to recover the goods.

If the seller has shipped conforming goods as agreed, the buyer has the *duty to accept* them and become the owner of the goods in accordance with concepts of title.[32] If the seller has shipped nonconforming goods but the buyer is still willing to accept them, the UCC provides the buyer with the opportunity to later revoke acceptance *only* if the nonconformity substantially impairs the value of the goods. The acceptance of nonconforming goods by the buyer triggers the buyer's obligation to pay consistent with the terms of the agreement.

Special Rules for Installment Contracts

Cash flow or other business reasons sometimes require delivery and billing in two or more separate lots. The UCC provides for such circumstances through use of an **installment contract**. In an installment contract, each lot must be accepted and paid for separately. This means that a buyer can accept one installment without giving up the right to reject any additional installments that are nonconforming. This is essentially an exception to the perfect tender rule because the standard for rejection is more restrictive and, thus, provides additional tender protection to the seller. In an installment contract, the buyer may reject an installment only if the nonconformity *substantially* impairs the value of that installment *and* the nonconformity cannot be cured. If a buyer subsequently accepts a nonconforming installment of the goods and does not notify the seller that she is canceling the contract, the UCC provides that the seller may assume the contract to be reinstated.

CONCEPT SUMMARY Performance of Sales Contracts

- Under the UCC, parties to a sales contract have an implied good faith obligation to be "honest in fact in the conduct of the transaction concerned."
- Except in the case of commercial impracticability, the seller must fulfill an obligation to perfectly tender goods in accordance with the contract or the buyer may reject.
- When nonconforming goods have been delivered and time exists that will allow conforming goods to be delivered before performance is due, the seller may cure by delivering the conforming goods.
- When nonconforming goods equal to or superior to the contracted-for goods have been delivered in good faith, the seller has the right to cure even if the time for performance has expired as long as the buyer is not injured by the delay.
- The buyer can accept the goods or reject them with seasonable notice, but if he accepts, his obligation to pay is then triggered.
- An installment contract permits delivery of goods in separate lots and payment at separate times, with the new right to accept or reject each time.

---

[32]UCC § 2-606 and § 2-607.

BREACH AND REMEDIES IN SALES AGREEMENTS

Although the UCC is grounded in the principle that the law should encourage the consummation of business transactions, it also defines what constitutes nonperformance, known as **breach,** and provides relief for parties that have acted in good faith and sustained damages through no fault of their own. These relief mechanisms are called **remedies**[33] in the UCC and are based on the goal of placing the innocent (nonbreaching) party back in the same position he would have been in if the contract *had been performed* by the parties as originally contemplated in the agreement.

Anticipatory Repudiation in the UCC

Recall that, under the common law, contracting parties have a right to cancel the contract even before any performance is due if it becomes clear that one party does not intend to perform as agreed. The UCC embraces that same right by recognizing that if one party communicates either in writing, orally, or by some action inconsistent with performance, this is a *repudiation* of the agreement. The UCC treats this as a breach even if performance was *not yet due.* The nonbreaching party may then either (1) suspend her own performance, treating the breach as final, and pursue any remedies available (remedies are discussed in the next section); or (2) suspend her own performance, wait for a period of time for the breaching party to *retract* the repudiation, and promise to perform.

Remedies Available to the Seller

A buyer breaches a sales contract when she does any one of the following: (1) rejects the goods despite the fact that the goods conformed to the contract specifications, (2) wrongfully revokes an acceptance, (3) fails to pay the seller in accordance with the contract, or (4) fails to meet her obligations under the contract. In the event of one or more of those instances, the UCC allows the seller to pursue certain remedies against the buyer to recover any losses and prevent future losses. Note that the UCC allows the seller more than one remedy as long as each remedy is *necessary* to help the nonbreaching party recover damages. The choice of remedies depends on *when* the breach occurs relative to whether the goods have been delivered.

Goods in Hands of Seller
When the breach has occurred before the goods were actually received by the buyer, the seller may:

1. Cancel the contract outright or discontinue his own performance (such as withholding or stopping delivery).
2. Resell the goods at fair market value to another party or dispose of the goods for recycling in accordance with reasonable commercial standards of the industry. Commercial standards vary depending on the nature of the goods and are subject to state law. If goods are not perishable, commercial standards and state law may require a public auction advertised over a period of time. Perishable goods are excluded from typical advertising requirements in an effort to mitigate damages.
3. Recover any incidental damages related to the exercise of the reselling remedy such as hard costs of resale (e.g., broker's commission, auction fees) and any difference in value between the original contract price and the resale price.[34]
4. If unable to sell the goods at fair market value, recover the full value of the contract from the buyer. If the seller exercises this remedy, he may no -longer resell the goods even if a new buyer is found.

Legal **Speak** ›))
Incidental Damages under the UCC Any commercially reasonable charges, expenses, or commissions incurred in stopping delivery or in transportation, care, and custody of goods after a buyer's breach.

---

[33]UCC § 2-701, et seq.
[34]UCC § 2-207(1).

Goods in Hands of Buyer   In the case of nonpayment after the buyer has accepted (or such time has passed that the buyer is assumed to have accepted) the goods, the seller may recover the *entire* contract price plus incidental damages. This is also true if the goods are damaged or destroyed, assuming the risk of loss has been passed to the buyer via contract terms or by virtue of the UCC.

In the case of wrongful rejection (rejecting conforming goods) or wrongful revocation of acceptance, the seller may *reclaim* the goods and exercise the remedies provided for in the UCC when the goods are in the hands of the seller, including the recovery of costs related to the reclamation.

Remedies Available to the Buyer

The primary way that a seller breaches a contract is by delivering *nonconforming* goods to the buyer or by failing to make timely delivery of all or part of the lot. A seller who has repudiated the contract prior to delivery of the goods (recall the doctrine of *anticipatory repudiation,* discussed earlier in this chapter) is also deemed to have breached the contract, and the buyer is entitled to pursue remedies. The UCC provides remedies to protect the buyer from further damages and compensate her for any losses suffered due to the breach.

Remedies Following Rejection of Goods   The UCC provides buyers with the immediate remedy of **rightful rejection** of all or part of the lot when the seller delivers nonconforming goods. In the case of rejection due to nonconformity, the buyer must give the seller *seasonable notification* of the rejection. By exercising the right of rejection, the buyer has canceled the contract and is thus discharged from performing (paying) under the agreement and may recover any money already paid (such as a deposit). Rejection also enables the buyer to pursue additional remedies to prevent any further losses and/or recover for losses incurred as a result of the breach.

Cover   Consider the dilemma of the buyer when the seller has not made a timely delivery or has delivered defective goods. No matter what the legal impact of the seller's actions, the buyer who requires the goods in order to conduct business operations must act immediately to prevent her own losses. The UCC provides the buyer with an option to take immediate steps by canceling the contract and purchasing *substitute* goods from another vendor (a right known as **cover**) in order to continue business operations. The UCC requires the covering party to purchase the goods in good faith and without unreasonable delay.[35] The right of cover also allows the covering party to bring a lawsuit to recover from the seller the difference between the *cost of cover* and the *original* contract costs. Covering parties may also recover incidental or consequential damages. However, if the buyer actually saved expenses because of the breach by the seller, those costs are deducted.

For example, suppose that on June 1, PartCo agrees to sell ToyCo goods based on the following memorandum drafted by ToyCo's manager:

1. *Item and Quantity:* 1,000 Type-A toy parts.
2. *Price:* $5 per toy part.
3. *Delivery:* On or before June 30 by Swift Trucking Company to ToyCo warehouse. Delivery charge of $500 to be paid by buyer.

On July 1, the parts have not arrived, but ToyCo has invested substantial sums in preparing its manufacturing operations to be ready in anticipation of the June 30 shipment

Legal Speak ·))
Consequential Damages under the UCC   Such damage, loss, or injury as does not flow directly and immediately from the act of the party, but only from some consequences or results of such act.[36]

---

[35]UCC § 2-712(1).
[36]UCC § 2-715(1).

date. Thus, ToyCo's manager opts to cancel the contract and contacts a local company, NewCo, to order the substitute goods (toy parts). NewCo's price per part is $7. However, because NewCo is a local company, the delivery charge will be only $100. The damages calculation is:

Cover damages:
$7 (reasonable price of substitute goods) less $5 (contract price) = $2 per part for 1,000 parts
Plus:
Incidental and consequential damages (if applicable)
Minus:
Costs saved by virtue of the seller's breach ($400 reduction on delivery charges)

Lawsuit for Money Damages   There may be certain instances in which the buyer properly rejects the goods but does not think it prudent or necessary to use the right to cover. In this case, the UCC gives the buyer the right to sue the breaching party for damages sustained due to the breach. If the buyer chooses this option (not to cover), the measure of damages is different than the covering damage measure. The major difference is the *point in time* used to calculate any losses. In a no-cover case, the recovery is derived by taking the difference between the contract price and the market price at the *time that the buyer learned* of the breach.

Specific Performance   Sometimes it is simply not feasible for the buyer to use cover or a suit for money damages as a remedy. This occurs for example, when the goods in question are *unique* and cannot be obtained elsewhere in the market, as in the case of a sales contract for a rare book, a particular work of art, or a unique coin collection. In these circumstances, the UCC provides the buyer with a remedy of **specific performance,** which allows the buyer to obtain a court order that compels the breaching party to perform his obligation under the contract.

Remedies Following Acceptance of Nonconforming Goods

Commercial conditions or special circumstances may sometimes make the buyer accept (knowing or unknowingly) nonconforming goods. The UCC recognizes certain situations in which even though the buyer has accepted the goods, there may still be a need to protect the buyer's rights by providing remedies for relief.

Revocation of Acceptance   Sometimes a buyer may not realize that the goods are *nonconforming,* and after a cursory inspection the buyer may *unknowingly* accept the goods. The UCC provides protection for such buyers, so long as they act within a reasonable time after discovery of the nonconformance. Buyers who have accepted the goods that turn out to be defective or nonconforming may still recover for any losses by **revoking acceptance**. For a buyer to effectively revoke acceptance, the UCC requires that the non-conformance must *substantially* impair the value of the goods and the buyer must notify the seller within a reasonable time after he discovers (or should have discovered) the breach.[37] Once a reasonable time (generally in accordance with industry standards) has passed after acceptance, the buyer is then barred from pursuing a remedy.

Lawsuit for Money Damages   The buyer may wish to accept the nonconforming goods with full knowledge that the tender of delivery was less than perfect. In this case, the UCC gives protection to the buyer by making it clear that the buyer does *not* give up the

---

[37]UCC § 2-607(3)(a).

right to sue the seller for the buyer's damages resulting from the seller's delivery of non-conforming goods.[38] Just as in a revocation of acceptance (discussed earlier), in order to preserve the right to sue for damages, the buyer must *notify* the seller within a *reasonable time* after the defect was or should have been discovered.

CONCEPT SUMMARY Breach and Remedies in Sales Agreements

- The UCC seeks to remedy breach by placing the nonbreaching party in the same situation she would have been in had the contract been executed as written.

- Faced with anticipatory repudiation by the other party, a party under the UCC can either withdraw and sue for damages or halt performance until the repudiation is retracted.

- If a buyer breaches before delivery by rejection of or nonpayment for conforming goods, then the seller may stop further performance, resell the goods, or, if unable to resell, seek damages. If the buyer's breach occurs after delivery, the seller may sue for the full contract price or reclaim the goods and collect incidental damages.

- If a seller breaches by delivering nonconforming goods, the buyer may reject the goods, seek cover and sue for damages incurred by the new purchase, not seek cover and sue for damages for the difference between the contract and market prices at the time of breach, or ask for specific performance. If the buyer accepts the nonconforming goods out of ignorance or necessity, he still retains the right to sue for damages incurred by the nonconformance.

CONTRACTS FOR INTERNATIONAL SALES OF GOODS LO 9-8

More than ever before in the history of commerce, business managers and owners are engaged in commercial transactions that reach beyond the borders of their own nation. Extraordinary advances over the last two decades in technology, shipping methods, and logistics control have lowered the global barrier to entry for many businesses. The focus in this chapter is on international transactions for the sale of goods by examining the international counterparts to the UCC: the U.N. Convention on Contracts for the International Sale of Goods (CISG) and the International Chamber of Commerce (INCO) terms. In Chapter 26, "International Law and Global Commerce," international law is covered in broad strokes to facilitate an understanding of sources of international law, foreign legal systems, trade protections, and public policy objectives of trading partners.

U.N. Convention on Contracts for the International Sale of Goods

In 1988, the United States became a signatory nation to a U.N. treaty that attempts to establish an international commercial code. The **U.N. Convention on Contracts for the International Sale of Goods (CISG)** governs sale of goods transactions between businesses in any of its 79 member countries.[39] Much like the UCC, the CISG exists to fill in terms of a sale of goods contract when the parties haven't otherwise agreed. Parties are free to negotiate the allocation of risk, insurance requirements, delivery, payment terms, choice of law, and the like to displace the CISG principles. It is particularly important for

---

[38]UCC § 2-714(1).

[39]http://www.uncitral.org/ In March 2013, Brazil became the 79th country to adopt the CISG. It will enter into force for Brazil in April 2014.

Legal Speak ›))
Choice of Law and Forum Clauses Terms of a contract that predetermine which nation's laws and court system will be used in a potential lawsuit under that contract.

managers to understand *choice of law and forum* principles in international contracts, because risk and expense of enforcement become increasingly important factors that should be considered in arriving at appropriate pricing, delivery proposals, and insurance needs.

If one party will have to travel significant distances or hire special counsel to enforce an agreement or recover for damages suffered, adjusting the price or delivery terms accordingly may sometimes help to reduce risk.

Coverage and Major Provisions of CISG

The CISG operates on the same fundamental principle as many commercial codes around the world (including the UCC) in that the law favors the completion of a transaction as agreed upon but also provides relief when one party has breached. The CISG covers parties that maintain a place of business in one of the signatory countries. Note that citizenship of shareholders, directors, or officers is not a factor under the CISG. The CISG covers contracts for the sale of goods between *merchants*. This is perhaps the biggest difference between the UCC and the CISG. The CISG provisions do *not* apply to transactions in which one party is a nonmerchant. Other major important provisions are discussed below.

No Writing Required   The CISG has no formal writing requirement (such as the UCC's statute of frauds) and specifically provides that contracts are not subject to requirements as to format. A totality of the circumstances, such as course of past dealing, evidence of oral or written negotiations between the parties, and industry practice may be sufficient to prove that an enforceable contract exists.

Offer and Acceptance   A contract for the sale of goods between businesses located in different CISG signatory countries begins with offer and acceptance. As with the UCC, the offer need not have complete terms in order to be valid. The offer requires only (1) a brief description of the goods, (2) quantity, and (3) price. Beyond those three terms, so

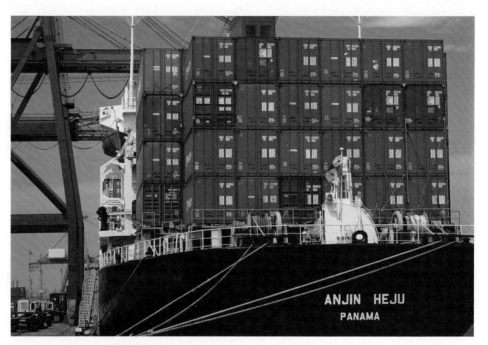

Many international sales transactions are governed by the U.N. Convention on Contracts for the International Sale of Goods.

long as there is some evidence that the parties intended to form a contract, nothing more is needed for a valid offer. Acceptance may be made within a reasonable time and is effective only when it is received by the offeror (thus, the offer may be withdrawn at any point prior to that time).

Remedies   The CISG provides for a party that has delivered nonconforming goods to be given an adequate opportunity to cure the problem. In general, the CISG gives sellers an absolute right and obligation to cure, and buyers must allow the seller the opportunity to cure even if the time for performance is past due. Of course, a buyer must give notice of the nonconformance in a timely manner in order to trigger the seller's cure obligations. If the seller does not cure, the CISG provides a right for the buyer to pursue remedies.

INCO: International Chamber of Commerce Terms

With respect to title, risk of loss, and delivery terms, sometimes the language barrier can lead to confusion among the parties and to disputes regarding a loss. The International Chamber of Commerce provides international abbreviations, known as **INCO terms,** to designate many of the responsibilities. INCO terms are generally used in conjunction with the CISG and are also used in domestic shipping contracts as well. For example, in the absence of any agreement between the parties, the CISG provides that risk passes at the point at which the seller has delivered the goods to a carrier. If the goods are not to be delivered, the risk of loss passes in accordance with the INCO term *EXW* ("ex works"). The INCO term EXW has the universal meaning that the parties understand the goods will not be delivered or transported by the seller. Rather, the seller need only make the goods available to the buyer at the seller's place of business and provide the buyer with appropriate documentation of title. There are 11 INCO terms in all. The most common ones are:

- *FCA ("free carrier"):* This term means that the seller provides transportation at the seller's expense only to the carrier named by the buyer.
- *FOB ("free on board"):* This term is always accompanied by the name of a port (e.g., FOB New York) and applies only when transportation is via freighter ship. It means that the seller's expense and risk of loss *end* when the seller delivers goods "over the ship's rail" to the freighter ship. The buyer is responsible for the freighter delivery charge and any losses occurring en route to delivery.

CONCEPT SUMMARY Contracts for International Sales of Goods

- The CISG, the international counterpart to the UCC, is a U.N. treaty that governs sales contracts between businesses located in signatory countries.
- Four major differences between the CISG and the UCC are (1) it does not apply to non-merchants, (2) it has no statute of frauds, (3) offers can be withdrawn at any point prior to the offeror's receiving the acceptance, and (4) the right to cure exists even after the performance period is over.
- INCO terms are standardized contractual terms and designations used in international sales contracts to avoid confusion due to language barriers and differing legal systems.
- Some INCO terms are also used in domestic transactions and can have different applications. For example, FOB is used both domestically and internationally and sometimes indicates dissimilar buyer and seller rights and obligations.

Sales contracts p. 232   Agreements to transfer title to real property or tangible assets at a given price.

Goods p. 232   Tangible personal property that is movable at the time of identification to a contract of sale.

Merchant p. 232   One that is regularly engaged in the sale of a particular good.

Open terms p. 234   Unspecified terms in a sales contract that do not detract from the validity of the contract so long as the parties intended to make the contract and other specified terms give a basis for remedy in case of breach.

Output contract p. 234   A contract in which the buyer agrees to buy all the goods that the seller produces for a set time and at a set price and the seller may sell only to that one buyer. The quantity for the contract is the seller's output.

Requirements contract p. 234   A contract in which the buyer agrees to buy whatever he needs from the seller during a set period and the buyer may buy only from that one seller. The quantity for the contract is what the buyer requires.

Merchant's firm offer p. 234   An offer in writing between merchants to buy or sell goods along with a promise without consideration to keep that offer for a stated amount of time or, if unstated, no longer than three months.

Purchase order p. 235   A form commonly used in sales contracts as an offer from the buyer; contains preprinted clauses along with blanks to accommodate the specifics of the transaction.

Acknowledgment form p. 235   A form commonly used in sales contracts as an acceptance from the seller in response to a purchase order; contains preprinted provisions and has blanks to accommodate the specifics of the transaction.

Battle of the forms p. 235   The conflict between the terms written into standardized purchase (offer) and acknowledgment (acceptance) forms, which differ in that one form favors the buyer and the other the seller. The UCC attempts to broker a truce in this battle while keeping the contract of sale intact.

Knockout rule p. 235   As applied in many states, the view that when a buyer and seller engage in a battle of the forms and different terms are exchanged,

both the seller's and buyer's differing terms drop out and substitute UCC gap fillers complete the contract.

Confirmation memorandum p. 237   A written verification of an agreement. Under the statute of frauds section of the UCC, a merchant who receives a signed confirmation memorandum from another merchant will be bound by the memorandum just as if she had signed it, unless she promptly objects.

Risk of loss p. 238   The risk of one party's having to bear the loss due to damage, destruction, or loss of goods bargained for under a sales contract.

Title p. 238   The legal right to ownership in a good and to all the privileges and responsibilities that ownership entails.

Shipment contract p. 239   A contract in which the seller is required to send the goods to the buyer via a carrier. When the carrier receives the goods, the seller has fulfilled his duty and the buyer assumes title and bears the risk of loss.

Destination contract p. 239   A contract in which the seller is required to deliver the goods to a chosen destination and not just to the carrier. When the goods have been tendered at the destination, the seller has fulfilled his duty and the buyer takes title and risk of loss.

Tender p. 239   An unconditional performance of the seller by delivering the purchased goods or otherwise making them available to the buyer.

FOB point p. 239   *Domestic:* A shipping term that indicates the place to which the seller must deliver goods. In the absence of a contract provision to the contrary, title and risk of loss pass to the buyer at this point. *International:* An INCO term indicating that goods are to be shipped via freighter ship and that title and risk of loss transfer to the buyer when the goods are delivered to the named ship.

Tender of delivery p. 243   Seller's obligation under which, for delivery of goods, tender occurs when the seller produces goods conforming to the contract and provides adequate notice of their delivery to the buyer.

Perfect tender rule p. 243   Rule that requires the seller to deliver her goods exactly as the contract requires in quantity, quality, and all other respects or risk the buyer's lawful rejection of the goods.

Cure p. 243   The right of a seller to replace non-conforming goods before final contract performance is due. If nonconforming goods were delivered in good faith and were considered equal to or superior to what was ordered, the seller may cure after final contract performance is due if the buyer will not suffer injury.

Assurance p. 244   A pledge or guarantee that gives confidence to one party that the other party is able to complete performance under a contract.

Commercially impracticable p. 244   Rule applied by the UCC when a delay in delivery or nondelivery has been made impracticable by the occurrence of an unanticipated event so long as the event directly affected a basic assumption of the contract.

Installment contract p. 247   A contract allowing delivery of goods and payments for goods at separate times, with the goods being accepted or rejected separately.

Breach p. 248   The failure to meet a contractual obligation.

Remedies p. 248   Either monetary, performance, or injunctive, the court-ordered means of enforcing rights and redressing wrongs after a breach.

Rightful rejection p. 249   The justified refusal to accept nonconforming goods under a sales contract.

Cover p. 249   A nonbreaching buyer's right to purchase substitute goods on the open market after a delivery of nonconforming goods from the original seller and to sue for the difference.

Specific performance p. 250   A court order compelling the breaching party to perform as the contract states when monetary damages would be an insufficient remedy.

Revoking acceptance p. 250   Remedy whereby the buyer, even after accepting the goods, can still revoke acceptance if the goods are nonconforming in a way that substantially affects their value and he notifies the seller of the revocation in a timely fashion.

U.N. Convention on Contracts for the International Sale of Goods (CISG) p. 251   Treaty that governs international sales contracts among businesses located in U.N.-member countries that have ratified it.

INCO terms p. 253   Standardized contractual terms and designations used in international and some domestic sales contracts to avoid confusion due to language barriers and differing legal systems.

THEORY TO PRACTICE

Bentley is a manager at a high-end printing company called Graphic Communications Inc. (GCI). GCI designs and produces posters and other materials for advertising purposes for a variety of clients, including a local symphony orchestra and Main Street University. After GCI received a large order from the university that required a special press, Bentley was assigned to locate a suitable press, negotiate the purchase terms, and arrange for delivery no later than July 1. Bentley negotiated a price with Armstrong Press Manufacturing for the Armstrong model 2000 printing press. The press was sufficiently large as to require that it be delivered in three separate pieces and then assembled on-site. One factor in choosing Armstrong as a vendor was that GCI had used Armstrong before for purchases of smaller presses and had been satisfied with its products and services. In those previous transactions, GCI had used its own standard preprinted purchase order, and no disputes developed.

Once the parties agreed on price, Bentley issued a preprinted purchase order. The purchase order was one page long and had very few terms. It contained only the price, description of the press, the date of the purchase order, a provision that agreed that all three pieces of the press would be delivered and operational by July 1, and Bentley's signature. After Armstrong received the purchase order, Armstrong's manager handwrote this phrase in the delivery section of the purchase order: "Acknowledged as a destination contract. To be delivered and assembled in three installments to GCI over the month of May." Armstrong's manager then signed the purchase order, faxed the purchase order back to Bentley, and began to process the order. Armstrong shipped the first part of the press using its own delivery service. Before delivery, the truck was involved in an accident, and the first part of the press was destroyed.

1. Is Armstrong's addition of the delivery term binding on GCI? Explain the UCC analysis governing the additional terms added by Armstrong.

2. Does the fact that the parties had a history of past dealings with each other impact your analysis in Question 1? Why or why not?

3. When does title to the goods pass in this contract? Who has the risk of loss? How is your answer related to your analysis of Question 1?

4. Is the purchase order sufficient to satisfy the statute of frauds? Why or why not?

5. Assume that Armstrong ships the first two parts of the press with no problem but anticipates a significant delay for the third part. Knowing that GCI requires the press to be ready on July 1, Armstrong substitutes a newer and more expensive version of the final piece of the press by June 15. Has Armstrong breached the contract? When it is delivered, must GCI accept the final piece because it is newer and more expensive than the goods it had bargained for?

6. In Question 5, if GCI accepts the replaced good but one week later discovers that the new press component is incompatible with the first two components, may GCI still reject the goods despite the fact that it has accepted them and one week's time has passed? What UCC provision covers this situation?

7. If GCI rejects the final shipment of goods, what are GCI's options in terms of a remedy?

MANAGER'S CHALLENGE

Managers have a responsibility to protect their company from legal liability or disputes as much as possible through the use of various prevention measures. In the Theory to Practice problem, the crux of the potential disputes depends on the comprehensiveness of the purchase order. Even if ultimately the press is delivered, GCI could have avoided a number of potential liabilities through inclusion of basic language of agreement in the purchase order. Assume that Bentley is required to submit a memorandum to her senior manager describing how the purchase order could be revised to provide protection for GCI by ensuring that any future purchases anticipate potential problems with the vendor. Be sure to provide a potential solution for each problem posed in Theory to Practice problem. A sample answer may be found on this textbook's website at www.mhhe.com/melvinleb2e.

CASE SUMMARY 9.1 :: Fisherman Surgical Instruments, LLC v. Tri-anim Health Services, Inc., 502 F. Supp. 2d 1170 (Kan. 2007)

REQUIREMENTS CONTRACTS AND GOOD FAITH

Fisherman makes high-end surgical instruments for use by medical professionals. Not long after the company opened, it contracted with a medical supply dealer, Tri-anim, to sell its instruments to doctors. The contract did not include quantity but did state that Tri-anim would buy from Fisherman based on "mutually agreed upon sales goals." The parties also agreed that Tri-anim would not sell products that competed with Fisherman's instruments. Shortly after Tri-anim began selling the products, surgeons complained that the quality of Fisherman's instruments was substandard. Tri-anim then began selling a competitor's products. It also canceled the contract with Fisherman, saying it was void under the UCC because the agreement did not specify the quantity of goods.

CASE QUESTIONS

1. Who prevails and why?

2. Is this a requirements contract or output contract?

3. If Tri-anim did not cancel the contract but instead bought nothing and sold nothing, would Fisherman have any cause of action against Tri-anim? If so, what would be the appropriate remedy?

CASE SUMMARY 9.2 :: General Motors Corp. v Acme Refining Co., 513 F. Supp. 2d 906 (E.D. Mich. 2007)

RIGHT OF REJECTION

Acme Refining collects, melts down, and resells scrap metal. In producing its cars, General Motors (GM) creates a massive amount of scrap metal that must be removed. Acme contracted to purchase and pick up scrap metal from GM's plant. The contract provided that the metal was to be taken "as-is, where-is." After removing 850,000 tons of metal from the GM plant, Acme realized the metal was corrupted by nonmetal products and waste oils, making smelting much more costly. Instead of rejecting the metal, Acme e-mailed GM over several weeks in an attempt to negotiate a lower price. Unable to bring down the price, Acme then rejected all the scrap metal.

CASE QUESTIONS

1. Was Acme's rejection lawful?
2. Did Acme give seasonable notification of rejection?

CASE SUMMARY 9.3 :: Glenn Distributors Corp. v Carlisle Plastics, Inc., 297 F.3d 294 (3d Cir. 2002)

COVER

Glenn Distributors sells closeout merchandise to discount stores. The merchandise consists of goods that have been changed or discontinued, so large quantities can be bought at bargain prices. Carlisle Plastics makes "Ruffies" name-brand trash bags. Glenn contracted to buy $990,000 worth of Ruffies bags from Carlisle, but Carlisle shipped Glenn only $736,000 worth of the bags and sold the others to a different buyer. Glenn claimed it was unable to cover because the only name-brand bag for that price was Ruffies and only Carlisle made Ruffies. Unable to cover, Glenn sued for $230,000 in lost profits.

CASE QUESTIONS

1. Did Glenn make reasonable efforts to cover?
2. Should Glenn have to cover the lost profits by buying products other than trash bags? Why or why not?

CASE SUMMARY 9.4 :: S.W.B. New England, Inc. v. R.A.B. Food Group, LLC, 2008 WL 540091 (S.D.N.Y. 2008)

SPECIFIC PERFORMANCE

SWB is a distributor of kosher food products in New England. SWB's only substantial competitor is Millbrook. SWB entered a contract to buy kosher products from Rokeach. Rokeach is the dominant kosher food supplier in the region and has established a trusted brand name in New England for kosher products. After the SWB-Rokeach contract was in place, Food Group purchased Rokeach. Food Group refused to honor the SWB-Rokeach contract and began to sell only to Millbrook. SWB brought suit, asking for specific performance from Food Group and Rokeach.

CASE QUESTIONS

1. What are the specific requirements for a court to grant specific performance to SWB?
2. Do these requirements fit this case?

BATTLE OF THE FORMS

Mozaffarian and his wife, each suing individually and as d/b/a three companies they owned, signed a credit agreement in which they expressly acknowledged receipt of, and agreed to be bound by, terms and conditions contained in an extrinsic (external) document, which they neither read nor requested a copy of to read. The credit agreement identified the terms and conditions as those contained on each invoice. After the credit application was approved, they then saw, for the first time, the terms and conditions, which contained a New York forum selection clause. Movado proved by a preponderance of the evidence that the terms and conditions of the extrinsic document were incorporated into the credit agreement and that the defendants

acknowledged receipt and agreed to be bound by the same. The credit agreement, which identified the terms and conditions as those contained on each invoice, was sufficient to put the defendants on notice that there was an additional document of legal import to the contract they were executing.

CASE QUESTIONS

1. Was the forum selection clause an additional term, a different term, a confirmatory writing, or a term incorporated into the document? Explain.
2. Does the fact that Mozaffarian et al. never requested to see the extrinsic document have any bearing on the case? Why or why not?

COMMERCIAL IMPRACTICABILITY

In 2007, real estate developer Igor Krivoruchko contracted with Ner Tamid Congregation of North Town, an Illinois not-for-profit corporation, to purchase property Ner Tamid owned on Rosemont Avenue in Chicago. After postponing the closing once, Krivoruchko refused to go forward with the deal because he said he could not obtain the kind of financing he hoped to get. The purchase contract contained no financing contingency clause because, believing he was "creditworthy" and had not had problems in the past with the lender with which he was dealing, Krivoruchko did not desire one. Ner Tamid sued for breach of contract, and Krivoruchko defended, in part claiming commercial impracticability because he could not obtain the financing he wanted due to an "unanticipated" and "unforeseeable" downturn in the economy.

CASE QUESTIONS

1. In its decision, the district court cited newspaper articles that discussed the volatility of the economy and specifically the real estate market. Do these articles act in any way to support or defeat Krivoruchko's claim?
2. Should a defense of commercial impracticability be effective under circumstances in which prices are affected by changes in the local or national economy? Explain.
3. How might Krivoruchko have protected himself under this contract?
4. How might Ner Tamid Congregation of North Town have protected itself under this contract?

Existence of a Sales Contract

1. Yes. This is a requirements contract, so Boston Hardware is obligated to purchase only what it requires (250 shovels).

2. Yes. The delivery terms would be supplied by the UCC because they are missing from the contract. Therefore, New York High School takes delivery at Big Apple's place of business. Big Apple needs only to have the desks available by September 1 for pickup by New York High School.

3. Yes. But for the patient's acquisition of the overlays, the dentist's services would have been unnecessary. This contract is predominantly one for goods.

4. No contract. Careful! While this is a merchant's firm offer for seven months, the UCC restricts a merchant's firm offer to no more than *three months* (see UCC § 2-205). Therefore, L.A.'s offer is no longer valid.

5. No contract. Midwest's return of the acknowledgment with the change in date of delivery would be considered a material change because the delivery date was such an important condition of the contract (holiday season).

Risk of Loss

1. Chase. In a shipment contract, the seller (Marshall) needs only to deliver the goods to the hands of the carrier. In this case, title passed to Chase when Marshall placed them in Mercury's hands. (*Note:* Of course, Chase may be able to sue Mercury for any losses, but Marshall is entitled to payment for the goods from Chase.)

2. Harlan Dairy Co. The fact that parties agreed to delivery and payment to be made at a specific destination indicates that this is a destination contract. In a destination contract, risk of loss is borne by the seller (Harlan) until the goods are tendered.

3. Holmes. Careful! Although this is a destination contract, Holmes delivered *nonconforming goods* (bowler hats instead of top hats). Therefore, Holmes did not complete performance, and the risk of loss never passed to Cardozo.

4. Smooth Lager. "FOB Distributor's Warehouse, Mobile, AL" indicates that the title and risk of loss will transfer when the goods are satisfactorily delivered to the buyer at the buyer's warehouse in Mobile, Alabama. Smooth Lager retains ownership and risk of loss until delivery occurs.

5. White. The buyer, White, took physical possession of the good, and, according to the UCC, risk of loss passes at that point so long as the seller is a merchant.

Buyer's Rights and Obligations

1. Grocer is obligated to buy eggs at market price from Farmer for the duration of the contract. Commercial impracticability is a narrow doctrine and generally does not apply in cases where changing economic conditions impact the contract.

2. Grocer is obligated to pay for the corn. Grocer's knowing acceptance of the nonconforming goods triggered his obligation to pay.

3. Grocer is obligated to pay for the skim milk because he failed to affirmatively notify the seller of his rejection in a timely manner.

4. Grocer is obligated to pay the fair market value for 100 chickens (not turkeys). Because the seller didn't deliver a perfect tender, Grocer could have (1) rejected the entire shipment, (2) accepted the entire shipment, or (3) accepted part of the shipment and rejected the rest. He opted for the last choice and, thus, is obligated only for the goods accepted.

10
CHAPTER

Torts and Products Liability

learning **objectives**

After studying this chapter, students who have mastered the material will be able to:

10-1 Articulate a basic definition of a tort and identify the source of law governing various types of torts.

10-2 Determine the classification of tort based on the conduct of the wrongdoer.

10-3 Give specific examples of how tort law applies in the business environment.

10-4 Apply the elements and defenses of the torts of defamation, trade libel, and product disparagement and discuss the applicability of each in the business environment.

10-5 Identify the differences in terms of liability for traditional print defamation and defamation in cyberspace.

10-6 Distinguish business competition torts from other intentional torts and understand their applicability in commercial relationships.

10-7 Recognize conduct that is classified as negligent and identify any potential defenses.

10-8 Provide alternate theories of liability and defense that can be applied when a product is the cause of an injury.

10-9 Articulate what must be proved in negligence and strict liability cases and appreciate how the levels of proof differ.

earning to recognize situations in which a business venture may have potential liability to another party is an important part of limiting risk in business operations. Tort law and products liability law set out certain conduct and standards of reasonableness and provide legal recourse when a violation of those standards results in an injury causing losses. Because business owners are ordinarily responsible for the intentional or accidental conduct of their employees who cause another party harm, it is essential for managers to understand ways in which to control risk and reduce liability. In this chapter, students will learn:

- The fundamental principles of tort law, types of torts, and how each applies in a business context.
- Rules governing intentional and business competition torts.
- How liability arises for negligent acts and the defenses to liability.
- Special rules governing strict liability and products liability.

OVERVIEW OF TORT LAW LO 10-1

A **tort**[1] is a civil wrong where one party has acted, or in some cases failed to act, and that action or inaction causes a loss to be suffered by another party. The law provides a remedy for one who has suffered an injury by compelling the wrongdoer to pay compensation to the injured party. Tort law is best understood as law that is intended to compensate injured parties for losses resulting in harm from some unreasonable conduct by another.[2] One who commits a tort is known as the **tortfeasor.** The tortfeasor's wrongful conduct is described as **tortious conduct.** Recall from Chapter 1, "Legal Foundations," that an individual may commit a criminal offense and a civil wrong in the very *same* act. While criminal statutes are intended to punish and deter the wrongdoer, the common law of torts is primarily intended to provide *compensation* for the victim. In some cases tort law also may be used to deter wrongful conduct in the future.

SOURCES OF LAW

For the most part, tort law is governed by state common law principles. Recall from Chapter 1, "Legal Foundations," that courts look to rules articulated by the American Law Institute (ALI) for guidance on applying common law legal principles. For tort law, these rules are known as the ***Restatement of Torts.*** The ALI has amended the Restatements twice, and, therefore, these sources of law are called the *Restatement (Second) of Torts* and the *Restatement (Third) of Torts.* Remember that courts are not bound by any of the Restatements, but they do

---

[1]The term *tort* originally derives from the Latin root *tortus,* meaning "twisted" or "wrested aside". As with many legal terms, Latin words were given a French twist in English common law via the Norman kings. Thus, the shortened term *tort* is a French root meaning "wrong."

[2]*Black's Law Dictionary.*

recognize them as widely applied principles of law. The Second Restatements have the benefit of volumes of case law and wide acceptance, and therefore references to the Restatements in this chapter refer to the Second Restatements unless otherwise noted.

Laws that cover individuals who are injured by a product, known as *products liability laws,* may take the form of state common law or state statutes that expressly impose liability for injuries that result from products. These statutes are based primarily on the Restatements and are relatively uniform from state to state.

CATEGORIES OF TORTS

LO 10-2, 10-3

Torts fall into one of three general categories: *intentional torts, negligence,* and *strict liability.* An **intentional tort** is one in which the tortfeasor was *willful* in bringing about a particular event that caused harm to another party. **Negligence** is an accidental (without willful intent) event that caused harm to another party. The difference between the two is the mind-set and intent of the tortfeasor. For example, suppose that Pangloss is the delivery van driver for Cultivate Your Garden Flowers Inc. One day while on a delivery he spots his archenemy crossing the street, so he accelerates his truck and hits him. In this case, Pangloss has committed an intentional tort (battery). If, on the other hand, Pangloss is late for his delivery, carelessly speeds around a turn, and accidentally hits a pedestrian crossing the street, he has committed the tort of negligence.

Legal Speak ›))
Willful Conduct
Intentional behavior directed by the "will."

Strict liability torts, in which a tortfeasor may be held liable for an act regardless of intent or willfulness, applies primarily in cases of defective products and abnormally dangerous activities (such as major construction demolition). Owning a wild animal or even some breeds of dogs can result in strict liability should the animal harm an individual, regardless of the precautions taken by the animal's owner.[3]

INTENTIONAL BUSINESS-RELATED TORTS

While the law provides relief for injured parties in a variety of circumstances, there are some intentional torts that are more important to business owners and managers because they have the potential to impact business relationships and operations.

Defamation

LO 10-4

The law recognizes an individual's or a company's reputation as a valuable asset by imposing liability on any party that makes false and defamatory statements affecting another party's reputation. In this context, the term *party* means an individual, business, or product. Just as in all civil lawsuits, the *untrue statements* must have caused the victim to suffer *damages.* Generally, we think of written defamation as **libel** and oral (spoken) defamation as **slander.** In order to recover for a defamation action, the plaintiff must prove four elements:

■ *Defamatory statement:* A *false* and defamatory statement concerning a party's reputation or honesty or a statement that subjects a party to hate, contempt, or ridicule. In order to qualify as defamatory, the statement must have a tendency to harm the reputation of the plaintiff.[4] Because many statements can be interpreted in more than one way, the law provides that the statement is defamatory so long as a defamatory interpretation is an objectively reasonable one and the plaintiff shows that at least one

---

[3]Numerous cities and municipalities have declared certain breeds of dogs such as pit bulls, rottweilers, and mastiffs to be dangerous animals, and many have even banned the ownership of such animals. See, for example, *Tracy v. Solesky,* 25 A.3d 1025, 421 Md. 192 (2011).

[4]*Restatement (Second) of Torts,* § 559.

of the recipients did in fact make that interpretation. Note that the statement must be false, not merely unkind. Moreover, if a statement was *pure opinion,* that statement is not defamatory. That is, a defamatory statement is one that must be *provable as false.*

■ *Dissemination to a third party:* In the Restatements, this requirement is referred to as *publication,* but in this context it does not literally require the statement to be published. Rather, this element requires that the statement must somehow reach the ears or eyes of someone other than the tortfeasor and the victim. For example, suppose a manager telephones one of his employees and says, "You are the one who stole $100 in petty cash, so you're fired." Even if the accusatory statement is false, the manager has not defamed the employee based on that action alone. No third party heard the statement, and, thus, the dissemination element is missing.

■ *Specificity:* The statement must be about a particular party, business, or product. Thus, any general statement about a profession as a whole cannot constitute defamation, but a false statement about a company can be the basis of a reputation claim.

■ *Damages:* In a business context, the aggrieved party must be able to prove that he or she suffered some pecuniary harm. Examples of damages in a defamation suit include situations in which the victim has lost a valuable client due to the tortfeasor's defamatory comment or the victim is unable to secure employment because of a tortfeasor's defamatory comment during a reference check.

Legal **Speak** ›))
Pecuniary Harm
Lost revenue or profits, both actual and potential.

Public Figure Standard   If the victim is a public figure, such as a candidate for political office or a celebrity, the defamation must have been committed with *malice* or reckless disregard for the truth. This "public figure" rule is based on the U.S. Supreme Court's landmark ruling in *New York Times v. Sullivan.*[5] The case involved a public official, a police commander, who sued *The New York Times* for defamation based on allegations printed in the newspaper that accused him of complicity in criminal activity. In announcing the public figure standard, the Court ruled that, in order for a public figure to prevail in a defamation case, the plaintiff must provide evidence that the defamer either had "actual knowledge" that the statement was false or made the defamatory statement with a "reckless disregard for the truth."

Defenses to Defamation

Truth   Truth is an absolute defense to a charge of defamation. If the statement made is truthful, no defamation has occurred.

Legal **Speak** ›))
Malice Typically defined as the intentional doing of a wrongful act with intent to harm. However, in the context of defamation evidence of ill will is not required for the plaintiff to prevail.

Privilege Defenses   If the injured party meets all of the requirements of a defamation claim, the defendant may still avoid liability if the defamatory statement falls into the category of *privileged statements.* Privilege is a defense that recognizes either a legal or public policy–based immunity from a defamation claim. It is divided into two subcategories: **absolute privilege,** where by the defendant need not offer any further evidence to assert the defense, and **qualified privilege,** where by the defendant must offer evidence of good faith and be absent of malice to be shielded from liability.

Absolute Privilege   Courts generally recognize three types of absolute privilege:

■ *Government officials:* The framers recognized the need for free debate among members of Congress and gave immunity in the Constitution via the "speech and debate clause," which shields members of Congress from liability for any statement made during a congressional debate, hearing, and so on, while in office. The U.S. Supreme Court later extended that protection to all federal officials.[6]

---

[5]376 U.S. 254 (1964).
[6]*Barr v. Matteo,* 360 U.S. 564 (1959).

- *Judicial officers/proceedings:* All states now recognize some protection of participants of a judicial proceeding for statements made during the proceeding. This includes judges, lawyers, and, in some cases, witnesses.
- *State legislators:* Similar immunity has been extended by the states to protect state legislators for statements made in the course of carrying out their duties.

Qualified Privilege   Courts also recognize certain qualified privileges that are grounded in public policy:

- *Media:* Employees of media organizations (e.g., television, radio, periodicals) are afforded a qualified protection from defamation liability. So long as the media has acted in good faith, *absent of malice,* and without a reckless disregard for the truth, the media is protected from liability through privilege as a defense for unintentional mistakes of fact in their reporting.
- *Fair report privilege:* If one relies on an official public document or a statement made by a public official and, when making an alleged defamatory statement, cites the document or public statement, no cause of action for defamation occurs unless the speaker knows the statement is false.
- *Employers:* An increasing number of states have extended some liability protection for employers who are providing a reference for an ex-employee. So long as the information is factual and the employer has not acted with malice, the employer's statement may be privileged.

In Case 10.1, a federal trial court applies a state employer-reference privilege statute.

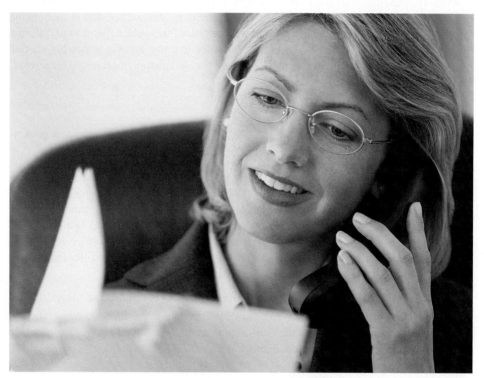

Some states provide statutory immunity from defamation claims for employers providing references for ex-employees, so long as the information is factual.

FACT SUMMARY Swift Transportation operates a trucking company and hired Belanger as a tractor-trailer driver. Swift has various safety policies, among them the "Forbidden Five," which are five infractions that can lead to immediate termination of its drivers. One such infraction is rear-ending another vehicle. In his third year of employment, Belanger was driving a Swift tractor-trailer on the Cross Bronx Expressway when he crashed into the back of another tractor-trailer, causing $40,000 in damage. Swift considers every accident preventable unless proved otherwise, so Belanger was immediately terminated for violating one of the Forbidden Five. Belanger claimed that the accident was not his fault, but a subsequent investigation by Swift's claims department concluded that the accident was preventable. Swift recorded the incident on a specialized database website (Data Website) that is operated by the U.S. government to promote highway safety through a readily available check on commercial driving records. When Belanger sought other truck-driving jobs, the companies looked on the Data Website and found out that, according to Swift, Belanger "did not meet the company's safety standards." Belanger sued Swift for defamation in the workplace. Swift defended that employer-to-employer references were privileged from liability for defamation unless Swift acted with malice. Belanger contended that (1) posting the information on the public Data Website resulted in a loss of the employer's reference privilege because it was not employer-to-employer and (2) Swift acted maliciously by not acknowledging Belanger's side of the story in its investigation.

SYNOPSIS OF DECISION AND OPINION The U.S. district court ruled in Swift's favor, citing two reasons. First, there was no reason why employer candor regarding employee references should not be protected from defamation suits when it occurs on the website since it was equally as important as it would be in a one-on-one discussion. Second, Swift's following of company procedures of immediate termination, independent investigation, and recording of the accident on Data Website did not indicate malice.

WORDS OF THE COURT: Defamation in an Employee Reference "Mr. Belanger offers no rationale for the distinction which he draws between a [Data Website]-type employer information clearinghouse and direct employer-to-employer contact addressing the candor concern underlying the [employer-to-employer reference] privilege. Here, employer forthrightness about employee driving records has obvious importance, as evidenced by the federal regulation compelling trucking companies to investigate applicant drivers' safety records before hiring." . . .

Malicious Defamation by the Employer "[T]he sparse record here contains no evidence capable of showing any improper motive in inputting the incident in the [Data Website] records. Mr. Belanger's evidence that he had received no contact from the defendant in response to his explanation of how the accident occurred provides no basis for a jury to reasonably find 'any improper or unjustifiable motive.'"

Case Questions

1. What is the public policy behind giving privilege to employer references?

2. Is it fair that Belanger has a permanent bad reference? Would you hire him?

Trade Libel and Product Disparagement Laws

In cases where a competitor has made a false statement that disparaged a competing product, an injured party may sue for **trade libel.** This tort requires that the statement (1) be a clear and *specific* reference to the disparaged party or product (e.g., using the actual brand name of the product), (2) be made with either knowledge that the statement was false or reckless disregard for the truth, and (3) be communicated to a third party (similar to defamation).

Some states have passed **product disparagement statutes** intended to protect the interest of a state's major industries, such as agriculture, dairy, or beef.[7] In perhaps the most famous product disparagement case, the Texas Cattle Ranchers Association sued Oprah Winfrey under a Texas law allowing recovery for any rancher who suffered damages as a result of false disparagement. On her television show, Winfrey agreed with statements made by one of her guests that alleged certain U.S. market hamburger meat could cause mad cow disease, which is fatal to humans. At the end of the segment, Winfrey took the position that she would cease eating any hamburgers. The ranchers showed evidence that beef sales dropped precipitously immediately after the broadcast and alleged that Winfrey's statements were false and caused the ranchers lost revenue. The jury rejected the cattle ranchers' claim as too broad and without sufficient evidence that the remarks alone were the cause of the losses.[8]

Fraudulent Misrepresentation

Recall the discussion of misrepresentation and fraudulent misrepresentation in Chapter 7, "Contract Formation." It is important to note that there are some important overlapping legal principles of tort and contract law. For example, in some cases contract law allows a contract to be canceled if one party made false representations concerning a *material fact.* This means that the misrepresented fact must involve an important aspect of the basis of the contract, such as a change in the value of the contract or an increase in one party's risk. Fraudulent misrepresentation (sometimes referred to simply as *fraud*) is *also* recognized as a tort in cases where the law provides a remedy to recover damages when the innocent party suffers a pecuniary loss as a result of the false representation. In cases of fraudulent misrepresentation, the law allows the innocent party to recover if (1) the misrepresentation was a material fact known to be false by the tortfeasor (or was a reckless disregard for the truth); (2) the tortfeasor intended to persuade the innocent party to rely on the statement, and the innocent party did, in fact, rely on it; and (3) damages were suffered by the innocent party. For example, Buyer asks Seller whether Seller's property is properly zoned for a manufacturing facility. In an effort to induce Buyer to purchase the property, Seller misrepresents that the property is zoned for manufacturing. Buyer then enters into a purchase agreement for the property with a 10 percent down payment, balance due in 30 days. Buyer then proceeds to spend money by hiring an architect to visit the site and draw plans for the new facility. The day after the agreement is signed, Seller applies to the zoning board for a change in zoning, hoping that it will be changed before Buyer completes the agreement by paying the balance owed. The zoning board does not change the status. In a case against Seller for fraud, Buyer would be entitled to cancel the contract *and* recover any losses in tort suffered as a result of Seller's fraudulent misrepresentation (such as the money spent on hiring the architect).

> **KEY** POINT
>
> Fraudulent misrepresentation (in both contracts and torts) must center on a *material fact;* that is, a fact that is significant or would impact the parties' rights or obligations in a transaction as opposed to a minor and inconsequential detail.

---

[7]For example, disparagement of Idaho potatoes is covered in Idaho Code § 6-2003. For a list of many such laws, see *Of Banana Bills and Veggie Hate Crimes: The Constitutionality of Agricultural Disparagement Statutes,* 34 Harv. J. Legis. 135 (1997).

[8]Affirmed in *Texas Beef Group v. Winfrey,* 201 F.3d 680 (5th Cir. 2000).

Protections for Online Content Providers

Along with holding the actual tortfeasor liable in a defamation case, the law imposes certain liability upon the publisher of the libelous statements as well. However, the law does not impose liability on the *distributor* of the publication (such as a bookstore or newsstand). For example, suppose a famous movie star is the subject of a gossip feature in a hypothetical tabloid called the *American Tattler*. The feature implies that the movie star was seen at a local restaurant and was so intoxicated that she could not control her conduct. In a lawsuit for defamation, the movie star proves that the story was false and that it led to her being fired by her movie studio. In terms of liability, both the author of the defamatory feature and the publication *(American Tattler)* may be liable for damages.

However, the rules pertaining to publishers of online content in cyberspace are different. In our movie-star example, suppose that instead of the *American Tattler* publishing the defamatory feature, a gossip columnist hired by America Online (AOL) had written it for an AOL entertainment news board. There would be no doubt of the liability of the author, but would AOL be liable as the "publisher"?

As Internet accessibility increased rapidly, courts struggled with this question. In a 1991 case, *Cubby Inc. v. CompuServe, Inc.*,[9] the plaintiffs filed a defamation action against CompuServe as a "publisher" of defamatory materials contained in an online publication called *Rumorville, USA*. Rumorville was composed, written, and edited by a third party who was not employed by CompuServe. The federal trial court in the southern district of New York held that CompuServe was *not* a publisher in the context of defamation law but rather was more akin to a bookstore and thus Internet service providers (ISPs) such as CompuServe were to be treated as "distributors." Consequently, CompuServe was not subject to liability for any defamatory statements so long as it did not "edit, review or reformulate" the publication.

However, not all courts took that view. A few years later, as the number of Internet service providers grew, a New York state trial court issued a very different ruling. In *Stratton v. Prodigy Services Company*, decided in 1995, the court ruled that an ISP could be held liable as a publisher of defamatory material. The case involved a Prodigy-maintained electronic bulletin board, available to its subscribers, called "Money Talk." Although Prodigy did not formally edit the postings, it had a policy that reserved the right to eliminate postings if they were objectionable. The plaintiff filed suit against Prodigy as a publisher of material that was allegedly libelous. In stark contrast to the *Cubby* court, a state trial court in New York ruled that Prodigy was a publisher in the context of a defamation claim and, therefore, could be liable for damages resulting from defamatory comments in its electronic bulletin board. The court held that Prodigy's "conscious effort to maintain editorial control" over the content was sufficient to qualify it as a *publisher* as that term is understood in defamation law.

In an apparent effort to address the pleas of ISPs for a uniform standard, Congress enacted the **Communications Decency Act (CDA) of 1996.**[10] This law extended immunity to the ISPs by protecting them from any defamation liability as a "publisher or speaker of any information provided by another information content provider". In effect, Congress made the policy choice that ISPs were to be treated as newsstand-like distributors.

One of the first cases to interpret this law was *Blumenthal v. Drudge and America Online, Inc.*[11] Although the case was decided by a trial court, the reasoning is often cited by appellate courts when applying the ISP safe harbor. The case involved a defamation lawsuit filed by a high-profile White House adviser (Blumenthal) against a controversial political journalist (Drudge) and America Online (AOL) because of spousal abuse and cover-up allegations in a column written by Drudge. The column was posted on an AOL news board as part of an agreement between Drudge and America Online. After Drudge posted a retraction and acknowledged that the allegations were false, Blumenthal sued Drudge and AOL for defamation. The trial court dismissed the case against AOL, citing the Communications Decency Act's safe-harbor provisions for ISPs. The court noted that even if AOL could conceivably be categorized as a *publisher* of defamatory material under previous cases, Congress specifically exempted ISPs such as AOL from civil suits for defamation.

[10]18 U.S.C.A. § 1462. Note that some portions of the CDA, namely Congress's attempt to regulate Internet pornography, were struck down as unconstitutional by various federal courts. However, this section survived judicial scrutiny.

[9]776 F. Supp. 135 (S.D.N.Y. 1991).

[11]992 F. Supp. 44 (D.D.C. 1998).

Every state has enacted a consumer fraud protection act. These acts punish very severely those who commit fraud, allowing victims of fraud, in many instances, to sue and collect treble damages.

Courts will also allow recovery for misrepresentations that are not intentional but are *negligent* misrepresentations. In most cases, the parties have to have some type of business relationship for the innocent party to recover. Any statement made by a party that turns out not to be accurate may still allow the innocent party to recover if the tortfeasor's statement was negligent. In the Buyer-Seller case discussed earlier, suppose that Seller had no actual knowledge of the zoning status for the property but made a statement that it was zoned for manufacturing. Buyer would still be able to recover despite the fact that Seller did not know that the statement was false. Seller is still liable because he was negligent in his duty to know such an important fact (negligence is discussed in detail later in this chapter).

False Imprisonment

The tort of false imprisonment is defined by the Restatements as the "intentional infliction of a confinement upon another party." In the business context, a merchant most commonly encounters these circumstances in cases of suspected retail theft. While the merchant has the right to briefly detain a suspected shoplifter, she must be cautious about giving rise to a false-imprisonment claim when detaining an individual or attempting to recover the merchandise. The Restatements provide for a **merchant's privilege**[12] to shield a merchant from liability for temporarily detaining a party who is *reasonably* suspected of stealing merchandise. This privilege, however, is very narrow. In order to gain protection under the privilege, the merchant must follow certain guidelines:

- *Limited detention:* The privilege applies only for a short period of time under the circumstances. Some courts have limited this time period to as few as 15 minutes. However, most courts follow a case-by-case analysis with the general framework that the detention may last the time duration necessary to confront the accused party, recover any goods stolen, and wait for the authorities to arrive (if necessary).

- *Limited to premises*: Generally, the privilege applies only if the suspected party is confronted on the merchant's premises or an immediately adjacent area (such as a parking lot).

- *Seizure of property*: The merchant or merchant's agent may seize alleged stolen property in plain view but may not search the accused shoplifter.

- *Coercion*: The merchant or merchant's agent (such as a store security guard) may not attempt to coerce payment, purport to officially arrest the detained party, or attempt to obtain a confession.

Table 10.1 provides an overview of other types of intentional torts and examples of each.

Business Competition Torts

Tort law also provides for the promotion of fairness in business dealings and for the reimbursement of a party that has suffered some damages as a result of a competitor's tortious acts. These common law torts arise when a tortfeasor (typically a competitor to the harmed party) interferes with an existing contract or hinders a prospective contract between two parties.

Tortious Interference with Existing Contractual Relationship   When one party *induces* another party to break an existing contract with a third party, the inducing party may be liable for any damages suffered by the innocent party as a result of breaking

---

[12]Also known as *shopkeeper's privilege*. See *Restatement (Second) of Torts,* § 120A.

TABLE 10.1 Other Intentional Torts

Tort	Definition	Example
Battery	Intentional touching of another person, without that person's consent, in a harmful or offensive manner.	An employee touches another employee, without consent, causing embarrassment, a feeling of harassment, or physical injury.
Intentional infliction of emotional distress	Extreme, outrageous, or reckless conduct that is intended to inflict emotional or mental distress (physical harm is not necessary).	A bill collector contacts a debtor's mother and threatens to physically harm and imprison the debtor son and to put a lien on the mother's house. The mother suffers two heart attacks after the threats persist.*
Trespass (land)	The act of entering another's land or causing another person or object to enter land owned by a private party without the owner's consent.	A survey crew mistakenly surveys the wrong property. While working, the crew damages landscaping. The landowner is entitled to compensation as a result of the crew's trespass.
Trespass (chattel†)	The act of interfering with another's use or possession of chattel (such as personal property).	An employee takes home his employer's drill for personal use without the employer's permission and with the intent to return it the next morning. The drill is broken while under the employee's control. The employee is liable for costs of repair/replacement and any lost profits resulting from the downtime.
Conversion	The civil counterpart to theft; intended to reimburse a party who suffered damages as a result of theft or any other substantial interference with the party's ownership, where fairness requires that the tortfeasor reimburse the injured party for the full value of the property.	The controller of a corporation embezzles corporate funds and covers up discrepancies on the financial statements. In addition to the controller's facing criminal charges, the controller's employer may sue her for conversion in an attempt to recover the embezzled funds.
Civil assault	The act of putting someone in fear and apprehension of immediate harmful or offensive contact (battery). No actual contact is required.	A worker yells at a customer and starts moving toward the customer in a hostile manner. If the customer reasonably believes that she is about to be struck, she has been civilly assaulted even if she runs away without being touched.

*Based on *George v. Jordan Marsh Co.*, 268 N.E.2d 915 (Mass. 1971).
† Chattel is the English common law term for personal property or equipment that is movable.

the contract. For the injured party to recover damages, the tortfeasor must have (1) had *specific knowledge* of the contract, (2) actively *interfered* with the contract, and (3) caused some identifiable damages (losses) to the injured party. Business owners and managers may encounter contract interference torts in the context of employment contract restrictions against working for competitors (known as a *restrictive covenant*[13]) or in defending an allegation of interference in the process of hiring a new employee away from a competitor. For example, Lee is a talented software programmer and signs a contract with Computer Researchers Inc. (CRI) for three years. The contract stipulates that Lee will not work for any of CRI's competitors during that time even if he is terminated or voluntarily resigns from CRI. After one year, one of CRI's competitors, Multi-Com, contacts Lee and attempts to convince him to leave CRI and work for MultiCom. During the negotiations, Lee shows MultiCom his contract with CRI, and MultiCom's manager then offers a higher salary and a $1,000 signing bonus to Lee. Lee resigns from CRI with two years left on his contract and goes to work for MultiCom. CRI must then spend several thousand dollars recruiting and training a new programmer to finish Lee's projects. In this case, many courts would consider holding MultiCom liable for CRI's damages because CRI was injured as a result of MultiCom's tortious interference with the CRI-Lee contract. Of course, CRI would also be entitled to recover damages from Lee for breaking the contract.

In Case 10.2, a state appellate court analyzes the conduct of the parties in determining whether a competitor tortiously interfered with a contract between an employer and an employee.

CASE 10.2 Mattison v. Johnston, 730 P.2d 286 (Ariz. App. 1986)

FACT SUMMARY Mattison owned Hidden Hills Beauty Salon and hired Drowne as a hair stylist in 1982. In 1984, Drowne signed a restrictive covenant contract agreeing not to work at any competing hair salon within one year of termination from Hidden Hills. Over the next 10 months, Johnston, the owner of a competing beauty salon located one-half mile from Hidden Hills, actively solicited Drowne to leave Hidden Hills and work for his salon. Eventually, Drowne quit Hidden Hills and began working for Johnston. Mattison sued Johnston for intentional interference with the restrictive covenant contract. Johnston claimed that he was simply engaging in standard business competition and that it was Drowne's individual choice to break her contract with Hidden Hills.

SYNOPSIS OF DECISION AND OPINION The Arizona state appellate court ruled in favor of Mattison. The court reasoned that Johnston had known about the restriction and actively continued to induce Drowne to breach the restrictive covenant. Competition is not a valid excuse for breaking a restrictive covenant that was created to avoid just such practices.

WORDS OF THE COURT: Intentional Interference "Johnston [and his partner] also contend that when a defendant is a competitor regarding the business involved in the contract, his interference with the contract may not be improper since competition is a valid defense to such action. However, Johnston failed to recognize that Mattison is claiming that they induced Drowne to break the restrictive covenant [and] not the at-will employment relationship. . . . [quoting the Restatements] 'Under these circumstances a defendant engaged in the same business might induce the employee to quit his job, but he would not be justified in engaging the employee to work for him in an activity that would mean violation of the contract not to compete.'"

Case Questions

1. What are the conflicting public policy concerns in this case?

2. Why would Mattison sue Johnston for interference rather than suing Drowne for breach?

---

[13]Restrictive covenants are covered in detail in Chapter 7, "Contract Formation."

Note that interference does not occur when a competitor merely offers a better price to a competitor's customer. For example, suppose that Chung is the owner of several self-service car washes and signs a two-year agreement with Mega Distributor for the supplying of snack vending machines in the lobby of each of Chung's car washes. Under the contract, Chung will receive 30 percent of the sales from the machines. Shortly thereafter, Chung is contacted by a sales rep from Start-Up Snacks and offered the same terms as the Mega contract except that Chung will receive 60 percent of the sales from the machines. Chung crunches the numbers and concludes that the increase in revenue will more than make up for any penalties incurred for breaching the Chung-Mega contract, so he breaks his contract with Mega and enters into a new contract with Start-Up. Despite the fact that Start-Up knew of the Mega contract, the level of interference is *not* sufficient to constitute a tort. In this case, Chung decided on his own to break the contract with Mega and was not *induced* to do so by Start-Up. It is important to note, however, that Mega could still sue Chung for failing to perform his obligations as agreed in the contract.[14]

 Self-Check Intentional Torts

Which tort, if any, fits each of the following facts?

1. Jason and Elaine are both being considered for a promotion to VP of sales. Jason starts a false rumor that Elaine doctored the books to make her accounts look better than they actually are. Because of the investigation and the need to fill the position, Elaine is dropped from consideration and Jason gets the promotion.

2. MOT Corporation does all of its banking with Second National Bank. MOT receives a 1 percent interest rate on its savings account and pays a fee of $.02 per check written. A representative of Third National Bank visits MOT's offices and tells the company that Third National pays 1.25 percent interest and has free corporate checking. MOT closes its accounts with Second National and moves all its banking business to Third National.

3. Wayne gets into his car after work, but it won't start. He returns to his office, and everyone has gone home. He takes the keys to a company vehicle and drives home intending to drive it back to the office in the morning. That night, a violent storm causes a tree branch to fall on the car, causing extensive damage.

4. Nancy has triplets attending eighth grade. Every once in a while she takes small quantities of paper, pens, paper clips, and other stationery supplies home from work and gives them to her kids for school use.

5. Frank is a used-car salesman. He is working with a customer who decides to buy a car. The price is agreed to, and the customer tells Frank that he will go to the bank to get a certified check. They shake hands. Frank then says, "You should know that this car used to be owned by Tiger Woods." The customer returns with the certified check, all paperwork is signed, and the customer drives the car home. The next day, the customer discovers that Tiger Woods never owned the car.

Answers to this Self-Check are provided at the end of the chapter.

---

[14]Based on *Restatement (Second) of Torts*, § 766, Illustration 3.

- A tort is a civil wrong and can be intentional, negligent, or strict liability.
- Defamation is a false statement that specifically concerns an individual, company, or product, is aired to a third party, and results in pecuniary harm to the victim.
- A victim of fraud must show intentional misrepresentation by the tortfeasor of a material fact, reliance on that fact, and damages resulting from that reliance.
- False imprisonment is an intentional tort unless the tortfeasor is a merchant who temporarily and reasonably detains a suspected thief.
- When actions exceed standard competitive practices, a company may be liable for intentional interference with a contract by a third party if the company had specific knowledge of a contract and intentionally disrupted its proper execution.

Legal Speak ›))
Induce To bring about or give rise to. In the context of tortious interference, liability is triggered if interference causes the harm.

Tortious Interference with Prospective Advantage In addition to providing protection against interference from third parties in existing contracts, the law also protects interference with *potential* contract (prospects) or other business relationships. The protections and definition of interference are similar to the existing contractual interference rules discussed earlier. However, because no contract actually exists, courts allow recovery for this tort only under limited circumstances in which the tortfeasor's conduct was highly anticompetitive. For example, assume that OldCo intends to sabotage NewCo's efforts to obtain a new customer through a competitive bidding process. An OldCo employee hacks into NewCo's computer and destroys the proposal forms. NewCo cannot submit the bid before the deadline and, thus, doesn't get the contract. Assuming that NewCo can prove it suffered damages, OldCo could be held liable for interference with prospective advantage.

LO 10-7 NEGLIGENCE

Tort law also applies when one party fails to act reasonably and harm occurs, even though that party did not intend to cause harm; the party is liable for any injuries or damages suffered by another party as a result of the unreasonable conduct. This category of tort is called *negligence.* Recall from the first section of this chapter that the primary difference between intentional torts and negligence is the mind-set of the tortfeasor. When a tortfeasor causes harm to an injured party by creating an *unreasonable risk of harm,* the law provides the injured party a remedy regardless of the tortfeasor's intent. The Restatements also recognize certain defenses that may be asserted in a negligence case.

Elements of Negligence

The law requires that specific elements be proved in order to recover in a lawsuit against a tortfeasor for negligence. The injured party must prove five fundamental elements by answering certain questions about the conduct in question:

- *Duty:* Did the tortfeasor owe a duty of care to the injured party?
- *Breach of duty:* Did the tortfeasor fail to exercise reasonable care?
- *Cause in fact:* Except for the breach of duty by the tortfeasor, would the injured party have suffered damages?
- *Proximate (legal) cause:* Was there a legally recognized and close-in-proximity link between the breach of duty and the damages suffered by the injured party?
- *Actual damages:* Did the injured party suffer some physical harm that resulted in identifiable losses?

Duty   The initial consideration in a negligence analysis is whether or not the tortfeasor owed the injured party a *legal* **duty.** The law imposes a general duty on all parties to act reasonably and not to impart unreasonable risk to others. In addition to having this general duty, some parties owe a special (heightened) duty of conduct to avoid liability for negligence.

General Duty of Reasonable Conduct   The law imposes a general duty on every party to act as a *reasonably prudent person* would under the circumstances. That is, everyone owes a duty to everyone else to act in a manner that does not impose unreasonable risk. The reasonably prudent person standard emphasizes that the conduct must be *objectively* reasonable. This means that at trial a fact finder (such as the jury) could conclude that a reasonably prudent person in the same circumstances should have realized that certain conduct would be risky or harmful to another person. In general, the scope of that duty is defined by *foreseeability.* In tort law, the term *person* in the reasonably prudent person standard is meant to be a generic term. The scope of duty is frequently defined by a particular industry or occupation. For example, the level of duty for a physician is defined by what a reasonably prudent *physician* would have done under the circumstances. It is important to understand that duty is an element that *expands* and *contracts* based upon whether or not it was foreseeable that the conduct in question would cause an unreasonable risk of harm. For example, Cain is a guest on a shock-host television show. The owners of the show arrange to have Abel surprise Cain on the show with an embarrassing secret. Cain is embarrassed and runs off the stage, and no further incident ensues. Three days later, Abel persists in calling Cain and harassing him about this secret. Cain then shoots and kills Abel later that afternoon. Cain is sentenced to a life term, so Abel's heirs sue the owners of the shock-host television show for negligence, claiming they owed Abel a duty to protect him from Cain. In this case, a court will likely rule that due to the time period between the show and the shooting (three days) and the fact that no incident occurred on the show or immediately thereafter, the duty owed to Abel ended when the show ended and did not extend to the time of the incident. This is primarily because it was not reasonably foreseeable under the factual circumstances of this case that Cain would act in such a rash manner then or thereafter.[15]

No General Duty to Act   The duty of care, discussed above, does *not* include a general duty to act or to rescue another. Tort law allocates liability based on a fundamental difference between some *act* by one party that harms or endangers another party, known as **misfeasance,** and the failure to act or intervene in a certain situation, known as **nonfeasance.** While injured parties may generally recover for misfeasance, injured parties may not hold a defendant liable for failing to act *unless* the parties had a **special relationship** to each other. Special relationships that are set out in the Restatements include those of a common carrier (such as a bus company) to its passengers, innkeepers to guests, employers to employees, a school to students, and a landlord to tenants.[16] One important special relationship of interest to business owners and managers is a business's duty to *warn* and *assist* any business visitors or patrons in regard to potential danger or harm (such as a slippery floor) on business premises. Therefore, businesses have a special relationship with their visitors and patrons that would allow recovery even in a case of nonfeasance. Suppose that Mitch is employed by a city as a lifeguard at a city beach. He sees Nicole in trouble in the surf and swims out to help her. Nicole is calm and cooperative, but while pulling her in, Mitch dislocates Nicole's shoulder because he fails to use an accepted or approved technique. He instead uses the "Mitch maneuver," an easier but unapproved and dangerous

---

[15]Based on *Graves v. Warner Brothers*, 656 N.W.2d 195 (Mich. App. 2002).

[16]*Restatement (Second) of Torts,* § 314A.

technique that he invented and hoped to make popular. Mitch has injured Nicole because he has acted badly. He is at fault due to his misfeasance, and both Mitch and the city will be liable to Nicole for her injuries. Now suppose, instead, that Mitch had not been paying attention and Nicole drowned because he was talking with friends and not doing his job. Nicole died because Mitch failed to act. By providing a lifeguard, the city has created a special relationship with swimmers at its beach, so Mitch is at fault due to his nonfeasance and, again, both Mitch and the city will be liable.

Landowners   Landowners owe a general duty to parties off the land from any unreasonable risks to them caused by something on the land. Courts use a reasonableness standard to determine the point at which the landowner should have acted. For example, the owner of GreenAcre plants several trees on the edge of his property, which is adjacent to a busy suburban street. One month later, one tree was dead with no green vegetation and with evidence of decaying bark and cracks in the roots. Eventually, the tree falls onto the road and injures a passerby. In this instance, a court may find that the landowner had a duty to inspect and remove the tree because it was foreseeable that the dead tree would be a risk to passersby if it fell.[17]

Landowners also owe a special duty to certain parties based on categories spelled out in the Restatements. It is important to understand that in a situation where a tenant is in possession of *leased space,* the tenant has the same special duties and level of liability that is imposed on landowners. Once a landlord/owner has given possession of the property to the tenant, the landlord is generally not held liable except for certain common areas (e.g., common stairwells, restrooms, or lobby).[18] The expected level of care varies by category. Table 10.2 sets out the categories of special relationship duties owed by landowners to licensees, invitees, and trespassers.

Breach of Duty   Once it has been established that one party owed another a general or special duty, the next factor to assess is whether or not that party fulfilled obligations. Failing to meet these obligations is known as a **breach of duty.** As discussed earlier, duties include (1) general obligations to act in a reasonable manner so as not to put another in harm's way and (2) special duties to certain parties, including the duty to inspect or duty to warn of defects. While the Restatements don't actually list events of breach, courts have traditionally looked to certain guideposts for determining whether a breach of duty has occurred.

Violation of Safety Statute   If the legislature has passed a statute intended to promote safety and one party violated the statute, there is a strong presumption that the party violating the statute has also breached her general duty to those who are protected by the law. Violations of safety statutes are sometime referred to as *negligence per se.* For example, the state legislature passes a law requiring that construction companies provide hard hats for all workers and visitors on a construction site. One day a prospective tenant visits an office building construction site to check on its progress, but there are not a sufficient number of hard hats available. The site manager allows the visitor on the site without a hard hat. The visitor is then injured by falling debris. In this case, the construction company has violated the state safety statute, and a court may find a breach of duty occurred without delving into a reasonably prudent person analysis.

---

[17]It should be noted that the Restatements do except "natural" conditions from the general duty. However, if a landowner planted shrubs or excavated land, this falls under the category of *artificial* and is not an exception to the landowner's general duty to persons off the property.

[18]There are exceptions to this rule, such as a situation in which the landlord transferred possession knowing of a certain defect but failed to warn the tenant about it.

TABLE 10.2 Special Relationship Duties Owed by Landowners

Special Relationship To	Definition	Example	Duties Owed
Licensee	Party has owner's consent to be on property for a nonbusiness purpose.	Social guest	Warn licensee of any known dangerous conditions on or about the premises. *No duty owed to licensee to inspect for hidden dangers.*
Invitee	Party is invited onto property by owner for business purposes or because landowner holds the premises open to the public.	Customer in a retail store	Warn invitee of any known dangerous conditions on or about the premises. Duty to inspect the premises for hidden dangers and take reasonable efforts to fix any defects.
Trespasser	Party enters premises without owner's consent.	Landscaping crew that accidentally mows wrong property	No duty to warn, inspect, or repair. Exception is a general duty of care when (1) owner has reason to know of regular trespass (such as a worn pathway) or (2) owner has reason to anticipate that young children might trespass on the property.

States also pass statutes intended to establish specific liability standards in certain circumstances. For example, *dram shop laws,* enacted in most but not all states, impose liability on the owners and employees of a public establishment where alcohol is being served. These laws allow a third party who has been injured or harmed by an intoxicated tortfeasor to recover damages against the owner or employee who served the obviously intoxicated patron.[19]

Common Law Standards of Behavior   When the state legislature has been silent, appellate courts in each individual state have usually developed a fairly extensive body of cases in their common law so that certain standards of behavior may be used in judging whether or not a breach occurred. Standards related to maintenance of property (such as clearing ice from sidewalks) and safety measures (such as keeping one's car in good repair if driving on public roads) are examples of nonstatutory standards for reasonable behavior.

Res Ipsa Loquitur   The doctrine of *res ipsa loquitur* (a Latin phrase meaning "the thing or matter speaks for itself") is deep-seated in American tort law. This doctrine allows an injured party to create a presumption that the tortfeasor was negligent by pointing to certain facts that infer negligent conduct without a showing of exactly how the tortfeasor

---

[19]Note that an increasing number of state legislatures have also imposed similar liability for all social hosts, including the serving of alcohol in a private home.

behaved.[20] An English judge first used this Latin phrase over a century ago in a case involving a pedestrian who was struck by a flour barrel that fell from a warehouse owned by the defendant. Although the injured party could not actually show how or why the barrel fell, the court held that the facts themselves were sufficient to impute a presumption of negligence.[21]

Assume that Kathy notices smoke coming out from under the hood of her car. She has the car towed to a mechanic, who determines that a valve cover gasket is leaking. She instructs him to make the necessary repairs. When she picks up the car, she pays the bill and drives off. One mile later, while stopped at a light, Kathy sees smoke coming from the hood again and gets out of the car just before it catches fire. The fire consumes the car, causing the engine to melt, and thus no specific cause for the fire can be determined. Kathy cannot prove exactly what the mechanic did wrong, but the car shouldn't have caught fire if the mechanic had repaired the car properly. She can use *res ipsa loquitur* to infer negligence.

Cause in Fact   After establishing that a breach of duty has occurred, the injured party must also prove that the tortfeasor's conduct was the **cause in fact** of the damages suffered by the injured party. In other words, there must be a *link* between breach of duty and damages. The overwhelming majority of courts use a simple test, known as the *but-for test,* to establish a link. Thus, the question that must be answered is this: "But for (except for) the breach of duty by the tortfeasor, would the injured party have suffered damages?" If the answer is no, then there is a link between the tortfeasor's conduct and the harm suffered by the injured party. The question can also be asked this way: "If the tortfeasor had complied with her legal duty, would the injured party have suffered damages?" Again, a no answer indicates a link and, thus, cause in fact. For example, suppose that Donald checks into Hotel's 20th-floor luxury suite. He watches a beautiful sunset while leaning on the balcony railing, but the railing snaps and Donald falls 20 stories. In a negligence analysis, one can reasonably conclude that Hotel owes Donald both a general duty and a special duty (innkeeper) and that the duty was breached because the rail was assumably defective in some way. For cause in fact, one asks: But for the breach of duty by Hotel, would Donald have suffered damages? The answer is clearly no because if Hotel hadn't breached its duty (e.g., had inspected and kept the railing in good repair), Donald would not have suffered damages. Thus, the breach of duty by Hotel was the *cause in fact* of Donald's injuries.

Scope of But-For Test   One problem in applying the but-for test is its overreaching broadness. Its application may result in holding a tortfeasor liable for injuries that occurred well beyond the foreseeable scope of the wrongdoing. For example, in the Donald-Hotel case, suppose that after Donald's balcony rail had snapped, Donald fell but the broken balcony rail also fell and penetrated the windshield of a car on the street below, injuring the driver. The injury causes the driver of the car to swerve, hit a pedestrian, and crash into an adjacent canal. A witness to the accident then attempts to rescue the driver of the car from the canal but drowns doing so. Five blocks away, a shopkeeper is so startled by the noise from the accident that she drops a priceless vase on her foot. In this set of accidental chain reactions, using the but-for test would impose liability on Hotel for each injury and damage, including Donald's fall, the driver of the car, the struck pedestrian, the drowned rescuer, and foot injuries from the destroyed vase. Nevertheless, a sense of fairness demands that the law cannot reasonably impose *all* of this liability on Hotel. At what point, if any, is the tortfeasor relieved from liability?

---

[20]*Restatement (Second) of Torts,* § 328(D).

[21]*Byrne v. Boadle,* 159 Eng. Rep. 299 (Eng. 1863). The court wrote, "[A] barrel could not roll out of a warehouse without some negligence, and to say the plaintiff who is injured by it must call witnesses . . . is preposterous."

The broad sweep of the but-for test requires a further step to establish liability. This step, known as **proximate (legal) cause,** is discussed next.

Proximate (Legal) Cause   In addition to showing that the tortfeasor's breach of duty was the cause in fact of the damages, the injured party must also prove that (1) the tortfeasor's conduct was also the closest-in-proximity cause of the damages and (2) the tortfeasor's liability wasn't canceled due to a superseding cause. These *proximate cause* concepts protect tortfeasors from liability for far-reaching and out-of-the-ordinary injuries resulting in damages from the tortious act.

Closest-in-Proximity   The majority of courts favor using *foreseeability* to define the scope of the risk. In the Donald-Hotel example discussed earlier, the jury would be charged with determining the scope of Hotel's liability. Liability would hinge on whether or not it was foreseeable that a faulty balcony railing would result in damages to be suffered by Donald (probable liability), the driver of the car (possible liability), the pedestrian (possible liability), the drowned rescuer (improbable liability), and the owner of the vase (very improbable liability). The Restatements define proximate cause as that which helps draw the line that determines when a tortfeasor is "not liable for harm different from harms whose risk made the [tortfeasor's] conduct tortious."

Unless the facts are so obvious as to not raise a question, the determination of proximate cause is a jury decision. In *Colaitis v. Benihana,*[22] a woman sued Benihana restaurant after her husband died from complications he suffered ducking from a shrimp tossed at him by a chef at the restaurant. The neck injury occurred in January, and after two operations, he died 10 months later. His death was attributed to an infection suffered following the first operation. Because he had been in good health and doctors testified that the neck injury resulted from dodging the shrimp tossed at him, the judge permitted the trial to go forward, ruling that proximate cause was an issue for the jury to determine. After a five-week trial, the jury found for Benihana.

The proximate cause concept theme was first enunciated in Landmark Case 10.3, perhaps the most famous case in American tort law.

Superseding Cause   Sometimes an *intervening* event takes place after the tortfeasor's negligent act. The intervening act may also contribute to the negligence by producing additional damages to the injured party. Some (but not all) intervening acts may be the basis for limiting a tortfeasor's liability. These acts are called *superseding causes* (i.e., supersede the tortfeasor's liability) and are also defined by *foreseeability.* For example, in the Donald-Hotel case, suppose that Donald fell only one story and sustained a broken wrist. While being driven to the hospital, a freak tornado hits the car that Donald is in and the wrist injury is made worse. In a case for damages related to the injury, even though the but-for test would impose liability on Hotel even for the aggravated broken wrist, Hotel's liability is discontinued (though not eliminated for the original injury) once the tornado hits as a superseding cause and Hotel is not liable for the aggravated injury. This limit applies because it was not reasonably foreseeable by Hotel that Donald would be injured by a tornado en route to the hospital.

Actual Damages   In order to recover in a negligence case, the tortfeasor must have caused another party **actual damages.** This means that the party alleging injury must prove that she suffered some type of physical harm derived from an injury caused by the tortfeasor. An injured party may not prevail if the injuries were limited to mental and/or emotional harm alone. However, once a party has proved some *physical* harm, she is eligible for a variety of other types of damages, including out-of-pocket economic losses (such as medical bills), pain and suffering, lost time from employment, and similar categories.

---

[22]Case # 15439/02, N.Y. Sup. Ct, 2006.

FACT SUMMARY   Palsgraf bought a railroad ticket for Rockaway Beach, New York, and was waiting on the platform for her train. A different train arrived on a platform 100 yards away, allowed passengers to board, and began to depart from the station. Running to catch the departing train, two commuters grabbed onto the side and tried to hoist themselves up and into the moving car. To aid one of the men, the conductor on the train pulled him onto the train but dislodged a package covered in newspaper that the passenger was carrying. The package, which turned out to be fireworks, fell to the platform and exploded. The blast shook the station with sufficient force that large iron scales (used to weigh freight on various trains) hanging over Palsgraf fell on her, resulting in a severe injury. Palsgraf sued the Long Island Railroad for the conductor's negligent conduct of pulling the commuter onto the train, which eventually caused the explosion and her injury from the falling scales.

SYNOPSIS OF DECISION AND OPINION   In a famous opinion written by Judge Benjamin Cardozo (who would later serve on the U.S. Supreme Court), the New York Court of Appeals ruled in favor of the Long Island Railroad. Cardozo reasoned that because the conductor *could not have known* that the man he was helping onto the train had a box full of fireworks, the action of the conductor was not a proximate-enough cause to incur liability for Palsgraf's injuries.

WORDS OF THE COURT: Proximate Cause   "[T]he orbit of the danger as disclosed to the eye of reasonable vigilance would be the orbit of the duty. One who jostles one's neighbor in a crowd does not invade the rights of others standing at the outer fringe when the unintended contact casts a bomb upon the ground. The wrongdoer as to them is the man who carries the bomb, not the one who explodes it without suspicion of the danger. Life will have to be made over, and human nature transformed, before prevision so extravagant can be accepted as the norm of conduct, the customary standard to which behavior must conform. . . . The risk reasonably to be perceived defines the duty to be obeyed, and risk imports relation; it is risk to another or to others within the range of apprehension."

Case Questions

1. Are all the other elements of a negligence tort satisfied in this case?

2. Who else might Palsgraf have sued? For what?

 Self-Check   Proximate Cause

Is proximate cause met in these situations?

1. A truck driver crashes into a guardrail. During the accident, a defective steering wheel rapidly spins around, breaking the driver's arm. The driver sues the maker of the steering mechanism.

2. A tenant hurts herself falling down defective steps. The tenant sues the landlord's insurance company, alleging that it knew the steps were defective but insured him anyway, thus discouraging him from fixing them.

3. An employer burns down his warehouse for the insurance money. An employee is arrested and falsely imprisoned by the police for the crime. The employee sues the employer for negligence.

4. A passenger is injured in an automobile accident. The passenger sues the liquor store that sold alcohol to the driver of the car, who was already visibly intoxicated.

Answers to this Self-Check are provided at the end of the chapter.

Punitive damages may be awarded but are rare because they can be awarded only when the tortfeasor's conduct was extremely reckless or willful and wanton.[23]

Many states allow a spouse or children of an injured party to recover damages related to the negligence. This includes loss of companionship or marital relations (known as *loss of consortium*). Moreover, if the injured party dies, his *estate* may sue for the damages that the injured party would have recovered if he had survived. Spouses and children may also recover damages for losses sustained by virtue of the death of an injured party.

Defenses to Negligence Claims

Once the elements of negligence are met, the analysis then shifts to potential defenses available to the tortfeasor. The two primary defenses to claims of negligence are *comparative negligence* and *assumption of the risk.*

Comparative Negligence   In cases where the injured party's conduct has played a factor in the harm suffered, the Restatements allow the tortfeasor to assert the defense of **comparative negligence.** This defense requires a jury to allocate the proportion of negligence committed by each party in terms of percentage (see Table 10.3). Ultimately, successfully asserting comparative negligence reduces (but does not eliminate) the final award to the plaintiff.

Note that comparative negligence is a cousin to the common law doctrine of *contributory negligence,* whereby even 1 percent of negligence on the part of the plaintiff was a complete bar to any plaintiff recovery. The overwhelming majority of states do not follow this standard because of its harshness on the injured party. Four states—Alabama, Maryland, North Carolina, and Virginia—along with the District of Columbia continue to recognize the contributory negligence defense. Indiana follows the contributory negligence rule in medical malpractice cases only.

Assumption of the Risk   When the injured party knew that a substantial and apparent risk was associated with certain conduct and the party went ahead with the dangerous activity anyway, the Restatements allow the tortfeasor to assert the defense of **assumption of the risk** so long as (1) the injured party/plaintiff knew or should have known (by virtue of the circumstances, warning signs, etc.) that a risk of harm was inherent in the activity and (2) the injured party/plaintiff voluntarily participated in the activity. Certain activities are considered to be "inherently dangerous" (such as bungee jumping or parachuting), and companies that are providers of these activities may have limited protection from liability if they acted reasonably in minimizing the dangers and made full disclosures of the risks to participants.

Legal Speak ›))
Estate In addition to land, assets, and personal property, a person's *estate* also consists of legal rights and entitlements after death, including the right to sue for the tortious conduct that caused the death.

Legal Speak ›))
Punitive Damages Monetary damages, generally a multiple of the actual damages, that are awarded partly to punish the tortfeasor and partly to deter others from acting in a similar manner.

TABLE 10.3 Comparative Negligence Formula

Suppose Abel is injured by Baker's conduct and suffers damages totaling $100,000. A jury finds that Baker was 80 percent responsible for the injury but that Abel also contributed to his own injury and was 20 percent responsible for the harm. How much does Abel ultimately recover?

Damages suffered × Percentage of Baker's negligence = Recovery amount

$$\$100,000 \times 80\% = \$80,000$$

---

[23]Punitive damages were sought in 12 percent of the estimated 25,000 tort and contract trials concluded in state courts in 2005. Punitive damages were awarded in 700 (5 percent) of the 14,359 trials in which the plaintiff prevailed. Among the trials in which punitive damages were requested by plaintiff winners, 30 percent received these damages. The median punitive-damage award among the 700 trials that resulted in punitive damages was $64,000 in 2005, and 13 percent of these cases had punitive awards of $1 million or more. (*Punitive Damage Awards in State Courts, 2005,* Special Report, U.S. Department of Justice, Office of Justice Programs, 2011.)

FACT SUMMARY Zeidman and Fisher were participants in a golf foursome at a charity tournament. On one hole where the view of the fairway was partially blocked, the foursome became concerned that they might inadvertently hit any players hidden by the blind spots on the fairway ahead of them. The group agreed that Zeidman would take a golf cart and ride ahead to see whether the course was clear for the group to hit. Zeidman made his observation and returned to his foursome in the cart. Because he intended on returning to his foursome to report that the group ahead was out of harm's way and because he never signaled to his group that it was safe to hit, Zeidman never entertained the possibility that one of his group would hit a shot. Before Zeidman returned, Fisher, becoming impatient, hit his shot while Zeidman was driving his cart back to the foursome. Fisher's shot was errant, and the ball struck Zeidman in the face, causing serious and permanent injuries. The trial court dismissed Zeidman's negligence lawsuit against Fisher on summary judgment, ruling that Zeidman had assumed the risk of participating in the golf match and this assumption of risk barred any recovery. Zeidman appealed.

SYNOPSIS OF DECISION AND OPINION The Pennsylvania Superior Court reversed the trial court's decision and ruled in favor of Zeidman. The court reasoned that the assumption-of-the-risk doctrine requires that the evidence show that the injured party (1) fully understood the specific risk, (2) voluntarily chooses to encounter it, and (3) manifested a willingness to accept the known risk. In this case, an objectively reasonable person may have assumed that no risk existed because Zeidman's agreed-upon task was to check whether the fairway was clear and then report to his own foursome if it was safe to hit. Because he had not yet completed this task, Zeidman did not manifest a willingness to accept a known risk.

WORDS OF THE COURT: Assumption-of-the-Risk Doctrine "In the circumstances of the present case, it is obvious that Zeidman, on returning from his forward observer mission, did not consciously assume the risk of friendly fire when, to the contrary, he had every right to anticipate none of his playing partners would attempt a tee shot until his return to the tee box. To grant summary judgment on the basis of assumption of the risk it must first be concluded, as a matter of law, that the party consciously appreciated the risk that attended a certain endeavor. . . . Accordingly, whether Zeidman is able to convince a jury that his version of events is true remains to be seen, he, in any event is entitled to his day in court."

Case Questions

1. If Zeidman had signaled to his partners that all was clear from the fairway and was then hit while returning in the cart, would Fisher be entitled to a summary judgment based on assumption of the risk?

2. What duty did Fisher owe Zeidman in the first place? Was it a special-relationship duty?

In Case 10.4, a state appellate court considers the assumption-of-the-risk defense in the context of leisure sports.

CONCEPT SUMMARY Negligence Analysis

- *Duty:* Did the tortfeasor owe a duty to the injured party?
- *Breach:* Did the tortfeasor breach the reasonably prudent person standard?
- *Causation:* Except for the tortfeasor's breach of duty, would the plaintiff have suffered the injury?
- *Proximate (legal) cause:* Was the breach the closest in proximity? Were there any superseding causes? Was the harm foreseeable?
- *Damages:* Did the injury to person or property result in losses?
- *Defenses:* Did the injured party contribute to the injury (comparative negligence)? Did the injured party know of the risk but go ahead anyway (assumption of the risk)?

STRICT LIABILITY TORTS

The tort liability theories covered so far in this chapter are based on either intent or negligence. The Restatements also provide for liability in certain cases where neither intent nor negligence need be proved. This category of tort is known as *strict liability* and is recognized in the Restatements primarily for abnormally dangerous activities and for defective products (discussed in the next section).[24] Strict liability is a concept rooted in the notion that the general public benefits when liability is imposed on those who engage in certain activities that result in harm to another party, even if the activities are undertaken in the most careful manner possible (without negligence).

Abnormally Dangerous Activities

The Restatements set out a six-factor test to determine whether abnormally dangerous activities trigger strict liability for any harm caused by the activity:

- Does the activity involve a high degree of risk of some harm?
- Is there a likelihood that the harm that results will be great?
- Is it possible to eliminate the risk by exercising reasonable care?
- Is the activity relatively common?
- Is the location of the activity appropriate to the risk?
- Is there any community value that outweighs the dangerous attributes?

Strict liability is imposed on businesses engaged in abnormally dangerous operations such as the use of explosives in building demolition.

---

[24]Strict liability is also imposed under the common law for the keepers of wild or dangerous animals.

For example, suppose that ChemicalCo produces 100 pounds of plastic explosives for use in the demolition of a building. It leases a railroad car and ships the explosives to its storage warehouse until the buyer can pick them up. Before the buyer picks them up, thieves break in and inadvertently ignite the explosives. The explosion causes damage to several buildings and an injury to a party standing in the surrounding area. Using the six-factor test, a court will likely impose strict liability on ChemicalCo due to the nature of the abnormally dangerous activity of storing explosives. Other strict liability cases have involved storage and use of toxic flammable liquids, nuclear power, and blasting for demolition or construction.

LO 10-8 # PRODUCTS LIABILITY

Products liability refers to the liability of any seller (including the manufacturer, retailer, and any intermediary seller such as a wholesaler) of a product that, because of a defect, causes harm to a consumer. Note that modern products liability law protects not only the actual purchaser but also any ultimate users who are harmed by the product's defect. In a products liability case, the injured party may pursue a legal remedy against the seller under one of three theories: (1) negligence, (2) warranty, or (3) strict liability.

Negligence

The negligence analysis covered earlier in this chapter may also be applied to the seller of a product. Although historically negligence was severely limited as a remedy because the law protected only the actual purchaser, a revised rule announced in the landmark case of *MacPherson v. Buick*[25] has been adopted in every state. Under the *MacPherson* rule, one who negligently manufactures a product is liable for *any injuries to persons* (and, in some limited cases, property) proximately caused by the negligence. For example, suppose that Holmes purchases a motorcycle from a dealer and gives it to his son Wendell. Wendell is injured on the motorcycle and sues the manufacturer for negligence. So long as Wendell can prove negligence, the manufacturer will be liable for Wendell's injuries despite the fact that Wendell was not the one who entered into the purchase agreement with the dealer or the manufacturer.

Courts have found that manufacturers have the duty of care regarding proper design, manufacturing, testing, inspection, and shipping. Retailers do not have as comprehensive a duty as the manufacturer but still have a duty to warn consumers of any product they know or suspect to be unreasonably dangerous.

Warranty

Historically, warranty laws were important protection for purchasers because they imposed liability even in the absence of negligence. When the seller makes a representation of fact about a product, this is known as an *express* warranty. If the seller has not made a specific representation about the product, the buyer may still be protected by a Uniform Commercial Code–imposed *implied* warranty. Warranties are set out in Article 2 (Sales) of the UCC and are discussed in detail in Chapter 22, "Consumer Protection Law."

LO 10-9 ## Strict Liability

The most appealing option for pursuing a products liability case is the doctrine of strict liability, because the injured party need not prove the elements of negligence. In *Greenman*

---

[25]111 N.E. 1050 (N.Y. 1916). The historical requirement that negligence suits could only be brought by the direct purchaser was known as *privity of contract.*

v. Yuba Power Products, Inc.,[26] the California Supreme Court decided a groundbreaking case that paved the way for adoption of a strict liability standard for product defects by ruling that "a manufacturer is strictly liable in tort when an article he places on the market, knowing that it is to be used without inspection for defects, proves to have a defect which causes injury to a human being." Two years after the *Greenman* case was decided, a similar doctrine of strict liability tort for the sellers of products was included in the *Restatement (Second) of Torts* in § 402A. The Restatements specifically indicate that liability still exists even if the seller used all possible care. Note that the term *seller* means not only the product's manufacturer but also all business parties through the chain of commerce, including the retailer.

Section 402A is a bedrock for strict products liability because a substantial majority of states have adopted the section that imposes special liability on the seller of a product that could harm the user. Specifically, § 402A imposes strict liability on the seller so long as the injured party can show that the product was in a *defective* condition and that the defect rendered the product *unreasonably dangerous*. Liability under § 402A is triggered only when:

- The seller is engaged in the business of selling such a product, and
- The product is expected to and does reach the user or consumer without a substantial change in the condition in which it is sold.

Section 402A's strict liability is imposed on the seller even though:

- The seller has exercised all possible care in preparation and sale of the product, and
- The user or consumer has not bought the product from or entered into any contractual relationship with the seller. (No privity of contract is required.)

Defining "Defect"   For a party to recover for an injury caused by a product, the product must have been defective and have created a danger that is outside the reasonable consumer's expectations. Courts have recognized several theories of unreasonably dangerous defects.

Design or Manufacturing Defect   A product may become dangerous if it is *designed* improperly in that foreseeable risks of harm posed by the product could have been reduced or avoided by some *alternative* design. Even products that are designed properly may still be rendered dangerously defective by some mistake made during the *manufacturing* process. For example, suppose CarCo designs a new car intended to have higher-than-average gas mileage. It achieves this by moving the gas tank to a different position on the car. The design, however, results in the gas tank rupturing during a rear-end crash. This is a classic design defect.[27] However, if CarCo designs the new car properly but one of the factory workers improperly installs the brakes and this eventually results in an injury, the product has been rendered unreasonably dangerous via a manufacturing defect.

Inadequate Warning   Products that are ostensibly safe may carry risks unknown to a reasonable consumer. In such cases, the law requires the product to carry sufficient warnings and instructions. Failure to warn may render the product unreasonably dangerous even absent any manufacturing or design defect. One common category of inadequate-warning cases involves prescription drugs, but the theory of unreasonable danger applies to all products that carry some danger in use (such as a lawn mower or snow thrower).

In Case 10.5, a company manufacturing a product free from any defects is sued because a dangerous product made by another company that its product is used with has caused injury and no warnings had been given.

---

[26]377 P.2d 897 (Cal. 1963).

[27]A case involving Ford Motor Company's design defect that caused rear-end explosions is featured in Chapter 5, "Business, Societal, and Ethical Contexts of Law."

FACT SUMMARY Barker was a mechanic who repaired cars, trucks, tractors, and similar vehicles from 1967 to 1995. Barker's work required him to use heavy machinery to grind, sand, and cut components such as brake linings and brake shoes. These components contained asbestos, which has been proved to cause disease in those who inhale the dust produced by the grinding and cutting of the components. The machines that Barker used to work on these components were manufactured by a predecessor company to Hennessy Industries. Barker died in 2008 from asbestos-related illnesses, and his wife sued Hennessy under a strict liability theory. Barker's wife argued that Hennessy was liable because it was aware that its product (machinery) was used in conjunction with the asbestos-containing products but failed to warn users of the danger. Hennessy argued that it could not be held liable for injuries caused by another manufacturer's product even if it was foreseeable that its machines would be used to repair products that contained asbestos. The trial court dismissed the suit because Hennessy showed that its machines were stand-alone products that did not contain asbestos or require asbestos to operate.

SYNOPSIS OF DECISION AND OPINION The California Court of Appeals upheld the trial court's decision in favor of Hennessy. The court held that a product manufacturer is liable in strict liability or negligence for harm caused by another manufacturer's product only when its own product contributes to the harm. Because Hennessy's product was not itself defective, Hennessy could not be held liable even when its product was used in conjunction with an independent defective product. Furthermore, strict liability does not require that a manufacturer foresee harm that may occur should its own safe product be used with another's unsafe or defective product.

WORDS OF THE COURT: Duty to Warn as a Basis for Strict Liability "On the basis of the undisputed evidence, the trial court properly determined that Hennessy did not owe Barker a duty of care to prevent or warn about the dangers of asbestos exposure. . . . While Hennessy did not dispute that Barker's death was caused by asbestosis and asbestos-related lung disease, the connection between Hennessy's conduct and Barker's injury was remote 'because [Hennessy] did not manufacture, sell, or supply any asbestos product that may have caused' Barker's disease. . . . Foreseeability of harm is therefore an inadequate basis for the imposition of strict liability on the manufacturer of a product that will be used in conjunction with a defective product. Here, the defective product is the asbestos-containing brake parts—not Hennessy's machines. Additionally, there was no evidence that the brake parts were dangerous only when used in combination with Hennessy's machines. A manufacturer does not owe 'a duty to warn about dangers arising entirely from another manufacturer's product, even if it is foreseeable that the products will be used together.'"

Case Questions

1. Who should have warned Barker of the dangers of working with asbestos?

2. A dissenting opinion was written, saying that the case should have gone to a jury because Hennessy knew that its machines and lathes could be used only with dangerous asbestos-related products. Do you agree or disagree with the dissent? Why?

3. What would have to be proved for a defense of assumption of risk to be effective had this gone to trial?

4. From an ethical perspective, do you agree or disagree with the court's decision? Explain.

Improper Packaging A product can be rendered unreasonably dangerous by a defect in the packaging. Cases that have recognized this theory of defect are primarily asserted against manufacturers of products that require safety-proof containers as well as food or beverage packages that clearly indicate whether the product has been tampered with (such as a seal on a bottle of juice). Perhaps the most famous case on improper packaging involved the well-publicized Tylenol scare in 1986. In *Elsroth v. Johnson & Johnson*,[28] a

---

[28]700 F. Supp. 151 (1988).

federal court in New York held that Johnson & Johnson, the manufacturer of Tylenol, was not liable for the death of a consumer who was the victim of tampering by an unknown third party. The estate of the consumer brought suit, claiming that improper packaging had led to the tampering when an unknown third party removed a package of Tylenol from a supermarket shelf, laced it with cyanide, and then somehow resealed the container and box so the tampering was not readily detectable. However, the court pointed to the fact that the Tylenol bottle featured a foil seal glued to the mouth of the container, a shrink-wrap seal around the neck and cap of the bottle, and a box sealed with glue in which the bottle was placed. Because Johnson & Johnson went above and beyond existing standards by using three different methods to prevent consumption of a tampered product, the company could not be held liable under § 402A.

Unavoidably Unsafe   Some products are inherently dangerous. That is, some products are designed and manufactured correctly, and adequate warning has been given, but the product is still dangerous (such as a handgun). Most courts have been reluctant to impose strict liability for damages resulting from handgun use in cases where the product was properly manufactured and designed. Until recently, cigarettes were in this same category, but some courts have recognized that, depending on the circumstances, a cigarette manufacturer may be held liable for the damages suffered by a smoker.[29]

Causation and Damages   Once it has been established that the product was unreasonably dangerous, the injured party need now prove only that the defective product was the cause of the injuries and that the product caused an actual injury that resulted in damages.

Seller's Defenses   Although strict liability imposes a relatively onerous burden on the seller, the law recognizes several defenses for a seller even if the injured party has established all of the required elements for liability.

Substantial Change   The Restatements draw a line of liability based on the condition of the product at the time it leaves the seller's control. For strict liability to apply, the product must reach the end user without substantial change. Thus, if a product leaves the manufacturing plant in a reasonable condition (not dangerous) and then is contaminated or damaged in the next stage of the commercial chain of delivery, any resulting harm is outside the strict liability model. Depending on the circumstances, of course, the manufacturer may still be liable for negligence but not under strict liability.

Assumption of the Risk   Although courts apply this defense narrowly,[30] it is still recognized as a defense for sellers in a strict product liability case. An injured party has assumed the risk if the party knew or should have known about the risk and disregarded this risk by continuing with the activity at issue for her own benefit. For example, suppose that WidgetCo owns a high-speed machine for producing widgets and a foreign object lodges in the machine while it is operating. The instructions warn to shut down the machine before removing the object, but the plant manager decides against a shutdown, fearing it would cost money from lost production time. If the plant manager is injured while removing the object from the operating machinery and sues the machine's manufacturer under a strict product liability theory, the manufacturer may successfully assert the assumption-of-the-risk defense.[31]

---

[29]*Williams v. Phillip Morris, Inc.,* 2002 WL 1677722 (N.D. Cal. 2002).

[30]See *Assumption of Risk and Strict Products Liability,* 95 Harv. L. Rev. 872 (1982).

[31]Based on *Micallef v. Miehle Co.,* 348 N.E.2d 571 (N.Y. Ct. App. 1976).

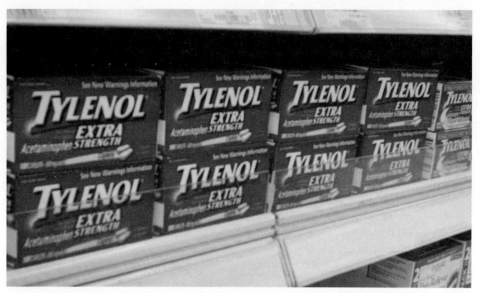

A court found that Tylenol's packaging was not defective and thus the company was not liable for any injuries resulting from third-party tampering.

Sometimes a large quantity of goods is sold to the public before a dangerous defect in the product is discovered. That product may then be recalled. If a consumer is made fully aware of a product recall due to a design or manufacturing defect but continues to use the product, assumption of risk may be asserted if injury and a lawsuit result.

Misuse of Product   In a case where the injured party may have *not* known of a certain risk but failed to use the product in a manner that an ordinarily prudent person would have then the seller may use product misuse as a defense. Courts have been reluctant to allow this defense unless the particular use of the product was so far from its ordinary use that it was not reasonably foreseeable by the seller.

Figure 10.1 provides an analysis of how liability is determined to apply or not apply under UCC §402A.

FIGURE 10.1   Section 402A Liability

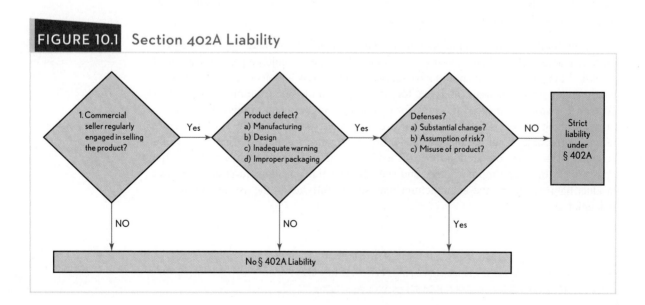

CONCEPT SUMMARY   Strict Liability and Product Liability

Strict liability:

- Applies to abnormally dangerous activities.
- Applies in the absence of negligence.
- Applies regardless of the care exercised by the tortfeasor.

Product liability:

- Makes a company liable for design or manufacturing defects that cause harm.
- Applies in the absence of proof of negligent design or manufacture.
- Requires that injured parties prove only the defect and injuries; causation is not required.
- Can apply if a warning of a known danger or defect is not issued.

KEY TERMS

Tort p. 261   A civil wrong in which one party's action or inaction causes a loss to be suffered by another party.

Tortfeasor p. 261   One who commits a civil wrong against another that results in injury to person or property.

Tortious conduct p. 261   The wrongful action or inaction of a tortfeasor.

Restatement of Torts p. 261   An influential document issued by the American Law Institute that summarizes the general principles of U.S. tort law and is recognized by the courts as a source of widely applied principles of law. ALI has amended the Restatements twice, resulting in the *Restatement (Second) of Torts and the Restatement (Third) of Torts.*

Intentional torts p. 262   A category of torts in which the tortfeasor was willful in bringing about a particular event that caused harm to another party.

Negligence p. 262   A category of torts in which the tortfeasor was without willful intent in bringing about a particular event that caused harm to another party.

Strict liability p. 262   A category of torts in which a tortfeasor may be held liable for an act regardless of intent or willfulness; applies primarily to cases of defective products and abnormally dangerous activities.

Libel p. 262   Written defamation, in which someone publishes in print (words or pictures), writes, or broadcasts through radio, television, or film an untruth about another that will do harm to that person's reputation or honesty or subject a party to hate, contempt, or ridicule.

Slander p. 262   Oral defamation, in which someone tells one or more persons an untruth about another that will harm the reputation or honesty of the person defamed or subject a party to hate, contempt, or ridicule.

Absolute privilege p. 263   A defense to a defamation claim whereby the defendant need not proffer any further evidence to assert the defense; provided to government officials, judicial officers and proceedings, and state legislatures.

Qualified privilege p. 263   A defense to a defamation claim whereby the defendant must offer evidence of good faith and be absent of malice to be shielded from liability; provided for the media and employers.

Trade libel p. 265   A tort in which a competitor has made a false statement that disparaged a competing product.

Product disparagement statutes p. 266   Statutes intended to protect the interest of a state's major industries, such as agriculture, dairy, or beef.

Communications Decency Act (CDA) of 1996 p. 267   Federal legislation that extends immunity to ISPs by protecting them from any defamation liability as a "publisher or speaker of any information provided by another information content provider."

Merchant's privilege p. 268   A narrow privilege, provided for in the Restatements, that shields a merchant from liability for temporarily detaining a party who is reasonably suspected of stealing merchandise.

Duty p. 273   A fundamental element that must be proved to recover in a negligence lawsuit against a tort-feasor: The injured party must prove that the tortfeasor owed him a duty of care.

Misfeasance p. 273   An act by one party that harms or endangers another party.

Nonfeasance p. 273   The failure to act or intervene in a certain situation.

Special relationship p. 273   In tort law, a heightened duty created between certain parties, such as that of a common carrier to its passengers, innkeepers to guests, employers to employees, businesses to patrons, a school to students, and a landlord to tenants and landowners.

Breach of duty p. 274   A fundamental element that must be proved to recover in a negligence lawsuit against a tortfeasor: The injured party must prove that the tortfeasor failed to exercise reasonable care in fulfilling her obligations.

Cause in fact p. 276   A fundamental element that must be proved to recover in a negligence lawsuit against a tortfeasor: The injured party must prove

that except for the breach of duty by the tortfeasor, he would not have suffered damages.

Proximate (legal) cause p. 277   A fundamental element that must be proved to recover in a negligence lawsuit against a tortfeasor: The injured party must prove a legally recognized and close-in-proximity link between the breach of duty and the damages suffered.

Actual damages p. 277   A fundamental element that must be proved to recover in a negligence lawsuit against a tortfeasor: The injured party must prove that she suffered some physical harm that resulted in identifiable losses.

Comparative negligence p. 279   A defense to claims of negligence in which the injured party's conduct has played a factor in the harm suffered and, thus, the proportion of negligence should be divided.

Assumption of the risk p. 279   A defense to claims of negligence in which the injured party knew that a substantial and apparent risk was associated with certain conduct and the party went ahead with the dangerous activity anyway.

THEORY TO PRACTICE

Computer Installers (CI) Inc. is a company that sells, installs, and maintains computer networks for organizations that have large numbers of users. CI entered into a contract with Big Time Firm (BTF) to replace the firm's computer network. CI's contract included routine installation tasks such as laying network cable and wiring in the various offices to facilitate numerous network users simultaneously, installing new PCs in one-third of the network user stations, and setting up an appropriate network server with sufficient backup capability. CI arrived on March 1 and began work on rewiring BTF's office to facilitate the new computer system. In the process of installing the new cabling for the network, a CI technician accidentally rewired the system that controlled the fire sprinklers and rendered the sprinklers inoperable.

Office Cleaners (OC) Inc. was cleaning BTF's offices at night on March 2. One of OC's employees left a lit cigarette in one of BTF's restrooms. That night, as a result of the lit cigarette, a small fire began in the restroom. Because the sprinklers were inoperable, the fire spread and caused damage to the entire office and equipment in the amount of $50,000.

1. What level of duty does CI owe to BTF, and has CI breached that duty?
2. To what extent is the concept of cause in fact versus proximate cause important in regard to CI's liability?
3. At what point, if any, is CI's liability cut off? Does OC assume full liability for the fire?
4. Assume that BTF had fired its night security guard on February 1 and never refilled the position. Thus, no guard was present when the fire started. Articulate a possible defense for CI and OC based on this fact.
5. Suppose that after the incident the sales manager of Data Management Inc., one of CI's competitors, is having lunch with Sheldon, the chief information officer of City Hospital. City Hospital had an existing contract with CI to maintain City Hospital's network. During lunch, Data Management's sales manager tells Sheldon about the fire incident and also states that, based on his personal knowledge, CI was a shoddy outfit that had a poor reputation in the industry. The sales manager then proposed a new Data Management information

system for City Hospital at a lower price than CI's. When Sheldon was reluctant to consider the offer, Data Management's sales manager offered to pay any penalty that City Hospital suffered as a result of canceling the CI contract. Sheldon cancels the contract with CI, citing customer service problems. What possible torts have been committed? What are the requirements for CI to recover damages?

Another context in which managers encounter tort law is the area of employment checks and references. Suppose that the technician installer employed by CI in the Theory to Practice problem was suspended for incompetence. The installer was so enraged that he threatened his fellow employees with bodily harm and was subsequently fired. The installer sought new employment and listed several CI managers as references on his application to a prospective employer. Consider the conundrum of the manager asked for a reference. How would you address the question? On the one hand, CI may be liable for any defamatory statements made by its managers in this situation. On the other hand, if CI simply refuses to say anything in a reference and it turns out that the installer is dangerous and assaults a colleague at his new workplace, an injured party could possibly claim that CI was negligent in not providing the new employer with important information about the ex-employee installer's potential for danger.

In groups or individually, develop a policy for CI managers on giving references for ex-employees that balances the concern of defamation with that of negligence in failing to inform a prospective employer about a potentially dangerous employee. Assume that your state has the same laws as Connecticut, and use the *Belanger v. Swift Transportation, Inc.*, case found earlier in this chapter to help develop a legally sound policy. A more comprehensive briefing of the case is available on this textbook's website at www.mhhe.com/melvinleb2e. Be sure to address (1) a brief overview of the background and a summary of the legal ramifications of not having a sound reference defamation policy and (2) how your policy fits into the privilege defense in the law. A sample answer may be found on this textbook's website at www.mhhe.com/melvinleb2e.

CASE SUMMARY 10.1 :: Maher v. Best Western Inn, 717 So. 2d 97 (Fla. App. 5th Dist. 1998)

SPECIAL RELATIONSHIPS

Maher is a blind woman who checked into a Best Western that welcomed pets like her Seeing Eye dog Ina. Shortly after Maher checked in with her parents, another motel patron walked by with two unleashed dogs—one German shepard and one pit bull. The two unleashed dogs attacked Ina, Maher, and her parents. Maher sued Best Western for negligence.

CASE QUESTIONS

1. What duty did Best Western owe Maher?
2. Was it *reasonable* for Best Western to do more to prevent the attack?
3. Would a bystander have had a duty to prevent the attack if it occurred on the street?

CASE SUMMARY 10.2 :: Wurtzel v. Starbucks Coffee Co., 257 F. Supp. 2d 520 (E.D.N.Y. 2003)

RES IPSA LOQUITUR

Wurtzel bought a cup of coffee in her local Starbucks and placed it in her car's cup holder. Shortly after leaving the store, she was making a turn when the lid came off the coffee and the liquid spilled over Wurtzel's right leg, burning her severely. Wurtzel never looked to see if the lid was on correctly and did not see the coffee spill or the clerk secure the lid to the cup. She sued Starbucks for negligence, invoking the doctrine of *res ipsa loquitur.*

CASE QUESTIONS

1. Was Starbucks clearly negligent without any need for witnesses?
2. Who else may have been negligent?

NEGLIGENCE PER SE

Bonifay and Fordham bought a box of .32-caliber bullets from a Wal-Mart in Florida. Four hours later, the two men robbed an auto-parts store and killed Coker with those bullets. When they bought the ammunition, both Bonifay and Fordham were under 21 years of age. The federal Gun Control Act makes it illegal to sell ammunition to anyone under 21. Coker's wife sued Wal-Mart for the wrongful death of her husband.

CASE QUESTIONS

1. Is Wal-Mart liable?
2. What if it was reasonable to assume that the two men were over 21?
3. Could Wal-Mart have foreseen the robbery any more than the train conductor could have foreseen the bag full of fireworks in *Palsgraf?*

STRICT PRODUCTS LIABILITY

Gorran suffered a heart attack after following the diet plan of *Dr. Atkins' New Diet Revolution.* Gorran claimed the heart attack was a result of the high-fat, high-protein diet advocated by Dr. Atkins. He sued the publisher for selling a defective product—a diet plan that causes a heart attack.

CASE QUESTIONS

1. Can a diet plan be considered a "product"?
2. Why would Gorran want to sue under products liability theory rather than just negligence?

ASSUMPTION OF RISK

In 1994, Aaris injured her right knee practicing a gymnastic stunt called the "cradle." The stunt requires that two cheerleaders face each other to form a "base" and launch a third cheerleader, the "flyer," into the air. After the flyer pikes, she descends toward the ground where the base cheerleaders are supposed to catch her. A fourth cheerleader acts as a spotter to assist in the catch. As the team practiced, the flyer kept landing awkwardly, even scratching the faces of the base cheerleaders. Aaris told her coach that they were having problems cradling the flyer, but the coach attributed their problems to "bad technique" and told them that they "need to keep on trying it over and over again." Aaris felt uncomfortable performing the stunt and asked: "Do we have to do this stunt?" Her coach responded: "You should be doing it every single time." Finally, while trying to do the stunt, the flyer wobbled and fell on Aaris, injuring Aaris's leg. In 1993, Aaris had received stunt training while she was on the freshman high school cheerleading squad. She had then participated in tryouts and made the junior varsity cheerleader team. Aaris received formal instruction in stunt technique and safety, and she knew that the stunts were dangerous. As a freshman, she injured her left knee performing a toe-touch stunt. Evidence showed that the flyer and the other base cheerleader had also received formal stunt technique and safety training. Aaris sued the coach and school for negligence. The coach and school district asserted the defense of assumption of risk.

CASE QUESTIONS

1. What must Aaris prove in order to hold her coach and the school district liable for her injuries?
2. For a defense of assumption of risk to be successful, what must the coach and school district prove?

DANGEROUS CONDITION AND COMPARATIVE NEGLIGENCE

Burton worked for a marketing and merchandising company that helped new retail businesses prepare for openings. She was brought in to work at a new CVS Pharmacy getting ready for its grand opening. While unloading trucks, Burton noticed a pothole about 10 or 15 feet from the store's back door. The pothole was approximately 1 foot wide and 2 inches deep. Burton informed her co-workers and CVS's management of the pothole and urged everyone to exercise caution. One week later, Burton was seriously injured when, while loading a vehicle, she stepped into the pothole, tripped, and fell to the ground. Burton filed suit against both CVS and its landlord, MDC.

CASE QUESTIONS

1. Can a property owner be liable for injuries when a dangerous condition is open and obvious? Does the owner have a duty to warn when the dangerous condition is open and obvious?
2. Can a property owner be liable for injuries when a dangerous condition is open and obvious and the injured party was well aware of the dangerous condition?
3. Does Burton's knowledge of the dangerous condition merely raise an issue of fact as to her own comparative negligence?

 Self-Check **ANSWERS**

Intentional Torts

1. Defamation. Specifically, it is slander because the statements Jason made were oral.
2. No tort has been committed. This is not a tortious interference with contract because Third Bank merely offered a better price for its services and MOT made the decision to switch.
3. Trespass to chattel. Wayne has interfered with his company's ability to use the car and will be responsible for the repairs and any damages suffered by the company because the car is unavailable.
4. Conversion. Nancy is stealing the stationery supplies and civilly is responsible for paying the company back for the full value of the supplies she has taken.
5. No tort has been committed. This is not a fraud because the deal had already been agreed to and the intentionally false statement was not material to the deal.

Proximate Cause

1. Yes. The injury (broken arm) was sufficiently proximate to the negligence (defective steering column). *McCown v. International Harvester Co.*, 342 A.2d 381.
2. No. Too many acts of intervening negligence on the part of the landlord. *Matthias v. United Pacific Ins. Co.*, 67 Cal. Rptr. 511, 514.
3. Yes. It was reasonably foreseeable that the employee would have been falsely arrested for the fire. The jury found that the employer had framed the employee. *Seidel v. Greenberg*, 260 A.2d 863, 871.
4. Yes. It was reasonably foreseeable and violated state dram shop laws. *Gonzales v. Krueger*, 799 P.2d 1318, 1321.

At approximately 5 p.m., a commercial truck driver for National Networks (Driver Alpha) caused a three-car automobile collision after his truck crossed the center median on I-57 in southern Illinois. Given the severity of the accident, the fire department closed I-57's northbound lanes for several hours, which created a 4- or 5-mile traffic jam stretching away from the original accident. Four hours later, traffic still was not moving because of the Driver Alpha accident. At 9 p.m., a car carrying brothers David and Paul approached the end of the stalled northbound traffic without incident. Moments later, Driver Omega, driving a truck for TLS, Inc., slammed into David and Paul's vehicle. The collision killed Paul and seriously injured David. The weather was clear, and Driver Omega was doing 55 mph on a flat, straight road when he hit David and Paul's car. No other accidents had occurred during the four hours.

David filed a personal-injury suit in state court against Driver Omega and TLS. Mary, as special administrator for Paul's estate, filed a similar suit against the same defendants. Shortly thereafter, Driver Omega and TLS filed third-party complaints against Driver Alpha, National Networks, and others (collectively, the "Driver Alpha defendants"), alleging that the Driver Alpha defendants' negligence in causing the first accident was the proximate cause of the second accident between Driver Omega and the two brothers. The plaintiffs amended their complaints to add the Driver Alpha defendants as direct defendants.

ENGAGEMENT QUESTIONS

1. Had there been a string of accidents over the four-hour period, could there then be enough doubt to make proximate cause a jury question?

2. Had the weather caused visibility problems or had the Bloods' accident occurred on a curve, could there then be enough doubt to make proximate cause a jury question?

3. The court cited precedent indicating that 10 to 15 minutes between accidents is an appropriate measure of timing regarding proximate cause. Do you agree, or is this too much or too little time? Explain.

4. Why is the need to establish proximate cause an important element in negligence actions?

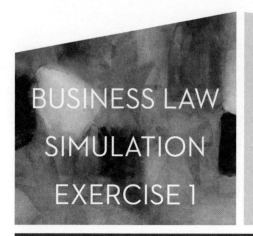

BUSINESS LAW SIMULATION EXERCISE 1

Restrictive Covenants in Contracts: Neurology Associates, LLP v. Elizabeth Blackwell, M.D.

learning objectives

After studying this simulation, students who have mastered the material will be able to:

1. Explain the legal doctrines that govern the use of restrictive covenants.

2. Interpret and apply the rules set forth in current case law.

3. Articulate a cogent argument for each party/side in the dispute.

4. Negotiate a tenable solution as an alternative to a judicial forum.

Chapters 6 through 9 provided you with a variety of legal doctrines and rules governing contract formation and performance and then illustrated how these doctrines and rules apply in the corporate sector context. This simulation is designed to help you understand how the various topics covered in the contract law chapters connect. By focusing on a simulated legal dispute, you will replicate a real-world experience by applying legal doctrines and using analytical and critical-thinking skills. This simulation is a sequential decision-making exercise structured around a model in which the participants assume a role in managing tasks and work toward a tenable solution.

The simulation is structured in three parts:

■ Part 1 is a hypothetical fact pattern describing events leading up to a legal dispute in the hypothetical U.S. state of Longville.

■ Part 2 is a set of two hypothetical case summaries from Longville appellate courts that provide a brief set of facts, several legal points, and short excerpts from the opinion itself. While these cases are hypothetical, they are based on actual cases from appellate courts in various states and represent the view of the majority of state courts in the United States.

■ Part 3 is an assignment sheet that will be provided to you by your instructor to be used in conjunction with this simulation.

Part 1: Stipulated Facts

1. In May 2008, Dr. Elizabeth Blackwell (Blackwell) had earned her medical doctor degree and completed all necessary requirements to receive a license to practice medicine in the State of Longville. She specialized in neurological medicine. Although she was offered professional opportunities in several large hospitals, she pursued an employment offer with Neurological Associates (NA), LLC. NA is a two-physician practice located in a small town in the southwestern area of the state of Longville and 20 miles north of Galway, the largest city in Longville. Although the pay was lower than that in the larger hospitals, Blackwell wanted to be close to her family and did not wish to engage in a practice that required the strenuous schedules associated with larger medical providers.

2. NA was managed by two partners, Dr. Richard Cohn (Cohn) and Dr. Jean Valjean (Valjean). While negotiating Blackwell's employment agreement, Cohn was the primary contact and the parties agreed to compensation terms, vacation, on-call duties (after hours), and a fringe benefit package. The employment agreement included an arbitration clause requiring that the parties agree to nonbinding arbitration in the event of a dispute arising from the agreement. It also provided for Blackwell to have paid time off to study for and take the examinations required to become board-certified in neurology. NA agreed to a $1,000 payment to be used for a course intended to help prepare candidates for the test. Blackwell began her employment with NA on June 1, 2008.

3. Immediately after hiring Blackwell, NA paid for Blackwell to accompany the partners to a medical conference at which they were scheduled to speak. At the conference, Cohn and Valjean introduced her to a number of physicians in hopes of building the referral base for the practice.

4. In July 2008, Cohn approached Blackwell and told her that he needed her to sign an additional document that was supposed to be part of her contract but that he had neglected to mention during negotiations. He explained

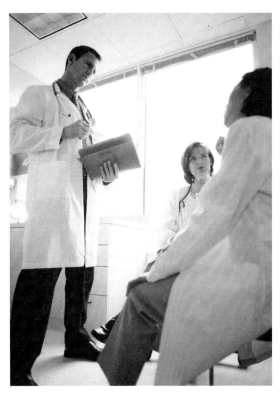

In this simulation exercise, a physician in a health care practice becomes involved in a dispute over a provision in her contract that restricted future employment.

that the document was standard procedure in medical practices and that he had been so busy during the negotiation period that he had forgotten to mention it to Blackwell. He went on to explain that Blackwell should sign the document by the end of the workday and that this would "make the lawyers happy."

5. The document was titled "Addendum to Contract—Restrictive Covenant and Noncompete Clause" and read in pertinent part:

> *Section 1: The parties hereby agree, in consideration of the exchange of good, valuable, and sufficient consideration, to be bound by the following provision:*
>
> *For a period of three years after the date of her separation from NA, Blackwell agrees that she will not contract with any provider of neurological services, nor compete in any way with NA, within a radius of 50 miles of NA's practice location. It is acknowledged*

that this restriction covers the entirety of the southwestern region of Longville.

6. Blackwell felt that she should have a lawyer review the document, but Cohn insisted the addendum was normal procedure and she needed to sign it quickly to make things "legal." He emphasized that he would have to have the signed document by the end of the day or that, as it was a condition of her employment, Blackwell's payroll check could not be processed until the document was signed. Blackwell reluctantly signed the document and submitted it to Cohn.

7. In August 2012, Blackwell began to have conflicts with Cohn and, to a lesser extent, Valjean. While Cohn and Valjean took frequent vacations during the summer, Blackwell was left to staff the practice alone. She felt overwhelmed and met with Cohn to discuss a more equitable work schedule. Cohn refused any negotiation, explaining that Blackwell was hired as a "workhorse" and that her salary was fair given the size of the practice and market. Cohn urged Blackwell to continue her hard work and not to complain about her work schedule. Eventually, explained Cohn, Blackwell would become a partner in the practice and would enjoy the fruits of her labor.

8. In September 2012, Blackwell continued to handle a very heavy caseload, seeing almost twice as many patients as Cohn or Valjean. In response to Blackwell's plea for additional staff, NA hired a new physician to help manage the caseload. Although Blackwell was initially relieved, the situation at work continued to deteriorate. The workload was such that Cohn kept denying Blackwell's request for time off to prepare for the upcoming board certification exam, advising her to put if off until the caseload lightened up a bit.

9. Blackwell began to receive phone calls from recruiters trying to lure her away from the practice to work at a new neurology clinic in Galway Hospital (located in the city of Galway). The recruiters offered a significant amount of money because there was a substantial shortage of neurologists in the southwest region of Longville. However, Blackwell never pursued these opportunities because she believed the restrictive covenant prevented her from working in Galway.

10. In January 2013, Blackwell was granted her paid leave to prepare for her board certification, and she took the exam in February 2013. However, after she returned to the practice, she began to feel even more isolated from the other physicians.

11. On March 1, 2013, Blackwell, fed up with NA, announced that she was giving NA 60 days' notice that she was leaving the practice to join Galway Hospital and that her resignation would be effective on May 1, 2013. She anticipated starting at Galway on June 1, 2013. Galway was forming a new neurology practice group, and it had offered to employ Blackwell as one of the founding physicians in the group.

12. Cohn immediately sent Blackwell a letter informing her that he accepted her resignation but that she had responsibilities under her contract that prevented her from accepting a new position with a competitor.

Part 2: State of Longville Case Law

Wellspan Hospital and Medical Group v. Phillip Bayliss, M.D.

Supreme Court of the State of Longville (2005)

Facts

- This is the leading case on restrictive covenants/ noncompete agreements in the context of medical practices in the state of Longville. It has not been modified or reversed since it was decided.

- Wellspan is a not-for-profit health care system located in Columbus County in the southeastern portion of the state of Longville. Bayliss is a physician specializing in OB/GYN services.

- Wellspan hired Bayliss as its medical director in 2000, at which time Bayliss signed an employment agreement that included a restrictive covenant under which Bayliss agreed not to engage in medical practice in Columbus County and five other contiguous counties (this covered the entire southeastern region of Longville) for a period of two years after the separation of employment between Wellspan and Bayliss.

- Wellspan invested over $1 million in equipping Bayliss's practice, hiring additional physicians, and undertaking promotional strategies intended on marketing the practice and increasing the number of referrals.

- Relations between Wellspan and Bayliss deteriorated when they disagreed over Wellspan's expansion strategy. In February 2004, Bayliss resigned his position at Wellspan and established his OB/GYN practice only 5 miles from the Wellspan practice. This was within the area covered under the restrictive covenant.

- The state's highest court considered the enforceability of Wellspan's restrictive covenant against Bayliss.

POINTS OF LAW AND OPINION EXCERPTS

Point (a)

The Longville state courts will enforce a restrictive covenant *only* if it is *reasonably necessary* to protect the legitimate interests of the employer, and courts either may strike down a covenant altogether or may reform (known as *bluelining*) a covenant if it is overbroad in some way.

Excerpt (a)

"Courts in the State of Longville have historically been reluctant to enforce contracts that place restraints on trade or on the ability of an individual to earn a living; however, postemployment noncompetition covenants are *not* per se unreasonable or unenforceable."

Point (b)

The threshold requirement for enforceability of a covenant is that the employer must be protecting a *legitimate business interest*. The primary legitimate business interests that Longville courts have held to be protectable in a covenant are (1) trade secrets or confidential business information, (2) customer goodwill, and (3) investments in the employee.

Excerpt (b1)

"A *trade secret* is legitimate business interest because it may include a compilation of information which is used in one's business that gives one an opportunity to obtain an advantage over competitors. A trade secret does not include an employee's aptitude, skill, dexterity, manual and mental ability, or other subjective knowledge. In addition, if a competitor could obtain the information by legitimate means, it will not be given protection as a trade secret."

Excerpt (b2)

"The interest protected under the umbrella of *goodwill* is a business's positive reputation. Goodwill represents a preexisting relationship arising from a continuous course of business which is expected to continue indefinitely. A business's goodwill is considered a protectible interest even when the goodwill has been acquired through the efforts of an employee. The concept of customer goodwill as a protectible interest has been applied to patient relationships when the noncompetition covenant at issue involves a health care professional. This court has cited the erosion of the ex-employer's patient relationships as one factor in the decision to enforce a restrictive covenant."

Excerpt (b3)

"A third protectible interest recognized by Longville courts is the *efforts and financial resources invested by an employer* to provide to its employees specialized training in the methods of the employer's business. In a past case, the defendant was a salesman of securities who had received extensive and continuous training from his employer, particularly with respect to methods and problems in the sale of mutual fund shares. He then voluntarily left his position with his employer and started his own business selling mutual fund shares. The court enforced the noncompetition covenant at issue, enjoining the defendant from engaging in the business of selling mutual fund shares in Pennsylvania. The court found merit in the argument that it would be inequitable for the defendant to start a new business in direct competition with his ex-employer after having received extensive, specialized training in the methods and problems of the business directly from his ex-employer."

Point (c)

A medical practice's patient referral base is a legitimate protectable business interest when a medical practice can demonstrate that it has invested in the production and generation of such a base.

Excerpt (c)

"A patient referral base is a protected interest, protecting the investments required to develop such a base is consistent with our holding in other employer–employee situations outside the health care field. In the context of a noncompetition covenant, we think that the referral bases of a specialized medical care institution are analogous to a physician's patient relationships or an employer's customer relationships. Viewed in such light, recognition of a patient referral base as a protected interest fits squarely within Longville case law."

Point (d)

If the threshold requirement of protectable interest is met, the next step in the analysis is to apply two *balancing tests:* (1) the employer's protectable interest balanced against the employee's interest in earning a living and (2) the employee and employer interests with the interests of the public.

Excerpt (d1)

"In weighing the competing interests of employer and employee, the court must engage in an analysis of *reasonableness.* First, the covenant must be reasonably necessary for the protection of the employer. In addition, the temporal and geographical restrictions imposed on the ex-employee must be reasonably limited."

Excerpt (d2)

"Regarding the second balancing test, in the context of noncompete agreements among physicians, the *interests of the public* are defined as a function of the availability of appropriate medical services to the community. Since there is no evidence of a lack of availability of OB/GYN physicians within the restricted area, the interests of the public are served and, thus, enforcement of the covenant against Bayliss does not result in public harm."

Held

Because Wellspan had shown that it had a legitimate business interest in protecting its patient referral base and because the court had determined that the restriction was tailored to those interests and that no public harm would be suffered by enforcement of the restriction, the court found *in favor of Wellspan.*

Regional General Hospital v. Anesthesiology Associates, Inc. Appellate Court of the State of Longville (2007)

Facts

- Anesthesiology Associates Inc. (AAI) is a medical practice that employs physicians and certified registered nurse anesthetists (employees). In January 2002, AAI entered into a contract with Regional General Hospital (Regional) to provide mutually agreed-upon services to Regional's patients.

- The employment agreements that AAI has with its employees contained a postemployment restrictive covenant wherein employees agreed to the following restrictions: (1) that for a period of two years from separation from AAI, ex-employees would not contract with or compete against AAI at any facility where AAI was currently the provider of anesthesiology services and (2) that for a period of one year from separation, ex-employees agreed not to contract or compete against AAI at any facility where AAI has provided services for the last 12 months ending on the period of the employee's departure date. Because AAI provided services to more than 35 hospitals in five different states, the geographic restrictions effectively covered a five-state region.

- Regional let the agreement with AAI expire and offered direct employment to several AAI employees. Fearing that employees of AAI would not accept these employment offers for fear of a lawsuit by AAI based on breach of the restrictive covenant, Regional filed suit against AAI seeking a declaratory judgment that the covenant was unenforceable because it was overly broad in scope and duration and unduly restricted AAI employees from accepting employment with Regional.

Legal Speak ›))
Declaratory Judgment A remedy used to determine the rights of the parties in a set of circumstances (such as the enforceability of a contract) and is binding on the litigants even though no damages were awarded.

POINTS OF LAW AND OPINION EXCERPTS

Point (a)

In accordance with the Longville Supreme Court's decision in *Wellspan v. Bayliss,* the court will enforce a restrictive covenant *only* if it is *reasonably necessary* to protect the legitimate interests of the employer.

Point (b)

In addition to serving a legitimate business interest, the restriction must be tailored narrowly enough so that it is reasonably necessary to protect the interest of the employer. If an employer does not compete in a particular geographic area, enforcement of a covenant in that area is not reasonably necessary for the employer's protection. Any restriction that is *overly broad in geographic scope and duration* renders it unenforceable, and courts have the authority to either pare back the restriction or set it aside entirely.

Excerpt (b1)

"In determining reasonableness of scope and duration, we must balance the interest the employer seeks to protect against the important interest of the employee in being able to earn a living in her chosen profession. The court finds that neither the time limitations, nor the territorial scope of the agreement are overly broad or unreasonable.

Furthermore, although the noncompete clause covers five states in scope, such restriction is reasonable given the *regional nature* of their current hospital clientele. In this case, the restrictions are narrowly tailored to be limited only to certain providers within that region."

Held

In favor of AAI. AAI's restrictive covenants in its employment agreements were reasonably related to AAI's business interests and were not overly broad.

Regulation in the Workplace

11
CHAPTER

Agency

learning **objectives**

After studying this chapter, students who have mastered the material will be able to:

11-1 Recognize, define, and give examples of an agency relationship.

11-2 Classify agents as either employees or independent contractors by applying the direction and control tests.

11-3 Explain the process for creating an agency relationship and the impact of that relationship on the liability of the principal.

11-4 List the sources of an agent's authority to bind the principal in contract and give examples of each source.

11-5 Apply the doctrine of respondeat superior and identify its impact and limits.

11-6 Define the duties that collectively comprise a fiduciary obligation owed by the agent to the principal.

11-7 Articulate the duties owed by a principal to the agent and to third parties.

11-8 List the two primary methods used to terminate agency relationships and give examples of each method.

11-9 Recognize the dangers of the principal's failing to notify third parties of an agent's termination.

gency relationships are fundamental to the business environment because they set out rules and standards for situations in which one party hires another party to act on the hiring party's behalf. Business owners and managers who understand the obligations and liabilities of such a relationship are in a favorable position to limit their company's liability to both the hired party and third parties. Understanding **agency law** is also a crucial first step to understanding laws that govern rights, duties, and obligations between employers and employees.

In this chapter, students will learn:

- The definition, categories, and sources of law that govern agency relationships.
- Liabilities, duties, and obligations that are created by an agency relationship.

DEFINITIONS AND SOURCES OF AGENCY LAW LO 11-1

Agency is a legal relationship in which the parties agree, in some form, that one party will act as an **agent** for another party, called the **principal,** subject to the control of the principal. Agency relationships are common and essential in the business environment and exist in a variety of forms. A common form of agency arises in an employer-employee relationship, but there are other important forms of agency as well.

In all agency relationships, the principal authorizes the agent to provide services or accomplish some task on behalf of the principal and under the principal's charge. Understanding agency law requires one to be aware of (1) legal requirements for *creating* an agency, (2) *liability* of a principal for the agent's conduct, and (3) *duties* and obligations of the parties. The principal and agent may be either individuals or entities (such as a corporation). Agency law generally exists on the state statutory level and is based on the ***Restatement (Second) of Agency.***[1] Some states have also retained some common law doctrines of agency that operate in tandem with the statutes.

CLASSIFICATION OF AGENTS LO 11-2

Agents are classified into one of three broad categories: (1) *employee agents,* (2) *independent contractor agents,* and (3) *gratuitous agents.* Understanding these categories is important for business owners and managers primarily because the liability of the

---

[1] Recall from Chapter 1, "Legal Foundations," that the American Law Institute promulgates the Restatements. It should be noted that the ALI has published the *Restatement (Third) of Agency;* however, no state has adopted its provisions. Therefore, all references to the Restatements in this textbook are to *Restatement (Second) of Agency.*

principal for acts of the agent depends on the agency relationship between the principal, the agent, and any relevant third parties.

Employee Agents

Individual employees who are authorized to transact business on behalf of the employer principal are called **employee agents.** Principals are liable for the actions or omissions (such as negligence) of employee agents. However, it is important to understand that not every employee is an agent. In order to be classified as an employee agent, the employee must have some source of authority to represent the employer. The nonagent employee relationship is sometimes referred to as the *master-servant relationship* to distinguish it from an employer-employee agent relationship. For example, at the local branch of Mega Bank, the teller is an employee agent of Mega Bank who is authorized to conduct certain limited transactions (such as cashing a check) on Mega Bank's behalf. The branch manager at Mega Bank is also an employee agent, and her agency is likely wider in scope to include approval of small business loans and similar transactions. The security guard at the local branch is also an employee but is not an employee agent since the guard does not have authority to transact business on Mega Bank's behalf. Therefore, the guard could be characterized as the servant in a master-servant relationship.

By contrast, an **independent contractor agent** is not considered an employee and has no legal protections of employees such as minimum-wage and overtime-compensation laws. An equally important factor is that the principal generally has no liability for actions and omissions of an independent contractor agent. In the business environment, professional service providers such as attorneys, outside accountants, and architects are all examples of independent contractors.

Agents who act on behalf of a principal without receiving any compensation are called **gratuitous agents.** To take a simple example, if you ask your roommate to pick up your laundry on your behalf as a favor, he is your gratuitous agent. In most respects, the rights and duties of gratuitous agents are the same as those of paid agents except that the duty of

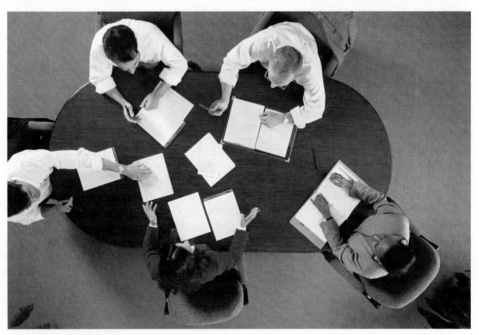

Business owners and managers depend on their agents to help carry out business operations.

care applicable to the gratuitous agent is not as great (an agent's duty of care is discussed later in this chapter).

Employee Agents versus Independent Contractors: Direction and Control

Although the parties themselves may agree to a certain classification, the status of an agent is not based on what the parties agreed to but is instead determined by the *actual* working relationship between principal and agent. Courts apply the *substance-over-form*[2] analysis to determine the classification of an agent. Fundamentally, the agent is classified based on the amount of *direction and control* that the principal has over the agent in terms of setting the agent's work schedule and pay rate and determining the level of day-to-day supervision required. In an employer-employee agent relationship, the employer principal typically sets work hours, decides what salary to pay, and exercises control over the employee agent's working conditions and responsibilities. Independent contractors usually work based on a deadline but typically choose their own schedule to accomplish that deadline. In terms of payment, independent contractors usually send an invoice on a monthly basis (sometimes longer) for services rendered rather than drawing a weekly or biweekly paycheck. Courts also use other criteria for determining the status of an agent that focus on the nature of the agent's duties. For example, an *independent occupation or profession* in which the agent has more than one customer or client (as in the case of accountants, attorneys, architects) indicates an independent contactor. On the other hand, if the principal provides tools or heavy equipment to the agent at the workplace, this generally indicates that the agent is an employee.

> **KEY POINT**
>
> The agent is classified based on the amount of *direction and control* that the principal has over the agent in terms of setting a work schedule, pay rate, and day-to-day supervision requirements.

Courts may also look to state common law or statutes for guidance in determining independent contractor status. For example, California courts consider (1) whether the worker is engaged in a distinct occupation or business, (2) whether, considering the kind of occupation and locality, the work is usually done under the principal's direction or by a specialist without supervision, (3) the skill required, (4) whether the principal or worker supplies the instrumentalities, tools, and place of work, (5) the length of time for which the services are to be performed, (6) the method of payment, whether by time or by job, (7) whether the work is part of the principal's regular business, and (8) whether the parties believe they are creating an employer-employee relationship.[3]

IRS's Three-Prong Test   Because so many questions regarding agency status occur in an employment tax context (e.g., is the employer liable to pay legally mandated employment taxes on a certain worker?), the Internal Revenue Service (IRS) has devised a three-prong test to determine an agent's status. While this test is not binding on courts, some appellate courts cite it as a useful tool in determining an agent's classification.[4] The IRS considers:

- *Behavioral* aspects of the agency. (Does the company control what the worker does and how the worker does the job assigned?)

---

[2]Recall that the substance-over-form standard is the equitable maxim discussed in Chapter 1, "Legal Foundations," whereby courts look to the intent of the parties involved and adhere to a standard of good faith and fair play instead of applying a technical and superficial standard or the parties' subjective intent.

[3]*Estrada v. FedEx Ground Package System,* 64 Cal. Rptr. 3d 327 (2007).

[4]This three-prong approach replaced the IRS's notorious 20-point test in 1997. The IRS specifically disclaims the 20-point test and takes the position that there is "no magic or set number of factors that makes the worker an employee or an independent contractor."

- The *financial arrangements* between principal and agent. (Are the business aspects of the worker's job controlled by the payer?)
- The type of *working relationship* the parties have in terms of benefits and promises of continuing employment.

The consequences of a business owner's or manager's misclassifying an employee can be severe. For example, suppose that Computer Warehouse Corporation (CWC) classifies five computer programmers as independent contractors even though CWC sets their schedule and supervises the work product. This continues for one year until the IRS audits CWC and determines that the programmers were actually employees. The IRS will then assess CWC back employment taxes, plus a penalty for the wrongful classification, plus interest owed to the government for the one-year period. Depending on the salaries and the length of time the employees were misclassified, the amount due could exceed several hundred thousand dollars of unplanned tax liability. This would also likely be followed by a Department of Labor audit to determine compliance with federal labor and wage statutes.

 Self-Check Agency Classification

What is More's agency classification?

1. More, an author, is hired by Henry VIII Publications to write a book tentatively titled *Utopia*. The parties agree that More will be paid a lump sum of $50,000 when the book is complete and that the manuscript will be due in six months.

2. More is hired by Henry to work as a computer consultant. The parties agree that More will be on-site at Henry's office on Mondays from 9 a.m. to 5 p.m. for eight consecutive weeks and will be paid each week upon receipt of an invoice by Henry's bookkeeper. More has eight other clients.

3. More is hired by Henry to work as a sales associate for his retail clothing store. The parties agree that More will work at the store Monday through Friday from 10 a.m. to 6 p.m. at a rate of $9 per hour plus a 15 percent commission on merchandise sold by More.

4. More is Henry's neighbor and agrees to do him a favor by transporting Henry's valuable rare coin collection to a local trade show.

5. More is hired by Henry to make telemarketing calls for Henry's media company. The parties enter into a written agreement titled "Independent Contractor Agreement" in which both parties agree that More will be an independent agent. Henry sets More's schedule and pays him $1,000 every other week plus a $500 bonus every year during the holiday season. More uses equipment owned by the media company.

6. More, a professional athlete, is hired by Henry, the owner of a major-league baseball franchise, to play baseball at an annual salary of $1 million. More's contract requires that he show up for all off-season camps, practices, and games for the entire length of the event. If he fails to show up, he agrees to reduction in pay via a fine. More is paid every other week, and Henry pays for More's health and retirement benefits.

Answers to this Self-Check are provided at the end of the chapter.

Classification of Workers

PROBLEM *While some agent classifications are clear, as the global economy evolves and new positions and types of occupations are created, managers face the difficult choice of classification without the benefit of clear guidelines from previous court cases or IRS rulings. If an agent is misclassified, the tax liability incurred may be substantial.*

SOLUTION File IRS Form SS-8.

Form SS-8 was created by the IRS to assist business owners and managers in complying with tax regulations regarding independent contractor status. Filing the form gives the principal/employer assurances that either (1) the classification by the employer is correct or (2) the classification needs to be changed and similar positions in the future should be classified in the same way. The other benefit to filing the form is that it may be evidence of good faith efforts to comply with the tax law. If the IRS determines that the principal/employer made a good faith mistake in classifying the agent, no penalty is imposed. If the IRS regards the principal/employer's classification as reckless or made without requisite good faith compliance efforts, penalties and interest are added to the assessment of back taxes.[5]

[5]Note that any intent, in any context, to purposefully (intentionally) evade tax due is a criminal offense.

OVERVIEW OF AN AGENCY TRANSACTION

LO 11-3

Before delving into the individual components of agency law, it is important to understand the function of an agency transaction from a larger perspective. Fundamentally, an agency transaction involves one party hiring another party to transact business on behalf of (or perform a task for) the hiring party. In a business context, this relationship is crucial because business owners and managers depend on agents to carry out the daily operations of the business.

Business owners and managers use agents to enter into contracts, perform necessary services, and advance their objectives in various ways. First, an agency relationship is typically created expressly by the parties with the duties of the agent being set out by the principal. Second, the parties perform their respective duties in accordance with their agreement and agency law. Finally, an agency transaction is ended by the termination of the agency by the parties. In some cases, the agency is terminated by operation of law (e.g., the principal hires the agent to paint a building, but the building is destroyed by fire before the agent begins to paint). Table 11.1 provides an overview of an agency transaction.

TABLE 11.1 Agency Transaction Overview

Creation of Agency	Performance of Obligations and Duties	Termination of Agency
Principal wishes to form agency and agent consents.	Agent performs as agreed and in accordance with fiduciary obligations. Principal's primary obligation is payment of the agent.	Express act of parties or operation of law.

Creation of an Agency Relationship

The Restatements define the creation of an agency relationship in terms of *consent* and *control*. Specifically, agency is described as a *fiduciary* relationship that results from manifestations of consent by the principal to the agent to act on the principal's behalf subject to her control. The agent must also give consent to perform the act.

Manifestations and Consent

The first step in creating an agency relationship is for the principal to **manifest** some offer to form an agency. **Consent** occurs when an agent agrees to act for the principal. In order to determine whether the parties have in fact manifested an offer of agency and acceptance by the agent, courts apply an objective standard. That is, given the parties' outward expressions, actions, and words, would a reasonable person believe that the principal intended that an agency be created and that the agent did in fact consent to the agency relationship? Courts do not look to the subjective intent of the parties as definitive. Rather, courts use the *objective* standard of what a reasonable person would have concluded about the manifestations and consent in the context of the relationship between the parties.

Control

In addition to giving consent, the parties must have an understanding that the principal is in control of the agency relationship. The control need not be total or continuous and need not extend to the way the agent performs, but there must be some sense that the principal is defining the tasks and objectives of the agency relationship.

Formalities

The law does not require any formal expression of an agency relationship between the parties. Most states do not require that the parties consent to the agency in writing. In fact, conduct alone can be the sufficient basis for formation of the agency relationship and can create rights and obligations of the principal and agent. However, a minority of states have a statutory equal dignity rule that specifies the formalities for certain principal-agent transactions.

In Case 11.1, an appellate court considers whether the conduct of the parties gave rise to an agency relationship.

CASE 11.1 Bosse v. Brinker Restaurant d/b/a Chili's Grill and Bar, 2005 Mass. Super. LEXIS 372

FACT SUMMARY Bosse was part of a group of four teenagers ordering and eating a meal at the Chili's restaurant in Dedham, Massachusetts. The tab for the meal came to $56, but the group fled from the restaurant without paying and drove off. A regular patron of the restaurant saw them leave without paying and followed them in his own car. The teenagers saw the patron following them, so they stopped their car and confronted him in a parking lot at a nearby retail center. The pursuing patron yelled that he had seen them skip out on their bill at Chili's and that they would not get away with it. The patron's car was unmarked; it bore no Chili's insignia. He wore civilian clothing and no uniform or other insignia of employment at Chili's.

The teenagers then fled the lot, and a high-speed chase ensued through residential side streets. During the chase, the patron used his cell phone to call a Chili's employee and provided him with a description of the teenagers' car and the path of the chase. The Chili's employee then related this information to a 911 dispatcher. In the course of the high-speed chase, the teenagers collided with a cement wall and were injured. The pursuing patron left the crash scene area and was never identified.

Bosse sued the restaurant owner, Brinker Restaurant Corp. doing business as Chili's Grill and Bar, for damages related to the crash. Bosse argued that the actions of the parties resulted in the Chili's patron being converted to an agent of Chili's, that he conducted his chase as an agent of the restaurant, and that the restaurant should be liable for the consequences of his negligent or reckless pursuit. Brinker filed a motion for summary judgment on the grounds that no genuine issue of fact existed regarding the lack of an agency relationship through express acts or implication.

SYNOPSIS OF DECISION AND OPINION The Massachusetts Superior Court granted Brinker's motion for a summary judgment. The court held that an agency relationship requires three elements: (1) consent, (2) right of control, and (3) agent's conduct that benefits the principal in some way. In this case, the court ruled that the evidence was insufficient to create a genuine issue whether Chili's authorized the patron to act as a posse to conduct a chase. No information indicates any preliminary communication between the patron and restaurant employees. The events were spontaneous and fast-breaking. No member of Chili's house staff joined in the pursuit, and, in fact, Chili's had an unwritten but express policy forbidding staff to pursue a tab-dodger out of the building. The court concluded that Chili's had no chance or desire to control the patron and that any benefit Chili's received was minimal at best.

WORDS OF THE COURT: Elements of an Agency Relationship "For these reasons no genuine issue of material fact emerges upon a claim of an agency relationship. The information generated by discovery does not permit an inference that Chili's consented to such a relationship; that it had the right of control necessary for such a relationship; or that it possessed a genuine interest or benefit in such a relationship. The burden of the plaintiffs is to establish at least a genuine question of the presence of all three elements. If the evidence had failed to materialize upon any one of those elements, the deficiency would be fatal to the lawsuit. The evidence appears to have failed to materialize upon all three of the elements. Consequently, the plaintiffs enjoy no reasonable expectation of proving an agency relationship. Full summary judgment is appropriate."

Case Questions

1. If the pursuing patron were actually an off-duty employee of Chili's, how would that impact your agency analysis?

2. When the pursuing patron called the Chili's employee with a description of the pursuit and that employee in turn called the police, wasn't that an act of consent by Chili's?

Overlay of Agency Law with Other Areas of Law

Note that the law of agency often overlays and interacts with other areas of the law, especially contracts and torts. It is important to understand that several areas of law may all be operating in tandem during a given transaction but that each area regulates a different aspect of the transaction. For example, although agency itself is not a contractual relationship, the parties to an agency often enter into contracts to accomplish a particular objective. While the contract governs the *terms* of performance for the parties, agency law governs the agent's authority to *bind* the principal to a third party. Contract law does not displace agency law. Rather, the two areas of the law operate together. This is also true concerning torts such as negligence. While negligence law guides us in defining what constitutes an act of negligence and provides defenses, agency law governs whether or not the *principal* is liable for any alleged negligence of the agent.

CONCEPT SUMMARY Overview of Agency Law

- Agency is a legal relationship in which the parties agree, in some form, that one party will act as an agent for another party, called the principal, subject to the control of the principal.
- Agency law generally exists on the state statutory level and is based on the *Restatement (Second) of Agency*.
- The agent is classified, applying a substance-over-form analysis, as either an employee or an independent contractor based on the amount of direction and control that the principal has over the agent in terms of work schedule, pay rate, and day-to-day supervision.

(continued)

- Liability of a principal for any acts or omissions of the agent and regulation by federal and state labor laws are related to the relationship between the principal, the agent, and any relevant third party.

- The law of agency operates in tandem with other areas of the law, especially contracts and torts.

LIABILITY OF THE PRINCIPAL FOR ACTS OF THE AGENT

LO 11-4

One of the most important aspects of agency law involves understanding the ways in which actions of an agent result in liability for the principal. For agency purposes, liability can arise either through a contract obligation or through vicarious liability (liability for another) in tort. Therefore, when a third party claims that the principal is liable for an agent's act, he is asserting that the principal is responsible for any legal consequences of that act (such as damages or losses suffered by the third party).

Authority

Creation of an agency relationship typically involves the agent's power to bind the principal to third parties (and third parties to the principal) in an agreement of some type. The power to bind the principal in a certain transaction is derived from the agent's *authority*. This authority arises primarily through one of three ways. The primary sources of an agent's power are (1) *actual authority,* (2) *apparent authority,* and (3) *ratification.*

Actual Authority   Typically, an agent's power to bind is through **actual authority,** which arises either when the parties expressly agree to create an agency relationship or when the authority is *implied* based on custom or course of past dealings. For example, the president of a corporation is thought of as having implied powers to bind the corporation to virtually all contracts that she determines are in the best interest of the corporation. The president need not obtain express approval from the board of directors for day-to-day transactions (although the president may be required by statute or by virtue of the organization's bylaws to obtain approval from the board prior to entering into certain contracts, such as a contract to sell all or most of the company's assets, and making other major decisions).[6]

Apparent Authority   An agent may also gain power to bind the principal from the *appearance* of legitimate authority to a third party this is known as **apparent authority.** Determining whether an agent has apparent authority can be difficult because it is a source of power that is not expressly authorized by the principal. The key to understanding this power is to determine whether a third party was objectively *reasonable* in her belief that the apparent agent is in fact authorized to act for the principal.[7] Apparent authority arises from the actions of a principal that lead a third party to believe that an agent has the authority to act on the principal's behalf. In Case 11.2, a state appellate court considered the creation of apparent authority in the context of settlement negotiations in a lawsuit.

Ratification   An agent can also have retroactive (after-the-fact) power to bind through **ratification.** Ratification occurs when the principal affirms a previously unauthorized act. That is, even though the agent did not have the authority to bind the principal initially, the

---

[6]The authority of officers to bind a corporation is discussed in detail in Chapter 16, "Corporations."

[7]*Restatement (Second) of Agency,* § 27.

FACT SUMMARY   Hannington, a graduate student at the University of Pennsylvania (Penn), brought suit against the university for breach of contract. Attorneys for both sides appeared to have reached a settlement when, just prior to trial, Hannington's attorney notified the court that a settlement had been reached and sent Penn a final draft of the settlement agreement. Penn agreed to the settlement terms and sent the settlement agreement back to Hannington's attorney with Penn's authorized signatures. However, Hannington refused to sign the settlement agreement, hired a new attorney, and opted to proceed to trial. The trial court refused to allow Hannington's case to go forward and held that Hannington's attorney had apparent authority to settle the case and Penn had reasonably relied on Hannington's attorney as being an agent authorized to settle the case. Hannington appealed.

SYNOPSIS OF DECISION AND OPINION   The Superior Court of Pennsylvania affirmed the trial court's decision and ruled in favor of Penn. The court held that under the doctrine of apparent authority, the innocent party, Penn, was entitled to rely on counsel's representations as they reasonably believed that Hannington's attorney had the authority to settle the case. Negotiations were ongoing for six months, so Penn had reason to believe that Hannington's attorney was in fact authorized to act for Hannington. Any subsequent dispute about settlement terms was between Hannington and his attorney and should not affect Penn.

WORDS OF THE COURT: Apparent Authority   "The doctrine of apparent authority permits a settlement agreement to be enforced where a third party reasonably believes that the principal's lawyer, the agent, has the authority to settle the case even though the lawyer fraudulently represents that he has such authority. . . . The fact that an agent has wronged his principal does not insulate the principal vis-à-vis an innocent third party who had no responsibility for the agent's conduct. . . . The doctrine of apparent authority applies to permit a settlement agreement to be enforced where a third party reasonably believes that the principal's lawyer, the agent, has the authority to settle the case, even where the lawyer does not have express authority to settle. . . . The Pennsylvania Superior Court will not presume that members of the Bar will disregard the requirement that they must obtain their clients' express consent prior to settling a case."

Case Questions

1. Suppose that in the middle of settlement negotiations, Hannington becomes frustrated with the impasse. He hires his neighbor, another attorney not yet involved in the case, to draft a settlement agreement and sends it to Penn. Is apparent authority created in this circumstance? Explain.

2. Since Hannington never actually signed the agreement, was it reasonable for Penn to assume that Hannington's attorney had obtained his express consent to the terms? Has the court effectively deprived Hannington of his right to proceed to trial?

---

principal may subsequently give after-the-fact authority by either (1) expressly ratifying the transaction or (2) not repudiating the act (i.e., not retaining the benefits while knowing that they resulted from an unauthorized act by the agent). For example, suppose that Manager is the general manager of an apartment complex and is the agent of Owner. After a series of burglaries, Manager hires InstallCo to install an expensive burglar alarm system in the complex. InstallCo has never done business with Manager previously but allowed him to sign an alarm service contract as Owner's agent. During the weeklong installation, Owner notices the workers on the site and asks Manager to fill him in on the details. It is at this point that the authority is either ratified or disclaimed. Owner never expressly gave Manager authority to contract with InstallCo, and given the expense, nature of the contract, and lack of past dealing, it is unlikely that any implied or apparent authority exists. Nonetheless, Owner may be pleased with Manager's decision and ratify (affirm) the transaction. Owner also ratifies the transaction if he does nothing to disaffirm the transaction (such as stopping InstallCo from continuing work), because Owner is still reaping the benefits of what he knows to have been an unauthorized transaction. Thus, if Owner learns of the transaction, says nothing, and receives the benefits, he may not now refuse to honor the contract on the basis that Manager lacked the agency power to bind Owner to a contract with InstallCo.

Agent's Contract Liability to Third Parties

An authorized agent who enters into a contract with a third party binds the principal to perform certain obligations, and the third party may legally enforce the contract against the principal. However, there are circumstances in which the agent may also be held liable to perform the contract in the event that the principal refuses to perform. An agent's liability to third parties in a contract hinges on whether the agency relationship is *fully disclosed, partially disclosed,* or *undisclosed.*

Fully Disclosed Agency   When the third party entering into the contract is aware of the identity of the principal and knows that the agent is acting on behalf of the principal in the transaction, then the agency relationship is a **fully disclosed agency.** In a fully disclosed agency relationship, only the principal is contractually obligated to the third party. Because the agent has no liability, third parties have no legal recourse against the agent if the principal fails to meet her obligations under the contract. For example, suppose that Abel is hired by Peters to locate and purchase a suitable piece of real estate for Peters's new warehouse. Abel locates the property and enters into a contract to purchase the property from Thompson. Abel signs the contract "Abel, as agent for Peters." In this case, if Peters changes his mind and decides not to complete the transaction, Abel has no liability because his agency was fully disclosed. Thompson's sole remedy is to pursue a breach of contract lawsuit against Peters.

Partially Disclosed Agency   If the third party knows that the agent is representing a principal but does not know the *actual identity* of the principal, the agency relationship is a **partially disclosed agency.** In some cases, the agent may identify the principal only as an "interested real estate buyer" or by some other generic terminology. In a partially disclosed agency relationship, both the principal and the agent may be liable for the obligations under the contract.[8] Because the principal is not identified, the third party must rely on the agent's good faith dealings and credit. Therefore, the law imposes liability on the agent in the event that the principal does not perform her contractual obligations. For example, in the Abel-Peters-Thompson transaction, suppose that Peters is a high-profile real estate developer and he hires Abel to purchase Thompson's land on Peters's behalf. Peters believes that Thompson may hold out for a higher price if he knows that the buyer is a wealthy land developer, so he instructs Abel not to make his identity known when entering into the real estate purchase contract with Thompson. Although Thompson is aware that Abel is an agent, he is not aware of the principal's identity. Abel signs the contract without any indication that Peters is the principal. If Peters later changes his mind and refuses to perform under the contract, Thompson may pursue remedies against Abel and/or Peters. If Thompson is successful in his case against Abel, Abel has the right of indemnification from Peters.

Undisclosed Agency   When a third party is completely unaware that an agency relationship exists and believes that the agent is acting on her own behalf in entering a contract, this is called an **undisclosed agency.** In an undisclosed agency relationship, the agent is fully liable to perform the contract. Because the third party has no reason to know that an agency exists, he relies on the agent's good faith dealings and credit. Therefore, the law imposes liability on the agent in the event that the principal does not perform the

[8]*Restatement (Second) of Agency,* § 321.

Legal **Speak** ›))
Indemnification
Right of reimbursement from another for a loss suffered due to a third party's act or default.

contractual obligations. For example, in the Abel-Peters-Thompson transaction, suppose that Peters is a high-profile real estate developer and he hires Abel to purchase Thompson's land on Peters's behalf. Peters believes that Thompson may hold out for a higher price if he knows that the buyer is a wealthy land developer. Moreover, Peters is sufficiently confident in his belief that his identity will drive up the price that he takes extraordinary efforts to keep his interest in the property confidential. He instructs Abel not to inform Thompson of his status as an agent and to enter into the real estate purchase contract with Thompson in Abel's individual name. Since Thompson is not aware that Abel is an agent, nor is he aware of the principal's identity, this is an undisclosed agency relationship. Therefore, if Peters later changes his mind and refuses to perform under the contract, Thompson may pursue remedies against Abel. In some states, if Thompson subsequently finds out that Peters is the actual principal, he may pursue legal remedies against Peters as well. In any case, if Abel is made to pay, Abel has the right to indemnification from Peters.

Tort Liability to Third Parties

LO 11-5

In some cases, a principal may be held liable for an agent's tort, most commonly the tort of negligence, even though the principal has not engaged in any wrongful conduct. This is particularly true when the agent is an employee. For example, suppose Pep's Pizza Parlor employs a driver to deliver its products. On the way to a delivery, the driver is negligent and injures a pedestrian. Pep's is held liable for damages suffered by the pedestrian even though it exercised all due care (checking the driver's record before hiring him, etc.). Liability for principals of agents who are classified as employees is derived from the doctrine of **respondeat superior**.[9] Note that respondeat superior also holds employers liable for negligent acts of both employee agents and nonagent employees. This is a form of *vicarious liability* because it involves one party's liability for the act of another party. However, principals are generally *not* liable for negligent acts of agents that are independent contractors. This question of liability is yet another reason why correct classification of agents by business owners and managers is crucial to controlling risk.

Legal Speak >))
Vicarious liability
Liability that a supervisory party (typically an employer) bears for the actionable conduct of a subordinate or associate (such as an employee).

Scope of Employment The doctrine of respondeat superior is limited by a requirement that in order for a principal (employer) to be liable for the employee's tort, the act must have occurred within the employee's *scope of employment*. Respondeat superior is a powerful tool for an injured third party because it allows the party to recover damages from the employer under the assumption that the employer's resources and insurance coverage are more abundant than those of the employee agent who committed the negligence. The scope of employment rule is an attempt to place some limitations on the principal's liability. Thus, for the principal to be liable, the agent's tortious conduct must have (1) been related to her duties as an employee of the principal, (2) occurred substantially within the reasonable time and space limits, and (3) been motivated, in part, by a purpose to serve the principal.

In Case 11.3, a state appellate court applies the scope of employment rule in a case where an employee agent committed an act of negligence while performing employment-related duties outside the traditional workplace.

Frolics and Detours The other exception to the respondeat superior doctrine occurs when an agent, during a normal workday, does something purely for her own reasons that are unrelated to employment. During this time, the employee's conduct is thought of as being

> **KEY** POINT
> The doctrine of respondeat superior stands for the proposition that a principal (employer) is liable for the servant's or agent's (employee's) tort when that act resulted in physical harm or injury and occurred within the employee's scope of employment.

---

[9]Literal Latin translation: "let the master answer"; *Collins Latin* (2008).

FACT SUMMARY Gatzke was employed as a district manager for Walgreen Company (Walgreen)[10] when he was assigned to supervise the opening and preliminary operations of a new Walgreen-owned restaurant in Duluth, Minnesota. This assignment required Walgreen to pay for Gatzke's temporary housing close to the new site. While on the Duluth assignment, Gatzke lived at the nearby Edgewater Motel for a period of several weeks. He used his motel room as a makeshift office and would use the desk in the room for routine paperwork including expense reports. Gatzke was a management-level salaried employee and, therefore, had no set work schedule.

On one workday, Gatzke and several employees had spent the entire day on-site at the new restaurant and then had a business dinner there until approximately midnight. Afterward, Gatzke and one of his colleagues went to a bar where they continued their discussion concerning the new restaurant over several cocktails in the span of one and one-half hours. Gatzke then returned to his motel room and began to fill out his expense report. The evidence showed that Gatzke accidentally dropped a lit cigarette in the trash can next to the desk in his room while filling out the reports. This started a fire, and although Gatzke escaped unharmed, the motel was severely damaged by the ensuing fire. Edgewater sued Walgreen, among other defendants, claiming that it was vicariously liable for the acts of Gatzke as its employee agent. Walgreen countered that Gatzke's negligent smoking was well outside the scope of his employment and the company cannot be held liable for the damages he caused.

SYNOPSIS OF DECISION AND OPINION The Minnesota Supreme Court ruled in favor of Edgewater and held that Gatzke's act of smoking was within his scope of employment under the circumstances. The court

pointed to the chain of events that led to the negligence and concluded that, in this context, Gatzke's actions—including the dinner meeting, the discussions over cocktails, and the filling out of the expense report—were all in furtherance of Walgreen's business. Short personal interruptions, such as smoking, do not necessarily take the employee agent outside his scope of employment.

WORDS OF THE COURT: Scope of Employment "The question of whether smoking can be within an employee's scope of employment is a close one, but after careful consideration of the issue we are persuaded by the reasoning of other courts which hold that smoking can be an act within an employee's scope of employment. It seems only logical to conclude that an employee does not abandon his employment as a matter of law while temporarily acting for his personal comfort when such activities involve only slight deviations from work that are reasonable under the circumstances, such as eating, drinking, or smoking.

"A mere deviation by an employee from the strict course of his duty does not release his employer from liability. An employee does not cease to be acting within the course of his employment because of an incidental personal act, or by slight deflections for a personal or private purpose, if his main purpose is still to carry on the business of his employer."

Case Questions

1. If the evidence showed that Gatzke had intentionally tried to commit arson, how would that impact the court's analysis?

2. Suppose that Gatzke had been writing out personal postcards and not filling out an expense report when he started the fire. Would Walgreen still be liable?

[10]No connection to the national drugstore chain Walgreens.

outside the zone that is governed by respondeat superior. The law recognizes this activity, called a **frolic,** as a protection for the principal against any harm suffered as a result of an agent's negligence while on the frolic. The frolic exception is sometimes thorny to apply because determining the precise times that the frolic began and that it ended can be a difficult. Moreover, if the conduct is a small-scale deviation that is normally expected in the workday, it is not considered a frolic but rather a simple **detour.** Detours are still within the ambit of respondeat superior. Courts use a case-by-case approach to applying the frolic doctrine because the conduct is judged based on the degree to which it is or is not within the scope of employment. To understand the difference between frolic and detour, consider the following two hypothetical cases.

Flash is employed by Apollo Messenger Service as the driver of its delivery van. During his workday, he is speeding in the delivery van and negligently injures a pedestrian. Suppose that at the time of the accident Flash is on his lunch break and driving the van to the local stadium to purchase tickets for his family to a ball game to be played that night. In this case, a court will likely rule that Apollo is not liable under respondeat superior because of the frolic exception. Alternatively, suppose that Flash was on his way to pick up a cup of coffee at the local coffee shop and he struck the pedestrian in the parking lot. The coffee stop would likely be considered a detour. Although he was not acting for the employer, the negligence would likely be imputed to Apollo because Flash made only a short stop that constituted a small-scale deviation from his employment duties. Because it can reasonably be expected that delivery van drivers will take short breaks during the workday, a court may find that Apollo is liable for Flash's conduct under respondeat superior.

Intentional Torts   Generally, intentional torts by an agent (such as committing an assault in the workplace) are thought to be outside the scope of employment, and, therefore, employers are not liable for such conduct unless the assault has a close connection to serving the principal. In a well-known decision on this topic, a state supreme court ruled that a sales associate employed by Nabisco who had assaulted the manager of a store in his territory was acting within his scope of employment because the original dispute involved shelf space at the store where the assault took place. The court held that because the agent employee was in the store on Nabisco business and the assault stemmed from his job as a sales associate, even an intentional tort such as battery could be covered by respondeat superior.[11] Thus, even unauthorized acts by an agent do not necessarily exempt the conduct from liability for the principal.

Negligent Hiring Doctrine

A majority of states recognize a tort-based theory of liability for employers for negligent or intentional torts of employees when the employer had *reason to know* that the employee may cause harm within his scope of employment. This liability theory is called the **negligent hiring doctrine,** and it requires employers to take reasonable steps (such as criminal background investigation and reference checks) to protect third parties, particularly customers and other employees, from harm at the hands of an employee. Courts are especially inclined to hold employers liable under this doctrine in cases where (1) the employees are required to have a high level of public contact, as occurs with service and maintenance personnel, real estate agents, or delivery persons, or (2) the employees are entrusted with caring for the sick, elderly, or other particularly vulnerable populations.

Negligent hiring occurs when, prior to the time the employee is actually hired, the employer knew or should have known of the employee's unfitness.[12] Liability generally focuses on the employer's methods of determining suitability for the position. For example, in *Abbot v. Payne*[13] a state appellate court in Florida held the owners of a pest control company liable for negligent hiring when the company's management failed to run a criminal background check on an employee who subsequently sexually assaulted a customer during a home service call. The employee had a record of multiple arrests for sexually related crimes, and the court found that the employer had a duty to screen the employee for

---

[11]*Lange v. National Biscuit Company,* 211 N.W.2d 783 (Minn. 1973).

[12]*Restatement (Second) of Agency,* §§ 401–411.

[13]457 So. 2d 435 (Fla. App. 1984).

any information that indicated that the employee should not have been placed in a position of trust with regular access to customer information and regular contact with the public on the employer's behalf. The doctrine also includes *negligent retention* if circumstances arose *after* the hiring process that should have given notice to the employer of a potential for an employee to cause harm.

Independent Contractors   Recall from earlier in this chapter that, as a general rule, principals are not liable for the negligent acts or omissions of an independent contractor agent. One important exception to this rule occurs when the principal has been negligent in hiring, and it is based on the *peculiar risk doctrine* that is rooted in the Restatements. The doctrine requires a principal to take reasonable steps to determine the fitness of an independent contractor agent to perform an inherently dangerous task. For example, a land developer that hires a demolition company to take down a large old building with dynamite has a legal obligation to ensure that the demolition company has reasonable safety measures in place, experienced personnel, proper safety licensing and permitting, and so on.

CONCEPT SUMMARY Principal and Agent Liability to Third Parties

	Contracts	
Agency Relationship	**Liability of Principal to Third Party**	**Liability of Agent to Third Party**
Fully disclosed (Third party knew of agency relationship and the identity of the principal.)	Full liability to perform contract obligations	None (so long as agent did not exceed scope of authority).
Partially disclosed (Third party knew of agency relationship but not the identity of the principal.)	Full liability to perform contract obligations	Full liability to perform contract obligations if the principal fails to meet contractual obligations. If agent is made to pay, she is entitled to reimbursement (indemnification) from the principal.
Undisclosed (Third party had no reason to know that any agency relationship existed.)	Full liability to perform contract obligations	Full liability to perform contract obligations if the principal fails to meet contractual obligations. In some states, if the third party finds out the identity of the principal, she may pursue the principal for remedies. In any case, if agent is made to pay, she is entitled to reimbursement (indemnification) from the principal.

	Torts	
Type of Tort	Liability of Principal to Third Party	Liability of Agent to Third Party
Intentional torts of employees	No liability unless the act was directly tied to the employee's responsibilities	Fully liable to third party for damages or losses
Intentional torts of independent contractor	No liability	Fully liable to third party for damages or losses
Negligence of employees	Vicariously liable under doctrine of respondeat superior for acts of all employees (including employee agents and employee servants) that resulted from harm within the employee's scope of employment.	Fully liable to third party for damages or losses
Negligence of independent contractors	No liability (except in cases of negligent hiring; see below).	Fully liable to third party for damages or losses
Negligent hiring of employees	Vicariously liable for damages or losses if employer could have foreseen possible harm by the employee through a determination of fitness for the position.	N/A
Negligent hiring of independent contractor	None except in cases where the principal hires a contractor for an inherently dangerous job that poses a peculiar risk	N/A

DUTIES, OBLIGATIONS, AND REMEDIES OF THE PRINCIPAL AND AGENT

LO 11-6, 11-7

Inherent in an agency relationship are certain duties and obligations of the parties. Agents owe duties to principals, and principals owe duties to agents. If either party fails to fulfill his duties and obligations, the law provides a remedy for the party suffering an injury or loss.

Agent's Duties to the Principal

The very essence of an agency relationship involves the creation of duties for the agent to act in good faith and in the principal's best interest at all times. These duties are automatic and need not be specifically agreed upon by the parties. The duties that define an agency relationship are collectively called a *fiduciary* duty, which requires the agent to act according to higher standards than nonfiduciaries in a transaction. Fiduciary duty consists of five subduties: *loyalty, obedience, care, disclosure,* and *accounting.*

Loyalty   The duty of loyalty is the centerpiece of fiduciary obligation. The law requires that the agent hold the principal's objectives paramount. Unless the principal has knowingly agreed to the contrary or extraordinary circumstances exist, the agent is obliged to advance the principal's interest over her own interests. The Restatements require the agent to act *solely* for the benefit of the principal in all matters connected with the agency. This includes obligations of the agent to refrain from *self-dealing,* or engaging in any competition or other conflicts of interest, and to keep information about the principal and transaction *confidential.* For example, suppose that Jingle, a real estate agent, is hired by Landis to market and sell a parcel of land. Landis expects to sell the land for $100,000, but Jingle knows the property's value to be higher. Unknown to Landis, Jingle forms a partnership with two friends and buys the land at the discounted price. Jingle has breached his duty of loyalty to Landis by engaging in self-dealing (benefiting from the undervalued property) and a conflict of interest. Jingle cannot represent both sides (taking a commission from both buyer and seller) without express permission from Landis.

The duty of loyalty applies universally to all agents irrespective of the scope of the agency. Therefore, all employees owe a duty of loyalty to their employers, but the specific implications of the duty vary with the position the employee occupies. If a clerk at a chain of retail stores mentions to a customer that "business is slow," it is unlikely that the employee violated the duty of loyalty, which includes keeping business information confidential. However, if the company's chief financial officer mentions to a friend at a neighborhood block party that "the company's revenues are dropping like a stone," this may constitute a breach of loyalty through discussion of confidential business information.

> **KEY** POINT
> The duty of loyalty is the centerpiece of fiduciary obligation: The agent is obliged to advance the principal's interest over her own interests.

Obedience   An agent also has the duty to obey *lawful instructions* from the principal and cannot substitute her own judgment for the judgment of the principal (unless specifically authorized). Instructions from the principal are considered to be manifestations of the principal's objectives. Note that agents who are instructed to conduct unlawful activities do not breach the duty of obedience by refusing to perform the illegal conduct.

Care   An agent has the duty to act with **due care** when conducting business on behalf the principal. This requires the agent to act in the same careful manner when conducting the principal's affairs as a reasonable person would in conducting her own personal affairs. The duty of care standard is similar to the standard discussed in Chapter 10, "Torts and Products Liability," in the context of negligence; that is, the duty expands and contracts based on the circumstances of the case and the position of the parties. Agents with specialized knowledge are held to a higher standard of care than are nonspecialists.

Gratuitous Agents   Recall from earlier in this chapter that gratuitous agents are agents that are not compensated for their work. A gratuitous agent is held to a lower duty of care than is a paid agent. For a gratuitous agent to breach his duty of care to the principal, he must have acted so recklessly that a reasonable person would regard the conduct as *grossly* negligent.

Disclosure   Agents have an ongoing duty to keep the principal informed and disclose any and all relevant facts to the principal. This duty is based on the notion that because agents may bind principals, it is essential that the agent provide as much information as possible to the principal. This includes all aspects of the relationship, such as keeping the principal informed during negotiations of a transaction. The duty also includes the obligation to disclose any pertinent negatives. This means that if

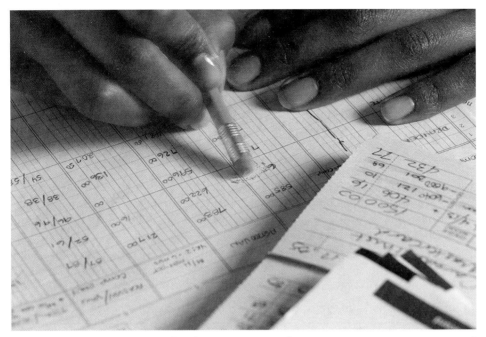

An agent owes the principal a duty to account for any money spent or received on behalf of the principal.

the agent has a lack of information about an important fact, he must disclose that lack. For example, suppose that Buyer is interested in purchasing the assets of BigCo and hires Agent to investigate the possibility of an acquisition and to determine the value of the company. Agent has an obligation to inform Buyer of any contact and information he may have about the transaction. Agent must also disclose the fact that he cannot verify the actual value of the assets and that his estimates are best guesses. The fact that Agent cannot verify actual value is a pertinent negative and must be disclosed.

Accounting   Unless the parties agree otherwise, the agent must keep appropriate written records for any money that the agent spends or receives in the course of the agent's representation. Known as the duty to **account,** this includes keeping records on data such as reimbursable expenses, checks or cash received on behalf of the principal, and any liabilities incurred in the course of the agent's conduct. The duty to account includes a prohibition against intermingling the principal's funds (or property) with the agent's own funds or possessions. For example, suppose that Penelope gives her agent, Julia, a check for $100,000 and instructs her to use it for a deposit on a warehouse that Penelope wishes to purchase for her business. Julia has a large personal tax bill that must be paid that same day, so she deposits the $100,000 in her personal account and writes a personal check to pay her tax bill using Penelope's money. She knows that her employment check will be arriving the next day, so she is confident that she will be able to pay the money back without Penelope's knowledge. Julia has breached her fiduciary duty by failing to keep a proper accounting through commingling the funds.[14]

---

[14]Julia has also committed the criminal offense of embezzlement, which is discussed in detail in Chapter 23, "Criminal Law and Procedure in Business."

Self-Check   Fiduciary Duty

Which fiduciary duty, if any, was breached?

1. Dorian is an employee of Gray Industries. His roommate works for a competitor to Gray. Dorian photocopies Gray's customer list and information and gives it to his roommate.

2. Dorian is a stockbroker for the Gray Family Trust with express authority to buy and sell stocks for the trust. Dorian knows that stock in High Flyers Inc. is overpriced and does not promise solid returns. However, he buys the stock in High Flyers because his commission will be higher than that for other stocks.

3. Gray hires Dorian to represent his interests as his agent in a business transaction and expressly instructs him not to sign any contracts with Grendel. Dorian attends a meeting and decides that a contract with Grendel would be a good deal for Gray. Dorian signs the contract on Gray's behalf.

4. Gray hires Dorian to sell widgets on Gray's behalf. Dorian accepts cash payments from Gray's customers but places the cash in his personal bank account for safekeeping and forgets to keep a record of the payments.

Answers to this Self-Check are provided at the end of the chapter.

Principal's Remedies for Breach

If an agent's breach of duty to the principal causes damages to the principal, the principal may recover those damages by suing the agent for the breach. If an agent's breach of duty resulted in the principal's becoming liable to a third party, then the agent must indemnify and hold harmless the principal from any losses as a result of the liability.

Rescission and Disgorgement   If the agent breaches the duty of loyalty, the principal's remedies also include the ability to *rescind* any transaction between the principal and agent. A court may also order the agent to return any funds earned as a result of the breaching conduct (this is known as *disgorgement*). For example, suppose that Coleridge hires Wordsworth as an employee in Coleridge's investment banking firm. Unknown to Coleridge, Wordsworth launches a competing firm and uses Coleridge's client lists to develop business for his own firm. In fact, in its first year, Wordsworth's new firm collected $100,000 in fees generated from client lists belonging to Coleridge. Because Wordsworth breached his duty of loyalty, not only is Coleridge entitled to out-of-pocket losses and damages but a court will also order disgorgement of Wordsworth's profits by ordering him to pay Coleridge $100,000 in addition to any other damages suffered by Coleridge as a result of Wordsworth's breach.

Unauthorized Acts of Agents   A principal is responsible for the acts of an authorized agent even if particular acts were unauthorized. The risk of loss from the unauthorized acts of a dishonest agent falls on the principal that selected the agent. Agency law presumes liability of a principal even when the agent acts less than admirably, exhibits poor business judgment, or commits fraud. In Case 11.4, a state appellate court analyzes the liability of principals for embezzlement by an authorized agent.

Duties and Obligations of the Principal to the Agent

When an agent acts on behalf of its principal, the agent may incur expenses, make payments, suffer an injury, or cause damages to third parties. In such cases, the

FACT SUMMARY Romanelli hired Schor as an accountant and financial adviser for his business and personal matters. Schor suggested opening new accounts at Citibank in order to obtain a lower interest rate on a line of credit. Romanelli, as principal of Romanelli, Inc., signed a business account application, corporate resolution, and signature card and gave it to Schor. Eventually, Romanelli changed his mind and instructed Schor not to open the account. However, unbeknownst to Romanelli, Schor added his signature to the Romanelli signature card and opened an account in the name of Romanelli, Inc. Over the next four years, Schor used this account to embezzle several hundred thousand dollars from Romanelli. Romanelli sued Citibank and others that participated in the transactions under the theory that Schor was not authorized to conduct business on Romanelli's behalf and that the banks were negligent in allowing him to do so. The trial court ruled in favor of Citibank and Romanelli appealed.

SYNOPSIS OF DECISION AND OPINION The New York appellate court affirmed the lower court's decision in favor of Citibank. The court ruled that laws of agency that made principals liable for authorized acts of agents also made the principals liable for *unauthorized* acts. The court reasoned that the common law has traditionally placed the risk on the principal because the principal is generally better-suited than a third party to control the agent's conduct.

WORDS OF THE COURT: Acts of Dishonest Agents "The risk of loss from the unauthorized acts of a dishonest agent falls on the principal that selected the agent. Plaintiffs' principal testified that he hired the accountant to act as a financial adviser for plaintiffs and gave him the checks to pay plaintiffs' taxes. The accountant, therefore, was plaintiffs' agent and was authorized to endorse the checks payable to plaintiffs and issue checks payable to the taxing authorities. The bank properly cashed the checks since the endorsement by the accountant was authorized by the principal."

Case Questions

1. Romanelli argued that Schor was acting outside his scope of authority and thus no liability for the principals exists. Does that strike you as convincing?

2. What remedy does Romanelli have against Schor?

principal has a duty to *reimburse and indemnify* its agents. This duty applies in the following cases:

- Payments made or expenses incurred within the agent's *actual authority.*
- Payments made by the agent for the principal's benefit but done *without authority,* so long as the agent acted under a mistaken good faith belief that he had the authority to act.
- Claims made by third parties on contracts entered into by an authorized agent and on the principal's behalf.
- Claims made by third parties for torts allegedly committed by the agent if the agent's conduct was within the agent's actual authority or the agent was unaware that the conduct was tortious.

The principal must provide the costs of a legal defense including attorney fees and any resulting liability settlement payment. In order to obtain the principal's protection, the agent must give the principal reasonable notice of the claim and cooperate with the principal in managing the defense (e.g., by appearing as a witness).

However, a principal does *not* have a duty to reimburse or indemnify the agent if the payments made or expenses incurred were (1) outside the agent's actual authority, (2) from losses resulting from the agent's negligence, or (3) from losses resulting from the agent's intentional tort or an illegal act.

Agent's Remedies for Breach

When a principal breaches a duty owed to an agent, the agent generally has the right to recover damages in court. The most common breach occurs when the principal refuses to reimburse or indemnify the agent. Assuming that the principal's obligation to do so is triggered by law but she still refuses to properly compensate the agent, the agent's sole remedy is to file suit in order to collect any money owed to the agent and to be reimbursed for out-of-pocket and incidental costs. As a practical matter, the principal and agent may have entered into some type of express agreement that spells out specific remedies the parties may exercise in the event of a breach. For example, suppose that Cardozo hires Holmes Inspection Company to perform an engineering inspection on a building Cardozo is considering buying. Cardozo agrees to pay Holmes $1,000 for services rendered, plus any out-of-pocket expenses, within 10 days of the inspection services. Although Holmes performs the services, Cardozo loses interest in the transaction and fails to pay Holmes the fee. Cardozo has breached his duty as a principal by failing to pay Holmes. Holmes may sue for damages and is entitled to the agreed-upon fee and reimbursement of the out-of-pocket expenses. However, suppose that Cardozo and Holmes signed a written agreement that included a *penalty clause* whereby Cardozo agreed to pay a late fee and 10 percent interest per month for every month the invoice was outstanding. In this case, Holmes not only may recover the fee and expenses by virtue of Cardozo's breach of his duty as a principal but may also recover the late fees and interest by virtue of their contractual agreement.

LO 11-8, 11-9 # TERMINATION OF THE AGENCY RELATIONSHIP

An agency relationship may be terminated in a variety of ways. Termination is an important issue for business owners and managers because the effect of a termination of the agency relationship also terminates the principal's duties and obligations to the agent and to third parties. It is equally important to understand the circumstances under which a third party must be notified of the termination in order to cut off the liability of the principal at a definite point. Failing to properly notify appropriate parties may result in *continued liability* of the principal for acts of the agent despite the termination. In general, an agency relationship is terminated either through **express acts** or through **operation of law.**

Express Acts

In a typical agency relationship, both the principal and the agent have the power to dissolve the agency at any time. Either party may end the agency through **termination** by simply communicating the desire to terminate the relationship. Termination by the principal is known as *revocation.* When the agent initiates the termination, it is known as *renunciation.* It is important to understand that the legal *power* of termination is not synonymous with the legal *right* of termination. Therefore, the principal may terminate the agreement (thereby revoking her authority for the agent to act in her place), but the termination may still be unlawful because the law did not give the principal the right to end the agreement before mutual performance. Thus, the agent may be entitled to damages as a result of the principal's conduct of wrongful termination. For example, suppose that Foley hires Paul to paint the lobby of Foley's office building. The parties agree that Paul will paint the lobby over a period of two weeks and that Foley will pay him $1,000 upon completion. Halfway through the work, Foley learns that a major tenant has filed for bankruptcy, so he calls Paul and tells him to stop work because he can no longer afford the costs of painting. In this case, Foley, as the principal, has the power to terminate the agency relationship by revocation. However, because Foley's actions are a

Eliminating Lingering Liability via Notification

PROBLEM *The effect of termination of an agency relationship is that the agent no longer has actual authority. However, agency law recognizes that in a case where a principal has terminated an agency by an express act, the agent may still have apparent authority to bind the principal to a contract with a third party. When the principal has acted in a way that would give a third party the belief that his agent has actual authority but then revokes the actual authority of the agent, the agent may still have lingering authority from the third party's perspective.*

For example, suppose that Sergio is employed as a buyer for High End Furniture Manufacturing Company (High End). One of Sergio's responsibilities is to order appropriate amounts of materials from Lumber Depot. Sergio would place the order by telephone with Lumber Depot and then he would pick up the materials in a rented truck for delivery to High End's workshop. Lumber Depot would issue an invoice and High End would pay within 30 days. This same transaction occurred approximately 10 times in six months. Assume that Sergio is terminated, but the next day he calls in an order to Lumber Depot from his home telephone. He then picks up the materials and absconds with them. This is a situation in which High End may still have liability to pay Lumber Depot based on Sergio's apparent authority. In order to terminate liability to a third party for the acts of Sergio, High End must notify the third party of the termination. This is especially true in cases where, as in the High End case, the pattern of repeated conduct (Sergio would order and pick up materials, Lumber Depot would issue an invoice, and then High End would pay) creates a reasonable belief that Sergio's authority was express and ongoing.

SOLUTION *Implement a third-party notification system to eliminate lingering authority and prevent liability based on apparent authority. Whenever an agency relationship has been terminated by an express act, the principal must notify any third parties (such as vendors or suppliers) who may be affected by the termination. Without a systematic approach in place, an employer may still be liable for the acts of the former agent even without the agent's having actual authority. Therefore, as part of its human resource management system, companies may put into place a third-party notification system whenever an agent employee has been terminated.*

In the High End–Sergio case, High End could avoid liability by making third-party notifications part of its procedure when terminating an employee (or any agent). While typical employee termination checklists focus on return of company property, final paycheck, and other administrative tasks, a solution to lingering authority may be as simple as adding notification to the list. If High End had sent an e-mail to the manager of Lumber Depot notifying her of Sergio's status, that would eliminate any liability for High End for apparent authority actions of Sergio. The e-mail need not be lengthy or detailed[15] but should be specific:

> Dear Lumber Depot Manager: Please note that, effective immediately, Sergio is no longer employed by High End. Any purchases made on High End's behalf must be accompanied by a purchase order signed by me until further notice. Sincerely, Vice President of High End.

This type of notice satisfies the termination notice required under agency law and, thus, eliminates any potential apparent authority claims by third parties based on Sergio's conduct.

[15]In order to avoid any potential liability for defamation, caution should be exercised in not giving any information about *why* the termination took place.

---

breach of the Foley-Paul contract,[16] Foley's termination is unlawful and Paul may recover any damages that he suffered as a result of the breach of contract.

More often than not, the parties in an agency relationship will have agreed to a fixed term for the representation. In that case, the agency relationship may be terminated by **expiration.**

---

[16]Recall from Chapter 7, "Contract Formation," that economic factors may generally not be used to excuse performance of a contract obligation (such as Foley's obligation to pay).

The expiration may be tied to a *time period* (principal hires agent for a one-year period) or an *event* (principal hires agent as a substitute worker only until an injured worker returns). Instead of setting a fixed time or event, the parties may agree to end the agency once the agency's *purpose* has been accomplished. For example, in the Foley-Paul agency relationship, discussed earlier, suppose that Foley did not attempt to terminate the agency but instead the painting services were finished on time. In this case, the agency ends automatically because the purpose of the agency, as originally contemplated by the parties, has been accomplished.

Operation of Law

Agency may also be terminated as provided for by statute or through certain common law doctrines. First, an agency relationship is terminated by the *destruction* of essential subject matter of the relationship. So long as the agent's role is predicated on some particular property being at the disposal of the principal and the property is no longer practically or legally available, agency is automatically terminated. For example, Foley hires Paul to paint the lobby of Foley's office building. The day after the two agree, Foley's building burns down. The Paul-Foley agency relationship is terminated.

An agency relationship is also terminated automatically if either the principal or the agent *dies,* files for *bankruptcy,* or does not have the requisite *mental capacity* to continue the relationship. However, it is important to note that exceptions exist to these common law doctrines. Increasingly, various jurisdictions have prescribed statutory exceptions to certain events of termination. For example, in the case of the death of a principal, some state statutes permit the agent to continue to have actual authority until the agent learns of the death. Therefore, so long as the agent is acting in good faith, the agent may continue his duties until he actually receives notice of the death of the principal.

CONCEPT SUMMARY Duties, Obligations, and Remedies of the Parties

- Agents owe a fiduciary duty to principals. This duty requires the agent to act according to higher standards than nonfiduciaries in a transaction, including the duties of loyalty, obedience, care, disclosure, and accounting.
- The duty of loyalty is the centerpiece of fiduciary obligation because the agent is obliged to advance the principal's interest over her own interest.
- If an agent's breach of duty to the principal causes damages to the principal, the principal may recover those damages from the agent.
- If an agent's breach of duty resulted in the principal's becoming liable to a third party, then the agent must indemnify and hold harmless the principal from any losses as a result of the liability.
- If an agent breaches the duty of loyalty, the principal may rescind any agreement between principal and agent and the agent may be liable to return profits earned as a result of the breach.
- Principals have a duty to reimburse and indemnify agents for expenses incurred, injuries suffered, or damages caused to third parties when the agent acted within actual authority or in good faith on behalf of the principal.
- A principal owes independent duties to third parties to use reasonable care in screening, hiring, informing, training, and supervising its agents.
- An agency relationship is terminated either through express acts (termination or expiration) or through operation of law (destruction of subject matter, death, bankruptcy, or mental capacity).

Agency law p. 303   The body of laws that governs the relationships created when one party hires another party to act on the hiring party's behalf.

Agent p. 303   One who agrees to act and is authorized to act on behalf of another, a principal, to legally bind the principal in particular business transactions with third parties pursuant to an agency relationship.

Principal p. 303   An agent's master; the person from whom an agent has received instruction and authorization and to whose benefit the agent is expected to perform and make decisions pursuant to an agency relationship.

Restatement (Second) of Agency p. 303   A set of principles, issued by the American Law Institute, intended to clarify the prevailing opinion of how the law of agency stands.

Employee agents p. 304   One of three broad categories of agents; includes, generally, anyone who performs services for a principal who can control what will be done and how it will be done.

Independent contractor agents p. 304   One of three broad categories of agents; includes, generally, anyone who performs services for a principal who has the right to control or direct only the result of the work and not the means and methods of accomplishing the result.

Gratuitous agents p. 304   One of three broad categories of agents; includes, generally, anyone who acts on behalf of a principal without receiving any compensation.

Manifest p. 308   Apparent and evident to the senses. In the context of agency law, courts apply an objective standard to determine whether the principal intended that an agency be created.

Consent p. 308   An agent's agreeing to act for the principal. In the context of agency law, courts apply an objective standard to determine whether the agent did in fact agree to the agency relationship.

Actual authority p. 310   A source of the agent's authority that occurs either when the parties expressly agree to create an agency relationship or when the authority is implied based on custom or the course of past dealings.

Apparent authority p. 310   A source of the agent's authority that occurs when there is an appearance of legitimate authority to a third party rather than express authorization by the principal.

Ratification p. 310   A retroactive source of the agent's authority that occurs when the principal affirms a previously unauthorized act by either (1) expressly ratifying the transaction or (2) not repudiating the act (i.e., the principal retains the benefits while knowing that they resulted from an unauthorized act by the agent).

Fully disclosed agency p. 312   A type of agency relationship in which the third party entering into the contract is aware of the identity of the principal and knows that the agent is acting on behalf of the principal in the transaction.

Partially disclosed agency p. 312   A type of agency relationship in which the third party knows that the agent is representing a principal but does not know the actual identity of the principal.

Undisclosed agency p. 312   A type of agency relationship in which a third party is completely unaware that an agency relationship exists and believes that the agent is acting on her own behalf in entering a contract.

Respondeat superior p. 313 (Latin for "let the master answer")   A common law doctrine under which a principal (employer) is liable for the tortious action of the servant or agent (employee) when that act resulted in physical harm or injury and occurred within the agent's scope of employment.

Frolic p. 314   An exception to the respondeat superior doctrine that occurs when an agent, during a normal workday, does something purely for her own reasons that are unrelated to her employment.

Detour p. 314   Conduct classified as a small-scale deviation that is normally expected in the workday and, therefore, is within the ambit of respondeat superior.

Negligent hiring doctrine p. 315   A tort-based theory of liability for employers for negligent or intentional torts of employees when the employer had reason to know that the employee may cause harm within his scope of employment.

Due care p. 318   A subduty of fiduciary duty that requires that the agent act in the same careful manner when conducting the principal's affairs as a reasonable person would in conducting her own personal affairs.

Account p. 319   A subduty of fiduciary duty that requires that the agent keep records such as a written list of transactions, noting money owed and money paid, and other detailed statements of mutual demands.

Express acts p. 322   Acts by which an agency relationship is terminated; can be either simple communication of the desire to terminate the relationship, the expiration of a fixed term, or satisfaction of purpose.

Operation of law p. 322   Method whereby an agency relationship is terminated as provided for in a statute or through certain common law doctrines covering the destruction of essential subject matter, death, bankruptcy, or lack of requisite mental capacity.

Termination p. 322   Method of ending an agency relationship whereby either the principal (revocation) or the agent (renunciation) simply communicate the desire to dissolve the relationship.

Expiration p. 323   Method of ending an agency relationship whereby the parties agree to a fixed term for the relationship.

THEORY TO PRACTICE

Cold Case Trucking (CCT) specializes in transportation of products that require refrigeration or freezing while being transported from the product's manufacturer to a wholesaler's warehouse. In an effort to improve its shipping logistics operations, CCT hired Crusoe, who had experience in operations logistics, as a consultant. CCT and Crusoe agreed that Crusoe would study CCT's operations by conducting interviews with employees and customers and then would design a new logistics plan and oversee its implementation. The parties agreed that Crusoe would give regular updates on his progress by attending weekly CCT management meetings. Because the CCT project was so time-intensive, Crusoe devoted 100 percent of his work time to CCT. The company also agreed to pay Crusoe $200 per documented hour for work on the project upon receiving an invoice from Crusoe and to make office space available at CCT's headquarters for Crusoe's exclusive use.

1. What is Crusoe's agent classification? What factors should CCT analyze in making this determination?

2. What is the source of Crusoe's authority to act as CCT's agent?

3. Assume that Crusoe is driving to interview one of CCT's customers for his study of CCT's logistical operations. While en route, he negligently hits a pedestrian. Is CCT liable for injuries to the pedestrian caused by its agent (Crusoe) under the doctrine of respondeat superior? Explain your analysis.

4. Suppose that Crusoe learns several important CCT trade secrets in the course of his agency and sells the information to a CCT competitor for $500,000. Which fiduciary duty has Crusoe breached? Explain your analysis. What are CCT's potential remedies against Crusoe?

5. Assume that part of Crusoe's agreement with CCT allowed Crusoe to use CCT's account at a local office supply store. Over a period of three months, Crusoe ordered any office machinery or supplies he needed for his work directly from the store. The store billed CCT directly and was paid (along with any other charges by authorized CCT employees) within 30 days of CCT's receipt of the bill. Suppose that a dispute arises between CCT and Crusoe about the quality of Crusoe's work and CCT terminates the consulting agreement. The next day Crusoe picks up a new computer from the office supply store, charges it to CCT's account, and absconds with it. Is CCT liable for payment to the office supply store for the computer? Explain your analysis.

6. What steps should CCT have taken to prevent possible liability in Question 5?

Legally astute managers are able to limit their company's risk by recognizing potential liability during business planning. Spotting potential legal issues and understanding when to contact counsel are important management skills. Suppose that in the Theory to Practice problem you are a CCT manager and that Crusoe presents his logistics and operations improvement plan at a management meeting. Part of Crusoe's plan involves converting the delivery truck drivers from employees to independent contractors. Crusoe claims that this will save employment taxes and limit CCT's liability for driver negligence. Crusoe recommends having the drivers sign independent contractor agreements and paying them based on a monthly fee rather than as hourly employees. After the meeting, you receive the following e-mail from the vice president of operations:

To: All managers

Fr: VP/Operations

Re: Crusoe's plan

Please give me any feedback or concerns you have about Crusoe's recommendations presented at today's management meeting. I will be drafting a summary memorandum for top-level management next week, and we will be moving to implementation of some or all of Crusoe's recommendations shortly.

Draft a three- to five-paragraph e-mail to your vice president concerning the proposal to convert drivers to independent contractors. Using your knowledge of agency law, be sure to raise any pertinent legal issues and discuss potential liability in explaining your concerns. Conclude the e-mail with a brief recommendation on how best to proceed.

CASE SUMMARY 11.1 :: Bishop v. Texas A&M University, 105 S.W.3d 646 (2002)

RESPONDEAT SUPERIOR

A drama club at Texas A&M University (TAMU) performed *Dracula*, which was directed and supervised by a faculty adviser employed by TAMU. Bishop, a student at TAMU, was playing Vlad the Impaler in the performance when, during the final scene, a fellow student missed the stab pad attached to Bishop's chest and stabbed him with a bowie knife. Bishop suffered a collapsed lung and brought suit against TAMU, alleging that, under the doctrine of respondeat superior, TAMU was liable for the injuries he sustained as a result of the negligence of its faculty adviser employee.

TAMU prohibited deadly weapons campuswide, and Bishop argued that the employee was negligent in using a real knife and in not ensuring that TAMU policies were being enforced.

CASE QUESTIONS

1. Do you believe TAMU should be held vicariously liable under the doctrine of respondeat superior in this case? Why or why not?

2. Assume that the directors were independent contractors rather than university-employed faculty. How does that affect your analysis? Explain.

PUBLIC POLICY

A crew of five pipe fitters was employed by a contractor and was ordered to put in a valve on a transfer pipe to a high-level nuclear waste tank. However, the crew had sufficient experience to realize that the wrong valve had been ordered. The valve to be used was rated at 1,975 pounds per square inch (psi) in a system of pipes that was to be tested at 2,235 psi. The crew was concerned that the underrated valve could cause nuclear contamination and injury to workers. The pipe fitters refused their supervisor's order to install the underrated valve, and they stopped work at the site until management relented and ordered the sturdier valve to be installed. One month later the company terminated the whole crew, citing financial cutbacks in the company.

CASE QUESTIONS

1. What exceptions displacing the employment-at-will doctrine could the pipe fitters assert?
2. What theory would be best advanced by the pipe fitters? Explain.

FIDUCIARY DUTY

Parker, a sports agent, represented David Toms, a professional golfer. Parker also represented Shaun Micheel and other professional golfers. Parker received a 20 percent commission on any endorsement contracts signed by Toms and a 25 percent commission on endorsement contracts signed by Micheel. In 2003, Parker was in the middle of negotiations with Cleveland Golf on Toms's behalf. After Micheel was the surprise winner at the PGA Championship, Parker convinced Toms that he should hold out for a more lucrative endorsement deal than was being offered by Cleveland, and he subsequently signed Micheel, instead of Toms, to the Cleveland Golf deal.

CASE QUESTIONS

1. What agency relationship exists between Toms and Parker?
2. If an agency relationship exists, when was a fiduciary duty created and what subduties apply to this case? Explain.
3. Is Parker's employer also liable for the actions of Parker? Why or why not?

INDEPENDENT CONTRACTOR STATUS

All employees who were hired by Federal Express (FedEx) as long-haul delivery drivers were required to sign an operating agreement that identified the driver as an independent contractor. Under the terms of the agreement, the driver would provide his own truck, mark the truck with the FedEx logo, pay all costs of operating and maintaining the truck, and use the truck exclusively in the service of FedEx, along with other specific obligations. The drivers brought a class action suit contending that for the purpose of their entitlement to reimbursement for work-related expenses, they were employees, not independent contractors.

CASE QUESTIONS

1. Should the drivers be classified as independent contractors?
2. What tests should the court apply to determine the status of the drivers?

Self-Check **ANSWERS**

Agency Classification

1. Independent contractor. Factors: (a) A publisher has very little direction and control of an author in terms of time and schedule; (b) lump-sum payment; and (c) no ongoing relationship.

2. Independent contractor. While More may appear at first glance to be an employee due to the schedule, consider that (a) More has eight such clients (he doesn't work exclusively for Henry); (b) More is paid through invoice; and (c) a short-term agreement exists with no promise of continuing employment.

3. Employee. Factors: (a) full direction and control over More's schedule; and (b) hourly wages (in addition to the commission).

4. Gratuitous agent.

5. Employee. While this may appear at first glance to be an independent contractor relationship because of the agreement, remember that courts apply a substance-over-form analysis in determining agency status. Consider that (a) More's schedule is set by Henry; (b) More is paid the same amount on a biweekly basis; (c) the annual holiday bonus may be evidence of continuing employment; and (d) More uses Henry's equipment to do his job.

6. Employee. Level of salary is not determinative in an agency classification analysis. More's schedule is set, Henry provides his pay and benefits, and More predominantly uses Henry's equipment to perform his work.

Fiduciary Duty

1. Loyalty. Dorian's actions were a conflict of interest and violated a duty to keep business information confidential.

2. Loyalty. Dorian's actions constitute self-dealing because he put his interest ahead of Gray's interests.

3. Obedience. Gray's instructions were clear and lawful, and Dorian violated his obligation to follow the instructions of the principal.

4. Accounting. Dorian's commingling of the cash he accepted on Gray's behalf with his own cash violated his fiduciary duty.

12 CHAPTER

Employment Relationships and Labor Law

learning objectives

After studying this chapter, students who have mastered the material will be able to:

12-1 Assess the origins and impact of the labor movement on modern labor law.

12-2 Explain the fundamentals and impact of the employment-at-will doctrine.

12-3 Describe the main statutory protections for workers and regulations on employers in the areas of wages and hours, retirement, health care, sudden job loss, work-related injuries, and workplace safety.

12-4 List the benefits provided by federal law for workers who are in need of a leave for medical purposes or a leave to care for an ill family member.

12-5 Identify federal statutes that impact labor-management relations and give examples of specific protections for workers that are set out in each law.

12-6 Explain the process for forming a certified labor union.

12-7 Describe the rights of and limits on workers in regard to engaging in collective bargaining and strikes and analyze the potential impact of a work stoppage.

12-8 Differentiate between an economic strike and an unfair labor practices strike.

12-9 Provide examples of illegal work stoppages.

The nature and character of the relationship between employer and employee is continually evolving. Modern day employees enjoy protection primarily from an extensive array of federal and state statutes and administrative regulations that are intended to guard against abusive or oppressive actions or policies of employers. This chapter covers laws related to the *well-being* of employees, and it examines *labor law,* which governs the rights of workers to organize and operate labor unions. A working knowledge of employment regulation and labor law is fundamental for business owners and managers for reducing the risk of liability in hiring and managing their workforce. Note that employment discrimination law is covered in the next chapter. In this chapter, students will learn:

■ Federal and state regulations related to employee wages and hours, retirement, health care, unemployment, workplace injuries and safety, and special laws and protections for employees who are minors.

■ Laws that guarantee workers the right to unionize and those that protect workers from being required to join a union.

■ Regulations that govern labor union practices and employer conduct in regard to dealing with proposed and established labor unions.

ORIGINS OF EMPLOYMENT REGULATION AND LABOR LAW   LO 12-1

As the American economy boomed with the dawn of the industrial age, employment opportunities shifted away from agriculture toward industrial production beginning in the mid-1880s. The Industrial Revolution was fueled in part by the availability of an abundant workforce consisting of immigrants and displaced farmers willing to work long hours for low wages. Conditions in the industrial plants were brutal and dangerous, and exploitation of unskilled labor was common and of little concern to politicians of that era. Workers who were injured on the job were terminated and given no compensation for medical care. In the absence of any compulsory education laws or financial alternatives, industrial labor families sent young children to work, including work in coal mines and slaughterhouses. Attempts by workers to organize or to bargain were met by industrialists with physical intimidation, assault, and job loss.

However, in the early 1900s, a growing labor movement, inspired by the increased political power of immigrant groups and a growing intolerance of the public for corporate abuses,[1]

---

[1]Upton Sinclair's classic novel *The Jungle,* which detailed employee abuses and described unthinkable sanitary conditions in turn-of-the-century Chicago meat factories, is cited in the legislative history for many worker protection statutes as a basis for the need for regulation. It is an example of how literature can influence the law.

forced the federal government to legislate federal protections for employees regarding working conditions, unionization, and child labor laws. Eventually, additional worker protections related to wages and hours, injuries on the job, workplace safety, and layoffs were added to the federal labor statutes.

LO 12-2 # EMPLOYMENT-AT-WILL DOCTRINE

The **employment-at-will** doctrine is a deep-seated common law rule that exists in some form in every U.S. jurisdiction.[2] Fundamentally, the doctrine permits employers to terminate an **at-will employee** with or without advance notice and with or without just cause, subject to certain exceptions. So long as the termination does not fall under one of the exceptions, the employer is insulated from a wrongful-termination lawsuit. The employment-at-will doctrine reflects the principal's wide latitude in decision making when exercising the power and right to terminate an employee. However, several important exceptions limit the applicability to the rule. The employment-at-will doctrine does not apply in cases where (1) the employee has an express contract, (2) courts have fashioned a common law exception, or (3) there is some specific statutory protection against job termination (such as antidiscrimination laws).

Express Contracts

One major exception to the employment-at-will rule occurs when an employee has an express contractual relationship with the employer that is intended to displace the employment-at-will rule. When the parties enter into a contract, the rights of the **contract employee** in the case of termination are spelled out in the contract. Typically, an employment contract will provide that employers may terminate the employee only for "good cause," such as a violation of a workplace rule or commission of a criminal act in the course of his employment. The contract ordinarily lists the events that cause termination, and the parties agree on any posttermination obligations. The parties may also formally agree to some type of severance pay in the event that the employer terminates the employee for any other reason than the causes listed in the contract.

Labor Contracts   While some employment agreements are contracts between managers and a business entity, some contracts give rights to nonmanagement employees as well. These contracts, called *collective bargaining agreements (CBAs)*, are negotiated by a labor union on behalf of a group of employees. CBAs often provide protection by prescribing a process that must be used by the employer before terminating an employee. The process is designed to ensure that employees are being treated consistent with the standards in the CBA. CBAs and labor unions are covered in detail later in this chapter.

Implied Contracts

An employment-at-will relationship may be converted to a contract relationship if the employer acted in a manner that would lead a reasonable person to believe that the employer intended to offer the employee protection from termination without cause. This protection, called an *implied contract,* arises in two circumstances. First, a manual or bulletin (such as an employee handbook) that is drafted and distributed by the employer may give rise to an implied contract theory if the manual extends some protections or process to the employee that she would not have under the employment-at-will doctrine. For example, if an employer designs a process in which supervisors use a system of progressive discipline before a termination may occur (e.g., warning for the first violation of a workplace

---

[2]One state, Montana, does not use the term *employment-at-will,* but a common law doctrine insulating employers from wrongful-termination claims under certain circumstances does exist.

rule, suspension for the second violation, and termination for the third violation), this may be the basis for an implied contract that displaces the employment-at-will rule. Second, an oral promise made by an employer that a reasonable person would believe extends protection against termination without cause may constitute an implied contract. Suppose, for example, that Rous-

seau has worked for 20 years at World Industries. At a luncheon honoring Rousseau, the president of World Industries says, "In honor of your excellent service, you have a job at this company until you wish to retire!" The next week, Rousseau is terminated. If a court determines that the language used by the president would lead a reasonable person to believe that Rousseau was more than just an employee at-will, World Industries may be liable for a wrongful-termination claim. Of course, any contract theory, express or implied, must be based on the standards in contract law for formation and performance of a contract that were covered in Unit Two.

Public Policy Exception

One important exception that displaces the employment-at-will rule recognizes that allowing employers to terminate an employee for certain reasons may contradict *public policy* (welfare of the general public). The public policy exception is a narrowly applied common law rule that places the public welfare ahead of the rights of an employer. This provision is best thought of as a backstop provision for situations in which no specific statute is applicable but the termination was inconsistent with the general public's well-being. In Case 12.1, a state appellate court considers whether or not a public policy exception applied to an employee who was terminated based on her safety-related complaints about a child care facility.

However, it should be stressed that courts have been *reluctant* to expand the narrow public policy exception. In *Bammert v. Don's Super-Valu, Inc.,*[3] the Wisconsin Supreme Court refused to apply the public policy exception when the wife of a police officer alleged that she was fired in retaliation for her husband's arresting her employer's wife. The court held that the public policy exception was too narrow to include specific retaliatory conduct when there was a dubious connection to any public policy objectives.

The *Bammert* decision illustrates an important point in understanding the public policy exception to the employment-at-will doctrine: its limit in scope. Absent a specific statutory protection (such as a whistle-blower law) the threshold for relief using a public policy justification is very high. Some examples include refusal to commit an illegal act (such as filing a false tax return), exercising a legal right (such as refusal to take a polygraph test), or performing an important act (such as the prevention of a violent crime). For example, in *Gardner v. Loomis Armored Inc.,*[4] the Washington Supreme Court ruled that an armored car guard who was fired after he violated company rules by leaving his armored car was entitled to be reinstated in his job. Gardner had left his truck to save a bank manager who was running from the bank and being chased by a knife-wielding bank robber. After locking the truck, he ran to her rescue and prevented harm to her. The court explained that there was no specific legal duty for Gardner to act; however, public policy and societal values encourage heroic conduct and assistance for those whose life is in danger.

Statutory Exceptions

Certain federal and state statutes also displace common law employment-at-will rules. Perhaps the best examples are the antidiscrimination laws that prohibit termination

---

[3]646 N.W.2d 365 (Wis. 2002).

[4]913 P.2d 377 (1996).

FACT SUMMARY   Jasper was hired as the director of Kid University (KU), a child care facility in Johnston, Iowa. She was paid an hourly wage, and there were no specific terms of employment. A short time after Jasper started her employment, the husband and wife owners of KU announced that the facility would need to cut staff in order to reduce overhead. Jasper complained that any staff cuts would place KU in jeopardy of violating state administrative regulations related to the minimum ratios between staff and children. The issue of the staff-children ratio was the source of considerable tension between Jasper and KU's owners. The owners insisted that Jasper find a way to cut staff expenses, and Jasper continued to assert that the current staffing was necessary for compliance with state regulations. The owners eventually proposed that Jasper and her assistant director begin to work in the classroom to help reduce staffing costs. However, Jasper protested any job responsibility change and asserted that the staffing ratio would still not be compliant with state regulations. Soon thereafter, KU terminated Jasper from her employment at the facility.

Jasper brought a wrongful-discharge suit against KU and its owners, claiming that her firing was based on her refusal to violate the staff-children ratio and that such a termination was a violation of public policy. The trial court found in favor of KU because Jasper was an employee at-will and had not demonstrated that KU violated "well-recognized and clearly defined public policy." The trial court held that the public policy exception could not apply because the staff-children ratio was an administrative rule and was not mandated by statute. The court of appeals reversed and found in Jasper's favor, holding that, even absent a statute, a clear public policy existed that child care centers be adequately staffed.

SYNOPSIS OF DECISION AND OPINION   The Iowa Supreme Court ruled in favor of Jasper and held that administrative regulations are a reliable source of public policy because of the strong similarities between statutes and administrative regulations. The court noted that administrative regulations are a means for the legislature to deal with the array of complex and technical problems it faces. The administrative regulations in this case were a direction by the legislature to the Department of Human Services to establish rules concerning proper staff-to-child ratios as a means of ensuring the health, safety, and welfare of children in child care facilities. Any termination that was a result of Jasper's insistence that the ratio be maintained was a violation of public policy and an exception to the employment-at-will doctrine rule.

WORDS OF THE COURT: Public Policy Exception   "We adhere to the common-law employment-at-will doctrine in Iowa. However, we joined the parade of other states twenty years ago in adopting the public-policy exception to the employment-at-will doctrine. In doing so, we recognized a cause of action in Iowa for wrongful discharge from employment when the reasons contravene public policy. . . . Without question, the protection of children is a matter of fundamental public interest. These factors satisfy the goal that the [child-staff ratio] regulation affects the public interest. . . . We conclude that the particular administrative rule at issue in this case supports a clear and well-defined public policy that gives rise for [a lawsuit based on] wrongful discharge."

Case Questions

1. KU pointed out that there was no evidence that it actually violated the regulation during Jasper's period of employment. Shouldn't an employer have to "act" before any public policy concerns justify an exception to the employment-at-will rule?

2. Does the court's ruling mean that all state administrative regulations are now the source of public policy considerations?

(and many other workplace actions) based on certain discriminatory motivations such as race or gender.[5] Other statutes prevent employers from terminating employees for specific reasons such as being absent due to jury duty[6] or attempting to form a union.

---

[5]Employment discrimination is covered in detail in Chapter 13, "Employment Discrimination."

[6]For example, a statute in Pennsylvania prohibits employers from terminating, demoting, or depriving employees of seniority or other benefits because they have responded to a jury summons or have served as a juror. See 42 Pa. Cons. Stat. § 4563.

State Whistle-Blower Statutes   Important statutory prohibitions for business owners and managers are derived from federal and state statutory protections of **whistle-blowers.** *Whistle-blower* is a colloquial term used in reference to an employee or agent who reports unlawful conduct or a statutory violation by his employer to the authorities. In general, employers may not terminate an employee for making a report to the authorities (i.e., "blowing the whistle") about the employer's conduct. Each state follows its own whistle-blowing statute, but, most commonly, whistle-blowers are protected when they report the violation of a law or standard by their employer to the authorities. Some states cover whistle-blowing only by government employees or employees of government contractors. Although certain jurisdictions limit whistle-blower protection to employees whose disclosures involve conduct that could result in some harm to the employees or the public at large, a minority of states have extended that protection to employees whose disclosures involve *any* illegal or improper conduct. Some jurisdictions, such as the state of New York, have set a relatively high threshold for whistle-blowers to gain statutory protection. New York statutes require that the disclosures be related to conduct "dangerous" to the public.

In any case, however, employers may terminate employees who are whistle-blowers if they can show that they terminated the employee for reasons that are *independent* of any whistle-blowing. For example, suppose that Padraig is an employee of Celtic Crystal Company (CCC). Over the past year, Padraig has been suspended twice for poor work and lateness. His manager warned him that any more instances of lateness would result in termination. On Monday, Padraig discovers that CCC has failed to take appropriate measures to remove a hazardous substance from the CCC warehouse. Padraig notifies the authorities that CCC is out of compliance. CCC learns of the complaint and its source on Tuesday. On Friday, Padraig is late for work and is terminated. Padraig is clearly protected as a whistle-blower in most jurisdictions. However, if CCC provides evidence that it intended to terminate Padraig prior to the whistle-blowing or that the decision, in light of Padraig's disciplinary record at CCC, was made independent of the whistle-blowing, CCC will most likely avoid liability for wrongful termination in violation of the whistle-blower statute.

Federal Whistle-Blower Statutes   Federal employees are protected from retaliation for whistle-blowing by the Whistleblower Protection Act of 1989.[7] The law also covers employees of companies that contract with the government to provide goods or services (e.g., a construction company building a federal highway). Additionally, some federal statutes give specific antiretaliation protections for employees who disclose conduct that violates the particular statute. For example, the False Claims Act protects employees who disclose that their firm has committed fraud in dealing with contracts with the federal government. Similarly, both the federal Fair Labor Standards Act and the Sarbanes-Oxley Act (regulation of corporations) provide whistle-blowers with specific statutory protections for reporting or testifying against their employer in an investigation, hearing, or trial.

EMPLOYMENT REGULATION

LO 12-3, 12-4, 12-5

Congress and state legislatures have passed laws intended to protect employees from oppressive or unfair practices in the workplace.[8] These employment protection laws are intended to safeguard the welfare of individual workers who have little or no bargaining power in the employer-employee relationship. Federal law often works in tandem with state law in regulating employers with respect to minimum wages, overtime pay, use of child labor, sudden job loss, workplace injuries, workplace safety, and medical leaves.

---

[7]5 U.S.C. § 1201.

[8]Note that although some municipalities have also passed worker protections that supplement the federal and state protections, the employer-employee relationship is typically considered the province of state and federal lawmakers.

CONCEPT SUMMARY Employment Relationships

- The employment-at-will doctrine holds that employers have the right to terminate an employee with or without advance notice and with or without just cause, subject to certain exceptions.

- An important exception to the employment-at-will rule occurs when an employee has an express contractual relationship with the employer.

- An employment-at-will relationship may be converted into an implied contract relationship if the employer acted in a manner that would lead a reasonable person to believe that the employer intended to offer the employee protection from termination without cause; the employer's action could be either a statement in a manual or bulletin or an oral promise.

- Certain federal and state statutes also displace common law employment-at-will rules, including statutes providing protection for whistle-blowers.

- The public policy exception is a narrow common law rule that places the public welfare ahead of the rights of an employer and prohibits employers from terminating an employee for certain reasons that contradict public policy.

Wages and Hours

The centerpiece of wage and hour law protections is the **Fair Labor Standards Act (FLSA)**[9] passed in 1938 and intended to cover all employers engaged in interstate commerce.[10] Although the statute is expansive, its primary provisions mandate (1) payment of a minimum wage,[11] (2) a maximum 40-hour workweek, (3) overtime pay, and (4) restrictions on children working in certain occupations and during certain hours. The FLSA and its regulations are administered and enforced by the U.S. Department of Labor.

Minimum Wage, Maximum Hours, and Overtime   The FLSA establishes a minimum wage to be paid to every employee covered under the act. Over the years Congress has raised the minimum wage to its current level of $7.25.[12] However, states are permitted to set a higher minimum wage level for employees working within a state's jurisdictional boundaries. A more controversial provision of the FLSA is the requirement for employees to be compensated for commuting time if their employer requires the employee to perform a significant amount of work during the commute. However, courts have applied this provision relatively narrowly. For example, in *Singh v. City of New York,*[13] a federal appellate court ruled against a New York City fire inspector who claimed that he should have been compensated under the FLSA for commuting time from his home to individual inspection sites. The court held that the mere carrying of inspection documents without any other active employment-related responsibility while commuting was not counted as work as defined in the FLSA.

40-Hour Workweek   In addition to setting the minimum wage, the FLSA sets a standard workweek at 40 hours in a seven-day period. Any hours worked by an employee over the standard workweek are entitled to **overtime compensation.** Overtime

---

[9]29 U.S.C. § 201.

[10]Given the interpretation by modern courts, the statute covers virtually all employers.

[11]The FLSA is sometimes called the *minimum wage law* but actually includes substantially more protections.

[12]For an update on the federal minimum wage, see this textbook's companion website at www.mhhe.com/melvinleb2e.

[13]524 F.3d 361 (2d Cir. 2008).

compensation is calculated by multiplying the hourly base rate of the employee times one and one-half. Thus, an employee making $10 per hour in her normal base pay is entitled to $15 per hour for overtime compensation. Note that all wage and hour laws under the FLSA assume a base unit of time of one week. For example, suppose that Mikhail has morning child care responsibilities and requests a schedule for seven hours a day on Monday through Friday and five hours on Saturday. Although Mikhail works six days per week, he is not entitled to overtime pay under the FLSA because his total hours did not exceed 40 in a one-week period. Employees are not entitled to overtime pay based on an eight-hour workday. If Mikhail were to work four days a week for 10 hours a day, no overtime would be earned.

Some workers receive a set weekly salary for a 37.5-hour workweek. Suppose that Kim works as a shipping clerk from 8 a.m. until 4:30 p.m., with a 60-minute lunch, on Monday through Friday. One day, her boss asks her to stay late to finish preparing a shipment, and she stays until 6:30 p.m. Kim is not entitled to overtime pay because she has worked only 39.5 hours in that week.

Exempt Employees

Perhaps the most important concept that business owners and managers should understand about the FLSA is that the act does not cover all employees. Employers are not bound by the FLSA for employees classified as **exempt employees.** The underlying concept behind the FLSA is to level the playing field for employees who are in an untenable bargaining position with employers. Consistent with that concept, the law imputes a certain level of bargaining power for professional and management-level employees and, therefore, exempts them from FLSA protections. When the FLSA was first enacted, the division between management and labor was relatively clear and classification was based on salary thresholds. However, as the lines between labor and management blurred during the rise of the information age and the general rise in the skill, education, and wages of workers, classification became increasingly problematic. To be considered exempt, an employee must make a minimum annual salary of $23,660 per year, or $455 per week *and* the employee must perform the duties of an exempt employee. Employees earning $100,000 are always presumed to be exempt. Typically, hourly workers are not considered exempt. However, being paid a salary does not automatically make an employee exempt. Exempt duties can be classified as either executive, administrative, or professional. Note that although the term white-collar employees is term is somewhat outdated, in the context of FLSA law, white-collar employees typically engage in employment that does not require physical labor, does not involve repetitive tasks, and are typically paid an annual salary and not on an hourly basis. In classifying an employee as covered or exempt, employers must take into account multiple factors:

- Education or skill level or certifications required for the position, salary level, and compensation method (i.e., commission versus hourly).
- Amount of physical labor required.
- Amount of repetitive tasks (performing an unskilled task over and over again, as does a clerk in a company mailroom).
- Degree of supervision required by the employer.

In Case 12.2, a federal trial court applies the FLSA to the workplace operations and practices of a well-known retail coffee shop chain.

Examples of employees who are *not* covered by the FLSA include (1) professionals who require specialized study and certifications, such as attorneys, physicians, teachers, and accountants; (2) management or supervisory employees; (3) computer programmers and engineers; and (4) employees subject to certain certification and regulatory requirements, such as insurance adjusters or dental hygienists.

FACT SUMMARY   Starbucks operates more than 6,500 retail coffee stores in the United States. Each store is staffed by "partners" including entry-level baristas, shift supervisors, assistant store managers (ASMs), and store managers. In October 2002, Starbucks changed the job description for ASMs to include routine tasks, including service, cleaning, and other nonmanagement tasks, and reclassified them for purposes of the FLSA from "exempt" to "nonexempt." This made all ASMs throughout the country eligible for overtime. Although Starbucks anticipated that ASMs would continue to work more than 40 hours after the reclassification, it did not increase store labor budgets and store managers were discouraged from allowing workers overtime. Several ASMs contended that the new job responsibilities could not be completed in 40 hours and that Starbucks managers enforced an unwritten policy of encouraging or allowing ASMs to work "off the clock" (perform the job responsibilities without being compensated) in order to control overtime costs. One ASM testified that a district manager informed her that her job needs to get done "regardless of how long it takes." Falcon and other ASMs filed suit claiming that Starbucks violated the FLSA. Starbucks contended that it had a written policy prohibiting off-the-clock work and filed a motion for summary judgment.

SYNOPSIS OF DECISION AND OPINION   The federal district court ruled in favor of Falcon and denied Starbucks's motion for summary judgment. The court held that significant evidence showed that either ASMs worked off-the-clock or time was taken off if they attempted to record all of their hours. There was a strong showing that (1) ASM job duties were not easily completed within 40 hours, while overtime was strongly discouraged, (2) labor budgets were not increased, and (3) manager bonuses were based, in part, on limiting overtime hours. Despite an official "time worked is time paid" policy, Starbucks created an environment that encouraged FLSA violations. A policy of discouraging overtime, while not unlawful, could, together with other factors, lead to a consistent pattern of violations.

WORDS OF THE COURT: Motivation to Violate the FLSA   "Plaintiffs have also provided significant evidence in support of their claim that [they] either worked off-the-clock or had time shaved off of their hours by Store Managers when they attempted to record all of the hours they actually worked. Finally, Plaintiffs have made a strong showing that Starbucks' general policy of requiring ASMs to perform job duties that could not easily be completed within 40 hours while, at the same time, strongly discouraging overtime after the reclassification, failing to increase labor budgets, and basing bonuses, at least in part, on labor hours created an environment that at least strongly motivated managers to commit the alleged FLSA violations."

Case Questions

1. What could Starbucks have done to be sure that its prohibition against off-the-clock work was enforced?

2. Why does the court consider it important that Starbucks did not increase store budgets when it reclassified the ASMs as nonexempt?

The consequences of misclassification may be severe. Unless an employee is clearly exempt from the FLSA coverage, she should be classified as a **covered nonexempt employee** under the FLSA provisions until such time as the employer has legal assurances that the employee is exempt. To understand the dilemma faced by employers over misclassification, suppose that Standish hires Alden as a customer service agent to handle complaints over the phone. Alden has a significant amount of practical experience and a diploma from a technical school. Standish agrees to pay Alden an annual base salary of $26,000. Because the work does not involve physical labor, Standish classifies Alden as exempt from

> **KEY POINT**
>
> Coverage by the FLSA is not determined by job title. Some employees have job titles that include the word *executive*, but they still qualify for FLSA coverage (e.g., executive secretary).

the FLSA. Over the course of the next six months, due to an increase in customer complaints, Standish works an average of 50 hours per week on the phones trying to resolve complaints. Because Standish classified Alden as an employee with an annual salary and exempt from the FLSA, he does not pay Alden any overtime compensation.

Assume that the Department of Labor audits Standish and reclassifies Alden as being covered by the FLSA because of his relatively low salary level, the minimal educational requirements for the position, and the repetitive task of answering customer calls. In addition to any fine levied against Standish for violating the FLSA, the Department of Labor will order Standish to pay Alden back pay for any time worked by Alden over the 40-hour workweek. Figure 12.1 represents a sample calculation of Standish's potential liability.

FIGURE 12.1 FLSA Liability

1. Calculate Alden's approximate hourly base rate:

   $26,000/52 weeks = $500 per week
   $500/40 hours = $12.50 per hour

2. Calculate Alden's overtime rate:

   $12.50 × 1.5 = $18.75

3. Calculate overtime pay owed:

   10 hr/wk × 24 wk (6 mo) = 240 hr
   $18.75 × 240 = $4,500

Because of the misclassification over six months, Standish owes Alden $4,500 in back pay, plus interest, as set out by the FLSA regulations.

 Self-Check   Exempt versus Covered (Nonexempt) Employees

Which employees are exempt from the FLSA protections?

1. An employee hired as a computer programmer at a software manufacturing company for an annual salary of $50,000.

2. An architect hired to work for a design-build construction company at a rate of $85,000 per year.

3. A cashier at a supermarket who is paid $10 per hour.

4. An assistant store manager whose duties also include routine work such as stocking shelves during busy seasons.

5. A secretary who is paid a salary of $500 per week and has set hours of employment.

6. An employee hired to sell life insurance for an insurance company who is paid a base salary of $15,000 plus a 10 percent commission on all insurance sold.

   Answers to this Self-Check are provided at the end of the chapter.

Child Labor Laws

The FLSA outlaws the once common practice of sending school-age children to work instead of to school by imposing restrictions on hiring workers under 18 years old. Table 12.1 sets out restrictions for the age requirements that have been issued by the Department of Labor pursuant to its FLSA authority. It is important to note that children in family agricultural jobs and child actors are not subject to the FLSA restrictions, but state statutes often require appropriate educational standards to be met through the use of tutors and home schooling.

TABLE 12.1	Child Labor Restrictions
Age	**Restriction**
Under 14	No employment except newspaper sale and delivery
14–15	Limited hours during school days in nonhazardous jobs (such as a busboy or dishwasher in a restaurant)
16–17	No limits on hours, but cannot work in dangerous jobs such as mining or heavy industry and other hazardous jobs as defined in FLSA regulations

A federal court found that when Starbucks reclassified a group of employees from exempt to nonexempt, it triggered significant liability under the FLSA.

Every state has passed a child labor statute to supplement the federal law. For example, while the FLSA sets no limits on the hours a 16- or 17-year-old may work, most states have implemented their own hour limits for this age group. The FLSA is silent regarding employment certificates, commonly called *working papers,* yet most states have mandated some sort of documentation policy. It is imperative that a manager be aware of both federal and state law requirements.

Retirement

Employers are not required to establish retirement plans for their employees, although as a competitive matter many often do so to attract and retain high-quality employees. If an employer does offer retirement benefits, they are typically offered in the form of a **pension** or through a **tax-deferred retirement savings account** such as a 401(k)[14] plan. In a pension plan, the employer promises to pay a monthly sum to employees who retire from the company after a certain number of years of service. The amount is ordinarily based on the length of service and the employee's final salary rate as of the date of retirement. In a retirement savings account, the employee commits to saving a certain percentage of base pay in an account that is controlled directly by the employee and not the employer. The employee then has the ability to allocate her savings via various investment vehicles that range from very safe to high risk. Some employers match the employee's contribution by paying an extra amount into the account based on a certain percentage of the employee's base salary. The major benefit for the employee is that retirement savings grow without triggering any tax liability until the employee is ready to make retirement withdrawals from the account.

Regulation of Pensions and Retirement Accounts   If employers establish either a pension fund or a retirement savings plan, the employer is subject to the requirements of a federal statute called the **Employee Retirement Income Security Act (ERISA)**[15] of 1974. The ERISA is a comprehensive set of laws and regulations that requires employers to make certain disclosures related to investment risk and provides transparency for plan beneficiaries. The ERISA establishes rules for conflict of interest (such as how much of a company's own stock can be held in a pension plan) and imposes certain fiduciary standards for investing and managing pension plans or administering retirement savings plans. Employers must adhere to record-keeping regulations and must treat all employees in accordance with a set of standardized vesting rules. The ERISA authorizes the Department of Labor to monitor pension and retirement savings plan administration. The department oversees the Labor Management Services Administration, in part to implement, administer, and enforce the ERISA.

Legal Speak ›))
Vesting An ERISA guideline stipulating that employees are entitled to their benefits from various employer-contributed benefit plans within a certain period of time, even if they no longer work for their employer.

Social Security

In addition to any pension or retirement plans offered by employers, workers are entitled to a retirement income from the federal government by virtue of the **Social Security Act (SSA) of 1935.** The SSA provides a broad set of benefits for workers that are funded by mandatory employment taxes paid by both employer and employee into a trust fund administered by the federal government. These employment taxes are mandated by the Federal Insurance Contributions Act (FICA).[16] Employees are entitled to retirement benefits based on how many credits they have earned during their working life. Credits are accrued as a worker progresses through her career no matter how many different employers the worker has over a lifetime. The SSA also provides for payments to be made when a worker becomes disabled, and it provides survivor benefits for spouses and children upon the death of a worker.

Health Care

Employers are not required to provide employees with health care insurance or plans. The Patient Protection and Affordable Care Act,[17] discussed in Chapter 2, "Business and the Constitution," and below, mandates that all citizens be covered by a health care plan by 2014. While it is hoped that businesses will provide their employees with health care

---

[14]The term *401(k)* is a shorthand reference to the Internal Revenue Code regulation that regulates tax-deferred savings plans.

[15]29 U.S.C. § 1001 et seq.

[16]29 U.S.C. § 1001 et seq.

[17]26 U.S.C. § 5000A

coverage, a business may choose not to provide coverage and pay a fee to the U.S. government instead. As a competitive matter, many companies do provide employees with a health care plan option whereby the employer and employee share the costs of the insurance plan. If the employer does provide a health care plan, two federal statutes regulate certain aspects of administering the plan. First, the Health Insurance Portability and Accountability Act (HIPAA)[18] sets administrative rules and standards designed to protect employee medical information and records from disclosure to a third party. Second, the Consolidated Omnibus Budget Reconciliation Act (COBRA)[19] mandates that employers provide continuous coverage to any employee who has been terminated even if the worker was terminated for cause.[20] The COBRA requires that the employer provide the exact same health coverage for up to 18 months. It's important to note that the COBRA does not require employers to *pay* for the health plan premiums of a former employee. The employee has full responsibility for payment of all insurance premiums and administrative fees.

Patient Protection and Affordable Care Act of 2010 and Health Care and Education Reconciliation Act of 2010

On March 23, 2010, the Patient Protection and Affordable Care Act (PPACA) was signed into law. One week later, on March 30, 2010, the Health Care and Education Reconciliation Act (HCERA) of 2010 was enacted, adding to and amending parts of the PPACA. Together they have overhauled the U.S. health care system. The legislation was the subject of intense debate and extended media coverage, but from a business manager's perspective, much of the law's mandate occurs in 2014. The law requires that employers with 50 or more full-time employees to purchase health care insurance for their employees by 2015 or face a penalty. It also offers small business owners (those employing fewer than 25 full-time workers) immediate tax incentives if they offer health care coverage to their employees and pay at least 50 percent of the total costs for their employees' coverage. In 2014, individuals not covered through their employer's policy are legally required to purchase health care insurance from a health care exchange that is set up by individual states (or groups of states). By 2018, employers that offer high-end health care plans (plans that cost more than $27,500 per year) to their employees will be required to pay an additional tax based on the total cost of the plan.

For an update on federal regulation of health care, see this textbook's website at www.mhhe.com/melvinleb2e.

Sudden Job Loss

After the Great Depression sent unemployment rates soaring to 20 percent and higher, Congress responded with the **Federal Unemployment Tax Act (FUTA)**[21] of 1935, which provided limited payments to workers who had been temporarily or permanently terminated from employment through no fault of their own. The FUTA established a state-administered fund to provide payments to workers who have suffered sudden job loss. Only the employer pays FUTA taxes. In order to obtain unemployment benefits, the worker must actively seek new employment and, if necessary, retraining in a different field. Unemployment compensation is intended to cover workers who lose their jobs because of economic difficulties and not intended to reward an employee who was terminated for cause. However, because states set their own standards and procedures, the exact eligibility

---

[18]29 U.S.C. § 1181 et seq.

[19]29 U.S.C. § 1161.

[20]In egregious cases, such as that of an employee who is terminated for theft from the company, COBRA benefits may not apply.

[21]26 U.S.C. § 3301 et seq.

requirements and the amount available vary among different jurisdictions. The amount paid to those qualified for assistance is generally nowhere near the gross or even net salary the displaced worker was making.

WARN Act   Employers that either intend to close down an entire facility or intend to lay off 50 or more workers are required to provide advance notice to employees in accordance with the **Worker Adjustment and Retraining Notification (WARN) Act.**[22] However, the WARN Act applies only to employers with at least 100 full-time employees, and if the closing or layoff will affect 50 or more employees. The law's requirements are triggered when the intended closing will result in permanent terminations or layoffs for six months or longer or when the company imposes a reduction in work time of 50 percent or more for six months or longer. The WARN Act requires the employer to provide each affected employee with at least 60-day written notice of the closing or layoff as well as notification of the local government where the facility is situated. Employers failing to comply with the WARN Act are subject to pay damages and attorney fees to displaced workers. A minority of states also provide additional statutory protections for workers displaced because of mass layoffs.

Workplace Injuries

While historically tort law was the only mechanism for compensating an employee who suffered an injury on the job or a job-related illness, all states now have **workers' compensation** statutes. These statutes establish a structure for an injured employee to be compensated through a statutorily mandated insurance program as the *exclusive* remedy for workplace injuries or illnesses. Employees with job-related injuries or illnesses are paid based on a percentage of the employee's salary at the time of the occurrence. Workers' compensation statutes typically require the establishment of a system for processing claims through the state workers' compensation board (or a similarly named agency), and the compensation is funded through employer-paid insurance policies. Companies may also be self-insured if they meet their individual state's requirements for establishing a fund that is sufficient to make payments to injured employees. The most important aspect of the workers' compensation system is that the employee is generally paid *regardless* of any issues related to fault or negligence of the employee, the employer, or any third party; however, certain defenses to a worker's compensation claim may be asserted by the employer. This plan ensures an injured worker a continuous income for an injury that requires her to stop working. In exchange for this compensation, the employee is barred from pursuing a negligence lawsuit related to the injury against the employer. The state statutes are often broad in terms of coverage, but most states exempt domestic workers and temporary or seasonal employees from protection.

Defenses to Workers' Compensation Claims   In many states, an injured worker is not entitled to workers' compensation if the injury is intentionally self-inflicted, was a result of a knowing violation of safety rules by the employee, resulted from the employee's willful misconduct or horseplay not condoned by the employer, or resulted from intoxication or illegal drug use. Should the employee fail to give the employer timely notice of the injury as determined by state statute, the claim is lost, and a failure to bring a claim within the state's statute of limitations can bar a claim.

Intentional Actions or Recklessness of Employer   Two important exceptions to the workers' compensation laws are cases in which (1) an employer has engaged in actions that intentionally created conditions that resulted in harm or (2) an employer acts

---

[22]29 U.S.C. § 2101 et seq.

with a reckless disregard for the safety of its employees. In these cases, the injured or ill party may bypass the workers' compensation system and sue the employer for a full recovery including punitive damages. As a practical matter, however, although an injured employee may recover a higher amount through litigation, the prospect of immediate compensation and the uncertainties and delays inherent in litigation mean that many people will opt to file a workers' compensation claim rather than pursue litigation. In any case, once the injured party files a workers' compensation claim, she is barred from suing her employer in any suit related to the injury.

Course of Employment   In order to trigger protection under workers' compensation laws, the injury must meet two main criteria: (1) The injury was accidental, and (2) the injury occurred within the course of employment. Accidental injuries are injuries that occur without any intent to cause harm or injure. The course of employment requirement varies by jurisdiction, but most state courts have interpreted the scope of employment requirement broadly and in favor of coverage of the injured worker. While cases where the employee is injured on the job at the worksite during regular business hours are clearly covered, off-premises activity is also covered so long as it is sufficiently related to the worker's employment. Even when the injury is indirectly related to the employee's job responsibilities, courts have been willing to extend workers' compensation coverage to the injured employee. Case 12.3 illustrates one state appellate court's willingness to extend workers' compensation rights to an employee who was injured during a criminal act.

Regulation of Workplace Safety

While workers' compensation laws are designed to protect workers who are injured, the federal statute intended to *prevent* workplace injuries is the **Occupational Safety and Health Act (OSHA),**[23] passed in 1970. The objective of OSHA statutes and regulation is to make the workplace as safe as possible for workers engaged in business operations through (1) setting national safety standards, (2) mandating information disclosure and warnings of hazardous working areas and assignments, (3) establishing record-keeping and reporting requirements, and (4) imposing a general duty upon employers to keep a workplace reasonably safe. The OSHA law has broad coverage encompassing virtually every private employer. Federal, state, and local government units are exempt.

Occupational Safety and Health Administration   The OSHA statute created the Occupational Safety and Health Administration, under the jurisdiction of the Department of Labor, to administer and enforce the statute. The administration has expansive enforcement authority, including routine or unscheduled worksite inspections, in carrying out the provisions of the law. Industries that are ultrahazardous (such as mining) are highly regulated by OSHA administrative rules. The administration also investigates complaints made by employees alleging that an employer violated safety standards. Employees making a complaint to the administration are protected from retaliation by the employer via the OSHA's whistle-blowing provisions.[24]

OSHA Provisions   The OSHA regulations have evolved into a complex and lengthy set of rules and standards because so many of the regulations are industry-specific. However, there are some provisions that apply to all employers. For example, employers with 11 or more employees are required to maintain records about the company's safety records

---

[23]29 U.S.C. § 553.

[24]Whistle-blowing protections were discussed in detail earlier in this chapter.

FACT SUMMARY   Sisco worked as a tow truck driver for Quicker Recovery, a towing company in Oregon that had a contract to provide towing services for a municipal police department. The contract required Quicker to provide a tow truck within 30 minutes of receiving the request for services. Sisco was dispatched to tow an impounded truck and was en route to the location when the police stopped him for speeding in the tow truck. Sisco refused to produce his driver's license or any other identification for the police and was arrested pursuant to a state statute allowing the police to arrest any traffic violator who cannot be identified sufficiently for purposes of issuing a citation. Sisco physically resisted arrest, but he was eventually subdued by officers who used an electronic stun gun to take him into custody. The day after the arrest, Sisco complained of neck pain and recurring spasms caused by the altercation with the officers. He claimed that the pain prevented him from carrying out his job responsibilities as a tow truck driver and submitted a workers' compensation claim. The Oregon Workers' Compensation Board determined that his neck injury was not a compensable work-related injury. Sisco appealed.

SYNOPSIS OF DECISION AND OPINION   The Court of Appeals of Oregon reversed the board's decision and ruled in favor of Sisco. The court held that the risk of proximate interaction with the officers after being stopped for speeding while responding to a tow call was sufficiently related to his employment. Therefore, the employee's injury did "arise out of" his employment for purposes of the Oregon Workers' Compensation Law, and thus the causal connection between the injury and the employment was sufficient to warrant compensation.

WORDS OF THE COURT: Work-Related Injury "To be compensable under the Oregon Workers' Compensation Law, an injury must arise out of and in the course of employment. The 'arise out of' [part] of the compensability test requires that a causal link exist between the worker's injury and his or her employment. The requirement that the injury occur in the course of the employment concerns the time, place, and circumstances of the injury. . . . Here, as the board acknowledged with respect to the 'time' and 'place' facets of that element, claimant was, in fact, responding to a tow call at the time that he was stopped, leading to the interaction that culminated in his injury. . . .

"[The] claimant's work environment exposed him to numerous and diverse risks and dynamics associated with driving and involving interactions with third persons, such as other drivers and law enforcement personnel. One obvious example is the risk of a tow truck driver being involved in an accident with another motorist, while speeding in response to a tow call, and then being assaulted by that motorist because of anger and frustration over the accident. . . . Similarly, the risk of proximate interaction with law enforcement officers after being stopped for speeding, while responding to a tow call, is manifestly a risk related to claimant's employment. Further—albeit (fortunately) only rarely—such interactions can escalate, sometimes resulting in physical injury. In that regard, the assessment of the injury-producing risk here is qualitatively no different than that pertaining to an assault by an angry motorist—or, for that matter, an assault by a coworker. Each is extraordinary—for example, being assaulted by a coworker is hardly the 'norm' in most employment environments—but each is 'a risk to which the work environment exposed [the] claimant.'"

Case Questions

1. Suppose Sisco's altercation occurred while he was en route to his house during an unpaid one-hour lunch break. Would Sisco still be eligible for compensation? Why or why not?

2. Would Sisco have been better served trying to articulate a negligence claim? Explain.

3. Doesn't public policy prevent a worker from claiming compensation for an incident involving a criminal act? Should the court take public policy considerations into account?

and to document the investigation of any accidents. These reports must be kept current and prepared for inspection by the administration without any subpoena or advance notice required. If an employee is killed in a work-related accident or if three or more employees

The OSHA statute was passed to prevent employee injuries in the workplace.

are hospitalized in one event, the employer is required to notify the administration as soon as possible and no later than eight business hours after the accident. Once notification is made, the administration dispatches an inspector to investigate the accident. If the employer is found to have been in violation of a specific or general safety standard, then the administration takes appropriate enforcement action, including levying fines, issuing cease-and-desist orders, and, in egregious cases, pursuing criminal charges against the company and its officers. In the event of a workplace death, the administration cooperates with local authorities that may also have jurisdiction, especially in criminal cases. In Case 12.4, a company is cited for a violation even though it acted in good faith and according to the custom and practice of the industry.

Under the OSHA rules, employees have a limited right to walk off the job when faced with a hazardous workplace condition. In *Whirlpool v. Marshall*,[25] the U.S. Supreme Court held that, despite the lack of any specific language in the OSHA statute that allows employees to walk off the job, the law permitted employees this right under the narrow circumstances in which (1) the employee faces a condition that he reasonably believes will result in serious injury or death and (2) the context makes it impractical for the employee to contact administration inspectors.

Family and Medical Leave Act

As American society has changed since the industrial revolution, so has society's need to provide for employees who are faced with choosing between caring for a loved one and losing a job, seniority, or a promotion. In response to pressures on the workforce to care for a family member, in 1993 Congress passed the **Family and Medical Leave Act (FMLA),**[26] which sets out the basic protections for workers who need a brief leave from work to care for themselves or an immediate family member. Some states have similar leave statutes that allow for additional time periods or provide additional medical leave protections to employees within the state's jurisdiction.

FMLA Scope and Coverage

The FMLA is administered by the Department of Labor and applies to employers that have 50 or more employees within 75 miles. For example, if BrewCorp operates three coffeehouses in Kansas City with 20 employees at each location, the company would be considered to have 60 employees within a 75-mile radius. An employee, to be eligible for benefits, must have worked for the company for at least 12 months and have worked 1,250 hours during the past 12 months. The law mandates that the employers provide up to 12 weeks of unpaid leave to employees for the purposes of caring for family medical matters during any 12-month period. An eligible employee may take an FMLA leave when the employee needs to care for a newborn or newly adopted baby or when a *serious health condition* affects the employee or the employee's spouse, child, or parent. For an employee to be eligible for an FMLA leave, the serious health condition must require continued treatments by a health care provider and must be of such severity as to

---

[25]445 U.S. 1 (1980).
[26]29 U.S.C. § 2601 et seq.

FACT SUMMARY   Corbesco was an industrial roofing company that was hired to install roofing and insulation at the Chenualt Air Base in Lake Charles, Louisiana. The job required several Corbesco workers to work on the roof of a hanger that was 60 feet high. Although the roof was essentially flat and there was little danger of slippage due to its slope, the nature of the work required the workers to kneel or stand on the edge of the roof. Thus, high winds posed a significant danger to the workers, and Corbesco regularly sought wind and weather forecasts from the National Weather Service. Roger Mathew, one of Corbesco's workers installing insulation on the roof, lost his balance after a wind gust caught the sheet of insulation he was holding and pulled him forward. Mathew fell 60 feet through the open structure of the hangar and was killed.

A compliance officer from the Occupational Safety and Health Administration (OSHA) inspected the hangar where Mathew had fallen and issued a citation that imposed a $1,000 penalty against Corbesco for failing to install a safety net under the roof. The regulation cited by the officer stated that "[s]afety nets shall be provided when workplaces are more than 25 feet above the ground or water surface, or other surfaces where the use of ladders, scaffolds, catch platforms, temporary floors, safety lines, or safety belts is impractical." Because the officer determined that the absence of a safety net at the hangar presented "a substantial probability that death or serious physical harm could result," he classified the violation as "serious." Corbesco appealed the penalty on the basis that the custom and practice of the industry was not to use safety nets for work on a flat roof. The company argued that the safety net rule was a "general regulation" and that the government was required to show that Corbesco had actual knowledge that it was required to furnish the safety nets. An administrative law judge affirmed the safety violation citation but reduced the penalty to $50, finding that Corbesco maintained a good safety program and that the

violation was not in bad faith. Corbesco appealed the judgment.

SYNOPSIS OF DECISION AND OPINION   The court of appeals found for OSHA, affirming the citation. Although the rule regarding safety nets was very general, it nevertheless put Corbesco on notice that safety nets were required when workers were more than 25 feet above the ground. The regulation also preempted any custom and practice of the industry.

WORDS OF THE COURT: "Interpretation of OSHA Regulations"   "[OSHA] did not violate Corbesco's right to due process because Corbesco had constructive notice that it was required to install safety nets under its crew while they were working on the edge of a flat roof some sixty feet above a concrete floor. [OSHA] frequently has said that a flat roof cannot serve as a temporary floor if workers must operate along the perimeter of such a roof as it does not provide fall protection; either a safety net or one of the alternate safety devices listed in [the safety regulation] must be used. A reasonable construction company in Corbesco's position would have known about these interpretations of this standard."

Case Questions

1. When a particular custom and practice of an industry have been established, is it necessary for OSHA to still regulate in that area? Why or why not?

2. OSHA determined that a flat roof cannot be considered a temporary floor. Corbesco argued otherwise. Is it fair to Corbesco that it is cited when the regulation is not specific and is open to interpretation?

3. OSHA officers had visited the site several times prior to the accident but had never informed Corbesco that safety nets were needed. As a government agency, OSHA has immunity from lawsuits for negligent or improper safety inspections. Is it right for OSHA to issue the citation when the agency had failed to notify Corbesco of the violation?

render the person unable to care for herself for three consecutive days. The employee must give 30 days' notice of his intent to take a leave unless an emergency arises, which allows reduced notice. All conditions that are covered under the FMLA must be properly documented by a physician and are subject to periodic reevaluation at the employer's request.

Some states have enacted laws reducing the size of the companies covered and some have expanded coverage to include organ donations and bone marrow transplants. Certain states have also extended coverage to include the care of grandparents, domestic partners, and others.

FMLA Protections Although the FMLA does not require employers to pay employees on leave, it does require that the employer maintain the employee's health care benefits uninterrupted throughout the leave period. The FMLA also affords employees certain protections related to job security: (1) Employers are restricted from taking or threatening any adverse job action against the employee because of an FMLA leave; (2) upon returning from the leave, employees are guaranteed employment in the same or a similar job at the same rate of pay; and (3) employers must reinstate an FMLA-leave employee immediately upon the employee's notification that the leave is over. The FMLA does *not* require, however, that returning employees be credited with seniority that was accrued while on leave.

> **KEY** POINT
>
> The FMLA requires that an employee returning from a medical leave be reinstated at the same rate of pay.

Key Employees If an employee's salary range is in the top 10 percent of all salaries in the company, the FMLA classifies him as a *key employee*. Although key employees are entitled to the FMLA protections, employers have a right not to reinstate the employee if reinstatement would cause a "substantial and grievous economic injury." However, courts apply this exception narrowly, and employers must comply with required notifications and procedures set out by the statute, including the duty to notify an employee who is taking the leave of her key-employee status and the limits of the FMLA protections.

CONCEPT SUMMARY Employment Regulation Laws

Federal Statute	General Provisions	Coverage
Fair Labor Standards Act (FLSA)	Wages and hours; child labor	Mandates (1) payment of minimum wage, (2) maximum 40-hour workweek, (3) overtime pay rate, and (4) restriction on children working in certain occupations and during certain hours.
Employee Retirement Income Security Act (ERISA)	Pensions and retirement funds	Subjects employers that establish retirement benefits to the requirements of ERISA laws and regulations, which primarily require employers to (1) make certain disclosures related to investment risk and (2) provide transparency to plan beneficiaries.
Social Security Act	Retirement income	Provides a broad set of benefits for workers, including a retirement income from the federal government; funded by mandatory employment taxes paid into a trust fund by both employer and employee and administered by the federal government.
Federal Unemployment Tax Act (FUTA)	Temporary and permanent unemployment	Provides limited payments to workers who have been temporarily or permanently terminated from employment through no fault of their own; funded by the employer only.

Federal Statute	General Provisions	Coverage
Workers' compensation statutes (state level)	Workplace injuries	Serves as a mandatory alternative to negligence lawsuits by offering compensation to an employee who suffered an accidental injury (in the course of employment) as the exclusive remedy for the injury; funded through employer-paid insurance policies.
Occupational Safety and Health Act (OSHA)	Workplace safety	Sets workplace rules and regulations, administered and enforced by the Occupational Safety and Health Administration, to promote the safety of workers and prevent workplace injuries.
Family and Medical Leave Act (FMLA)	Medical leaves	Requires that an employee returning from a medical leave taken to care for himself or an immediate family member be reinstated at the same rate of pay.

EMPLOYEE PRIVACY

The privacy of employees while they are at the workplace or are off-site performing work-related tasks is an issue of growing concern because many employers regularly monitor employee behavior in some form. In a study coauthored by the American Management Association and the ePolicy Institute, 73 percent of employers reported that they monitored employee e-mail messages and 48 percent regularly employed video surveillance. Ten percent even monitored social-networking sites.[27] Other issues related to employee privacy include telephone and voice-mail monitoring and drug and alcohol testing in various employment contexts. As a general matter, an employee's right to privacy in the workplace is very limited. However, employees may have some limited rights that are typically afforded by a statute.

Monitoring of E-Mail and Internet Usage

An employee's activities while using an employer's computer system are not protected by any privacy laws. All computer use is ordinarily subject to employer monitoring, including the right to:

■ Track websites visited by employees.

■ Count keystrokes and mouse clicks.

■ Block employees from visiting specific Internet sites.

■ Limit the amount of time an employee may spend at a specific website.

A company's information technology services may use filters, keystroke-recording software, and other detection devices for determining whether the use of e-mail is inconsistent with company policy. At large companies, part of the management team may include compliance officers assigned to coordinate monitoring and ensure that employees are following all company e-mail and Internet policies.

Employer Liability   Employers are increasingly employing elaborate employee monitoring measures primarily to limit their risk of vicarious liability (liability for the act of an employee) in areas such as defamation and employment discrimination. For example, in the AMA/ePolicy survey cited earlier, 15 percent of the companies surveyed had faced a lawsuit triggered by employee e-mail. Companies typically adopt specific guidelines

---

[27]See *The 2007 Electronic Monitoring & Surveillance Survey* (New York: American Management Association, 2007).

and policies for e-mail and Internet use and inform employees that all Internet and e-mail usage is subject to monitoring.

Telephone and Voice Mail

While the right of an employer to monitor e-mail and Internet usage of workplace computers for business reasons is very expansive, employees are afforded certain protections for telephone calls and voice mail by the **Electronic Communications Privacy Act (ECPA).**[28] The ECPA updated existing wiretap laws and restricts an employer from monitoring an employee's personal calls (even those from the workplace) without the employee's consent. Employers may monitor business calls but must disconnect the moment they recognize that a call is personal. Employers are also restricted from accessing an employee's office voice mail without the employee's consent. However, the ECPA has two exceptions that severely limit its protections for employees. First, the business-extension exception permits an employer to monitor employee electronic communications on company-owned devices so long as this is done in the ordinary course of business. Second, the ECPA allows an employer to avoid liability if the employee consents to the monitoring. Some employers now routinely require employees to consent to monitoring as a condition of employment.

Drug and Alcohol Testing

Employee privacy protection from use of regular or random drug or alcohol tests in the workplace is governed primarily by state statutes, and these laws vary considerably. Some states permit employee testing so long as the employer follows certain procedural safeguards intended to ensure confidentiality, safety, and accuracy. Other states permit testing only when the employee's job carries a great deal of risk to the employee or the public or when a worker has been involved in a work-related accident in which drug use is suspected.

Americans with Disabilities Act Considerations One important issue that arises with drug and alcohol testing is the rights of an employee under the Americans with Disabilities Act (ADA). The ADA, which is discussed in detail in Chapter 13, "Employment Discrimination," prohibits discrimination on the basis of a physical disability. If the testing uncovers a former drug addiction (or current alcoholism), under certain circumstances the employee is protected from discipline or termination under the ADA.

The ADA also places restrictions on medical examinations and tests. Employers may require a medical examination only after a job offer has been made. The job offer may be made contingent upon passing the medical test, so the test must be administered after all other hiring information is obtained and found satisfactory. If an employer requires medical testing, the tests must be administered to all prospective employees and may not be used to target those with disabilities or to determine whether women are pregnant. Data obtained through medical testing must be kept in a separate file and be available only to those with a demonstrable "need to know."

In Case 12.5, a company requires a medical test too soon and is sued by two prospective employees.

Polygraph Testing

In 1988, Congress passed the **Employee Polygraph Protection Act,**[29] which prohibits most private sector employers from requiring a polygraph (lie detector) test as a condition of employment. Additionally, employers are prohibited from taking or threatening action against current employees who refuse to take the test. However, the act permits employers to use polygraph tests when investigating losses attributable to theft or other economic loss

---

[28]18 U.S.C. § 2510, et seq.

[29]29 U.S.C. § 2001, et seq.

FACT SUMMARY   Leonel and two other applicants were given conditional offers of employment by American Airlines. The offers of employment were contingent upon passing background checks and medical examinations. Prior to the background checks being completed, American sent Leonel and the other applicants to its on-site facility for the required medical exams, and each applicant filled out a medical questionnaire. Although Leonel and the other applicants were HIV-positive, they did not disclose their condition or related medications on the questionnaire. After blood tests revealed that the applicants were HIV-positive, American rescinded the employment offers, citing each applicant's failure to disclose relevant information on the medical questionnaires. Leonel and the other applicants filed suit under the Americans with Disabilities Act (and similar state statutes), arguing that the medical exams were premature. The trial court ruled in favor of American Airlines.

SYNOPSIS OF DECISION AND OPINION   The Court of Appeals for the Ninth Circuit reversed the trial court and ruled in favor of Leonel and the other two applicants. The court held that the ADA and California state statutes prohibit the use of medical testing prior to such time as the application process was completed. The court rejected American's argument that the expedited medical examinations were necessary to remain competitive for the best candidates.

WORDS OF THE COURT: Premature Medical Testing
"Here, it is undisputed that American's offers were subject to both medical and non-medical conditions when they were made to the appellants and the appellants were required to undergo immediate medical examinations. Thus the offers were not real, the medical examination process was premature and American cannot penalize the appellants for failing to disclose their HIV-positive status—unless the company can establish that it could not reasonably have completed the background checks before subjecting the appellants to medical examinations and questioning. It has not done so. As justification for accelerating the medical examinations, American's Manager of Flight Service Procedures, Julie Bourk-Suchman, explained that the company found it important to minimize the length of time that elapsed during the hiring process in order to compete for applicants. But competition in hiring is not in itself a reason to contravene the ADA's and FEHA's (California's Fair Employment and Housing Act) mandates to defer the medical component of the hiring process until the non-medical component is completed."

Case Questions

1. Why should medical tests be given only after all nonmedical tests are completed satisfactorily?

2. Why did the court determine that American had not truly tendered a conditional offer of employment?

3. At what point would a true conditional offer of employment have been appropriate?

---

or when the employee is in the security or pharmaceutical industry. The law does not apply if the employer is a federal, state, or local government entity. Note that some state statutes give employees added protections related to the use of polygraph tests such as limiting their use to preemployment screening only.

LABOR UNIONS AND COLLECTIVE BARGAINING   LO 12-6

Another source of legal protections for workers is labor unions. Although union membership peaked in the early 1950s, when nearly one-third of American workers were unionized, in 2012 the percentage of wage and salary workers who were members of a union was 11.3 percent, down from 11.8 percent in 2011.[30] Today most labor unions in America are members of one of the two larger umbrella organizations: the American Federation of Labor–Congress of Industrial Organizations (AFL-CIO) and the Changes to Win Federation, which split from the AFL-CIO in 2005.

---

[30]U.S. Department of Labor, Bureau of Labor Statistics, *Economic News Release, Union Members Summary,* January 23, 2013.

Labor Law

The **National Labor Relations Act (NLRA),**[31] originally passed in 1935, is the center-piece of labor-management regulation statutes. It provides general protections for the rights of workers to organize, engage in **collective bargaining,** and use economic weapons (such as a strike) in the collective bargaining process. Collective bargaining is the process of negotiating an agreement on behalf of an entire workforce instead of individuals' negotiating privately on their own behalf (or not negotiating at all). The statute also contained an enabling provision that formed the **National Labor Relations Board (NLRB)** to administer, implement, and enforce the law's wide-sweeping provisions. In addition to the traditional administrative agency duties of implementation and enforcement, the NLRB monitors union elections for fraud and sets guidelines for employers and unions in regard to fair labor practices.

In general, the NLRA covers all employers whose business activity involves some aspect of interstate commerce. As a practical matter, under modern interpretation by the courts, this means that the NLRA coverage is practically universal. Some workers are specifically exempted by statute, including railroad and airline employees.[32] To be eligible for protection under the NLRA, the worker must be a *current* employee (not an applicant or retiree).

Labor-Management Relations

> **KEY** POINT
> The NLRA provides general protections for the rights of workers to organize and engage in collective bargaining.

Through amendments to the NLRA since its enactment, Congress clarified and reformed the legal standards applicable to employers and unions to ensure fairness to both labor and management in resolving differences. These laws deemed certain labor practices illegal, thus making them *unfair* labor practices under the NLRA.

Labor Management Relations Act

Passage of the NLRA brought about a wave of industrial strikes that impacted daily commercial activity across the United States. This created a backlash sufficient to cause Congress to limit certain union practices and rights by amending the NLRA with the **Labor Management Relations Act**[33] in 1947. The amendment prohibited employers and employees from agreeing that union membership is *required* as a condition for employment. The law also authorizes states to enact **right-to-work laws,** which make it illegal for employers to agree with unions that union membership be required for *continuing* employment. In sum, this permitted states to outlaw what had become a common part of labor-management agreements: forcing employees to join or continue membership in a union as a condition of employment. The law also made clear that employers had the right to voice their reasons for opposition to formation of a union and gave a specific authorization for the president of the United States to suspend a strike for up to 80 days in times of national emergency.[34]

Labor-Management Reporting and Disclosure Act

In response to increasing allegations of corruption in major trade unions, Congress enacted the **Labor-Management Reporting and Disclosure Act** in 1959,[35] which established a system of reporting and checks intended to uncover and prevent fraud and corruption among union officials. The law (1) regulates the internal operating procedures of a union, including election processes,

---

[31]29 U.S.C. § 151 et seq. This law is also called the *Wagner Act,* and it displaced an earlier attempt at labor regulation, the Norris-LaGuardia Act, which proved ineffective.

[32]Separate statutes govern railroad and airline labor-management regulations.

[33]29 U.S.C. § 141 (also known as the *Taft-Hartley Act*).

[34]Labor unions waged an extensive lobbying campaign to oppose the bill, but the provision related to the right to suspend a strike in the event of national emergency was popular with the citizenry who still had Word War II in vivid memory. President Truman vetoed the law, but Congress overrode the veto.

[35]29 U.S.C. § 1154 (also known as the *Landrum-Griffin Act*).

procedures, and rights of members at membership and officer meetings; (2) requires extensive financial disclosures by unions; and (3) gives the NLRB additional oversight jurisdiction for internal union governance.

Union Formation

While major labor unions such as the AFL-CIO are a well-known part of the American landscape, regional unions or even unions that have only one employer are recognized by the NLRA as well. If an employer has not already recognized a union, and a group of employees decide that they wish to form a **collective bargaining unit** to deal with labor-management matters such as negotiating a contract, the NLRA sets out a procedure for forming a union.

Authorization Cards   Typically, a group of employees organize an effort to have other workers sign **authorization cards** indicating that they wish to form a local union and/or join an existing union. At least 30 percent of the authorization cards must be signed by employees in a certain bargaining unit. Employees may bargain collectively only if they have a mutuality of interests (similar nonmanagement jobs, worksites, and conditions). Bargaining units may be recognized as employees of a single employer or those of an entire region or industry.

Election   Once the union organizers obtain authorization cards from at least 30 percent of the members of a bargaining unit, the authorization cards are filed with the NLRB. The formal union certification process begins when the NLRB sets a date for an **election** (vote to elect or reject unionization) by the entire bargaining unit. During the period of time prior to the election, union organizers are permitted to *campaign,* for example, by distributing flyers and leaflets to employees. However, employers still have a right to *limit* any union campaign activities that take place on the employer's property and/or during the regular workday so long as they can justify the limits as being based on business reasons (such as safety or interference with business operations) and not simply an effort to stop unionization. One appellate court has held, for example, that employer restrictions on distribution of pro-union literature during an unpaid lunch hour in an employee cafeteria were overly restrictive and not sufficiently related to legitimate business objectives.[36] Although employers may not impose overly burdensome restrictions on employees engaging in pro-union campaigns, employees cannot use threats or coercion in their efforts to convince other bargaining-unit employees to unionize. In a 1992 case, the Supreme Court ruled that nonemployee union organizers may *not* distribute pro-union flyers in a company-owned parking lot without permission of the company.[37] Misconduct during a campaign constitutes an unfair labor practice and results in the NLRB or a court setting aside any election results as well as taking other enforcement action (and sometimes criminal charges).[38] Employers also have a right to campaign *against* unionization, but they are subject to regulatory restrictions designed to prevent employers from using economic pressure to influence employee voting. The NLRA regulations prohibit employers from using threats of termination or demotions or incentives (such as a bonus or additional vacation time) in exchange for a nonunion vote.

Certification   After a legally sound election is held, a simple majority of pro-union votes is required for the NLRB to **certify** the collective bargaining unit as a union. The employer must then recognize the union as the exclusive bargaining representative of the workers and is required to bargain in good faith with the union thereafter. Table 12.2 summarizes the union formation process.

---

[36]*International Transportation Service v. NLRB,* 449 F.3d 160 (D.C. Cir. 2006).

[37]*Lechmere, Inc. v. NLRB,* 502 U.S. 527 (1992).

[38]*Associated Rubber Co. v. NLRB,* 296 F.3d 1055 (11th Cir. 2002).

TABLE 12.2 Forming a Union

Authorization Cards	Filing with NLRB	Campaign	Election	Certification or Rejection
A group of employees, with a mutuality of interests, organize an effort to have other workers sign authorization cards; 30 percent of the collective bargaining unit must sign in order to proceed to the next step.	Authorization cards are filed with the NLRB, and a formal union certification process begins when the NLRB sets a date for an election.	Union organizers campaign according to fair labor practices. Management is also permitted to engage in certain practices to campaign against unionization.	Entire bargaining unit votes to either elect or reject unionization. A simple majority is required to certify the union.	If a simple majority voted *for* unionization, the union is certified. The employer must recognize the union as the exclusive bargaining representative of the workers and is required to bargain in good faith with the union thereafter. If a simple majority voted *against* unionization, the union is rejected.

Reform Efforts   Beginning in 2007, several efforts have been made to amend the NLRA with the Employee Free Choice Act (sometimes referred to by the media as the *Card Check Act*), which would provide workers an option of procedures for having a union certified as the legal representative of the bargaining unit. The most controversial provision of the law would authorize the NLRB to certify unions either when an NLRB-supervised election results in a majority of pro-union votes or when the bargaining unit can show that over 50 percent of the employees in the bargaining unit have signed an authorization card. The proposed law is supported by labor unions on the basis that it protects the unionization process from employers that are resistant to collective bargaining. Employers are generally against the law on the basis that it puts undue pressure on employees to sign authorization cards and the employees' cards would not be secret. The proposed law has not yet received sufficient support for congressional passage. In 2011, the Secret Ballot Protection Act[39] was introduced in the House of Representatives, but it has not yet garnered enough congressional support to become law. A direct response to the *card-check* process, the proposed law would preserve a worker's right to cast private votes.[40] For an update on any amendments to the NLRA, check this textbook's website at www.mhhe.com/melvinleb2e.

LO 12-7   Collective Bargaining

Collective bargaining is the process of negotiating terms and conditions of employment for employees in the collective bargaining unit. These terms are typically negotiated, and if a collective bargaining agreement is reached, the parties enter into a binding contract. The NLRA regulations set out certain guidelines for which terms must be negotiated and which terms are not subject to the bargaining requirements. Union contracts typically include terms related to wages, benefits (such as health care insurance and pension accounts), work hours, overtime procedures, and promotion systems, as well as procedures for handling disciplinary violations, suspensions, terminations, and layoffs.

Good Faith Bargaining Requirements   The NLRA requires that both parties engage in good faith negotiations. This is not a requirement that one side or the other

---

[39]H.R. 1176.

[40]In response to the Employee Free Choice Act's pending status, four states—Arizona, South Carolina, South Dakota, and Utah—have amended their state constitutions to guarantee their workers the right to secret ballots when voting for or against union representation.

concede a particular term. Rather, the parties are obligated to demonstrate that they are engaged in moving toward an agreement. Tactics by either side that are intended to delay, stall, or hinder the process or to undermine the union through economic pressure on workers constitute unfair labor practices, and the NLRB may opt to intervene and conduct labor negotiations or pursue enforcement action for unfair labor practices if appropriate.

Grievances   Union contracts normally specify the means of arbitrating union **grievances** against an employer action or practice. Enforcement is initiated when an affected union member files an employee grievance. The union is given the exclusive authority to invoke the arbitration provisions of the agreement, and it conducts the proceedings before the arbitrator on behalf of the employee. The arbitrator's decision is always subject to review by courts that are applying federal standards related to fairness and good faith. However, a court will not set aside an an arbitrator's decision simply because the court disagrees with it. Courts give great deference to arbitrators and will intervene only in cases of fundamental unfairness in some procedural or substantive way.

If the union chooses not to bring a grievance to arbitration, the individual union member is normally *not* authorized to pursue a lawsuit against the employer to enforce contract provisions. The union has broad discretion in deciding when to seek arbitration on the basis of a union member grievance.

Strikes and Other Work Stoppages

LO 12-8, 12-9

The NLRA specifically provides that union employees can commence a **strike** in order to induce the employer to concede certain contract terms during collective bargaining. Certain occupations, though, may be restricted from striking via statute if allowing a strike would significantly jeopardize public health or safety (such as air traffic controllers, law enforcement, or emergency services). Although the right to strike is protected, the NLRA also provides guidelines on when, where, and how a strike may be carried out. Most strikes are commenced when the employer-union negotiations have reached an impasse and the union membership has determined that extreme action is necessary to continue the bargaining process. During an impasse, the union leadership will call for the members to vote for "strike authorization" to be given to leadership if the employer refuses to continue the bargaining process. Although most strikes occur in a collective bargaining context, unions may also commence a strike against an employer that is engaging in unfair labor practices.

Poststrike Rehiring   While a strike is a potent economic weapon of a union, its impact on striking union members can be harsh. Workers are cut off from any pay, medical benefits, and other compensation until the strike is over. Moreover, employers have no *legal* obligation to rehire striking workers or provide retroactive pay in cases of a strike for economic reasons. Although, as a practical matter, rehiring of striking workers and partial or full retroactive pay is frequently guaranteed by the poststrike contract agreement, it is still a risk for some workers. However, if a strike is commenced due to an *unfair labor practice* rather than for *economic* reasons, the striking employees are entitled to immediate restatement with back pay once they unconditionally return to work. Economic strikes typically arise in the context of union members' failing to agree with the employer on wages or benefits. In Case 12.6, a federal appeals court distinguishes between economic strikes and unfair labor practice strikes.

From the perspective of the union, however, a strike also has the potential to result in significant economic harm for the employer company. Because the NLRA also gives other employees the right to refuse to cross a picket line, a strike can be devastating to the revenue of the employer if the strike requires a full or partial shutdown of business operations.

Strikers have the right to engage in **picketing** at the employer's facilities, although there is no right to picket at the actual property site owned by the company. Picketing must be

FACT SUMMARY Midwestern Personnel Services (MPS) provided cement and transport truck drivers to River City Holdings (River City), a construction materials company that serviced a variety of locations in different states. MPS contracted to supply drivers to River City for a project at a union job site. The contract for the project guaranteed that MPS would supply River City with unionized drivers. MPS obtained driver-employee signatures on union authorization cards by advising drivers that membership in an out-of-state union, which MPS had selected, was required to keep their jobs at MPS. Eventually, the drivers became dissatisfied with the out-of-state union and formed a local union for collective bargaining purposes. When MPS refused to recognize the local union on the basis that the agreement with the out-of-state union remained in effect, the drivers went on strike. MPS subsequently refused the employees' unconditional offer to return to work and hired replacement workers. The National Labor Relations Board (NLRB) concluded that the employees' strike at MPS was based on MPS's unfair labor practices, rather than an economic dispute, and ordered the drivers reinstated with back pay. MPS appealed.

SYNOPSIS OF DECISION AND OPINION The U.S. Court of Appeals for the Seventh Circuit ruled in favor of the employees and affirmed the NLRB's findings. The court held that the strike was clearly based on MPS's unfair labor practices and, thus, the employees were entitled to reinstatement with back pay. The court noted that MPS unlawfully assisted the out-of-state union by negotiating with and recognizing it without any indication of uncoerced majority support by the employees. Further, the union authorization cards were unlawfully obtained by threats of termination, and the refusal to reinstate the employees was itself an unfair labor practice.

WORDS OF THE COURT: Unfair Labor Practice Strikes "Under [the NLRA], unfair labor practices strikers are entitled to immediate reinstatement with back pay once they unconditionally offer to return to work, whereas economic strikers may be permanently replaced. An unfair labor practices strike does not lose its character as such if economic motives contribute to its cause, however; it remains an unfair labor practices strike so long as the employees are motivated in part by unfair labor practices. . . . In determining whether management–labor cooperation has crossed over from permissible cooperation to unlawful coercion, courts consider a confluence of factors, with no one factor being dispositive. This nonexclusive list of factors includes whether the employer solicited contact with the union; the rank and position of the company's solicitor; whether the employer silently acquiesced in the union's drive for membership; whether the employer shepherded its employees to meetings with a prospective union; whether management was present at meetings between its employees and a prospective union; whether the signing of union authorization cards was coerced; and whether the employer quickly recognized the assisted union after the employees signed authorization cards yet exhibited prejudice against another union selected by the employees. . . . Normally a court defers to the credibility determinations of the NLRB unless there is some extraordinary reason why the court should ignore them, for instance if those findings are inherently incredible or patently unreasonable. . . . We conclude that substantial evidence in the record as a whole supports the Board's conclusions that the strike was an unfair labor practices strike."

Case Questions

1. Why does the court criticize MPS for recognizing the out-of-state union as the exclusive bargaining representative of the workers?

2. Suppose that MPS did recognize the local union and, subsequently, MPS and the local union negotiations reached an impasse over wages. Does MPS have any legal obligations to rehire the striking workers? Explain.

peaceful and not interfere with the operations of the employer. Picketing cannot be used to prevent or harass customers or nonstriking employees.

Unions may also call for union member and public boycotts of the employer's product or services as a method of pressuring management to engage in negotiations or concede a disputed point in a collective bargaining contract. If other unions recognize the boycotts, the economic impact on the employer may be significant.

The NLRA provides unionized workers with the right to strike and picket in a peaceful manner in front of the employer's facilities.

LEGAL/ETHICAL REFLECTION *and* DISCUSSION

In 2012, the possible demise of the Twinkie made national headlines. In January 2012, Hostess Brands Inc., the maker of Twinkies, Wonder Bread, Drakes Cakes, and other well-known products, filed for Chapter 11 bankruptcy protection, which would have allowed for a restructuring and survival of the company. After unsuccessful negotiations with the union, Hostess petitioned the court in November 2012 and was granted approval to close the business and sell its assets. Hostess asserted that closing the company was necessary due to skyrocketing costs and cited the Bakery Union's strike and collective bargaining agreements, which covered approximately 15,000 of Hostess's 18,500 employees, as the biggest factors.

1. Hostess faced growing competition and increasing costs and wanted to modify wages.

The unions resisted, and the company ultimately closed. The union was doing its job, yet thousands of people lost employment and thousands of tax dollars were lost to cities where plants were located. If you were a union leader, how would you justify this?

2. Unions arose at a time when employees were vulnerable and needed protection. Since so many state and federal employment regulating statutes have been enacted, and employer practices are so public through the media and the Internet, are unions as necessary as they once were?

Note: In March 2013, the Metropouloses, a family of entrepreneurs, were approved to purchase control of Hostess brands, which will allow Twinkies and other Hostess products to survive.

Illegal Work Stoppages and Boycotts

The term *strike* implies a statutorily authorized work stoppage under the NLRA. Other types of work stoppages (or slowdowns) are illegal, and employers may terminate employees, unionized or not, for engaging in illegal work stoppages. Most importantly, if peaceful picketing turns violent or union members threaten management, then the strike becomes an illegal work stoppage and union members engaged in that conduct are not protected under the NLRA. Other illegal work stoppages include:

- *Wildcat strikes:* When individual union members or small groups of union members go on strike for short bursts of time without union authorization, this is called a *wildcat strike.* Wildcat strikes are illegal, but sometimes the form of a wildcat strike is subtle, as occurs when a group of employees simultaneously use sick time to perpetrate a work stoppage or slowdown.

- *Sit-in strikes:* Any occupation of an employer's facility for the purpose of a work stoppage is illegal.

- *Strike during cooling-off period:* The NLRA allows a federal court to enforce a strike prohibition for a period of 80 days if a strike threatens national public health or security. During this cooling-off period, the government facilitates negotiations between the parties, and any strike during this time is illegal.

- *Secondary boycotts:* Efforts to increase the pressure on an employer involved in collective bargaining by directing a strike against a third party (such as a supplier or customer of the employer) is illegal. For example, suppose that Trade Union (TU) is at an impasse with BigCo. In addition to striking against BigCo, TU organizes a picket line in front of the headquarters of one of BigCo's main customers, SellerCo, with signs stating "Boycott SellerCo. They support unfair labor practices." TU's action toward SellerCo is a secondary boycott and constitutes an unfair labor practice.

Lockouts and Replacement Workers   Employers who are faced with the prospect of a strike have several options under the law. First, any employer that reasonably anticipates a strike by a group of employees may employ a **lockout** by shutting down the business and preventing employees from working, thus depriving them of their employment and putting economic pressure on the union's members before the union can do the same to the employer through a strike. For example, suppose that in the BigCo-TU negotiations discussed earlier the parties are at an impasse in contract negotiations in October. BigCo is concerned that TU may be waiting until BigCo's busy holiday season in December before commencing a strike in order to exert maximum economic pressure on BigCo.[41] Under these circumstances, BigCo is permitted to shut down its plant immediately, locking out union members, in hopes of driving the union to the bargaining table in an effort to reach an agreement well ahead of their busy season. Some lockouts are not permitted under the NLRA. Any time an employer lacks a *legitimate business reason* for employing a lockout, it may be an unfair labor practice. Additionally, any time a lockout is used for undermining the collective bargaining process or disrupting union organizing efforts, the practice is illegal.

> **KEY** POINT
> Lockouts are a permissible labor practice so long as a legitimate business reason underlies the lockout.

Second, employers who are subject to a strike may hire nonunion **replacement workers** in order to continue operations during the strike. When the strike is over, employers may either retain the replacement workers or discharge them (without liability) in favor of returning workers.

 Self-Check   Unfair Labor Practices

Which of these actions may constitute an unfair labor practice under the NLRA?

1. Management refuses to recognize a certified union on the basis that several employees in the union have presented a petition that indicates that 40 percent of the employees in the proposed bargaining unit oppose unionization.

---

[41]Based on the Supreme Court's decision in *American Shipbuilding Company v. NLRB,* 380 U.S. 300 (1965).

2. During a union-vote campaign, management throws an antiunion dinner banquet party and invites all employees and their families to attend. During the banquet, management gives speeches and points out the benefits of working in a nonunionized workplace.

3. During a union-vote campaign, pro-union employees distribute leaflets to fellow employees in the employee locker room as they leave the plant at the end of their shift.

4. Management at a school supplies manufacturing company is at an impasse with a certified union over contract terms. Because the managers fear that the union will call a strike just before their fall busy season, they shut down the plant and lock out employees.

5. Workers strike in a right-to-work state over stalled salary negotiations during collective bargaining. After the strike is settled, management refuses to rehire some of the striking employees. They assert that they must be rehired due to the state's right-to-work statute.

6. A certified union strikes over management's refusal to abide by the terms of an existing collective bargaining agreement. Once the dispute is resolved in arbitration, management refuses to rehire half of the striking workers.

Answers to this Self-Check are provided at the end of the chapter.

KEY TERMS

Employment at-will p. 332   Deep-seated common law principle that employers have the right to terminate an employee with or without advance notice and with or without just cause, subject to certain exceptions.

At-will employee p. 332   Any employee who is not a contractual employee; may be terminated at an time and for any reason except in cases where public policy is violated or the termination is illegally discriminatory or is prohibited by statutory or common law exceptions.

Contract employee p. 332   An employee who works under an agreement that defines when the employee begins employment and when the employment ends.

Whistle-blower p. 335   An employee or agent who reports legal misconduct or a statutory violation by her employer to the authorities.

Fair Labor Standards Act (FLSA) p. 336   A federal law enacted in 1938 and intended to cover all employers engaged in interstate commerce; mandates payment of a minimum wage, a maximum 40-hour workweek, overtime pay, and restrictions on children working in certain occupations and during certain hours.

Overtime compensation p. 336   A higher rate of pay for the hours that nonexempt employees work in excess of 40 hours in one seven-day workweek; calculated at one and one-half times the employee's hourly base rate.

Exempt employees p. 337   Classification of employees who are not covered by FLSA protections; generally consists of employees whose responsibilities are primarily executive, administrative, or professional.

Covered (nonexempt) employees p. 338   Employees who are protected by the FLSA and other statutes.

Pension p. 340   A retirement benefit in which the employer promises to pay a monthly sum to employees who retire from the company after a certain number of years of service. The amount is ordinarily based on the length of service and the employee's final salary rate.

Tax-deferred retirement savings account p. 341   A retirement savings plan in which the employee commits to saving a certain percentage of base pay in an account that is controlled directly by the employee. The funds grow tax-free until they are withdrawn.

Employee Retirement Income Security Act (ERISA) p. 341   A federal law enacted in 1974 consisting of a comprehensive set of laws and regulations that requires employers to make certain disclosures related to investment risk, thus providing transparency for plan beneficiaries.

Social Security Act (SSA) of 1935 p. 341   A federal law providing a broad set of benefits for workers, including a retirement income; funded by mandatory employment taxes paid into a trust fund by both employer and employee and administered by the federal government.

Federal Unemployment Tax Act (FUTA) p. 342   A federal law enacted in 1935 that established a state-administered fund to provide payments to workers who have suffered sudden job loss; funded through employment taxes shared by employer and employee.

Worker Adjustment and Retraining Notification (WARN) Act p. 343   A federal law enacted in 1989 to protect employees by requiring most employers with 100 or more employees to pro vide at least 60-day written notification of facility closings and mass layoffs of employees.

Workers' compensation p. 343   State statutes that provide an employee who is injured in the course of employment with a partial payment in exchange for mandatory relinquishment of the employee's right to sue the employer for the tort of negligence; funded through employer-paid insurance policies.

Occupational Safety and Health Act (OSHA) p. 344   A federal law enacted in 1970 that sets forth workplace rules and regulations to promote safety of workers and prevent workplace injuries.

Family and Medical Leave Act (FMLA) p. 346   A federal law enacted in 1993 that requires certain employers to give time off to employees to take care of their own or a family member's illness or to care for a newborn or adopted child.

Electronic Communications Privacy Act (ECPA) p. 350   A federal law enacted in 1986 that extends legal protection against wiretapping and other forms of unauthorized interception and explicitly allows employers to monitor employee communications on company equipment as long as this is done in the ordinary course of business or the employee consents to the monitoring.

Employee Polygraph Protection Act p. 350   A federal law that prohibits most private sector employers from requiring a polygraph test as a condition of employment.

National Labor Relations Act (NLRA) p. 352   A federal law enacted in 1935 that provides general protections for the rights of workers to organize, engage in collective bargaining, and take part in strikes and other forms of concerted activity in support of their demands. Also known as *Wagner Act*.

Collective bargaining p. 352   The process of negotiating terms and conditions of employment for employees in the collective bargaining unit.

National Labor Relations Board (NLRB) p. 352 An independent federal agency created by the NLRA and charged with administering, implementing, and enforcing NLRA provisions, as well as monitoring union elections for fraud and setting guidelines for employers and unions in regard to fair labor practices.

Labor Management Relations Act p. 352   A federal law, enacted in 1947 as an amendment to the NLRA, that prohibits requiring employees to join or continue membership in a union as a condition of employment. Also known as *Taft-Hartley Act*.

Right-to-work law p. 352   A state law prohibiting employers from requiring that employees join a union to continue working and that nonunion employees contribute to certain union costs such as the cost related to collective bargaining.

Labor-Management Reporting and Disclosure Act p. 352   A federal law enacted in 1959 that established a system of reporting and checks intended to uncover and prevent fraud and corruption among union officials by regulating internal operating procedures and union matters. Also known as *Landrum-Griffin Act*.

Collective bargaining unit p. 353   An employee group that, on the basis of a mutuality of interests, is an appropriate unit for collective bargaining.

Authorization cards p. 353   Signed statements by employees indicating that they wish to unionize and/or are electing to be represented by an existing union.

Election p. 353   A vote to elect or reject unionization by the entire bargaining unit.

Certify p. 353   In labor law, to recognize a collective bargaining unit as a union. The NLRB's certification process occurs when a legally sound election reveals a simple majority of pro-union votes.

Grievance p. 355   In labor la w, a complaint filed with or by a union to challenge an employer's treatment of one or more union members.

Strike p. 355   A concerted and sustained refusal by workers to perform some or all of the services for which they were hired in order to induce the employer to concede certain contract terms during collective bargaining or to engage in fair labor practices.

Picketing p. 355   A union's patrolling alongside the premises of a business to organize the workers, to gain recognition as a bargaining agent, or to publicize a labor dispute with the owner or whomever the owner deals with.

Lockout p. 358   The shutdown of a business by the employer to prevent employees from working, thus depriving them of their employment and putting economic pressure on the union's members before the union can do the same to the employer through a strike.

Replacement workers p. 358   Nonunion employees hired by a company in order to continue its operations during a strike.

Collegiate Banner Company (CBC) is a manufacturer and distributor of flags and banners bearing the names, logos, mottos, and mascots of American colleges and universities. Its products are purchased for retail sale by college bookstores as well as large-scale retail outlet sports equipment chains. CBC's administrative headquarters and sole manufacturing facility are located in different buildings on the same site. Its total workforce is 121 employees, with 76 employees located in the plant and the remaining 45 employees working in the office. CBC classifies its employees into two broad categories: administrative employees and trade employees. The breakdown is illustrated in the table below.

1. Name the FLSA classification (covered or exempt) for each position in the table below, and give your analysis for each classification.
2. Suppose that Falstaff is a plant manager and exercises his right to take a leave under the FMLA. When Falstaff returns, he is told that the replacement plant manager has increased efficiency in the plant by 30 percent and that he is being reassigned

Administrative Employees

Position	Primary Duty	Pay Range	Location	Number of Employees
Executive managers	Business planning and operations	$150,000 and above	Office	5
General manager	Hiring, supervision, and evaluation of professional staff	$75,000–$100,000	Office	10
Professional staff	Operational functions such as accounting, customer service, marketing, logistics, and human resources	$50,000–$100,000	Office	15
Support staff	Support managers and professional staff with administrative tasks such as scheduling, document and report preparation, answering calls, and keeping track of expenses	$20,000 (entry level) to $75,000 (president's administrative assistant)	Office	15

Trade Employees

Position	Primary Duty	Pay Range	Location	Number of Employees
Plant supervisor	Day-to-day supervision of line managers and employees in the manufacturing facility	$30/hour	75% plant 25% office	1
Line manager	Supervision of line workers in various sections of the plant; responsible for evaluation, efficiency reports, and ensuring quality control	$25–$30/hour	90% plant 10% office	10
Skilled tradesperson	Work involving use of specialized equipment for product designs and layouts	$20–$25/hour	Plant	20
Tradesperson	Line work of repetitive tasks required to manufacture the product	$12–$20/hour	Plant	30
Delivery truck driver	Loading and delivering of product to retailers or wholesalers	$12–$25/hour	Plant	15

as a skilled tradesperson because no other jobs are available. Has CBC violated the FMLA? Could CBC limit its liability by informing Falstaff that he is a key employee? What is the impact of key-employee classification in this case?

3. Assume that CBC management is concerned about productivity and hires a consultant to restrict its company computers from accessing certain websites in the month of March during the national college basketball playoffs. Has CBC violated the employees' rights to privacy?

4. Suppose that several employees are interested in forming a union. Which groups of people have sufficient mutuality of interests to form a collective bargaining unit under the NLRA? Can any administrative employees be recognized as a collective bargaining unit? Why or why not?

5. Assume that workers employed as tradespersons obtain sufficient authorization cards and the NLRB schedules an election. One of the organizers of the union effort passes out union fliers in the plant cafeteria during an unpaid lunch hour. The plant manager halts the practice on the basis that no union solicitation is permitted on CBC's property. Has CBC committed an unfair labor practice by prohibiting the distribution of the fliers? Suppose that the pro-union organizer distributed the fliers while the tradespersons were on the line working. Could CBC ban that practice? Why or why not?

6. Assume a union for skilled tradespersons is certified but CBC refuses to recognize the union. The union workers strike and picket outside of CBC's headquarters. They also organize a picket line in front of several Sports Outlet stores because Sports Outlet is a major retail store customer of CBC. Are these two pickets (one in front of CBC and one in front of Sports Outlet) permitted under the NLRA? Why are they different? If the union workers cease the strike and offer unconditionally to come back to work, must CBC reinstate them? Is this an economic strike? Why or why not?

MANAGER'S CHALLENGE

Companies that have a unionized workforce must incorporate union considerations into their business planning. Managers may be faced with difficult choices if union members are threatening to strike. Assume that you are employed as a general manager at CBC in the Theory to Practice problem and that the delivery truck drivers are unionized. You receive a voice mail from an executive manager informing you that negotiations over a union contract for the delivery truck drivers have stalled and that the union has threatened to hold a strike vote. She requests that you (individually or in small groups) compose a two- to three-page memorandum that describes the advantages and disadvantages from CBC's perspective of (1) a lockout, (2) a strike, with CBC hiring replacement workers, or (3) further negotiations. Be sure to address legal, ethical, economic, and employee-relations implications. A sample answer may be found on this textbook's website at www.mhhe.com/melvinleb2e.

CASE SUMMARY 12.1 :: Bonilla v. Baker Concrete Construction, 487 F.3d 1340 (2007)

COMPENSATION FOR COMMUTING

Bonillo was one of several workers hired by Baker Concrete to work on construction at the Miami airport. During construction, airport security required the workers to pass through a security gate and ride in an airport-authorized bus to the site. Baker Concrete paid the workers for being at the site from 7:30 a.m. until 4 p.m. Because of the security requirements, the workers had to arrive at the airport an hour early in order to get to the site on time, and their commute home was extended 15 additional minutes. The workers sued, contending that under the Fair Labor Standards Act they should have been compensated for time spent being transported to and from the employee parking area to the construction site.

CASE QUESTIONS

1. Who prevails and why?
2. Explain your analysis and construct a hypothetical situation in which the losing party may have prevailed.

OVERTIME

Mitchell was employed by the retail clothing chain Abercrombie & Fitch as a manager-in-training (MIT). As an MIT, Mitchell was scheduled to work a fixed, preset, five-day, 40-hour workweek and was paid an annual salary. Other than a high school diploma and general retail experience, there are no specific requirements for the MIT position. Mitchell's daily tasks consisted of a general exposure to principles in retail management, including human resource practices and operational tasks such as setting up displays. Mitchell's hours fluctuated from week to week, sometimes well beyond 40 hours, and she argued that she was entitled to overtime compensation under the FLSA.

CASE QUESTIONS

1. Given the stipulated facts, could Mitchell be considered a nonexempt employee entitled to overtime compensation? Why or why not?
2. Would your answer change if Mitchell was promoted to the position of manager? Explain.

UNFAIR LABOR PRACTICES

WinCo operates a grocery store in California on a 10-acre lot. In accordance with company policy, WinCo allows no solicitors on its premises except for allowing scouts to sell cookies. When a local union was campaigning for the upcoming election, nonemployee union representatives came on the premises and passed out pro-union literature in the company parking lot and in the employee cafeteria during an unpaid lunch hour. WinCo forced the organizers to vacate the premises, and the union complained.

CASE QUESTIONS

1. Does WinCo have the right to limit the local union's campaign activities on its property? What would WinCo have to prove in order to do so? Cite an example.
2. Would the union's actions have any impact on the upcoming election? Explain.

WARN ACT

Childress was one of 106 employees employed by Darby Lumber. When Darby was sold to a new company, the new company quickly ran into financial problems. As a result, the new employer informed the employees that there would be a major layoff. The next day Darby shut down its mill and laid off 88 employees, including Childress. The other 18 employees continued operations at the mill for several weeks until they, too, were laid off.

CASE QUESTIONS

1. Could the WARN Act apply to Darby given the stipulated facts? Why or why not?
2. Suppose the layoffs were for a period of five months. Are the law's requirements triggered? Explain.

COMPENSATION FOR ON-CALL TIME

Casserly and the other plaintiffs were employed as physician assistants at the State Correctional Facility at Canon City, Colorado. Each was assigned to a single facility for full-time duties requiring not less than 40 hours per week. In addition, on a rotating basis, each plaintiff was required to provide emergency medical services to inmates after regular working hours. During on-call periods, the plaintiffs were required to respond to any of seven facilities covering an 8-mile radius within 20 minutes of receiving a call. The number and frequency of calls received during any on-call shift were not predictable. The need to respond immediately to medical calls required the plaintiffs to maintain a constant state of readiness. They did not engage in recreational activities during these hours, nor did they use this time for their own personal purposes. The plaintiffs testified that they did not shower, walk for recreation, cook meals, eat in restaurants, entertain guests, perform yard work, or attend sporting events during their on-call hours. They could not be alone with their children. Some even rented motel rooms in Canon. Casserly and the other physician assistants were paid $1.75 per hour for their on-call time but were paid at one and one-half their regular rate of pay for the hours they were physically present at a facility responding to a call.

CASE QUESTIONS

1. Since the on-call employees had to remain in a constant state of readiness, was their time for their benefit or for the employer's benefit?
2. Are the physician assistants justly compensated by the $1.75 per hour, or are they entitled to one and one-half times regular pay under the FLSA? Should they be paid at the one-and-one-half rate even when sitting home?

FAMILY AND MEDICAL LEAVE ACT

Sullivan was employed by the USPS. In January 2009, he requested leave under the Family and Medical Leave Act (FMLA). In support of his request, he submitted a physician's certification that he suffered from frequent and painful attacks of gout in his feet and ankles that would require his absence from work for 5 to 10 days every month in 2009. A USPS committee, including the FMLA coordinator, reviewed the certification and decided to exercise the agency's right to obtain a second medical opinion. Sullivan was sent a letter notifying him that he was required to obtain the second medical evaluation. He was told when and where to report for the examination and advised that failure to appear could result in the denial of his FMLA request. Sullivan did not report for the examination. USPS informed Sullivan that his failure to appear was considered a failure to act in good faith but gave him an opportunity to explain his absence. He claimed that he didn't receive the notification letter. This reason was deemed not credible because the FMLA director had confirmed delivery of the letter. He was told that his application was denied and no leave would be approved in 2009. Sullivan still submitted 6 to 7 additional FMLA-leave requests in 2009 and approximately 14 FMLA-leave requests in 2010. All were denied for failure to show entitlement. He was disciplined twice for noncompliance with rules, and after 45 unscheduled absences for which he did not follow agency leave-requesting procedures he was terminated for failure to comply with the agency's leave regulations.

CASE QUESTIONS

1. Even though Sullivan supplied a physician's certification, did the agency have the right to require a second medical evaluation?
2. How could Sullivan have avoided the conflict and qualified for leave?

WHISTLE-BLOWER PROTECTION

Haynes, an animal keeper at the Zoological Society of Cincinnati (Zoo), was assigned to the bear and walrus area and was responsible for feeding and taking general care of the animals. Haynes lodged several complaints with her supervisors about the unsafe conditions in her assigned areas, but Zoo failed to address her concerns. One afternoon a co-worker, Stober, stopped in front of the den of a male polar bear and offered the bear a grape through the bars of the bear's cage. The bear pulled Stober's hand through the bars and bit off a portion of her arm. Haynes, who was with Stober when the attack occurred, gave a statement to authorities about the incident and blamed lack of personnel training and poor conditions inside the bear den as factors contributing to Stober's injuries. The next day Haynes was demoted to an entry-level position at the birdhouse and then, a few days later, was suspended without pay for insubordination. Haynes sued Zoo, asserting that Zoo had demoted and suspended her in retaliation for reporting alleged unsafe working conditions to authorities. Zoo countered that Haynes was a member of a union and therefore could not avail herself of whistle-blower protections that were afforded to other employees.

CASE QUESTIONS

1. Should Haynes be prevented from asserting a whistle-blower claim because she is a member of a union?
2. Could Haynes claim the public policy exception in regard to this termination? Why or why not?

 Self-Check **ANSWERS**

Exempt versus Covered (Nonexempt) Employees

1. Exempt. Computer programmers are specifically exempted by statute (despite the lower-than-$100,000 salary).
2. Exempt. Professional with advanced study and certification.
3. Covered. Hourly wage earner with repetitive work tasks.
4. Covered. See *Falcon et al. v. Starbucks* on page 338.
5. Covered. Nonprofessional with no advanced study or certification requirements.
6. Exempt. White-collar employees are likely to be regulated by state insurance laws.

Unfair Labor Practices

1. Unfair labor practice. Once an election has taken place, if a simple majority (51 percent) of the bargaining unit vote to unionize, the union is certified and must be recognized even if 40 percent oppose unionization.
2. Probably not an unfair labor practice. Management is permitted to campaign against unionization in such a way—so long as there are no financial incentives (such as bonuses) offered. Management may not threaten employees with pay cuts, demotions, or the like during the campaign.
3. Given that the workers are leaving at the end of the shift and that the fliers are distributed in the employee locker room, this is likely a permissible labor practice even though it takes place on the employer's premises.
4. This is a lockout. So long as there is a legitimate business reason, lockouts are permitted by the NLRA.
5. Right-to-work statutes protect workers only from having to join a union to guarantee continued employment and from having to share certain union costs. Right-to-work statutes do not guarantee anyone the right to a job.
6. Refusal to hire is an unfair labor practice because the workers were striking over an unfair labor practice (refusing to abide by an existing collective bargaining contract) rather than for economic reasons. See *NLRB v. Midwestern Personnel Services, Inc.* on page 357.

13
CHAPTER

Employment Discrimination

learning **objectives**

After studying this chapter, students who have mastered the material will be able to:

13-1 Define the term *employment discrimination* and articulate the origins of antidiscrimination law.

13-2 Explain the role of the Equal Employment Opportunity Commission (EEOC).

13-3 List and describe the protections afforded under the major federal antidiscrimination statutes.

13-4 Identify the protected classes under Title VII and explain why membership in a protected class is essential in an employment discrimination claim.

13-5 Apply three theories of discrimination and name the U.S. Supreme Court cases used to establish the standards for each theory.

13-6 Explain the concepts of a prima facie case and shifting of the burden of proof.

13-7 Describe the provisions of the Americans with Disabilities Act (ADA) and its impact on business operations.

13-8 List and describe the major defenses available to employers.

13-9 Apply the U.S. Supreme Court's standards necessary for a lawful affirmative action program.

13-10 Explain the role of state law in employment discrimination cases.

One of the most frequent legal challenges encountered by business owners and managers involves laws that prohibit *discrimination* in the workplace. Lawsuits related to employment discrimination have increased dramatically in the last 20 years, and managers frequently find themselves involved in employment discrimination claims as a witness, supervisor, defendant, or plaintiff/victim. Discrimination can be intentional or unintentional, and even a policy that applies to everyone equally can result in some form of discrimination. This area of law has developed very rapidly over the last 50 years, and the numerous statutes, along with standards and tests developed by courts to apply the rules, combine to form a relatively complex body of law from a variety of sources. In this chapter, students will learn:

- The definition, source, and statutory framework of discrimination law.

- Theories of discrimination and employer defenses.

- The role of affirmative action in the workplace.

- Additional workplace antidiscrimination laws imposed by the states.

DEFINITION, SOURCE OF LAW, AND STATUTORY ORIGINS   LO 13-1, 13-2

Recall from previous chapters that one of the major exceptions to the employment at-will doctrine, whereby employers may discharge employees with or without cause without triggering liability, occurs when a statute prohibits the employer's action. One of the major categories of statutes that prohibit employers from terminating employees is antidiscrimination statutes that bar any job action (such as termination) based on certain discriminatory motives. The term **employment discrimination** has a broad-based definition encompassing workplace-related discrimination that includes (1) the hiring process; (2) treatment of employees in terms of promotions and demotions, work schedules, working conditions, and assignments; and (3) disciplinary action such as reprimands, suspension, or termination. Historically, U.S. common law had recognized virtually no protections for employees from discrimination based on race, color, gender, religion, national origin, age, disabilities, and other characteristics. For example, until the Equal Pay Act of 1963, employers could arbitrarily pay men and women, doing the same work, at different levels with no consequences. One year later, Congress passed the most sweeping antidiscrimination protections for workers in U.S. history as part of the Civil Rights Act of 1964. In addition to federal statutes, legislation enacted in some states provides additional antidiscrimination protections in the workplace.

Equal Employment Opportunity Commission (EEOC)

An important part of the Civil Rights Act of 1964 was the creation of an agency to monitor employer compliance with the statute. The administrative agency[1] charged with carrying out federal workplace antidiscrimination laws is the **Equal Employment Opportunity Commission (EEOC).** The EEOC is a five-member commission whose members are appointed by the president with approval of the Senate. As an administrative agency, the EEOC uses its rulemaking authority, investigatory powers, and enforcement action as necessary to administer the statutory mandates established by Congress. The EEOC plays two important roles in ensuring discrimination victims' protection under various statutes. First, filing a complaint with the EEOC is the first step for a party claiming unlawful employment discrimination (procedures for asserting a discrimination claim are discussed later in this chapter). Second, in certain cases the EEOC will sue on *behalf* of an aggrieved employee. This is a powerful method of enforcing antidiscrimination laws because it gives aggrieved employees the full resources of the federal government, which can be particularly crucial when bringing an individual claim of employment discrimination against a large employer.

However, as a practical matter, the EEOC can pursue only a fraction of the claims that are made by employees. In 2010, 99,922 charges were filed; in 2011, 99,947 charges were filed; and in 2012, 99,412 charges were filed with the agency.[2] The agency therefore focuses on cases that have some important legal significance or that involve employer conduct that was particularly egregious or was in bad faith (e.g., attempting to prevent an employee's claim with a threat of termination or demotion).

LO 13-3 FEDERAL WORKPLACE ANTIDISCRIMINATION STATUTES

The primary federal antidiscrimination statutes are (1) **Title VII** of the Civil Rights Act of 1964[3] and its subsequent amendments, especially the Civil Rights Act of 1991;[4] (2) the **Age Discrimination in Employment Act (ADEA) of 1967;**[5] and (3) the **Americans with Disabilities Act (ADA) of 1990,**[6] which was last amended in 2009. The **Equal Pay Act of 1963** is actually part of the Fair Labor Standards Act but contains some antidiscrimination provisions as well.

These statutes may be categorized into two classes that are helpful in understanding their purpose: (1) laws that require the person in the protected class to receive *equal treatment* to that of nonclass members and (2) laws that require the person in the protected class to receive *special treatment.* For example, Title VII of the Civil Rights Act of 1964 requires women to be treated equally with men. In contrast, the Americans with Disabilities Act

---

[1]An administrative agency is a statutorily created body with responsibilities related to the formation, implementation, and enforcement of regulations intended to administer a federal law. Administrative agencies and law are covered in detail in Chapter 18, "Administrative Law."

[2]www.eeoc.gov/eeoc/statistics/enforcement/charges.cfm.

[3]42 U.S.C. § 2000e et seq.

[4]42 U.S.C. § 1981a et seq.

[5]29 U.S.C. § 620 et seq.

[6]42 U.S.C. § 12002 et seq.

(discussed later in this chapter) requires that persons with certain disabilities be given special treatment via reasonable accommodations by their employer, when possible.

To illustrate the contours of the federal antidiscrimination statutes, suppose that Prescott is seeking employment as an internal accountant and provides a résumé and supporting application materials to WidgetCo, a manufacturing firm with 50 employees. This hypothetical is used throughout the chapter to discuss possible scenarios involving various employment discrimination theories and defenses.

TITLE VII

LO 13-4, 13-5, 13-6

Title VII of the Civil Rights Act of 1964 and its amendments make up the centerpiece of antidiscrimination statutes. Even when interpreting antidiscrimination statutes that are not part of Title VII, courts often apply the antidiscrimination law using the Title VII statutory model and application procedures. Title VII applies to any private sector employer with 15 or more full-time employees, as well as to labor unions, employment agencies, state and local governments, and most federal government employees. The law covers a comprehensive set of job-related transactions including hiring and firing, promotion and demotion, disciplinary actions, work schedule, pay rate, job assignment, and other employer actions. Referred to simply as *Title VII*, the law prohibits discrimination in the workplace on the basis of an employee's race, color, national origin, gender, or religion. These classifications are known as **protected classes.** In 1978, Congress amended Title VII to specifically add pregnancy as a protected class as well.[7]

Protected Classes

It is important to understand that one fundamental tenet of federal antidiscrimination laws is that not all discrimination is illegal. Under Title VII or any other antidiscrimination laws, statutory protection is extended only to those who have been discriminated against based on their membership in a protected class. For example, in our Prescott hypothetical, discussed earlier, suppose that Prescott was hired by WidgetCo as an accountant. Prescott shows up on the first day wearing a T-shirt and blue jeans. His manager points out that his attire is not consistent with company dress policy and requests that he leave and return in more formal business attire. Prescott refuses to comply with his manager's request, so he is terminated. For purposes of understanding employment discrimination statutes, there are two important questions. First, was Prescott discriminated against? The answer is clearly yes. Prescott was terminated not for his poor performance but for wearing certain attire. Thus, it can be said that Prescott was the victim of anti-blue-jeans discrimination. However, the second question is more important: Was Prescott discriminated against based on his membership in a *protected class?* In other words, did WidgetCo terminate Prescott based on his color, race, national origin, religion, or gender? The answer is clearly no. Because this particular type of discrimination was not based

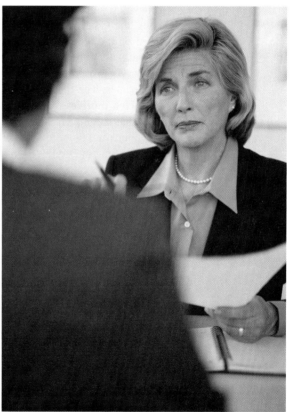

Antidiscrimination laws cover job-related transactions such as the hiring process.

---

[7]Pregnancy Discrimination Act of 1978, 42 U.S.C. § 2000(e)k.

on Prescott's association with a protected class, WidgetCo's discriminatory action (his termination) is not prohibited by Title VII.

It is also important to note that the plaintiff need not be in a *minority* within the protected classes in order to be covered by Title VII. While the majority of discrimination cases filed are based on discrimination related to a minority within a protected class, the statute protects against any discrimination based on association with a protected class and does not require that the plaintiff be a member of a certain ethnic category. For example, in *McDonald v. Santa Fe Train,*[8] the U.S. Supreme Court held that racial discrimination against white employees violates Title VII if the employer was motivated by race. However, there are certain instances in which an employer's preference for certain minority class members in an employment decision is *permitted* by an affirmative action plan (discussed later in this chapter).

> **KEY** POINT
>
> For an employee to be protected under Title VII, the employer's discriminatory decision must have been based on the employee's membership in a *protected class.*

Theories of Discrimination

For several years following the passage of the Civil Rights Act of 1964, courts struggled with having to apply such a massive statutory scheme in the workplace with virtually no comparable protections in the history of labor law to use as precedent. The result was that federal courts applied the statutes unevenly and variously, which resulted in overly broad or overly narrow interpretations of the law. Beginning in 1971, the Supreme Court began to develop guidance for the courts on how to apply Title VII. In a number of landmark cases, the Court developed several theories of discrimination that plaintiffs may pursue based on the type of discrimination alleged. These cases also provided the lower courts with a system of tests that are used to apply the various theories of discrimination. Thus, the three most common theories and attendant tests are sometimes referred to by their case names. The theories are (1) **disparate treatment** (*McDonnell Douglas*[9] standard); (2) **mixed motives** (*Hopkins*[10] standard); and (3) **disparate impact** (*Griggs*[11] standard). Note that subsequent amendments to Title VII have added statutory language consistent with the case law on disparate treatment and disparate impact. Nonetheless, the theories are still commonly referred to by their case names.

Disparate Treatment   Disparate treatment is overt and intentional discrimination. Simply put, when an employer treats an employee (or potential employee) differently based on her membership in a protected class, this constitutes discrimination under Title VII. This theory of discrimination may be proved through the use of either *direct* or *indirect* evidence. Direct evidence is evidence that proves a fact without any further inference or presumption. For example, suppose in our working hypothetical that Prescott is a woman who applied for the position at WidgetCo After the interview, the manager informs her that she will not get the position and states: "I think you are the most qualified applicant, but we prefer a man in that role, because this job may involve night work and I would be concerned about a woman's safety." Here, WidgetCo is treating Prescott differently based on a protected class—gender. Even though the manager's decision seems to be based on a true concern for Prescott's well-being, the fact that Prescott is being deprived of an employment opportunity solely because she is a woman violates Title VII.

---

[8]427 U.S. 273 (1976). The case involved a lawsuit brought by a white employee who was terminated for allegedly stealing from the company. The same incident involved a black employee who was also alleged to have stolen from the company but was given only a reprimand.

[9]*McDonnell Douglas Corp. v. Green,* 411 U.S. 792 (1973).

[10]*PriceWaterhouse v. Hopkins,* 490 U.S. 228 (1989).

[11]*Griggs v. Duke Power Co.,* 401 U.S. 424 (1971).

Overt and intentional discrimination does not have to be with evil intent. For example, in *Vaughn v. Edel*[12] a federal appellate court ruled that special efforts made by an employer to avoid a discrimination charge resulted in a Title VII violation. The case involved a black woman who, despite low productivity, was given satisfactory work ratings from her supervisor. The supervisor testified that he had intentionally overstated his satisfaction with the employee's performance on her annual evaluation because a top-level manager was concerned about a possible discrimination claim. Eventually, the company undertook a cost-cutting study that revealed the employee's poor performance, and she was terminated as a result of the study. The court held in favor of the employee and ruled that the employer's decision not to apply the usual evaluation procedures was a racial decision and violated Title VII.

However, as one could imagine, direct evidence of discrimination became increasingly rare in favor of a more subtle form of discrimination. In *McDonnell Douglas Corp. v. Green,* the Supreme Court crafted an alternative method of disparate treatment proof that plaintiffs could use to obtain relief under Title VII. This method of proof is usually referred to as the *McDonnell Douglas* standard, and it contemplates a burden-shifting analysis (explained below).

The *McDonnell Douglas* standard has three stages. In the first stage the plaintiff must establish a *prima facie*[13] case of discrimination.

To establish a claim of discrimination that satisfies the prima facie requirement under the *McDonnell Douglas* standard, the Supreme Court created a four-prong disparate treatment test that lower courts adapt to fit the type of discrimination at issue. The plaintiff must establish that:

1. She is a member of a protected class.
2. She applied for and was qualified for the job (or promotion, etc., depending on the factual circumstances of the controversy) and met the employer's legitimate expectations.
3. She was rejected by the employer.
4. The employer continued to seek applicants or filled the position with a person outside the protected class.

Legal **Speak** ›))
Prima Facie Case
Establishing certain evidence that is sufficient to prevail in a discrimination claim without proving additional facts, unless disproved or rebutted by the opposing party.

In cases involving types of discriminatory action unrelated to hiring or promotion, the appropriate prong is adjusted accordingly. For example, in a wrongful-termination claim, the plaintiff would have to satisfy prongs 2 and 3 (candidate was qualified and rejected despite the qualification) by proving that she was terminated by her employer despite qualifications and performance and that, following the discharge, she was replaced by someone with comparable qualifications who was not in the same protected class.

Once the plaintiff makes out a prima facie case, the second stage of the *McDonnell Douglas* standard requires the **burden of proof** to *shift* to the employer, who then must articulate a *legitimate, nondiscriminatory* reason for the discriminatory action. If the employer does provide a legitimate, nondiscriminatory reason for firing the plaintiff, the third stage of the standard

> **KEY** POINT
>
> As in all civil cases, the initial burden of proof rests upon the plaintiff to prove her case. Once the plaintiff establishes a prima facie case, a presumption is created that the employer discriminated against the employee. However, this presumption is rebuttable (refutable) because the burden of proof then shifts to the employer to provide a nondiscriminatory reason for the decision. If the nondiscriminatory reason is plausible and supported by the evidence, this creates a presumption that the employer is not liable for discrimination. The burden then shifts once again back to the employee, who then has the opportunity to offer evidence that tends to prove that the reason offered by the employer is a pretext.

---

[12]918 F.2d 517 (5th Cir. 1990).

[13]A Latin phrase meaning "at a first view," which, according to the authoritative *Collins Latin Gem,* is sometimes mistakenly translated as "on its face."

contemplates that the burden then *shifts back* to the employee to show that the reason given by the employer is not the actual reason for the employment action. A false reason under these circumstances is called a **pretext.** It should be noted that issues related to proving discrimination and pretext are *fact* questions for the jury to decide. In a disparate treatment case, the plaintiff is alleging intentional discrimination, the employer is asserting a legitimate reason for its action, and it is up to the jury as the finder of fact to decide which version of facts is more compelling and believable.

Suppose that in the Prescott hypothetical case she was African-American and was hired by WidgetCo as a junior accountant. After three years, she was promoted to senior accountant and given a pay raise. When a manager's position was posted a year later, Prescott applied and was hopeful that with her four years of experience and other qualifications, she would get the promotion. However, she was passed over for this position and for several subsequent openings for management positions. Eventually, she learned that two managers who had been promoted ahead of her each had only one year of experience and that all of the managers promoted ahead of her were either white or male. Prescott's disparate treatment claim under the *McDonnell Douglas* standard's four-prong test would likely be sufficient to establish a prima facie case because (1) Prescott was in a protected class; (2) she had applied for and was qualified for the promotion; (3) she was not promoted; and (4) WidgetCo promoted less experienced individuals. At this point, the burden of proof *shifts* to WidgetCo to provide a legitimate, nondiscriminatory reason for not promoting Prescott. Suppose that WidgetCo submits employee records that indicate that Prescott was late for work three times in the last two years and the company cites that as its legitimate reason. The burden of proof then *shifts back* to the employee/plaintiff to provide evidence that WidgetCo's reason is merely a pretext for discriminatory action. For example, Prescott could provide evidence of pretext by citing attendance records of others in the company to prove that a record of only three incidents of lateness did not disqualify other employees from bring promoted.

In Case 13.1, a federal appellate court applies the *McDonnell Douglas* standard for disparate treatment and provides an example of the burden-shifting analysis and when an employee must prove pretext.

Mixed Motives   Although the Supreme Court made it easier for plaintiffs to assert their Title VII rights under a disparate treatment theory, employers were being consistently insulated from liability from Title VII by asserting legitimate, subjective-based reasons (such as inability to work as a member of a team) to defeat a Title VII claim. Even when these cases involved unlawful discriminatory reasons for the employment action, so long as the employer could cite even one legitimate reason, the employee could *not* recover under a disparate treatment theory. To alleviate this problem, the Supreme Court articulated an alternative theory of protection under Title VII when the cause of the employment action was motivated by both legitimate *and* discriminatory motives. The mixed motives theory was articulated in *PriceWaterhouse v. Hopkins.*[14]

The case involved Hopkins, a woman employed as an associate at the global accounting and consulting firm of PriceWaterhouse (now PriceWaterhouseCoopers). Like many professional service firms, associates are eventually proposed for partnership in the firm after a certain length of time. Hopkins was proposed for partnership, and, as part of the process, the firm's partners were asked to write evaluations of Hopkins and make a recommendation as to whether the firm should offer her partnership. In general, associates who are not voted in as partners are either terminated or held over for reconsideration in the next year. Hopkins's evaluations were mostly positive, with partners praising

---

[14]490 U.S. 228 (1989).

FACT SUMMARY Aquino, a man of Chinese-Filipino origin, worked on a Honda assembly line. His time at Honda was tumultuous, and he had been suspended on numerous occasions for disciplinary violations. Upon returning from a suspension in 2001, Aquino was assigned to an engine installation station. Concurrent with Aquino's assignment, Honda experienced a number of cases of vehicle tampering and vandalism. A Honda manager conducted an investigation and concluded that Aquino was the only person with access to the tools necessary to conduct the vandalism. Upon Honda's complaint, Aquino was arrested, but the charges were eventually dropped due to insufficient evidence. Nonetheless, Honda terminated Aquino's employment after an internal investigation confirmed its initial conclusions on the matter. Aquino filed suit, claiming his termination was based on the fact that he was the only nonwhite employee assigned to the unit.

SYNOPSIS OF DECISION AND OPINION The Sixth Circuit Court of Appeals ruled in Honda's favor and dismissed Aquino's claims. The court noted that during the second part of the *McDonnell Douglas* analysis the burden shifted to Honda to prove it had a legitimate, nondiscriminatory reason to dismiss Aquino. The court reasoned that Honda's reasonable belief that Aquino committed the vandalism met this burden. The court also pointed out that when the burden shifted back to Aquino to show this was pretextual,

he could not offer any evidence of pretext. Therefore, Aquino did not meet his burden, and, as a result, Honda was justified in terminating his employment.

WORDS OF THE COURT: Pretext "McDonnell Douglas's third step requires the plaintiff to introduce evidence to create a genuine issue of material fact that (1) the defendant's stated reasons had no basis in fact, (2) the stated reasons were not the actual reasons, or (3) the stated reasons were insufficient to explain the defendant's actions.... Aquino attempt[ed] to meet his burden by trying to discredit Honda's stated reason through innuendo and flat denial. [He asserted] (but d[id] not introduce evidence to corroborate the assertion) that Honda manipulated the evidence of the incidents.... Aquino may or may not have been the author of the vandalism, but that is essentially beside the point; what the court must assess here is whether Aquino has introduced evidence that Honda's accusation (and therefore its stated reason) was baseless, malicious, or pretextual."

Case Questions

1. Why did Aquino have the burden of proving that Honda's reason for discharging him was a pretext? Didn't he already prove a prima facie case?

2. Considering the criminal charges against him were dropped, what would Aquino need to have shown in order to meet his burden that Honda's reasons for dismissing him were pretextual?

---

her role in securing a large government client. They also evaluated her as extremely competent, bright, and hardworking. However, a significant number of partners were concerned about her interpersonal skills. She was abrasive, shouted at the staff, and used foul language in public. Several partners, though, went further and criticized her using gender-stereotypical, demeaning comments, such as advising Hopkins to "act more like a lady" or "take a course in charm school." One partner even made a suggestion that Hopkins should "walk more femininely, talk more femininely, dress more femininely, and wear makeup" if she wanted to improve her chances for partnership. As a result of these negative comments, the firm initially opted to hold Hopkins over for one more year but eventually notified her that she would not be placed for a partnership vote again. Hopkins sued under Title VII using a theory of disparate treatment, but the firm pointed to the documented legitimate reasons relating to Hopkins's inability to work as a team member. In essence, the case involved both legitimate reasons for the job action that were mixed with illegitimate discriminatory motives as evidenced by the evaluations written by the partners.

Legal Speak ›))
Preponderance of the Evidence More likely than not. A lower standard of proof as compared to "clear and convincing evidence."

Ultimately, the Supreme Court adopted a new theory and framework for certain intentional discrimination: *mixed motives.* Under this theory, an employee is protected under Title VII in a case where legitimate motives are mixed with illegitimate motives if the employee proves the protected-class membership was a *substantial factor in the decision-making process.* Once established, the burden then shifts to the employer to offer evidence that it would have made the same employment decision regardless of the protected characteristics. In the Hopkins case, the Court held that Hopkins had met her burden of proving that gender was a substantial factor in the firm's decision-making process because the language of the evaluations was so closely tied to gender discrimination.[15] The Court also held that the employer's burden need only be proved by a preponderance of the evidence.

Disparate Impact

Even when an employer is not motivated by discriminatory intent, Title VII prohibits an employer from using a facially neutral practice (i.e., one that applies to all employees regardless of class membership) that has an unlawful *adverse impact* on members of a protected class. When it first announced this theory in *Griggs v. Duke Power Co.,*[16] the Supreme Court recognized that *intent* was *not* always a necessary element to prove discrimination and that certain evaluation techniques for employee selection, promotion, and assignment—such as written tests, height and weight requirements, educational requirements, and oral candidate interviews—could be administered uniformly to all candidates yet still impact certain protected-class members adversely. The Court ruled that some testing mechanisms operate as "built-in headwinds" for minority groups and are unrelated to measuring job capability.

The disparate impact framework is similar to that of intentional discrimination cases in that the plaintiff must first prove a prima facie case by showing that certain methods resulted in statistically significant differences that adversely impacted members of a protected class. To satisfy this requirement, the plaintiff frequently provides statistical data related to a testing measure. The EEOC's *Uniform Guidelines on Employee Selection Criteria* defines adverse impact as occurring when members of a protected class are selected at a rate less than 80 percent of that of the highest-scoring group.[17] For example, suppose that Prescott's mother is Cuban and, therefore, Prescott can be considered Latino in the national-origin class under Title VII. Prescott was required to take a test for the accounting position at WidgetCo Of all candidates taking the exam, Asian candidates faired best, with 10 of 20 candidates passing the test. Among Latino candidates as a group, only 3 out of 20 candidates passed. Because the number of Latino candidates who passed was less than 80 percent of the number who passed among the highest-scoring group (Asians), this would be important evidence in Prescott's disparate impact claim of discrimination. Once the prima facie elements are established, the burden of proof then shifts to the employer to provide evidence that the challenged practice is *job-related* for the position in question and is a *business necessity.* However, even if the employer shows a valid business necessity, the plaintiff may still prevail if he proves that the employer refused to adopt an alternative practice that would satisfy the employer's interests without having the adverse impact.

Despite the EEOC guidelines and federal court decisions, disparate impact is still a very thorny area of discrimination law. In Case 13.2, which received abundant media coverage, the U.S. Supreme Court weighed a disparate treatment claim by an employee in which

---

[15]In the majority opinion, Justice Brennan opined that "if an employee's flawed 'interpersonal skills' can be corrected by a soft-hued suit or a new shade of lipstick, perhaps it is the employee's sex and not her interpersonal skills that has drawn the criticism."

[16]401 U.S. 424 (1971).

[17]29 CFR § 1607.4(D).

FACT SUMMARY   The city of New Haven, Connecticut, administered an objective written examination to any fire department employee who aspired to be promoted. The examination was designed and administered by a professional testing service company that specialized in race-neutral examinations for police and fire agencies. In fact, when designing the examination, the company deliberately oversampled[18] minority firefighters to ensure that the results would not unintentionally favor white candidates.

Nonetheless, the results of the exam were such that white candidates had outperformed minority candidates. After considerable debate, the city discarded the test results, fearing that minority candidates who had underperformed in the exam would file a disparate impact–based lawsuit. Ricci was a white firefighter who placed highly on the promotion exam, and he filed a Title VII lawsuit against the city based on a disparate treatment claim. The city defended on the basis that it acted on a good faith belief that canceling the examination results was necessary to comply with Title VII's *disparate impact* provisions. The trial court and the court of appeals ruled in favor of the city, and Ricci appealed to the U.S. Supreme Court.

SYNOPSIS OF DECISION AND OPINION   The U.S. Supreme Court reversed the lower courts and ruled in favor of Ricci. The Court held that the city's action in discarding the examination results violated Title VII's prohibition against disparate treatment because all of the evidence demonstrated that the city had rejected the test results solely on the basis that the higher-scoring candidates were white. According to the Court, if

employers act in good faith to design a legitimate test to be race-neutral, the fact that the numbers come out differently than the employer expects is not, in and of itself, enough to discard the results of the test. Employers must provide some strong factual evidence that any discriminatory measures taken (such as discarding test results on the basis that higher-scoring candidates were of a particular race) were necessary to avoid liability. Such was not the case here, and, therefore, the city's actions violated Title VII.

WORDS OF THE COURT: Discarding Test Results   "[Employers] may not take the . . . step of discarding the test altogether to achieve a more desirable racial distribution of promotion-eligible candidates—absent a strong basis in evidence that the test was deficient and that discarding the results is necessary to avoid violating the disparate impact provision. Restricting an employer's ability to discard test results (and thereby discriminate against qualified candidates on the basis of their race) also is in keeping with Title VII's express protection of bona fide promotional examinations."

Case Questions

1. The employer in this case is a municipal government agency. Does this case apply to private employers as well? Why or why not?

2. Given the Court's ruling, what's an example of circumstances where an employer *could* discard the results of a promotion test?

[18]*Sample* is a term used in research studies meaning data from a cross-section profile of the population studied that represents the population as a whole.

---

the discriminatory treatment was based on an employer's concern over a disparate impact lawsuit that involved promotion examinations given by the fire department in New Haven, Connecticut.

Sexual Harassment

Because Title VII includes gender as a protected class, federal law extends protection to employees who are being sexually harassed. Unwelcome sexual advances, requests for sexual favors, and other verbal or physical conduct of a sexual nature are considered violations of Title VII if the conduct (1) occurs in the context of explicit or implicit conditions of an individual's employment or as a basis for any employment decisions or (2) unreasonably interferes with an individual's work performance or creates an offensive work environment. Generally, a victim of sexual harassment alleges one of two theories. In the *quid pro quo* theory (derived from the Latin phrase meaning "something for something else"), for example, the harasser demands sexual favors as a condition of continued employment or a prerequisite for a promotion or pay raise. More commonly, sexual harassment takes the form of a *hostile work environment.* Under this theory, a violation of Title VII occurs when the conduct of the harasser (or group of harassers) is of such a severe and crude nature that it interferes with the victim's ability to perform the job. Additionally, if the behavior is abusive and the abuse led the employee to quit, the employee is still permitted to bring an action against the harasser.[19] Note that this is different from a typical discrimination case in which the employer must have actually taken some adverse action for a violation to occur. While there is no formula for determining a hostile work environment, courts have deemed certain behaviors as a violation of Title VII. These include (1) initiating a discussion of sexual acts, activities, or physical attributes in workplace areas (such as the employee cafeteria); (2) engaging in unnecessary or excessive physical contact; (3) using crude, demeaning, or vulgar language; and (4) displaying pornographic pictures or movies. In determining whether a hostile work environment has been created, courts will generally require that the harassment be severe and pervasive. This means that if an inappropriate incident occurred but was not subsequently repeated, that onetime incident will likely not support a claim for harassment.

More recently, the U.S. Supreme Court has developed sexual harassment doctrines related to the liability of an *employer* for harassment committed by the victim's co-worker or supervisor, and the Court has also made clear that sexual harassment prohibitions apply to same-sex harassment. In *Faragher v. City of Boca Raton,*[20] the Court held that an employer that (1) failed to make employees aware of its sexual harassment policy, (2) failed to have any system in place meant to deter harassment, or (3) failed to enforce an existing policy could be liable for sexual harassment even when the employer had no *actual* knowledge of the illegal conduct. In that case, Faragher, a lifeguard employed by the city of Boca Raton, was subjected to a stream of harassment, sexual pranks, requests for sexual favors, and other crude behavior by her co-workers. Faragher made her supervisors aware of the harassment, and, in fact, supervisory personnel themselves engaged in occasional verbal harassment of Faragher. However, Faragher never complained to the city manager, who supervised the Beach Safety Division where Faragher was employed. Nor did Faragher's immediate supervisor notify the city manager of the complaints. Nonetheless, the Court held that the city was liable under Title VII because it had failed to distribute its policy on or make any serious effort to deter sexual harassment. Moreover, the city had no system in place where by Faragher could report the harassment, nor did it have any other policy enforcement mechanisms. Thus, the Court held the city liable despite the fact that the city manager did not have actual knowledge of the harassment. In *Oncale v. Sundowner Offshore Services, Inc.,*[21] the Court held that an employee on an oil rig who was subject to homosexual advances by his co-workers was protected under Title VII. The Court made clear that Title VII was gender-neutral and recognized sexual harassment as a form of discrimination regardless of the gender of the victim or the harasser.

> **KEY** POINT
>
> Although the *Ricci* case has many legal dimensions, its immediate impact on employers is that discarding results of a race-neutral employment or promotion test, even if done to avoid disparate impact liability, may give rise to a disparate treatment claim by affected employees or promotion candidates.

---

[19]*Harris v. Forklift Systems, Inc.,* 510 U.S. 17 (1993).

[20]524 U.S. 775 (1998).

[21]523 U.S. 75 (1998).

What is the best potential theory of discrimination for the plaintiff to pursue?

1. Lian, an American of Chinese descent, is employed as an architect in a large regional firm. His evaluations by his superiors have been mostly positive for two years apart from the consistent exception that he arrived late for client meetings on a frequent basis. On one evaluation, his superior wrote, "I thought Asians were supposed to be efficient. What happened here?" One month later, Lian is denied a promotion based on his record of "tardiness and other general considerations."

2. The city of Oz advertises for police officers. It requires that applicants be a minimum of 6 feet tall and weigh a minimum of 180 pounds.

3. Dothard applies for a position as a firefighter. She is excluded because she cannot lift the free-weight requirement mandated in the job description. Over the past five years, men have passed the test 50 percent of the time and women have passed 20 percent of the time.

4. Pettigrew, a woman, was an insurance adjuster at a company that had a rule that no adjusters were allowed to enroll in law school because the employer perceived doing so as a conflict of interest. The company was aware of several adjusters who were in fact enrolled in law school, but it did not act against them. Pettigrew enrolled in law school, and when the company found out about it, she was terminated. The other adjusters were all male.

5. Bronte was employed as a bookkeeper at the nation's largest toy store, where she worked with Barnes. Barnes had a reputation as the office comedian and, over the course of several months, had made various jokes related to Bronte's figure and recommended that she come on casual day dressed in sexy lingerie. Bronte tried to laugh at the jokes, but was in fact very upset about the remarks. When she confronted Barnes about the behavior, he advised her to "lighten up" and told her that he was equally sarcastic toward male employees. Bronte quit one day later.

Answers to this Self-Check are provided at the end of the chapter.

Figure 13.1 illustrates the steps in a Title VII analysis.

Remedies

Title VII provides aggrieved employees with a broad range of remedies to compensate for unlawful discrimination. These remedies include an injunction (a court order to cease from engaging in a particular unlawful practice or an order compelling a party to act), reinstatement, compensatory damages in the form of back pay, retroactive promotions, and requirements that the employer take certain actions in order to remedy

In *Ricci v. DeStefano,* the Supreme Court ruled that the city of New Haven, Connecticut, violated Title VII when it discarded test results of a promotion examination for firefighters based on considerations related to race.

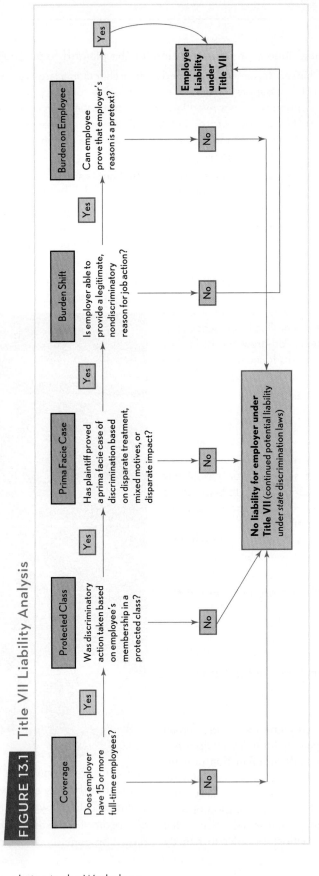

FIGURE 13.1   Title VII Liability Analysis

Coverage

Does employer have 15 or more full-time employees?

Yes

Protected Class

Was discriminatory action taken based on employee's membership in a protected class?

Yes

Prima Facie Case

Has plaintiff proved a prima facie case of discrimination based on disparate treatment, mixed motives, or disparate impact?

Yes

Burden Shift

Is employer able to provide a legitimate, nondiscriminatory reason for job action?

Yes

Burden on Employee

Can employee prove that employer's reason is a pretext?

Yes

No

No

No

No

No

Employer Liability under Title VII

No liability for employer under Title VII (continued potential liability under state discrimination laws) patterns or practices resulting in discrimination. Punitive damages (intended to deter future conduct of employers) are available only when a plaintiff proves that a private employer acted with malice, in retaliation, or with reckless disregard to the employment discrimination laws.

AGE DISCRIMINATION IN EMPLOYMENT ACT

Among the fastest-growing varieties of employment discrimination claims are those based on age. Under the Age Discrimination in Employment Act (ADEA), employers that have 20 or more employees are prohibited from discriminating against employees on the basis of their age once employees have reached age 40. The ADEA is similar to Title VII in that the protected employees are not entitled to special treatment but are included as members of a protected class when employers discriminate against them in favor of a *substantially younger* employee. Courts use a Title VII–based analysis for evaluating age claims. For example, *disparate treatment* under the ADEA requires that the employer's intentional discrimination against the employee based on the employee's age be proved using a modified *McDonnell Douglas* standard for establishing a prima facie case. Therefore, plaintiffs may make ADEA claims based on only (1) protected-class membership (40 or over), (2) satisfactory job performance (based on employer's legitimate expectations), (3) adverse job action such as termination or demotion, (4) replacement with someone substantially younger (or more favorable treatment to someone substantially younger), or (5) other evidence that indicates that it is *more likely than not* that the employee's age was the reason for the adverse employment action.[22]

If the employee makes a prima facie case, then the employer must present a nondiscriminatory reason for the adverse employment action. Once the employer presents the nondiscriminatory reason, then it is up to the employee to convince the fact finder that the reason the employer gave is false (pretextual) and the real reason is age discrimination.

The ADEA also acts to prohibit mandatory retirement policies. Exceptions are made for certain executives and those with high policymaking positions,[23] federal law enforcement officers, pilots, air traffic controllers, and firefighters.[24] States are also permitted to set defensible police and firefighter retirement ages.[25] If an employer can prove a BFOQ, discussed later in this chapter, age may be taken into consideration regarding mandatory retirement.[26]

Substantially Younger Requirement

If a plaintiff is attempting to prove age discrimination based upon the fact that younger employees are treated more favorably, then the plaintiff must prove that the younger employees are *substantially younger.* The federal courts vary greatly in their interpretation of what constitutes substantially younger, but many courts follow the general rule that the age difference must be at least 10 years in order to qualify as substantially younger.[27]

One important distinction of an ADEA claim is that it is irrelevant whether the younger employee is a member of the protected class or not. For example, let's assume Prescott is hired at WidgetCo and is 50 years old. He is terminated and replaced by another employee

---

[22]*Robin v. Espo Engineering Corp.,* 210 F.3d 1081 (7th Cir. 2000).

[23]29 U.S.C. § 631(c)(1).

[24]5 U.S.C. § 8335.

[25]29 U.S.C. § 623(j).

[26]29 U.S.C. § 623(f)(1).

[27]*Pitasi v. Gartner Group, Inc.,* 184 F.3d 709 (7th Cir. 1999).

who is 40 years old. Both employees are members of the protected class (40 years old and older), but because someone substantially younger has replaced Prescott, he may still pursue his claim by proving that the reason he was replaced was based on age discrimination. Suppose, however, that Prescott is a 69-year-old employee and is replaced by a 67-year-old employee. That age difference is not sufficient to make a claim of age discrimination.

The ADEA protects only older employees. In fact, the U.S. Supreme Court has said that the ADEA does not prohibit employers from discriminating against employees under 40 years old in favor of those in the intended protected class.[28]

Disparate impact claims under the ADEA, which do not require proof of an intent to discriminate, are rare, but disparate impact (similar to a *Griggs*-type standard based on statistical evidence of exclusion) was specifically recognized as an ADEA discrimination theory by the U.S. Supreme Court in *Smith v. City of Jackson, Miss.*[29] In that case, the Court held that the ADEA authorizes disparate impact claims but that the employer's burden to show the reasonableness of the business practice at issue is *minimal.* That is, the employer does *not* have to meet the higher standard of proof required in Title VII disparate impact cases: that the practice at issue was a *business necessity.* Thus, it is easier for employers to prevail in an ADEA disparate impact action than in a disparate impact alleging (for example) race discrimination under Title VII.

LO 13-7 AMERICANS WITH DISABILITIES ACT

One of the most significant federal antidiscrimination laws that impacts business owners and managers is the Americans with Disabilities Act (ADA).[30] The ADA was originally passed in 1990, but it was amended in 2008 to settle some of the more controversial court interpretations related to the *definition* of disability. Fundamentally, the ADA seeks to eliminate discriminatory employment practices against disabled persons that would prevent otherwise-qualified individuals from obtaining or continuing employment, being promoted, or obtaining benefits available to nondisabled employees. The ADA requires that employers with 15 or more employees make **reasonable accommodations** for a disabled employee in the workplace so long as the accommodations do not cause the employer to suffer an undue hardship.

Documented-Disability Requirement

In order to qualify for an accommodation, the employee must have a documented **disability.** The ADA defines disability as a *physical* or *mental* impairment that substantially limits a person's ability to participate in *major life activities.* Courts have ruled that certain disabilities, such as blindness, cancer, heart disease, paraplegia, and acquired immune deficiency syndrome (AIDS), all fit squarely into the disability category. However, the definition and interpretation of the disability requirement has been the subject of considerable uncertainty since the passage of the original version of the ADA. Because Congress did not specify examples of major life activities in the original ADA statute, courts and the EEOC struggled to establish appropriate limits.

In a series of cases beginning in 1999, the Supreme Court narrowed the definition of what disabilities were covered under the ADA and ruled that any condition that could be corrected, such as severe myopia causing poor vision,[31] was not a disability covered by the act. In subsequent years, the Court ruled that carpal tunnel syndrome was also not covered because it could not be considered so debilitating as to interfere with any major life activity.[32]

---

[28]*Gen. Dynamics Land Sys. v. Cline,* 540 U.S. 581 (2004).

[29]125 S. Ct. 1536 (2005).

[30]42 U.S.C. § 1201.

[31]*Sutton v. United Airlines,* 527 U.S. 471 (1999).

[32]*Toyota Motor Manufacturing v. Williams,* 534 U.S. 185 (2002).

ADA Amendments Act of 2008

As the narrow interpretation of ADA solidified in federal courts, Congress passed an amendment to the ADA that effectively reversed the Supreme Court's efforts to read the disabilities category as a narrow class of ailments. The ADA Amendments Act of 2008 (ADAAA) became effective for any ADA discrimination occurring on or after January 1, 2009. The ADAAA expanded the definition of disability with specific statutory definitions intended to urge courts to interpret the definition of disability "in favor of broad coverage of the individuals under this Act, to the maximum extent permitted by terms of the Act."[33]

Although the basic definition of disability under the original ADA was left in place, the ADAAA expanded the statutory protections to specifically cover disabilities that had been excluded from coverage by virtue of the Supreme Court's ADA case law the ADAAA includes a requirement that courts make a determination of one's disability without regard for the ability to correct the condition with "medication, artificial aids" and other "assistive technology." However, for an individual to be protected under the ADAAA, the plaintiff must still have a physical or mental impairment that substantially limits one or more major life activities.[34]

"Regarded-as" Test

Even if an individual does not meet the definitional requirements of disability under the ADA, employees may still be protected by the ADA under an alternative theory of the act known as the *regarded-as* test. Like the definitional scope of the disability requirement in the ADAAA, the regarded-as standard has been substantially broadened by Congress as well. The standard applies when an employee is *regarded as having impairment* by her employer (even if the impairment is not *actually* a disability). For example, Babak is diagnosed with a chronic medical condition, but the condition doesn't require any accommodation in the workplace. Babak applies for a promotion to supervisor but is denied because his manager is fearful that Babak's condition will limit his energy level and impact his ability to fulfill his role. Under the ADAAA, Babak would be protected by the statute even though his condition is not a disability as defined in the ADA. This is true because Babak's employer *regarded him as* disabled by virtue of his condition.[35]

Reasonable Accommodations

Once an employee has established that she has a covered disability, the ADA requires an employer to make *reasonable accommodations* that allow the employee to perform essential job functions. The ADA states that reasonable accommodations may include (1) existing facilities made readily available to individuals with disabilities and (2) job restructuring, part-time or modified work schedules, reassignment to vacant positions, and provision of readers or interpreters. Courts have held that accommodations such as installing wheelchair ramps, making training manuals or other materials available in oral form, modifying work assignments or a work schedule, and providing sound amplification are all reasonable.

---

[33]42 U.S.C. § 12002(4)(a).

[34]The statute also requires that there be "a record of" the disability. As one commentator has pointed out, this requirement is nearly obsolete and unaffected by the ADAAA. See A. Long, *Introducing the New and Improved Americans with Disabilities Act: Assessing the ADA Amendments Act of 2008,* 103 Nw. UL Rev. Colloquy 106 (2008).

[35]There is an ongoing debate as to the coverage of the regarded-as test in light of the passage of the ADAAA. This explanation and example are based on EEOC guidance and public information contained on the website. For updates on how the ADAAA is being applied by the courts, see this textbook's website at www.mhhe.com/melvinleb2e.

However, the statute does not require the employer to provide accommodations that constitute an *undue hardship* on the employer. The statute defines an undue hardship as one that would result in significant difficulty or expense in the context of the overall resources of the employer, the number of persons employed, the effect on expenses or resources, or the impact of the accommodation upon the operation of the facility. For example, Gant is disabled and unable to walk stairs. He is employed as an accountant in a local real estate firm that occupies a converted Victorian house as its headquarters. Gant informs his employer that an elevator will need to be installed in the Victorian house, because he occasionally needs to visit the upstairs to collect documents necessary to perform his job. It is likely that Gant's employer could demonstrate an undue hardship for Gant's elevator request. However, if Gant requests that his employer assign an employee to regularly bring documents from the upper floors to Gant's desk, this would likely be a reasonable accommodation.

The fact that an employer is required to provide reasonable accommodations does not mean that the employer must provide a specific accommodation demanded by the employee. If any of multiple accommodations would work appropriately, the employer is free to choose among them, taking into account cost and convenience.[36]

Federal courts continue to struggle to define the range of reasonable expectations and the limits of undue hardship in a variety of settings. In Case 13.3, the U.S. Supreme Court analyzed the reasonable-accommodations request in the context of professional sports.

EQUAL PAY ACT

In 1963, President Kennedy signed the Equal Pay Act (EPA) into law, making it illegal for employers to pay unequal wages to men and women who perform substantially equal work. Technically, the EPA is an amendment to the Fair Labor Standards Act,[37] and is therefore not always categorized as an antidiscrimination statute. Nonetheless, the EPA does prevent discrimination by requiring an employer to provide equal pay for men and women who perform equal work unless the difference is based on a factor other than gender.[38]

To establish a prima facie case, a plaintiff must demonstrate that (1) the employer pays different wages to employees of the opposite sex; (2) the employees perform equal work on jobs requiring equal skill, effort, and responsibility; and (3) the jobs are performed under similar working conditions.[39] If a prima facie case is established, the burden shifts to the employer to prove that the wage differential is justified by a preponderance of the evidence under one of four affirmative defenses: (1) a seniority system; (2) a merit system; (3) a system pegging earnings to quality or quantity of production; or (4) any factor other than sex. Equal Pay Act claims are often combined with Title VII claims of sex discrimination in compensation. Courts, however, have found separate essential elements and standards of proof for the two statutory claims.

Lilly Ledbetter Fair Pay Act of 2009

The Lilly Ledbetter Fair Pay Act (Ledbetter Act) effectively reversed the U.S. Supreme Court's decision in *Ledbetter v. Goodyear Tire & Rubber Co.*[40] In the *Ledbetter* case, a 19-year-veteran of Goodyear Tire & Rubber Co. sued the company when she learned that for much of her career male counterparts had been paid more for doing the same

---

[36]*Stewart v. Happy Herman's Cheshire Bridge, Inc.,* 117 F.3d 1278 (11th Cir. 1997).

[37]29 U.S.C. § 206(d).

[38]At the time of the EPA's passage in 1963, women earned only 59 cents for every dollar earned by men. Although enforcement of the EPA as well as other civil rights laws has helped to narrow the wage gap, disparities remain.

[39]*Corning Glass Works v. Brennan,* 417 U.S. 188 (1974).

[40]550 U.S. 618 (2007).

FACT SUMMARY   Martin is a professional golfer who is afflicted with a degenerative circulatory disorder recognized as a disability under the Americans with Disabilities Act (ADA). The disorder causes Martin severe pain due to an obstruction of blood flow between his legs and his heart. The Professional Golf Association (PGA) Tour[41] rules require that players in tournaments walk the course. However, because walking caused Martin pain, anxiety, and generally worsened his condition, he could not walk the course. As a collegiate athlete, Martin obtained a waiver for the walking rule from the National Collegiate Athletic Association. When Martin turned professional and tried to qualify for the PGA Tour, he requested that he be permitted to use a golf cart. Although PGA Tour rules prohibit players from using golf carts on the final two stages of the qualifying tournaments, Martin petitioned for a waiver on the basis that he was covered by the ADA. The PGA rejected his request on the grounds that it was not a reasonable accommodation. The PGA asserted that walking was a fundamental part of golf and waiving it for any reason would *fundamentally* alter the nature of the competition. They argued that the fatigue from walking is a critical factor in the outcome of tournaments. Martin countered by noting that even with the use of a cart he would be required to walk 1 mile during each round of golf and, because his disability causes him pain and fatigue, the use of the cart would not allow him an advantage over other players.

SYNOPSIS OF DECISION AND OPINION   The U.S. Supreme Court ruled in Martin's favor and held that the PGA was required to accommodate Martin's disability under the ADA. The Court found that because nothing in the Official Rules of Golf expressly prohibits the use of carts, the PGA's walking rule was not an essential part of the game. The Court also reasoned that the actual fatigue from walking four rounds of golf was insignificant (noting expert testimony indicating that walking the golf course burns fewer calories than are contained in one Big Mac). Thus, the Court concluded that waiving the rule for Martin would not fundamentally alter the game.

WORDS OF THE COURT: Reasonable Accommodation   "[The PGA Tour's] refusal to consider Martin's personal circumstances in deciding whether to accommodate his disability runs counter to the clear language and purpose of the ADA. . . . [T]he ADA was enacted to eliminate discrimination against 'individuals' with disabilities, and to that end, the Act requires without exception that any 'policies, practices, or procedures' . . . be reasonably modified for disabled 'individuals' as necessary to afford access unless doing so would fundamentally alter what is offered. To comply with this command, an individualized inquiry must be made to determine whether a specific modification for a particular person's disability would be reasonable under the circumstances as well as necessary for that person, and yet at the same time not work a fundamental alteration. . . . As we have demonstrated, however, the walking rule is at best peripheral to the nature of [golf], and thus it might be waived in individual cases without working a fundamental alteration. . . . Martin 'easily endures greater fatigue even with a cart than his able-bodied competitors do by walking.' The purpose of the walking rule is therefore not compromised in the slightest by allowing Martin to use a cart. A modification that provides an exception to a peripheral tournament rule without impairing its purpose cannot be said to 'fundamentally alter' the tournament. What it can be said to do, on the other hand, is to allow Martin the chance to qualify for and compete in the [PGA Tour]. . . . As a result, Martin's request for a waiver of the walking rule should have been granted."

Case Questions

1. Why was the PGA so reluctant to allow Martin to use a golf cart, especially considering carts are allowed in other tournaments?

2. Do you agree with the Court's reasoning that allowing Martin to use a golf cart during tournaments does not give him an advantage? Why or why not? Are there any scenarios in which it might and, as a result, would alter the fundamental nature of the game?

3. Given the Court's reasoning, would a request to double the size of the hole so that a partially blind competitor could see it when putting fundamentally alter the game? Explain your answer.

[41]The PGA Tour is golf's most competitive and lucrative professional competition.

work that she did. Although the Supreme Court did not deny that Ledbetter had been discriminated against, it ruled that she should have filed suit within 180 days of *receiving* her first unfair paycheck, not 180 days from the time she *learned* of the difference in pay. The ruling upended long-standing practice in courts across the country that had held that the 180-day-period begins when an employee becomes *aware* of his or her plight. Under the Supreme Court's framework, any employer that could hide pay discrimination for six months could effectively avoid liability under the law and leave workers with no recourse. Because pay information is often confidential, pay discrimination is difficult to detect. Thus, if employers are insulated from liability after 180 days, they have little incentive to correct pay discrimination. The Ledbetter Act declared that each discriminatory paycheck, not simply the employee's first check, resets the period of time during which a worker may file a pay discrimination claim. The Ledbetter Act therefore ensures that employees subject to wage discrimination on the basis of race, color, national origin, gender, religion, age, or disability have the opportunity to challenge *every* discriminatory paycheck that they receive.

CONCEPT SUMMARY Federal Employment Discrimination Statutes

- Title VII of the Civil Rights Act of 1964 applies to any private sector employer with 15 or more full-time employees as well as of the labor unions, employment agencies, state and local governments, and most to federal government.
- Title VII prohibits discrimination in the workplace on the basis of membership in a protected class. The protected classes are race, color, national origin, gender, pregnancy, and religion.
- There are three basic theories of discrimination: (1) disparate treatment (the *McDonnell Douglas* standard); (2) mixed motives (the *Hopkins* standard); and (3) disparate impact (the *Griggs* standard).
- Disparate treatment is overt and intentional discrimination and occurs when an employer treats an employee differently based on membership in a protected class.
- Under the *McDonnell Douglas* test a plaintiff must make a prima facie case showing that (1) the plaintiff is a member of a protected class, (2) the plaintiff was qualified for and applied for a job, (3) the plaintiff was rejected, and (4) the position was filled by a nonclass member. Then the burden shifts to the employer to show a legitimate nondiscriminatory reason for the action. Finally, the burden shifts back to the individual to show that the reason given by the employer was not the actual reason for its action.
- The mixed motives theory articulated in *Hopkins* protects employees when legitimate motives are mixed with illegitimate motives and an employee is discriminated against. Under this theory, the employee must prove that membership in a protected class was a substantial factor in the decision-making process. The burden then shifts to the employer to offer evidence that it would have made the same employment decision regardless of membership in a protected class.
- The disparate impact test articulated in *Griggs* prohibits an employer from using a facially neutral practice that has an adverse impact on members of a protected class.
- Under the disparate impact theory a plaintiff must prove that the evaluation methods resulted in statistically significant differences that adversely impacted members of a protected class.
- Title VII provides for various remedies, including injunctions, reinstatement, compensatory damages, retroactive promotions, and remedial actions by the employer.

- The Age Discrimination in Employment Act (ADEA) prohibits employers from discriminating against employees on the basis of their age if (1) the employee is 40 years old or over; (2) the employee's job performance is satisfactory; (3) the employee is adversely affected by the job action; and (4) better treatment is given to someone substantially younger.

- The Americans with Disabilities Act (ADA) seeks to eliminate discriminatory employment practices against disabled persons by requiring that employers with 15 or more employees make reasonable accommodations to allow the disabled employee to perform essential job functions, so long as the accommodations do not cause the employer to suffer an undue hardship.

- The Equal Pay Act (EPA) makes it illegal for employers to pay unequal wages to men and women who perform substantially equal work unless the difference is based on a factor other than sex.

PROCEDURES FOR ASSERTING A CLAIM

Federal antidiscrimination statutes prescribe a specific procedure for employees alleging employment discrimination. First, an aggrieved employee must file a **complaint** against the employer with the local office of the EEOC (generally within 180 days of the adverse job action). The EEOC then notifies the employer and commences a preliminary investigation. As an administrative agency, the EEOC may use its authority to obtain documents, statements from witnesses, and other evidence that will aid in the investigation. Courts have granted the EEOC wide latitude in investigating discrimination claims, including the authority to have access to confidential employer files.

During and immediately after the investigation, the EEOC is required by statute to engage in **conciliation negotiations.** This means that the EEOC has an affirmative statutory duty to make good faith efforts in favor of settlement of the case instead of a lawsuit.

If efforts at conciliation fail, the EEOC may choose to file suit against the employer on the employee's behalf or may decide not to take any action at all. After 180 days have passed from the time of the complaint, the employee may demand that the EEOC issue a *right-to-sue letter.* This letter entitles the employee to file a lawsuit in a federal court. Note that even though all employment discrimination claims must begin with the EEOC, ultimately the employee will have an opportunity to present his case in court. This is true even if the EEOC decides that the case has no merit and declines to investigate.

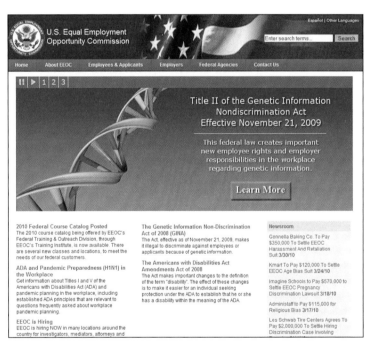

Employees alleging discrimination by their employer must first file a complaint with the EEOC, which then notifies the employer of the allegations and begins a preliminary investigation.

EMPLOYER DEFENSES

Earlier in the chapter, we saw that the burden-shifting scheme in a discrimination case is subject to the employer offering either a nondiscriminatory motive for the action in question or asserting a legally recognized *defense*. Each antidiscrimination statute has its own set of defenses, but there is some level of commonality among employer defenses.

Business Necessity

Perhaps the broadest defense to employment discrimination is when a business can justify discrimination on the basis that it is *legitimately necessary* to the business operations of the company. The **Business necessity test,** is a defense used to rebut a *disparate impact* claim when a certain practice or procedure has impacted a particular protected class. For example, suppose MovingCo requires all of its workers to be able to lift 100 pounds. During the application process, the applicants are required to pick up a 100-pound piece of furniture. After one year, the test resulted in more women than men being eliminated from job consideration. If sued under a disparate impact theory, MovingCo has a strong business necessity defense so long as the standard was applied neutrally to all candidates. Another common business necessity is a particular level of education, such as a requirement by an accounting firm that all of its professionals have at least a bachelor of science degree in accounting.

Bona Fide Occupational Qualification

Federal antidiscrimination statutes allow employers to hire and employ on the basis of religion, gender, or national origin in certain instances when the classification is a **bona fide occupational qualification (BFOQ)** that is reasonably necessary to the normal operation of the particular business or enterprise.[42] Note that the statutes do not allow race to be used as a BFOQ. The ADEA has a similar BFOQ defense. Although the ADA does not have an express BFOQ provision, the statutory scheme allows exclusion of persons with disabilities if the person, with or without reasonable accommodation, cannot perform essential job functions (a concept similar to BFOQ).

Classic examples of BFOQ classifications are religion for the employment of clergy and the use of gender to hire a movie actor. In cases that are not as clear, the employer must prove that members of the excluded class cannot safely and effectively perform *essential* job duties. Courts have held that BFOQ cannot be based on paternalism (protecting women from work in potentially dangerous positions such as mining, construction, or law enforcement). Customer preference generally is not a sufficient justification for a BFOQ. When an oil company refused to promote a woman because many foreign companies will not do business with women, the Ninth Circuit Court of Appeals stated, "No foreign nation can compel the non-enforcement of Title VII here."[43]

This rule is subject to qualification. When customer modesty must be protected, as in female locker rooms, or when the privacy of medical patients is involved, gender may be a valid BFOQ.

In Landmark Case 13.4, a major airline is sued by a male applicant who was denied a job because of a BFOQ in part created based on customer preference.

Seniority

Federal antidiscrimination statutes also provide a defense for employers using a seniority system as the basis for certain job decisions. For an employer to assert this defense, the seniority system must be based on objective elements of seniority (actual number of years

---

[42]42 U.S.C. § 2000e-2(e).

[43]*Fernandez v. Wynn Oil Co.*, 653 F.2d 1273 (9th Cir. 1981).

FACT SUMMARY   Diaz was denied a job as a flight attendant with Pan American Airlines because the airline had a policy that only a woman could be hired as a flight attendant. Diaz filed a complaint with EEOC, alleging that Pan Am's policy was a violation of Title VII because he faced hiring discrimination based on his gender. Pan Am argued that gender was a bona fide occupational qualification (BFOQ) for the position because expert studies had determined that women were better in nontechnical aspects of the job, such as reassuring anxious passengers. Pan Am also argued that passengers preferred women as flight attendants and that customer preference in this case should also be considered as part of its BFOQ defense. The trial court found for Pan Am.

SYNOPSIS OF DECISION AND OPINION   The Court of Appeals for the Fifth Circuit reversed the trial court's ruling and held in favor of Diaz. The court rejected Pan Am's arguments and ruled that the EEOC guidelines require that BFOQ defenses based on gender be interpreted narrowly. In this case, the court held that Pan Am's assertion that women were better in nontechnical aspects of the job may be important but is not directly relevant in a BFOQ analysis. Similarly, the court also ruled that customer preference for a certain gender is not consistent with EEOC's guidelines.

WORDS OF THE COURT: Sex Discrimination and Customer Preference   "The primary function of an airline is to transport passengers safely from one point to another. While a pleasant environment, enhanced

by the obvious cosmetic effect that female stewardesses provide as well as, according to the finding of the trial court, their apparent ability to perform the non-mechanical functions of the job in a more effective manner than most men, may all be important, they are tangential to the essence of the business involved. No one has suggested that having male stewards will so seriously affect the operation of an airline as to jeopardize or even minimize its ability to provide safe transportation from one place to another.

"Similarly, we do not feel that the fact that Pan Am's passengers prefer female stewardesses should alter our judgment. On this subject, EEOC guidelines state that a BFOQ ought not be based on 'the refusal to hire an individual because of the preferences of co-workers, the employer, clients or customers.'"

Case Questions

1. If customers truly overwhelmingly prefer one gender over another in certain jobs, is it fair or appropriate to force the public to be uncomfortable or unhappy in order to prevent sexual discrimination?

2. Why did the court decide that sex was not a BFOQ to qualify as a flight attendant?

3. Would the decision be the same if, instead of sex, the BFOQ was based on race, national origin, or religion? Why or why not?

4. Whether sex discrimination can be a BFOQ is interpreted narrowly by the EEOC, whose guidelines were adopted by the circuit court. Identify situations in which sex could be defended successfully as a BFOQ.

---

on the job) and the employment decisions must have been made in good faith and pursuant to that established objective system. The employee/plaintiff has the burden of proving improper motivation behind the employer's adoption or use of the system.

Employee Misconduct

Employers are not required to overlook misconduct when complying with antidiscrimination statutes. When an employee commits an act of misconduct, so long as that act has been identified to the employee as misconduct, employers may discipline the employee in accordance with the company's general practices without liability for discrimination. If the employer's practices and procedures are set forth in a workplace publication (usually in the employee handbook or a similar company document), misconduct is a powerful defense. The U.S. Supreme Court has even extended that protection to employers when the employer discovered the misconduct *after* the adverse employment action.[44] So long as the employer shows that the misconduct was sufficiently grave as to warrant the adverse employment action (such as termination for theft of a petty cash account), employers may use after-acquired evidence of misconduct as a defense.

LO 13-9   ## AFFIRMATIVE ACTION PROGRAMS

Affirmative action as it is understood today includes, but goes beyond, outreach attempts to recruit minority applicants, special training programs, and the reevaluation of the effect of selection criteria. Affirmative action in employment began during World War II when President Franklin D. Roosevelt issued an executive order banning racial, religious, and gender discrimination in the defense industry. Executive Order 11246,[46] issued by President Lyndon B. Johnson in 1965, extended affirmative action's reach by requiring that employers who have a contract with the federal government for services and supplies initiate good faith efforts to implement an affirmative action plan in their companies. Although most employers are not subject to the executive order, social pressures and/or threat of litigation has induced many employers to adopt voluntary affirmative action plans. Affirmative action may also be imposed on an employer by courts as a judicial remedy when they find that the employer acted in a pattern of egregious discrimination against employees.

LEGAL/ETHICAL REFLECTION *and* DISCUSSION

In *Ludtke v. Kuhn*,[47] Ludtke, a female accredited sports reporter, sued Major League Baseball (MLB) and the New York Yankees to gain rights to access the Yankees' locker room. She asserted that she was denied information available to male reporters and this impacted her ability to do her job. MLB and the Yankees claimed that if woman were allowed in the locker room, the players' privacy and modesty would be improperly affected and the wholesome image of baseball would be impacted. Ludtke prevailed, and now men's locker rooms are open to both sexes in all sports. Certain personal areas and showers are still restricted for all reporters. Male reporters are not permitted in women's locker rooms.

1. Do you agree with this decision?

2. Does this mean that women are entitled to more privacy than men?

3. It is an accepted BFOQ that spas and health clubs may still require same-sex attendants. Why should such a distinction be made?

4. Should male reporters have the same equal opportunity and be permitted into female sports locker rooms? Why or why not?

5. Professional soccer, basketball, and football teams had already permitted female access to their locker rooms prior to this suit, and male sports reporters supported the right of women to have equal access. Should these facts affect your decision?

[47]461 F. Supp. 86 (S.D.N.Y. 1978).

---

[44]*McKennon v. Nashville Banner Publishing Co.*, 513 U.S. 352 (1995).

[45]*Coleman v. Donahoe*, 667 F.3d 835 (7th Cir. 2012)

[46]41 CFR § 60.1, § 60.2.

Legality

Although federal antidiscrimination statutes do not require employers to give preferential treatment to minority employees, the Supreme Court has upheld the constitutionality of Executive Order 11246 and has allowed certain affirmative action plans to apply to private employers as a condition to a contract with the federal government. State and local governments soon followed suit with affirmative action plans aimed at addressing inequalities in the workplace and in education.[48] Affirmative action does not require absolute equality. Companies must work to ensure that their employee workforce reflects the available qualified workforce with respect to race and gender. Therefore, a local company in a city whose population is 75 percent white and 25 percent black (assuming all are qualified) may have an employee workforce that is 75 percent white and 25 percent black. As long as the company advertises openings properly and conducts legal and appropriate hiring policies, the company is in compliance. Should a discrepancy exist, a company may be approved, through a plan, to allow preferences in hiring until the proper goal is met. In *Adarand Constructors, Inc. v. Pena,*[49] the Supreme Court ruled that state and local government affirmative action plans in race-based or gender-based preferences for hiring contractors would be subject to the *strict scrutiny* standard. Recall from Chapter 2, "Business and the Constitution," that the strict scrutiny standard is the highest level of scrutiny and more often than not results in a finding of unconstitutionality. However, the Court's ruling made clear that a state and local government affirmative action program is constitutional so long as it (1) attempts to remedy an actual past practice of discrimination and (2) does not employ a system of quotas (e.g., hiring according to a mathematical formula based on race). One of the most misunderstood issues under affirmative action involves quotas. Many businesses and organizations wrongly adopted mathematical quotas as a simplistic means of compliance; however, the Supreme Court has ruled that the strict use of quotas not only is prohibited under affirmative action but is unconstitutional.[50]

STATE ANTIDISCRIMINATION STATUTES

LO 13-10

In addition to complying with federal antidiscrimination statutes, certain employers are also subject to regulation under a state antidiscrimination statutory scheme. Each state has its own statutes that are often modeled after the federal statutes (although they have different titles, such as the Human Relations Act). In addition, states also have their own administrative agencies (modeled after the EEOC) charged with enforcing and adjudicating discrimination cases.

State antidiscrimination statutes sometimes differ substantially from federal laws in two ways that impact business owners and managers. First, state statutes tend to cover more employers, with some states imposing antidiscrimination statutes on small businesses with just *one* employee. Many federal statutes cover only employers (unions, etc.) with 15 or more employees. Second, while federal statutes are relatively conservative in exactly

---

[48]The Supreme Court decided several cases specifically related to admissions by state-sponsored universities beginning in 1978. Most recently, in *Gruttinger v. Bollinger,* 539 U.S. 306 (2003), the Court held that affirmative action in admissions is constitutional so long as the minority status of the applicant is used as a plus factor and not in accordance with a rigid formula reserving certain seats for minority applicants.

[49]515 U.S. 200 (1995).

[50]*Wygant v. Jackson Board of Education,* 106 S. Ct. 1842 (1986): Laying off white employees to hire minorities to achieve the goal violates the Equal Protection Clause; and *Regents of the University of California v. Bakke,* 438 U.S. 265 (1978): A medical school's strict racial admission quota violated the Fourteenth Amendment.

what constitutes a protected class, some states have expanded protected-class membership, most notably to discrimination based on sexual orientation or gender transformation. In Case 13.5, a state appellate court compares New Jersey's state statutory antidiscrimination protections with the protections under Title VII.

CASE 13.5 Enriquez v. West Jersey Health Systems, 777 A.2d 365 (N.J. Super. Ct. App. Div. 2001)

FACT SUMMARY Enriquez, a biological male, was hired as a medical director for an outpatient treatment center operated by West Jersey Health Systems. Soon after his employment began, Enriquez began an external transformation from male to female. This transformation was a result of Enriquez's gender identity disorder. During the transformation, Enriquez was approached by co-workers and managers who voiced discomfort with her transformation. A Health Systems manager, citing Enriquez's obligation to contribute to a productive work atmosphere, requested that Enriquez halt the transformation process and go back to her prior appearance. When her contract came up for renewal, Enriquez was told that her contract would not be renewed unless she ceased the transformation. After Enriquez refused, her contract was not renewed and she was informed that the termination was permanent. After the termination, Enriquez completed the surgical portion of her transformation.

SYNOPSIS OF DECISION AND OPINION The New Jersey Superior Court found for Enriquez. The court held that while Title VII does not bar discrimination based on sexual orientation or gender identity disorders, New Jersey's Law Against Discrimination (LAD) does. The court reasoned that since the LAD makes it unlawful to discriminate against someone based upon sex and affectional or sexual orientation, individuals who were transsexual or affected by a gender identity disorder were also considered to be members of a protected class and were protected from discrimination.

WORDS OF THE COURT: Coverage under LAD "Title VII of the Civil Rights Act of 1964 does not

contain language barring discrimination based on one's affectional or sexual orientation. Moreover, the federal courts construing Title VII have unanimously concluded that discrimination on the basis of gender dysphoria is not sex discrimination. Basically, the federal courts conclude that discrimination on the basis of sex outlaws discrimination against women because they are women, and against men because they are men. . . . We disagree with [this] rationale. . . . A person who is discriminated against because he changes his gender from male to female is being discriminated against because he or she is a member of a very small minority whose condition remains incomprehensible to most individuals. . . . It is incomprehensible to us that our Legislature would ban discrimination against heterosexual men and women; against homosexual men and women; against bisexual men and women; against men and women who are perceived, presumed or identified by others as not conforming to the stereotypical notions of how men and women behave, but would condone discrimination against men or women who seek to change their anatomical sex because they suffer from a gender identity disorder. We conclude that sex discrimination under the LAD includes gender discrimination so as to protect plaintiff from gender stereotyping and discrimination for transforming herself from a man to a woman."

Case Questions

1. Why couldn't this case have been covered by Title VII on the basis of gender?

2. If Enriquez's employment with Health Systems were not terminated, would she still have a claim for discrimination? Would the conduct of her co-workers and managers have been sufficient to prevail on a discrimination suit? Why or why not?

Employment discrimination p. 367 Workplace-related discrimination in the hiring process and treatment of employees; encompasses everything from promotions and demotions to work schedules, working conditions, and disciplinary measures.

Equal Employment Opportunity Commission (EEOC) p. 368 A five-member federal administrative agency that administers congressional mandates that ensure adequate protection for victims of discrimination; accepts and investigates worker complaints and, in certain cases, will sue on behalf of employees.

Title VII p. 368 The section of the Civil Rights Act of 1964 that serves as the centerpiece of antidiscrimination law; covers a comprehensive set of job-related transactions and prohibits discrimination in the workplace on the basis of an employee's race, color, national origin, gender, religion, or pregancy. The law applies to any private sector employer with 15 or more full-time employees and to unions, employment agencies, state and local governments, and most of the federal government.

Age Discrimination in Employment Act (ADEA) of 1967 p. 368 A federal statute that prohibits employers from discriminating against employees on the basis of their age once employees have reached age 40.

Americans with Disabilities Act (ADA) of 1990 p. 368 A federal statute that seeks to eliminate discriminatory employment practices against disabled persons; requires that employers with 15 or more employees make reasonable accommodations for a disabled employee in the workplace as long as the accommodations do not cause the employer to suffer an undue hardship.

Equal Pay Act of 1963 p. 368 A federal statute that makes it illegal for employers to pay unequal wages to men and women who perform substantially equal work.

Protected classes p. 369 The classifications of individuals that are specified in Title VII, including color, race, national origin, religion, gender, and pregnancy.

Disparate treatment p. 370 Theory of employment discrimination predicated on overt and intentional discrimination; includes being treated differently because of one's membership in a protected class.

Mixed motives p. 370 Theory of employment discrimination in which the cause of the adverse employment action was motivated by both legitimate and discriminatory motives.

Disparate impact p. 370 Theory of employment discrimination in which employee evaluation techniques that are not themselves discriminatory have a different and adverse impact on members of a protected class.

Burden of proof p. 371 A party's duty to prove a disputed assertion or charge.

Pretext p. 372 A false reason offered to justify an action.

Reasonable accommodations p. 380 Accommodations, required under the Americans with Disabilities Act, that allow disabled individuals to adequately perform essential job functions.

Disability p. 380 A physical or mental impairment that substantially limits a person's ability to participate in major life activities.

Complaint p. 385 A form that an aggrieved employee files against his employer with the EEOC that details how the employee was discriminated against.

Conciliation negotiations p. 385 The required attempts by the EEOC to settle a discrimination case instead of filing a lawsuit.

Business necessity test p. 386 A defense used to rebut disparate impact claims when a business can prove that a certain skill, ability, or procedure is absolutely necessary to the operation of the business. Discrimination is permitted even if a protected class is adversely affected.

Bona fide occupational qualification (BFOQ) p. 386 A provision in certain federal antidiscrimination statutes that allows discrimination based on religion, gender, or national origin when it can be shown that such discrimination is reasonably necessary to the business operation.

Affirmative action p. 388 An action plan designed to maintain equal employment opportunities and to remedy past employment discrimination of women, persons of color, persons with disabilities, and other underutilized protected classes.

Hudson runs a successful business operation called Cleaning Inc. and employs a workforce of over 100 people in various positions. The company has contracts with several companies to provide office-cleaning services. One employee, Curt, had been with the company for almost two years when he applied for a supervisory position. The position involved higher pay and better benefits. Although he was qualified to be a site supervisor, Curt was not promoted. Cleaning Inc. explained that *only* a woman could be hired because the position involved regular searches of the women employees' locker room to look for any items reported stolen from cleaning sites.

1. If Curt files suit against Cleaning Inc. for discrimination, what statute will he be relying on and what is his probable theory of discrimination?

2. What would Curt need to prove in order to shift the burden to Cleaning Inc.?

3. What is the company's best defense to a charge of discrimination?

4. In order to file the complaint against Cleaning Inc., what procedures must Curt follow? May he file a lawsuit immediately?

5. Assume that Curt was not promoted because he was undergoing a series of sex change procedures and that other employees were uncomfortable with him. Is Curtis protected under federal antidiscrimination statutes? Why or why not?

6. Same facts as in Question 5, but assume Curtis filed suit in a state that had a statute similar to New Jersey's antidiscrimination law (as seen in the *Enriquez v. West Jersey Health Systems* case). Would Curtis be covered under the state law? Why or why not?

Recall from page 376 that employers may be liable for sexual harassment under the *Faragher* case when the employer has not taken affirmative steps to deter harassment or failed to have a structure in place to enforce sexual harassment policies, such as a system for deterring and reporting sexual harassment. Assume you are a manager at Cleaning Inc. (as in the Theory to Practice problem) and you receive the following e-mail from the company's vice president of operations:

I just read an article about a company that was sued under the sexual harassment laws. I know we have a good policy, but we need a system in place for claims and compliance. Please draft a two- to three-page memorandum that outlines how to implement a system that will (1) help deter sexual harassment, (2) ensure that our policy is well known by the employees, and (3) provide a procedure for initiating and investigating complaints.

A sample answer may be found on this textbook's website at www.mhhe.com/melvinleb2e.

MISCONDUCT

Dumas was an African-American employee of UPRC, which employed him as a regional manager. UPRC, a rail freight company, was named in a discrimination claim by a co-worker of Dumas. During the EEOC investigation, Dumas supported his co-worker's claims by offering statements verifying discriminatory practices at UPRC. After the co-worker's claim was settled, UPRC conducted a routine audit that found that Dumas had falsified his track inspection records over a period of time in the past. UPRC immediately terminated Dumas.

CASE QUESTIONS

1. Does Dumas have a valid employment discrimination claim?

2. If so, what theories would be best advanced by Dumas?

ADEA

Harding was the CEO of Head Hunters International (HHI). After HHI was bought by MonsterCareers.com (MCC), the two firms were integrated. Soon after the merger, MCC informed Harding that his performance was lacking and he was terminated from his position. Harding later found out that Carey, a relative newcomer to MCC, was being promoted to his position. Harding, who is 51, alleged discrimination on the basis of his age because Carey is 42.

CASE QUESTIONS

1. Does Harding have a claim for employment discrimination under ADEA? Why or why not?
2. Would your answer change if Carey was 24, 39, or 45? Explain.

ADA

Barnett, a baggage loader for U.S. Airways (USA), injured his back while loading an inordinately heavy suitcase. His doctor diagnosed him with a permanently slipped disk and recurring back spasms. Barnett's condition is permanent, and he is considered to be disabled under the ADA. Upon returning to work, USA offered to reassign him from baggage loader to luggage deliverer, a job in which he would drive the baggage carts from plane to plane. However, Barnett wanted a position in the mailroom sorting mail. USA denied Barnett's request because it operated on a strict seniority system for filling vacancies.

CASE QUESTIONS

1. Does Barnett have a cause of action under the ADA? Why or why not?
2. Has USA fulfilled its duty of reasonable accommodation?

STATE ANTIDISCRIMINATION PROTECTION

Hope, a homosexual who was infected with HIV, was hired as a cook in a youth correctional facility in California. While there, he was continually the subject of derogatory comments made by male guards and a supervising cook because of his sexual orientation. These comments were numerous in number and spoken in front of co-workers. Moreover, while other cooks received assistance in cleaning their stations, Hope received no such help and often his co-workers would throw their trash in his station. During his first five years of employment, Hope's medical condition never affected him. However, he eventually started to miss work because of the side effects of his medication, combined with the stress from the harassment he was subjected to. After informing his supervisors of his condition, he was put on administrative leave and later terminated for abusing sick leave policy.

CASE QUESTIONS

1. Is Hope a member of a protected class under Title VII?
2. Can he bring a federal claim for employment discrimination?
3. Suppose California has a state antidiscrimination statute that protects sexual orientation. Would Hope have a state claim for discrimination? Why or why not?
4. Had Hope not been terminated, would he have had a claim? Why or why not?

PRETEXT AND SEX DISCRIMINATION

Diane Schroer was a male-to-female transsexual. Born male, Schroer has a female gender identity, an internal, psychological sense of herself as a woman. Prior to changing her name and presenting herself as a woman, Schroer applied for the position of specialist in terrorism and international crime with the Congressional Research Service (CRS) at the Library of Congress. The terrorism specialist provides expert policy analysis to congressional committees, members of Congress, and their staffs and requires a security clearance. Schroer was well qualified for the job. She had many contacts around the world and held master's degrees in history and international relations. During Schroer's 25 years in the U.S. Armed Forces, she was a colonel and held important command and staff positions in the Armored Cavalry, Airborne, Special Forces, and Special Operations units and in two combat operations. She directed the U.S. Special Operations Command, a 120-person classified organization that tracked and targeted high-threat international terrorist organizations. She analyzed sensitive intelligence reports, planned a range of classified and conventional operations, and regularly briefed senior military and government officials, including the vice president, the secretary of defense, and the chairman of the Joint Chiefs of Staff. She held a top-secret security clearance for the seven years prior to her job application.

Schroer was the highest-rated of all 18 candidates. The selection committee unanimously recommended that Schroer be offered the job, which she accepted. Schroer then asked for a meeting and disclosed to Preece, the assistant director for Foreign Affairs, Defense and Trade, who was the selecting official for the position, that she would be undergoing an impending sex change. Soon afterward, Preece rescinded the job offer, claiming that it could take too long to have the necessary security clearance reissued, that there was a lack of trustworthiness because Schroer did not make her disclosure at the beginning, and that Schroer's contacts might not remain available to her. It was also believed that her operation would distract Schroer from doing her job. Preece never determined the effect of Schroer's sex change on her clearance and never checked the continued viability of her contacts. Schroer brought suit based on sex discrimination.

CASE QUESTIONS

1. What should Preece have done after being informed by Schroer of her imminent sex change?
2. Were Preece's reasons for rescinding the job offer defendable or a pretext for discrimination?
3. Is stereotyping discrimination based on sex? Why or why not?

RACE DISCRIMINATION

Bradley was a black male who worked as a delivery man for Pizzaco, doing business as Domino's. He was fired for noncompliance with Domino's no-beard policy. The no-beard policy was established nationwide by Pizzaco's franchisor, Domino's Pizza, Inc. Bradley alleged that he suffered from psuedofolliculitis barbae (PFB), a skin condition affecting approximately 50 percent of African-American males and causing half of those affected to be unable to shave at all. Bradley claimed that the no-beard policy deprived him and other African-American males suffering from PFB of equal employment opportunities in violation of Title VII. Domino's defended the policy, saying that it was common sense that the better its people looked, the better its sales would be. Domino's also stated that any exceptions would make the policy too difficult to enforce. A survey was introduced showing that 20 percent of those surveyed would react negatively to a delivery man with a beard. The EEOC contended that Domino's failed to show business justification for its inflexible no-beard policy, and the commission sought injunctive relief to enjoin Domino's ongoing policy. (Bradley was shown to have only a mild case of PFB and could have been cleanshaven, so he was found not to be entitled to relief and was not part of this suit.)

CASE QUESTIONS

1. Is customer preference a persuasive argument for this policy? Why or why not?

2. Is this a disparate treatment or disparate impact case?

3. What would Domino's have to have proved to successfully support a business necessity claim?

4. How could a manager allow an exception for an employee claiming PFB yet maintain the no-beard policy for other employees?

 Self-Check **ANSWERS**

Theories of Discrimination

1. Mixed motives. This is similar to the *Price Waterhouse* case. There are legitimate reasons for the denial of promotion (tardiness) mixed with potentially illegitimate reasons (based on national origin stereotyping).

2. Disparate impact. This facially neutral policy will have an unfair impact on women since the majority of women will not meet the height and weight requirements.

3. Disparate impact. Based on the EEOC guidelines, a disparate impact claim could be made because women are impacted in a disparate manner. The fire department must show that the free-weight requirement is a business necessity in order for it to be valid.

4. Disparate treatment. A neutral workplace rule (prohibition) was applied (or not applied) differently to men than to women. The *McDonnell Douglas* framework applies here.

5. Sexual harassment via hostile work environment theory so long as there is evidence that the behavior was so crude as to interfere with the plaintiff's job function and led her to resign.

The plaintiff was a janitorial supervisor who, while performing his job, ventured into the break room to clean and restock it. One of the company's employees had just put money into a vending machine, but her chips were stuck. She asked the plaintiff and a security guard for assistance. As they tilted the machine, the plaintiff felt an injury in the back of his foot. He had ruptured his Achilles tendon. The plaintiff's job did not in any way involve repair or maintenance of the vending machines. The plaintiff filed a claim for workers' compensation.

ENGAGEMENT QUESTIONS

1. Would it influence the decision if the vending machine featured a prominent sign stating that tilting the machine was dangerous and could cause injury?

2. Would it influence the decision if the employer had a written policy stating that vending machines were not to be struck, moved, or tipped?

3. Intended that "a reasonable jury could conclude that an employee hired to perform janitorial services is expected by his employer to assist other employees with problems they encounter in the workplace, especially in areas in which the janitorial employee regularly performs janitorial services." Do you agree with that statement? Why or why not?

4. How can a company protect itself from potential liability for injuries from conduct not directly or obviously an integral part of an employee's job responsibilities?

BUSINESS LAW SIMULATION EXERCISE 2

Employment Discrimination: John Falstaff v. Revere Furniture Company

learning objectives

After studying this simulation, students who have mastered the material will be able to:

1. Explain the legal doctrines that govern employers in the context of antidiscrimination statutes.

2. Interpret and apply the rules set forth in current case law.

3. Articulate a cogent argument for each party/side in the dispute.

4. Negotiate a tenable solution as an alternative to a judicial forum.

The chapters in this unit covered a variety of legal doctrines and rules governing labor and employment discrimination law as well as examples of how these doctrines and rules apply in the workplace. This simulation is designed to help you understand how the various topics covered in the employment discrimination chapter connect. By focusing on a simulated legal dispute, you will gain virtually real-world experience in applying legal doctrines and using analytical and critical-thinking skills. This simulation is a sequential decision-making exercise structured around a model in which the participants assume a role in managing tasks and work toward a tenable solution.

The simulation is structured in three parts:

■ Part 1 is a hypothetical fact pattern describing events leading up to a legal dispute in the hypothetical U.S. state of Longville, which is located in the jurisdiction of the fictitious U.S. Court of Appeals for the 14th Circuit.

■ Part 2 contains (1) a statutory excerpt from the actual Americans with Disability Act Amendment Act (ADAAA) and (2) two case summaries from hypothetical appellate courts, each of which provides a brief set of facts, several legal points, and short excerpts from the opinion itself. While these cases are hypothetical, they are based on actual cases from federal appellate courts and represent the view of the majority of federal courts.

■ Part 3 is an assignment sheet handout that will be provided to you by your instructor.

Part 1: Stipulated Facts

1. Paul Revere Furniture Company (Revere) is a manufacturer and retailer of high-end furniture based in Longville. Revere sells its products at its retail outlets across the United States and employs a workforce of approximately 800 employees in 30 states. Its largest retail outlet is adjacent to its headquarters in Longville.

2. On July 1, 2010, John Falstaff (Falstaff) applied for a position at Revere as a floor manager in Revere's Longville store. Falstaff applied for the position after finding out about the opportunity on Revere's website. The position description is shown in Exhibit A.

3. After an interview with Constance Howe (Howe), Revere's regional vice president who supervised all floor managers in the retail stores in the Longville region, Falstaff was hired for the position on July 5, 2010. At the time of hire, Falstaff filled out a personnel form on which he reported that he was in good general health with no injuries or conditions that would prevent him from performing his job, including the physical tasks, and that his weight was approximately 215 pounds and his height was approximately 6 feet.

4. From his start date through May 2011, Falstaff received favorable reviews for his performance as floor manager, and no policy violations were noted in the file. In late June 2011, Falstaff called in sick for three consecutive days, complaining of a back injury. Revere's standard operating procedure required the regional vice president to contact any manager who called in sick more than two consecutive days. Howe telephoned Falstaff, who explained that he had strained his back and was having severe back pain that prevented him from being able to stand or sit comfortably for more than one hour. Falstaff also acknowledged that the pain was subsiding and that he anticipated being able to return to work after one more day of rest. Howe wished Falstaff the best and advised him that he had only two more sick days left. Howe also informed Falstaff that he should consider filing a claim for

In this simulation exercise, an employee of a furniture company claims that he was terminated due to a disability.

disability insurance if his condition did not improve soon.

5. Despite his assurances, Falstaff did not return to work as promised and called in sick for a sixth day. Howe then contacted Falstaff and directed him to see a company-hired physician for a determination as to whether Falstaff could return to work or whether he should be certified as disabled for purposes of filing a claim of disability with Revere's insurance carrier.

6. On July 1, Falstaff was examined by Dr. William Jefferson, a physician hired by the company. Dr. Jefferson concluded that Falstaff was not disabled and had suffered a mild sprain in his lower back region. Dr. Jefferson prescribed ice, over-the-counter pain relief, and a period of two weeks of light duty, during which Falstaff would not be required to lift anything over 10 pounds. After that, Dr. Jefferson advised that Falstaff

would be ready to return to his regular duties as floor manager.

7. On July 2, Falstaff returned to work on light-duty status. Howe assigned Falstaff to desk duties only and instructed other floor managers that Falstaff was not to engage in any lifting of objects that weighed 10 or more pounds.

8. During the next three months, Falstaff's attendance at work was spotty. Although he never called in sick to work, he arrived late six times, took an extended lunch hour three times, and left work early nine times. On each occasion, Falstaff would explain his absence using the excuse that his back was causing him too much pain to sit up and that even the light lifting required on the floor was difficult for him. When Falstaff was at work, he would complain loudly to subordinates and customers that the company was making him work and that working was making his condition worse.

9. Falstaff's absences and workplace complaints also began to affect his performance. His monthly reports to Howe had been chronically late, as were his payroll records. This resulted in several complaints by sales employees about Falstaff's performance. On September 1, 2011, Howe issued Falstaff a "Corrective Action" letter advising that Falstaff's performance was not satisfactory and outlining the specific violations, including the late reports, his attendance problems, and his inappropriate workplace comments. The letter also warned Falstaff that failure to take corrective action to improve would result in termination.

10. After receiving the letter, Falstaff sent an e-mail to Howe claiming that the poor performance was due to "increasing back pain" and that he had developed "shortness of breath" when exerting any physical labor such as moving the furniture displays as required.

11. During this same period of time (June–September), Falstaff's weight increased significantly, from 215 pounds to 320 pounds. As Falstaff's weight increased, he was increasingly reluctant to perform any physical tasks and would order subordinates to move furniture, arrange "Manager's Special" displays, and do other physical activities. During his shift, Falstaff would frequently stay in the manager's office, never coming out to the showroom.

12. In October 2011, Falstaff sought help from his own physician. Falstaff's physician, Dr. Amanda King, examined Falstaff and diagnosed him with a strained lower back. However, in her report, she also made note that "the most significant factor in patient's health is his obesity. His weight increases the strain on his lower back, limits his range of motion, and leaves him short of breath after just a few steps. His weight severely impacts or eliminates his ability to stand for significant periods of time and to pick up anything over 5 lbs." Falstaff sent Dr. King's report to Howe.

13. In two phone conversations with Falstaff over several days after Dr. King's report, Howe indicated that she was concerned that Falstaff may not be able to fully perform the duties required. Falstaff indicated that he could still effectively manage the store so long as other employees were assigned to do any heavy lifting in Falstaff's store.

14. In December 2011, Revere terminated Falstaff. Revere cited lower-than-expected revenue for the previous fiscal year as the primary reason for cutting back its workforce. On his discharge slip, Howe wrote that the reasons for Falstaff's termination were strategic need to cut costs and poor job performance.

15. Falstaff alleges that his termination violated the ADAAA.

Paul Revere Furniture Company—Employment Opportunity

Position: Store floor manager (Longville)

Pay Scale: Based upon experience

General Description: Floor managers are responsible for ensuring overall productive and efficient operations of a retail store location. This includes supervising a sales force of 4–6 people, keeping appropriate corporate records, resolving customer complaints, joining the sales team on the showroom floor during busy holiday seasons, tracking inventory, setting up "Manager's Special" displays, and doing occasional physical work related to tracking and placing merchandise in showrooms in a fashion conducive to maximizing sales.

Physical Requirements: Applicants must be in good overall health sufficient to meet physical requirements of (1) long periods of standing without a break (1–2 hours) and (2), when necessary, occasional climbing, kneeling, bending, stooping, balancing, reaching, and lifting of items (such as furniture) in excess of 50 pounds.

Qualifications:

- High school diploma or G.E.D. required.
- Two years of experience working as a supervisor in a large retail setting is preferred.
- Ability to fulfill physical requirements.
- No convictions for felonies or any theft-related offenses.
- Reliable transportation to work.

Applications: Applications are available on our website at www.revere.com/employment.

Part 2: Statutory and Case Law

Statute: *United States Code*

Excerpt from Americans with Disabilities Act Amendments Act (ADAAA)

§ 1: This Act shall become effective January 1, 2009

§ 2: Definition of disability

As used in this Act:

(1) **Disability:** The term "disability" means, with respect to an individual—
   (A) a physical or mental impairment that substantially limits one or more major life activities of such individual;
   (B) a record of such an impairment; or
   (C) being regarded as having such an impairment on major life activities.

(2) **Major life activities:** In general, for purposes of paragraph (1), major life activities include, but are not limited to, caring for oneself, performing manual tasks, seeing, hearing, eating, sleeping, walking, standing, lifting, bending, speaking, breathing, learning, reading, concentrating, thinking, communicating, and working.

(3) **Major bodily functions:** For purposes of paragraph (1), a major life activity also includes the operation of a major bodily function such as brain, respiratory, circulatory, and endocrine.

(4) **Regarded as having such an impairment:** For purposes of paragraph (1)(C), an individual meets the requirement of "being regarded

as having such an impairment" if the individual establishes that he or she has been subjected to an action prohibited under this Act because of an actual or perceived physical or mental impairment whether or not the impairment limits or is perceived to limit a major life activity.

(5) **Exclusions:** Paragraph (1)(C) shall not apply to impairments that are transitory and minor.

A transitory impairment is an impairment with an actual or expected duration of 6 months or less.

(6) **Rules of construction regarding the definition of disability:** The definition of "disability" in paragraph (1) shall be construed in favor of broad coverage of individuals under this Act, to the maximum extent permitted by the terms of this Act.

Case Law

Grindle v. Watkins Motor Lines
14th Circuit Court of Appeals (2007)

Facts

- Grindle was hired as a dockworker by Watkins Motor Lines in 2005. The job description provided that applicants must be able to lift packages over 50 pounds on a repetitive basis and that the job involved daily loading and unloading of heavy freight, standing for eight hours at a time, and tolerance for outdoor weather on the loading dock. At the time of hire, Grindle weighed 345 pounds, and he reported on his application that he had no medical conditions that he was aware of.

- Over a period of one year, a supervisor at Watkins disciplined Grindle several times for failing to load his freight in a timely manner. Grindle had several written reprimands for this violation in his file and was placed on probation. Under the Watkins employee handbook, Grindle faced termination if his performance did not improve.

- Grindle complained to his manager that Watkins's loading-time goals were impossible to meet as Grindle was not physically able to perform the tasks in the time given. After a third letter of reprimand in April 2006, Grindle asked his manager for a different set of time goals, but Watkins's management refused this option.

- The day after his request for a time schedule adjustment was denied, Grindle saw a physician because he was unable to sleep due to the fear that he would lose his job. During the visit, Grindle's physician reported that Grindle's weight, which was now at 450 pounds, was classified as obese and that extended lifting and standing caused potential injury. The physician advised Grindle not to engage in these strenuous work activities until he had lost at least 75 pounds.

- When Grindle returned to work, he again requested a time schedule adjustment, citing his physician's report and recommendation. Again, Watkins refused any adjustment.

- Shortly thereafter, Grindle was terminated due to his inability to perform the job duties for his position. After receiving a right-to-sue letter from the EEOC, Grindle filed suit against Watkins, claiming that the company was required under the ADA to accommodate his obesity as a disability.

POINTS OF LAW AND OPINION EXCERPTS

Point (a)

A claim of disparate treatment under the ADA will be analyzed under the *McDonnell Douglas* standard.

Excerpt (a)

"We have held that claims under the ADA are analyzed under the framework set forth in *McDonnell Douglas v. Green*. In order to establish a prima facie case under the ADA, the plaintiff must prove that (1) the defendants are subject to the ADA; (2) the plaintiff is disabled within the meaning of the Act; (3) the plaintiff could have performed the job if accommodations had been provided; (4) the plaintiff was subject to an adverse employment action because of the disability."

Point (b)

The threshold requirement to qualify as an ADA-covered disability is that the disability must be physical or mental impairment that substantially limits one or more of the major life activities of the individual.

Excerpt (b1)

"An impairment, for purposes of the ADA, is any 'physiological disorder, or condition, cosmetic disfigurement, or anatomical loss affecting one or more of [various] body systems such as: musculoskeletal; special sense organs; respiratory, including speech organs; cardiovascular; reproductive, digestive, genito-urinary; hemic and lymphatic; skin; and endocrine.'"

Excerpt (b2)

"Examples of normal life activities in past cases in this circuit include seeing, walking, lifting a child, communicating with co-workers and sleeping."

Point (c)

Abnormal physical characteristics in height or weight that have no physiological cause are not considered disabilities under the ADA.

Excerpt (c1)

"We observed in previous cases that physical characteristics that are not the result of a physiological disorder are not considered impairments for the purposes of determining either actual or perceived disability."

Excerpt (c2)

"For example, in one previous case, we held that a plaintiff-firefighter's claim that he was disciplined because his weight did not meet a union standard failed because 'obesity, except in special cases where the obesity relates to a physiological disorder, is not a physical impairment within the meaning of the statutes.'"

Point (d)

This circuit declines to follow a minority of courts' rulings that adopts a medical-based formula (such as body mass index) to determine whether certain levels of obesity rise to the level of disability. Without any physiological cause, obesity is not covered as a disability.

Excerpt (d1)

"We specifically decline to follow some trial courts application of a body mass index or other height-weight calibrations because such calculations belie our previous holding in which we repeatedly emphasized that a physical characteristic must relate to a physiological disorder in order to qualify as an ADA impairment."

Held

Because Grindle had not shown that his obesity was a result of some physiological condition or that it prevented him from engaging in normal life activities as required in the ADA, the court found in favor of Watkins.

Adams v. Salt River Master Carvers
2nd Circuit Court of Appeals (2009)

Facts

- Adams was employed as a welding technician by Salt River Master Carvers, an employer covered by the ADA. His position required strenuous physical activity.
- Approximately one year after his employment began, Adams was diagnosed by his family doctor as an insulin-dependent type 2 diabetic. His doctor prescribed medication and a strict eating regimen requiring daily insulin injections and certain types of food at certain times of the day related to the time of the insulin injection.
- In January 2009, Adams informed his supervisor of his condition, submitted the doctor's report and recommendations, and requested that his schedule be adjusted to accommodate four to six breaks per day from his eight-hour work shift. He said this was necessary or else he would become too dizzy and lightheaded and could pose a safety risk.
- Salt River then required Adams to see a company-hired physician. The company physician agreed with the diabetes diagnosis but recommended that Adams have only one insulin injection per day and that he be given two breaks for eating to balance the insulin. The doctor also recommended that Adams not be assigned any more than an 8-hour shift in any 24-hour period.
- A Salt River manager then met with Adams and told him that he was "concerned with Adams's ability to get the job done" and that diabetes had "slowed him down considerably." Salt River then implemented the company physician recommendations regarding Adams's work assignment.
- In March 2009, amid the continuing economic turbulence, Salt River announced that workforce reduction terminations were necessary. Adams, despite having more seniority than most of his co-workers, was terminated on March 31, 2009, with Salt River citing the work reduction plan as the reason.

POINTS OF LAW AND OPINION EXCERPTS

Point (a)

Because the alleged discrimination took place after January 1, 2009, the provisions of the ADA Amendments Act (ADAAA) of 2008 apply to this case.

Point (b)

The ADAAA significantly broadened the definition of disability necessary for protection under the ADA. Specifically, under the ADAAA, a disability is any impairment that substantially limits a major life activity. That statute specifically adds several activities that have yet to be formally recognized. They include eating, sleeping, standing, lifting, bending, and reading.

Excerpt (b1)

"Under both the ADA and the ADAAA, our analysis of whether the impairment is substantially limiting is based on the nature and severity of the impairment, the duration or expected duration of the impairment, as well as the permanent or long-term impact of the impairment."

Excerpt (b2)

"We conclude that Adams's diabetes substantially limits his life activity of eating. The record is replete with statements, both by Adams and his doctors, that to manage his disease Adams is required to strictly monitor what, and when, he eats. Adams stated that these restrictions constrain him every day, 'whether it's a workday, a weekend or a holiday.' He cannot eat large meals or skip meals, and must eat a snack every few hours. He must schedule each day's blood tests, medications, and food intake. He 'sometimes become[s] weak and dizzy without warning,' and only when he eats something do these sensations quickly subside. If he fails to follow his diet regimen for more than a meal or two, his blood sugar rises to a level that aggravates his disease. Adams's doctor testified that controlling diabetes is like being on a chemical roller coaster."

Point (c)

Even if the physical impairment was not actually a disability, Salt River's conduct indicates that the company regarded Adams as disabled. The regarded-as standard was also expanded under the ADAAA and would be applicable to this case.

Excerpt (c1)

"This court has held that an individual need not actually have a physical impairment to state a claim under the ADA . . . as long as that individual is 'regarded as having such an impairment.' To be 'regarded as' having a disability, a plaintiff must prove he is regarded as having an impairment that substantially limits one or more major life activities. A plaintiff must allege that the employer perceived that the employee suffered from an impairment that would be covered under the statute."

Excerpt (c2)

"Evidence in this case shows that Salt River management was 'concerned with Adams's ability to get the job done' and that they had concluded that the diabetes had 'slowed him down considerably.' "

Point (d)

The correlation of the discrimination and the termination may, coupled with other factors, constitute a pretextual reason for the discharge.

Excerpt (d1)

"When an employer offers inconsistent explanations for an adverse employment decision a genuine issue of material fact is raised with regard to the veracity of the nondiscriminatory reason. Here, the defendants have offered various explanations for Adams's termination including financial reasons, poor performance, and inappropriate conduct. The allegations regarding Adams's poor performance and inappropriate conduct are questionable in light of their failure to raise these issues prior to the proceedings in the trial court."

Held

In favor of Adams. The ADAAA covers Adams's disability under both the disparate treatment discrimination theory and the regarded-as theory.

Business Entities, Securities Regulation, and Corporate Governance

14

CHAPTER

Choice of Business Entity, Sole Proprietorships, and Partnerships

learning **objectives**

After studying this chapter, students who have mastered the material will be able to:

14-1 Articulate the factors that business owners should consider when selecting a business entity.

14-2 Identify methods through which sole proprietorships and partnerships may be capitalized (funded).

14-3 List the elements required to form a general partnership and the statutory requirements for forming a limited partnership.

14-4 Recognize the effect and role of the RUPA for general partnerships and the RULPA for limited partnerships.

14-5 Distinguish between personal and tax liability for general partners and limited partners.

14-6 Differentiate the consequences of partner separation versus dissolution.

14-7 Recognize the role of franchises in business.

All business ventures operate as a legally recognized form of business entity.[1] Business owners and managers who have a fundamental knowledge of the structure, advantages, and risks associated with each form of business entity are more effective at focusing on business opportunities while limiting potential liability. Most states recognize at least six forms of business entities. In addition to providing an overview of the forms of business entities and factors used to determine the best choice of entity for a given business, this chapter focuses on the law governing two basic forms of entity: sole proprietorships and partnerships. Other forms of entities are covered in the next two chapters. In this chapter, students will learn:

- The factors to be considered in determining what business form fits which business type.

- Fundamental principles of the law governing sole proprietorships.

- Legal regulation for formation and governance of partnerships, including personal liability of partners for business debts and other liabilities.

- Rules governing the separation of partners from the partnership and procedures for dissolving a partnership.

---

[1] Business entities are sometimes referred to as *business organizations*.

CHOOSING A BUSINESS ENTITY

LO 14-1

The best choice of business entity is primarily driven by the risk, tax, and operational objectives of the owner(s) and the type of business operations contemplated. Choosing a business entity is an important part of business planning for both start-up entrepreneurs and the managers of a business supervising the launch of an additional venture that supplements the existing business. Each form of entity has its attendant advantages and drawbacks and a variety of legal consequences for the *owners*, known as **principals,** of the business. In choosing a business entity, principals should consider at least the following factors:

- *Formation:* How easy is the entity to form and maintain? Must there be more than one principal? What annual filings or fees are required, and what formalities need be followed?

- *Liability:* To what extent are the principals *personally* liable for debts and other contract or tort liabilities of the business entity itself? To take a simple example, suppose Gardner owns a consulting business and rents office space from Landlord under a five-year lease agreement. After one year, Gardner loses a large client and can no longer afford the office space. He cancels his lease and moves his office to the basement of his home. If the assets of the consulting business are insufficient to pay a court judgment in favor of the damaged party (Landlord), does Landlord, as the injured party, have a claim for the balance against Gardner's personal assets (such as a personal bank account or stock portfolio)?

- *Capitalization:* How will the business entity fund its operations? May the principal(s) sell ownership rights in the business to raise capital?
- *Taxation of income:* How will tax authorities treat the entity? Will the entity itself pay taxes, or are the taxes passed through to the principals?
- *Management and operation:* How, and by whom, will the business venture be operated? Will the principals be involved in day-to-day operations of the business? What duties do the principals owe to the business and to each other? How will the profits and losses be split? If a principal decides to leave the business entity, may the remaining principals continue to operate?

Table 14.1 sets out the most common forms of business entities.

Sole Proprietorships

LO 14-2

The easiest single-person ownership entity to form and maintain is a **sole proprietorship.** A sole proprietorship requires only a minimal fee, involves a straightforward filing requirement with the appropriate state government authority, and typically requires no annual filings. Its ease of formation and maintenance makes this entity a top choice for start-up businesses with relatively low annual revenues and expenses. An individual planning to conduct a sole proprietorship business under a trade name, rather than her individual name (i.e., "Gates IT Consulting" rather than "Joan Gates") will also file a "doing business as,"

TABLE 14.1 Common Forms of Business Entities

Name of Entity	Brief Description	Coverage in Text
Sole proprietorship	One-person entity in which the debts and liabilities of the business are also personal debts and liabilities of the principal.	Chapter 14
Partnerships: General Limited	Two or more principals that agree to share profits and losses in an ongoing business venture. Debts and liabilities of the business are also personal debts and liabilities of the general partners. Limited partners have limited liability.	Chapter 14
Limited liability partnership	Two or more principals that agree to share profits and losses in an ongoing business venture. The principals have heightened liability protection from debts and liabilities of the partnership.	Chapter 15
Limited liability company	Two or more principals in an ongoing business venture with potentially favorable tax treatment and limited liability for the principals.	Chapter 15
Corporation	One or more principals that invest money in exchange for ownership (stock). The principals generally have no personal liability for debts and liabilities of the business.	Chapter 16

Principals in start-up business ventures have several alternatives when selecting a business entity.

or DBA, certificate (a DBA name is sometimes known as a *fictitious name*) with a local or state office. There may be additional licenses required by the state and city where the business operates (sales tax licenses, etc.). These requirements vary by jurisdiction.

Sole proprietorships are limited in their options for raising money and are typically capitalized through a proprietor's personal resources or a private or commercial loan that is secured by the proprietor's personal assets.[2] A sole proprietorship business is not subject to corporate income taxation, and no tax return is filed on behalf of the business. Rather, the principal reports business income and expenses on her own individual tax return and pays taxes on business income (or deducts business losses) based on her own individual tax rate. It is important to note that although most sole proprietorships are relatively small in terms of assets and revenues, sole proprietorships are not restricted in terms of the number of employees can operate in as many locations as the principal desires.

The chief drawback to this form of entity is a complete *lack of protection* of the principal's personal assets for unpaid debts and liabilities of the business. All debts and liabilities of the business are also *personal debts and liabilities* of the principal. For example, suppose Redfern is the principal of Redfern Catering, a sole proprietorship. Redfern Catering has approximately $5,000 in assets. One of Redfern's employees negligently uses spoiled ingredients in a soup that is served to customers. Marshall is a customer who develops food poisoning and obtains a court judgment against Redfern Catering to compensate him for damages that resulted from medical bills in the amount of $50,000. Assuming that Redfern Catering had no insurance coverage for this event, Marshall would have $45,000 of judgment unpaid after exhausting the business of its assets ($50,000 judgment minus $5,000 assets). Thus, Redfern would be *personally* liable to Marshall for the remaining unpaid

---

[2]A secured loan is one in which the borrower grants the lender legal rights to something of value until the loan is paid back in full (e.g., a car secures a car loan).

[3]Note that all states prohibit certain assets from being seized to satisfy a judgment, such as the principal's home residence. Some states also exempt retirement portfolios as well.

judgment. This means that Marshall could execute the judgment against Redfern by using a judicially sanctioned process for seizing funds from Redfern's personal bank account, stock portfolio, and other assets. As a result of this lack of protection, sole proprietors often purchase comprehensive liability insurance for the business in amounts sufficient to cover potential tort liabilities such as the one described in the Redfern-Marshall example.

Termination A sole proprietorship is terminated either by an express act of the principal or by operation of law in the case of the death or personal bankruptcy of the proprietor. Although a sole proprietor may sell the assets of her business to another party, the proprietor's *ownership* interest in a sole proprietorship cannot pass to her heirs through a gift or an estate. In Case 14.1, a state appellate court analyzes the moment of termination of a sole proprietorship in the context of successor liability.

CASE 14.1 Vernon v. Schuster, 688 N.E.2d 1172 (Ill. 1997)

FACT SUMMARY James Schuster was a sole proprietor doing business as Diversey Heating and Plumbing and contracted with Vernon to install and maintain a boiler in his building. Schuster also promised Vernon a 10-year warranty, and the parties agreed to a long-term service agreement whereby Schuster was to perform an annual prewinter inspection of the boiler and render any service needed for upkeep. Schuster performed the services for a period of three years, but he died in October 1993 before performing the prewinter inspection on Vernon's boiler. After Schuster died, his son Jerry Schuster began to operate Diversey and serve Diversey customers. In February 1994, Vernon discovered that the boiler was broken beyond repair and needed to be replaced. Vernon brought a breach-of-warranty lawsuit against Jerry Schuster on the basis that he had continued the sole proprietorship that his father had started and therefore Jerry Schuster should honor the warranty given by James Schuster. Jerry Schuster maintained that he had no responsibility to honor a warranty provided by a predecessor business. The trial court dismissed most of the lawsuit, holding that Jerry Schuster could not be held liable for the obligations of his father's sole proprietorship interest. The appellate court reversed on the basis that Jerry Schuster's business was merely a continuation of his father's business and thus he could potentially have continued liability.

SYNOPSIS OF DECISION AND OPINION The Illinois Supreme Court found in favor of Schuster and held that a sole proprietor does not have a legal identity separate from that of the individual who owns it. Although the sole proprietor may do business under a fictitious name, the principal does not create an entity

distinct from the person operating the business. In this case, Diversey Heating has no legal existence. It was only a pseudonym for James Schuster. Once he died, Diversey Heating ceased to exist. Now Diversey is only a pseudonym for Jerry Schuster. The court also rejected Vernon's theory that Schuster's business fell within the "continuation" exception to the rule of successor nonliability because Vernon failed to show that the new entity had a common identity of ownership with the previous entity.

WORDS OF THE COURT: Termination of a Sole Proprietorship's Obligations "Once sole proprietor James Schuster died, he could not be the same sole proprietor as defendant [Jerry Schuster], who became a sole proprietor after his father's death. James Schuster and defendant [Jerry Schuster], one succeeding the other, cannot be the same entity. Even if defendant [Jerry Schuster] inherited Diversey from his father, defendant [Jerry Schuster] would not have continued his father's sole proprietorship, but rather would have started a new sole proprietorship."

Case Questions

1. A dissenting opinion in this case argued that Jerry Schuster did carry on his father's business and should be liable for obligations of the continued business. Does that strike you as reasonable? Shouldn't a warranty be valid so long as the business that provided the warranty is still operating?

2. If Jerry Schuster changed the name of the business but still used the tools and equipment he inherited from his father, how would that impact your analysis of this case?

An entity with *more* than one principal has a number of additional choices. The simplest multiple-person business entity is a **partnership.** There are two traditional subcategories of partnerships: general partnerships and limited partnerships. Most partnerships are **express partnerships,** in which the principals agree to some ongoing business relationship. In some cases, however, even though the parties did not intend on being partners, the law recognizes the relationship as a partnership and imposes the same liability on the principals as would be imposed if the parties had formed an express partnership. Two other related types of partnerships are limited liability partnerships (LLPs) and limited liability limited partnerships (LLLPs). These are hybrid forms of partnership (having characteristics common to several different entities) and are covered in detail in Chapter 15, "Limited Liability Companies and Limited Liability Partnerships."

General Partnerships   Unlike most business entities, general partnerships are not created by filing a form with a government agency. Instead, the law recognizes two or more principals as being a general partnership if they have *demonstrated* an intent to carry on as co-owners of a business for profit. While some general partnerships have extensive written agreements detailing the internal operations of the business and the rights and responsibilities of the principals, others operate without any written agreement at all. In the absence of an agreement, the Revised Uniform Partnership Act (RUPA) governs a general partnership. Just like the Uniform Commercial Code, the RUPA is a *model statute* drafted and occasionally revised by the National Conference of Commissioners on Uniform State Laws. To date, approximately 40 states have adopted all or substantial portions of the RUPA. States that have not yet adopted the RUPA operate under the RUPA's predecessor, the Uniform Partnership Act (UPA).[4] The RUPA should be thought of as a default set of laws that apply only when the principals have not expressly agreed otherwise (similar to the UCC's gap-filler function). The RUPA also contains certain agency principles including fiduciary duties of partners to each other and to the partnership. In addition to the RUPA, the common law plays a role in general partnership law in certain cases where principles of general fairness must be applied and the RUPA doesn't contemplate that particular situation.[5]

Formation   No formal document or government filing is necessary to form a general partnership. In fact, it is important to note that the parties may not actually *intend* to be partners, but the law still recognizes their relationship as an **implied partnership.** For example, suppose that Carl and Jan are neighbors and during a block party Carl mentions that his family's secret salad dressing was popular with the neighbors and friends. Jan loves the dressing and offers to help Carl sell the dressing at local gourmet stores in exchange for 50 percent of the profits. Carl agrees so long as he is responsible for making the dressing and Jan is responsible for providing bottles and labels, transporting, and selling. Here, despite the fact that the parties may have intended to have an informal arrangement, legally they have created a general partnership. This is important because this arrangement gives rise to potential liability for both Carl and Jan even though they never intended to assume such risks. In Case 14.2, a state appellate court analyzes whether a romantic relationship created an implied partnership in business.

Conversely, even if the parties *label* themselves as general partners and draft a partnership agreement, this does not, in and of itself, form a general partnership.[6] Fundamentally,

---

[4]Louisiana is the only state not to adopt the UPA or the RUPA.

[5]RUPA § 104(a) refers to this, stating, "Unless displaced by particular provisions of this [act], the principles of law and equity supplement this act."

[6]Recall the equitable maxim from Chapter 1, "Legal Foundations," relating to the law recognizing substance over form.

FACT SUMMARY Waddell and Rustin entered into a romantic relationship soon after meeting in 1999. Waddell maintained that their association started as personal and also grew into a business partnership. Rustin denied that they were ever express or implied business partners. At the time the two met, Rustin and his brother owned and operated a store called "Lots of Christmas," and Waddell began working at the store in 2000. One year later, Rustin started a construction and excavation business. Both at the Lots of Christmas store and at the construction company, Waddell claimed that she had management and oversight over business projects, had access to the company checkbook, paid company bills, helped Rustin choose construction projects, and even changed the store's name from "Lots of Christmas" to "Aluminum Decor and More" to improve sales. Waddell testified that she did not receive any pay checks for her work, but that the couple ran the businesses as partners. When the personal relationship ended, Waddell brought suit claiming that she was entitled to a percentage of the profits because the relationship had been an implied partnership. The trial court ruled that no implied partnership was created.

SYNOPSIS OF DECISION AND OPINION The Court of Appeals of Tennessee affirmed the trial court and held in favor of Rustin. The court ruled that because there was no written partnership agreement between Waddell and Rustin, Waddell bore the burden of proving the existence of a partnership by clear and convincing evidence. Given that Waddell had no experience in construction or excavation when they met and that Rustin had engaged in construction work for years, it was clear that his efforts had made the business viable. Waddell did not contribute equipment, experience, or capital. Therefore, the court held that one cannot reasonably conclude that Waddell's relationship with Rustin rose to the level of an implied partnership.

WORDS OF THE COURT: Implied Partnership "Rustin acknowledges, as do we, that Waddell performed certain work related to Rustin's business enterprises. However, it cannot be said of this case that the parties' prosperity was due in equal part to Waddell's efforts. Rustin and his brother ran the store prior to Waddell's relationship with Rustin. Waddell's work at the Store is better characterized as helping out rather than the contribution of an equal partner. Notwithstanding Waddell's activities related to certain houses or cabins, the record shows that Rustin, with his experience in construction and excavation, clearly was the primary driver of the construction enterprise. Waddell testified that she contributed no real property; personal property; money; formal training in interior design; excavation experience; or construction experience to any partnership."

Case Questions

1. Given the court's ruling, what could Waddell have done differently to ensure that she would have had partner status?

2. At what point does a personal relationship rise to an implied partnership?

---

a general partnership is thought of as (1) an association of two or more people or entities, (2) who are co-owners and comanagers of the business and (3) share in the profits of an ongoing business operation. General partnerships typically use the designation *GP* at the end of their business name to signify the general partnership as their form of entity.

Sometimes, the parties wish to have only a limited-in-time relationship instead of an ongoing business entity. This relationship is generally referred to as a **joint venture** and is governed by the same legal principles as a general partnership.

Liability of the Principals Much like sole proprietors, general partners have no protection of their personal assets for unpaid debts and liabilities of the partnership. However, the RUPA imposes *additional* liability on general partners by making all general partners **jointly and severally liable** for unpaid debts and liabilities of the partnership. This means that general partners' personal assets are at risk both together (jointly) and separately

An express partnership is created when two or more principals agree to share profits in an ongoing business relationship.

(severally) for all debts and liabilities of the partnership regardless of the source of the debt or liability. In the Redfern Catering example discussed earlier suppose that Redfern and Colgate formed a general partnership to operate the catering business as Redfern-Colgate Catering, GP. Marshall obtains a judgment against the business for medical damages related to food poisoning. Marshall must first exhaust all of the assets of the partnership. If the assets are not enough to satisfy the judgment, Marshall may then attempt to collect the unpaid portion of the judgment from the personal assets of Redfern and Colgate together or separately because Redfern and Colgate have joint and several liability for the entire debt. Thus, Marshall may choose to collect 50 percent from Redfern and 50 percent from Colgate or any combination thereof (60/40, 70/30, etc.). Suppose that Redfern has no assets and moves to Key West to become a shrimper. In this case, Marshall may choose to collect the *entire* unpaid judgment from Colgate. However, because generally the partners share in losses as well as profits, Colgate could try to pursue Redfern through a civil suit for 50 percent of the loss he suffered in paying out the judgment to Marshall. This joint and several liability rule may *not* be altered by the parties' agreement, nor may the principals limit their liability based on the principals' agreement to split profits and losses on a percentage basis. So, in the Redfern-Colgate partnership, suppose that they agreed at the start of the catering business that Colgate would receive 30 percent of the profits. Colgate may *not* assert that his liability to Marshall is limited to 30 percent of the total unpaid judgment.

Capitalization General partnerships are generally funded either through debt (i.e., borrowing money from the principals, a commercial lender, or a private individual third party) or through a sale of equity (selling a percentage of ownership rights in the partnership and any profits of the business). Partnerships may not, however, sell ownership rights through the public markets

> **KEY** POINT
>
> General partners' personal assets are at risk for the full amount of the debts and liabilities of the partnership jointly (all partners together) and severally (each and every partner separately) regardless of their percentage of ownership interest in the partnership.

The principals in the hypothetical Redfern-Colgate Catering, GP, have joint and several liability for all debts and liabilities of the partnership.

such as the New York Stock Exchange. Sometimes general partners hedge their financial investment through a combination of debt and equity. The concepts of debt and equity are discussed in detail in Chapter 17, "Regulation of Securities, Corporate Governance, and Financial Markets."

Taxation of Partnership and Principals   Just as in the case of a sole proprietorship, a partnership is a **pass-through entity.** This means that the partnership entity pays no level of corporate tax. Rather, profits are taxed *after* they pass through the business and are distributed to the individual partners. The income is reported on the individual general partner's *personal tax return* (the familiar tax form 1040) and taxed based on the individual rate of the general partner. In fact, the partnership entity itself does not file a tax return, but it does file an *information return* for purposes of providing the government with documentation regarding how much, when, and to whom profits were paid. Of course, partners also report business partnership losses on their individual tax returns and are permitted to deduct those losses to offset certain types of income.

Operation and Management of the Partnership   Absent an agreement by the parties, the RUPA also governs certain internal operations of the general partnership. For example, unless the parties agree otherwise, each partner receives an equal share of the partnership profit payments regardless of the partner's involvement in the success of the business. The same rule applies to losses. Absent an agreement to the contrary, general partners have the general power to *bind* the partnership to a contractual obligation (e.g., a lease for office space) even if the other general partners have no knowledge of the transaction.

Note that partners who provide labor to the partnership are not entitled to any compensation (other than a share of profits) for this work unless the principals have agreed ahead of time to certain compensation terms. For example, assume that in the Redfern-Colgate general partnership, Redfern works in the kitchen 80 hours per week while Colgate spends no time working on behalf of the partnership. Absent any advance agreement between the partners, Redfern is not entitled to any compensation for the kitchen work.

Fiduciary Obligations   General partners have a set of duties that ensure they are acting in the best interest of the partnership. These duties are known as **fiduciary duties.**[7] They are very similar to the duties owed by an agent to a principal that were discussed in Chapter 11, "Agency." Fundamentally, the RUPA sets out these duties as threefold: (1) loyalty, (2) care, and (3) good faith. The loyalty standard prohibits a general partner from engaging in competition with the interests of the partnership and also prohibits other conflicts of interest with the partnership such as using the partnership property for personal gain at the expense of the interests of the entity. Partners must also exercise due care in handling the affairs of the partnership and treat business affairs with the same diligence as they would apply in treating their own personal business affairs. The good faith standard requires that partners exercise appropriate discretion in dealing with other partners and third parties concerning the partnership's business enterprise operations.

Limited Partnerships
A limited partnership is an entity that exists by virtue of a *state statute* that recognizes one or more principals as managing the business enterprise while other principals participate only in terms of contributing capital or property. A limited partnership has at least one general partner (managing principal) and at least one limited partner (investing principal). In the absence of an agreement, the Revised Uniform Limited Partnership Act (RULPA) governs a limited partnership. However, the RULPA actually works in tandem with the RUPA. That is, when an issue of liability or operation arises, the written partnership agreement governs. If there is no agreement or the agreement is silent on this issue, then the RULPA resolves the issue. If the RULPA does not provide rules on a particular issue, courts may sometimes look to the RUPA for guidance.

Formation   To form limited partnership, the general partner files a **certificate of limited partnership** with the state government authority[8] (usually in the secretary of state's office). Generally, the certificate is not overly complex. It requires routine information such as the name, address, and capital contribution of each partner. Although the RULPA does not formally require a partnership agreement, the vast majority of limited partnerships have one. The agreement details the rights, obligations, and relationships between partners. These partnerships typically use the designation *LP* at the end of their business name to signify the limited partnership as their form of entity. Figure 14.1 presents a sample certificate of limited partnership.

Personal Liability of Principals   Each general partner in a limited partnership is *personally liable* for all of the partnership's debts and liabilities, just as if the general partners were in a general partnership. However, limited partners do *not* have the same automatic personal liability of a general partner.[9] Rather, the limited partner's liability is limited to whatever the limited partner *contributed* to the partnership. For example, suppose that Redfern initially operates Redfern Catering as a sole proprietor but decides to expand his business operations. He decides to raise capital through the selling of some ownership interest in his business. Redfern convinces Macduff to invest $20,000 in Redfern Catering. However, Macduff has substantial personal assets he wishes to protect and no interest in running the day-to-day operations of the business. The two form Redfern Catering LP, with Redfern as the general partner and Macduff as the limited partner. In an effort to cut costs, Redfern negligently uses spoiled ingredients, and a customer, Marshall, is sickened.

---

[7]RUPA § 404.

[8]RULPA § 201.

[9]RULPA § 403(b).

D

The Commonwealth of Massachusetts
William Francis Galvin
Secretary of the Commonwealth
One Ashburton Place - Room 1717, Boston, Massachusetts 02108-1512

Limited Partnership Certificate
(General Laws Chapter 109, Section 8)

(1) The exact name of the limited partnership:

Redfern Catering, LP

> Basic information including name, purpose, and address of the partnership. Note that Redfern Catering is using the LP (limited partnership) designation.

(2) The general character of the business of the limited partnership:

Catering services

(3) The street address of the limited partnership in the commonwealth at which its records will be maintained:

1000 Restaurant Avenue
Boston, MA 02108

> State statutes require that all business entities have a physical address within the state jurisdiction. Out-of-state entities use a resident agent to satisfy this requirement. Some commercial services offer resident agent services for a fee. Attorneys sometimes serve as resident agents for their business clients. A resident agent typically provides services such as accepting legal documents (such as a complaint in a lawsuit) for the partnership. In-state partnerships simply use a partner as their resident agent (as in the case of Redfern Catering, LP).

(4) The name and street address of the resident agent:

Francis Redfern   1000 Restaurant Avenue
                                    Boston, MA 02108

(5) The name and business address of each general partner:

Francis Redfern
1000 Restaurant Avenue
Boston, MA 02108

(6) The latest date on which the limited partnership is to dissolve: October 10, 2030

> Most states require the partners to select an ending date for the partnership but allow the partners to continue the partnership after the ending date by simply filing an additional form extending the date.

(7) Additional matters:

Alexandra Macduff

Signed *(by all general partners)*: _____

Consent of resident agent:

> The resident agent consents to serve in compliance with responsibilities set out by the state statute.

I **Francis Redfern** _____ ,
resident agent of the above limited partnership, consent to my appointment as resident agent pursuant to G.L. c109 Section 8 (a) (3)*

or attach registered agents consent hereto.

Marshall obtains a judgment against Redfern Catering LP, but after the assets of the partnership are exhausted, Marshall is still owed a balance from the judgment. Because Redfern is a general partner, Marshall may recover the balance from Redfern's personal assets but *not* from Macduff as a limited partner.

There are some exceptions to the liability rule spelled out in the RULPA. The primary exception occurs when a limited partner acts *illegally* or *negligently* within the scope of partnership duties. When a limited partner engages in wrongful conduct on behalf of the limited partnership and causes an injury resulting in damages, the limited partner is personally liable to pay damages to the injured party.

Capitalization Limited partnerships are generally funded either through debt (i.e., borrowing money from the principals, a commercial lender, or private individual third parties) or through a sale of equity (selling a percentage of ownership rights in the partnership and any profits of the business). Limited partnerships may not, however, sell ownership rights through the public markets such as the New York Stock Exchange (NYSE). Although not considered publicly traded equity, when limited partnership interests are sold to the public (usually through a broker-dealer with contacts in the investment community), they are subject to strict federal securities laws and state securities laws commonly known as *blue sky laws*. Securities law is discussed extensively in Chapter 17, "Regulation of Securities, Corporate Governance, and Financial Markets."

Taxation of Partners and Partnership Limited partnerships are pass-through entities just like general partnerships. The same rules apply for taxation as in a general partnership. That is, profits or losses are reported in the principal's personal tax return, and tax is paid in accordance with the individual partner's individual tax rate. The general partner is responsible for filing an *information return* with taxing authorities, but limited partnerships do not pay corporate taxes. As in the case of general partnerships, this information return informs tax authorities of profits or losses of the partnership entity.

Management and Operation of the Partnership One of the primary differences between general partners and limited partners is the extent to which they are permitted to be involved in day-to-day operations of the business. General partners manage the business and are permitted to bind the partnership. Limited partners may *not* participate in daily management of the business, do not have authority to bind the partnership, and remain primarily investors. Limited partners who do engage in daily management and operations *jeopardize* their limited partnership status. Under the RULPA, limited partners may engage in consulting and contribute expertise but may not engage in management activities such as supervision of employees.[10]

Although sometimes limited partners are referred to colloquially as *silent partners*, limited partners have the right to access partnership information (such as inspection of financial records) about the business and general information about the partnership's operations (such as contracts the partnership has executed). The partnership agreement may expand the limited partner's role in management (though not to the point where the limited partner's role constitutes day-to-day involvement in running the business) and may also expand her rights and prerogatives, such as the right to remove a general partner or the right to block admission of new partners. These provisions in a partnership agreement are relatively common because they allow the limited partner to better protect her investment.

> **KEY** POINT
> Limited partners may *not* participate in daily management of the business, do not have authority to bind the partnership, and remain primarily as investors.

Limited partnerships also differ from general partnerships in terms of the default rule for sharing profits and losses. Recall from our earlier discussion that the RUPA contemplates

---

[10]RULPA § 303(b), (c).

that partners, absent agreement to the contrary, share equally in profits and losses. However, in a limited partnership, the partners share in profits and losses in proportion to "the value of contributions made by each partner to the extent they have been received by the partnership and have not been returned."[11] For example, suppose Pablo, Vincent, and Frida form a limited partnership for the purpose of starting an art auction house. The partnership is initially structured as follows:

Partner	Initial Capital Contribution	Role
Pablo	$20,000	General partner; salaried employee
Vincent	$45,000	Limited partner
Frida	$45,000	Limited partner

The partnership agreement provides for a salary for Pablo but is silent on distribution of profits and losses. Frida has an immediate need for cash, so the parties agree to return $10,000 of her investment. Under the RULPA, profits and losses are now allocated with 20 percent to Pablo, 35 percent to Frida, and 45 percent to Vincent.

In some cases, the principals in a partnership make specific agreements and label themselves as limited partners. This labeling is not sufficient to maintain a limited partner status (and, thus, protection from certain liabilities). The focus of the inquiry is the principals' *conduct*. The question is not how they *labeled* themselves or how they signed certain documents or what they called themselves. Rather, the question is this: Did the principals *operate* as a limited partnership? Case 14.3 is an example of the substance-over-form analysis applied to partnership law.

Family Limited Partnerships   Another type of partnership is a family limited partnership. A family limited partnership is simply a limited partnership that is used for estate planning for families of considerable wealth. The actual process and legal procedures governing family limited partnership transactions are a very complex area of tax and estate law. The fundamental purpose of a family limited partnership is to enable wealthy members of one generation to distribute assets (in the form of an IRS-recognized gift) to heirs using a method that allows the distributing generation to claim a much lower market value than the actual market value of the gift. It also allows the distributing generation to transfer assets out of their large estate into the smaller estates of their heirs and avoid estate taxes upon their death. Some states have amended their RULPA statutes to accommodate the special circumstances of a family limited partnership with respect to partner dissociation (discussed next).

LO 14-6 ## Partner Dissociation and Dissolution of the Partnership

When a partner no longer wishes to be a principal in the partnership, she may choose to leave the partnership. The RUPA[12] uses the term **dissociation** to describe this act of separation, while the RULPA uses the term **withdrawal.** Both the RUPA and RULPA give the partners substantial rights that govern withdrawal under the partnership agreement,

---

[11]RULPA § 403(c).

[12]The rules governing dissociation and dissolution are perhaps the biggest difference between the UPA and RUPA. Under the UPA, such events cause an automatic dissolution of the partnership. The RUPA allows the partnership to continue under certain circumstances.

FACT SUMMARY   Dormilee Morton inherited the assets of her husband's construction company, consisting primarily of heavy equipment and building materials. Using these assets, her son, Steven Morton, began to run the day-to-day operations of the business, but the business failed in a period of five years. During that time, Steven Morton was responsible for all tax filings and signed the tax returns indicating that Morton Construction was a limited partnership. On Mrs. Morton's personal tax return, she indicated that she was a "silent partner" in Morton Construction. However, during the same years, Mrs. Morton signed for bank loans as "Dormilee Morton and Steven Morton d/b/a Morton Construction Company." She also provided additional capital for the business when needed. Her home phone number and home address were listed as the principal place of business for Morton Construction.

The IRS assessed Morton Construction over $40,000 in back taxes and penalties for failing to pay federal employment taxes during a four-year period. Because Steven Morton and the business were without assets, the IRS pursued Mrs. Morton as a general partner in the business. Morton defended on the basis that she had been nothing more than a limited partner, as indicated on the tax returns, and was thus insulated from liabilities of the partnership.

SYNOPSIS OF DECISION AND OPINION   The court ruled against Mrs. Morton and upheld the judgment in favor of the IRS's tax assessment against the personal assets of Mrs. Morton as a general partner. The court concluded that the notations on the tax returns in and of themselves are not determinative for

the status of an entity. Mrs. Morton participated in the business in the same way as a general partner would and, thus, had no limited liability status. In coming to this conclusion, the court cited several factors that indicated the business was run as a general partnership: her contribution of all capital assets, her taking a 50 percent business loss on previous tax returns, her granting the bank a security interest in their equipment, and her willful ignorance of business mail that arrived at her own home.

WORDS OF THE COURT: Substance over Form
"[T]he court concludes that she was not, in fact, a limited partner. The business was a general partnership or, at least, a joint venture. The mere marking on the tax returns of 'limited partner' has no effect when it is clear that no limited partnership, either *de facto* or *de jure*, exists. Thus, the reasons are twofold for denying Mrs. Morton's [emphatic declaration] that she was a limited partner in Morton Construction Company: (1) utter failure to comply with the [state] statutory requirements for establishing a limited partnership; and (2) her general involvement in the business."

Case Questions

1. What could Dormilee Morton have done to strengthen her status as a limited partner?

2. Both Mortons testified that Mrs. Morton was involved in only a very small part of the business and that Steven had taken charge of all financial and tax affairs. Do you think it is fair to hold a widow responsible for the misdealing or ineptness of her son in this case?

---

but they differ significantly if the partners have not agreed to displace the RUPA and RULPA provisions.

Dissociation under the RUPA   The RUPA lists 10 specific events that are events of dissociation, but the majority of dissociations are the result of one of the following three events: (1) voluntary separation from the partnership, whereby one partner gives specific notice to withdraw from the partnership; (2) expulsion by the *unanimous* vote of the other partners; or (3) the partner's inability to carry out her duties to the partnership (as in the case of incapacity or death) or inability to have an economic stake in the business (as in the case of an individual partner filing for bankruptcy protection). The RUPA makes a distinction between *rightful* and *wrongful* dissociation. When a partner exercises a rightful dissociation, she is no longer liable for the debts and liabilities incurred by the partnership. Although the partner is still liable for predissociation liability, she no longer

Legal Speak ›))
De Facto   Existing in fact; having effect even though not formally recognized.
De Jure   Existing in or by right of law.

CONCEPT SUMMARY Sole Proprietorships versus Partnerships

	Sole Proprietorships	Partnerships, LP and GP
Formation	Low start-up costs and minimal filing. One-person entity.	Minimal filing requirements. Partnership agreement may result in some legal fees. GP has two or more partners. LP must have at least one general partner and one or more limited partners.
Liability of principal(s)	All debts and liabilities of the business are the personal liabilities of the sole proprietor. All of the proprietor's assets are at risk to satisfy business debts and liabilities.	GP: Each general partner is jointly and severally liable for debts and liabilities of the partnership. All personal assets of a general partner are at risk. LP: Personal assets of the limited partners are not at risk for debts and liabilities of the entity.
Capital	Proprietor uses personal assets or bank loan secured by personal assets.	Partners each contribute capital as needed. The partnership agreement governs how and when additional calls for partners' contributions are made. Bank loans secured by partnership assets and/or personal guarantees.
Taxes	All income taxes of the business are paid at the proprietor's individual tax rate and reported on the proprietor's individual income tax return. Miscellaneous state and local taxes to operate business.	No taxation at the partnership entity level. All income tax of the business passes through the partnership, is distributed to the partners, and is paid at the individual tax rate of the receiving partner. Partnership files information return to inform IRS of profits or losses. Miscellaneous state and local taxes to operate business.
Management and control	One-person entity.	Management and control as outlined in partnership agreements or under RUPA/UPA if not agreed upon. Limited partner cannot have day-to-day involvement. Fiduciary duties are owed by partners.
Designation	John Doe d/b/a Doe Consulting Services	Doe Partners, GP Doe Partners, LP

owes any fiduciary duty to the partnership or the remaining principals. A wrongful dissociation occurs if a partner's withdrawal violates the partnership agreement or if a partner withdraws from a partnership before the expiration of a previously agreed-upon time has elapsed. In the event of a wrongful termination, the wrongfully dissociated partner "is liable to the partnership and to the other partners for damages caused by the dissociation."[13] For example, suppose that Abel, Baker, and Cain are general partners in ABC Landscape Design and have no written agreement about the partnership. Abel is knowledgeable in the operation of specific equipment crucial to the success of the business. ABC enters into a contract to provide services to several large office centers. After a few months, Abel withdraws from the partnership to pursue another career. As a result, the partnership cannot perform the services on time and breaches several agreements while attempting to locate a replacement to operate the equipment. Abel would be liable for damages suffered by the partnership.

When a partner dissociates herself (rightfully or wrongfully) from the partnership, the partnership does *not* automatically dissolve. In fact, the RUPA leans toward the notion that the partnership can continue.[14] If the remaining principals wish to continue operating the business partnership, they must purchase the partnership interest of the dissociating partner based on a formula contained in the RUPA. Again, it is important to note that these are RUPA default rules and that a partnership agreement often fixes the method or formula for determining the buyout price.

There may be certain cases where the remaining principals wish to dissolve the partnership after dissociation. The dissolution does not actually end the partnership but rather triggers the process of **winding up.** Only after windup is complete is the partnership officially considered terminated. Windup is the period of time necessary to settle the affairs of the partnership and includes activities such as discharging the partnership's liabilities, settling and closing the partnership's business, marshaling the assets of the partnership, and distributing any net proceeds to the partners.

Withdrawal under the RULPA   Because the overwhelming majority of limited partnerships operate under a partnership agreement that spells out detailed rules for withdrawal of a general or limited partner, the RULPA does not play as significant a role as does the RUPA for general partnerships. However, the RULPA does set down default rules for withdrawal of partners in the event that the written agreement does not cover withdrawal or its consequences sufficiently. A *general partner* may withdraw at any time without causing dissolution of the partnership. The withdrawal does not result in automatic dissolution provided that (1) the partnership still has at least one remaining *general partner* and (2) all of the partners (both general and limited) agree in writing to continue the partnership.

If the partner's withdrawal does not result in dissolution of the partnership, the partnership must pay the departing partner the fair market value of her interest in the limited partnership within a reasonable time after withdrawal.[15]

In contrast, *limited* partners are subject to restrictions on withdrawal. Absent an agreement in writing to the contrary, the general rule is that limited partners may *not* withdraw from a partnership before the partnership termination time agreed on by the partners.

> **KEY** POINT
> The dissociation (under the RUPA in a general partnership) or withdrawal (under the RULPA in a limited partnership) does not result in automatic dissolution so long as the remaining partners wish to continue.

---

[13]RUPA § 602(c).

[14]RUPA § 606(a).

[15]RULPA § 604.

If the limited partnership agreement does not provide for a certain time before termination, limited partners may withdraw with at least six months' prior written notice to the other partners. Some states have passed additional restrictions, including an absolute prohibition of withdrawal, intended to address special circumstances in family limited partnerships.

✅ Self-Check   Rules for Dissociation/Withdrawal

Is there a basis for rightful dissociation/withdrawal?

1. Under RUPA, a general partnership that owns a diner has 10 partners. One partner never works, only shows up to eat, and harasses servers. Seven partners vote to throw him out.

2. Under RUPA, a tax lawyer who is a partner in a small law firm wants to start a new career at the IRS. She informs her colleagues of her departure at the end of the year, just before the busy tax season.

3. Under RULPA, a limited partner in a partnership that owns a baseball team decides he no longer wants to be part of the steroid scandals, so he withdraws.

4. Under RULPA, a limited partner in a juice company wants to leave and get into the wind-powered energy business. The partnership agreement allows limited partners to leave so long as they do not invest in another beverage company for three years.

Answers to this Self-Check are provided at the end of the chapter.

Other Events of Dissolution   Dissociation is not the only way that a partnership may be dissolved. A partnership may also be dissolved when the partnership has reached its agreed-upon term (a certain date set out in the filings and/or partnership agreement) or when dissolution is mandated by court order or, in the case of a general partnership, agreed to by unanimous consent of the partners. Note that dissolving a limited partnership does not require unanimous consent of all partners. Rather, unanimous consent of each general partner and consent of any limited partner that owns a majority of the rights to receive a distribution as a limited partner is sufficient to dissolve the partnership.

CONCEPT SUMMARY Partner Dissociation or Withdrawal and Dissolution of the Partnership

■ The RUPA lists a variety of events of dissociation, including voluntary separation, expulsion, incapacity, and death, that are termed *rightful* dissociations.

■ In a rightful dissociation, the withdrawing partner is no longer liable for postdissociation liabilities of the partnership. In a *wrongful dissociation* (e.g., one that violates the partnership agreement), the withdrawing partner is liable for any damages the withdrawal caused.

■ The RULPA plays a less significant role in a limited partnership context because so many limited partnerships operate under detailed agreements.

■ Under the RULPA, a general partner may withdraw at any time without causing dissolution. Limited partners are subject to restrictions on withdrawal.

■ Partnerships may also be dissolved upon reaching the agreed-upon term, by court order, or by unanimous consent of the parties.

Franchises: A Method rather than an Entity

An existing entity that wishes to distribute its products to a broader market without the overhead costs of retail space, equipment, and employees can do so through the use of a **franchise.** A franchise should be thought of as a *method* of conducting business that centers on a contractual relationship rather than as a business entity. Federal statutes define a franchise as an arrangement of a continuing commercial relationship for the right to operate a business pursuant to the franchisor's trade name or to sell the seller's branded goods. A franchise involves the **franchisor,** a business entity that has a proven track record of success, selling to a **franchisee** the right to operate the business and use the business's trade secrets, trademarks, products, and so on. The franchisor assists the franchisee with financing, supplies, training, and other aspects of running a successful operation.

Franchise Agreements   The parties are typically bound to each other via a franchise agreement. The franchise agreement covers some of the following terms that govern the relationship between franchisee and franchisor: (1) the term (time limit) of the agreement; (2) franchise fees, payment terms, and ongoing investment or buying requirements; (3) territory rights that usually provide the franchisee with an exclusive geographic area; (4) commitments from the franchisor for training, ongoing management support, and advertising; (5) commitments from the franchisee to follow operating protocol; (6) royalties and other fees that the franchisee must pay; and (7) franchisee termination and/or cancellation policies.

FTC Regulation   The Federal Trade Commission (FTC) is the federal regulatory authority that oversees the regulation of franchisors. The FTC regulations are primarily designed to ensure full disclosure of all information relating to a franchise company prior to a franchisee investment. The FTC regulations are very detailed, but almost all focus on mandatory disclosures about the financial condition of the franchise, success

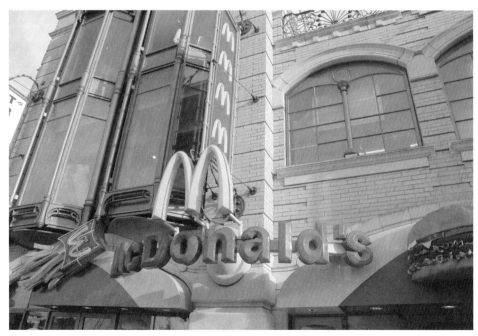

McDonald's worldwide market success was accomplished through franchising.

rates, and other important information used by potential franchisees faced with making the decision to invest in the franchise. The disclosure process is lengthy and complex and almost always requires the counsel of an attorney skilled in franchise law.

State Regulation   Most states have implemented their own individual franchise rules and minimum disclosure requirements to supplement the federal legislation. These additional requirements usually entail filing a registration statement with a state regulatory agency (the state-level equivalent of the FTC). The registration statements are public documents and often require detailed disclosures and biographical information on the principals of the franchisor.

KEY TERMS

Principals p. 409   Owners of a business entity.

Sole proprietorship p. 410   One-person business entity with minimal filing requirements.

Partnership p. 413   Multiple-person business entity in which the partners conduct an ongoing business relationship and share profits and losses.

Express partnership p. 413   Partnership formed when the parties have agreed to conduct a partnership on certain terms and conditions.

Implied partnership p. 413   Partnership formed when the parties have acted like general partners even though the parties did not agree or intend to form a partnership.

Joint venture p. 414   Business relationship between two or more parties for a limited-in-time venture.

Jointly and severally liable p. 414   Legal principle that imposes liability on general partners both together (jointly) and separately (severally) for debts and liabilities of the partnership.

Pass-through entity p. 416   A business entity that does not pay corporate taxes, such as a partnership. Rather, any profits are taxed at individual rates after they pass through the business and are distributed to the partners.

Fiduciary duties p. 417   Under the Revised Uniform Partnership Act, general partners' duties of loyalty, care, and good faith; intended to ensure that the partners are acting in the best interest of the partnership.

Certificate of limited partnership p. 417   The document filed with the state government authority by the general partner to form a limited partnership; requires routine information such as the name, address, and capital contribution of each partner.

Dissociation p. 420   Term used by the RUPA to describe the act of separation of one partner from the partnership.

Withdrawal p. 420   Term used by the RULPA to describe the act of separation of one partner from the partnership.

Winding up p. 423   After dissolution, the process of paying the debts of the partnership and liquidating and/or distributing the remaining assets.

Franchise p. 425   A business arrangement (not a form of business entity) of continuing commercial relationship for the right to operate a business pursuant to the franchisor's trade name or to sell the seller's branded goods.

Franchisor p. 425   A business entity that has a proven track record of success and ability to franchise its products.

Franchisee p. 425   Individual or business with the legal right to operate a franchised business and use the business's trademarks and trade secrets.

Demuth is a sole proprietor of a business that specializes in designing and manufacturing custom-made medical instruments for health care professionals. Several hospitals and physician practice groups approach Demuth and ask him to design and produce a highly specialized surgical instrument that is currently unavailable in the market from larger manufacturers. Demuth, unable to finance the research and development costs, convinces Warren, a private investor, to fund the project. Demuth also recruits Oakley, a physician, to lend her medical expertise. Demuth drafted a letter to Warren and Oakley thanking them for their confidence in the project and setting out certain terms for the venture. The letter was very brief and stated that the parties were equal participants in the business venture intended to develop and manufacture a certain surgical instrument. Demuth would contribute his expertise, laboratory workspace, and manufacturing facilities to the project. Warren would contribute $100,000 as a capital contribution, and Oakley would contribute medical expertise, research knowledge, and $10,000 in capital. The letter ended with a statement that the business venture would last for five years unless the parties mutually agreed on extending the term. Profits or losses would be calculated annually, and each party was to be paid in equal shares for any profits or bear equal losses. Warren and Oakley each wrote "Agreed" and signed and dated the letter on the bottom. Demuth then went on to hire a top engineer and purchased equipment to work on the Demuth-Warren-Oakley project.

After a year of slow progress on the project, Demuth was concerned that the initial capital contribution was not going to be sufficient to carry the venture into its second year. Demuth approached Warren for an additional $100,000. Warren, who was disgruntled about the slow progress, refused. Demuth, anxious about keeping the venture afloat, negotiated a *loan* on behalf of the business with Strand, another private investor. Without the knowledge of the other principals, Demuth signed the promissory note "Demuth-Oakley-Warren Partnership, by Demuth, Partner."

1. What form of entity have Demuth, Warren, and Oakley formed? What law governs the operation of the partnership and the rights of the partners?

2. If the venture becomes insolvent (runs out of money to pay its regular monthly bills), will Demuth, Warren, and/or Oakley be liable for any, some, or all of the debt owed to Strand? If, just after the venture becomes insolvent, Demuth files for personal bankruptcy, will Warren and Oakley now be liable 100 percent for the debt owed to Strand?

3. Assume that when Oakley found out about the loan to Strand, she was so angered that she gave notice to Demuth that she was withdrawing from the partnership before the agreed-upon five-year period. What is the legal impact of Oakley's dissociation on the partnership? Is the partnership automatically dissolved? Is Oakley still liable for the Strand debt and to any creditors to which the partnership owed money?

4. In Question 3 above, suppose that Demuth and Warren decide they cannot continue without Oakley's expertise and they dissolve the partnership. In the process, they are forced to breach several contracts with their vendors. What is Oakley's postdissociation liability to Demuth and Warren for any damages suffered by breaching the vendor contracts?

5. Suppose that, instead of the conflict that developed, the parties ended up being profitable on the venture and they were eager to continue the business. What are the factors that the parties should consider when choosing a business entity that suits the company's needs now and in the future?

A basic understanding of business entities is important when individuals are considering a start-up venture, such as the one contemplated in the Theory to Practice problem, or when a company wishes to start a new business, joint venture, or partnership with another company or individual that leverages its existing business. Suppose you are a manager of Network Associates Corp., a company that retails, installs, and maintains computer networks for business clients. You receive the following e-mail from your senior manager:

> Our company has been approached by NewComp Inc. to form a business relationship that will involve our company being the exclusive supplier of NewComp computer networking products for the northeast

and mid-Atlantic regions of the United States. This could be a lucrative opportunity for us. To avoid any liability problems for Network Associates, we are considering a new entity, separate and apart from the corporation. I will be consulting our counsel and analyzing whether the return will be worth the liability and investment risk. To assist me in my analysis, please write a two- to three-page memorandum that gives me some basic information on (1) what factors we should consider when selecting an entity and (2) whether, if we just begin doing business jointly without any formal agreement, we are exposing ourselves to liability unnecessarily?

A sample answer to this question may be found on this textbook's website at www.mhhe.com/melvinleb2e.

PARTNERSHIP LIABILITY

Lewis and Holland bought a run-down home in Memphis, Tennessee, to renovate and then sell for a profit. The two agreed that Lewis would live in the house during the renovations. In this time period, 20-year-old Amanda Conklin visited the house, where Lewis provided her with alcohol and illicit drugs. As a result of the use of this combination, Conklin died. Lewis attempted to conceal the death by placing her in the car in the garage of the home under construction. Police discovered Conklin's body a month and a half later and arrested Lewis. Conklin's estate sued Holland for civil damages related to Conklin's death under the theory that Holland and Lewis were partners in the co-ownership of the property and, as Lewis's partner, Holland was liable for whatever Lewis did upon the land they co-owned as general partners.

CASE QUESTIONS

1. Was there a partnership?
2. What was the partnership formed to do?
3. As a practical matter, why would Conklin's estate sue Holland instead of Lewis for partnership liability?

FIDUCIARY DUTY

Salmon and Meinhard were partners who entered into a 20-year leasing agreement to operate Hotel Bristol in midtown Manhattan. In exchange for his capital contribution, Meinhard would receive 40 percent of the profits for the first five years and 50 percent every year after until the 20th year, when the lease ended. All losses would be born equally. Salmon alone would "manage, lease, underlet and operate" the hotel. At first, the two lost money, but after 20 years the hotel was very profitable. Just before the lease was about to end, the owner of the hotel (who also owned the five lots surrounding the hotel) approached Salmon and encouraged him to lease the whole city block, including the hotel, for a term of 80 years. Salmon agreed to the expansion plan and drafted the agreements so that the new arrangement began the day after the Meinhard-Salmon lease ended.

Under the new arrangement, Salmon had sole control of the hotel and the rest of the block. Meinhard sued Salmon for breach of fiduciary duty. Salmon asserted that their original partnership had ended when the 20-year lease expired and that he owed Meinhard no duty because they were not partners in the new venture. In its opinion, the court wrote: "Many forms of conduct permissible in a workaday world for those acting at arm's length, are forbidden to those bound by fiduciary ties. A trustee is held to something stricter than the morals of the market place. Not honesty alone, but the punctilio of an honor the most sensitive, is then the standard of behavior."

CASE QUESTIONS

1. Whom did the court side with?
2. What duty did Meinhard claim was breached?
3. Does fiduciary duty end when the partnership expires?

GOOD FAITH

Rahemtulla met Hassam at his religious congregation. Hassam visited Rahemtulla and his wife many times at their home before he pitched his idea to open a steak house restaurant in the Howard Johnson's Inn. Hassam owned the inn along with several other partners. Hassam told the Rahemtullas that revenues from the steak house could be over $2 million a year. Hassam knew that Rahemtulla had absolutely no experience in the food and beverage industry but offered to help him. Rahemtulla quit his job in the corporate sector and borrowed $100,000 using his house as collateral. The $100,000 was Rahemtulla's capital contribution in the partnership. The two entered into a partnership and signed a lease with the Howard Johnson's Inn partnership for the restaurant space. The restaurant opened and Rahemtulla began to co-operate it with Hassam. From the beginning, the restaurant was losing money, and Hassam began to make unilateral decisions that would help cut expenses. The restaurant was dealt a serious financial setback when authorities refused to approve a liquor license for the restaurant, thus lowering revenue potential. After several months, Rahemtulla complained that he had been cheated by Hassam, whose financial reward came from the lease without any concern about the restaurant operations. Hassam blamed Rahemtulla for incompetence in managing the venture. Rahemtulla sued Hassam for breach of fiduciary duty and dealing in bad faith.

CASE QUESTIONS

1. What duties did Hassam owe Rahemtulla?
2. Does it matter that Rahemtulla made foolish decisions when he trusted his friend?
3. What is the potential conflict when Hassam creates a partnership to lease from another partnership he is part of?

DUTY OF LOYALTY

Technology Crosser Ventures (TCV), LP, is a venture capital fund that invests as a limited partner in technology companies that require an infusion of capital. Among the partners are Testler, Hoag, and Kimball. One of the companies they invested in was Spree.com. The partnership was structured to allow Spree, a corporation, to be the general partner with TCV as the limited partner. As part of the partnership agreement, Testler would represent TCV as a member of the board of directors of Spree.com. On August 24, 2000, *The Wall Street Journal* reported a story about TCV and its partners that depicted Testler, Hoag, and Kimball discussing their investments at Testler's office. The paper quoted Testler saying, "What do we want to do with this puppy? The cash runs out soon." Hoag then asked, "They're going to be looking at us for more capital, aren't they?" Kimball added, "I don't want to be supporting them until who knows when." The three men were talking about Spree.com. Spree became insolvent (unable to pay bills as they became due) not long after the article appeared. Spree sued TCV, arguing that the article made it impossible for the company to get more investors. Spree sued Testler for breach of loyalty and due care.

CASE QUESTIONS

1. Who prevails and why?
2. Does this case show potential problems with venture capital firms as limited partners?
3. Was TCV in "control" of Spree.com because it held the purse strings?

FIDUCIARY DUTY

In February 1992, author Thomas Clancy formed Jack Ryan Limited Partnership (JRLP), named after Clancy's fictional hero. Clancy's only partner in the venture was his wife, King. JRLP's purpose was to generate revenue related to the writing, publishing, and sale of certain novels. Each partner owned a half interest in JRLP. The partnership agreement had standard provisions imposing the duty of diligence but also contained a specific provision that allowed each partner to compete freely on an individual basis with the interests of JRLP. Specifically, each partner gave up the right to claim that the other partner breached the duty of care by participating in a competing venture. Clancy had the absolute right to withdraw the use of his name for the series of novels at any time. By 1996 Clancy and King were divorced but remained partners in the highly profitable JRLP entity. In 2001, Clancy announced that he was exercising his right to withdraw the right to use his name for the series starting in 2004. When Clancy did finally withdraw the right to use his name, King filed suit against him, alleging that Clancy's withdrawal of the right to use his name was a breach of fiduciary duty that he owed to King and was done out of ill will toward her stemming from the divorce. Clancy countered that he had the right to conduct the partnership as he thought best and pointed to the partnership agreement's provision on insulation from liability for due care.

CASE QUESTIONS

1. Are there any circumstances under which there could be a *good faith* reason for Clancy to withdraw the right to use his name?
2. Why didn't the provision effectively waiving a breach-of-duty-of-care lawsuit by one partner against another govern this dispute?

✓ Self-Check **ANSWERS**

Rules for Dissociation/Withdrawal

1. No. In order to expel a partner, assuming the absence of a partnership agreement, the RUPA requires *all* partners to vote to expel.

2. Probably not. Her departure at the end of the year just before the busy tax season may result in the partnership's being unable to perform the services on time and possibly breaching agreements while attempting to locate a replacement. Under the RUPA, the departing lawyer may be liable for damages suffered by the partnership.

3. No. Under the RULPA, *limited* partners are subject to restrictions on withdrawal. Absent an agreement in writing to the contrary, the general rule is that limited partners may *not* withdraw from a partnership before the partnership termination time agreed on by the partners. If the limited partnership agreement does *not* provide for a certain time of termination, limited partners may withdraw with at least six months' prior written notice to the other partners. Some states have passed additional restrictions, including an absolute prohibition of withdrawal intended to address special circumstances in family limited partnerships.

4. Yes, so long as the partner acts in good faith. Partnership agreements always displace any RUPA or RULPA rules.

15 CHAPTER

Limited Liability Companies and Limited Liability Partnerships

learning **objectives**

After studying this chapter, students who have mastered the material will be able to:

15-1 Identify the sources and level of laws that govern LLC and LLP entities.

15-2 Explain the function of an operating agreement and the fundamental structure of an LLC.

15-3 Distinguish between the formation and management of an LLC and the formation and management of an LLP.

15-4 Determine the rights of principals upon withdrawal from an LLC.

15-5 Articulate the legal protections from personal liability afforded to the principals in an LLC and LLP.

15-6 Identify the tax treatment schemes of an LLC and LLP.

15-7 Provide the primary methods for capitalizing limited liability entities.

This chapter continues the discussion of forms of business entities and laws that govern business organizations by focusing on limited liability companies (LLCs) and limited liability partnerships (LLPs). The use of these entities has grown rapidly since states first began to recognize them in the late 1970s. They have become a common part of the modern business environment because they offer flexibility advantages for certain business ventures. In this chapter students will learn:

- Background and laws related to operation of a limited liability company (LLC) and a limited liability partnership (LLP).

- Legal liability of principals in an LLC and LLP.

OVERVIEW OF LLCs AND LLPs

LO 15-1, 15-2, 15-3

Prior to the development of LLCs and LLPs, principals who wished to avoid the double taxation of a corporation but still desired liability protection for their personal assets had few choices. In 1977, the Wyoming legislature gave businesses the choice of new hybrid entities that were designed to have characteristics of a partnership while providing full protections afforded to the principals of a corporation. The first hybrid entity was known as a **limited liability company (LLC).** After the Internal Revenue Service began to classify the LLC as a partnership for tax purposes in 1988, many states followed suit and passed their own limited liability statutes primarily modeled on Wyoming's statute. The Uniform Limited Liability Company Act (ULLCA) is the model statute used by the vast majority of state legislatures. A subsequent IRS ruling in 1997 made the selection of the LLC even more attractive because the IRS eliminated strict operating requirements that previously had to be met for an entity to qualify as a partnership for tax purposes. Now all states recognize and provide both procedural (formation) and internal default rules (in the event the parties do not agree otherwise) for the LLC. However, LLC statutes can vary considerably from state to state. Note that a minority of states do not permit partnership taxation at the *state* income tax level. Beginning in 2008, some states began to adopt statutes based on the Revised Uniform Limited Liability Company Act (RULLCA). The revised version attempts to clarify some of the more technical aspects of LLC governance, such as the handling of deadlocks, sufficiency of operating agreements, and rights of members who depart the LLC. As of 2013, only eight states and the District of Columbia had adopted the RULLCA.

The growth in popularity of limited liability companies led state legislatures to consider the liability dilemma of general partners, and they consequently expanded liability protection for general partners in a partnership. In 1991, Texas enacted

Beginning in 1977, state legislatures began to authorize hybrid forms of business entities that afforded favorable tax treatment and limited liability for principals.

the first **limited liability partnership (LLP)** statute, which provided limited protection to general partners. By 1996, many states adopted a more extensive shield for general partners from liability for LLP debts and other liabilities. Now, about half of all states provide the same level of liability protection to a general partner in an LLP as is provided to a limited partner in a limited partnership entity.

While LLCs and LLPs are similar in many ways to corporations and partnerships, the legal terminology for describing procedural and governance aspects of these entities is different. It is important to understand the differences to avoid any confusion about the form of entity.

Limited Liability Companies (LLCs)

A limited liability company is an entity whose primary characteristics are that it offers its principals the same amount of liability protection afforded to principals of a corporate form of entity and it offers pass-through tax treatment for its principals without the restrictions on ownership and scope required for other pass-through entities (such as an S corporation, discussed in detail in the next chapter). For example, suppose that Developer Inc. wants to start a land use project to build a commercial office building. It wishes to partner with Garrett, the owner of several pieces of property in the area under consideration. Both the principals of Developer Inc. and Garrett wish to have pass-through tax treatment but also wish to have as much protection as possible from liability of personal assets. Because Developer Inc. is a corporate principal, the parties cannot choose a pass-through corporate entity. They can, however, achieve these objectives by forming an LLC. In an LLC, owners are known as *members*.

Formation   An LLC is formed by filing **articles of organization** (also called **certificates of organization**) with the state public filing official in the secretary of state's corporation bureau. Although historically LLCs were required to file fairly extensive articles, modern-day trends require the same type of information as included on a corporation's articles of incorporation. Most states require only basic information such as the name of the entity, the location of its principal place of business, and the names of its members. A number of states also require a contemporaneous filing with tax authorities to notify them of the existence of the LLC. A sample certificate of organization for an LLC is presented in Figure 15.1.

Most importantly, LLCs are frequently governed by agreement of the parties in the form of an **operating agreement.**[1] If the parties do not execute an operating agreement, the state LLC statute sets out default rules. Operating agreements, similar to partnership agreements, cover many of the internal rules for the actual operation of the entity. One of the primary benefits of an LLC is that it affords its members a great deal of flexibility in terms of the rights and responsibilities of each member. This flexibility includes:

- *Structure of governance and responsibility of members:* The agreement will typically set forth a structure for managing the entity through a single member or a board of "managing members" (akin to a board of directors), and the agreement will define their responsibilities in terms of day-to-day operations of the entity. This provision will also spell out voting rights of members, procedures for voting, transactions that require a vote of the general members (such as the sale of the LLC assets to another company), and procedures for admission of any new members.

- *Death, incapacity, and dissolution:* Members often agree to a series of "what ifs" of managing an LLC through their operating agreement. If a member can no longer perform the duties required by the agreement, this section details a procedure for handling the circumstance of a member's death or incapacity. The procedure is typically different for managing members and members, but in most cases the operating agreement allows the venture's remaining members to choose whether or not to continue. In the event the members choose not to continue, the procedure for dissolution (including preferences of members in terms of who gets paid first after liquidation) is typically outlined in the agreement.

Liability   Another important feature of an LLC is its limited liability of its members. LLC members are insulated from personal liability for any business debt or liability if the venture fails. For example, suppose that Phillips is the managing member of Active Wear LLC and signs a five-year lease agreement with Landlord on behalf of Active Wear. One year into the lease, Active Wear has a downturn in business, is forced to breach the lease, and moves out hoping to convert to an online business model. Landlord's rights are against the LLC entity only. Landlord may not obtain a judgment against Phillips or collect back rent or other damages from Phillips's personal assets.

However, two important factors moderate this limited liability. First, landlords and other creditors will often require a **personal guarantee** from the members whereby the members pledge personal assets to guarantee payment obligations of the business venture.[2] Second, a court may discard the protection in a case where the court finds that fairness demands that the LLC members should compensate any damaged party when the entity is without resources to cover the full amount owed (e.g., in a case where the members engaged in fraud).

> **KEY** POINT
> Although LLC members are insulated from personal liability for any business debt or liability, creditors often require LLC members to sign personal guarantees and, in cases of fundamental unfairness, a court may disregard the LLC protections.

---

[1] Some states call this document an "LLC agreement" or other similar names.

[2] Personal guarantees are discussed in more detail in the next chapter.

FIGURE 15.1   Sample LLC Certificate of Organization

PENNSYLVANIA DEPARTMENT OF STATE
CORPORATION BUREAU

Certificate of Organization
Domestic Limited Liability Company
(15 Pa.C.S. § 8913)

Name Daniel J. Webster, Esquire Address 1000 Professional Avenue, Suite 120 City State Zip Code Philadelphia, PA 19130	Document will be returned to the name and address you enter to the left. ⇐

Typically, a business attorney
will prepare this document
for the LLC and assist the
principals with administrative
start-up.

Fee: $125

    In compliance with the requirements of 15 Pa.C.S. § 8913 (relating to certificate of organization), the undersigned, desiring to organize a limited liability company, hereby certifies that:

1. The name of the limited liability company (*designator is required, i.e., "company", "limited"* or *"limited liability company" or abbreviation*):

Redfern Catering, LLC

Basic information about the
LLC and its registered
location. Note that an LLC
may opt to use a commercial
registered office provider
(similar to resident agent
services) for a fee. The provider
typically provides services
such as accepting legal
documents (e.g., a complaint
in a lawsuit) for the LLC.

2. The (a) address of the limited liability company's initial registered office in this Commonwealth or (b) name of its commercial registered office provider and the county of venue is:

(a) Number and Street	City	State	Zip	County
One Alpha Drive,	Elizabethtown,	PA	17022	Lancaster

(b) Name of Commercial Registered Office Provider		County
c/o: None		

3. The name and address, including street and number, if any, of each organizer is (*all Organizers must sign on page 2*):

Name	Address
Francis Redfern	One Alpha Drive, Elizabethtown, PA 17022
Alexander Colgate	10 Flamingo Drive, Dania Beach, FL 33004

Organizers are those who
start up the LLC initially.
Once the LLC is formed,
they become *members*.

FIGURE 15.1   Sample LLC Certificate of Organization

DSCB:15-8913-2

4. *Strike out if inapplicable term*
   A member's interest in the company is to be evidenced by a certificate of membership interest.

These provisions allow the LLC's organizers to choose (1) whether the LLC actually has to issue a certificate to evidence a member's interest and (2) whether the LLC is to be manager-managed or member-managed.

5. *Strike out if inapplicable:*
   Management of the company is vested in a manager or managers.

6. The specified effective date, if any, is: **October 10, 2014**
                          month   date   year   hour, if any

LLCs are sometimes used by professional service firms (such as a law firm or a group of architects). If the LLC wishes to restrict the business to members with professional licenses in a certain field, the profession is inserted here.

7. *Strike out if inapplicable:* The company is a restricted professional company organized to render the following restricted professional service(s):

Not applicable

The organizers may add additional provisions of LLC management unique to the company by attaching a sheet to the certificate of organization.

8. For additional provisions of the certificate, if any, attach an 8½ × 11 sheet.

IN TESTIMONY WHERE OF, the organizer(s) has (have) signed this Certificate of Organization this

_____ day of_____, _____ .

_____
                Signature

_____
                Signature

_____
                Signature

Signature of all organizers.

Taxation   Another attractive advantage of an LLC is the various tax treatment alternatives. Although many LLCs are typically treated as a pass-through entity, the LLC's members may also elect to be taxed as a corporation if they consider the corporate tax structure more favorable. Recall from the discussion in previous chapters of pass-through entities that their advantages are primarily (1) the ability to flow through to the investors the tax deductions and losses that are typically generated by an emerging company or a company with significant up-front debt and (2) the ability to distribute earnings without incurring double-level taxation (i.e., without having a tax imposed on both the entity and the member).

Capitalization   LLCs are capitalized primarily through debt via private lenders or commercial lenders or through a sale of equity ownership in the LLC itself. The operating agreement of the LLC often controls the amount and methods of capitalizing the business.

Management and Operation   LLC statutes typically assume that the members will agree on the specifics of managing the venture through a management agreement. Some states require the entire agreement to be in writing, some require only certain parts of the agreement to be in writing, while other states have no writing requirement at all. Most states distinguish between a **member-managed LLC** and a **manager-managed LLC.** In a member-managed LLC, the management structure of the entity is similar to a general partnership with all the members having the authority to bind the business. In a manager-managed LLC, a named manager (or managers) generally has the day-to-day operational responsibilities, while the nonmanaging members are typically investors with little input on the course of business taken by the entity except for major decisions (such as a merger). In a manager-managed LLC, nonmanaging members generally do not have the authority to act on behalf of the business venture. The choice of manager-managed or member-managed is generally made on the public filing of the articles of organization and is available to third parties for purposes of checking the authority of an individual to bind the LLC.

As in many business relationships, the managers of an LLC owe the *fiduciary duties* of care and loyalty to the LLC's other members. Controlling members (those with veto power or the ownership stake to block decisions by other members) also owe a duty of loyalty to the other members. LLC statutes regarding fiduciary duties vary by state and can be strengthened or pared back by the operating agreement. In fact, the modern trend is to specifically eliminate any liability for a breach of the duty of care. However, managers and controlling members (i.e., members with ownership sufficient to decide or veto internal operational matters) must adhere to the duty of loyalty, are prohibited from self-dealing, and must act in good faith when dealing with the LLC's business matters.

> **KEY POINT**
> Managing members and controlling members owe a fiduciary duty to other members.

LO 15-4   Dissolution of LLCs and Dissociation of Members

LLC laws define **dissolution** of an LLC as a liquidation process[3] triggered by an event that is specified in the operating agreement (such as the death of a key member) or by the decision of the majority of membership interests (or the percentage called for in the operating agreement) to dissolve the company. The members of an LLC may have also agreed to a maximum term for conducting business in the operating agreement. If the term expires but the members want the LLC to continue, they must have a unanimous vote to fix an additional term *or* the majority of LLC member interests may vote to continue the LLC at will (with no fixed term and subject to dissolution at any time). **Dissociation** occurs when an individual member decides to exercise the right to withdraw from the partnership. Generally, upon a dissociation the remaining members may either continue the LLC or

---

[3]Liquidation includes preserving assets of a business, paying creditors, and then distributing any remaining profits to the individual members.

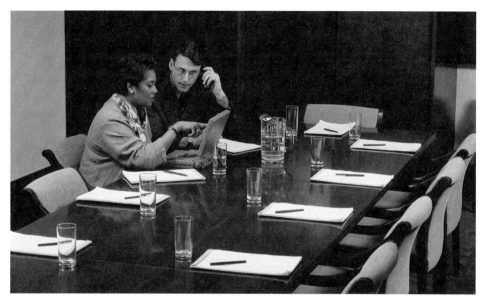

Members of an LLC can prevent disputes from occurring by planning for events, such as death or dissociation of a member, in their operating agreement.

decide to trigger dissolution. Of course, the parties may agree to their own unique set of rules through the operating agreement. Agreeing ahead of time on what will happen if one member decides to withdraw and reducing the agreement to writing is a strategic way to avoid future disputes. Case 15.1 illustrates the dangers of failing to address an important issue in an operating agreement when a court takes up a dispute between the members of an LLC and a departing member.

Limited Liability Partnerships (LLPs) LO 15-5, 15-6, 15-7

Most states recognize limited liability partnerships through their partnership statutes. Recall that the chief danger of being a general partner is the amount of potential liability for acts of other general partners or the debts and liabilities of the partnership itself. LLP statutes provide general partnerships with the right to convert their entity and gain the protective shield ordinarily only afforded to limited partners or corporate shareholders. Although the origins of LLP laws were rooted in protection of professional service firm partnerships (law, accounting, etc.), the use of LLPs is much more widespread now as some family businesses have also used the LLP form as a way to handle issues unique to the transition from one generation to another.

Formation   Limited liability partnerships are formed when a general partnership files a **statement of qualification** with the appropriate public official. The conversion of the partnership must be approved by a majority of the ownership. The statement includes the name and street address, an affirmative statement electing to become an LLP, an effective date, and the signatures of at least two of the partners. Some states also require a filing to inform tax authorities of the existence of the entity. Once approved, the filing becomes part of the public record.

Liability   Of all of the business entities that we have discussed thus far, the LLP has the greatest variance of liability protection under state law. While the general idea behind being an LLP is that all partners have liability protection for debts and liabilities of the partnership, some states impose conditions on these limits. In cases where a partner has engaged in some misconduct or tortious conduct (such as negligence), the LLP acts to shield only the personal assets of *other* partners—never the partner who committed the misconduct or negligence.

FACT SUMMARY   Lieberman was a member and vice president of Wyoming.com, LLC (Wyoming), with a $20,000 ownership stake in the LLC at the time of formation in 1994. After a dispute between the parties in 1998, Lieberman was terminated as vice president by the other LLC members. Lieberman served Wyoming with a "notice of withdrawal" and demanded that Wyoming pay for Lieberman's "share of the company" in the amount of $400,000. Wyoming held a meeting of remaining members and voted to accept Lieberman's withdrawal and continue operating the LLC. Wyoming then notified Lieberman that they accepted his withdrawal but offered him only $20,000 because that was his initial ownership stake. Lieberman rejected the $20,000 offer. Because the operating agreement was silent on the issue of dissociation, Wyoming filed suit asking for a declaratory judgment of its rights against Lieberman.

SYNOPSIS OF DECISION AND OPINION   The Wyoming Supreme Court ruled that Lieberman did not have the right to force Wyoming to buy his interest even after the notice of withdrawal. Lieberman's withdrawal is recognized as a dissociation under the state LLC statute, but there was no contractual provision (via the operating agreement) between the members related to a buyout of a dissociating member's financial interest in the venture. The operating agreement only provided a method for calculating a member's interest in the case of *dissolution*. Nor does the state LLC statute provide for a buyout in the case of a dissociated member. Therefore, even though Lieberman is a dissociated member, he may not demand a buyout, nor may Wyoming force him to sell his interest. Lieberman continues to keep his interest in the LLC until dissolution.

WORDS OF THE COURT: Limited Rights   "Lieberman has withdrawn as a member of Wyoming.com and all remaining members unanimously accepted his withdrawal as a member. Lieberman is thus no longer a member of Wyoming.com. . . . Because the members of Wyoming.com failed to contractually provide for a buy-out, Lieberman remains a [financial interest] holder in Wyoming.com, LLC. There are no further rights or obligations of the parties for this court to construe with regards to this situation."

Case Questions

1. Based on the court's decision, what specific rights did Lieberman lose when he withdrew as a member of the LLC?

2. What kind of language and methodology could be included in an operating agreement that could have prevented this dispute?

Legal Speak ›))
Declaratory Judgment   A binding court judgment that establishes the rights and other legal relations of the parties without providing for enforcement. In this case, Wyoming limited its legal risks and unknowns in relation to Lieberman by obtaining a court decision before taking any further action regarding Lieberman's rights in the LLC.

In Case 15.2, a federal appeals court analyzes the potential personal liability of partners after an LLP has been dissolved.

Some states provide liability shields for LLP partners *only* when the liability arises from some *negligence* by another partner but not for other types of liabilities such as those resulting from a breach of contract. For example, suppose that the LLP state statutes of New Chipperville provide for liability protection for partners when one partner acts negligently. Two accountants, Milton and Cowley, form a limited liability partnership called MC Tax Services LLP in New Chipperville. On behalf of the LLP, the partners sign a lease for space with Landlord and invest several thousand dollars from their own assets for start-up capital. One year later, Milton commits a serious error on a client's tax return, and the client sues the firm for malpractice and obtains a $50,000 judgment against the LLP. Because of the negative attention of this case, MC Tax Services loses several large clients and can no longer make its lease payments to Landlord, and the partnership dissolves. Assume that the judgment is not covered by insurance and exceeds the assets of the LLP. Under the law of New Chipperville, the client may pursue Milton's individual assets to pay the $50,000 judgment but not Cowley's. The liability shield protects Cowley for any acts of his partner when the liability results from a *tort* (in this case professional malpractice, a form of negligence). However, Cowley is still liable to Landlord for defaulting on the lease because the liability resulted from a *contractual* obligation.

FACT SUMMARY   Chargois and Ernster (C&E) were individuals who formed and registered a limited liability partnership to operate their law practice in 2002. In an attempt to solicit business, C&E developed a website in June 2003 that included a link using Dillard Department Stores' corporate name and trademarked logo. C&E had represented several Dillard customers, and the website gave potential clients access to content created by C&E that allegedly documented acts of illegal profiling by Dillard. Dillard sued C&E for trademark infringement, cyber piracy, and various business torts.

In 2004, while the litigation continued, Chargois and Ernster executed a separation agreement that provided for dissolution of the partnership. C&E's registration as an LLP was not renewed with state authorities, and the registration expired later that same year. However, the defunct LLP entity remained a party to the Dillard litigation, and no party was substituted on its behalf. On November 2, 2004, the court entered a final judgment ordering "Chargois & Ernster, L.L.P." to pay Dillard $143,500.

Dillard could not collect on the judgment because the entity had been dissolved and had no assets. Dillard sought a declaration that the two principals were personally liable, jointly and severally, for the 2004 final judgment entered against C&E. Chargois and Ernster argued that they were shielded from any partnership liability or debt by the state LLP statute. The trial court granted judgment for Dillard in the amount of $143,500 against Chargois and Ernster, jointly and severally, and each appealed.

SYNOPSIS OF DECISION AND OPINION   The U.S. Court of Appeals for the Fifth Circuit ruled in favor of Dillard and held Chargois and Ernster personally liable for the judgment owed to Dillard. The court rejected arguments that the partners were insulated from liability because C&E's debt was incurred when the infringing website was created in June 2003, at which time C&E was still a registered limited liability partnership. Instead, the court found that the debt was incurred when the judgment was entered on November 2, 2004, at which time the LLP had lost its liability-limiting attributes and no longer protected Chargois and Ernster.

WORDS OF THE COURT: Timing of a Liability   "Although the terms 'debt' and 'incurred' are not defined by the [statute], a plain reading of the statute's text supports Dillard's proffered interpretation. Neither partner was necessarily aware in June 2003 that displaying the Dillard's mark on the law firm website would ultimately lead to a partnership debt. The underlying conduct gave rise to the possibility of a future debt, but to say that a debt was 'incurred' at that time unrealistically distorts the meaning of the word. After all, [C&E's] conduct may have gone undetected, it may have been adjudged perfectly innocent, or Dillard's may have opted not to sue. Under any of those scenarios, no debt would ever have been incurred, let alone incurred in June 2003. It was only when the district court entered judgment against [C&E] in November 2004 that a payable debt came into existence. It was then that [C&E] incurred the debt within the meaning of the provision."

Case Questions

1. Should two partners who have agreed to separate be forced to continue the LLP's existence for a certain period of time?

2. Could it be argued that the debt actually was incurred once C&E had notice that they had infringed on Dillard's trademark?

[4]The reported citation of this case includes Evanston Insurance Company as a party for procedural reasons. For sake of clarity, the case citation has been abbreviated.

Consider the plight of someone who has suffered damages due to another's negligence but cannot recover compensation because of the protection of an LLP. In the Milton-Cowley example discussed earlier, suppose that the client who was damaged by Milton's error cannot actually recover the judgment awarded to him because Milton is without assets. Because Cowley is not liable, the client is left with a court order that is worthless. In order to be sure that parties have at least some ability to recover, an increasing number of states require that the LLP and individual partners carry and maintain a certain amount of *liability insurance* as a condition of LLP formation.

Taxation   LLPs are treated as pass-through entities. They are not subject to tax; any income is taxed only when it is distributed to its partners. Because it is not a taxable entity, an LLP files an information return that informs federal and state tax authorities of the profits and losses of the LLP. All income or losses are reported on the partners' individual tax returns. Any losses are deductible and may sometimes help to reduce taxes on other sources of revenue in the individual's tax return.

Capitalization   LLPs are capitalized in the same way as a partnership: through debt via private or commercial lenders or by a sale of partnership equity for ownership in the LLP itself. The partnership agreement of the LLP often controls the amount and methods of capitalizing the business and the procedures for collecting additional contributions from partners as necessary (a process known as a *capital call*). Additional capital contribution requirements are frequently the subject of a partnership agreement. There are some cases in which the partnership has the right to "call" for more money contributions from each partner in order to keep the partnership afloat. Although terms vary, partners that are not in a position to make a call contribution may be forced to sell their interest in the partnership.

Management and Operation   Although not required by statute, limited liability partnerships will frequently have a partnership agreement that sets out the management and operational structure. LLPs are sometimes governed by one or more managing partners and/or some type of executive committee elected by the other partners. The day-to-day operations and powers of the partners and board of partners are spelled out in the partnership agreement as well. The election procedures, qualifications, compensation, meeting times, and other organizational matters are typically addressed in the partnership agreement. In most states, the default agreement is the governing RUPA or UPA provision.

CONCEPT SUMMARY   LLCs and LLPs

	Limited Liability Company (LLC)	Limited Liability Partnership (LLP)
Personal liability of principals	LLC members and managers are not personally liable for any debts or liabilities of the LLC so long as state law conditions are met.	LLP partners are generally not liable for the debts of the partnership or the liabilities of the other partners. Partners are personally liable for their own negligence.
Organization/ start-up expenses	Articles of organization. Legal fees are usually based on number of members and complexity of organization.	Statement of qualification. Legal fees are usually based on number of members and complexity of organization.
Management and control	Managed through managing member(s) (no officers, directors, or shareholders). Members abide by operating agreement for management and control issues.	Managed through managing partner(s) and/or executive committee (no officers, directors, or shareholders). Members abide by partnership agreement for management and control issues.

	Limited Liability Company (LLC)	Limited Liability Partnership (LLP)
Capital	Typically sells shares of financial interest in the LLC and/or secures private or commercial loans.	Private or commercial loans. Personal financial contributions of partners may be required in partnership agreement.
Taxes	Option of being treated as a corporation or as a pass-through entity. May also have to pay miscellaneous state and local taxes to operate business.	Pass-through taxation treatment (no tax is paid on income to the entity, but when the entity distributes dividends, tax is paid at the individual partner's individual tax rate). May also have to pay miscellaneous state and local taxes to operate business.
Designation	Doe Group, LLC	Doe and Associates, LLP

KEY TERMS

Limited liability company (LLC) p. 433   A multiperson form of business entity that offers liability protection for its principals along with various tax options.

Limited liability partnership (LLP) p. 434   Form of business entity that provides the same level of liability protection to a general partner in an LLP as is provided to a limited partner in a limited partnership form of entity.

Articles of organization p. 435   Document filed to create an LLC; in most states, requires only basic information such as the name of the entity, the location of its principal place of business, and the names of its members. *Also called* certificate of organization.

Operating agreement p. 435   Document that governs an LLC; sets out the structure and internal rules for operation of the entity.

Personal guarantee p. 435   Pledge from LLC members of personal assets to guarantee payment obligations of the business venture.

Member-managed LLC p. 438   LLC management structure similar to that of a general partnership, with all the members having the authority to bind the business.

Manager-managed LLC p. 438   LLC management structure in which the members name a manager (or managers) who generally has the day-to-day operational responsibilities while the nonmanaging members are typically investors with little input on the course of business taken by the entity except for major decisions.

Dissolution p. 438   In the context of an LLC, a liquidation process triggered by an event that is specified in the operating agreement (such as the death of a key member) or by the decision of the majority of membership interests (or the percentage called for in the operating agreement) to dissolve the company.

Dissociation p. 438   Process in which an individual member of an LLC exercises the right to withdraw from the partnership.

Statement of qualification p. 439   Document filed to form a limited liability partnership by converting a general partnership.

Beverly Hills Autos (BHA) LLC is a retail car dealership organized as a limited liability company and engaged in the business of selling various brands of luxury automobiles and SUVs in several dealership locations. The LLC was structured as a manager-managed LLC with two managing members and six other members who were primarily investors. The parties had an operating agreement that provided the structure and authority of managing members, included a provision eliminating liability for a breach of the duty of care, and stated that the members agreed to abide by the default LLC statute in their state based on the Uniform Limited Liability Company Act (ULLCA) for terms not in the agreement. One of the nonmanaging members, Luciano, began a conversation with the owner of another car dealership and eventually negotiated a merger agreement. However, the managing members were out of town, and Luciano signed the agreement on behalf of the partnership without the managers' knowledge. When the managing members learned of the merger, they immediately attempted to cancel the contract on behalf of BHA.

1. Will a court support BHA's attempt to cancel the contract? What will be BHA's likely theory of the case?
2. Assume that the managing members agreed with the transaction and signed on in agreement. Given BHA's choice of business entity, what are the options for financing this transaction?
3. Would an LLP be a better form than an LLC for BHA? Why or why not?
4. Assume that Luciano didn't bring the opportunity to the LLC members but rather purchased the competing dealership with another partner outside the LLC. Subsequently, Luciano offers to sell the dealership to BHA at a premium over what he paid for it. Has Luciano breached his fiduciary duty? If so, which one?
5. If Luciano decides to exercise his dissociation rights, what is the impact on the remaining members of the LLC? Is dissolution of the LLC triggered by Luciano's dissociation?

Members in an LLC typically begin negotiating an operating agreement by meeting and developing a list of concerns and objectives that are addressed in an LLC operating agreement. Assume that you are a founding principal in Beverly Hills Auto in the Theory to Practice problem. Individually or in groups, develop a one-page bullet-point memorandum that outlines concerns that the BHA members may have. Be sure to address issues related to profit and loss split; managing members; insurance; day-to-day operations; meetings; voting rights; procedures for death, disability, or bankruptcy of a member or managing member; and a procedure in case of deadlock. A sample answer may be found on this textbook's website www.mhhe.com/melvinleb2e.

LIABILITY OF LLC MEMBER

Flahive is the managing member of Flahive Oil and Gas, LLC. The LLC entered into an agreement with Kaycee to mine oil and gas from Kaycee's property. During the mining, Kaycee alleged that Flahive's process was flawed and resulted in contamination of Kaycee's property. After discovering that the LLC was without assets, Kaycee sued Flahive individually. Flahive defended on the basis that the contract was between the LLC and Kaycee and that he has no personal liability.

CASE QUESTIONS

1. Can the court disregard the LLC entity in this situation?
2. Does fairness demand that Flahive be personally responsible for the LLC's negligence?

PERSONAL GUARANTEES OF LLC MEMBERS

Four physicians formed an LLC to operate a medical practice. They capitalized the venture with a bank loan to the LLC. Each physician signed a personal guarantee to secure a proportionate part of the loan (25 percent each). A dispute developed that led two of the physicians to depart and move to another practice. The bank became concerned that the loan was in jeopardy, so it brought suit against the remaining physicians in the practice to recover the amount due under the loan from them. While the bank sued the remaining physicians, the departing physicians were engaged in litigation with the remaining physicians over mismanagement of their former practice. The remaining physicians contended that the bank could not enforce the personal guarantees until disputes among the physicians were resolved because the LLC may still have assets if the litigation is successful.

CASE QUESTIONS

1. Does the bank have to wait until the litigation is complete to enforce the personal guarantees against the physicians? Why or why not?
2. What is the impact of the departing physicians' dissociation from the LLC?

INVOLUNTARY WITHDRAWAL

Lambrecht was a founding member of an accounting firm, Jordan & Company. He and other members of his firm formed an LLC for purposes of acquiring and maintaining real estate for the firm's offices. The LLC members signed an operating agreement that required withdrawal from the LLC upon termination from Jordan & Company and specified that the ex-member would be entitled to only the balance in his or her capital account. In November 2000, Lambrecht assaulted a colleague in the office and was eventually charged with battery. Jordan & Company terminated Lambrecht and offered approximately $3,000 as payment for his capital account. Lambrecht refused to accept the payment and disputed that he was required to withdraw, claiming that the operating agreement covered only voluntary cessation of employment. Lambrecht also claimed that the agreement to pay the capital account balance was unfair and that any payment should be based on market value.

CASE QUESTIONS

1. May the LLC members force Lambrecht to withdraw?
2. Is it fair to base the payment on the capital account balance (typically very small) rather than fair market value (typically a larger amount) when the withdrawal is forced?

LLP INNOCENT PARTNERS

Wheeler, Lawson, and Snyder formed an LLP for their law practice. Wheeler was the managing partner for the LLP and oversaw the firm's business affairs, including malpractice insurance coverage. When applying to First American Title for the firm's malpractice insurance, Wheeler made a material misrepresentation on the insurance application. Both Wheeler and Lawson engaged in unethical and illegal conduct by failing to properly administer client trust funds and using the funds for their own benefit. Snyder was located at a separate office and had little contact with his partners and no knowledge of their misrepresentations or illegal conduct. Eventually, the firm was sued for malpractice and damages by various clients. First American Title paid out several claims and then sought recovery from each of the partners and canceled their policy based on the misrepresentation by Wheeler. Snyder argued that he should not be liable for the negligent or intentional acts of his partners.

CASE QUESTIONS

1. Does the LLP shield protect Snyder's personal assets from negligence committed by other partners?
2. Should Snyder have been more active in regard to being aware of his partners' deeds? Did he have a duty to inquire?

16
CHAPTER

Corporations

learning objectives

After studying this chapter, students who have mastered the material will be able to:

16-1 Identify the sources and level of law governing the formation and internal matters of corporations.

16-2 Recognize the liability associated with improper formation by a promoter.

16-3 Explain the primary methods for capitalizing a corporation.

16-4 Categorize corporate entities on the basis of how their income is taxed and understand the concept of flow-through taxation.

16-5 Describe the fundamental structure and roles of officers, directors, and shareholders in the corporate form of entity and understand the functions of each role and how the structure is governed.

16-6 Identify the major fiduciary duties owed by insiders of a corporation to its shareholders and give examples of each duty.

16-7 Apply the business judgment rule to an alleged breach of fiduciary duty by an insider.

16-8 Distinguish between a shareholder derivative suit and a direct action suit.

16-9 Identify circumstances under which a court will pierce the veil and explain the impact on the principals.

This chapter continues the discussion of business entities that provide liability protection for principals. The principals of some business ventures form a *corporation* to achieve their objectives and gain flexibility not found in other entities. Although the corporate form is sometimes associated with large multinational corporations, in fact many corporations are relatively small, with a limited number of principals (sometimes just a single owner). In this chapter, students will learn:

- The governing source of law and categories of corporations.

- Rules governing the formation of a corporation.

- Personal liability of the principals for corporate liabilities and debts.

- How corporations are capitalized, taxed, and structured.

- The duties of corporate managers, such as officers and directors, to the owners of the corporation.

CORPORATE ENTITIES LO 16-1, 16-2

A **corporation** is a fictitious legal entity that exists as an independent "person" separate from its principals. Although this corporate "person" is a legally created fiction, it is a well-established and deeply seated principle of American law. Recall from Chapter 2, "Business and the Constitution," that the U.S. Supreme Court has ruled that

corporations are entitled to full First Amendment protection for political speech. In a business context it is also important to note that a corporation, like an individual person, may file suit or be sued and may form a contract or breach a contract. In contrast to sole proprietorships and partnerships, the obligations of corporations are separate and distinct from the personal obligations of their principals.

Corporations are created through a state law filing, and their formation is governed through *state statutes*. State statutes vary in their corporate formation and governance rules, but each state has a specific law, often called the **business corporation law** or something similar, that covers such matters as the structure of the corporation, oversight of the activity of the corporation's managers, rights of the principals in the case of the sale of assets or ownership interests, annual reporting requirements, and other issues that affect the internal rules of the business venture. Over half of the states have adopted all or substantial portions of a model act known as the **Revised Model Business Corporation Act (RMBCA)**[1] drafted by the American Law Institute. While state statutes regulate the internal governance of a corporation, federal laws regulate the offering or trading of

---

[1] The American Law Institute also issued *Principles of Corporate Governance* in 1994.

ownership interests to the public and set certain standards for internal governance for some companies.[2]

Categories of Corporations

Corporations may be classified into one or more categories that reflect their overall purpose, capitalization (how they are funded), location, and structure. The two major categories are *privately held corporations,* which are owned exclusively by a group of private individuals, and *publicly held corporations,* which sell their ownership interests via public stock exchanges.

Privately Held versus Publicly Held   The most common category is a **privately held corporation.** Privately held corporations are those that do not sell ownership interests through sales via a broker to the general public or to financial institutions or public investors. Privately held corporations have substantial flexibility in terms of their internal operating procedures and do not generally have to comply with rigorous corporate structures or formalities. For example, in lieu of an actual meeting, privately held corporations often use a single document signed by each principal to dispose of necessary tasks such as electing directors or issuing stock. This document is known as a *unanimous consent resolution.* Many states give privately held corporations the option of electing to become a *closely held* or *family-held* entity. This option further restricts the number or type of owners that a corporation may have, but it gives even more flexibility on how the business venture may be organized and managed.

Note that even though many privately held corporations have a relatively small number of shareholders, there is no limit in terms of revenue. It is not uncommon for corporations with revenues in the eight-figure range to be privately held. Often, the flexibility of a privately held corporation outweighs any desire of the principals to capitalize the business through a sale to the general public.

When a privately held corporation wishes to fund capitalization through the sale of ownership interests to the general public and commercial investors, the principals pursue an Initial Public Offering (IPO) and then continue their corporate existence as a publicly held corporation. After the IPO, the corporation trades (buys and sells) stocks through a public stock exchange (the New York Stock Exchange, or NYSE, is perhaps the most famous and influential, but many more exist). A publicly held corporation is subject to a substantial amount of federal and state regulation, primarily through securities laws and corporate governance statutes such as the Sarbanes-Oxley Act. A publicly held corporation is subject to close scrutiny by a variety of regulatory agencies because investors across the globe depend on regulation to ensure integrity among the insiders managing the corporation. Regulation of publicly held corporations is discussed extensively in Chapter 17, "Regulation of Securities, Corporate Governance, and Financial Markets."

Other Categories   Besides being classified as publicly held or privately held, corporations may fall into one of the following categories:

- *Domestic:* In the state of its incorporation, a corporation is referred to as a *domestic* corporation.
- *Foreign:* A corporation that transacts business in a state other than its state of incorporation is known as a *foreign* corporation in the other state. For example, WidgetCo is incorporated in Florida and sells its widgets in Florida and Georgia. In Florida, WidgetCo is referred to as a domestic corporation. In Georgia, it is referred to as a foreign corporation.

---

[2]Federal securities law is discussed in detail in Chapter 17, "Regulation of Securities, Corporate Governance, and Financial Markets."

- *Alien:* A corporation formed outside the United States that transacts business in the United States is referred to as an *alien* corporation.
- *Nonprofit: Nonprofit* corporations are those that do not have profit-seeking owners but rather exist to perform some service to the public at large. (Examples include charities, educational institutions, and certain hospitals).
- *Public: Public* corporations are those formed by a government body to serve the public at large, such as public mass transit companies. Public corporations have a similar structure to a private corporation but have no owners. Be sure not to confuse *publicly held* corporations (discussed earlier) with public corporations.
- *Professional: Professional* corporations are those in which the ownership is restricted to a particular profession licensed in a certain field. These corporations have a corporate structure but are open only to members in good standing of a particular profession. For example, law firms that are organized as a professional corporation may be owned only by attorneys admitted to the practice of law who are currently active and in good standing.

Formation

Compared to other entities, a corporation has perhaps the most formal filing and reporting requirements. Principals that wish to form a corporation do so by filing a document with a state authority, usually the corporation bureau of the secretary of state's office, that sets out the corporation's name and purpose, number of shares issued, and address of the corporation's headquarters. This document, known as the **articles of incorporation,**[3] sets in motion the incorporation process. In addition to requiring the articles of incorporation, state statutes often require filings with tax authorities to notify them of a corporation's existence.

Visit Connect for examples of articles of incorporation from various states.

State authorities then review the articles, and if they are in satisfactory form, the authorities register the document in public archives and the venture is considered formed. In most states, the date of incorporation is actually made retroactive to the date of filing with the state authorities.

Preincorporation Activity: Liability of Promoters

In most cases, an individual or group of individuals begin to carry out a business venture's activity before actually filing the articles of incorporation. These activities may include arranging for necessary capital through a loan, recruiting personnel, leasing property, and arranging to have the business incorporated. The individual who performs these activities is known as a *promoter.* If the promoter makes a contract on behalf of a not-yet-formed corporation, she may have some degree of *personal liability* to perform under the contract. Generally, the promoter is personally liable when she knows (and the other party has *no reason* to know) that the corporation is not in existence on the day of the signing. The RMBCA provides that anyone purporting to act on behalf of a corporation, knowing incorporation has not yet occurred, is jointly and severally liable for all liabilities created by the acts. For example, Edgar anticipates opening a private detective agency and enters into a one-year lease agreement for office space with Landlord, signing on behalf of the yet-to-be-formed Edgar Detective Agency Inc. One month later, Edgar's financing falls through, and he abandons the idea. Edgar would be a promoter and personally liable for the lease payments (or any penalty for breaching the lease contract) to Landlord.

---

[3]In a minority of states, this is known as the *corporate charter.*

However, a promoter's personal liability *ceases* at the moment that the corporation is formed and has adopted the contract. In the Edgar-Landlord contract, suppose that Edgar signs on behalf of the corporation, incorporates the business venture the next day, and opens up a bank account. For the first month's rent, Edgar pays the rent via company check. Because the corporation has been formed and, by virtue of accepting a company check, Landlord has adopted the contract, Edgar's personal liability has been extinguished. If Edgar abandons the business after six months, his personal assets are not subject to the Landlord's reach.

Case 16.1 illustrates the risks of preincorporation activity by promoters.

Choice of State of Incorporation

One of the first considerations for principals forming a corporation is choosing in what state to incorporate the business venture. Most corporations with a relatively small number of principals choose to incorporate in the state in which they will locate their

---

CASE 16.1 Branch v. Mullineaux et al., 2010 N.Y. slip op. 31850(U), Supreme Court of New York County

FACT SUMMARY Branch agreed to provide $75,000 in short-term financing to three individuals, Mullineaux, Gefter, and Satsky (MGS), for purposes of starting up a venture called "Stereo House" in which the principals would profit by arranging parties in a luxury beach house in the Hamptons (Long Island, New York) and charging guests to attend these events. Branch entered into an agreement with MGS whereby they agreed that the yet-to-be-formed venture would pay back the money to Branch at an interest rate of 10 percent over four months. After Branch provided the funding and entered into the agreement, MGS allegedly formed the Stereo House entity but did not open a bank account, did not execute the proper legal documents, and did not ratify any of the Branch transactions. The venture was ultimately unsuccessful, and Stereo House was unable to pay back the majority of the loan. Branch sued MGS as individuals under a theory of promoter liability. MGS defended by claiming that the $75,000 was an investment and therefore the entire amount was at risk without any liability on MGS's part.

SYNOPSIS OF DECISION AND OPINION The New York court held in favor of Branch. The court ruled that because the agreement was executed prior to formation of the entity, MGS created individual liability to Branch. MGS were liable as individuals since promoters who execute preincorporation contracts in the name of a proposed corporation are personally liable on the contract unless the parties have

agreed otherwise. In this case, it was undisputed that the corporate entity did not exist at the time that the agreement was entered into. Thus, as preincorporation promoters, MGS were personally liable for the agreement executed prior to the incorporation of an entity, even if the entity would otherwise be considered the contracting party.

WORDS OF THE COURT: Liability of Promoters "Indeed, a corporation which did not exist at the time the contract was entered into, cannot be bound by the terms thereof unless the obligation is assumed in some manner by the corporation after it comes into existence by adopting, ratifying, or accepting it. [W]hen a promoter executes a contract on behalf of a nonexistent corporation, the promoter is presumed to be personally liable under that contract absent proof of the parties' contrary intent or until there has been a novation between the corporation and the other contracting party. Here, defendants have proffered no evidence that the Stereo House entity adopted, ratified or accepted the agreement they made with plaintiff. Thus, there is no basis for the court to overcome this presumption and shift the individual [MGS's] liability for repayment to [the Stereo House entity]."

Case Questions

1. What steps should MGS have taken to help limit their promoter liability?
2. Isn't Branch's loss a risk of doing business? Why should MGS be individually liable?

---

principal office and operate the business venture. Some corporations choose the state of Delaware as the state of incorporation because of the advantages of that state's permissive rules on the flexibility of how a corporation's managers (in the form of officers and directors, discussed later) operate the business. For the most part, publicly held corporations decide that incorporation in Delaware is a wise choice because the Delaware statutes give officers and directors of those corporations wide latitude in decision making that does not require shareholder consent. Delaware has also adopted statutes that offer officers and directors strong protections

from shareholder lawsuits that allege managerial negligence has resulted in damages to shareholder interest. This protection, known as the **business judgment rule,** is discussed in more detail later in this chapter. Moreover, Delaware has a well-established body of case law that allows more reliability in corporate planning. Note that despite some myths to the contrary, Delaware's tax structure is *not* favorable to out-of-state corporations that incorporate in Delaware. Although Delaware has no sales tax on retail merchandise, this rule applies to in-state sales only. Thus, an out-of-state business that uses Delaware to incorporate but does not sell any products or services in Delaware has no tax advantage at all. In fact, in the big picture, corporations with a relatively small number of principals will end up paying more in taxes considering the assessment of business franchise taxes or fees in both Delaware and the state where most of the business venture's activity takes place.

Capitalization

LO 16-3

Corporations have perhaps the widest range of options when considering how to finance their operations. They may be funded through debt or through the the of equity (ownership interests) in a variety of forms.

Debt   Corporations often borrow money from either commercial lenders (such as banks) or private investors to fund day-to-day operations, and this is usually evidenced by a loan agreement and a promissory note. For larger projects, corporations may also use more sophisticated forms of debt such as issues of bonds or debentures. Bonds are debt money issued by a corporation to the general public with promises to pay the bondholders back at a specified rate of interest for a specified length of time and to repay the entire loan upon the expiration of the bond (known as the *maturity date*). Note that bondholders are not shareholders but, rather, become creditors of the corporation. Bonds are secured through the corporation's pledging of certain assets. Debentures function essentially the same as bonds, but instead of pledging some specific piece of property, a corporation issues debentures on the strength of the general credit of the corporation. Both privately held and publicly held corporations may issue bonds. Even relatively small corporations use bonds to finance expansion or the building of a new facility, and bonds can range in amount from several hundred million dollars to as little as $500,000 (bonds of the latter amount are referred to as *micro bonds*). The primary advantage of bonds and debentures is that their rate of interest is usually lower than than that of a commercial bank loan. However, the process can be lengthy and is a more complex legal transaction than a conventional bank loan or a loan through a private individual.

Equity   Corporations also sell equity to capitalize their operations. For modest amounts of funding, corporations may turn to private investors or groups of investors. Sometimes a corporation will hire a registered broker-dealer that drafts a document describing the company and the intended use of the funds and distributes it to qualified individuals who are seeking investment opportunities that have relatively high risk in hopes of higher returns. This process constitutes the issuance of a security and, thus, is highly regulated. Securities law is discussed extensively in Chapter 17, "Regulation of Securities, Corporate Governance, and Financial Markets."

Venture Capital Firms   When a corporation seeks a more significant amount of capital, the corporation may turn to a *venture capital* firm. Venture capital is funding provided by a group of professional investors for use in a developing business. These firms are frequently focused on one industry (e.g., health care or the technology sector). The major advantage of venture capital is that these firms often have substantial resources and are also a source of expertise in operations and expansion of the corporation. However, in exchange for this, principals usually insist on substantial control over the corporation via its board of directors and even its officers. Venture capitalists are not thought of as long-term investors. They will usually require an "exit strategy" whereby the venture capital firm exits the corporation with a substantial return. This exit strategy may be to take the company public through an initial public offering or to get the company to grow to a point at which a competitor would be willing to pay a substantial premium to purchase the corporation.

Public Offerings   Privately held corporations may find that their expansion plans require even more capital than can be raised using private investors. In that case, some companies opt to proceed through a very complex and time-consuming process of converting the corporation from privately held to publicly held by engaging in an initial public offering (IPO). At that point, the corporation may raise equity by selling its shares to the general public and to financial institutions.

Initial Organizational Meeting

After filing the articles of incorporation, the principals typically hold an organizational meeting. This allows the principals to resolve any pending issues and to amend the articles of incorporation to reflect any changes in the principals' strategy since the time of formation. Specifically, the principals will address such issues as:

- *Bylaws:* Although state statutes govern some of the internal rules of a corporation, there are still some issues left to the principals. These rules are generally articulated in the corporation's bylaws. The bylaws typically specify the date, time, and place for the annual shareholders' meetings, the number of officers and directors of the corporation, the process for electing the board of directors, and a listing of each officer along with a description of that officer's duties (responsibilities and liability of officers and directors are discussed later in this chapter). Note that the bylaws are not filed with the state filing official, and thus are not public, but are kept in the corporate records.

- *Board of directors and officers:* In some cases, the members of the board of directors are reported in the articles of incorporation. If they are, the principals may make changes at this organizational meeting by holding another election for the board by the owners of the corporation. Officers are also identified at this meeting, and, depending on the bylaws, the officers are appointed by the board or, in some special cases, elected by the board.

- *Issuance of shares:* The organizational meeting also often involves the official issuance of ownership interests consistent with the articles of incorporation filing. The ownership interests are referred to as *shares* and are evidenced by a stock certificate that indicates the owner's name and the number of shares issued. Therefore, owners of a corporation are referred to as **shareholders.** The issuance of shares is usually recorded in a stock register which is kept by the secretary of the corporation along with other corporate records of the business (such as meeting minutes, resolutions, etc.). In a privately held corporation, the stock certificates and register are not public documents and are kept with the corporate records in the corporation's registered place of business.

Commencement of Business and Corporate Formalities

Once the corporation has been properly formed and postformation organizational matters have been attended to, the corporation's officers commence business operations. As a practical matter, the business entity may have already commenced operations under the promoter, and thus the business operations are simply continued by the newly formed corporate entity. Even after commencement of business operations, officers and directors have a responsibility to comply with state statutory requirements regarding shareholders' and directors' meetings, filing of annual reports, and disclosures to shareholders, and they must use their best efforts to keep corporate records and bylaws up to date. These responsibilities are examples of corporate formalities. Failing to attend to corporate formalities may subject the principals to personal liability (discussed in detail later in this chapter).

Liability   Perhaps the most attractive feature of a corporation is its limited liability for the personal assets of its owners and, with certain exceptions, for its officers and directors. In general, shareholders, directors, and officers of a corporation are insulated from personal liability in the event that the corporation runs up large debts or suffers some liability. This liability protection is often referred to as the **corporate veil.** For example, Roscoe and Pound are shareholders of Roscoe Corporation, and obtain a credit card from Express Credit. They use it in good faith to make purchases to operate the business. For several years, Roscoe Corporation conducts business and pays its debts regularly. However, industry conditions worsen for Roscoe Corporation, and it defaults on payment to Express Credit. Assuming that Roscoe Corporation has no assets, any attempt to collect the credit card debt from Roscoe or Pound individually will be thwarted by the protection of the corporate veil.

While this appears to be a boon for shareholders, officers, and directors at first glance, there are two important factors that temper the liability issue. First, most lenders, such as banks, will require a *personal guarantee* from the principals to back any loan given to a corporation with personal assets. Second, in some cases courts will discard the corporate veil and allow parties to reach through the corporation to access the personal assets of one or more shareholders. This is known as **piercing the corporate veil**. Piercing the corporate veil is covered later in this chapter.

Personal Guarantees   As one would imagine, banks, landlords, and other creditors are fully aware of the limited liability provided by the corporate veil. Thus, if a corporation is a start-up or has limited assets, these creditors will almost always require that the shareholders give a personal guarantee. A personal guarantee allows the creditor to obtain a judgment against the personal assets of one or more shareholders in the event of a default by the corporation. Personal guarantees are frequently *in addition* to any collateral that is pledged by shareholders or the corporation itself. For example, suppose that Chef Perrier wishes to start his own restaurant and forms Le Chef Inc. as the sole shareholder. For Le Chef Inc. to obtain a lease, the landlord will require a contract with Le Chef Inc. and *also* with Perrier personally. For the company to obtain a loan from the local bank to purchase equipment, inventory, and furniture, the bank will require that (1) Le Chef Inc. agree to a loan repayment schedule; (2) Le Chef Inc. give the bank a right to claim the equipment and inventory as collateral; and (3) Chef Perrier provide a personal guarantee of the loan.

Preformation	Legal Formation	Postformation	Start of Business Operations	Corporate Formalities
1. Principals* decide that the corporate entity is advantageous to business objectives. 2. Promoter drafts articles of incorporation according to the principals' needs. 3. Promoter is personally liable for any preformation debts or activities on behalf of the future corporation.	1. Promoter files articles of incorporation with state agency. 2. Upon approval by state agency, the corporation is legally recognized as a business entity. 3. Promoter is no longer personally liable for debts or actions on behalf of the corporation.	1. Principals hold initial organizational meeting to approve bylaws, elect directors, and appoint officers. 2. Officers and directors formally issue stock certificates as evidence of shares in the corporation. 3. Shareholders typically sign a shareholders' agreement in which the parties agree to certain procedures for selling or transferring stock, etc.	Officers and directors oversee the start of business operations.	1. Officers and directors are responsible for complying with annual meeting, reporting, and filing requirements. 2. Bylaws and shareholders' agreement are subject to ongoing review and adjustment when necessary.

*While *principals* is used here, this summary applies equally to corporations that have only a single principal.

LO 16-4 ## Taxation

For multiperson ventures, it is not uncommon for the tax-related needs of the individuals to differ. For example, Abel, Baker, and Cain wish to form NewCo.com. The corporate form may favor Abel, while the interests of Baker may be better served by a partnership. Before selecting an appropriate form of entity, the parties try to anticipate the best way to minimize taxes while maintaining an appropriate degree of liability protection.

C Corporations   Every C corporation is considered a legal, taxable entity that is separate from the owners for income tax purposes. Therefore, corporations pay tax on their earnings, and then shareholders pay tax on any corporate earnings distributed to them in the form of dividends. This system is known as *double taxation:* The taxation occurs at both (1) the corporate level, when income is earned by the corporation, and (2) the individual level, when it is distributed as a dividend (profit) to the shareholder.

S Corporations   Corporations that qualify for and elect *Subchapter S* treatment offer flow-through (also known as *pass-through*) tax treatment. The term *Subchapter S* is simply a designation named after the section of the Internal Revenue Code that details requirements to qualify for flow-through tax treatment as a corporation. Subject to certain exceptions under the tax laws, Subchapter S corporations are not subject to tax at the entity level: The taxable income or loss of the business operated by the entity flows through to the entity's shareholders. As a result, Subchapter S corporations can offer investors numerous tax benefits. Of particular importance are:

- *Use of losses to limit tax liability:* the ability to flow through to the investors the tax deductions and losses that are typically generated by an emerging company during its early years.

- *Avoidance of double taxation:* the ability to distribute earnings without incurring double-level taxation (i.e., without having a tax imposed on both the entity and the equity holder).

The primary reason that some corporations do *not* choose an S election is that the tax code allows only certain types of corporations to have that status and, thus, the favorable tax treatment. However, only C corporations are entitled to certain tax deductions (amounts used to pay for employee benefits, for example). Thus, even small entities that qualify for S corporation status may opt to be a C corporation if it reduces their overall tax liability.

In order to qualify as an S corporation, the enterprise must meet the following criteria:

- *Limited classification:* An S corporation must be a domestic corporation with no non-resident or alien shareholders.

- *Single class of stock:* An enterprise cannot be an S corporation if it has more than a single class of stock (except a differentiation of voting and nonvoting stock, explained later in this chapter).

- *No corporate shareholders:* An enterprise cannot be an S corporation if any of its shareholders is a corporation, a partnership, or a discretionary trust.

- *Limited scope of business:* Banks and insurance companies may not elect to be an S corporation.

- *Limited number and type of shareholders:* An enterprise cannot be an S corporation if it has more than 100 shareholders. Only individuals, estates, and certain trusts may be shareholders.

- *80 percent subsidiaries:* An enterprise cannot be an S corporation if it owns more than 80 percent of the stock of a subsidiary corporation.

- *Unanimous consent:* All shareholders must consent to S corporation status.

Figure 16.1 provides a comparison of the tax implications of C corporations and S corporations.

FIGURE 16.1 Taxation of C Corporations and S Corporations

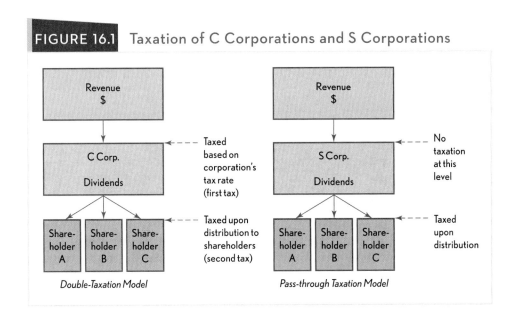

CONCEPT SUMMARY Corporate Form of Entity

Personal liability of principals	Corporations exist as a separate legal "person." Officers, directors, and shareholders are not personally liable for any debts or liabilities of the corporation (absent fraud). Corporate veil protection.
Organization and start-up expenses	Formation procedures are relatively easy if the entity is privately held and has limited shareholders. Bylaws, shareholders' agreement, and resolutions are drafted by an attorney, resulting in higher costs. Publicly held companies or "private offerings" involve extensive legal documentation and higher fees.
Management and control	Shareholders elect directors. Directors appoint officers. Officers have day-to-day control over management with directors' oversight. Shareholders must vote on significant corporate decisions (merger, sale of significant assets, or stock issuance). Bylaws are the internal operating rules of the entity.
Capital	Capital may be raised by the sale of shares (equity) or by a loan from a bank (debt). Some corporations may also raise money by issuing bonds and other debt instruments.
Taxes	A C corporation pays taxes at the corporate rate on all income of the entity. When the entity distributes profits to shareholders *(dividends),* the income is taxed again at the shareholder's individual rate. This is known as *double taxation.* An S corporation has *pass-through* taxation treatment. No tax is paid on income to the entity, but when the entity distributes dividends, tax is paid at the individual shareholder's rate. Subchapter S shareholders may also have to pay miscellaneous state and local taxes to operate the business.
Designations	Doe, Inc. Doe Corporation Doe Company

STRUCTURE, MANAGEMENT, AND OPERATION

LO 16-5, 16-6

Fundamentally, corporations are structured around an allocation of power based on three categories: *shareholders, directors,* and *officers.* Shareholders are the owners of the corporation and act principally through electing and removing directors and approving or withholding approval of major corporate decisions. **Directors** are responsible for oversight and management of the corporation's course of direction. **Officers** carry out the directors' set course of direction through management of the day-to-day operations of the business. Although this allocation of power is based on the RMBCA, many states allow a corporation to alter the structure as necessary to meet the needs of the entity. Very large corporations and very small corporations often manage their operations using a modified form of this structure. For example, in some cases a corporation has only one or two shareholders, each of whom acts as a director and an officer. This structure is essentially useless, so they may opt to adopt a slightly different structure through the bylaws and/or an agreement among the shareholders as to the rights and responsibilities of each shareholder.

Shareholders

Shareholders are the owners of the corporation. While shareholders do not directly manage the corporation, most states give shareholders certain rights to protect their ownership interests. Most importantly, shareholders, assuming a majority of the ownership consent, have the power to elect and remove directors at the annual shareholders' meetings. State statutes also give rights to shareholders to veto any fundamental changes to the corporation that are proposed by the directors and officers. Examples of fundamental changes are selling substantial assets, engaging in a merger, issuing more capital stock, pursuing venture capital financing, and issuing a bond. Shareholders also must approve any changes in the structure of the corporation through amending the articles of incorporation or bylaws. For example, Widget Manufacturing Inc. is structured as follows:

Name	Percentage of Total Stock Owned	Role
Abel	10	Officer, director, shareholder
Baker	10	Officer, director, shareholder
Cain	20	Director, shareholder
David	20	Shareholder
Elias	40	Shareholder

Suppose that Abel and Baker locate what they believe to be an excellent opportunity to merge with a larger competitor. They will need to convince either Cain and David or Elias to approve the transaction in order to move ahead. If they are able to convince only Cain or David and Elias resists the transaction, Elias and the remaining shareholder would have the ability to block the merger from taking place. Note also that some corporations, particularly closely held corporations, issue *voting stock* to some shareholders and *nonvoting stock* to other shareholders. This is done to ensure that a certain shareholder or group of shareholders can control the corporation, but it still allows other shareholders the ability to receive payments from the corporation's profit (called *dividends*) and other benefits of ownership. For example, in the Widget Manufacturing Inc. example above, suppose that Elias was the father of Abel, Baker, Cain, and David. He wishes to be sure that his heirs receive dividends in certain proportions but does not yet wish to cede control of the corporation to them. Elias could issue nonvoting stock to Abel, Baker, Cain, and David but still retain the power to elect and remove them as directors or to void any transaction. However, it is important to note that shareholders cannot bind the corporation, nor can shareholders demand that the directors take a certain action or adopt a certain policy.

Board of Directors

While shareholders have the power to veto transactions, it is the board of directors that actually sets the strategy and policies of the corporation. The board of directors also has an important oversight function, and state statutes contemplate that the body be *independent* from the shareholders and officers. Most planning initiatives that result in a change to the

The board of directors typically makes use of committees to carry out its work and oversight responsibilities.

corporation, such as an acquisition of another corporation's assets or stock, are overseen by the board prior to submitting the plan to shareholders for approval.

Election of Directors   Shareholders elect directors. In most corporations directors hold office for one year, but the bylaws can set any term. The bylaws also set the procedures and requirements for an election in terms of time and date, notification to shareholders, and the number of shareholders who must be present to hold a vote (known as the *quorum requirement*). Some states require at least three directors except in the case of a closely held corporation, where the number of directors is equal to the number of shareholders. Therefore, a one-person corporation requires only one director. Other states (such as Delaware) have abolished any minimum number of directors. The number of directors is typically set out in the corporation's bylaws.

Removal of Directors   Directors may be removed by a shareholder vote or, less frequently, by a court order. Absent a contrary provision in the articles of incorporation, shareholders may remove a director with or without cause.[4] The removal process is usually set out in the bylaws, but in almost all cases the shareholder vote must take place at a properly called shareholders' meeting. Most states also allow a *court* to order a director to be removed, but only for *cause* (such as fraud). This is a rare event but would be necessary if the director at issue is also a shareholder with sufficient voting power to defeat removal votes by minority shareholders.

Meetings   Acts of the board of directors take place only at official meetings that occur at a regular annual or semiannual time as specified in the corporation's bylaws or by a statute. Special meetings to handle pressing matters may also be called so long as a notification procedure is followed in accordance with the bylaws. The votes of a majority of the directors who are present at a meeting are required to take action. Most states allow

---

[4]RMBCA § 8.08(a).

board action to take place without a meeting if the directors act through unanimous written consent (all directors agree in writing to the action) or the directors agree to meet via a communication means through which all directors can hear and speak with one another at the same time (such as through videoconferencing or webcam). For routine matters such as approving the choice of the corporation's auditing firm or legal counsel, corporations often choose these alternate routes to board action.

Committees   Much of the board's work is done through its committees. Each committee consists of a small group of board members who are charged with overseeing or performing a given task and making recommendations to the full board. Examples of such committees are a compensation committee (investigates appropriate compensation for its officers, etc., and makes a recommendation), an audit committee (oversees the proper reporting of earnings and other audit functions), and an election committee (supervises the procedures for director elections).

Officers

The corporation's officers are appointed by, and may be removed by, the board of directors. The officers carry out the day-to-day operations of the corporation and execute the strategy and mandates set out by the board of directors. As a practical matter, officers work closely with the directors in setting the course of a corporation's path, but major changes in the corporation may not be taken through officer action alone. Although some states still require the traditional officer roles to be filled (president, vice president, secretary, and treasurer), the current trend is to allow the titles and responsibilities of the officers to be set by the bylaws or the board of directors.[5] Officers have both express and implied authority. Express authority comes from the bylaws or through a board of directors' resolution that gives specific authority to a particular officer. For example, the board of directors may pass

Tim Cook, CEO of Apple, follows in Steve Jobs's shoes by using annual shareholders meetings as an event to launch products.

---

[5]See *Delaware General Corporate Law* § 142(a).

a resolution authorizing the treasurer of a corporation to open a bank account or to start a money market account for surplus cash on hand. Officers may also have inherent authority, based on their position, to act on behalf of the corporation. Recall from Chapter 11, "Agency," that certain corporate officers have *implied authority* to be an agent of the corporation. This is an important concept in corporate law because it helps define the powers of corporate officers.

President Traditionally, the president has the implied power to bind the corporation in ordinary business operation transactions and to oversee nonofficer employees. Therefore, the president of a manufacturing corporation has the authority to enter into a distribution contract with wholesalers or to hire and fire a receptionist, for example.

Vice President Depending on the size and scope of the corporation, the vice president may have some limited implied authority. For example, a vice president for marketing would likely have implied authority to bind the corporation to a vendor of advertising. The implied authority of a vice president may also include additional powers to bind the corporation in ordinary business transactions if such authority is a routine practice in a certain industry.

Treasurer Aside from the routine tasks of collecting the accounts receivable and paying the accounts payable, the treasurer has little or no other implied authority.

Secretary The secretary has the implied authority to certify the records and resolutions of the company. When the board of directors passes a resolution, it is the secretary who affixes his signature to it, which confirms that the document is genuine. Third parties in a particular transaction may rely on this certification. For example, suppose that Antonin, the secretary of MusicCo, delivers a forged resolution to a bank that authorizes MusicCo to borrow $50,000. The resolution has Antonin's signature affixed to it with a statement that the resolution was duly passed at a board of directors' meeting. The bank loans the money to MusicCo based on the resolution. MusicCo then becomes financially insolvent and attempts to avoid repaying the loan on the basis that MusicCo's directors did not in fact authorize the loan. The bank would prevail because, by virtue of Antonin's implied authority, it had the right to rely on Antonin's certification as secretary.[6]

Fiduciary Duties of Officers and Directors

Officers, directors, and controlling shareholders of a corporation (known as *insiders*) are in a unique position of trust to guide the corporation in a certain direction. Officers and directors owe the corporation's shareholders several well-defined fiduciary duties: the **duty of care** and the **duty of loyalty.** Breaching these duties may result in *personal liability* for the officer or director. Officers and directors must act carefully when they act on behalf of the corporation and must also not put their *own* interests ahead of the corporation's interests. The duty of loyalty also applies to *controlling shareholders* in relation to other shareholders. The duty of care is tempered by a protection for officers and directors when they have acted in good faith but still made an unwise decision that resulted in some loss to the corporation. This protection is known as the *business judgment rule.*

Duty of Care Fundamentally, officers and directors must exercise the degree of skill, diligence, and care that a reasonably prudent person would exercise under the same circumstances. Most states define the duty of care through a three-part test. First, the officers and directors must always act in good faith. Second, they must also act with the care that an objectively prudent person in a like position would exercise under similar circumstances.

---

[6]Based on *In re Drive-In Development Corporation,* 371 F.2d 217 (7th Cir. 1966).

Third, they must carry out their duties in a manner that is reasonably calculated to advance the best interests of the corporation. This duty applies to all directors and officers regardless of whether the corporation is large or small or whether the directors are paid or unpaid. Courts have held that a director breaches her duty of care when she has failed to fulfill her role in oversight. This may occur in several ways:

- *Negligence:* When a director doesn't read reports, financial records, or other information provided by the corporation or doesn't attend meetings, this weighs heavily in favor of a finding of a breach of duty.

- *Failure to act with diligence:* Directors have the obligation to question any suspicious activity by the corporation or its officers. If the issue is outside their field, they must investigate it by consulting outside experts (such as a CPA or an attorney). They must attempt to have more than just a cursory understanding of the inner workings of the corporation and must monitor the corporation and the business practices of its officers.

- *Rubber stamp:* Directors have the duty to be sure that any transaction proposed by the officers (or by other directors) is, from the *best information* available to them at the time, in the best interest of the corporation and is not imprudent. They have a duty to determine whether the proposed action will impact the corporation in a negative way, and thus they cannot act as a "rubber stamp." If they disagree with a decision being made by other directors, they must register their dissent in the record of the meeting.

This is not to say that directors cannot rely on the expertise and assurances of others. Under the RMBCA, directors still fulfill their duty of care even though they did not personally verify the records or other information provided to them by officers or outside experts. Directors may rely on opinions, reports, statements, and financial records if they are presented by the officers of a corporation whom the directors "reasonably believes . . . to be reliable and competent in these matters."[7] Directors may also rely on professionals such as attorneys and auditors or on board committees so long as that reliance is reasonable in terms of the directors' belief in the source's competence.

Business Judgment Rule   At first glance, the duty of care looks onerous. When a corporation engages in a certain transaction or in a certain course of conduct that generates losses, some shareholders may inevitably believe it was the fault of the directors' lack of care. The business judgment rule protects officers and directors from liability for decisions that may have been unwise but did not breach the duty of care. This rule insulates directors and officers from liability when, based on reasonable information at the time, the transaction or course of action turns out badly from the standpoint of the corporation. Directors and officers often seek protection of this rule when an individual shareholder or group of shareholders files a lawsuit against them. LO 16-7

Although the RMBCA does not include a business judgment rule, every state has adopted the rule (either by including it in their statutes or recognizing its applicability in common law) as a defense to a breach-of-the-duty-of-care claim against a director. Fundamentally, directors must have acted in *good faith* to insulate themselves from liability for breach of care. Most courts define good faith by requiring directors and officers to clear three hurdles in order to obtain the protection of the business judgment rule:

- *No private interest:* In order to claim protection under the business judgment rule, the director must have had no financial self-interest in the disputed transaction or decision. Being a shareholder of a merging company or a supplier to a corporation may be dangerous territory for a director because a transaction with the merger partner or supplier may have some degree of self-dealing contamination that will deprive the director of any business judgment rule protection.

---

[7]RMBCA § 8.30(b).

- *Best information:* An important prerequisite to protection by the business judgment rule is the requirement that directors be active in keeping themselves informed on all material aspects of the decision or transaction at issue. Directors and officers have a duty to be diligent in investigating any proposal, decision, or transaction, and this includes, when appropriate, consulting outside experts.

- *Rational belief:* The third requirement that directors and officers must meet in order to be protected under the rule is that the decision or approval of the transaction must have been the product of some reasoned decision making based on rational beliefs. This rational-belief requirement means that courts focus on the process of the decision making. Directors' and officers' decision-making procedures must be set up in a way that allows careful decisions to be made regarding the best interests of the corporation. Boards will often form committees to carry out their work, and often this committee structure itself is a significant step in establishing a procedure that helps preserve the business judgment rule protection.

> **KEY** POINT
>
> To have protection under the business judgment rule, directors and officers must exercise good faith, have no private financial self-interest, and use diligence to acquire the best material information related to a proposed decision.

Despite the fact that Delaware is generally thought of as a state that has fairly broad business judgment rule protection, Landmark Case 16.2, which sent shockwaves through corporate boardrooms nationwide, illustrates the importance of the duty to investigate all *material* facts of a proposed transaction before approving it.

 Self-Check   Business Judgment Rule

Will these directors be protected by the business judgment rule?

1. Directors of a bank consult with legal, banking, and industry experts concerning a proposed merger. They set up a directors' subcommittee to investigate the merger and ultimately approve moving ahead after two months of deliberation. The day after the merger, a substantial drop in the stock price of the bank takes place and shareholders lose nearly 30 percent of the value of their investment.

2. The company president recommends to the board that NewCo hire Dewey, Cheatham, and Howe as their auditing firm. In the same meeting as the recommendation, the directors approve the firm. One year later, it is revealed that the audits were fraudulent and that the president had been looting the company resulting in several millions of dollars in losses.

3. Shareholders of a major league baseball franchise corporation sue the directors because the team refuses to schedule night games. The shareholders argue that the revenue lost from night games is responsible for the poor financial performance of the company. The directors refuse to schedule night games because they believe it would have a deteriorating effect on the neighborhood.

4. The company vice president recommends that the directors of the corporation purchase a parcel of prime real estate on which to build a new office building for the company. Four of the six directors are members of a real estate partnership that owns that property. Without any disclosures, the directors vote unanimously to approve of the purchase and the decision is made the same day as the vice president's recommendation. One month later, it was revealed that the price paid by the corporation was 20 percent above fair market value for the property.

Answers to this Self-Check are provided at the end of the chapter.

FACT SUMMARY Van Gorkom was an officer, director, and shareholder of Trans Union Corporation. Trans Union's stock was traded on the New York Stock Exchange (NYSE) and had never sold for higher than $39 per share. Prior to announcing his retirement, Van Gorkom sought to sell his shares to Pritzker, an individual investor, for $55 per share. Because Van Gorkhom's holdings in Trans Union were substantial, he was required to get the approval of Trans Union's board of directors for the sale to Pritzker. Van Gorkom proposed the sale to the board in an oral presentation. Most of the other officers opposed the sale on the basis that the price was too low given the value of the company. Indeed, the chief financial officer advised the directors that the price was in the "low range." The directors did not review the terms of the Van Gorkom–Pritzker agreement, did not perform any valuation analysis on the company, and did not consult any of the company's investment bankers. After Van Gorkom pressured the directors by informing them that Pritzker would withdraw the offer within three days, the board deliberated for several hours and approved the transaction. A group of shareholders brought a lawsuit against the directors of Trans Union based on a breach of the duty of care that resulted in the stock being sold at a value well under its actual worth. The directors sought protection under the business judgment rule, claiming they relied on Van Gorkom's representations and the NYSE stock price.

SYNOPSIS OF DECISION AND OPINION The Delaware Supreme Court ruled *against* the directors, holding that they could not be afforded the protection of the business judgment rule. The court's decision was primarily based on conclusion that the directors had failed to obtain all material information and had not conducted any investigation about the transaction. The court pointed to the fact that the board never even reviewed the Van Gorkom–Pritzker agreement, nor had the board undertaken anything more than a cursory inquiry into the actual value of the corporation.

WORDS OF THE COURT: Duty to Be Informed "We do not say that the Board of Directors was not entitled to give some credence to Van Gorkom's representation that $55 was an adequate or fair price. [T]he directors were entitled to rely upon their chairman's opinion of value and adequacy, provided that such opinion was reached on a sound basis. Here, the issue is whether the directors informed themselves as to all information that was reasonably available to them. Had they done so, they would have learned of the source and derivation of the $55 price and could not reasonably have relied thereupon in good faith.

"None of the directors, management or outside, were investment bankers or financial analysts. Yet the Board did not consider recessing the meeting until a later hour that day (or requesting an extension of Pritzker's deadline) to give it time to elicit more information as to the sufficiency of the offer, either from inside management or from Trans Union's own investment banker, Salomon Brothers, whose Chicago specialist in merger and acquisitions was known to the Board and familiar with Trans Union's affairs. Thus, the record compels the conclusion that the Board lacked valuation information adequate to reach an informed business judgment as to the fairness of $55 per share for sale of the Company."

Case Questions

1. Assume that the directors were highly sophisticated business executives. Should they have to consult others on issues about which they already have sufficient knowledge (such as the company's valuation)?

2. Note that, in light of Van Gorkom, many states (including Delaware) passed statutes that extended the scope of the business judgment defense. Should the business judgment rule protect directors even when they fail to verify the statements of internal management concerning a corporate transaction that is being touted to officers as advantageous to the corporation?

Duty of Loyalty An additional fiduciary duty owed to shareholders by officers, directors, and controlling shareholders is the *duty of loyalty.* Shareholders that have some degree of control over corporate decisions also owe this duty, and it is principally a duty intended to prevent oppression of minority shareholders. The duty of loyalty is primarily focused on providing protection to shareholders when a transaction occurs in which the possibility of self-dealing is present.

Prohibition against Certain Self-Dealing   Self-dealing in this context occurs when an officer, director, or controlling shareholder has a personal financial stake in a transaction that the corporation is engaged in and that individual helps to influence the advancement of the transaction. For example, recall our working hypothetical structure for Widget Manufacturing Inc.:

Name	Percentage of Total Stock Owned	Role
Abel	10	Officer, director, shareholder
Baker	10	Officer, director, shareholder
Cain	20	Director, shareholder
David	20	Shareholder
Elias	40	Shareholder

Suppose that Cain owns port properties and leases warehouse space to industries using the port. Abel, as president of the corporation, searches for a warehouse for Widget Manufacturing's storage needs, and he identifies several potential properties. Abel writes a report for the board of directors describing the advantages and disadvantages of each property. Because Cain is an officer and director, this transaction has at least the *potential* to conflict with the best financial interests of the corporation. This potential for conflict, however, is not a breach of the duty of loyalty automatically. The RMBCA provides that a self-dealing transaction is not a breach of the duty of loyalty so long as a majority of disinterested parties (those with no self-interest conflicts) approve it after *disclosure* of the conflict.[8] In the Widget Manufacturing example, Cain would simply need to disclose his interest in the property and abstain from influencing other directors about the vote. After disclosure, the vote of Abel and Baker to approve the transaction insulates Cain from a charge of breaching his duty of loyalty to Widget's other shareholders.

Even if the transaction was not formally approved as provided in RMBCA, the modern trend has been for courts to allow such transactions so long as they are, under the circumstances, fair to the corporation and performed in good faith.

Corporate Opportunity Doctrine   The duty of loyalty also requires disclosure and good faith when an insider (i.e., director, officer, or controlling shareholder) learns of a potentially lucrative business opportunity that could enrich her individually but is related to the corporation's business. That is, an insider may not *usurp* for herself a business opportunity that belongs to the corporation or would benefit the corporation in some direct way.

To determine when an opportunity belongs to a corporation and is therefore off-limits to insiders who are officers, directors, or controlling shareholders unless they have followed specific disclosure steps courts use several questions: (1) Did the corporation have a current interest or expected interest in the opportunity (such as an existing contract to purchase a piece of property)? (2) Is it fair to the corporation's shareholders to allow another to usurp a certain interest? (3) Is the opportunity closely related to the corporation's existing or prospective business activities? In answering these questions, courts will take into consideration whether the officer, director, or controlling shareholder learned of the opportunity

Legal **Speak** ›))
Usurp In the context of the corporate opportunity doctrine, to *usurp* is to seize a particular opportunity for oneself when the opportunity rightfully belongs to the corporation.

---

[8]RMBCA § 8.60.

because of his role in the corporation and whether a party used corporate resources to take advantage of the opportunity.

Officers, directors, and controlling shareholders who become aware of a business opportunity belonging to the corporation must disclose the opportunity to the corporation in total. That is, all plans and relevant information on the opportunity must be presented to the board of directors. If the board, for whatever reasons, rejects the opportunity, the insider is then free to pursue the opportunity with no fear of liability.

For example, in our Widget Manufacturing Inc. example, suppose that the directors all discuss the need for a new warehouse facility and they authorize Abel to find a suitable lot on which to build. While Abel pursues this objective, Cain's neighbor makes him aware of a parcel of land that would fit Widget's needs in terms of space, zoning, workforce population, access, and price. Cain purchases the property for himself at a price of $100,000. He then tells a commercial real estate broker to contact Abel and advise him that the property is on the market for $200,000. In this case, because Cain was an insider who knew of a business opportunity that would benefit Widget Manufacturing and knew that the corporation was in the market for a parcel of land, he had an obligation to disclose the opportunity to the corporation first rather than buying it.

However, suppose that, instead of buying the lot, Cain discloses the opportunity to the corporation's board of directors. If the directors reject that opportunity to purchase, then Cain is free to make the purchase and even to sell it or lease it to Widget Manufacturing at a profit. Failing to follow the disclosure rules is a breach of the duty of loyalty.

CONCEPT SUMMARY Fiduciary Duties of Officers, Directors, and Controlling Shareholders

- Officers, directors, and controlling shareholders (sometimes called *insiders*) owe corporate shareholders the fiduciary duties of care (use of skill, diligence, and care to advance the best interests of the corporation) and loyalty (prohibition against self-dealing or conflicts of interests).
- The business judgment rule protects insiders from liability for breach of the duty of care so long as the insider acted in good faith, was diligent about making a well-informed decision, and had no financial self-interest in the decision.

Breach-of-Fiduciary-Duty Lawsuits by Shareholders

LO 16-8

One objective of this chapter is to focus on the rights of shareholders and the standards for fiduciary duties owed to shareholders by insiders such as officers, directors, and controlling shareholders. But how do shareholders actually enforce their rights in a corporation? Shareholders enforce their rights and fiduciary duties through the use of a lawsuit in the form of a shareholder's *derivative action* or a shareholder's *direct action.*

In a derivative suit, an individual shareholder (or a group of shareholders) brings a lawsuit against an insider in the name of the corporation itself. Most derivative lawsuits are brought because the shareholder alleges a breach of fiduciary duty of care or loyalty by an insider. There are several special procedural requirements for a derivative action, but the most important of them is that the shareholders must first make a formal demand on the board of directors to take corrective action and must allow sufficient time for correction. Only if the board refuses to act may the shareholder commence a derivative suit.

Shareholders may also file a direct action (where the shareholder is bringing suit on her own behalf) in cases where the shareholder alleges oppression of minority shareholders or where a question of voting rights or shareholder inspection rights arises.

Limiting Director Liability   A corporate board typically has several measures in place designed to limit the directors' liability. They include appointing oversight committees to monitor executive management and consulting with outside professional firms to ensure validity of the information and data used by the board in its decision making. In a more controversial method, directors approve a *limited liability provision* in their corporate charter (articles of incorporation or bylaws) that eliminates any liability for ordinary negligence on the part of directors and officers. In Case 16.3, a group of shareholders sued the officers and directors of their corporation for breach of fiduciary duty. The court's analysis focuses on the validity of a limited liability provision.

CASE 16.3   H. Carl McCall, Trustee of the New York Common Retirement Fund et al., Derivatively on Behalf of Columbia/HCA Healthcare Corporation v. Scott et al., 239 F.3d 808 (6th Cir. 2001)[9]

FACT SUMMARY   McCall and other investors are shareholders who brought a derivative lawsuit against Richard L. Scott as board chairman and all other officers and directors of Columbia/HCA Healthcare Corporation (Columbia) alleging various breach-of-fiduciary-duty claims in connection with allegations of health care insurance fraud by Columbia executives and employees. The shareholders claimed that the board had intentionally and/or recklessly disregarded fraudulent activities of senior management. This included management's attempts to improperly boost revenue through systematic o verbilling for a period of two years. The shareholders argued that given their experience in the industry, Columbia board members must have ignored red flags that would have indicated that questionable and/or fraudulent billing practices were being carried out by Columbia. The directors defended by citing a provision in the corporate charter that purported to limit the liability of the directors in the case of an allegation of the breach of duty of care so long as they did not act in bad faith.

SYNOPSIS OF DECISION AND OPINION   The Sixth Circuit Court of Appeals ruled in favor of the shareholders, reasoning that the provision in the charter was unenforceable in the face of such gross, ongoing negligence by the directors in failing to notice or investigate the illegal conduct of the corporation's officers. The board's gross negligence included willful ignorance of certain known risks that could have revealed the fraud. This included (1) failure to act in the face of unusual audit information, (2) failure to launch an inquiry after the board was notified that Columbia was under federal investigation, and (3) inadequate response to a story printed in *The New York Times* about the questionable billing practices at several companies, including Columbia.

WORDS OF THE COURT: Director Liability for Illegal Corporate Activities   "Liability on the part of a director for breach of the duty of care for failing to give appropriate attention to potentially illegal conduct may arise from an unconsidered failure of the board to act in circumstances in which due attention may have prevented the loss. Unconsidered action can form the basis for liability . . . and the magnitude and duration of the alleged wrongdoing is relevant in determining whether the failure of the directors to act constitutes bad faith."

Case Questions

1. If the corporation's officers have carefully covered up the wrongdoing, is it still fair to hold directors liable for failing to detect the illegal activities?

2. Is it ethical for directors to include a waiver of liability for shareholder suits in their corporate charter? Is it sound public policy for courts to recognize a limited liability provision in a charter? Why or why not?

[9]Modified in part by 250 F.3d 997 (6th Cir. 2001).

Piercing the Corporate Veil

A court will sometimes discard the corporate veil when it believes that fairness demands doing so. Although there is no single rule on when the corporate entity may be disregarded, courts typically examine the entire spectrum of facts to determine whether the corporate form has been abused. However, four factors in particular have been adopted by many courts as guideposts for determining whether to pierce the corporate veil.

- *Inadequate capitalization:* One important factor courts examine in deciding whether to pierce the veil is whether or not a corporation has been adequately capitalized. When a corporation is merely a shell with nothing invested, courts are inclined to pierce the corporate veil as a matter of fairness. Similarly, if the corporation had initial capitalization but the shareholders siphoned the profits and assets, a court will view it as an inadequately capitalized corporation.

- *Nature of the claim:* When the claim involves a voluntary creditor, such as a trade creditor who provides a corporation with inventory based on credit, courts are generally not inclined to pierce the corporate veil because the creditor had an opportunity to mitigate the risk of loss (e.g., by requiring a personal guarantee). On the other hand, courts are more likely to pierce the corporate veil when the claim involves some sort of tort, such as negligence by the corporation's employees or even the principals themselves. This is essentially because the victims of negligence (such as a pedestrian struck by a delivery truck operated by a corporate employee) have become *involuntary* creditors and have never had the opportunity to mitigate the risk of loss.

- *Evidence of fraud or wrongdoing:* If the shareholders, officers, or directors have committed fraud or have engaged in some type of serious and willful wrongdoing, this is an important factor in a court's decision to pierce the corporate veil. Misrepresentations to creditors regarding important facts about the financial condition of the company or lying to investors about potential liabilities of the corporation are examples of fraud that could lead to a piercing of the veil.

- *Failing to follow corporate formalities:* Another important factor used by the courts in deciding whether piercing would be appropriate is the corporation's adherence to the statutes, rules, and practices governing a corporation. For example, corporations that file articles of incorporation but never bother to follow up with required or standard practices are in danger of losing their corporate veil protection. Specifically, courts may look at whether there is a proper separation between the corporation and the individual shareholder(s), whether stock certificates were ever issued, whether shareholders' meetings were ever held, and whether proper corporate records (such as minutes of the meetings, resolutions, and stock register) were maintained. For example, suppose that two brothers, Abel and Cain, formed AC Inc. by filing articles of incorporation. Because they are brothers, they decided to split the profits 50-50 and, wishing to save the expense of hiring an attorney, never kept up with corporate formalities after the articles were filed. In the event that a claim is made against AC Inc., Abel and Cain have potentially exposed their personal assets to claimants if AC Inc. does not have sufficient assets to pay the claim.

> **KEY** POINT
>
> The corporate veil that shields the personal assets of principals from corporate debts and liabilities may be pierced in certain cases of inadequate capitalization, fraud, or failure to follow corporate formalities.

In Case 16.4, an appellate court analyzes a claim in which one party has asked the court to pierce a corporate veil.

FACT SUMMARY Shelby Property Investors (Shelby) was a company engaged in developing and selling residential real estate that was chiefly managed by Essad, one of three principals in the entity. Florence Cement Company (Florence) contracted with Shelby to perform concrete and asphalt work at one of Shelby's properties. Ultimately, Shelby's real estate venture did not yield a profit, but Shelby was able to pay all subcontractors on the job except one—Florence. When Florence sued to recover $114,557 it was owed, Shelby was without assets. Florence sought to pierce Shelby's corporate veil and hold the principals personally liable. Florence argued that the evidence suggested that Shelby (1) was not an authentic business entity because of the principals' mixing personal and business transactions and (2) had engaged in fraud by misrepresenting facts to its bank concerning a loan used to pay subcontractors. The trial court ruled that piercing the corporate veil was not warranted.

SYNOPSIS OF DECISION AND OPINION The Court of Appeals of Michigan reversed the trial court's decision and ruled in favor of Florence on the issue of piercing the corporate veil. The court pointed to Shelby's company history, which indicated that the principals treated their own liabilities as Shelby's liabilities and vice versa and intentionally undercapitalized Shelby, causing Shelby to be continuously insolvent, including at the time it contracted with Florence. Essad also falsified the sworn statement in the final loan draw request to the bank, and this constituted use of Shelby for fraudulent purposes. Therefore, Florence satisfied the elements for piercing the corporate veil.

WORDS OF THE COURT: Factors Favoring Corporate Veil Piercing "Shelby was defendants' alter ego. [The principals] made no distinction between their own debts and Shelby's debts. [The principals] did not treat Shelby as a separate entity. Such a failure is a hallmark of a claim for piercing the corporate veil. Essentially, where members do not treat an artificial entity as separate from themselves, neither will this Court.

"The facts of this case further show that defendants used Shelby to commit a wrong or fraud. Essad falsified the sworn statement that he submitted to [the bank] for the final draw of the remaining loan proceeds. It is undisputed that the request for the draw stated that Shelby "OWES NO MONEY FOR THE IMPROVEMENT OTHER THAN AS SET FORTH ABOVE." However, Essad knew that Shelby owed Florence more than the $142,000 indicated on this request for the draw because Essad had signed the contract with Florence on behalf of Shelby. Thus, the evidence overwhelmingly shows that Essad knowingly falsified the request for the draw, which amounted to fraud. And, as such, Essad clearly used Shelby to commit a wrong or fraud."

Case Questions

1. What steps could Shelby's principals have taken to help prevent any piercing of their corporate veil?

2. If Essad had not committed the fraudulent bank transaction, would the court have allowed the veil to be pierced? Why or why not?

Corporation p. 447   A fictitious legal entity that exists as an independent "person" separate from its principals.

Business corporation law p. 447   Often the title for a specific state law that covers such matters as the structure of the corporation, oversight of the activity of the corporation's managers, rights of the principals in the case of the sale of assets or ownership interests, annual reporting requirements, and other issues that affect the internal rules of the business venture.

Revised Model Business Corporation Act (RMBCA) p. 447   Model act drafted by the American Law Institute and adopted by over half of the states as a template for compiling their own statutes governing corporations.

Privately held corporation p. 448   A corporation that does not sell ownership interests through sales via a broker to the general public or to financial institutions or investors.

Articles of incorporation p. 449   The document filed with a state authority that sets in motion the incorporation process, includes the corporation's name and purpose, number of shares issued, and address of the corporation's headquarters.

Business judgment rule p. 451   A principle that protects corporate officers and directors from liability when they have made an unwise decision that results in a loss to the corporation but they have acted in good faith, had no private financial self-interest, and used diligence to acquire the best information related to the decision.

Shareholders p. 452   The owners of a corporation; act principally through electing and removing directors and approving or withholding approval of major corporate decisions.

Corporate veil p. 453   The liability protection afforded to shareholders, directors, and officers of a corporation whereby they are insulated from personal liability in the event that the corporation runs up large debts or suffers some liability.

Piercing the corporate veil p. 453   Action in which a court discards the corporate veil and holds some or all of the shareholders personally liable because fairness demands doing so in certain cases of inadequate capitalization, fraud, and failure to follow corporate formalities.

Directors p. 456   Individuals responsible for oversight and management of the corporation's course of direction.

Officers p. 456   Individuals appointed by the board of directors to carry out the directors' set course of direction through management of the day-to-day operations of the business.

Duty of care p. 460   A fiduciary duty owed to shareholders by officers and directors; requires that the fiduciaries exercise the degree of skill, diligence, and care that a reasonably prudent person would exercise under the same circumstances, acting in good faith and in a manner that is reasonably calculated to advance the best interests of the corporation.

Duty of loyalty p. 460   A fiduciary duty owed to shareholders by officers, directors, and controlling shareholders; requires that the fiduciaries put the corporation's interests ahead of their own and do not engage in self-dealing or conflicts of interests.

Adams and Barker were two individual scientists engaged in research related to inventing a patentable pharmaceutical product. Once they had gained critical mass for the project, they convinced Barker's old college roommate, Cornelius, to invest $100,000 in exchange for an ownership share in a newly formed company called Pharma Corporation (Pharma). The parties agreed that Adams and Barker would continue product development until the company was ready to apply for a patent and then Cornelius would use his contacts to find a manufacturer to produce and market the patented drug. Pharma was structured as follows:

Name	Stock Owned (%)	Role
Adams	35	President, director
Barker	35	Vice president and secretary, director
Cornelius	30	Shareholder

The parties hired counsel to incorporate Pharma, issue stock certificates, and draft bylaws. The corporate records were then turned over to Barker, and she filed them in her desk drawer. No additional formalities were followed, and the records were not maintained, nor were any directors' or shareholders' meetings held.

In year 2, Pharma's application for a patent was rejected. The rejection required Adams and Barker to hire an additional expert to help with research and would put the project behind by approximately 16 months. Adams hired Elliot, a well-known scientist, to help with the project. At this point, though, Pharma's financial resources were drying up. Trying to keep the company afloat, Adams began to pay certain Pharma bills with his personal credit card and Baker sometimes wrote personal checks for lab equipment.

1. What category of corporation is Pharma, and what are the options in terms of structure and raising capital?

2. Would Pharma be eligible to be an S corporation? If one of the shareholders objected, could the other two vote to become an S corporation without the third?

3. Did Adams have the right to hire Elliot without the others' consent? Suppose that Cornelius believes that Elliot is not a good hire for Pharma. Can he fire Elliot?

In year 3, the financial condition of Pharma continued to worsen. A representative of the dominant pharmaceutical company in the market, Multi-Drug (MD), approached Adams and Barker with an acquisition offer. MD offered to pay $50,000 to buy all of Pharma's assets and offered a five-year employment agreement with MD to both Adams and Barker. On the same day as the offer, Adams and Barker sent a one-page e-mail to Cornelius informing him that they had voted to approve the sale of assets of Pharma to MD and the transaction would take place in one business day.

4. Suppose Cornelius is unhappy with the transaction. Does he have any say in the matter? Does he have the power to stop the sale?

5. Have Adams and Barker breached their fiduciary duties to Cornelius? If so, what duties, specifically, and how were they breached?

6. Are Adams and Barker protected by the business judgment rule? Why or why not?

7. What type of lawsuit, derivative or direct, would be filed by Cornelius to:

   a. Force Adams and Barker to have a shareholders' meeting and formal vote.

   b. Recover against Adams and Barker for damages Cornelius suffered as a result of an alleged breach of duty.

In the Theory to Practice problem, the principals have made a series of errors that could result in the piercing of the corporate veil. Corporations of all sizes can make similar mistakes if they are not diligent. Suppose that you receive an e-mail from a senior manager who read a newspaper article about the liability of one company's principals in a case where the court had pierced the corporate veil. She asks you to write her a two-page memorandum that recommends a standard operating procedure and policy aimed at preserving your company's corporate veil. Use the mistakes made by Pharma as one guide for avoiding potential liability.

A sample answer may be found on this textbook's website at www.mhhe.com/melvinleb2e.

CASE SUMMARY 16.1 :: Miner v. Fashion Enterprises, Inc., 794 N.E.2d 902 (2003)

PIERCING THE CORPORATE VEIL

Karen Lynn, Inc. (Lynn Corporation), was a wholly owned subsidiary of Fashion Enterprises, Inc. This meant that the sole shareholder of Lynn Corporation was the corporate entity of Fashion Enterprises, Inc. Lynn Corporation entered into a 10-year lease for retail space in Chicago with Miner with no personal guarantees or guarantee by Fashion Enterprises. The company defaulted on the lease by not making rental payments, and Miner obtained a court judgment against Lynn Corporation. The corporation was without assets, and Miner asked the court to pierce the corporate veil and allow the judgment to be enforced against its sole shareholder, Fashion Enterprises, Inc. The trial court dismissed the suit, holding that Miner was entitled to only the assets of Lynn Corporation. Miner appealed.

CASE QUESTIONS

1. Who prevails and why?
2. What factors would the court weigh in deciding whether to pierce the veil?

CASE SUMMARY 16.2 :: Goldman v. Chapman and Region Associates, 44 A.3d 938 (N.Y. 2007)

CORPORATE VEIL PROTECTION

Chapman was the sole shareholder, officer, and director of Region Associates (Region). In 2001, Goldman obtained a judgment against Region in the amount of $209,320 as a result of Goldman's lawsuit against Region (but not Chapman individually). Goldman attempted to collect the judgment from Region but was unsuccessful because Region was without any substantial assets. After exhausting all efforts to collect the judgment from Region, Goldman filed suit asking the court to allow him to pierce Region's corporate veil and collect the judgment from Chapman's personal assets.

CASE QUESTIONS

1. Who prevails and why?
2. Did Chapman use the law to perpetrate an injustice?
3. Is it fair that Goldman is stuck with a worthless judgment and that Chapman may simply start a new company.

SHAREHOLDER RIGHTS

Morrison and Gugle incorporated a company, opened a retail store together, and agreed to a half owner-ship each. Each shareholder was an officer (Gugle as president, Morrison as secretary and treasurer), and each was a director. Additionally, each was an active employee of the business. Gugle and Morrison had a variety of business disputes, and eventually Gugle, as president, fired Morrison. After the termination, Morrison demanded the right to inspect corporate records and financial documents, but Gugle refused to provide any information or access to the records, citing her authority to do so as president of the corporation. Morrison sued Gugle for, among other counts, breach of fiduciary duty.

CASE QUESTIONS

1. Who prevails and why?
2. Does the president have the power to fire a fellow officer and director who is also half owner of the corporation?
3. What fiduciary duty, if any, was breached here?

BUSINESS JUDGMENT RULE

H. Ross Perot became the single largest shareholder and a director of General Motors as a result of GM's acquisition of Perot's highly successful company Electronic Data Systems (EDS). A rift grew between Perot and GM's other directors, and after appointing a subcommittee of directors to study possible alter-natives, GM's directors offered to purchase back Perot's stock at a significant premium over market value. In exchange for the payment, Perot agreed to leave his director's seat, not compete with any GM subsidiary (particularly EDS), and cease any criticism of GM's directors. A group of GM share-holders sued the directors under the theory that the directors had breached their fiduciary duty by wast-ing corporate assets in buying Perot's silence. The directors asserted the business judgment rule as a defense.

CASE QUESTIONS

1. Who prevails and why?
2. What fiduciary duty is at issue?

LIABILITY OF DIRECTORS

Koerner, Inc., was found to have violated a copyright owned by Burdick. Burdick brought suit against each of Koerner's directors on the basis that the directors had financially benefited from the copyright infringement and, therefore, were liable for the copyright infringe-ment damages by virtue of their membership on the board of directors. The directors argued that there was no evidence of day-to-day involvement, intent, or any specific knowledge of the infringement by the directors and, thus, they were not personally liable.

CASE QUESTIONS

1. Who prevails and why?
2. Does the corporate veil protect directors in these circumstances?

Self-Check **ANSWERS**
Business Judgment Rule

1. Yes. The directors fulfilled their duties by consulting outside experts and appointing an oversight subcommittee. They acted in good faith and had a rational belief that the merger was in the interests of the company.

2. No. The directors have the obligation to investigate the auditing firm and not to rubber stamp the decision of the president. This is either gross negligence or willful ignorance. Either way, the directors violated their duty of care and were not acting with the best information and, thus, cannot be shielded by the business judgment rule.

3. Yes. Even if the directors' explanation is a result of poor business judgment, it is not an act of bad faith and is done with a rational belief. Thus, the directors are protected by the business judgment rule.

4. No. The four directors violated the corporate opportunity doctrine by failing to disclose their financial interest in the real estate. This is an act of bad faith, and, therefore, those four directors are not shielded by the business judgment rule.

17
CHAPTER

Regulation of Securities, Corporate Governance, and Financial Markets

learning objectives

After studying this chapter, students who have mastered the material will be able to:

17-1 Articulate factors that differentiate, and the laws that regulate, the primary and secondary securities markets.

17-2 Apply the legal test for what constitutes a security.

17-3 Distinguish between classifications of equity and debt instruments and give an example of each.

17-4 Recognize the fundamental reason behind securities regulation and have a working knowledge of the legal process leading to issuance of original securities.

17-5 Describe the role of the Securities and Exchange Commission (SEC) in securities law compliance and enforcement.

17-6 List the major categories of securities and transactions that are exempt from registration requirements.

17-7 Articulate the ethical and legal duties of corporate insiders.

17-8 Identify the legal standard necessary to bring a securities fraud suit against directors and officers in light of the Private Securities Litigation Reform Act.

17-9 Explain the role of state blue-sky laws in securities regulation.

17-10 Show an awareness of the impact of the Sarbanes-Oxley Act on a corporation's officers and directors and its corporate governance.

17-11 Articulate key protections afforded by regulation of the financial markets.

The options that various business entities have for funding operations were covered in the previous chapters in this unit. This chapter focuses on the entities that sell ownership of a venture, known as *equity,* to investors who are interested in receiving a return on their investment based on the success of the business. Other entities find it advantageous to raise money by issuing *debt* instruments to public investors who wish to receive a fixed rate of return regardless of the profitability of the business entity. The issuance and trading of equity and debt instruments to public investors is highly regulated by federal and state *securities law.* In addition to securities regulation, federal laws impose mandates on corporate governance procedures in certain corporations and regulate broad financial markets.

The actions of business owners and managers who are engaged in raising capital or operate in the financial markets, as well as corporate governance of publicly held entities, are subject to the scrutiny of regulatory authorities, and the consequences of noncompliance can be severe.

Specifically, students will learn:

- The background and scope of the primary and secondary securities markets and the role of regulatory agencies in enforcement.
- Classifications of securities and rules that regulate their issuance, sale, and trading and provide exemptions from certain securities laws for qualified ventures.
- Legal mandates associated with corporate governance and regulation of the broader financial market.

OVERVIEW OF THE SECURITIES MARKET   LO 17-1

Securities transactions occur in two settings: (1) the *primary market,* in which businesses sell original issues and reissues of securities to raise capital and (2) the *secondary market,* in which investors buy and sell issued securities among themselves. Both of these markets are governed by federal and state **securities law,** and various securities regulations require registration and disclosures and prescribe certain procedures intended to give investors confidence in the value of a particular security.

In the primary market, issuers raise capital by selling securities in public markets (to the general investment community) or in private placements (to limited groups of investors, such as venture capitalists or institutional investors). Issuing securities to the public markets for the first time is known as an *initial public offering (IPO).* A company is said to "go public" when it decides to sell its voting common shares for the first

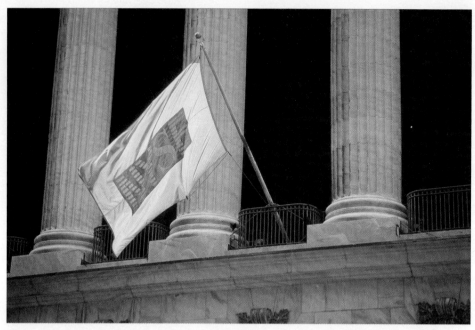

Companies may raise money through issuing securities to investors via a public exchange such as the New York Stock Exchange (NYSE). The NYSE is the world's largest stock exchange, with almost $28.5 trillion in market capitalization.

time to outside investors through public markets such as the New York Stock Exchange (NYSE). The sale is made through the use of a mandatory registration statement that discloses important facts about the offering to potential investors.

In the secondary market, the trading of already-issued securities does not raise capital for the issuing business. Rather, investors sell to other investors in hopes of making a profit or preventing a loss. Once a company has sold shares to the public, it becomes subject to extensive reporting requirements to federal regulators. In theory, this secondary market provides cash flow for investors to continue their investments in primary markets.

Not all securities offerings and transactions are subject to the full burden of the federal and state regulatory schemes. Some securities transactions are exempt from full registration, and the law allows a fast-track system for securities that fall into the category of relatively small offerings or private placements. These exemptions are not automatic. The issuer or trader of a security must craft the security transaction to conform to the exemption requirements according to federal and state laws.

LO 17-2   Security Defined

Given the regulatory requirements that are triggered by a securities transaction, business owners and managers need a working knowledge of the instruments and transactions that federal and state laws define as securities and securities offerings. The regulations include registration and disclosure requirements, specific requirements to exempt a securities offering from the federal securities scheme, liability for misrepresentation or omissions in the offering materials, antifraud protections for buyers of securities, and criminal sanctions under certain circumstances for those engaged in fraud while selling or trading securities.

Federal Securities Law   Stocks and bonds are well-known types of securities that are regulated by securities statutes. In addition, partnership interests, stock options, warrants, agreements to invest, participation in a pool of assets, certain types of promissory notes, and many other arrangements that might commonly be considered investments are regulated by securities laws.

Federal securities statutes define a security in two ways: (1) by recognizing specific forms of securities, such as notes, stocks, treasury stocks, transferable shares, bonds, and debentures, and (2) by providing a catchall definition of other investment transactions in a more *generic* sense, including participation in profit-sharing agreements; collateral trust certificates; preorganization certificates or subscriptions; investment contracts; and a fractional, undivided interest in gas, oil, or other mineral rights. Even some *business plans,* depending on the language and circumstances, may constitute a securities offering. Note that certain types of debt instruments, such as a promissory note secured by a home mortgage or by accounts receivable or other business assets, are *not* securities.

Based on these definitions, the general standard for determining whether an arrangement or offering is defined as a security is quite broad: A security is any *investment* that involves a person giving something with an *expectation of profit* through the efforts of a *third party.* In Landmark Case 17.1, the U.S. Supreme Court articulated a four-part test that helped to give lower courts a framework for defining a security and securities offering.

Modern Application of the *Howey* Test

Although the four parts of the *Howey* test remain intact, federal courts have added further clarification that has expanded the definition of what constitutes a securities offering. Courts now apply a sweeping standard including the investment itself, commonality, profit expectations, and the efforts of others.

Investment   The investment may be cash or a noncash instrument for which the investing party receives only the speculative promise of a return and not any tangible commodity or assets.

Commonality   Courts have ruled that an investment scheme satisfies this requirement either through *horizontal commonality* (multiple investors have a common expectation of profit in the investment) or via *vertical commonality* (a single investor has a common expectation of profit with the *promoter* of her investment).

Profit Expectations   The expectation of a return on investment (profitability) must be the primary reason for the investment.

Efforts of Others   The efforts of the promoter(s) or agents of the promoter(s) must be the primary sources of revenue that results in profits. Note that *Howey* actually required that the investor not be involved in any way with generating the profits. However, the modern trend is for courts to allow some *limited passive involvement* by the investor so long as the promoter/agent has been the primary source of the efforts.

CONCEPT SUMMARY Modern *Howey* Test

Investment	Commonality	Promoter
Cash or noncash instrument. Investor's primary motive is expectation of profit.	Multiple investors in single transaction (horizontal). Single investor in single transaction (vertical).	Uses investor money to generate profits primarily by promoter's efforts. *Modern rule:* Limited passive action by investor OK.

FACT SUMMARY Howey owned 100 acres of real estate that were used to grow citrus. In an attempt to raise capital for improvements in his citrus operations, Howey offered an investment opportunity to third-party investors. Investors could purchase a certain tract of the real estate and enter into a service agreement whereby Howey would provide services related to care and harvesting of the citrus crop on the real estate. Investors were not required to enter into the service agreement, but investors that did sign a service agreement were given a percentage of the profits from the harvest. Approximately 80 percent of the investors entered into the service contract. The Securities and Exchange Commission (SEC), the federal regulatory agency that enforces federal securities laws, charged Howey with several violations of federal securities law, alleging that the investment constituted an investment contract and was, therefore, required to be registered as a security. Howey argued that the investment opportunity was a contractual agreement and not a securities offering because the service agreement was not mandatory. Howey claimed that the transaction was simply a real estate purchase with an optional profit sharing opportunity. The trial court and circuit court of appeals both ruled in favor of Howey. The SEC appealed to the U.S. Supreme Court.

SYNOPSIS OF DECISION AND OPINION The Court ruled in favor of the SEC and developed what has become a guidepost test for determining what constitutes a security subject to federal regulation. The so-called *Howey* test has a four-part analysis. Courts examine whether (1) the investment opportunity at issue is an investment of money, (2) the money is invested in a common enterprise, (3) the investor does so with expectations of profits, and (4) the profits are generated *solely* by the efforts of persons other than the investor. In this case, the combination of the purchase of land along with the service contract satisfied the four requirements because the investors had no desire to occupy or develop the property themselves. Rather, the Court pointed out, the investors were attracted by the prospects of a return on their investment.

WORDS OF THE COURT: Investment Contracts as Securities "[A]n investment contract for the purposes of the Securities Act means a contract, transaction or scheme whereby a person invests his money in a common enterprise and is led to expect profits solely from the efforts of the promoter of a third party, it being immaterial whether the shares in the enterprise are evidenced by formal certificates or by nominal interests in the physical assets employed in that enterprise."

Case Questions

1. Could Howey adjust the business model and retool the opportunity without triggering securities regulation? How?

2. Recall from the facts that the service contract was optional and approximately 20 percent of the investors purchased the real estate only. Does that 20 percent of investors satisfy the four-part test? Was it enough to satisfy the test that all investors had the mere *opportunity* to enter into the service agreement?

 Self-Check The *Howey* Test

Do these opportunities constitute a securities offering under the *Howey* test?

1. Smith offers to sell earthworms to third-party investors. The investors enter into a contract whereby, after the purchase, Smith will raise the worms in such a way as to promote massive reproduction and he guarantees to repurchase the worms from the investors at a certain rate based on the actual sale price to third-party farmers. Thus, an investor can purchase a certain dollar amount of worms, have Smith raise the worms and locate a farmer buyer, and then have Smith repurchase the worms from the investor at a higher price than the investor's original price based on the sale price to the farmer.

2. Utley offered to sell one-half acre beachfront lots to the public at $50,000 per lot. After the completion of a sale, Utley offered to perform services as a general contractor for purposes of building a shore house on the lot. Among the buyers of the lots, 20 percent of the owners hired Utley to build the houses, but the other 80 percent either hired their own contractors or left the land undeveloped. Once the houses were built, Utley offered to find a buyer for a 10 percent commission on a complete sale.

3. Alliance was a leasing company that devised an opportunity for third-party investors in which the investors paid money to Alliance for the purchase of commercial or kitchen equipment. Alliance then acted as an agent to arrange an equipment lease with the business lessee who needed the equipment. Alliance entered into a joint venture agreement with the investors to sell them the equipment and to broker a lease between the investor and a lessee. The lease agreement provided for lease payments to be paid by the lessees directly to the investor on a monthly basis over a two-year period, at the end of which a balloon payment (the entire principal) would be due. Alliance represented that the investors would earn a 14 percent rate of return on their investment and that risk was low.

Answers to this Self-Check are provided at the end of the chapter.

CATEGORIES OF SECURITIES

LO 17-3

Securities fall into one of two general categories: **equity** or **debt.** Each category includes an inventory of *instruments* that are tangible representations of the security and that define the rights of the owner of the security. Some securities have restrictions on the ownership rights (such as the right to sell the security to another party).

Equity Instruments

Equity instruments represent an investor's ownership interests in which financial return on the investment is based primarily on the performance of the venture that issued the securities. However, equity holders have no specific right or guarantee on the investment. Therefore, investors with equity interests may profit considerably from a company that is consistently profitable. However, if the company fails, the equity interest becomes worthless and the investor is without any legal recourse (assuming that no fraud or malfeasance occurred that led to the company's demise) to recover her original investment. Two prevalent forms of equity instruments issued by corporations are *common stock* and *preferred stock.*

Common Stock   The most frequently used form of equity instrument is **common stock** (also called **common shares**), which entitles the equity owner to payments based on the current profitability of the company. The payments are known as *dividends,* and the decision on whether to pay dividends to equity owners, as well as how much to pay, rests with the company's board of directors. Common stock owners also have the right to payment in the event that the corporation is sold for a profit or the company is dissolved (assuming any value is left in the company). In certain companies, common stock may be *voting* or *nonvoting.* A nonvoting common stockholder is entitled to all benefits of ownership except the right to vote for directors or on major corporate decisions. However, most common stockholders are typically entitled to full voting rights. Rights and duties of shareholders, directors, and officers were discussed in detail in

Legal Speak ›))
Subordinate In the context of stock ownership rights, a subordinate position is a lower or secondary position in terms of being entitled to profits or assets. For example, common stockholders are subordinate to preferred stockholders.

Legal Speak ›))
Senior in Priority When a business must liquidate assets because it fails and either dissolves or files for bankruptcy protection, payments to creditors and shareholders are made according to priority. Thus, those that are "senior" in priority get paid first.

Chapter 16, "Corporations." While common stockholders share in the profits, they also bear the greatest risk of loss because they are typically *subordinate* to all creditors and preferred stockholders if the corporation files for bankruptcy protection or simply dissolves with limited assets.

Preferred Stock   An alternative form of equity that has less risk than common stock because it has certain quasi-debt features is **preferred stock.** Perhaps the biggest advantage of preferred stock is that preferred stockholders have preference rights over common stockholders in receiving dividends from the corporation. In the event that the corporation fails or files for bankruptcy, preferred stockholders are ahead of common stockholders when trying to recover their losses from the liquidation proceeds. Preferred stock may be voting or nonvoting.

Debt Instruments

Debt is another common tool for raising capital. Holders of debt instruments, which include promissory notes, bonds, and debentures, are generally entitled to receive payments that are *senior in priority* to those of preferred or common stockholders. *Promissory notes* are the most commonly used debt instrument. The note simply represents a promise to pay back a certain sum of money (principal) plus accrued interest over an agreed-upon time period. The lender is paid back with principal and interest payments, typically monthly, in accordance with the terms of the note. *Bonds* are debt instruments that are issued by a corporation and are secured by certain assets of the company. *Debentures* are unsecured debt instruments that are issued by a corporation and are backed by the pledge of the corporation's general credit. Investors holding debt instruments are primarily interested in a fixed rate of return regardless of the profitability of the corporation and expect repayment of the debt after a certain period of years.

Use of Bonds and Debentures   Bonds and debentures represent the borrowing of money from investors to raise capital for the corporate issuer of the debt instrument. Larger corporations prefer bonds as a method of splitting up their long-term debt, and they blend the use of bonds with conventional borrower-lender (bank) loans for short-term debt. Because bonds are debt instruments, investors expect fixed payments at regular intervals until the bond *matures,* at which time the principal amount of the bond, known as its *face amount,* is paid to the investor.

Although bonds are thought of as capital-raising tools of major corporations, some newer bond issues, known as *micro bonds,* streamline paperwork, reduce fees, and are appealing to smaller business ventures that wish to take advantage of bond financing in the $500,000 to $1,000,000 range.

connect |BUSINESS LAW
Visit Connect to learn about how smaller companies use micro bonds in a link to the article from *Entrepreneur* magazine.

LO 17-4, 17-5   # SECURITIES REGULATION

Fundamentally, all securities regulation has the same rationale: protecting investors and ensuring public confidence in the integrity of the securities market. Note that securities laws are not meant to provide insurance for losses or to punish a venture's principals simply because the business does not earn a profit. The underlying premise of all securities regulation is **disclosure.** Much of the regulation concerning fraud or securities sales boils down to whether the seller or issuer has made truthful and sufficiently full disclosures about the security itself. Securities law is primarily a matter of federal statutes and regulations, but all states have similar disclosure and fraud laws within state borders.

The Securities and Exchange Commission (SEC) is an independent federal administrative agency that is charged with regulating the issuing and trading of securities.

Securities and Exchange Commission

The **Securities and Exchange Commission (SEC)** is the federal administrative agency charged with rulemaking, enforcement, and adjudication of federal securities laws. Unlike many administrative agencies, the SEC is an *independent agency* that does not have a seat in the president's cabinet and is not subject to direct control by the president. Five commissioners, appointed by the president and subject to advice-and-consent approval by the Senate, compose the SEC. Commissioners may be removed for misconduct, but no commissioner has been removed since the SEC was formed by Congress in 1934. In addition to being a source of expert information on securities laws, the SEC has wide-ranging executive, legislative, and judicial powers.

The SEC's executive powers include the power to investigate potential violations of securities laws and regulations. The SEC also has a variety of administrative enforcement mechanisms, such as issuing a cease and desist order.[1] In egregious cases, the SEC initiates criminal charges against an individual and/or company that has allegedly violated securities law. The SEC's legislative authority is granted by Congress and allows the SEC to draft and publish securities regulations and interpretations of statutes, rules, and court decisions. Pursuant to its legislative powers, the SEC also issues interpretative letters and no-action letters to advise the securities investment and trading community on how the SEC will treat a proposed transaction. These letters are not binding on the SEC, but they do carry significant weight with courts and are crucial to the day-to-day operations of publicly held companies. The SEC's judicial powers are primarily rooted in its role as a hearing tribunal for enforcing certain securities violations, including alleged indiscretions of brokers in their business dealings. The SEC has the power to suspend or revoke professional licenses of brokers and others regulated by securities laws.

---

[1] An administrative order requiring a certain party to halt unlawful activity.

Though it is the primary regulatory authority of the securities markets, the SEC works closely with many other institutions, including Congress, other federal agencies, self-regulatory organizations (such as stock exchanges), state securities regulators, and various private sector organizations. The chair of the SEC is one of four members[2] of the President's Working Group on Financial Markets.

The agency is composed of several divisions and departments. The highest-profile divisions are Enforcement and Corporation Finance because they are primarily responsible for investigation and enforcement action against violators. Much of the SEC's day-to-day work is done through its 11 regional offices, which are spread throughout the United States.

Figure 17.1 shows the SEC's organizational structure.

EDGAR   An important function of the SEC is to maintain a national clearinghouse for public corporation disclosures and filings required by federal securities laws. This clearinghouse is made available to the public through the SEC's computer database known as EDGAR. In addition to providing access to EDGAR, the SEC's website serves as a source of information to educate investors on risks and SEC procedures.

FIGURE 17.1   Structure of the Securities and Exchange Commission

Source: www.sec.gov/images/secorg.pdf.

---

[2]The other members are the chair of the Federal Reserve, the chair of the Commodities Futures Trading Commission, and the secretary of the Treasury.

The Securities Act of 1933

The primary scope of the **Securities Act of 1933**[3] (the "33 Act") is the regulation of original issuance (and reissuance) of securities to investors by business venture issuers. The 33 Act mandates (1) a registration filing for any venture selling securities to the public, (2) certain disclosures concerning the issuer's governance and financial condition, and (3) SEC oversight over the registration and issuance of securities. The system is designed to give potential investors a transparent view of the business entity's financial information, potential liabilities, management practices, and other pertinent information that a business venture is required to disclose in its registration materials. The 33 Act also provides defrauded investors with remedies against issuers that violate the statutory requirements. Congress has also provided *special exemptions* for issuance of securities to relatively small groups of qualified investors. These exemptions are discussed in the next section of this chapter.

> **KEY** POINT
>
> The Securities Act of 1933 covers the processes of issuing and reissuing securities to the public. The law requires registration and certain disclosures and authorizes the SEC to oversee the transactions.

Preregistration Documentation The 33 Act and the SEC regulations require extensive documentation even before the registration statement is filed. This documentation requires the expertise of a variety of professionals, but ultimately it consists of legal documents that are drafted by highly specialized attorneys skilled in securities law. Required documentation before registration includes a *letter of intent* (issuer indicates management and board approval of the issuing of shares); *comfort letters* (including an opinion letter from the issuer's corporate counsel, verifying the business venture's adherence to corporate formalities, and a letter of compliance and opinion from the business venture's accounting firm, verifying the accuracy of the business's financial records); and an *underwriting agreement,* in which the issuer enters into an agreement with a syndicate of underwriters[4] specifying the amount of securities offered, the compensation for the underwriters, and terms related to representations and warranties of the issuer and underwriters.

Registration Registering a security is a relatively complex process that is divided into four phases. First, as discussed above, the issuer assembles preregistration documents. Second, the issuer begins the prefiling period while the registration statement is being prepared. The form of the registration statement is prescribed by SEC regulations and is broken down into two parts. The first part is the **prospectus,** which is intended to give investors a realistic view of the issuer's business, risk factors, financial position, financial statements, and disclosures concerning directors, officers, and controlling shareholders. The second part of the registration statement is *supplemental information* that documents and supports the prospectus. Once the prospectus is drafted, the next phase of registration is the *SEC review* of the statement. During these first two phases of the registration process, the securities may not be marketed or sold to the public. In the third phase, the registration statement is submitted and the SEC has 10 days to review it for incomplete or misleading disclosures. In phase four, the SEC may issue a *refusal order* that prevents the registration from taking effect. Even after the SEC's 10-day review period has expired, the SEC can issue a *stop order* if it determines there was a defect in the disclosures. If the SEC does not act, the registration statement becomes effective 20 days after it was filed. During the SEC review phase, the security may not be sold, but it may be *marketed* to

---

[3]15 U.S.C. § 77a et seq.

[4]In this context, an underwriter is a professional in the securities market that agrees to facilitate the sale of stock to the public for a fee.

the public subject to strict SEC regulations. Once the registration statement has become effective, the securities are permitted to be sold to the public. After the offering's contemplated registration statement expires, securities may still be sold and marketed to investors, but investors must receive a prospectus and the marketing materials are still subject to the SEC's oversight. Table 17.1 illustratates the phases of Securities Registration under the 33 Act.

Exemptions from Registration While the SEC regulations pertaining to registering securities are intended to protect investors, the process itself is extremely onerous and expensive for issuers who are engaged in a relatively small offering. In order to assist business ventures seeking smaller amounts of capital from the public investment community, the securities laws allow a number of **exemptions** from registration for smaller issuers. For a number of economic, legal, and other practical reasons, *most businesses offer their securities on an exempt basis.* From a federal standpoint, the most common exemption is one for *nonpublic* offerings to a limited number of sophisticated investors who have prior business relationships with the issuer or who privately negotiate their securities purchases. Another common exemption, known as a regulatory *safe harbor,* involves offerings with specified dollar limitations and/or limitations on the number of *nonaccredited investors.* While the security may be exempt from the burdensome regulations of the 33 Act, as a condition for establishing an exemption a seller of securities is still required to make available or prepare and deliver *certain disclosures* to prospective investors. The breadth and content of these disclosures vary depending upon the particular requirements for registration or exemption imposed by law. The following securities are common examples of securities that are exempt from full registration requirements:

- Commercial paper (such as promissory notes that are purchased by sophisticated investors and investment banks) with a maturity date of less than nine months.
- Securities of charitable organizations.

TABLE 17.1 Phases of Securities Registration

Phase 1 Pre-registration	Phase 2 Registration Statement	Phase 3 SEC Review	Phase 4 SEC Response
Proposed issuer assembles pre-registration documents such as letters of intent, comfort letters, and an underwriting agreement.	Proposed issuer drafts prospectus with disclosures and financial information and submits the statement to the SEC.	The SEC reviews the registration statement over a period of 10 days.	The SEC may either: (1) Issue a refusal order during the 10-day review period or issue a stop order after the review period. Proposed issuer must revise and resubmit. (2) Take no action, and the registration becomes effective 20 days after the original SEC filing. The security may now be sold to the public.

- Annuities and other issues of insurance companies.
- Government-issued securities such as municipal bonds.
- Securities issued by banks and other institutions subject to government supervision.
- In certain cases under Regulation D (explained next), securities issues of up to $5 million in any 12-month period.

In addition to the exemption for some *types* of securities, the securities laws also exempt certain *transactions* that an issuer may use to sell the security. Some of the more common transaction exemptions fall under a securities law provision known as **Regulation D.** Regulation D exemptions apply to *limited* offers that involve a relatively small amount of money or offers that are made in a limited manner. Within Regulation D, the exemptions are often referred to by their rule number:

- Rule 504 exempts a noninvestment company offering up to $1 million in any 12-month period.
- Rule 504a exempts offerings up to $500,000 in any 12-month period by certain companies.
- Rule 505 exempts a private noninvestment company offering up to $5 million in any 12-month period.
- Rule 506 exempts private noninvestment company offerings in unlimited amounts that are not generally advertised or available to the general public.

Another commonly used exemption is known as a **private placement,** in which the issuer accepts investments only from those who meet the standards for *accredited investors.* Accredited investors are those who have sufficient experience, business savvy, and knowledge of the market for the law to impute that they have a certain cognizance of investment risk and the ability to protect their own interests. These investors must meet personal net worth or income requirements in order to qualify. Exempt private placement offers are still required to make important disclosures to potential investors about the business and its principals. In a private placement, these disclosures are made through the use of a *private placement memorandum.* The Securities Act of 1933 exempts private placement transactions under Section 4(2). The most common are:

- Offerings up to $5 million that are made solely to accredited investors in any 12-month period and are not advertised.
- Purely local offerings, in which purchase is restricted to residents of the same state as the company and resale is barred to nonresidents for nine months.

Liability for Violations   The 33 Act, and its subsequent amendments, imposes both civil and criminal penalties on offerors and sellers of securities who violate the act's provisions. The penalties include (1) rescission of the investment by the investor, (2) civil penalties and fines, and (3) incarceration for egregious cases. The SEC has broad authority to pursue civil and criminal sanctions when an offering is accomplished by false or misleading means. Table 17.2 provides specific remedies and penalties for noncompliance with securities issuance regulations.

> **KEY** POINT
> Exemption from registration does not exempt issuers from appropriate disclosures to investors and financial transparency.

Defenses   If a corporation fails to comply with the 33 Act, it may avoid liability or penalties by successfully asserting one of two defenses: (1) The omission or misrepresentation in the registration or offering was not *material* (i.e., the omission or misrepresentation was so minor that it did not affect the value of the offering or injure an investor), or (2) the investor had *knowledge* about the omission or misrepresentation and proceeded

TABLE 17.2   33 Act Liabilities and Penalties

Violation	Remedy/Penalty
Noncompliance with registration requirements	Investors who purchased unregistered securities are entitled to rescind the investment and to be paid back in full.
Fraud in registration statement or offering	Investors may recover damages from the issuer if they relied on the statements in considering the purchase.
Fraud in any transaction or offering	The issuer is subject to criminal penalties, including substantial fines and incarceration.

with the investment *assuming the risk.* If the violator is not actually the issuer of the stock but a third party involved in the transaction (such as an underwriter), that party may avoid liability by proving she acted with *due diligence* in verifying the veracity and completeness of the required disclosures.

Materiality　The definition of materiality is significant because the import and truthfulness of information presented in a prospectus is at the very heart of statutory disclosure requirements. Courts use a total-mix test to determine whether or not an omission or representation is material. Even when the most important information is omitted from the prospectus, an omission cannot be considered material if the total mix of information was already reasonably available to the investing public. Thus, if an investor should have known about a particular fact that was available in the total mix of information, she cannot later claim that the undisclosed fact was a material omission.

Bespeaks Caution Doctrine　One of the most powerful defenses for an issuer is the judicially created bespeaks caution doctrine. This defense allows an issuer who included specific and narrowly tailored cautionary disclosures in the prospectus to negate any allegedly misleading or overly optimistic prediction. However, an issuer cannot be protected through the bespeaks caution doctrine if the cautionary statements were overly broad or too general. Rather, courts require that the cautionary language be specifically tailored to the prediction.

In Case 17.2, an appellate court considers the bespeaks caution doctrine in the context of an investment in the Trump Taj Mahal hotel and casino in Atlantic City.

LO 17-7   The Securities Act of 1934

While the 33 Act regulates the *issuance* of securities to the public by a corporation, the **Securities Act of 1934**[5] (the "34 Act") regulates the sale of securities between investors *after* an investor purchased them from a business entity issuer. Therefore, the 34 Act's authority is over brokers, dealers, securities associations, brokerage firms, and other business entities that are engaged in the sale of securities between investors. Similar to the 33 Act, this statute requires registration with the SEC for issuers who wish to have their securities offered on a *national exchange,* such as the New York Stock Exchange, and compels all sellers of securities to fully disclose all pertinent details to potential investors. The 34 Act also regulates the relationship between existing stockholders and the corporation by requiring disclosure of information concerning (1) the financial performance of the company, (2) corporate governance procedures, and (3) any changes that increase or decrease risk that have occurred since the last report (such as the company being named as a defendant in a lawsuit).

---

[5] 15 U.S.C. § 78a et seq.

FACT SUMMARY   Trump and his codefendants offered securities to the public in order to finance the purchase, construction, and operation of the Trump Taj Mahal, which was billed as the most lavish casino resort in Atlantic City. The prospectus accompanying the bonds estimated the costs for completion and disclosed the plan for securing the entire financing package, which included bond proceeds, capital from Trump, and various loans and lines of credit. The prospectus stated: "The Partnership believes that the funds generated from the operation of the Taj Mahal will be sufficient to cover all of its debt service (interest and principal)." The prospectus also contained numerous cautionary statements on factors including the intense competition in the casino industry, the absence of an operating history for the Taj Mahal, and the possibility that the enterprise may become unable to repay the interest on the bonds in the event of a mortgage default and subsequent liquidation of the Taj Mahal. When Kaufman and other investors discovered that Trump and his codefendants planned to file for reorganization under Chapter 11 of the bankruptcy code, they filed a suit alleging that the Taj Mahal offering's prospectus contained material misstatements and omissions and constituted fraud. The trial court ruled in favor of Trump and held that the cautionary statements that surrounded each representation barred any misrepresentation claim. Kaufman appealed.

SYNOPSIS OF DECISION AND OPINION   The U.S. Court of Appeals for the Third Circuit affirmed the trial court's ruling in favor of Trump. The court applied the bespeaks caution doctrine, whereby cautionary language in a prospectus negates the materiality of an alleged

misrepresentation. The court held that the defendants had included substantive statements that were tailored to address specific future projections and estimates or opinions in the prospectus. The bespeaks caution doctrine means that cautionary statements included in a prospectus may render the challenged predictive statements or opinions immaterial as a matter of law.

WORDS OF THE COURT: Bespeaks Caution Doctrine   "Because of the abundant and meaningful cautionary language contained in the prospectus, we hold that [Kaufman has] failed to state an actionable claim regarding the statements that the Partnership believed it could repay the bonds. We can say that the prospectus here truly bespeaks caution because, not only does the prospectus generally convey the riskiness of the investment, but its warning and cautionary language directly address the substance of the statement of [Kaufman's] challenge. That is to say, the cautionary statements were tailored precisely to address the uncertainty concerning the partnership's ability to repay the bondholders."

Case Questions

1. Kaufman claimed that the prospectus failed to disclose the fact that the average casino "win" would have to top $1.3 billion per day in order to pay the debt back. Should Trump have disclosed that fact? Do issuers have a duty to disclose negative information in the prospectus?

2. Is the bespeaks caution doctrine consistent with the 33 Act's overall goal of transparency and disclosure in a securities issuance? Why or why not? Could the doctrine be modified to be more favorable to an investor?

Section 10(b)   Section 10(b) of the 34 Act is the primary *antifraud* provision covering the trading of securities. The section makes it a criminal offense to engage in any fraud, directly or indirectly, in connection with the purchase and sale of any security. Its scope is very broad, and the SEC strictly enforces this section, often referred to as *Rule 10(b)(5)*. Although the term *10(b)(5)* is perhaps best known for its use by the SEC in prosecuting insider-trading cases, in reality this section is a very expansive antifraud provision intended to cover all actions, conspiracies, or schemes that could potentially result in an investor's being defrauded, damaged, or misled.

Insider Trading   The SEC has become increasingly aggressive about the enforcement of Rule 10(b)(5) with respect to **insider trading.** Essentially, when a corporate insider has access to certain information not available to the general investor public, the insider may not trade in the company's stock on the basis of the inside information. Insiders include executives, managers, corporate counsel, consultants, employees, brokers, accountants, vendors, partners, and even majority shareholders. In 1988, Congress passed the **Insider Trading and Securities Fraud Enforcement Act,** which raised the criminal and civil penalties for insider trading, increased the liability of brokerage firms for wrongful acts of their employees, and gave the SEC more power to pursue violations of Rule 10(b)(5).

In Case 17.3, a federal appeals court applies the insider-trading provisions to an insider who bought stock in Microsoft based on information he had obtained from his own company's work on the X-Box.

CASE 17.3   U.S. v. Bhagat, 436 F.3d 1140 (9th Cir. 2006)

FACT SUMMARY   Bhagat was employed as an engineer by NVIDIA, a publicly held corporation located in Silicon Valley that manufactured graphics processors and media communication devices. On Sunday, March 5, 2000, the chief executive officer of NVIDIA sent an e-mail to all company employees announcing that NVIDIA had entered into a contract with Microsoft to develop and manufacture 3-D graphics for Microsoft's X-Box. The e-mail contained a prediction that the deal would result in nearly $2 billion in revenue over the next five years. On Monday, March 6, NVIDIA's management sent out several follow-up e-mails, including one from the vice president of marketing that was entitled "Xbox shhhh" and gave specific instructions to keep the information confidential. NVIDIA's management imposed an employee trading blackout (i.e., employees were not permitted to purchase or sell any NVIDIA stock) for several days. Employees were also required to cancel any open or outstanding orders for NVIDIA stock.

Bhagat arrived at his office on that same Monday morning, and approximately 20 minutes after the trading-blackout e-mail was sent, he purchased a large quantity of NVIDIA stock—his largest purchase in three years. After the news about NVIDIA's contract with Microsoft was released, NVIDIA's stock rose sharply and Bhagat reaped a substantial profit. On the same day that he purchased his stock, Bhagat contacted two friends, who also purchased unusually large quantities of NVIDIA. The Securities and Exchange Commission (SEC) investigated the trade, and Bhagat claimed that he had read his e-mail only after he had bought the stock and that, by the time he tried to cancel the transaction, he was told it was too late to do so. Bhagat was convicted by a jury of insider trading, securities tipping, and lying to the SEC investigators. Bhagat appealed on the grounds that the government

presented no direct evidence that Bhagat had read his e-mail prior to executing the trade.

SYNOPSIS OF DECISION AND OPINION   The U.S. Court of Appeals for the Ninth Circuit upheld Bhagat's convictions. The court held that even without direct evidence that Bhagat read any of the e-mails prior to purchasing the stock, the jury was allowed to infer Bhagat's insider knowledge by virtue of the fact that he had probably read his company e-mail upon entering the office, as a normal, reasonable person would. The court rejected Bhagat's contention that his trades were made on "general strength of the stock" and questioned his credibility based on his testimony at trial that he had tried to cancel the transaction once he read the trading-blackout e-mail but could not recall the branch of the brokerage house he called or the name, or even the gender, of the representative he spoke with.

WORDS OF THE COURT: Insider Knowledge   "The government offered significant evidence to support the jury's conclusion that Bhagat was aware of the confidential X-Box information before he executed his trades. The X-Box e-mails were sent prior to his purchase. The e-mails were found on his computer. Bhagat was at his office for several hours prior to executing his trade, which provided him the opportunity to read the e-mails. Finally, Bhagat took virtually no action to divest himself of the stock, or to inform his company that he had violated the company's trading blackout. The fact that this evidence was all circumstantial does not lessen its sufficiency to support a guilty verdict."

Case Questions

1. Is Bhagat liable as an insider even though he was a relatively low-level employee? Why?

2. What role did Bhagat's credibility play in this case?

Tipper-Tippee Liability Although Rule 10(b)(5) clearly applies to insiders using internal corporate information to profit or prevent a loss in their own stock portfolios, the rule also extends specifically to outside parties who learn of the insider information and trade stock on the basis of the information. This is known as *tipper-tippee liability* (and can even be extended to other parties whom the tippee told about the internal information) and is a criminal offense under the 34 Act. Rule 10(b)(5) is violated if (1) the information released by the tipper constituted a breach of the tipper's *fiduciary duty* to the company, (2) the tipper obtained some personal *benefit* by giving the tip, (3) the tippee knew or should have known that the information was *wrongfully disclosed,* and (4) the tippee ben-*efited* from the information. For example, suppose that Charles, the executive assistant to the chief financial officer at a public company, discovers information that is likely to adversely impact the price of the stock of the company. Because Charles owns no stock in the company, there is no possibility of direct 10(b)(5) liability for insider trading. How-ever, suppose that Charles knows that his *neighbor* owns stock in the company and offers his neighbor the information in exchange for a fee. When the neighbor hears the insider information, he sells all of his stock in the company. The next day, the stock price falls by 50 percent. Both Charles (as tipper) and the neighbor (as tippee) are liable for violating rule 10(b)(5) under the tipper-tippee theory. Charles benefited by earning the fee, and the neighbor benefited by selling the stock on the basis of the inside information.

In Case 17.4, famous football coach Barry Switzer was charged with insider trading for inadvertently overhearing insider information while attending his son's sporting event. Although this case was decided by a trial court in 1984, the decision was never reversed and the reasoning has been adopted by other federal courts as late as 2005, including a U.S. circuit court of appeal. It has also been cited in 53 law journal articles.

Section 16 While Rule 10(b)(5) prohibits insider trading using information based on insider or tipper-tippee knowledge, **Section 16** of the 34 Act imposes restrictions and report-ing requirements on ownership positions and stock trades made by certain corporate insid-ers named in the statute. It was most recently amended in 1991 to clarify certain provisions and extend its reporting requirements, but fundamentally Section 16 mandates transparency of all stock trades by insiders and prohibits insiders from earning short-swing profits.

Section 16(a) classifies any person who is an executive officer, a director, or a share-holder owning 10 percent or more of a company's total stock as an *insider* and requires such insiders to file regular reports with the SEC disclosing their stock ownership and trad-ing of their company's stock. This reporting requirement allows the SEC and the invest-ment community to monitor unusual stock activity, such as whether a company's chief executive officer sells substantial portions of his stock in the company during a short time frame. Although an insider's stock sale could be the result of outside influences unrelated to the company, many investors would see it as a sign of trouble. The SEC regularly inves-tigates such activity as it may be indicative of stock manipulation.

Section 16(b) includes a clawback provision that allows a corporation to recapture any profits earned by an insider on a purchase or sale of the company's stock that occurred within a six-month period. These earnings are called *short-swing profits,* and the prohibi-tion against them is intended to deter insiders from profiting by manipulating the stock's short-term performance. Section 16(b) is a strict liability statute because it applies even if the insider did not use any insider information or intend any stock manipulation in real-izing a short-swing profit.

Section 10(b)(5) and Section 16 in Tandem To understand how the two primary regulations of insiders work in tandem, consider the following example: Suppose that RocketCo is a publicly held corporation subject to the provisions of the 34 Act. Armstrong is the company's chief financial officer, and Shepard is on the board of directors.

FACT SUMMARY Although Barry Switzer is best known for his success as a professional and college football coach, he also had significant involvement in various business ventures in Oklahoma and Texas. While attending his son's track meet in 1982, Switzer was filling time between events and lay down in the bleachers to sunbathe. Sitting in bleachers in front of Switzer was Platt, an executive at Texas International Corporation (TIC). Switzer and Platt knew each other and had greeted one another earlier in the track meet, but Platt was unaware of Switzer's presence in the bleachers at that time. Within earshot of Switzer, Platt discussed some of the challenges and troubles of TIC with his wife, who was sitting next to him in the bleachers. The 20 minute conversation included highly confidential information about one of TIC's subsidiary companies named Phoenix.

The next day, Switzer, without expressly mentioning what he had overheard, convinced several investors to form a partnership for purposes of buying Phoenix stock. Switzer, both as an individual and as a partner with other investors, purchased large amounts of Phoenix stock. Before overhearing Platt's conversation, neither Switzer nor his partners ever heard of Phoenix. Ultimately, Switzer and his partners earned a substantial profit from the purchase and sale of the Phoenix stock.

After an investigation of Phoenix, the SEC filed a complaint alleging that Switzer was a tippee and tipped others on insider information. They charged that Switzer and his partners violated Rule 10(b)(5) of the 34 Act by engaging in insider trading because Switzer had used the information that he overheard from Platt while lying in the bleachers. The SEC requested that the court order Switzer and his partners to return the profits realized in the Phoenix stock transactions.

SYNOPSIS OF DECISION AND OPINION The U.S. District Court for the Western District of Oklahoma ruled in favor of Switzer and his partners. The court held that Switzer's conduct did not meet the requirements for Rule 10(b)(5) liability under the tipper-tippee theory. The court pointed out that (1) it was not clear that Platt's casual conversation with his wife constituted a breach of duty and (2) Switzer and his partners had no reason to know whether the information they received was material or confidential.

WORDS OF THE COURT: Improper Purposes Requirement "Platt did not breach a duty to the shareholders of Phoenix, and thus [SEC] failed to meet its burden of proof [required] to prove tipper/tippee liability. Moreover, even if SEC was able to prove this breach, Switzer's conduct does not rise to the level of a 10(b)(5) violation. Switzer [and his partners] could not have known that the information was material, non-public information disseminated by a corporate insider for an improper purpose, and thus are not liable as tippees under rule 10(b)(5)."

Case Questions

1. Although Platt did not intend on disclosing the information to Switzer, could Platt's choice to discuss confidential corporate matters with his spouse in a public place where he could easily be overheard constitute the requisite breach of duty required for a tipper-tippee case?

2. The SEC never appealed this case. Do you believe that the SEC prosecuted Switzer because of his high profile?

3. Did Switzer's partners have a legal and/or ethical duty to inquire about the source of Switzer's information?

The company has invested several million dollars on a 10-year research project to produce an alternate fuel product that will result in substantially lower pollution. As of the end of the last year, Armstrong and Shepard each owned 10,000 shares of RocketCo's stock. This year, they traded as follows:

January 1	Armstrong purchases 1,000 shares at $10/share.
	Shepard purchases 5,000 shares at $10/share.
March 1	Shepard purchases 5,000 additional shares at $10/share.
May 1	Shepard purchases 1,000 additional shares at $20/share.
	Armstrong sells 1,000 shares at $20/share.
November 1	Shepard sells all of his shares of RocketCo at $25/share.
December 1	RocketCo stock drops to $2/share.

ImClone Insider Tips: Ethical Dilemmas and Choices

ImClone Systems was a publicly traded biopharmaceutical company founded by Samuel Waksal, who also served as the company's CEO and chairman of the board. In December 2001, ImClone and the public markets were anxiously awaiting FDA approval on an experimental cancer treatment drug called Erbitux that ImClone had developed. Because of his position at ImClone, Waksal had advance knowledge that the FDA would not be giving approval for the use of the drug. Before the public announcement by the FDA, Waksal called his stockbroker, Peter Bacanovic at Merrill Lynch (now a subsidiary of Bank of America), and ordered him to sell substantial amounts of ImClone stock from his personal portfolio. Waksal also urged his immediate family to sell their ImClone stock as well.

Television personality and media conglomerate owner Martha Stewart, pictured here with her attorney outside a federal courthouse, was convicted of obstruction of justice in connection with the SEC's investigation of insider trading at ImClone Systems.

Bacanovic had other brokerage clients who owned ImClone stock, including Martha Stewart, the star of her own media conglomerate and the CEO and chair of the board for the publicly traded holding company for her empire, Martha Stewart Living/Omnimedia. Bacanovic instructed his assistant, Douglas Faneuil, to tip Stewart to the fact that Waksal had sold a substantial portion of ImClone stock. After the tip, Stewart instructed Bacanovic to sell all her ImClone shares. The next day, ImClone announced publicly that the FDA had not approved the use of Erbitux, and ImClone's stock dropped by more than 20 percent. By selling when she did, Stewart avoided losses of over $45,000.

According to government documents, when the SEC launched an investigation of Waksal and ImClone, Bacanovic and Stewart fabricated an alibi for the sell orders and told investigators that Stewart had decided earlier that the stock should be sold once it reached a certain price. Stewart also told investigators that she did not recall anyone telling her about the Waksal sale. However, Bacanovic's assistant, Faneuil, faced with criminal charges, testified for the government against Stewart and Bacanovic. In 2004, Stewart and Baconovic were convicted of obstructing justice in a securities fraud investigation and were sentenced to prison and made to pay substantial fines. Stewart was barred from serving on any board of a publicly held company. Waksal and some of his family members were also convicted of securities fraud related to insider trading and sentenced to seven years in jail.[6]

1. Stewart was not an insider of ImClone, and she received the tip from her stockbroker. Does she have an ethical obligation to ask where the tip came from or why the broker was recommending selling the stock? Does the fact that Stewart was an officer and director of a publicly traded corporation require her to use higher ethical standards when buying and selling stock of other companies?

[6]See SEC Release 2003–69 dated June 4, 2003.

(continued)

2. Given the relatively small amount of money involved, do you think that Stewart's sale manipulated the stock in a way that hurt other investors?

3. When Faneuil was ordered to commit an illegal act by tipping Stewart, what were his options as a practical matter? If he was told to tip Stewart or he would be fired from his job, does that affect the ethical decision-making model?

4. Some commentators have argued for the repeal of insider-trading laws because these laws impede economic efficiency. If insider-trading laws were repealed, how would that impact your analysis as to whether Waksal, Stewart, Bacanovic, and Faneuil acted ethically?

5. Ultimately, Stewart was convicted not for securities fraud but for lying to investigators about the transaction. Given the nature of the transaction and the limited harm it caused other investors, did the government act ethically in pursuing her case? If she weren't a celebrity, would the government have acted in the same way?

Assume further that on October 30, both Armstrong and Shepard learned in advance of public knowledge that the Environmental Protection Agency (EPA) failed to give regulatory approval to RocketCo's new alternative fuel and that improvements to the formula would likely take many more years of research and testing. After the public disclosure by the EPA of the adverse decision on November 30, RocketCo's stock price dropped precipitously.

■ *10(b)(5) liability:* Because Armstrong and Shepard are both unquestionably insiders, the information about the EPA's adverse decision cannot be used as the basis for selling RocketCo stock. The timing of Shepard's sale of a substantial portion of RocketCo's stock gives rise to an inference that the insider information precipitated the sale of the stock. If he engaged in insider trading, Shepard faces potential civil liability to injured shareholders as well as possible criminal liability and SEC enforcement action under the 34 Act. Because there is no indication that Armstrong's May sale of the stock was related to the EPA's adverse decision, she does not face 10(b)(5) liability.

■ *Section 16(a) coverage:* Armstrong and Shepard are both statutory insiders of RocketCo and, therefore, are required to report each and every trade to the SEC. Indeed, Section 16(a) is designed to alert investors and the SEC to potential wrongdoing when an insider takes abrupt action in trading, as in the case of Shepard's selling of all of his stock.

■ *Section 16(b) liability:* Because Shepard did not profit from a short swing (his last purchase was in May and he did not sell until November), he does not have Section 16(b) liability. Armstrong's sale of 1,000 shares in May would trigger liability under Section 16(b) because she reaped profits of $10 per share when selling within six months of her purchase. Therefore, the corporation would be entitled to recapture the $10,000 profit realized by Armstrong's short swing. Note that it is irrelevant that Armstrong did not use insider information to make the profit. Section 16(b) short-swing liability is a *strict liability* provision.

LO 17-8 ## Other Important Federal Statutes

While the disclosure and registration requirements in the 1933 and 1934 acts are aimed at protecting investors, other federal statutes are focused on protecting publicly held companies from frivolous litigation by investors.

Private Securities Litigation Reform Act of 1995   In the early 1990s, the securities regulation community and publicly held companies became concerned about what they believed to be an increasingly unwarranted number of lawsuits that they characterized as abusive. Indeed, a number of law firms specialized in the initiation of litigation on behalf of alleged defrauded shareholders. While the shareholders recovered minimal amounts, sizable legal fees were awarded to law firms. The lawsuits were frequently based on glowing predictions of future growth and other such public comments by company executives. Congress, in an attempt to curtail this type of litigation, passed the **Private Securities Litigation Reform Act (PSLRA) of 1995.**[7] The PSLRA has made it more difficult to pursue litigation under the securities laws that is based solely on commentary by the company's executives. The PSLRA provides *safe harbors* from lawsuits that shield the company and its officers and directors so long as the principals acted in *good faith* and *disclosed* all relevant facts. The law also requires that in order for a shareholder to prevail in a suit based on statements of corporate executives that turned out to be incorrect or to be misrepresentations, the shareholder must prove **scienter** as an essential element of the case. Courts have traditionally required shareholder plaintiffs to *itemize* particular facts that give rise to a strong inference that the defendant acted with the required deceptive state of mind. The law defined suits as frivolous if the "shareholder derivative actions [are] begun with [the] hope of winning large attorney fees or private settlements, and with no intention of benefiting [the] corporation on behalf of which [the] suit is theoretically brought."

In Case 17.5, the U.S. Supreme Court made clear that shareholders have the substantial hurdle of scienter to pass in order to pursue their fraud claim against insiders.

Legal Speak ⟩⟩
Scienter In the context of securities litigation, scienter means specific intent to deceive, manipulate, or defraud.

Securities Litigation Uniform Standards Act of 1998   After the passage of the PSLRA, corporate concerns about shareholder litigation continued because shareholders could still engage in litigation by suing corporations in state courts, under *state* securities statutes, for inadequate or overly optimistic statements. Congress responded by enacting the **Securities Litigation Uniform Standards Act of 1998.**[8] The law, which took the form of an amendment to the 34 Act, is intended to prevent private parties from instituting certain lawsuits in federal *or* state court that are based on the statutory or common law of any state that punishes "a misrepresentation or omission of a material fact" or the use of "any manipulative device or contrivance" concerning the purchase or sale of a covered security.

Securities Regulation by States: Blue-Sky Laws

LO 17-9

State securities laws are commonly known as **blue-sky laws,** named after the original state statutory protection of investors from unsavory issuers selling nothing more than "blue sky." Blue-sky laws are frequently constructed to match federal securities statutes. In theory, these state statutes are intended to cover purely intrastate securities offerings (those in which the issuers and all potential investors are within one state's borders), but, as a practical matter, state securities regulations are an additional safeguard for investors when the federal government declines to exercise its jurisdiction over a particular securities offering. A majority of states have adopted all or substantially all of the Uniform Securities Act. Typical provisions include prohibition against fraud in the sale of securities, registration requirements for brokers and dealers, exemptions, civil liability for issuers failing to comply, and state court remedies for defrauded investors.

---

[7] 15 U.S.C. § 78u.

[8] 15 U.S.C. § 77z et seq.

FACT SUMMARY   Tellabs, Inc., manufactures specialized equipment for fiber optic networks. The shareholders alleged that Notebaert, Tellabs' CEO, "falsely reassured public investors that Tellabs was continuing to enjoy strong demand for its products and earning record revenues" when, in fact, Notebaert knew the opposite was true. The shareholders of Tellabs alleged that Notebaert knowingly misled the public in several ways. First, he made statements indicating that demand for Tellabs' flagship networking device, the TITAN 5500, was continuing to grow, while demand for that product was actually dropping. Second, Notebaert made a series of overstated revenue projections when, in reality, demand for the TITAN 5500 was drying up and production of the TITAN 6500 was behind schedule. The shareholders alleged that, based on Notebaert's optimistic assessments, market analysts recommended that investors buy Tellabs' stock. Not long after these statements, Tellabs disclosed that demand for the TITAN 5500 had significantly dropped. Simultaneously, the company substantially lowered its revenue projections for the second quarter of 2001. The next day, the price of Tellabs stock, which had reached a high of $67, plunged to a low of $15.87. A group of shareholders filed a lawsuit alleging that Tellabs and Notebaert had engaged in securities fraud in violation of Section 10(b) of the 34 Act.

The trial court dismissed the complaint, ruling that although the shareholders had alleged that Notebaert's statements were misleading, they had not provided specific instances of Notebaert's conduct that inferred *scienter*. The appellate court reversed, concluding that the shareholders had sufficiently alleged that Notebaert acted with the requisite state of mind. Tellabs and Notebaert appealed to the U.S. Supreme Court.

SYNOPSIS OF DECISION AND OPINION   The U.S. Supreme Court reversed the appellate court and ruled in favor of Tellabs and Notebaert. The Court reasoned that under the PSLRA, the complaint must allege a *strong* inference of scienter. To qualify as a "strong inference" within the meaning of the PSLRA, an inference of scienter must be more than merely plausible or reasonable—it must be cogent and at least as compelling as any opposing inference of nonfraudulent intent. Note that the Court did *not* rule on whether Notebaert's statements did or did not qualify as evidence of scienter. Rather, it vacated the lower court's judgment because the trial court had not used the correct standard to ascertain the inference of scienter.

WORDS OF THE COURT: Strong Inference of Scienter Required   "The strength of an inference cannot be decided in a vacuum. The inquiry is inherently comparative: How likely is it that one conclusion, as compared to others, follows from the underlying facts? To determine whether the plaintiff has alleged facts that give rise to the requisite 'strong inference' of scienter, a court must consider plausible nonculpable explanations for the defendant's conduct, as well as inferences favoring the plaintiff. The inference that the defendant acted with scienter need not be irrefutable, i.e., of the 'smoking-gun' genre, or even the 'most plausible of competing inferences,' yet the inference of scienter must be more than merely 'reasonable' or 'permissible'—it must be cogent and compelling, thus strong in light of other explanations. A complaint will survive, we hold, only if a reasonable person would deem the inference of scienter cogent and at least as compelling as any opposing inference one could draw from the facts alleged."

Case Questions

1. After reading this case, do you think that application of the PSLRA is consistent in balancing the rights of shareholders with curbing frivolous litigation?

2. Would you qualify Notebaert's statements as intentionally misleading or just overly optimistic? What's the difference?

REGULATION OF CORPORATE GOVERNANCE AND FINANCIAL MARKETS

LO 17-10, 17-11

In addition to regulating the issuing and trading of securities, federal and state statutes also regulate certain internal governance procedures of publicly held corporations. **Corporate governance** is the process used by the officers and directors to establish lines of responsibility, approval, and oversight among key stakeholders and set out rules for making corporate decisions. While corporations have traditionally resisted any form of direct government regulation of internal corporate decision making, public scandals have caused Congress to impose certain mandates meant to ensure public confidence in the publicly traded markets and to protect investors. Professionals from outside firms that conduct services for publicly held corporations, notably accounting firms, are also subject to certain regulatory requirements when they conduct audits of public corporations. Most recently, the financial crisis that began in 2008 continues to spur regulatory reforms via Congress and through administrative agencies in the area of corporate governance, specifically that of firms and institutions involved in the financial markets.

The Sarbanes-Oxley Act of 2002

In the wake of the infamous corporate fraud and malfeasance scandals beginning in 2000—most memorably Enron,[9] MCI WorldCom, Global Crossing, HealthSouth, and Tyco—a public outcry and a growing lack of investor confidence in corporate financial disclosures caused Congress to overhaul the entire corporate governance regulatory structure by passing the **Sarbanes-Oxley (SOX) Act of 2002.**[10] Most commentators agree that the SOX Act provided the most sweeping and comprehensive amendments to the 33 and 34 acts in securities law history. While substantial portions of SOX are aimed at solving specific mechanism failures in auditing and other accounting procedures, the law also imposes higher levels of fiduciary responsibilities on those involved in corporate governance. It was widely believed that a lack of oversight by gatekeepers, such as auditors and federal regulators, was a leading factor in the fraud and malfeasance that caused the high-profile demise of these large, publicly held corporations.

> **KEY** POINT
>
> The Sarbanes-Oxley (SOX) Act of 2002 was passed in response to revelations of corporate fraud and malfeasance in publicly held companies. The law aims to solve specific mechanism failures in accounting methods and requires higher levels of fiduciary responsibilities for those involved in corporate governance.

The SOX Act was intended to impose stricter regulation and controls on how corporations do business through regulation of three broad areas: *auditing, financial reporting,* and internal *corporate governance.* The SOX Act also provided for an additional enforcement apparatus and increased penalties for violation of existing securities laws.

Reforms in the Accounting Industry   As various corporate fraud and mismanagement scandals came to the public's attention, incidents of public corporations misreporting important financial information spiked[11] and Congress replaced the accounting industry's self-regulation of auditing with a new federal agency called the Public Company Accounting Oversight Board (PCAOB). The PCAOB implements, administers, and enforces the SOX Act mandates. Accounting firms that audit public companies accessing U.S. capital markets are required to register with the PCAOB and are subject to its oversight and enforcement authority. The PCAOB also establishes regulations that standardize certain auditing procedures and ethical parameters.

Recall from our discussion of Enron in Chapter 5, "Business, Societal, and Ethical Contexts of Law," that one major contributing factor in the company's collapse was the questionable independence of the Andersen auditing partner assigned to Enron. The SOX Act seeks to increase auditor independence through setting mandatory rotation of auditing partners, banning accounting firms from providing nonauditing consulting services for public companies for which they provide auditing, and restricting accounting firm

---

[9]A business ethics case study on Enron is featured in Chapter 5, "Business, Societal, and Ethical Contexts of Law."

[10]15 U.S.C. § 7241.

[11]From 1990–1997, the number of publicly held corporations that misreported their revenue and had to restate earnings averaged 49 per year. In 2002, 330 corporations restated earnings.

Former MCI WorldCom CEO Bernard Ebbers, seen here after his arrest on securities fraud charges, was a central figure in the corporate scandals that led to passage of the Sarbanes-Oxley Act of 2002.

KEY POINT

The SOX Act imposes stricter regulation and controls on how corporations do business by regulating three broad areas: *auditing, financial reporting,* and internal *corporate governance.*

employees involved in auditing from leaving the auditing firm to go to work for an audit client.

Financial Reporting The SOX Act makes key corporate officers more accountable for financial reporting by requiring that chief executive officers and chief financial officers personally certify the accuracy of all required SEC filings. These two corporate officers must also ensure that the certification is based on reliable and accurate information through the maintenance of internal financial fraud detection controls that are subject to review by outside auditors. The SOX Act regulations set standardized financial reporting formats and restrict certain types of accounting methods that are not transparent to auditors, such as using special offshore tax entities to hold corporate assets.

Corporate Governance The SOX Act requires that public companies maintain audit committees composed entirely of independent directors and specifies that the committee must contain at least one director with sufficient financial acumen to probe audits in depth. Audit committees have substantial regulatory obligations under the SOX Act. These obligations include (1) using their authority to engage, monitor, and terminate the company's outside auditing firm; (2) implementing a system of controls that involves a comprehensive examination of the audit reports and methods used by the company and outside auditors to properly report information that truly reflects the financial condition of the company; and (3) establishing a structure that facilitates direct communication between the audit committee and the auditors (not using corporate officers as go-betweens).

The SOX Act also requires public companies to establish a code of ethics and conduct for their top financial officers, and it prohibits certain practices such as a public corporation's lending money to its officers and directors (with some narrow exceptions). In addition, officers and directors are obligated to disclose their own buying and selling of company stock within a certain time frame. To prevent the secret looting of a company by its officers, the act includes what is known as a *clawback provision:* the requirement that executive performance bonuses be retroactively forfeited back to the company if the bonuses were tied to any financial reports that were later deemed false or were issued without appropriate controls.

Enforcement under SOX

The SOX Act also greatly expanded the scope and methods of enforcing securities law. The SEC's jurisdiction, enforcement alternatives, and enforcement budget were substantially increased by the SOX Act.

Emergency Escrow Recognizing that many of the remedies in the SOX Act are largely useless if the corporation's assets have been looted by insiders engaged in fraud, the law specifically gives the SEC the authority to intervene in any extraordinary payments made by a company that may be the subject of an SEC investigation. Upon approval by a federal court, the SOX Act allows the SEC to force any extraordinary corporate payouts into a government-controlled emergency escrow fund, where they are held pending further investigation by authorities. This is a powerful weapon in the SEC's enforcement arsenal because the SOX Act does not require any formal allegation of wrongdoing as a prerequisite for intervening in an extraordinary payment. For example, in a 2005 case, *SEC v. Gemstar-TV Guide International, Inc.,*[12] a federal appeals court held that the SEC was reasonable in intervening when a corporation's board of directors authorized multibillion-dollar payments to its executives who were resigning under fire after the company had to revise its past earnings statements sharply downward. The court held that the payments to two executives, totaling $37 million, constituted an extraordinary payment and triggered the SEC's right to intervene and the court's right to approve the SEC's request for an emergency escrow. The court pointed out that although the SEC had not launched a formal investigation, the substantial revision of earnings statements coupled with the fact that insiders were departing the company in the wake of the scandal was sufficient to give the SEC intervention rights under the SOX Act.

Substantial Penalties Violators of the SOX Act are subject to both civil penalties and criminal prosecution. For example, officers who certify a required financial report filing knowing that the report either is inaccurate or was not subject to required controls before the certification are subject to criminal penalties of up to $1 million in fines and 10 years of incarceration. For cases in which the certification was used as part of a larger fraudulent scheme, the penalties increase to $5 million in fines and 20 years of incarceration. The SOX Act also specifically directs the U.S. Sentencing Commission to amend sentencing guidelines to provide for harsher penalties for those convicted of securities fraud statutes.

Whistle-Blowers Parties that communicate information relating to any illegal conduct in financial reporting or corporate governance are protected against any retaliation by the company. Audit committees must have a structure in place to process and investigate any whistle-blower[13] complaints and any party that engages in retaliation is subject to civil action and federal criminal prosecution.

The Dodd-Frank Act also created a $300 billion fund to reward whistle-blowers who provide significant information about securities fraud to regulatory authorities. Employees of publicly held entities may collect a bounty of 10 to 30 percent of the monetary sanctions collected in the action if the information they provide to government agencies results in a penalty exceeding $1 million. The SEC has the discretion to base the whistle-blower award on the significance of the information provided, the level of assistance provided by the whistle-blower, and the government's interest in deterring securities fraud.

Document Destruction Rules The SOX Act created new provisions for punishing individuals who destroy the evidence that might be relevant to the investigation of any violation of federal securities laws. Anyone who alters, destroys, or conceals relevant documents is subject to up to 20 years of incarceration. The law applies universally to any party who has control over the documents and covers any actions performed either before, during, or after any formal investigation is commenced.

Conspiracy to Commit Fraud The definition of *securities* fraud was expanded by the SOX Act, and the creation of a new federal criminal law outlawing *conspiracy* to commit fraud has made pursuing criminal fraud charges against officers and directors substantially easier for government prosecutors. The law also extended the statute of limitations for civil lawsuits filed by defrauded investors attempting to recover lost money.

---

[12]401 F.3d 1031 (9th Cir. 2005).

[13]*Whistle-blower,* a term used to describe an employee or agent who reports some legal misconduct or statutory violation to the authorities, is discussed in detail in Chapter 12, "Employment Relationships and Labor Law."

- The SOX Act imposes regulations on publicly held corporations in broad areas: auditing, financial reporting, and corporate governance.
- The PCAOB is the body created by the SOX Act as an oversight board for firms performing audits of public companies.
- Certain corporate officers are responsible for certifying the accuracy and completeness of financial reports and disclosures.
- The SOX Act requires a public corporation to form an audit committee, prescribes the composition of the committee, and imposes substantial responsibility on the committee to prevent and detect fraud.
- Enforcement provisions of the SOX Act include (1) authorization of the SEC to intervene in any extraordinary payments made by a company and to hold the payments in an emergency escrow fund until further investigation is conducted; (2) enhanced criminal penalties for violations, especially for destruction of documents; (3) protection of whistle-blowers; and (4) expansion of the definition of securities fraud by outlawing any conspiracy to commit fraud.

Troubled Assets Relief Program (TARP)

As the financial crisis that began in 2008 unfolded, increasing fears of a disastrous global financial meltdown and substantial public pressure caused Congress to provide direct loans to corporations most acutely impacted by the crisis. These loans were intended primarily for large corporations in the financial services and insurance sectors (such as Citigroup and AIG), but federal loans were also extended to companies in other troubled industries, such as auto manufacturers.[14] However, as a condition of the loan, recipients were required to abide by corporate governance and executive compensation mandates. The loan program and its mandates were created in the **American Recovery and Reinvestment Act of 2009,**[15] which established the **Troubled Assets Relief Program (TARP)** to administer the loans. In general, TARP loan recipients agreed to (1) impose restrictions on compensation (including bonuses) of officers, (2) form an independent compensation committee, and (3) give shareholders more say on compensation of officers and directors. The TARP provisions empower the Department of the Treasury to recover any bonuses paid that are inconsistent with the law's requirements.

TARP Today   A key provision of TARP is the recipient's agreement to abide by certain rules and practices until all TARP money has been paid back. This restriction led several recipients to repay the funds relatively soon. TARP recipients are required to apply for release from the program after showing that their financial condition is sufficiently stable. Within a year of passage of TARP, more than 50 banks were approved to pay back TARP funds, including a $25 billion payment from JPMorgan Chase and a $3.6 billion payment from Capital One Financial. Still, some of the largest TARP payouts, to companies such as American Insurance Group (AIG), have not been repaid to the government. The special inspector general of the TARP program has estimated that the TARP program will last until at least 2017. Table 17.3 lists some of the restrictions on TARP recipients.

---

[14]These loans were dubbed by the media as "bailouts."
[15]Pub. L. No. 111-5, 123 Stat. 115 (2009).

TABLE 17.3 Select TARP Rules

- *Compensation:* The company's compensation plan cannot be structured in such a way as to encourage artificial inflation of the company's stock price. TARP recipients are also severely restricted with respect to paying bonuses to senior executives.

- *Corporate governance:* The board of directors must establish an active compensation committee that is composed entirely of independent directors and monitors executive compensation to ensure that it is consistent with TARP regulations. The chief executive officer and the chief financial officer must both sign compliance certifications verifying executive compensation. The law also requires that TARP recipients provide shareholders with a *nonbinding* vote on any compensation plan recommended by the board of directors.

- *Luxury expenditures:* TARP recipients must adhere to regulations that cease or curb any company expenditures that are regarded as excessive, including high-price office renovations and exorbitant travel and entertainment expenses such as the use of private jets.

Financial Market Regulation

Companies that do business in the financial markets are regulated by a complex structure of federal regulatory schemes that are enforced through a variety of administrative agencies and regulatory bodies. The Securities and Exchange Commission, the Federal Reserve, the Office of the Comptroller of the Currency, and the Federal Trade Commission all have some degree of jurisdiction over various aspects of transactions in the global financial markets. The regulated financial transactions include commercial and consumer loans, investments, credit, insurance, and commodities exchange.

Regulator Shopping   As the financial crisis that began in 2008 became more serious, lawmakers became concerned that the complexity of the regulatory scheme for financial markets was contributing to undetected fraud and extreme risks by financial institutions. Moreover, it had become apparent that the patchwork of administrative agency and regulatory body jurisdiction enabled companies to hide losses and conceal fraudulent activity. The system even allowed for *regulator shopping* in certain sectors of the financial markets. For example, when mortgage company giant Countrywide Financial Corporation started its subprime-mortgage program in 1996, it was jointly regulated by the Federal Reserve and the Office of the Comptroller of the Currency. Countrywide's subprime-mortgage program allowed home buyers with a relatively low credit score to qualify for a mortgage by paying a higher interest rate and paying a monthly premium to insure the loan in the case of default. The program also featured "teaser rates" that made the initial payments artificially low, but substantially larger payments were required as the loan's interest rate increased after each reset period (typically one to five years after the loan was made). Defaults on the teaser rate loans are widely cited as a significant contributing factor in the financial crisis and the deepening of the recession that began in 2008. Although Countrywide was the leading lender of subprime mortgages, similar practices were widespread in the lending industry at that time. When Countrywide's senior executives became frustrated with regulatory authorities that were pressuring Countrywide to reexamine its risk level for subprime loans, Countrywide's management decided to convert its corporate organizational structure in 2007 so that it could fall under the jurisdiction of the Office of Thrift Supervision (OTS). The OTS was widely regarded in the industry as a weaker regulator that took a hands-off approach to questions on risk standards enforcement.[16] As subprime loan payments adjusted upward and the economy worsened, cash-strapped borrowers began defaulting on their mortgages in record proportions. When credit markets tightened in 2008, Countrywide quickly became insolvent and unable to fund its operations. Facing bankruptcy, the once mighty lender and market share leader in mortgage loans was forced to sell its assets to Bank of America at less than a quarter of its previous market value. It was reported in the financial press that the OTS had ignored warning signs about Countrywide's risky practices and gave far too much deference to the company's aggressive accounting practices. Several Countrywide executives, including its founder Angelo Mozilo, were charged with fraud and insider trading, and other top-level employees are the subjects of a continuing federal investigation. In 2010, Congress eliminated the OTS and transferred its functions to other agencies.

Regulatory Reform of Financial Markets

In 2010, at the urging of the Obama administration and chief government regulators, Congress passed a new law with sweeping reforms of the financial regulatory system. The law was designed to address the systemic failure of previous regulatory systems and agencies to detect the financial crisis that began in 2008 and sent global financial markets reeling and thus to prevent a recurrence of such a crisis. The law, named the **Wall Street Reform and Consumer Protection Act,** overhauled the regulation of U.S. financial services and markets.

Financial Stability Oversight Council

The law created a new independent body with a board of regulators to address dangerous risks to the global financial markets posed by risky investments or actions of large financial institutions. The Financial Stability Oversight Council is composed of nine members, eight of whom already direct various agencies involved in the financial system (e.g., the chairman of the Federal Reserve) and one of whom is independent. The council has the power to break up companies deemed to pose a threat to the nation's financial stability even if those companies are not insolvent. The council also has the power to compel the Federal Reserve to assume an oversight position in regard to certain institutions that pose global risks to the financial markets. These institutions have been dubbed by commentators as "too big to fail" and were a central issue in the financial crisis that began in 2008.

Bureau of Consumer Financial Protection

The law also created a federal administrative agency called the Bureau of Consumer Financial Protection that has direct oversight of companies providing mortgages, credit cards, savings accounts, and annuities. The bureau also has the authority to write new regulations that add additional layers of protection for consumers regarding disclosures, fees, and restrictions on certain lending practices.

BUSINESS LAW

Visit Connect for an update on the Wall Street Reform and Consumer Protection Act and other regulatory reforms of the financial markets.

Other Provisions

The law has also (1) given shareholders greater power to limit executive officer compensation, (2) increased the authority and budget of the SEC for more enhanced oversight of sophisticated investment vehicles such as hedge funds and derivatives, (3) increased the power and oversight jurisdiction of the Federal Reserve, and (4) created an Office of National Insurance.

---

[16]The OTS was also the regulatory authority that failed to prevent numerous institutions under its authority from failing, including Washington Mutual Bank.

Securities law p. 475 The body of federal and state laws governing the issuance and trading of equity and debt instruments to public investors.

Equity p. 479 Ownership interest in a corporation whereby financial return on the investment is based primarily on the performance of the venture.

Debt p. 479 A common tool for raising capital; includes promissory notes, bonds, and debentures that offer investors a fixed rate of return, regardless of the profitability of the corporation, and repayment after a certain period of years. Debt is senior in priority to equity instruments.

Common stock (common shares) p. 479 A form of equity instrument that entitles the equity owner to payments based on the current profitability of the company.

Preferred stock p. 480 A form of equity instrument that has less risk than common stock because it has certain quasi-debt features. Preferred stockholders have preference rights over common stockholders in receiving dividends from the corporation.

Disclosure p. 480 The process in which companies are to release all information, positive or negative, that might bear on an investment decision; serves as the underlying premise of all securities regulation and is required by the Securities and Exchange Commission to protect investors and ensure public confidence in the integrity of the securities market.

Securities and Exchange Commission (SEC) p. 481 The independent federal administrative agency charged with rulemaking, enforcement, and adjudication of federal securities laws.

Securities Act of 1933 p. 483 Federal legislation that covers the processes of issuing and reissuing securities to the public; requires registration and certain disclosures and authorizes the Securities and Exchange Commission to oversee the transactions.

Prospectus p. 483 The first part of the security registration statement prescribed by Securities and Exchange Commission regulations; intended to give investors a realistic view of the issuer's business, risk factors, financial position, financial statements, and disclosures concerning directors, officers, and controlling shareholders.

Exemptions p. 484 For smaller issuers of securities, types of offerings or transactions in selling a security that are not subject to certain Securities and Exchange Commission regulations on registration; intended to assist business ventures seeking smaller amounts of capital from the public investment community.

Regulation D p. 485 A securities law provision that exempts an issuer from registration on the basis of certain transactions; applies to limited offers that involve a relatively small amount of money or offers that are made in a limited manner.

Private placement p. 485 A securities law provision that exempts an issuer from registration when the issuer accepts investments only from those who meet the standards for accredited investors.

Securities Act of 1934 p. 486 Federal legislation that regulates the sale of securities between investors after an investor purchased them from a business entity issuer.

Insider trading p. 487 Illegal securities trading in which a corporate insider uses information not available to the general investor public as the basis for trades in the company's stock.

Insider Trading and Securities Fraud Enforcement Act p. 488 Federal legislation passed in 1988 that raised the criminal and civil penalties for insider trading, increased the liability of brokerage firms for wrongful acts of their employees, and gave the Securities and Exchange Commission more power to pursue violations of insider trading.

Section 16 p. 489 Provision of the Securities Act of 1934 that imposes restrictions and reporting requirements on ownership positions and stock trades made by certain corporate insiders named in the statute.

Private Securities Litigation Reform Act (PSLRA) of 1995 p. 493 Federal legislation making it more difficult to pursue litigation under the securities laws that is based solely on commentary by company executives; intended to protect publicly held companies from frivolous litigation.

Scienter p. 493 Specific intent to deceive, manipulate, or defraud.

Securities Litigation Uniform Standards Act of 1998 p. 493 An amendment to the Securities Act of 1934 that prevents private parties from instituting certain lawsuits in federal or state court that are based on the statutory or common law of any state that punishes "a misrepresentation or omission of a material fact" or the use of "any manipulative device or contrivance" concerning the purchase or sale of a covered security.

Blue-sky laws p. 493   State securities laws intended to cover purely intrastate securities offerings.

Corporate governance p. 494   The process used by corporate officers and directors to establish lines of responsibility, approval, and oversight among key stakeholders and set out rules for making corporate decisions.

Sarbanes-Oxley (SOX) Act of 2002 p. 495   Amendments to the '33 and '34 Securities Acts that imposes stricter regulation and controls on how corporations do business, through regulation of auditing, financial reporting, and internal corporate governance.

American Recovery and Reinvestment Act of 2009 p. 498   Federal legislation that created a loan program and underlying mandates for corporations most acutely impacted by the financial crisis that began in 2008; also established the Troubled Assets Relief Program (TARP) to administer the loans.

Troubled Assets Relief Program (TARP) p. 498   A program established by the American Recovery and Reinvestment Act of 2009 to purchase assets and equity from financial institutions and thereby strengthen the U.S. financial sector.

Wall Street Reform and Consumer Protection Act p. 500   Federal legislation designed to overhaul the regulation of U.S. financial services and markets.

THEORY TO PRACTICE

Four individuals are the collective owners, directors, and shareholders ('principals') of Cool Runnings Manufacturing Company (CRMC), which designs and manufactures snow sports equipment such as snowboards, racing skis, and related products. The principals built the company over a 10-year period from start-up to over $20 million in annual revenue. Six months ago, the principals met and decided to embark on an aggressive expansion plan with the objective of doubling CRMC's production capacity in five years.

This plan required approximately $50 million to fund the purchase of real estate, equipment, expanded payroll, additional taxes, and marketing expenses. One reason for this expansion plan was to develop a new snowboard product, the Tectonic Board, which early marketing research indicated would become one of CRMC's best-selling products. The principals were under pressure to develop this new product because of an overall slump in sales. However, given CRMC's current facilities and budget, the product was currently only halfway through the design phase and not expected on the market for at least three more years. The demand for CRMC's existing brands of snowboards was slowly, but steadily, declining. In fact, the company's profits had been so stagnant that it could

not reasonably afford to borrow the entire amount of the expansion cost given its recently diminishing cash flow. However, because of the development of the Tectonic Board, the principals are hopeful that they can attract capital by selling stock to investors.

1. What are the alternatives for financing this expansion plan? Should CRMC consider a bond? Why or why not? Would selling equity be more or less advantageous than issuing a bond?

2. Assume that the principals decide to issue stock to the public in order to raise money. They know of five investors that may be interested in this opportunity, so they send each a copy of the business plan for CRMC's expansion along with a cover letter explaining the price of the stock and giving instructions on how to buy the stock. Has CRMC committed a violation of securities laws by sending out the business plan and cover letter? Could that constitute the sale of a security?

3. Suppose that, instead of sending the business plan as in Question 2 above, the principals consulted counsel and informed her that they wish to develop a prospectus and distribute it to a limited number of high-net-worth investors. Must the securities be registered before marketing or selling them? If not, what exemption(s) could they fall into?

Assume that the principals proceed as in Question 3 and send the plan to 15 high-net-worth potential investors. During face-to-face and videoconference meetings with the investors, the CEO made the following statements in response to investor questions:

Question: Is CRMC's financial position currently sound, or are there threats to your financial well-being?

CEO: CRMC's cash flow is expected to increase steadily because the Tectonic Board is the board for a new generation of boarders. Our research shows that it has potential to bring us a sizable return on our investment.

Question: What stage of development is the Tectonic Board in?

CEO: If all goes well, it will be on store shelves in less than one year.

Question: Is there a current demand for your existing snowboard products?

CEO: We have had very strong sales. However, like every product, they have their ups and downs. They're likely to be on the upside shortly.

4. Based on these statements, one investor purchases a substantial amount of stock. If the business venture fails before the Tectonic is released, will the investor have any recourse against CRMC and its CEO based on the statements made by the CEO? Why or why not?

5. If an investor files a fraud suit against CRMC and its CEO, would the statements alone be sufficient to pass the PSLRA standards for scienter?

6. Do any of the statements themselves constitute the required elements under PSLRA? What type of conduct, if coupled with the statements, could meet the scienter standard?

MANAGER'S CHALLENGE

From the facts in the Theory to Practice problem one can see the potential complications and hazards of selling equity as a form of raising capital. Assume that the principals approach you as their senior manager and ask that you devise a potential plan to raise money without actually issuing securities. Individually, or in a small group, draft an "Opportunity Plan" that describes a process by which CRMC could raise money without being subject to securities laws. The effectiveness of your Opportunity Plan will depend on your knowledge of the *Howey* test to be sure that the opportunity does not qualify as a security that is subject to registration. A sample answer may be found on this textbook's website at www.mhhe.com/melvinleb2e.

CASE SUMMARY 17.1 :: Nursing Home Pension Fund v. Oracle Corp., 380 F.3d 1226 (9th Cir. 2004)

SCIENTER

Software giant Oracle released its newest product, the 11i Suite, in 2000. The company issued press releases and disseminated other information to the public that touted the software as a significant achievement that would enhance its revenue. Over the next 12 months, executive management continued making overly optimistic forecasts about the software and earnings. During that same period, Oracle's CEO, Larry Ellison, sold nearly $1 billion worth of his personal stock in Oracle.

Shortly after Ellison's sale was completed, Oracle released negative news about earnings and it became obvious that the 11i Suite sales were substantially below expectations. The stock price dropped sharply.

CASE QUESTIONS

1. Does the timing of the insider sale and the release of the negative earnings statement constitute sufficient scienter to clear the PSLRA's scienter hurdle?

2. Who prevails and why?

MATERIAL MISSTATEMENTS

Vantive is a manufacturer of client management software designed for use by sales representatives from various industries. Vantive is also a retailer and provides support services for the software. After a successful public offering in 1995, the company's stock sold for $6 per share and soon rose to as high as $35 per share. When the tech sector slumped in 1998, the stock dropped to less than $15 per share over an eight-month period. During this eight-month period, management forecast strong gains in income by using a model that recognized millions of dollars in revenue based on software licenses that would *not* actually be realized unless the licensees were successful in selling *sublicenses* for the software. A group of shareholders brought suit under 10(b)(5).

CASE QUESTIONS

1. Were the forecasts sufficient to constitute a material misstatement of fact and an omission that violated securities laws? Explain.
2. Is Vantive protected by the PSLRA?

EXEMPT SECURITIES

FSC was a securities brokerage firm that sold limited partnership interests to Mark and 27 other investors. All investors executed a *subscription agreement* in which each investor revealed his or her income and represented that he or she had the opportunity to review relevant information, including risk factors, and was sufficiently knowledgeable and savvy to understand the implications of the investment. However, FSC managers never actually reviewed the completed subscription agreements, and all who applied to be investors were admitted. When the interests dropped in value, Mark sued to rescind the contract on the basis that the securities were not registered and that he was not a qualified investor. FSC defended that the offering qualified under the 33 Act safe-harbor provision of Regulation D.

CASE QUESTIONS

1. Should Mark prevail?
2. Is it relevant that FSC never reviewed the subscription agreement?

GOOD FAITH IN PSLRA

Fleming is a publicly held company involved in litigation with another company over a trade dispute. During the litigation, the officers of Fleming disclosed the litigation and the relevant factual basis for the litigation in its SEC-required disclosure materials. The litigation resulted in a $200 million jury verdict against Fleming, causing Fleming's stock to drop precipitously. After an appellate court reversed part of the verdict and Fleming settled the case for $20 million, the stock regained some of its previous value but never returned to its pre-litigation levels. A group of shareholders sued Fleming's officers and directors, claiming that the disclosure of litigation was not detailed enough, did not disclose the potential downside risks of a losing jury verdict, and thus constituted a misleading statement and omissions in violation of the 1934 Securities Act. Fleming's officers defended that they disclosed all known facts of the litigation and were protected by the Private Securities Litigation Reform Act's safe-harbor provisions because they acted in good faith and disclosed all the facts they were privy to at the time.

CASE QUESTIONS

1. Who prevails and why?
2. Should Fleming's officers be protected by the PLSRA?

 Self-Check **ANSWERS**

The *Howey* Test

1. This question is based on *Smith v. Gross*, 604 F.2d 639 (9th Cir. 1979), in which the court decided that the earthworm scheme did constitute a securities offering. It fit all elements of the *Howey* test and had vertical commonality because the investor profited from the work of the promoter.

2. Careful! This question first appears to be a replica of the *Howey* case's facts, but there are substantial differences in the investment opportunities. Utley's plan would likely *not* constitute offering a security. He was offering developing and real estate services, but they were not a requirement for purchasing the property. Owners of the property may simply have purchased it for their own vacation use and not as an investment with expectations of return. Utley's services did not have the required commonality, nor did investors necessarily benefit from Utley's efforts.

3. This question is based on *SEC v. Alliance Lease Corp.*, 2000 LEXIS 5227 (S.D. Cal. 2000), in which the court held that Alliance's leasing plan was a securities offering under the *Howey* standards. The investment opportunity had both vertical and horizontal commonality, and the investors profited primarily due to the efforts of Alliance in arranging the leases.

THE BUSINESS JUDGMENT DEFENSE

A minority shareholder of a corporation that owns a major-league baseball franchise was disappointed with the company's performance, which he alleged was due to mismanagement by its directors and its majority shareholder. The corporation had sustained operating losses for four consecutive years, and the shareholder alleged that the losses were directly attributable to the board's decision not to install lights in the home stadium. The shareholder complained that all of the company's competitors (i.e., other major-league baseball teams) had lights installed in order to facilitate night games, thereby expanding attendance and revenue. Attendance at games for teams that had installed lights had as much as doubled since night games began. The minority shareholder brought suit against the majority shareholder and the board of directors, alleging mismanagement and negligence. The corporation's directors asserted the business judgment defense and contended that the board had generally agreed with the majority shareholder's beliefs that lights should not be installed because (1) lights would have a deteriorating effect on the neighborhood and (2) baseball was traditionally a daytime sport and daytime games were part of the corporation's business model. The trial court dismissed the shareholder suit in favor of the corporation, and the shareholders appealed.

ENGAGEMENT QUESTIONS

1. Are the reasons given by the board for not installing lights legitimate? Was there any fraud or conflict of interest? Do the directors have any ethical responsibility to the residents of the surrounding neighborhood as secondary stakeholders?

2. Does the business judgment rule require that the board's decision be legitimate? Is legitimate the same as "rational"? Why or why not?

3. This case was decided before the landmark *Smith v. Van Gorkom* case in Chapter 16 , "Corporations" (page 463). How would you apply the holding in that case to these facts? Who would prevail?

4. In deciding not to install lights, has the board and the majority shareholder put their own interests ahead of the corporation's interest? Is that a breach of their fiduciary duty? Why or why not?

5. Is it possible that installing the lights would *not* increase the profitability of the team? If so, how does that impact your analysis?

UNIT **FIVE**

Regulatory Environment of Business

18
CHAPTER

Administrative Law

learning **objectives**

After studying this chapter, students who have mastered the material will be able to:

18-1 Explain the purpose of administrative law.

18-2 List and articulate the primary functions of an administrative agency.

18-3 Give examples of several administrative agencies that regulate business.

18-4 Identify the primary sources of law that provide authority and set limits for administrative agencies.

18-5 Discuss how the Administrative Procedures Act (APA) and enabling statutes interrelate to provide an agency with its jurisdiction and scope of authority.

18-6 Identify and explain the steps used in administrative rulemaking.

18-7 Define the powers of administrative agencies in the areas of licensing, inspection, and adjudication.

18-8 Describe the limits on agency powers imposed by the legislative, executive, and judicial branches of the government.

18-9 Name two federal public disclosure statutes and describe how these statutes make administrative agencies more accountable to the public.

M uch of the law's reach over business occurs through federal and state agencies that create regulations based on legislatively set policy objectives and then administer the policies through monitoring and enforcement actions. The various laws that prescribe or regulate this process are known as *administrative laws*. The regulations are created and carried out by *administrative agencies*, and business owners and managers encounter these agencies at various levels. Although these agencies have broad powers, they are still limited by the Constitution, statutes, and judicial review. In this chapter, students will learn:

- The definition and role of administrative law in the U.S. legal system.

- The functions and scope of administrative agencies and the limits on these agencies' powers.

- Ways in which administrative agencies are accountable to the public.

- The role of state administrative law.

DEFINITION, FUNCTION, AND SOURCES OF ADMINISTRATIVE LAW   LO 18-1

Administrative law is the body of law, drawn from various sources, that defines and regulates federal regulatory agencies and limits the exercise of authority by these agencies. Federal regulatory agencies are bodies that function within a particular executive branch *department* (such as the Internal Revenue Service functioning within the Department of the Treasury) and *nondepartment* agencies (such as the Environmental Protection Agency). The federal government also has *independent agencies* (such as the Securities and Exchange Commission) that have been designated by Congress as independent of the executive branch and do not exist by virtue of the authority of the president or a department. Departments are headed by a *cabinet secretary* who reports directly to the president. Department agencies, nondepartment agencies, and independent agencies are either headed by *administrators* or composed of *commissioners* and headed by the commission chair. These department, nondepartment, and independent agencies are collectively referred to as **administrative agencies.**

Primary Functions of Administrative Agencies   LO 18-2, 18-3

Administrative agencies have a wide range of functions related to the formation, implementation, and enforcement of regulations intended to administer a federal law. Although the agencies are primarily thought of as part of the executive branch and, therefore, exercise *executive powers* to enforce federal laws related to a particular agency's jurisdictional expertise, they also exercise important *legislative* and *judicial* functions as well.

Policymaking One of the most important functions of an administrative agency is its responsibility of making policy that is consistent with implementation of federal law. When Congress passes a piece of legislation, it is often crafted in broad strokes that may include findings of fact and/or objectives of the law. However, the practical aspects of implementing the laws often require more complex and detailed policies. Administrative agencies are frequently charged by Congress to study potential solutions to a problem and then to exercise a legislative function by creating legally enforceable rules, known as *administrative regulations,* that purport to satisfy Congress's will by filling in the details of the statute. This policymaking function is known as **rulemaking.**

Administrative agencies also use a system of adjudicatory bodies established within the administrative agency to decide cases that involve an alleged violation of the agency's rules. These adjudicatory bodies are staffed with administrative law judges who are actually employees of the particular regulatory body. This judicial function is known as **adjudication.**

The rulemaking and adjudication powers and processes are discussed in detail later in the chapter.

Investigation and Enforcement Many administrative agencies also have an agency enforcement division devoted to investigating alleged violations of the agency's administrative regulations and recommending enforcement actions such as fines and other sanctions. Agencies have a wide range of discretion as to when and how they enforce regulations against a violator. Administrative agencies also monitor compliance with regulatory requirements through inspection of facilities and grounds of business sites under their jurisdiction.

Licensing and Permitting Some administrative agencies also are responsible for licensing and permitting in a wide variety of areas, including licenses for professionals and industries. Examples include the Securities and Exchange Commission which issues licenses to certain individuals involved in public trading of stocks, and the Federal Communications Commission which licenses television and radio stations. Agencies also issue permits, such as those issued by the Environmental Protection Agency to control air and water pollution.

Distribution of Federal Statutory Benefits to the Public When Congress confers a benefit to the citizenry at large, administrative agencies are the portal used by the law to actually distribute those benefits. Agencies are involved in the application process and distribute benefits according to law. These benefits include loan guarantees for students, medical care for the poor and elderly, compensation for workers laid off by their employers, and many other federal programs. For example, the Social Security Administration is responsible for distributing retirement and medical benefits to eligible citizens.

Figure 18.1 is an organizational chart that shows the major federal administrative agencies.

LO 18-4 ## Sources of Administrative Law

Administrative law is not thought of as a *separate* body of statutes that govern administrative agencies. Rather, administrative law is a combination of four distinct sources of law that operate in tandem.

U.S. Constitution The U.S. Constitution places limits on the type of powers that agencies may exercise and also places limits on the methods that agencies may employ in carrying out their duties. Examples of provisions of the Constitution that limit agency powers include the Due Process Clause; doctrines derived from the principle of separation of powers, including the nondelegation doctrine; and the Fourth Amendment protections against certain warrantless searches by agency personnel.

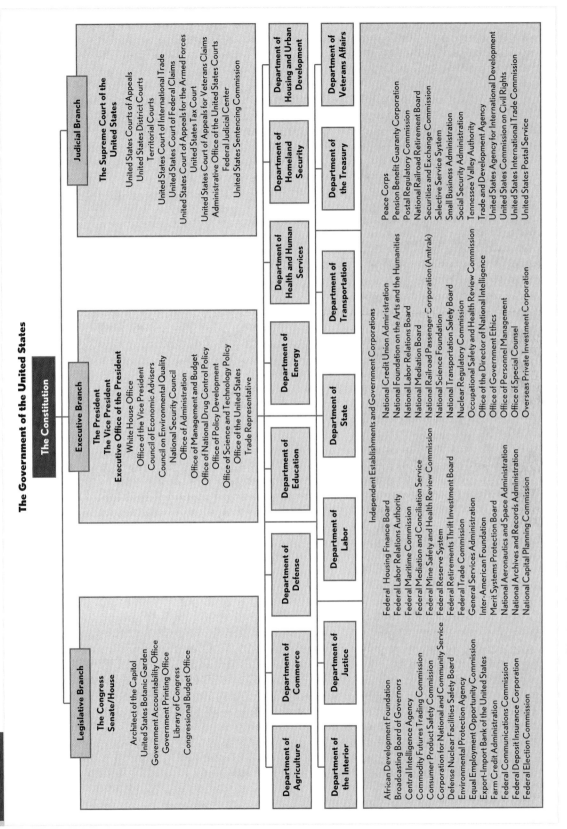

The Government of the United States

The Constitution

Legislative Branch

The Congress
Senate/House

Architect of the Capitol
United States Botanic Garden
Government Accountability Office
Government Printing Office
Library of Congress
Congressional Budget Office

Executive Branch

The President
The Vice President
Executive Office of the President
White House Office
Office of the Vice President
Council of Economic Advisers
Council on Environmental Quality
National Security Council
Office of Administration
Office of Management and Budget
Office of National Drug Control Policy
Office of Policy Development
Office of Science and Technology Policy
Office of the United States
Trade Representative

Judicial Branch

The Supreme Court of the
United States

United States Courts of Appeals
United States District Courts
Territorial Courts
United States Court of International Trade
United States Court of Federal Claims
United States Court of Appeals for the Armed Forces
United States Tax Court
United States Court of Appeals for Veterans Claims
Administrative Office of the United States Courts
Federal Judicial Center
United States Sentencing Commission

Department of Agriculture
Department of the Interior
Department of Commerce
Department of Justice
Department of Defense
Department of Labor
Department of Education
Department of State
Department of Energy
Department of Health and Human Services
Department of Transportation
Department of Homeland Security
Department of the Treasury
Department of Housing and Urban Development
Department of Veterans Affairs

Independent Establishments and Government Corporations

African Development Foundation
Broadcasting Board of Governors
Central Intelligence Agency
Commodity Futures Trading Commission
Consumer Product Safety Commission
Corporation for National and Community Service
Defense Nuclear Facilities Safety Board
Environmental Protection Agency
Equal Employment Opportunity Commission
Export-Import Bank of the United States
Farm Credit Administration
Federal Communications Commission
Federal Deposit Insurance Corporation
Federal Election Commission

Federal Housing Finance Board
Federal Labor Relations Authority
Federal Maritime Commission
Federal Mediation and Conciliation Service
Federal Mine Safety and Health Review Commission
Federal Reserve System
Federal Retirements Thrift Investment Board
Federal Trade Commission
General Services Administration
Inter-American Foundation
Merit Systems Protection Board
National Aeronautics and Space Administration
National Archives and Records Administration
National Capital Planning Commission

National Credit Union Administration
National Foundation on the Arts and the Humanities
National Labor Relations Board
National Mediation Board
National Railroad Passenger Corporation (Amtrak)
National Science Foundation
National Transportation Safety Board
Nuclear Regulatory Commission
Occupational Safety and Health Review Commission
Office of the Director of National Intelligence
Office of Government Ethics
Office of Personnel Management
Office of Special Counsel
Overseas Private Investment Corporation

Peace Corps
Pension Benefit Guaranty Corporation
Postal Regulatory Commission
National Railroad Retirement Board
Securities and Exchange Commission
Selective Service System
Small Business Administration
Social Security Administration
Tennessee Valley Authority
Trade and Development Agency
United States Agency for International Development
United States Commission on Civil Rights
United States International Trade Commission
United States Postal Service

Source: http://bensguide.gpo.gov/files/gov_chart.pdf.

Administrative Procedures Act (APA)   The Administrative Procedures Act (APA)[1] of 1946 is a federal statute that imposes specific procedural structures and due process requirements on administrative agencies' duties of rulemaking, adjudication, and other agency functions. The APA also provides for judicial review of agency actions and determinations.

Enabling Statutes   Congress will sometimes choose to create a new administrative agency to carry out the details of macro objectives set by the law. When Congress wishes to establish an administrative agency, it passes a federal law called an **enabling statute.** Enabling statutes are important because they are the source of an agency's authority and establish the agency's scope and jurisdiction over certain matters. For example, in 1970 Congress passed the Occupational Safety and Health Act,[2] which established the Occupational Safety and Health Administration (OSHA) and set this agency's mission as *prevention* of workplace injuries and assurance of safe working conditions for employees. The enabling act portion of the law placed OSHA under the authority of the Department of Labor and provided for the jurisdiction necessary to study and develop workplace safety regulations as well as the agency's authority to investigate, enforce, and adjudicate matters involving those regulations. Enabling acts are also used by Congress to *charge* an agency with certain additional responsibilities or to provide additional authority for the agency in a particular area of need.

> **KEY** POINT
>
> *Administrative law* is a combination of several different sources of law. The primary sources are the Constitution, the Administrative Procedures Act (APA), and enabling statutes. Common law also plays a minor role.

Common Law   Prior to the establishment of the APA, a body of common law that regulated administrative agencies existed. While much of the common law has been codified through the APA, courts sometimes still refer to the common law in applying or interpreting the APA.

LO 18-5, 18-6 # SCOPE OF ADMINISTRATIVE AGENCY POWER

Legal Speak ⟩⟩
Codified A common law doctrine that was previously not expressed in a code but has now been arranged into an ordered, written code is referred to as being *codified*.

Administrative agencies are often granted broad powers by Congress to accomplish objectives set out in an enabling statute. These powers include policymaking through *rulemaking; enforcement, licensing, and inspection;* and *adjudication.*

Rulemaking

Administrative agencies are charged with developing *rules* designed to facilitate the federal government's administration of the law and programs as set down in federal statutes. The rulemaking process is set out in the APA and is supplemented by the enabling statutes passed by Congress. In practice, many of an agency's rulemaking duties are carried out through *informal* rulemaking procedures that are permitted under the basic structure of the APA.[3] Despite its name, informal rulemaking actually involves a procedure set down in the APA that is centered on the concepts of notice, public comment, publication of a final rule, and the opportunity to challenge a rule in court. *Formal* rulemaking is used only when Congress has specifically indicated in the enabling statute that the agency rules must be made "on the record after a hearing." In the case of formal rulemaking, the agency is required to engage in an extensive hearing process outlined in the APA[4] to develop the rules. Formal rulemaking is very cumbersome and rarely used.

---

[1] 5 U.S.C. §§ 551–706.

[2] 29 U.S.C, §§ 651–678.

[3] APA § 553.

[4] APA §§ 556 and 557.

Many administrative agencies employ scientists to conduct research and provide data and conclusions to policymakers.

Agency Study and Research   Depending on the mandates in the enabling statute, the agency begins to study and research the various alternatives for achieving the goals set by Congress. In some cases, such as in environmental regulation, much of the study and research function is performed by government scientists or outside contractor experts who provide data and conclusions to regulatory policymakers in the agency. In addition to working with scientists, outside experts, and policymakers, regulatory agencies also typically employ a significant number of attorneys who ensure that the rulemaking process is compliant with various sources of administrative law. Agencies may also have separate divisions unrelated to rulemaking for enforcement, licensing, and other functions. These nonrulemaking functions are described later in this chapter.

Notice: Publication of the Proposed Rule   After research and study, the agency drafts a proposed rule that purports to achieve one or more objectives set out in the enabling statute. The APA requires that notice of proposed rulemaking be published in the *Federal Register* and that the notice must include "actual terms, substance and description" of the proposed rule.[5] In theory, this requirement puts parties that have some stake in the rule on notice that the rule will become law unless the regulatory agency is persuaded otherwise or a court challenge is brought.

Agencies are also required to publicly disclose any studies, reports, data, or other pertinent material that the agency relied upon in creating the proposed rule. Figure 18.2 is an excerpt from the *Federal Register.* It sets out a proposed rule by the Environmental Protection Agency under the authority of the Clean Air Act.

Legal Speak ›))
Federal Register A daily publication distributed by the federal government (found in major libraries) primarily for announcing proposed agency rules, final agency regulations, and other administrative agency or executive branch announcements, such as executive orders.

_____

[5]APA § 553.

Federal Register / Vol. 75, No. 13 / Thursday, January 21, 2010 / Proposed Rules   3423

ENVIRONMENTAL PROTECTION AGENCY

40 CFR Part 55

[EPA–R10–OAR–2009–0799; FRL–9095–7]

Outer Continental Shelf Air Regulations Consistency Update for Alaska

AGENCY: Environmental Protection Agency (EPA).

ACTION: Proposed rule.

SUMMARY: EPA is proposing to include in the regulations the revised applicability dates in the emissions user fees provision in 18 AAC 50.410. Requirements applying to Outer Continental Shelf ("OCS") sources located within 25 miles of States' seaward boundaries must be updated periodically to remain consistent with the requirements of the corresponding onshore area ("COA"), as mandated by section 328(a)(1) of the Clean Air Act ("the Act"). The portion of the OCS air regulations that is being updated pertains to the emission user fee requirements for OCS sources operating off of the State of Alaska. The intended effect of approving the OCS requirements for the State of Alaska is to regulate emissions from OCS sources in a manner consistent with the requirements onshore. The change to the existing requirements discussed below is incorporated by reference into the regulations and is listed in the appendix to the OCS air regulations.

DATES: Written comments must be received on or before *February 22, 2010.*

ADDRESSES: Submit your comments, identified by Docket ID Number EPA–R10–OAR–2009–0799, by one of the following methods:

A. *Federal eRulemaking Portal: http://www.regulations.gov:* Follow the on-line instructions for submitting comments;

B. *E-Mail: greaves.natasha@epa.gov;*

C. *Mail:* Natasha Greaves, Federal and Delegated Air Programs Unit, U.S. Environmental Protection Agency, Region 10, 1200 Sixth Avenue, Suite 900, Mail Stop: AWT–107, Seattle, WA 98101;

D. *Hand Delivery:* U.S. Environmental Protection Agency Region 10, Attn: Natasha Greaves (AWT–107), 1200 Sixth Avenue, Seattle, Washington 98101, 9th Floor. Such deliveries are only accepted during normal hours of operation, and special arrangements should be made for deliveries of boxed information.

Please see the direct final rule which is located in the Rules section of this **Federal Register** for detailed instructions on how to submit comments.

FOR FURTHER INFORMATION CONTACT: Natasha Greaves, Federal and Delegated Air Programs Unit, Office of Air, Waste, and Toxics, U.S. Environmental Protection Agency, Region 10,

1200 Sixth Avenue, Suite 900, Mail Stop: AWT–107, Seattle, WA 98101; telephone number: (206) 553–7079; e- mail address: *greaves.natasha@epa.gov.*

SUPPLEMENTARY INFORMATION: For further information, please see the direct final action, of the same title, which is located in the Rules section of this **Federal Register.** EPA is incorporating 18 AAC 50.410 as amended through June 18, 2009 as a direct final rule without prior proposal because EPA views this as noncontroversial and anticipates no adverse comments. A detailed rationale for the approval is set forth in the preamble to the direct final rule. If EPA receives no adverse comments, EPA will not take further action on this proposed rule. If EPA receives adverse comments, EPA will withdraw the direct final rule and it will not take effect. EPA will address all public comments in a subsequent final rule based on this proposed rule. EPA will not institute a second comment period on this action. Any parties interested in commenting on this action should do so at this time. Please note that if we receive adverse comments on an amendment, paragraph, or section of this rule and if that provision may be severed from the remainder of the rule, EPA may adopt as final those provisions of the rule that are not the subject of an adverse comment.

Administrative Requirements

Under the Clean Air Act, the Administrator is required to establish requirements to control air pollution from OCS sources located within 25 miles of States' seaward boundaries that are the same as onshore air control requirements. To comply with this statutory mandate, EPA must incorporate applicable onshore rules into part 55 as they exist onshore. 42 U.S.C. 7627(a)(1); 40 CFR 55.12. Thus, in promulgating OCS consistency updates, EPA's role is to maintain consistency between OCS regulations and the regulations of onshore areas, provided that they meet the criteria of the Clean Air Act. Accordingly, this action simply updates the existing OCS requirements to make them consistent with requirements onshore, without the exercise of policy discretion by EPA. For that reason, this action:

• Is not a "significant regulatory action" subject to review by the Office of Management and Budget under Executive Order 12866 (58 FR 51735, October 4, 1993);

• Is certified as not having a significant economic impact on a substantial number of small entities under the Regulatory Flexibility Act (5 U.S.C. 601 *et seq.*);

• Does not contain any unfunded mandate or significantly or uniquely affect small governments, as described in the Unfunded Mandates Reform Act of 1995 (Pub. L. 104–4);

• Does not have Federalism implications as specified in Executive Order 13132 (64 FR 43255, August 10, 1999);

• Is not an economically significant regulatory action based on health or safety risks subject to Executive Order 13045 (62 FR 19885, April 23, 1997);

• Is not a significant regulatory action subject to Executive Order 13211 (66 FR 28355, May 22, 2001);

• Is not subject to requirements of Section 12(d) of the National Technology Transfer and Advancement Act of 1995 (15 U.S.C. 272 note) because application of those requirements would be inconsistent with the Clean Air Act; and

• Does not provide EPA with the discretionary authority to address, as appropriate, disproportionate human health or environmental effects, using practicable and legally permissible methods, under Executive Order 12898 (59 FR 7629, February 16, 1994).

In addition, this rule does not have tribal implications as specified by Executive Order 13175 (65 FR 67249, November 9, 2000), because it does not have a substantial direct effect on one or more Indian tribes, on the relationship between the Federal Government and Indian tribes, or on the distribution of power and responsibilities between the Federal Government and Indian tribes, nor does it impose substantial direct compliance costs on tribal governments, nor preempt tribal law.

Under the provisions of the Paperwork Reduction Act, 44 U.S.C. 3501 *et seq.*, an agency may not conduct or sponsor, and a person is not required to respond to, a collection of information unless it displays a currently valid OMB control number. OMB has approved the information collection requirements contained in 40 CFR part 55 and, by extension, this update to the rules, and has assigned OMB control number 2060–0249. Notice of OMB's approval of EPA Information Collection Request ("ICR") No. 1601.07 was published in the **Federal Register** on February 17, 2009 (74 FR 7432). The approval expires January 31, 2012. As EPA previously indicated (70 FR 65897– 65898 (November 1, 2005)), the annual public reporting and recordkeeping burden for collection of information under 40 CFR part 55 is estimated to average 549 hours per response, using the definition of burden provided in 44 U.S.C. 3502(2).

List of Subjects in 40 CFR Part 55

Environmental protection, Administrative practice and procedures, Air pollution control, Hydrocarbons, Incorporation by reference, Intergovernmental relations, Nitrogen dioxide, Nitrogen oxides, Outer Continental Shelf, Ozone, Particulate matter, Permits, Reporting and recordkeeping requirements, Sulfur oxides.

Dated December 14, 2009.

Michelle L. Pirzadeh,

Acting Regional Administrator, Region 10.

[FR Doc. 2C10–1108 Filed 1–20–10: 8:45 am]

BILLING CODE 6560–50–P

Public Comment Once the proposed rule has been published in the *Federal Register*, the agency must then give time for the public to comment. In fact, the APA requires that the affected parties be allowed to participate in the rulemaking through submission of their own research and findings and that the agency make a good faith effort to study anything submitted and to consider the arguments made in the comment period. In cases that impact a particular region of the country, agencies sometimes choose to meet public comment requirements by holding public hearings at strategic times and locations during the comment period. In practice, many of the comments and much of the evidence submitted on proposed rules are generally delivered by representatives from, among others, (1) various factions from business and industry (such as the National Manufacturers Association); (2) professional associations that represent large blocks of constituents (such as the National Association of Realtors); and (3) public advocacy groups (such as the Natural Resources Defense Council). For example, suppose the Securities and Exchange Commission proposes new rules relating to corporate reporting disclosure requirements for publicly held companies.[6] The SEC would likely expect various groups representing publicly held companies, as well as the executives of the affected companies, to comment urging the SEC to make the requirements the least burdensome possible. On the other hand, the SEC is also likely to receive comments from consumer advocacy and shareholder watchdog groups urging the agency to adopt even stricter disclosure requirements.

Protection of Small Business Owners The Regulatory Flexibility Act (RFA) of 1980, as amended by the Small Business Regulatory Enforcement Fairness Act (SBREFA) of 1996, requires agencies to ask for and consider regulatory proposals that address the size of the businesses or other organizations subject to regulation. When a proposed regulation will have a significant economic impact on a substantial number of small businesses, the RFA requires, among other things, that agencies analyze and take into consideration small business concerns. Under the RFA, when an agency issues a rule that will have a significant economic impact on a substantial number of small entities, the agency must provide small businesses the opportunity to participate in the rulemaking. Providing the opportunity to participate may include soliciting and receiving comments from small businesses. The participation of small businesses helps agencies fulfill their statutory objectives while reducing, as much as possible, the burden on small businesses.

Revision or Final Publication After the comment period has ended, the agency may either revise the rule or simply publish the final rule in the *Federal Register*. If the agency revises the rule between the time that it was originally proposed and the time that it is published as final, there is generally *no* legal obligation to provide an additional comment period. As a practical matter, agencies publishing controversial proposed rules may opt for a second comment period, but there is no legal mandate to do so. One exception to this rule occurs when the agency's revised rule is a *substantial* or *material alteration* of the originally proposed rule. Courts have given agencies broad latitude in publishing a revised final rule *without* an additional comment period so long as the revisions are a *logical outgrowth* of the originally proposed rule. Revisions that stay within the original scope of the proposed rule do not trigger the requirement of a second comment period. In Case 18.1, a federal court of appeals applied the logical-outgrowth test and the APA to the Internal Revenue Service's decision to revise a proposed rule and publish it as final without an additional comment period.

---

[6] A publicly held company's stock is sold to the general public via a public exchange such as the New York Stock Exchange. Such companies are regulated by a variety of federal agencies and are discussed in detail in Chapter 17, "Regulation of Securities, Corporate Governance, and Financial Markets."

FACT SUMMARY The Internal Revenue Service (IRS) proposed a rule concerning the allocation of membership dues paid to nonprofit organizations under which certain nondues revenue was to be treated as taxable revenue. According to the proposed rule, the IRS intended to determine tax liability from this revenue using a seven-factor test. After the comment period, the IRS replaced the seven-factor test with a new allocation method that the IRS considered to be more fair and consistent. The new method carved down the factors used in the original rule, and a new *three-factor test* was published as a final rule without any additional comment period.

The American Medical Association (AMA) is a nonprofit corporation that charges its members dues that cover a variety of services. The AMA also publishes several journals from which the AMA derives revenue. Under the IRS's three-factor test for allocation, the AMA's tax liability increased significantly. After the IRS assessed the AMA's tax liability under the three-factor test, the AMA brought a lawsuit claiming that the new three-factor allocation regulation was invalid because the IRS had never given the proper public notice required by the APA when the agency departed from its original seven-factor test.

SYNOPSIS OF DECISION AND OPINION The Seventh Circuit Court of Appeals ruled in favor of the IRS, holding that the APA authorizes two types of notice for proposed rules: either a notice that specifies the "terms and substance" of the contemplated regulation or a notice that merely identifies the "subject and issues involved" in the process. Because this language is used to clearly indicate that the notice need not identify every precise proposal the agency may ultimately adopt, the notice is adequate if it simply apprises interested parties of the issues to be addressed in the rulemaking process.

The court reasoned that the IRS's publication of the original proposed seven-factor rule was not binding on the agency and that the IRS's change in policy was a *logical outgrowth* of the original proposal and not a wholly new approach to the issue of proper allocation standards. In fact, the final three-factor test was contained within the original seven-factor test, and thus the AMA and all other similarly situated organizations had adequate notice of the pending rule.

WORDS OF THE COURT: Logical-Outgrowth Test "[A] final rule is not invalid for lack of adequate notice if the rule finally adopted is a logical outgrowth of the original proposal. . . . [A] rule will be invalidated if no notice was given of an issue addressed by the final rules[,] . . . [if the] issue was only addressed in the most general terms in the initial proposal, or where a final rule changes a preexisting agency practice. While an agency must explain and justify its departures from a proposed rule, it is not straitjacketed into the approach initially suggested on pain of triggering a further round of notice-and-comment. The AMA was given a meaningful opportunity to comment on the IRS's dues allocation rules, and those rules will not be invalidated for lack of proper notice."

Case Questions

1. Under the logical-outgrowth test used by the court, would the outcome have been different if the IRS simply published a proposed rule saying that it was going to alter the calculation of membership dues by tax-exempt organizations and did not provide further details or methods? Why or why not?

2. Given the standard used by the court, can you think of an example of a change that would *not* be considered a logical outgrowth provided that the appropriate notice was initially given?

If the agency's view has not been swayed during the comment period, the agency will publish the proposed rule in the *Federal Register* as final.[7] When publishing the final rule, the agency is required by the APA to include "a concise general statement of basis and purpose." This statement is used to meet the legal requirement that the decision be based on *reasoned decision making* and not made arbitrarily or capriciously. The agency must also state its conclusions on major issues of fact or policy that were used in its decision making

[7] APA § 552(a)(1)(D).

when issuing the final rule. Agencies also typically include an effective date in the final rule as well. Once it is in effect, the rule is called a **regulation** and is published in the Code of Federal Regulations (CFR).

In 1990, Congress passed the Negotiated Rulemaking Act,[8] which provides an alternative to normal rulemaking policies in cases where it is possible that various cooperating parties could ultimately reach an *agreement* on the negotiated proposed rule. The law provides guidelines for administrative agencies to engage in a formal negotiation procedure intended to draft rules that have the support of affected parties even prior to publication. The negotiations are conducted through committees composed of representatives from the agency and parties that have an interest in the rule. However, the act does not relieve the agency of the responsibility to properly publish and establish a comment period for the negotiated proposed rule. Nor does the act require that the agency end up actually publishing the negotiated rule instead of an agency-made rule.

Judicial Challenges   After the final rule is published, the APA allows adversely affected parties to challenge the final rule in court.[9] Courts apply the *arbitrary and capricious* standard when reviewing a final rule. That is, for the rule to pass judicial muster, the evidence must show that the agency made its final decision based on a consideration of relevant factors without any clear errors of judgment and that its process was consistent with the APA procedural requirements. The right to judicial review of final rules is a relatively narrow one, and courts give great *deference* to agency authority in the area of rulemaking. Judicial review as a limit on nonrulemaking agency action and authority is discussed in the next section.

Legal **Speak** ›))
Arbitrary and Capricious Failure to exercise honest judgment instead of reasoned consideration of all relevant factors.

CONCEPT SUMMARY Steps in the Rulemaking Process

1. Enabling statute	Congress passes a statute establishing an agency or charging an agency with new authority.
2. Agency study	Agency-selected experts research and review issues as set forth in the enabling statute.
3. Proposed rule published	Based on agency findings, the proposed rule is articulated and published in the *Federal Register* to give notice to parties affected by the rule.
4. Public comment	Parties that have an interest in the rule may respond directly to the agency with comments.
5. Rule revised (if necessary)	Agency reconsiders the rule based on public comments and revises the rule if necessary. If revised, the rule need *not* be published unless it is radically different from the original.
6. Final rule published	Final version of the rule is published in the *Federal Register* and has the full force and effect of law. The rule becomes part of the Code of Federal Regulations (CFR).
7. Judicial challenges	Individual parties may challenge the rule in court under certain circumstances.

---

[8] 5 U.S.C. §§ 561–570.
[9] APA §§ 701–706.

LO 18-7 Enforcement, Licensing, and Inspection

In terms of **enforcement,** the U.S. Supreme Court has ruled that agencies have broad discretion in *when* and *whom* to regulate. This authority, known as the agency's *prosecutorial discretion,* has been held as practically unreviewable by the judiciary. While enabling statutes can sometimes narrow the agency's authority, courts are still highly deferential to an agency's decision on when and how to enforce its regulations. Absent a showing that the agency engaged in a patent abuse of discretion in enforcement, parties challenging administrative agency actions have a substantial obstacle to overcome in order to justify judicial interference. Agencies have a separate division (apart from rulemaking) that carries out enforcement responsibilities through the use of investigators and the agency's Office of General Counsel.

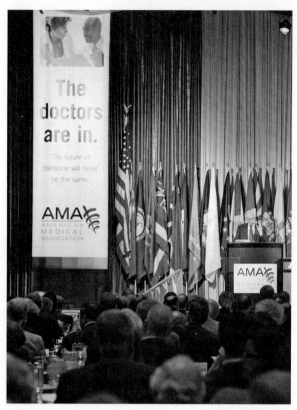

The American Medical Association ultimately failed in its claim that the IRS's rulemaking procedure was flawed.

Administrative agencies also regulate and administer laws through **licensing.** Agencies are frequently delegated the statutory power to issue, renew, suspend, or revoke a license to conduct a certain business. Once a company is licensed, the agency may impose fines or impose restrictions upon the *licensee* for any violation of agency regulations. One of the more high-profile examples of an agency that regulates through licensing is the Federal Communications Commission (FCC), which issues licenses for use of broadcast frequencies. Administrative agencies at the state level often issue *occupational licenses* and regulate professionals such as attorneys and physicians, as well as occupations such as those of hairstylists and contractors. State administrative agencies are discussed in more detail later in this section.

Some agencies also monitor compliance with administrative regulations by conducting **inspections** of businesses and individuals within their jurisdiction. Recall from Chapter 2, "Business and the Constitution," that government agents are restricted from engaging in unreasonable searches without a search warrant. Administrative agencies are, of course, covered by the same restriction, and ordinarily an agency must secure an *administrative warrant* before government agents may enter and inspect a business to monitor compliance with an administrative regulation. However, certain businesses are classified as *pervasively regulated,* and, therefore, the Supreme Court has fashioned an exception to the warrant requirement that covers situations in which the agency conducts regularly scheduled inspections pursuant to a rule. For example, MillCo operates several mills that are subject to a hypothetical enabling statute called the Mill Control Act (MCA). The MCA provides that all mills must be maintained in a certain way and that the administrative agency with jurisdiction over the MCA should promulgate rules that include monthly inspections to ensure compliance. Any inspections of MillCo's facilities pursuant to the rule would generally not require a warrant because MillCo qualifies as a pervasively regulated business as defined in the MCA.

> **KEY** POINT
>
> Courts are highly deferential to agency decisions involving how and when an agency enforces a regulation.

Even in cases where courts have held that administrative agencies are required to obtain an administrative warrant to conduct an inspection of a business, the Supreme Court has held that agencies are subject to a lower standard of probable cause to obtain the warrant than the standard the government must meet to obtain a criminal warrant. In Case 18.2, a federal appeals court considers the difference between an administrative warrant and a criminal warrant.

Also within the agencies' enforcement powers is the right to require businesses subject to the agency's jurisdiction to (1) keep certain records for inspection, (2) turn over relevant documents that may be useful in determining compliance with a particular rule, and (3) request statements or other information from the business's principals or managers.

Adjudication

Many (but not all) administrative agencies have authority to *adjudicate* matters under their jurisdiction. Adjudication is a hearing in which the government and the private party each present evidence in a quasi-judicial setting. In most agencies, the presiding officer is an **administrative law judge (ALJ)** who is typically an attorney employed by the agency to adjudicate disputes.

CASE 18.2 Trinity Marine Products v. Secretary of Labor Elaine Chao, 512 F.3d 198 (5th Cir. 2007)

FACT SUMMARY Compliance officers from the Occupational Safety and Health Administration (OSHA)[10] arrived at the facilities of Trinity Marine Products to conduct an inspection pursuant to their authority under the Occupational Safety and Health Act. Trinity's managers turned the OSHA inspectors away, so OSHA obtained an administrative warrant and returned with federal marshals. After the threat of arrest by the marshals, Trinity officials allowed the search under protest. Trinity later brought an action against OSHA, contending that the warrant had been issued without probable cause and that administrative warrants could not be legally executed by using force against nonconsenting parties. Trinity argued that refusal by a party to honor an administrative warrant should trigger a contempt-of-court proceeding to determine the validity of the warrant and that the government may not use force or arrest to enforce an administrative warrant.

SYNOPSIS OF DECISION AND OPINION The Fifth Circuit Court of Appeals ruled in favor of OSHA, reasoning that the standards for probable cause were lower for administrative warrants than for criminal warrants and that federal statutes and case law allowed administrative warrants to be executed using a reasonable degree of force. In this case, the government had shown that it had sufficient information to justify an inspection and, because Trinity

would not honor the warrant, that use of the marshals to gain entry was appropriate and consistent with the statutory intent that allows OSHA to "investigate and inspect without delay."

WORDS OF THE COURT: Probable Cause for Administrative Warrants "[A]dministrative warrants are distinguishable from traditional criminal warrants in a number of ways. They have, for instance, a different—linguistically idiosyncratic—'probable' cause standard: Probable cause may be based either on specific evidence of an existing violation, as in the traditional criminal context, or on a lesser showing that 'reasonable legislative or administrative standards for conducting an inspection are satisfied with respect to a particular establishment.' "

Case Questions

1. Would Trinity's case against OSHA have been stronger if the inspectors showed up with the marshals and forcibly searched the premises without first attempting to inspect without a warrant? Why or why not?

2. What are some examples of situations in which the probable cause standard for administrative warrants would not be met?

[10]OSHA is an administrative agency under the auspices of the Department of Labor.

Recall from Chapter 2, "Business and the Constitution," that federal adjudicatory powers are constitutionally vested exclusively in federal courts. However, federal courts have permitted agency adjudication when it occurs in the context of public rights disputes (a private party dispute with an agency over the agency's action or inaction) or when two private parties are disputing rights that arise within an area of the agency's jurisdiction.[11]

Appeals The losing party in an ALJ case generally has an automatic appeal to the administrative head of the agency, who may overturn or affirm the ALJ's ruling. An adverse decision from the agency may also be challenged in a federal trial court. Court challenges are discussed in detail in the next section of this chapter.

CONCEPT SUMMARY Scope of Administrative Agency Power

- Administrative agencies have broad powers, including rulemaking, enforcement, licensing, and adjudication.
- Agencies develop rules to be used in facilitating the government's administration of the law.
- The rulemaking process involves agency research, publication of a proposed rule in the *Federal Register,* a period for public comment on the proposed rule, and either revising the rule for additional comment or publishing a finalized rule.
- Agencies must use a reasoned decision-making process that is not arbitrary or capricious.
- After a final rule is published, the APA allows adversely affected parties to challenge the rule in court. However, courts give great deference to the agency's decisions.
- Agencies have prosecutorial discretion in deciding when and whom to regulate.
- Administrative agencies also regulate and administer laws through the licensing process, in which they issue, renew, suspend, or revoke a license to conduct certain types of business.
- Some agencies also monitor compliance with regulation by conducting inspections of businesses and individuals within their jurisdiction.
- Administrative agencies have the authority to adjudicate matters under their jurisdiction by holding a hearing between the government and private parties in front of an administrative law judge.

LO 18-8 # LIMITS ON ADMINISTRATIVE AGENCIES

Although the powers delegated to administrative agencies are broad, it is important to remember that all administrative agencies, including independent agencies, are limited in their authority by the three-part system of the federal government. The legislative, executive, and judicial branches all have various means of power that limit the authority of administrative agencies.

---

[11]Some agencies use their adjudication power to actually set policy as an alternative method to their traditional rulemaking authority when they wish to take a particular course of action in a given case. This is a controversial method of making policy, but the U.S. Supreme Court has allowed agencies to use adjudication instead of rulemaking in instances where the adjudication promotes a fundamental fairness. However, the Court made clear that this was a relatively narrow power that may be exercised only when fundamental fairness to the parties requires it.

Executive Branch

From a structural perspective, administrative agencies are extensions of the *executive branch's* authority to carry out the legislative mandates, and the Supreme Court has acknowledged that the president of the United States has some inherent general right to exercise power over administrative agencies in a variety of ways. Although this inherent power is notoriously vague, from an administrative law perspective, the president's power is derived from the Appointments Clause[12] and from direct power through executive orders and, to a lesser degree, through budgetary control.

Appointments Clause   The Constitution gives the president the power to appoint "officers of the United States" consistent with the Appointments Clause in Article II. Although subject to confirmation by the Senate, the president has the exclusive right to nominate principal officers such as *cabinet members* or *commissioners* of independent agencies that report directly to the president. Although not specifically articulated in the Constitution, the Supreme Court has held that the president also has the power to remove any principal officers at any time with or without cause and without any congressional approval. However, Congress sometimes passes an enablement act with a *restriction* on the president's power to remove a particular officer of the government. Federal courts have held that this limiting type of statutory restriction is constitutional so long as the restrictions do not impair the president's ability to carry out his constitutional duty.[13] In fact, Congress has designated certain agencies, such as the Securities and Exchange Commission (SEC) and the Federal Trade Commission (FTC), as *independent* of the president's direct powers, and the heads and commissioners of independent agencies may be removed only for good cause (such as corruption) but not for mere differences in policy views between the agency and the president.

Direct Power   For the last several decades, presidents have exercised *direct power* over administrative agencies to accomplish the president's public policy objectives. For example, in 1982, in response to what President Reagan perceived as a regulatory system that was so burdensome on certain industries that it impacted the industrial output of the country, he issued an executive order requiring that all federal administrative agencies submit to cost-benefit analysis along with any proposed regulation as part of a mandatory review process by the Office of Management and Budget (OMB). OMB was assigned to encourage agencies to be as cost-conscious as possible when imposing regulatory schemes on certain industries. This executive order is thought of as direct power over the agencies because the OMB reports directly to the president.

Congress

Although the U.S. Supreme Court narrowed congressional review of agency actions in the famous 1983 case of *INS v. Chadha*,[14] Congress still retains significant power to influence, amend, or void actions of an administrative agency. For example, Congress may exercise its constitutionally granted *power of the purse* over government funding of particular agencies, or it may simply enact legislation that restricts an agency's authority or pass a new law to overrule an administrative regulation. In 1996, Congress amended the APA[15] to restore its

---

[12]U.S. Constitution art. II, § 2, cl. 2.

[13]*Morrison v. Olsen*, 487 U.S. 654 (1988).

[14]462 U.S. 919 (1983). The Court held that a decades-old congressional procedure for overruling agency regulations, known as a *legislative veto*, violated the bicameralism and presentment requirements of the U.S. Constitution.

[15]The APA was amended by the Contract with America Advancement Act in 1996, which provides for congressional authority to review administrative regulations. The amendment was intended to reestablish congressional power to nullify agency regulations by addressing the constitutional problems with the legislative veto as outlined in *INS v. Chadha*, 5 U.S.C. § 801 et seq. (2008).

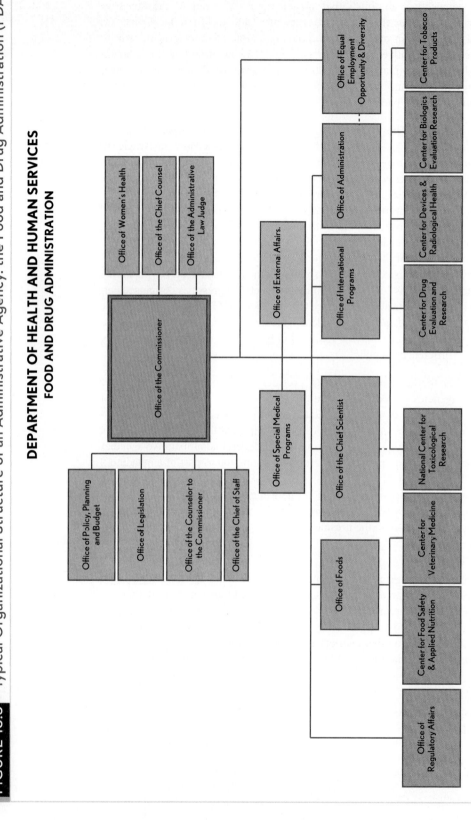

DEPARTMENT OF HEALTH AND HUMAN SERVICES
FOOD AND DRUG ADMINISTRATION

Office of Women's Health

Office of the Chief Counsel

Office of the Administrative Law Judge

Office of the Commissioner

Office of Policy, Planning and Budget

Office of Legislation

Office of the Counselor to the Commissioner

Office of the Chief of Staff

Office of External Affairs.

Office of Special Medical Programs

Office of the Chief Scientist

Office of Administration

Office of International Programs

Office of Equal Employment Opportunity & Diversity

Office of Foods

Office of Regulatory Affairs

Center for Food Safety & Applied Nutrition

Center for Veterinary Medicine

National Center for Toxicological Research

Center for Drug Evaluation and Research

Center for Devices & Radiological Health

Center for Biologics Evaluation Research

Center for Tobacco Products

Source: www.fda.gov/AboutFDA/CentersOffices/OrganizationCharts/ucm282075.htm.

own authority to cancel an agency's final rule if (1) both houses agree, (2) they pass a resolution to overrule within 60 days, and (3) the overruling resolution is presented to the president.

Congress also has oversight over administrative agencies by virtue of the Senate's power of *advice and consent*[16] in the appointment of certain high-ranking agency officers. Although Congress may not appoint administrative officials,[17] as a practical matter it still wields broad influence over appointments by virtue of the political realities involved in agency-head selection. Ultimately, Congress has the power to remove an administrative agency head via impeachment by the House of Representatives and removal by the Senate.

Judicial Review

The APA sets various standards of review for cases where administrative agency actions are challenged in a federal court.[18] Of course, courts will set aside any agency action that is inconsistent with the Constitution. But the APA also authorizes courts to void agency actions if the agency has exceeded its *statutory authority* or if agency actions have been taken without adhering to the statutorily established *procedure.*

Statutory Interpretation by Agencies

Because Congress uses very broad objectives when it passes an enabling act and other laws, administrative agencies must sometimes interpret an ambiguous statute in order to carry out their duties or take administrative action. In 1984, the Supreme Court adopted the *Chevron* test[19] as the framework to analyze the validity of administrative agency statutory interpretation and action. First, courts look to the language of the statutory authority given to the agency by Congress. If the agency's interpretations or actions conflict with the plain-language meaning of the statute, then a court may hold that the agency's interpretation or actions were unlawful. If, however, the statute is silent or ambiguous on the agency's authority, the court applies the **arbitrary and capricious standard** to determine whether the agency's actions were lawful. A heightened standard, known as the *substantial evidence test,* applies only in a relatively small number of cases where the formal rulemaking process was required by the enabling act.

Applying the Arbitrary and Capricious Standard

In order to meet the judicial review requirements, agencies must provide evidence that a *reasoned decision-making* process was used rather than an action that was *arbitrary and capricious.* This standard applies to all agency actions, including rulemaking, adjudication, enforcement, inspection, and licensing. Arbitrariness and capriciousness is found when the agency has taken action that is not based on a consideration of relevant factors, including viable alternatives available to the regulatory agency, or is a result of a clear error of judgment by the agency. The APA specifically requires that courts review only the information that the agency had available to it at the time it took the action in question.

Although the power of courts to set aside an administrative agency's action is clear, courts have traditionally been sparing in the use of this power. The U.S. Supreme Court has consistently held that judicial deference to administrative agencies is an important part of administrative law and that a court should not substitute its judgment for that of the agency.[20]

---

[16]U.S. Constitution art. II, § 2, cl. 2 (the Appointments Clause).

[17]*Buckley v. Valeo,* 424 U.S. 1 (1976).

[18]APA § 706 et seq.

[19]*Chevron USA, Inc. v. NRDC,* 104 S. Ct. 2778 (1984).

[20]*Citizens to Preserve Overton Park, Inc. v. Volpe,* 401 U.S. 402 (1971).

The Court provided guidance for lower courts in applying the arbitrary and capricious standard in *Motor Vehicle Manufacturing Association v. State Farm Mutual Automobile Association.*[21] In that case, the Court ruled that agency action was arbitrary and capricious if the agency (1) relied on factors that Congress has not intended it to consider, (2) failed to consider an important aspect of the problem, (3) offered an explanation for its decision that runs counter to the evidence before the agency, or (4) offered an explanation that is so implausible that it could not be ascribed to a difference in view or the product of agency expertise.

The arbitrary and capricious standard received significant media attention when it was the central issue in a case challenging the Department of Interior's six-month ban on deepwater drilling in the wake of the Deepwater Horizon (BP) oil spill disaster. The government's drilling moratorium suspended drilling on 33 exploratory wells and halted the issuing of any new permits. In a June 2010 ruling by the U.S. district court in Louisiana, the government's drilling moratorium was found to be arbitrary and capricious, and the court issued an injunction against the government's action. Judge Martin Feldman wrote that "[t]he court is unable to divine or fathom a relationship between the findings [of the government agency] and the immense scope of the moratorium." The court invalidated the agency's actions based on its conclusion that the government failed to "cogently reflect the decision to issue a blanket, generic, indeed punitive, moratorium."[22] Ultimately, the Secretary of the Interior withdrew the moratorium. Note that the legal aspects of the Deepwater Horizon oil spill are covered in more detail in Chapter 19, "Environmental Law."

In Case 18.3, the U.S. Supreme Court applies the *Motor Vehicle Manufacturing* reasoning to a decision by the Federal Communications Commission (FCC) to change its view on the use of fleeting expletives on the public airwaves.

CASE 18.3 Federal Communications Commission v. Fox Television Stations, Inc., 129 S.Ct. 1800 (2009)

FACT SUMMARY The Federal Communications Commission (FCC) had traditionally followed a restrained enforcement policy for the use of profanity in broadcasts when the indecent material was of a fleeting and isolated nature. In 2001, the FCC further clarified its policy by acknowledging that although the First Amendment protects indecent speech, the government had a compelling interest in regulating profanity during certain hours when viewers were likely to include children. The FCC gave guidance to its media licensees (including Fox Television) that an indecency violation would be judged using a two-prong test: (1) whether the material describes or depicts sexual or excretory organs or activities and (2) whether the broadcast is patently offensive (explicit or graphic description or depiction of sexual or excretory organs or activities).

In 2003, the FCC applied the test to an incident on an awards show in which U2 lead singer Bono gave an acceptance speech that included the phrase "This is really, really, f---ing brilliant." The FCC ruled that the expletive did not constitute a violation of the FCC's indecency policy and reaffirmed its policy of enforcement restraint on fleeting expletives.

Five months after deciding the Bono incident was not indecent, the FCC abruptly changed its course and instituted a zero-tolerance rule for any use of certain words that were inherently indecent no matter what the context or brevity. In 2006, the FCC issued a decision that imposed fines on Fox Broadcasting for two incidents involving the use of fleeting expletives in two different broadcasts. The first occurred during the *2002 Billboard Music Awards* when pop singer and actress

---

[21]463 U.S. 29 (1983).

[22]*Hornbeck Offshore Services, LLC v. Salazar,* U.S.D.C. Civil Action 10-1663 (E.D. Louisiana).

Cher stated: "People have been telling me I'm on the way out every year, right? So f--- 'em." The second incident involved the *2003 Billboard Music Awards,* during which celebrity Nicole Richie, a presenter on the show, stated: "Have you ever tried to get cow s--- out of a Prada purse? It's not so f---ing simple."

Fox brought an action seeking to have the new standard invalidated on the basis that the agency had been arbitrary and capricious in its actions by adopting a new standard for the enforcement of profanity regulations involving the use of fleeting expletives. The Second Circuit Court of Appeals ruled in favor of Fox. The court held that although the arbitrary and capricious standard is a narrow one and agency decisions should be given deference by courts, the FCC had not supplied any reasoned analysis for the radical departure from its previous policies. The FCC appealed the case to the U.S. Supreme Court.

SYNOPSIS OF DECISION AND OPINION   In a 5-4 decision, the U.S. Supreme Court reversed the lower court's decision and ruled in favor of the FCC. The Court held that the FCC's actions were not arbitrary and capricious and that the court of appeals had misapplied the *State Farm* standard. The majority found the FCC's reasoning for expanding the scope of its enforcement activity to be rational and consistent with reasoned decision making. Moreover, the Court held that certain scientific criteria were not required and that the FCC's repeated reliance on context showed it had not adopted a presumption that all uses of the words were indecent.[23]

WORDS OF THE COURT: Empirical Data Not Always Required   "There are some propositions for which scant empirical evidence can be marshaled, and harmful effect of broadcast profanity on children is one of them. One cannot demand a multiyear

controlled study, in which some children are intentionally exposed to indecent broadcast (and insulated from all other indecency), and others shielded from all indecency. It is one thing to set aside agency action under the Administrative Procedure Act because of failure to adduce empirical data that can readily be obtained [such as cost-benefit analysis of mandatory restraints in autos, at issue in the *State Farm* case]. It is something else to insist upon obtaining the unobtainable. Here it suffices to know that children mimic the behavior they observe—or at least the behavior that is presented to them as normal and appropriate. Programming replete with one-word indecent expletives will tend to produce children who use (at least) one-word expletives. Congress has made the determination that indecent material is harmful to children, and has left enforcement of the ban to the Commission. If enforcement had to be supported by empirical data, the ban would effectively be a nullity."

Case Questions

1. Would the FCC have avoided this case if it published its intent to change policy in the *Federal Register,* solicited public comments and opinions on the matter, and then decided to make the reversal in policy? Why or why not?

2. Although the Court concludes that certain empirical data cannot be "marshaled," couldn't the FCC have provided studies, publications, etc., that examine the impact of indecent language on children? Shouldn't the FCC be required to attempt to obtain empirical data?

[23]Note that apart from its administrative law analysis, the Court was also concerned about potential First Amendment questions. It instructed the lower court to consider the issue on remand. The First Amendment is discussed in Chapter 2, "Business and the Constitution."

 Self-Check   Arbitrary and Capricious

Is the agency's action arbitrary and capricious?

1. After a series of deadly vehicle accidents on the nation's highways that were caused by underinflated tires, the National Highway Traffic Safety Administration (NHTSA)—the administrative agency charged with regulating the nation's highways to make them safer—proposed a rule requiring automobile manufacturers to include tire pressure monitoring systems (TPMSs), which would warn drivers that they have underinflated tires, as standard equipment on all new cars. The rule states that manufacturers must provide a TPMS that warns drivers when one tire is 30 percent or more underinflated. Despite the fact that a 20 percent standard proved to be more reliable and

(continued)

safer, the NHTSA settled on the 30 percent standard because of its slightly lower cost. A safety advocacy group challenged the rulemaking decision to adopt the 30 percent standard.

2. Pursuant to a congressionally set objective of improving and maintaining the quality of public bodies of water, the Clean Water Act authorizes the Environmental Protection Agency (EPA) to issue permits to and regulate any facility discharging pollutants into waters of the United States. OilCo is a company specializing in refining pure Alaskan crude oil, which is found only in the town of Barren Ground, Alaska. Barren Ground is one of the few places in the United States that has perfect, pollutant-free, water due to the town's remote location. OilCo wishes to build three new refining plants in Barren Ground that each use a state-of-the-art refining system. However, the system requires cooling via a saline-based solution. OilCo applied for a permit to discharge its used coolant into Barren Ground Bay, but the EPA granted OilCo a discharge permit with a maximum pollution level of 0. This meant OilCo could not discharge any of its coolant without first treating it to the point at which it is no longer a pollutant but rather pure water. This process would be very expensive to implement and run for OilCo, so OilCo challenged the EPA ruling on the permit.

3. The Federal Energy Regulatory Commission (FERC) is an administrative agency responsible for permitting new power plants. Under the Save the Waters Act, the FERC is responsible for establishing a permitting process and issuing permits to individuals and companies wishing to construct hydroelectric power plants. Under the established process, a company must obtain a permit in order to gather information, conduct feasibility studies, and create architectural plans. The information gathered can be used for subsequent applications for licenses to construct and operate the plants. Clean Green Electric Co. (CGEC) wants to build two hydroelectric power plants on the Raging Waters River in Colorado in an area outside Small Town. CGEC applied for a permit to begin gathering information about the feasibility of locating the power plants outside Small Town. However, the FERC denied the company's permit application based in part on information from two prior permits CGEC had obtained for construction of the same power plants at the same site. CGEC challenged the ruling, arguing that the FERC should consider only information in the most recent permit application.

Answers to this Self-Check are provided at the end of the chapter.

LO 18-9 PUBLIC ACCOUNTABILITY

Because administrative agencies are granted broad powers and discretion, Congress has developed several safeguards to make agencies accountable to the public and to make their work as transparent as possible. This is accomplished through statutorily authorized citizen suits as well as mandatory-disclosure and open-meeting laws.

Private Citizen Suits

In addition to limits imposed on federal administrative agencies by the executive, legislative, and judicial branches, many enabling statutes contain provisions authorizing any member of the public at large who is directly affected by a particular agency action (or inaction) to bring a lawsuit against violators of a particular regulation and/or the administrative agency itself for failing to fulfill a duty imposed by statute. These suits are called **citizen suits** and are particularly prevalent in statutes related to protection of the

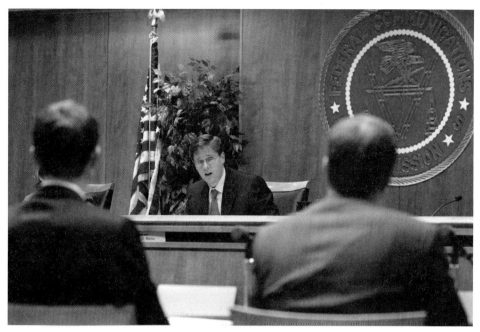

The U.S. Supreme Court ruled that the FCC's decision to institute a zero-tolerance rule for fleeting expletives in broadcasts was "entirely rational" and not arbitrary or capricious.

environment.[24] As a practical matter, organized activist groups such as, in the case of environmental regulation, the Sierra Club or the Natural Resources Defense Council (NRDC) often file citizen suits.

In terms of suits against the government, it is important to realize that citizen suits cannot be used to attack the *substance* of a regulation that has been properly promulgated. Citizen suit provisions may be used only to compel the agency to act in a manner consistent with the enabling act or another federal statute. For example, suppose that Congress passed an enabling statute that required the Occupational Health and Safety Administration (OSHA) to promulgate regulations that provide a safe procedure for the removal of asbestos[25]-laden ceiling tiles within one year of the date of the law's passage. The OSHA properly promulgates a regulation pursuant to the statute, but an activist group, Friends of Workers (FOW), believes that the regulations do not do enough to protect employees in workplaces with asbestos. If FOW files a citizen suit against the OSHA claiming that the OSHA failed to carry out the enabling act's objectives, most courts would dismiss the suit because FOW is challenging the substance of the regulation. However, suppose that the OSHA fails to provide any regulations within the statutorily prescribed one-year period. In that case, FOW would be able to bring a citizen suit against the OSHA to compel it to promulgate the regulation.

> **KEY** POINT
>
> *Citizen suits* may be brought against a private party (as a violator) or against the administrative agency for failing to act in a manner consistent with the enabling statute's requirements.

---

[24]See, for example, *Bennett v. Spear,* 520 U.S. 154 (1997), interpreting the citizen suit provisions of the Endangered Species Act, 16 U.S.C. § 1540.

[25]Asbestos is a human-made material that was commonly used to make ceiling and floor tiles until the 1980s when governmental health agencies determined that asbestos dust was linked to cancer.

Federal Disclosure Statutes

One way that administrative agencies are accountable to the public is through transparency, which requires public access to informational records held by the government and disclosures concerning open hearings and other business conducted by federal agencies. Congress provides two primary mechanisms to achieve these transparency objectives: the *Freedom of Information Act (FOIA),* which gives the public the right to examine a great many government documents, and the *Government in the Sunshine Act,* which requires that certain agency meetings be open to the public.

Freedom of Information Act (FOIA)

The Freedom of Information Act (FOIA— frequently pronounced "foy-a") was passed by Congress in 1966 (and expanded by amendments in 1974)[26] to open up certain agency records for public inspection. Fundamentally, the FOIA requires agencies to publish certain matters and, upon the request of an individual or agency (such as a media outlet), to allow public inspection of all other records created or obtained by the agency in the course of doing its work. In order to ensure agency cooperation in complying with the FOIA, the law allows private parties to sue the agency if the records are wrongfully withheld.

However, the FOIA also contains nine separate categories of exceptions designed to protect legitimate interests. The most commonly excluded records are documents that contain (1) sensitive national defense or foreign policy information; (2) agency personnel matters or agency policies on purely administrative issues, such as schedules, performance reviews, records related to personnel, medical files, and other private matters; and (3) trade secrets and privileged commercial information, such as a secret process or device submitted by a business to the agency. For example, assume that ProductCo applies to the Environmental Protection Agency for a permit to discharge waste products into a stream after they are treated for pollution by a secret cleaning process designed by ProductCo's scientists. This process would likely need to be identified in ProductCo's permit application and, thus, would be within the orbit of the FOIA. However, it would fall into the trade secret exception and would be protected from disclosure to the public at large.

In Case 18.4, an appellate court considers whether daily calendars of government officials that contain personal entries are records subject to FOIA disclosure.

Government in the Sunshine Act

The Government in the Sunshine Act requires that agencies announce their meetings at least one week in advance and open the meetings to the public unless a meeting falls within one of the Sunshine Act exceptions. However, the law does not apply to meetings that are purely consultative in character or that concern investigatory or adjudication matters.

ADMINISTRATIVE LAW AT THE STATE LEVEL

Business owners and managers should also expect to encounter state administrative agencies as well as federal agencies. Although our discussion has focused primarily on federal administrative law, state agencies also have broad executive, legislative, and adjudication discretion in matters of state administrative law. Indeed, many state agencies exist to accomplish substantially the same objectives as those of federal agencies, but they operate at a comparatively micro level, with state administrative law more tailored to the needs of the particular state. California, for example, supplements existing federal air pollution regulations with additional state regulations designed to reduce smog problems in its major cities.

States often have their own versions of federal agencies. For example, all states have a department of revenue (or some similarly named agency) that is the state's version of the

---

[26]5 U.S.C. § 552.

FACT SUMMARY In February 2001, the U.S. Department of Agriculture (USDA) published notice of a proposed rule regulating exposure to Listeria, a dangerous, food-borne bacterium that can be found in ready-to-eat meat and poultry. The USDA later issued an interim final rule that Consumer Federation of America (CFA) regarded as significantly weaker than the originally proposed rule. CFA suspected that the interim final rule was the result of pressure applied by industry representatives during lobbying meetings with agency officials.

Seeking to learn whether USDA officials had met exclusively, or nearly exclusively, with industry representatives who favored the weakening of the original proposed rule, CFA filed a Freedom of Information Act (FOIA) request for access to the public calendars of five senior USDA officials and one USDA administrative assistant. When the USDA failed to provide a substantive response within the statutory time period, CFA filed suit in district court to compel production of the calendars.

Ultimately the USDA took the position that the calendars were not "agency records" as defined in the FOIA and therefore that CFA had no right to access. The trial court agreed and ruled that the officials' appointment calendars were not agency records. CFA appealed.

SYNOPSIS OF DECISION AND OPINION The D.C. Circuit Court of Appeals ruled in favor of CFA and held that the calendars were agency records under the FOIA and were subject to public access. The court ruled that since the USDA calendars were continually updated, distributed to employees, and used to conduct agency business, the calendars were included under the FOIA. The court pointed out that unlike a personal diary containing an individual's private reflections on his or her work—but which the individual does not rely upon to perform his or her duties—the USDA calendars were in fact relied upon by both their authors and their authors' colleagues to facilitate the day-to-day operations of the department's work. The court also ruled that the administrative assistant's calendar was *not* an agency record covered by the FOIA because it was not distributed among senior officials and was more of a personal time schedule.

WORDS OF THE COURT: Personal Information and Agency Records "USDA protests that, because the calendars contain personal as well as business entries, they cannot be considered 'agency records.' There is no doubt that the presence of such information may be relevant in determining the use of a document. But as we said in [previous cases], the inclusion of personal information does not, by itself, take material outside the ambit of FOIA. Were that not true, an official could avoid disclosure of the only documentation of a meeting held with industry officials during the pendency of a rulemaking—the very information that CFA seeks in this case—simply by adorning the document with personal entries. In [a previous case], we held that [a government official's] daily agendas were agency records, notwithstanding that the personal information contained in the agendas [was] identical to that found in [his] appointment calendars, which we found to be personal records. The distinguishing factor was that the agendas were distributed to staff for their use in determining [his] availability for meetings."

Case Questions

1. What did CFA expect to uncover through the use of the FOIA?

2. If government officials know that they will have to reveal their personal calendars, wouldn't that potentially chill necessary debate within or outside the agency?

Internal Revenue Service. States frequently have agencies devoted to the regulation of parties within the state's borders in regard to the sale of securities (selling a business entity's stock to the public), protection of the environment, regulation of banking and insurance companies, workplace safety, consumer protection, and labor and employee antidiscrimination regulations. Federal and state agencies also share information and work together on joint operations. State administrative law is very similar to the federal scheme in terms of how regulations are developed, implemented, and enforced.

Administrative law p. 509   A body of law and regulations that governs the organization and operation of administrative agencies.

Administrative agencies p. 509   Governmental bodies that have the authority to implement and administer particular regulations; include department, nondepartment, and independent agencies.

Rulemaking p. 510   The legislative function of administrative agencies, whereby they create legally enforceable rules in order to fill in the details of a statute.

Adjudication p. 510   The judicial function of administrative agencies, whereby the agencies make policy. Administrative law judges hear cases brought before the specific agency.

Enabling statute p. 512   A law passed by Congress when it is establishing an administrative agency; serves as the source of the agency's authority and describes the agency's scope and jurisdiction over certain matters.

Regulation p. 517   A rule that is in effect and is published in the Code of Federal Regulations and that has the force of a law.

Enforcement p. 518   The function of administrative agencies whereby they investigate alleged violations of their administrative regulations and recommend enforcement actions; generally carried out through an agency's Office of General Counsel. In deciding when and whom to regulate, the agencies have prosecutorial discretion that is practically unreviewable by the judiciary.

Licensing p. 518   The task of issuing a license authorizing a business or industry to do something.

Inspection p. 518   The act of monitoring a business's compliance with administrative regulations. An administrative agency ordinarily secures a warrant and then enters and inspects the business's premises.

Administrative law judge (ALJ) p. 519   An individual, typically an attorney, who is employed by an agency to adjudicate disputes.

Arbitrary and capricious standard p. 523   The broad judicial benchmark used to determine whether an agency's actions were a result of a reasoned decision-making process.

Citizen suits p. 526   Lawsuits that are initiated by members of the public who are directly affected by an agency action and are brought against violators of the regulation and/or the administrative agency itself for failing to fulfill a duty imposed upon it.

Main Line Restaurant Group (MLRG) is a company that owns and operates a national chain of Italian-themed restaurants. Each of its restaurants is equipped with a series of hoods that ventilate smoke from a wood-burning pizza oven to the outside via a roof vent.

In 2013, Congress passed a statute, as part of a broader air pollution control law, that authorized the appropriate administrative agency to implement rules intended to decrease the amount of pollution caused by debris in the air from commercial use of wood-burning ovens.

1. What administrative agency would likely have jurisdiction under this statute?

2. When Congress passes a law such as the one described above, what is this type of statute called?

Assume that the appropriate administrative agency studies the issues presented in the pollution control law and proposes a rule that all wood-burning ovens used in a commercial establishment must either be replaced by gas ovens or be retrofitted with a certain pollution control device that will cost $15,200 per hood. Although a similar, lower-cost device is available, the agency did not view costs as a barrier to implementation when proposing the rule. The proposed rule also requires the hoods to be installed within five years.

3. What options does MLRG have for effecting a change in the proposed rule so that it includes the lower-cost device as an option?

Assume that the agency published a revised final rule that includes an amendment allowing the use of the lower-cost device but also includes an added provision that shortens the implementation deadline from the original five years to one year.

4. Is the administrative agency required to publish the amended rule again and allow a second comment period before it finalizes the rule? What rule would govern this analysis?

5. Assume that the administrative agency is not required to republish and allow an additional comment period what are MLRG's options for challenging the rule at this point?

6. What standards will a court use to judge the validity of the final rule?

MANAGER'S CHALLENGE

The following guide is excerpted from a federal administrative agency publication that sets out guidance for submitting public comments. Based on this guide, draft a two-page letter to the appropriate administrative agency on MLRG's behalf, explaining why you would urge the agency to change the proposed rule, in the Theory to Practice problem, concerning wood-burning ovens.

SUGGESTIONS FOR SUBMITTING COMMENTS

There are four general areas that you may wish to comment on concerning regulations:

1. *The need for the rule.*
2. *Other options.* If the agency has proposed or discussed requirements, you may be able to think of other things the agency could do that would solve the problem in a less costly way for your firm or industry. One option that has often been suggested is for the agency to give small firms more time to comply with a regulation, such as a change to a food label. Another option may be for the agency to identify a goal companies must meet, but to allow each firm to achieve the stated goal in its own way. Another option may be to request an exemption for certain types of businesses for which the requirements are not applicable. Because the quality and persuasiveness of your comment affects the agency's decision, including data, logical

reasoning, and other information to support your comment always helps.

3. *Benefits of the rule.* You may want to explain (in detail if possible) whether you think a specific requirement would achieve the intended results. For example, you may want to provide detailed information documenting whether your industry has a particular problem. Furthermore, you may want to comment on the degree to which a proposed requirement is already common practice, and how much a federal rule would change practices in your industry.

4. *Costs of the rule.* In many cases, the regulatory options and costs of the rule will be the areas that you will know most about and may want to include in your submission. The following chart gives examples of costs that your company or industry may experience as a result of a regulation.

COST FACTOR CHART

The factors outlined below can be used for commenting on each proposed requirement in the codified section. This chart is only a suggestion for submitting comments. You are free to comment in any manner you wish or not at all. You may also, for example, respond by plant, firm, industry group, or in any other manner.

A sample answer may be found on this textbook's website at www.mhhe.com/melvinleb2e.

Category	Explanation	Examples
1. What new capital equipment or materials will you have to buy to comply with the regulation?	Estimate the actual cost of new capital equipment or materials that you will have to purchase (one time or annually) and any loss of equipment that can no longer be used.	Chemicals for new tests will cost $40 per test for each of the 4 tests per week. The depreciated value of an extruder that will no longer be able to be used is $7,500.

(continued)

Category	Explanation	Examples
2. What is the size of your firm?	Estimate the size of your firm either by number of employees or by annual sales. A range may be given.	Our firm has 200 full-time employees and 20 part-time employees. Annual sales are between $10 and $50 million.
3. What products do you make?	Describe the type of products that your firm makes that are covered by the potential regulation.	Our firm makes 2 varieties of herbal supplements in 3 sizes each. We make 4 flavors of Larry's Ice Cream in 2 sizes each.
4. What are your average annual profits?	Again, *do not report sensitive information*, but you may wish to provide an approximate annual amount that you can use to finance new requirements.	My firm makes between $20,000 and $50,000 per year.
5. Who owns your firm? How many plants do you have?	Explain whether or not you are a subsidiary of a larger firm.	We are a solely owned firm with 2 plants.

Source: www.regulations.gov

CASE SUMMARY 18.1 :: Int'l Union, United Mine Workers of America v. Mine Safety and Health Admin., 407 F.3d 1250 (D.C. Cir. 2005)

LOGICAL-OUTGROWTH TEST

The secretary of the Mine Safety and Health Administration proposed a new rule intended to increase safety of workers by ensuring proper ventilation in mines. The proposed rule required a minimum velocity of 300 feet per minute (fpm) to be kept through the ventilation regulator to ensure adequate mine ventilation. During the comment period, empirical data were submitted that suggested that requiring *minimum flow* was the safest alternative and, thus, the agency would not set a *maximum flow*. However, when the final rule was published, it provided for a maximum airflow of 500 fpm. A mining company challenged the final rule because there was no comment period to discuss maximum airflows.

CASE QUESTIONS

1. Is the maximum-airflow rule a logical outgrowth of the proposed rule? Why or why not?
2. Is the agency required to republish the rule?

ARBITRARY AND CAPRICIOUS

CBS Corp. presented a live broadcast of the National Football League's Super Bowl XXXVIII on February 1, 2004. The broadcast included a 15-minute halftime program produced by MTV Networks and headlined by singer and actress Janet Jackson and singer Justin Timberlake. During the performance Mr. Timberlake, in an unscripted act, ripped off a piece of Ms. Jackson's bustier in what the network called a "wardrobe malfunction," which resulted in Ms. Jackson's bare breast being broadcast for nine-sixteenths of one second. While CBS had implemented a five-second audio delay to account for any profane language, it had no such video delay and the images were broadcast in real time. The FCC issued CBS a Notice of Liability for indecency and fined it $550,000 for the incident, claiming it was willful. CBS claimed that the ruling was arbitrary and capricious, based upon prior FCC decisions in similar circumstances. The FCC argued that it had enforced a valid indecency rule even though prior rule changes failed to specifically address indecent *images*.

CASE QUESTIONS

1. Is the FCC's decision arbitrary and capricious? Why or why not?
2. Should CBS be found liable? Why or why not?

JUDICIAL REVIEW

Paul Holowecki was employed by Federal Express Corporation (FedEx) when FedEx implemented two new performance programs that tie employee compensation and continued employment to certain performance measures. Holowecki, along with other FedEx employees over the age of 40, claimed that the incentive programs unlawfully discriminated against older employees. Under the Age Discrimination in Employment Act (ADEA), claimants must file a *charge* with the Equal Employment Opportunity Commission (EEOC) and then wait a statutorily defined period of time before filing suit in federal court. However, the ADEA does not define what constitutes a charge. The EEOC, using its authority to implement procedures necessary to carry out its objectives, promulgated a rule that states a "charge shall mean a statement filed with the Commission by or on behalf of an aggrieved person which alleges that the named prospective defendant has engaged in or is about to engage in actions in violation of the Act." Before filing suit, Holowecki submitted an intake questionnaire with the EEOC and filed a six-page affidavit. FedEx claimed that the questionnaire and affidavit did not constitute a formal charge against the company because they were only one step in a formal complaint procedure. FedEx argued that the EEOC's interpretation of the definition of "charge" was outside the agency's statutory authority.

CASE QUESTIONS

1. Who prevails and why?
2. Will the court defer to the EEOC's interpretation?
3. What is the standard used by the courts in cases such as this one?

ARBITARY AND CAPRICIOUS

In response to outbreaks of mad cow disease, the Food and Drug Administration and the U.S. Department of Agriculture (USDA) implemented a number of regulations to protect American consumers and cattle herds. Chief among them was a regulation banning cattle imports from countries in which mad cow disease was known to exist. Shortly after the ban went into effect, the USDA partially reversed course and published a proposed rule allowing certain low-risk products into the United States. During the comment period, some groups objected to the proposed rule due to evidence of potential contamination even in low-risk products.

The agency then published its final rule, which modified existing regulations to allow the import of low-risk products. The Ranchers Cattlemen Action Legal Fund United Stockgrowers of America challenged the agency's decision to allow low-risk products as arbitrary and capricious even though the agency had held several comment periods.

CASE QUESTIONS

1. Is the decision arbitrary and capricious? Why or why not?
2. Does the fact that the agency held several comment periods impact your analysis?

CITIZEN SUITS

Little Canyon Mountain had been an "open-use" park adjacent to private properties since 1985. In 2003, a federal agency's environmental assessment resulted in a plan for limited off-road-vehicle access in a certain area of the park. This plan was called the *fuels-reduction project*. The U.S. Bureau of Land Management (BLM) has regulatory authority to change off-road-vehicle use designations when these vehicles are "causing or will cause considerable adverse effects upon soil, vegetation, wildlife, wildlife habitat, cultural resources, historical resources, threatened or endangered species, wilderness suitability, other authorized uses, or other resources." After this plan was implemented, the BLM received numerous complaints from adjacent landowners regarding off-road-vehicle use in that area of the park. Gardner and Concerned Citizens for Little Canyon Mountain sued the BLM and argued that the 2003 environmental assessment for the fuels-reduction project by a BLM specialist was reason to require action by the BLM to close Little Canyon Mountain to off-road vehicles.

CASE QUESTIONS

1. Is Gardner challenging the substance of a regulation or how a regulation was promulgated?
2. What is Gardner's main concern, and what is he asking the court to do?

Arbitrary and Capricious

1. The agency's decision is likely to be considered arbitrary and capricious. The NHTSA is charged with making the nation's highway's safer, and by ignoring the fact that a four-tire, 20 percent TPMS is safer and more reliable and choosing a slightly cheaper, less safe alternative, the agency is not making a reasoned decision. See *Public Citizen, Inc. v. Mineta,* 340 F.3d 39 (2d Cir. 2003).

2. The EPA's decision is *not* arbitrary and capricious because the EPA is tasked with improving or maintaining the nation's water quality under the CWA. Therefore, its decision to issue OilCo a permit with an effluent limitation of 0 is perfectly reasonable because that is the level necessary to maintain water quality in that region. See *Texas Oil & Gas Ass'n v. United States EPA,* 161 F.3d 923 (5th Cir. 1998).

3. The FERC's decision is *not* arbitrary and capricious because there were no changed circumstances. The same power plants and the same sites were involved; therefore, the FERC could rely on the prior permits and information from their review to determine whether or not to issue another permit for this site. See *Symbiotics, L.L.C. v. FERC,* 110 Fed. Appx. 76 (10th Cir. 2004).

19 CHAPTER

Environmental Law

learning objectives

After studying this chapter, students who have mastered the material will be able to:

19-1 Explain the impact of environmental regulation on business.

19-2 Identify the origins and sources of environmental law.

19-3 Describe the role of the Environmental Protection Agency and state agencies in implementation and enforcement of environmental laws.

19-4 Explain the role of citizen suits in enforcing environmental regulations.

19-5 Describe the primary objectives and provisions of major federal statutes that protect the environment.

19-6 Provide examples of various industries regulated by the air and water pollution laws related to disposal of waste and hazardous materials.

19-7 Articulate potential liability of various parties under the federal environmental cleanup statutes.

19-8 Distinguish between removal and remedial cleanup efforts in the context of environmental regulation.

nvironmental law is a collection of federal, state, and local laws that protect natural resources and promote a healthier environment for the public at large. Whether it be federal regulation of industrial plants or a city ordinance prohibiting the use of certain pesticides by landscapers within municipal limits, business owners and managers from across the spectrum of commercial sectors encounter environmental law and regulation in their daily operations and in their business planning. In this chapter, students will learn:

- Environmental law's origins, sources, and enforcement mechanisms.

- Major federal environmental statutes that apply to business operations.

- Laws that impose liability on private individuals and businesses for environmental cleanup costs.

IMPACT OF ENVIRONMENTAL LAW ON BUSINESS LO 19-1

Business owners and managers all too often assume that environmental law and regulation is a concern only for owners of large industrial plants that produce smokestack pollution or dump waste into rivers. Yet it is clear that environmental laws must be thought of as having broad coverage and that an understanding of environmental law is important in limiting a company's liability and maintaining regulatory compliance. Any assumption that environmental laws are not pertinent to a particular business's operation may be costly in terms of liability and may forgo opportunities for proactive business planning and risk control.

As the American public becomes increasingly concerned over threats to the environment and related issues such as oil spills and greenhouse gases, governments at the federal, state, and local level have broadened environmental regulation and liability for environmental cleanups. Local businesses such as dry cleaners, bakeries, mechanicshops, gas station, landscaping firms, contracting firms, and a host of others are subject to various environmental laws.

Liability for environmental cleanup is another concern for business owners and managers if their business operations involve ownership of land. Certain federal statutes (discussed in detail later in this chapter) create liability for owners of property that is contaminated even if the owner did not contribute to the contamination. This strict liability concept is an important factor when planning a land purchase.

ORIGINS AND SOURCES OF ENVIRONMENTAL LAW LO 19-2

The origins of environmental protections were primarily based on the common law doctrine of **nuisance.** In a suit for nuisance, an aggrieved party sues to compel a polluter to cease polluting based on the aggrieved party's right to enjoy her property without interference from a third party. Local zoning ordinances are generally designed to prevent nuisance by segmenting a municipality into zones–industrial, residential, and so forth. However, this common law doctrine was a protection of a party's *individual property rights*. Historically, the federal government left regulation of the environment to state and local authorities. This resulted in a patchwork of standards, with some areas of the country allowing heavy industrial pollution while other areas regulated or banned such pollution. Because pollution does not respect state boundaries, it became apparent that federal statutes would be necessary to achieve meaningful environmental protections.

Modern environmental protection statutes at both the federal and state levels have largely supplanted any common law protections. In addition, local municipalities often have environmental ordinance standards related to safety and local public policy (such as proper disposal of engine oil or other hazardous waste by a local mechanic). Environmental protection statutes are wide-ranging, but federal and state statutes that impact businesses are primarily designed to (1) ensure that government agency decisions have the least possible impact on the environment, (2) promote clean air and water through regulation and permits, (3) regulate the use and disposal of solid and hazardous waste, (4) clean up property or waterways that are contaminated with hazardous waste, and (5) protect wildlife and endangered species.

LO 19-3 GOVERNMENT ENFORCEMENT

Federal environmental laws are primarily administered, implemented, and enforced by the U.S. Environmental Protection Agency (EPA). The EPA, created in 1970, works in tandem with other administrative agencies in handling a broad range of environmental concerns at the federal level. For example, the U.S. Fish and Wildlife Service primarily enforces statutes protecting endangered species. However, if the use of pesticides is responsible for depleting the population of certain endangered species, the EPA will work to use environmental regulation to halt the use of the pesticides. Other agencies that have certain environmental regulation jurisdiction include the Food and Drug Administration (FDA) and the Nuclear Regulatory Commission (NRC).

Like all administrative agencies, the EPA has broad powers to implement and enforce environmental laws by promulgating rules,[1] permitting, issuing advisory opinions, and investigating potential violations of federal environmental protection statutes, as well as using traditional enforcement tools such as administrative fines and penalties, civil suits and, in egregious cases, criminal complaints.

In addition to the EPA and other federal agencies, each state has its own environmental agency to implement and enforce state environmental statutes. In certain municipalities, a local environmental agency may exist to enforce local ordinances such as illegal dumping. The names of the agency vary among jurisdictions, but titles such as Department of Environmental Protection or Department of Natural Resources, or some variation of the two, are common. An important feature of many federal environmental laws is that state governments are often mandated to work in conjunction with (or under the supervision of) the EPA when implementing and enforcing federal environmental statutes such as the Clean Water Act.

LO 19-4 Citizen Suit Provisions and Watchdog Groups

Perhaps more than in any other area of the law, citizen interest organizations (also called *watchdog groups*) have contributed to the enforcement of environmental statutes and

---

[1]Recall from Chapter 18, "Administrative Law," that administrative agencies are authorized by statute to implement binding legal regulations after following a rulemaking process.

policy. These citizen interest organizations and individual citizens are statutorily authorized to file a lawsuit against either a polluter who is in violation of environmental statutes or regulations or a government agency or unit (such as the EPA or a municipality) that is not taking legally mandated steps to carry out environmental law enforcement. Individuals and groups derive this authority to file enforcement lawsuits by virtue of **citizen suit provisions** that are a part of many federal and state environmental statutes.

When an environmental statute authorizes citizen suits, it generally requires that notice of a citizen suit be given the agency with jurisdiction over the matter and allows the agency to decide whether to initiate agency action instead of allowing the citizen suit to go forward. A private citizen or group cannot profit from an enforcement action, and frequently the initiator of the suit seeks only to have a court order preventing or requiring a certain action. Typically, citizen suit provisions in environmental law spell out a procedure that gives the appropriate government agency and the polluter specific notice of the complaint and provides a period of time (usually 60 days) for action by the agency or compliance by the violator. If the time period expires without any action, the citizen suit may be filed in court. Citizen suits may not be commenced against a polluter if the government agency is already prosecuting the same violator. Some of the more common initiators of environmental law citizen suits include the Sierra Club, the Natural Resources Defense Council, and the Environmental Defense Fund. Local environmental watchdog groups in different regions of the United States tend to focus on a particular concern unique to the region (e.g., the Spotted Owl Defense League of Oregon).

In Case 19.1, an appellate court analyzes the procedure used in a citizen suit under the Clean Water Act.

NATIONAL ENVIRONMENTAL POLICY ACT

LO 19-5

One the first attempts at comprehensive legislation to address environmental regulation was the **National Environmental Policy Act (NEPA)**[2] enacted in 1969. The law was intended to serve as a national charter for environmental regulation, but its focus is on planning and prevention rather than achieving a certain result (such as cleaner water) according to scientific standards. The NEPA established a process that must be followed by federal agencies in making decisions that have the potential to have a significant impact on the environment. The NEPA also created the Council on Environmental Quality to oversee the NEPA procedures and to make periodic progress reports to the Congress and the president.

NEPA Coverage and Procedures

The NEPA procedures are triggered when a federal agency takes any action that may reasonably be considered as having an impact on the environment. This action may be in the form of an agency's issuing a permit or license or engaging in rulemaking. The NEPA is also activated when Congress passes a law that requires federal funding (such as federal highway or bridge construction). Note that actions by private individuals, businesses, and state and local governments are not regulated by the NEPA. However, all states have enacted parallel statutes (laws similar to the NEPA statute but covering a wider range of parties) to cover state and local government actions as well.

Procedural Steps

Federal agencies are required to incorporate the NEPA procedural steps into their decision-making process at the earliest possible opportunity by identifying the purpose of and need for a promised project, possible alternatives, and the environmental impact of certain

---

[2]42 U.S.C. § 4321 et seq.

FACT SUMMARY Gaston owned a metals smelting facility in South Carolina and operated it until 1995. After 1995, Gaston continued to treat contaminated storm water at the facility and to release this treated water into a lake on Gaston's property. However, the lake's water overflow discharged into other waterways and spread pollutants that resulted from the contact of rainwater with scrap metal stored by Gaston on its property. Friends of the Earth is an environmental citizen action group whose members include owners of property affected by the Gaston pollutants. Although Gaston attempted to solve the problem, the company continued to miss compliance deadlines for reducing the pollutants being discharged into the waterways. Friends sent Gaston a notice letter that alleged its noncompliance with the statute and named over 300 specific violations committed by Gaston. The Clean Water Act required that this statutory notice be sent prior to bringing a citizen suit. Ultimately, Friends brought a citizen suit, and the trial court imposed a $2.3 million fine on Gaston based on the violations alleged by Friends in the required prelawsuit notice and on additional violations that were uncovered during the discovery phase of the litigation. Gaston appealed the trial court's decision, arguing that the imposition of the citizen suit fine was not authorized by the statute because much of the penalty was related to pollutants that were not identified in the original notice letter.

SYNOPSIS OF DECISION AND OPINION The Fourth Circuit Court of Appeals reversed the civil fines imposed by the trial court on Gaston for all violations except the ones that were articulated in the Friends' citizen suit notice. The court held that the notice letter

provision in the statute has the legislative objective of bringing a polluter into regulatory compliance by means of citizen suit provisions. That objective would be frustrated if courts were to impose civil fines on a polluter based on violations that were unknown to the violator at the time of the notice letter. However, the court upheld several fines that were related to the allegations contained in the notice letter from Friends.

WORDS OF THE COURT: Purpose of the Notice Letter Requirement "This regulation provides, in relevant part, that the notice shall include sufficient information to permit the recipient to identify the specific standard, limitation, or order alleged to have been violated. Notice given by a citizen plaintiff under the Clean Water Act thus must provide the alleged violator with enough information to attempt to correct the violation and avert the citizen suit. . . .

"Our conclusion is not altered by the fact that when the plaintiffs sent their notice letter, they did not have access to information that they later acquired in discovery in this case. The plaintiffs' lack of information before their suit was filed cannot excuse the deficiencies in the notice letter, because those deficiencies prevented attainment of the legislative objectives of encouraging pre-suit governmental involvement and securing violator compliance."

Case Questions

1. Did Gaston escape a substantial civil fine based on a statutory technicality?

2. What could Friends have included in the notice letter that might help it prevail in a future case where the true extent of the violations is unknown?

---

actions. Once this step has been accomplished, the agency must categorize the action into one of three classifications based on its level of environmental impact:

- *Categorical exclusion (CE):* The CE category is used for those actions that have little or no potential for significant environmental impact. A CE classification may also be mandated by a particular statute, thereby having the effect of exempting certain actions from any further environmental assessment.

- *Environmental assessment (EA):* Projects and actions in which the environmental impact is unknown are classified in the EA category. Actions classified as EA require the agency to produce a public document setting forth the need for the proposed action, alternatives, the environmental impact of the proposed action and its alternatives, and

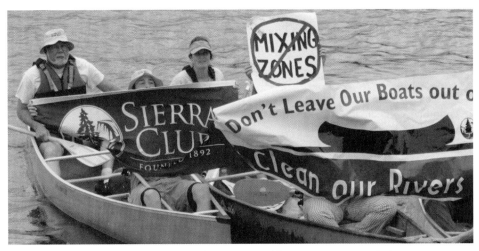

Citizen suit provisions in many environmental laws permit watchdog groups such as the Sierra Club to file suit against alleged polluters or the government to enforce the statute.

a list of agencies and persons consulted. The EA is used to determine whether the action requires preparation of a more extensive report called an *environmental impact statement*. If, however, based on the EA, the agency makes a finding of no significant impact, the agency may proceed with the proposed action.

■ *Environmental impact statement (EIS):* The EIS category is used for actions classified as having the potential for *significant impact* on the environment. If an EA provides evidence that some significant environmental impact is at issue, the agency must prepare a draft of an EIS and publish it for public comment. The EIS is an expanded form of an EA that includes (1) a description of the proposed action, (2) a statement of significant issues and specific forecasting of what environmental risks are involved with the proposed action, (3) alternatives to the actions and an assessment of environmental risk of the alternatives, (4) financial assessments of the promised actions and alternatives, and (5) plans for reducing or preventing environmental harm. Once the public and interested constituencies have commented on the EIS, the agency revises the EIS as necessary and issues a final EIS. The final EIS also sets out the agency decision on environmental impact and its chosen alternative for pursuing the agency action.

As a practical matter, the NEPA process gives public notice and affords consumer interest groups, businesses, and private citizens a chance to influence the agency's decision. The NEPA contains a citizen suit provision whereby private individuals and organizations may sue a federal agency directly to force compliance with the NEPA procedures.

CONCEPT SUMMARY National Environmental Policy Act

■ The National Environmental Policy Act (NEPA) of 1969 established a process that must be followed by federal agencies when they are making decisions that may reasonably impact the environment or when Congress passes a law that requires federal funding.

■ Federal agencies are required to incorporate NEPA procedural steps into their decision-making process by identifying the purpose of and need for a promised project, possible alternatives, and the environmental impact.

(continued)

- Once the procedural steps are accomplished, the agency must categorize the action into one of three classifications based on its level of environmental impact: (1) categorical exclusion (little or no potential impact), (2) environmental assessment (unknown impact), or (3) environmental impact statement (potentially significant impact).
- The NEPA process gives public notice and affords consumer interest groups, businesses, and private citizens a chance to influence the agency's decision or directly force compliance via citizen suit provisions.

LO 19-6 # THE CLEAN AIR ACT

Enacted in 1963, the **Clean Air Act (CAA)**[3] is a considerably complex statute aimed at improving outdoor air quality in the United States. The CAA replaced earlier legislation that had proved ineffective. The law has been amended several times since its original passage, most recently in 1997 to expand its coverage and provide a system of market-based incentives and enforcement options intended to encourage voluntary compliance with air standards. As its starting point, the CAA authorized the EPA to establish the National Ambient Air Quality Standards (NAAQS) that set permissible levels of certain air pollutants such as carbon monoxide, lead, and particulate matter (microscopic ash and dirt that are the ingredients for smog). Although the statute itself is multifaceted, its basic structure focuses on **stationary sources of air pollution** (such as an industrial manufacturing plant) and **mobile sources of air pollution** (motor vehicles).

Stationary Sources of Air Pollution

An important feature of the CAA is that *state legislatures* are required to determine the best way to achieve the NAAQS. State governments have a uniquely local understanding of state industries, geography, and demographics and are usually in the best position to decide on a solution. Each state is required to develop a collection of regulations that help to achieve a reduction in each pollutant to below the maximum level set in the NAAQS. This plan takes the form of a mandated **State Implementation Plan (SIP),** and the SIP must be submitted to the EPA within certain time frames set out in the statute. If the SIP is not acceptable, the EPA may either impose sanctions on the state (such as withholding certain federal funding) or step in to implement its own plan.

SIPs also feature a program for issuing **operating permits** to existing stationary sources that emit pollutants at special levels. Operating permits include information on which pollutants are being released, how much is being released, and steps the source is taking to reduce pollution, including technological requirements and methods to monitor the pollution. SIPs also include the requirements for obtaining a *preoperating permit* for any new source of pollutants being planned. Preoperating permits require the applicant to show that the construction of a stationary source has incorporated *state-of-the-art* technology to control the NAAQS pollutants. The CAA regulations also require a new source permit when a plant owner makes *substantial modifications* to an existing stationary source. Sometimes an issue arises as to what constitutes modification. This is an important factor in business planning because certain modifications may trigger additional regulatory measures and permit requirements.

Market-Based Approaches

One relatively controversial part of the CAA is the law's **market-based approach.** This approach was implemented by the 1990 amendments to the CAA and is accomplished through (1) *emission trading* via the permitting process and (2) a *cap and trade* plan intended

---

[3]42 U.S.C. §§ 7401–7671.

to achieve lower levels of pollutants that contribute to acid rain.[4] Although the plans have separate procedural systems, they are both considered market-based approaches. Under these approaches, businesses have certain *choices* as to how they reach their pollution reduction goals, including pollution allowances that can be traded, bought, and sold. In that same vein, a business may be allowed to expand its pollution output in one area if it is able to offset the increase by reducing another pollutant in greater measure than the one being expanded.

Economic Incentive Theory   The emission-trading scheme embraces the economic incentive theory that overall pollution reduction will result if businesses have an economic and competitive incentive, rather than a mandate, to invest in modern equipment and plants. Proponents argue that this approach results in businesses investing in more efficient plants that will yield clean air units to sell or trade to an out-of-compliance buyer. As emitting pollution becomes more expensive, every company will be forced to modernize to stay competitive in the market. For example, suppose that Citadel Manufacturing Company and Guardian Operations Inc. operate manufacturing plants that emit pollutants regulated by the CAA. Each company obtains a permit to emit 50 units of pollutant X and 50 units of pollutant Y per year. Citadel decides to modernize its plant at a cost of $1 million. The modernization results in a significant reduction in pollutant X, so now Citadel emits only 10 units per year. Guardian, on the other hand, claims it does not have the resources to modernize and its current plant will emit 80 units of pollutant X. In a market-based approach, Guardian may choose to comply by either purchasing 30 units of pollutant X emission credit from Citadel or reducing its use of pollutant Y to offset the additional units of pollutant X. If using the offset method, Guardian would have to reduce its use of pollutant Y at least 31 units (an amount greater than the exceeding pollutant). In this example, proponents of the market-based approach would point out that (1) this approach does not force burdensome mandates that may bankrupt a company, such as requirements to purchase expensive equipment; (2) eventually Guardian will likely begin to consider investing in new technology so as not to be dependent on sellers of pollution units; and (3) the overall pollution reduction is the same under this approach as it would be under a mandate approach.

> **KEY** POINT
>
> A market-based approach was instituted by the 1990 CAA amendments to give businesses alternative methods of complying with pollution standards.

Critics of this approach argue that it results in clean air being treated as a commodity rather than as a natural resource. Opponents of market-based solutions argue that the government could achieve greater reductions in pollution through the use of gradual statutory mandates to improve pollution control and government-backed loans to help companies purchase equipment.

Mobile Sources of Air Pollution

While substantial gains have been made in reducing pollution from motor vehicles over the past few decades, the internal combustion engine remains a significant source of hazardous pollutants. The EPA has issued standards intended to limit motor vehicle emissions through its Transport and Air Quality (TAQ) Program. The TAQ Program regulates (1) tailpipe emissions, (2) fuel economy, (3) performance standards, and (4) the composition and distribution of fuels, particularly gasoline, used in motor vehicles.

Tailpipe Emissions   The CAA initially set the first federal tailpipe emission standards, but granted California authority to set even tighter emission standards due to the state's higher-than-average levels of air pollution. The 1990 amendments gave states the choice of

---

[4]*Acid rain* is a broad term referring to a mixture of wet and dry components from the atmosphere that contains significant amounts of nitric and sulfuric acids. Governmental agencies have concluded that acid rain poses significant threats to the environment and specific ecosystems.

either adopting the federal standards or using the California standards, but states may not adopt their own standards. Both the federal and California standards require an inspection and maintenance program to ensure that car manufacturers limit the exhaust emissions of five major pollutants that emit from tailpipes, including hydrocarbons and carbon monoxide. The difference between the two sets of standards is that the California standards have stricter miles-per-gallon (mpg) requirements and lower levels of allowable pollution.

Fuel Economy Standards   Fuel economy standards set average mile-per-gallon requirements for motor vehicles and are determined by the year of the motor vehicle's production and its classification (car versus light truck). These regulations are called Corporate Average Fuel Economy (CAFE) standards, and they were enacted by Congress in 1975 with the purpose of reducing energy consumption by increasing the fuel economy of cars and light trucks. Regulating the CAFE standards is the responsibility of the National Highway Traffic Safety Administration (which sets the standards) and the EPA (which specifies a required standard calculation method for average fuel economy). The CAFE standards were overhauled in 2007 by the Energy Independence and Security Act,[5] which increased the mandated average for cars from 27.5 miles per gallon (mpg) to 35.5 mpg by 2020. However, in 2009, President Obama directed the regulatory agencies to explore a more rapid increase to the CAFE standards. In 2011, the government came to an agreement with the 13 largest automakers to increase CAFE standards for cars and light trucks to 54.5 mpg by model year 2025.

Performance Standards   The TAQ Program also requires that motor vehicle manufacturers obtain a Certificate of Conformity from the EPA that certifies that a vehicle's useful life is at least 10 years or 100,000 miles for passenger cars and up to 365,000 miles for heavy trucks. The useful-life standards are intended to make sure that manufacturers have designed the motor vehicle's emission system to last a certain period of time. Performance standards also include requirements for certain in-vehicle diagnostic systems that would allow a mechanic to detect an otherwise hidden defect in the emission control systems.

Fuel Composition and Distribution   The manufacturing and transportation of gasoline, diesel fuel, and fuel additives is regulated by the EPA under authority of the CAA. The EPA uses a registration system to ensure that any fuel product is tested and certified as safe for public health and is used in compliance with CAA regulations. In addition to requiring a complete ban on the use of lead-based gasoline beginning in 1995, the law also includes a requirement that gasoline components contain certain detergents to reduce emissions.

CONCEPT SUMMARY The Clean Air Act

- The Clean Air Act is aimed at improving outdoor air quality based on National Ambient Air Quality Standards that set permissible levels of certain air pollutants.
- The basic structure of the statute focuses on pollution from either stationary sources (manufacturing plants) or mobile sources (motor vehicles).
- State legislatures are required to determine the best way to achieve the NAAQS for stationary sources in the form of a mandated State Implementation Plan (SIP) that must be submitted to the EPA.
- SIPs also feature a program for issuing operating permits to existing stationary sources that emit pollutants at special levels, preoperating permits for any new source of pollutants being planned, and new source permits for substantial modifications to an existing source.

---

[5]42 U.S.C. § 17001 et seq.

- A market-based approach embraces an economic incentive theory and was instituted by the 1990 CAA amendments to give businesses a choice of methods for complying with pollution standards.
- The EPA has issued standards intended to limit mobile source emissions through its Transport and Air Quality Program, which regulates (1) tailpipe emissions, (2) fuel economy standards, (3) performance standards, and (4) fuel composition and distribution.

WATER POLLUTION CONTROL

The pollution of waterways is one of the biggest challenges facing environmental policy-makers. Waterways take the form of surface water (such as lakes or rivers) or groundwater (subsurface water, such as that used for wells). Because water travels through jurisdictional boundaries and may be subject to various legal property rights,[6] water pollution and conservation regulation is necessarily addressed by a combination of federal, state, and local statutes and rules.

The Clean Water Act

Water quality standards are set primarily by and regulated through the **Clean Water Act (CWA),**[7] a federal statute that is implemented and enforced by the EPA in tandem with the U.S. Army Corps of Engineers and state agencies. Much like the CAA, the CWA has been amended in significant ways to stem pollution from industrial, municipal, and agricultural sources.

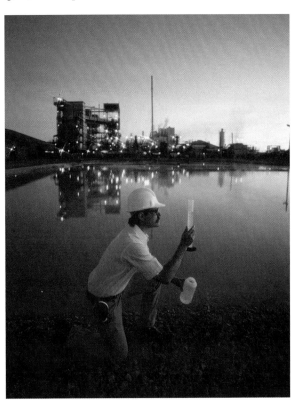

Waterways are protected by an array of environmental regulation statutes, including the Clean Water Act.

Water Quality Regulation Each state sets water quality standards, subject to EPA review, for the navigable waterways within the state's borders. State agencies set scientifically measurable standards consisting of several criteria intended to improve the quality of surface water. The standards are set according to the designated use of the water source. Sources in which the designated uses are swimming or fishing must have the quality standards set high. Once the state has set its standards, it must monitor whether its water sources are meeting those standards and disclose the results through a mandatory reporting system. If progress toward achieving the standards is too slow or nonexistent, the state must propose a new strategy to meet the quality standards. The EPA must approve any new strategies and may step in and impose its own strategy if it determines that the state is out of compliance with the CWA.

Permitting Pollution emission into the waterways from sources such as industrial plants is regulated through the EPA's National Pollution Discharge Elimination System. The system establishes permitting procedures for businesses and individuals that require discharge of some material into a water source in order to operate their facilities. A permit is required regardless of the quality of the receiving water or whether the discharge actually causes

---

[6]The legal term for water ownership rights is *riparian rights.*

[7]33 U.S.C. § 1251 et seq.

pollution. Permits are issued as either *individual* permits, which are specifically tailored to an individual facility, or *general* permits, which cover multiple facilities within a certain category. Individual permits are often issued to business facilities, while general permits are issued for all discharges in a specific geographic area (such as a city-designated development zone).

In order to obtain a permit, existing sources of pollution are required to install pollution control technology that is the best *practical* control technology. This means that the cost of implementation is given equal weight to that of the effectiveness of pollution control. New applicants for permits are required to employ the best *available* control technology, which means that the permit applicant must install the most technologically advanced control methods on the market regardless of cost. The EPA has established timetables for existing sources to adopt best *available* control technology as well.

Liability for Oil Spills

Largely in response to a 10-million-gallon oil spill that resulted when the *Exxon Valdez* oil tanker ran aground, Congress passed the **Oil Pollution Act (OPA)**[8] in 1990. The OPA increased the EPA's authority to prevent and respond to disastrous oil spills in public water sources. The law also imposed a tax on oil freighters in order to fund the national Oil Spill Liability Trust Fund, which is available to fund up to $1 billion per spill. Energy companies are required to file environmental impact plans with the U.S. Department of Interior, which has oversight authority over all oil drilling. The OPA was intended to promote contingency planning between government and industry to prevent and respond to a spill event. The OPA also increased penalties for noncompliance and broadened the government's response and enforcement authority. The law caps the liability of responsible parties at $75 million per spill, plus removal costs. However, in case of gross negligence, the cap does not apply.

Deepwater Horizon (BP) Oil Spill   The largest offshore oil spill in U.S. history began on April 20, 2010, after an explosion aboard the BP-controlled oil drilling platform *Deepwater Horizon.* The *Deepwater Horizon* was situated in the Gulf of Mexico approximately 40 miles southeast of the Louisiana coast. The explosion killed 11 people working on the platform and created an oil spill that the National Oceanic and Atmospheric Administration estimated was leaking almost 5,000 barrels (210,000 gallons) per day. BP tried several methods for controlling the leak, but the logistics of such a deep-sea operation resulted in a number of failed attempts to control the leaking.

Connect | BUSINESS LAW

Visit Connect for an update on the legal aspects of the *Deepwater Horizon* oil spill.

The gusher continued for nearly three months and resulted in an estimated 4.9 million barrels spilled into the Gulf of Mexico, making it the largest aquatic oil spill in history. The Gulf's coastal communities, whose income comes primarily from fishing and tourism, were devastated. BP faced sharp criticism for its handling of the crisis, and the Justice Department launched a criminal investigation into the incident. Although BP acknowledged its liability in the accident, the company alleged that other contractors on the oil rig were also negligent in the spill. By 2012, BP had paid a civil fine and costs totaling $4.5 billion and pleaded guilty to 11 felony counts related to the deaths of the oil rig's crew. Several BP executives were charged with various crimes, including lying to investigators about how many gallons were leaking at the very beginning of the spill.

Of course, the incident spurred hundreds of lawsuits. Most of the lawsuits were consolidated into one class action case according to federal court rules. In 2012, BP entered into a settlement agreement and agreed to pay $7.8 billion to resolve the class action litigation. In Case 19.2, a federal court considers the fairness of the settlement agreement proposed by the parties to resolve the lawsuit.

---

[8]33 U.S.C §§ 2702–2761

FACT SUMMARY After the *Deepwater Horizon* explosion and spill affected the health and economic well-being of Gulf Coast residents, hundreds of lawsuits were filed against BP. In August 2010, the Judicial Panel on Multidistrict Litigation centralized all federal actions in the U.S. District Court for the Eastern District of Louisiana pursuant to federal statutes. Eventually, hundreds of cases with thousands of individual claimants would be consolidated with this multidistrict litigation. The parties engaged in an extraordinary amount of discovery within a compressed time period to prepare for trial. This included taking 311 depositions, producing approximately 90 million pages of documents, and exchanging more than 80 expert reports. Depositions were conducted on multiple tracks and on two continents. In February 2011, settlement negotiations began in earnest for the proposed settlement agreement, and by September 2012 both parties moved for final approval from the court. The court ordered a Fairness Hearing in order to determine approvability of the agreement. Some plaintiffs argued that it was not fair that BP would obtain a broad classwide release as well as a signed individual release from each claimant that accepts a payment pursuant to the settlement agreement.

SYNOPSIS OF DECISION AND OPINION In a lengthy opinion, the court ruled that the proposed settlement agreement was fair and approved it. The court pointed out that the agreement included extensive compensation for individual and business losses, including compensation for claims related to property damage, economic losses of fisheries and other small businesses on the coastline, the rebuilding of wetlands, and vessel repair, as well as compensation for other losses caused by the spill. The court also found that the agreement created an effective method for advertising news of the settlement to affected residents and businesses and provided an infrastructure designed to pay claims quickly.

WORDS OF THE COURT: Fair Settlement "Proponents of a class settlement must show by a preponderance of the evidence that the settlement is fair, reasonable, and adequate. The Fifth Circuit has articulated six factors to guide a court's review of whether a settlement is fair, reasonable, and adequate:

(1) the existence of fraud or collusion behind the settlement;

(2) the complexity, expense, and likely duration of the litigation;

(3) the stage of the proceedings and the amount of discovery completed;

(4) the probability of plaintiffs' success on the merits;

(5) the range of possible recovery; and

(6) the opinions of the class counsel, class representatives, and absent class members.

Because the public interest strongly favors the voluntary settlement of class actions, there is a strong presumption in favor of finding the settlement fair, reasonable, and adequate. The preference for settlement over the expenditure of scarce judicial resources gains added force under the OPA statute, which is designed to catalyze settlements."

Case Questions

1. Do you agree with the court that the public interest is served best by settlement in these kinds of cases? Why or why not?

2. What is a fair sum to pay business owners who suffered damages through loss of tourism because of the spill? Isn't it impossible to determine how much a particular business *could* have made?

Drinking Water

The **Safe Drinking Water Act (SDWA)**[9] is a federal statute that sets minimum quality and safety standards for every public water system and every source of drinking water in the United States. This includes rivers, lakes, reservoirs, springs, and subsurface water wells. The SDWA's standards vary based on the size and usage of the system. The statute requires

---

[9]42 U.S.C. § 300.

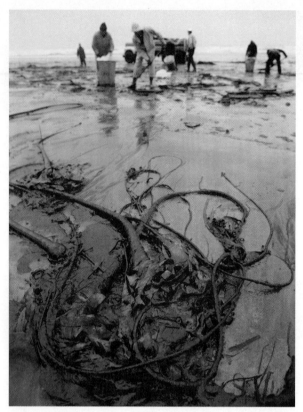

Passed shortly after the *Exxon Valdez* oil spill, the Oil Pollution Act imposes liability on responsible parties for cleanup costs and economic damages suffered by business owners and residents of affected areas.

the EPA to balance both *costs* and *health* benefits in setting the standards. Public water agencies are required to test and monitor water sources and systems at various points. A report of the results must be given to the state regulatory agency on a regular basis. The SDWA also requires states to oversee programs to certify that water system operators engage in safe practices and that they have the technical and financial capacity to ensure a consistent supply of safe drinking water as well as the ability to respond quickly to any defects in the water system.

CONCEPT SUMMARY   Water Pollution Control

- Water pollution and conservation regulation is addressed by a combination of federal, state, and local statutes and rules.
- Water quality standards are set and regulated through the Clean Water Act.
- Each state sets water quality standards, subject to EPA review, for the navigable waterways within the state's borders and monitors whether the standards are being met.
- Pollution emission into waterways is regulated through the EPA's National Pollution Discharge Elimination System, which establishes procedures for issuing permits (either individual permits or general permits), which required regardless of the quality of the receiving water or actual pollution.
- Existing sources of pollution are required to install the best practical control technology, whereas new applicants are required to employ the best available technology in order to obtain a permit.
- The Safe Drinking Water Act is a federal statute that sets minimum quality and safety standards for every public water system and every source of drinking water in the United States.
- Congress increased the EPA's authority to prevent and respond to disastrous oil spills in water sources through the Oil Pollution Act.

REGULATION OF SOLID WASTE AND HAZARDOUS MATERIALS DISPOSAL

Although hazardous waste was historically within the jurisdiction of state legislatures, several debacles in the early 1970s in which toxic waste was discovered to have polluted community water sources resulted in congressional action in the form of a comprehensive federal statute. Although the handling, proper disposal, and liability for cleanup of abandoned solid waste and hazardous materials are regulated by federal law, states still play a crucial role in enforcement. Solid waste is generally garbage, refuse, sludge from a waste treatment plant, and sewage. Hazardous materials are chemical compounds and other inherently toxic substances (such as cleaning fluids and pesticides) used primarily in industry, agriculture, and research facilities.

Resource Conservation and Recovery Act

The **Resource Conservation and Recovery Act (RCRA)**[10] is intended to regulate *active and future facilities* that produce solid waste and/or hazardous materials. The RCRA created a "cradle-to-grave" procedure for handling waste from its origins to its transportation, treatment, storage, and disposal. Like many other environmental laws, the RCRA established reporting requirements and procedures and provides for civil penalties and citizen suits. In egregious cases, the RCRA also includes criminal provisions for prosecution of intentional violations.

The RCRA bans the open dumping of solid waste and authorizes the EPA to set standards for municipal waste landfill facilities. The law specifies special procedures that must be employed for disposal of certain types of municipal waste such as refrigerators (which often contain potentially toxic refrigerant solution). The regulations govern the location, design, operation, and closing of a landfill site and require regular testing for groundwater contamination.

Waste that is (or becomes) hazardous is also regulated by the RCRA. The statute regulates both those who generate the pollution and those transporting the waste. A generator is defined by the law as any facility whose processes create hazardous waste. A transporter is an entity that moves hazardous waste from one site to another via ground, water, or air transportation. These regulations include a mandatory tracking system in which the use of a standardized hazardous waste manifest form establishes a chain of custody for the waste to ensure accountability. The RCRA also imposes a permit system for facilities that treat, store, or dispose of hazardous waste.

Universal waste (batteries, fluorescent bulbs, and mercury-containing equipment such as thermostats) is included under the RCRA, but the EPA has issued federal rules that make compliance easier for business owners who are disposing of universal waste in the ordinary course of operations. The rules allow universal waste to be transported by common carrier rather than a more expensive hazardous waste carrier that has been certified by the EPA. Used tires, oil, and batteries are also covered by the RCRA, and the EPA has established special guidelines for disposal of motor vehicle waste products by repair and service facilities.

> **KEY** POINT
>
> The Resource Conservation and Recovery Act (RCRA) is intended to regulate *active and future facilities* that produce solid waste and/or hazardous materials. It created a "cradle-to-grave" procedure that includes handling regulations for waste from its origins to its transportation, treatment, storage, and disposal.

Toxic Substances Control Act

The **Toxic Substances Control Act (TSCA)**[11] is a federal statute that gives the EPA jurisdiction to control risks that may be posed by the manufacturing, processing, using, and disposing of chemical compounds. The TSCA's scope is very broad: It covers every chemical substance except pesticides, tobacco, nuclear material, and items already regulated under the Food, Drug and Cosmetic Act.[12]

The TSCA has both reporting and regulatory components. Specifically, the statute provides for (1) an EPA-maintained inventory of every chemical substance that may be legally manufactured, processed, or imported into the United States; (2) EPA authority to require companies to conduct specific screening tests that may reveal risks to public welfare; (3) EPA regulation on the use, labeling, and control measures of the substance; (4) record-keeping requirements; and (5) an obligation to report any potential adverse impact that the manufacturer, processor, or importer may become aware of in the course of operations.

---

[10]42 U.S.C. § 6901 et seq.

[11]15 U.S.C. § 2601.

[12]Includes food, food additives, pharmaceuticals, and cosmetics. This law is discussed in detail in Chapter 22, "Consumer Protection Law."

- The Resource Conservation and Recovery Act is intended to regulate active and future facilities that produce solid waste and/or hazardous materials, and it created a "cradle-to-grave" procedure for handling waste.
- The Toxic Substances Control Act is a federal statute that gives the EPA broad jurisdiction to control risks that may be posed by the manufacturing, processing, using, and disposing of chemical compounds.
- Although the handling, proper disposal, and liability for cleanup of abandoned solid waste and hazardous materials are regulated by federal law, states play a crucial role in enforcement.

COMPREHENSIVE ENVIRONMENTAL RESPONSE COMPENSATION AND LIABILITY ACT

LO 19-7

While the environmental laws that we have discussed focus on controlling and reducing existing or new sources of pollution, toxic waste contamination that had been generated prior to the enactment of waste control statutes and then abandoned by the polluter became a major hurdle to achieving environmental safety for the public. To confront the problem, Congress passed the **Comprehensive Environmental Response Compensation and Liability Act (CERCLA)**[13] in 1980.

Superfund

The CERCLA is commonly referred to as the **Superfund** because its main provisions center on the notion that cleanup operations for abandoned toxic waste sites (including both land and water sites) are to be funded by a self-sustaining quasi-escrow fund administered by the federal government. Superfund was initially funded by fees and taxes levied upon substances that contain hazardous components, primarily in the petroleum and chemical industries. However, the statutory scheme also replenishes the fund by allocating financial responsibility to parties that are statutorily responsible for all or part of the cleanup costs. Therefore, the cleanup of a particularly toxic site could be conducted, and then the EPA could sue a statutorily responsible party for the cleanup costs. Critics of the law argue that the Superfund is consistently underfunded and that taxpayers bear a disproportionate amount of the cleanup costs. Proponents argue that the Superfund model is the most effective way to halt further damage from abandoned toxic waste sites while identifying polluters and assessing financial liability.

In 1986, the CERCLA was amended by the **Superfund Amendments and Reauthorization Act (SARA)**.[14] Although SARA's provisions were primarily clarifications and technical definitional adjustments, the law contained a new requirement for states to establish emergency response commissions to draft emergency procedures for a hazardous chemical accident and implement them in the event of such an accident. All states must maintain and revise the plan as necessary, as well as fund a hazardous materials response unit. The act also requires businesses to disclose the presence of certain chemicals within a community and imposes an affirmative obligation to notify authorities of any spills or discharges of hazardous materials. For continuity, this textbook uses the term *Superfund* to refer to all of the provisions of CERCLA and SARA *combined.*

---

[13]42 U.S.C. § 9601.

[14]42 U.S.C. § 9601e.

Removal and Remedial Responses

The Superfund law established a two-front approach to handling hazardous substance cleanup: (1) **removal,** whereby authorization is given for actions to address releases or imminent releases of hazardous materials; and (2) **remedial,** whereby the EPA identifies the most hazardous waste sites and establishes a National Priorities List (NPL) for cleanup. In determining what sites are eligible, the EPA considers the overall potential harm to public health. To date, the EPA has placed over 25,000 sites around the country on the NPL. Once on the NPL, the EPA begins the remedial enforcement process by investigating the site, identifying parties that may be liable for cleanup costs, assessing the toxicity of the site, and determining the best remedial measure to accomplish cleanup. Figure 19.1 provides a map of Superfund sites on the NPL.

> **KEY** POINT
>
> The Superfund law addresses hazardous substance cleanup in two ways: (1) removal (for imminent releases) and (2) remedial (long-term cleanup projects).

Liability of Principally Responsible Parties (PRPs)

The sharpest teeth of the Superfund law are (1) it is retroactive and, therefore, applies to any disposal made prior to its enactment in 1980 and (2) it imposes broad strict liability standards for cleanup costs on certain businesses and individuals that fit the statute's definition of a *principally responsible party* (*PRP*). The Superfund also specifically imposes *joint and several* liability on PRPs. There are three classes of PRPs:

- Current owners of the site.
- Any owner or operator of the site at the time when the hazardous substances were disposed at the site.
- Any business that accepts hazardous substances for transport to the site and selected the site (such as a waste hauler).

Legal Speak ›))
Joint and Several Liability The legal principle that makes two or more parties liable for an entire debt either individually or jointly in any proportional combination.

FIGURE 19.1 Superfund Sites

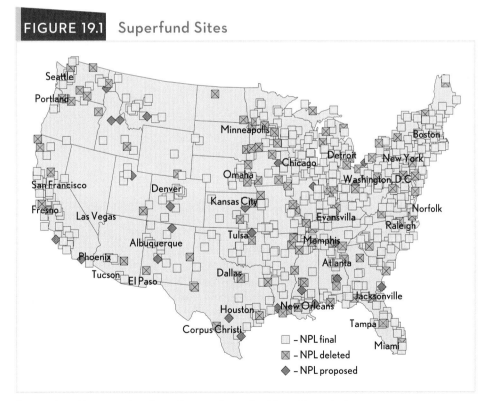

Source: http://toxmap.nlm.nih.gov/toxmap/superfund/mapControls.do.

For example, suppose that a parcel of commercial real estate is listed on the NPL because the groundwater is contaminated due to a leak in an underground storage tank. The EPA investigates the parcel and finds records of three previous owners: GasCo (used it for a retail gasoline station), ChairCo (used it for warehouse storage of furniture), and its current owner, DevelopCo (using it for real estate development), which has plans to build a retail storefront. The EPA determines that hazardous materials were stored in underground tanks by GasCo. Subject to certain defenses (discussed next), both GasCo and DevelopCo have joint and several liability for the cleanup costs. Suppose further that GasCo has been dissolved or was liquidated under the bankruptcy law and it no longer exists as an entity. Under the Superfund law, the EPA can hold DevelopCo, the parcel's current owner as of the NPL listing, liable for the *full* amount of the cleanup costs even though DevelopCo never contributed to the contamination.

Consent Decrees

Once the EPA has contacted the PRPs, the agency begins negotiations centered on PRP liability and cleanup operations. The parties draft a series of nonbinding agreements in order to evidence their good faith in moving the cleanup process ahead. If negotiations result in a settlement being reached before cleanup efforts are commenced or are complete, the EPA and PRP enter into a binding agreement, called a *consent decree,* that lays out how the cleanup plan will be implemented and who bears which costs. If the EPA believes the PRP is not negotiating in good faith or is stalling, it may cease negotiations, implement a cleanup plan, and pursue a civil suit against the PRP to recover the entire amount of the cleanup costs. The EPA may also begin enforcement actions against the PRP that may result in civil fines or, in extreme cases, criminal prosecution.

Allocation of Liability

When the EPA enters into a consent decree with a PRP, the PRP has the right to sue third parties such as transporters, other polluters, and municipalities to recover a portion of the cleanup costs related to the polluter's action. However, allocating liability among multiple polluters is a difficult process. In Case 19.3 an appellate court considers the scope of authority and discretion of courts engaged in a Superfund allocation analysis.

Defenses to Liability

As you may imagine, the Superfund law has come under fire by business advocacy groups for its potential to devastate innocent property owners and lenders. As a result, Congress carved out several defenses to liability for parties that meet certain criteria.

Secured Creditors

Suppose, in the DevelopCo case hypothetical, that during EPA's investigation DevelopCo defaults on its mortgage payments and its financial lender forecloses on the property. Because the lender is now the owner, does that subject the bank to liability under Superfund? Probably not. To protect lenders (such as banks) that have become owners of contaminated property through foreclosure, the Superfund law contains a provision that excludes any such lender from liability for cleanup costs. Lender-owners may avoid liability so long as the lender was (1) an owner by virtue of the contaminated property being used as collateral for a loan and (2) not participating in the management of the facility prior to foreclosure. The EPA has issued specific guidelines to define what activities constitute participating in management.

Innocent Landowners

A current owner of a site that is listed on the NPL may avoid liability for cleanup costs so long as the owner establishes that she purchased the

FACT SUMMARY   For decades, two public landfills in Connecticut accepted industrial waste, including municipal solid waste from various municipalities. The EPA declared the landfills to be Superfund sites because they were leaking chemicals and threatening the local water supply. The EPA began the remedial enforcement process by investigating and identifying various principally responsible parties (PRPs) that contributed to the pollution, and it entered into consent decrees for them to contribute to the cost of cleanup. The PRPs, which were all corporations that had disposed of waste in the landfills, formed a coalition to represent their common interests and sued several municipalities for contribution to the cleanup costs. In a long, complicated litigation, a special master was appointed by the court to try to mediate a settlement. The special master came to certain conclusions about which parties contributed how much waste. At trial, the district court did not follow the conclusion of the special master and allocated much of the liability to the municipalities that ran the landfills. The municipalities appealed.

SYNOPSIS OF DECISION AND OPINION   The U.S. Court of Appeals for the Second Circuit affirmed the district court's ruling. Appellate courts will not overturn a district court's allocation of remediation costs in Superfund cases unless there is an abuse of discretion. It was within the right of the court not to follow all of the findings of the special master and to allocate more costs to the municipalities than recommended by the master. For the court to abuse its discretion, it would have to have committed an error of law or be clearly wrong in its finding of facts.

The allocation of costs in such complicated proceedings may produce varying results; the court chose a method of allocation that was proper based on the evidence.

WORDS OF THE COURT: Court's Discretion under CERCLA   "Because [CERCLA's] expansive language affords a district court broad discretion to balance the equities in the interests of justice, the appellate court will not overturn the district court's allocation of response costs absent an abuse of that discretion. A district court abuses or exceeds the discretion accorded to it when (1) its decision rests on an error of law (such as application of the wrong legal principle) or a clearly erroneous factual finding, or (2) its decision—though not necessarily the product of a legal error or a clearly erroneous factual finding—cannot be located within the range of permissible decisions. . . . A district court must give 'some deference' to a master's recommendation where the master has 'direct and extensive' knowledge about the particular circumstances of a given case. A district court that extends some deference to the master will consider his recommendation and the factors influencing it, but will not regard the recommendation as the alpha and omega of the analysis. . . . The Federal Rules of Civil Procedure expressly permit a district court to 'modify' a special master's report. . . . [A] plaintiff may recover any necessary costs of response incurred consistent with the national contingency plan. . . . [CERCLA] does not limit courts to any particular list of factors. The court may consider the state of mind of the parties, their economic status, any contracts between them bearing on the subject, any traditional equitable defenses as mitigating factors and any other factors deemed appropriate to balance the equities in the totality of the circumstances."

Case Questions

1. Suppose the coalition sues the companies that transported the waste? Are they liable as PRPs? Why or why not?

2. Do you think that courts should have broad discretion when engaging in a Superfund allocation analysis? Why or why not?

property without knowledge of the contamination. The owner must submit evidence that she conducted *all appropriate inquiries* into the previous ownership, using a reasonable amount of investigation to determine whether any contamination was present. So long as the owner complies with land use restrictions, takes reasonable steps to limit the impact of the hazardous substances on the general public, and cooperates with government agencies, she may avoid cleanup liability under the statute.

Prospective Purchasers   In 2002, Congress enacted the Small Business Liability Relief Act,[15] which provides a defense to Superfund liability for a party that purchased the property *with knowledge* of the contamination. The statute provides for limited liability so long as the owner agrees to take reasonable steps to limit the impact of the contamination, prevent further contamination, and notify authorities of any imminent or actual pollutant release.

 Self-Check   PRP Liability

Who has PRP liability?

The EPA placed a parcel of land known as Noxious Flats on the NPL in 2009 due to contamination caused by chemicals from cleaning solvents and from lead paint. Using the information in the following table, determine whether each party has PRP liability:

Party	Relationship to Noxious Flats	Hazardous Substance Use
Richmond Industries	Owned the property from 1970 to 1979 and operated an industrial plant.	After use of industrial cleaning solvents, stored the used solvents in an underground tank.
Bright Paint Company	Leased the property from Richmond from 1979 to 1985.	Dumped paint production waste into a hole in the ground and buried it.
Warehouse Storage Inc.	Purchased the property from Richmond in 1986 without any environmental investigation; installed concrete over the entire property and built warehouse spaces for lease.	No contamination by Warehouse Storage. Richmond's underground tank ruptured in 1988 and caused groundwater contamination. Warehouse Storage had no knowledge of the rupture.
The Factory Restaurant	Leased the property from Warehouse Storage from 1995 to 2008; built an upscale restaurant as part of a community revitalization project to turn blighted industrial areas into retail and restaurant zones. Lessor hired an environmental service company to survey the property before signing the lease, and no contamination was detected.	No contamination.
First Neighborhood Bank	Foreclosed on Warehouse Storage Inc., which defaulted on its loan in 2008.	None.

Answers to this Self-Check are provided at the end of the chapter.

---

[15]42 U.S.C. § 9607(r).

Avoiding Environmental Liability in Land Acquisitions

PROBLEM *A land acquisition may result in Superfund liability for the purchasing business even if the acquirer did not contaminate the property.*

Suppose that Chef Kuo is looking for a new location for expanding her restaurant operations. She locates a potential property, but when visiting the site, Kuo notices that it is adjacent to inactive railroad tracks. In the past, Kuo recalls an article in the local newspaper that reported on some railroad yards in the area that were contaminated by a toxic substance called PCB that was buried beneath the tracks when they were put down many years ago. Kuo is convinced that this property is ideal for her newest restaurant but is concerned about any potential environmental liability. Yet, at this early stage of the acquisition, she does not wish to invest in an expensive assessment.

SOLUTION *Engage a qualified firm to perform an environmental transaction screen.*

When considering a property for acquisition or lease, a simple transaction screen can be conducted to provide the buyer with more data on potential environmental problems with the property. Prior to signing any agreement committing to the purchase, Kuo should engage an environmental services consulting firm to conduct a transaction screen. This screen (also called an *Environmental Phase I*) is a minimal, relatively inexpensive assessment that typically consists of (1) record checks for ownership, code violations, or environmental agency actions; (2) an interview with the current site owner; and (3) a site visit for obvious signs of potential environmental liability (such as an aboveground port for an underground tank). In Kuo's case, if the transaction screen indicates potential contamination, Kuo may choose either to abandon the transaction entirely and continue her search or to invest more money in further assessments (Phase II and Phase III) that include soil and groundwater testing to determine the presence of contamination and, if necessary, recommend a process for remediation of the contamination. These advanced assessments are much more expensive, so Kuo will have to decide if the costs of assessment (and possible remediation) are sufficiently equal to the benefits of putting her restaurant on that site.

It is also important for business owners and managers to be sure that the firms they are hiring are *qualified* within the meaning of federal and state statutory definitions. In order to assert an innocent purchaser defense, the company must have relied on the report of a qualified environmental professional. Federal and state statutes lay out the standards for qualification. To qualify under the EPA standards, an environmental professional must (1) be certified by the federal government to perform environmental inspections, (2) be a licensed engineer or geologist, (3) have at least a bachelor's-degree level of education, and (4) have 10 years of relevant work experience.

CONCEPT SUMMARY Superfund Response

- If there is an immediate threat of hazardous materials release, the Superfund law requires immediate *removal* efforts. Local authorities respond pursuant to their Superfund emergency plan.
- In cases of long-term contamination of a land or water site, the Superfund law requires the EPA to determine suitability for placement on the National Priorities List (NPL).
- For sites listed on the NPL, government authorities then investigate the site's chain of ownership to determine any principally responsible parties (PRPs) and assess cleanup alternatives.

(continued)

- Government officials negotiate with PRPs to determine contributions for cleanup. If an agreement is reached, the parties enter into a binding agreement called a consent decree. If the negotiations fail, the government typically files a Superfund lawsuit to collect cleanup costs from PRPs.

Table 19.1 sets out the major environmental laws.

TABLE 19.1 Major Environmental Laws	
National Environmental Policy Act (NEPA) of 1969	Establishes a process that must be followed by federal agencies when making decisions that may reasonably impact the environment or when federal funding is involved.
Clean Air Act (most recently amended in 1997)	Improves outdoor air quality based on National Ambient Air Quality Standards that set permissible levels of certain air pollutants. The law focuses on pollution from both stationary sources (manufacturing plants) and mobile sources (motor vehicles).
Clean Water Act	Sets water quality standards and regulates disposal of pollutants into public waterways.
Resource Conservation and Recovery Act (RCRA)	Regulates *active and future facilities* that produce solid waste and/or hazardous materials; uses a "cradle-to-grave" procedure that includes handling regulations for waste from its origins to its transportation, treatment, storage, and disposal.
Comprehensive Environmental Response Compensation and Liability Act (CERCLA), commonly referred to as *Superfund*	Addresses hazardous substance cleanup in two ways: (1) removal (for imminent releases) and (2) remedial (for long-term cleanup projects).

WILDLIFE PROTECTION

Wildlife and aquatic life are protected by a series of specialized federal statutes, including the Marine Mammal Protection Act and the Migratory Bird Conservation Act. These laws impact industries such as fisheries or logging because they restrict certain activities even on private lands to meet the objective of protecting wildlife. Perhaps the most important wildlife protection is the **Endangered Species Act (ESA).**[16] The ESA is administered jointly by agencies in the U.S. Department of Commerce and the U.S. Department of the Interior.

---

[16]16 U.S.C. § 1531.

Nuisance p. 537   A common law legal action for redressing harm arising from the misuse of one's property that is based on the aggrieved party's right to enjoy his property without interference from a third party.

Citizen suit provisions p. 539   Laws that authorize private individuals or watchdog groups to file environmental enforcement lawsuits.

National Environmental Policy Act (NEPA) p. 539   Federal legislation enacted in 1969 that established a process federal agencies must follow when making decisions that have the potential to have a significant impact on the environment.

Clean Air Act (CAA) p. 542   Federal legislation enacted in 1963 to improve, strengthen, and accelerate programs for the prevention and abatement of air pollution; focuses on stationary and mobile sources in the United States.

Stationary sources of air pollution p. 542   Fixed-site emitters of air pollutants fossil-fueled power plants, petroleum refineries, petrochemical plants, food processing plants, and other industrial sources.

Mobile sources of air pollution p. 542   Nonstationary sources of air pollutants automobiles, buses, trucks, ships, trains, aircraft, and various other vehicles.

State Implementation Plan (SIP) p. 542   A mandated state plan for complying with the federal Clean Air Act that is submitted to the Environmental Protection Agency; consists of a collection of regulations that help to achieve a reduction in pollution.

Operating permits p. 542   Licenses issued by authorities to existing stationary sources that permit pollution emission at certain levels.

Market-based approach p. 542   An approach to pollution control that gives businesses a choice of methods based on economic incentives for complying with pollution standards; instituted by the 1990 amendments to the Clean Air Act.

Clean Water Act (CWA) p. 545   Federal legislation that regulates water quality standards and aims to stem water pollution from industrial, municipal, and agricultaral sources; implemented and enforced by the EPA.

Oil Pollution Act (OPA) p. 546   Federal legislation enacted in 1990 to streamline and strengthen the Environmental Protection Agency's ability to prevent and respond to catastrophic oil spills in water sources.

Safe Drinking Water Act (SDWA) p. 547   Federal legislation that sets minimum quality and safety standards for every public water system and every source of drinking water in the United States.

Resource Conservation and Recovery Act (RCRA) p. 549   Federal legislation enacted in 1976 to regulate active and future facilities that produce solid waste and/or hazardous materials.

Toxic Substances Control Act (TSCA) p. 549   Federal legislation that gives the Environmental Protection Agency jurisdiction to control risks that may be posed by the manufacturing, processing, using, and disposing of chemical compounds.

Comprehensive Environmental Response Compensation and Liability Act (CERCLA) p. 550   Federal legislation enacted in 1980 to create a tax on the chemical and petroleum industries and provide broad federal authority to respond directly to releases or threatened releases of hazardous substances that may endanger public health or the environment. Also called *Superfund.*

Superfund p. 550   Another name for the CERCLA, derived from that act's main provisions whereby cleanup operations for abandoned toxic waste sites are to be funded by a self-sustaining quasi-escrow fund to be administered by the federal government.

Superfund Amendments and Reauthorization Act (SARA) p. 550   A 1986 amendment to the CERCLA that requires that states establish emergency response commissions to draft emergency procedures for a hazardous chemical accident and implement them in the event of such an accident; requires that businesses disclose the presence of certain chemicals within a community; and imposes an obligation on businesses to notify authorities of any spills or discharges of hazardous materials.

Removal p. 551   Under the Superfund law, an approach to handling hazardous substance cleanup whereby authorizization is given for actions to address releases or imminent releases of hazardous materials.

Remedial p. 551   Under the Superfund law, an approach to handling hazardous substance cleanup whereby the Environmental Protection Agency identifies the most hazardous waste sites and generates a National Priorities List.

Endangered Species Act (ESA) p. 556   Federal legislation enacted in 1973 that established a procedure for identifying imperiled species and preserving them from extinction.

Regional Cuisine Publications Corporation (RCPC) is the publisher of a monthly magazine that features recipes and articles on culinary traditions from various regions in the United States. RCPC began in the South and expanded into the mid-Atlantic and New England markets in the last 10 years. Part of RCPC's business model was that the actual name of the magazine distributed in a certain region took on that region's name (*Southern Cuisine, New England Cuisine,* etc.). Although RCPC began its business by contracting with outside vendors that supplied magazine-quality paper, as it expanded circulation, RCPC sought to reduce its rising paper costs by producing its own paper in-house. RCPC's management has located a small production facility that had been owned by Paper Production Inc. since 1950. RCPC begins to consider purchasing the facility and property.

1. In investigating the purchase of the facility, what environmental laws will RCPC need to be aware of? In what way could environmental regulation affect the costs of the transaction?

2. Assume that the facility emits certain pollutants into the air. RCPC wishes to partially reconstruct the facility after its purchase for purposes of being able to run the facility for longer periods of time. Does this trigger any regulatory concerns?

3. Suppose that the facility emits more of a certain pollutant than permitted by the EPA standards. What are RCPC's options under the CAA's market-based approach?

4. Assume that the facility discharges waste from the paper production process into an adjoining river and, because Paper Production was struggling financially, the company never upgraded its technology. If RCPC purchases the facility, will it be required to upgrade the waste discharge technology under the Clean Water Act? What is the standard set by the CWA for upgrading technology?

5. What type of precautionary measures should RCPC's management take to be sure to limit potential Superfund liability prior to any purchase of the site?

Assume that, in the Theory to Practice problem, RCPC wishes to pursue negotiations for the purchase of the facility and that you are a junior manager at RCPC. You receive the following e-mail from your senior manager:

> We are pursuing the purchase of the paper facility, but we are concerned about environmental liability due to potential groundwater contamination. Please write a two- to three-page memorandum that recommends two environmental consulting firms in the area to conduct an assessment. We want to be sure that these firms are qualified as defined by the law.

Research (1) what qualifications are required by our state environmental agency or the EPA, (2) determine which firms in our area are qualified, and (3) provide a brief description in your memorandum of each firm based on its website.

After rereading the Solutions for Managers feature in this chapter, write a two- to three-page memorandum in response to your senior manager's request. Note that a link to EPA's standards (as well as a sample answer to this Manager's Challenge) may be found on this textbook's website at www.mhhe.com/melvinleb2e.

CLEAN WATER ACT

El Paso Gold Mines owns 100 acres of land bought in 1968 near Cripple Creek, Colorado. Though El Paso did not engage in mining activity on the land, the land contained a collapsed mine shaft built in 1910. The shaft is connected to a 6-mile-long drainage tunnel that is connected to other old mines draining into Cripple Creek. A citizens' watchdog group, the Sierra Club, brought suit alleging that El Paso violated the Clean Water Act by discharging pollutants (zinc and manganese) from a source, the mine shaft, into the creek without a discharge permit.

CASE QUESTIONS

1. Does the Sierra Club have an actionable claim under the Clean Water Act? Why or why not?
2. If El Paso wanted to use the land for mining activity, would the company be required to obtain a permit? If so, what would need to be done in order to obtain the permit?

SUPERFUND

The Paoli Rail Yard covers about 30 acres in Paoli, Pennsylvania, and consists of an electric train repair facility owned by Amtrak and operated by Philadelphia-based Southeastern Pennsylvania Transportation Authority (SEPTA). Prior to Amtrak's acquisition of the property, the site was owned by the Pennsylvania Railroad Company from 1939 until 1967, Penn Central Transportation until 1976, and Conrail until 1982. All previous owners are now defunct. In 1979, a toxic chemical known as PCB was discovered in the rail yard, and the EPA declared the yard a Superfund site. The EPA then began the remedial enforcement process and brought an action against potentially responsible parties.

CASE QUESTIONS

1. Do any of the prior owners of the rail yard have PRP liability?
2. Could SEPTA or Amtrak have taken action to avoid liability? Explain.

RESOURCE CONSERVATION AND RECOVERY ACT

Paxton, a proprietor, intended to set up a recycling facility on one of his properties. He then contracted with Wal-Mart to recycle or dispose of various lamps and bulbs that contained spent mercury and other products that contained lead. Instead of recycling the items, Paxton crushed or shredded them and left them piled on the property. The state determined that there were hazardous waste violations, and it filed suit.

CASE QUESTIONS

1. What federal statute(s) could apply to this case? Explain.
2. Citing the RCRA "cradle-to-grave" procedure, do you think Wal-Mart was contributory in violation of the statute? Why or why not?

CASE SUMMARY 19.4 :: Beverly E. Black and James A. Black v. George Weston & Stroehmann Bakeries, Inc., U.S. Dist. Ct. (W.D.N.Y. 2008)

CLEAN AIR ACT

Black, a realtor, owned adjacent rental properties in a New York neighborhood. On the same block, Stroehmann Bakeries owned and operated a bakery. Black alleged that the bakery had emitted "noxious discharges" and that these emissions had coated his properties with mold and mold residue. As a result, Black's properties were discolored, causing a loss of rental income and resale value. An investigation was conducted, and the agency concluded that the bakery was the source of the mold growth found on Black's properties.

CASE QUESTIONS

1. What standard was used to determine whether or not the discharges constituted a violation of the Clean Air Act?
2. What common law doctrine could Black have possibly pursued in an attempt to compel Stroehmann to cease polluting?

CITIZEN SUITS

In the late 1990s, the city of New York confronted growing concerns surrounding the mosquito-borne West Nile virus by implementing an aerial and ground spraying program. The program consisted of spray planes and trucks that would douse the city with malathion, a controversial neurotoxin pesticide, in an attempt to eradicate mosquitoes carrying the potentially fatal virus. The plan was controversial because of the exposure of the general public to the potentially hazardous pesticide. The No Spray Coalition, a group of local organizations and individuals, filed suit to halt the insecticide spraying, alleging that such spraying violated the Clean Water Act.

CASE QUESTIONS

1. What would No Spray have to prove in order to have an actionable claim under the CWA?
2. Explain the significance of citizen suit provisions and watchdog groups in the context of this case.

Self-Check **ANSWERS**

PRP Liability

1. *Richmond Industries* is liable as a PRP because it owned the plant at the time of disposal of the cleaning solvents in the tank. Note that, under Superfund, it is *irrelevant* that the disposal was made prior to the Superfund law's enactment (Superfund is retroactive) and that no actual *contamination* took place while Richmond owned the parcel.

2. *Bright Paint* is liable as a PRP. Same rationale as above.

3. *Warehouse Storage Inc.* is probably not liable as a PRP. No disposal took place under its ownership. The contamination occurred under its ownership, but Warehouse never disposed of any solid waste or hazardous materials.

4. *The Factory Restaurant* has no liability as a disposer of materials. If the EPA placed Noxious Flats on the NPL while The Factory Restaurant was operating on the site, the business is still shielded from liability under the Superfund as an innocent lessor because it performed an environmental assessment prior to entering into the lease.

5. *First Neighborhood Bank* has no liability as a PRP. The bank is shielded because it is a secured creditor that did not actively participate in ownership or operation prior to the foreclosure.

20

CHAPTER

Antitrust and Regulation of Competition

learning **objectives**

After studying this chapter, students who have mastered the material will be able to:

20-1 Articulate the fundamental purpose and source of law for antitrust regulation.

20-2 Identify the main federal statutes in antitrust law.

20-3 Distinguish and explain the differences between the per se standard and the rule of reason standard.

20-4 List and articulate the primary ways that businesses use horizontal and vertical restraints of trade.

20-5 Recognize when a business has achieved a monopoly and explain the restrictions on a monopoly business under antitrust law.

20-6 Explain why the *U.S. v. Microsoft* case is an important part of antitrust law.

20-7 Articulate the role of more modern antitrust statutes in regulating competition.

ven in a free market economy, business owners and managers depend on certain regulation of competition in the marketplace. This regulation allows for innovation and entrepreneurial effort to thrive without the threat of being eliminated from the marketplace by larger competitors that have already established a market share. The law also promotes competition among businesses, which allows consumers to receive the benefits of competitive pricing. This chapter covers regulation of competition, which is primarily accomplished through antitrust laws enforced by the federal government. Specifically, students will learn:

- The background, scope, and purpose of laws that regulate competition.
- The statutory model for antitrust laws.
- How antitrust laws are applied to various anticompetitive actions by businesses.

BACKGROUND, PURPOSE, AND SOURCE OF ANTITRUST LAW   LO 20-1

The purposes of antitrust law are to prevent, punish, and deter certain anticompetitive conduct and unfair business practices. Original notions of antitrust law come from the shifting of the U.S. economy from predominantly family agriculture and small merchants into the Industrial Revolution era, in which the historically famous robber barons of the late

19th century accumulated and wielded such market power that other companies could not compete on a level playing field. These business entities were known as *trusts* (the most famous being Rockefeller's Standard Oil Trust) and ultimately resulted in a few companies being able to manipulate prices, thereby causing limited choices and high prices for consumers. President Theodore Roosevelt, the renowned trustbuster, led a movement that resulted, eventually, in federal regulation of trusts that were engaged in anticompetitive behavior. Antitrust laws are exclusively federal statutes, and the agencies charged with enforcement of these laws are the Department of Justice (U.S. Attorney's Office) and the Federal Trade Commission. Violators of antitrust laws are subject to both *civil penalties* and *criminal sanctions,* including incarceration.

Modern-day antitrust enforcement is concerned primarily with protecting the *competitive process* rather than protecting individual competitor companies. The underlying theory is that protection of this process will ultimately benefit consumers.

FEDERAL STATUTES AND ENFORCEMENT   LO 20-2

The statutory scheme of federal antitrust law is actually a combination of five different laws. The **Sherman Act**[1] (1890) is the centerpiece of antitrust

---

[1] 15 U.S.C. §§ 1–7.

law and it prohibits contracts, combinations, and conspiracies in restraint of trade and also prohibits monopolization. The **Clayton Act,**[2] enacted in 1914 and significantly amended in 1936 by the **Robinson-Patman Act** and in 1950 by the **Celler-Kefauver Antimerger Act,** deals with specific types of restraints, including exclusive dealing arrangements, tie-in sales, price discrimination, mergers and acquisitions, and interlocking directorates. These restraints are covered in detail later in this chapter.

Both the U.S. Department of Justice and the Federal Trade Commission (FTC) enforce various antitrust laws. The **Federal Trade Commission Act**[3] of 1914, administered solely by the FTC, is a catchall enactment that has been construed as including all the prohibitions of the other antitrust laws.

In addition to providing for government enforcement of antitrust statutes, the laws also permit an aggrieved party to file a private enforcement action against an alleged antitrust violator. Some antitrust statutes allow a party that suffered damages by virtue of any antitrust violation the right to a private suit in the federal courts for *triple* the damages sustained plus reasonable attorney fees and a court order restraining future violations. These statutes are intended to provide a significant financial deterrent to antitrust infraction and to compensate parties injured through anticompetitive behavior.

> **KEY** POINT
>
> Antitrust matters are covered by federal law, with the Sherman Act as the primary governing statute.

LO 20-3   SHERMAN ANTITRUST ACT

Thought of as the central piece of federal antitrust law, the Sherman Act is divided into two parts. First, the act provides prohibitions against restraints of trade. The Sherman Act prohibits "[e]very contract, combination in the form of trust or otherwise, or conspiracy, in restraint of trade or commerce."[4] The second part of the act covers monopolization. The Sherman Act provides a remedy against "[e]very person who shall monopolize, or attempt to monopolize . . . any part of the trade or commerce among the several States."[5] This prohibition does not make a monopoly illegal automatically. Only a monopoly that has been *acquired* or *maintained* through prohibited conduct is illegal. The Sherman Act has both civil and criminal penalties.

To understand the distinction between the sections, consider the difference between single-firm conduct (only one business engaged in a certain transaction or behavior) and multifirm conduct (more than one business engaged in a certain transaction or behavior). Multifirm conduct tends to be seen as more likely than single-firm conduct to have an anticompetitive effect and is regulated under Section 1 of the act. Single-firm conduct is less likely to be considered as restraining trade, but under certain circumstances, for example, using market domination to eliminate a competitor, it is covered by Section 2 of the act.

Per Se Standard versus Rule of Reason Standard

While the sweeping language of the Sherman Act, taken literally, could reasonably be read as a blanket ban on virtually every commercial agreement, the U.S. Supreme Court has long held that the statute applies only to those parties who have acted in some *unreasonable manner* that resulted in an identifiable anticompetitive behavior. The Court has developed two standards for use by federal courts in deciding whether or not a certain transaction or action violates the Sherman Act: the **per se standard** and

---

[2]15 U.S.C. §§ 12–27.

[3]15 U.S.C. §§ 41–58.

[4]15 U.S.C. § 1.

[5]15 U.S.C. § 2.

The Sherman Act was created to limit the ability of corporate giants such as Standard Oil Trust, founded by John Rockefeller (left), to monopolize markets and control major industries. President Theodore Roosevelt, depicted in an editorial cartoon of the era (right), became known as the nation's trustbuster.

the **rule of reason standard.** Some concerted activities are so blatantly anticompetitive that they are considered *per se* violations. Collusion among competitors to set artificially high prices—a practice known as *price-fixing*—is a clear example of a per se violation. The per se standard has been developed into a comparatively complicated body of law and tests for federal courts to apply. But the case law still gives business owners and managers relatively clear guidance on what constitutes blatant violations of the Sherman Act that have no competitive justification. In effect, the per se rule means that if a company has committed a per se violation of the act, as articulated in the body of case law, the violator has no defense. The per se standard also promotes more consistent enforcement by regulatory authorities.

Legal Speak ›))
Per Se A Latin term literally meaning "of, in, or by itself," that is, without any additional facts needed to prove a point.

For example, suppose that SportCo operates a chain of sporting goods stores in the southeastern United States. SportCo's president contacts the owner of Main Street Athletic Gear, and the two agree not to undercut each other on the price of baseballs. They set the price at 30 percent higher than fair market value. These two have colluded against consumers by fixing an artificially high price for a product. Because the SportCo-Main Street agreement is blatantly anticompetitive, it is a per se violation of the Sherman Act.

Rule of Reason

Despite the substantial body of case law that makes up the various rules used in applying the per se standard, the economic complexities of the global business community, technology, and individual industry practices are too unique to be assessed using a strict per se standard. Recognizing the need to assess a certain transaction's impact on the broader

FIGURE 20.1

Chain of
Commercial
Supply

marketplace, the Court developed a second standard known as the *rule of reason.* Even if a transaction is not considered a per se violation, the action or transaction in question must also meet the alternate standard. The rule of reason requires that a fact finder (judge or jury) embark on an examination into market complexities and industry practices in order to determine whether or not the parties' actions violate the Sherman Act. Under this standard, a business alleged to have committed a violation may offer evidence that its actions were reasonable because they were justified and necessitated by economic conditions. In essence, the rule of reason contemplates a scale in which the court weighs any anticompetitive harm suffered against marketwide benefits of the actions. Through this examination, a court may determine whether such justification is merely a *pretext* for advancement of the violator's economic benefit or whether, in fact, the economic benefits outweigh the burdens.

For instance, in our SportCo-Main Street example discussed earlier, suppose that instead of agreeing to set a price, the president of SportCo offered to lead efforts to form Retail Business Association (RBA) with Main Street and other area retailers for the purpose of sharing ideas, information, and data. Depending on the form and content of the information sharing, the RBA may be a violation of antitrust laws. However, RBA would argue that the rule of reason (not per se) should apply, and the association would have to offer legitimate business reasons and economic justifications. If a court finds that any anticompetitive harm caused by RBA is outweighed by marketwide *benefits* of its actions, RBA's formation does not violate the Sherman Act.

LO 20-4

Per Se Sherman Act Violations: Restraints

The U.S. Supreme Court and other federal appellate courts have developed a body of case law that deems certain actions or transactions as per se violations of the Sherman Act. Certain per se violations arise through the use of **horizontal restraints.** In a horizontal restraint of trade, one company partners with a *competing* company (i.e., one located horizontally on the chain of commercial supply, such as a competing retailer or competing manufacturer) to take action resulting in the elimination or reduction of competition from other competitors. Businesses may also commit a per se violation of the Sherman Act through use of a **vertical restraint.** In this type of restraint of trade, one company colludes with another company (other than a competitor) along the chain of commercial supply (see Figure 20.1), such as a manufacturer colluding with a retailer on the price of a product.

Horizontal Restraints

Although any concerted agreement among competitors to reduce competition or attempt to manipulate the competitive market is a horizontal restraint and a per se violation of antitrust law, the most common types of prohibited horizontal restraints are horizontal price-fixing, allocation of markets or customers, and boycotts.

Meeting of the Minds   One crucial component of a horizontal restraint is some meeting of the minds among the parties about the restraint. The statute requires the conspiring parties to *agree* to and then commit an *overt act.* As one would imagine, any illegal agreement is not likely to be explicit (or certainly not in writing), so courts have permitted proof of meeting of the minds to be satisfied through *circumstantial* evidence regarding the timing of any communication between the parties and their subsequent restraining actions.

In one of the most famous essays in the history of economic thought, *The Wealth of Nations,* Adam Smith wrote in 1766 that "people in the same trade seldom meet together even for merriment or diversity, but the conversation ends in a conspiracy against the public or in some contrivance to raise prices." This famous quote was used by prosecutors in a high-profile antitrust case against Alfred Taubman, the chairman of the well-known auction firm Sotheby's Holding, Inc., and Sir Anthony Tennant, chief executive of Christie's International. In the case, no direct evidence (such as a witness) of the agreement existed, but prosecutors used business calendars and other data to build a timeline and alleged that the two men met on 12 occasions and then engaged in an unusual course of action concerning policies on commissions that each firm followed after the last of the 12 meetings. Both executives were convicted in December 2001.

Price-Fixing   Any agreement by competitors to fix the price for buying or selling a particular good or any agreement by competitors to fix the quantity of goods to be produced, offered for sale, or bought is a per se violation of the Sherman Act. For example, suppose NewCo and OldCo are competitors in the market selling computer chips. They may not agree to set the price at $250 per package of 50. Doing so would be a barefaced attempt to increase their profits by leaving the consumer with no options. Nor may they agree to limit the production or sale of computer chips to 100,000 per month in order to manipulate the supply and demand curve that is essential to a market economy.

There are, of course, some instances in which conduct by competitors with respect to pricing policies does not constitute price-fixing. In some industries, price-leading (cutting or increasing prices based on the actions of a competitor) is commonplace. Although this may appear to be price-fixing, the element of agreement is usually not satisfied because the competitors are not taking these actions in concert. For example, suppose that Economy Jet begins to cut its airfare on the route from Boston to New York City. It is almost inevitable that all other airlines would cut their fares on that route as well. If Economy Jet cuts its price, there can be no legitimate conclusion that the parties intended to act to restrain competition.

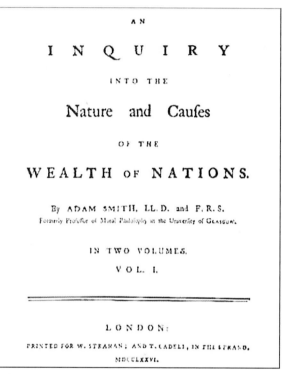

Adam Smith's *The Wealth of Nations* is often cited in support of the notion that frequent meetings and conversations by competitors are circumstantial evidence of anticompetitive collusion.

In the past decade, the U.S. Supreme Court has narrowed the use of the per se standard and expanded the use of the rule of reason analysis in certain cases of horizontal price-fixing. In Case 20.1, the Court used the rule of reason standard in evaluating a joint venture alleged to have engaged in price-fixing.

Market Allocation   Agreements among competitors dividing markets by territory or by customers are anticompetitive and illegal per se. Such arrangements are blatantly restrictive because they leave no room for competition of any kind. Thus, competing firms may not divide among themselves the geographic areas in which they sell, nor may they distribute customers or allocate the available market. All such understandings, whether direct or indirect, are unlawful.

Boycotts   When competing firms agree to a *concerted* refusal to deal with a third party (whether it be buying from or selling to the party), this may be considered a per se

FACT SUMMARY Historically, Texaco and Shell Oil have competed with one another in the global markets as refiners of crude oil and suppliers of gasoline to retail service stations. In 1998, the two companies formed a joint venture, Equilon, to consolidate their operations in the western United States. Texaco and Shell agreed to share expenses and profits from the jointly controlled new entity. Although the Equilon entity engaged in the refinement of crude oil into gasoline, the actual end product was sold to retailers under the brand names of Texaco and Shell at a mutually agreed-upon price.

The retailers of Texaco and Shell products brought a class action lawsuit against Texaco and Shell, alleging that creating the joint venture was a per se violation of the Sherman Act because it ended any price competition between the two and amounted to a horizontal price-fixing scheme.

SYNOPSIS OF DECISION AND OPINION The U.S. Supreme Court ruled in favor of Texaco and Shell, holding that the rule of reason standard should apply. The Court reasoned that per se liability applies only to agreements that are so plainly anticompetitive that no study of the industry is needed to establish their illegality. In this case, the market analysis was relevant.

The Court held that the joint venture agreement was *not* horizontal price-fixing because the challenged pricing policy was simply price-setting by a single entity, Equilon, and not a pricing agreement between competing entities with respect to their competing products.

WORDS OF THE COURT: Narrow Per Se Rules "[T]his Court has long recognized that Congress intended to outlaw only unreasonable restraints. Instead, this Court presumptively applies a rule of reason analysis, under which antitrust plaintiffs must demonstrate that a particular contract or combination is in fact unreasonable and anticompetitive before it will be found unlawful. Per se liability is reserved for only those agreements that are so plainly anticompetitive that no elaborate study of the industry is needed to establish their illegality. Accordingly, we have expressed reluctance to adopt per se rules where the economic impact of certain practices is not immediately obvious."

Case Questions

1. Does this case mean that competitors may simply create a joint venture to avoid any liability for price-fixing?

2. Why did the retailers allege that forming this joint venture was anticompetitive behavior?

Sherman Act violation. Although the U.S. Supreme Court has narrowed this doctrine and has applied the rule of reason in some limited cases, a concerted agreement to boycott a supplier or consumer group is still a very risky proposition. In *United States v. Colgate,* decided in 1919, the U.S. Supreme Court held that a *unilateral* boycott does not fall under the Sherman Act. However, even the so-called *Colgate* doctrine has been narrowed. In order to pass anticompetitive muster, the boycott must be truly unilateral with no other party having direct or indirect involvement.

 Self-Check   Horizontal Restraint

What type of horizontal restraint is at issue?

1. Two gasoline service stations are located on opposite sides of the same street. The two owners agree not to undercut each other on gas prices.

2. Two suppliers agree not to sell their product to a certain retailer because they believe that the retailer is undercutting other larger retailers in price and that this has impacted the larger retailers' purchases from the two suppliers.

3. Two retailers of active-wear clothing agree that one will sell only in the Miami market and the other only in the Atlanta market.

Answers to this Self-Check are provided at the end of the chapter.

Vertical Restraints

Vertical price-fixing occurs when a seller attempts to control the resale price of a product at a lower level in the supply chain. Although concerted action or agreement between a manufacturer and a retailer to fix the price at the retail level is not considered a per se violation of the Sherman Act, courts apply a rule of reason analysis to determine whether any antitrust laws were violated. In the 2007 case of *Leegin Creative Leather Products v. PSKS, Inc.,*[6] the U.S. Supreme Court held that all vertical price restraints were now to be judged by the rule of reason. The case involved a manufacturer of leather apparel that would not sell its products to retailers that sold its apparel at a discount. When the manufacturer discovered that a retailer was discounting the leather apparel by 20 percent, the retailer was cut off from supply. The retailer sued the manufacturer, contending that its policies amounted to a vertical restraint. The trial and appellate courts applied the traditional per se analysis, but the U.S. Supreme Court reversed the decision and instituted a rule of reason policy for vertical price restraints after being convinced that such restraints can have pro-competitive effects.

Nonprice Restraints   The U.S. Supreme Court has applied the rule of reason to non-price vertical restraints since its 1977 landmark antitrust decision in *Continental T.V. v. GTE Sylvania.*[7] Vertical restraints that do not involve price-fixing generally involve some type of restraint on the distribution of a product in the marketplace. Although business entities have always had the right to *unilaterally* assign exclusive territories to their distributors and to limit the number of distributors that are authorized to sell their product in a specific geographic area, certain agreements between sellers and distributors relating to sales of a product outside the exclusive territory may give rise to an allegation of an unlawful vertical restraint. Such restraints are frequently an attempt to control the *intrabrand competition* (i.e., the setting of different prices by different distributors for the same product) of a seller's product among various distributors, with the intent of boosting the product's *interbrand competition* (i.e., its relative competitiveness with similar products made by other sellers). For example, Raleigh is the manufacturer of expensive watches and sells the products through both Connelly and Sicius as exclusive distributors. Raleigh's interest is in making sure that Connelly and Sicius don't compete with each other in the same geographic market (intrabrand competition) because Raleigh wants to be sure that the pricing for the watches is in line with the pricing and the market share of Raleigh's competing companies (interbrand competition). Therefore, Raleigh attempts to impose a restriction that limits its distributors to specific geographic territories and prohibits them from selling outside those territories. These restraints on Connelly and Sicius help ensure that Raleigh watches will continue to thrive in the marketplace. Any arrangement Raleigh makes with Connelly and Sicius is considered a vertical restraint. Because courts use the rule of reason standard for vertical restraints, Raleigh's plan could still survive judicial scrutiny if it was justified on the grounds that it does not have a negative impact on competition in the watch-manufacturing industry.

Tying Agreements   Tying agreements occur when a seller refuses to sell a certain product (the tying product) unless the buyer also purchases a different product (the tied product) from the seller. Typically, this occurs when a seller has a substantial share of the market for the tying product and is attempting to leverage the power of the tying product to gain market share for another of the seller's products. This tying arrangement model violates the Sherman Act. For example, Kahlo's firm has a substantial share of the cable modem market but has recently introduced a new brand of Ethernet cable (used to connect

---

[6]127 S. Ct. 2705 (2007).

[7]433 U.S. 36 (1977).

the cable modem to a computer). If Kahlo requires her distributors to purchase the Ethernet cable as a condition of the sale of the cable modems, she has used her market share to tie the cable modems to the Ethernet cable. Note also that tying arrangements may be a violation of the Clayton Act (discussed later in this chapter).

The most difficult question in analyzing a tying agreement is where to draw the line between legitimate parallel product enhancements and anticompetitive market manipulation. A producer of shoes is clearly entitled to "tie" the right shoe with the left shoe, but what about products that have separate, albeit related, functions? This problem has resulted in courts' developing a **soft per se analysis** for determining the legality of a tying arrangement. In *U.S. Steel v. Fortner Enterprises*,[8] the U.S. Supreme Court provided guidance for lower courts by setting out a four-part test. For a tying arrangement to be illegal, the government (or plaintiff) must show that (1) the agreement involves two separate and distinct items rather than integrated components of a larger product, service, or business system; (2) the tying product cannot be purchased unless the tied product is also purchased; (3) the seller has sufficient economic power in the market to appreciably restrain competition; and (4) a "not insubstantial" amount of commerce in the tied product is affected by the seller's tying agreement.

Criminal Liability

Antitrust violators are subject to criminal prosecution. The Antitrust Criminal Penalty Enhancement and Reform Act of 2004[9] enhanced penalties for violations of antitrust laws. The maximum fine for individuals was set at $1 million, and the maximum fine for corporations was raised to $100 million. The Sherman Act also provides for a prison sentence of up to 10 years for those convicted of willful antitrust violations.

CONCEPT SUMMARY Restraints of Trade

- Horizontal restraints (acting in concert with a competitor that is on same level of distribution) include:
    a. *Price-fixing:* Agreement between competitors to fix actual prices is generally illegal per se.
    b. *Market allocation:* Agreement between competitors to divide markets or geographic regions is illegal per se.
    c. *Boycotts:* Concerted refusal to sell or buy from an individual, firm, or group may be illegal per se or by the rule of reason, depending on the specific facts.
- Vertical restraints (acting in concert with another party on a different distributional level) include:
    a. *Vertical price-fixing.* Agreement between buyer and seller with respect to the price of resale of the product is judged by the rule of reason standard.
    b. *Exclusive selling, territorial, and dealing agreements.* Relationship between buyer and seller related to an exclusive franchise and/or a specified territory is governed by the rule of reason and the Clayton Act.
    c. *Tie-ins.* Sellers that tie a second product to the first product are acting illegally per se if the seller possesses sufficient market power to render the tie-in coercive.
- Antitrust laws also carry criminal penalties including fines and incarceration.

---

[8]429 U.S. 610 (1977).

[9]Pub. L. No. 108-257, 118 Stat. 661 (codified as amended in scattered sections of 15 U.S.C.).

ANTITRUST LAW AND PROFESSIONAL SPORTS

A recurring debate in antitrust law centers on whether professional sports leagues are legitimate joint ventures or whether the owners are a conspiracy to restrain trade. This includes the history of Major League Baseball's infamous exemption cases and the National Football League's attempts to offer exclusive contracts for merchandising.

Major League Baseball

The history of Major League Baseball's exemption from the Sherman Act dates back to a 1922 U.S. Supreme Court case in which the Court ruled that the business of putting on an "exhibition" of baseball did not involve interstate commerce and was therefore not subject to the provisions of the Sherman Act.[10] The Court reaffirmed the exemption in the 1952 case *Toolson v. New York Yankees*.[11] In Case 20.2, the Court reexamined its rulings on the exemption of Major League Baseball in one of the most famous cases in antitrust law.

CASE 20.2   Flood v. Kuhn, 407 U.S. 258 (1972)

FACT SUMMARY   Curt Flood was a professional baseball player who was traded by the St. Louis Cardinals to the Philadelphia Phillies. For a variety of reasons, Flood was unhappy with the trade; refused to report to his new team and was forfeiting a significant salary. Flood sent a letter to Kuhn, the commissioner of Major League Baseball, demanding free agency. Kuhn declined to grant Flood free agency on the basis of the "reserve clause" in Flood's contract. The reserve clause was a standard provision in every player's contract whereby the player agreed that upon the contract's expiration the rights to the player were retained by the team that originally signed him. As a practical matter, the clause allowed a team to retain the rights of a player indefinitely. Therefore, the clause prevented Flood from negotiating with another team and gave St. Louis the right to trade him to a new team or renew his contract. Flood sued Major League Baseball, contending that the reserve clauses in the contracts were illegal under the Sherman Act. Flood argued that the previous cases exempting baseball from antitrust laws should be reversed because modern-day baseball is now part of interstate commerce through radio and television broadcasts.

SYNOPSIS OF DECISION AND OPINION   The U.S. Supreme Court held for Kuhn and upheld the exemption primarily based on the doctrine of stare decisis. Although the Court acknowledged that it is reasonable to conclude that baseball is now engaged in interstate commerce, it did not reverse its earlier decisions because of what the Court concluded was Congress's "positive inaction" to the earlier decisions exempting Major League Baseball from the antitrust laws. The Court was unwilling to disturb 50 years of precedent when it was clear that Congress had adequate opportunity and yet did not act to introduce legislation intended to remediate the baseball exemption. The Court also made clear that no other professional sports could be considered exempt from antitrust law.

WORDS OF THE COURT: Congressional Silence "The Court has emphasized that since 1922 baseball, with full and continuing congressional awareness, has been allowed to develop and to expand unhindered by federal legislative action. Remedial legislation has been introduced repeatedly in Congress but none has ever been enacted. The Court, accordingly, has concluded that Congress as yet has had no intention to subject baseball's reserve system to the reach of the antitrust statutes. This, obviously, has been deemed to be something other than mere congressional silence and passivity."

Case Questions

1. Should stare decisis be such a powerful doctrine that it trumps modern societal realities (such as baseball's growing use of interstate commerce via radio and television)?

2. Do you agree that, as a public policy matter, Major League Baseball should have an exemption from antitrust laws? Why or why not?

---

[10]*Federal Baseball Club v. National League,* 259 U.S. 200 (1922).

[11]346 U.S. 356 (1953).

Although Flood lost his case before the Supreme Court, it inspired other players to seek free-agency status, and the availability of free agency in general became the norm in baseball over a period of two decades. The passage of the Curt Flood Act of 1998[12] added a new provision to existing antitrust statutes that applied only to professional baseball players and eliminated the broad antitrust exemption for baseball. Still, although it permitted players to bring an antitrust action against the league, the law was full of restrictions and limitations on when and how the players could pursue an antitrust claim (e.g., the suit cannot be related to franchise expansion or relocation). Some commentators have suggested that the law generated congressional boasting but did not have any significant impact on Major League Baseball's antitrust exemption.[13]

National Football League

Since the first challenge in 1957,[14] the U.S. Supreme Court has declined to provide the National Football League with a baseball-type exemption. In 2010, the Supreme Court gave its latest guidance on the topic in *American Needle, Inc. v. National Football League.*[15] The case involved the NFL's licensing contract for merchandising of its teams' logos for shirts, hats, sweatshirts, and other attire and memorabilia. Although the NFL had previously extended nonexclusive merchandise rights to multiple companies, in December 2000 the NFL changed course and granted an exclusive contract to Reebok to produce and sell trademarked merchandise for *all* of the league's 32 teams. One of the companies frozen out by the new arrangement, American Needle, Inc., sued the NFL, claiming that the Reebok agreement was a result of collusion between the 32 teams that amounted to an illegal conspiracy under the Sherman Act. The NFL argued that although the teams were separately owned and operated, the league itself was a single entity for purposes of merchandising and therefore was incapable of such a conspiracy and thus effectively exempt from Sherman Act liability. Although a federal appellate court ruled in favor of the NFL, the Supreme Court unanimously reversed the appellate court's decision and held in favor of American Needle. Using a rule of reason analysis, Justice John Paul Stevens, himself a former antitrust lawyer, wrote, "When teams license such property, they are not pursuing the common interests of the whole league, but, instead, the interests of each 'corporation itself.'" The Court ruled that although the NFL teams did have some common objectives, they were also competitors not only on the field but as corporations. The teams compete to attract fans, increase gate receipts, and secure contracts with management and player personnel. Therefore, the Court rejected the NFL's single-entity theory and held that the league was subject to the Sherman Act.

LO 20-5 # MONOPOLIZATION

A monopoly holder has inherent power in setting prices without any chance of losing market share due to competition. Antitrust laws designed to combat this problem are known as **structural-offense laws** because the offenses generally do not involve a behavioral aspect (such as price-fixing). Section 2 of the Sherman Act was designed to prevent business monopolies, but it does not *prohibit* a business entity from becoming a monopoly. Rather,

---

[12]15 U.S.C. § 26b (2006).

[13]For an excellent explanation and summary of commentary on the Curt Flood Act, see N. Grow, *Reevaluating the Curt Flood Act,* 87 Neb. L. Rev. 747 (2008).

[14]*Radovich v. National Football League,* 352 U.S. 445 (1957).

[15]130 S.Ct. 2201 (2010).

the statute outlaws *affirmative action* toward monopolizing or attempting to monopolize a part of trade or commerce. The Sherman Act also prohibits the use of *monopoly power* to create an anticompetitive market in a particular industry. In the landmark monopoly case *U.S. v. Grinnell*,[16] the U.S. Supreme Court defined monopolization as "the willful acquisition or maintenance of power in a relevant market as opposed to

growth as a consequence of superior product, business acumen or historical accident." Thus, for a business entity to violate Section 2 of the Sherman Act, it not only must possess monopoly power but also must have an overt intent to monopolize.

Monopoly Power

A business entity that has the power to fix prices or to exclude competitors in a given market is said to have monopoly power. The focus for determining whether or not an entity has monopoly power is the entity's share of the relevant market. Although the Court has not laid down a bright-line test for what percentage of market share is required for determining that a monopoly exists, firms that have had as little as 50 percent of the market have been found to have monopoly power. Courts may also look at other factors, such as the existence in the industry at issue of barriers to entry of new competitors, in their analysis.

The *Microsoft* Case

LO 20-6

One of the most famous monopoly cases was *U.S. v. Microsoft,* in which the federal government sued Microsoft for anticompetitive behavior in the development and distribution of its Internet browser software called Explorer. The government alleged that Microsoft used its monopoly in the computer operating system market to eliminate competition from a more popular Internet browser, called Navigator, sold by Netscape. The trial court ruled against Microsoft and ordered the radical remedy of requiring Microsoft to reorganize its operating system entity separate and apart from its entity responsible for Explorer.

On appeal, the D.C. Circuit Court of Appeals issued an opinion that affirmed much of the trial court's decision but reversed some key rulings as well. Most significantly, the appellate court vacated the order that required the company to break apart. While the court affirmed the finding by the trial court that Microsoft fundamentally employed illegal anticompetitive means to maintain and further its monopoly of the operating system market, the court reversed and remanded for reconsideration the finding that Microsoft illegally attempted to monopolize the browser market, ruling that the appropriate standard was the rule of reason analysis.[17]

The Consent Order At the same time, a number of individual states and companies that had been damaged by Microsoft's actions, such as Sun Microsystems, were also suing Microsoft. However, before the new trial, the Department of Justice and many of the states came to terms and settled the case by entering into a consent order. The order required Microsoft to provide competitors with the detailed technical information needed to make competing products, such as e-mail and multimedia players, work seamlessly with its Windows operating system. Microsoft also agreed to make Windows available under a standard licensing agreement (without any tying product) to computer manufacturers.

In 2002, U.S. District Judge Colleen Kollar-Kotelly approved the settlement, ruling that the consent order was in the public interest and rejecting arguments by some states that the

Legal Speak ⟨))
Consent Order An agreement between the government and a party that spells out detailed conditions and compliance measures that the party agrees to take in exchange for the government's not pursuing a court action.

---

[16]384 U.S. 563 (1966).

[17]*U.S. v. Microsoft,* 253 F.3d 34 (D.C. Cir. 2001).

order wasn't tough enough on Microsoft. This ruling was widely viewed as a victory for Microsoft, and, once their appeal to a higher court failed, the states ended their legal battle against the software giant.

Intent to Monopolize

Once a court has determined that a particular business entity holds monopoly power, the next question centers on the entity's willful intent to acquire or maintain the monopoly. This analysis requires a court to examine whether or not the alleged monopolizer has engaged in a course of conduct that would reasonably lead one to conclude that the entity has purposefully furthered or attempted to maintain monopoly power. It is a difficult standard to spell out because each case and each industry have their own complexities. However, it is important to note that the courts have not required a showing that the entity engaged in predatory practices against a competitor (although this would clearly be a sign of intent to maintain or expand a monopoly) in order to have liability under the Sherman Act. For example, an appellate court has held that a national aluminum manufacturer and distributor violated Section 2 of the Sherman Act simply by acquiring every new opportunity relating to the production or marketing of aluminum.

Attempted Monopolization

Because actual monopoly power is relatively rare, the Sherman Act also prohibits *attempts* by a business to gain monopoly power—that is, a business entity that does not yet have monopoly power pursues an anticompetitive course of conduct designed to achieve it. The analysis of attempted monopolization focuses on a three-part test. First, the entity must have had a demonstrable and specific intent to achieve a monopoly. Second, the entity must have acted in an anticompetitive manner designed to injure its actual or potential competition. Third, there must exist a dangerous probability that monopoly power would in fact be achieved.

CLAYTON ACT

The Clayton Act (and its amendments) curb certain anticompetitive practices that are not specifically covered by the Sherman Act. Congress clearly intended the Clayton Act to be a vehicle for attacking practices that monopolists had historically used to create monopoly power. As a result, the act is designed as a preventive statute. Both the Department of Justice and the Federal Trade Commission enforce the Clayton Act.

Tying Arrangements and Exclusive Dealing

One important provision of the Clayton Act prohibits tying arrangements and exclusive dealing agreements involving the sale or leasing of *commodities*. Any agreement that involves services, real estate, or intangible property must be attacked under the Sherman Act. The tying arrangement model discussed earlier in this chapter in the context of the Sherman Act is the same model that is covered by the Clayton Act. Any tying arrangement that requires a buyer to purchase one product (the tied product) as a condition of buying another product (the tying product) from the same seller is considered anticompetitive. Some courts have held that the standard for finding an antitrust violation under the Clayton Act is less rigorous than that required under the Sherman Act. These courts have held that the proof of the seller's economic power in the market, necessary to establish a Sherman Act violation, is *not* required for a Clayton Act tying violation.

Exclusive dealing agreements are also covered in Section 3 of the Clayton Act. As discussed earlier in this chapter, an exclusive dealing agreement (such as a franchise) is a form of vertical restraint. Such agreements fall under the Clayton Act because they are arrangements between buyers and sellers in which the buyer agrees to handle one seller's product exclusively or to purchase its entire product line from the same seller. Not all such arrangements violate the Clayton Act (franchise agreements, for example, are exclusive dealing arrangements that don't violate antitrust laws). Only agreements that may "substantially lessen the competition or tend to create a monopoly" violate the act.

Mergers and Acquisitions

Historically, a business entity could gain monopoly power by merging with a competitor or acquiring the competitor through a buyout. The Clayton Act was designed to prevent this monopoly strategy. The act prohibits business entities from acquiring the stock or assets of their competitors when the action will substantially lessen competition or tend to create a monopoly.

FEDERAL TRADE COMMISSION ACT

In the same year that the Clayton Act was passed, Congress also broadened antitrust coverage through the Federal Trade Commission Act (FTCA). The law is designed as a catchall statute that prohibits all unfair and deceptive methods of competition. Any anticompetitive conduct that falls outside the scope of other antitrust laws may still violate the FTCA. The law also gives broad powers to the Federal Trade Commission to investigate any complaints or instances of unfair competition.

Search Bias: FTC Investigates Google

Because the FTCA is so broad, the FTC often uses it when the agency is investigating a case in which the facts are not yet fully developed. The FTC recently used its powers under the FTCA to launch an investigation into Google's content practices. Competitors (including Yelp.com) complained that Google's algorithm and design of its search engine were aimed at excluding or demoting the websites of actual or potential competitors. The FTC named this allegation "search bias" and focused on Google's alleged practice of delivering its own results in a manner that unfairly provides Google an advantage over its competitors. In January 2013, after a nearly two-year investigation, Google and the FTC agreed to a settlement in which Google agreed to provide a mechanism to ensure that competitors are not being excluded or demoted unfairly in search results. The FTC issued a statement announcing the settlement and explained that the commission would not take any further action on the issue of search bias because the evidence did not demonstrate that Google's actions had stifled competition in violation of antitrust laws. Google now faces similar antitrust claims in the European Union.

HART-SCOTT-RODINO ANTITRUST IMPROVEMENTS ACT OF 1976

LO 20-7

The Hart-Scott-Rodino Act is a preventive statute that requires business entities that are contemplating mergers involving dollar amounts of a certain size to give advance notice to the FTC and the Department of Justice of their intention. This provides the Department of Justice with veto power on a proposed merger if the transaction would violate any of the antitrust laws (including the Sherman Act).

ROBINSON-PATMAN ACT

Although the Clayton Act covers the anticompetitive arrangement known as *price discrimination*, the Robinson-Patman Act, enacted in 1936, amended the Clayton Act provisions to provide for broader regulatory authority to curb price discrimination. As a practical matter, the Robinson-Patman Act is enforced almost exclusively by the FTC.

Price Discrimination

Section 2(a) of the act makes it illegal for a business entity to discriminate in price "between different purchasers of commodities of like quality or grade." This discrimination, however, is illegal only when the discrimination results in an effect that may substantially lessen competition, tend to create a monopoly, or injure, destroy, or prevent competition with any person who either grants or knowingly receives the benefit of such discrimination.

To violate Section 2(a), a business entity must have made two or more sales to different purchasers at different prices. This means that quoting a discriminatory price or refusing to sell except at a discriminatory price is not a violation of the act.

Defenses There are essentially two defenses to a price discrimination claim, and both are centered on the fact that some price discrimination may be legitimate. First, any time a seller has different manufacturing, shipping, or operational costs that vary from buyer to buyer, no violation of antitrust laws occurs. Second, if a seller conducts a good faith campaign to meet the lower price of a competitor and this results in price discrimination between several buyers, the seller has not violated antitrust laws.

KEY TERMS

Sherman Act p. 563 The centerpiece of the statutory scheme of federal antitrust law; prohibits contracts, combinations, and conspiracies in restraint of trade and prohibits monopolization.

Clayton Act p. 564 A federal antitrust law enacted in 1914 as a preventive statute that deals with specific types of trade restraints, including exclusive dealing arrangements, tie-in sales, price discrimination, mergers and acquisitions, and interlocking directorates.

Robinson-Patman Act p. 564 A federal antitrust law enacted in 1936 that amends the Clayton Act provisions by providing for broader regulatory authority to curb price discrimination.

Celler-Kefauver Antimerger Act p. 564 A federal antitrust law enacted in 1950 that amends the Clayton Act provisions by severely restricting anticompetitive mergers resulting from the acquisition of assets.

Federal Trade Commission Act p. 564 A federal law enacted in 1914 that established the Federal Trade Commission, which administers the act; intended as a catch-all statute that has been construed as including all the prohibitions of the other antitrust laws.

Per se standard p. 564 (*per se:* Latin for "of, in, or by itself," i.e., without any additional facts needed to prove a point) A standard used by federal courts in deciding whether a certain transaction or action violates the Sherman Act; applied in cases of concerted activities that are blatantly anticompetitive.

Rule of reason standard p. 565 A second standard used by federal courts in deciding whether or not certain transaction or action violates the Sherman Act, contemplating a scale in which the court weighs any anticompetitive harm suffered against marketwide benefits of their actions.

Horizontal restraints p. 566 Per se violations of the Sherman Act in which the restraining of trade involves agreements between competitors to take action that results in the elimination or reduction of competition from other competitors.

Vertical restraints p. 566 Violations of the Sherman Act (judged by the rule of reason) in which the restraining of trade involves agreements between noncompetitors on different distributional levels in the chain of commercial supply.

Vertical price-fixing p. 569 Price-fixing in which a seller attempts to control the resale price of a product at a lower level in the supply chain.

Soft per se analysis p. 570 An approach developed by the courts for determining the legality of a tying arrangement: An arrangement in which a seller ties a second product to the first product is illegal per se if the seller possesses sufficient market power to render the tie-in coercive.

Structural-offense laws p. 572 Antitrust laws designed to combat the problem of monopolization by outlawing affirmative action toward monopolizing or attempting to monopolize a part of trade or commerce.

THEORY TO PRACTICE

SurgiPro is a company engaged in the manufacture and sale of surgical instruments to physician groups and hospitals. After several decades in the market, SurgiPro has a 75 percent market share in the surgical instrument industry. SurgiPro was approached by Medical Devices Corporation (MDC), a competitor of SurgiPro with only a 5 percent market share. MDC proposed that the two companies cease undercutting each other on the retail price of scalpels. MDC also proposed that each company sell only 1,000 scalpels per month at a set price of no lower than $15 per scalpel. MDC reasoned that the sale of scalpels had such a low profit margin that the only way either SurgiPro or MDC could make a profit on the product would be through this plan. An executive at SurgiPro agreed to consider the plan.

1. Have the parties committed a violation of any antitrust laws? What laws may apply in this situation, and is the fact that SurgiPro agreed to consider the plan significant?

2. How is the plan that MDC is proposing best characterized in the context of antitrust law?

Assume that SurgiPro rejects MDC's proposal and instead proposes that they agree that SurgiPro will sell its products only to customers in the mid-Atlantic states and that MDC will sell only in southern states.

3. Which, if any, antitrust laws does SurgiPro's proposal violate?

4. If SurgiPro and MDC are sued by a competitor, should the court use the per se standard or the rule of reasons? Why?

Suppose that both SurgiPro and MDC purchase raw materials for their products from SupplyCo. SurgiPro notifies SupplyCo that it will no longer purchase the supplier's raw materials unless SupplyCo ceases its sales to MDC. SupplyCo agrees because it does not want to lose the substantial revenue from SurgiPro.

5. Which, if any, antitrust laws does this action violate?

6. Assume that SurgiPro wishes to merge with MDC. What antitrust laws will need to be considered before entering into a merger agreement?

MANAGER'S CHALLENGE

Midlevel managers are sometimes required to prepare a memorandum for an executive manager that helps the executive manager prepare for a meeting (a "prep memo") with another company's principals. Assume you receive the following e-mail from your executive manager:

I will be meeting with a representative of MDC tomorrow. Please draft a two-page prep memo that provides information on entering into a joint venture with MDC for selling scalpels. We could share in

expenses of manufacturing and distributing scalpels and split the profits equally. The memo should address how this venture could be structured and whether or not we could still use the brand names. I read an article in *The Wall Street Journal* about antitrust issues in a similar agreement between Texaco and Shell. Perhaps that will help you in preparing the memo.

Prepare a two-page prep memo for your executive manager. A sample answer may be found on this textbook's website at www.mhhe.com/melvinleb2e.

PREDATORY PRICING

Covad is in the business of providing DSL Internet service to consumers in the southern region of the United States. BellSouth is the regional telephone company covering the area and also offers DSL Internet service. Covad and BellSouth entered into an agreement whereby Covad would lease BellSouth's phone lines used in Covad's DSL service. Covad alleged that, after the contract was executed, BellSouth engaged in predatory pricing. Covad sued BellSouth for violation of the Sherman Act, claiming that BellSouth's efforts were an attempt to further a monopoly and squeeze Covad out of the market.

CASE QUESTIONS

1. Who prevails and why?
2. What section of the Sherman Act is at issue here?
3. How should the court apply the statute to this case?

TYING

Grumman Systems accused Data General of violating the Sherman Act based on Data General's tying the sale of its copyrighted software with a requirement that the buyer enter into an agreement to purchase Data General's support services for the software. Data General defended on the basis that the support services were an integral part of its software and not a separate product.

CASE QUESTIONS

1. Is this tying arrangement a violation of antitrust laws? Explain your answer.
2. Is this an example of a horizontal or vertical restraint?

ANTICOMPETITIVE ACTION

IBM manufactures and sells computers and related equipment. It also has a leasing division. Greyhound was a leasing company that would purchase "second-generation" computers from IBM at up to a 75 percent discount (depending on how old the equipment was) and then lease them to its customers at a relatively inexpensive price. In fact, because Greyhound could buy at such a high discount, it was able to undercut IBM's standard lease rates. Although IBM had about 82 percent of this leasing market, IBM became concerned when its leasing market share fell. It determined that the main reason for its loss in the leasing market was that companies like Greyhound were able to offer better terms to consumers. IBM phased in reduced discount rates so that the maximum discount was 12 percent. Greyhound sued IBM, alleging monopolization in violation of the Sherman Act.

CASE QUESTIONS

1. Who prevails and why? Explain your answer.
2. Are there any similarities between this case and the *Microsoft* case?

HORIZONTAL RESTRAINTS

Tanka was a student athlete attending the University of Southern California (USC). When she decided to transfer to UCLA, the athletic director at USC invoked an NCAA rule that allowed USC to prevent Tanka from playing sports at UCLA for one year. The NCAA rule only applied to student-athlete transfers within a particular conference.

Tanka sued USC and the NCAA, claiming that the rule amounted to a horizontal restraint violating the Sherman Act.

CASE QUESTIONS

1. Who prevails and why?
2. Should the rule of reason be used in this analysis? Explain.

PER SE VIOLATIONS

HRM, a manufacturer of the prescription drug Cardizem CD, and Andrx, the manufacturer of a generic version of the drug, were embroiled in a patent infringement dispute in 1996. Andrx counterclaimed with allegations of unfair competition. After a year of extensive settlement negotiations, the parties entered into an agreement whereby Andrx, which had obtained FDA approval to market its generic version, agreed that it would not market the generic version in the United States for a certain period of time in exchange for payments by HRM of up to $40 million per year. Both parties agreed to drop the claims from the 1996 lawsuits against each other.

The parties fulfilled the agreement faithfully, and Andrx waited until June 1999 to market its generic drug. After its release, the generic drug sold for a much lower price than Cardizem CD and captured a substantial portion of the market. A group of plaintiffs filed a class action lawsuit against HRM and Andrx, alleging that their settlement agreement was a per se violation of the Sherman Act as it was a form of horizontal price restraint.

CASE QUESTIONS

1. Who prevails and why? Explain your reasoning.
2. What type of illegal restraint is being alleged by the plaintiffs in this case?

 Self-Check **ANSWERS**

Horizontal Restraint

1. Price-fixing.
2. Boycott.
3. Market allocation.

21
CHAPTER

Creditors' Rights and Bankruptcy

learning objectives

After studying this chapter, students who have mastered the material will be able to:

21-1 Distinguish between unsecured creditors and secured creditors and determine the rights of each set of creditors.

21-2 Apply the framework for a secured transaction for personal property under UCC Article 9 in a business context.

21-3 Articulate the process of obtaining a secured interest in real estate.

21-4 Describe the role of sureties and guarantors in a secured loan transaction.

21-5 Explain the various nonstatutory options and legal ramifications for a business facing financial distress.

21-6 Determine the rights, protections, and obligations of both creditors and debtors under federal bankruptcy laws.

21-7 Distinguish and explain the various bankruptcy options for debtors under Chapter 7, Chapter 11, and Chapter 13 of the Bankruptcy Code.

21-8 Explain the impact of the Bankruptcy Abuse Prevention and Consumer Protection Act on creditors and debtors.

The financial crisis that drove the markets sharply downward in 2008 is perhaps the most prominent confirmation of the fact that global commerce depends on credit. Creditors are one of the most important components of the global economy because they provide merchants and consumers with the opportunity to purchase goods and inventory, acquire real estate and other assets, and expand business operations without spending large sums of cash to fund current business operations. In order to encourage creditors to extend appropriate commercial credit to merchants and consumers, the law gives certain protection to creditors. At the same time, the law also provides statutory protections and other alternatives for borrowers in times of financial crisis. Business owners and managers frequently engage in extending or receiving credit, and understanding the legal ramifications in both circumstances is pivotal to protecting the interests of creditors and debtors. In this chapter, students will learn:

- Laws that govern the relationship between creditors and borrowers and how they apply in a business context.

- Legal ramifications of alternatives for a business facing a financial crisis.

- Fundamental principles of the federal Bankruptcy Code and its applicability to business.

CREDITORS' RIGHTS   LO 21-1

Although people typically think of commercial lenders and banks as being creditors, the scope of creditors is much wider, including manufacturers, suppliers, and retailers. While most creditors have little problem collecting money owed to them, there are certain times that the creditor must take legal action to recover the debt. Laws that protect creditors' rights come primarily from common law and statutory law at the state level. Bankruptcy laws, discussed later in this chapter, are primarily federal statutes. The level of protection varies in part based on whether or not the credit was secured by some type of collateral. Credit that is not collateralized is known as **unsecured debt.** When the borrower has pledged collateral in order to obtain credit, the creditor is known as a **secured creditor.**

Unsecured Creditors

Businesses often use unsecured debt in the form of a loan or line of credit primarily to help fund short-term operations. Examples include private loans from another party, loans from a bank or other commercial lender, and credit cards. In each of these cases, credit is extended based on the borrower's creditworthiness rather than as a result of the borrower's promise to pledge collateral.

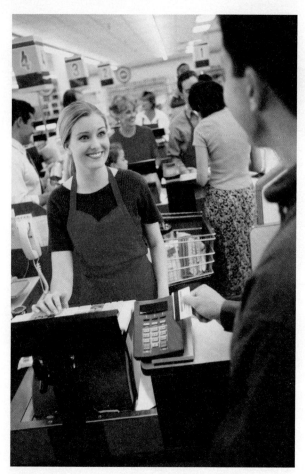

A credit card is the most common form of unsecured credit used in consumer transactions.

Unsecured creditors are offered very little protection if the borrower defaults on paying back the loan. Note that interest rates on unsecured loans tend to be higher than those on loans based on secured credit.

When a borrower fails to pay back the loan or make payments toward the loan as agreed, the unsecured creditor's exclusive legal remedy is to bring a lawsuit against the borrower and obtain a judgment from the court. Essentially, the basis of such a debt collection lawsuit is breach of contract in that the borrower failed to fulfill his obligations under the contract (repayment). Once the creditor has obtained a judgment, either the borrower must pay the full amount of the judgment or the creditor may pursue a court order. The latter option allows the creditor to use a judicially created procedure to seize any property or assets of the borrower.[1] Certain assets, however, are exempt from seizure (such as the borrower's primary residence). Additionally, a creditor's lawsuit or execution of a judgment must be halted if the borrower files for protection under the Bankruptcy Code (discussed later). As a result, unsecured creditors have very little practical way to collect debts owed. Certain consumer loans and credit card debt are also subject to state and federal statutory regulation regarding late fees, interest rates, disclosures, and credit reporting practices. These regulations are discussed in greater detail in Chapter 22, "Consumer Protection Law."

Secured Creditors

When credit is secured by a pledge of collateral by the borrower, the creditor has more viable alternatives to collect the debt. The alternatives depend on the category of secured creditor.

SECURED TRANSACTIONS UNDER ARTICLE 9 OF THE UCC

LO 21-2

One common way that a creditor attempts to ensure full payment by the borrower is by creating a *secured-party relationship* whereby the borrower pledges certain property of value to secure the debt owed. When personal property (e.g., goods or other assets such as cash) or fixtures to real estate (e.g., light fixtures or a built-in reception desk) are intended to serve as the collateral, Article 9 of the Uniform Commercial Code provides a uniform set of rules to govern the transaction. With some variations, Article 9 has been adopted in all states, and it gives business owners and managers some degree of reliability in planning a loan transaction. Note that loans collateralized with real estate (also known as *real property*) are governed not by Article 9 but rather by statutes related to mortgages, discussed in the next section.

In essence, Article 9 provides a framework for secured transactions by recognizing the rights of the creditor, known as the **secured party,** against other creditors of the borrower and against the borrower himself in the event of a default in payment. In the

---

[1]In most states, the judgment is executed through use of the sheriff's department, and the seized assets are sold at auction (known as a *sheriff's sale*).

UCC, a borrower is known as the **debtor.** Article 9 also provides a procedure for the secured party to establish priority in the collateral over other creditors; this procedure is known as **perfecting** the interest in the collateral. The rights of the secured party are known as a **security interest.** There are two Article 9 requirements in order for a creditor to obtain the *full* benefit of a security interest: the security agreement and perfection.

Security Agreement

Typically, the parties will enter into a security agreement that specifies the parties, describes the collateral, articulates the obligations of the debtor (primarily payment), and states the remedies available to the secured party in the event of default. In the event the agreement is silent on a particular matter, Article 9 acts to fill that void by providing a standard set of rules.

Perfection

Perfection of a security interest is the act of establishing the secured party's rights ahead of the rights of other creditors. Although Article 9 does not define the term *perfection,* it does describe an order of priority among creditors and the actions that a secured party must take to establish these rights. Perfection occurs at the moment of (1) taking physical possession of the collateral, (2) officially filing a statement of notice with a state and/or local government office, or (3) taking legal control of the collateral (such as establishing joint authority over a brokerage account whose funds are being used to collateralize a loan).

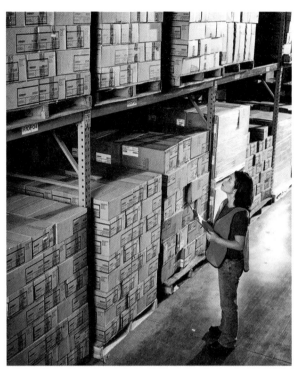

Secured credit transactions, such as a loan for which the debtor's inventory is used as collateral, are typically governed by a security agreement between the parties.

REAL ESTATE

LO 21-3

When real estate (also called *real property*[2]) is being used to collateralize a loan, the creditor takes an interest in the collateral through use of a **mortgage.** A mortgage is a written document that specifies the parties and the real estate and is filed with a state and/or local government agency, thereby becoming a public record that others can look up. This filing is intended to give notice to the public and other creditors of the secured party's interest in the real estate collateral. The creditor is known as the **mortgagee,** and the borrower is the **mortgagor.** A mortgage is typically accompanied by a **promissory note.** The promissory note is a contract in which the borrower promises to pay back the creditor at a certain rate of interest over a specified period of years (usually 15, 20, or 30 years). State statutes primarily govern the relationship between mortgagor and mortgagee. These statutes define the procedure that the creditor must follow in order to pursue certain remedies against the debtor. In the most extreme measure, a creditor declares the loan in default and institutes a **mortgage foreclosure** in an effort to take title and possession of the real estate in hopes of selling the property to pay off the debt owed. In the wake of the mortgage foreclosure

---

[2]Although some sources cite technical differences between these terms, according to *Black's Law Dictionary,* the term *real estate* is generally synonymous with *real property.*

crisis that began in 2007, Congress passed the Mortgage Forgiveness Debt Relief Act.[3] The intent of the law was to assist homeowners in avoiding foreclosure by offering them certain guarantees and tax breaks from the government when they refinanced a mortgage loan. Properties owned by business entities, or by individuals for business purposes (such as a seashore rental property), are not eligible for relief under this law.

LO 21-4 SURETIES AND GUARANTORS

Another common method for helping to secure a loan is to require a *third party* to back up the promises made by the debtor regarding repayment of the loan. In some cases, a creditor may be willing to extend a loan to a borrower, but the borrower's creditworthiness may be either questionable or too brief to qualify for the credit required. In such a case, the creditor will usually require that a third party with sufficient creditworthiness and assets also sign the loan agreement and become jointly liable with the debtor for his promise to repay the loan (thus the commonly used term *cosigning*). When a party agrees to be *primarily* liable to pay the loan, she is known as a **surety.** When a party agrees to be liable *only* if the debtor actually defaults, she is known as a **guarantor.** For example, in order to secure a loan for the purchase of a new car, Bank requires Cain to have a cosigner because Cain's credit is insufficient to qualify for the loan. Cain convinces Abel to be his cosigner, and Bank requires Abel to cosign as a surety. In the first year of the loan, Abel is late in making payments and eventually becomes 60 days' past due. Bank now has the option of pursuing remedies against either Cain or Abel to pay the debt. Because Abel has more assets, he is likely the best party to pursue. However, suppose that Abel signed as a *guarantor* instead of a surety. In that case, Bank would have to pursue full remedies against Cain by obtaining a court judgment and attempting to collect as much as possible (such as repossessing the car for resale) before Bank could pursue Abel. In the event Bank cannot recover the full amount from remedies against Cain, *only then* is Cain liable for the balance owed.

Personal Guaranties for Business Loans

Business owners and managers often encounter suretyship and guaranty concepts in the context of a **personal guaranty** of a business loan. When a business borrows money, for example, to expand operations or to fund an acquisition of some type, the creditor will often require that the owners (sometimes referred to as the *principals* of a business entity) of small and midsize companies give their personal guaranty to back up the business loan. This means that in the event of a default by the business entity debtor, the principals have pledged their personal assets (such as individual bank accounts, equity in a property, or other assets) if the assets of the business are insufficient to repay the loan. Creditors realize that without this guaranty, the principals of a debtor corporation can simply walk away from the debt without any personal liability for the loan. As a result, creditors often wish to make the principals more accountable by securing a business loan with both a security interest in certain collateral *and* the personal guaranties of the principals. For example, suppose that Caulfield is the principal of Rye Inc., a manufacturing firm specializing in production of high-quality baseball catcher's mitts, with annual revenues of $25 million. Rye has been successful over the past 10 years. Now Caulfield wishes to expand his operations to start to manufacture other baseball equipment and plans to fund the expansion with a loan from Big Bank. Although Rye's operations have been profitable in the past and it will likely have no problem in repaying the loan from existing revenues, Big Bank not only will require a security interest in any collateral owned by Rye but also will likely require Caulfield to personally guaranty the loan as an additional measure of security. From Big Bank's perspective, the personal guaranty gives it maximum leverage over Caulfield in the event of a default by Rye.

---

[3]Pub L. No. 110-142 (2007).

Determine the status of each creditor.

1. ExtremeCo, a manufacturer of a line of extreme gear such as snowboards, gives Retailer merchandise for her inventory on credit. ExtremeCo requires Retailer to sign an agreement that describes the inventory as collateral and specifies that Retailer will pay ExtremeCo monthly based on sales of ExtremeCo's product. ExtremeCo files a statement of interest in the collateral with the appropriate government agency.

2. Office Galaxy sells office supplies to a local insurance agency. Office Galaxy delivers the goods on the 1st of the month and sends an invoice on the 15th of each month to the manager of the insurance agency.

3. BigBank lends WidgetCo $100,000 to purchase land in order to build a new warehouse. Widget-Co uses the land itself as collateral.

4. BigBank lends WidgetCo $50,000 to fund the hiring of seasonal employees during the holiday rush. BigBank requires the principals of WidgetCo to sign a promissory note agreeing that they will pay the note from personal assets if WidgetCo defaults on payments.

Answers to this Self-Check are provided at the end of the chapter.

CONCEPT SUMMARY Creditors' Rights

- Unsecured creditors give loans based on creditworthiness without the security of collateral and must bring a lawsuit in the case of default.

- A secured creditor can retain the collateral given to secure his loan; no lawsuit is necessary under the UCC if there is a security agreement and the interest has been perfected.

- A creditor uses real estate as collateral with a mortgage. In the case of default, the debtor goes into foreclosure, and the creditor sells the real estate to cover his losses.

- A debtor can obtain a loan with collateral or creditworthiness by getting a third party to pay off the loan for him (surety) or to pay off the loan if he defaults (guarantor). A business without credit can get a loan by using a creditworthy individual as a personal guaranty.

ALTERNATIVES FOR INSOLVENT BORROWERS   LO 21-5

When a business venture no longer has adequate assets to maintain its operations and can no longer pay its bills as they become due in the usual course of trade and business, it is considered **insolvent.** A company's specific response to insolvency is largely dependent on the type of financial crisis. For example, if the insolvency is a result of *temporary* poor cash flow but the receivables will likely provide enough cash to continue operations in the future, then bankruptcy may not be the best option (or even an option at all, depending on the assets-debt ratio of the struggling venture). On the other hand, if the venture is cash-starved because of, for example, a particularly burdensome union contract and has no realistic way to recover from the financial crisis without some statutory protection from creditors, then the law provides the venture with the ability to hold creditors off while the business reorganizes and drafts a plan on how the venture intends to continue its operations in the future. This plan could include a reformation of the problematic union contract. When a business becomes insolvent, its principals have several choices in dealing with the venture's debt. Some of these options do not involve any statutory protections and, therefore, may have legal ramifications for the business and its principals.

Out of Existence

Out of existence (also known as the "lights-out option") is a nonstatutory option in which the venture simply ceases operations without paying creditors. Usually the debtor company files an out-of-existence certificate or articles of dissolution with the state corporation bureau and simply ceases doing business. However, the debts are still valid obligations of the company, and a creditor may pursue a debt collection lawsuit in an attempt to collect any available cash or assets to satisfy the debt. In fact, some states require that all creditors be notified before the business is recognized as legally dissolved. Out of existence is a particularly dangerous option if the debt has been secured through a *personal guaranty* by principals of the business (discussed earlier). However, if the debtor has no assets, no personal guaranties exist, and the debt is not substantial enough to make legal methods to collect economically viable for creditors, the lights-out option is the quickest and least expensive option.

Workout: Accord and Satisfaction

When the principals of a business venture wish to continue operations of a business that is underperforming and is in poor financial condition, they may hire a professional (sometimes called a *turnaround specialist*) to help revise its business model and to negotiate with commercial lenders with the objective of setting the company on sound financial footing. At the same time, in order to avoid collection lawsuits from certain suppliers and creditors, the business venture must also attempt to settle past debts. These various steps of turning around a business are often referred to by creditors as a **workout.**

Recall our discussion in Chapter 8, "Contract Performance: Conditions, Breach, and Remedies," concerning **accord and satisfaction.** When a company or individual is facing a financial crisis, the debtor may approach the creditor and offer to settle the debt for less than the amount owed. Thus, a legal contract is created between debtor and creditor whereby the creditor agrees to accept a sum less than owed in exchange for releasing the debtor from all legal liability. This may allow the debtor some additional time to seek an infusion of capital or collect a large receivable and thus continue its operations without the threat of a creditor's collection lawsuit or involuntary bankruptcy (discussed later). This option is sometimes used in conjunction with an *out-of-existence* strategy when the debtor's principals are seeking to have a personal guaranty discharged but have no intent to continue operations.

LO 21-6 BANKRUPTCY

Of course, there are circumstances when the debtor's best option is protection from creditors via the Bankruptcy Code. The concept of forgiveness of debt and protection of borrowers from creditors has deep historical roots that some scholars have traced back to the Old Testament. The underlying concept and public policy objectives behind bankruptcy protection is to give a debtor a "fresh start" and to prevent creditors from gaining unfair advantage over each other in being paid. In the United States, the need for bankruptcy laws was recognized in Article I of the U.S. Constitution.[4] For the most part, bankruptcy proceedings are a matter of federal law. State courts can have some limited involvement in issues that involve the borrower, usually called the *debtor* in a bankruptcy context, in one way or another, but they generally do not have any jurisdiction over bankruptcy proceedings. The law of bankruptcy is found within the federal statutes ("Bankruptcy Code"[5]). The starting place for all bankruptcy matters is the federal bankruptcy court.

---

[4]Article I, § 8, gives Congress the responsibility to "establish . . . uniform Laws on the subject of Bankruptcies throughout the United States."

[5]See Title 11 of the United States Code.

The Bankruptcy Code is divided into chapters, and often the reference to someone filing for bankruptcy protection is known as "filing for Chapter 11." The most common forms of bankruptcy are Chapter 7 (liquidation of debtor's assets and discharge of debts), Chapter 11 (reorganization), and Chapter 13 (debt adjustment and repayment of consumer debt). Other chapters contain definitions, describe procedural aspects of bankruptcy, and contain special provisions for bankruptcies by municipalities, stockbrokers, and railroads. Congress amended the Bankruptcy Code in 2005 with the Bankruptcy Abuse Prevention and Consumer Protection Act, which imposed additional requirements on those seeking protection under the Bankruptcy Code. The specific provisions of the 2005 amendment are covered later in this chapter.

Automatic Stay

Filing for bankruptcy protects the debtor through an immediate **automatic stay.** The automatic stay is a legal prohibition of creditors' either initiating or continuing any debt collection action against the debtor or her property. The stay is a powerful legal tool because it stops all collection efforts, all harassment, and all foreclosure actions. It permits the debtor to attempt a repayment or reorganization plan or simply to be relieved of the financial pressures resulting from a financial crisis. The stay also allows the bankruptcy court to deal with the debtor's assets and creditors in a single forum where the rights of all concerned may be heard at once.

> **KEY** POINT
> An automatic stay halts creditors, including government agencies, from all collection efforts, including litigation.

Bankruptcy Trustee

The Bankruptcy Code provides for the appointment of a **bankruptcy trustee** in certain cases. A trustee is appointed in cases where the debtor seeks liquidation and discharge of

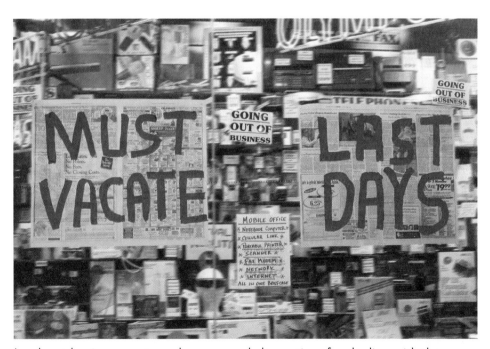

Insolvent business ventures have several alternatives for dealing with the business's debts, including filing for protection from creditors under the Bankruptcy Code.

debts (Chapter 7) or in cases where the debtor is a consumer attempting to repay much of the debt over a period of time (Chapter 13). The trustee, often an attorney highly skilled in bankruptcy law, is charged with the duty of collecting the debtor's available assets, known as the **bankruptcy estate,** and reducing them to cash for distribution, preserving the interests of both the debtor and creditors. Federal law gives the trustee extensive authority and power to accomplish this objective. For example, the bankruptcy trustee may void certain transfers that are considered to be an unfair advantage of one creditor over another. These are known as **voidable transfers.**

The most common voidable transfer is a *preferential transfer.* A preferential transfer occurs when the debtor makes a payment to satisfy a *prebankruptcy petition* debt to a creditor within 90 days of the petition. If the creditor received more than it would have under the liquidation proceedings, the trustee may void the transfer and have the assets taken back from the creditor and placed back into the bankruptcy estate. Preferential transfers to *insiders* (including relatives, partners, officers, and directors of an individual or corporate debtor) are also voidable. Under certain circumstances, any insider transfers made within one year of the petition filing can be voided and placed back into the bankruptcy estate. Additionally, a transfer is voidable as a *fraudulent transfer* if it occurs when a debtor transfers property to a third person within one year of the petition filing with intent to delay, hinder, or defraud creditors. For example, suppose that Eyre is the sole owner of Jane's Pretzel Company (JPC). After several years of reasonable success in business, JPC experiences financial difficulty and owes its creditors $100,000 with only $5,000 in assets. JPC files for Chapter 7 liquidation and discharge. After JPC files the petition, the trustee is appointed and discovers several transfers out of the ordinary course of business. First, two weeks before JPC's petition for bankruptcy, Eyre paid off the entire balance owed to an important vendor on a loan secured by Eyre's personal guaranty. If the trustee determines that the vendor obtained more than it would have from the distribution of JPC's assets under the Bankruptcy Code (which is likely in this situation given the assets versus the debts), the payment can be voided and the money would be put back into the bankruptcy estate. Second, Eyre had borrowed $20,000 from her brother-in-law and, despite the fact that the loan was to be paid over five years, Eyre paid back the entire amount one month before filing for bankruptcy.

> **KEY** POINT
>
> The bankruptcy trustee has the legal power to void any transfer of money that the debtor made for the benefit of insiders.

That transaction would be classified as an insider preferential transfer, and the trustee would void the transfer and recover the payment from Eyre's brother-in-law on behalf of the bankruptcy estate.

LO 21-7 DEBTOR'S OPTIONS

When filing for protection under the Bankruptcy Code, the debtor chooses one of three main options: Chapter 7, Chapter 11, or Chapter 13.

Chapter 7: Liquidation and Discharge

Chapter 7 bankruptcy is perhaps the most extreme measure a business or individual can take. In essence, the debtor agrees to have most of her property liquidated and then the cash distributed to creditors. In exchange, the bankruptcy court gives legal protection to the debtor by discharging any remaining debts. For example, suppose WidgetCo has $50,000 in debts and only $10,000 in nonexempt assets. The bankruptcy court will distribute the $10,000 to creditors, and the remaining debt ($40,000) will be discharged. WidgetCo will be out of business, but its principals will get a fresh start and will not have to pay any of the debts incurred. Chapter 7 outlines a very specific procedure for discharge of debt.

Bankruptcy Petition   The proceedings are started in the bankruptcy court by the filing of a bankruptcy petition. The petition can be either *voluntary* or *involuntary*. A **voluntary bankruptcy petition** is filed by the *debtor* and includes the names of creditors; a list of debts; and a list of the debtor's assets, income, and expenses. In order to qualify for protection under Chapter 7, the debtor's income must be less than the average income in her home state (this requirement is known as the *means test*). An **involuntary bankruptcy petition** is one that is filed *against* a debtor by a group of three or more creditors with an unsecured aggregate claim of at least $11,625 who claim that the debtor is failing to pay the debt as it comes due. This is an extreme measure, and involuntary petitions are relatively rare. This option poses some risk for the creditors because the Bankruptcy Code allows a company to recover damages against creditors who attempt to drive a debtor into bankruptcy but are unsuccessful.

Automatic Stay   As discussed earlier, the filing of a petition gives protection to the debtor immediately. This means that creditors must suspend all collection activity as of the day the petition was filed. Note that the suspension is temporary and designed to give the bankruptcy court the time to decide the validity of the petition.

Order for Relief   Once the court determines the validity of the petition, an order for relief is granted, the automatic stay effectively becomes *permanent,* and the bankruptcy proceeds.

Appointment of Trustee   Once the order of relief is granted, the court appoints an interim bankruptcy trustee to oversee the case. A permanent trustee is elected at the first meeting of creditors. Once appointed, the trustee creates a bankruptcy estate. Note that the trustee is a representative of the court and *not* a representative of the debtor or of the creditors. The trustee has the responsibility of administering the bankruptcy proceedings in accordance with the law.

Meeting of Creditors and Administering of the Estate   Within 30 days of the order of relief, the court calls for a meeting of creditors. The debtor (usually along with an attorney) must appear and submit to questioning by the creditors regarding the debtor's assets, financial affairs, and any attempt to conceal assets or income. After the meeting of creditors and election of the trustee, the trustee takes possession of the bankruptcy estate. The estate consists of the debtor's interest in real, personal, tangible, and intangible property no matter where that property is located at the time the petition is filed. Property acquired *after* the petition does not become part of the bankruptcy estate. The trustee's responsibility is to collect all assets that are legally required to be liquidated for the benefit of the creditors. Trustees separate exempt and nonexempt property, recover any improper transfers of funds before or during the filing of the petition, sell or otherwise dispose of the property, and finally distribute the proceeds to creditors.

In the case where the debtor is an individual, not all property is subject to liquidation. The debtor is entitled to hold on to certain assets. These assets are known as *exempt assets.* Note that in a Chapter 7 bankruptcy of a business entity, there are no exempt assets. All assets must be liquidated. For individuals, some examples of exemptions are:

■ Up to $22,975 in equity in the debtor's primary residence (homestead exemption).

■ Interest in a motor vehicle up to $3,675.

■ Interest up to $575 for a particular item, household goods, and furnishings (aggregate total limited to $12,250).

■ Interest in jewelry up to $1,550.

■ Right to receive Social Security and certain welfare benefits; alimony and child support; education savings accounts; and certain pension benefits.

■ Right to receive certain personal injury and other awards up to $22,975.

Distribution and Discharge   Once the trustee has administered the bankruptcy estate, the trustee then distributes the proceeds to creditors in an order of priority set by the Bankruptcy Code. Secured creditors are paid first and in full so long as the value of the collateral equals or exceeds the amount of their security interests. Unsecured creditors are paid from the remaining proceeds of the bankruptcy estate (if any). The order of payment for unsecured debtors is specified in the Bankruptcy Code (see Table 21.1).

Note that some debts are *nondischargeable.* These include:

- Claims for federal, state, and local taxes (including fines and penalties related to the taxes) within two years of the petition filing.
- Debts incurred within 60 days of the petition for luxury goods of more than $1,000 from a single creditor or cash advances in excess of $1,000 obtained by a debtor using credit cards or revolving lines of credit.
- Alimony, maintenance, and child support.
- Debts related to willful or malicious injury to a person or property.
- Debts related to court-ordered punitive damages against the debtor.
- Student loan debts, unless the debtor can prove "undue hardship."

Under what circumstances can a debtor have a student loan debt discharged for hardship? In Case 21.1, a federal court gives some guidance on answering that question.

Chapter 11: Reorganization

Although located in the Bankruptcy Code, Chapter 11 differs greatly from a liquidation bankruptcy. Chapter 11 is best thought of as temporary protection for a corporation[6] from creditors while the corporation goes through a planning process to pay creditors and continue business without the need to terminate the entity completely. Chapter 11 is an acknowledgment that, as a matter of public policy, it is better to allow a business entity the opportunity to revise its business practices without the pressure of creditors who could halt the business operations and shut down the company—actions that could result in job costs and in some creditors not getting paid anything at all.

TABLE 21.1   Order of Priority for Unsecured Creditors

1. Administration expenses—court costs and trustee and attorney fees.
2. Involuntary bankruptcy expenses incurred from date of filing to order of relief.
3. Unpaid wages and commissions earned within 90 days, limited to $10,950 per claimant.
4. Unsecured claims for contributions for employee benefits, 180 days prior to filing and $10,950 per employee.
5. Claims by farmers or fishermen up to $5,400.
6. Consumer deposits up to $2,425 before the petition in connection with the purchase, lease, or rental of property.
7. Paternity, alimony, maintenance, and support debts.
8. Certain taxes and penalties due to government units, such as income and property taxes.
9. Claims of general creditors.

---

[6]Individual debtors are also eligible for relief under Chapter 11, but such cases are rare.

FACT SUMMARY Jones graduated from a large university in Georgia with a degree in history and a minor in economics in the 1980s. Although Jones was supposed to enter the army upon graduation, he gained admission to law school and earned his law degree. However, Jones could not pass the bar examination after several attempts. He spent the next 14 years in various positions including the army, substitute teaching, writing, and social work. Jones then returned to school to get a master of education degree in the teaching of visual arts. Jones continued his education with yet another master's degree in divinity in 2005. At age 52, Jones held a bachelor's degree, a juris doctor, and two master's degrees. He borrowed heavily for his education and, at the time of the bankruptcy petition, had defaulted on 18 student loans worth $140,000 of debt. Note that Jones's undergraduate and law school debts were discharged in a previous bankruptcy hearing. Jones argued that the debt was so high that to pay the debt would cause "undue hardship," and he asked the court to discharge the loan. His creditor maintained that Jones did not meet the undue-hardship standard.

SYNOPSIS OF DECISION AND OPINION The bankruptcy court ruled in favor of the creditor and refused to discharge Jones's student loans. The court reasoned that as a healthy, educated, employable man, paying the money back would not amount to undue hardship.

WORDS OF THE COURT: Undue-Hardship Standard "In order to demonstrate undue hardship, the Chapter 7 debtor must demonstrate: (1) that the debtor cannot maintain, based on current income and expenses, a "minimal" standard of living for herself and her dependents if forced to repay the loans; (2) that additional circumstances exist indicating that this state of affairs is likely to persist for a significant portion of the repayment period for student loans; and (3) that the debtor has made good faith efforts to repay the loans. . . . Mr. Jones is a relatively healthy, 52-year-old individual with no dependents. He has no medical or psychiatric condition that prevents him from employment. Although he is presently unemployed, he has not demonstrated that he has made diligent efforts to secure stable employment now or in the past. His present employment situation does not exist because he is unemployable. On the contrary, Mr. Jones is a highly educated individual who has marketable skills in a variety of areas: e.g., legal, managerial, correctional, religious, literary and artistic."

Case Questions

1. If Jones had been unable to work due to illness or injury, would that be sufficient to meet the undue-hardship standard set out by the court?

2. Note that one court did not find undue hardship enough to discharge student loans for a "46-year-old part-time legal secretary, raising her 14-year-old child and living with her sister, and who had psychiatric problems and had twice attempted suicide" [*In re Brightful*, 267 F.3d 324 (3d Cir. 2001)]. Why would Congress and courts be reluctant to allow the discharge of student loans without meeting this difficult test?

The fundamental proceedings of a Chapter 11 case are very similar to those of a Chapter 7 case, discussed earlier. A petition is filed either voluntarily or involuntarily, the automatic stay provision is triggered, and, if the petition is proper, the order of relief then sets the reorganization process in motion. A creditor committee is appointed, and the committee can consult with the debtor and/or the trustee to formulate the repayment plan.

The major difference, however, is that unlike the case in a Chapter 7 proceeding, the debtor generally continues to *operate the business* in a Chapter 11 case. The bankruptcy court may also opt to appoint a trustee to oversee the basic management of the business entity and report back to the court. This process, known as **debtor in possession (DIP),** gives great power to the debtor to rehabilitate the business entity.

DIP Powers   In many ways, the executives in a DIP business entity have an ideal situation from a workout perspective. While the stigma of Chapter 11 may cause difficulty in raising new capital, the Bankruptcy Code gives the DIP power to void prepetition preferential payments and to cancel or assume prepetition contracts (including leases, supplier contracts, and service contracts). The so-called **strong-arm clause** of the Bankruptcy Code allows the DIP to avoid any obligation or transfer of property that the debtor would otherwise be obligated to perform.

For larger companies, a DIP's power is most important in the context of *union contracts* known as collective bargaining agreements. The Bankruptcy Code sets forth standards and procedures under which a collective bargaining contract can be rejected if the debtor has first proposed necessary contractual modifications to the union and the union has rejected them without good cause.

Reorganization Plan   The centerpiece of a Chapter 11 case is the **reorganization plan.** It is a plan, generally filed by the debtor, which articulates a specific strategy and financial plan for emerging from financial distress. The DIP has the exclusive right to draft the plan within 120 days after the Chapter 11 petition. The court must approve the plan before it becomes binding on the creditors. The plan must be submitted to the creditors for a vote and generally must designate "classes" of claims and interests (such as secured versus unsecured) and provide an adequate means for partial payment to creditors. Creditors are given the opportunity to accept or reject the plan, but if they reject the plan, the Bankruptcy Code allows the debtor to request that the court force the creditors to accept the plan (the wording in the code is known as the **cram-down provision**). So long as the plan is fair, equitable, and feasible from the court's perspective, the court will require creditors to accept the plan even over their objections. The plan is binding on all parties upon its approval by the court. It is important to note that a Chapter 11 filing may be converted during any stage (even before the plan is submitted) to a Chapter 7 filing. Most financially distressed business entities will attempt a recovery using the generous provisions of Chapter 11 before deciding to liquidate. On the other hand, some companies do, in fact, turn around and emerge very strong from a Chapter 11 filing.

Chapter 13: Repayment Plan

Also known as the "wage-earner plan," this form of bankruptcy is limited to *individuals* who have a substantial debt, and it *cannot* be used to cover any business debt (even as a sole proprietor). Chapter 13 allows debtors with a regular source of income to catch up on mortgage, car, tax, and domestic support payments; repay an adjusted debt to certain creditors over time (typically five years); and still keep all of their assets. It is less expensive and less complicated than reorganization or liquidation proceedings and can be accomplished only by filing a voluntary bankruptcy petition. Payments are typically made to the bankruptcy trustee, who distributes them to creditors. Unsecured creditors frequently are paid less than they are owed, depending on the circumstances of the case.

BANKRUPTCY ABUSE PREVENTION AND CONSUMER PROTECTION ACT

LO 21-8

In 2005, Congress passed legislation intended to curb perceived abuses of statutory bankruptcy protection by enacting the Bankruptcy Abuse Prevention and Consumer Protection Act (BAPCPA). While the congressional sponsors of the bill touted its public policy benefits of making the consuming public more responsible with debt, the law was widely criticized by bankruptcy attorneys and judges as unnecessarily burdening the debtor, the trustee, and the court with more paperwork and expenses while not curbing abuse.[7] The law overhauled the Bankruptcy Code for the first time since 1994 and, fundamentally, made it more difficult for debtors to seek protection under Chapter 7. The major provisions of the law are (1) a *means test* for the debtor; (2) proof of the debtor's income; (3) higher priority for alimony and support payments by the debtor; and (4) credit counseling for the debtor.

---

[7]See Judge Monroe's comment in *In re Sosa,* 336 B.R. 113 (Bankr. W.D. Tex. 2005); "the legislation's adoption in its title of the words 'consumer protection' is the grossest of misnomers."

Means Test

The most important change was to increase the statutory requirements for eligibility under Chapter 7 straight liquidation by adding a "means test" that is determined by comparing the applicant's current monthly income to the median income for the applicant's state. If the applicant's income is more than the median, the applicant would not be eligible for Chapter 7. Thus, a substantial number of bankruptcy applicants who previously would have been eligible for a discharge of substantially all debts must now repay them under a Chapter 13 filing. For example, the state of Maryland's median family income for a family of one is $52,762 and $72,417 for a family of three. Therefore, if the debtor applies for a Chapter 7 bankruptcy seeking to discharge debts but her income is above the median, the petition would be denied and the debtor would have only Chapter 13 (debt repayment) as an option.

In Case 21.2, the U.S. Supreme Court analyzes the BAPCPA's provisions related to the means test.

CASE 21.2   Ransom v. FIA Card Services, 131 S.Ct. 716 (2011)

FACT SUMMARY Ransom filed for Chapter 13 bankruptcy relief in 2006. His filings included $82,500 worth of unsecured credit card debt owed to FIA Card Services. In his repayment plan, Ransom proposed repayment of 25 percent of his outstanding debt to FIA over a five-year period. Despite the fact that he owned his car outright (no debt), Ransom listed his reasonably necessary living expenses and claimed a standard amount provided for in the Bankruptcy Code for a car: $471 per month and $210.55 for maintenance costs. FIA objected to the plan based on the fact that Ransom owned his car outright and was not required to make payments. Allowing the car deduction, FIA argued, amounted to allowing Ransom to avoid paying at least $28,000 of his FIA debt. The bankruptcy court denied confirmation of Ransom's plan, and the appellate court affirmed the decision.

SYNOPSIS OF DECISION AND OPINION The U.S. Supreme Court ruled in favor of FIA and held that Ransom could not take the car-ownership deduction. The Court ruled that the Bankruptcy Abuse Prevention and Consumer Protection Act of 2005 required courts to apply a *means test* to help ensure that debtors who can pay back their creditors actually do so with the help of the Bankruptcy Code. The means test depends on accurate reporting of reasonably necessary living expenses. Since Ransom had no actual loan or lease payment due, he was not entitled to claim a car-ownership deduction. The Court rejected Ransom's argument that the language in the statute regarding applicability of the car-ownership deduction was ambiguous. The Court also explained that Ransom was entitled to "ownership costs" but that the car-ownership deduction was limited to debtors who were required to make loan or lease payments for their car.

WORDS OF THE COURT: Purpose of the Means Test "Ransom next contends that denying the ownership allowance to debtors in his position 'sends entirely the wrong message, namely, that it is advantageous to be deeply in debt on motor vehicle loans, rather than to pay them off.' But the choice here is not between thrifty savers and profligate borrowers, as Ransom would have it. Money is fungible: The $14,000 that Ransom spent to purchase his Camry outright was money he did not devote to paying down his credit card debt, and Congress did not express a preference for one use of these funds over the other. Further, Ransom's argument mistakes what the deductions in the means test are meant to accomplish. Rather than effecting any broad federal policy as to saving or borrowing, the deductions serve merely to ensure that debtors in bankruptcy can afford essential items. The car-ownership allowance thus safeguards a debtor's ability to retain a car throughout the plan period. If the debtor already owns a car outright, he has no need for this protection."

Case Questions

1. Does the Court's decision encourage responsible actions by the debtor? Does this encourage debtors to take on new debt instead of driving an old car, as Ransom suggested?

2. How did the Bankruptcy Abuse Prevention and Consumer Protection Act of 2005 affect this case?

Proof of Income

Debtors must provide the bankruptcy trustee copies of recent tax returns and pay stubs or other income verification on a timely basis. If the debtor has failed to file a tax return for the previous year, she may be required to file a return as a condition of bankruptcy approval.

Alimony and Support

The BAPCPA gives alimony and support obligations a higher priority than certain other creditors.

Credit Counseling

Prior to filing for bankruptcy, the debtor must complete a short (approximately one-hour) credit-counseling seminar and must also complete a longer course, known as Credit Education, prior to actually receiving a discharge of debts.

Table 21.2 is a summary and comparison of various bankruptcy options.

TABLE 21.2 Bankruptcy Options

Chapter 7 (Liquidation) Individuals and Businesses	Chapter 11 (Reorganization) Individuals and Businesses	Chapter 13 (Consumer Debt Adjustment) Individuals Only
1. Petition	1. Petition	1. Petition
2. Automatic stay	2. Automatic stay	2. Automatic stay
3. Order of relief or dismissal (apply means test)	3. Debtor in possession	3. Most debts paid back over five years
4. Creditor committee	4. File plan	4. Some unsecured debts reduced, some unsecured debts discharged
5. Trustee	5. Creditors approve a "cram down"	
6. Administration of bankruptcy estate	6. Emerge from Chapter 11 or convert to Chapter 7	
7. Distribution		
8. Discharge		

CONCEPT SUMMARY Bankruptcy and Alternatives

- Upon a filing for bankruptcy, in most cases a trustee is appointed by the bankruptcy court to protect the remaining bankruptcy assets, known as the estate.
- The trustee has the legal power to void fraudulent or preferential transfers that the debtor made to certain creditors before filing bankruptcy.
- Once a business becomes insolvent, it can either file bankruptcy, dissolve itself out of existence, or, if it wants to stay in business, work out terms of accord and satisfaction to pay creditors.
- A business debtor in Chapter 7 has its assets liquidated and debts discharged by the court.
- To avoid lost jobs and unpaid creditors, some companies enter Chapter 11, wherein a debtor in possession (DIP) tries to rehabilitate the company and partially compensate creditors under a reorganization plan.
- An individual can develop a repayment plan in Chapter 13 bankruptcy in order to use his income to slowly pay back debts while not having to liquidate assets.

Unsecured debt p. 581   Credit that is not collateralized.

Secured creditor p. 581   A creditor that extends credit based on collateral pledged by the borrower.

Secured party p. 582   The creditor in a secured transaction.

Debtor p. 583   The borrower in a secured transaction.

Perfecting p. 583   Procedure by which the secured party establishes priority in the collateral over other creditors, as provided by Article 9 of the Uniform Commercial Code.

Security interest p. 583   The rights of the secured party in a transaction.

Mortgage p. 583   A written document that specifies the parties and the real estate being used to collateralize a loan and that is filed with a state and/or local government agency.

Mortgagee p. 583   The creditor in a transaction in which real estate is being used to collateralize a loan.

Mortgagor p. 583   The borrower in a transaction in which real estate is being used to collateralize a loan.

Promissory note p. 583   A contract in which the borrower promises to pay back the creditor at a certain rate of interest over a specified period of years.

Mortgage foreclosure p. 583   A remedy against a debtor in which a creditor declares the loan in default and takes title and possession of the collateralized real estate in hopes of selling the property to pay off the debt owed.

Surety p. 584   A third party that agrees to be primarily liable to pay a loan.

Guarantor p. 584   A third party that agrees to be liable to pay a loan only if the debtor actually defaults.

Personal guaranty p. 584   In a business loan, a pledge given by the principals of a business to repay the loan with their personal assets if the assets of the business are insufficient to do so in the event of a default by the business entity debtor; serves as a safeguard for creditors.

Insolvent p. 585   Condition in which a business venture no longer has adequate assets to maintain its operations and can no longer pay its bills as they become due in the usual course of trade and business.

Workout p. 586   The process in which a debtor meets a loan commitment by satisfying altered repayment terms; intended to turn around a business when the principals wish to continue operations and the business is underperforming and is in poor financial condition.

Accord and satisfaction p. 586   A legal contract between debtor and creditor whereby the creditor agrees to accept a sum less than owed in exchange for releasing the debtor from all legal liability.

Automatic stay p. 587   A legal prohibition of creditors' either initiating or continuing any debt collection action against the debtor or her property.

Bankruptcy trustee p. 587   An individual, often an attorney highly skilled in bankruptcy law, appointed in Chapter 7 or Chapter 13 cases and charged with the duty of taking control of the bankruptcy estate and reducing it to cash for distribution, preserving the interests of both the debtor and the creditors.

Bankruptcy estate p. 588   The debtor's available assets in a bankruptcy proceeding.

Voidable transfers p. 588   In bankruptcy proceedings, certain transfers that are considered an unfair advantage of one creditor over another.

Voluntary bankruptcy petition p. 589   A petition filed in the bankruptcy court by the debtor that includes the names of creditors, a list of debts, and a list of the debtor's assets, income, and expenses.

Involuntary bankruptcy petition p. 589   A petition filed in the bankruptcy court against a debtor by a group of three or more creditors with an unsecured aggregate claim of at least $11,625 who claim that the debtor is failing to pay the debt as it comes due.

Debtor in possession (DIP) p. 591   A Chapter 11 bankruptcy process in which the debtor generally remains in control of assets and business operations in an attempt to rehabilitate the business entity.

Strong-arm clause p. 592   Provision of the Bankruptcy Code that allows the debtor in possession to avoid any obligation or transfer of property that the debtor would otherwise be obligated to perform.

Reorganization plan p. 592   A plan, generally filed by the debtor, that articulates a specific strategy and financial plan for emerging from financial distress; serves as the keystone of a Chapter 11 case.

Cram-down provision p. 592   A term used in reference to the Chapter 11 provision that allows the debtor to request that the court force the creditors to accept a plan that is fair, equitable, and feasible.

Yankee Export Company (YEC) is a purveyor of U.S. products for several European food market chains. YEC's annual revenue is approximately $10 million, and the company employs approximately 20 people, including YEC's only shareholders, directors, and officers: Moss and Whippany. Moss is the day-to-day manager of the venture, while Whippany is mostly an investor with no management duties other than giving consultation on business matters when asked by Moss. For several years, the venture was profitable, but due to a rapid increase in the value of the U.S. dollar against European currencies, YEC began to have cash flow problems. Its products were becoming more expensive for its European customers, and orders dropped slowly over a period of a year. When it appeared that YEC would be unable to generate enough cash to cover monthly expenses, Moss called for a meeting with Whippany and with YEC's accountants. The parties agreed that the rise of the dollar had a negative impact on all U.S. exports and that YEC was at the beginning of a financial challenge. The company's assets were approximately $200,000. The current major debts are set out in the following YEC Creditor Table.

1. Identify the probable category of each creditor. What are the rights of each creditor in the event that YEC defaults on its obligation to that particular creditor?

2. If Moss and Whippany believe the financial crisis is temporary, what are their best nonstatutory options to continue the business if it becomes insolvent? What statutory option(s) do they have?

3. If Moss and Whippany do not believe the financial crisis is recoverable, what nonstatutory and statutory options does YEC have? What are the advantages and drawbacks of each option? If the building lease were not personally guaranteed by Moss and Whippany, how would this fact change your analysis?

4. Which creditors are bound by the provisions of UCC Article 9?

5. Does the fact that YEC has 20 employees add any ethical obligations that should be considered in Moss and Whippany's decision making concerning the future of the company?

6. Suppose that the landlord begins to start eviction proceedings due to YEC's payment default. How could YEC stop the eviction?

7. If YEC files for Chapter 7, what debts are potentially dischargeable? Assuming any assets are left, in what order would the creditors be paid?

YEC Creditor Table

Creditor	Reason	Amount
IRS	Back taxes.	$35,000
Ag Industries	U.S. trade creditor from which YEC buys its inventory.	$20,000 balance secured with a promissory note and perfected security interest in inventory
Landlord	Five years left on the office building lease.	$50,000 per year (backed by personal guarantees of Moss and Whippany)
Office Leasing Company	Two years left on equipment lease.	$500 per month
Company credit card	Office supplies and miscellaneous items.	$8,000 balance
Whippany	Whippany gave YEC a $15,000 personal loan evidenced only by a promissory note.	$11,000 balance payable on a monthly basis for 36 more months at 8% interest

Sometimes managers and owners are one and the same, and playing both roles can be a difficult line to walk. Relationships between parties in a business entity are governed by legal duties (these duties were discussed in Unit Four) owed to one another. Yet the manager/owner must also be sure to be attuned to the other legal requirements and the relationships between the company and third-party creditors or vendors. Suppose that, in the Theory to Practice problem, Moss and Whippany decide to try to maintain YEC's operations for one more month and then make a final decision on whether or not to seek bankruptcy. Whippany sends an e-mail to Moss requesting that Moss authorize immediately the full payment by YEC of Whippany's personal loan. Draft a two paragraph e-mail that Moss could send to Whippany that analyzes (1) the legal risks and consequences of honoring Whippany's request, (2) the potential harm to relationships with other creditors, and (3) the ethical implications of paying back the loan early. A sample answer may be found on this textbook's website at www.mhhe.com/melvinleb2e.

CASE SUMMARY 21.1 :: In re Fehrs, 391 B.R. 53 (Bankr. D. Idaho, 2008)

VOIDABLE TRANSFERS

In 2002, Fehrs met and began living with her boyfriend, Murrietta. They also lived with her teenage son from a former marriage, Jae. Fehrs bought a housing lot at 464 Second Street and another at 117 Terrill Loop, both in the city of Mullan, Idaho. Fehrs and Murrietta contracted with Peter Axtman to build them a house at 464 Second Street. As construction began, problems arose. Soon Murrietta and Fehrs broke up, and Axtman filed a lawsuit against Fehrs for what he was owed for his services. Two months after the suit was filed, Fehrs transferred her property at 117 Terrill Loop to her son Jae in exchange for $1. Fehrs said she made the transfer because Jae was always drinking and partying with friends at 117 Terrill Loop and she did not want to be liable if anything should happen. Two months later Fehrs filed for bankruptcy.

CASE QUESTIONS

1. Why do you think Fehrs sold the lot to her son?
2. What can the trustee do to make sure Axtman gets all he is owed?

CASE SUMMARY 21.2 :: Ellison v. Comm'r of Internal Revenue Service, 385 B.R. 158 (S.D. W. Va. 2008)

AUTOMATIC STAY

Ellison ran a small company, and both he and his company filed for bankruptcy in 1994. The court issued an automatic stay to creditors. A month later the IRS contacted Ellison about unpaid taxes from 1993. Although Ellison consented to the tax being assessed, the IRS continued to pursue payment of the back taxes even after the bankruptcy petition was filed. Ellison filed suit against the IRS for the violation of her automatic stay rights under the bankruptcy code.

CASE QUESTIONS

1. Will Ellison not have to pay these taxes, or can they be discharged?
2. Does the IRS have any defense to pursuing the debt during the automatic stay period?
3. If Ellison wins, what does that say about the power of an automatic stay?

NONDISCHARGEABLE DEBTS

Fedderson ran Big Al's restaurant, which was doing poorly. In a last-ditch effort to make more money, he bought a $2,000 ice cream machine for Big Al's on his personal credit card. Sixty days later Fedderson filed for bankruptcy. The credit card company argued that the ice cream machine debt should not be discharged because it is a luxury good that was bought too close to the bankruptcy petition.

CASE QUESTIONS

1. Should the ice cream machine debt be discharged?
2. Should it matter to the court that Fedderson should have known that he would be insolvent in two months and that trying to stop financial catastrophe with an ice cream machine was foolish?

CHAPTER 11 AND COLLECTIVE BARGAINING AGREEMENTS

In October, Northwest Airlines declared Chapter 11 bankruptcy and sought to renegotiate a collective bargaining agreement with the flight attendants' union. The contract would need to be changed for Northwest to reorganize and try to save the company. After several months of negotiations, the union finally rejected a March 1 proposal. Northwest's DIP asked the court to unilaterally enforce the terms of the rejected agreement because the union had failed to agree to reasonable terms.

CASE QUESTIONS

1. What is the name of the power that Northwest is asking the court to exercise?
2. What must the court find about the union's rejection to permit unilateral enforcement?
3. Should it matter that Northwest easily reached agreements with both the pilots' and mechanics' unions?

MEANS TEST

When Charmaine Richie filed for Chapter 7 bankruptcy, she had been making a living through odd jobs over the past year yielding an income of $22,608. The median income is $37,873 for her home state of Wisconsin. Just prior to her bankruptcy petition filing, Richie completed a master's degree in outdoor therapeutic recreation administration, which qualified her to work as a therapist for the handicapped in a camp or outdoor clinical setting. A job in this field would likely have brought Richie well above the median income and disqualify her for protection under a Chapter 7 bankruptcy. Additionally, Richie had been looking for jobs in her field but only in the Racine-Kenosha area of Wisconsin, where there were very few opportunities. She was qualified to work at many other jobs that would have brought her above the median, but she wanted employment only in her chosen field and in her home geographic area.

After her petition was filed, the bankruptcy trustee requested the court to reject the Chapter 7 petition and convert the case to a Chapter 13 petition, whereby Richie would have to pay all or much of her debt. The trustee alleged that Richie was abusing the Chapter 7 bankruptcy means test because she was *capable* of earning more money but did not. Moreover, Richie filed bankruptcy immediately after graduate school, when her future earning potential was relatively high. Richie argued that moving elsewhere to work would be a burden and having a different full-time job would hurt her future prospects for getting a job in her chosen field.

CASE QUESTIONS

1. Should Richie be forced to relocate or work in another field in order to use bankruptcy laws?
2. Richie lacks the ability to pay because she has not engaged in a broad employment search, does not wish to work outside her chosen field, and does not wish to work within her chosen field outside her geographic area. Should her creditors bear the burden of her choices?

 Self-check **ANSWERS**

Creditor Status

1. ExtremeCo has a perfected (by filing) security interest in Retailer's inventory.
2. Office Galaxy is an unsecured creditor.
3. BigBank is a secured creditor as mortgagee, with WidgetCo as mortgagor.
4. BigBank is an unsecured creditor of WidgetCo, *but* the debt is collateralized through personal guarantees in the event of default.

---

22 CHAPTER

Consumer Protection Law

learning objectives

After studying this chapter, students who have mastered the material will be able to:

22-1 Explain the role of the Federal Trade Commission in terms of various statutory consumer protections.

22-2 Articulate the standards used to define false advertising and other deceptive practices and identify specific consumer protection laws applied to bulk e-mail.

22-3 Define *warranty* and give an example of a warranty.

22-4 Distinguish between express warranties and implied warranties, explain the protections afforded by each type of warranty, and articulate the standards for disclaiming a warranty.

22-5 Name and explain the federal statutory protections afforded to consumers for faulty or unsafe products and for food and drug safety.

22-6 Identify the parties in a credit transaction and understand the role of federal statutory laws in consumer credit transactions.

22-7 List the various components of the Truth in Lending Act and give specific examples of regulatory requirements.

22-8 Explain the protections afforded to consumers by federal statutes regulating the collection of consumer debt.

Since the height of the American industrial revolution, the body of law that protects consumers in transactions with merchants and creditors has grown dramatically. As the law becomes increasingly concerned with protecting consumers, statutes and administrative regulations that form a body known as **consumer law** have become progressively more important in their impact on business owners and managers. Individuals and businesses are subject to regulation at the federal, state, and local levels in a wide variety of consumer transactions. In this chapter, students will learn how the law protects consumers in three areas:

- Unfair and deceptive trade practices.
- Product quality and functionality.
- Credit and collection of consumer debts.

UNFAIR OR DECEPTIVE SALES PRACTICES LO 22-1

Until the early 20th century, the only legal protection that consumers had against unscrupulous sellers that engaged in deceit during a sale was a common law suit for fraud. In 1914, Congress passed the **Federal Trade Commission Act (FTCA),**[1] one of the very first statutory

---
[1] 15 U.S.C. § 41 et seq.

protections for American consumers. The FTCA established an administrative agency called the **Federal Trade Commission (FTC)** and charged the FTC with the broad mandate of preventing unfair and deceptive acts or practices in commercial transactions. Courts have been very deferential to the FTC's wide-ranging authority over advertising, price disclosures, and representations made during the sales process of consumer goods. Under this authority, the FTC has promulgated regulations that define a deceptive practice as one that is likely to *mislead* a reasonably prudent consumer and that resulted in some sort of *detriment* to the consumer.

FALSE ADVERTISING LO 22-2

Deceptive advertising is a significant source of consumer complaints. FTC regulations and memorandums provide several specific examples of prohibited deceptive advertising, such as making *expressly false statements* in an advertisement about a product's quality, ingredients, or effectiveness. Note that in addition to violating the FTC's regulations, expressly false advertisements may also give rise to a breach of warranty (discussed later in this chapter). The FTC rule also prohibits the use of fake testimonials or endorsements and the use of fake pictures of the product performing in a manner that is inaccurate.

Bait and Switch

Regulatory authorities have become increasingly aggressive about investigation of complaints by consumers of bait and switch ploys. In bait and switch scheme, a seller advertises an item for sale at a particularly good price (30 percent off retail) or on favorable terms (zero down, zero interest), but the seller has no intention of actually selling that product at that price or on those terms. When the consumer comes to the business after seeing the advertisement, the seller discourages the purchase of the advertised item and instead tries to convince the buyer to purchase a different item for a higher price or on less favorable terms. The seller's techniques for discouraging the purchase of the product vary (such as lying about whether the product was sold out or was ever available), but the end result is the same: The buyer walks out of the store with a more expensive product than the advertised product. For example, suppose that Widget Depot, a merchant, advertises a sale as follows: "Classic Widgets on sale: 40% off retail value! Clearance sale" (the bait). When Copperfield shows up a day later at Widget Depot and asks for a Classic Widget, he is referred to the manager. The manager gives a false explanation to Copperfield that the Classic Widget is out of stock and more would have to be retrieved from an off-site facility. This means Copperfield would have to wait one week for a Classic Widget. However, the manager offers Copperfield an alternative: For his trouble and time, she will sell him the newly introduced Ultimate Widget, which is currently in stock at an introductory price of 5 percent off the normal retail price. The manager goes on to explain that although the Ultimate Widget is more expensive than the Classic Widget (especially given the 40 percent Classic Widget discount), the Ultimate Widget could be trusted to last longer than the Classic. Thus, the dishonest manager reasoned, the Ultimate was actually a better deal than the Classic. Copperfield relies on the manager's advice and buys the Ultimate Widget. Under most state statutes, the conduct of Widget Depot's manager was unlawful as a bait and switch scheme.

The Federal Trade Commission (FTC) has broad authority to ensure that merchant advertising is not deceptive or misleading.

Pricing

Pricing is an important component of advertising and is also subject to consumer protection regulations. Some of the more common examples of deceptive advertising via pricing are:

- Misrepresenting the prices of a competitor.
- Artificially inflating the original retail price of a product when featuring it as a sale item in order to make it appear that the original price was higher than it actually was.
- Using phrases such as "clearance priced" or "marked down for sale" when the items are not being sold at reduced rates.

Financial Institutions

In addition to the FTC, the Office of the Comptroller of the Currency (OCC) also pursues violations of the Federal Trade Commission Act if the deceptive advertising involves a financial institution such as a bank. For example, in one case, California-based Providian National Bank agreed to pay fines and restitution totaling $300 million for deceptive advertising. The case centered on Providian's credit card "payment protection plan" program. The program involved an agreement for the cardholder to pay a monthly fee for an insurance plan, which Providian advertised would cover the cardholder's monthly minimum amount due if the cardholder suffered involuntary unemployment, hospitalization, or disability. Providian's advertising materials promised that the cardholder would not have to pay monthly credit card payments for up to 18 months from the time of unemployment, hospitalization, or disability. However, Providian failed to adequately disclose that in the case of involuntary unemployment, consumers were covered under the plan *only* for the number of months in which the consumer paid credit protection fees, rather than the advertised 18 months. Authorities also took issue with Providian's claim that its credit card had no annual fee. In practice, Providian waived the annual fee of $60 only if the consumer signed up for the aforementioned credit protection plan—at a cost of $156 per year.[2]

Telemarketing

Public concern about deceptive telemarketing practices targeting elderly victims in the 1990s resulted in Congress enacting several statutes regulating telemarketing firms and practices. The primary statutes are the **Telephone Consumer Protection Act**[3] and the **Telemarketing and Consumer Fraud and Abuse Prevention Act.**[4] These laws (1) allow consumers to *opt out* of receiving unwanted calls from telemarketers, (2) ban the use of unsolicited recorded calls and faxes, (3) regulate 900-number calls to prevent consumers from unknowingly generating charges, (4) prohibit telemarketers from making false representations, and (5) require disclosure of all the material terms of a proposed transaction. The laws prescribe *how* and *when* a telemarketer may obtain permission to obtain payment from the consumer's checking, savings, or credit accounts. It also prohibits any harassment, threats, or deceit by the telemarketer.

Do Not Call List   The FTC established the Do Not Call Registry whereby consumers may sign up to be on a list that protects them from certain

Visit Connect to learn where you can register for the Do Not Call list.

unsolicited calls by telemarketers. Some organizations are exempt from the Do Not Call list prohibitions. They include (1) charitable organizations, (2) certain political organizations, and (3) businesses with whom the consumer has had past commercial contacts.

---

[2]Comptroller of the Currency and Administrator of National Banks Press Release, NR 2000-49.

[3]47 U.S.C. § 227.

[4]15 U.S.C. § 6101 et seq.

Odometers

The U.S. Department of Transportation estimates that odometer rollback, the process of physically altering a vehicle's odometer in order to make it appear as if the vehicle had traveled fewer miles than it actually had, is a $3-billion-a-year enterprise.[5] Odometer fraud is perpetrated both easily and surreptitiously, and it was often impossible for a consumer to detect. The **Federal Odometer Act**[6] makes it a crime to change vehicle odometers and requires that any faulty odometer be plainly disclosed in writing to potential buyers. The law sets out regulations that (1) define and prohibit odometer tampering, (2) prohibit buying or installing any device used for tampering, (3) prescribe procedures for odometer repair, (4) require certain disclosures related to the actual mileage of the vehicle when it is sold to a new owner, (5) give jurisdiction for the implementation and enforcement of the law to the secretary of transportation, and (6) impose a record-keeping requirement on vehicle dealers and distributors.

In addition to giving the secretary of transportation the authority to enforce the statute, the law provides victims of odometer tampering with a remedy of *triple* the actual damages suffered. However, the lawsuit must take place within two years of the date of purchase.

State Statutes

In addition to federal statutes, each state has adopted consumer protections by enacting state laws aimed at preventing unfair or deceptive trade practices within state borders. The statutes often empower the state attorney general to pursue violators using enforcement mechanisms such as civil lawsuits and, in extreme cases, criminal charges. Many states have created specific task forces to police merchants' and other sellers' compliance with consumer protection statutes in regard to transactions that take place primarily within the state's borders. Enforcement powers are usually given to the state's law enforcement authorities: the state attorney general and local district attorneys. State statutes often give aggrieved consumers the right to bring a lawsuit directly against any violator to recover damages. Therefore, federal agencies and state authorities are thought of as having concurrent (overlapping) jurisdiction.

State statutory protections often fill gaps in federal protections. For example, the New Jersey Consumer Fraud Act covers certain transactions that would not be within the coverage of a federal statute. In Case 22.1, a New Jersey appellate court applies a state consumer fraud statute to a real estate transaction.

CASE 22.1 Vagias v. Woodmont Properties, 894 A.2d 68 (N.J. Super. Ct. 2006)

FACT SUMMARY   Vagias hired Dingle as his realtor and told her that he was in the market to buy a house in Montville Township, New Jersey. Vagias communicated to Dingle that he desired that particular municipality due to the favorable reputation of the township's schools. Dingle showed Vagias a house in a development called Woodmont Court at Montville, and Vagias inquired as to whether this house was actually located within the jurisdictional limits of Montville Township. Dingle and a representative of the builder, neither of whom were familiar with the township boundaries, assured Vagias that the house was in Montville Township and Vagias purchased the home for $740,000. When Vagias attempted to enroll his son in the school system, he learned that his house was actually located outside the Montville Township limits. Vagias sued to have the sale rescinded on the basis of Dingle's and the homebuilder's misrepresentation concerning location. Vagias argued that he had paid a premium for the house based on the reputation of the school system in a

---

[5]See *Secretary of Transportation's Report to the Congress on the Federal Odometer Act* (2006).
[6]49 U.S.C. § 32701 et seq.

certain township. Woodmont argued that the misrepresentations were not intentional and that Vagias suffered no loss in the value of the home.

SYNOPSIS OF DECISION AND OPINION The Superior Court of New Jersey ruled in favor of Vagias. The court held that Vagias specified that location in Montville Township was a prerequisite to purchasing a house at Woodmont and, therefore, that location became a part of the basis of the bargain. Under the New Jersey Consumer Fraud Act, Dingle's misrepresentation need not be an intentional misrepresentation. Dingle and Woodmont knew of Vagias's concerns and made an affirmative misrepresentation. That is all that is necessary to prevail in a New Jersey Consumer Fraud Act case.

WORDS OF THE COURT: No Intent Required "[W]hen [the real estate agent] told [Vagias] that the house was in 'Montville' she made an affirmative misrepresentation. Her intent is not an issue for purposes of the Act. If she provided plaintiffs with affirmative misinformation on what she knew was a critical issue in their decision to purchase the house, she violated the Act. . . . Further, she was not an innocent bystander making a casual comment. She was assisting plaintiffs in choosing a house to buy, and she received a commission on the sale. [Thus] Dingle's statements were not idle comments or mere puffery."

Case Questions

1. Had Dingle not known that Vagias was specifically looking for a home in Montville Township yet had still made her statements, would the outcome of the case have been different? Why or why not? Explain your answer.

2. If Vagias paid market value for his home still been able to send his son to a highly rated elementary school, and the only detriment imposed upon him was a lower social status due to the location of the home, how would that affect your analysis?

LEGAL IMPLICATIONS *in* CYBERSPACE

Regulation of Online Advertising

As use of the Internet by consumers increased in the late 1990s, *spam*—unsolicited e-mails advertising a product or service—became so increasingly problematic that state legislatures took the early lead in regulating spam and establishing tough criminal penalties for illegal spam suppliers. Thirty-three states passed some form of legislation that attempted to regulate unsolicited e-mails. California's law was one of the toughest because it required online marketers to obtain a consumer's permission *prior* to sending e-mail solicitations. Virginia went a step further and made sending certain unsolicited e-mails a felony and indicted two men for running a large illegal bulk e-mail operation. Some states, such as New York, passed antispam legislation as part of a larger package of identity theft laws. Then New York Attorney General Eliot Spitzer[7] grabbed headlines by indicting a man, dubbed the "Buffalo Spammer," for sending 825 million spam messages.

However, there was no *federal* statute regulating unsolicited e-mail until Congress passed the **Controlling the Assault of Non-Solicited Pornography and Marketing Act of 2003,**[8] better known as the CAN-SPAM Act. The new law supplanted sometimes-tougher state statutes, but it still outlawed the dubious methods used by certain spam suppliers and provided for criminal sanctions in severe cases. The statute also prohibits online marketing providers from falsifying the "from" name and information in the subject line designed to fool consumers into opening an unsolicited e-mail message. It also requires the sender to provide a physical address of the producer of the e-mail and specifically label any pornographic links with adult-content warnings. The law imposes an affirmative obligation on the sender to notify the recipient of procedures to opt out of receiving any future e-mail from the sender. One controversial provision of the law required the FTC to start a "do-not-spam" list modeled on the Do Not Call list. However, the FTC resisted the notion of

[7]Mr. Spitzer was later elected governor of New York, but resigned in the wake of a prostitution scandal.

[8]15 U.S.C. § 7701 et seq.

(continued)

creating such a list based on technology and privacy grounds, and the list was never implemented.

The CAN-SPAM Act allows e-mail recipients the right to bring a lawsuit directly against the spammer as a compliance mechanism in egregious cases and in cases where the plaintiff can prove that the spam produced actual damages (such as a shutdown of a retail store's computer server that caused loss of profits or repair charges). The FTC has been aggressively enforcing the law against the most serious offenders and pursuing criminal charges where appropriate. For example, in June 2007, two spammers were convicted under the CAN-SPAM Act for sending out millions of e-mail messages with highly offensive pornographic images. The defendants were sentenced to five years in prison and ordered to pay $1.3 million from the profits of their front company.[9] The FTC has also used its enforcement authority to file civil complaints against companies that are engaged in spamming as part of their marketing strategy. The FTC is particularly strict in its enforcement of the CAN-SPAM Act when pursuing companies whose primary market is Internet pornography.[10]

In 2005, the FTC issued a report that indicated that the volume of spam had leveled off since the law was enacted, with a marked decrease in sexually explicit e-mail, which reached fewer mailboxes. Critics of the CAN-SPAM Act contend that the decrease is due primarily to enhanced technology improvements in e-mail filtering and that the act is ineffective and difficult to enforce. One report featured in *PC Magazine* concluded that less than 1 percent of spam complied with the CAN-SPAM Act. Responding to some industry criticism of the effectiveness of the law, the FTC revised its regulations in 2008 to widen its jurisdiction and specifically prohibit spam distributors from charging a consumer a fee in order to process an opt-out request.

[9]*United States v. Shaffer*, 472 F.3d 1219 (10th Cir., 2007). The defendants were also convicted of mail fraud and racketeering.

[10]See *FTC Cracks Down on Illegal X-Rated Spam*, Federal Trade Commission Bulletin 2005-07-20.

CONCEPT SUMMARY Unfair and Deceptive Trade Practices

- The Federal Trade Commission (FTC) is charged with preventing unfair and deceptive acts or practices in commercial transactions. In doing so, the FTC has wide-ranging authority over advertising, price disclosures, and representations made during the sales process of consumer goods.

- In bait and switch schemes, a seller advertises an item for sale at a very good price or on favorable terms but in reality has no intention of actually selling that product at that price or on those terms. Instead, when the consumer comes to the business after seeing the advertisement, the seller discourages the purchase of the advertised item and tries to convince the buyer to purchase a different item for a higher price or on less favorable terms.

- Pricing is also subject to consumer protection regulations, including a ban on misrepresentations of the prices of a competitor, artificially inflating the original retail price of a product when featuring it as a sale item, and using phrases such as "clearance priced" or "marked down for sale" when the items are not being sold at reduced prices.

- The FTC established the Do Not Call Registry whereby consumers sign up to be on a list that protects them from certain unsolicited calls by telemarketers.

- The Federal Odometer Act makes it a crime to change vehicle odometers and requires that any faulty odometer be plainly disclosed in writing to potential buyers.

- The Controlling the Assault of Non-Solicited Pornography and Marketing (CAN-SPAM) Act of 2003 regulates the sending of unsolicited e-mail (spam) by prohibiting certain online marketing practices, including falsifying the "from" name and information in the subject line, and mandating that senders provide a physical address of the producer of the e-mail.

WARRANTIES

Consumers have certain statutory protections related to the quality and functionality of products sold by merchants. These protections are derived primarily from *products liability* statutes and *commercial law* statutes, which provide for *warranty* protection. Some of these statutes overlap with other consumer protection laws. Products liability statutes often operate in tandem with laws related to negligence; thus, products liability law is discussed in detail in Chapter 10, "Torts and Products Liability."

A **warranty** is a seller's (or lessor's) promise to a consumer concerning the quality and/or functionality of a product. Warranties are recognized as legally enforceable promises under state statutory laws that are based on Article 2 of the Uniform Commercial Code. Recall that in Chapter 9, "Contracts for the Sale of Goods," Article 2 was covered in the context of formation and performance of *sales contracts*. The focus of this chapter is the *warranty provisions* of Article 2 that protect consumers. When the seller makes a representation of *fact* about a product, this is known as an **express warranty.** If the seller has not made a specific representation about the product, the buyer may still be protected by a UCC-imposed **implied warranty.**

Express Warranty

In some cases a seller expressly represents that the goods have certain *qualities* or a certain level of *efficiency*. If the goods turn out not to have these qualities, the buyer may sue for a breach of the express warranty. As a practical matter, many of these seller representations are made through advertising. In one famous case,[11] the supreme court in the state of Washington held that a car manufacturer breached an express warranty when it advertised in its brochures that the car had "shatter proof glass" that would not fly or shatter even upon the "hardest impact." After a small pebble struck the windshield and resulted in shattered glass and injuries to the driver, the court ruled in favor of the injured driver, stating that the buyer had *reasonably relied* on those representations and had no reason to suspect they were false.

Because many express warranties arise in the context of advertising, the UCC makes a distinction between factual promises and "puffery." Puffery is a *nonfactual* statement commonly used in advertising with such claims as "This car gets great gas mileage" or "Sweater made from finest wool." Of course, neither of these statements is fact-based because there is no method to verify words such as "great" or "finest." Thus, neither of these statements constitutes an express warranty. However, if the statements are changed slightly to "This car gets 35 miles per gallon when driven on the highway" or "Sweater is 100% Irish wool," then these statements may be considered factual promises to the buyer, thus creating an express warranty from the seller.

 Self-Check Express Warranty

Has an express warranty been created?

1. Randall has been the victim of several robberies in his store. He purchases a chemical weapon spray called Repel that was advertised to "instantly stop attackers" and "incapacitate groups of people instantly." Randall is robbed and attempts to use Repel to stop the crime, but the robber is not stopped. Rather, he becomes enraged and assaults Randall during the robbery.

2. Juliet sees a newspaper advertisement by a car manufacturer: "The sexiest convertible on the market."

(continued)

---

[11]*Baxter v. Ford Motor Co.,* 12 P.2d 409 (Wash. 1932).

3. Benjamin buys a watch that bears this sticker on the packaging: "100% waterproof."

4. Jenner watches a TV ad for running shoes that shows scenes of a jogger in a park and then switches the scene to the same runner on a snow-covered hiking trail. The catchphrase "A sneaker for all seasons" flashes on the screen. No mention is made of the shoes' suitability for use on a particular surface. Jenner purchases the shoes, and when he runs on a snowy trail, they fall apart and Jenner suffers foot injuries as a result.

Answers to this Self-Check are provided at the end of the chapter.

Implied Warranties

Even in cases where the seller makes no express promise about the goods, the UCC imposes several *implied warranties.* Implied warranties apply only in specific circumstances and have certain limits as to their protections of buyers.

Merchantability
The implied warranty of merchantability[12] applies to every sale of a product from a *merchant* to a buyer (note that the buyer may or may not be a merchant) and requires the seller to warrant that the product is fit for its ordinary use. For purposes of the UCC, a merchant is one who is regularly engaged in the sale of that product. Thus, if you purchase a new or used lawn mower from your neighbor (an accountant), no implied warranty exists. Merchants must also conform to the industry safety standards in packaging and labeling the goods in order for the goods to qualify as merchantable. This UCC requirement also applies to food and drink to be consumed either on the merchant's premises or somewhere else.

Fitness for a Particular Purpose
An implied warranty also arises when a seller promises that the product is fit for a particular purpose.[13] In order for this warranty to be created, the buyer must prove that the seller knew of the buyer's desire to use the product in a specified way (not necessarily in its ordinary way) and the buyer relied on the seller's advice and recommendation. For example, suppose that Buyer consults with Salesperson and indicates that she requires a new set of boots for a hiking trip that will involve walking through small streams. Salesperson recommends that Buyer purchase brand A boots for the hiking trip. Buyer purchases the boots, but when she is hiking, it turns out the boots are not waterproof and they fall apart on the first day of hiking through a small stream. Buyer's boots are destroyed, and she suffers injuries to her feet that require medical care. Because no express promise was made concerning the boots, Buyer must turn to an implied-warranty theory. In this case, Buyer will be able to recover based on a breach of *implied* warranty of fitness for a particular use.

Warranty Disclaimers and Limitations

The UCC allows a seller to **disclaim** both implied and express warranties under certain conditions. However, in order to disclaim a warranty, the seller must do so in a conspicuous writing by using, for example, capital letters, bold print, or a larger font that stands out from the rest of the writing. Although the UCC does not require specific language to disclaim warranties, courts have held phrases such as "with all faults" or "as is" as sufficient to disclaim a warranty. However, the UCC does require that any disclaimer of the warranty of merchantability actually use the word "merchantability" in the disclaimer.

Sellers may also, under certain circumstances, *limit the remedies* of a buyer who has suffered damages because of a seller's breach of warranty. This limitation of remedies is

---

[12]UCC § 2-314(2).
[13]UCC § 2-315.

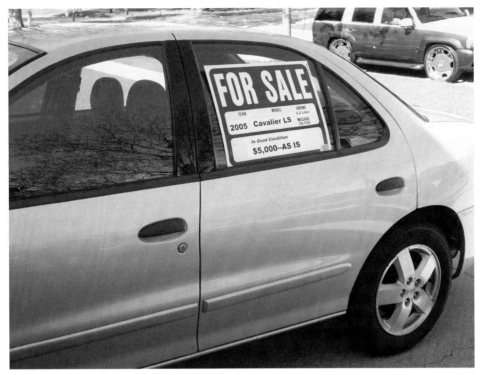

In order to disclaim express or implied warranties, a seller must conspicuously use disclaimer language such as "with all faults" or "as is."

primarily used when the only harm suffered by the buyer was the loss of the use of the product. In such cases, the seller may attempt to limit the remedy to replacement or repair of the product and cut off any consequential damages (as might arise, e.g., if the buyer suffered loss of profit due to the defective product). However, the UCC makes clear that any attempt to limit damages when a *personal injury* is involved will be automatically void. It is important to note that the Magnuson-Moss Act, discussed later in this chapter, *restricts* certain disclaimers and limitations of remedies by sellers.

In Case 22.2, an appellate court considers whether alleged hearing loss from an iPod can be the basis of a breach-of-warranty claim.

Magnuson-Moss Warranty–Federal Trade Commission Improvement Act

LO 22-5

The Magnuson-Moss Warranty–Federal Trade Commission Improvement Act,[14] generally referred to by its short title, the *Magnuson-Moss Act,* regulates warranties given by a seller or lessor to a consumer. As with other consumer protection statutes, the Magnuson-Moss Act does *not* apply to purely merchant transactions, in which the buyer and seller are regularly engaged in the sale of goods. A consumer is defined as one who purchases or leases a good with the intent of using it for *personal* reasons rather than resale or use in a business. The Magnuson-Moss Act does *not* mandate that sellers offer a warranty to a buyer. However, if the seller or lessor does offer a **written express warranty,** the transaction is subject to the provisions of the statute. It is important to note that the Magnuson-Moss Act did not create any additional implied warranties upon which consumers can base a lawsuit; rather,

---

[14]15 U.S.C.A. § 2301.

FACT SUMMARY Apple's iPod comes with a set of earbud headphones that are detachable from the iPod unit. The iPod may also be used to play music through different headphones or through various speaker systems. Apple includes the following warning with each iPod:

Avoid Hearing Damage

Warning: Permanent hearing loss may occur if earphones or headphones are used at high volume. You can adapt over time to a higher volume of sound, which may sound normal but can be damaging to your hearing. Set your iPod's volume to a safe level before that happens. If you experience ringing in your ears, reduce the volume or discontinue use of your iPod.

Birdsong sought to bring a class action suit against Apple, alleging that the iPod is capable of producing 115 decibels, and the class members were iPod owners who had allegedly suffered hearing loss using the iPod earbud set at the highest decibel level. Birdsong's theory of liability (among other claims) was based on Apple's breach of implied warranty of merchantability. The trial court dismissed Birdsong's suit, and he appealed.

SYNOPSIS OF DECISION AND OPINION The Court of Appeals for the Ninth Circuit upheld the decision in favor of Apple. The court rejected Birdsong's theory that the iPod was not merchantable because it comes with stock earbuds that are designed to be placed deep into the ear canal rather than over the ears, which increases the danger of hearing damage. The court pointed out that the ordinary use of the iPod was to listen to music and that the product was fit for that use. There was no allegation of malfunction, and Birdsong did not allege that the iPods failed to do anything they were designed to do, nor did he allege that he had suffered or is substantially certain to suffer inevitable hearing loss or other injury directly from iPod use.

WORDS OF THE COURT: Ordinary Purpose "The plaintiffs admit that the iPod has an 'ordinary purpose of listening to music,' and nothing they allege suggests iPods are unsafe for that use or defective. The plaintiffs recognize that iPods play music, have an adjustable volume, and transmit sound through earbuds. The [complaint] includes statements that (1) the iPod is capable of playing 115 decibels of sound; (2) consumers may listen at unsafe levels; and (3) iPod batteries can last 12 to 14 hours and are rechargeable, giving users the opportunity to listen for long periods of time. Taken as true, such statements suggest only that users have the option of using an iPod in a risky manner, not that the product lacks any minimum level of quality."

Case Questions

1. If the iPod is capable of playing at a certain level of sound, isn't it foreseeable that users would assume that a high level of sound was "ordinary" use?

2. If Apple did not provide the warning, how would that impact your analysis?

---

it created a *federal cause of action* for the breach of consumer warranties contained in state statutes. This is accomplished by permitting consumers to bring a lawsuit directly against a seller to recover damages as a result of the seller's violating the statute. However, the statute does allow the seller to resolve disputes using an alternative dispute resolution system (such as binding arbitration) so long as the seller made appropriate disclosures about the dispute resolution requirement at the time of the transaction. The Federal Trade Commission is responsible for implementing and enforcing the Magnuson-Moss Act's requirements.

Legal Speak ◄))
Federal Cause of Action A statutorily created right to sue a violator in federal court. Such statutes typically give federal courts specific subject matter jurisdiction over violations of a statute.

Labeling Requirements If the product being warranted costs $10 or more, the Magnuson-Moss Act requires that the warranty itself contain a label stating the conditions of the warranty. Sellers and lessors of products that carry a full-warranty label must honor a repair or replacement promise for defects. A full warranty must also include a term of duration (e.g., "full one-year warranty"). A limited-warranty label means only that the seller does not bind itself to promises of full warranty in some way (e.g., "limited warranty: engine transmission not covered by warranty").

The Magnuson-Moss Act also requires that warranties be written conspicuously and in plain and clear language. The language must be specific to the parts, products, characteristics, or functionality covered by the warranty.

Restrictions on Disclaimers and Limitations   The Magnuson-Moss Act preempts state law and imposes a restriction on disclaimers made by sellers and lessors. The statute modifies rules on disclaimers that were allowed by state law with respect to the implied warranty of merchantability and the implied warranty of fitness for a particular use. If the transaction is covered by the Magnuson-Moss Act (because it involves a *written, express* agreement), the seller may *not* disclaim any implied warranties. Sellers are permitted to set a time frame on the implied warranties so long as the expiration date corresponds with the expiration of any express warranties. If the seller wishes to limit certain damages, the Magnuson-Moss Act requires that such limits be conspicuously featured in the warranty. Typically, the seller complies with this conspicuous-disclosure requirement by featuring the limitation language in **bold** type or setting it apart in some other way in the document. Figure 22.1 provides an example of a warranty disclaimer and limitation of remedies.

> **KEY** POINT
> The Magnuson-Moss Act does not mandate that sellers offer a warranty to a consumer-buyer, nor does it create any additional implied warranties. If the seller does offer a warranty, the transaction is subject to the provisions of the statute.

Consumer Product Safety Act

Congress passed the **Consumer Product Safety Act (CPSA)**[15] in response to a growing number of injuries and deaths being caused by products, particularly toys, sold to consumers.[16] The statute created the Consumer Product Safety Commission as the federal regulatory agency and as a national information clearinghouse intended to achieve the statute's objective of making consumer products safer. The commission researches, institutes, and enforces safety standards for consumer products that pose a potential risk of injury. If the commission determines that a product defect poses an ongoing threat to consumer safety, the manufacturer may be required to institute a recall. As a practical matter, manufacturers that detect a potential problem with one of their consumer products will typically issue a recall order immediately, without an order from the commission, in an effort to stem potential liability. The commission also has traditional regulatory agency authority to enforce regulations and

---

FIGURE 22.1   Sample Disclaimer and Limitation of Remedies

Disclaimer of warranties
The buyer agrees to take the Widget Board with **all faults** and **as is.** The seller does not make any express warranties about the Widget Board and **expressly disclaims the implied warranty of merchantability** and **disclaims** any other **implied warranty** created by law including the **implied warranty of fitness for a particular use.**

Limitation of remedies
Seller's sole obligation and Buyer's **sole remedy** for any damages related to the failure of the Widget Board to perform are **limited to adjustment or replacement** of any part causing the failure or at the **Seller's option** to refund the purchase amount to the Buyer.

---

[15]15 U.S.C. § 2051 et seq.

[16]Just prior to enactment of the statute, the U.S. Department of Health, Education, and Welfare reported that consumer products were causing approximately 30,000 deaths, 110,000 permanent injuries, and 20 million injuries that required medical treatment per year. Familiar toys such as Etch-a-Sketch had caused serious lacerations due to broken glass from the toy's screen for dozens of children.

halt any action inconsistent with the CPSA's objectives. In 2001, the commission instituted action against multinational manufacturer Cosco, Inc., a well-known maker of baby care products, when the company failed to report problems with its baby strollers, car seats, and cribs. After an investigation revealed that Cosco's products had resulted in more than 300 injuries and two deaths to infants and small children, the commission levied a $1.3 million fine against Cosco—one of the largest in the agency's history. The CPSA also gives individual consumers the right to bring a lawsuit directly against a manufacturer that violates the statute.

Other CPSA Protections   Subsequent amendments to the CPSA expanded the commission's jurisdiction to include more specific categories of consumer products. The agency now administers the Flammable Fabrics Act[17] (regulates material used in clothing, especially children's sleepwear), the Child Protection and Toy Safety Act[18] (set standards for components used to make toys, such as a ban on lead paint), the Poison Prevention Packaging Act[19] (set standards for disclosing use of poisons in consumer products, such as detergents and cleansers), and the Refrigerator Safety Act (passed after several media reports of children who were suffocated after climbing in old refrigerators in refuse lots).

FOOD AND DRUG SAFETY

The **Food, Drug and Cosmetic Act (FDCA)** is the federal statute that created the **Food and Drug Administration (FDA)** to regulate the testing, manufacturing, and distributing of foods, medications (including over-the-counter medications and prescription drugs), medical devices, and cosmetics. A major component of the FDCA is the requirement that makers of certain food ingredients, additives, drugs, or medical devices obtain formal FDA approval prior to selling the product to the general public. The application process is very rigorous and evaluates data supplied by the applicant as well as independent evidence from FDA scientists or government contractors. When the FDA has approved a drug for public use, any advertising for the drug is subject to FDA regulation in terms of what representations may be made and what disclosures must be included. FDA regulations also govern *labeling* of food packages.

FDA Regulations and Enforcement: Food Safety

The FDA regulations define specific *food safety* processes, procedures, and standards, such as the requirement that employees handling food wear rubber gloves and hair netting. The statute also sets out a broader catchall standard by outlawing any generally *adulterated* food that has potential for public harm. The FDA defines adulterated food as that which contains a "filthy, putrid, or decomposed substance" or any food "unfit for consumption."

The FDA also investigates any public outbreaks of illness related to food contamination. During its investigation of such outbreaks, the FDA uses its broad enforcement powers to detect and prevent any further contamination. These powers include seizure of contaminated products, mandatory recalls, civil enforcement lawsuits, fines, and criminal prosecution for egregious cases. One of the largest fines ever levied by FDA was against Odwalla Juice Company in 1998. The Odwalla juice case is featured as a Capstone Case Study in the back of this textbook.

> **KEY** POINT
>
> The FDA enforces both specific and general standards for food safety. While certain regulations set out specific purity or safety standards, a catchall provision sets out a general standard banning all adulterated food.

---

[17]15 U.S.C. § 1191.

[18]15 U.S.C. § 1262(e).

[19]15 U.S.C. § 2079.

- A warranty is a seller's legally enforceable promise to a consumer concerning the quality and/or functionality of a product.

- Express warranties are created (generally through advertising) when the seller promises that the goods have certain qualities or a certain level of efficiency.

- Puffery is a non-fact-based statement used in advertising that does not create an express warranty.

- The implied warranty of merchantability applies to every sale of a product from a merchant to a buyer and requires the seller to warrant that the product is fit for its ordinary use.

- An implied warranty is created when a seller promises that the product is fit for a particular purpose. In order for the warranty to arise, the buyer must prove that the seller knew of the buyer's desire to use the product in a specified way and the buyer relied on the seller's advice and recommendation.

- In order to disclaim a warranty, the seller must do so in a conspicuous writing by using, for example, capital letters, bold print, or a larger font that stands out from the rest of the writing.

- The Magnuson-Moss Act is a federal statute that regulates warranties given by a seller or lessor to a consumer. If the seller or lessor offers a written warranty, the transaction is subject to the provisions of the statute. If an express warranty is given, the seller may not disclaim implied warranties.

- Under the Magnuson-Moss Act, if the product being warranted costs $10 or more, the act requires that warranties be written conspicuously and in plain and clear language and be specific to the parts, products, characteristics, or functionality covered by the warranty.

- The Food, Drug and Cosmetic Act (FDCA) created the Food and Drug Administration (FDA) to regulate the testing, manufacturing, and distributing of foods, medications, and medical devices. A major component of the FDCA is the requirement that makers of certain food ingredients, additives, drugs, or medical devices obtain formal FDA approval before selling the product to the general public.

CREDIT TRANSACTIONS

Credit is one of the most important components of a stable economy.[20] The use of credit by consumers in the business environment is widespread and primarily exists in the form of loans and credit cards. A consumer credit transaction takes place between a **creditor**[21] (typically a financial institution, but any party regularly extending credit to consumers is considered a creditor) and a **borrower** (sometimes referred to as a *debtor*). Merchants are considered creditors when they regularly engage in extending credit terms to a patron. It is important for business owners and managers to be aware that establishing a credit relationship with a consumer borrower triggers protections for the borrower via federal and state statutes. There is a large body of administrative law that regulates credit transactions as well.

---

[20]A primary factor in the financial crisis that began in September 2008 was an extreme and abrupt tightening of the credit markets by financial institutions that were reeling from losses in a variety of industries but especially from increasingly high default rates on home mortgage loans. This, in turn, made consumer credit (such as a mortgage or car loan) more difficult to obtain and contributed to a slowing in consumer spending. The inability of consumers and businesses to obtain credit is one of many factors that deepened the crisis and led to a precipitous rise in unemployment.

[21]In some contexts, the creditor is known as a *lender*.

Consumer Credit Regulation

The centerpiece of federal statutory regulation of credit transactions is the **Consumer Credit Protection Act (CCPA).**[22] The CCPA has been amended several times and now has six components that regulate credit transactions between a creditor and a borrower. These components include consumer protections in the areas of disclosure of credit terms, credit reporting, antidiscrimination laws for credit applicants, and collection of debts from consumers.

LO 22-7 ## Truth in Lending Act

The **Truth in Lending Act (TILA)**[23] is the part of the CCPA that requires lenders to disclose to borrower applicants certain information about the loan or terms of credit. It also mandates uniform methods of computation and explanation of the terms of the loan or credit arrangements. The primary objective behind the TILA is to allow consumers access to reliable information related to interest rates and other important terms and to provide a standardized reporting system for consumers to compare loan offers. The TILA's scope is limited to credit extensions made to consumers and used primarily for personal, family, or household purposes.

The TILA covers only creditors that are *regularly* engaged in extending credit for goods and services (such as banks, department stores, suppliers, wholesalers, and retailers) plus those that are regularly engaged in *arranging* credit that is for personal, family, or household goods (such as a mortgage broker). For example, suppose Armstrong wishes to renovate the kitchen in his home and plans to finance the renovation through a loan. If Armstrong applies for a home improvement loan from his local bank, the transaction is covered under the TILA and the bank would be required to strictly comply with the act's requirements. However, suppose that, instead, Armstrong convinces his retired uncle, Rogers, to make a five-year loan. Rogers's attorney drafts a promissory note and sends it to Armstrong for signature. The Rogers-to Armstrong loan transaction is *not* covered under the TILA, and Armstrong is without any statutory disclosure protection.

> **KEY** POINT
>
> The TILA covers only creditors that are regularly engaged in extending credit for goods and services or in arranging credit that is for personal, family, or household goods.

The TILA also authorized the Federal Reserve Board to set regulations with procedures and protections that help achieve the objectives of the act. The most important regulation for business owners and managers is **Regulation Z,** which requires that certain written disclosures be made prior to the time that a credit transaction is consummated. The two most important terms in a TILA disclosure statement are the *finance charge* and the *annual percentage rate(APR)*. These two terms are different ways of expressing the same disclosure: the total amount of interest that the consumer will pay over the life of the loan or credit extension. The finance charge must be stated in a dollar amount that represents the *sum* of interest charges that will be paid along with the required payment of principal to pay the loan back. The APR is written as a mathematical percentage that is used to determine the interest rate being paid by the consumer. Because the finance charge and APR are so important, Regulation Z requires that their disclosure must be *more conspicuous* than other disclosures. The regulation also requires that fees may not be hidden within a finance charge. Therefore, transaction charges, loan origination fees,[24] and charges for required life

---

[22]15 U.S.C. § 1601 et seq.

[23]15 U.S.C. § 1605.

[24]Sometimes called *points,* loan origination fees are essentially prepaid interest. A loan at 7 percent with 1 point means that, upon receiving the loan, the borrower pays the creditor 1 percent (1 point) of interest based on the initial principal amount of the loan. Then the borrower repays the principal plus 7 percent in interest per year for the life of the loan.

insurance (if the borrower dies, the policy pays off the creditor) must all be disclosed, if applicable. If a creditor fails to comply with the TILA's disclosure requirements in any way, the debtor has the right to cancel any contract associated with the loan without any further obligation to the creditor. The creditor is also required to notify the debtor of her statutory right to cancel the contract for any reason within *three business days* of the transaction. Failing to provide proper notice of a cancellation right extends that right for up to three years from the date of the contract. As a practical matter, creditors can avoid liability by being sure that their notice of the right to cancel is consistent with the format prescribed by the Federal Reserve Board.

In Case 22.3, an appellate court considers a consumer's claim that the required cancellation notice was inadequate and, therefore, she was entitled to cancel the loan contract one year after signing it. Figure 22.2 and Figure 22.3 are sample TILA disclosure statements similar to the one that would have been used by the plaintiff in Case 22.3.

Other Federal Statutory Protections

The CCPA and the TILA have been amended several times to include additional protections for consumers related to credit discrimination, credit card issuers, and consumer leases.

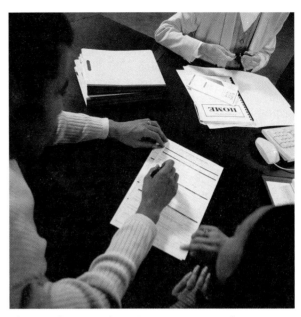

The Truth in Lending Act requires creditors to make certain disclosures about a loan transaction (such as fees), and allows consumers to cancel the loan contract for any reason within three business days of the transaction.

Consumer Financial Protection Bureau   As part of its sweeping overhaul of the U.S. financial market regulatory system, Congress created the Consumer Financial Protection Bureau (CFPB) to consolidate positions from other agencies that had responsibilities for oversight and regulation of consumer lending. The CFPB is an independent agency housed within the Federal Reserve. Fees paid by banks fund the agency, which is charged with setting rules to curb unfair practices in regard to consumer loans and credit cards. The CFPB provides consumer protection through education, enforcement, and dissemination of information to the public that is based on studies the agency has performed. For example, the CFPB recently launched an investigation into the impact of financial products such as accounts with banks and credit unions that are marketed to students through colleges and universities. According to the CFPB's press release, it intends to use the information gathered to determine whether these products are in the best interest of students. Regulation of the financial markets is covered in detail in Chapter 17, "Regulation of Securities, Corporate Governance, and Financial Markets."

Antidiscrimination   Denying an applicant credit on the basis of discriminatory factors relating to the applicant's race, religion, national origin, color, gender, age, or marital status is unlawful under the **Equal Credit Opportunity Act,**[25] which was passed in 1974. The statute was driven primarily by the civil rights movement of the late 1960s and early 1970s to prevent what was then a relatively common practice of considering gender or race in credit decisions. The law also applies to charging higher interest rates based on discriminatory factors.

---

[25]15 U.S.C. § 1691.

FACT SUMMARY   In March 2003, Palmer obtained a debt-consolidation loan from Champion that was secured by a second mortgage on her home. (This type of loan is also known as a *home equity loan.*) On the day the loan closing took place, she signed several loan documents as well as the required TILA disclosures. Several days later, Palmer received copies of these documents by mail along with the "notice of her right to cancel" disclosure required by the TILA. The notice of her right to cancel provided that Palmer could "cancel the transaction for any reason within three business days of (1) the date of the transaction, (2) the date she received her TILA disclosures, or (3) the date she received the notice of right to cancel." The notice also provided that if she was to cancel the transaction by mail or telegraph, the cancellation had to be postmarked no later than April 1, 2003. Palmer did not cancel the transaction within the allotted time period. However, in August 2004 she filed for cancellation of the transaction under the extended three-year statute of limitations under the TILA, claiming that Champion failed to make TILA disclosures because the time frames in the cancellation notice were too confusing.

SYNOPSIS OF DECISION AND OPINION   The U.S. Court of Appeals for the First Circuit affirmed the trial court's decision and dismissed Palmer's claim. The court reasoned that the notice of right to cancel provided by Champion complied with the TILA disclosure requirements and that an objectively reasonable consumer would not find the notice confusing. Therefore, Palmer's right to rescind was not extended by a failure to follow TILA procedures.

WORDS OF THE COURT: Objectively Reasonable Notice   "[I]n the TILA context . . . we, like other courts, have focused the lens of our inquiry on the text of the disclosures themselves rather than on plaintiffs' descriptions of their subjective understandings. . . . This emphasis on objective reasonableness, rather than subjective understanding, is also appropriate in light of the sound tenet that courts must evaluate the adequacy of TILA disclosures from the vantage point of a hypothetical average consumer—a consumer who is neither particularly sophisticated nor particularly dense. . . . Thus, we turn to the question of whether the average consumer, looking at the Notice objectively, would find it confusing. We conclude that she would not. . . . It clearly and conspicuously indicates that the debtor can rescind 'within three (3) business days from whichever of [three enumerated] events occurs last.' . . . We fail to see how any reasonably alert person—that is, the average consumer—reading the Notice would be drawn to the April 1 deadline without also grasping the twice-repeated alternative deadlines. . . . Because we find the Notice clear and adequate, and because the plaintiff otherwise concedes receiving all the required disclosures, her right of rescission under the TILA had long expired by the time she commenced this action."

Case Questions

1. Given the language of the time frame notice, do you agree with the court's statements that it was clear and that objectively reasonable consumers would not be confused by it? Why or why not?

2. Examine Figure 22.3. This is a notice that is similar to the notice Palmer received. Does it affect your analysis?

Credit Cards   In May 2009, Congress overhauled the statutory scheme governing consumer credit card transactions. The **Credit Card Accountability Responsibility and Disclosure Act of 2009 (CARD Act)**[26] increases the power and oversight authority of the Federal Trade Commission over credit card issuers. The CARD Act was primarily intended to protect consumers from unreasonable surprises when interest rates increase and credit card fees are imposed and to restrict marketing and card-issuing practices targeted to younger (18 to 21 years of age) consumers. Among other requirements, credit card issuers:

■ Are prohibited from issuing a credit card to any consumer under the age of 21 unless the consumer submits either the signature of a cosigner over the age of 21 who has the means to repay debts incurred by the consumer or financial information indicating an independent means (regular income) of repaying any debts. Special rules exist for credit cards issued to college students.

---

[26]Pub. L. No. 111-24, H.R. 627 (amending 15 U.S.C. § 1601 et seq.).

FIGURE 22.2 Sample Home Equity Loan TILA Disclosure

August 17, 2005

HOME EQUITY ("Account")
TRUTH IN LENDING DISCLOSURE
(Contract)

```
FIRST FINANCIAL BANK
100 E LANCASTER AVE
DOWNINGTOWN, PA 19335    ("Lender')
```

"you" and "your" mean the recipient of this disclosure. "we", "us" and "our" mean the Lender listed above. "e" means an estimate.

IMPORTANT FACTS ABOUT OUR HOME EQUITY INTEREST ONLY LINE OF CREDIT

RETENTION OF INFORMATION. This disclosure contains important information about our home equity line of credit, Interest Only Line ("Account"). You should read it carefully and keep a copy for your records.

AVAILABILITY OF TERMS. All of the terms described below are subject to change. If these terms change (other than the annual percentage rate) and you decide, as a result, not to enter into an agreement with us, you are entitled to a refund of any fees you paid to us or anyone else in connection with your application.

SECURITY INTEREST. We will take a security interest in your home (collateral). You could lose your home if you do not meet the obligations in your agreement with us.

POSSIBLE ACTIONS. We can terminate your Account, and require you to pay us the entire outstanding balance in one payment if; you engage in fraud or material misrepresentation in connection with the Account; or, you do not meet the repayment terms; and/or, your action or inaction adversely affects the collateral or our rights in the collateral.

We can refuse to make additional extensions of credit or reduce your credit limit if: the value of the dwelling securing the Account declines significantly below its appraised value for purposes of the Account; or, we reasonably believe you will not be able to meet the repayment requirements due to a material change in your financial circumstances; or, you are in default of a material obligation in the agreement; or, government action prevents us from imposing the annual percentage rate provided for or impairs our security interest such that the value of the interest is less than 120 percent of the credit line; or, a regulatory agency has notified us that continued advances would constitute an unsafe and unsound practice; and/or, the maximum annual percentage rate is reached.

The initial agreement permits us to make certain changes to the terms of the agreement at specified times or upon the occurrence of specified events.

MINIMUM PAYMENT REQUIREMENTS. You can obtain advances of credit for 10 years (the "Draw Period"). During the Draw Period, payments will be due monthly. Your minimum periodic payment will be equal to the accrued interest as of the closing date of each billing statement. Although principal payments are not required, pay down on the unpaid principal balance can be made at any time without penalty.

BALLOON PAYMENT. After the Draw Period ends you will no longer be able to obtain credit advances. You will be required to pay the entire balance that you owe after the expiration of the Draw Period in a single balloon payment.

MINIMUM-PAYMENT EXAMPLE. As an example, the minimum interest only payment on a balance of $10,000 at an **ANNUAL PERCENTAGE RATE** of 8% would vary between 120 monthly payments of $61.37 and $67.95. This would be followed by one final payment of $10,067.95.

FEES AND CHARGES. To open and maintain your Account, you must carry insurance on the property securing your Account and pay us the following fees:

Mortgage or Trust Deed Preparation	$ _____	Appraisal	$ _95.00 to $235.00 (Waived)_
Title Search	$ 35.00 (Waived)	Abstract	$ _____
Title Insurance	$ _____	Recording Fees	$ _66.50 (Waived)_
Survey	$ 3.00 to $6.00 (Waived)	Document Preparation Fee	$ _175.00_

*Payable at Application   **Payable at closing   ***Chargeable as a credit advance to your account   ****Based on a $10,000.00 representative amount of credit
If you tell us you have decided not to enter into the Account within three days of receiving this Disclosure in person, or within six days after the day we mail it to you, as the case might be, any fees or charges you might have already paid will be refunded.

TAX DEDUCTIBILITY. You should consult a tax advisor regarding the deductibility of interest and charges for the Account.

OTHER PRODUCTS. If you ask, we will provide you with information on our other available home equity Accounts.

MINIMUM TRANSACTION REQUIREMENTS. Credit advances must be in increments of $500.00.

VARIABLE RATE FEATURE. The Account has a variable rate feature. The annual percentage rate (corresponding to the periodic rate) and minimum payment can change as a result. The annual percentage rate includes only interest and no other costs. The annual percentage rate is based on the value of an index. The index is the Wall Street Journal published Prime Rate (if published in a range, the highest number in the range will be used) and is published in the Wall Street Journal.

RATE CHANGES. The annual percentage rate can change monthly. The maximum **ANNUAL PERCENTAGE RATE** that can apply is 18.000%. Apart from this rate cap, there is no limit on the amount by which the rate can change in any one-year period.

MAXIMUM-RATE AND PAYMENT EXAMPLE. If the **ANNUAL PERCENTAGE RATE** equaled the 18.000% maximum and you had an outstanding balance of $10,000.00, your minimum payment would be $152.88. This annual percentage rate could be reached the first time your interest rate changes, unless your initial rate is equal to the maximum, in which case it would be reached immediately.

HISTORICAL EXAMPLE. The following table shows how the annual percentage rate and the minimum payments for a single $10,000.00 credit advance would have changed based on changes in the index over the past 15 years. The index values are from July of each year. While only one payment amount per year is shown, payments would have varied during each year of the Draw Period.

The table assumes that no additional credit advances were taken, that only the minimum payments were made, and that the rate remained constant during each year. It does not necessarily indicate how the index or your payments will change in the future.

YEAR	INDEX (%)	MARGIN* (%)	ANNUAL PERCENTAGE RATE (%)	MINIMUM PERIODIC PAYMENTS ($)
1990	10.000%	00.50%	10.500%	$86.30
1991	8.500%	00.50%	9.000%	$73.97
1992	6.000%	00.50%	6.500%	$53.42
1993	6.000%	00.50%	6.500%	$53.42
1994	7.250%	00.50%	7.750%	$63.70
1995	8.750%	00.50%	9.250%	$76.03
1996	8.250%	00.50%	8.750%	$71.92
1997	8.500%	00.50%	9.000%	$73.97
1998	8.500%	00.50%	9.000%	$73.97
1999	8.000%	00.50%	8.500%	$69.86
2000	9.500%	00.50%	10.000%	$00.00
2001	6.750%	00.50%	7.250%	$00.00
2002	4.750%	00.50%	5.250%	$00.00
2003	4.000%	00.50%	4.500%	$00.00
2004	4.250%	00.50%	4.750%	$00.00

*This is a margin we have used recently

FIGURE 22.3   Sample Home Equity Loan Notice of Right to Cancel

HOME EQUITY LINE OF CREDIT
NOTICE OF RIGHT TO CANCEL

LENDER: Main Street Bank	DATE 10/01/2010
	LOAN NO. 5931569013
	TYPE Equity Line

BORROWERS/OWNERS Eva St. Clair

ADDRESS 123 Stowes Lane
CITY/STATE/ZIP New Town, MA
PROPERTY 10 Main Street, Unionville, MA

We have agreed to establish an open-end credit account for you, and you have agreed to give us a mortgage/lien/security interest on your home as security for the account. You have a legal right under federal law to cancel this account, without cost, within THREE BUSINESS DAYS after the latest of the following events:

(1)   The opening date of the account, which is 02/20/2009   ; or
(2)   The date you received your Truth in Lending disclosures; or
(3)   The date you received this notice of your right to cancel the account.

If you cancel the account, the mortgage/lien/security interest on your home is also cancelled. Within TWENTY CALENDAR DAYS of receiving your notice, we must take the necessary steps to reflect the fact that the mortgage/lien/security interest on your home has been cancelled. We must return to you any money or property you have given to us or to anyone else in connection with this account.

You may keep any money or property we have given you until we have done the things mentioned above, but you must then offer to return the money or property. If it is impractical or unfair for you to return the property, you must offer its reasonable value. You may offer to return the property at your home or at the location of the property. Money must be returned to the address below. If we do not take possession of the money or property within TWENTY CALENDAR DAYS of your offer, you may keep it without further obligation.

HOW TO CANCEL

If you decide to cancel this account, you may do so by notifying us, in writing, at

Main Street Bank
Unionville, MA

You may use any written statement that is signed and dated by you and states your intention to cancel, or you may use this notice by dating and signing below. Keep one copy of this notice no matter how you notify us because it contains important information about your rights.

If you cancel by mail or telegram, you must send the notice no later than MIDNIGHT of October 5, 2010   (or MIDNIGHT of the THIRD BUSINESS DAY following the latest of the three events listed above). If you send or deliver your written notice to cancel some other way, it must be delivered to the above address no later than that time.

I WISH TO CANCEL

_____   _____
CONSUMER'S SIGNATURE   DATE

The undersigned each acknowledge receipt of two copies each of <u>NOTICE OF RIGHT TO CANCEL.</u>

Each borrower/owner in this transaction has the right to cancel. The exercise of this right by one borrower/owner shall be effective as to all borrowers/owners.

Eva St. Clair 10/1/10	_____
BORROWER/OWNER Eva St. Clair DATE	BORROWER/OWNER DATE
_____	_____
BORROWER/OWNER DATE	BORROWER/OWNER DATE

- Must comply with rules that require institutions of higher education (such as colleges and universities) to publicly disclose any contract of agreement made with a credit card issuer. Credit card issuers may not offer college students tangible items (gifts) to induce them to apply for credit cards.

- Must give 45 days' advance notice of any impending raise in rates.

- Must mail credit statements at least 21 days before the bill's due date (extended from 14 days in the previous law).

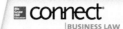

Visit Connect for more information on how the CARD Act affects college students.

Existing Regulations under the TILA   The CARD Act added to already existing disclosure and transaction regulations under the TILA. Those existing measures were left intact. The existing provisions of the TILA include:

- Protection of consumers when a card is used to buy what turns out to be a faulty product by requiring the card issuer to investigate and, depending on the results of the investigation, credit the consumer's account.

- A limitation of the consumer's liability for unauthorized charges of a total amount of $50. As a practical matter, consumers usually get even more favorable treatment than the law allows because many major credit card companies now have a policy of waiving any charges they determine to be fraudulent. If the card is reported stolen to the issuer *prior* to any unauthorized charge, the consumer has no liability for charges. Although credit card companies are permitted to send unsolicited cards to consumers, fraudulent or unauthorized use prior to the acceptance of the offer will not result in liability to the addressee/consumer.

- A statutory procedure for consumers who are claiming a billing error[27] or disputing a charge on their account. The procedure includes a time frame and a requirement that the credit issuer attempt to investigate the dispute and resolve it in good faith. The TILA also prohibits the credit issuer from charging the consumer interest on the charge while the dispute is being investigated.

Although the overwhelming majority of the cases featured in this textbook are appellate court decisions, Case 22.4 is a municipal court (local court) case, included here to illustrate the types of creditor abuses that spurred enactment of the CARD Act.

Identity Theft   In 2003, Congress gave some protections to consumers who were victims of *identity theft.* Identity theft occurs when a criminal assumes the identity of an individual for purposes of making fraudulent credit transactions in the victim's name. The **Fair and Accurate Credit Transactions (FACT) Act**[28] requires that credit bureaus stop reporting any fraudulent account information from the time a consumer alleges identity theft until the conclusion of an investigation period. The FACT Act also contains provisions that established a national fraud alert system so that consumers have a timely way to guard their credit once they suspect identity fraud has occurred.

Consumer Leases   In addition to its regulation of debt incurred in purchasing products or services, the TILA regulates the *leasing relationship,* whereby a creditor lessor typically gives the possession and use of equipment or a motor vehicle to a consumer debtor in exchange for monthly payments over an agreed-upon period of time. When the leasing period expires, the consumer either returns the goods or exercises an option to purchase the goods at a predetermined price. Consumer leasing is regulated by the **Consumer Leasing Act (CLA),** which covers lessors engaged in leasing or those arranging leases for

---

[27]These protections were added to the TILA by the Fair Credit Billing Act (15 USCA § 1681 et seq.).

[28]Pub. L. No. 108-159, 117 Stat. 1952 (Dec. 4, 2003) (amending 15 U.S.C. § 1681).

FACT SUMMARY Discover brought a collection lawsuit in the amount of $5,564.28 against Owens after she defaulted on her credit card agreement. Owens had obtained the Discover card in 1996 with a credit limit of $1,900 and subsequently charged $1,460. However, her credit card agreement allowed Discover to add fees and increase her interest rate in certain circumstances, such as when she paid late or less than the minimum amount due. Owens became disabled and experienced severe financial difficulty. Although she stopped using the credit card and made payments regularly, Discover continued to assess fees consistent with the credit card agreement. In sum, despite never using the credit card and paying $3,492 toward an original debt of $1,900, with all of the fees and accrued charges, Owens nevertheless faced a $5,564.28 outstanding balance at the time of the collection suit.

SYNOPSIS OF DECISION AND OPINION The court ruled in favor of Owens, holding that the terms of Discover's credit card agreement provisions were unreasonable and the six-year accumulation of over-limit fees was manifestly unconscionable.[29] The court pointed out that this was not a case where a debtor recklessly used her credit card to purchase items beyond the agree-upon credit limit. Rather, the bulk of the balance owed was due to fees, charges, and substantial increases in the finance rate. Moreover, Discover had a duty to mitigate its damages once it became clear that Owens would never be in a position to make the required payments.

WORDS OF THE COURT: Credit Card Company Practices "This court is all too aware of the widespread financial exploitation of the urban poor by overbearing credit-card companies. Defendant has clearly been the victim of plaintiff's unreasonable, unconscionable, and unjust business practices. This court has broad legal and equitable powers, and now brings them to bear for the debtor in this case."

Case Questions

1. The court conceded that Discover had complied with existing federal regulations regarding disclosures of fees and so forth. Given this fact, is the court sacrificing legal principles in favor of a paternalistic approach? Is this good public policy?

2. Suppose that Owens had chosen to close the account and notified Discover that she was defaulting on the account and could not pay. Would she have been in a better position than if (as she actually did) she kept paying as much as she could afford (the minimum amount due or less) over a period of six years?

3. How could Discover have known that Owens, as the court said, would "never be in a position" to pay the full amount owed?

[29]Recall from Chapter 6, "Overview and Language of Contracts," that unconscionability is a narrow doctrine used only when one party has used bargaining power to oppress the other party.

---

consumers in the ordinary course of business. Many of the CLA's provisions mirror the statutory protections afforded to consumer debtors in a loan transaction, such as requirements on APR disclosure and on standardization of certain information.

Credit Reports Because creditors rely so heavily on credit bureaus (private companies that compile data about a consumer's credit history as well as current liabilities), Congress gave consumers federal statutory protection in the **Fair Credit Reporting Act (FCRA)**.[30] The FCRA sets privacy rights for consumer credit reports and requires that the credit bureaus give individual consumers complete and timely access to their own credit reports. In order to ensure that the credit report is accurate, the FCRA requires each of the credit bureaus to provide individual consumers with a copy of their own credit report, free of charge, once per year. Additionally, any time the report is used in a credit-making decision (such as a loan application), the consumer has the right to obtain a free copy of the

[30]15 U.S.C. § 1681 et seq.

credit report used in the decision making. The FCRA also provides a dispute resolution system designed to allow consumers the right to challenge any information on their credit report if the information is incorrect. Further, the FCRA requires that credit bureaus remove any entry that is obsolete. The FCRA defines obsolete as any negative information (such as an account that was closed by the creditor and placed for collection) that is over 7 years old and a bankruptcy filing that occurred more than 14 years prior to the date of the report.

CONSUMER DEBT COLLECTION

LO 22-8

As discussed in the previous section, consumer credit transactions are heavily regulated in an effort to protect consumers and help level the playing field between creditors and debtor consumers. Similarly, when a creditor's agent is collecting a debt owed to the creditor by virtue of an extension of consumer credit, the collection process is subject to regulation. Agents involved in debt collection for consumer debts are directly regulated by a federal statute called the **Fair Debt Collection Practices Act (FDCPA).**[31] The FDCPA applies only to *agents* of the debtor that are attempting to collect the debt from the consumer. These agents typically take the form of a collection agency, but others that are collecting consumer debts on behalf of the debtor (such as attorneys) may also be subject to the FDCPA under certain conditions.[32] A creditor that is attempting to collect her own debt is *not* subject to the act. However, both creditors and collection agencies are subject to additional state statutory and regulatory requirements as well.

FDCPA Requirements

The FDCPA requires that the collection agency make known certain rights of the debtor in a **validation disclosure** when making the initial to inquire about the debt. This disclosure notice must inform the debtor that he has 30 days to dispute the debt. The law also requires that the collection agency investigate any disputed debt and obtain written verification of the debt from the original creditor.

In addition to requiring validation disclosure, the FDCPA prohibits certain conduct in the course of attempting to collect a debt. First, the law limits the contact that a debt collector may have with third parties such as employers. Second, certain methods are unlawful. Specifically, the FDCPA prohibits collector contact (1) at inconvenient times, such as early morning or late night calls, or at inconvenient places, such as the debtor's place of employment or sites of social events; (2) after the collector is informed that the debtor is represented by an attorney; or (3) after the debtor gives written notice that she refuses to pay the debt and requests the agent to cease contact. The FDCPA also prohibits any harassing, intimidating, or misleading tactics by collection agents, such as making threats of incarceration, posing as an attorney or law enforcement agent, or using abusive, degrading language.

Enforcement

Federal statutes that govern consumer debt collection are enforced primarily by the Federal Trade Commission (FTC). The FTC uses a system of penalties, cease and desist orders, and civil lawsuits to enforce the FDCPA. However, the law also provides individual consumers with a statutory cause of action so that a debtor may sue a collection agent directly for any damages suffered, plus attorney fees incurred in bringing suit. On the state level, state attorneys general often have authority to prosecute collection agents engaged in abusive collection tactics within their state's jurisdiction.

---

[31]15 U.S.C. § 1692 (became Title VII of the Consumer Credit Protection Act).

[32]*Heintz v. Jenkins,* 514 U.S. 291 (1995).

Consumer law p. 601　The statutory and administrative body of law that protects consumers engaging in transactions with merchants and creditors.

Federal Trade Commission Act (FTCA) p. 601　A statute that created the Federal Trade Commission and prohibited deceptive trade practices.

Federal Trade Commission (FTC) p. 601　An agency charged with the broad mandate of preventing unfair and deceptive acts or practices in commercial transactions.

Telephone Consumer Protection Act and Telemarketing and Consumer Fraud and Abuse Prevention Act p. 603　Two statutes that regulate telemarketing firms and practices; allow consumers to opt out of unwanted calls from telemarketers, ban the use of unsolicited recorded calls and faxes, and prohibit telemarketers from making false representations.

Federal Odometer Act p. 604　A law that makes it a crime to change vehicle odometers and requires that any faulty odometer be plainly disclosed in writing to potential buyers.

Controlling the Assault of Non-Solicited Pornography and Marketing Act of 2003 p. 605　A federal statute that regulates the sending of unsolicited e-mail (spam) by prohibiting certain practices, such as falsifying the "from" name and information in the subject line, and requiring the sender to provide a physical address of the producer of the e-mail. Also called *CAN-SPAM Act*.

Warranty p. 607　A seller's (or lessor's) legally enforceable promise to a consumer concerning the quality and/or functionality of a product.

Express warranty p. 607　A warranty that arises when a seller makes a representation of fact about a product.

Implied warranty p. 607　A warranty that exists even when the seller does not make a specific representation about the product.

Disclaim p. 608　To renounce a legal right or claim.

Written express warranty p. 609　A warranty whose terms are put in writing for the consumer.

Consumer Product Safety Act (CPSA) p. 611　The federal statute that created the Consumer Product Safety Commission, with the aim of making consumer products safer.

Food, Drug and Cosmetic Act (FDCA) p. 612　The federal statute that created the Food and Drug Administration and that requires the makers of certain food ingredients, additives, drugs, or medical devices to obtain formal FDA approval before selling the product to the general public.

Food and Drug Administration (FDA) p. 612　The federal agency that regulates the testing, manufacturing, and distributing of foods, medications, and medical devices.

Creditor p. 613　Any party that regularly extends credit and to which a debt becomes owed.

Borrower p. 613　The party to whom credit is extended and who owes the debt.

Consumer Credit Protection Act (CCPA) p. 614　Federal legislation that regulates credit transactions between a creditor and a borrower and provides consumer protections in the areas of disclosure of credit terms, credit reporting, antidiscrimination laws, and collection of debts from consumers; serves as the centerpiece of federal statutory regulation of credit transactions.

Truth in Lending Act (TILA) p. 614　The part of the Consumer Credit Protection Act that requires lenders to disclose to borrower applicants certain information about the loan or terms of credit and mandates uniform methods of computation and explanation of the terms of the loan or credit arrangements.

Regulation Z p. 614　The part of the Truth in Lending Act requiring that certain written disclosures be made prior to the time that a credit transaction is consummated.

Equal Credit Opportunity Act p. 615　Federal legislation, passed in 1974, that prohibits discrimination of a credit applicant based on the applicant's race, religion, national origin, color, gender, age, or marital status.

Credit Card Accountability Responsibility and Disclosure Act of 2009 (CARD Act) p. 616　Federal legislation that protects consumers from unreasonable interest rate increases and credit card fees and requires card issuers to give a 45-day advance notice of any impending rate increase.

Fair and Accurate Credit Transactions (FACT) Act p. 619　Federal legislation that requires credit bureaus to stop reporting any fraudulent account information from the time a consumer alleges identity theft until the conclusion of the investigation.

Consumer Leasing Act (CLA) p. 619　Federal legislation that regulates lessors engaged in leasing or arranging leases for consumers in the ordinary course of business.

Fair Credit Reporting Act (FCRA) p. 620   Federal legislation that sets privacy rights for consumer credit reports and requires that the credit bureaus give individual consumers complete and timely access to their own credit reports.

Fair Debt Collection Practices Act (FDCPA) p. 621 A federal statute that regulates agents of the creditor involved in debt collection for consumer debts and that requires the collection agency to make known certain rights of the debtor.

Validation disclosure p. 621   A notice in which a collection agency, when making initial contact with a debtor, makes known certain rights of the debtor, including the fact that he has 30 days to dispute the debt; required under the Fair Debt Collection Practices Act.

THEORY TO PRACTICE

Outdoor World Inc. is a retailer of sporting goods gear, equipment, and accessories for use in outdoor sports and camping. Outdoor World carries two brands of tents, the Extreme Tent and the Tectonic Tent. The Extreme is more popular and less expensive, but the manufacturers of the Tectonic have promised financial incentives to Outdoor World for selling a certain amount of Tectonics.

1. Suppose the manager of Outdoor World places this advertisement in the newspaper: "Extreme Tents 50% off—This week only." Willen, in the market for a tent, sees the advertisement and arrives at Outdoor World the next day. The manager explains to Willen that the Extreme is temporarily out of stock and tries to sell him the Tectonic instead. Does the manager's conduct constitute a deceptive trade practice? What law governs unfair trade practices?

2. In Question 1 above, assume that Willen informs the manager that he is moving to Iceland and will require a tent that can maintain a certain degree of warmth. Although there is no specific reference to such a quality on the label, the manager assures Willen that he, himself, is an avid camper and has used the Tectonic recently and he states that it will maintain warmth. Did the manager create a warranty? What kind of warranty?

3. In Question 2 above, assume that Willen purchased the Tectonic and that the agreement of sale for the tent contains this provision: "All implied warranties are hereby excluded." Is Willen still protected by any warranty? Which one(s)?

4. Assume that Outdoor World wishes to begin a marketing campaign by sending its existing customers e-mail advertisements of sales and new items. What kinds of requirements should Outdoor World be aware of in order to comply with the CAN-SPAM Act?

5. After a downturn in the economy and a tightening of consumer credit, Outdoor World decides to offer qualified customers credit for consumer purchases. What is the legal impact of this decision?

6. One year after Outdoor World began the credit accounts for its patrons, one customer defaults. The manager calls the customer to try to collect the debt owed. Is the manager subject to the provisions of the Fair Debt Collection Practices Act? Why or why not?

MANAGER'S CHALLENGE

Managers are often involved in business planning discussions where having sufficient legal acumen enables them to limit the company's liability while maximizing opportunities. Assume that you are one of group of midlevel managers in the Theory to Practice problem and that you receive this e-mail from the chief operating officer of Outdoor World:

> Given the decline in customers who are buying new outdoor sports accessories, senior management is considering a plan to begin selling preowned sporting equipment at discount prices. However, we want to make sure that we understand the liability exposure in tandem with the cost-benefit analysis. Lead a small group discussion among the midlevel managers about the opportunities and threats that such a plan would involve, and write a two-page summary memorandum of your conclusions.

A sample answer may be found on this textbook's website at www.mhhe.com/melvinleb2e.

TRUTH IN LENDING ACT

Barrer obtained a credit card with Chase in 2004 and accepted the cardmember agreement. In February 2005, Chase mailed a Change in Terms Notice to Barrer that notified him of an increase in the annual percentage rate from 8.99 percent to 24.24 percent in certain events, including payment default and persistently late payments. The notice provided a right for Barrer to reject these terms in writing, but he did not. In April 2005, Barrer's APR jumped to 24.24 percent. Chase claimed that it increased the rate because of information obtained from a credit agency about Barrer's being an increased credit risk, even though that condition was not listed in the notice as an event qualifying for a rate increase.

CASE QUESTIONS

1. Do Chase's actions comply with the TILA? Why or why not?
2. Shouldn't Barrer be liable for failing to reject the new terms?

FAIR DEBT COLLECTION PRACTICES ACT

Myers owed over $11,000 to an automobile finance company in 2001. LHR was hired to collect the debt, and an LHR agent contacted her with threats of a lawsuit and garnishment of her wages. Myers negotiated a settlement whereby LHR accepted approximately $3,000 as complete payment for the debt. Myers wire-transferred the money to LHR to satisfy the debt, and later received a letter saying the debt was paid in full. However, Myers later found out that her settled debt was still reported to the credit agencies by LHR and this adversely affected her credit rating. Despite the settlement, LHR agents continued to call Myers, threatening to sue her, garnish her wages, and report her to government authorities for tax evasion.

CASE QUESTIONS

1. Were LHR's actions lawful under the FDCPA? Why or why not?
2. If LHR's actions were not lawful, what could it have done to comply with the act?

CONSUMER FRAUD ACT

From 1995 to 2001, McDonald's, the famous fast-food chain, sponsored promotional games including "Monopoly Games at McDonald's," "The Deluxe Monopoly Game," and "Who Wants to be a Millionaire." For each of these promotional games, McDonald's conducted an extensive marketing and advertising campaign through which it represented that all customers had a fair and equal chance to win and it specified the odds of winning. However, the FBI investigated McDonald's based upon claims that the game pieces required to win the high-value, "million-dollar" prizes were compromised and were being diverted to friends and family of personnel who had access to these pieces. Yet throughout this investigation, and even after individuals pleaded guilty to conspiracy charges related to the diversionary practices, McDonald's continued its advertising practices. Phoenix, a Burger King franchisee, sued under the CFA, claiming that the advertisements stating everyone has a fair and equal chance to win are false and deceptive.

CASE QUESTIONS

1. Does Phoenix have a claim under the Consumer Fraud Act? Why or why not?
2. Would there be any other factors affecting whether or not Phoenix had a claim?

CASE SUMMARY 22.4 :: American Suzuki Motor Corp. v. Carney, 37 Cal. App. 4th 1291 (Cal. App. 1995)

IMPLIED WARRANTIES

Carney purchased a Suzuki Samurai SUV. Although Carney had never experienced any safety issues with his Suzuki, several SUV rollover incidents made him wary of continuing to drive the vehicle. Carney sued for a refund based on a theory of breach of implied warranty, citing an automotive expert who tested the Suzuki Samurai and concluded that it has a higher rollover risk because of its high center of gravity, narrow tread width, and light weight.

CASE QUESTIONS

1. Which implied warranty is Carney claiming here, and what is the legal standard for such warranties?
2. Can Suzuki disclaim this warranty? Why or why not?

CASE SUMMARY 22.5 :: Hauter v. Zogarts, 534 P.2d 377 (Ca. 1975)

WARRANTIES

Zogarts makes the "Golfing Gizmo" that Hauter received as a gift from his mother for his 13th birthday. The Gizmo is billed as a "completely equipped backyard driving range" and consists of a golf ball attached to a cord that causes the ball to come back to the player after it is struck. The Gizmo's box reads "COMPLETELY SAFE BALL WILL NOT HIT PLAYER." Hauter read the safety manual and used the Gizmo a dozen times. In one hit, however, he hit too far under the ball, the cord tangled, and the ball struck Hauter in the temple.

Hauter suffered severe permanent injuries. Hauter sued Zogarts for breach of express and implied warranty. Zogarts defended by pointing out that the photos of the man using the Gizmo properly were a disclaimer that it was "completely safe" only when used in that way.

CASE QUESTIONS

1. What words on the box could have created the express warranty?
2. Is the phrase "completely safe" a verifiable fact, or is it puffing?

 Self-Check **ANSWERS**

Express Warranty

1. Express warranty created by specific advertised promises such as "instantly stops" and "incapacitates."

2. No express warranty—puffing, not promises.

3. Express warranty created by verifiable promise of fact.

4. Although advertisements can create warranties by what they show, it is unlikely that any express warranty was created here because no express promise was made about quality.

---

23 CHAPTER

Criminal Law and Procedure in Business

learning objectives

After studying this chapter, students who have mastered the material will be able to:

23-1 Explain the origins and sources of criminal law and procedure.

23-2 Distinguish between criminal law and criminal procedure.

23-3 Compare criminal law with civil law.

23-4 Articulate the underlying tenets of criminal law and the requirements for criminal liability.

23-5 Identify circumstances in which business managers and owners may be liable for criminal violations by a corporation.

23-6 Give specific examples of white-collar-crime laws that may impact a business entity and/or its owners and managers.

23-7 Explain the steps in the criminal justice system.

23-8 Name and explain the various constitutional procedural protections afforded to those accused of a crime.

23-9 Understand the exclusionary rule and how it applies to business.

One way that the government regulates the practices and operations of business owners and managers is through **criminal law.** This chapter focuses on how criminal law, criminal procedure, and the criminal justice system impact the legal environment of business. In this chapter, students will learn:

- The origins and sources of criminal law.
- Elements and examples of criminal acts.
- The steps in the criminal justice system.
- Legal protections for those accused of committing a crime.

ORIGINS AND SOURCES OF CRIMINAL LAW AND PROCEDURE

LO 23-1

Crime in the United States is ordinarily dealt with by state authorities, predominantly under state statutory law. While each state has its own system of criminal law, there is an increasing body of federal criminal law. Thus, the federal criminal justice system exists alongside (sometimes overlapping) the state systems. Much of American criminal law is derived from English criminal law that existed primarily as common law with some statutory mandates. However, in the 1960s, state legislatures began to assemble various statutes addressing criminal culpability and integrating state common law to form more comprehensive criminal codes.

MODERN CRIMINAL LAW: THE MODEL PENAL CODE

Nearly two-thirds of the states have enacted criminal codes based on the **Model Penal Code (MPC)** adopted by the American Law Institute (ALI) in 1962.[1] The vocabulary and formation of the MPC have been very influential in shaping criminal law notions, even in states where the MPC has not been formally adopted. However, many states have retained certain portions of their common law within their criminal codes as well.

In 1971, the congressionally appointed National Commission on Reform of Federal Criminal Laws issued a model federal criminal code that consolidated and clarified existing statutory law. However, it has long been settled that there are no federal common law crimes.[2] Although a state criminal statute and a federal criminal statute may outlaw identical or substantially identical conduct, state law and federal law may coexist unless the federal statute contains specific language that preempts state law.[3]

---

[1]Recall from Chapter 1, "Legal Foundations," that the ALI is an organization of attorneys, judges, and law professors that produces model statutes to promote consistency in the application of the law from state to state.

[2]*U.S. v. Hudson and Goodwin,* 11 U.S. 32 (1812).

[3]*Goldstein v. California,* 412 U.S. 546 (1973).

CRIMINAL LAW VERSUS CRIMINAL PROCEDURE

While *criminal law* defines the boundaries of behavior and sanctions for violating those boundaries, **criminal procedure** refers to the legal process and safeguards afforded to individuals (and in some cases business entities) during criminal investigations, arrests, trials, and sentencing. Criminal *law* consists of a body of law that, for the purposes of preventing harm to society, declares what conduct is criminal and prescribes the punishment to be imposed for such conduct. Criminal *procedure* sets limits on the government's authority in applying criminal law. Criminal procedure is covered in detail later in this chapter.

Criminal Law versus Civil Law

Recall the distinctions between civil law and criminal law covered in Chapter 1, "Legal Foundations." Civil laws are designed to compensate parties (including businesses) for damages as a result of another's conduct. Criminal statutes are a protection of *society,* and the violation of a criminal law results in a penalty to the violator, such as a fine or imprisonment. It is important to remember that these categories are not mutually exclusive; one can violate a criminal law and commit a civil wrong in the very same act. For example, suppose that Mcduff is an accountant for Shakespeare Book Company (SBC) and steals $100,000 from the business by creating a fake employee on the company's books and secretly paying the fake employee's salary to himself. Upon discovery, SBC notifies the authorities, and Mcduff will likely be charged with various criminal offenses such as grand theft and fraud. If he is convicted, he will likely be incarcerated for an extended period of time. Although sometimes courts order restitution as part of a criminal sentence, SBC may also choose to file a civil lawsuit against Mcduff individually in order to recover the losses due to Mcduff's commission of the tort[4] of conversion (the civil counterpart of theft). SBC may also be entitled to compensation from Mcduff for other incidental expenses it incurred as a result of the theft (such as costs of detecting the theft). If SBC is successful in obtaining a civil judgment against Mcduff, the company may then attempt to recover its losses by tapping Mcduff's personal assets.

> **KEY** POINT
>
> Criminal *law* defines the boundaries of behavior and sanctions for violating those boundaries; criminal *procedure* refers to legal protections of citizens during criminal investigations, arrests, trials, and sentencing.

Burden of Proof   One significant difference between a criminal case and a civil case is the **burden of proof.** In a civil case, the plaintiff needs to prove only by a **preponderance of the evidence** that the defendant committed a civil wrong. This means that the fact finder need not be completely convinced that the plaintiff's arguments in the case should prevail. Rather, the fact finder need be convinced only that the defendant's liability was *more likely than not* for the plaintiff to meet her burden of proof. In criminal cases, where the stakes may involve an individual's liberty, the standard of proof is much higher. In a criminal case, the government must prove its case **beyond a reasonable doubt.** Thus, a fact finder must be convinced that the defendant's criminal liability is not in doubt to a reasonable person.

General Principles of Criminal Law

There are two important underlying tenets to criminal law: *legality* and *punishment.* The principle of **legality** is a protection of individuals from being charged with some unspecified general offense. Legality simply requires that crimes be specifically proscribed by law in advance of the conduct sought to be punished. This includes the notion that the

---

[4]Torts were covered in detail in Chapter 10, "Torts and Products Liability."

Constitution bars both Congress and state legislatures from enacting retroactive criminal statutes (known as *ex post facto* laws). Statutes that fail to give fair warning that a particular conduct is unlawful may be struck down by the courts as too vague. The principle of **punishment** is based on the concepts that (1) criminal law acts as a *deterrent,* (2) it *removes* dangerous criminals from the population, and (3) *rehabilitation* is an important part of the criminal justice system. Punishments are applied using a sentencing system that follows a general range of years prescribed by the legislature. After conviction, a sentence is imposed by the court based on the individual trial judge's discretion and assessment of the severity of the crime and mitigating circumstances. However, starting in the 1980s, public dissatisfaction with an actual or perceived view that courts were not imposing sufficiently stiff penalties spurred federal and state legislatures to pass laws requiring courts to assess penalties based on statutorily prescribed **sentencing guidelines.** These guidelines have had the impact of severely restricting judicial discretion. This same movement is also responsible for a spate of statutes that include mandatory minimum sentences for certain offenses as well as minimum sentences for repeat offenders (some states adopted a "three strikes" law, which requires a 25-year sentence for a third felony conviction). Despite criticism by many prominent judges, attorneys, and legal scholars on various fronts, state and federal legislators continue to generally support the concept of sentencing guidelines and mandatory minimums.

Criminal Liability

From a legal perspective a crime has two parts: a physical part, in which the defendant committed an *act* or *omission,* and a mental part which involves the defendant's subjective *state of mind.* Thus, an analysis of criminal liability involves three fundamental questions: First, did the defendant actually commit the prohibited act? Second, did the defendant have a culpable state of mind? Third, does the law give the defendant a palpable defense (such as a self-defense claim to a homicide charge)?

Act Requirement   The **act requirement,** also called by its Latin name, *actus reus,* requires the government to prove that a defendant's actions objectively satisfied the elements of a particular offense. The act requirement is based on the fundamental criminal law tenet that evil thoughts alone do not constitute a criminal act. Rather, there must be some overt conduct (either an act or an omission), and it must be voluntary. Courts generally follow the rule that an act is voluntary unless it is demonstrated that the defendant acted based on physical compulsion, reflex, or certain physiological or neurological diseases. An act by omission occurs when a crime is defined in terms of *failure* to act. For example, if the chief financial officer fails to disclose data required by federal securities law, she has committed an omission that satisfies the act requirement.

Mental Requirement   The mental element, also called by its Latin name, *mens rea,* which translates literally into "guilty mind," requires that the defendant have a requisite degree of culpability with regard to each element of a given crime. The fundamental underpinning is that an act does not make a person guilty unless his mind is guilty.[5] The words contained in a criminal statute to express the guilty mind requirement include *intentionally, knowingly, maliciously, willfully,* and *wantonly.* However, some criminal statutes set the intent requirement at mere recklessness or negligence and not actual intent as the level of culpability. Thus, an act or omission in which the defendant's conduct deviated from the standard of conduct so grossly that a reasonable person would judge it as criminal may also satisfy the mental element requirement.

_____

[5]Expressed as the common law Latin maxim: *Actus not facit reum nisi mens sit rea* (*Collins Latin,* 2009).

Uttering forged instruments

"Whoever **utters** and **publishes** as true a false, forged or altered record, deed, instrument or other writing mentioned in § 831.01 (i.e., "letter of attorney, policy of insurance, bill of lading, bill of exchange or promissory note, or an order, acquittance, or discharge for money or other property") **knowing** the same to be false, altered, forged or counterfeited, with **intent** to injure or defraud any person, shall be guilty of a felony of the third degree."

Courts and legislatures have also established certain rules for applying the mental element requirement in cases of *mistake*. Certain statutes also impose *strict liability,* whereby the mental element is assumed by certain conduct so that the defendant's culpable state of mind need not be proved.

Figure 23.1 illustrates the typical language of the act requirement and the intent requirement with an example from a Florida criminal statute prohibiting forgery.

Defenses   Even when the requisite mental state and criminal act standards are proved, the law provides for certain defenses based on unique circumstances of the crime. **Self-defense** is an example of a defense to a criminal charge of homicide in that the law recognizes that certain cases necessitate the use of deadly force to repel an attack in which the defendant reasonably feared that death or substantial harm was about to occur either to the defendant or to a third party. The rules governing self-defense are complex and vary from state to state, especially on the question of whether the defendant is required to retreat before using deadly force. The defense afforded by the self-defense doctrine is at its height when it involves use of deadly force to repel an attack in the victim's home or place of business.

The other major category of defense is **mental incapacity.** As you may imagine, this defense is very controversial and is sometimes colloquially called the *insanity defense.* That term is potentially misleading because in certain jurisdictions incapacity covers a wide variety of conditions in addition to insanity. Although mental incapacity has a variety of definitions depending on the jurisdiction, the MPC requires the defendant's actions to be related to some type of mental disease or defect.[6] The MPC also specifically rules out any sociopathic personality disorders as the basis for a mental incapacity case.

Less frequently asserted defenses include *duress,* in which a defendant committed a crime in response to another person's threat to inflict personal injury (threats to property or reputation are insufficient), and *intoxication,* which generally depends on whether the intoxication was voluntary or involuntary. If voluntary, the criminal act is excused only if the defendant was so intoxicated that he could not form the requisite mental intent (guilty mind) to have criminal culpability. If involuntary, the defense is broader but still requires proof that the intoxication rendered the defendant unable to understand that his conduct constituted a crime.

Types of Crimes

Crimes may be classified in several different ways. **Felonies** are crimes that generally carry *one year or more* of incarceration as the penalty. **Misdemeanors** are crimes that carry

---

[6]MPC § 4.01(1).

up to one year of incarceration as the penalty. Frequently, states also have degrees (or grades) of crimes within each of those categories that further delineate the seriousness of the crime. Thus, a premeditated murder would be referred to as a first-degree felony, whereas shoplifting a shirt may be defined as a second- (or third-) degree misdemeanor. Many states also have a classification of crimes known as *summary offenses* or *infraction offenses,* which are minor crimes that carry no threat of jail (for first offenders) such as a charge of underage alcohol use.

Crimes are also sometimes classified based on the victim or result of the crime. Crimes in which the prepetrator has used force or violence, such as murder or sexual assault, are classified as *violent crimes.* Crimes that involve offensive or disorderly conduct in public are referred to as *public order crimes.* This category also includes crimes that have no direct victim but that society has judged to be detrimental to public well-being, such as crimes related to narcotics, prostitution, or obscenity. Crimes that involve damage to or stealing of property (such as theft, vandalism, or arson) are usually referred to as *property crimes.* When crimes take place in the business environment, they are classified as *white-collar crimes.*

CRIMINAL LAW AND BUSINESS ENTITIES   LO 23-5

While any discussion of criminal law necessarily focuses on criminal culpability of individuals, business owners and managers should have a fundamental knowledge of how criminal law may be applied to business entities. This knowledge helps business owners and managers to reduce risk and add value to the business by taking affirmative steps to limit criminal culpability for the business and its principals.

The modern trend in criminal law is to expand the scope of criminal statutes to include criminal culpability for corporations and their principals. Courts have allowed liability to exist for corporations so long as the prosecutor can prove that the corporation's agents (not just executive management) were engaged in criminal conduct on behalf of the company. Recall from Chapter 16, "Corporations," that courts have recognized that corporations exist as a separate legal "person." Criminal statutes have embraced the concept that a corporation may be charged with a crime along with, or apart from, its principals or agents. The Model Penal Code provides for criminal liability for business entities if any one of the following applies:

1. The criminal act by the business's agent is within the *scope of her employment,* and the statute imposes liability on the business for such an act (e.g., the agent shreds documents related to potentially unlawful conduct, creating liability under obstruction of justice).
2. The criminal omission is the failure to perform a specific duty imposed by law (e.g., the agent fails to make important disclosures in a report to investors).
3. The crime was authorized by one of the corporation's top-level managers (e.g., a chief financial officer orders an internal accountant to file a false corporate tax return).

Congress has specifically included business entities in criminal statutes in areas that impact business, including fraud, obstruction of justice, health and safety requirements, sale of ownership interests (securities law), disclosure requirements, environmental regulations, and antitrust or other anticompetition laws.

Individual Liability for Business Crimes

Congress and state legislatures have also expanded criminal culpability for individual officers and directors (and sometimes majority owners) for corporate crimes committed within the scope of their employment. These principals are often included in criminal statutes that require officers and directors to act as responsible corporate officers in complying with statutes and being diligent about adhering to standards set out in statutes and regulations.

Because of the inherent difficulties in terms of proof, most statutes do not require the specific mental intent (guilty mind) that is required for other crimes. Since the mid-1970s, legislative bodies have begun to impose what amounts to strict liability statutes for corporate officers even when the officer in question did not have any actual knowledge that a crime had taken place.

In 2002, the Sarbanes-Oxley Act imposed significant criminal liability for officers, directors, and majority shareholders of corporations that falsify financial disclosures and provides up to 20 years of incarceration for any employee who destroys documents relevant to a government agency investigation. The Sarbanes-Oxley law is discussed in detail in Chapter 17, "Regulation of Securities, Corporate Governance, and Financial Markets." Case 23.1 provides an example of individual officer liability for business crimes.

CONCEPT SUMMARY Criminal Law

- Criminal law is based on state and federal laws that started as common law crimes but were codified into statutes based on the Model Penal Code.
- While some actions involve both criminal and civil liability, civil laws protect individuals by redressing injuries and criminal laws protect society as a whole by punishing wrongdoers.
- Criminal liability requires both a bad act (*Actus reus*) *and* a guilty mind (*mens rea*).
- Even when a requisite mental state and bad act are proved, the accused can offer a defense such as mental incapacity, duress, or self-defense to avoid criminal liability.
- Corporations and their managers can be guilty of the crimes of their employees if the crime was committed for some corporate advantage or benefit of the company.

LO 23-6 # WHITE-COLLAR CRIME

White-collar crimes usually signify criminal violations by corporations or individuals, including fraud, bribery, theft, and conspiracy committed in the course of the offender's occupational duties. Typically, these crimes are set out in state and/or federal statutes.

Fraud

Perhaps the most common white-collar crime is fraud. *Fraud* is a broad general term used to describe a transaction in which one party made false representations of a matter of fact (either by words or conduct) that were intended to deceive another. In certain cases, active concealment of a material fact (versus an affirmative false representation) may also constitute fraud. The basic elements of criminal fraud are (1) a false representation (or concealment) concerning a material fact and (2) another party relied on the false misrepresentation of the fact and suffered damages as a result. A material fact is one that is essential to the agreement or one that affects the value of the transaction. For example, suppose that Rasputin applies for a loan to start his business. Because his finances are in dire straits, Rasputin submitts a false set of tax returns to the bank loan officer. Based on this information, the bank lends Rasputin the money. Rasputin has committed a fraud upon the bank. Bank fraud of this nature is a felony punishable under state and, depending on the bank, federal criminal statutes.

In 1990, Congress passed the **Mail Fraud Act**[7] with the intent of giving federal prosecutors significant leverage in prosecuting white-collar criminals. The statute criminalizes any fraud in which the defrauding party uses the mail or any wire, radio, or television in

---

[7]10 U.S.C. § 1341.

FACT SUMMARY   LaGrou's warehouse in Chicago stored frozen meat for various food companies in the region. Its cold storage facility held more than 20 million pounds of poultry, pork, and beef. That building also had a severe rodent problem, as evidenced by rat droppings that could be found in every corner of the warehouse and nests found in boxes of meat. The company organized employee "rat patrols" that would catch up to 50 rats a day, but more would enter each night. Packing areas had puddles of beef blood mixed with rat hair and feces, and meat boxes showed rat trails with teeth marks. According to government investigators, employees would mark rat-infested boxes with "MM" for Mickey Mouse, but the boxes were not discarded. The warehouse was referred to by employees as an "amusement park for rats" and a "house of horrors for the City of Chicago." Evidence indicated that Stewart, president of LaGrou, knew of the rat infestation for a period of three years. Stewart told the employees to keep catching rats but refused to perform a full extermination because he determined that it would be too expensive. After notification that U.S. Department of Agriculture inspectors had scheduled a visit, Stewart had the employees work through the night to throw away boxes of rat-infested meat. Yet the USDA inspectors still found the rats, the filth, and the discarded meat. Stewart was charged with violating federal criminal laws prohibiting the sale of adulterated meat. At trial, Stewart defended that he did not have the requisite knowledge for criminal liability because he had no actual knowledge of any specific meat contamination.

SYNOPSIS OF DECISION AND OPINION   The Seventh Circuit Court of Appeals ruled against Stewart

and LaGrou. The court held that knowledge of *any* rat problem was sufficient and that Stewart was liable for all the violations that he was in charge of preventing. The court ruled that the government need not prove that Stewart had actual knowledge of specific meats that were contaminated. Stewart had a responsibility to install systems to ensure sanitation standards. The court affirmed the trial court's order that Stewart must contribute personal assets to the $8.2 million in fines and serve five years on probation.

WORDS OF THE COURT: Liability for Criminal Conduct of Others   "The conditions at LaGrou's cold storage warehouse at 2101 Pershing Road in Chicago were enough to turn even the most enthusiastic meat-loving carnivore into a vegetarian. . . . In this case, the government needed to prove that agents of the LaGrou corporation knowingly stored meat, poultry, and food products under unsanitary conditions. LaGrou's president, Jack Stewart, and the Pershing Road warehouse manager, David Smith, were both well aware of the rodent infestation problem and other insanitary conditions at the warehouse, yet persisted in storing and distributing meat, poultry, and food products there."

Case Questions

1. What if Stewart was never told about the rat problem. Did he have a responsibility to find out?

2. What about the workers who shipped the contaminated meat each day? Should they be guilty of some crime? What about the government inspectors who let the warehouse operate for three years? Who is most culpable?

---

perpetrating the fraud. This comprehensive approach to criminalizing fraud is based on Congress's authority to regulate mail and interstate commerce. It also covers any *organization* of a scheme to defraud by false pretenses. For example, in the Rasputin example discussed earlier, suppose that Rasputin sets up an elaborate scheme to fool investors into thinking that he has invented a new product that will bring in several millions of dollars of revenue. He designs a brochure and mails it to several wealthy individuals. At this point, Rasputin has committed mail fraud even though he has not actually induced any investors. The ease of prosecution for mail fraud has made it a primary tool used by prosecutors in white-collar crime investigations.

Another form of fraud is *embezzlement*. Embezzlement is appropriately categorized as fraud (and not as theft) because it involves fraudulent concealment of financial records to perpetrate theft. Embezzlement occurs when someone in a position of trust creates fraudulent records to disguise the theft. For example, suppose that Rasputin is the controller of WidgetCo. Over the period of a month, Rasputin transfers small amounts of Widget's money to his personal checking account and adjusts the monthly financial statements to indicate that the money was in WidgetCo's account. This act constitutes embezzlement because of the cover-up aspect of the scheme. If Rasputin had come into his office one morning, stole cash from the safe, and walked out never to return, this would likely constitute theft because no scheme was involved.

Ponzi Schemes

A Ponzi scheme is a fraudulent investment operation that pays returns to investors from their own money or money paid by subsequent investors rather than from any actual profit earned. The scheme is named after Charles Ponzi, who became notorious for using the technique in 1903. A Ponzi scheme usually offers returns that other investments cannot match in order to entice new investors. This is generally accomplished in the form of short-term returns that are either abnormally high or unusually consistent. The perpetuation of the returns that a Ponzi scheme advertises and pays requires an ever-increasing flow of money from investors in order to keep the scheme going. The system is destined to collapse because the earnings, if any, are less than the payments. The authorities uncover some schemes before they collapse if an investor suspects that she is a victim and reports the investments to authorities. As more investors become involved, the likelihood of the scheme coming to the attention of authorities increases.

For example, suppose that High Return Investments (HRI) prints advertising brochures that promise a 30 percent return on an investment in just one month—an extraordinary return by any measure. HRI states that it uses a "complex offshore investment strategy that is the result of years of study and testing." No matter how fancy the brochures are, it is difficult to attract any large initial investments without a track record. Thus, HRI convinces a few investors to take the risk with small amounts of money. Instead of investing the money, HRI then takes out a loan and repays the initial investors with the promised 30 percent return one month later. This is where HRI sets the trap: Initial investors now invest larger sums, and new investors want a piece of the action. It is no longer necessary to take out a loan because sufficient capital from eager new investors is flowing into HRI's hands. The cascading effect then allows HRI to pay back any loans used to perpetrate the scheme and take handsome bonus fees for managing the money. HRI covers its tracks by producing false investment statements for its investors showing high returns. When one or more investors request a withdrawal, there is sufficient cash to pay out. But HRI's scheme cannot last forever. Typically HRI's schemers will end up in one of two scenarios: (1) HRI disappears with the investment money, or (2) the scheme collapses because too many investors demand their returns at the same time. The second scenario typically happens when investor confidence in the equities markets deteriorates and investors withdraw money from market-based investments in favor of cash and other safer forms. For example, when the financial crisis of 2008 began to shake investor confidence, it unraveled the largest Ponzi scheme ever operated by a single person. Federal prosecutors claim that a 20-year scheme, operated by well-known investment manager Bernard Madoff, cost his investors billions of dollars. Madoff's scheme is examined in detail in the Business Ethics Perspective.

Conspiracy

Conspiracy is an agreement by two or more persons to commit a criminal act. It is itself a punishable offense: All parties to the agreement are subject to prosecution. Because the crime is complete upon agreement, there is a very low threshold for satisfying the criminal act requirement. Conspiracy requires a specific *intent* to achieve the object of the conspiracy but does not require that the act actually be carried out. The MPC contemplates

Epic Fraud: Bernie Madoff's Multibillion-Dollar Ponzi Scheme

OVERVIEW Bernie Madoff founded Bernard L. Madoff Investment Securities firm in 1960 and was its chairman until his arrest in 2008. Madoff's firm originally thrived, and he rose to become one of the chief figures in the financial markets. During the 1980s Madoff was a rising star in the investment community and eventually served as chairman of the board of directors of the National Association Securities Dealers (NASD), the self-regulating industry organization overseeing securities brokers and dealers. Madoff was also influential in Washington, D.C., and regularly donated hundreds of thousands of dollars to candidates and political committees, including influential U.S. senators. During his rise, Madoff also gained a reputation as a generous philanthropist who donated significant sums of money to charities ranging from cancer research to the American Jewish Congress. In fact, it was his association with so many charities and nonprofits that allowed his Ponzi scheme to continue unabated for nearly 20 years.

MADOFF'S PONZI SCHEME Madoff began his scheme during the recessionary pressures of the early 1990s. His investors were defecting as Madoff's returns shrank, and Madoff set on a course to reverse that trend. He designed a fake investment strategy, which he named "split-strike conversions," and marketed investment funds using this strategy with a promise of a 10 to 12 percent return per month on an investment no matter how volatile the stock market was. In reality, Madoff planned an elaborate hoax in which he deposited all incoming investor money in a business account controlled exclusively by him, printed up bogus statements that were intended to dupe investors into having confidence that their investments were safe and were returning high yields, developed an infrastructure of in-house analysts to convince investors of the firm's sophistication, and paid out strategically timed profits to certain investors that were designed to entice additional investment. The scheme was calculated to lure investors with consistent returns between 10 and 12 percent annually and increase investor confidence in

Madoff's methods. The hoax worked. In a short period of time, investors were knocking down Madoff's door to get in. Madoff set up a screening system and was very selective in his choice of clients, giving his firm an air of inimitability, sophistication, and safety. A key part of Madoff's scheme depended on his emphasis on secrecy. He insisted that investment managers not list him on their own reports to individual investors. Madoff justified the secrecy requirements on the basis that his investment strategy was a valuable trade secret and he was simply being vigilant about protecting his investors.

PHILANTHROPY AS PART OF THE SCHEME Madoff's reputation in the philanthropic community allowed him access to large charity fund endowments, and many of his clients were nonprofit institutions. These institutions were a crucial part of the scheme because Madoff knew that charities generally did not make withdrawals from their invested endowments even in times of financial strife. Nonprofits typically allow their endowments to grow, and they withdraw funds only in rare circumstances. This allowed Madoff the ability to funnel money where needed and when needed to continue perpetrating his fraud.

Madoff's scheme continued to grow because investors were more than willing to invest large sums of money, sometimes personal fortunes in the billion-dollar category, and he always had a plentiful supply of cash when investors would make periodic withdrawals. Of course, Madoff earned sizable commissions for his work and lived an opulent lifestyle with private jets, a Palm Beach mansion, and a yacht on the French Riviera.

FEEDER FUNDS As the pressure of the scheme demanded more cash to support the fraud, Madoff extended his fraud into Europe, Asia, and Latin America. A key component to the success of the scheme was a steady flow of new investor dollars from a group of super investors. Madoff depended on these super investors, who not only invested their own holdings but also funneled other wealthy investors to Madoff's firm. These

(continued)

super investors created what Madoff termed *feeder funds* to channel billions of dollars in investment cash into Madoff's fictitious investment fund. In return, the managers of the feeder funds were rewarded with handsome commissions. After the scheme collapsed, the government alleged that feeder fund investment managers Jeffery Picower and Stanley Chais were both involved in directing investor money to Madoff's firm and were paid commission fees for bringing in investor cash and made extraordinary returns on their own personal investments with Madoff at rates much higher than other investors were paid. By early 2008, Madoff's firm had 4,800 clients—all clamoring to invest more money.

THE COLLAPSE In December 2008, the ongoing financial and credit crisis began to put pressure on Madoff's firm as clients demanded their investments be returned in order to cover their cash flow needs and to move their wealth into safer investments. As the demands mushroomed, Madoff quickly ran out of cash and could not turn to any financial institutions for credit. On December 10, when he could no longer stem the financial and legal catastrophes, Madoff confessed his scheme to his family and turned himself in to authorities the next day. The news of Madoff's arrest sent shock waves from Wall Street to Palm Beach as investors came to grips with the plot. Those who had invested all or substantially all of their assets with Madoff were wiped out overnight. Sophisticated money managers, wealthy investors, and large charities were all among Madoff's victims, and the news shook investor confidence even more, contributing to further declines in the market. In perhaps the most tragic case of the Madoff scheme, French millionaire investor Terry Villochet, who had invested his family's substantial wealth with Madoff, lost billions in the scheme. Facing certain bankruptcy, Villochet committed suicide two weeks after learning of Madoff's arrest.

EARLY WARNINGS As early as 1999, a financial analyst named Harry Markopolos did an in-depth study of Madoff's investments at the request of a client. Markopolos was astonished at what he found and began to document at least two dozen red flags that indicated fraud. Markopolos was skeptical of the three-person accounting firm used by Madoff to verify the authenticity of the investments. Although Markopolos brought this information to government authorities, the subsequent investigations by the Securities and Exchange Commission (SEC) did not reveal any fraud. In the meantime, Madoff restructured his firm and agreed not to be involved in the actual sales of securities. However, Madoff was too deep into the scheme to halt it, and as volatility in the market increased in 2000–2001, investors continued to seek Madoff's consistent returns.

AFTERMATH In March 2009, Madoff pleaded guilty to 11 felonies, including fraud and perjury. He was given the maximum sentence of 150 years of incarceration. Madoff's accountant was also charged and cooperated with authorities in exchange for leniency. Prosecutors are still investigating allegations that certain investors had insider knowledge of the scheme. Hundreds of investors have filed lawsuits against a variety of banks, accounting firms, investment managers, and financial advisers.

The SEC was heavily criticized during a congressional hearing into the Madoff matter. Congress inquired why Markopolos had not been taken more seriously and how it was that the SEC did not have the expertise and system checks to discover the fraud earlier. Federal prosecutors froze all of Madoff's assets, and a federal court appointed a trustee to recover any funds that were unlawfully transferred before the collapse.

1. What factors caused Madoff to go from a legitimate and respected investor to a con man? Was it purely greed?

2. Madoff claimed that his scheme was simply a stopgap measure to bridge the 1990 recession and that he had intended to go back to legitimate methods once the economy improved. If this were true, would it remove the ethical taint from the scheme?

3. How was Madoff able to fool some of the most sophisticated investors for so long?

4. Consider the ethical decision making of the investment managers who were funneling other investors to Madoff. Did they have an ethical obligation to inquire how Madoff was making the returns?

Bernie Madoff, seen here being escorted by U.S. marshals after being sentenced to 150 years in jail, perpetrated the largest and longest Ponzi scheme in U.S. history.

5. Madoff used the notion that his investment strategy was a trade secret to ward off any investor inquiries. If you were doubtful about the strategy but upon inquiry were denied any details of the strategy, would that affect your decision to invest?

6. Consider the ethics of self-regulation of broker-dealers. Does self-regulation depend on adherence to high ethical standards? In the Madoff case, did he get the benefit of the doubt as a Wall Street insider? Why do you suppose that the SEC was not more aggressive with Madoff?

conspiracy as a crime that requires two guilty minds. Therefore, both parties must actually *manifest* intent to commit the criminal act for a conspiracy to occur.

Racketeer Influenced and Corrupt Organizations Act (RICO)

The federal Racketeer Influenced and Corrupt Organizations Act[8] (RICO) was enacted in 1970 with the objective of providing the government with a powerful tool to fight the rising tide of organized crime. One purpose of the RICO law was to prevent organized crime from infiltrating legitimate business operations. The statute makes it a criminal offense for anyone associated with an enterprise to conduct or participate in its affairs through a pattern of racketeering activity. Although racketeering is generally understood to mean an organized conspiracy to commit the crimes of extortion or coercion, state and federal legislatures have added to the definition by including conduct such as engaging in illegal gambling, narcotics trafficking, and prostitution.

---

[8]18 U.S.C. §§ 1961–1968.

The modern trend is for authorities to use the RICO statute in an expansive manner, including criminal conduct that is not traditionally related to organized crime. Because RICO laws define racketeering in such broad terms, including crimes such as wire fraud, mail fraud, and securities fraud, prosecutors have been increasingly willing to bring RICO cases in white-collar crimes and political corruption cases. Although the penalties under RICO are stiff, the real teeth of the law are found in its forfeiture provisions. They allow prosecutors to seize the defendant's personal assets if the government can prove that the assets were obtained using profits from criminal activity. This is a powerful tool because it has the effect of bankrupting the racketeering enterprise while an individual convicted under the statute is incarcerated.

Insider Trading

In the wake of the financial crisis that began in 2008, the government has become increasingly aggressive about the enforcement of **insider-trading laws.** These laws are federal securities statutes that prohibit corporate insiders who have access to certain information that is not available to the general investment public from trading their company's stock based on the insider knowledge. Insiders can be executives, managers, corporate counsel, consultants, certain employees, brokers, and even majority shareholders. In 1988, Congress passed the Insider Trading and Securities Fraud Enforcement Act that raised the criminal and civil penalties for insider trading, increased the liability of brokerage houses for wrongful acts of their employees, and gave the government more authority to pursue insider-trading violations. Insider-trading laws and other laws regulate the issuance and trading of certain business ownership interests (such as stocks) and are discussed in detail in Chapter 17 "Regulation of Securities, Corporate Governance, and Financial Markets."

Bribery

Bribery generally involves a scheme to pay a government official money in order to obtain favorable treatment for a personal or business transaction. Bribery is covered in both federal and state statutes. Note that bribery is an offense that requires only the *offer* of a bribe. It is not necessary that the transaction actually takes place. For example, suppose that Whitaker is the owner of a construction company and bids on a contract to build a firehouse in the city. Whitaker promises a city councilman that she will pay him 10 percent of the total profit in the contract if the councilman will vote to give Whitaker the contract. The offer itself is unlawful even if the councilman does not go along with the scheme. Of course, if the councilman does go along with the bribe (known as a *kickback* in these circumstances), he too will be culpable for bribery (and perhaps several other *public trust* laws).

Obstruction of Justice

Prosecutors have been increasingly willing to prosecute white-collar criminals under federal laws prohibiting the obstruction of justice[9] for any conduct that is related to attempting to cover up evidence of wrongdoing. Cover-ups take many forms, including (1) lying to investigators, (2) altering documents, (3) shredding or concealing documents or any media such as videotape, and (4) inducing other witnesses to lie or influencing witnesses to refrain from cooperating with authorities. Note that an obstruction of justice charge may stand *independently,* and prosecutors need not charge or convict the defendant with the underlying crime. For example, suppose that prosecutors interview Rasputin during the criminal investigation of insider trading at Rasputin's firm. Rasputin lies about his involvement in the insider trading to the authorities. When it is found out that Rasputin lied, prosecutors charge Rasputin with obstruction of justice. Rasputin may be convicted of the

---

[9]18 U.S.C. § 1001 et seq.

obstruction charge even if prosecutors do not have sufficient evidence to charge Rasputin with the underlying crime (insider trading).

In one of the most famous cases of a company being charged with obstruction, federal prosecutors charged the accounting firm Arthur Andersen with obstruction, alleging that individuals within the firm shredded documents related to the collapse and fraudulent practices of the Enron corporation. A federal grand jury also indicted individual employees of Arthur Andersen for obstruction. The Enron and Arthur Andersen cases are discussed in detail in Chapter 5, "Business, Societal, and Ethical Contexts of Law."

Foreign Corrupt Practices Act (FCPA)

The **Foreign Corrupt Practices Act (FCPA)**[10] of 1977 is a criminal statute that was enacted principally to prevent corporate bribery of *foreign officials* in business transactions. The law prohibits a company and its officers, employees, and agents from giving, offering, or promising anything of value to any foreign (non-U.S.) official with the intent of obtaining or retaining business or any other competitive advantage. This prohibition is interpreted broadly in that companies may be held liable for violating the antibribery provisions of the FCPA whether or not they took any action within U.S. borders. Thus, a U.S. company can be liable for the conduct of its overseas employees or agents even if no money was transferred from the United States and no U.S. citizen participated in any way in the foreign bribery.

A foreign official is any officer or employee of a foreign government, regardless of rank; employees of government-owned or government-controlled businesses; foreign political parties; party officials; candidates for political office; and employees of public international organizations (such as the United Nations or the World Bank). This list can include owner-employees as well. Even if the improper payment is not accepted, just offering it violates the FCPA. Likewise, other FCPA violations include instructing, authorizing, or allowing a third party to make a prohibited payment on a company's behalf; ratifying a payment after the fact; or making a payment to a third party knowing or having reason to know that it will likely be given to a government official. Prohibited payments include not only cash and cash equivalents but also gifts, entertainment, travel, and the like. The FCPA is discussed in greater detail in Chapter 26, "International Law and Global Commerce."

 Self-Check   White-Collar Crime

What white-collar crimes are at issue in the following circumstances?

1. WidgetCo applies for a permit to do business in Venezuela. The government official denies the permit, and a WidgetCo executive pays for a lavish meal at a four-star restaurant while discussing the permit application.

2. InvestCo advertises a return of 15 percent on any investments in its Super Duper Fund. Even when the market drops dramatically, Super Duper continues to perform at this level for 18 consecutive months. In its disclosures, InvestCo reports that its auditing firm is headed by an InvestCo officer's son-in-law.

3. WidgetCo and PlankCo agree to illegally fix prices so that the lack of competition drives the prices of their products artificially high. The companies begin the process to set prices but abandon the plan at the last moment.

4. Evidence exists that WidgetCo's CEO was funneling money from the corporation with the help of several other executive managers. The funds came from an investment fraud scheme in which each executive played a part to perpetrate the scheme and use WidgetCo as a front business to help bolster their scheme with investors.

Answers to this Self-Check are provided at the end of the chapter.

---

[10]28 U.S.C. § 1602 et seq.

FACT SUMMARY After the collapse of the Soviet Union in 1991, the people of the country of Azerbaijan reclaimed its independence and moved toward a market-based economy via a system of privatization. Among the privatization efforts were the sale of SOCAR, the state-owned oil company, through the use of a public voucher system designed to ensure investors a fair chance at bidding on state-owned assets. Bourke was approached by Kozeny about participating in an investment opportunity that would lead to the purchase of SOCAR. Kozeny, dubbed the "Pirate of Prague" by *Fortune* magazine, was an entrepreneur known for his crooked transactions in a similar privatization effort during the Czech Republic's reforms in the mid-1990s. The media had reported that Kozeny and his partner engaged in massive fraud during the privatization of the state-owned industries in the Czech Republic, including engaging in insider trading, purchasing state secrets, and participating in various other unsavory business practices.

Bourke and Kozeny became partners and developed an elaborate investment scheme designed to ensure that they would have exclusive rights to purchase SOCAR. When the Azeri government expressed doubts about privatization of SOCAR, Bourke recruited several other wealthy businessmen and a former U.S. senator to help persuade the government that privatization would be in the country's best interest. Without the knowledge of some of the partners, these efforts included Kozeny's bribes to Azeri government officials. Kozeny, Bourke, and others were indicted for violation of the Foreign Corrupt Practices Act (FCPA) and other violations of federal law. Kozeny became a fugitive and never faced trial, but Bourke was convicted of conspiracy to violate the FCPA. He appealed on the basis that he had no actual knowledge of the bribery and had not willfully avoided Kozeny's corrupt actions.

SYNOPSIS OF DECISION AND OPINION The Court of Appeals for the Second Circuit upheld Bourke's convictions. The court pointed to evidence of conversations that indicated that Bourke was fully cognizant of the plan to offer bribes to Azeri officials and had on a number of occasions inquired of fellow business associates whether "Vikter [Kozeny] was paying enough." Given Kozeny's reputation and Bourke's actions to avoid detection under the FCPA, it was clear that, at the very least, Bourke willfully ignored and avoided the FCPA violations that were occurring in the partnership's efforts to buy SOCAR.

WORDS OF THE COURT: Conscious Avoidance "While the government's primary theory at trial was that he had actual knowledge of the bribery scheme, there is ample evidence to support a conviction based on the alternate theory of conscious avoidance. The testimony at trial demonstrated that Bourke was aware of how pervasive corruption was in Azerbaijan generally. Bourke knew of Kozeny's reputation as the "Pirate of Prague." Bourke created the American advisory companies to shield himself and other American investors from potential liability from payments made in violation of FCPA, and joined the boards of the American companies instead of joining the [venture's] board. In so doing, Bourke enabled himself to participate in the investment without acquiring actual knowledge of [the venture's] undertakings."

Case Questions

1. What steps could Bourke have taken to be sure that he was not involved in FCPA violations?

2. If bribery is a normal way of economic life in some parts of the world, how might the FCPA impact the competitiveness of American companies?

Several law firms have recently alerted their clients of stepped-up FCPA enforcement by the Justice Department and the Securities and Exchange Commission, including a massive investigation in 2012 that resulted in Pfizer paying a $15 million fine for bribes paid by Pfizer employees to officials in Italy, Russia, and several eastern European countries.[11] In Case 23.2, a federal appeals court reviews the conviction of an American business partner of Vikter Kozeny, the notorious "Pirate of Prague," under the FCPA.

---

[11]See, for example, J. Coopersmith, *DOJ and SEC Continue Enforcement Trend,* Davis Wright Tremaine, LLP, Client Briefing, October 12, 2012.

THE CRIMINAL JUSTICE SYSTEM

LO 23-7

The criminal justice system is best thought of as one process that operates in two phases: **investigation** and **adjudication.** This section describes the nuts and bolts of the criminal justice process. Procedural safeguards that are afforded to those suspected or accused of crimes constitute *criminal procedure* and are discussed in the next section of this chapter.

Investigation

During the investigation phase, the authorities become aware of an alleged criminal act and begin an investigation by gathering physical evidence and interviewing witnesses and potential suspects. Because most criminal acts are handled at the state level, most enforcement of criminal law is conducted by state or local police agencies. Violations of federal laws are investigated by various federal law enforcement agencies, including the Federal Bureau of Investigation (FBI). In a business context, investigators from federal regulatory agencies such as the Securities and Exchange Commission (SEC) or the Internal Revenue Service (IRS) may also undertake specialized criminal investigation. During this initial stage, investigators may also ask a court to authorize a search warrant in an effort to obtain more evidence. A warrant may be issued only based on **probable cause.** Once the authorities believe that sufficient evidence creates enough probable cause to indicate the culpability of a suspect, they will, depending on the circumstances, either obtain an *arrest warrant* or, more commonly, *arrest* the suspect by taking him into physical custody. If the criminal violation is a minor one, the authorities may simply issue a *citation,* whereby the violator may resolve the charge by paying a fine or may contest the charge in court. If an actual arrest has taken place, the authorities may continue their investigation by gathering more physical evidence, interviewing new witnesses, and attempting to further interview the suspect. The investigators then file formal criminal charges against the suspect and prepare a brief report for a local magistrate and prosecutors. The suspect, now charged, is referred to as the *defendant* and is formally read the charges by a magistrate. The magistrate then sets bail (if appropriate) and, if necessary, appoints an attorney to represent the defendant. Frequently, the prosecutor will review the investigator's report (and sometimes conduct additional investigation) and then decide whether she can prove the charges in a court of law based on available evidence. The prosecutor decides whether to (1) proceed with prosecuting the defendant on the original charge, (2) amend the charges as necessary, (3) drop the charges altogether due to lack of evidence. The actual title of the prosecutor varies between jurisdictions, but local prosecutors are typically employed by the district attorney, state prosecutors are employed by the state's attorney general, and federal prosecutors work for the U.S. attorney general under the authority of the U.S. Department of Justice.

Legal **Speak** ⟩⟩
Bail The security, in the form of cash or a bond, given to the court to ensure the appearance of a defendant in court at a later date. If the defendant appears in court, the bail is returned. If he flees, the bail is forfeited.

Adjudication

If the prosecutor elects to proceed with the charges, the defendant is entitled to a **preliminary adjudication.** Some jurisdictions use the *grand jury* system, while others use a *preliminary hearing* in front of a local magistrate. In each case, the prosecutor presents evidence of the defendant's guilt, and the decision maker (either the grand jurors or the magistrate) determines whether probable cause exists to hold the defendant over for trial. If the prosecutor cannot offer sufficient evidence of probable cause, the charges are dismissed. As a practical matter, very few cases are dismissed at this stage.

The defendant is notified that he is held over for trial through either an *indictment* (in the case of a grand jury) or formal filing of an *information* (in the case of a magistrate). The defendant is then entitled to an arraignment in a state trial court, at which he is informed of the final charges and is asked to enter a *plea* of guilty, not guilty, or no contest,[12] An overwhelming majority of defendants plead not guilty at this stage, even if they intend on negotiating an eventual guilty plea with the prosecutor. Following the arraignment, the prosecutor and defense counsel will typically enter into a plea-bargaining negotiation. This involves the parties agreeing to concessions from each side that will avoid trial and result in a voluntary plea of guilty or no contest by the defendant. All states also have some type of pretrial intervention for first-time offenders of nonviolent crimes, whereby the defendant typically agrees to fulfill certain conditions (community service, drug rehabilitation, etc.) in exchange for the charges being dismissed at a later date. If a plea agreement cannot be reached, the case proceeds to trial. In a trial, the finder of fact (usually a jury in a criminal trial)[13] weighs the evidence and determines whether the prosecutor has proved the charges against the defendant beyond a reasonable doubt. If the jury finds the defendant guilty, this results in a *conviction.* If the jury finds the defendant not guilty, this results in an *acquittal* and the defendant cannot be prosecuted for the same charges again. If the jury is deadlocked (unable to reach a consensus decision), this results in a *mistrial* and the prosecutor decides whether or not to refile charges against the defendant a second time. If the defendant is convicted, he may file an *appeal* setting out the basis for having the conviction reversed.

If the defendant is convicted, the judge sets a future date for *sentencing.* In the interim, the court considers requests and reports by authorities, victims of the defendant's crime, character witnesses for the defendant, and sentencing guidelines (or statutory mandatory minimum sentences) in determining the defendant's punishment.

CONCEPT SUMMARY The Criminal Justice Process

Investigative Phase	Adjudicative Phase
1. Investigate possible crime.	1. Preliminary adjudication (via grand jury or magistrate depending on jurisdiction).
2. Interview witnesses.	2. File indictment (known as "information" depending on jurisdiction) or drop charges due to insufficient evidence.
3. Obtain search warrants if necessary.	3. Defendant enters plea and enters plea negotiations if necessary.
4. Obtain arrest warrant or take suspect into custody or issue a citation for minor infractions.	4. If no plea agreement is reached, defendant goes to trial.
5. Defendant is formally charged.	5. Conviction or acquittal of the defendant.
6. Local judicial authority sets bail and appoints defense counsel if necessary.	6. Sentencing (if convicted).

---

[12]In a plea of no contest, sometimes called by its Latin form *nolo contendere,* the defendant does not admit or deny the charges but is willing to accept the sanctions as if guilty.

[13]Recall from Chapter 3, "The American Judicial System, Jurisdiction, and Venue," that the finder of fact may be either a jury *or* a judge.

CRIMINAL PROCEDURE

Recall from the beginning of this chapter the differences between criminal law and criminal procedure. While criminal law defines the boundaries of behavior and sanctions for violating those boundaries, *criminal procedure* refers to legal safeguards to protect the rights of individuals (and in some cases business entities) during investigation by the government, arrest, trial, and sentencing. The protections are primarily provided by the U.S. Constitution's Bill of Rights. For purposes of understanding criminal procedure in a business environment, our focus is on protections found in the Fourth, Fifth, and Sixth Amendments. While the Constitution regulates many aspects of criminal procedure, as a practical matter state and federal legislatures also enact statutes and rules setting forth certain procedures that authorities must follow during investigation, arrest, criminal trial, and sentencing. State constitutions may also provide *additional* criminal procedure protections for a state's citizens. For example, one state may be more apt to require a higher level of probable cause for arrest than is prescribed by the federal rules or courts. Of course, states may not repeal the federal constitutional rights of individuals.

Warrant A court order authorizing an official to do something she would otherwise be prohibited from doing. The most common are warrants for arrest, search, or seizure.

Searches and Arrest

The Fourth Amendment to the U.S. Constitution protects individuals (and sometimes businesses) from unreasonable search and seizure by government agents and permits warrants to be issued only if probable cause exists. The U.S. Supreme Court has developed a large body of law to guide courts in determining the appropriate boundaries of searches and arrests by authorities. First, the Court has held that the Fourth Amendment applies to both *searches* and *arrests*. However, a warrant is usually required before a search takes place (with certain exceptions). A warrant for arrest is generally not required in order to take a suspect into custody. Second, the Constitution requires that an impartial magistrate issue a search or arrest warrant only if probable cause has been established. Third, whether or not a search or arrest warrant exists, the action taken by authorities must always be *reasonable* and consistent with constitutional protections. Fourth, the authorities may conduct *limited,* warrantless searches in certain cases. For example, police may conduct short, pat-down searches even without probable cause when the officer has a reasonable suspicion[14] that criminal activity is taking place or when the officer's safety is an issue.

Although the Fourth Amendment requires authorities to obtain a warrant before searching a citizen, the Supreme Court has allowed the police to conduct a limited pat-down search when an officer has reasonable suspicion that criminal activity is taking place.

Expectation of Privacy A fundamental part of the protections provided by the Fourth Amendment is that its protections are based on whether an individual's *reasonable expectation of privacy* has been violated by government authorities. The courts have held that individuals have the highest expectations of privacy in their own homes. However, once an individual goes into the public (such as driving a car on a public highway), the privacy expectations are diminished and Fourth Amendment protections become more limited in scope. Examples of evidence that is *not* protected under reasonable expectation of privacy include trash that has been set

---

[14]Reasonable suspicion has been described as a standard that is lower than probable cause but "more than just a hunch"; *Terry v. Ohio,* 392 U.S. 1 (1968).

out on the public curb for pickup, or any apparently abandoned property, and things a person says or does in public. In terms of the abandoned property example, note that if the evidence has been disposed of but is still located on the real estate (land) of the owner, then the owner may still have a reasonable expectation of privacy. For example, Scofield is being investigated for tax fraud. The authorities observe Scofield putting out large bags of paper for trash pickup.

They wait until midnight and then take the bags from the curbside outside Scofield's residence. When Scofield is brought to trial, the prosecutor introduces the discarded papers as evidence of tax fraud. If Scofield claims his Fourth Amendment rights were violated, it is likely that he would lose that argument because courts have consistently held that public papers disposed of as garbage are abandoned property and not subject to reasonable expectations of privacy. Suppose, though, that the real estate at issue was a country home with a long driveway and that trash collectors actually traveled onto the property to collect the garbage. If the authorities entered the land without a warrant and confiscated the bags of discarded papers, a court may very well find the search to be illegal.

Plain View Doctrine   Courts have held that authorities generally do not commit a Fourth Amendment violation when a government agent obtains evidence by virtue of seeing an object that is in his plain view and the agent has the right to be in the position to have that view. This is called the **plain view doctrine.** For example, suppose that during a routine traffic violation stop, a police officer observes an illegal handgun lying on the seat next to the driver. The officer may then arrest the driver and confiscate the weapon without a warrant because the plain view search is not prohibited by the Fourth Amendment. The plain view doctrine also allows authorities to use simple mechanical devices that are available to the general public, such as a flashlight or a camera with telephoto lenses to enhance their view. However, courts have limited authorities' ability to obtain information by means of special high-tech devices that are not available to the general public. For example, in a 2001 case, the U.S. Supreme Court held that the use of a thermal imager (a device used to produce images of relative amounts of heat escaping from a structure) by authorities on a public sidewalk outside a residence was *not* covered by the plain view doctrine and constituted an illegal search.[15] The Court reasoned that because the data could not be obtained through use of the naked eye or basic equipment available to the general public, the action constituted a search even though government authorities had not physically entered the house.

The courts have adopted a similar position regarding aerial observations made by authorities. That is, so long as the plane or helicopter is in public navigable airspace, anything the police can see with the naked eye or basic equipment such as binoculars will be considered in plain view. In *Dow Chemical Co. v. U.S.,*[16] the Supreme Court ruled that the use of an airplane by government agents to fly over one of Dow's chemical plant complexes for purposes of taking investigative photographs with a zoom lens fit into the plain view exception and did not require a warrant because a zoom lens was readily available for purchase by the public.

---

[15]*Kyllo v. U.S.,* 553 U.S. 27 (2001). The case involved the use of a device by U.S. Drug Enforcement Agency officials to obtain information on a suspected marijuana-growing operation in a residence. The agents obtained a warrant based on the fact that the thermal imager revealed that the garage of the residence was emitting extraordinary levels of heat. Indeed, Kyllo had been using heat lamps to grow marijuana in the garage, and he was eventually convicted at trial. The Supreme Court reversed the conviction on the basis that the thermal search evidence was obtained in violation of the Fourth Amendment. Justice Scalia wrote famously that allowing the authorities to use advanced technology would "leave the homeowner at the mercy of advancing technology— including the technology that could discern all human activity in the home."

[16]476 U.S. 227 (1986).

Searches of Business Premises Courts have been very reluctant to extend reasonable-expectation-of-privacy rights to the workplace. This is particularly true when the business is highly regulated. Recall from Chapter 18, "Administrative Law," that certain businesses are classified as *pervasively regulated* and, therefore, are not entitled to full Fourth Amendment protections. Instead, the U.S. Supreme Court has fashioned an exception to the Fourth Amendment warrant requirements that applies when an agency is conducting regularly scheduled inspections pursuant to an administrative rule. Even in cases where courts have held that administrative agencies are required to obtain an *administrative warrant* to conduct an inspection of a business, the Court has held that agencies are held to a lower standard of probable cause to obtain the warrant than would be required if the government were obtaining a criminal warrant.

Self-Incrimination

The Fifth Amendment provides that no person "shall be compelled in any criminal case to be a witness against himself." This means that individuals have the right not to offer any information or statements that may be used against them in a criminal prosecution. If an individual believes that any statement or testimony may incriminate her in a criminal case, she may decline to testify on Fifth Amendment grounds. Note that the right of self-incrimination also protects those called as witnesses in other types of matters. For example, suppose that in the tax fraud hypothetical case discussed earlier, the government prosecutes Scofield for tax evasion. During the trial, the prosecutor issues a subpoena to Montgomery, Scofield's business partner. If Montgomery has a belief that any questions asked of him as a witness in Scofield's trial may uncover evidence of his own criminal culpability, he may refuse to testify at Scofield's trial even though Montgomery is not under investigation.

The Fifth Amendment right against self-incrimination also applies while authorities are *investigating* crimes. Generally, the context is that government authorities are interviewing an individual in the course of a criminal investigation. Although most case law surrounding this right deals with police interrogations of a suspect, in a business context business owners and managers should realize that agents of regulatory agencies, such as the Internal Revenue Service, are bound by the same guidelines as agents of police agencies are when interviewing suspects during a criminal investigation. An important element of this protection is that it is limited to *custodial* interrogations, in which the interviewee has been taken into custody or deprived of his freedom in some significant way. In this event, the authorities are required to give affirmative preinterview warnings to the suspect that he has the right not to make any statements and that any statement that is given may eventually be used as evidence against him in a criminal trial.

For example, suppose that an FBI agent telephones Barrabas and requests a meeting in Barrabas's office. The agent explains that he is investigating a fraud scheme involving government contracts. Barrabas agrees to the meeting, and during the conversation he admits to certain incriminating facts. The admission will likely be admissible as evidence despite the failure of the agent to provide the self-incrimination warning. Because the statement was made voluntarily in a noncoercive setting (Barrabas's office) and because Barrabas could have stopped the interview at any time, the interview may not be considered custodial and Barrabas's Fifth Amendment protections are not triggered. Alternatively, if the agent had arrested Barrabas and transported him to a local FBI field office, the agent would be required to give the warnings about self-incrimination.

The warning requirements were set out in Landmark Case 23.3, perhaps the most famous case in criminal procedure.

Production of Business Records

Business records such as letters, memorandums, e-mail exchanges, inventory accounts, financial documents, and the like are often at the very crux of cases where government

FACT SUMMARY Ernesto Miranda was a suspect in the knifepoint rape of an 18-year -old woman. Two police officers took Miranda into custody and detained him at a police station. They interviewed Miranda for two hours and obtained a full confession from him. The officers never told Miranda that he had the constitutional right to an attorney and the right to remain silent or that whatever he said could be used against him later at his trial. Only after Miranda confessed did the police have him sign a statement that said the confession was made voluntarily and with full knowledge of his legal rights. After being convicted on the strength of the confession, Miranda appealed, arguing that being interviewed in police custody is inherently coercive if the suspect is unaware of his rights. Thus, his confession was not, in fact, voluntary.

SYNOPSIS OF DECISION AND OPINION The U.S. Supreme Court ruled in favor of Miranda. In a decision that sent shock waves through the law enforcement community, the Court held that Miranda's confession was inherently involuntary and, thus, could not be used at his trial. The Court ordered a retrial. Even though the police did not physically force Miranda to confess, anything he said while trapped in a police interrogation room without knowing that he could have a lawyer or just stay quiet was inherently involuntary and violated the Fifth Amendment. The Court reasoned that because police always have inherent power in any custodial interrogation of a suspect, unless the suspect is informed of his rights beforehand, any confession would be presumed involuntary and coerced and not admissible in court.

WORDS OF THE COURT: Coercive Environment "It is obvious that such an interrogation environment is created for no purpose other than to subjugate the individual to the will of his examiner. This atmosphere carries its own badge of intimidation. To be sure, this is not physical intimidation, but it is equally destructive of human dignity. . . . Today, then, there can be no doubt that the Fifth Amendment privilege is available outside of criminal court proceedings and serves to protect persons in all settings in which their freedom of action is curtailed in any significant way from being compelled to incriminate themselves. We have concluded that without proper safeguards the process of in-custody interrogation of persons suspected or accused of crime contains inherently compelling pressures which work to undermine the individual's will to resist and to compel him to speak where he would not otherwise do so freely. In order to combat these pressures and to permit a full opportunity to exercise the privilege against self-incrimination, the accused must be adequately and effectively apprised of his rights and the exercise of those rights must be fully honored."[17]

Case Questions

1. Do the Miranda warnings really matter? If you ask for a lawyer or will not talk, doesn't that mean you have something to hide? What would you do if you were a suspect?

2. What if the suspect is not in the police station? Is he still in "custody" in a police car? Pulled over for speeding? Sitting in his office with the police in front of him? When do the police stop talking to the suspect and start "interrogating" such that they need to give the Miranda warnings?

[17]What happened to Ernesto Miranda? On retrial he was found guilty based on other evidence. He spent over a decade behind bars. When he was paroled, he earned income selling police "Miranda cards" that he had autographed. In 1976, he was killed in a bar fight. *See* George C. Thomas, *Missing Miranda's Story,* 2 Ohio St. J. Crim. L. 677, 683–684 (2005).

---

authorities are investigating potential criminal activity in the business environment. Although the U.S. Supreme Court has held that certain business records may be classified as private papers and are protected by the Fifth Amendment, this protection has been severely narrowed over the last several decades. In 1984, the Court ruled that certain business records of a sole proprietor could be considered private papers because a sole proprietor is a form of business entity that is essentially the alter ego of the individual.[18] The Court reasoned that because there was no legal separation between the business and the sole owner (unlike a corporation, which exists as a separate legal "person"), the owner's

[18]*U.S. v. Doe,* 465 U.S. 605 (1984).

FACT SUMMARY   Braswell was the sole shareholder and officer in two companies engaged in brokering (buying and selling) timber, land, oil interests, and machinery. The only other directors in the companies were his wife and his mother. Federal authorities that were investigating Braswell's business subpoenaed his business records. Braswell refused to hand over the documents, claiming that he was asserting his Fifth Amendment right against self-incrimination. Braswell argued that when a business is so small that it is nothing more than a person's "alter ego," the Fifth Amendment safeguards should apply.

SYNOPSIS OF DECISION AND OPINION   The U.S. Supreme Court ruled against Braswell and compelled him to hand over the books and records. The Court held that a corporation can act only through its officers and employees and when an officer or employee acts as a records custodian for that company, then he is not entitled to Fifth Amendment protection because he is no longer acting as a private individual but as part of a corporation. The Fifth Amendment protects only private individuals.

WORDS OF THE COURT: Corporate Records   "Artificial entities such as corporations may act only through their agents, and a custodian's assumption of his representative capacity leads to certain obligations, including the duty to produce corporate records on proper demand by the Government. Under those circumstances, the custodian's act of production is not deemed a personal act, but rather an act of the corporation. Any claim of Fifth Amendment privilege asserted by the agent would be tantamount to a claim of privilege by the corporation—which of course possesses no such privilege."

Case Questions

1. If a corporation has been recognized as a legal "person" for First Amendment purposes, shouldn't the Fifth Amendment protect it too?

2. What if Braswell's company was a sole proprietorship rather than a corporation? What if he ran it alone out of his apartment? When should the Fifth Amendment start or stop protecting him?

records were considered personal and subject to Fifth Amendment protections. However, the Court has also made clear that records of a *corporation* are not subject to Fifth Amendment safeguards because that business entity is separate and distinct from its owners and does not qualify for self-incrimination protections.

In Case 23.4, the U.S. Supreme Court considers where to draw the line between personal and business records.

Trial

The Sixth Amendment provides that in all criminal prosecutions the accused shall enjoy the right to a *speedy trial.* Although the U.S. Supreme Court has not set out specific time periods in which a trial must take place, it has given guideposts for state courts in applying the speedy trial guarantee. Courts apply a balancing test in which both the prosecutor's and the defendant's conduct is examined to determine reasons for delay. Ordinarily, a court weighs the length of the delay versus the severity of the crime. A general rule is that a delay of eight months or more is presumptively unconstitutional. The federal criminal justice system operates according to an infrastructure established by the **Speedy Trial Act,**[19] which sets out specific time periods in which an accused must be brought to trial. If the time limits are exceeded, the courts must dismiss the charges.

The Sixth Amendment also contains other important procedural rights such as a right to a jury trial for serious crimes (generally any offense that carries more than six months' incarceration as a penalty), the right to a public trial, and the right to confront witnesses through cross-examination.[20]

---

[19] 18 U.S.C. 3161.

[20] Cross-examination and other trial terminology are discussed in detail in Chapter 3, "The American Judicial System, Jurisdiction, and Venue."

Double Jeopardy   Although the role of the Fifth Amendment is usually thought of in the context of self-incrimination, it also protects a defendant from being subject to prosecution twice for the same offense. This guarantee is known as a prohibition of **double jeopardy.** In essence, the doctrine prevents prosecutors from retrying a defendant on the same charges after a jury has acquitted her.

LO 23-9   ## Exclusionary Rule

Trial courts are required to exclude presentation of any evidence that is obtained as a result of a constitutional violation. This is known as the *exclusionary rule.* For example, if a law enforcement officer wrongfully searches a suspect's house without first obtaining a search warrant, any evidence obtained in that search may not be used against the suspect if he is arrested and brought to trial. One important exception in the business environment is that the exclusionary rule applies only when violations of the Constitution occur and not when a government agency violates its own *internal procedures.* For example, suppose that a government agent secretly records a conversation with a suspected tax evader during a meeting in the agent's office. The suspect offers the agent a bribe. However, the agent violated internal agency rules because he had failed to obtain a supervisor's permission to record any conversations with taxpayers. When the suspect is tried, she asserts that the recording cannot be introduced at trial because it is barred by the exclusionary rule. The U.S. Supreme Court has *rejected* such an argument and held that the exclusionary rule bars only evidence obtained in violation of a constitutional provision. In this case, an agency rule was violated, but no constitutional violations took place and, thus, the exclusionary rule does not apply.[21]

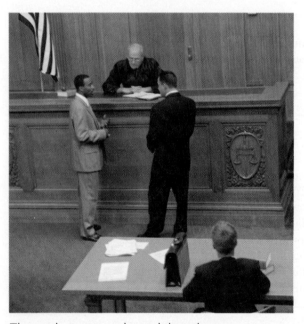

The exclusionary rule prohibits the use of evidence during a criminal trial that was obtained in violation of a defendant's constitutional rights.

Even evidence that is only indirectly obtained in violation of a defendant's rights is subject to the exclusionary rule because it is considered the *fruit of the poisonous tree.* This means that once original evidence is shown to have been unlawfully obtained, all evidence that stems from the original evidence (called *derivative evidence*) is also excluded. For example, suppose an agent of the Securities and Exchange Commission is investigating Falstaff for criminal fraud. The agent illegally searches the handbag of Falstaff's secretary and discovers evidence that Falstaff is concealing incriminating documents in his garage at home. Using the illegally obtained evidence, the agent then obtains a search warrant for Falstaff's home and discovers the incriminating documents. Because the agent's original evidence (obtained from Falstaff's secretary) was obtained in violation of the secretary's constitutional rights, a court would likely hold that the fruit of the poisonous tree doctrine rendered the warrant invalid and barred use of all evidence derived from the warrant (the incriminating documents) in a criminal trial against Falstaff.[22]

The exclusionary rule itself is controversial because it tends to benefit the guilty by excluding key evidence that would help convict them. Many legal

---

[21]Based on *U.S. v. Caceres,* 440 U.S. 741 (1979).

[22]See *Silverthorne Lumber Company v. U.S.,* 251 U.S. 385 (1920).

commentators have filled volumes of journals and treatises on the topic, but ultimately the exclusionary rule is justified by its proponents on the basis that it acts as a deterrent to violations of the Constitution by government authorities and the integrity of the judiciary requires that courts not be made a party to lawless invasions of constitutional rights of citizens by permitting unhindered government use of unlawfully obtained evidence. Nonetheless, the Supreme Court has fashioned several exceptions to the exclusionary rule intended to differentiate between abuse by the authorities of an individual's constitutional rights and those cases where the government has made an innocent mistake in obtaining evidence. Perhaps the most important exception to the rule occurs when the government can show that authorities were acting in *good faith* in obtaining evidence based on a search warrant issued by an authorized judge that was later found to be unsupported by an appropriate level of probable cause. In that case, even though the evidence is derived from a warrant that was granted but that was later found to have been a constitutional violation, the prosecutor may still introduce the evidence yielded from the search so long as the authorities were acting in good faith and reasonable reliance on the search warrant.

The exclusionary rule does have its limits, however. In Case 23.5, the U.S. Supreme Court considers the good faith exception in the context of a police clerical error.

CASE 23.5 Herring v. United States, 555 U.S. 135 (2009)

FACT SUMMARY   In July 2007, an investigator from the Coffee County (Alabama) Sheriff's Department learned that Herring was in the department's impound lot to retrieve personal items from his impounded truck. Police were familiar with Herring through past interactions, so they checked for any outstanding warrants for his arrest. Due to a clerical error, officers were incorrectly informed that an active warrant existed for Herring's arrest, and, pursuant to the warrant, they took him into custody shortly after his visit to the impound lot. During a search incidental to the arrest, officers discovered illegal narcotics and an illegal firearm in Herring's possession. Subsequently, the police records clerk discovered the oversight and officers became aware that the warrant for Herring's arrest had, in fact, been recalled several months before.

Herring was indicted on drug and firearm charges, and he filed a motion to have the narcotics and the gun excluded from evidence on the grounds that the search was conducted in violation of the Fourth Amendment since the warrant had been rescinded and the police had no probable cause for the arrest. The trial court denied the motion to suppress, citing the good faith exception to the exclusionary rule from *U.S. v. Leon*. The appellate court affirmed the ruling and held that since arresting officers were entirely innocent of any wrongdoing or carelessness,

the benefit of suppressing the evidence was marginal or nonexistent.

SYNOPSIS OF DECISION AND OPINION   The U.S. Supreme Court upheld the ruling of the lower courts in favor of the government. The Court applied the good faith exception to the exclusionary rule as set out in *U.S. v. Leon*. The majority emphasized that the Court had never held that the exclusionary rule was an individual right but, rather, that it applied only when application of the rule resulted in appreciable deterrence to law enforcement overreaching. In Herring's circumstances, the Court found that the conduct of the arresting officers did not rise to the level of culpability required for courts to apply the exclusionary rule. For a record-keeping error by the police to qualify for exclusion, the conduct would have to be *reckless* or a result of *knowingly* false entries. In this case, the officers were acting in objectively reasonable reliance on the subsequently invalidated warrant, and therefore the search of Herring fell squarely into the good faith exception recognized in previous cases. The Court held that the exclusionary rule is triggered only by police conduct that is sufficiently deliberate that exclusion can meaningfully deter it and sufficiently culpable that such deterrence is necessary to the integrity of the criminal justice system.

(continued)

A *dissenting opinion* argued that the exclusionary rule should be applied more broadly because its main objective is to compel respect for the constitutional guaranty in the only effectively available way—by removing the incentive to disregard it.

WORDS OF THE COURT [MAJORITY]: Scope of Exclusionary Rule "[Herring's] claim that police negligence automatically triggers suppression cannot be squared with the principles underlying the exclusionary rule, as they have been explained in our cases. In light of our repeated holdings that the deterrent effect of suppression must be substantial and outweigh any harm to the justice system, we conclude that when police mistakes are the result of negligence such as that described here, rather than systemic error or reckless disregard of constitutional requirement, any marginal deterrence does not 'pay its way.' In such a case, the criminal should not 'go free because the constable has blundered.' "[23]

Case Questions

1. How does this decision square with the exclusionary rule's objective of deterring police conduct?

2. Can you think of examples of police mistakes that could rise to the level at which the exclusionary rule would apply?

[23]The Court used this famous passage from Judge Benjamin Cardozo's opinion criticizing the federal exclusionary rule, which was not then applicable to the states, from *People v. Defore,* 242 N.Y. 13 (1926). Cardozo would later become an associate justice of the U.S. Supreme Court.

LEGAL IMPLICATIONS *in* CYBERSPACE

Computer Crimes and Internet Regulation

There are three major classes of criminal activity through use of a computer: (1) engaging in unauthorized use of a computer, which might involve stealing a user name and password or accessing the victim's computer via the Internet through a backdoor created by a Trojan horse[24] program; (2) creating or releasing a malicious computer program (e.g., computer virus, worm, Trojan horse); and (3) harassing and stalking in cyberspace.

Congress responded to the continued growth of computer crime with the **Computer Fraud and Abuse Act**,[25] which was most recently amended in 2001 by the Patriot Act. In essence, the law prohibits unauthorized use of computers to commit seven different crimes: (1) espionage; (2) the accessing of unauthorized information; (3) the accessing of a nonpublic government computer; (4) fraud by computer; (5) damage to a computer; (6) trafficking in passwords; and (7) extortionate threats to damage a computer.

[24]A Trojan horse is a virus that appears to perform one function yet actually performs another, such as the unauthorized collection, exploitation, falsification, or destruction of data.
[25]18 U.S.C. § 1030.

Obscenity in Cyberspace: The Communications Decency Act

The Internet has an element of entrepreneurial spirit associated with it, and many new companies and new business models were created to take advantage of the rapid growth of consumers in cyberspace. At the same time, it is clear that a significant number of business models benefiting from the boom are those associated with distribution of pornography. In the midst of some high-profile media stories involving the ease of access to online pornography by minors, Congress attempted to curb online content with the Communications Decency Act (CDA) in 1996. The CDA was intended to ban material that was "patently offensive" or "indecent" from being online if the content providers knew that children would have access to the material.

Challenges to the CDA

Shortly after the CDA was enacted, the American Civil Liberties Union (ACLU) filed a lawsuit challenging the act as an unconstitutional infringement on free speech. The case, *ACLU v. Reno* (called *Reno I*), was decided by the Supreme Court in 1997. It was the first time that the U.S. Supreme Court had to apply existing obscenity standards in cyberspace. One important element of the case was the Court's recognition of cyberspace as a unique medium that cannot be equated to broadcast media (such as radio or television) or any printed media (such as magazines or newspapers). This distinction was a key part of the Court's analysis that government was not entitled to as much deference in regulation of the Internet as the government is entitled to with other media. That said, the Court went on to strike down much of the act's substance, reasoning that the CDA's prohibition against "patently offensive" material being distributed on the web is too vague to pass constitutional muster.

Congressional Response to *Reno I*: Child Online Protection Act of 1998

Although the Court struck down much of the CDA, the opinion did set out, for the first time, the Court's view on the government's regulation of the Internet. The Court ruled that although the government had the right to regulate Internet traffic, the means employed by Congress was too broad a sweep. Using *Reno I* as a roadmap on constitutionality, Congress passed a similar piece of legislation the next year: with the Child Online Protection Act of 1998 (COPA).

The ACLU again filed a lawsuit challenging the COPA as unconstitutional. The new case, *ACLU v. Reno (Reno II)*, was decided by the U.S. Court of Appeals for the Third Circuit in 2000. The court of appeals ruled in favor of the ACLU and struck the statute down as still too overly broad. In 2003, the Supreme Court upheld the court of appeals' decision and adopted much of the court of appeals' reasoning.

CONCEPT SUMMARY Criminal Procedure

- The Fourth Amendment requires the authorities to obtain a warrant before searching areas where a citizen has a reasonable expectation of privacy.

- The Fifth Amendment protects an individual from involuntary self-incrimination before, during, and after an investigation and trial, but it does not protect a person from disclosing business records made in the person's capacity as corporate agent. The Fifth Amendment does not protect corporations.

- Anything said during custodial interrogation is presumed to be involuntary unless and until the person has been read the Miranda warnings.

- The exclusionary rule bans evidence obtained in violation of the Constitution from being used at trial.

KEY TERMS

Criminal law p. 627   The body of law that, for the purpose of preventing harm to society, defines the boundaries of behavior and prescribes sanctions for violating those boundaries.

Model Penal Code (MPC) p. 627   A statutory text adopted by the American Law Institute in 1962 in an effort to bring greater uniformity to state criminal laws by proffering certain legal standards and reforms.

Criminal procedure p. 628   The body of constitutional protections afforded to individuals and business entities during criminal investigations, arrests, trials, and sentencing.

Burden of proof p. 628   The responsibility of producing sufficient evidence in support of a fact or issue and favorably convincing the fact finder of that fact or issue.

Preponderance of the evidence p. 628 The burden of proof used in civil cases, under which the fact finder need be convinced only that the defendant's liability was more likely than not.

Beyond a reasonable doubt p. 628 The heightened burden of proof used in criminal cases, under which a fact finder must be convinced that the defendant's criminal liability is not in doubt to a reasonable person.

Legality p. 628 A principle of criminal law that protects individuals from being charged with some unspecified general offense; requires that crimes be specifically proscribed by law in advance of the conduct sought to be punished.

Punishment p. 629 A principle of criminal law that imposes a hardship in response to misconduct; based on the concepts that criminal law acts as a deterrent, it removes dangerous criminals from the population, and rehabilitation is an important part of the criminal justice system.

Sentencing guidelines p. 629 Statutorily prescribed standards for determining the punishment that a convicted criminal should receive on the basis of the nature of the crime and the offender's criminal history.

Act requirement p. 629 For criminal liability, the requirement that the government prove that a defendant's actions objectively satisfied the elements of a particular offense. Also called *actus reus.*

Self-defense p. 630 A defense to avoid criminal liability whereby the defendant's actions are related to the necessity of using deadly force to repel an attack in which the defendant reasonably feared that death or substantial harm was about to occur either to the defendant or to a third party.

Mental incapacity p. 630 A defense to avoid criminal liability whereby the defendant's actions are related to some type of mental disease or defect.

Felonies p. 630 Crimes that generally carry one year or more of incarceration as the penalty.

Misdemeanors p. 630 Crimes that carry up to one year of incarceration as the penalty.

Mail Fraud Act p. 632 Federal legislation enacted in 1990 as a comprehensive approach to criminalizing any fraud in which the defrauding party uses the mail or any wire, radio, or television in perpetrating the fraud.

Insider-trading laws p. 638 Federal securities statutes that prohibit corporate insiders who have access to certain information that is not available to the general investment public from trading their company's stock based on the insider knowledge.

Foreign Corrupt Practices Act (FCPA) p. 639 A federal criminal statute enacted principally to prevent corporate bribery of foreign officials in business transactions.

Investigation p. 641 The initial phase of the criminal justice process in which authorities become aware of an alleged criminal act and begin gathering physical evidence and interviewing witnesses and potential suspects.

Adjudication p. 641 A phase of the criminal justice system in which the prosecutor, after investigation, elects to proceed with the charges.

Probable cause p. 641 A reasonable amount of suspicion supported by circumstances sufficiently strong to justify a belief that a person has committed a crime.

Preliminary adjudication p. 641 A hearing at which the prosecutor presents evidence of the defendant's guilt and the decision maker (either the grand jurors or a magistrate) determines whether sufficient probable cause exists to hold the defendant over for trial.

Plain view doctrine p. 644 A doctrine stating that authorities generally do not commit a Fourth Amendment violation when a government agent obtains evidence by virtue of seeing an object that is in plain view of the agent.

Speedy Trial Act p. 647 A federal statute that sets out specific time periods in which an accused must be brought to trial.

Double jeopardy p. 648 Situation in which a defendant could be subject to prosecution twice for the same offense; prohibited by the Fifth Amendment.

Computer Fraud and Abuse Act p. 650 Federal legislation that prohibits unauthorized use of computers to commit espionage, the accessing of unauthorized information or of a nonpublic government computer, fraud by computer, damage to a computer, trafficking in passwords, and extortionate threats to damage a computer.

Dania Beach Antique Supply (DBAS) Inc. is a wholesaler of antique merchandise. DBAS employs expert buyers who purchase antiques in Europe, then makes any cosmetic improvements necessary (such as cleaning), and resells the merchandise to retail antique shops in the United States. Grendel is a senior-level executive at the company in charge of its primary warehouse, located in Fort Lauderdale, and a smaller facility at the Port of Miami. One of Grendel's responsibilities is to oversee worker safety in the facilities, as the processing of the antiques sometimes involves use of industrial machinery and cleaning solvents.

It was well known among DBAS employees that the Fort Lauderdale warehouse had less than ideal working conditions. The air-conditioning was often broken, and during the summer months the indoor temperature was in excess of 100 degrees. The cleaning solvents were left unattended, and the noxious fumes made working hazardous. When workers complained to Grendel, he purchased small fans to be placed in the facility but declined to overhaul the air-conditioning, claiming that the expense was too high and that the company was struggling financially. Grendel also ordered that the cleaning solvents be properly disposed of, but the on-site manager never carried out the order. In the meantime, several employees were hospitalized for heat exhaustion during their shift, and several others were made sick by the fumes from the cleaning solvents.

1. Assume that one worker notifies the Occupational Safety and Health Administration (OSHA) and that an OSHA agent informs Grendel that an investigation will be undertaken into the allegations of workplace hazards. Grendel immediately hires an air-conditioning repair company to fix the air-conditioning system. He also tells the on-site manager to destroy any maintenance records of the warehouse air-conditioning system history of inspections and repairs. What

potential criminal culpability would DBAS, Grendel, and the on-site manager have at this point? Do Grendel's preinvestigation actions constitute a criminal act? Do Grendel's actions after OSHA's notification of an investigation constitute a crime in and of themselves? Is the on-site manager criminally liable for carrying out Grendel's orders?

2. Suppose that Grendel is charged with a crime related to the workplace hazards and he defends by showing evidence that he ordered subordinates to take care of the hazards but his directions were never carried out. Is that a valid defense? If Grendel had second thoughts about his orders to destroy maintenance records and he called the manager to reverse his previous directions, would he still have criminal liability for attempting the cover-up?

3. Assume that during the investigation, OSHA agents make a midnight visit to Grendel's residence and remove documents from Grendel's trash bin on the public curb in front of his house. The documents contain incriminating evidence. Is the OSHA search illegal? Does the exclusionary rule apply in this case?

4. Assume that OSHA has information indicating that Grendel wrote about having a guilty conscience about the working conditions in the warehouse. If, during the criminal investigation of Grendel, OSHA issues a subpoena for Grendel's personal diary is Grendel's diary protected from inspection via the Fifth Amendment?

5. If OSHA investigators use cameras with telephoto lenses (that are available to the general public) to take pictures of the broken air-conditioning unit adjacent to the warehouse from the public sidewalk, does that require OSHA to obtain a search warrant?

A common element in cases where corporate executives are found guilty of criminal charges related to corporate activity is a lack of a systematic compliance procedure in the company's infrastructure. Senior managers are responsible for having systematic, internal controls in place that will help ensure compliance with federal and state statutes. Assume that you are a DBAS employee in the Theory to Practice problem and that both Grendel and the on-site warehouse manager are fired. You receive the following e-mail from the new vice president of operations:

Congratulations! You are being promoted to on-site manager at the Fort Lauderdale warehouse. The primary order of business is to develop a system of checks to be sure we are doing everything we can to avoid hazardous work conditions for our employees. Draft a two- to three-page memorandum that sets out

a specific system for compliance. The system should address (1) how complaints from workers will be handled; (2) procedures for inspecting the facility, reporting problems, and ensuring follow-up; (3) a clear chain of command; and (4) a response plan to handle hazards that require immediate response.

A sample answer may be found on this textbook's website at www.mhhe.com/melvinleb2e.

CASE SUMMARY 23.1 :: Bear Sterns & Co. V. Wyler, 182 F. Supp. 2D 679 (N.d. Ill. 2002)

PRODUCTION OF BUSINESS RECORDS

Bear Sterns had done business with Wyler, a Dutch businessman. A venture capitalist and resident of the Netherlands, Wyler kept offices in Toronto and Barbados. After the relationship soured, Bear Sterns sued Wyler for inducing one of its managing directors to make false statements and breach his fiduciary duties. In discovery, Bear Sterns requested that Wyler

disclose any business records that related to that fraudulent inducement. Wyler invoked his Fifth Amendment right against self-incrimination.

CASE QUESTIONS

1. Will the court force Wyler to disclose the documents? Are they business records?
2. Does the Fifth Amendment apply in civil suits?

CASE SUMMARY 23.2 :: Dollar S.S. Co. v. United States, 101 F.2d 638 (9th Cir. 1939)

CRIMINAL LAW AND BUSINESS ENTITIES

A harbor patrolman was hit by a bucket of garbage "consisting of cabbage, orange peel, celery, tea leaves, and water" thrown from a steamer named the *President Coolidge* in Honolulu harbor. Unable to find the actual sailor who had dumped the trash, the government charged the ship owner under a federal law making off-loading garbage into navigable waters illegal. The ship's owner, however, had taken measures to prevent

such dumping, such as issuing orders to the crew about its prohibition, hanging several warning signs in obvious places in both English and Chinese, and locking the "slop chutes" to prevent their use while in the harbor.

CASE QUESTIONS

1. Will the steamship company be criminally liable? Should it be even though it did everything to prevent the crime?
2. If the company should not be liable, what is the best way to prevent this crime?

CASE SUMMARY 23.3 :: United States v. Stewart, 323 F. Supp. 2d 606 (S.D.N.Y. 2004)

INSIDER TRADING

A wealthy businesswoman bought several thousand shares of a pharmaceutical company that was set to come out with a groundbreaking new cancer drug. She was a social friend of the company's CEO. On her way to vacation in Mexico, she received information from her broker that the CEO was selling all his shares. She eventually found out that the Food and Drug Administration was set to reject the cancer drug. She then

sold all her shares and saved her own portfolio from devastation.

CASE QUESTIONS

1. Is the woman guilty of insider trading? Why?
2. Would you do what she did or just wait around to lose all your money?
3. Should the CEO get to sell his shares?

FOREIGN CORRUPT PRACTICES ACT

Phillip Morris buys tobacco for its cigarettes from all around the world, including from South American growers in Venezuela. Phillip Morris entered a contract with La Fundacion Del Nino (the Children's Foundation) of Caracas, Venezuela, wherein the cigarette company would give the charity, which helped poor Venezuelan children, $12.5 million. In exchange, the Venezuelan government would put price controls on the country's tobacco crop.

CASE QUESTIONS

1. What criminal law did Phillip Morris possibly violate? Why?
2. Should the criminal law have a problem with money going to poor Venezuelan children and work for poor Venezuelan farmers?

EXCLUSIONARY RULE

The police received information that Yenzer, a fugitive, would be at a local dentist's office the next day. The police arrived at the dentist's office in hopes of capturing Yenzer, but she was not there. The receptionist informed them that Yenzer's appointment had been rescheduled for the next week. The police requested the exact date and time, and the dentist's receptionist complied. The police returned to the office at the rescheduled appointment time and arrested Yenzer when she arrived. Subsequent to her arrest, the police discovered evidence of additional crimes committed by Yenzer and charged her with various felonies. The Health Insurance Portability and Accountability Act (HIPAA) of 1996 prohibits dental offices from disclosing any information (including appointment times) about patients to third parties without the patient's permission. At trial, Yenzer argued that all evidence discovered after the dentist-office arrest should be excluded because the arrest was made as a result of a HIPAA violation.

CASE QUESTIONS

1. Is Yenzer's dental appointment time protected by the Fourth Amendment? Why or why not?
2. Did the police go too far in this case by requesting confidential information from the dentist's receptionist? Isn't the exclusionary rule intended to deter unlawful conduct by authorities?

 Self-Check **ANSWERS**

White-Collar Crime

1. FCPA. Buying a lavish meal for foreign government officials is prohibited.
2. Fraud (Ponzi scheme).
3. Conspiracy.
4. RICO.

24

CHAPTER

Personal Property, Real Property, and Land Use Law

learning **objectives**

After studying this chapter, students who have mastered the material will be able to:

24-1 Distinguish between tangible property and intellectual property.

24-2 Define and give examples of personal property used in business.

24-3 Explain the concepts of title, bundle of rights, and ownership by possession.

24-4 Identify the individual rights that landowners have in real property.

24-5 List and give examples of the three major forms of real estate ownership interests most commonly held by businesses and individuals.

24-6 Articulate and give examples of the duties, rights, and remedies of landlords and tenants in an agreement to lease real property.

24-7 Identify the differences in legal protections for tenants in commercial leases versus those in residential leases.

24-8 Distinguish between a sublease and an assignment and explain how each can be used in business planning objectives.

24-9 Give examples of two types of laws that regulate the use of real property by its owners.

24-10 Explain the government's rights and limits when exercising eminent domain.

aws governing the ownership and use of property have deep historical roots and are an integral part of the American legal system. Business owners and managers regularly encounter property law issues in business planning and operations. Examples include decisions on whether to own or lease certain property, rights of the property owners, landlord-tenant laws, and government restrictions on how property is used. In this chapter, students will learn:

- Categories of various types of property that are important to conducting business operations.
- Various levels of property ownership rights, responsibilities, and restrictions.
- Specific laws governing legal relationships between landlords and tenants.
- Methods used by the government to regulate the use of certain property.

DEFINITION AND CATEGORIES OF PROPERTY   LO 24-1

The term *property* in a legal sense is defined broadly a person's set of legal rights over others to use the property exclusively. While the casual meaning of the word *property* is often used in connection with real estate, the law of property recognizes two distinct categories: tangible property (such as real estate or goods) and intellectual property (such as patents). Laws covering tangible

property are discussed in this chapter, while intellectual property laws, also very important to business owners and managers, are covered in the next chapter.

TANGIBLE PROPERTY   LO 24-2

Tangible property, of course, is property that can be touched and physically possessed. The two forms of tangible property are **personal property** and **real property.**

Personal Property

Personal property is both tangible and *movable*. In a business context, goods, vehicles, inventory, and equipment for business operations, such as computers, are all examples of personal property. Personal property may be *owned* or *leased*. Leasing, which is governed by state statutory law modeled after the Uniform Commercial Code,[1] is discussed later in this section. Personal property rights of ownership, possession, and transfer are the subject of a blend of state statutes and common law principles.

---

[1] Recall from Chapter 1, "Legal Foundations," that the UCC is a "model" statute drafted by a group called the National Conference of Commissioners of Uniform State Laws (NCCUSL). Each state legislature makes its own decisions about whether to adopt the UCC in total, in part, or not at all (Louisiana is the only state to have rejected the UCC in its entirety).

Personal Property: Rights of Ownership and Ownership by Possession

The legal term for ownership rights in property is **title.** Normally, title is obtained by a grant of title by the current owner to a new owner, usually through a purchase or gift. Title is thought of as a *bundle of rights* related to the personal property. That is, the titleholder is permitted exclusive use of the personal property and has the rights to sell, lease, or prohibit another from using the property.

> **KEY** POINT
>
> Property ownership is fundamentally a bundle of rights whereby the titleholder has exclusive control, possession, and use of the property.

There are some instances, however, when the law allows a party to take title solely on the basis of *possession.*

Found Articles   The finder of lost property obtains title to the good by possession, except against the **actual owner.** Suppose that Commuter finds a gold wristwatch on a public sidewalk while walking to a commuter train station. She takes the watch to Station Manager, who, after asking each passenger in the area if he or she is the owner of the watch, is unable to find the true owner. Station Manager then keeps the watch from Commuter on the basis that Commuter is not the original owner. Assuming the true owner is not found, a court would likely find that Commuter has title over Station Manager and everyone else except for the original owner.[2]

Adverse Possession   Each state has a statute that applies to personal property held for an extended period of time by a possessor who is not the true owner. Once the statutory period has passed, the possessor of the goods is protected from any suit to recover the property except one by its true owner. The rule of adverse possession is also applied in a real property context and is explained in further detail later in this chapter.

Good Faith Purchasers   In some cases, a buyer will purchase a good or other personal property from someone who has physical possession of the property, but does not have title to the property (as is the case, e.g., with stolen goods). Under these circumstances, even if the buyer had no reason to know the good was stolen, the buyer does *not* acquire valid title. This situation is governed by the property law maxim that a seller cannot convey valid title unless she has valid title in the first place. Therefore, if the good was stolen, the actual owner may recover the property even from a good faith buyer.

Bailments   In a bailment relationship, although a possessor does not gain title via possession, the nonowner is still a rightful possessor of the goods. A bailment relationship is created when the *bailor* (owner of the property) entrusts a *bailee* to temporarily hold the property, usually for the parties' mutual benefit. If the parties intend to create a bailment relationship, the bailee owes a duty of *care* and a duty to act reasonably in protecting the property. For example, suppose that Franz brings his gold pocket watch to Max, a jeweler, for repair. Leaving the watch with Max created a bailment relationship. That is, Franz entrusted Max with his watch for their mutual benefit (Franz gets his watch fixed; Max earns income). Assume that Max has to leave the store in a rush that night and accidentally leaves the door open. The store is burglarized, and Franz's watch is stolen. Max would be liable for the cost of the watch due to his breach of the duty of care as bailee. On the other hand, suppose Max locked up the watch in a vault before he left, but a burglar with special skills broke into the vault and took the watch. In that case, most courts would find that Max had exercised due care and reasonableness and, therefore, is not liable for the theft.[3] Other common examples of a bailment relationship are coat check services, dry cleaning, and valet parking.[4]

In Case 24.1, a state appellate court analyzes the limits of bailment liability.

---

[2]Based on the landmark English common law case *Armory v. Delamirie,* 1 Strange 505 (K.B. 1722).

[3]Based on examples in Ray A. Brown, *The Law of Personal Property,* 3d ed. (Chicago: Callaghan and Company, 1975).

[4]Note that courts distinguish between a "self-check" parking lot (no bailment) and a valet parking lot, where an agent of the lot actually takes physical possession of the car via keys, etc. (bailment).

FACT SUMMARY Smith was employed by Ziva Jewelry, Inc. (Ziva), as a traveling salesman. In connection with his employment, Smith drove his own car to meet with potential customers and traveled with samples of expensive jewelry, which he typically kept locked in the trunk. In August 2000, while returning from a trade show, Smith stopped to get his car washed at a car wash owned and operated by Car Wash Headquarters (CWH). Smith left his keys with a CWH employee, watched the car as it went through the tunnel, and observed an employee driving the car a short distance to the drying area. Smith did not alert any CWH employee to the contents of the trunk. After the car was dried, the attendant signaled to Smith that the service was complete. As Smith paid the cashier, someone jumped into Smith's vehicle and drove off. Although the police located Smith's car in just 15 minutes, the jewelry, valued at over $850,000, was gone and was never recovered. Ziva sued CWH, alleging that CWH, as bailee, took possession of Smith's car and of the jewelry inside and that CWH failed to exercise due care to safeguard and return the bailed car and contents to Smith. The trial court granted CWH's motion for a summary judgment on the grounds that no bailment of the jewelry had been created. Ziva appealed.

SYNOPSIS OF DECISION AND OPINION The Supreme Court of Alabama affirmed the trial court's summary judgment in favor of CWH. The court held that Ziva could not establish that CWH expressly or impliedly agreed to take responsibility for the jewelry hidden inside Smith's trunk. Since Ziva acknowledged that the jewelry was not plainly visible, there was no reason for the employees to foresee that the trunk contained expensive jewelry. The court ruled that Ziva could not claim that CWH knew or that it should have reasonably foreseen or expected that it was taking responsibility for over $850,000 worth of jewelry when it accepted Smith's vehicle for the purpose of washing it.

WORDS OF THE COURT: Acceptance by the Bailee "Thus, there is no evidence indicating that CWH expressly or impliedly accepted responsibility for the jewelry in the trunk of Smith's vehicle. Without express or implied acceptance by the purported bailee, a bailment cannot arise."

Case Questions

1. If Smith's car was never recovered, would CWH be liable as a bailee for the car?

2. When a bailee takes a car as part of a bailment relationship, isn't the bailee also assuming liability for what is inside?

CONCEPT SUMMARY Personal Property

- Personal property is both tangible and movable and can be owned or leased. Examples of personal property include inventory and business systems such as telephones or computers.

- Title is the legal form of ownership of property and provides the titleholder exclusive rights to sell, lease, or prohibit others from using the property.

- Finders of lost property obtain title to the good by possession, except against the actual owner.

- Sellers cannot convey better title than what they have; therefore, if a buyer purchases stolen goods, the actual owner may still recover the property. It is irrelevant that the buyer who purchased the goods did so in good faith and did not know they were stolen.

- Bailments are created when the bailor (owner of the property) entrusts a bailee to temporarily hold the property. Common examples of bailments are coat checks and repair shops.

Leased Personal Property: UCC Article 2A

Businesses often choose to *lease* personal property, especially equipment, rather than purchase it outright. In an *equipment lease,* the lessor (owner of the property) gives the lessee (the party leasing the property) the exclusive right to possess and use the equipment for a

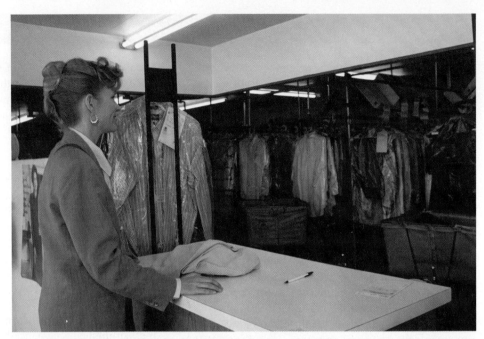

A bailment relationship is created when the owner of the property (bailor) temporarily entrusts it to another party (bailee) usually for their mutual benefit, as occurs when a customer gives clothes to a dry cleaner.

fixed period of time. The lessee often makes a monthly payment to the lessor, but at the end of the lease term the equipment is returned to the lessor. As a business matter, leasing is often an attractive alternative because the business can use the equipment on an exclusive basis without the investment required to purchase the equipment. There may also be tax advantages for the lessee in some cases. Examples of equipment that a business may lease are information systems equipment, telephones, furniture, and even heavy machinery used for manufacturing or construction. Note that leases fall into an area governed by both principles of property law and certain principles of commercial law. Lease agreements are a form of personal property contract and are governed by state statutory laws that are modeled after Article 2A of the Uniform Commercial Code. Article 2A covers many of the same subjects as the article governing the sale of goods, such as defining what constitutes a lease agreement, requiring certain lease agreements to be in writing, and allocating the risk of loss (i.e., which party is responsible if the equipment is destroyed) to one party or the other based on the circumstances of the transaction.

Real Property: Source of Law

The source of law that governs real property ownership is primarily state statutes, although some common law principles still exist. The statutes that regulate the legal relationship between residential landlord and tenant are based primarily on a model act known as the Uniform Residential Landlord-Tenant Act (URLTA). Note that when a landlord leases real property to a business, this is known as a *commercial* landlord-tenant agreement and is not governed by the URLTA. The landlord-tenant relationship is explored more fully later in this chapter.

LO 24-4 Ownership Rights

The ownership rights to a parcel (piece) of *real property,* also called *real estate,* includes the land and any structures built upon it, as well as plant life and vegetation. The structures are known as the property's *improvements*. The ownership rights also extend to anything that is affixed, known as *fixtures,* to the structure, such as plumbing, heating and cooling systems, and the like. Similar to the ownership rights in personal property, the ownership rights in a parcel of real property are thought of as a *bundle of rights*. This includes the right to sell, gift, lease, and control the property and its improvements. Ownership of real property is typically evidenced by a *deed.* Traditional property ownership rights are said to extend from "the soil upward into Heaven."[5] Generally, this means that certain rights are attached to the land that fit into four categories: (1) rights related to the *use and enjoyment* of the land; (2) *subsurface* rights; (3) *water* rights; and (4) *airspace* rights.

Use and Enjoyment of the Land

Generally, landowners have the right to use and enjoy the use of their property without interference from others. This interference is known as *nuisance* and occurs when one party creates *unreasonable conditions* that affect the landowner's use or enjoyment of the property. In many nuisance cases, a residential or business property owner sues a manufacturing company that owns a nearby plant for producing pollutants, making excessive noise, or emitting foul odors. Most courts apply the unreasonableness factor by examining the *nature* of the parcels of property at issue. In an area that is zoned for heavy industrial use, courts are reluctant to impose liability on a plant owner under the nuisance theory. Areas that are zoned for retail, office, or residential use are more likely to have legal protection from such nuisances.

Subsurface Rights

Landowners have rights to the soil and, most importantly, to any mineral, oil, or natural gas within the soil. These subsurface rights may be severed from the bundle of rights owned by the landowner and be sold to a third party.

Water Rights

Also known as *riparian* rights, landowners have the right to reasonable use of any streams, lakes, and groundwater (water contained in soil) that are fully or partially part of their real property. *Reasonable use* means that the landowner is entitled to only as much of the water as she can put to beneficial use upon her land while balancing the rights of others who have riparian rights in the same stream or lake (such as an adjacent landowner).

Airspace Rights

The law contemplates ownership of airspace by drawing an imaginary line emanating from the borders of the property into the sky. Perhaps the most significant exception to this rule is that courts have held that landowners may not use this right to prevent airplane flights over their property.[6] Most airspace rights cases involving businesses arise when one property owner builds a building that somehow interferes with the air rights of another. Consider the dilemma of a resort hotel when faced with a next-door neighbor that builds a building so tall that it blocks the sun from the resort's pool. In Case 24.2, the Florida Supreme Court considers the novel question of whether a famous Miami Beach resort's airspace rights included solar rights as well.

Real Property: Forms of Ownership Interests

LO 24-5

In most cases, real estate owners are entitled to the same general bundle of rights as that discussed in the section on personal property. However, some forms of ownership limit those general rights, and, therefore, it is necessary to understand the various *forms of ownership*. These are known as **ownership interests.** There are seven legally recognized interests; however, we will examine four common ownership interests that are important

---

[5]From English common law cases that cite the Latin phrase *cujus est solum, ejus usque ad coelum.*
[6]*U.S. v. Causby,* 328 U.S. 256 (1946).

FACT SUMMARY The Fontainebleau Hotel was in the process of constructing a 14-story addition to its resort hotel. After completion of eight stories, one of Fontainebleau's competitors, the Eden Roc Hotel, which owned adjoining property to the Fontainebleau, filed suit asking a court to issue an order prohibiting further construction of the addition. Eden Roc alleged that in the winter months, beginning at 2 o'clock in the afternoon and continuing until sunset, the shadow caused by the new addition would extend over Eden Roc's resort cabanas, main swimming pool, and several designated sunbathing areas. Eden Roc argued that this interference with sunlight and air violated its air rights and was causing Eden Roc to lose profits because its resort was now less desirable for guests wishing to use the pool facilities. Eden Roc also alleged that the construction plan was based on ill will between the owners of the resorts.

SYNOPSIS OF DECISION AND OPINION The Florida Supreme Court ruled in favor of the Fontainebleau on the basis of the general property law rule that property owners may use their property in any reasonable and lawful manner. The court noted that landowners are not obliged to use their property in a way that would prevent injury to a neighbor. The court also pointed out that modern American courts have consistently rejected the historical English law doctrine of "ancient lights," which provides a right to the free flow of light and air from adjoining land, as unworkable in current commercial life. Therefore, the court held that there is no legal right to the flow of air or light and that there is no cause of action so long as the structure serves a legitimately useful purpose.

WORDS OF THE COURT: Air and Solar Rights "[T]here . . . [is] no legal right to the free flow of light and air from the adjoining land, it is universally held that where a structure serves a useful and beneficial purpose, it does not give rise to a cause of action . . ., even though it causes injury to another by cutting off the light and air and interfering with the view that would otherwise be available over adjoining land in its natural state, regardless of the fact that the structure may have been erected partly for spite."

Case Questions

1. If Eden Roc could prove that the addition was completely out of spite, would this additional fact affect the court's decision?

2. The court also notes that individuals could build as high as or in any way that they wanted provided that doing so does not violate any laws, restrictions, or regulations. If the Fontainebleau was in violation of any code or regulation, would the outcome of the case have been different? Why or why not?

---

to business owners and managers: (1) *fee simple;* (2) *life estate;* (3) *leasehold estate;* and (4) *easements.*

Fee Simple   The term **fee simple** actually encompasses three distinct interests,[7] all centered on the basic concept that fee simple ownership interests are the highest level of general rights associated with real estate. *Fee simple absolute* means that the rights are *unrestricted* (of course, always subject to the restrictions imposed by law, such as zoning), infinite in duration, and inheritable by the owner's heirs. *Fee simple defeasible* is a fee simple right with certain restrictions. If one of these restrictions is violated, the property ownership automatically falls back *(reverts)* to the original owner. The right of reversion is why we think of the original owner as maintaining a partial ownership interest even after that owner has granted ownership interests to a third party. The restrictions primarily either limit the property to a *particular use* (e.g., it may be used only for certain charitable purposes) or entail the fulfillment of some *condition* or requirement related to the real estate (e.g., a municipality grants a contractor an interest in a 1,000-acre city-owned lot on the condition that the contractor build a landfill for public use on a 200-acre portion of the property).

Legal Speak ›))
Heirs Individuals who are legally entitled to inherit a decedent's property.

Legal Speak ›))
Defeasible Capable of being canceled.

---

[7]A minority of states also recognize a fourth interest of *fee tail,* which ensures that certain real estate will remain within the current owner's family.

The Florida Supreme Court ruled that the famous Fontainebleau hotel in Miami Beach, seen here, had the right to construct an addition to its property despite the fact that the addition blocked the sunlight to an adjacent resort hotel.

Life Estate   A **life estate** is simply an ownership interest that lasts for the lifetime of a particular person. The person who has a life estate interest is known as a *life tenant* because the life tenant may *not* sell, pledge, or convey the building in any way during ownership. However, life tenants do have day-to-day ownership duties such as paying taxes and repair/maintenance costs. A *life estate defeasible* is a life estate with a restriction attached in some way. Life estates are sometimes used as part of a business *succession* plan designed for the transition of the ownership of a family-owned business from one generation to the next. For example, suppose that Blake has built a successful family business with assets that include a valuable piece of real estate, including a modern warehouse facility. Blake uses 75 percent of the warehouse for his business and leases the other 25 percent of the space to tenants. Blake Jr. is the sole heir and has helped run the business for many years. Blake wishes to pass the business and all of the business's property on to Blake Jr. upon his death. Blake also wishes to use the rental income from the warehouse lease to help support his spouse for as long as she lives. To achieve both objectives, Blake may use the following language as part of his estate and business succession planning documents:

> If I die before my spouse, I, Blake, grant and convey my entire interest in Warehouse Real Estate to my spouse for her lifetime, on the condition that Blake Jr.'s business will pay no rent for use of the property; then to Blake Jr. in fee simple absolute.

In analyzing this language, we can determine that Blake intends to have his widowed spouse be the sole owner of the warehouse property during her lifetime but only on the condition that Blake Jr. is not charged any rent (a *life estate defeasible*). After her death, Blake Jr. inherits the real estate with ownership rights in fee simple absolute. This ensures that the benefit flows to Blake's spouse without additional burden on Blake Jr.'s ability

> **KEY** POINT
> *Fee simple absolute* is the highest level of ownership because it allows the titleholder unrestricted ownership rights.

to run the family business. Blake's spouse cannot sell her interest in the warehouse real estate, and this ensures that Blake Jr. will eventually receive the property with no restrictions on use and that the continuity between generations in the business will be preserved.

Leasehold Estate   A **leasehold estate** ownership interest affords the least amount of rights because it grants only a *qualified right* to use the real estate in an exclusive manner for a *limited* period of time. The most common form of leasehold estate is the *landlord-tenant agreement,* whereby the landlord gives the tenant a qualified right to possess and use the real estate for a specified period of years that is often spelled out in a written lease.[8] This is a qualified right because the landlord retains the right to enter under certain circumstances. This leasehold estate is known as a *tenancy for years.* At the expiration of the time period, the leasehold estate expires automatically, and the tenant no longer has any ownership interests. A landlord and tenant may also wish not to fix a specific time period but rather to have a month-to-month[9] agreement that continues to renew automatically for that time period (in this case, one month) until one party or the other gives advance notice that she wishes to terminate the lease. Notice must be given at least one complete time period ahead (in this case, one month's notice would be required). This leasehold estate is known as a *periodic tenancy.* In a business context, it is not unusual for parties to use both types of leasehold estates to achieve certain business objectives. For example, suppose that Browning is an architect with a thriving practice in commercial renovation planning. She enters into a five-year lease for office space in a small office building owned by Gilbert. Toward the end of the lease's term, Gilbert approaches Browning about renewing the lease agreement for an additional five years. However, Browning informs Gilbert that she plans to expand her firm and anticipates hiring new employees over the next five years. This expansion will require Browning to move into larger office space in the future. Gilbert offers a solution by agreeing to lease on a month-to-month basis. This gives Gilbert the opportunity to locate a new suitable tenant and Browning the opportunity to find larger space without any legal commitment beyond a one-month notice period. Note that, typically, Browning would have to pay a higher monthly rental payment under the monthly agreement than she would pay if she signed another five-year lease. However, it is likely a valuable return on investment given the flexibility afforded to her in a monthly lease. Based on their business objectives, the parties shifted their leasehold estate interest from a tenancy for years (the five-year lease) to a periodic tenancy (a month-to-month) lease.

Easements   An **easement** is a privilege to use the real estate owned by another. A common example of an easement is the grant given by property owners to utility companies for the privilege to install and maintain gas and water lines. Easements can arise by (1) an *express* grant (usually expressed in writing on the property deed); (2) *implication* or *necessity,* in which a property is landlocked between other properties and the owner must cross through the property of another to gain access to her property; or (3) *prescription,* in which the privilege is gained through adverse possession (discussed in the next section). Generally, easements are transferred with the property when the real estate is sold to another party so long as the new owner had reason to know of the easement (as is the case when the easement was expressly granted in a deed and has been publicly recorded with the appropriate government office).

A similar legal concept occurs when the landowner grants a *license.* A license is permission to use the property but is revocable at any time at the owner's discretion. The owner's right of revocation is the difference between an easement and a license.

---

[8] A real estate lease is a form of contract and is, therefore, subject to the statute of frauds, which provides that certain contracts must be in writing to be enforceable. The statute of frauds is discussed in detail in Chapter 7, "Contract Formation."

[9] The parties will sometimes agree to even shorter time periods, such as week to week.

Self-Check Ownership Interests

What is Swineburne's ownership interest?

1. Swineburne approaches Carroll with the idea of starting a charity soup kitchen. Carroll donates a parcel of real estate to Swineburne by providing this agreement: *"I convey this parcel to Swineburne in fee simple."* Swineburne uses the property to build a luxury resort hotel.

2. Swineburne approaches Carroll with the idea of starting a charity soup kitchen. Carroll donates a parcel of real estate to Swineburne by providing this agreement: *"I convey this parcel to Swineburne in fee simple provided that it be used for charitable purposes."* Swineburne uses the property to build a luxury resort hotel.

3. Swineburne approaches Carroll with the idea of starting a charity soup kitchen. Carroll agrees to rent a parcel of real estate to Swineburne for $1 a month on a month-to-month basis. The next day, Carroll gets an offer to purchase the real estate parcel for twice its market value on the condition that Carroll convey the real estate within five days. Carroll tells Swineburne to vacate the premises immediately.

4. Swineburne approaches Carroll with the idea of starting a charity soup kitchen. Carroll donates a parcel of real estate to Swineburne by providing this agreement: *"I convey this parcel to Swineburne for his life, and then to Carroll Jr. in fee simple absolute."* Swineburne uses the property to start a soup kitchen but dies shortly thereafter. Swineburne Jr. continues the soup kitchen. Carroll Jr. then informs Swineburne Jr. that she is selling the real estate and therefore Swineburne Jr. must vacate.

5. Swineburne approaches Carroll with a request that Carroll allow Swineburne to have the use of the driveway of a commercial office building owned by Carroll, which is on a parcel of property adjacent to Swineburne's charity soup kitchen. The driveway would allow easier access for trucks delivering supplies to the soup kitchen. Carroll executes and records a new deed with the statement: *"On the parcel of my commercial office building, I convey an easement for use of the driveway to Swineburne."* Carroll subsequently sells the property to Blago. Blago informs Swineburne that he may no longer use the driveway.

Answers to this Self-Check are provided at the end of the chapter.

Adverse Possession

In some cases, a party may gain title to real estate through the doctrine of adverse possession. In order to gain title to a parcel of property through adverse possession, the acquiring party must demonstrate that she has possessed it in a certain way for a certain period of time. These requirements are often spelled out in a particular state's statutory or common law. In general, the requirements are that the party must have met a three-prong test. Gaining title requires that the adverse possession must have been *open, notorious, and visible; exclusive and actual;* and *continuous.*

Open, Notorious, and Visible Possession The true holder of title cannot be relieved of that title unless she could reasonably be expected to know that another person has taken possession of the real estate and that the adverse possessor *intended* to assert a claim to its ownership. Examples of cases where courts have held that this prong was satisfied include those in which the adverse possessor had (1) demonstrated that the true owner had actual or imputed knowledge that the adverse party had taken possession of the land; (2) erected a fence or other enclosure around the property; or (3) paid taxes or other maintenance fees in connection with the land.

Exclusive and Actual Possession The adverse possessor must also show that she was in exclusive control of the property and did not share control or possession of the property with the true owner or the public generally. This means that at least a reasonable percentage of the land claimed by the adverse possessor must be in actual use.

Continuous Possession The adverse possession of the property must be continuous for a period of time set down by state statute or common law. About two-thirds of states require 15 years or longer, but some states allow a shorter period if the adverse possessor pays the taxes on the property. This does not mean that the adverse possessor is required to spend every consecutive day on the property. Rather, it means that the adverse possessor cannot *abandon* the property for a period of time. If the owner retakes possession within the prescribed time period, the adverse possessor's use stops and this prong cannot be satisfied unless the true owner abandons the property again in the future.

In Case 24.3, an appellate court considers a business owner's claim of title to a parcel of property through adverse possession.

CASE 24.3   2 North Street Corporation v. Getty Saugerties Corporation, 68 A.D.3d 1392 (N.Y. App. Div. 2009)

FACT SUMMARY 2 North Street is a corporation that owned a parcel of real estate used for a shopping center and a parking lot. Getty owned the adjacent lot, on which it had operated a gas station. A fence runs close to the boundary line between the properties but lies entirely on Getty's property. A narrow 0.129-acre strip of land exists between the boundary line and the fence. 2 North maintained the strip of land from the time the company purchased the property. For a period of approximately 23 years, 2 North paid a contractor to continuously maintain the strip's grass. The contractor also planted vegetation, removed rubbish and debris, and deposited snow plowed from 2 North's parking lot upon it. Getty never questioned the activities of the contractor, nor did anyone representing Getty grant the contractor permission to perform them. In 2007, 2 North brought an action seeking a declaration that it owned the strip of land through adverse possession. Getty objected on the basis that 2 North's use of the strip was not open and notorious enough to constitute notice to others claiming an adverse and hostile interest in the land. The trial court ruled in favor of 2 North, and Getty appealed.

SYNOPSIS OF DECISION AND OPINION The appellate division of the Supreme Court of New York affirmed the lower court's decision and held in favor of 2 North. The court ruled that 2 North had met its statutory burden of establishing that the character of the possession was hostile under a claim of right, actual, open and notorious, exclusive, and continuous for the statutory period of 10 years. The court was convinced that 2 North initially believed that it owned the strip and exclusively maintained it as its own even though the strip was not included in its deed description. This evidence of 2 North's continuous use and maintenance of the strip exemplified its possession as open and notorious, constituting notice to others that it was claiming an adverse and hostile interest in it.

WORDS OF THE COURT: Improvement Requirement "[The statute also requires] 'usual cultivation or improvement.' [Evidence of] this mandate will vary with the nature and situation of the property and the uses to which it can be applied and must consist of acts such as are usual in the ordinary cultivation and improvement of similar lands by thrifty owners. Notwithstanding [Getty's] assertions to the contrary, the [contractor's] activities on behalf of [2 North] and its predecessor over a period of 27 years were consistent with the nature, location and potential use of this property—a narrow strip of grass between two commercial businesses."

Case Questions

1. Was 2 North's use "notorious" given the fact that it is likely that Getty didn't realize that the land strip was on its property? What does one have to do to use property in a notorious fashion?

2. Should Getty be compensated for the strip of land taken by adverse possession? Should there be an offset for all of the money invested by 2 North in maintenance?

SALE OF REAL ESTATE

The most common way for commercial real estate to be transferred is through a sale.[10] Typically, the seller and buyer agree on essential terms about the purchase and enter into an agreement of sale for the purchase of real estate. The agreement usually provides for a period of time devoted to due diligence, specifies a tentative settlement date (also called the *closing date*), and is supported by a cash deposit to be held by an escrow agent. The due diligence time period varies based on the complexity of the transaction. During this time the buyer will (1) arrange for financing through a financial institution or a private lender (such as a relative); (2) conduct an inspection of the property to be sure that the parties are aware of any physical defects, zoning issues, and other items that may affect the use or price of the property; and (3) have an attorney or title agent check to be sure that the seller has clear title to the property and will be able to convey the property without any legal obstacles. The agreement of sale spells out the timelines as well as the rights and obligations of the parties during the due diligence period. After the due diligence period has expired, the parties attend a settlement meeting at which the buyer presents payment and the seller conveys title to the property via a deed.

Legal Speak ›))
Escrow Agent A neutral third party designated to hold a sum of money while the parties fulfill conditions in a contract.

LAWS GOVERNING LANDLORD-TENANT AGREEMENTS

LO 24-6, 24-7

An agreement between a landlord and a tenant for the rental of property is called a **lease** and is an example of the intersection between property law and contract law. As such, the sources of law governing leases range from state statutory protections of residential tenants to common law principles governing certain contracts. While the law of contracts is covered fully in Unit Two of this textbook, some references to contract law are necessary in a discussion of property law. Additionally, while statutes that cover residential leases often feature protections for the tenants from arbitrary and wrongful acts of the landlord (such as a wrongful eviction), laws that govern the relationship between landlord-tenant agreements in a *commercial lease* (i.e., a lease for property that is to be used for commercial purposes such as a retail store in a shopping center) tend not to offer as much protection for business tenants. This is ordinarily because commercial leases are thought of as *negotiated* between the parties and, since both parties are engaged in business, a degree of sophistication is imputed to the tenant that is not present in a residential lease. Indeed, because many agreements for property between landlords and businesses are documented in the form of a lease, most issues regarding landlord and tenant rights and duties are spelled out in the lease. However, in cases where the parties have not specifically agreed on certain terms, the common law provides a basic set of rules.

> **KEY** POINT
>
> The law tends to offer more protection to residential tenants than to commercial tenants because a certain level of business and legal acumen is imputed to business owners and managers.

Because business managers and owners are frequently on the front lines in negotiating a lease, it is important to have an understanding of the basic legal framework governing landlord-tenant agreements.

Tenant Rights

Fundamentally, tenants have the rights of *possession, quiet enjoyment,* and *habitability.* The right to possession simply means that the landlord must deliver the legal right to possess the property to the tenant at the commencement of the lease agreement. In most

---

[10]Other methods to transfer (mainly noncommercial) real estate are through a tax sale (for nonpayment of taxes), inheritance, gift, and adverse possession.

states, the law requires the landlord to make reasonable efforts to give property access to the tenant by ensuring that any previous tenant has vacated and that the tenant has keys to the premises.[11] *Quiet enjoyment* is the tenant's right to use the premises without interference from the landlord. For example, Barclay leases a retail space to Jimenez. Barclay also owns the property next door to the leased property. One week after Jimenez takes possession of the space, Barclay begins to renovate the property next door and allows the contractor to place a construction dumpster in Jimenez's back lot. In this case Barclay has actually occupied a part of the property leased to Jimenez and, thus, has breached the tenant's right to quiet enjoyment.

Related to the right of quiet enjoyment is the tenant's right to have the leased space in a reasonable condition, known as the right of *habitability*. Note that the right of habitability is mostly applicable in the residential lease context. Essentially, this is a protection of the tenant's right to occupy leased premises that are not in such an unreasonably poor or unsafe condition that a person cannot live there. Although an increasing number of courts are imposing this common law duty in a commercial context, some courts are still *reluctant* to protect this right for commercial tenants unless the circumstances are extreme (e.g., the condition of the premises violates a state or local building safety code).[12]

Tenant Remedies

Legal Speak ·))

Escrow In a tenant remedy context, escrow is an amount of money delivered by the tenant to a third party (such as an attorney) to be held by the third party until the dispute between landlord and tenant is resolved.

In the event that a landlord breaches a duty or promise to a tenant, the tenant has a variety of legal alternatives to compensate the tenant. These legal alternatives are known as **tenant remedies.** In the case of a violation of the tenant's right of possession, the tenant either may terminate the lease and sue the landlord for damages or may continue the lease and recover damages after the landlord is able to give possession. In the case of violation of the right of either quiet enjoyment or habitability, the tenant generally may choose to terminate the lease and/or to sue for damages (particularly if the violation occurs after possession has taken place). In some extreme cases under a violation of the right of habitability, tenants are permitted to withhold rent and pay the amounts due into escrow until any legal dispute is resolved. If the tenant cannot feasibly use the premises for their intended use because of landlord neglect or inaction, the tenant may claim to have been *constructively evicted* and may vacate the premises and terminate the lease without any further liability to the landlord.

Tenant Duties

For the most part, in a commercial lease context, the tenant's duties under the common law are to pay the rent as agreed upon and to act reasonably in care and use of the property. This duty of reasonableness includes refraining from disturbing other tenants, obeying reasonable landlord rules, complying with health and safety codes, and notifying the landlord when repairs are necessary on the premises.

Landlord Rights and Remedies

If a tenant violates the duty to pay rent (whether the tenant is using or has abandoned the premises) or the duty to act reasonabley in the use of the property, the common law allows several remedies to help the landlord recover damages. Depending on the circumstances, the landlord may keep any *security deposit* held by the landlord and/or may *evict* (remove) the tenant from the premises. Most lease agreements typically call for the landlord to hold a certain amount of money to secure the landlord in the event that any damage is committed during the lease term and to give the landlord an option to recover part of any

---

[11]*Restatement (Second) of Property* § 6.2.

[12]*Restatement (Second) of Property* § 5.1.

monies owed as a result of the tenant's abandoning the premises (with or without notice) before the lease term ends. The right of the landlord to keep the security deposit is highly regulated by statute in both residential and commercial real estate leases. At the end of the lease period, the landlord is typically required to return the security deposit to the tenant after subtracting the cost of any damages and giving an itemized list of the claimed damages to the tenant. The landlord must also act within a reasonable *time* after the end of the lease. The maximum period of time that the landlord may hold the deposit after the end of the lease is set by state statute and ranges between 15 and 45 days.[13] In addition to taking action to recover damages via the security deposit, a landlord may also remove the tenant through *eviction.* This is an extreme remedy and may be used only when some significant violation of the tenant's duties has occurred. For example, a tenant that pays rent a few days late one month may *not* be evicted for violating the duty to pay. In order to evict a tenant, the landlord must follow statutorily prescribed procedures for eviction. This generally includes filing a lawsuit of eviction at a local court for a summary hearing on the issue. If the court agrees, the landlord is permitted to proceed with the eviction with assistance of county authorities such as the sheriff's office.

Assignment and Subletting

LO 24-8

Absent an agreement to the contrary, the parties in a lease agreement may transfer their interest to a third party. A landlord may sell her property to another party (who must honor the lease agreement) during the lease term, and a tenant may *assign* or *sublet* the premises. If the tenant wishes to transfer his interests (right to possess and use the premises) to a third party for the *entire* remaining length of the term, this is called an **assignment.** The third party in an assignment is known as the *assignee.* If the tenant transfers anything less than the remaining term, this is known as a **sublease.** The third party in a sublease is called a *subleasee.* In both cases, the tenant remains bound to the original lease agreement, and if the assignee or subleasee fails to pay rent, the original tenant is still liable for the payments. The original tenant's liability is extinguished only if the landlord has released the tenant from that particular obligation. The assignee or subleasee receives the full legal benefits of tenancy, including the right to sue the landlord if the landlord violates any of her duties such as the right to quiet possession (discussed earlier in this section). While landlords often insist that lease agreements contain *antiassignment clauses* that restrict a tenant's right to assign or sublet, there are certain cases where this right may be seen as a mutually beneficial way to achieve mutual business objectives.

CONCEPT SUMMARY Landlord-Tenant Agreements

- A lease is an agreement between a landlord and a tenant for the rental of real estate.
- Generally, statutes are more protective of the tenant in residential leases than in commercial leases.
- Tenants have three basic rights: (1) possession, (2) quiet enjoyment, and (3) habitability. The right of possession is the tenant's right to possess and occupy the property, and the right of quiet enjoyment and habitability is the tenant's right to have the property be in safe, livable condition.

(continued)

---

[13]For example, in Maryland landlords have 45 days to return security deposits to residential tenants. See Md. Real Property Code Ann. § 8-203. Conversely, in Florida landlords have 15 days to return a security deposit if they are not pursuing a damage claim against the tenant, but if they are going to impose a claim, they have 30 days to notify the tenant. See Fla. Stat. § 83.49.

- The duties of a tenant are to pay the rent and to act reasonably in care and use of the property. Acting reasonably includes not disturbing other tenants and notifying the landlord of any needed repairs so that the property remains safe.

- Both the tenant and landlord have remedies available to them in instances where the other party breached the lease agreement or did not fulfill her duties. For example, tenants may be able to withhold rent or sue for damages, and landlords may be able to evict the tenant and/or keep the security deposit.

- Tenants may also assign or sublease their interests in a property. Assignments are for the full term of the original lease, and subleases are for any period of time less than the full term. Similarly, landlords may sell their property to a third party, who must honor any current remaining lease agreements.

LO 24-9 REGULATION OF COMMERCIAL LAND USE

State and local governments frequently pass statutes and ordinances that impose regulation on how a landowner may use a particular parcel of real estate. These regulations come in several forms, but the two types of regulations that are most crucial in business planning and operations are *zoning* ordinances and *environmental* regulations.

Zoning Ordinances

Zoning is generally done at the local level in the form of local ordinances passed by the county or municipal government. Counties, cities, boroughs, townships, villages, parishes, and the like are all forms of local government that pass ordinances. The power to pass zoning ordinances is well established in the law. Recall our discussion in Chapter 2, "Business and the Constitution," about the government's *police powers*. When a local government passes a zoning ordinance, it is exercising its police powers to advance legitimate objectives of the municipality as a whole. The Supreme Court has recognized such power,[14] but the Court has also set limits on the government's control of private property.

Use Regulation   From a business perspective, one of the most important types of zoning regulation is ordinances that establish various districts for particular uses of property. The municipality is typically divided into zones, in each of which only certain use of the land is permitted. These zones include areas for industrial, retail, and residential uses. Some municipalities divide their land uses further, specifying such uses as light industrial, warehouse, and so on.

Enforcement and Appeals   A local administrative agent such as a zoning officer or building inspector employed by the municipality typically enforces local use ordinances. A zoning board or commission is often appointed by the local government to handle appeals from decisions of the zoning officer and to consider applications for parties that wish to have an exception to one of the zoning laws. These exceptions are known as *variances*. Local governments vary greatly in their guidelines for permitting a variance, but, typically, if the variance does not harm the surrounding neighborhood or interfere with any local interests, the board will permit the variance.

Limits on Zoning Regulations   Courts have ruled that the law sets limits on a local government's right to regulate private property usage through a variety of constitutional protections of property owners. First, if the zoning is so overreaching that it deprives the

---

[14]*Village of Euclid v. Ambler Realty Co.,* 272 U.S. 365 (1926).

Maximum Leverage in a Lease to Reach Business Objectives

PROBLEM *When a business is considering leased-space alternatives to locate its operations, one important business objective is planning for expansion while minimizing risks.*

To achieve this objective, a business may lease space that is larger than its current needs but will be needed to implement a 10-year expansion plan. However, the current cash flow of the business supports only a smaller leased area. For example, suppose that the management of Extreme Widget, Inc. (EWI), a manufacturer of high-performance widgets, locates a facility that is 10,000 square feet. Although EWI's current needs and financial ability support only 5,000 square feet, the management team is anxious to secure the space because of its ideal location and competitive rental rate. EWI is also embarking on an expansion plan that will require at least another 5,000 square feet of space over the next five years. EWI's objectives are to (1) secure the 10,000-square-foot parcel, (2) reduce the risk and liability of the added expenses by having alternatives for generating additional revenue to support the additional space until it is needed, and (3) provide EWI with maximum flexibility in case expansion plans must be put on hold.

SOLUTION *Negotiate a subletting clause with an option for an assignment.*

One method of using the law to help achieve business objectives would be for EWI's management to approach the landlord of the facility and propose the inclusion of a *sublease and assignment clause* in a five-year lease. The clause could include the following provisions:

- EWI has the right to negotiate a sublease for up to 5,000 square feet of the facility, with EWI remaining primarily liable to the landlord on the lease.

- EWI has the option of assigning all or part of the lease so long as the landlord has the opportunity to review the financial condition and creditworthiness of the proposed assignee. The landlord may accept or reject the candidate based on creditworthiness.

- If the landlord accepts the assignee, EWI remains primarily liable under the lease for a period of one year and then is released from any obligations of the lease.

This solution achieves EWI's objectives by providing maximum flexibility to expand (or contract) while reducing the financial risks associated with leasing 10,000 square feet of property. The landlord also derives a benefit from the agreement because he now has a five-year lease in place for 10,000 square feet and the right to reject any proposed assignee.

Businesses in expansion mode may use subletting and assignment rights when leasing a property to maximize expansion opportunities while minimizing legal risk.

owner of all economic value of her property, the zoning will be categorized as a *taking* and the government is required to pay the owner the market value of the property as required in the Constitution's *Takings Clause*.[15] This is known as the power of *eminent domain* and is discussed in more detail in the next section. Second, under certain circumstances, those affected by a zoning ordinance are entitled to some procedural due process, such as a hearing by the local government.[16] Finally, a zoning law cannot discriminate because doing so violates the Equal Protection Clause of the Fourteenth Amendment. Courts in most states have also generally allowed zoning related to *aesthetics* so long as aesthetics is only one factor, not the sole factor, in a municipality's zoning decision.

Environmental Regulation

An increasing concern for business owners and managers is federal, state, and local regulation of land use based on the government's interest in advancing sound environmental policy. In general, governments may impose environmentally based land use regulations so long as they advance some substantial and legitimate state interest. For example, statutes aimed at preservation of open land areas have been found to be a legitimate government regulation of private property. Courts have generally held that wetland and coastland preservation ordinances that restrict the owner's right to develop, fill, or dredge the land are a legal use of the government's police powers. However, the Supreme Court curtailed this type of regulation by ruling that if the regulation completely depleted all economic value from the property, that act would constitute a government *taking* under the eminent domain power and trigger the government's obligation to pay compensation to the property owner. For example, suppose that Developer purchases 20 acres of Florida beachfront property with the intent to develop the acreage into a resort. In response to concerned environmental groups, the state of Florida then passes a statute that restricts development along the coast running from the ocean to 1,000 yards inland. In Developer's case, this would amount to a loss of two prime acres of beachfront property, but Developer would have use of the remaining 18 acres. Developer sues for compensation because its partial loss of revenue was due to the state regulation. Most courts would rule against Developer because the government interest in preserving coastland has been held legitimate in the past and because Developer lost only part of the revenue stream and additional revenue is too speculative. On the other hand, if the state's statute had been more overreaching and resulted in Developer losing all economic value of the property, Developer would be entitled to compensation from the government.[17]

Of course, apart from understanding environmentally based land use regulations, business owners and managers must also be knowledgeable about a separate body of federal and state law aimed at broader environmental policies. These broad-based concerns, such as laws that regulate pollution, operation of factories, solid waste, and toxic chemicals are discussed in detail in Chapter 19, "Environmental Law."

LO 24-10   # EMINENT DOMAIN

It is important to understand the difference between a legitimate government land use *regulation* and a government *taking* of property that triggers a constitutional requirement to compensate the landowner. The authority of the state and federal government to take private property is called the power of *eminent domain,* which is derived from the Fifth Amendment provision that states: "[N]or shall private property be taken for public use without just compensation."

---

[15]U.S. Constitution, Fifth Amendment.

[16]U.S. Constitution, Fourteenth Amendment (Due Process Clause).

[17]Based on the facts in *Nollan v. California,* 483 U.S. 825 (1987).

Procedure

Eminent domain is traditionally invoked using a *condemnation proceeding*. Once a government has decided that certain real estate is necessary for public use, the government typically begins to negotiate sales agreements with the private property owners of the area(s) to be taken. If the negotiations fail, the government will formally institute a judicial proceeding to condemn the real estate. The court will be sure that procedural rights are being afforded to the property owner and will determine the fair market value of the real estate. Once the court has entered its order, the condemnation is complete and the government now holds title to the real estate.

Public Use

Note that the Constitution uses the phrase *public use* in the text. Typically, public use may mean the building of public highways, schools, public hospitals, and other traditional public government functions. However, the Supreme Court has construed the public use language very broadly for uses outside the traditional uses so long as the government can demonstrate that its actions were rationally related to some conceivable public purpose. This broad construction has been the source of controversy. For example, suppose that the government condemns a blighted area of a city in hopes of developing the condemned area into a thriving example of urban renewal that brings along new retail and office buildings. The plan calls for condemnation of some areas adjacent to the blight that have single-family houses and thriving small, neighborhood businesses. Because the government does not intend to build any facilities for public use, is the taking unconstitutional? The Supreme Court took up that very issue in Case 24.4. It was perhaps the most important eminent domain decision since 1954.[18]

---

[18]The urban renewal interest was first sanctioned by the Supreme Court in *Berman v. Parker,* 348 U.S. 26 (1954).

CASE 24.4 Kelo v. City of New London, 545 U.S. 469 (2005)

FACT SUMMARY   The city of New London devised an economic development plan that was projected to create more than 1,000 jobs and increase tax and other revenue. The plan called for a waterfront conference hotel; a marina; and various retail, commercial, and residential properties. The city's development authority designated a large area composed of adjacent parcels of real estate to be condemned in order to redevelop the property consistent with the redevelopment plan. The city's agent purchased some of the property from willing sellers and gave notice that the city would institute condemnation proceedings via the power of eminent domain to acquire the remaining property from unwilling owners. The city purchased all but nine parcels of real estate and brought condemnations against nine property owners including Kelo, the named plaintiff. Although the city conceded that the condemned properties were not part of the blighted areas (in fact some

had recently been renovated), they were condemned simply because of their location in the proposed development area. The lower courts' decisions were mixed, and the U.S. Supreme Court accepted the case on appeal to decide the question of whether the city's plan qualified as a public use within the meaning of the Takings Clause of the Fifth Amendment to the U.S. Constitution.

SYNOPSIS OF DECISION AND OPINION   The Court ruled in favor of the city and articulated guideposts for appropriate use of the Takings Clause. The Court affirmed the principle that the government is not permitted to take one party's private property for the sole purpose of transferring it to another private party and acknowledged that the city would not be able to take the property if the city planned on bestowing it to a private development company or individual or if any

(continued)

benefits from the plan would be realized only by private individuals. However, the city's development plan did not contemplate any direct bestowment of property rights upon private individuals or companies. Moreover, even though some of the uses would be private in nature, the Court ruled that the standard to be used is the broader interpretation of the property being used for a *public purpose*. The Court found that the overall elimination of blight is a legitimate public purpose and held that the city's plan was a valid exercise of the city's eminent domain power.

WORDS OF THE COURT: Public Purpose   "[T]his 'Court long ago rejected any literal requirement that condemned property be put into use for the general public.' Indeed, while many state courts . . . endorsed 'use by the public' as the proper definition of public use that narrow view steadily eroded over time. Not only was the 'use by the public' test difficult to administer . . ., but it proved to be impractical given the diverse and always evolving needs of society. Accordingly, when this Court began applying the Fifth Amendment to the States at the end of the 19th Century, it embraced the broader and more natural interpretation of public use as 'public purpose.' . . . Without exception, our cases have defined [this] concept broadly, reflecting our long-standing policy of deference to legislative judgments in this field. . . . Given the comprehensive character of the plan [and] the thorough deliberation that preceded its adoption . . . [it] unquestionably serves a public purpose."

Case Questions

1. In dissenting opinions, members of the Court argued that this decision makes all private property vulnerable to being taken and transferred to another private owner (against established principles the Court mentioned earlier) so long as the property is upgraded in some way. Moreover, they argued that this decision is advantageous to large corporations or individuals with political power or connections, while those with few resources are disadvantaged. Do you agree? Why or why not?

2. Would the case have been decided differently if the project built only a large industrial park? Why or why not?

KEY TERMS

Personal property p. 657   Any movable or tangible object that can be owned or leased (e.g., computers, inventory, furniture, jewelry); includes everything except real property.

Real property p. 657   Land, or anything growing on, attached to, or erected on the land. Examples of real property include parcels of land, homes, warehouses, stores, and crops.

Title p. 658   The legal term for ownership in property; confers on the titleholder the exclusive use of personal property and the rights to sell, lease, or prohibit another from using the property.

Actual owner p. 658   The individual who is recognized as having primary or residual title to the property and is, therefore, the ultimate owner of the property.

Ownership interests p. 661   The various forms of real property ownership. Some forms limit the rights that owners of real estate have.

Fee simple p. 662   The broadest property interest in land, which endures until the current holder dies without heirs.

Life estate p. 663   An ownership interest in real estate that lasts for the lifetime of a particular person.

Leasehold estate p. 664   The qualified right to use real estate in an exclusive manner for a limited period of time. The most common form is a landlord-tenant agreement.

Easement p. 664   The privilege to use real estate owned by another.

Lease p. 667   An agreement between a landlord and a tenant for the rental of property.

Tenant remedies p. 668   The legal alternatives available to tenants as compensation in the event a landlord breaches a lease; include termination of the lease, a suit for damages, and withholding of rent.

Assignment p. 669   A tenant's transfer of his interests to a third party for the entire term remaining on the lease.

Sublease p. 669   A tenant's transfer of her interests to a third party for anything less than the term remaining on the lease.

THEORY TO PRACTICE

Restaurant Supply Inc. (RSI) is a wholesale supplier of food and nonfood kitchen products for restaurants and hotels. Last year, RSI signed up a large hotel chain as a new client. In order to fill the needs of their new client, the principals of RSI decided to expand by constructing a new warehouse in an industrially zoned section of the city. RSI also received a tax credit for installing alternative energy sources in its new warehouse, so it invested $50,000 in a new solar panel system to be placed on the roof of the warehouse to serve as a source of power, with traditional gas and electric as a backup system. RSI eventually finished construction of the warehouse and the solar panels and immediately moved its food and nonfood inventory into the warehouse. A few months after RSI moved into its new warehouse, the property adjacent to RSI's was sold to a glue factory.

1. Assume the glue factory ran 24 hours per day on a seven-day schedule and produced noxious fumes. Eventually, RSI began to suspect that the fumes were tainting the taste of the food that was being stored in RSI's warehouse. RSI then filed suit to stop the glue factory from discharging the noxious fumes. What is RSI's possible legal theory against the glue factory? What factors will a court use to analyze RSI's claim? Does the glue factory have any defenses?

2. Assume that the glue factory shuts down its operations in order to expand and upgrade its facilities to prevent the emission of the noxious fumes. In the process, the glue factory adds several stories to its building. The additional stories result in a blockage of sun, which subsequently results in RSI's solar panels being rendered useless. RSI files suit against the glue factory for interference in RSI's property rights. What property right violation has RSI alleged? What case in the text gives you some guidance on this question? Is the RSI case distinguishable from that case? Who prevails in the RSI–glue factory case and why?

3. Assume that in preparation for the building renovation the glue factory conducted a survey and found that RSI's driveway was actually built 15 feet too wide and encroached on the glue factory's property. Since the time it built the warehouse, RSI has maintained the road, removed snow, and so on. One day RSI gets a letter from the owner of the glue factory demanding that the driveway be ripped up and repaved consistent with the correct property line. Could RSI use the doctrine of adverse possession to refuse the demand? What are the standards that courts use to analyze ownership via adverse possession?

4. Suppose that RSI is owned by Abel and that his son, Abel Jr., is the top manager in charge of business operations. When planning how the business will pass from Abel to his son upon Abel's death, Abel wishes to have the ownership of the warehouse pass to his spouse for her lifetime and then to Abel Jr. What type of ownership interest could Abel use to accomplish this objective? What restrictions would his spouse have once she inherits the warehouse?

5. Assume that RSI wishes to increase its solar panel usage by purchasing large brand A panels and installing them on the rooftop of the warehouse. However, a city ordinance exists that bans the use of brand A panels because they tend to make a building look less attractive. What is this type of ordinance called? Is this type of ordinance legal? Why or why not? Assuming that the ordinance is legal, are there any alternatives that RSI could pursue with local authorities?

Managers provide valuable input and analysis for business operation expansion planning efforts. We've seen how various legal issues related to ownership and use of property can impact those planning efforts. Assume that, in the Theory to Practice problem, you are part of a three-person management team for RSI and have received the following e-mail from your senior manager:

> RSI is developing expansion plans that include new facilities in the southwestern United States. At this time, we are considering leasing office and operational space in several large cities but are interested in a particular 25,000-square-foot facility that has an ideal location and rental rate. However, at this time, we need only 10,000 square feet. The landlord has said that she is willing to negotiate lease terms but that we must lease the entire 25,000-square-foot space. RSI wants to expand but keep risk and financial exposure at a minimum.

Research alternatives for possible subleasing or assigning of the unused space to third parties, and develop a short presentation (no more than five PowerPoint slides) that could be presented to the landlord on proposed lease terms that would help RSI accomplish its objectives. Be sure to include a listing of the advantages of this arrangement for the landlord and for RSI. A sample answer may be found on this textbook's website at www.mhhe.com/melvinleb2e.

CASE SUMMARY 24.1 :: Singer Co. v. Stott & Davis Motor Express, Inc., and Stoda Corp., 79 A.2d 227 (N.Y. App. Div. 1981)

BAILMENTS

Stoda Corporation operated a warehouse used by Singer to store 133 air-conditioner units. Upon storing the goods in the warehouse, officers and managers of Singer inspected the warehouse and observed that it had a network of sprinkler systems. A fire broke out at Stoda's warehouse, the sprinkler system failed to activate, and the fire destroyed all of the Singer goods.

Singer sued, claiming Stoda's negligence in storing goods in a warehouse without adequate fire protection breached its bailment duties.

CASE QUESTIONS

1. Who prevails and why?
2. What is the standard that the bailee (Stoda) owes to the bailor (Singer)?

CASE SUMMARY 24.2 :: Chaplin v. Sanders, 676 P.2d 431 (Wash. 1984)

ADVERSE POSSESSION

In 1957, Hibbard decided to clear his land in order to open a trailer park. Because there was no clear boundary between Hibbard's property and the adjoining property to the east, Hibbard cleared the property up to a large drainage ditch and installed an access road to the left of the ditch to signify the property line. Hibbard opened a trailer park facility, and later that year, McMurray, the owner of the eastern parcel, had a survey conducted. McMurray informed Hibbard that the access road encroached on his property by 20 feet. Subsequently, Hibbard sold the trailer park to Gilbert and noted in the sales contract that (1) the driveway encroached 20 feet on McMurray's property, (2) Gilbert agreed not to claim ownership of the property, and (3) Gilbert agreed he would remove the blacktop if ever requested to do so. From 1967 to 1976, the property changed ownership several times but no mention was made of the encroachment or contract provision from the Hibbard-Gilbert sale. In 1976, Sanders purchased the trailer park and was given notice of the encroachment and provision but mistook the road to which the notice referred. Since the development of the trailer park, the road had been continuously used, and the area between the drainage ditch and road had been maintained by the various trailer park property owners (through means such as planting flowers and mowing the grass) and used by residents for picnics. Sanders also installed underground wiring and surface poles in the area.

Two years later Chaplin purchased the eastern lot from McMurray, had a survey conducted, and had architects design buildings for development based on the true property line from the survey. Washington requires a 10-year period of use in order to establish adverse possession.

CASE QUESTIONS

1. Are all of the elements for adverse possession met so that Sanders now has title to the disputed parcel? Why or why not?
2. What is the appropriate starting time from which to measure ownership in order to satisfy Washington's statutory requirement for 10 years of possession?

CASE SUMMARY 24.3 :: Dayenian v. American National Bank and Trust Co. of Chicago, 414 N.E.2d 1199 (Ill. App. Ct. 1980)

ASSIGNMENTS AND SUBLEASES

Dayenian entered into a two-year lease agreement for an apartment with Monticello Realty Corporation on July 14. On October 26 of that year she signed a portion of the lease headed "Assignment," which stated that she assigned all her rights, title, and interest in the lease to Lambert from December 1 onward but that she was not relieved of any liability under the lease. Lambert accepted this on November 8, by signing a section titled "Acceptance of Assignment," and that same day Monticello Realty executed a portion of the lease entitled "Consent to Assignment," which consented on the condition that Dayenian remain liable for payment of rent. In March of the following year, Lake Shore Drive Development Company mailed Lambert

a notice of intent to convert the apartment building to a condominium; the notice provided for a right of first refusal to purchase the apartment if he responded. Lambert never acted upon this notice, and in May the developer entered into a contract to sell the apartment to another party. Dayenian sued, claiming that she should have been given the right of first refusal because she was the tenant of the apartment at the time the notice to convert was sent and that the transfer to Lambert was a sublease.

CASE QUESTIONS

1. Is the transfer an assignment or a sublease? Why?
2. What do the courts look to in making this determination?

LANDLORD-TENANT AGREEMENTS

Jones operated a gas station, which he leased from Amoco Oil Company under a franchise agreement. The lease was a standard form signed by Jones in order to obtain the franchise. The lease required Jones to return the premises in substantially the same condition as received, less ordinary wear and tear, and also required him to perform necessary upkeep and maintenance on the premises, including clearing sidewalks. Although the lease did not indicate which party was responsible for fire insurance, it did note that Amoco could terminate the lease upon destruction of the premises. Early one morning a no-fault fire broke out, gutting parts of the station and causing $118,850 in damage. After the fire, Amoco terminated the lease and leveled the station. Amoco then sued Jones for not returning the station in substantially the same condition as he received it.

CASE QUESTIONS

1. Does Jones have an obligation to rebuild the gas station? Why or why not?
2. Why would Amoco terminate the lease?

CONSTRUCTIVE EVICTION

Scene-In-Action (Scene) rented a building from Automobile Supply Co. (Auto) for Scene's business of manufacturing electrical advertising signs. The space was also used to house administrative offices of the business. Included in the lease was a provision requiring Auto to supply heat to the premises. The heat provision included language to the effect that efficient heat was necessary to keep the building comfortable in order to produce signs and carry on normal office tasks. Soon after the lease was signed, the building was without heat for several hours on numerous occasions throughout two months. Scene made repeated complaints about the situation to Auto, but Auto failed to fix the problem. The problems continued, and as the temperature dropped during the height of winter, there were many days when the temperature inside was below 50 degrees. As a result of the lack of heat, a number of Scene's employees would not return to work, claiming they were ill and unable to work in the cold conditions. Unable to carry on business, Scene terminated the lease, claiming it was constructively evicted because it had been deprived of the beneficial use and enjoyment of the premises. Auto countersued for payments owed, claiming Scene could have vacated the premises earlier but instead stayed and maintained business operations without paying rent. Thus, Scene was not constructively evicted.

CASE QUESTIONS

1. Who prevails and why? Do the conditions support a constructive eviction theory?
2. Suppose that the landlord had made good faith efforts to fix the problem but was unable to for a period of three months. How would that impact your analysis?

✅ Self-Check **ANSWERS**

Ownership Interests

1. Swineburne owns the property in fee simple absolute and is permitted to use the property for any lawful use, including a luxury resort.

2. Swineburne's ownership was in fee simple defeasible (restricted by Carroll's "provided that" language in the agreement). When he violated the restriction, the ownership rights reverted back to Carroll.

3. Swineburne's interest is in the form of a periodic (month-to-month) tenancy. Therefore, Carroll must give Swineburne at least one month's notice before terminating the lease.

4. Swineburne was a life tenant, so all ownership interests are extinguished upon his death. Carroll Jr. is then the owner in fee simple absolute and has the right to terminate Swineburne Jr.'s use of the real estate.

5. Swineburne has an express easement to use the driveway. Blago had reason to know of the easement at the time of purchase (via the easement statement recorded on the deed); therefore, he must honor Swineburne's easement.

25 CHAPTER

Intellectual Property

learning **objectives**

After studying this chapter, students who have mastered the material will be able to:

25-1 Define *trade secret* and other protectable business information and articulate the various legal implications for misappropriation of that information.

25-2 Classify trademarks based on their level of distinctiveness and give examples of trademarks, trade dress, and service marks.

25-3 Express how federal laws aimed at regulating trademarks in cyberspace apply to domain names.

25-4 Identify and understand the impact of trademark infringement and dilution.

25-5 Articulate the fundamental requirements for copyright protection, the legal ramifications of copyright infringement, and the impact of technology on copyright law.

25-6 Apply the fair use defense and give examples from case law.

25-7 Explain the process for obtaining and maintaining a patent and articulate the basic requirements for an invention to have patent protection.

25-8 Identify and understand the remedies for acts of patent infringement.

The formal protection of intellectual property has been a foundation of U.S. law since the ratification of the Constitution. In Article I, Section 8, of the U.S. Constitution, Congress is specifically authorized to protect intellectual property "by securing for limited Times to Authors and Inventors the exclusive Right to their respective Writings and Discoveries." A study published in the *Harvard Business Review* found that intellectual property represents approximately 70 percent of an average firm's value, and that number has nearly doubled in one decade.[1] This chapter discusses the increasingly important legal concepts of intellectual property protection that will help business owners and managers to make informed decisions on how best to protect their own intellectual property and prevent infringing upon the intellectual property rights of others. In this chapter, students will learn:

■ Legal protections for trade secrets and other business information.

■ Statutory and common law requirements for protection of trademarks, service marks, and trade dress.

■ Requirements for protection under federal copyright laws, consequences of infringement, and application of the fair use test.

■ Overview of protections for inventors through patent law and statutory requirements for obtaining a patent.

TRADE SECRETS AND PROTECTION OF BUSINESS INFORMATION LO 25-1

Among the most valuable assets of any firm are its secret processes, formulas, methods, procedures, and lists that allow the firm to have a competitive advantage in its trade. It is important to understand that many types of trade secrets, business information, and business methods may *not* be protectable by patent or copyright laws. In fact, patent applicants generally rely on trade secret law to protect their inventions while patent applications are in progress. Businesses from across the spectrum of sectors turn to trade secret protection laws to protect some or all of their valuable creative ideas. Examples of technical and business information material that can be protected by trade secret law include customer lists, designs, instructional methods, manufacturing processes and product formulas, and document-tracking processes.

Courts use several factors under the common law of the majority of states to determine whether certain material constitutes a trade secret:

■ The extent to which the information is known outside the claimant's (i.e., the firm claiming that the information is a trade secret) business.

---

[1] K. Rivet and D. Kline, *Discovering New Value in Intellectual Property,* Harv. Bus. Rev., January 2000, p. 58.

- Measures taken by the claimant to guard the confidentiality of the information.
- The value of the information to competitors.
- The amount invested (in terms of time and money) in developing the information.
- The efforts to maintain trade secret confidentiality among the claimant's employees and third-party vendors (such as auditing firms).

TRADE SECRET PROTECTIONS

Trade secret protections are provided by state statutes and/or state common law. The Uniform Trade Secrets Act (UTSA)[2] defines trade secrets as information or articles that are to be kept secret because of their particular value. A trade secret is a formula, pattern, compilation, program, device, method, technique, or process that meets the following criteria:

- Derives *independent economic value,* actual or potential, from not being generally known to, and not being readily ascertainable by proper means by, other persons who can obtain economic value from its disclosure or use.
- Is the subject of efforts that are reasonable under the circumstances to maintain its secrecy. Economic value must be identified by the owner, and secrecy must be kept.

Misappropriation

Most state statutes use the definition of **misappropriation** from the UTSA: (1) the acquisition of a trade secret of another by a person who knows or has reason to know that the trade secret was acquired by improper means or (2) any disclosure or use of a trade secret of another without express or implied consent.

Criminal Sanctions

While the UTSA does not contain any criminal sanctions, many states have added a separate set of statutes that make certain trade secret misappropriation a criminal offense. For example, in 1997, a district attorney in California prosecuted several executives and employees of Avant! Corporation, a firm that designed software related to semiconductor chips. The prosecutor was alerted to the case after a competitor of Avant! sued the firm in an action brought under California's Trade Secret Act, alleging that Avant! employees stole computer code from one of Avant!'s primary competitors.[3] Ultimately, Avant! accepted a plea bargain from the prosecutor that forced the company and seven individuals to pay $35 million in fines and resulted in incarceration for five of the defendants. The **Economic Espionage Act** is a federal statute passed in 1996 providing criminal penalties for domestic and foreign theft of trade secrets.

Exclusive Rights for Unlimited Duration

Perhaps the most significant advantage of trade secret protection over other forms of intellectual property (such as patents) is that protection for trade secrets does not expire after a fixed period of time. A trade secret owner has the right to keep others from misappropriating and using the trade secret for the duration of the firm's existence. Although sometimes the misappropriation is a result of industrial espionage, most trade secret cases involve people who have taken their former employer's trade secrets for use in a new start-up business or by a new employer.

---

[2]The UTSA is a model law drafted by the American Law Institute for use by state legislatures. For more information on the ALI and model laws, see Chapter 1, "Legal Foundations."

[3]*Cadence Design Systems, Inc. v. Avant!,* 253 F.3d 1147 (9th Cir. 2002). The parties settled the civil suit for $265 million.

Trade secret protection endures so long as the requirements for protection continue to be met. The protection is lost if the owner fails to take reasonable steps to keep the information secret. For example, Sam discovers a new method for manipulating images in multimedia works. He demonstrates his new method to a number of other developers at a multimedia conference. Sam may have lost his trade secret protection for the image manipulation method because he failed to take appropriate steps to keep his method secret.

Trade secret owners have recourse only against misappropriation. Discovery of protected information through independent research or reverse engineering (taking a product apart to see how it works) is *not* misappropriation.

 Self-Check   Trade Secrets

Which of the following may be protectable as a trade secret?

1. A list of customers compiled by a firm that includes buying patterns, purchaser contact information, and preferred products of each customer.

2. A system used by a medical practice for scheduling patients for doctor's office visits.

3. The formula for a new brand of fruit drink at a beverage supply company.

4. The process used by an accounting firm to draft financial statements in accordance with generally accepted accounting procedures (GAAP).

5. New software that helps a manufacturer speed up the design process for new products.

Answers to this Self-Check are provided at the end of the chapter.

TRADEMARKS, SERVICE MARKS, AND TRADE DRESS   LO 25-2

A **trademark** is a nonfunctional, distinctive word, name, shape, symbol, phrase, or combination of words and symbols that helps consumers to distinguish one product from another.[4] The Lanham Act[5] is the federal statute that protects an owner's registered trademark from use without the mark holder's permission. The key requirement to a protectable trademark is *distinctiveness* that indicates the product's source. For example, the name and logo of Coca-Cola comprise one of the most famous trademarks in the world. Consumers have confidence in the product, and the Coca-Cola trademark distinguishes the product from competing colas. Other famous marks include McDonald's golden arches and Nike's swoosh. While trademarks are typically associated with products, **service marks** are used to identify business services. Examples of famous service marks include Hilton Hotels (accommodation) and Greyhound Lines (transportation).

Trade Dress

Businesses are increasingly eager to extend trademark protection beyond words and symbols and to gain protection for a product's shape or the color combination of its packaging. These beyond-the-mark features are called **trade dress.** Traditionally, courts have allowed trade dress protection for sounds, scents, textures, shapes, and color combinations for businesses such as restaurants.[6] More recently, the U.S. Patent and Trademark Office (USPTO) has granted protection to trade dress characteristics so long as the mark holder proves that the trade dress provides an exclusive link to the source product in the

---

[4]15 U.S.C. § 1127 (2006).
[5]15 U.S.C. § 1052 (2006).
[6]*Two Pesos, Inc. v. Taco Cabana, Inc.,* 112 S. Ct. 2753 (1992).

consumer's mind. For example, beginning in 2005, after having secured trademark registration for the two-dimensional iPod symbol and the cobranded "Made for iPod" symbol, Apple applied for trademark protection of the actual three-dimensional shape of the product. Apple provided the USPTO with evidence that (1) it had spent millions of dollars on advertising targeted to building an association between iPod's shape and Apple, (2) there was a widespread consumer familiarity with the iPod's design, and (3) many consumers automatically linked the iPod's shape with Apple. In 2008, the USPTO granted Apple's application for trademark registration. Figure 25.1 shows the sketches submitted by Apple to the USPTO.

Trademarks as a Business Asset

The primary objective of trademark protection is to provide the mark holder with a means of preventing others from fooling consumers into buying a product that they erroneously believe is produced by the mark holder. Businesses invest significant resources in their trademarks to build consumer loyalty to a particular brand. Designs, color schemes, shapes, and other features all play a role in creating a link in the buying public's mind. Trademarks allow consumers to quickly identify a product and distinguish it from similar or competing products. The Lanham Act is designed to prevent business competitors from getting a "free ride" on the shoulders of a more famous brand. For example, if a small economy-car manufacturer could use the name or symbols associated with Rolls-Royce, the smaller company would deprive the mark holder of its investments in the mark and gain name recognition at no cost.

Classifications of Trademarks

As discussed earlier, trademark protection is based on distinctiveness. For a trademark to be distinctive, it must identify the source of a particular product (or service for service marks). Courts classify marks based on their level of distinctiveness, and this classification determines their level of protection. The more distinctive the mark, the more protection the mark has under the Lanham Act.

Arbitrary or Fanciful   A mark that has no direct connection to the product is categorized as arbitrary or fanciful. An arbitrary mark is a real word being used as part

FIGURE 25.1   Apple iPod Trademark Registration

Apple secured trademark protection for the iPod symbol (top left), its cobranded product symbol (bottom left), and the shape of the iPod (right).

Google is one of the strongest and most distinctive trademarks in the world.

of a mark that has nothing to do with the word's literal meaning (e.g., Apple or Amazon). A fanciful mark is one that centers upon a word made up with the intention of being used as a distinctive term. For example, Google's name and symbol were created by the company's founders and have no obvious connection to an Internet search engine. Therefore, Google fits into the fanciful category.

Suggestive Marks that suggest the product or service without literally describing it are considered highly distinctive. Courts classify a mark as suggestive if imagination, thought, and perception are required to understand how it is tied to the underlying product or service. For example, the trademark "Under Armour" suggests a product used under something for protection. Understanding the actual product however, requires a leap of imagination, thought, or perception. Suggestive marks are similar to arbitrary marks in that they tend to be highly distinctive and are given a high level of protection.

Descriptive A descriptive mark is one that makes specific reference to features, qualities, or characteristics of a product or service and is not inherently distinctive. Courts have held marks such as After Tan (moisturizing lotion for use after sunbathing), Tender Vittles (cat food), and Car Freshener (air deodorizer for cars) as descriptive marks because no leap of imagination is required to connect the mark with the product. Because descriptive marks are not inherently distinctive, they are not protected under the Lanham Act unless they have acquired a **secondary meaning.** Descriptive-mark holders must provide evidence that the general public connects the mark with the mark holder's product or service rather than with the ordinary meaning of the term.

Standards for Secondary Meaning A secondary meaning is created when the consuming public primarily associates a mark with a *particular* product rather than any alternate meaning. For example, Microsoft attempted to protect the term *Windows* as a mark for its revolutionary operating system for many years. In order to attain that right, Microsoft was required to show that much of the consuming public more often associated that term with its operating system rather than panes of glass.

In Case 25.1, a federal court of appeals analyzes the requirements for a secondary meaning.

FACT SUMMARY   Custom Vehicles registered the trademark Work-N-Play for one of its products. Work-N-Play vehicles were vans designed to be both a mobile office and, upon conversion that took the owner approximately one hour, a camper. Later, Forest River manufactured a van with a ramp door from the rear cargo section that had space fitted for a snowmobile, motorcycle, or ATV. Forest River named the van Work and Play (without registering it as a trademark). Custom filed suit for trademark infringement, but the district court held that no infringement had taken place.

SYNOPSIS OF DECISION AND OPINION   The U.S. Court of Appeals for the Seventh Circuit affirmed the trial court's decision in favor of Forest, ruling that Custom's mark was *descriptive* but had not acquired a secondary meaning. Sales of Custom's product were relatively small, and there was no evidence that the mark would have any brand recognition. Thus, the mark was not sufficiently "famous" to be afforded trademark protection.

WORDS OF THE COURT: Secondary Meaning "A trademark, like a patent, carries a presumption of validity. However, in the case of a registered descriptive mark, the presumption is that it has acquired secondary meaning. But the act of registration merely begins the process that leads to the presumption. Bare registration is not enough. Trademarks cannot be 'banked' or 'warehoused'—that is, an individual or entity cannot register thousands of names, unrelated to any product or service that it sells, in the hope of extracting a license fee from sellers of products or services for which one of the names might be apt. [The registrant] of a name must certify that the product is in use in commerce—defined as the bona fide use of a mark in the ordinary course of trade, and not made merely to reserve a right in a mark—within six months after the trademark is registered. Within those six months, the use of the trademark in one commercial sale is not enough to place the trademark in the ordinary course of trade, unless the sale is large enough to seize the attention of the relevant market."

Case Questions

1. Should Custom have waited until it sold more of this product before it registered Work-N-Play as a trademark?

2. Why must a descriptive mark acquire a secondary meaning in order to have protection?

LEGAL IMPLICATIONS *in* CYBERSPACE   LO 25-3

Domain Names, Trademarks, and Cybersquatting

The explosive growth of consumer Internet use caused concern among trademark holders on a number of fronts. Chief among them was the practice of individuals who legally registered domain names that were also words associated with a famous trademark. Once the domain name was secured, the individual would offer the domain name at an extraordinarily inflated rate to the trademark owner. This practice became known as *cybersquatting* and was the subject of considerable media attention in the 1990s and early 2000s. Congress responded to this practice by passing a federal statute designed to curb some of the more unscrupulous cybersquatters. That law, the Anti-cybersquatting Consumer Protection Act (ACPA), gave specific statutory remedies to trademark owners to recover trademark-related domain names from users who acted in bad faith. **Bad faith** is a dishonesty of belief or purpose. In this context, the bad-faith requirement may be met in a number of ways but is typically satisfied when the registrant has no legitimate reason for the use of the domain name or the registrant is using the domain name to profit or confuse consumers. In Case 25.2, a federal court outlines nine examples of bad faith under the ACPA.

FACT SUMMARY   People for the Ethical Treatment of Animals (PETA) is the high-profile nonprofit organization devoted to educating the public at large and attempting to prevent the abuse of animals for corporate gain. Doughney registered PETA.org, claiming he was head of an organization called People Eating Tasty Animals and, thus, was entitled to use the name. Doughney's website contained links to furriers and others that would be in direct conflict with PETA's mission. PETA filed suit against Doughney, alleging, among other things, that his use of PETA.org violated the ACPA.

SYNOPSIS OF DECISION AND OPINION   The court ruled in favor of PETA, granted it summary judgment, and ordered Doughney to cease use of the PETA.org domain name. The court pointed out nine examples of bad-faith action taken by Doughney and held that his actions violated the ACPA. The court rejected Doughney's claim that the website was merely a parody of the PETA organization because of the likelihood of confusion. In fact, Doughney admitted that "many people" would initially assume that they were accessing an authentic site sponsored by PETA.

WORDS OF THE COURT: Bad Faith   "[Under the ACPA], there are nine factors a court must consider in making a determination of whether the Defendant had a bad faith intent. Applying these factors, it appears that Doughney had the requisite bad faith intent.

"First, Defendant possessed no intellectual property rights in 'PETA.ORG' when he registered the domain name in 1995. Second, the 'PETA.ORG' domain name is not the Defendant, Michael T. Doughney's legal name or any name that is otherwise used to identify the Defendant. Third, Defendant had not engaged in prior use of the 'PETA.ORG' domain name in connection with the bona fide offering of any goods or services prior to registering 'PETA.ORG.' Fourth, Defendant used the PETA mark in a commercial manner. Fifth, Defendant clearly intended to confuse, mislead and divert Internet users into accessing his website, which contained information antithetical, and therefore harmful to the goodwill represented by the PETA mark. Sixth, on Doughney's 'PETA.ORG' website, Doughney made reference to seeing what PETA would offer him if PETA did not like his website. Seventh, Defendant, when registering the domain name 'PETA. ORG,' falsely stated that 'People Eating Tasty Animals' was a non-profit educational organization and that this website did not infringe any trademark. Eighth, Defendant has registered other Internet domain names which are identical or similar to either marks or names of famous people or organizations he opposes. Ninth, the PETA mark used in the 'PETA.ORG' domain name is distinctive and famous and was so at the time Defendant registered this site in September 1995."

Case Questions

1. Was there any indication that Doughney was cybersquatting?

2. Could Doughney have avoided liability by making changes to his website or business model? What changes may help shield him from liability?

BUSINESS ETHICS PERSPECTIVE

Name for a King's Ransom

1. Do you think that registering a domain name with the sole intent of selling the domain name is ethical? Isn't this just the market economy at work?

2. If one individual buys a domain name from another, with the intent of reselling it to another party, is that a different ethical decision than in Question 1?

3. Are there any circumstances in which a party could ethically obtain the domain name of a famous trademark?

LO 25-3 ACQUIRING RIGHTS FOR TRADEMARK PROTECTION

Holders acquire rights to trademark protection either through (1) use in commerce or (2) registration of the mark with the USPTO. Acquiring rights through use in commerce carries a significant risk that the mark holder's rights will not be fully realized nationwide, so most holders opt to register the mark (see Solutions for Managers: Advantages of Trademark Registration).

KEY POINT

Trademark holders may acquire rights in the mark through use in commerce or through USPTO registration.

A mark holder typically uses the symbol™ (or℠) to indicate that the mark is not yet registered with the USPTO, but the holder is indicating that he considers the mark distinctive enough to be protected and, in some cases, that the application for registration is pending. Once the mark has been approved by the USPTO, it is considered registered and the mark holder now uses the well-known symbol® to indicate completed registration.

A mark may be registered with USPTO only if the holder has a bona fide intent to use the mark in commerce. Once the mark is registered, the mark holder has nationwide rights to its use. However, even with registration, the mark may still be used by anyone who used the mark in commerce *prior* to registration.

| BUSINESS LAW

Have an idea for a trademark? Visit Connect to try a trademark registration search.

In essence, different parties can have trademark protection simultaneously. For example, if Robert begins to use a trademark for a specialty coffee in his coffee shop in Boston but does not use it in any other market, he has acquired the right to use it in *Boston only* because he was the first to put it into commerce. However, if National Brand Coffee (NBC) wants to use the very same trademark, NBC may register it with the USPTO and be entitled to nationwide rights except the right to use it in the Boston geographic market. So both Robert and NBC have rights to the same trademark, but the rights extend only to the appropriate geographic area.

Policing the Mark

One important aspect of trademark law is that mark holders have an obligation to protect their rights by "policing" their marks. Famous-mark holders often employ watch services and other methods to identify potential infringers of their marks, and they typically have a system set up that includes sending a cease and desist letter and, if necessary, litigating in support of their policing efforts. For example, Volkswagen posts its policing policy on website and makes clear that it employs an aggressive system designed to halt any unauthorized use of its mark. Jeep runs advertising in national publications to distinguish its product from other sport utility vehicles. In order to be protected, a trademark must be in use and stay distinctly tied to a product in the consuming public's mind. If a word becomes so generic that it has lost is distinctiveness, the rights are lost through genericization. Although the most famous case is perhaps Bayer's loss of the right to protect the mark *aspirin*,[7] marks such as *zipper* and *elevator* were also lost to genericization. Brands that are working to avoid genericization include Google, Xerox, and Band-Aid.

Applications and the USPTO

Registration of a mark is not automatic. A mark holder must submit to an approval process through the USPTO, which examines the mark for distinctiveness, checks for any similar marks that are already registered, and ensures compliance with trademark registration standards (e.g., secondary meaning for descriptive marks). The USPTO also has the right to reject applications for marks that are immoral or scandalous. Some famous rejections include:

---

[7]287 F.2d 492 (2d Cir. 1961).

- Twitter's initial application in 2009 to trademark the term *tweet* was rejected because of insufficient evidence of secondary meaning. However, by 2012, Twitter acquired full trademark rights in "tweet."
- Chippendales' application to trademark its famous "cuffs-and-collar only" configuration worn by its waiters was rejected as not inherently distinctive. The USPTO was not sufficiently persuaded by the affidavit of an expert on American burlesque theater who stated that the Chippendales costumes are associated with "iconic characters" that make the costumes distinctive.
- The application of reality television personality Michael Sorrentino to register his *Jersey Shore* nickname "The Situation" was rejected by the USPTO because the mark was too close to a previously registered mark issued to a Memphis retailer who sold apparel and shoes.

SOLUTIONS FOR MANAGERS

Advantages of Trademark Registration

PROBLEM *The common law and statutory law protections in the area of trademark protection result in too much uncertainty regarding a business's ability to use the mark.*

SOLUTION *Register your trademark as soon as possible with the USPTO.*

Although this may require attorney fees, the return on investment may well be worth it. The major advantages to registration are:

- Registration gives a party the right to use the mark nationwide, subject to any geographic exceptions.

- Registration constitutes nationwide constructive notice to the public of trademark ownership.

- Registration enables a party to bring an infringement suit in federal court.

- Registration allows a party to potentially recover treble (triple) damages, attorney fees, and other remedies.

- Registered trademarks may, after five years, become "incontestable," at which point the exclusive right to use the mark is conclusively established.

Registering a trademark with the USPTO provides maximum nationwide protection and gives the mark holder the right to enforce its rights in federal court.

LO 25-4 Trademark Infringement

Infringement occurs when a party uses a protected mark without the mark holder's consent. For a mark holder to prevail on a claim of trademark infringement under the Lanham Act, she has the burden of proving that the infringement would likely cause confusion among reasonable consumers (called the *likelihood of confusion* standard). In determining whether a likelihood of confusion exists, many courts apply a balancing test that has largely grown from a model set out by the U.S. Court of Appeals for the Second Circuit in the important infringement case *Polaroid Corp. v. Polarad Elect. Corporation*.[8] The factors are (1) strength of the mark (how famous is it?), (2) similarity between marks, (3) proximity of the products and their competitiveness with each other, (4) evidence that the mark holder may be preparing to launch a product for sale in the market of the alleged infringer's product (a technique known in trademark law as *bridging the gap*), (5) evidence of actual consumer confusion, (6) evidence of bad faith by the infringer, (7) respective quality of the products, and (8) sophistication of consumers in the relevant market. The application of the *Polaroid* test is not mechanical but rather focuses on the ultimate question of whether, looking at the products in their totality, consumers are likely to be confused.

> ### KEY POINT
>
> For a trademark holder to prevent another from using the holder's mark, the holder must prove that the use of the mark by another will be likely to cause consumer confusion as to the source of the goods. Courts use the eight-factor *Polaroid* test to assess likelihood of confusion.

In Case 25.3, an appellate court analyzes whether the use of a trademark in a song title and lyrics constitutes infringement.

Trademark Dilution

In addition to bringing an infringement claim under the Lanham Act, holders of famous marks may also enforce their rights via the **Federal Trademark Dilution Act** of 1995[9] as amended by the Trademark Dilution Revision Act (TDRA)[10] of 2006. In a dilution claim, evidence of consumer confusion is *not* necessary in order for the mark holder to prevail. Dilution occurs either through blurring or tarnishment. Blurring dilutes the distinctive quality of the mark through its identification with goods that are not alike. Dilution by blurring may be found regardless of the presence or absence of actual or likely confusion, of competition, or of actual injury. For example, consider the hypothetical products of Red Bull brand pianos or Ford brand tennis shoes. Consumers would not necessarily be confused about the origin, but each dilutes the distinctive quality of a famous mark. Dilution by tarnishment occurs when an association arising from the similarity between a mark or trade name and a famous mark harms the reputation of the famous mark with something that a consumer might find objectionable or unflattering (e.g., Apple brand cigarettes).[11]

The TDRA specifies six nonexhaustive factors for courts to consider in determining whether there is dilution by blurring:[12]

- The degree of similarity between the mark and the famous mark.
- The degree of inherent or acquired distinctiveness of the mark.
- The extent to which the owner of the famous mark is engaging in substantially exclusive use of the mark.
- The degree of recognition (fame) of the mark.

---

[8]287 F.2d 492 (2d Cir. 1961).

[9]15 U.S.C. § 1125.

[10]15 U.S.C. § 1125.

[11]15 U.S.C. § 1125(c)(2)(C) (2006).

[12]15 U.S.C. § 1125(c)(2)(B)(i)-(vi) (2006).

FACT SUMMARY　Barbie is the famous doll manufactured by Mattel with roots beginning in the 1950s. Mattel has invested significant resources in the worldwide marketing and development of the doll, and it has used the Barbie trademark on a variety of accessories for decades. This included development of a Ken doll, and the toy couple went on to become a common reference in pop culture. In 1997, the Danish band Aqua produced a song called "Barbie Girl" in which one band member impersonated Barbie by singing in a high-pitched, doll-like voice in a musical conversation with another band member called Ken. The chorus included:

> I'm a Barbie girl, in my Barbie world
>
> Life in plastic, it's fantastic
>
> You can brush my hair, undress me everywhere
>
> Imagination, life is your creation
>
> Come on Barbie, let's go party!

Mattel brought an action against Aqua's record label, MCA, for trademark infringement (among other claims) for use of the Barbie mark. The trial court granted summary judgment to MCA, ruling that no infringement had occurred.

SYNOPSIS OF DECISION AND OPINION　The Court of Appeals for the Ninth Circuit ruled in favor of MCA. The court distinguished between use of a mark on a product and use of a mark in a song title and explained that although consumers frequently look to the title of a work to determine what it is about, they do not regard titles of artistic works in the same way as they do the names of ordinary commercial products. The court adopted a rule that literary titles do not violate the Lanham Act unless the title has no artistic relevance to the underlying work whatsoever or, if it has some artistic relevance, unless the title explicitly misleads as to the source or the content of the work.

WORDS OF THE COURT: No Infringement　Applying [the literary title rule] to our case, we conclude that MCA's use of Barbie is not an infringement of Mattel's trademark. Under the first prong of [the rule], the use of Barbie in the song title clearly is relevant to the underlying work, namely, the song itself. As noted, the song is about Barbie and the values Aqua claims she represents. The song title does not explicitly mislead as to the source of the work; it does not, explicitly or otherwise, suggest that it was produced by Mattel. The only indication that Mattel might be associated with the song is the use of Barbie in the title[.]

Counterclaim Dismissed:　"After Mattel filed suit, Mattel and MCA employees traded barbs in the press. . . . MCA filed a counterclaim for defamation based on the Mattel representative's use of the words 'bank robber,' 'heist,' 'crime' and 'theft.'. . . In context, all these terms are nonactionable rhetorical hyperbole. The parties are advised to chill."

Case Questions

1. Given the rule adopted by the court, can you think of an example in which a literary title would violate the Lanham Act?

2. Why did the court distinguish between use of a mark on a product and use of a mark in a song title?

- Whether use of the mark by the alleged infringer was intended to create an association with the famous mark.

- Any actual association between the mark and the famous mark.

In addition to setting out statutory blurring standards, the TDRA also requires the mark holder to prove that his mark is famous by offering evidence that it is widely recognized by the general consuming public of the United States.

CONCEPT SUMMARY Trademarks

- A trademark is a word, symbol, or phrase used to identify a seller's product and distinguish it from other products.

- Businesses invest significant resources in trademark design; trade marks are among a company's most valuable assets.

(continued)

- Trademark protection is a combination of state law and a federal statute known as the Lanham Act.

- Trademark protection is obtained either through initial use in commerce or registration with the USPTO.

- Managers should focus special attention on policing their firm's mark, that is, having a policy in place and taking steps to prevent others from using the mark.

- In order to prove infringement, the mark owner must prove that use of the mark by another could cause consumer confusion or that the use of the mark dilutes or tarnishes the mark.

COPYRIGHT LAW: PROTECTIONS OF ORIGINAL EXPRESSIONS

LO 25-5

Black's Law Dictionary defines a copyright as "the right of literary property as recognized and sanctioned by positive law." Copyright protection is an intangible right granted by the Copyright Act of 1976[13] (a federal statute) to the author or originator of an *original* literary or artistic production, whereby the artist is invested, for a specified period (see Table 25.1), with the sole and exclusive privilege of multiplying copies of the work and with the right to profit from its publication and sale.

The Copyright Act allows creators to obtain a copyright by having an "original work of authorship fixed in any tangible medium of expression, not known or later developed, from which [it] can be perceived, reproduced, or otherwise communicated, either directly or with the aid of a machine or device."[14]

Protected works include literary works, musical works, dramatic works, choreographic works, motion pictures, sound recordings, and pictorial or graphical works. Works that *cannot* be protected include ideas, procedures, processes, systems, methods of operation, concepts, principles, and discoveries, no matter how they are explained, illustrated, or described.[15]

Fundamentally, in order to gain copyright protection, a work must meet a three-part test: (1) **originality,** (2) some degree of **creativity,** and (3) fixed in a **durable medium.**

Originality and Creativity Requirements

The meaning of the word *original* has brought about the most controversy in interpreting the requirements of the Copyright Act. What is to be considered original, and what guidelines should be used to determine originality? The courts have ruled that an original work of authorship is a work that is original to the *author,* which means that the author must use *her own creative capabilities* to create the work or medium. Does this mean that a compilation of noncopyrightable facts (such as names and telephone numbers) can be copyrighted as long as one author put the collaboration together first or in a creative way? In *Feist Publications, Inc. v. Rural Telephone Service,*[16] the landmark case on copyright originality and creativity, the U.S. Supreme Court gave some guidance as to what level of creativity was necessary to meet the originality requirements. The Court ruled that, although compilations of facts could be copyrightable, there had to be some *creative* element used that made the compilation an original work. For example, the White Pages of a telephone directory do not meet the creativity requirement because they are simply

---

[13]17 U.S.C. § 101 et seq.

[14]17 U.S.C. § 102(a).

[15]Note that ideas, procedures, systems, and the like may be covered by intellectual property protections other than copyright law.

[16]499 U.S. 340 (1991). This case was the beginning of the phone book battles. Once *Feist* was decided, several different publication companies began to compete with telephone companies for Yellow Pages advertising. This one decision spurred a new niche in the publishing industry.

TABLE 25.1 Copyright Protection Periods

Copyright Owner	Copyright Duration
Sole author or originator	70 years from death of the author or originator
Publisher or other party (works for hire)	First of (1) 120 years from the date of creation or (2) 95 years from the date of publication
More than one author or originator	70 years from the death of the last surviving author or originator

arranged alphabetically. One federal appellate court has even held that the Yellow Pages listings of a telephone directory do not meet the originality requirement.[17]

Durable Medium

To be protected, a work must be fixed in a *durable medium.* This underscores the copyright law's requirement that the work must be more than just an idea or thought process. In fact, the work must be in a tangible form, such as writing, digital, video, and so forth. Copyright protections extend automatically to a work once created. Although there is no need to register the work with the United States Copyright Office to obtain protection, registration is a prerequisite to actually *enforcing* the holder's rights in court.

COPYRIGHT INFRINGEMENT

LO 25-6

When a copyright holder pursues a party that it believes has infringed on its copyright, the aggrieved party will generally pursue one of three *theories of infringement.* These theories have been developed by the federal courts to analyze copyright infringement cases. These theories are *direct, indirect* (also known as *contributory*), and *vicarious* infringement.

Direct Infringement

Direct infringement occurs when the copyright owner can prove that she has legal ownership of the work in question and that the infringer copied the work without permission. While the first element is straightforward, the second element is more complex than appears at first glance. In the context of the copyright protections afforded by law, it is clear that the word *copied* must have an expansive definition rather than a narrow one (i.e., *copy* means more than "exact replica"). At the same time, of course, the definition cannot be so expansive as to foreclose any works of the same category.

Courts have developed the *substantial similarity standard* to guide the definition of *copy* under copyright laws. Thus, a copyright holder need prove only that the infringer copied plots, structures, and/or organizations that made the infringing work substantially similar to the copyrighted work.

Indirect Infringement

Indirect infringement (also known as *contributory infringement*) involves three parties: the copyright owner, the direct infringer, and the *facilitator* of the infringement. The theory of indirect infringement is one that holds the facilitator liable for damages. Therefore, before pursuing a theory of indirect infringement, the copyright owner must identify the direct infringer. Normally, for the facilitator to be liable, that party must have knowledge

Legal Speak ·))
Direct and Imputed Knowledge Direct knowledge implies that a party has firsthand, actual knowledge of a fact. Imputed knowledge is gained from circumstances or a relationship with a third party in which a diligent party "should have known" about the fact at issue.

---

[17]*BellSouth Advertising v. Donnelley Information Publishing,* 999 F.2d 1436 (11th Cir. 1993).

(direct or imputed) of the infringement and/or contribute to the infringement in some material way. In the famous case of *A&M Records, Inc. v. Napster, Inc.,*[18] a federal appeals court held that Napster's business model of facilitating a peer-to-peer community for sharing of digital music files constituted contributory infringement because Napster had the ability to locate infringing material listed on its search engines and the right to terminate users' access to the system. Digital file sharing is discussed more extensively later in this section (see Legal Implications in Cyberspace: Copyrights in the Digital Age).

Vicarious Infringement

The final copyright infringement theory, **vicarious infringement,** is similar to the indirect infringement theory in that they both involve third parties not involved in actual direct infringement. Vicarious liability is based on agency law (see Chapter 11, "Agency") and can be used as a theory of liability when the infringing party (the agent) is acting on behalf of or for the benefit of another party (the principal). In that case, the principal party is vicariously liable. The copyright owner will be entitled to remedies against the principal to the same extent as against the direct infringer. Vicarious liability most often occurs in an employer-employee circumstance in which the employee is acting with authority from the employer and commits an act of infringement that benefits the employer.

The **No Electronic Theft (NET) Act**[19] of 1997 increased the criminal penalties for violation of the Copyright Act. The NET Act provides for criminal liability for anyone infringing on a copyright by making a reproduction or distribution, including by electronic means, of one or more copies of a copyrighted work with a total retail value of more than $1,000. Penalties include maximum fines of $250,000 and potential incarceration.[20]

Defense to Infringement Claims: Fair Use

Copyright owners do not enjoy unlimited rights to their work. Rather, the law balances public interests with the property rights of copyright owners. The most common and powerful defense is **fair use.** A landmark case on the fair use defense is *Universal Studios v. Sony,*[21] in which the U.S. Supreme Court ruled that Sony's manufacturing and selling of Betamax (the first videocassette tape recording format for use in home videocassette recorders, or VCRs) was *not* **per se** infringement. After Sony had started producing videotape recorders (sold under the brand name Betamax) in a price range that many consumers could afford, Universal saw the mass distribution of this product as a threat to its business and market share. Universal sued Sony on an infringement theory, claiming that consumers were using the Sony product to copy its copyrighted movies. The Court made clear that Congress did not give absolute control over all uses of copyrighted materials. Some uses were *permitted,* and because the device could still be used for "substantial non-infringing uses," the Court held that Sony was not liable for contributory infringement. This *fair use exception,* known as the *Sony defense* or the *Betamax doctrine,* was used, unsuccessfully, as the basis for the defense in the *A&M Records v. Napster* case (discussed previously in this chapter) and was reexamined by the U.S. Supreme Court in the *MGM v. Grokster* case (discussed later in the chapter).[22] Fair use has also been extended to the use of a work for parody or satirical purposes.[23]

---

[18]239 F.3d 1004 (2001).

[19]17 U.S.C. § 506.

[20]A catalyst for this law was a criminal case brought against an MIT student who posted copyrighted software on the web free of charge for anyone to download. The government could not obtain a conviction in the case because the existing law (prior to the NET Act) imposed criminal liability only when the infringement was undertaken for private *financial* gain. The NET Act eliminated the financial gain requirement for a criminal conviction. See *U.S. v. LaMacchia,* 871 F. Supp. 535 (D. Mass. 1994).

[21]464 U.S. 417.

[22]See Legal Implications in Cyberspace: Copyrights in the Digital Age.

[23]*Campbell v. Acuff-Rose Music, Inc.,* 510 U.S. 569 (1994).

The term *fair use* has now been codified in the Copyright Act with four specific (though nonexclusive) guideposts: the *purpose* and *nature* of the use, the nature of the *work* itself, the *amount* and substantiality of the material used, and the *effect* of the use on the market.

Purpose and Nature of the Use

If the use of the work is to further education or scholarship, courts are more likely to be sympathetic to an assertion of fair use. This does not mean, however, that whole sections of textbooks or copied videotapes may be used with impunity. Also, if the use is for some commercially profitable purpose, this will weigh heavily against the infringer. This is not to say that commercial use is a complete bar to assertion of fair use.

Nature of the Work

If the copyrighted material has not yet been put into the public domain, fair use is a difficult defense. This is not to say that a complete bar to nonpublic works exists; newsworthy and factual information is still subject to fair use.

Amount and Substantiality Used

Courts essentially analyze the totality of the circumstances regarding the amount of copyrighted material used compared to the entire work at issue. Short phrases and limited use of the copyrighted work are often protected by the fair use defense.

Market Effect

Courts are reluctant to allow fair use as a defense (even if the use fits the other three categories) if a copyright holder demonstrates that the *value* of a copyrighted work will be diminished by allowing its use. Fair use cannot impair the marketability or economic success of the copyrighted work.

 Self-Check   Fair Use

Which of these situations would constitute fair use?

1. A manager photocopies an article of interest from *The Wall Street Journal* and distributes it to three co-workers who also may be interested.

2. A company buys one copy of a training manual from a publisher and then distributes photocopies of entire chapters to its workforce.

3. An executive rents a DVD on motivation from her local video/DVD store. The next day, she shows the DVD during work hours to her management team in order to inspire the team members to adopt certain leadership practices.

4. A firm that arranges corporate training sessions buys a DVD that features former General Electric CEO Jack Welch speaking on problem-solving skills for executives. The firm shows 30 minutes of this DVD at the beginning of each of its eight-hour training sessions called "Solutions for Solving," for which it charges $500 per person for the entire session.

Answers to this Self-Check are provided at the end of the chapter.

RIAA Lawsuits

In addition to aggressively pursuing file-sharing services such as Napster and Grokster, the motion picture and music recording industry has filed thousands of infringement lawsuits against individuals engaged in file sharing. The Recording Industry Association of America (RIAA) has invested substantial resources in tracking down and recovering damages from individual infringers. In a 2009 case that garnered substantial media attention, a jury imposed damages of $1.92 million against Jammie Thomas-Rasset in a federal court in Minnesota. The award was the result of a lawsuit filed by RIAA against Thomas-Rasset that alleged she downloaded more than 1,700 copyrighted songs.

Legal **Speak** ›))
Infringement The unlawful use of another's intellectual property.

Copyrights in the Digital Age

Technology has created new challenges for legislatures and courts struggling with applying copyright law in the digital age.

Computer Software   In order to settle uncertainty in the computer science field about the ability to copyright computer software, Congress amended the Copyright Act with the Computer Software Copyright Act.[24] This law, passed in 1980, specifically defined computer software programs as literary works and, thus, entitled to protection. However, the nature of computer software brings with it a good deal of uncertainty in terms of copyright protection. In 1986, the landmark case of *Whelan v. Jaslow*[25] gave the first guidance by an appellate court on the issue of copyright protection for software and indicated that courts were willing to extend broad protection to computer programs, including both the "look and feel" of a program's displays and also the program's structure, sequence, and organization. More recently, courts have been carving back this broad protection and adopting a more sophisticated test. One appellate court also made clear that patents, not copyrights, would be the most suitable form of intellectual property protection to protect the dynamic aspects of writing computer software programs.[26]

Evolution of Copyright Law and Technology

The revolutionary technological gains and the increasing popularity of the information superhighway has led to significant threats to copyright holders such as record labels and movie studios. In the past, copyright infringement of movies and music was limited because the technology that existed to copy these media was not capable of producing mass copies, except through a sophisticated criminal network. In short, the average consumer was limited in what he could copy and distribute, and thus copyright

[24]17 U.S.C.A. § 117.

[25]797 F.2d 1222 (3d Cir. 1986).

[26]*Computer Associates International v. Latai, Inc.,* 982 F.2d 693 (2d Cir. 1992).

holders had little fear that day-to-day consumer infringement would impact their revenue stream from sales of the original. However, when the digital age truly arrived, copyright holders responded by lobbying Congress for additional protections in the area of copyright laws.

Digital Millennium Copyright Act   Congress passed the Digital Millennium Copyright Act (DMCA) in 1998 in an attempt to modernize copyright law to deal with the new challenges that had emerged in the digital age. The DMCA was controversial because it added substantial protections for copyright holders of digital products and gave immunity to Internet service providers (ISPs) for certain copyright liability. Some of the major provisions of the DMCA are:

- Civil and criminal penalties established for anyone who produces, sells, or distributes any product or service that circumvents antipiracy software or other antipiracy technology.

- Restriction of import or distribution of analog video recorders and camcorders that lack antipiracy features.

- No liability of ISPs for copyright infringement by their users (such as posting copyrighted software on an ISP's electronic bulletin board) so long as the ISP does not have actual knowledge of the infringing material.

File Sharing   Technology changed the status quo rapidly. The late 1990s saw the introduction of two very important technological advances: (1) the popular music file format known as MP3 (essentially, compressed digital files) and (2) the increasing speed advancements of the Internet. These two additions changed the once hourslong process of transferring music and movies over the Internet to a process that took just a few minutes or less. The MP3 file popularity grew very quickly. This, in turn, brought about the ability to upload and download music and video files from one private personal computer to another. The ability to upload and download hundreds of files a day led to the establishment of peer-to-peer

(P2P) networking and, of course, entrepreneurs who have leveraged this technology into profit. The pioneer of P2P file-sharing communities was Napster. As discussed, the Ninth Circuit Court of Appeals effectively shut down Napster after the court ruled that Napster's business model was inherently illegal because Napster had imputed knowledge of copyright infringement. However, other Napster-like services were thriving under a business model whereby the P2P provider could not have any actual knowledge of copyright infringement. The motion picture and recording industries doggedly pursued each of these companies by suing them under a contributory infringement theory. Of course, Napster eventually reemerged as a pay-for-subscription service. Ultimately, the issue of what level of intent was necessary to constitute infringement was decided by the U.S. Supreme Court in Landmark Case 25.4.

LANDMARK CASE 25.4   Metro-Goldwyn-Mayer Studios v. Grokster, Ltd., 545 U.S. 913 (2005)

FACT SUMMARY   After the Napster decision, a number of other P2P file-sharing communities emerged with a slightly different business model. One famous firm, Grokster, used a business model whereby it would be *impossible* for Grokster to know if the files being shared were an infringing use. Thus, Grokster argued, no Napster-like imputed liability could attach and no contributor infringement existed. According to Grokster (and many other such firms that were emerging), its business was precisely the same business that Sony was in when selling the Betamax and thus Grokster was entitled to the same type of fair use exception—"capable of substantial non-infringing uses"—as was articulated by the Supreme Court in the *Sony* case. When MGM studios sued Grokster (and others including StreamCast, the distributor of Morpheus software), both the federal trial court and the federal court of appeals *agreed* with Grokster and allowed Grokster to use the *Sony* exception in their rulings against MGM.[27]

SYNOPSIS OF DECISION AND OPINION   The Supreme Court unanimously held that Grokster *could* be liable for inducing copyright infringement and reversed the court of appeals ruling. The Court specifically ruled that anyone who distributes a device with the intent to promote its use to infringe copyright is liable for the resulting acts of infringement (contributory) by third parties. Although there was some disagreement among the justices about the *Sony* defense, ultimately the Court held that the lower courts had misapplied the *Sony* exception because there was ample evidence that Grokster had acted with intent to cause copyright infringement via the use of its software.

WORDS OF THE COURT: Evidence of Intent   "Three features of this evidence of intent are particularly notable. First, each company showed itself to be aiming to satisfy a known source of demand for copyright infringement, the market comprising former Napster users. StreamCast's internal documents made constant reference to Napster, it initially distributed its Morpheus software through an OpenNap program compatible with Napster, it advertised its OpenNap program to Napster users, and its Morpheus software functions as Napster did except that it could be used to distribute more kinds of files, including copyrighted movies and software programs. Grokster's name is apparently derived from Napster, it too initially offered an OpenNap program, its software's function is likewise comparable to Napster's, and it attempted to divert queries for Napster onto its own Web site. Grokster and StreamCast's efforts to supply services to former Napster users, deprived of a mechanism to copy and distribute what were overwhelmingly infringing files, indicate a principal, if not exclusive, intent on the part of each to bring about infringement."

Case Questions

1. Why was the Court so concerned about the Open Nap program offered by StreamCast and Grokster?

2. Why do you think the Court refused to apply the *Sony* exception in this case?

[27] *Metro-Goldwyn-Mayer Studios v. Grokster, Ltd.,* 380 F.3d 1154 (9th Cir. 2004).

- Copyright protection is an intangible right granted by the Copyright Act to the author or originator of an original literary or artistic production.
- In order to obtain copyright protection, the work must be a result of some creative capability by the author or originator, and it must be fixed in a durable medium (such as in writing).
- There are three theories of infringement: direct, indirect (contributory), and vicarious.
- A powerful defense is fair use of copyrighted material, for which a court will examine the purpose and nature of the use, the nature of the work, the amount used, and the market effect of the use.

PATENTS: LEGAL PROTECTION OF INVENTIONS AND PROCESSES

A patent is a statutorily created monopoly right that allows an inventor the exclusive entitlement to make, use, license, and sell her invention for a limited period of time. Patent rights are important in the entire business community but are particularly vital to the manufacturing, technology, and pharmaceutical sectors. Patents are often an important part of these firms' planning because their business model depends on the benefits of obtaining a patent—the full legal protection of their ideas, methods, and inventions. Once a patent is obtained, a competitor is barred from profiting off the patented device or process during the life of the patent. Thus, a patent can be a firm's most important and valuable asset.

Understanding the fundamentals and discarding the myths of patent laws are important for managers. The most common myth is an assumption that nearly any new idea or invention is "patentable" (able to obtain patent law protection). This assumption is *not* true and may be an expensive lesson to learn. In fact, in order to be patented, the idea or invention must meet stringent criteria set down in federal statutes. The patent application procedure is often very expensive because one must almost always obtain counsel that specializes in patent law. Such law firms, known colloquially as *intellectual property* (or simply IP) *firms,* are often more expensive than expert counsel in other areas of the law given the specialized nature of their services.

Even if one is successful in obtaining a patent, enforcing the patent via an infringement suit is an even more expensive undertaking. According to a study in *The New York Times,* the median cost for enforcing a patent (assuming an infringement suit is necessary) is around $1.2 million. This significant cost factor must be considered in a company's patent management strategy.

LO 25-7 FUNDAMENTALS OF PATENT LAW

Patent law in the United States dates back to 1790 and is governed by the Patent Act established by the same Congress that ratified the U.S. Constitution. Of course, the law has been amended since then, but the basic standards have not changed much. There are three different categories of patents:

- *Utility patents* constitute a broad category that covers the invention of any new and useful process, machine, article of manufacture, or composition of matter or any new and

Avoiding Intellectual Property Liability: Landmines on the Web

PROBLEM *Managers who oversee an Internet-based marketing model are often barraged with conflicting information and advice about trademark and copyright law.*

By taking simple and inexpensive precautions, managers can help protect their company from infringement liability.

SOLUTION 1 *Limit your linking.*

Courts have allowed the use of a typical hypertext link so long as the use is reasonable under the circumstances. Inline imaging, framing, and even deep linking have all been given legal protection so long as the essence of the copyright and trademark laws is protected. However, an attempt to use a link to create confusion of the consumer that ultimately could result in the consumer's being directed to a competing business would constitute infringement.

For example, let's suppose that MuseumTicketsRUs is a registered trademark of a company that sells tickets to museum exhibits in major cities and that it hosts a website, MuseumTicketsRUs.com. A second firm, Artists.com, hosts a website that provides links to all museum websites, all museum online stores, art supply stores, and the like. If Artists.com simply provides a link to MuseumTicketsRUs, then no copyright or trademark infringement has taken place. However, if Artists.com uses MuseumTicketsRUs's logo, similar name, or other similar identifying characteristics and uses the link to direct a consumer-user to a competing site with which Artists.com has a commission-based agreement, this would clearly constitute infringement and expose Artists.com to significant legal liability. Thus, it is a good idea to take steps to avoid any consumer confusion by, for example, displaying a disclaimer stating that the originating site with the link is *not* related to or a part of the linked site.

Deep linking (i.e., linking to an embedded site) may be cause for additional concerns if the embedded site skips through advertising that the web page host has placed on the original site. It is a good practice to use links only to originating web pages (home pages) or at the very least to offer links to *both* the originating home page and the deep-linked page in close proximity, with labels for the user that describe the content of the page. Moreover, if the linked site has taken technical steps to prevent linking or given notice that it does not sanction deep linking, this should give managers pause because they may be crossing the line of reasonableness into infringement.

The ultimate protection against infringement, of course, is obtaining express permission to deep link or image. The owner of the site will often give you permission so long as your site is not a competitor or a site that may tend to tarnish its image (such as adult-content sites). A simple form for this permission is shown below.

Agreement and Permission to Use

This Agreement, made this _____ day of January, 2014, between MuseumTicketsRUs (Owner) and Artists.com (User), acknowledging sufficient consideration, the parties agree as follows:

1. Owner permits User to link, deep link, inline image, or frame Owner's website (www.MuseumTicketsRUs.com) from User's website (www.Artists.com).

2. User shall be entitled to use this permission until such time as Owner gives User 48 hours' notice via e-mail to cease the use of the link. Owner has the absolute and unconditional power to revoke this permission at any time and for any reason.

3. Upon such notice, User agrees to cease the use of any and all links to Owner's website as soon as possible.

4. Owner shall not be entitled to any compensation under this Agreement.

Signed: _____ (Owner)   Date:

_____ (User)   Date:

(continued)

A significant amount of litigation has ensued over the use of copyrighted photos in thumbnail size as a means of providing a website-content preview for consumers using an Internet search engine or linking to another page via the thumbnail image. The idea, of course, is to allow consumers who are searching for a particular image to scan multiple images and choose the appropriate one, rather than having to link to the actual pages to view the photos, thus saving the consumer user time.

Copying the image of another is clearly infringement. For example, if Best Furniture, a large retailer of patio furniture, takes photographs of its products and displays them on its website, the use of those photos by a competing retailer on the retailer's own website (or in a catalog for that matter) is clearly illegal. However, let's suppose that a website that is hosted by Patio and Deck Contractors Inc. provides thumbnail images of Best Furniture's patio furniture photos on its website with a link to Best Furniture's site as a service to Patio and Deck Contractors' customers. In this instance, the use of the images is legal under the fair use exception to the Copyright Act.

An overwhelming majority of courts have ruled that use of thumbnail photograph images by Internet websites has "transformed" the original photograph in such a way as to make the use of the images legal.

---

useful improvement. An important subcategory of utility patents is the business method patent, which is discussed in more detail later in this section.

The patent issued to the Wright brothers in 1906 for their flying machine began a new era in global commerce.

- *Design patents* cover primarily the invention of new ornamental designs for manufacture.
- *Plant patents* are the least frequently issued type of patents and cover the invention or discovery of asexually or sexually reproducible plants (such as flowers).

A patent for inventions or processes (utility and business method patents) lasts for a period of 20 years from the date of filing the application with the USPTO. A design patent lasts for 14 years.

In order to be patented, an invention must be *novel* and *nonobvious* and be a *proper subject matter* for protection under the patent law.

Novelty Standard

An invention or process must be unique and original, and a patent applicant must show that no other identical invention or process exists. The statute delineates the guidelines for this **novelty standard** based on a three-prong test. The first prong is the public use test and requires that the invention or process *not already be* in public use. The second prong governs priority for inventors of the same invention or process. The United States recognizes the first inventor-to-file rule in which patent rights are granted to the first inventor to file a patent application. The first inventor to file then has priority over other inventors of the same product. The final prong requires a determination by the USPTO that the applicant filed the patent within a reasonable time of the invention. Landmark Case 25.5 sets out the public use test of the novelty standard.

FACT SUMMARY DuPont chemical company produced a chemical known as Surlyn in 1964. Before DuPont found a commercial use for it, Butch Wagner, who was in the business of selling re-covered golf balls, began to experiment with Surlyn as a golf ball cover. In November 1964 he developed the formula so that it was suitable to give unprecedented durability to a golf ball, and he began to sell the Surlyn-covered balls that same year. Wagner never applied for a patent. Subsequently, Dunlop obtained a patent for Surlyn-covered golf balls, and when RAM began to produce the same type of golf balls, Dunlop sued RAM for infringement. RAM defended its use by challenging Dunlop's patent as invalid because Wagner had made the invention public 10 years earlier via his sale of many Surlyn-covered balls to a group of regular customers. Dunlop countered that Wagner had concealed an important ingredient and, thus, had concealed the actual invention from the public. The trial court agreed with RAM, holding that Wagner's public use barred Dunlop from obtaining a patent.

SYNOPSIS OF DECISION AND OPINION The appellate court affirmed the ruling of the trial court against Dunlop. The court held that Wagner's golf balls coated with the Surlyn-based invention were in public use because Wagner had marketed and sold the items as best he could as a sole proprietor. The court also ruled that the fact that Wagner did not reveal a key ingredient of the invention to the public was not relevant. Thus, Dunlop could not pass the first prong of the novelty standard (public use test) and was not entitled to a patent.

WORDS OF THE COURT: Public Use Test "The patent claims are broad enough to encompass any golf ball cover made principally of Surlyn, and there is no doubt that Wagner had made a large number of such golf balls and successfully placed them in public use. The only novel feature of this case arises from the fact that Wagner was careful not to disclose to the public the ingredient that made his golf ball so tough. . . . But in this case, although Wagner may have failed to act diligently to establish his own right to a patent, there was no lack of diligence in his attempt to make the benefits of his discovery available to the public. . . . [T]he evidence clearly demonstrates that Wagner endeavored to market his golf balls as promptly and effectively as possible. The balls themselves were in wide public use."

Case Questions

1. What factors did the court consider in ruling that Wagner's use was public?

2. What is Dunlop's theory as to why Wagner's conduct did not make the prior use public?

Nonobviousness Standard

The **nonobviousness standard** requires that an invention must be something more than that which would be obvious, in light of publicly available knowledge, to one who is skilled in the relevant field. In other words, a patent cannot be granted for minimal improvements that were relatively obvious to those in the field. For example, Joanna adds a small extender switch to her lawn mower (an existing patented invention) that will make it easier for taller people to kill the engine. Joanna is not entitled to a new patent because the invention is essentially a minimal (also called *de minimus*) improvement and relatively obvious.

Patentable Subject Matter Standard

Note that not all processes and inventions that are nonobvious and novel are patentable. The **patentable subject matter standard** bars laws of nature, natural phenomena, and abstract ideas from being patentable. Albert Einstein's theory of relativity was groundbreaking. It was new and nonobvious beyond question. But should this natural phenomenon be patentable? The patent system was not intended to cover every novel and nonobvious idea. The courts have held that some mathematical algorithms, materials common to nature (penicillin, for example), and unapplied ideas are not patentable. Ultimately, patent laws cover processes and ideas based on human ingenuity.

Business Method Patents   Because of the exclusion of certain subject matter from patent protection, courts have historically struggled with the notion of giving patent protection to a process developed by a business in the name of efficiency or some competitive advantage. Some courts rejected novel, useful, and commercially successful business methods as nonpatentable subject matter. However, in 1998, a federal appeals court helped settle many issues related to business method patents and provided guidance for other courts in the landmark case of *State Street Bank & Trust Co. v. Signature Financial Group*.[28] The *State Street* court articulated a cogent legal theory whereby business methods may be patentable so long as they accomplish something practically useful in a novel and nonobvious way. The case also provided a road map for the emerging Internet business community to plan Internet business models in such a way as to be eligible for patent protection. More recently, the U.S. Supreme Court upheld the notion that business methods, such as a system that institutions could use to hedge the seasonal risks of buying energy, were patentable.[29]

Design Patents   Patent laws also protect inventors of any new, original, and ornamental design for an article of manufacture. Design patents are subject to the same requirements as those for utility or business method patents (novelty and nonobvious), and the design must be primarily ornamental (not primarily functional). Design patents are mainly concerned with protecting the appearance of an article. The shape of the classic Coca-Cola bottle is a famous example of a design based primarily on appearance, not function.

LO 25-8   INFRINGEMENT, NOTICE, AND REMEDIES

Infringement is defined in the Patent Act in this way: "[W]hoever without authority makes, uses or sells any patented invention, within the United States during the term of the patent therefore, infringes the patent." Anyone who "actively induces infringement" of a patent is considered an infringer as well. Infringement occurs in one of two ways: as *literal infringement* or through *equivalence*.

Literal Infringement

The courts have developed three rules for determining whether **literal patent infringement** has occurred. The **rule of exactness** applies when the infringer makes, uses, or sells an invention that is exactly the same as the patent holder's claims in the patent application, thus infringing on the patent. An infringement also occurs if the infringing device does *more* than is described in the patent application of the protected invention. This literal infringement is known as the **rule of addition.** Under the **rule of omission,** however, when the alleged infringing invention lacks an essential element of the patent holder's claims in the patent application, infringement has *not* occurred.

Equivalence

The rule of omission is subject to abuse because individuals may avoid infringement liability by omitting an element of the patented device and substituting another element that is substantially similar but not exact. To prevent this abuse, the Supreme Court developed a doctrine that allowed courts to find infringement if the invention performs *substantially*

---

[28]149 F.3d 1368 (Fed. Cir. 1998). The case involved a challenge to a patent issued to Signature for a process that facilitated a method whereby several mutual funds pooled their investments into a single fund that achieved management cost savings over many other funds.

[29]*Bilski v. Kappos*, 130 S.Ct. 3218 (2010).

Computer Software and Internet Business Methods

Computer Programs   Of course, technology continues to give us new challenges as to what is and what is not patentable material. In the early 1970s, the Supreme Court took the view that computer programs and the machines that process them are nothing more than glorified algorithms and, therefore, not patentable. But in 1981, the Court decided *Diamond v. Diehr*[30] and "clarified" (some would say reversed) its position, ruling that some computer programs could be patented. Eventually, the courts developed a test to determine whether algorithm-based computer programming was patentable. The test was designed to investigate whether the computer-related process was applied in some fashion to physical elements or processes. In other words, did the algorithm allow a certain physical transformation to take place? If the computer programs were accompanied by some physical transformation, then they were patentable.

Internet Business Method Patents   After the court opened the door to business method patents in the 1998 *State Street* case (discussed earlier), many Internet-based businesses applied for patents. According to the USPTO, the number of patent applications for Internet business methods has increased nearly 800 percent. One of the most famous Internet business method patents was granted to Amazon for its "One-Click" ordering system that stores a customer's billing and shipping information so it does not have to be reentered on subsequent visits to the site. In a highly publicized case during the technology boom of the late 1990s, Amazon (still a relative newcomer in the bookselling business at the time) sued mega-bookseller Barnes and Noble over Barnes and Noble's use of an "Express Lane" option on its website that was similar to Amazon's patent in that the feature allowed consumers to "buy it now with just 1 click." Barnes and Noble defended on the basis that the patent should not have been issued because the invention was too obvious. After a preliminary defeat in the federal courts for Amazon,[31] the parties settled the dispute in March 2002. Although Amazon lost on what was essentially thought of as a procedural issue, one important victory was that it did *not* lose the patent on the basis of nonobviousness. Therefore, the court signaled that Internet business methods, so long as they fit the requirements for other utility and method patents, were protectable.

In some cases though, courts have been reluctant to enforce business method patents in the technology sector when the process described in the patent is too narrow due to the lack of technology at the time of the patent. In 2002, a California college professor sued Netscape, Microsoft, and AOL for infringing on a patent he obtained relating to efficiency in website interactivity. The federal appeals court affirmed the ruling of the trial court, which found that the professor's patents were invalid altogether and that the patent description was too generic to be enforceable.[32]

[30] 450 U.S. 175 (1981). The case involved a patent application for a computer program that facilitated molding uncured synthetic rubber into cured rubber. According to the patent application, the process differed from the previously employed method because of the use of specific mathematical formulas, which would allow for more accurate measuring of material heating and feeding times. The patent was rejected by the USPTO because the patent examiner did not find that the process met the subject matter requirements of the Patent Act.

[31] *Amazon.com, Inc. v. Barnesandnoble.com, Inc.,* 239 F.3d 1343 (Fed. Cir. 2001).

[32] *Netscape Corp. v. Konrad,* 295 F.3d 1315 (Fed. Cir. 2002).

the same function in substantially the same way to achieve the same result. The doctrine, known as the **doctrine of equivalence,** however, is limited to an evaluation of whether any of the key elements of the claim have been interchanged with known equivalents.

The Patent Act sets forth appropriate measures that must be taken to properly inform users that an article is patented. This is often done by placing the word *patent,* the abbreviation *pat.,* or the patent number on the specific article. If no marking is identifiable, then the patentee is unable to collect damages from infringers unless they were properly warned and still continued to infringe.

Patent infringers are subject to the following damages:

- *Actual damages:* Examples include profit from lost sales and royalties for any sale made by the infringer.
- *Prejudgment interest:* It is not uncommon for years to pass before an infringer is spotted; thus, revenue from possible sales may have been withheld from the patentee for a long period of time.
- *Attorney fees:* The prevailing party may receive reasonable attorney fees when the infringer has acted in bad faith (i.e., had received notice that the invention was patented and yet continued his infringing conduct).

CONCEPT SUMMARY Patents

- A patent is a government-sanctioned monopoly right that allows an inventor the exclusive rights over an invention or method for a limited period of time.
- In order to be patented, the invention or method must be novel and nonobvious and be of proper subject matter (natural phenomena are not protected under patent laws).
- Some business methods are patentable so long as they accomplish something practically useful in a novel and nonobvious way.
- Infringement may occur either through literal means or through equivalence.

TABLE 25.2 Intellectual Property Protections

Type	Coverage	Source of Law	Example	Duration
Trade secrets	Secret processes, formulas, methods, procedures, and lists that provide the owner with economic advantage.	State statutes based on Uniform Trade Secret Act and/or state common law	Customer lists with contact information, buying patterns, and credit histories	Life of the owner (entity or individual)
Trademarks, service marks, trade dress	Words, symbols, or phrases that identify a particular seller's product or service and distinguish it from other products and services. Trade dress extends trademark protection to the shape or color scheme of a product.	Federal statute (Lanham Act) and some state and federal common law	Google (trademark) Hilton Hotels (service mark) iPod's shape (trade dress)	Unlimited so long as the owner actively protects ("polices") the use of the mark
Copyrights	Authors and originators of literary or artistic production.	Federal statute (Copyright Act of 1976, as amended)	Rights of a recording artist and writer of a song	*Author:* 70 years from death of the author *Work for hire:* 120 years from date of creation or 95 years from publication
Patents	Inventors, for exclusive rights to make, use, license, or sell an invention.	Federal statute (Patent Act)	Rights to a newly discovered pharmaceutical	20 years from date of filing except for design patents (14 years)

Misappropriation p. 682 (1) The acquisition of a trade secret of another by a person who knows or has reason to know that the trade secret was acquired by improper means or (2) the disclosure of a trade secret to another without express or implied consent.

Economic Espionage Act p. 682 A federal statute passed in 1996 that provides criminal penalties for domestic and foreign theft of trade secrets.

Trademark p. 683 A nonfunctional, distinctive word, name, shape, symbol, phrase, or combination of words and symbols that helps consumers to distinguish one product from another.

Service mark p. 683 A word, symbol, or phrase used to identify a particular seller's services and distinguish them from other services.

Trade dress p. 683 A product's distinctive design, packaging, color, or other characteristic that makes it unique from other products or goods.

Secondary meaning p. 685 A requirement for a descriptive trademark to gain protection; acquired when the consuming public primarily associates the mark with a particular product or service rather than with the ordinary meaning of the term.

Bad faith p. 686 A dishonesty of belief or purpose; in the legal context, a concept in which a malicious motive on the part of the defendant in a lawsuit is necessary in order for the plaintiff to recover. Under the Anticybersquatting Consumer Protection Act, the court looks to nine factors in making a determination of bad-faith intent.

Federal Trademark Dilution Act p. 690 A federal law enacted in 1995, and amended in 2006, that permits mark holders to recover damages and prevent others from diluting distinctive trademarks.

Originality p. 692 For copyright protection, the requirement that the author must use his own creative capabilities to create the work or medium.

Creativity p. 692 For copyright protection of a compilation, the requirement that there must be some creative element used that made the compilation an original work.

Durable medium p. 692 For copyright protection, the requirement that the work must be in a tangible form, such as writing, digital, video, and so forth.

Direct infringement p. 693 A theory of copyright infringement under which the copyright owner proves that she has legal ownership of the work in question and that the infringer copied the work in a substantially similar manner without permission.

Indirect infringement p. 693 A theory of copyright infringement under which a third-party facilitator is liable for damages when the facilitator has knowledge of the infringement and/or contributes to the infringement in some material way. Also called *contributory infringement.*

Vicarious infringement p. 694 A theory of copyright infringement that applies when there has been a direct infringement and a third-party facilitator is in a position to control that infringement and benefits financially from it.

No Electronic Theft (NET) Act p. 694 A federal law enacted in 1997 that provides for criminal liability for anyone who willfully infringes on a copyright.

Fair use p. 694 A defense against copyright infringement under which the court examines the purpose and nature of the use, the nature of the work, the amount used, and the market effect of the use to determine whether the use is permitted.

Per se p. 694 (Latin for "of, in, or by itself") A standard used by courts when no additional facts are needed to prove a point.

Novelty standard p. 700 A standard requiring that an invention or process must be unique and original to be patented and that the patent applicant must show that no other identical invention or process exists.

Nonobviousness standard p. 701 A standard requiring that to be patented, an invention must be something more than that which would be obvious, in light of publicly available knowledge, to one who is skilled in the relevant field.

Patentable subject matter standard p. 701 A standard that bars laws of nature, natural phenomena, and abstract ideas from being patentable subject matter.

Literal patent infringement p. 702 Patent infringement in which the invention or process violates either the rule of exactness or the rule of addition.

Rule of exactness p. 702   The principle that literal patent infringement has occurred when the infringer makes, uses, or sells an invention that is exactly the same as the patent holder's claims in the patent application.

Rule of addition p. 702   The principle that literal patent infringement has occurred when the infringing device does more than is described in the patent application of the protected invention.

Rule of omission p. 702   The principle that infringement has not occurred when the alleged patent-infringing invention lacks an essential element of the patent holder's claims in the patent application.

Doctrine of equivalence p. 703   A doctrine that allows courts to find patent infringement when an invention, compared with a patented device, performs substantially the same function in substantially the same way to achieve the same result.

THEORY TO PRACTICE

WidgetCo is a manufacturer and wholesaler of a line of widget products with annual revenue of $50 million. Maurice, a midlevel manager at WidgetCo, supervises a work team responsible for assessing quality assurance for the widgets before they are shipped to various retailers around the United States. Maurice and his group have been highly successful in developing a quality assurance process, including the development of training manuals, a video series for new employees, and specific checklists and procedures to ensure that any defective or substandard widgets are detected and repaired prior to shipping.

1. Which forms of intellectual property protections are available to WidgetCo to protect the quality assurance process and materials that Maurice's team has developed?

2. What are the major advantages and disadvantages of each protection?

3. Compare the facts of the hypothetical in this Theory to Practice with the standards for qualification of a trade secret. Could the process be considered a trade secret under these standards?

4. What steps could the company take to achieve its objective of having the process protected under trade secret laws and avoid misappropriation?

5. If WidgetCo wants copyright protection for its manuals and training video series, how will it obtain protection under the Copyright Act? If the manuals are simply a compilation of facts known in the industry, are they protectable?

MANAGER'S CHALLENGE

One major consideration in protecting a trade secret is the efforts by the company to keep the secret confidential. Develop a written policy for WidgetCo (in the Theory to Practice problem) to help ensure that these trade secrets and materials will be protected and kept confidential under the Uniform Trade Secrets Act. What considerations should management take into account when developing a policy on trade secrets? Be sure to think about primary stakeholders (such as employees who may depart with the trade secrets) and secondary stakeholders (such as third-party visitors or outside auditors that may be privy to the processes and materials). Note that this is not intended to be a legal document. Rather, the policy should be thought of as a draft statement of internal control on trade secrets, processes, and materials. A sample answer may be found on this textbook's website at www.mhhe.com/melvinleb2e.

TRADE SECRET

Harvey Bennett, Inc., is a company that developed a method designed to be taught to infants on how to survive in the water. The company developed a course in this technique, called *swim-float-swim,* and generated revenue by training and certifying instructors who then teach the technique to the public at large for a fee. The instructors are trained extensively on the nearly 2,000 procedures necessary to accomplish the technique. All instructors signed a nondisclosure form and an agreement not to compete. When several of the instructors resigned and formed a venture called Aquatic Survival, Bennett filed suit claiming, among other allegations, misappropriation of the swim-float-swim system.

CASE QUESTIONS

1. Does the swim-float-swim technique qualify as a trade secret?
2. What factors would the court use to assess whether the technique is a trade secret? Discuss.

TRADEMARKS/SERVICE MARKS

Reed Elsevier operated a website that allowed users to identify an attorney by using a variety of criteria, including geographic location, practice expertise, and so forth. The website, www.lawyers.com, was first used in commerce by Reed in 1998. Later, Reed applied to have lawyers.com registered as a service mark.

CASE QUESTIONS

1. Is the mark too generic for protection?
2. If the court determines the mark is primarily descriptive, what further obstacle must Reed overcome in order to obtain protection for the mark?

PATENTS

KSR designs and manufactures auto parts and sells them to auto manufacturers (not consumers), and it developed a pedal device for Ford vehicles. KSR received a patent on the pedal device. KSR also sold products to General Motors (GM), and, in order to make the pedal device compatible for GM cars, KSR added an electronic throttle control to the pedal device. Teleflex claimed to have a patent for the pedal device that could be connected to such a throttle and, therefore, sued KSR for patent infringement. KSR defended on the basis that the device produced for GM was simply a combination of two existing products and could not be patentable.

CASE QUESTIONS

1. What do you think Teleflex's specific theory of infringement was?
2. Which element of patentability does KSR claim Teleflex is missing in the combined device?

COPYRIGHT

Darden filed an application with the Copyright Office, seeking to register his website, which he titled, "APPRAISERSdotCOM." He described APPRAISERSdotCOM as a derivative work based on "U.S. Census black and white outline maps" and "clip art." Darden's application identified "graphics, text, colors, and arrangement" as the material that he added to the preexisting work and for which he claimed copyright protection. Additionally, Darden filed a separate application for registration of the work "Maps for APPRAISERSdotCOM." Darden described his "maps" work as a derivative work that, similar to the APPRAISERSdotCOM work, was based on preexisting U.S. Census black-and-white outline maps.

CASE QUESTIONS

1. Determine whether Darden's compilation is protectable using the *Feist* doctrine.
2. Does Darden's idea contain the necessary elements for copyright protection? Discuss.

✅ Self-Check **ANSWERS**

Trade Secrets

1. This type of customer data is protectable as a trade secret because of its potential value to a competitor.
2. The system is probably not protectable unless it is something highly unique. But the basis of scheduling medical appointments is not typically protectable.
3. Formulas are protectable.
4. Unless the process is highly unique, it is not protectable because it is based on a public source.
5. Software source coding is protectable.

Fair Use

1. Covered by fair use. Limited amount used, noncommercial use, and minimal market effect support the fair use defense.
2. Not covered by fair use. Market effect and commercial nature of the use would exclude it from the fair use defense.
3. Probably not fair use. The market effect would determine this question, but the commercial nature and the fact that it is the entire DVD would weigh against fair use as a defense.
4. Not fair use. Commercial nature, profit motive, amount and substantiality used, and market effect would bar any use of fair use in this case.

26

CHAPTER

International Law and Global Commerce

learning **objectives**

After studying this chapter, students who have mastered the material will be able to:

26-1 Distinguish between international public law and international private law.

26-2 Give examples of and explain the various sources that compose the body of international law.

26-3 Explain the role of the various international courts.

26-4 List the different categories of national legal systems used in the world and give an example of a country in each category.

26-5 Apply the standards of the Convention on the Recognition and Enforcement of Foreign Arbitral Awards.

26-6 Explain the various methods of alternate dispute resolution in an international context.

26-7 Articulate several specific laws that regulate international commercial law and understand when each law applies.

26-8 Identify the methods used to enforce the rights of intellectual property holders in foreign countries.

Rapid developments in technology, improvements in export logistics, and creation of additional transportation lines have all been catalysts that propelled our modern global economy. Although large multinational firms have had international business relationships and systems for decades, the new global marketplace has been expanded dramatically to include midsize and smaller firms that see international markets as an accessible vehicle for market share growth. Of course, while the potential return may be significant, the risks, especially legal risks, increase substantially in an international business transaction. A working knowledge of international law helps business owners and managers with global interests reduce risk and increase profits. In this chapter, students will learn:

- The definition and sources of international law.
- International dispute resolution methods.
- Commercial and intellectual property regulation in an international context.

DEFINITION, SOURCES, AND SYSTEMS OF INTERNATIONAL LAW   LO 26-1

International law has traditionally been defined in very broad terms and not limited simply to rules that are applied to settle disputes in court. Rather, international law is influenced by a combination of law, religious tenets, and diplomatic relations between nations. This broad definition makes enforcement of international laws challenging, and adherence to international law is sometimes based on expectations of reciprocal behavior rather than legal sanctions.

Most legal sources define modern international law as a body of *rules* and *principles* of action binding on countries, international organizations, and individuals in their relations with one another.[1]

Public Law versus Private Law

One important distinction necessary to understanding international law is that it may be categorized as either **public international law**, which primarily addresses relations between individual countries and international organizations, and **private international law**, which focuses on regulation of private individuals and business entities.

SOURCES OF INTERNATIONAL LAW   LO 26-2

In one sense, the primary source of international law is the body of law in each individual country. However, international law can also provide

---

[1] *Restatement (Third) of the Foreign Relations Law of the United States* § 102.

individual countries with some degree of harmonized standards that increase reliability and encourage fairness, due process, and barrier-free trade among nations. Therefore, treaties, customs, and judicial decisions are also considered to be sources of international law.

Treaties A treaty is any agreement between two or more nations to cooperate in a certain manner. Treaties may be related to defense, trade, extradition, and other matters between countries. Although treaties have been in use since before the Roman Empire, most existing modern-day treaties were created after World War II. More recently, the **Vienna Convention on the Law of Treaties**, effective in 1980, has become one of the standards used by courts and other tribunals when interpreting treaty law.[2]

Customs Along with treaty law, customary international law is a primary source of law affecting individuals and businesses engaged in international transactions. Customary law follows the basic principle of international law that individual conduct is permitted unless expressly forbidden. Therefore, prohibitions as well as affirmative practices must be proved by the state relying on them.

Judicial Decisions Most treaties and national laws recognize both an international tribunal, such as the International Court of Justice (discussed later), and a ruling by a national court applying international law principles. One important concept related to judicial decisions as a source of international law is *comity*. **Comity** is the general notion that nations will defer to and give effect to the laws and court decisions of other nations. However, comity is not a legal doctrine that requires courts to accept the judgments of foreign courts. Rather, it is rooted in the idea that reciprocal treatment is a necessary element of international relations. In Case 26.1, a federal court considers the concept of comity when ruling on whether a foreign court's judgment is enforceable in the United States.

KEY POINT
The three primary sources of international law are treaties, customs, and judicial decisions.

INTERNATIONAL ORGANIZATIONS

International organizations play a unique role in the development of international law. These organizations are typically structured through use of multinational representation and are created and regulated by treaty. Perhaps the most famous organization is the **United Nations (U.N.)**, which was created after World War II to facilitate common international concerns on defense, trade, protection of human rights, and other matters. From a business perspective, the U.N. has made significant achievements in harmonizing laws related to the sale of goods between businesses in different countries and other international business transactions. The U.N. Commission on International Trade Law developed the **U.N. Convention on Contracts for the International Sale of Goods (CISG)**, which is used to set rules for certain business transactions. The CISG is discussed in more detail later in this chapter.

Other important international organizations include:

- The World Trade Organization (WTO), which promotes and has certain authority over disputes involving trade barriers.
- The International Monetary Fund (IMF), which is intended to promote stability of world currencies and provide temporary assistance for countries to help prevent the collapse of their economies.

---

[2]The U.S. has not yet ratified the Vienna Convention, but the U.S. government has recognized it as an authoritative source to guide tribunals in matters related to treaty law.

FACT SUMMARY   La Ligue Contre Le Racisme et L'Antisemitisme (LICRA) and L'Union des Etudiants Juifs de France, citizens of France, are nonprofit organizations dedicated to eliminating anti-Semitism. Yahoo!, Inc., operates various Internet websites and services that any computer user can access at the uniform resource locator (URL) www.yahoo.com. Yahoo! subsidiary corporations operate regional Yahoo! sites and services in many other nations, including France.

Yahoo!'s auction site allows anyone to post an item for sale and solicit bids from any computer user around the globe. Yahoo! monitors the transaction through limited regulation by prohibiting particular items from being sold (such as stolen goods, body parts, prescription and illegal drugs, weapons, and goods violating U.S. copyright laws or embargoes). Yahoo! informs auction sellers that they must comply with Yahoo!'s policies and may not offer items to buyers in jurisdictions in which the sale of such items violates the jurisdiction's applicable laws. Yahoo! does not actively regulate the content of each posting, and individuals are able to post, and have in fact posted, highly offensive memorabilia, including Nazi objects.

LICRA filed suit against Yahoo! in France based on a French law banning the sale of Nazi- and Third Reich–related goods through auction services. The French court concluded that the Yahoo.com auction site violated the French Criminal Code, which prohibits exhibition of Nazi propaganda and artifacts for sale.

Yahoo! contends that such a ban would infringe impermissibly upon its rights under the First Amendment to the U.S. Constitution. Accordingly, Yahoo! filed a lawsuit in a U.S. federal district court seeking a declaratory judgment that the French court's orders are neither cognizable nor enforceable under the laws of the United States.

SYNOPSIS OF DECISION AND OPINION   The district court ruled in favor of Yahoo!, holding that U.S. courts were not bound by judgments of foreign courts when the judgment is inconsistent with the Constitution and laws of the United States. The court reasoned that because the display of Nazi memorabilia could not be prohibited in the United States because of First Amendment concerns, a U.S. court cannot honor a foreign judgment that would violate the Constitution were it to be applied in the United States. Moreover, although France has the sovereign right to regulate what speech is permissible in France, U.S. courts may not enforce a foreign order that violates the protections of the U.S. Constitution by regulating protected speech that occurs simultaneously within U.S. and French borders. The court based its authority on the concept of comity.

WORDS OF THE COURT: Comity   "[According to our federal law] [n]o legal judgment has any effect, of its own force, beyond the limits of the sovereignty from which its authority is derived. Although the United States Constitution and implementing legislation require that full faith and credit be given to judgments of sister states, territories, and possessions of the United States, the extent to which the United States, or any state, honors the judicial decrees of foreign nations is a matter of choice, governed by the comity of nations. Comity is neither a matter of absolute obligation, on the one hand, nor of mere courtesy and good will, upon the other."

Case Questions

1. Why did Yahoo! choose to obtain a declaratory judgment from a U.S. court rather than appeal the ruling in the French courts?

2. In effect, isn't the U.S. court ruling that the U.S. Constitution protects American companies even when they do business in a foreign country that does not recognize the concepts embodied by our First Amendment?

[3] It is important to note that an appellate court subsequently reversed the decision of this court on procedural grounds. The appellate court let stand the court's substantive reasoning regarding the concept of comity and ultimately agreed with much of the trial court's holding but ruled that the case should be dismissed on grounds unrelated to the comity analysis. *Yahoo! v. La Ligue Contre Le Racisme et L'Antisemitisme*, 433 F.3d 1199 (7th Cir. 2006).

■ The Organization for Economic Cooperation and Development (OEDC), which coordinates aid to developing countries and takes steps toward eliminating bribery and other corruption from developing economies.

INTERNATIONAL COURTS

International courts play a role in the development and interpretation of international law, but their power to enforce a ruling on sovereign nations can be tenuous and their jurisdiction may be limited.

The **International Court of Justice** (also known as the *World Court*) is the judicial branch of the United Nations. It is based in the Netherlands and its main functions are to settle legal disputes submitted to it by member states and give advisory opinions on legal questions submitted to it by duly authorized international organs, agencies, and the U.N. General Assembly. This court should not be confused with the International Criminal Court, which also potentially has global jurisdiction. Established in 1945 by the U.N. Charter, the World Court began work in 1946 as the successor to the Permanent Court of International Justice. The Statute of the International Court of Justice, similar to that of its predecessor, is the main constitutional document constituting and regulating the Court.

The Court's workload is characterized by a wide range of judicial activity. The Court has dealt with relatively few cases in its history, but there has clearly been an increased willingness to use the Court since the 1980s, especially among developing countries. The United States withdrew from compulsory jurisdiction in 1986, and so it accepts the court's jurisdiction only on a case-by-case basis. The U.N. Charter authorizes the U.N. Security Council to enforce rulings, but such enforcement is subject to the veto power of the five permanent members of the Security Council.

The **European Court of Justice** sits in Luxembourg and is the final arbiter of the codes governing European Union (EU) member countries. The court is composed of judges from each EU member country and is structured in a civil law tradition, so most of its procedures and decisions are based on treaties governing EU countries regarding commercial regulations, protections, and guarantees. National courts of EU members are

The World Court, seen here in session in The Hague, Netherlands, is one of the principal international courts.

obliged by treaty to honor the decisions of the court and are obligated to apply EU laws (known as *community laws*).

Sovereign Immunity

One of the oldest doctrines of international law is that of **sovereign immunity**. In general, this doctrine holds that, with some exceptions, nations are exempt from jurisdiction by other nations' courts. The **Foreign Sovereign Immunities Act (FSIA)** is a federal statute that incorporates this concept by explicitly prohibiting U.S. courts from rendering judicial actions against foreign nations or their government officials unless (1) the foreign nation has waived its immunity either explicitly or by implication, (2) the foreign nation is engaged in some commercial enterprise on U.S. soil, or (3) the foreign nation's actions have a direct effect on U.S. interests.

One implication of the FSIA for U.S. businesses occurs in the context of companies that provide services to foreign governments. To what extent are they protected by federal law, such as employment discrimination protections, when they are carrying out their contractual obligations to the foreign government? A federal appeals court considers that question in Case 26.2.

LEGAL SYSTEMS OF NATIONS

LO 26-4

Legal systems of the world may be thought of as falling into one of the following broad categories: civil law, common law, religious-based law (such as Sharia law or Talmudic law), and mixed law systems (which refers not to a single system but to a combination of systems).

Civil Law Systems

Countries using **civil law systems** have drawn their body of law largely from the Roman law heritage, which uses written law as the highest source, and have opted for a systematic codification of their general law. They rely heavily on written codes to define their laws and do not favor the notion of courts filling in any gaps in the statutes. Rather, courts apply the code law to individual cases without the mandate of following cases that were decided by previous courts considering the same questions. Most European, Latin American, African, and Asian countries use civil law systems.

Common Law Systems

The common law system takes on a variety of cultural and legal forms throughout the world. Although there are differences from country to country, this category generally includes countries whose law, for the most part, is technically based on English common law concepts and legal organizational methods that strongly favor use of case law, as opposed to legislation, as the ordinary means of expressions of general law. If there is no case law to guide the court, common law systems allow courts to fill in the gaps not covered by statutes and may create new law consistent with public policy. Common law jurisdictions adhere to the concept of judicial review, whereby a court may strike down a law passed by the legislature if the law is found to violate some other overriding principle of law (such as the U.S. Constitution). As you may imagine, the common law tradition is used by countries that were once colonies or protectorates of Great Britain, including the United States, Canada, and Australia.

Religious-Based Legal Systems

Religious-based legal systems are legal doctrines and guidelines directly based on certain religious tenets. For example, the Sharia, derived from the Qur'an (the scared text of Islam) regulates many aspects of life for Muslims, including crime, politics, business

FACT SUMMARY Vance International is a U.S. company that provides security services to corporations and foreign sovereigns, including the Kingdom of Saudi Arabia. Vance was hired to augment the security provided to a princess of the Saudi royal family while the princess underwent medical treatments in California. The Saudi military was responsible for protection, and Saudi military officers supervised all security at the site.

Butters, a woman employed by Vance as a security officer, was assigned to the Saudi detail and, on several occasions, Butters temporarily worked as an acting supervisor in a security command post. Vance managers recommended to the Saudis that Butters be promoted to serving a full rotation in the command post, but the Saudi authorities rejected that recommendation. Their rejection was based on the Saudi military supervisor's contention that the appointment of a woman for that post was unacceptable under Islamic law and that Saudis would consider it inappropriate for their officers to spend long periods of time in a command post with a woman present.

Butters brought suit against Vance for gender discrimination in the loss of the promotion, and Vance asserted immunity under the Federal Sovereign Immunities Act because it was carrying out orders of the Saudi government. Butters argued that Vance fell under one of the exceptions to the FSIA because the company was engaged in a commercial activity.

SYNOPSIS OF DECISION AND OPINION The Fourth Circuit Court of Appeals ruled in favor of Vance. The court reasoned that Vance was entitled to immunity from suit under the Foreign Sovereign Immunities Act because Vance's client, the Kingdom of Saudi Arabia, was responsible for Butters' not being promoted. The court held that the action here was not exempt from the FSIA as "commercial activities" because the relevant act was quintessentially an act peculiar to sovereigns and that Vance was entitled to derivative immunity under the FSIA because it was following Saudi Arabia's orders not to promote Butters.

WORDS OF THE COURT: Impact of Sovereign Immunity "Any type of governmental immunity reflects a trade-off between the possibility that an official's wrongdoing will remain unpunished and the risk that government functions will be impaired. The resolution of immunity questions inherently requires a balance between the evils inevitable in any available alternative. FSIA immunity presupposes a tolerance for the sovereign decisions of other countries that may reflect legal norms and cultural values quite different from our own. Here Saudi Arabia made a decision to protect a member of its royal family in a manner consistent with Islamic law and custom. The Act requires not that we approve of the diverse cultural or political motivations that may underlie another sovereign's acts, but that we respect them."

Case Questions

1. How far does the FSIA immunity go? If one of Vance's employees was ordered by Saudi officials to physically detain Butters and she was injured, would Vance still be protected by the FSIA against any liability resulting from Butters's injury?

2. When the court states that the "FSIA immunity presupposes a tolerance for the sovereign decisions of other countries that may reflect legal norms and cultural values quite different from our own," what legal norms and cultural values is it referring to?

transactions, family, sexuality, and hygiene. The Sharia is the centerpiece of Islamic law, which is now the most widely used religious-based legal system. Islamic law is interpreted by religious leaders and is carried out by a government body.

Mixed Legal Systems

Mixed legal systems (also known as *hybrid* or *composite legal systems*) include not only political entities in which two or more systems apply cumulatively or interactively but also entities in which there is a combination of systems as a result of more or less clearly defined fields of application. For example, Saudi Arabia uses Islamic-based law to regulate personal conduct of its citizens and visitors and uses a civil law system to regulate business transactions and other areas of the law.

INTERNATIONAL DISPUTE RESOLUTION

The parties to an international dispute are typically corporations or government entities, rather than private individuals, while domestic dispute resolution can involve relatively small claims by individuals. Many countries, recognizing that different considerations apply to international disputes, have provided for a separate legal regime to govern international dispute resolution.

Arbitration

Arbitration is considered international if the parties to the arbitration are of different nationalities or the subject matter of the dispute involves a state other than the country in which the parties are nationals. An international arbitration usually has no connection with the country in which the arbitration is being held, other than the fact that it is taking place on its territory.

The major difference between international and domestic arbitrations is that international arbitration awards have very wide enforceability in many countries. This is largely attributable to the acceptance of international treaties such as the 1958 **Convention on the Recognition and Enforcement of Foreign Arbitral Awards**, which allows for the enforcement of arbitration awards in many major countries provided that the arbitration is international.

International Arbitration Forums

Prominent bodies that administer arbitrations include the International Chamber of Commerce's (ICC's) International Court of Arbitration in Paris, the London Court of International Arbitration (LCIA), and the American Arbitration Association (AAA). Each of these institutions has formulated its own arbitration rules; namely, the ICC Rules of Arbitration, the LCIA Rules, and the AAA International Arbitration Rules. Except for the AAA, which provides that its International Arbitration Rules apply only in the absence of any designated rules, the other two sets of institutional rules are applied to the arbitrations administered by the arbitration bodies.

All the institutional rules govern the commencement of the arbitration, exchange of arbitration pleadings, appointment and removal of arbitrators, and hearing and interim measures of protection, among other rules. If parties have not agreed on the number of arbitrators, one arbitrator is appointed, although the arbitration institution may appoint three arbitrators if it appears that the dispute warrants it.

In terms of the choice of arbitrator, the LCIA Rules provide that it, alone, is empowered to appoint arbitrators, although arbitrators will be appointed with due regard to any criteria for selection agreed to by the parties in writing. The ICC Rules of Arbitration allow parties to nominate, by agreement, an arbitrator for the ICC court's confirmation; while the AAA International Arbitration Rules require only that parties notify the AAA of any *designation* of an arbitrator.

When the forum of the arbitration has not been agreed to, the LCIA generally determines it according to the parties' contentions and the circumstances of the arbitration. However, the LCIA Rules provide that in such situations, the seat of the arbitration will be London unless, on the basis of the parties' written comments, the LCIA deems another seat more appropriate in view of the circumstances.

Under the ICC Rules of Arbitration, a document known as the *Terms of Reference,* containing a summary of the parties' claims, a list of issues to be determined, and applicable procedural rules, must be drafted and submitted to the arbitrator and the opposing party. Although time-consuming, discussion of agreed issues is designed to encourage settlement. Also, arbitration awards must be submitted to the ICC court for approval. There are no similar requirements under the LCIA Rules and the AAA International Arbitration Rules.

Ad Hoc Arbitration Rules

Rules such as those set out in the U.N. Commission on International Trade Law (UNCITRAL) Arbitration Rules serve to bridge the gap for parties who are unwilling to incur additional expense to use the services of an arbitration body but who do not wish to spend time agreeing to the details of a procedure to govern their arbitration.

ALTERNATIVES TO THE ICC: THE WORLD INTELLECTUAL PROPERTY ORGANIZATION

There are arbitration institutions other than the ICC, some with regional specialization and some with subject matter specialization. The World International Property Organization (WIPO) in Geneva, Switzerland, created an arbitration center for arbitration related to intellectual property such as patents, trademarks, and copyrights. Some advantages of the WIPO center are:

- The WIPO lists best practices regarding nomination of arbitrators, including a list system, thus encouraging the parties to agree on people based on their *qualifications*.
- The WIPO explicitly states that, when nominating arbitrators, it will take into account any preferences expressed by the parties, *and* it has created a mechanism to implement this in practice: a database of names and it detailed qualifications.
- The WIPO rules explicitly cater to multiparty arbitrations.

INTERNATIONAL MEDIATION

The growing popularity of mediation and conciliation, both of which first took root in the United States but have gained increasing support in other jurisdictions, reflects a high degree of frustration with the cost and delays often associated with traditional dispute resolution procedures. Mediation and conciliation both involve a consensual (rather than adjudicative) process, often with the involvement of a neutral third party. Such forms of dispute resolution may loosely be described as third-party-assisted negotiation.

Mediation and conciliation are now widely used in many countries, including the United States, Canada, Australia, South Africa, New Zealand, Germany, Holland, and Switzerland, as well as in the Hong Kong region of China. They are also gaining acceptance in the United Kingdom through the establishment of organizations dedicated to their promotion and use, such as the London-based Center for Dispute Resolution, although conciliation has long been practiced in the United Kingdom by the Advisory Conciliation and Arbitration Service in the field of employment-law disputes.

LO 26-7 ## INTERNATIONAL COMMERCIAL LAW

Although this chapter has focused thus far on the sources and processes for a broad-based category of international law disputes, *commercial transactions and trade practices* are also governed by various sources of international (and U.S.) law.

Foreign Corrupt Practices Act (FCPA)

The **Foreign Corrupt Practices Act (FCPA)**[4] of 1977 was enacted principally to prevent corporate bribery of foreign officials. This act has three major parts: (1) It requires the keeping by corporations of accurate books, records, and accounts; (2) it requires issuers registered with the Securities and Exchange Commission to maintain a responsible internal

---

[4]28 U.S.C. § 1602 et seq.

accounting control system; and (3) it prohibits bribery by American corporations of foreign officials.

The FCPA was amended by Congress in 1988 in response to numerous criticisms. One of the changes enacted a *knowing* standard in order to find violations of the act. A person's state of mind is knowing with respect to conduct, a circumstance, or a result if the person is aware that he is engaging in the conduct, that the circumstance exists, or that the result is substantially certain to occur or if the person has a firm belief that the circumstance exists or that the result is substantially certain to occur. The 1998 amendment to the FCPA brought it into compliance with the Organization for Economic Cooperation and Development's agreement on bribery.

The centerpiece of the FCPA is its antibribery provision. The law prohibits a company and its officers, employees, and agents from giving, offering, or promising anything of value to any foreign (non-U.S.) official with the intent to obtain or retain business or any other advantage. This prohibition is interpreted broadly in that companies may be held liable for violating the antibribery provisions of the FCPA whether or not they took any action in the United States. Thus, a U.S. company can be liable for the conduct of its overseas employees or agents even if no money was transferred from the United States and no American citizen participated in any way in the foreign bribery.

Foreign officials include any officers or employees of a foreign government, regardless of rank; employees of government-owned or government-controlled businesses; foreign political parties and party officials; candidates for political office; and employees of public international organizations (such as the United Nations or the World Bank). This can include owner-employees as well. Even if the improper payment is not consummated, just offering it violates the FCPA. Likewise, instructing, authorizing, or allowing a third party to make a prohibited payment on a company's behalf, ratifying a payment after the fact, and making a payment to a third party knowing or having reason to know that it will likely be given to a government official constitute FCPA violations. This includes not only cash and cash equivalents but also gifts, entertainment, travel expenses, accommodations, and anything else of tangible or intangible value.

 Self-Check   Foreign Corrupt Practices Act

Which proposed transactions violate the FCPA?

1. WidgetCo applies for a permit to do business in Venezuela. The government official denies the permit, and a WidgetCo executive pays for a lavish meal at a four-star restaurant while discussing the permit application with the official.

2. WidgetCo applies for a permit to do business in Venezuela. The government official denies the permit, so WidgetCo hires a consultant in Venezuela who is the brother of the government official. WidgetCo pays the consultant $100,000 to handle the permit process although the permit itself costs only $1,000.

3. WidgetCo applies for a permit to do business in Venezuela. A government official denies the permit, so WidgetCo hires a consultant in Venezuela who is the brother of the government official and pays a reasonable fee for services plus reimbursement of traveling expenses. The consultant submits a handwritten invoice for the reimbursements totaling $100,000.

4. WidgetCo applies for a permit to do business in Venezuela. A government official denies the permit, so WidgetCo hires a consultant in Venezuela who is the brother of the government official and pays a reasonable fee for services plus reasonable reimbursement of traveling expenses. When the permit is finally approved, WidgetCo executives send the consultant a case of California wine as a thank-you gift.

Answers to this Self-Check are provided at the end of the chapter.

U.N. Convention on Contracts for the International Sale of Goods (CISG)

In 1988, the United States became a signatory nation to a U.N. treaty that attempts to establish an international commercial code. The *U.N. Convention on Contracts for the International Sale of Goods (CISG)* governs transactions between any of its 79 ratifying countries (as of March 2013). Much like America's Uniform Commercial Code, the CISG exists to fill in the terms of a sale of goods contract when the parties haven't otherwise agreed. Parties are free to negotiate the allocation of risk, insurance requirements, delivery, payment terms, choice of law, and the like to displace the CISG principles. It is particularly important for managers to understand *choice of law and forum* principles in international contracts, because risk and expense of enforcement become increasingly important factors that must be considered in arriving at appropriate pricing and delivery proposals. If one party will have to travel significant distances or hire special counsel to enforce an agreement or recover for damages suffered, adjusting the price or delivery terms accordingly may sometimes help to reduce the risks.

Legal Speak ›))

Choice of Law and Forum Clauses Terms of a contract that predetermine what nation's laws and court system will be used in a potential lawsuit under that contract.

Coverage and Major Provisions of the CISG

The CISG operates on the same fundamental principle as many commercial codes around the world (including the Uniform Commercial Code[5] followed by most American states) in that the law favors the completion of a transaction as agreed upon but also provides relief when one party has breached. The CISG covers parties that maintain a place of business in one of the signatory countries. Note that citizenship of shareholders, directors, or officers is not a factor under the CISG. Generally, the CISG covers contracts for the sale of goods between *merchants*. This is perhaps the biggest difference between the UCC and the CISG. The CISG provisions do *not* apply to transactions in which one party is a nonmerchant. Other major important provisions are discussed below.

No Writing Required   The CISG has no formal writing requirement (such as the UCC's statute of frauds) and specifically provides that contracts are not subject to requirements as to format. A totality of the circumstances, such as course of past dealing, evidence of oral or written negotiations between the parties, and industry practice, may be sufficient to prove that an enforceable contract exists.

Although the CISG eliminates any formal writing requirement, it still allows individual countries to impose a writing requirement through an Article 96 declaration. The United States has not made such a declaration. In Case 26.3, a federal court grapples with a dispute in which one country has made an Article 96 declaration and one country has not.

Offer and Acceptance   A contract for the sale of goods between businesses located in different CISG signatory countries begins with offer and acceptance. As with the UCC, the offer need not have complete terms in order to be valid. The offer requires only a brief description of the goods, quantity, and price. Beyond those three terms, so long as there is some evidence that the parties intended to form a contract, nothing more is needed for a valid offer. Acceptance may be made within a reasonable time and is effective only when it is received by the offeror (thus, the offer may be withdrawn at any point prior to that time).

Remedies   The CISG provides for a party that has delivered nonconforming goods to be given an adequate opportunity to cure the problem. In general, the CISG gives sellers an absolute right and obligation to cure, and buyers must allow the seller the opportunity to

---

[5]The Uniform Commercial Code was covered in Chapter 9, "Contracts for the Sale of Goods."

FACT SUMMARY Forestal Guarani S.A. is an Argentina-based manufacturer of various lumber products, including wood finger joints. Daros International, Inc., is a New Jersey–based import-export corporation. In 1999, Forestal and Daros entered into an oral agreement for Daros to sell Forestal's wood finger joints to third parties in the United States. Pursuant to that agreement, Forestal sent Daros the finger joints along with an invoice for $1.86 million. However, Daros paid Forestal a total of only $1.46 million. When Forestal sued to recover the amount owed, Daros admitted that it had paid Forestal $1.46 million in exchange for the finger joints but denied that it owed Forestal any additional money. Daros argued that under the CISG, which governed its relationship with Forestal, there was no liability because the absence of any written contract precluded Forestal's claims since Argentina had exercised its rights in an Article 96 declaration. The trial court granted a summary judgment claim in favor of Daros, finding that Argentina's declaration was sufficient to extinguish Forestal's claim.

SYNOPSIS OF DECISION AND OPINION The U.S. Court of Appeals for the Third Circuit reversed the decision of the trial court and ruled in favor of Forestal. Although the court acknowledged that the issue of whether a contract must be in writing under these circumstances was a case of first impression, it rejected the trial court's conclusion that Forestal's claim was extinguished by virtue of the Article 96 declaration. The court held that when one country has adopted an Article 96 declaration and the other country has not, choice of law principles must be considered and the trial court should have taken the course of past conduct into account before granting a summary judgment motion.

WORDS OF THE COURT: Evidence of a Contract "Daros contended that Forestal had submitted no 'credible evidence' of a contract with Daros. The [trial court] agreed with that contention, concluding that there was no evidence that the parties ever had any contract at all. It is undisputed, however, that Forestal sold wooden finger-joints to Daros and that Daros gave Forestal money in exchange. Indeed, Daros nowhere denies that the parties at the very least had a verbal contract for those sales.

Furthermore, Forestal submitted an accountant's certification, with supporting documentation, as well as invoices in an effort to substantiate its claim that it is owed money. There is also deposition testimony indicating that the parties had a contract. The [trial court] did not expressly refer to some of these materials in its opinion, and we do not know why it evidently disregarded them. In short, we cannot say at this stage that there is no genuine question of material fact as to whether the parties had or did not have some sort of contractual relationship and whether Forestal can prove as much under whatever law actually controls this case."

Case Questions

1. After reading this case, do you think that the United States should opt for an Article 96 declaration? Why or why not?

2. Do the advantages of a statute of frauds rule (e.g., certainty) outweigh the advantages of a no writing requirement (e.g., flow of commerce)?

cure even if the time for performance is past due. Of course, a buyer must give notice of the nonconformance in a timely manner in order to trigger the seller's cure obligations. If the seller does not cure, the CISG provides a right for the buyer to pursue remedies.

INCO: International Chamber of Commerce Terms

With respect to title, risk of loss, and delivery terms, sometimes the language barrier can lead to confusion among the parties and to disputes regarding a loss. The International Chamber of Commerce provides international abbreviations, known as **INCO terms**, to designate many of the responsibilities. INCO terms are generally used in conjunction with the CISG. For example, in the absence of any agreement between the parties, the CISG provides that risk passes at the point at which the seller has delivered the goods to a carrier. If the goods are not to be delivered, the risk of loss passes in accordance with the

INCO term *EXW ("ex works")*. The INCO term EXW has the universal meaning that the parties understand the goods will not be delivered or transported by the seller. Rather, the seller need only make the goods available to the buyer at the seller's place of business and provide the buyer with appropriate documentation of title. There are 11 INCO terms in all. Some of the more common ones are:

- *FCA ("free carrier"):* This term means that the seller provides transportation at the seller's expense only to the carrier named by the buyer.
- *FOB ("free on board"):* This term is always accompanied by the name of a port (e.g., FOB New York) and applies only when transportation is via freighter ship. It means that the seller's expense and risk of loss *end* when the seller delivers goods "over the ship's rail" to the freighter ship. The buyer is responsible for the freighter delivery charges and any losses occurring en route to delivery.

CONCEPT SUMMARY Contracts for International Sales of Goods

- The CISG, the international counterpart to the UCC, is a treaty that governs sales contracts between businesses located in signatory countries.
- Four major differences between the CISG and the UCC are that it does not apply to nonmerchants, it has no writing requirement, offers can be withdrawn at any point prior the offeror's receiving the acceptance, and the right to cure exists even after the performance period is over.
- INCO terms are standardized contractual terms and designations used in international sales contracts to avoid confusion due to language barriers and differing legal systems.

ENFORCING INTELLECTUAL PROPERTY
LO 26-8 RIGHTS ABROAD

While the laws of intellectual property protection are well settled in the United States, as U.S. companies become increasingly dependent on foreign sales and operations, global agreements have turned ever more important as well. The international law protection of intellectual property rights has primarily taken the form of multilateral agreements. However, as a practical matter, while many countries have improved intellectual property rights protection significantly over the past several decades, these agreements are still voluntary. Even when the government of a country agrees to abide by them (sometimes to avoid trade sanctions), the agreements are sometimes difficult to enforce in certain parts of the world. At the very least, enforcement of rights abroad significantly impacts the cost-benefit analysis of pursuing infringement claims in terms of additional fees and expenses related to foreign litigation.

Comprehensive Agreements

While U.S. firms are motivated to be committed to stronger intellectual property protection abroad, some countries' intellectual property trade agreements often lack a meaningful mechanism to ensure that signatory countries are actually fulfilling their obligations. Thus, the United States and other similarly situated countries backed the adoption of multinational minimal standards for intellectual property protection and an enforcement structure empowered with the ability to allow trade embargoes and other remedies designed to ensure that signatory countries comply with the agreement. As part of the **General Agreement on Tariffs and Trade (GATT)**, administered by the multinational World Trade Organization (WTO), the agreement to set these standards is known as the

The WTO (also called OMC, the abbreviation for its French name) plays an important role in protection of intellectual property in global commerce.

Agreement on Trade-Related Aspects of Intellectual Property (TRIPS). TRIPS covers minimum requirements and standards for all areas of intellectual property protections and also provides an infrastructure for enforcement and dispute resolution.

Agreements on Trademarks

International trademark policy is governed primarily by two agreements: the *Paris Convention* and the *Madrid Protocol.* The Paris Convention was the first multinational agreement to establish minimum requirements for trademark protection, and a general agreement by its signatories established protections against unfair competition. The **Madrid Protocol**, a 2003 agreement that was a descendant of the earlier Madrid Agreement, aims to help reduce the burden of multinational companies that desire multinational protection of their trademarks by providing a uniform, single-source process. Although important, these international agreements are not so specific as to actually require fundamental enforcement from signatory countries, and thus trademark protection may still be dubious and uneven in certain regions. Efforts to harmonize trademark laws on a regional level have been more successful.[6]

Agreement on Copyrights

Copyright protection in foreign countries is covered in the **Berne Convention** agreement. Fundamentally, this agreement requires that foreigners from signatory countries must be granted protection via reciprocity (known as *national treatment*) under the copyright laws of any other member country. For example, if Samuel, an American, distributes his novel in Great Britain (or in any signatory country), British courts are bound by the convention agreement to protect Samuel's rights under British law in the same way as would apply if Samuel were a citizen of Great Britain.

---

[6]The European Union established Community Trademark System to make trademark registration and protection more uniform in member states.

Agreement on Patents

The most important multilateral agreement on patents is the **Paris Convention** agreement. This agreement requires the approximately 160 member countries that signed the agreement to protect the same inventor rights under *any* member country's patent laws as those enjoyed by citizens of that member country. That is, each member agrees to extend national rights (or give full protection to) foreign inventors. However, risks still remain for the foreign inventor because the Paris Convention does not specify common standards for patentability and some jurisdictions may not allow certain inventions, which were patentable in the United States, to obtain patent protection in their own country due to noncompliance with its domestic law.

KEY TERMS

Public international law p. 711   Category of international law principles that primarily addresses relations between individual countries and international organizations.

Private international law p. 711   Category of international law principles that focuses on regulations of private individuals and business entities.

Vienna Convention on the Law of Treaties p. 712 One of the standards used by courts and other tribunals when interpreting treaty law.

Comity p. 712   The general notion that nations will defer to and give effect to the laws and court decisions of other nations.

United Nations (U.N.) p. 712   An international organization created after World War II to facilitate common international concerns on defense, trade, protection of human rights, and other matters.

U.N. Convention on Contracts for the International Sale of Goods (CISG) p. 712   A trade agreement developed by the U.N. Commission on International Trade Law to establish uniform rules for drafting certain international sales contracts.

International Court of Justice p. 714   The judicial branch of the United Nations, charged with settling legal disputes submitted to it by member states and giving advisory opinions on legal questions submitted to it by duly authorized international organs, agencies, and the U.N. General Assembly. Also known as *World Court.*

European Court of Justice p. 714   The court that functions as the final arbiter of the codes governing European Union member states.

Sovereign immunity p. 715   Long-standing doctrine of international law that holds that, with some exceptions, nations are exempt from jurisdiction by other nations' courts.

Foreign Sovereign Immunities Act (FSIA) p. 715 A federal statute that incorporates the concept of sovereign immunity by explicitly prohibiting U.S. courts from rendering judicial actions against foreign nations or their government officials unless the foreign nation has waived its immunity, is engaged in a commercial enterprise on U.S. soil, or has taken actions that have a direct effect on U.S. interests.

Civil law systems p. 715   Systems of law that are drawn largely from the Roman law heritage, which uses written law as the highest source, and opt for a systematic codification of general law principles.

Convention on the Recognition and Enforcement of Foreign Arbitral Awards p. 717   An international treaty established in 1958 that allows for the enforcement of arbitration awards in many major countries, provided that the arbitration is international.

Foreign Corrupt Practices Act (FCPA) p. 718 Federal legislation enacted in 1977 that prohibits corporate bribery of foreign officials, requires corporations to keep accurate books, records, and accounts, and requires issuers registered with the Securities and Exchange Commission to maintain a responsible internal accounting control system.

INCO terms p. 721   Standardized contractual terms and designations used in international sales contracts to avoid confusion due to language barriers and differing legal systems.

General Agreement on Tariffs and Trade (GATT) p. 722   A treaty designed to facilitate international trade; administered by the World Trade Organization.

Agreement on Trade-Related Aspects of Intellectual Property (TRIPS) p. 723   A multinational agreement that covers minimum requirements and standards for all areas of intellectual property protection and provides an infrastructure for enforcement and dispute resolution.

Madrid Protocol p. 723   A multinational agreement that aims to facilitate multinational protection of trademarks through the use of a uniform, single-source process.

Berne Convention p. 723   A multinational agreement covering copyright protection; requires that foreigners from signatory countries be granted protection, via reciprocity, under the copyright laws of any other member country.

Paris Convention p. 724   A multinational agreement covering patents; requires signatory countries to protect the same inventor rights under any member country's patent laws as those enjoyed by citizens of that member country.

THEORY TO PRACTICE

Cold Call Company (CCC) is a cellular phone manufacturer and distributor based in Miami, Florida. The firm has a significant market share in the southeastern United States and began to expand into South America as a natural supplement to its existing market. CCC entered into a written distribution agreement with Telefonica, a Brazilian-based provider of cell phone service and retailer of cell phone units with stores throughout Latin America. Telefonica agreed to buy 25,000 units over 12 months at US$5 per unit. The agreement also contained a provision whereby the parties agreed to ICC dispute resolution in the event of a dispute arising out of the distribution agreement. After several months, a dispute developed, and Telefonica filed suit against CCC in a federal district court in Miami.

1. What source(s) of international law(s) would generally govern this international business relationship?

2. When CCC asks the court to dismiss the case due to the ICC clause, Telefonica claims that the clause is invalid because it will have to travel to Europe to resolve the dispute and that is too burdensome. How will the federal court rule, and what case have you studied in this chapter that supports your answer?

   Assume further that the CCC-Telefonica agreement provides that all shipments are "FOB Port of Rio de Janeiro, Brazil." During one shipment, a batch

of 1,000 units is accidentally destroyed when being loaded on the freighter in Miami.

3. Under the CISG, who bears the risk of this loss? When did title pass?

   Assume that an executive at Telefonica arranges a golf outing with a politician in Argentina on behalf of the distribution manager of CCC. The Telefonica executive explains that it is customary in Argentina for business owners to entertain local politicians and that it is a necessary part of securing appropriate licenses for the CCC-Telefonica distribution relationship in Argentina. One day after the golf outing, the Telefonica executive sends a bill to CCC for the golf expenses, including equipment, food, and drinks ordered by the group.

4. If CCC pays the bill, will the company potentially violate any U.S. laws? If so, does the law apply to these circumstances? Will CCC be at a competitive disadvantage if it follows the law?

   Suppose that CCC refuses to pay the bill and that the Argentinean government prohibits CCC from exporting any products to Argentina. CCC loses a significant portion of its investment with Telefonica as a result of the ban.

5. Does CCC have recourse against the Argentinean government in U.S. courts? Why or why not? What legal doctrine controls this question? Could this be an exception?

MANAGER'S CHALLENGE

One important responsibility of a manager is to be vigilant about protecting his company from liability. One such liability in the international law context is a potential violation of the Foreign Corrupt Practices Act (FCPA). Individually or in small groups, take on the role of a CCC manager (from the Theory to

Practice problem), and draft a two-page memorandum to your senior manager on a proposed policy for CCC employees to help them avoid any violations of the FCPA. The policy should contain at least 5 red-flag situations in which CCC may be in danger of violating the act. For example, paying for entertainment of a government official when the official has some decision-making role is a red-flag situation in which CCC employees must recognize potential FCPA violations and act with restraint. A sample answer may be found on this textbook's website at www.mhhe.com/melvinleb2e.

CASE SUMMARY 26.1 :: TermoRio v. Electricrificadora del Atlantico S.A., 2006 WL 695832 (D.D.C. 2006)

ARBITRATION ENFORCEMENT

Electranta is a power company owned by the Colombian government. Electranta became involved in a dispute with TermoRio, a U.S. company doing business in Colombia. The dispute was arbitrated consistent with International Chamber of Commerce rules, and TermoRio was awarded US$60 million in damages. However, TermoRio could not convince the Colombian courts to enforce the award, and the government of Colombia refused to pay

TermoRio then filed suit in the U.S., attempting to have a federal court declare the acts of the Colombia courts unlawful and recognize the arbitration award.

CASE QUESTIONS

1. Under the Convention on the Recognition and Enforcement of Arbitral Awards, do the U.S. courts have authority to decide this case?
2. What do the ICC rules provide?

CASE SUMMARY 26.2 :: Plaintiffs A, B, C v. Zemin, 224 F. Supp. 2d 52 (N.D. Ill. 2003)

SOVEREIGN IMMUNITY

Several Chinese ex-patriots now living in the United States are members of a religious movement, Falun Gong, which is outlawed in China, and they brought suit against the Chinese government. Members of this movement are subject to arrest by Chinese government officials in the Falun Gong Control Office without any further charge, and the lawsuit maintained that they were subject to severe torture resulting in permanent physical

damage. The suit named the former president of China and officials of the Control Office as defendants, but the defendants never responded to the lawsuit.

CASE QUESTIONS

1. May the federal court issue a default judgment against the defendants?
2. What role does the doctrine of sovereign immunity play in this case?

CASE SUMMARY 26.3 :: Chateau des Charmes Wines Ltd. v. Sabate, 328 F.3d 528 (9th Cir. 2003)

CONTRACTS FOR THE INTERNATIONAL SALE OF GOODS

Sabate, a France-based company, sold wine corks to Chateau, a Canadian winery, via Sabate's U.S. subsidiary. The parties made the agreement by telephone, and no written contracts exist. After several transactions and the sale of over 1.2 million corks, Sabate began to send an invoice with each shipment that included a forum selection clause naming France as the agreed-upon location to resolve disputes. Chateau sued Sabate

in a U.S. court over the poor quality of the corks. Sabate moved to dismiss because the forum selection clause required the dispute to be litigated in France. Chateau claimed that the forum selection clause was added after the terms were agreed upon and, thus, was invalid and not part of the original contract.

CASE QUESTIONS

1. Is Chateau's silence upon receiving the invoices binding on the company under the Convention on Contracts for the International Sale of Goods?
2. Would your answer be the same under the UCC?

FOREIGN SOVEREIGN IMMUNITIES ACT

Altmann, a U.S. resident, filed suit in a federal district court against the Republic of Austria to recover a series of paintings that Altmann claims were wrongfully appropriated from her uncle just prior to World War II. The paintings had been held in her uncle's Vienna home until the German annexation of Austria in 1938. Altmann's uncle fled Austria, fearing persecution, and left half of his estate to Altmann in his will. The paintings were discovered by an Austrian journalist who alerted Altmann to the fact that her uncle's paintings were being held by the Austrian government in its art gallery archives. The Austrian government moved to dismiss the case based on the FSIA, but Altmann contended (among other arguments) that because the Austrian government's actions were taken *prior* to passage of the FSIA, they were outside the scope of the statute's immunity protection.

CASE QUESTIONS

1. Do sovereigns have immunity protection for actions prior to the FSIA's enactment?
2. Is it fair to allow Austria protection under these circumstances? Why or why not?

DISPUTE RESOLUTION

DiMercurio was a fisherman who was injured when a commercial shipping vessel owned by a Massachusetts company, Rosalie & Matteo Corporation, sank. DiMercurio prevailed in a personal injury suit against Rosalie & Matteo, but the company was without assets and could not pay the $350,000 judgment. Rosalie & Matteo subsequently assigned to DiMercurio all rights it had against its London-based insurance company, Sphere Drake, under an insurance policy issued to Rosalie & Matteo Corporation. DiMercurio then took his claim directly to Sphere Drake, demanding that the insurer pay the $350,000 judgment. Sphere Drake sought to invoke the arbitration process specified in the policy, which called for arbitration of all coverage disputes to be held in London under convention rules. DiMercurio challenged the validity of the arbitration provision, contending that it was overly burdensome on the arbitrating parties given that he would have to travel to London.

CASE QUESTIONS

1. Recall that in the Brower v. Gateway case in Chapter 4, "Resolving Disputes: Litigation and Alternative Dispute Resolution Options," the court held that Gateway's inclusion of an arbitration clause in a terms and conditions agreement was invalid because of the choice of ICC as the arbitration forum. Is this case distinguishable?
2. Give examples of types of agreements that you would consider too one-sided to be valid.

 Self-Check **ANSWERS**

Foreign Corrupt Practices Act

1. Violates FCPA's prohibition of offering anything of value (meal at a four-star restaurant) with intent to obtain the permit.
2. Violates FCPA's prohibition of paying a third party to pay off the government official (a consultant).
3. Violates FCPA's prohibition of paying cash equivalents (travel) in connection with the permit.
4. Violates FCPA's prohibition of after-the-fact (ratification) payments related to the permit application.

SEARCH AND SEIZURE/ EXCLUSIONARY RULE

When federal authorities became suspicious that the defendant was using his home for a large-scale marijuana indoor growth facility, two law enforcement agents used a thermal-imaging device from a public street outside the defendant's home. The use of the device indicated that the roof over the garage and a side wall of the house were relatively hot compared to the rest of the house and substantially warmer than neighboring homes. Based on informant tips, utility bills, and the thermal imaging, a federal judge issued a search warrant. Federal agents found an indoor growing operation that comprised more than 100 plants and that involved the defendant's use of high-intensity lamps to facilitate the cultivation process.

The defendant moved to suppress the evidence based on his Fourth Amendment right that guarantees that security of "persons, houses, papers, and effects, against unreasonable searches and seizures, shall not be violated." The government argued that the agents' use of the thermal imager was not a search because the device was used from a public street, was nonintrusive, and fell within a plain view doctrine exception. The trial court ruled against the defendant on the suppression of evidence, and the defendant appealed.

ENGAGEMENT QUESTIONS

1. Recall from Chapter 23, "Criminal Law and Procedure in Business," that the U.S. Supreme Court ruled that aerial observations by authorities are typically permissible. Does a thermal imager fit into that category? Is a thermal imager available to the general public?

2. Note that the Fourth Amendment lists what security guarantees (e.g., papers) are provided. Does this search fit into one of those categories?

3. If the defendant had been growing marijuana at his business's warehouse, how would that change your Fourth Amendment analysis?

4. The defendant is undoubtedly the distributor of large amounts of illegal drugs. Should he be protected by the exclusionary rule? Why or why not?

5. What other types of devices could potentially be used for plain view searches? For example, are devices used by scientists to enhance images unreasonable searches if used by law enforcement agents?

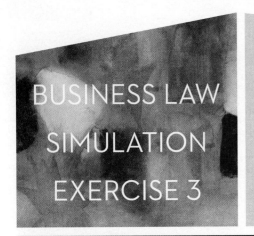

BUSINESS LAW SIMULATION EXERCISE 3

Trademarks in Cyberspace: Cool Runnings v. BigBuy.com

learning objectives

After studying this simulation, students who have mastered the material will be able to:

1. Explain the legal doctrines that govern trademark protection and infringement.

2. Interpret and apply the rules set forth in current case law.

3. Articulate a cogent argument for each party/side in the dispute.

4. Negotiate a tenable solution as an alternative to a judicial forum.

This simulation is designed to help you understand how the various topics covered in Chapter 25, "Intellectual Property," connect. By focusing on a simulated legal dispute, you will gain real-world experience in applying legal doctrines and using analytical and critical-thinking skills. This simulation is a sequential decision-making exercise structured around a model in which the participants assume a role in managing tasks and work toward a tenable solution.

The simulation is structured in three parts:

■ Part 1 is a hypothetical fact pattern describing events leading up to a legal dispute in the hypothetical U.S. state of Longville.

■ Part 2 is a statutory excerpt and a set of two hypothetical case summaries from two federal trial courts, both situated in Longville. Each summary provides a brief set of facts, several legal points, and short excerpts from the opinion itself. While these cases are hypothetical, they are based on actual cases from federal courts in various circuits.

■ Part 3 is an assignment sheet handout that will be provided to you by your instructor for use in conjunction with this simulation.

Part 1: Stipulated Facts

1. BigBuy.com Inc. is a company with a website that facilitates a web-based discount wholesaler business model that targets consumers wishing to buy products in bulk. In early 2008, BigBuy.com began developing a new marketing device that featured pop-up advertising. In October 2009, the company launched "BargainNow" as integrated software for BigBuy users.

2. BigBuy.com made the BargainNow software available to computer users, at no charge, as part of a larger package of software that users downloaded from BigBuy's website. The BargainNow software uses an internal directory of website addresses, search terms, and keyword algorithms to generate pop-up advertisements in response to a user's Internet activity.

3. The advertisements generated are randomly drawn from a list of BigBuy's advertising clients. In essence, BigBuy's software operates behind the scenes monitoring a user's Internet activity and then responds according to keywords the software identifies as part of a user's activity, such as words entered in an Internet search engine query or websites visited whose domain names match information contained in the BigBuy internal directory.

4. The pop-ups occur only a few seconds after the user has reached a retail website and, thus, present the user with a choice: to close the pop-up and continue navigating the website or to click on the promotion and navigate away from the original retailer's website to a competitor's website.

5. Cool Runnings Corporation is a large retailer of skateboards and snowboards with a USPTO registered trademark for "Cool Runnings" and sole and exclusive use of the mark. The company sells its products both from a catalog system with a 1-800 number and via its website at www.coolrunnings.com.

6. In January 2010, BigBuy landed an advertising client that is a major competitor to Cool Runnings and, pursuant to its business model, BigBuy installed www.coolrunnings.com and keywords such as *snowboards* and *skateboards* into its internal directory. Note that it did *not* install the keywords Cool *Runnings* in the directory.

This simulation exercise involves a trademark dispute between a snowboard retailer and an Internet advertising company.

Part 2: Statutory and Case Law
Statute: *United States Code*
Excerpt from Trademark Dilution Revision Act

Section 1: The owner of a famous mark . . . shall be entitled to an injunction against another person who, at any time after the owner's mark has become famous, commences use of a mark or trade name in commerce that is likely to cause dilution by blurring or dilution by tarnishment of the famous mark, regardless of the presence or absence of actual or likely confusion, of competition, or of actual economic injury.

Section 2: There are six nonexhaustive factors for courts to consider in determining whether there is dilution by blurring:

- The degree of similarity between the mark and the famous mark.
- The degree of inherent or acquired distinctiveness of the mark.
- The extent to which the owner of the famous mark is engaging in substantially exclusive use of the mark.
- The degree of recognition (fame) of the mark.
- Whether use of the mark by the alleged infringer was intended to create an association with the famous mark.
- Any actual association between the mark and the famous mark.

Case Law

1-800 Lenses, Inc., v. WhenU.com
Federal District Court, Eastern District of Longville (2010)

Facts

- 1-800 Lenses, Inc. (800-Lenses) sells and markets replacement lenses and related products through its website, located at www.1800Lenses.com, and also through telephone and mail orders. 800-Lenses obtained USPTO registration for the mark "1-800 LENSES" and the 1-800 LENSES logo.
- 800-Lenses has expended considerable sums on marketing these marks; in 2001, 800-Lenses spent $27,118,000 on marketing. Since the founding of 800-Lenses in 1995, the company has continuously used its service marks to promote and identify its products and services in the United States and abroad.
- 800-Lenses is the sole owner of the 1800-Lenses.com website.
- WhenU.com is a software company that has developed and distributes, among other products, the "SaveNow" program, a proprietary software application.
- The SaveNow program is computer software that operates only on the Microsoft Windows operating system. The SaveNow software, when installed, resides on individual computer users' computer desktops. When a computer user who has installed the SaveNow software browses the Internet, the SaveNow software scans activity conducted within the SaveNow user's Internet browser, comparing URLs, website addresses, search terms, and web-page content accessed by the SaveNow user with a proprietary directory, using algorithms contained in the software.
- Entering a URL into the browser will trigger the SaveNow software to deliver a pop-up advertisement. When a user types in "1800-Lenses.com," the URL for 800-Lenses' owned website, the SaveNow software recognizes that the user is interested in the eye-care category, and it retrieves from an Internet server a pop-up advertisement from that category.
- 800-Lenses filed a trademark infringement claim after discovering that the SaveNow software produced pop-up advertising for Lenses Warehouse, a WhenU.com customer and competitor of 800-Lenses.

POINTS OF LAW AND OPINION EXCERPTS

Point (a)

The Lanham Act, a federal statute, prohibits the *use in commerce,* without consent, of any registered mark in connection with the sale, offering for sale, distribution, or advertising of any goods in a way that is likely to cause confusion.

Excerpt (a1)

"A trademark is 'used in commerce' for purposes of the Lanham Act when it is used or displayed in the sale or advertising of services and the services are rendered in commerce, or the services are rendered in more than one state or in the United States and a foreign country and the person rendering the services is engaged in commerce in connection with the services."

Excerpt (a2)

"WhenU (defendant) *uses* 1-800 Lenses (plaintiff) mark in commerce. First, in causing pop-up advertisements for a competitor to appear when SaveNow users have specifically attempted to access plaintiff's website—on which plaintiff's trademark appears—defendants are displaying plaintiff's mark in the advertising of a competitor's services. SaveNow users that type plaintiff's website address into their browsers are clearly attempting to access plaintiff's website because of prior knowledge of the website, knowledge that is dependent on plaintiff's reputation and goodwill. SaveNow users that type 1-800 Lenses into a search engine in an attempt to find the URL for plaintiff's website are exhibiting a similar knowledge of plaintiff's goods and services, and pop-up advertisements that capitalize on this are clearly using plaintiff's mark. Thus, by causing pop-up advertisements to appear when SaveNow users have specifically attempted to find or access plaintiff's website, defendants are 'using' plaintiff's marks that appear on plaintiff's website."

Excerpt (a3)

"WhenU.com also *uses* the mark by including Plaintiff's URL, www.1800Lenses.com, in the proprietary WhenU.com directory of terms that triggers pop-up advertisements on SaveNow users' computers. In so doing, WhenU.com 'uses' Plaintiff's mark by including a version of Plaintiff's 1-800 LENSES mark, to advertise and publicize companies that are in direct competition with the Plaintiff."

Point (b)

Confusion for purposes of the Lanham Act is shown when there is a likelihood that an appreciable number of ordinarily prudent purchasers are likely to be misled, or indeed simply confused, as to the source of the goods in question or when consumers are likely to believe that the challenged use of a trademark is somehow sponsored, endorsed, or authorized by its owner. Thus, "confusion" for purposes of the Lanham Act includes confusion of any kind, including confusion as to source, sponsorship, affiliation, connection, or identification.

Excerpt (b1)

"It is black letter law that actual confusion need not be shown to prevail under the Lanham Act, since actual confusion is very difficult to prove and the Act requires only a likelihood of confusion as to source. In order to support a claim of infringement, a plaintiff must show a probability, not just a possibility, of confusion; a likelihood of confusion is actionable even absent evidence of actual confusion."

Excerpt (b2)

"Confusion that occurs prior to a sale may be actionable under the Lanham Act. For example, *initial interest confusion* occurs when a consumer, seeking a particular trademark holder's product, is instead lured away to the product of a competitor because of the competitor's use of a similar mark, even though the consumer is not actually confused about the source of the products or services at the time of actual purchase."

Excerpt (b3)

"Federal courts assess the likelihood of consumer confusion by examining (1) the strength of plaintiff's mark, (2) the similarity between the plaintiff's and defendant's marks, (3) proximity of the parties' services, (4) the likelihood that one party will 'bridge the gap' into the other's product line, (5) the existence of actual confusion between the marks, (6) the good faith of the defendant in using the mark, (7) the quality of the defendant's services, and (8) the sophistication of the consumers."

Point (c)

A mark holder may also be entitled to an injunction if it dilutes a famous mark under the Trademark Dilution Revision Act.

Excerpt (c1)

"The TDRA each outlines several nonexclusive factors the court may consider in determining whether a mark is famous such as (1) the duration, extent, and geographic reach of advertising and publicity of the mark, and (2) the amount, volume, and geographic extent of sales of goods or services offered under the mark, and (3) whether the mark is registered."

Excerpt (c2)

"For a dilution claim to succeed under TDRA, the mark used by the alleged diluter must be identical, or nearly identical, to the protected mark. Although no longer requires actual dilution, the new law does not eliminate the requirement that the mark used by the alleged diluter be identical, nearly identical, or substantially similar to the protected mark. For marks to be nearly identical to one another, they must be similar enough that a significant segment of the target group of customers sees the two marks as essentially the same."

Excerpt (c3)

"In the dilution context, the 'similarity of the marks' test is more stringent than in the infringement context."

Held

WhenU.com infringed the 1-800 Lenses trademark by using the 1-800 LENSES mark or confusingly similar terms as an element in the SaveNow proprietary directory. Ruling in favor of 800-Lenses.

TRUCK RENTAL INTERNATIONAL INC. V. WEB MARKETING LLC, FEDERAL DISTRICT COURT, WESTERN DISTRICT OF LONGVILLE (2009)

Facts

- Truck Rental International (TRI) Inc. claimed that Web Marketing LLC's pop-up advertising model infringed upon TRI's trademark. TRI alleged that Web Marketing's pop-up advertisements, which crowd the computer user's screen and block out TRI's website display, in effect, infringe on TRI's registered trademark.
- The SuperSavings program is computer software that operates only on the Microsoft Windows operating system. The SuperSavings software, if installed, resides on individual computer users' computer desktops. When a computer user who has

installed the SuperSavings software browses the Internet, the SuperSavings software scans activity conducted within the SuperSavings user's Internet browser, comparing URLs, website addresses, search terms, and web-page content accessed by the SuperSavings user with a proprietary directory, using algorithms contained in the software.

■ The average computer user who conducts a web search for the TRI website would expect the TRI website to appear on her computer screen; however, in this case, the computer screen fills with the advertisement of a TRI competitor.

■ The user must then click and close the pop-up advertisement window in order to get to her destination, the TRI website. While at first blush this detour in the user's web search seems like a siphoning off of a business opportunity, the fact is that the computer user consented to this detour when the user downloaded Web Marketing's computer software from the Internet. In other words, the user deliberately or unwittingly downloaded the pop-up advertisement software.

POINTS OF LAW AND OPINION EXCERPTS

Point (a)

A fundamental prerequisite for claims of trademark infringement pursuant to unfair competition is proof that the defendant used one of the plaintiff's protected marks in commerce.

Excerpt (a1)

"Web Marketing's pop-up advertisement software resides in individual computers as a result of the invitation and consent of the individual computer user and, thus, the advertisements do not use, alter, or interfere with TRI's trademarks and copyrights. Alas, computer users must endure pop-up advertising along with her ugly brother unsolicited bulk e-mail, 'spam,' as a burden of using the Internet."

Excerpt (a2)

"Domain names, like trade names, do not act as trademarks when they are used to identify a business entity; in order to infringe they must be used to identify the source of goods or services and 'where . . . the pure machine-linking function is the only use at issue, there is no trademark use and there can be no infringement.' Likewise in the instant case, Web Marketing's incorporation of TRI's URL and 'Truck Rental International' in the SuperSavings program is not a trademark use because Web Marketing merely uses the marks for the 'pure machine-linking function' and in no way advertises or promotes TRI's web address or any other TRI trademark."

Point b

In order to have a claim for trademark infringement under the Lanham Act, the mark owner must show that the defendant used the mark in a manner likely to confuse consumers.

Excerpt (b1)

"Consumer confusion is *not* established merely because trademarks are simultaneously visible to a consumer. Such comparative advertising does not violate trademark law, even when the advertising makes use of a competitor's trademark. A use of a rival's mark that does not engender confusion about origin or quality is permissible. For example, previous cases have held that the use of *'If You Like ESTEE LAUDER . . . You'll Love BEAUTY USA'* on a product's packaging and point of sale advertising is lawful comparative advertising. Thus, the appearance of Web Marketing's ads on a user's computer screen at the same time as the TRI web page is a result of how applications operate in the Windows environment and not consistent with evidence of intent to confuse the consumer."

Excerpt (b2)

"The SuperSavings program does not hinder or impede Internet users from accessing TRI's website. The SuperSavings program resides within the user's computer and does not interact or communicate with TRI's website, its computer servers, or its computer systems. Further, the SuperSavings program does not change the underlying appearance of the TRI website. In addition, the SuperSavings program is installed by the computer user who can decline to accept the licensing agreement or decline to download the program. Thus, the user controls the computer display the moment the Web Marketing ad pops up, and the user may also have other programs with pop-up windows notifying the user of an event within the computer system. The SuperSavings program is, therefore, no different than an e-mail system that pops a window up when the registered user receives a new e-mail message."

Held

In favor of Web Marketing. While pop-up advertisements seize the user's computer screen with a window of advertisement, blocking out the object of his search and his document and requiring the user to click several times to clear the computer screen, the advertisements do not meet the use and consumer confusion requirements necessary to prove trademark infringement.

CAPSTONE CASE STUDY 1
Coffee Wars: Starbucks v. Charbucks[1]

Overview and Objectives

Two years after opening their family-owned coffee bean roastery, Jim and Annie Clark had become accustomed to long workweeks and bootstrap financing. By 1997, their Black Bear Micro Roastery was finally growing, and the Clarks were hopeful that their new specialty blend, Charbucks, would give their uniquely dark-roasted coffee bean a catchy name to remember. Soon after launching the new blend, Annie Clark received a phone call from an insistent in-house lawyer at coffee giant Starbucks that threatened the very existence of the Clarks' company. Starbucks claimed that the Charbucks name and label infringed on its trademark, and it demanded that the Clarks cease the use of the name Charbucks and that any existing products with that name be removed from supermarket shelves. But the Clarks insisted that they had been careful to design the label with Black Bear Micro Roastery logos and that the name was tied to the dark-roasting process and not to anything related to the name Starbucks. Despite their beliefs that no infringement had taken place, the Clarks entered into settlement negotiations to avoid the legal costs associated with defending a trademark lawsuit. After the settlement negotiations failed, Starbucks sued Black Bear Micro Roastery and the stage was set for a coffee war that pitted a multinational powerhouse against a Main Street merchant. This case study emphasizes use of legal insight and business strategy, gives context for evaluating business ethics, and requires the application of trademark law.

Review Legal Concepts

Prior to reading the case, briefly review the following legal concepts that were covered in the textbook: legal insight and business strategy (p. 6), business, societal, and ethical contexts of law (p. 127), and trademark law (p. 683). Think of these areas of the law as you read the case study facts and questions.

[1] An earlier version of this case study appeared in the *Journal of Legal Studies Education* (29 J. Legal Stud. Educ. 27). Permission by Sean P. Melvin.

THE BLACK BEAR MICRO ROASTERY

Jim and Annie Clark were native New Englanders who shared a passion for coffee and an entrepreneurial spirit. After three years of research, they launched Black Bear Micro Roastery in 1995 with a mission of creating a unique methodology for roasting gourmet coffee beans through use of advanced technology and the "traditional Yankee work ethic." The company was situated in the lakes region of New Hampshire and targeted connoisseur coffee drinkers, primarily in the New England area, who appreciated the micro-roastery approach of producing small, high-quality batches of coffee beans. The beans were sold via mail order, from the Black Bear website, and through New England specialty stores and supermarkets. Eventually, Black Bear also sold its products through its own retail outlet and café in Portsmouth, New Hampshire.

True to their belief in the micro-roastery concept and their entrepreneurial courage, the Clarks invested their life savings in the company. In order to start the business, the couple sold many of their assets and refinanced the mortgage on their home for extra cash. They enlisted their teenage daughters as their labor force and committed to seven-day workweeks. The family business was the centerpiece of their family's livelihood.

As with many start-ups, business for Black Bear was slow and rocky at first. The price of green coffee beans had fluctuated unexpectedly, and the 1997 Teamsters strike at United Parcel Service had eaten into profit margins. Undeterred, Jim and Annie Clark kept the company going until it began to grow ever so slowly. In order to develop a niche in the gourmet coffee market, Black Bear began to develop unique blends with catchy names that were easy to remember. This included blends such as "Country French," "Kenya Safari," and "Mocha Java."

Charbucks

By April 1997, Black Bear had developed a loyal following from which it often solicited feedback and suggestions for new products. One common theme from customers was a desire for a blend with a darker-roasted bean that yielded a richer taste. Responding to that customer demand, Black Bear developed a darker-roasted blend and named it "Charbucks Blend." The *Char* was a reference to the new, darker-roasted coffee bean blend.

Charbucks Blend was sold in packaging that showed a picture of a black bear above the large-font printed words "Black Bear Micro Roastery." The label also informed consumers that the coffee was roasted and "Air Quenched" in New Hampshire, and it contained the catchphrase "You wanted it dark . . . You've got it dark!" There was no similarity between the Starbucks famous logo, a circular shape with the graphic of a mermaidlike siren encompassed by the phrase "Starbucks Coffee," and the Charbucks label except for the partial word *bucks.*

A CALL FROM GOLIATH

It didn't take long for Starbucks to get word of Charbucks Blend. Just four months after making their first sale of their new blend, the Clarks received a call from Starbucks' in-house counsel. In what Annie Clark described as an unmistakably threatening phone call, Starbucks' counsel insisted that Charbucks Blend was a violation of Starbucks' trademark rights and demanded that Black Bear cease the use of the name and take steps to completely remove Charbucks from the marketplace. Starbucks followed up with a formal demand to cease and desist and alleged that Black Bear's use of *Charbucks* was disparaging, diluted Starbucks' mark, and violated federal trademark law.

The Clarks held a family meeting to discuss the matter. While they agreed that they had done nothing wrong, they decided that a trademark battle with Starbucks could bankrupt their family business even if they eventually prevailed in court. The risk was too high, so they decided to pursue negotiations for settlement. They hired an attorney who sent Starbucks a letter on

Starbucks sued a small company in a battle over the use of the word "Charbucks."

behalf of Black Bear denying any liability for trademark infringement but also offering to engage in settlement negotiations given the limited time and financial resources that the Clarks had at their disposal. Starbucks hired outside counsel to negotiate a settlement agreement. In the event that settlement negotiations failed, Starbucks made it clear to Black Bear that it intended to file suit for trademark infringement. The negotiations dragged on for three years, and Black Bear's legal bills were soaring. Starbucks offered to compensate Black Bear for some of its legal expenses and costs of compliance (e.g., changing advertising, removing the products), but the parties could not agree on the amount or on a mutually acceptable public statement. On July 2, 2001, nearly four years after the first phone call about the dispute, Starbucks filed suit against Black Bear in the U.S. District Court for the Southern District of New York, alleging trademark dilution, trademark infringement, and violation of Section 43(a) of the Lanham Act (the federal trademark law). Starbucks demanded both damages and injunctive relief.

Starbucks' Strategy

The Clarks breathed a sigh of relief after learning that Zurich, the insurance carrier that issued Black Bear's general commercial liability insurance policy, determined that their company was covered under the policy for this particular lawsuit and that coverage for their legal defense costs against Starbucks would be provided. This allowed them the opportunity to have their day in court without the fear that Starbucks would use the litigation process to drive Black Bear out of business. Both sides were ordered to mediation, but little progress was made and the case looked headed for the courtroom.

However, soon after the mediation attempts failed, Starbucks employed a more aggressive litigation strategy. Its outside counsel notified Black Bear's counsel that unless the case was resolved, Starbucks would move to amend lawsuit to drop a claim for certain damages listed in the original complaint. The impact of this amendment was that Zurich would be able to withdraw coverage for Black Bear's defense on the basis that the remaining claims in the lawsuit were exempt from Black Bear's policy. Still, the Clarks would not settle the claim. Three months later, Starbucks followed through on its promise to amend the complaint, and Zurich soon notified the Clarks of its decision to terminate coverage for defense of the Starbucks case once the amendment was approved by the court. Ultimately, however, the court denied Starbucks' attempt to amend the complaint, finding that the amendment was designed primarily for affecting settlement negotiation leverage. Zurich was therefore compelled to continue covering the costs of Black Bear's defense.

In March 2005, a two-day trial was held in the matter of *Starbucks Corp. v. Wolfe's Borough Coffee, Inc., dba Black Bear Micro Roastery* in the U.S. District Court for the Southern District of New York. Starbucks relied primarily on the testimony of its expert, Warren Mitofsky, a scientist who had conducted a consumer survey and concluded that the number-one association of the nature of the name Charbucks in the mind of the consumers was with the brand Starbucks. However, Mitofsky also conceded that his survey had been conducted entirely by telephone and that any measurement of reaction to the familiarity with other visual cues, such as the Charbucks Blend label, could not be accomplished through a telephone survey. The trial court issued an opinion and order ruling in favor of Black Bear and dismissed all of the counts of Starbucks' complaint. The court held that Starbucks did not meet its burden of proving that *actual dilution* had taken place and that Starbucks could not prevail on the trademark infringement claim because there was no likelihood that consumers would confuse the Charbucks mark with the Starbucks mark.

For the time being, David had battled back Goliath—but the giant continued the fight in the appellate courts.

The Trademark Dilution Revision Act (TDRA)

In January 2006, Starbucks filed an appeal of the trial court's decision. While the appeal was pending, Congress amended the trademark laws by passing the Trademark Dilution Revision Act (TDRA) of 2006. The TDRA was passed primarily in response to the U.S. Supreme Court's decision in *Moseley v. V Secret Catalogue, Inc.,* in which the Court established the burden of proof for trademark holders by requiring evidence of *actual dilution.* Starbucks then argued that under the TDRA the test for dilution was substantially easier to meet because the statute rejects actual dilution in favor of a more relaxed *likelihood of dilution* standard. In its appeal, Starbucks contended that the TDRA definition of dilution by blurring and/or tarnishment was directly related to its claims against Black Bear and that the case should now be evaluated in light of changes made by the TDRA.

The appellate wheels of justice were grinding slowly in this case. The appellate court ordered a rehearing by the trial court in light of the TDRA. The trial court again entered a judgment in favor of Black Bear for substantially the same reasons detailed in the first opinion. Not surprisingly, Starbucks appealed.

In a December 2009 opinion, the U.S. Court of Appeals for the Second Circuit handed down its decision and affirmed much of the trial court's ruling. Specifically:

- Although the appellate court agreed with the trial court's conclusion that the Charbucks package design was significantly different in imagery, color, and format from Starbucks' logo and signage, the appellate court also held that the trial court had used the incorrect analytical framework for dilution by blurring as set out in the TDRA. Therefore, the appellate court remanded this one issue back to the trial court.

- The appellate court affirmed the trial court's ruling that Starbucks did not provide sufficient evidence that dilution had occurred through tarnishment because Black Bear's intent was clearly to promote a positive image for its brand of coffee rather than referring to it as a way to harm the reputation of Starbucks' coffees.

- The appellate court also affirmed the trial court's ruling that no infringement had occurred under the federal trademark statute and agreed with Black Bear's argument that the coexistence of the Starbucks mark and Charbucks Blend for 11 years with no report of a single customer becoming confused is a powerful indication that there is no confusion or likelihood of confusion.

Connecting Legal and Ethical Concepts: Questions for Discussion

Chapter 1, "Legal Foundations"

1. What lessons can managers learn from this case in terms of avoiding trademark liability and of decision making when enforcing a trademark?

2. Consider the Charbucks dispute from a cost-benefit perspective. What was the return on Starbucks' investment to pursue Black Bear for trademark infringement? Even if Black Bear's defense was covered by insurance, did the investment of time by the Clarks yield a sufficient return?

3. At what point, if any, does the cost-benefit analysis suggest that a settlement agreement would have yielded the most return for each party?

Chapter 5, "Business, Societal, and Ethical Contexts of Law"

1. Consider Starbucks' litigation strategy. When it used legal maneuvering to attempt to get Zurich to withdraw, was that ethical? Was it a legitimate

hard-nosed business practice, or did Starbucks use its resources in an attempt to force Black Bear into settlement?

2. Starbucks invests substantial resources into its theme of being a responsible company. On its website, the company announces, "We've always believed that businesses can—and should—have a positive impact on the communities they serve." How does that statement square with its strategy in the Charbucks litigation? Is there any ethical conflict between a company's stated objective to be a good corporate neighbor and its obligation to its stakeholders to protect its intellectual property?

3. Even if Black Bear was legally entitled to use *Charbucks,* is it ethical to use a name that sounds so close to someone else's famous coffee trademark?

Chapter 25, "Intellectual Property"

1. The TDRA defines blurring as an "association arising from the similarity between a mark and a famous mark that impairs the distinctiveness of the famous mark." How should the trial court rule on the issue of dilution by blurring given the new language in the TDRA?

2. Should the court have given more weight to the testimony of Starbucks' expert? Although the survey was conducted by telephone, shouldn't consumer confusion in the similar sounds (*Charbucks* versus it *Starbucks*) be sufficient to show blurring?

3. What legal issues must a famous-mark holder consider in preserving its trademark?

ASSIGNMENT: Find Black Bear a Trademark

Think of several names and a mark that Black Bear could have used for dark-roasted coffee beans instead of Charbucks. Conduct a preliminary search on the USPTO's website (www.uspto.gov) and on a commercial domain name website such as www.register.com to see if the name or mark is available. Use your knowledge of dilution law to be sure that your trademark is viable and protectable.

Overview and Objectives

In 1996, a deadly strain of bacteria broke out among residents of some West Coast states and eventually spread into western Canada. When the bacteria was traced to juice products made by the Odwalla Juice Company in California, the company's loyal customers and market analysts were shocked in disbelief. Odwalla had prided itself on being a socially responsible company that was passionate about producing the healthiest juice on the market.

The events that followed the outbreak provide an example of how vastly different areas of the law impact corporate strategy during a corporate crisis and how business ethics principles help drive the decision-making process. The objective of this case study[1] is to attempt to understand legal and ethical implications using a comprehensive and practical approach. In analyzing this case, students hone skills in constructing a business strategy for handling a crisis by (1) spotting the multifaceted legal and ethical challenges of the crisis, (2) recognizing the strengths and weaknesses in Odwalla's responses, and (3) using legal insight and ethical decision-making models to craft a response.

Review Legal Concepts

Prior to reading the case, briefly review the following legal concepts that were covered previously in this textbook: food and drug safety (p. 612), products liability (p. 282), negligence (p. 272), criminal law (p. 584), and business ethics (p. 127). Think of these areas of the law as you read the case study facts and questions.

THE ODWALLA JUICE COMPANY'S ORIGINS

Odwalla Juice Company was started in 1986 by a group of health-conscious friends living together in the San Francisco Bay area. Starting with a hand juicer and organically grown fruit, the owners produced fresh juice in the back shed of one of the founders' homes and sold their juice by delivering it daily to area restaurants.

Perhaps the most essential part of their business model was their claim that their juice was fresh from the fruit, without the pasteurization process that was used by other juice producers. In fact, Odwalla was one of the pioneers of a wider movement in the United States favoring more organic food consumption. Odwalla's founders held the belief that pasteurization—the process of heating the juice to a certain temperature for purposes of killing any bacteria that had developed during growing, picking, or processing—affected the taste of the juice and was unnecessary. Instead, Odwalla used an acid-based rinsing process to kill bacteria. Producing fresh organic fruit juice as a central component of its business model, Odwalla developed a loyal following of consumers who desired the freshest juice possible, and its sales grew exponentially. By the mid-1990s, Odwalla was selling nearly $90 million worth of juice per year.

"SOIL TO SOUL"

Odwalla's founders were at the forefront of the corporate social responsibility movement that can be traced to the mid-1980s. Indeed, as one of the founders was fond of saying, they embraced a "Zen-like philosophy" in all of their dealings, and community was an important factor in the equation. The company employed a *soil to soul* metaphor to describe its commitment to using fresh organic fruit (soil) to nurture the "body whole" (soul) of its consumers. Odwalla's reputation as a socially responsible, growth-oriented company flourished as it received awards from *Business Ethics* magazine in 1995 for Outstanding Corporate Environmentalism and from *Inc.* magazine in 1996 as Employer of the Year.

CRISIS ON THE COAST

In early October 1996, an outbreak of *E. coli*[2] struck several West Coast states, including California and Washington, and reached into western Canada as well. *E. coli* is a potentially deadly bacterium that develops

---

[1]A complete bibliography for this case study may be found on this textbook's website at www.mhhe.com/melvinleb2e.

[2]For purposes of this case study, *E. coli* is shorthand for *E. coli O157:H7*, which is the name of a strain of bacteria that lives in the digestive tracts of humans and animals. *E. coli* has been found in uncooked meat, raw milk or dairy products, and raw fruits and vegetables that have not been properly pasteurized or processed.

The Odwalla juice company faced a corporate crisis, which included legal issues and ethical questions, after its product was tied to an *E. coli* outbreak.

as a result of contamination of food products or processing. On October 30, 1996, health officials in the state of Washington notified Odwalla that they were investigating a possible link between the *E. coli* outbreak and Odwalla apple and carrot juice. After learning of the potential link, Odwalla's executive management team had an emergency meeting to discuss their response. Although there was no demonstrable link at this point, Odwalla's executive management team decided to mobilize a voluntary recall of products containing apple or carrot products. This was a major financial commitment involving the removal of Odwalla products from nearly 4,600 retail outlets in seven states in just 48 hours. Odwalla claimed that it spent $6.5 million on the recall effort.

Odwalla's corporate crisis took a tragic turn when, in November 1996, a 16-month-old child died from *E. coli* after drinking Odwalla apple juice. As many as 60

other consumers were hospitalized with *E. coli*–related illnesses in a period of just one month. At the height of the outbreak, government investigators confirmed that the Odwalla products were in fact the source of the *E. coli* contamination. Odwalla implemented a media strategy that included issuing daily statements to the press, holding internal conference calls where by managers were informed of updates, and setting up a website to disseminate information. Odwalla publicly promised to pay for all medical expenses of injured consumers and to reevaluate its manufacturing process immediately.

FALLOUT

Odwalla's brand name was decimated by the crisis. Immediately after the outbreak, Odwalla's stock price dropped 34 percent and sales of its juice products fell 90 percent in one month. The outbreak triggered numerous investigations by federal and state authorities. Customers filed negligence lawsuits, claiming that Odwalla had known that the acid-rinse method was ineffective and that scientific studies had shown that the method was effective in killing bacteria that caused *E. coli* only 8 percent of the time. After it had been shown that pasteurization was a widely used practice in the industry (although not required by federal or state laws) and that Odwalla management had ignored its own head of quality assurance's warning about potential contamination sources in the factory, the Food and Drug Administration levied a $1.5 million fine, the largest in the agency's history at that time.

Immediately after the recall, Odwalla was widely praised by the media and commentators for its handling of the crisis. The company decided that, despite mounting financial pressures from lawsuits and fines, no employees would be laid off and that it would continue to donate to community charities. Odwalla hired a public relations firm that constructed a standard explanation that the contamination was unforeseeable and that all appropriate safety measures were in place. The public largely believed Odwalla's explanations because its reputation for social responsibility was ironclad in its consumers' minds. Even the parents of the child whose *E. coli*–related death had ignited the crisis were quoted as saying that they didn't blame the company for her death and that Odwalla had done everything it could have under the circumstances.

However, during the discovery process in one of the lawsuits filed by an injured consumer, it was revealed that Odwalla had more knowledge of a potential health hazard prior to the outbreak than had been previously reported. A report surfaced that indicated that the U.S. Army had rejected Odwalla's proposal to sell its juice in U.S. Army commissaries after an army inspector found uncommonly high levels of bacteria in a sample and concluded that the risk of contamination was extraordinarily high. The army rejection had taken place four months prior to the *E. coli* outbreak. Responding to the army's findings, Odwalla's head of quality assurance recommended that the company add an additional layer of contamination protection by employing a chlorine-based washing system for the fruit. His recommendations were rejected, however, due to management's concern that the chlorine wash would affect the taste of the juice. After the army disclosures were made public, Odwalla settled several lawsuits despite its earlier resistance to a nonlitigation solution.

Soon after the settlement, *The Seattle Times* wrote a scathing editorial about Odwalla's course of action. The editorial predicted that Odwalla would forever be known as "the careless provider of poisoned fruit juice." Odwalla's stock was now trading at its lowest level ever, and the company was incurring massive debt to cover litigation costs and technology upgrades.

ODWALLA TODAY

After the fallout from the *E. coli* crisis, Odwalla invested heavily in quality assurance technology and eventually became an innovator of a "flash-pasteurization" process that killed all bacteria but kept the fresh taste and quality of the juice intact. Just two years after the crisis began, the readers of *San Francisco Magazine* voted Odwalla "Best Brand." Although the company looked poised for a comeback, it had accrued substantial debt and was forced to begin exploring the possibility of merger opportunities. After a merger with East Coast juice maker Fresh Samantha in 2000, Odwalla ended up as part of a large acquisition by the Minute Maid division of the Coca-Cola Company in October 2001. Today, Odwalla remains a subsidiary of Coca-Cola and has over 650 employees. Its management continues to focus on its "soil to soul" model, and Odwalla now features 25 organic products within eight product lines, including smoothies, soy shakes, and food bars.

Connecting Legal and Ethical Concepts: Questions for Discussion

Chapter 5, "Business, Societal, and Ethical Contexts of Law"

1. Is there a disconnect between Odwalla's corporate social responsibility model and its actions or course

of conduct? In what ways did Odwalla's course of conduct differ from its stated social goals?

2. Because Odwalla was not specifically required to use the pasteurization process at the time, what ethical considerations factor into the decision on whether or not to use pasteurization?

3. Does the fact that the industry standard at the time was to subject juice to pasteurization impact the ethical decision-making analysis?

Chapter 10, "Torts and Products Liability"

1. Did the manufacturing or *design process* of the juice render it an unreasonably dangerous product under the Restatements? Why or why not?

2. Are there any other ways in which the product could have been defective aside from manufacturing or design?

3. What defenses, if any, could Odwalla use to rebut a claim of a defective product?

Chapter 10, "Torts and Products Liability"

1. Are there any incidents of negligence indicated in the case (either pre- or postcontamination)?

2. In the context of a negligence analysis, what legal duties did Odwalla owe to its consumers? Does it owe any special duty to consumers?

3. Does failing to comply with industry standards at the time of the contamination constitute a breach of duty?

Chapter 22, "Consumer Protection Law"

1. What federal statute regulates Odwalla's processes and procedures?

2. Because the FDA required no specific pasteurization standards at the time, should Odwalla be fined for failing to use such a system?

3. If Odwalla had not voluntarily recalled the juice, what options did the FDA have in response to the outbreak?

Chapter 23, "Criminal Law and Procedure in Business"

1. Apply the Model Penal Code sections on criminal liability for business entities to the Odwalla case. Do the facts in the case indicate that Odwalla's action rose to the level of criminal culpability? If yes, what defense, if any, is available to Odwalla?

2. Odwalla's managers consistently issued statements denying that they had any actual or constructive knowledge that Odwalla's processing systems were

dangerous. Do any facts in the case study contradict those statements? Are these facts sufficient to establish the elements of criminal intent on the part of the executives who made the denials?

ASSIGNMENT: Devise Odwalla's Strategy

Odwalla ordered a voluntary recall that was expensive and potentially devastating to the company before an affirmative link was found. Assume you were one of the managers at the Odwalla emergency meeting held after the *E.coli* outbreak. What were Odwalla's options? Using the legal decisions in business analytical model in Chapter 1, "Legal Foundations," and the ethical decision-making paradigm in Chapter 5, "Business, Societal, and Ethical Contexts of Law," as a starting point, devise a strategy that includes the appropriate balance between (1) representing the best interests of the primary and secondary stakeholders, (2) protecting the company's future, (3) minimizing the risk of public harm, and (4) fulfilling the corporation's commitment to corporate social responsibility.

Overview and Objectives

In August 2001, the Federal Bureau of Investigation arrested eight individuals involved in a nationwide scheme to defraud the McDonald's Corporation and its customers by fraudulently manipulating McDonald's promotional prize contests over a period of five years. Although no McDonald's employees were implicated in the scam, the arrests sparked class action litigation by customers and competitors against McDonald's under a variety of legal theories. The events that led up to the arrests and the legal and ethical implications of McDonald's response to the revelations of the fraud are examined in this case study.[1]

Review Legal Concepts

Prior to reading the case, briefly review the following legal concepts that were covered in the textbook: standing (p. 97), arbitration (p. 110), consumer fraud (p. 603), contracts agreement (p. 168), unjust enrichment (p. 168), agency (p. 310), criminal law (p. 631), and business ethics (p. 123). Think of these areas of the law as you read the case study facts and questions.

MCDONALD'S PROMOTIONAL GAMES

McDonald's is perhaps the most familiar fast-food restaurant name in the world. The business began in 1940 with a restaurant opened by brothers Richard and Maurice McDonald in San Bernardino, California. Their introduction of the "Speedee Service System" in 1948 established the principles of the modern fast-food restaurant. The present company dates it founding to the opening of one of the first McDonald's franchises by Ray Kroc. Eventually, Mr. Kroc purchased the McDonald brothers' shares and began a worldwide expansion. The company was listed on the public stock market in 1965, and there are now more than 32,000 McDonald's restaurants around the world.

Marketing Strategies One of McDonald's most successful marketing strategies has been to use various cash games of chance based on themes from popular television shows such as *Who Wants to Be*

a *Millionaire?* and another promotional cash game based on the popular board game *Monopoly*. McDonald's operates these games as part of a consolidated national and international advertising and marketing effort. Industry experts have lauded McDonald's games as highly effective in attracting more customers and encouraging more visits by offering the opportunity to win instant prizes ranging from food to cash prizes of $1 million. Each of the promotional games has low-value, midvalue, and high-value prizes. In order to win a prize, a McDonald's customer obtains a game piece, which may be (1) received at a restaurant, either attached to food containers (such as french fry boxes and drink cups) or unattached and handed out separately, (2) found in an advertising insert of a newspaper, (3) received by direct mail, or

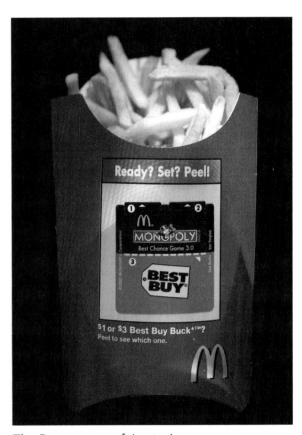

The Department of Justice's announcement of arrests related to a fraud scheme involving game pieces from McDonald's *Monopoly* promotional game sparked legal and ethical challenges for the fast-food giant.

[1]A complete bibliography for this case study may be found on this textbook's website at www.mhhe.com/melvinleb2e.

(4) obtained by requesting a game piece via the mail. Customers have the opportunity to become instant winners or to win by collecting specific game pieces. Low-value prizes include food items and low-dollar cash prizes. High-value prizes include vehicles and cash prizes up to $1 million. Customers can either win the cash prize by obtaining an instant $1 million–winner game piece or by collecting a sufficient number of certain game pieces.

Simon Marketing

Simon Marketing, Inc., an international marketing company headquartered in Los Angeles, was originally hired by McDonald's to develop its highly successful Happy Meals prize and promotional campaigns in the 1980s. Simon eventually became the exclusive company handling McDonald's promotional games, including "Monopoly Game at McDonald's," "Hatch, Match and Win," "When the USA Wins, You Win," and "Who Wants to Be a Millionaire?" In order to claim a high-value prize, the winner was required to redeem the winning game piece through Simon's security procedures. After receiving a game piece claim, Simon would confirm the legitimacy of the game piece and notify McDonald's that the claim was legitimate. McDonald's then distributed the prize to the winner.

In addition to verifying winning game pieces, Simon was also responsible for the printing and distribution of game pieces. As part of its agreement with McDonald's, Simon provided security measures to ensure the integrity of promotional games. Simon entrusted its security chief, retired police officer Jerome Jacobson, with the responsibility of ensuring the games' integrity and with disseminating the high-value pieces through legitimate channels.

Arrests and Indictments

In August 2001, the U.S. Attorney's Office filed criminal charges against eight people in Georgia, South Carolina, Florida, Texas, Indiana, and Wisconsin as part of a nationwide investigation into a plot to defraud the public by diverting winning game pieces from various McDonald's cash award giveaways. Dubbed "Operation Final Answer" by government investigators, the Department of Justice alleged that the group had been responsible for more than $20 million worth of winning game pieces that were diverted from proper delivery and then fraudulently claimed by winners pretending to be legitimate. The ringleader of the plot was 58-year-old Jerome Jacobson, the director of security at Simon Marketing. Jacobson devised a way to remove high-price game pieces prior to their distribution to retail McDonald's restaurants. Jacobson concocted a system

of recruiters (none of whom were Simon or McDonald's employees) who solicited others willing to falsely claim that they were legitimate winners of the McDonald's games. Prosecutors alleged that Jacobson sold $1 million prize pieces from the games and charged the fake winner $50,000 in cash plus a commission for the recruiter. On midvalue prizes and luxury vehicle prizes, the recruiters would sell the winning game pieces to other family members or friends. Among those arrested were a husband and wife whose son acted as one of Jacobson's recruiters.

After Jacobson agreed to cooperate with federal authorities in exchange for leniency, the government announced criminal indictments of 51 more individuals involved in the scam. Eventually, Jacobson pled guilty and was sentenced to 37 months in prison, assessed $750,000 in fines, and ordered to pay $13.4 million in restitution.

Civil Suits

Two weeks after the government announced the indictment, the first civil lawsuit was filed against McDonald's. By October 2001, so many civil suits had been filed against it that McDonald's asked the federal courts to consolidate all of the litigation into a single proceeding. Lawsuits alleged various claims, including violation of consumer fraud protection laws, unjust enrichment, and breach of contract. In many cases, the plaintiff sought class action[2] status.

In one case filed in an Illinois trial court, a customer sued McDonald's and Simon under the state consumer fraud statute and sought class action status. The plaintiffs alleged that McDonald's and Simon's actions constituted deceptive conduct and omissions of material terms from their promotional games. They pointed to evidence that McDonald's had been made aware of the fraud being conducted by Jacobson but had continued to market its promotional games, including publishing the odds of winning, for at least an additional eight months. However, because of Jacobson's scheme, the plaintiffs alleged that their actual odds of winning a substantial prize were zero.

Other cases centered on a theory of unjust enrichment. In these cases, plaintiffs alleged that McDonald's promotional games were highly successful and resulted in increased revenue for McDonald's and Simon. The plaintiffs pointed to evidence that McDonald's had a

---

[2]A class action lawsuit is a method for conducting a lawsuit in which a large group of persons with a well-defined common interest (class) has a representative of the group litigate the claim on behalf of the larger group, without the need to join every individual member of the class.

spike in sales during certain promotions. They alleged that McDonald's continued to use the promotion even after it knew that the integrity of the game was compromised and, therefore, that any profits made were caused by the fraud. Because customers were induced to purchase McDonald's products through the promotion, McDonald's was unjustly enriched by retaining the profits from the products.

McDonald's was also sued by its competitors over the scandal. In *Phoenix of Broward, Inc. v. McDonald's Corporation,*[3] the owner of a Burger King franchise in Fort Lauderdale, Florida, filed suit against McDonald's for false advertising and unfair competition. The owner alleged that McDonald's had enticed customers away from Burger King by employing the promotional game. Because the promotional materials represented that each customer had a fair chance to win the high-value prizes, Phoenix alleged that McDonald's actual knowledge that the game was rigged and its course of conduct, after learning of the FBI investigation, in continuing the promotion constituted unfair competition. Phoenix also claimed that the fraudulent game promotion yielded an unnatural spike in profits for McDonald's and that the Burger King franchise suffered damages as a result of McDonald's conduct.

MCDONALD'S STRATEGY

On the day the Justice Department announced the arrest of Jacobson and seven others, McDonald's announced that it was suspending the game entirely pending an internal investigation of the matter. It also announced a campaign to regain any lost public trust by launching an immediate $10 million promotional giveaway. The promotion allowed customers to win prizes of up to $1 million from promotional game pieces during a week-long period beginning in late August 2001.

Immediately after the arrests, McDonald's terminated its 25-year relationship with Simon by unilaterally canceling its contract with the agency. The move was devastating to Simon because McDonald's represented two-thirds of the agency's annual revenue.[4] After the revelations of fraud, Simon's other major client, Philip Morris,[5] which contracted with Simon to run promotional campaigns for its Kraft and Marlboro brands, also terminated its relationship with Simon. In

less than one week, the value of Simon's public shares plunged 78 percent, and the company was facing dozens of lawsuits and a criminal investigation.

Aggressive Litigation   McDonald's employed what can aptly be described as an aggressive litigation strategy by vigorously defending lawsuits while also pursuing Simon for reimbursement of the costs being incurred by McDonald's because of the fraudulent act of Simon's employee.

For each case that it defended that was related to the fraud, either McDonald's challenged the *standing* of the plaintiffs to bring an action against McDonald's based on the fraud or it sought a court order to compel *arbitration* based on the published rules of the game.

Phoenix Case   In the *Phoenix* case, McDonald's asserted that Phoenix did not have standing in a case alleging unfair competition because McDonald's actions were unrelated to any provable harm suffered by Phoenix's restaurant. Phoenix alleged that McDonald's misrepresented customers' chances to win high-value prizes but also alleged that as a result of this false advertising, the fraudulent promotion induced customers who would have eaten at Phoenix's Burger King restaurants (and not any other fast-food restaurants) to eat at McDonald's. Ultimately the courts agreed with McDonald's and dismissed the lawsuit, holding that Phoenix's allegations of the link between the false advertising (McDonald's games) and the injury suffered by Phoenix (decrease in Burger King's sales) was too vague to have standing to sue.

Customer Lawsuits   While McDonald's was successful at repelling suits by competitors, its attempts to halt lawsuits by its customers had mixed results. The stakes for customer lawsuits were becoming increasingly high as each plaintiff requested class action status. In each customer case, McDonald's argued that the plaintiff was bound by the terms of the Official Contest Rules published by McDonald's in conjunction with each of its promotional cash giveaway games. The rules included an arbitration clause whereby participants in the game promotion agreed to resolve any disputes by final and binding arbitration. The clause called for the arbitration to be held at the regional office of the American Arbitration Association (AAA) located closest to the participant.

In *Popovich v. McDonald's,*[6] a federal district court ruled that the arbitration clause included in the official rules was invalid because the arbitration costs were too

---

[3]489 F.3d 1156 (11th Cir. 2007).
[4]In the year prior to the scandal, Simon's annual revenue was $768 million.
[5]Philip Morris changed its name to Altria in 2003.

[6]189 F. Supp. 2d 772 (2002).

prohibitive. Popovich argued that the fees associated with an arbitration proceeding rendered the arbitration agreement an ineffective way to enforce his statutory rights of recovery from McDonald's for its fraudulent conduct. Popovich submitted evidence that, under the AAA rules, his claim would have to be arbitrated using the high-fee *commercial* procedures instead of the much lower cost *consumer* procedures. In ruling in favor of Popovich, the court held that because Popovich sought $20 million in damages for his potential class action, the fees required by the AAA would be between $48,000 and $126,000. The court concluded that, in the context of this claim, the arbitration costs were prohibitive and the clause was thus unenforceable.

An alternate theory was advanced by the plaintiff in *James v. McDonald's Corp.*[7] In that case, James argued that she should not be forced to arbitrate her claims because she never entered into an agreement to arbitrate her dispute. The plaintiff claimed that she was not aware of the rules, much less any rules that deprived her of a jury trial. She maintained that customers cannot be expected to read every container of food they purchase in order to know that they are entering into a contract. She also argued that, even if she was found to be bound by the rules, the arbitration clause in the rules was invalid because it was overly burdensome due to the high upfront costs required to pursue a claim through the AAA. However, the court ultimately ruled against James, found the arbitration clause to be valid, and refused to allow her lawsuit to go forward in the courts. In rejecting James's claim that the costs were too burdensome, the court pointed out that James had not submitted evidence that she considered applying for a fee waiver from the AAA that could have reduced the fees significantly.

SIMON LAWSUIT AND COUNTERSUIT

Two months after McDonald's terminated its relationship with Simon, its parent company filed a $1.9 billion lawsuit against McDonald's in which the company alleged breach of contract, fraud, and defamation. Simon alleged that, after learning of the nearly yearlong FBI investigation, McDonald's ran a fraudulent campaign to intentionally destroy Simon for its own public relations and financial benefit. The lawsuit also accused McDonald's of orchestrating a smear campaign through McDonald's representatives' contacting other Simon clients and urging them to quit doing business with Simon. Simon alleged that McDonald's

abrupt termination of their contract was unwarranted and unlawful and resulted in substantial losses.

McDonald's responded with a $105 million countersuit against Simon for negligence in failing to detect the fraud scheme and for breach of contract. McDonald's contended that its contract with Simon required Simon to repay McDonald's for any losses it incurred as a result of Simon's conduct. Given the losses from the embezzlement and the subsequent giveaway that was required to restore public confidence, McDonald's argued that it was entitled to be reimbursed by Simon.

SETTLEMENTS AND AFTERMATH

After aggressively battling litigants in the courtroom for a year, McDonald's reevaluated its two-front litigation strategy. The company engaged in settlement negotiations with customer lawsuit plaintiffs and was able to structure an agreement with Simon's insurance carrier that ultimately helped settle the class action claims filed against it by various customers. One year later, McDonald's agreed to a final settlement with Simon.

Customer Class Actions The uncertainties surrounding the arbitration clause and expenses of litigating a class action case resulted in a change in McDonald's strategy. Beginning in April 2002, McDonald's and Simon began to settle the various class action complaints filed by consumers by tapping the proceeds from Simon's liability insurance policies. Eventually, McDonald's settled a similar class action consumer suit filed in Canada.

Simon Litigation In an August 2003 filing with the Securities and Exchange Commission, McDonald's reported that it had agreed to pay Simon $16.6 million to settle all claims that were raised in the lawsuit.[8] However, in the meantime, Simon had effectively eliminated a majority of its ongoing promotion business operations and was in the process of disposing of its assets and settling liabilities related to the fraud. During the second quarter of 2002, the company ceased operations altogether except for attempting to find a buyer for its remaining assets. A September 2009 filing indicated that the company had reduced its workforce to 4 employees (from 136 employees in 2001). Although the company was not successful in finding a buyer for many years, in

---

[7] 417 F.3d 672 (7th Cir. 2005).

[8] Simon also sued Philip Morris and Simon Marketing's auditing firms (KPMG, PricewaterhouseCoopers, and Ernst & Young). Each case was settled before trial with a favorable outcome for Simon.

December 2009, Simon's remaining directors issued public disclosures that they had formed a committee to investigate the potential of an acquisition or combination with another company.

Connecting Legal and Ethical Concepts: Questions for Discussion

Chapter 4, "Resolving Disputes: Litigation and Alternative Dispute Resolution Options"

1. In the *Phoenix* case, the court ruled that competitors didn't have standing to sue McDonald's for fraud in the promotional games. Would competitors have standing to sue McDonald's Would customers have standing?

2. Could the arbitration clause used by McDonald's in its rules fit into any of the four grounds for unenforceability under the Federal Arbitration Act?

Chapter 5, "Business, Societal, and Ethical Contexts of Law"

1. Consider the ethical dilemma of McDonald's if it was approached by government authorities and informed that the promotion's integrity was suspect because of possible embezzlement. However, in order to gather additional evidence, investigators requested that McDonald's take no action until arrests were made. What was McDonald's ethical duty at this point? If it continued to run the game with knowledge of the fraud, no matter what its motives, wouldn't that expose the company to significant liability?

2. Is there a conflict in this case between McDonald's duties to primary stakeholders and its duties to secondary shareholders?

3. Was McDonald's decision not to discontinue the promotion in the face of ongoing fraud more of a principles-based approach or a consequences-based approach to ethical decision making?

4. Was the use of class action litigation ethically justified in this case? Were the civil suits an attempt to redress harm or a boon for law firms that specialize in class action litigation? Were the plaintiffs more interested in shaking down McDonald's or in justice?

Chapter 6, "Overview and Language of Contracts"

1. Why did trial courts consider the rules' contractual language binding on participants of the games when it was obvious that most customers hadn't actually read the rules? Had the customers agreed to the terms of the rules contract simply by purchasing a soft drink? Why or why not?

2. Assuming that offer and acceptance are satisfied, what consideration supports a customer-McDonald's contract?

3. Could the inclusion of an arbitration clause by McDonald's in an advertisement amid logos and trademarks be considered bad faith and held invalid as unconscionable?

Chapter 11, "Agency"

1. What was the agency status and relationship between McDonald's and Simon? Based on your answer, what duties did the parties owe each other? Were any duties breached?

2. To what extent was Simon liable for the embezzlement scheme of its employee Jacobson? Were Jacobson's actions within the scope of his employment? Why or why not?

Chapter 22, "Consumer Protection Law"

1. Could McDonald's conduct, specifically its continuing operations after being informed of possible fraud in its promotional games, constitute deceptive advertising and a deceptive sales practice under FTC regulations?

2. Suppose that one lawsuit that was brought against McDonald's was in New Jersey and the state court applied the New Jersey Consumer Fraud Act in the same way the appellate court applied it in *Vagias v. Woodmont Properties* (Case 22.1). Would McDonald's be liable under the state law? Why or why not?

3. Would your answers to Questions 1 and 2 above be the same if McDonald's halted the promotion as soon as it learned of the FBI investigation?

Chapter 23, "Criminal Law and Procedure in Business"

1. Do Jacobson's actions amount to fraud? Embezzlement? Theft?

2. Ultimately, the government charged Jacobson and his co-conspirators with mail fraud and wire fraud. Why do you think the government did not charge them with embezzlement?

3. Could the executives of Simon be held criminally liable for the embezzlement perpetrated by Jacobson? Why or why not?

ASSIGNMENT: Devise a Strategy for McDonald's

Assume you are one of the managers called to a confidential meeting to discuss McDonald's strategy after notification by government authorities that its promotional games were being rigged by a Simon insider. What are McDonald's options? Using the legal decisions in business analytical model in Chapter 1, "Legal Foundations," and the ethical decision-making paradigm in Chapter 5, "Business, Societal, and Ethical Contexts of Law" as a starting point, devise a strategy that includes the appropriate balance between (1) representing the best interests of its primary and secondary stakeholders, (2) protecting the future of the company, (3) minimizing the risk of public harm, and (4) addressing factors related to corporate social responsibility. Memorialize your strategy in a two-page memorandum.

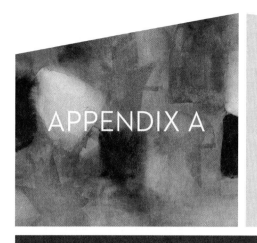

The Constitution of the United States of America

Preamble

We the People of the United States, in Order to form a more perfect Union, establish Justice, insure domestic Tranquility, provide for the common defense, promote the general Welfare, and secure the Blessings of Liberty to ourselves and our Posterity, do ordain and establish this Constitution for the United States of America.

Article I

Section 1 All legislative Powers herein granted shall be vested in a Congress of the United States, which shall consist of a Senate and House of Representatives.

Section 2 The House of Representatives shall be composed of Members chosen every second Year by the People of the several States, and the Electors in each State shall have the Qualifications requisite for Electors of the most numerous Branch of the State Legislature.

No Person shall be a Representative who shall not have attained to the age of twenty five Years, and been seven Years a Citizen of the United States, and who shall not, when elected, be an Inhabitant of that State in which he shall be chosen.

Representatives and direct Taxes shall be apportioned among the several States which may be included within this Union, according to their respective Numbers, which shall be determined by adding to the whole Number of free Persons, including those bound to Service for a Term of Years, and excluding Indians not taxed, three fifths of all other Persons.[1] The actual Enumeration shall be made within three Years after the first Meeting of the Congress of the United States, and within every subsequent Term of ten Years, in such Manner as they shall by Law direct. The Number of Representatives shall not exceed one for every thirty Thousand, but each State shall have at Least one Representative, and until such enumeration shall be made, the State of New Hampshire shall be entitled to choose three, Massachusetts eight, Rhode-Island and Providence Plantations one, Connecticut five, New York six, New Jersey four, Pennsylvania eight, Delaware one, Maryland six, Virginia ten, North Carolina five, South Carolina five, and Georgia three.

When vacancies happen in the Representation from any State, the Executive Authority thereof shall issue Writs of Election to fill such Vacancies.

The House of Representatives shall chuse their Speaker and other Officers; and shall have the sole Power of Impeachment.

Section 3 The Senate of the United States shall be composed of two Senators from each State, chosen by the Legislature thereof,[2] for six Years; and each Senator shall have one Vote.

Immediately after they shall be assembled in Consequence of the first Election, they shall be divided as equally as may be into three Classes. The Seats of the Senators of the first Class shall

---

[1]Changed by the Fourteenth Amendment.
[2]Changed by the Seventeenth Amendment.

be vacated at the Expiration of the second Year, of the second Class at the Expiration of the fourth Year, and of the third Class at the Expiration of the sixth Year, so that one third may be chosen every second Year; and if Vacancies happen by Resignation, or otherwise, during the Recess of the Legislature of any State, the Executive thereof may make temporary Appointments until the next Meeting of the Legislature, which shall then fill such Vacancies.[3]

No Person shall be a Senator who shall not have attained to the Age of thirty Years, and been nine Years a Citizen of the United States, and who shall not, when elected, be an Inhabitant of that State for which he shall be chosen.

The Vice President of the United States shall be President of the Senate, but shall have no Vote, unless they be equally divided.

The Senate shall chuse their other Officers, and also a President pro tempore, in the Absence of the Vice President, or when he shall exercise the Office of President of the United States.

The Senate shall have the sole Power to try all Impeachments. When sitting for that Purpose, they shall be on Oath or Affirmation. When the President of the United States is tried, the Chief Justice shall preside: And no Person shall be convicted without the Concurrence of two thirds of the Members present.

Judgment in Cases of Impeachment shall not extend further than to removal from Office, and disqualification to hold and enjoy any Office of honor, Trust or Profit under the United States: but the Party convicted shall nevertheless be liable and subject to Indictment, Trial, Judgment and Punishment, according to Law.

Section 4 The Times, Places and Manner of holding Elections for Senators and Representatives, shall be prescribed in each State by the Legislature thereof; but the Congress may at any time by Law make or alter such Regulations, except as to the Places of chusing Senators.

The Congress shall assemble at least once in every Year, and such Meeting shall be on the first Monday in December, unless they shall by Law appoint a different Day.[4]

Section 5 Each House shall be the Judge of the Elections, Returns and Qualifications of its own Members, and a Majority of each shall constitute a Quorum to do Business; but a smaller Number may adjourn from day to day, and may be authorized to compel the Attendance of absent Members, in such Manner, and under such Penalties as each House may provide.

Each House may determine the Rules of its Proceedings, punish its Members for disorderly Behaviour, and with the Concurrence of two thirds, expel a Member.

Each House shall keep a Journal of its Proceedings, and from time to time publish the same, excepting such Parts as may in their Judgment require Secrecy; and the Yeas and Nays of the Members of either House on any question shall, at the Desire of one fifth of those Present, be entered on the Journal.

Neither House, during the Session of Congress, shall, without the Consent of the other, adjourn for more than three days, nor to any other Place than that in which the two Houses shall be sitting.

Section 6 The Senators and Representatives shall receive a Compensation for their Services, to be ascertained by Law, and paid out of the Treasury of the United States. They shall in all Cases, except Treason, Felony and Breach of the Peace, be privileged from Arrest during their Attendance at the Session of their respective Houses, and in going to and returning from the same; and for any Speech or Debate in either House, they shall not be questioned in any other Place.

No Senator or Representative shall, during the Time for which he was elected, be appointed to any civil Office under the Authority of the United States, which shall have been created, or the Emoluments whereof shall have been encreased during such time; and no Person holding any Office under the United States, shall be a Member of either House during his Continuance in Office.

Section 7 All Bills for raising Revenue shall originate in the House of Representatives; but the Senate may propose or concur with Amendments as on other Bills.

Every Bill which shall have passed the House of Representatives and the Senate, shall, before it becomes a Law, be presented to the President of the United States; If he approves he shall sign it, but if not he shall return it, with his Objections to that House in which it shall have originated, who shall enter the Objections at large on their Journal, and proceed to reconsider it. If after such Reconsideration two thirds of that House shall agree to pass the Bill, it shall be sent, together with the Objections, to the other House, by which it shall likewise be reconsidered, and if approved by two thirds of that House, it shall become a Law. But in all such Cases the Votes of both Houses shall be determined by Yeas and Nays, and the Names of the Persons voting for and against the Bill shall be entered on the Journal of each House respectively. If any Bill shall not be returned by the President within ten Days (Sundays excepted) after it shall have been presented to him, the

---

[3]Changed by the Seventeenth Amendment.
[4]Changed by the Twentieth Amendment.

Same shall be a Law, in like Manner as if he had signed it, unless the Congress by their Adjournment prevent its Return, in which Case it shall not be a Law.

Every Order, Resolution, or Vote to which the Concurrence of the Senate and House of Representatives may be necessary (except on a question of Adjournment) shall be presented to the President of the United States; and before the Same shall take Effect, shall be approved by him, or being disapproved by him, shall be repassed by two thirds of the Senate and House of Representatives, according to the Rules and Limitations prescribed in the Case of a Bill.

Section 8 The Congress shall have Power To lay and collect Taxes, Duties, Imposts and Excises, to pay the Debts and provide for the common Defence and general Welfare of the United States; but all Duties, Im-posts and Excises shall be uniform throughout the United States.

To borrow Money on the credit of the United States;

To regulate Commerce with foreign Nations, and among the several States, and with the Indian Tribes;

To establish an uniform Rule of Naturalization, and uniform Laws on the subject of Bankruptcies throughout the United States;

To coin Money, regulate the Value thereof, and of foreign Coin, and fix the Standard of Weights and Measures;

To provide for the Punishment of counterfeiting the Securities and current Coin of the United States;

To establish Post Offices and post Roads;

To promote the Progress of Science and useful Arts, by securing for limited Times to Authors and Inventors the exclusive Right to their respective Writings and Discoveries;

To constitute Tribunals inferior to the supreme Court;

To define and punish Piracies and Felonies committed on the high Seas, and Offences against the Law of Nations;

To declare War, grant Letters of Marque and Reprisal, and make Rules concerning Captures on Land and Water;

To raise and support Armies, but no Appropriation of Money to that Use shall be for a longer Term than two Years;

To provide and maintain a Navy;

To make Rules for the Government and Regulation of the land and naval Forces;

To provide for calling forth the Militia to execute the Laws of the Union, suppress Insurrections and repel Invasions;

To provide for organizing, arming, and disciplining, the Militia, and for governing such Part of them as may be employed in the Service of the United States, reserving to the States respectively, the Appointment of the Officers, and the Authority of training the Militia according to the discipline prescribed by Congress;

To exercise exclusive Legislation in all Cases whatsoever, over such District (not exceeding ten Miles square) as may, by Cession of particular States, and the Acceptance of Congress, become the Seat of the Government of the United States, and to exercise like Authority over all Places purchased by the Consent of the Legislature of the State in which the Same shall be, for the Erection of Forts, Magazines, Arsenals, dock-Yards, and other needful Buildings;—And

To make all Laws which shall be necessary and proper for carrying into Execution the foregoing Powers, and all other Powers vested by this Constitution in the Government of the United States, or in any Department or Officer thereof.

Section 9 The Migration or Importation of such Persons as any of the States now existing shall think proper to admit, shall not be prohibited by the Congress prior to the Year one thousand eight hundred and eight, but a Tax or duty may be imposed on such Importation, not exceeding ten dollars for each Person.

The Privilege of the Writ of Habeas Corpus shall not be suspended, unless when in Cases of Rebellion or Invasion the public Safety may require it.

No Bill of Attainder or ex post facto Law shall be passed.

No Capitation, or other direct, Tax shall be laid, unless in Proportion to the Census of Enumeration herein before directed to be taken.[5]

No Tax or Duty shall be laid on Articles exported from any State.

No Preference shall be given by any Regulation of Commerce or Revenue to the Ports of one State over those of another: nor shall Vessels bound to, or from, one State, be obliged to enter, clear, or pay Duties in another.

No Money shall be drawn from the Treasury, but in Consequence of Appropriations made by Law; and a regular Statement and Account of the Receipts and Expenditures of all public Money shall be published from time to time.

No Title of Nobility shall be granted by the United States: And no Person holding any Office of Profit or Trust under them, shall, without the Consent of the Congress, accept of any present, Emolument, Office, or Title, of any kind whatever, from any King, Prince, or foreign State.

---

[5]Changed by the Sixteenth Amendment.

Section 10 No State shall enter into any Treaty, Alliance, or Confederation; grant Letters of Marque and Reprisal; coin Money; emit Bills of Credit; make any Thing but gold and silver coin a Tender in Payment of Debts; pass any Bill of Attainder, ex post facto Law, or Law impairing the Obligation of Contracts, or grant any Title of Nobility.

No State shall, without the Consent of the Congress, lay any Imposts or Duties on Imports or Exports, except what may be absolutely necessary for executing its inspection Laws: and the net Produce of all Duties and Imposts, laid by any State on Imports or Exports, shall be for the Use of the Treasury of the United States; and all such Laws shall be subject to the Revision and Controul of the Congress.

No State shall, without the consent of Congress, lay any Duty of Tonnage, keep Troops, or Ships of War in time of Peace, enter into any Agreement or Compact with another State, or with a foreign Power, or engage in War, unless actually invaded, or in such imminent Danger as will not admit of delay.

Article II

Section 1 The executive Power shall be vested in a President of the United States of America. He shall hold his Office during the Term of four Years, and, together with the Vice President, chosen for the same Term, be elected, as follows

Each state shall appoint, in such Manner as the Legislature thereof may direct, a Number of Electors, equal to the whole Number of Senators and Representatives to which the State may be entitled in Congress: but no Senator or Representative, or Person holding an Office of Trust or Profit under the United States, shall be appointed an Elector.

The Electors shall meet in their respective States, and vote by Ballot for two Persons, of whom one at least shall not be an inhabitant of the same State with themselves. And they shall make a List of all the Persons voted for, and of the Number of Votes for each; which List they shall sign and certify, and transmit sealed to the Seat of the Government of the United States, directed to the President of the Senate. The President of the Senate shall, in the Presence of the Senate and House of Representatives, open all the Certificates, and the Votes shall then be counted. The Person having the greatest Number of Votes shall be the President, if such Number be a Majority of the whole Number of Electors appointed; and if there be more than one who have such Majority, and have an equal Number of Votes, then the House of Representatives shall immediately chuse by Ballot one of them for President; and if no Person have a Majority,

then from the five highest on the List the said House shall in like Manner chuse the President. But in chusing the President, the Votes shall be taken by States, the Representation from each State having one Vote; A quorum for this purpose shall consist of a Member or Members from two thirds of the States, and a Majority of all the States shall be necessary to a Choice. In every Case, after the Choice of the President, the Person having the greatest Number of Votes of the Electors shall be the Vice President. But if there should remain two or more who have equal Votes, the Senate shall chuse from them by Ballot the Vice President.[6]

The Congress may determine the Time of chusing the Electors, and the Day on which they shall give their Votes; which Day shall be the same throughout the United States.

No Person except a natural born Citizen, or a Citizen of the United States, at the time of the Adoption of this Constitution, shall be eligible to the Office of President; neither shall any Person be eligible to that Office who shall not have attained to the Age of thirty five Years, and been fourteen Years a Resident within the United States.

In Case of the Removal of the President from Office, or of his Death, Resignation, or Inability to discharge the Powers and Duties of the said Office, the Same shall devolve on the Vice President, and the Congress may by Law provide for the Case of Removal, Death, Resignation or Inability, both of the President and Vice President, declaring what Officer shall then act as President, and such Officer shall act accordingly, until the Disability be removed, or a President shall be elected.[7]

The President shall, at stated Times, receive for his Services, a Compensation, which shall neither be encreased nor diminished during the Period for which he shall have been elected, and he shall not receive within that Period any other Emolument from the United States, or any of them.

Before he enter on the Execution of his Office, he shall take the following Oath or Affirmation:—"I do solemnly swear (or affirm) that I will faithfully execute the Office of President of the United States, and will to the best of my Ability, preserve, protect, and defend the Constitution of the United States."

Section 2 The President shall be Commander in Chief of the Army and Navy of the United States, and of the Militia of the several States, when called into the actual Service of the United States; he may require the Opinion, in writing, of the principal Officer in each

---

[6]Changed by the Twelfth Amendment.
[7]Changed by the Twenty-Fifth Amendment.

of the executive Departments, upon any Subject relating to the Duties of their respective Offices, and he shall have Power to grant Reprieves and Pardons for Offences against the United States, except in Cases of Impeachment.

He shall have Power, by and with the Advice and Consent of the Senate, to make Treaties, provided two thirds of the Senators present concur; and he shall nominate, and by and with the Advice and Consent of the Senate, shall appoint Ambassadors, other public Ministers and Consuls, Judges of the supreme Court, and all other Officers of the United States, whose Appointments are not herein otherwise provided for, and which shall be established by Law; but the Congress may by Law vest the Appointment of such inferior Officers, as they think proper, in the President alone, in the Courts of Law, or in the Heads of Departments.

The President shall have Power to fill up all Vacancies that may happen during the Recess of the Senate, by granting Commissions which shall expire at the End of their next Session.

Section 3 He shall from time to time give to the Congress Information of the State of the Union, and recommend to their Consideration such Measures as he shall judge necessary and expedient; he may, on extraordinary Occasions, convene both Houses, or either of them, and in Case of Disagreement between them, with Respect to the Time of Adjournment, he may adjourn them to such Time as he shall think proper; he shall receive Ambassadors and other public Ministers; he shall take Care that the Laws be faithfully executed, and shall Commission all the Officers of the United States.

Section 4 The President, Vice President and all civil Officers of the United States, shall be removed from Office on Impeachment for, and Conviction of, Treason, Bribery, or other high Crimes and Misdemeanors.

Article III

Section 1 The judicial Power of the United States, shall be vested in one supreme Court, and in such inferior Courts as the Congress may from time to time ordain and establish. The Judges, both of the supreme and inferior Courts, shall hold their Offices during good Behaviour, and shall, at stated Times, receive for their Services, a Compensation, which shall not be diminished during their Continuance in Office.

Section 2 The judicial Power shall extend to all Cases, in Law and Equity, arising under this Constitution, the Laws of the United States, and Treaties made, or which shall be made, under their Authority;—to all Cases affecting Ambassadors, other public Ministers

and Consuls;—to all Cases of admiralty and maritime Jurisdiction;—to Controversies to which the United States shall be a party;—to Controversies between two or more States;—between a State and Citizens of another State;[8] —between Citizens of different States;—between Citizens of the same State claiming Lands under Grants of different States, and between a State, or the Citizens thereof, and foreign States, Citizens or Subjects.

In all Cases affecting Ambassadors, other public Ministers and Consuls, and those in which a State shall be Party, the supreme Court shall have original Jurisdiction. In all the other Cases before mentioned, the supreme Court shall have appellate Jurisdiction, both as to Law and Fact, with such Exceptions, and under such Regulations as the Congress shall make.

The Trial of all Crimes, except in Cases of Impeachment, shall be by Jury: and such Trial shall be held in the State where the said Crimes shall have been committed; but when not committed within any State, the Trial shall be at such Place or Places as the Congress may by Law have directed.

Section 3 Treason against the United States, shall consist only in levying War against them, or in adhering to their Enemies, giving them Aid and Comfort. No Person shall be convicted of Treason unless on the Testimony of two Witnesses to the same overt Act, or on Confession in open Court.

The Congress shall have Power to declare the Punishment of Treason, but no Attainder of Treason shall work Corruption of Blood, or Forfeiture except during the Life of the Person attainted.

Article IV

Section 1 Full Faith and Credit shall be given in each State to the public Acts, Records, and judicial Proceedings of every other State. And the Congress may by general Laws prescribe the Manner in which such Acts, Records and Proceedings shall be proved, and the Effect thereof.

Section 2 The Citizens of each State shall be entitled to all Privileges and Immunities of Citizens in the several States.

A Person charged in any State with Treason, Felony, or other Crime, who shall flee from Justice, and be found in another State, shall on Demand of the executive Authority of the State from which he fled, be delivered up, to be removed to the State having Jurisdiction of the Crime.

---

[8]Changed by the Eleventh Amendment.

No Person held to Service or Labour in one State, under the Laws thereof, escaping into another, shall, in Consequence of any Law or Regulation therein, be discharged from such Service or Labour, but shall be delivered up on Claim of the Party to whom such Service or Labour may be due.[9]

Section 3 New States may be admitted by the Congress into this Union; but no new State shall be formed or erected within the Jurisdiction of any other State; nor any State be formed by the Junction of two or more States, or Parts of States, without the Consent of the Legislatures of the States concerned as well as of the Congress.

The Congress shall have Power to dispose of and make all needful Rules and Regulations respecting the Territory or other Property belonging to the United States; and nothing in this Constitution shall be so construed as to Prejudice any Claims of the United States, or of any particular State.

Section 4 The United States shall guarantee to every State in this Union a Republican Form of Government, and shall protect each of them against Invasion; and on Application of the Legislature, or of the Executive (when the Legislature cannot be convened) against domestic Violence.

Article V

The Congress, whenever two thirds of both Houses shall deem it necessary, shall propose Amendments to this Constitution, or, on the Application of the Legislatures of two thirds of the several States, shall call a Convention for proposing Amendments, which, in either Case, shall be valid to all Intents and Purposes, as Part of this Constitution, when ratified by the legislatures of three fourths of the several States, or by Conventions in three fourths thereof, as the one or the other Mode of Ratification may be proposed by the Congress; Provided that no Amendment which may be made prior to the Year One thousand eight hundred and eight shall in any Manner affect the first and fourth Clauses in the Ninth Section of the first Article; and that no State, without its Consent, shall be deprived of its equal Suffrage in the Senate.

Article VI

All Debts contracted and Engagements entered into, before the Adoption of this Constitution, shall be as valid against the United States under this Constitution, as under the Confederation.

The Constitution, and the Laws of the United States which shall be made in Pursuance thereof; and all Treaties made, or which shall be made, under the Authority of the United States, shall be the supreme Law of the Land; and the Judges in every State shall be bound thereby, any Thing in the Constitution or Laws of any State to the Contrary notwithstanding.

The Senators and Representatives before mentioned, and the Members of the several State Legislatures, and all executive and judicial Officers, both of the United States and of the several States, shall be bound by Oath or Affirmation, to support this Constitution; but no religious Test shall ever be required as a Qualification to any Office or public Trust under the United States.

Article VII

The Ratification of the Conventions of nine States, shall be sufficient for the Establishment of this Constitution between the States so ratifying the Same.

Done in Convention by the Unanimous Consent of the States present the Seventeenth Day of September in the Year of our Lord one thousand seven hundred and eighty seven and of the Independance of the United States of America the Twelfth. In witness whereof We have hereunto subscribed our Names.

Amendments

[The first 10 amendments are known as the "Bill of Rights."]

Amendment 1 (Ratified 1791) Congress shall make no law respecting an establishment of religion, or prohibiting the free exercise thereof; or abridging the freedom of speech, or of the press; or the right of the people peaceably to assemble, and to petition the Government for a redress of grievances.

Amendment 2 (Ratified 1791) A well regulated Militia, being necessary to the security of a free State, the right of the people to keep and bear Arms, shall not be infringed.

Amendment 3 (Ratified 1791) No Soldier shall, in time of peace be quartered in any house, without the consent of the Owner, nor in time of war, but in a manner to be prescribed by law.

Amendment 4 (Ratified 1791) The right of the people to be secure in their persons, houses, papers, and effects, against unreasonable searches and seizures, shall not be violated, and no Warrants shall issue, but upon probable cause, supported by Oath or

---

[9]Changed by the Thirteenth Amendment.

affirmation, and particularly describing the place to be searched, and the persons or things to be seized.

Amendment 5 (Ratified 1791)

No person shall be held to answer for a capital, or otherwise infamous crime, unless on a presentment or indictment of a Grand Jury, except in cases arising in the land or naval forces, or in the Militia, when in actual service in time of War or public danger; nor shall any person be subject for the same of-fence to be twice put in jeopardy of life or limb; nor shall be compelled in any criminal case to be a witness against himself, nor be deprived of life, liberty, or property, without due process of law; nor shall private property be taken for public use, without just compensation.

Amendment 6 (Ratified 1791)

In all criminal prosecutions, the accused shall enjoy the right to a speedy and public trial, by an impartial jury of the State and district wherein the crime shall have been committed, which district shall have been previously ascertained by law, and to be informed of the nature and cause of the accusation; to be confronted with the witnesses against him; to have compulsory process for obtaining Witnesses in his favor, and to have assistance of counsel for his defence.

Amendment 7 (Ratified 1791)

In Suits at common law, where the value in controversy shall exceed twenty dollars, the right of trial by jury shall be preserved, and no fact tried by a jury, shall be otherwise re-examined in any Court of the United States, than according to the rules of the common law.

Amendment 8 (Ratified 1791)

Excessive bail shall not be required, nor excessive fines imposed, nor cruel and unusual punishments inflicted.

Amendment 9 (Ratified 1791)

The enumeration in the Constitution, of certain rights, shall not be construed to deny or disparage others retained by the people.

Amendment 10 (Ratified 1791)

The powers not delegated to the United States by the Constitution, nor prohibited by it to the States, are reserved to the States respectively, or to the people.

Amendment 11 (Ratified 1795)

The Judicial power of the United States shall not be construed to extend to any suit in law or equity, commenced or prosecuted against one of the United States by Citizens of another State, or by Citizens or Subjects of any Foreign State.

Amendment 12 (Ratified 1804)

The Electors shall meet in their respective states, and vote by ballot for President and Vice-President, one of whom, at least, shall not be an inhabitant of the same state with themselves; they shall name in their ballots the person voted for as President, and in distinct ballots the person voted for as Vice-President, and they shall make distinct lists of all persons voted for as President, and of all persons voted for as Vice-President, and of the number of votes for each, which lists they shall sign and certify, and transmit sealed to the seat of the government of the United States, directed to the President of the Senate;—The President of the Senate shall, in the presence of the Senate and House of Representatives, open all the certificates and the votes shall then be counted;—The person having the greatest number of votes for President, shall be the President, if such number be a majority of the whole number of Electors appointed; and if no person have such majority, then from the persons having the highest numbers not exceeding three on the list of those voted for as President, the House of Representatives shall choose immediately, by ballot, the President. But in choosing the President, the votes shall be taken by states, the representation from each state having one vote; a quorum for this purpose shall consist of a member or members from two-thirds of the states, and a majority of all the states shall be necessary to a choice. And if the House of Representatives shall not choose a President whenever the right of choice shall devolve upon them, before the fourth day of March next following, then the Vice-President shall act as president, as in the case of the death or other constitutional disability of the President.[10] —The person having the greatest number of votes as Vice-President, shall be the Vice-President, if such number be a majority of the whole number of Electors appointed, and if no person have a majority, then from the two highest numbers on the list, the Senate shall choose the Vice-President; a quorum for the purpose shall consist of two-thirds of the whole number of Senators, and a majority of the whole number shall be necessary to a choice. But no person constitutionally ineligible to the office of President shall be eligible to that of Vice-President of the United States.

Amendment 13 (Ratified 1865)

Section 1 Neither slavery nor involuntary servitude, except as a punishment for crime whereof the party shall have been duly convicted, shall exist within the United States, or any place subject to their jurisdiction.

---

[10]Changed by the Twentieth Amendment.

Section 2 Congress shall have power to enforce this article by appropriate legislation.

Section 1 All persons born or naturalized in the United States, and subject to the jurisdiction thereof, are citizens of the United States and of the State wherein they reside. No State shall make or enforce any law which shall abridge the privileges or immunities of citizens of the United States; nor shall any State deprive any person of life, liberty, or property, without due process of law; nor deny to any person within its jurisdiction the equal protection of the laws.

Section 2 Representatives shall be apportioned among the several States according to their respective numbers, counting the whole number of persons in each State, excluding Indians not taxed. But when the right to vote at any election for the choice of electors for President and Vice President of the United States, Representatives in Congress, the Executive and Judicial officers of a State, or the members of the Legislature thereof, is denied to any of the male inhabitants of such State, being twenty-one[11] years of age, and citizens of the United States, or in any way abridged except for participation in rebellion, or other crime, the basis of representation therein shall be reduced in the proportion which the number of such male citizens shall bear to the whole number of male citizens twenty-one years of age in such State.

Section 3 No person shall be a Senator or Representative in Congress, or elector of President and Vice President, or hold any office, civil or military, under the United States, or under any State, who, having previously taken an oath, as a member of Congress, or as an officer of the United States, or as a member of any State legislature, or as an executive or judicial officer of any State, to support the Constitution of the United States, shall have engaged in insurrection or rebellion against the same, or given aid or comfort to the enemies thereof. But Congress may by a vote of two-thirds of each House, remove such disability.

Section 4 The validity of the public debt of the United States, authorized by law, including debts incurred for payment of pensions and bounties for services in suppressing insurrection or rebellion, shall not be questioned. But neither the United States nor any State shall assume or pay any debt or obligation incurred in aid of insurrection or rebellion against the United States, or any claim for the loss or emancipation of any slave; but all such debts, obligations and claims shall be held illegal and void.

Section 5 The Congress shall have power to enforce, by appropriate legislation, the provisions of this article.

Section 1 The right of citizens of the United States to vote shall not be denied or abridged by the United States or by any State on account of race, color, or previous condition of servitude.

Section 2 The Congress shall have power to enforce this article by appropriate legislation.

The Congress shall have power to lay and collect taxes on incomes, from whatever source derived, without apportionment among the several States, and without regard to any census or enumeration.

The Senate of the United States shall be composed of two Senators from each State, elected by the people thereof, for six years; and each Senator shall have one vote. The electors in each State shall have the qualifications requisite for electors of the most numerous branch of the State legislatures.

When vacancies happen in the representation of any State in the Senate, the executive authority of such State shall issue writs of election to fill such vacancies: *Provided,* That the legislature of any State may empower the executive thereof to make temporary appointments until the people fill the vacancies by election as the legislature may direct.

This amendment shall not be so construed as to affect the election or term of any Senator chosen before it becomes valid as part of the Constitution.

Section 1 After one year from the ratification of this article the manufacture, sale, or transportation of intoxicating liquors within, the importation thereof into, or the exportation thereof from the United States and all territory subject to the jurisdiction thereof for beverage purposes is hereby prohibited.

Section 2 The Congress and the several States shall have concurrent power to enforce this article by appropriate legislation.

Section 3 This article shall be inoperative unless it shall have been ratified as an amendment to the Constitution by the legislatures of the several States, as provided in the Constitution, within seven years from the

---

[11]Changed by the Twenty-Sixth Amendment.

date of the submission hereof to the States by the Congress.[12]

The right of citizens of the United States to vote shall not be denied or abridged by the United States or by any State on account of sex.

Congress shall have power to enforce this article by ap propriate legislation.

Section 1 The terms of the President and Vice President shall end at noon on the 20th day of January, and the terms of Senators and Representatives at noon on the 3d day of January, of the years in which such terms would have ended if this article had not been ratified; and the terms of their successors shall then begin.

Section 2 The Congress shall assemble at least once in every year, and such meeting shall begin at noon on the 3d day of January, unless they shall by law appoint a different day.

Section 3 If, at the time fixed for the beginning of the term of the President, the President elect shall have died, the Vice President elect shall become President. If a President shall not have been chosen before the time fixed for the beginning of his term, or if the President elect shall have failed to qualify, then the Vice President elect shall act as President until a President shall have qualified; and the Congress may by law provide for the case wherein neither a President elect nor a Vice President elect shall have qualified, declaring who shall then act as President, or the manner in which one who is to act shall be selected, and such person shall act accordingly until a President or Vice President shall have qualified.

Section 4 The Congress may by law provide for the case of the death of any of the persons from whom the House of Representatives may choose a President whenever the right of choice shall have devolved upon them, and for the case of the death of any of the persons from whom the Senate may choose a Vice President whenever the right of choice shall have devolved upon them.

Section 5 Sections 1 and 2 shall take effect on the 15th day of October following the ratification of this article.

Section 6 This article shall be inoperative unless it shall have been ratified as an amendment to the Constitution by the legislatures of three-fourths of the

several States within seven years from the date of its submission.

Section 1 The eighteenth article of amendment to the Constitution of the United States is hereby repealed.

Section 2 The transportation or importation into any State, Territory, or possession of the United States for delivery or use therein of intoxicating liquors, in violation of the laws thereof, is hereby prohibited.

Section 3 This article shall be inoperative unless it shall have been ratified as an amendment to the Constitution by conventions in the several States, as provided in the Constitution, within seven years from the date of the submission hereof to the States by the Congress.

Section 1 No person shall be elected to the office of the President more than twice, and no person who has held the office of President, or acted as President, for more than two years of a term to which some other person was elected President shall be elected to the office of the President more than once. But this Article shall not apply to any person holding the office of President when this Article was proposed by the Congress, and shall not prevent any person who may be holding the office of President, or acting as President, during the term within which this Article becomes operative from holding the office of President or acting as President during the remainder of such term.

Section 2 This Article shall be inoperative unless it shall have been ratified as an amendment to the Constitution by the legislatures of three-fourths of the several States within seven years from the date of its submission to the States by the Congress.

Section 1 The District constituting the seat of Government of the United States shall appoint in such manner as the Congress may direct:

A number of electors of President and Vice President equal to the whole number of Senators and Representatives in Congress to which the District would be entitled if it were a State, but in no event more than the least populous State; they shall be in addition to those appointed by the States, but they shall be considered, for the purposes of the election of President and Vice President, to be electors appointed by a State; and they shall meet in the District and perform such duties as provided by the twelfth article of amendment.

Section 2 The Congress shall have power to enforce this article by appropriate legislation.

---

[12]Repealed by the Twenty-First Amendment.

Amendment 24 (Ratified 1964) **Section 1** The right of citizens of the United States to vote in any primary or other election for President or Vice President, for electors for President or Vice President, or for Senator or Representative in Congress, shall not be denied or abridged by the United States or any State by reason of failure to pay any poll tax or other tax.

Section 2 The Congress shall have power to enforce this article by appropriate legislation.

Amendment 25 (Ratified 1967) **Section 1** In case of the removal of the President from office or of his death or resignation, the Vice President shall become President.

Section 2 Whenever there is a vacancy in the office of the Vice President, the President shall nominate a Vice President who shall take office upon confirmation by a majority vote of both Houses of Congress.

Section 3 Whenever the President transmits to the President pro tempore of the Senate and the Speaker of the House of Representatives his written declaration that he is unable to discharge the powers and duties of his office, and until he transmits to them a written declaration to the contrary, such powers and duties shall be discharged by the Vice President as Acting President.

Section 4 Whenever the Vice President and a majority of either the principal officers of the executive departments or of such other body as Congress may by law provide, transmit to the President pro tempore of the Senate and the Speaker of the House of Representatives their written declaration that the President is unable to discharge the powers and duties of his office, the Vice President shall immediately assume the powers and duties of the office as Acting President.

Thereafter, when the President transmits to the President pro tempore of the Senate and the Speaker of the House of Representatives his written declaration that no inability exists, he shall resume the powers and duties of his office unless the Vice President and a majority of either the principal officers of the executive department or of such other body as Congress may by law provide, transmit within four days to the President pro tempore of the Senate and the Speaker of the House of Representatives their written declaration that the President is unable to discharge the powers and duties of his office. Thereupon Congress shall decide the issue, assembling within forty-eight hours for that purpose if not in session. If the Congress, within twenty-one days after receipt of the latter written declaration, or, if Congress is not in session, within twenty-one days after Congress is required to assemble, determines by two-thirds vote of both Houses that the President is unable to discharge the powers and duties of his office, the Vice President shall continue to discharge the same as Acting President; otherwise, the President shall resume the powers and duties of his office.

Amendment 26 (Ratified 1971) **Section 1** The right of citizens of the United States, who are eighteen years of age or older, to vote shall not be denied or abridged by the United States or by any State on account of age.

Section 2 The Congress shall have power to enforce this article by appropriate legislation.

Amendment 27 (Ratified 1992) No law, varying the compensation for the services of the Senators and Representatives, shall take effect, until an election of Representatives shall have intervened.

Excerpts from the Sarbanes-Oxley Act of 2002

15 U.S.C. § 7241. Corporate Responsibility for Financial Reports

(a) Regulations required

The Commission shall, by rule, require, for each company filing periodic reports under section 78m (a) or 78o (d) of this title, that the principal executive officer or officers and the principal financial officer or officers, or persons performing similar functions, certify in each annual or quarterly report filed or submitted under either such section of this title that—

(1) the signing officer has reviewed the report;

(2) based on the officer's knowledge, the report does not contain any untrue statement of a material fact or omit to state a material fact necessary in order to make the statements made, in light of the circumstances under which such statements were made, not misleading;

(3) based on such officer's knowledge, the financial statements, and other financial information included in the report, fairly present in all material respects the financial condition and results of operations of the issuer as of, and for, the periods presented in the report;

(4) the signing officers—

(A) are responsible for establishing and maintaining internal controls;

(B) have designed such internal controls to ensure that material information relating to the issuer and its consolidated subsidiaries is made known to such officers by others within those entities, particularly during the period in which the periodic reports are being prepared;

(C) have evaluated the effectiveness of the issuer's internal controls as of a date within 90 days prior to the report; and

(D) have presented in the report their conclusions about the effectiveness of their internal controls based on their evaluation as of that date;

(5) the signing officers have disclosed to the issuer's auditors and the audit committee of the board of directors (or persons fulfilling the equivalent function)—

(A) all significant deficiencies in the design or operation of internal controls which could adversely affect the issuer's ability to record, process, summarize, and report financial data and have identified for the issuer's auditors any material weaknesses in internal controls; and

(B) any fraud, whether or not material, that involves management or other employees who have a significant role in the issuer's internal controls; and

(6) the signing officers have indicated in the report whether or not there were significant changes in internal controls or in other factors that could significantly affect internal controls subsequent to the date of their evaluation, including any corrective actions with regard to significant deficiencies and material weaknesses.

(b) Foreign reincorporations have no effect

Nothing in this section shall be interpreted or applied in any way to allow any issuer to lessen the legal force of the statement required under this section, by an issuer having reincorporated or having engaged in any other transaction that resulted in the transfer of the corporate domicile or offices of the issuer from inside the United States to outside of the United States.

(c) Deadline

The rules required by subsection (a) of this section shall be effective not later than 30 days after July 30, 2002.

15 U.S.C. § 7262. Management Assessment of Internal Controls

(a) Rules required

The Commission shall prescribe rules requiring each annual report required by section 78m (a) or 78o (d) of this title to contain an internal control report, which shall—

(1) state the responsibility of management for establishing and maintaining an adequate

internal control structure and procedures for financial reporting; and

(2) contain an assessment, as of the end of the most recent fiscal year of the issuer, of the effectiveness of the internal control structure and procedures of the issuer for financial reporting.

(b) Internal control evaluation and reporting

With respect to the internal control assessment required by subsection (a) of this section, each registered public accounting firm that prepares or issues the audit report for the issuer shall attest to, and report on, the assessment made by the management of the issuer. An attestation made under this subsection shall be made in accordance with standards for attestation engagements issued or adopted by the Board. Any such attestation shall not be the subject of a separate engagement.

15 U.S.C. § 1519. Destruction, Alteration, or Falsification of Records in Federal Investigations and Bankruptcy

Whoever knowingly alters, destroys, mutilates, conceals, covers up, falsifies, or makes a false entry in any record, document, or tangible object with the intent to impede, obstruct, or influence the investigation or proper administration of any matter within the jurisdiction of any department or agency of the United States or any case filed under title 11, or in relation to or contemplation of any such matter or case, shall be fined under this title, imprisoned not more than 20 years, or both.

Absolute privilege A defense to a defamation claim whereby the defendant need not proffer any further evidence to assert the defense; provided to government officials, judicial officers and proceedings, and state legislatures.

Acceptance The offeree's expression of agreement to the terms of the offer. The power of acceptance is created by a valid offer.

Accord and satisfaction A doctrine that allows one party to create an agreement, or accord, with the other party to accept a substitute performance in order to satisfy the original performance; the completion of the new duty discharges the old one.

Account A subduty of fiduciary duty that requires that the agent keep records such as a written list of transactions, noting money owed and money paid, and other detailed statements of mutual demands.

Acknowledgment form A form commonly used in sales contracts as an acceptance from the seller in response to a purchase order; contains preprinted provisions and has blanks to accommodate the specifics of the transaction.

Act requirement For criminal liability, the requirement that the government prove that a defendant's actions objectively satisfied the elements of a particular offense. Also called *actus reus*.

Actual authority A source of the agent's authority that occurs either when the parties expressly agree to create an agency relationship or when the authority is implied based on custom or the course of past dealings.

Actual damages A fundamental element that must be proved to recover in a negligence lawsuit against a tortfeasor; the injured party must prove that she suffered some physical harm that resulted in identifiable losses.

Actual owner The individual who is recognized as having primary or residual title to the property and is, therefore, the ultimate owner of the property.

Adjudication (Administrative) The judicial function of administrative agencies, whereby the agencies make policy. Administrative law judges hear cases brought before the specific agency.

Adjudication (Criminal) A phase of the criminal justice system in which the prosecutor, after investigation, elects to proceed with the charges.

Administrative agencies Governmental bodies that have the authority to implement and administer particular regulations; include department, nondepartment, and independent agencies.

Administrative law Refers to both the law made by administrative agencies and the laws and regulations that govern the creation, organization, and operation of administrative agencies.

Administrative law judge An individual, typically an attorney, who is employed by an agency to adjudicate disputes.

Affirmative action An action plan designed to maintain equal employment opportunities and to remedy past employment discrimination of women, persons of color, persons with disabilities, and other underutilized protected classes.

Age Discrimination in Employment Act (ADEA) of 1967 A federal statute that prohibits employers from discriminating against employees on the basis of their age once employees have reached age 40.

Agency law The body of laws that govern the relationships created when one party hires another party to act on the hiring party's behalf.

Agent One who agrees to act and is authorized to act on behalf of another, a principal, to legally bind the principal in particular business transactions with third parties pursuant to an agency relationship.

Agreement Any meeting of the minds resulting in mutual assent to do or refrain from doing something.

Agreement on Trade-Related Aspects of Intellectual Property (TRIPS) A multinational agreement that covers minimum requirements and standards for all areas of intellectual property protection and provides an infrastructure for enforcement and dispute resolution.

Ambiguous terms Contract terms that are vague and indefinite. In contract law, these terms are construed by the court against the interest of the side that drafted the agreement.

Amendments Changes made to the Constitution since its ratification.

American Recovery and Reinvestment Act of 2009 Federal legislation that created a loan program and underlying mandates for corporations most acutely impacted by the financial crisis that began in 2008; also established the Troubled Assets Relief Program (TARP) to administer the loans.

Americans with Disabilities Act (ADA) of 1990 A federal statute that seeks to eliminate discriminatory employment practices against disabled persons; requires that employers with 15 or more employees make reasonable accommodations for a disabled employee in the workplace as long as the accommodations do not cause the employer to suffer an undue hardship.

Answer Defendant's formal response to each paragraph of the complaint.

Anticipatory repudiation Doctrine under which, when one party makes clear that he has no intention to perform as agreed, the nonbreaching party is entitled to recover damages in anticipation of the breach rather than waiting until performance is due. Also called *anticipatory breach*.

Apparent authority A source of the agent's authority that occurs when there is an appearance of legitimate authority to a third party rather than express authorization by the principal.

Arbitrary and capricious standard The broad judicial benchmark used to determine whether an agency's actions were a result of a reasoned decision-making process.

Arbitration Method of alternatives dispute resolution in which the parties present their sides of the dispute to one or more neutral parties who then render a decision; often involves a set of rules designed to move from dispute to decision quickly.

Articles The main provisions of the Constitution that set out the government's structure, power, and procedures.

Articles of organization Document filed to create an LLC; in most states, requires only basic information such as the name of the entity, the location of its principal place of business, and the names of its members. *Also called* certificate of organization.

Assignment The transfer of one party's current rights under a contract to a third party, thereby extinguishing original party's rights.

Assumption of the risk A defense to claims of negligence in which the injured party knew that a substantial and apparent risk was associated with certain conduct and the party went ahead with the dangerous activity anyway.

Assurance A pledge or guarantee that gives confidence to one party that the other party is able to complete performance under a contract.

At-will employee Any employee who is not a contractual employee; may be terminated at an time and for any reason except in cases where public policy is violated or the termination is illegally discriminatory or is prohibited by statutory or common law exceptions.

Authorization cards Signed statements by employees indicating that they wish to unionize and/or are electing to be represented by an existing union.

Automatic stay A legal prohibition of creditors' either initiating or continuing any debt collection action against the debtor or her property.

Bad faith A dishonesty of belief or purpose; in the legal context, a concept in which a malicious motive on the part of the defendant in a lawsuit is necessary in order for the plaintiff to recover. Under the Anticybersquatting Consumer Protection Act, the court looks to nine factors in making a determination of bad-faith intent.

Bankruptcy A procedure by which a debtor's assets are reorganized and liquidated by a court order to pay off creditors and free the debtor from obligations under existing contracts.

Bankruptcy estate The debtor's available assets in a bankruptcy proceeding.

Bankruptcy trustee An individual, often an attorney highly skilled in bankruptcy law, appointed in Chapter 7 or Chapter 13 cases and charged with the duty of taking control of the bankruptcy estate and reducing it to cash for distribution, preserving the interests of both the debtor and the creditors.

Bargained-for exchange The aspect of consideration that differentiates contracts from illusory promises by holding that a performance or return promise is bargained for only if it was exchanged for another promise.

Battle of the forms The conflict between the terms written into standardized purchase (offer) and acknowledgment (acceptance) forms, which differ in that one form favors the buyer and the other the seller. The UCC attempts to broker a truce in this battle while keeping the contract of sale intact.

Bench trial Trial without a jury, in which the judge is both the finder of law and the finder of fact.

Berne Convention A multinational agreement covering copyright protection; requires that foreigners from signatory countries be granted protection, via reciprocity, under the copyright laws of any other member country.

Beyond a reasonable doubt The heightened burden of proof used in criminal cases, under which a fact finder must be convinced that the defendant's criminal liability is not in doubt to a reasonable person.

Bilateral contract A contract involving two promises and two performances.

Bill of Rights The first 10 amendments to the Constitution that preserve the rights of the people from unlawful acts of government officials, establish and protect freedom of speech and religion, and so on.

Black's Law Dictionary The leading legal dictionary.

Blue-sky laws State securities laws intended to cover purely intrastate securities offerings.

Bona fide occupational qualification (BFOQ) A provision in certain federal antidiscrimination statutes that allows discrimination based on religion, gender, or national origin when it can be shown that such discrimination is reasonably necessary to the business operation.

Borrower The party to whom credit is extended and who owes the debt.

Breach Condition that exists when one party has failed to perform her obligation under the contract. If the breach is material, the nonbreaching party is excused from his performance and can recover monetary damages.

Breach of duty A fundamental element that must be proved to recover in a negligence lawsuit against a tortfeasor: The injured party must prove that the tortfeasor failed to exercise reasonable care in fulfilling her obligations.

Burden of proof The responsibility of producing sufficient evidence in support of a fact or issue and favorably convincing the fact finder of that fact or issue.

Business ethics Recognizing right and wrong business behavior and acting responsibly to the business's stakeholders.

Business necessity defense A defense used to rebut disparate impact claims when a business can prove that a certain skill, ability, or procedure is absolutely necessary to the operation of the business. Discrimination is permitted even if a protected class is adversely affected.

Capacity For the formation of a valid contract, the requirement that both parties have the power to contract. Certain classes of persons have only limited powers to contract, including minors and those with mental incapacity.

Cause in fact A fundamental element that must be proved to recover in a negligence lawsuit against a tortfeasor: The injured party must prove that except for the breach of duty by the tortfeasor, he would not have suffered damages.

Celler-Kefauver Antimerger Act A federal antitrust law enacted in 1950 that amends the Clayton Act provisions by severely restricting anticompetitive mergers resulting from the acquisition of assets.

Certificate of limited partnership The document filed with the state government authority by the general partner to form a limited partnership; requires routine information such as the name, address, and capital contribution of each partner.

Certify In labor law, to recognize a collective bargaining unit as a union. The NLRB's certification process occurs when a legally sound election reveals a simple majority of pro-union votes.

Charging of the jury Instructions given from the judge to the jury explaining how to work through the process of coming to a factual decision in the case.

Citation The special format used by the legal community to express where a statute or case law can be found.

Citizen suit provisions Laws that authorize private individuals or watchdog groups to file environmental enforcement lawsuits.

Citizen suits Lawsuits that are initiated by members of the public who are directly affected by an agency action and are brought against violators of the regulation and/or the administrative agency itself for failing to fulfill a duty imposed upon it.

Civil laws Laws designed to compensate parties for money lost as a result of another's conduct.

Civil law systems Systems of law that are drawn largely from the Roman law heritage, which uses written law as the highest source, and opt for a systematic codification of general law principles.

Civil litigation A dispute resolution process in which the parties and their counsel argue their views of a civil controversy in a court of law.

Clayton Act A federal antitrust law enacted in 1914 as a preventive statute that deals with specific types of trade restraints, including exclusive dealing arrangements, tie-in sales, price discrimination, mergers and acquisitions, and interlocking directorates.

Clean Air Act (CAA) Federal legislation enacted in 1963 to improve, strengthen, and accelerate programs for the prevention and abatement of air pollution; focuses on stationary and mobile sources in the United States.

Clean hands An equitable doctrine whereby a party seeking to enforce a breach of contract against the opposing party must prove that he has no fault in causing the breach. Clean hands are shown by proving that one is prepared to tender performance.

Clean Water Act (CWA) Federal legislation that regulates water quality standards and aims to stem water pollution from industrial, municipal, and agricultaral sources; implemented and enforced by the EPA.

Closing arguments Attorneys' summations of the case, during which each attorney tries to convince the jury to decide the case in her party's favor; occurs after testimony is completed and evidence has been submitted.

Collective bargaining The process of negotiating terms and conditions of employment for employees in the collective bargaining unit.

Collective bargaining unit An employee group that, on the basis of a mutuality of interests, is an appropriate unit for collective bargaining.

Comity The general notion that nations will defer to and give effect to the laws and court decisions of other nations.

Commerce Clause The constitutional clause giving Congress the power to regulate commerce.

Commercially impracticable Rule applied by the UCC when a delay in delivery or nondelivery has been made impracticable by the occurrence of an unanticipated event so long as the event directly affected a basic assumption of the contract.

Common law Law that has not been passed by the legislature but rather is made by the courts and is based on the fundamentals of previous cases with similar facts.

Common stock (common shares) A form of equity instrument that entitles the equity owner to payments based on the current profitability of the company.

Communications Decency Act (CDA) of 1996 Federal legislation that extends immunity to Internet service providers by protecting them from any defamation liability as a "publisher or speaker of any information provided by another information content provider."

Comparative negligence A defense to claims of negligence in which the injured party's conduct has played a factor in the harm suffered and, thus, the proportion of negligence should be divided.

Compensatory damages Damages that are meant to make the injured party whole again. In contract law, they are an attempt to place the nonbreaching party in the position he would have been in had the contract been executed as agreed. Also called *direct* or *actual damages*.

Complaint The first formal document filed with the local clerk of courts when the plaintiff initiates a lawsuit claiming legal rights against another.

Complaint (Discrimination) A form that an aggrieved employee files against his employer with the EEOC that details how the employee was discriminated against.

Comprehensive Environmental Response Compensation and Liability Act (CERCLA) Federal legislation enacted in 1980 to create a tax on the chemical and petroleum industries and provide broad federal authority to respond directly to releases or threatened releases of hazardous substances that may endanger public health or the environment. Also called *Superfund*.

Computer Fraud and Abuse Act Federal legislation that prohibits unauthorized use of computers to commit espionage, the accessing of unauthorized information or of a nonpublic government computer, fraud by computer, damage to a computer, trafficking in passwords, and extortionate threats to damage a computer.

Conciliation negotiations The required attempts by the EEOC to settle a discrimination case instead of filing a lawsuit.

Concurrent jurisdiction Situation in which two different courts each have subject matter jurisdiction to hear a case.

Condition An event that must occur before a contract obligation is triggered.

Confirmation memorandum A written verification of an agreement. Under the statute of frauds section of the

UCC, a merchant who receives a signed confirmation memorandum from another merchant will be bound by the memorandum just as if she had signed it, unless she promptly objects.

Consent An agent's agreeing to act for the principal. In the context of agency law, courts apply an objective standard to determine whether the agent did in fact agree to the agency relationship.

Consequential damages Damages that repay the injured party for any foreseeable but indirect losses that flow from the breach of contract.

Consideration The mutual exchange of benefits and detriments; for the formation of a valid contract, the requirement that each party receives something of value (the benefit) from the other and that each party gives up something of value (the legal detriment) to the other, resulting in a bargained-for exchange.

Constitutional law The body of law interpreting state and federal constitutions.

Consumer Credit Protection Act (CCPA) Federal legislation that regulates credit transactions between a creditor and a borrower and provides consumer protections in the areas of disclosure of credit terms, credit reporting, antidiscrimination laws, and collection of debts from consumers; serves as the centerpiece of federal statutory regulation of credit transactions.

Consumer law The statutory and administrative body of law that protects consumers engaging in transactions with merchants and creditors.

Consumer Leasing Act (CLA) Federal legislation that regulates lessors engaged in leasing or arranging leases for consumers in the ordinary course of business.

Consumer Product Safety Act (CPSA) The federal statute that created the Consumer Product Safety Commission, with the aim of making consumer products safer.

Contractual employee An employee who works under an agreement that defines when the empl-oyee begins employment and when the employment ends.

Controlling the Assault of Non-Solicited Pornography and Marketing Act of 2003 A federal statute that regulates the sending of unsolicited e-mail (spam) by prohibiting certain practices, such as falsifying the "from" name and information in the subject line, and requiring the sender to provide a physical address of the producer of the e-mail. Also called *CAN-SPAM Act*.

Convention on the Recognition and Enforcement of Foreign Arbitral Awards An international treaty established in 1958 that allows for the enforcement of arbitration awards in many major countries, provided that the arbitration is international.

Corporate governance The process used by corporate officers and directors to establish lines of responsibility, approval, and oversight among key stakeholders and set out rules for making corporate decisions.

Counsel Another term for *attorney*.

Counterclaim A claim filed by a defendant who believes that the plaintiff has caused her damages arising out of the very same set of facts as articulated in the complaint.

Counteroffer An action terminating an offer whereby the offeree rejects the original offer and proposes a new offer with different terms.

Country of origin principle General agreement between the United States, Canada, and the European Union governments to apply the law of the country in which the defendant's servers are located.

Court A judicial tribunal duly constituted for the hearing and determination of cases.

Covenant not to compete Type of contract in which one party agrees not to compete with another party for a specified period of time.

Cover A nonbreaching buyer's right to purchase substitute goods on the open market after a delivery of nonconforming goods from the original seller and to sue for the difference.

Covered (nonexempt) employees Employees who are protected by the FLSA and other statutes.

Cram-down provision A term used in reference to the Chapter 11 provision that allows the debtor to request that the court force the creditors to accept a plan that is fair, equitable, and feasible.

Creativity For copyright protection of a compilation, the requirement that there must be some creative element used that made the compilation an original work.

Credit Card Accountability Responsibility and Disclosure Act of 2009 (CARD Act) Federal legislation that protects consumers from unreasonable interest rate increases and credit card fees and requires card issuers to give a 45-day advance notice of any impending rate increase.

Creditor Any party that regularly extends credit and to which a debt becomes owed.

Criminal law The body of law that, for the purpose of preventing harm to society, defines the boundaries of behavior and prescribes sanctions for violating those boundaries.

Criminal laws Laws designed to protect society that result in penalties to the violator such as fines or imprisonment.

Criminal procedure The body of constitutional protections afforded to individuals and business entities during criminal investigations, arrests, trials, and sentencing.

Cross-claim A claim filed by a defendant who believes that a third party is either partially or fully liable for the damages that the plaintiff has suffered and, therefore, should be involved as an indispensable party in the trial.

Cross-examination The opportunity for an attorney to ask questions in court, limited to issues brought out on direct examination, of a witness who has testified for the opposing party.

Cure The right of a seller to replace nonconforming goods before final contract performance is due. If nonconforming goods were delivered in good faith and were considered equal to or superior to what was ordered, the seller may cure after final contract performance is due if the buyer will not suffer injury.

Damages Money lost as a result of another's conduct.

Debt A common tool for raising capital; includes promissory notes, bonds, and debentures that offer investors a fixed rate of return, regardless of the profitability of the corporation, and repayment after a certain period of years. Debt is senior in priority to equity instruments.

Debtor The borrower in a secured transaction.

Debtor in possession (DIP) A Chapter 11 bankruptcy process in which the debtor generally remains in control of assets and business operations in an attempt to rehabilitate the business entity.

Defendant The party alleged by the plaintiff to have caused the plaintiff to suffer damages.

Delegation The transfer of one party's current duties under a contract to a third party to perform, with the original party remaining liable for any breach.

Deliberations The process in which jurors discuss, in private, the testimony and evidence presented at trial and vote to reach their verdict.

Deposition Method of discovery in which a witness gives sworn testimony to provide evidence prior to trial.

Destination contract A contract in which the seller is required to deliver the goods to a chosen destination and not just to the carrier. When the goods have been tendered at the destination, the seller has fulfilled his duty and the buyer takes title and risk of loss.

Detour Conduct classified as a small-scale deviation that is normally expected in the workday and, therefore, is within the ambit of respondeat superior.

Detrimental reliance Situation in which the offeree acts, based on a reasonable promise made by the offeror, and would be injured if the offeror's promise is not enforced.

Direct examination The first questioning of a witness during a trial, in which the witness is questioned by the attorney for the party presenting the witness.

Direct infringement A theory of copyright infringement under which the copyright owner proves that she has legal ownership of the work in question and that the infringer copied the work in a substantially similar manner without permission.

Disability A physical or mental impairment that substantially limits a person's ability to participate in major life activities.

Discharge In contract law, the removal of all legal obligations under the agreement.

Disclaim To renounce a legal right or claim.

Disclosure The process in which companies are to release all information, positive or negative, that might bear on an investment decision; serves as the underlying premise of all securities regulation and is required by the Securities and Exchange Commission to protect investors and ensure public confidence in the integrity of the securities market.

Discovery Process for the orderly exchange of information and evidence between the parties involved in litigation (or in some cases arbitration) prior to trial.

Disparate impact Theory of employment discrimination in which employee evaluation techniques that are not themselves discriminatory have a different and adverse impact on members of a protected class.

Disparate treatment Theory of employment discrimination predicated on overt and intentional discrimination; includes being treated differently because of one's membership in a protected class.

Dissociation Term used in the RUPA to describe the act of separation of a partner from the partnership. Also, the process in which an individual member of an LLC exercises the right to withdraw from the partnership.

Dissolution In the context of an LLC, a liquidation process triggered by an event that is specified in the operating agreement (such as the death of a key member) or by the decision of the majority of membership interests (or the percentage called for in the operating agreement) to dissolve the company.

Diversity of citizenship Situation in which opposing parties in a lawsuit are citizens of different states or one party is a citizen of a foreign country; the case is placed under federal court jurisdiction if the amount in controversy exceeds $75,000.

Divisible contract A contract that can be broken up into independent parts, each part able to stand alone.

Doctrine of equivalence A doctrine that allows courts to find patent infringement when an invention, compared with a patented device, performs substantially the same function in substantially the same way to achieve the same result.

Doctrine of stare decisis The principle that similar cases with similar facts under similar circumstances should have similar outcomes.

Double jeopardy Situation in which a defendant could be subject to prosecution twice for the same offense; prohibited by the Fifth Amendment.

Due care A subduty of fiduciary duty that requires that the agent act in the same careful manner when conducting the principal's affairs as a reasonable person would in conducting her own personal affairs.

Due process The principle that the government must respect all of the legal rights that are owed to a person according to the law.

Due Process Clause The constitutional clause protecting individuals from being deprived of "life, liberty, or property" without due process of law.

Durable medium For copyright protection, the requirement that the work must be in a tangible form, such as writing, digital, video, and so forth.

Duress The use of any form of unfair coercion by one party to induce another party to enter into or modify a contract; basis for avoiding a contract.

Duty A fundamental element that must be proved to recover in a negligence lawsuit against a tortfeasor: The injured party must prove that the tortfeasor owed him a duty of care.

Easement The privilege to use real estate owned by another.

Economic Espionage Act A federal statute passed in 1996 that provides criminal penalties for domestic and foreign theft of trade secrets.

Election A vote to elect or reject unionization by the entire bargaining unit.

Electronic Communications Privacy Act (ECPA) A federal law enacted in 1986 that extends legal protection against wiretapping and other forms of unauthorized interception and explicitly allows employers to monitor employee communications on company equipment as long as this is done in the ordinary course of business or the employee consents to the monitoring.

Employee agents One of three broad categories of agents; includes, generally, anyone who performs services for a principal who can control what will be done and how it will be done.

Employee Polygraph Protection Act A federal law that prohibits most private sector employers from requiring a polygraph test as a condition of employment.

Employee Retirement Income Security Act (ERISA) A federal law enacted in 1974 consisting of a comprehensive set of laws and regulations that requires employers to make certain disclosures related to investment risk, thus providing transparency for plan beneficiaries.

Employment at-will Deep-seated common law principle that employers have the right to terminate an employee with or without advance notice and with or without just cause, subject to certain exceptions.

Employment discrimination Workplace-related discrimination in the hiring process and treatment of employees; encompasses everything from promotions and demotions to work schedules, working conditions, and disciplinary measures.

Enabling statute A law passed by Congress when it is establishing an administrative agency; serves as the source of the agency's authority and describes the agency's scope and jurisdiction over certain matters.

Endangered Species Act (ESA) Federal legislation enacted in 1973 that established a procedure for identifying imperiled species and preserving them from extinction.

Energy bank Business model adopted by Enron Corporation, after deregulation of the energy markets, in which Enron purchased energy from one source at a discount rate and sold it to markets where demand was greatest for energy.

Enforceability The ability of a properly formed contract to be enforceable in a court of law; determined by examining whether the contract is a product of genuine assent and is in writing (under certain circumstances).

Enforcement The function of administrative agencies whereby they investigate alleged violations of their administrative regulations and recommend enforcement actions; generally carried out through an agency's Office of General Counsel. In deciding when and whom to regulate, the agencies have prosecutorial discretion that is practically unreviewable by the judiciary.

Entire contract A contract in which each component of the contract is dependent on every other component.

Enumerated powers Those powers that are explicitly granted to the three branches of government in the Constitution.

Equal Credit Opportunity Act Federal legislation, passed in 1974, that prohibits discrimination of a credit applicant based on the applicant's race, religion, national origin, color, gender, age, or marital status.

Equal Employment Opportunity Commission (EEOC) A five-member federal administrative agency that administers congressional mandates that ensure adequate protection for victims of discrimination; accepts and investigates worker complaints and, in certain cases, will sue on behalf of employees.

Equal Pay Act of 1963 A federal statute that makes it illegal for employers to pay unequal wages to men and women who perform substantially equal work.

Equitable maxims Common law rules that guide courts in deciding cases and controversies and are intended to be broad statements of rules based on notions of fairness and justice.

Equitable relief Relief granted in the form of either specific performance ("do it") or an injunction ("stop doing it") when monetary damages are insufficient due to the unique or irreversible consequence of the breach.

Equity Ownership interest in a corporation whereby financial return on the investment is based primarily on the performance of the venture.

Ethics A conscious system used for deciding moral dilemmas.

European Court of Justice The court that functions as the final arbiter of the codes governing European Union member states.

Executed contract A contract that is completed.

Executive branch Established under Article II of the Constitution and consists of the president and vice president.

Executive order An order made by the president which carries the full force of law. They are issued to enforce or interpret federal statutes and treaties.

Executory contract A contract that is not yet completed.

Exempt employees Classification of employees who are not covered by FLSA protections; generally consists of employees whose responsibilities are primarily executive, administrative, or professional.

Exemptions For smaller issuers of securities, types of offerings or transactions in selling a security that are not subject to certain Securities and Exchange Commission regulations on registration; intended to assist business ventures seeking smaller amounts of capital from the public investment community.

Expert evaluator The neutral fact-finder in expert evaluation who reviews documents and evidence provided by each party and draws on her range of experience and expertise in the industry to offer an opinion on the merits and value of the claim and recommend a settlement amount.

Expiration Method of ending an agency relationship whereby the parties agree to a fixed term for the relationship.

Express acts Acts by which an agency relationship is terminated; can be either simple communication of the desire to terminate the relationship, the expiration of a fixed term, or satisfaction of purpose.

Express contract A contract that is created when the parties have knowingly and intentionally agreed on the promises and performances.

Express partnership Partnership formed when the parties have agreed to conduct a partnership on certain terms and conditions.

Express warranty A warranty that arises when a seller makes a representation of fact about a product.

Fair and Accurate Credit Transactions (FACT) Act Federal legislation that requires credit bureaus to stop reporting any fraudulent account information from the time a consumer alleges identity theft until the conclusion of the investigation.

Fair Credit Reporting Act (FCRA) Federal legislation that sets privacy rights for consumer credit reports and requires that the credit bureaus give individual consumers complete and timely access to their own credit reports.

Fair Debt Collection Practices Act (FDCPA) A federal statute that regulates agents of the creditor involved in debt collection for consumer debts and that requires the collection agency to make known certain rights of the debtor.

Fair Labor Standards Act (FLSA) A federal law enacted in 1938 and intended to cover all employers engaged in interstate commerce; mandates payment of a minimum wage, a maximum 40-hour workweek, overtime pay, and restrictions on children working in certain occupations and during certain hours.

Fair use A defense against copyright infringement under which the court examines the purpose and nature of the use, the nature of the work, the amount used, and the market effect of the use to determine whether the use is permitted.

Family and Medical Leave Act (FMLA) A federal law enacted in 1993 that requires certain employers to give time off to employees to take care of their own or a family member's illness or to care for a newborn or adopted child.

Federal courts Courts that adjudicate matters dealing primarily with national laws, federal constitutional issues, and other cases that are outside the purview of state courts.

Federal Odometer Act A law that makes it a crime to change vehicle odometers and requires that any faulty odometer be plainly disclosed in writing to potential buyers.

Federal question Some issue arising from the Constitution, a federal statute or regulation, or federal common law.

Federal system System in which a national government coexists with the government of each state.

Federal Trade Commission An agency charged with the broad mandate of preventing unfair and deceptive acts or practices in commercial transactions.

Federal Trade Commission Act (FTCA) A federal law enacted in 1914 that established the Federal Trade Commission, which administers the act; intended as a catchall statute that has been construed as including all the prohibitions of the other antitrust laws.

Federal Trademark Dilution Act A federal law enacted in 1995 that permits mark holders to recover damages and prevent others from diluting distinctive trademarks.

Federal Unemployment Tax Act (FUTA) A federal law enacted in 1935 that established a state-administered fund to provide payments to workers who have suffered sudden job loss.

Fee simple The broadest property interest in land, which endures until the current holder dies without heirs.

Felonies Crimes that generally carry one year or more of incarceration as the penalty.

Fiduciary duties Under the Revised Uniform Partnership Act, general partners' duties of loyalty, care, and good faith; intended to ensure that the partners are acting in the best interest of the partnership.

Fifth Amendment Provides that no person "shall be compelled in any criminal case to be a witness against himself," guaranteeing individuals the right to remain silent both during the investigation and during any subsequent judicial proceedings.

FOB point *Domestic:* A shipping term that indicates the place to which the seller must deliver goods. In the absence of a contract provision to the contrary, title and risk of loss pass to the buyer at this point. *International:* An INCO term indicating that goods are to be shipped via freighter ship and that title and risk of loss transfer to the buyer when the goods are delivered to the named ship.

Food and Drug Administration (FDA) The federal agency that regulates the testing, manufacturing, and distributing of foods, medications, and medical devices.

Food, Drug and Cosmetic Act (FDCA) The federal statute that created the Food and Drug Administration and that requires the makers of certain food ingredients, additives, drugs, or medical devices to obtain formal FDA approval before selling the product to the general public.

Forbearance The giving up of a legal right as consideration in a contract.

Foreign Corrupt Practices Act (FCPA) Federal legislation enacted in 1977 that prohibits corporate bribery of foreign officials, requires corporations to keep accurate books, records, and accounts, and requires issuers registered with the Securities and Exchange Commission to maintain a responsible internal accounting control system.

Foreign Sovereign Immunities Act (FSIA) A federal statute that incorporates the concept of sovereign immunity by explicitly prohibiting U.S. courts from rendering judicial actions against foreign nations or their government officials unless the foreign nation has waived its immunity, is engaged in a commercial enterprise on U.S. soil, or has taken actions that have a direct effect on U.S. interests.

Formal contract A contract that meets one or more specific requirements of construction.

Fourth Amendment Protects individual citizens' rights to be secure in their "persons, houses, papers and effects."

Franchise A business arrangement (not a form of business entity) of continuing commercial relationship for the right to operate a business pursuant to the franchisor's trade name or to sell the seller's branded goods.

Franchisee Individual or business with the legal right to operate a franchised business and use the business's trademarks and trade secrets.

Franchisor A business entity that has a proven track record of success and ability to franchise its products.

Fraudulent misrepresentation Situation in which one party has engaged in conduct that meets the standards for misrepresentation and that party has actual knowledge that the representation is not true; basis for avoiding a contract.

Frolic An exception to the respondeat superior doctrine that occurs when an agent, during a normal workday, does something purely for her own reasons that are unrelated to her employment.

Frustration of purpose Doctrine that excuses a party from performance if, before a breach, a state of things that was the basis for forming the contract no longer exists, by no fault of either party.

Fully disclosed agency A type of agency relationship in which the third party entering into the contract is aware of the identity of the principal and knows that the agent is acting on behalf of the principal in the transaction.

General Agreement on Tariffs and Trade (GATT) A treaty designed to facilitate international trade; administered by the World Trade Organization.

Genuine assent The knowing, voluntary, and mutual approval of the terms of a contract by each party; required for a contract to be enforceable.

Good faith In contract law, the duty to honestly adhere to the contract's common purpose. Under this obligation neither party can do anything to prevent the other party from enjoying the "fruits of the contract." Instead, both must try to make the deal work as written.

Goods Tangible personal property that is movable at the time of identification to a contract of sale.

Gratuitous agents One of three broad categories of agents; includes, generally, anyone who acts on behalf of a principal without receiving any compensation.

Grievance In labor la w, a complaint filed with or by a union to challenge an employer's treatment of one or more union members.

Guarantor A third party that agrees to be liable to pay a loan only if the debtor actually defaults.

Horizontal restraints Per se violations of the Sherman Act in which the restraining of trade involves agreements between competitors to take action that results in the elimination or reduction of competition from other competitors.

Hung jury A jury that cannot come to a consensus decision on which party should prevail in a case.

Illusory promise A promise that courts will not enforce because the offeror is not truly bound by his vague promise or because a party cannot be bound by his promise due to the lack of a bargained-for exchange. Promises of gifts and deathbed promises are two examples.

Implied contract A contract in which the agreement is reached by the parties' actions rather than their words.

Implied partnership Partnership formed when the parties have acted like general partners even though the parties did not agree or intend to form a partnership.

Implied warranty A warranty that exists even when the seller does not make a specific representation about the product.

Impossibility Doctrine that excuses performance when an essential part of the contract has become impossible because a crucial, irreplaceable thing has been destroyed; a crucial person has died; a crucial means of performance no longer exists; or a crucial action has become illegal.

Impracticability Doctrine that excuses performance when an extreme circumstance occurs or reveals itself that destroys the value of the performance to the party and that circumstance was not the fault of either party and was not reasonably foreseeable.

In personam jurisdiction Another term for *personal jurisdiction.*

In rem jurisdiction Jurisdiction over real or personal property when the property itself is the principal subject of the lawsuit.

Incidental beneficiary Someone who, while not a party to the contract, stands to benefit from the contract simply because she may be in the right place at the right time. The contract was not entered into to benefit her specifically and she has no enforceable rights under the contract.

INCO terms Standardized contractual terms and designations used in international and some domestic sales contracts to avoid confusion due to language barriers and differing legal systems.

Independent contractor agents One of three broad categories of agents; includes, generally, anyone who performs services for a principal who has the right to control or direct only the result of the work and not the means and methods of accomplishing the result.

Indirect infringement A theory of copyright infringement under which a third-party facilitator is liable for damages when the facilitator has knowledge of the infringement and/or contributes to the infringement in some material way. Also called *contributory infringement.*

Informal contract A contract that is not required to be under seal by statute or to possess a certain form or language.

Injunctive relief A court order to refrain from performing a particular act.

Insider trading Illegal securities trading in which a corporate insider uses information not available to the general investor public as the basis for trades in the company's stock.

Insider Trading and Securities Fraud Enforcement Act Federal legislation passed in 1988 that raised the criminal and civil penalties for insider trading, increased the liability of brokerage firms for wrongful acts of their employees, and gave the Securities and Exchange Commission more power to pursue violations of insider trading.

Insider-trading laws Federal securities statutes that prohibit corporate insiders who have access to certain information that is not available to the general investment public from trading their company's stock based on the insider knowledge.

Insolvent Condition in which a business venture no longer has adequate assets to maintain its operations and can no longer pay its bills as they become due in the usual course of trade and business.

Inspection The act of monitoring a business's compliance with administrative regulations. An administrative agency ordinarily secures a warrant and then enters and inspects the business's premises.

Installment contract A contract allowing delivery of goods and payments for goods at separate times, with the goods being accepted or rejected separately.

Intended beneficiary Someone who, while not a party to the contract, stands to benefit from the contract because the contracting parties intended that he receive a benefit. He has enforceable rights under the contract.

Intentional torts A category of torts in which the tortfeasor was willful in bringing about a particular event that caused harm to another party.

Intermediate-level scrutiny The middle level of scrutiny applied by courts deciding constitutional issues through judicial review; upheld if the government shows that a regulation involves an important government objective that is furthered by substantially related means.

International Court of Justice The judicial branch of the United Nations, charged with settling legal disputes submitted to it by member states and giving advisory opinions on legal questions submitted to it by duly authorized international organs, agencies, and the U.N. General Assembly. Also known as *World Court.*

Interrogatory Method of discovery in which one party submits written questions to the opposing party to gather evidence prior to trial.

Investigation The initial phase of the criminal justice process in which authorities become aware of an alleged criminal act and begin gathering physical evidence and interviewing witnesses and potential suspects.

Involuntary bankruptcy petition A petition filed in the bankruptcy court against a debtor by a group of three or more creditors with an unsecured aggregate claim of at least $11,625 who claim that the debtor is failing to pay the debt as it comes due.

Irrevocable offers Offers that cannot be withdrawn by the offeror; include offers in the form of an option contract, offers that the offeree partly performed or detrimentally relied on, and firm offers by a merchant under the Uniform Commercial Code.

Joint venture Business relationship between two or more parties for a limited-in-time venture.

Jointly and severally liable Legal principle that imposes liability on general partners both together (jointly) and separately (severally) for debts and liabilities of the partnership.

Judicial branch Established under Article III of the Constitution and consists of the Supreme Court and other federal courts.

Judicial review The power of the judiciary to declare a legislative or executive act unconstitutional.

Judiciary A collection of federal and state courts existing primarily to adjudicate disputes and charged with the responsibility of judicial review.

Jurisdiction The legal authority that a court must have before it can hear a case.

Jurisprudence The science and philosophy of law that defines various approaches to the appropriate function of law and how legal doctrines should be developed and applied.

Jury selection The process of asking potential jurors questions to reveal any prejudices that may affect their judgment of the facts.

Knockout rule As applied in many states, the view that when a buyer and seller engage in a battle of the forms and different terms are exchanged, both the seller's and buyer's differing terms drop out and substitute UCC gap fillers complete the contract.

Labor Management Relations Act A federal law, enacted in 1947 as an amendment to the NLRA, that prohibits requiring employees to join or continue membership in a union as a condition of employment. Also known as Taft-Hartley Act.

Labor-Management Reporting and Disclosure Act A federal law enacted in 1959 that established a system of reporting and checks intended to uncover and prevent fraud and corruption among union officials by regulating internal operating procedures and union matters. Also known as Landrum-Griffin Act.

Lapse of time An event covered under operation of law in which a contract may be terminated once either the offeror's expressed time limit has expired or a reasonable time has passed.

Law A body of rules of action or conduct prescribed by controlling authority and having legal binding force.

Lease An agreement between a landlord and a tenant for the rental of property.

Leasehold estate The qualified right to use real estate in an exclusive manner for a limited period of time. The most common form is a landlord-tenant agreement.

Legality (Contracts) For the formation of a valid contract, the requirement that both the subject matter and performance of the contract must be legal.

Legality (Criminal) A principle of criminal law that protects individuals from being charged with some unspecified general offense; requires that crimes be specifically proscribed by law in advance of the conduct sought to be punished.

Legislative branch Established under Article I of the Constitution and consists of the House of Representatives and the Senate.

Legislative history The records kept by the legislature, including the debates, committee and conference reports, and legislative findings of fact used when creating a law, which can be used to show the legislature's intent.

Libel Written defamation, in which someone publishes in print (words or pictures), writes, or broadcasts through radio, television, or film an untruth about another that will do harm to that person's reputation or honesty or subject a party to hate, contempt, or ridicule.

Licensing The task of issuing a license authorizing a business or industry to do something.

Life estate An ownership interest in real estate that lasts for the lifetime of a particular person.

Limited liability company (LLC) A multiperson form of business entity that offers liability protection for its principals along with various tax options.

Limited liability partnership (LLP) Form of business entity that provides the same level of liability protection to a general partner in an LLP as is provided to a limited partner in a limited partnership form of entity.

Liquidated damages Reasonable estimates of the actual damages that will result if the contract is breached that are agreed to by the parties ahead of time.

Literal patent infringement Patent infringement in which the invention or process violates either the rule of exactness or the rule of addition.

Lockout The shutdown of a business by the employer to prevent employees from working, thus depriving them of their employment and putting economic pressure on the union's members before the union can do the same to the employer through a strike.

Lucid Sane and thinking clearly.

Madrid Protocol A multinational agreement that aims to facilitate multinational protection of trademarks through the use of a uniform, single-source process.

Mail Fraud Act Federal legislation enacted in 1990 as a comprehensive approach to criminalizing any fraud in which the defrauding party uses the mail or any wire, radio, or television in perpetrating the fraud.

Mailbox rule Principle stating that the acceptance of an offer is effective upon dispatch of the acceptance via a commercially reasonable means and not when the acceptance is received by the offeree; governs common law contracts.

Manager-managed LLC LLC management structure in which the members name a manager (or managers) who generally has the day-to-day operational responsibilities while the nonmanaging members are typically investors with little input on the course of business taken by the entity except for major decisions.

Manifest Apparent and evident to the senses. In the context of agency law, courts apply an objective standard to determine whether the principal intended that an agency be created.

Market-based approach An approach to pollution control that gives businesses a choice of methods based on economic incentives for complying with pollution standards; instituted by the 1990 amendments to the Clean Air Act.

Material Something that is important to the contract by being necessary and generally indispensable to the contract.

Maximizing profits A corporate ethical philosophy in which a company strives to make as much money as possible with an emphasis on not breaking the law. Ethics and corporate social responsibility are often secondary concerns.

Med-arb Method of alternative dispute resolution whereby the parties begin with mediation and, if mediation fails in a fixed time period, the parties agree to submit to arbitration.

Mediation Method of alternative dispute resolution in which a mediator attempts to settle a dispute by learning the facts of the matter and then negotiating a settlement between the two adverse parties.

Member-managed LLC LLC management structure similar to that of a general partnership, with all the members having the authority to bind the business.

Mental incapacity Category of individuals who have limited capacity to enter into a contract; includes anyone who is unable to understand the nature and consequences of the contract and anyone who is unable to act in a reasonable manner in relation to the transaction when the other party has reason to know of his condition.

Merchant One that is regularly engaged in the sale of a particular good.

Merchant's firm offer An offer in writing between merchants to buy or sell goods along with a promise without consideration to keep that offer for a stated amount of time or, if unstated, no longer than three months.

Merchant's privilege A narrow privilege, provided for in the Restatements, that shields a merchant from liability for temporarily detaining a party who is reasonably suspected of stealing merchandise.

Minimum contacts A defendant's activities within or affecting the state in which a lawsuit is brought that are considered legally sufficient to support jurisdiction in that state's courts.

Minitrial A condensed version of the case is presented to the top management from both sides, with an expert neutral party conducting the trial, allowing them to see and hear facts and arguments so more meaningful negotiations can take place.

Minors Category of individuals who have limited capacity to enter into a contract; includes those younger than the majority age of 18. Until a person reaches her majority age, any contract that she may enter into is voidable at the minor's option.

Mirror image rule Principle stating that the offeree's response operates as an acceptance only if it is the precise mirror image of the offer.

Misappropriation (1) The acquisition of a trade secret of another by a person who knows or has reason to know that the trade secret was acquired by improper means or (2) the disclosure of a trade secret to another without express or implied consent.

Misdemeanors Crimes that carry up to one year of incarceration as the penalty.

Misfeasance An act by one party that harms or endangers another party.

Misrepresentation Situation in which one party to an agreement makes a promise or representation about a material fact that is not true; basis for avoiding a contract.

Mistake In contract law, an erroneous belief that is not in accord with the existing facts.

Mixed motives Theory of employment discrimination in which the cause of the adverse employment action was motivated by both legitimate and discriminatory motives.

Mobile sources of air pollution Nonstationary sources of air pollutants automobiles, buses, trucks, ships, trains, aircraft, and various other vehicles.

Model Penal Code (MPC) A statutory text adopted by the American Law Institute in 1962 in an effort to bring greater uniformity to state criminal laws by proffering certain legal standards and reforms.

Model state statutes Statutes drafted by legal experts to be used as a model for state legislatures to adopt in their individual jurisdictions in order to increase the level of uniformity and fairness across courts in all states.

Money damages Sums levied on the breaching party and awarded to the nonbreaching party to remedy a loss from breach of contract.

Moral minimum A corporate ethical philosophy in which a company strives to act as ethically as possible as long as a reasonable profit is made. Ethics and corporate social responsibility are priorities.

Morals Generally accepted standards of right and wrong in a given society.

Mortgage A written document that specifies the parties and the real estate being used to collateralize a loan and that is filed with a state and/or local government agency.

Mortgagee The creditor in a transaction in which real estate is being used to collateralize a loan.

Mortgage foreclosure A remedy against a debtor in which a creditor declares the loan in default and takes title and possession of the collateralized real estate in hopes of selling the property to pay off the debt owed.

Mortgagor The borrower in a transaction in which real estate is being used to collateralize a loan.

Motion A request made by either party that asks the court to issue a certain order (such as a motion for summary judgment). Motions may be made before, during, and after the trial.

Mutual assent For the formation of a valid contract, the broad underlying requirement that the parties must reach an agreement using a combination of offer and acceptance and that the assent must be genuine.

Mutual consent Circumstance under which contracting parties may be discharged from their obligation although neither party has fully performed because they agree to cancel the contract.

Mutual mistake An erroneous belief held by both parties that concerns a basic assumption on which a contract was made.

National Environmental Policy Act (NEPA) Federal legislation enacted in 1969 that established a process federal agencies must follow when making decisions that have the potential to have a significant impact on the environment.

National Labor Relations Act (NLRA) A federal law enacted in 1935 that provides general protections for the rights of workers to organize, engage in collective bargaining, and take part in strikes and other forms of concerted activity in support of their demands. Also known as Wagner Act.

National Labor Relations Board (NLRB) An independent federal agency created by the NLRA and charged with administering, implementing, and enforcing NLRA provisions, as well as monitoring union elections for fraud and setting guidelines for employers and unions in regard to fair labor practices.

Necessary and Proper Clause The constitutional clause giving Congress the general implied authority to make laws necessary to carry out its other enumerated powers.

Negligence A category of torts in which the tortfeasor was without willful intent in bringing about a particular event that caused harm to another party.

Negligent hiring doctrine A tort-based theory of liability for employers for negligent or intentional torts of employees when the employer had reason to know that the employee may cause harm within his scope of employment.

No Electronic Theft (NET) Act A federal law enacted in 1997 that provides for criminal liability for anyone who willfully infringes on a copyright.

Nominal consideration Consideration that is stated in a written contract even though it is not actually exchanged.

Nonfeasance The failure to act or intervene in a certain situation.

Nonobviousness standard A standard requiring that to be patented, an invention must be something more than that which would be obvious, in light of publicly available knowledge, to one who is skilled in the relevant field.

Novation A type of substitute agreement in which the duties of the contract remain the same but a new, third party assumes the duties of an original party, discharging the original party from further obligations. (*Note*: Many courts use novation for new parties and new terms or substitute agreements.)

Novelty standard A standard requiring that an invention or process must be unique and original to be patented and that the patent applicant must show that no other identical invention or process exists.

Nuisance A common law legal action for redressing harm arising from the misuse of one's property that is based on the aggrieved party's right to enjoy his property without interference from a third party.

Objective intent For an offer to have legal effect, the requirement that, generally, the offeror must have a serious intention to become bound by the offer and that the terms of the offer must be reasonably certain.

Occupational Safety and Health Act (OSHA) A federal law enacted in 1970 that sets forth workplace rules and regulations to promote safety of workers and prevent workplace injuries.

Offer A promise or commitment to do (or refrain from doing) a specified activity. In contract law, the expression of a willingness to enter into a contract by the offeror's promising an offeree that she will perform certain obligations in exchange for the offeree's counterpromise to perform.

Oil Pollution Act (OPA) Federal legislation enacted in 1990 to streamline and strengthen the Environmental Protection Agency's ability to prevent and respond to catastrophic oil spills in water sources.

Omitted terms Contract terms that are left out or absent. In contract law, courts may supply a reasonable term in a situation where the contract is silent.

Open terms Unspecified terms in a sales contract that do not detract from the validity of the contract so long as the parties intended to make the contract and other specified terms give a basis for remedy in case of breach.

Opening statements Attorneys' presentations of their theories of the case and what they hope to prove to the jury; made at the onset of the trial.

Operating agreement Document that governs an LLC; sets out the structure and internal rules for operation of the entity.

Operating permits Licenses issued by authorities to existing stationary sources that permit pollution emission at certain levels.

Operation of law (Agency) Method whereby an agency relationship is terminated as provided for in a statute or through certain common law doctrines covering the destruction of essential subject matter, death, bankruptcy, or lack of requisite mental capacity.

Operation of law (Contracts) Termination of an offer by the occurrence of certain happenings or events, which generally include lapse of time, death or incapacity of the offeror or offeree, destruction of the subject matter of the contract prior to acceptance, and supervening illegality.

Ordinances Local statutes passed by local legislatures.

Original jurisdiction Jurisdiction that enables a court to be the first court to hear the case. The case must be filed first in this court.

Originality For copyright protection, the requirement that the author must use his own creative capabilities to create the work or medium.

Output contract A contract in which the buyer agrees to buy all the goods that the seller produces for a set time and at a set price and the seller may sell only to that one buyer. The quantity for the contract is the seller's output.

Overtime compensation A higher rate of pay for the hours that nonexempt employees work in excess of 40 hours in one seven-day workweek; calculated at one and one-half times the employee's hourly base rate.

Ownership interests The various forms of real property ownership. Some forms limit the rights that owners of real estate have.

Paris Convention A multinational agreement covering patents; requires signatory countries to protect the same inventor rights under any member country's patent laws as those enjoyed by citizens of that member country.

Parol evidence rule Interpretation rule stating that any writing intended by the parties to be the final expression of their agreement may not be contradicted by any oral or written agreements made prior to the writing.

Partially disclosed agency A type of agency relationship in which the third party knows that the agent is representing a principal but does not know the actual identity of the principal.

Partnership Multiple-person business entity in which the partners conduct an ongoing business relationship and share profits and losses.

Party A person or entity making or responding to a claim in a court.

Pass-through entity A business entity that does not pay corporate taxes, such as a partnership. Rather, any profits are taxed at individual rates after they pass through the business and are distributed to the partners.

Past consideration A promise made in return for a detriment previously made by the promisee; does not meet the bargained-for exchange requirement.

Patentable subject matter standard A standard that bars laws of nature, natural phenomena, and abstract ideas from being patentable subject matter.

Pension A retirement benefit in which the employer promises to pay a monthly sum to employees who retire from the company after a certain number of years of service. The amount is ordinarily based on the length of service and the employee's final salary rate.

Per se (Latin for "of, in, or by itself") A standard used by courts when no additional facts are needed to prove a point.

Per se standard (*per se:* Latin for "of, in, or by itself," i.e., without any additional facts needed to prove a point) A standard used by federal courts in deciding whether a certain transaction or action violates the Sherman Act; applied in cases of concerted activities that are blatantly anticompetitive.

Perfect tender rule Rule that requires the seller to deliver her goods exactly as the contract requires in quantity, quality, and all other respects or risk the buyer's lawful rejection of the goods.

Perfecting Procedure by which the secured party establishes priority in the collateral over other creditors, as provided by Article 9 of the Uniform Commercial Code.

Personal guarantee Pledge from LLC members of personal assets to guarantee payment obligations of the business venture.

Personal guaranty In a business loan, a pledge given by the principals of a business to repay the loan with their personal assets if the assets of the business are insufficient to do so in the event of a default by the business entity debtor; serves as a safeguard for creditors.

Personal jurisdiction The court's authority over the parties involved in the dispute.

Personal property Any movable or t-angible object that can be owned or leased (e.g., c-omputers, inventory, furniture, jewelry); includes everything except real property.

Picketing A union's patrolling alongside the premises of a business to organize the workers, to gain recognition as a bargaining agent, or to publicize a labor dispute with the owner or whomever the owner deals with.

Plain view doctrine A doctrine stating that authorities generally do not commit a Fourth Amendment violation when a government agent obtains evidence by virtue of seeing an object that is in plain view of the agent.

Plaintiff The party initiating a lawsuit who believes the conduct of another party has caused the plaintiff to suffer damages.

Preamble The introductory part of the Constitution that states its broad objectives.

Precedent Applying the law made in previous appellate court opinions to current cases with similar facts; binding on the trial courts.

Preemption The concept that primary sources of law are applied consistent with a hierarchy and that a law higher in the hierarchy will overrule and make void a conflicting law lower in the hierarchy. Federal law preempts conflicting state law. State law preempts conflicting city and county law.

Preexisting duty A duty that one is already legally obligated to perform and, thus, that is generally not recognized as a legal detriment.

Preferred stock A form of equity instrument that has less risk than common stock because it has certain quasi-debt features. Preferred stockholders have preference rights over common stockholders in receiving dividends from the corporation.

Preliminary adjudication A hearing at which the prosecutor presents evidence of the defendant's guilt and the decision maker (either the grand jurors or a magistrate) determines whether sufficient probable cause exists to hold the defendant over for trial.

Preponderance of the evidence The burden of proof used in civil cases, under which the fact finder need be convinced only that the defendant's liability was more likely than not.

Pretext A false reason offered to justify an action.

Pretrial conference A meeting between the attorneys for the parties and the judge in the case several weeks prior to trial, with the objectives of encouraging settlement and resolving any outstanding motions or procedural issues that arose during the pleadings or discovery stage.

Principal An agent's master; the person from whom an agent has received instruction and authorization and to whose benefit the agent is expected to perform and make decisions pursuant to an agency relationship.

Principals Owners of a business entity.

Private international law Category of international law principles that focuses on regulations of private individuals and business entities.

Private laws Laws recognized as binding between two parties even though no specific statute or regulation provides for the rights of the parties.

Private placement A securities law provision that exempts an issuer from registration when the issuer accepts investments only from those who meet the standards for accredited investors.

Private Securities Litigation Reform Act of 1995 (PSLRA) Federal legislation making it more difficult to pursue litigation under the securities laws that is based solely on commentary by company executives; intended to protect publicly held companies from frivolous litigation.

Probable cause A reasonable amount of suspicion supported by circumstances sufficiently strong to justify a belief that a person has committed a crime.

Procedural laws Laws that provide a structure and set out rules for pursuing substantive rights.

Product disparagement statutes Statutes intended to protect the interest of a state's major industries, such as agriculture, dairy, or beef.

Promissory estoppel Theory allowing for the recovery of damages by the relying party if the promisee actually relied on the promise and the promisee's reliance was reasonably foreseeable to the promisor.

Promissory note A contract in which the borrower promises to pay back the creditor at a certain rate of interest over a specified period of years.

Prospectus The first part of the security registration statement prescribed by Securities and Exchange Commission regulations; intended to give investors a realistic view of the issuer's business, risk factors, financial position, financial statements, and disclosures concerning directors, officers, and controlling shareholders.

Protected classes The classifications of individuals that are specified in Title VII, including color, race, national origin, religion, gender, and pregnancy.

Proximate (legal) cause A fundamental element that must be proved to recover in a negligence lawsuit against a tortfeasor: The injured party must prove a legally recognized and close-in-proximity link between the breach of duty and the damages suffered.

Public international law Category of international law principles that primarily addresses relations between individual countries and international organizations.

Public laws Laws derived from a government entity.

Public policy Part of the legality requirement for a valid contract; necessitates that the terms be consistent with public policy objectives.

Punishment A principle of criminal law that imposes a hardship in response to misconduct; based on the concepts that criminal law acts as a deterrent, it removes dangerous criminals from the population, and rehabilitation is an important part of the criminal justice system.

Purchase order A form commonly used in sales contracts as an offer from the buyer; contains preprinted clauses along with blanks to accommodate the specifics of the transaction.

Qualified privilege A defense to a defamation claim whereby the defendant must offer evidence of good faith and be absent of malice to be shielded from liability; provided for the media and employers.

Quasi-contract A classification that permits a contract to be enforceable in cases where no express or implied contract exists and one party suffers losses as a result of another party's unjust enrichment.

Quasi in rem jurisdiction Jurisdiction over real or personal property when the lawsuit has to do with personal liabilities not directly associated with the property.

Ratification A retroactive source of the agent's authority that occurs when the principal affirms a previously unauthorized act by either (1) expressly ratifying the transaction or (2) not repudiating the act (i.e., the principal retains the benefits while knowing that they resulted from an unauthorized act by the agent).

Rational basis The lowest level of scrutiny applied by courts deciding constitutional issues through judicial review; upheld if the government shows that the law has a reasonable connection to achieving a legitimate and constitutional objective.

Real property Land, or anything growing on, attached to, or erected on the land. Examples of real property include parcels of land, homes, warehouses, stores, and crops.

Reasonable accommodations Accommodations, required under the Americans with Disabilities Act, that allow disabled individuals to adequately perform essential job functions.

Reformation Contract modification in which the court rewrites the contract to conform to the parties' actual intentions when the parties have imperfectly expressed their agreement and the imperfection results in a dispute.

Regulation A rule that is in effect and is published in the Code of Federal Regulations and that has the force of a law.

Regulation D A securities law provision that exempts an issuer from registration on the basis of certain transactions; applies to limited offers that involve a relatively small amount of money or offers that are made in a limited manner.

Regulation Z The part of the Truth in Lending Act requiring that certain written disclosures be made prior to the time that a credit transaction is consummated.

Rejection An action terminating an offer whereby the offeree rejects the offer outright prior to acceptance.

Remand To send a case back to the lower court from which it came for further action consistent with the opinion and instructions of the higher court.

Remedial Under the Superfund law, an approach to handling hazardous substance cleanup whereby the Environmental Protection Agency identifies the most hazardous waste sites and generates a National Priorities List.

Remedies Either monetary, performance, or injunctive, the court-ordered means of enforcing rights and redressing wrongs after a breach. Also, judicial actions, which can be monetary or equitable, taken by courts that are intended to compensate an injured party in a civil lawsuit.

Removal Under the Superfund law, an approach to handling hazardous substance cleanup whereby authorization is given for actions to address releases or imminent releases of hazardous materials.

Reorganization plan A plan, generally filed by the debtor, that articulates a specific strategy and financial plan for emerging from financial distress; serves as the keystone of a Chapter 11 case.

Replacement workers Nonunion employees hired by a company in order to continue its operations during a strike.

Request for admissions A set of statements sent from one litigant to an adversary for the purpose of determining what facts are in dispute and which facts both parties accept as true.

Requests for production Requests aimed at producing specific items to help one party discover some important fact in the case.

Requirements contract A contract in which the buyer agrees to buy whatever he needs from the seller during a set period and the buyer may buy only from that one seller. The quantity for the contract is what the buyer requires.

Rescission Cancellation of a contract that occurs when both parties agree to discharge each other from all duties under the contract and end the agreement, no matter what has been done or left undone.

Resource Conservation and Recovery Act (RCRA) Federal legislation enacted in 1976 to regulate active and future facilities that produce solid waste and/or hazardous materials.

Respondeat superior (Latin for "let the master answer") A common law doctrine under which a principal (employer) is liable for the tortious action of the servant or agent (employee) when that act resulted in physical harm or injury and occurred within the agent's scope of employment.

Restatement of Torts An influential document issued by the American Law Institute that summarizes the general principles of U.S. tort law and is recognized by the courts as a source of widely applied principles of law. ALI has amended the Restatements twice, resulting in the *Restatement (Second) of Torts* and the *Restatement (Third) of Torts*.

Restatement (Second) of Agency A set of principles, issued by the American Law Institute, intended to clarify the prevailing opinion of how the law of agency stands.

Restatements of the Law A collection of uniform legal principles focused in a particular area of the law, which contains statements of common law legal principles and rules in a given area of law.

Restitution A remedy that restores to the plaintiff the value of the performance that he has already rendered to the breaching party and by which the breaching party has been unjustly enriched.

Revocation An action terminating an offer whereby the offeror decides to withdraw the offer by expressly communicating the revocation to the offeree prior to acceptance.

Revoking acceptance Remedy whereby the buyer, even after accepting the goods, can still revoke acceptance if the goods are nonconforming in a way that substantially affects their value and he notifies the seller of the revocation in a timely fashion.

Rightful rejection The justified refusal to accept nonconforming goods under a sales contract.

Right-to-work law A state law prohibiting employers from requiring that employees join a union to continue working and that nonunion employees contribute to certain union costs such as the cost related to collective bargaining.

Risk of loss The risk of one party's having to bear the loss due to damage, destruction, or loss of goods bargained for under a sales contract.

Robinson-Patman Act A federal antitrust law enacted in 1936 that amends the Clayton Act provisions by providing for broader regulatory authority to curb price discrimination.

Rule of addition The principle that literal patent infringement has occurred when the infringing device does more than is described in the patent application of the protected invention.

Rule of exactness The principle that literal patent infringement has occurred when the infringer makes, uses, or sells an invention that is exactly the same as the patent holder's claims in the patent application.

Rule of omission The principle that infringement has not occurred when the alleged patent-infringing invention lacks an essential element of the patent holder's claims in the patent application.

Rule of reason standard A second standard used by federal courts in deciding whether or not certain transaction or action violates the Sherman Act, contemplating a scale in which the court weighs any anticompetitive harm suffered against marketwide benefits of their actions.

Rulemaking The legislative function of admin- istrative agencies, whereby they create legally enforceable rules in order to fill in the details of a statute.

Safe Drinking Water Act (SDWA) Federal legislation that sets minimum quality and safety standards for every public water system and every source of drinking water in the United States.

Sales contracts Agreements to transfer title to real property or tangible assets at a given price.

Sarbanes-Oxley Act (SOX Act) of 2002 Amendments to the 1933 and 1934 Securities Acts that imposes stricter regulation and controls on how corporations do business, through regulation of auditing, financial reporting, and internal corporate governance.

Scienter Specific intent to deceive, manipulate, or defraud.

Secondary meaning A requirement for a descriptive trademark to gain protection; acquired when the consuming public primarily associates the mark with a particular product or service rather than with the ordinary meaning of the term.

Secondary sources Sources of law that have no independent authority or legally binding effect but can be used to illustrate a point or clarify a legal issue.

Section 16 Provision of the Securities Act of 1934 that imposes restrictions and reporting requirements on ownership positions and stock trades made by certain corporate insiders named in the statute.

Secured creditor A creditor that extends credit based on collateral pledged by the borrower.

Secured party The creditor in a secured transaction.

Securities Act of 1933 Federal legislation that covers the processes of issuing and reissuing securities to the public; requires registration and certain disclosures and authorizes the Securities and Exchange Commission to oversee the transactions.

Securities Act of 1934 Federal legislation that regulates the sale of securities between investors after an investor purchased them from a business entity issuer.

Securities and Exchange Commission (SEC) The independent federal administrative agency charged with rulemaking, enforcement, and adjudication of federal securities laws.

Securities law The body of federal and state laws governing the issuance and trading of equity and debt instruments to public investors.

Securities Litigation Uniform Standards Act of 1998 An amendment to the Securities Act of 1934 that prevents private parties from instituting certain lawsuits in federal or state court that are based on the statutory or common law of any state that punishes "a misrepresentation or omission of a material fact" or the use of "any manipulative device or contrivance" concerning the purchase or sale of a covered security.

Security interest The rights of the secured party in a transaction.

Self-defense A defense to avoid criminal liability whereby the defendant's actions are related to the necessity of using deadly force to repel an attack in which the defendant reasonably feared that death or substantial harm was about to occur either to the defendant or to a third party.

Sentencing guidelines Statutorily prescribed standards for determining the punishment that a convicted criminal should receive on the basis of the nature of the crime and the offender's criminal history.

Separation of powers The system of checks and balances created by the Constitution whereby the three branches have unique powers that allow them to resolve conflicts among themselves, thus ensuring no one branch exceeds its constitutional authority.

Service mark A word, symbol, or phrase used to identify a particular seller's services and distinguish them from other services.

Sherman Act The centerpiece of the statutory scheme of federal antitrust law; prohibits contracts, combinations, and conspiracies in restraint of trade and prohibits monopolization.

Shipment contract A contract in which the seller is required to send the goods to the buyer via a carrier. When the carrier receives the goods, the seller has fulfilled his duty and the buyer assumes title and bears the risk of loss.

Slander Oral defamation, in which someone tells one or more persons an untruth about another that will harm the reputation or honesty of the person defamed or subject a party to hate, contempt, or ridicule.

Social Security Act (SSA) of 1935 A federal law providing a broad set of benefits for workers, including a retirement income; funded by mandatory employment taxes paid into a trust fund by both employer and employee and administered by the federal government.

Soft per se analysis An approach developed by the courts for determining the legality of a tying arrangement: An arrangement in which a seller ties a second product to the first product is illegal per se if the seller possesses sufficient market power to render the tie-in coercive.

Sole proprietorship One-person business entity with minimal filing requirements.

Sovereign immunity Long-standing doctrine of international law that holds that, with some exceptions, nations are exempt from jurisdiction by other nations' courts.

Special relationship In tort law, a heightened duty created between certain parties, such as that of a common carrier to its passengers, innkeepers to guests, employers to employees, businesses to patrons, a school to students, and a landlord to tenants and landowners.

Specific performance A court order compelling the breaching party to perform as the contract states when monetary damages would be an insufficient remedy.

Speedy Trial Act A federal statute that sets out specific time periods in which an accused must be brought to trial.

Stakeholder Any individual or entity affected by a business's operations; includes the business's owners, investors, employees, customers, suppliers, and the wider community.

Standing Requirement that, to maintain a lawsuit against another party, the party asserting the claim must have suffered an injury in fact and the harm must be direct, concrete, and individualized.

State appellate courts State-level courts of precedent, concerned primarily with reviewing the decisions of trial courts.

State common law The governing body of law of contracts for services or real estate.

State courts Courts that adjudicate matters dealing primarily with cases arising from state statutory, state common, or state constitutional law.

State Implementation Plan (SIP) A mandated state plan for complying with the federal Clean Air Act that is submitted to the Environmental Protection Agency; consists of a collection of regulations that help to achieve a reduction in pollution.

State long-arm statutes State statutes intended to allow a court to reach into another state and exercise jurisdiction over a nonresident defendant due to the defendant's conduct or other circumstances.

Statement of qualification Document filed to form a limited liability partnership by converting a general partnership.

State statutory law The body of law governing contracts for goods or products; based on the Uniform Commercial Code.

State trial courts The first courts at the state level before which the facts of a case are decided.

Stationary sources of air pollution Fixed-site emitters of air pollutants which includes fossil-fueled power plants, petroleum refineries, petrochemical plants, food processing plants, and other industrial sources.

Statute of frauds The law governing which contracts must be in writing in order to be enforceable.

Statute of limitations A time frame, which begins when injury occurs, within which a lawsuit must be filed or the lawsuit will be barred.

Statutory law The body of law created by the legislature and approved by the executive branch of state and federal government.

Statutory scheme The structure of a statute and the format of its mandates.

Strict liability A category of torts in which a tortfeasor may be held liable for an act regardless of intent or willfulness; applies primarily to cases of defective products and abnormally dangerous activities.

Strict scrutiny The most stringent standard of scrutiny applied by courts deciding constitutional issues through judicial review when the government action is related to a fundamental right or is based on a suspect classification; upheld if the government shows a compelling need that justifies the law being enacted and no less restrictive alternatives exist.

Strike A concerted and sustained refusal by workers to perform some or all of the services for which they were hired in order to induce the employer to concede certain contract terms during collective bargaining or to engage in fair labor practices.

Strong-arm clause Provision of the Bankruptcy Code that allows the debtor in possession to avoid any obligation or transfer of property that the debtor would otherwise be obligated to perform.

Structural-offense laws Antitrust laws designed to combat the problem of monopolization by outlawing affirmative action toward monopolizing or attempting to monopolize a part of trade or commerce.

Subject matter jurisdiction The court's authority over the dispute between the parties.

Sublease A tenant's transfer of her interests to a third party for anything less than the term remaining on the lease.

Substantial performance Performance of the essential terms of the contract such that performance can be considered complete less damages for anything still unperformed.

Substantive laws Laws that provide individuals with rights and create certain duties.

Substitute agreement (modification) An agreement that replaces the original contract when the two parties agree to different duties, The new duties then replace and dissolve the obligations of the original contract.

Summary jury trial An abbreviated trial conducted before a jury and a sitting or retired judge at which attorneys present oral argument without witness testimony and the decision is nonbinding.

Summons Formal notification to the defendant that she has been named in the lawsuit and that her answer must be filed within a certain period of time.

Superfund Another name for the CERCLA, derived from that act's main provisions whereby cleanup operations for abandoned toxic waste sites are to be funded by a self-sustaining quasi-escrow fund to be administered by the federal government.

Superfund Amendments and Reauthorization Act (SARA) A 1986 amendment to the CERCLA that requires that states establish emergency response commissions to draft emergency procedures for a hazardous chemical accident and implement them in the event of such an accident; requires that businesses disclose the presence of certain chemicals within a community; and imposes an obligation on businesses to notify authorities of any spills or discharges of hazardous materials.

Supremacy Clause The constitutional clause that makes clear that federal law is always supreme to any state law that is in direct conflict.

Surety A third party that agrees to be primarily liable to pay a loan.

Tax-deferred retirement savings account A retirement savings plan in which the employee commits to saving a certain percentage of base pay in an account that is controlled directly by the employee. The funds grow tax-free until they are withdrawn.

Telephone Consumer Protection Act and Telemarketing and Consumer Fraud and Abuse Prevention Act Two statutes that regulate telemarketing firms and practices; allow consumers to opt out of unwanted calls from telemarketers, ban the use of unsolicited recorded calls and faxes, and prohibit telemarketers from making false representations.

Tenant remedies The legal alternatives available to tenants as compensation in the event a landlord breaches a lease; include termination of the lease, a suit for damages, and withholding of rent.

Tender An unconditional performance of the seller by delivering the purchased goods or otherwise making them available to the buyer.

Tender of delivery Seller's obligation under which, for delivery of goods, tender occurs when the seller produces goods conforming to the contract and provides adequate notice of their delivery to the buyer.

Termination Method of ending an agency relationship whereby either the principal (revocation) or the agent (renunciation) simply communicate the desire to dissolve the relationship.

Third-party beneficiary Someone who, while not a party to a contract, stands to benefit from the existence of the contract. (See *Incidental beneficiary* and *Intended beneficiary* in this glossary.)

Title VII The section of the Civil Rights Act of 1964 that serves as the centerpiece of antidiscrimination law; covers a comprehensive set of job-related transactions and prohibits discrimination in the workplace on the basis of an employee's race, color, national origin, gender, religion, or pregancy. The law applies to any private sector employer with 15 or more full-time employees and to unions, employment agencies, state and local governments, and most of the federal government.

Title The legal term for ownership in property; confers on the titleholder the exclusive use of personal property and the rights to sell, lease, or prohibit another from using the property.

Tort A civil wrong in which one party's action or inaction causes a loss to be suffered by another party.

Tortfeasor One who commits a civil wrong against another that results in injury to person or property.

Tortious conduct The wrongful action or inaction of a tortfeasor.

Toxic Substances Control Act (TSCA) Federal legislation that gives the Environmental Protection Agency jurisdiction to control risks that may be posed by the manufacturing, processing, using, and disposing of chemical compounds.

Trade dress A product's distinctive design, packaging, color, or other characteristic that makes it unique from other products or goods.

Trademark A nonfunctional, distinctive word, name, shape, symbol, phrase, or combination of words and symbols that helps consumers to distinguish one product from another.

Treble Damages Triple damages; often awarded in fraud cases.

Trial Stage of litigation that occurs when the case cannot be settled, generally taking place in front of a judge as the finder of law and with a jury as a finder of fact.

Trial de novo A completely new trial.

Troubled Assets Relief Program (TARP) A program established by the American Recovery and Reinvestment Act of 2009 to purchase assets and equity from financial institutions and thereby strengthen the U.S. financial sector.

Truth in Lending Act (TILA) The part of the Consumer Credit Protection Act that requires lenders to disclose to borrower applicants certain information about the loan or terms of credit and mandates uniform methods of computation and explanation of the terms of the loan or credit arrangements.

U.N. Convention on Contracts for the International Sale of Goods (CISG) A trade agreement developed by the U.N. Commission on International Trade Law to establish uniform rules for drafting certain international sales contracts.

U.S. courts of appeal The intermediate appellate courts in the federal system, frequently referred to as *circuit courts of appeal;* consist of 13 courts, each of which reviews the decisions of federal district courts in the state or several states within its circuit.

U.S. district courts Federal courts that serve the same primary trial function as state trial courts but address issues involving federal matters.

U.S. Supreme Court The ultimate arbiter of federal law that not only reviews decisions of the federal courts but also reviews decisions of state courts that involve some issue of federal law.

Unconscionability A defense that may allow a party to potentially avoid a contract on the grounds that she suffered a grossly unfair burden that shocks the objective conscience.

Undisclosed agency A type of agency relationship in which a third party is completely unaware that an agency relationship exists and believes that the agent is acting on her own behalf in entering a contract.

Undue influence A defense that gives legal relief to a party who was induced to enter into a contract through the improper pressure of a trusted relationship.

Unenforceable contract A contract that meets the elements required by law for an otherwise binding agreement but is subject to a legal defense.

Unilateral contract A contract involving one promise followed by one performance, which then triggers a second performance from the offeror.

Unilaterally altered Term pertaining to a contract in which one party changes a term of the offer or acceptance after the contract was made and without the consent of the other party, who is then discharged from performing.

Unilateral mistake An erroneous belief held by only one party about a basic assumption in the terms of an agreement.

United Nations (U.N.) An international organization created after World War II to facilitate common international concerns on defense, trade, protection of human rights, and other matters.

Unsecured debt Credit that is not collateralized.

Utilitarian Model of moral philosophy which holds that an action is ethically sound if it produces positive results for the most.

Valid contract A contract that has the necessary elements and, thus, can be enforceable.

Validation disclosure A notice in which a collection agency, when making initial contact with a debtor, makes known certain rights of the debtor, including the fact that he has 30 days to dispute the debt; required under the Fair Debt Collection Practices Act.

Values management Managerial system that emphasizes prioritizing moral values for the organization and ensuring that behaviors are aligned with those values.

Venue A determination of the most appropriate court location for litigating a dispute.

Verdict The final decision of a jury in a case.

Vertical price-fixing Price-fixing in which a seller attempts to control the resale price of a product at a lower level in the supply chain.

Vertical restraints Violations of the Sherman Act (judged by the rule of reason) in which the restraining of trade involves agreements between noncompetitors on different distributional levels in the chain of commercial supply.

Vicarious infringement A theory of copyright infringement that applies when there has been a direct infringement and a third-party facilitator is in a position to control that infringement and benefits financially from it.

Vienna Convention on the Law of Treaties One of the standards used by courts and other tribunals when interpreting treaty law.

Void contract A contract that lacks one or more of the basic required elements of a contract or that has not been formed in conformance with the law from the outset of the agreement and, thus, cannot be enforced by either party.

Voidable contract A contract that one party may, at its option, either disaffirm or enforce.

Voidable transfers In bankruptcy proceedings, certain transfers that are considered an unfair advantage of one creditor over another.

Voluntary bankruptcy petition A petition filed in the bankruptcy court by the debtor that includes the names of creditors, a list of debts, and a list of the debtor's assets, income, and expenses.

Wall Street Reform and Consumer Protection Act Federal legislation designed to overhaul the regulation of U.S. financial services and markets.

Warranty A seller's (or lessor's) legally enforceable promise to a consumer concerning the quality and/or functionality of a product.

Whistle-blower An employee or agent who reports legal misconduct or a statutory violation by her employer to the authorities.

Winding up After dissolution, the process of paying the debts of the partnership and liquidating and/or distributing the remaining assets.

Withdrawal Term used by the RULPA to describe the act of separation of one partner from the partnership.

Worker Adjustment and Retraining Notification (WARN) Act A federal law enacted in 1989 to protect employees by requiring most employers with 100 or more employees to provide at least 60-day written notification of facility closings and mass layoffs of employees.

Workers' compensation State statutes that provide an employee who is injured in the course of employment with a partial payment in exchange for mandatory relinquishment of the employee's right to sue the employer for the tort of negligence; funded through employer-paid insurance policies.

Workout The process in which a debtor meets a loan commitment by satisfying altered repayment terms; intended to turn around a business when the principals wish to continue operations and the business is underperforming and is in poor financial condition.

Written express warranty A warranty whose terms are put in writing for the consumer.

Zippo **standard** The legal framework used by trial courts in determining personal jurisdiction when one party is asserting minimum contacts based on a certain level of Internet activity by the defendant.

Chapter 1
© Eric Audras/PhotoAlto/PictureQuest, 5; © The McGraw-Hill Companies, Inc./Jill Braaten, photographer, 11; © Bettmann/Corbis, 12.

Chapter 2
Image is in the public domain. Title page of the first printing of the Federalist Papers, 1788, 38; © AP Photo, 45; © AP Photo/California Nurses Association, 55.

Chapter 3
© Comstock/PunchStock, 66; © MCT via Getty Images, 70; © The McGraw-Hill Companies, Inc./John Flournoy, photographer, 83.

Chapter 4
© Digital Vision/Getty Images, 98; © Tim Pannell/Corbis, 106; © fStop/Getty Images, 112.

Chapter 5
© Photodisc/PunchStock, 131; © AP Photo/Pat Sullivan, 135; © Jack Star/PhotoLink/Getty Images, 141.

Chapter 7
© Thinkstock/Getty Images, 168 left; © Photodisc/Getty Images, 168 right; © Creatas Images/PictureQuest, 174.

Chapter 8
© Brand X/Fotosearch, 207; © Bob Wickham/Getty Images, 210; © Frank Micelotta/PictureGroup via AP Images, 215.

Chapter 9
© Getty Images, 233; © Royalty-Free/Corbis, 246; © Royalty-Free/Corbis, 252.

Chapter 10
© Flying Colours Ltd./Getty Images, 264; © Image Source/Corbis, 281; © Roberts Publishing Services/Joshua Roberts. All rights reserved, 286.

Business Law Simulation Exercise 1
© Ryan McVay/Getty Images, 295.

Chapter 11
© C. Borland/PhotoLink/Getty Images, 304; © Stockbyte/Getty Images, 319.

Chapter 12
© The McGraw-Hill Companies, Inc./Jill Braaten, photographer, 340; © Royalty-Free/Corbis, 346; © The McGraw-Hill Companies, Inc./Christopher Kerrigan, photographer, 357.

Chapter 13
© Ryan McVay/Getty Images, 369; © Royalty-Free/Corbis, 377.

Business Law Simulation Exercise 2
© cultura/Corbis/RF, 399.

Chapter 14
© Randy Faris/Corbis, 411; © Stockbyte/Getty Images, 415; © Banana Stock/PunchStock, 416; © The McGraw-Hill Companies, Inc./John Flournoy, photographer, 425.

Chapter 15
© AP Photo/Nati Harnik, 434; © Royalty-Free/Corbis, 439.

Chapter 16
© Copyright 1997 IMS Communications Ltd./Capstone Design. All Rights Reserved, 458; © AP Photo/Paul Sakuma, 459.

Chapter 17
© Royalty-Free/Corbis, 476; © AP Photo, 481; © AP Photo/Kathy Willens, 491; © AP Photo/Mary Altaffer, 496.

Chapter 18
© Comstock/PictureQuest, 513; © AP Photo/Nam Y. Huh, 518; © Chris Kleponis/Bloomberg via Getty Images, 527.

Chapter 19
© AP Photo/Rick Bowmer, 541; © Creatas Images/Jupiterimages, 545; © D. Falcone/PhotoLink/Getty Images, 548.

Chapter 20
© Associated Press, 565 left; © Bettmann/Corbis, 565 right; Image is in the public domain. Title page from 1st edition of Wealth of Nations in 1776, 567.

Chapter 21
© PunchStock/SuperStock, 582; © Anderson Ross/Brand X/Corbis, 583; © Imagestate Media (John Foxx), 587.

Chapter 22
© The McGraw-Hill Companies, Inc./John Flournoy, photographer, 602; © Roberts Publishing Services/Joshua Roberts. All rights reserved, 609; © Keith Brofsky/Getty Images, 615.

Chapter 23
© AP Photo/Kathy Willens, 637; © Stockbyte/Getty Images, 643; © Brand X Pictures, 648.

Chapter 24
© PhotoLink/Getty Images, 660; © AP Photo, 663; © AP Photo/Paul Sakuma, 671.

Chapter 25
© AP Photo/Paul Sakuma, 685; © Paul J. Richards/AFP/Getty Images, 689; © AP Photo/U.S. National Archives Records Administration, 700.

Chapter 26
© AP Photo/Peter Dejong, 714; © KEYSTONE/Fabrice Coffrini, 723.

Business Law Simulation Exercise 3
© Doug Berry/Corbis, 731.

Capstone Case Study 1
© Greg Kuchik/Getty Images, 738.

Capstone Case Study 2
© Jeff Greenberg/Alamy, 742.

Capstone Case Study 3
© Tim Boyle/Getty Images, 745.

Page numbers followed by n refer to notes.

A

Aaris v. Las Virgenes Unified School District, 289
Abbot v. Payne, 315
Abolin v. Farmers American Mutual Life Insurance, 204n
ACLU v. Reno, 650
Adams v. Salt River Master Carvers, 402–404
Adarand Constructors, Inc. v. Pena, 389
Advanced Technology Services, Inc. v. KM Docs. LLC, 160
ALS Scan, Inc. v. Digital Serv. Consultants, Inc., 92
Altmann v. Republic of Austria, 727
A&M Records v. Napster, Inc., 694
Amazon.com, Inc. v. Barnesandnoble.com, Inc., 703n
American Express v. Italian Colors Restaurant, 113
American Medical Association v. United States Internal Revenue Service, 516
American Needle, Inc. v. National Football League, 571
American Shipbuilding Company v. NLRB, 358n
American Suzuki Motor Corp. v. Carney, 625
Amoco Oil Co. v. Jones, 678
Angel v. Murray, 183n
Aquino v. Honda of America, Inc., 373
Arizona Cartridge Remanufacturers Association v. Lexmark, 198–199
Arizona v. United States, 10
Armory v. Delamirie, 658n
Arthur Andersen LLP v. United States, 138
Asahi Metal Industrial Company v. Superior Court of California, 77
Associated Rubber Co. v. NLRB, 353n
Austin Hill Country Realty, Inc., d/b/a Re/Max Austin Hill Country Realtors, et al. v. Palisades Plaza, Inc., d/b/a The Palisades, 220
Automobile Supply Co. v. Scene-In-Action, 678
AutoNation USA Corporation v. Leroy, 120

B

Bad Frog Brewery, Inc. v. N.Y. State Liquor Authority, 52
Baltimore & Ohio Railroad Company v. United States, 169n
Bammert v. Don's Super-Valu, Inc., 333
Barker v. Hennessy, 284
Barr v. Matteo, 263n
Barrer v. Chase Bank USA, 624

Bartus v. Riccardi, 244n
Batson v. Kentucky, 107
Baxter v. Ford Motor Co., 607n
Bear Sterns & Co. v. Wyler, 654
Belanger v. Swift Transportation, Inc., 265, 289
BellSouth Advertising v. Donnelley Information Publishing, 693n
Bennett v. American Electric Power Services Corp., 182
Bennett v. Shidler, 707
Bennett v. Spear, 527n
Berman v. Parker, 673n
Best Van Lines, Inc. v. Walker, 92
Beverly E. Black and James A. Black v. George Weston & Stroehmann Bakeries, Inc., 560
Bibb v. Navajo Freight Lines, 44
Bickford v. Onslow Memorial Hospital Foundation, 89
Bilski v. Kappos, 702n
Biomedical Systems Corp. v. GE Marquette Medical Systems, Inc., 199
Birdsong v. Apple, Inc., 610
Bishop v. Texas A&M University, 327
Blumenthal v. Drudge and America Online, Inc., 267
Bonilla v. Baker Concrete Construction, 362
Bosse v. Brinker Restaurant dba Chili's Grill and Bar, 308–309
Bradley v. Pizzaco of Nebraska, Inc., 394
Branch v. Mullineaux et al., 450
Braswell v. United States, 647
Bridgestone Americas Holding, Inc. v. Mayberry, 104–105
Brower v. Gateway 2000, Inc., 120, 193n
Brown v. Entertainment Merchants Association, 43, 56
Brundridge v. Fluor Federal Services, Inc., 328
Buckley v. Valeo, 523n
Burdick v. Koerner, 472
Burton v. MDC PGA Plaza Corp., 291
Butters v. Vance International, Inc., 716
Byrne v. Boadle, 276n

C

Cadence Design Systems, Inc. v. Avant!, 682n
Calder v. Jones, 77
Campbell v. Acuff-Rose Music, Inc., 694n
Car Transportation Brokerage Company v. Blue Bird, No. 08-16103, 245
Cargill v. Monfort of Colorado, Inc., 26
Carlill v. Carbolic Smoke Ball Co., 172n
Carnival Cruise Lines v. Shute, 79

Casserly v. U.S. State, 364
CBS Corp. v. Fed. Commc'n Comm'n, 533
Central Hudson Gas v. Public Service Commission, 52, 53, 54, 63
Chambers v. Travelers Companies, 162
Chaplin v. Sanders, 676–677
Chateau des Charmes Wines Ltd. v. Sabate, 726
Chattler v. U.S., 155
Chevron USA, Inc. v. NRDC, 523n
Childress v. Darby Lumber, Inc., 363
Cipollone v. Liggett Group, Inc., et al., 61
Citizens to Preserve Overton Park, Inc. v. Volpe, 523n
Citizens United v. Federal Election Commission, 54
City of Philadelphia v. Fleming Companies, Inc., 505
Clancy v. King, 430
Clemens v. McNamee, 79–80
Coker v. Wal-Mart Stores, Inc., 289
Colaitis v. Benihana, 277
Coleman v. Donahoe, 388n
Computer Associates International v. Latai, Inc., 696n
Conklin v. Holland, 428
Connally v. General Construction, 26
Consumer Federation of America v. Department of Agriculture, 529
Continental T.V. v. GTE Sylvania, 569
Corbesco, Inc. v. Dole, 347
Corning Glass Works v. Brennan, 382n
Covad Communications Co. v. BellSouth Corp., 578
Cubby Inc. v. Compuserve, Inc., 267
Custom Vehicles v. Forest River, 686
Cybersell, Inc. v. Cybersell, Inc., 83

D

Dalton v. Educational Testing Service, 226
Darden v. Peters, 708
Data General Corporation v. Grumman Systems Support Corporation, 578
Day v. Case Credit Corp., 26
Dayenian v. American National Bank and Trust Co. of Chicago, 677
Del Monte Corp. v. Martin, 229
Deutsche Bank Sec., Inc. v. Montana Bd. of Invs., 93

Page numbers followed by n refer to notes.

Arthur Andersen, 137–139, 639
Articles of organization (LLC), 435
Assent, 169
Assignment
    contract rights, 221, 225
    landlord-tenant, 669, 677
Assumption of risk
    definition, 288
    negligence, 279
    products liability, 285–286
Attorneys as in-house counsel, 6
Audio Home Recording Act, 696
Audit reforms (SOX Act), 495–496
Authority, in agency, 310–312
Avant! Corporation, 682

B

Bad faith, 686, 705
Bail, 641
Bailments, 658, 676
Ballot initiative, 54n
Ballot propositions, 45, 54
Bankruptcy
    alimony, 594
    automatic stay
        basic provisions, 587
        case summary, 597
        Chapter 7, 589
        definition, 595
    Bankruptcy Abuse Prevention
        and Consumer Protection Act
        (BAPCPA), 592–594
    case summaries
        automatic stay, 597
        means test, 599
        nondischargeable debts, 598
        reorganization (Chapter 11), 598
        voidable transfers, 597
    Chapter 7: liquidation and discharge,
        588–589
    Chapter 11: reorganization, 598
        basic provisions, 590–592
        case summary, 598
        definition, 595
    child support, 594
    contract performance, 212, 224
    cram down provision (Chapter 11), 592,
        595
    credit counseling, 594
    debtor in possession (Chapter 11),
        591–592, 595
    debtor's options, 588–592
    distribution and discharge (Chapter 7),
        590
    estate, 588, 595
    fraudulent transfer, 588
    income, proof of, 594
    involuntary bankruptcy petition, 589, 595
    liquidation and discharge (Chapter 7),
        588–589

means test, 593, 599
meeting of creditors (Chapter 7), 589
nondischargeable debts (case summary),
    598
overview, 586–588
preferential transfer, 588
reorganization (Chapter 11)
    basic provisions, 590–592
    case summary, 598
    definition, 595
repayment plan (Chapter 13), 592
strong-arm clause, 592, 595
trustee, 587–588, 595
voidable transfers
    basic provisions, 588
    case summary, 597
    definition, 595
voluntary bankruptcy petition, 589, 595
Bankruptcy Abuse Prevention and Con-
    sumer Protection Act, 592–594
Battle of the forms, 235, 254
Bench trials, 106, 117
Bender, H. H., 192n, 221n
Benton, Jeremy, 125n
Berne Convention, 723, 725
"Beyond a reasonable doubt" standard, 628,
    652
Bilateral contracts, 154, 161
Bill of Rights
    background, 38
    business, implications for, 51–55
    definition, 59
    states, applicability to, 56
Bills, 9
Binding rulings, 66, 67, 68
Bipartisan Campaign Reform Act, 54
Black Bear Micro Roastery, 737–740
Black's Law Dictionary, 5, 23
Blue sky laws, 493, 502
Bonds, 480
Bonusgate scandal (AIG), 139–141
Boycotts, 357–358
Branches of government, 37–38
Breach of contract, 17, 213–215, 224
Breach of warranty, 110
Brennan, Jr., William J., 374n
Bribery, 638
Briefs, 67
British common law, 11
British Petroleum (BP), 546
Burden of proof (criminal law), 628, 651
Business and law
    Bill of Rights, 51–55
    Congressional powers, 38
    counsel's role, 6–7
    criminal law, 631–632
    dispute resolution, 95–96
    environmental law, 537
    intentional torts, 262–272
    jurisdiction, 73
    laws that impact business, 13
    legal decisions by managers, 20–23

legal theory and practice, 5–8
model laws, 15
overview, 5–6
stare decisis, 12–13
strategic planning, 6
Business Corporation Law, 469
"Business corporation law," 447
Business entities
    choice of, 409–410
    criminal law, 631–632, 654
    franchises; *see* Franchise
    joint ventures, 414, 426
    limited liability company; *see* Limited
        liability company (LLC)
    limited liability partnership; *see* Limited
        liability partnership (LLP)
    partnerships; *see* Partnerships
    sole proprietorships, 410–412, 426
    summary of types, 410
    trusts, 563
Business judgment rule
    case summary, 472
    definition, 451, 469
    duty of care, 461–462
Business lawyers, 6
Business records, production of, 645–647

C

Calamari, J. D., 192n, 221n
CAN-SPAM Act, 605
Capacity, in contracts, 185–187, 197
Capital One Financial, 498
Card Check Act, 354
Care, duty of
    agency law, 318, 325
    corporations, 460–461, 469
    due care, duty of, 438
Case of first impression, 14
Case precedents; *see* Precedents
Case studies
    coffee wars (Starbucks and Charbucks),
        737–740
    fraud (McDonald's promotional games),
        745–750
    juice contamination (Odwalla), 741–744
Causey, Rick, 136
Celler-Kefauver Antimerger Act, 576
Central Hudson test
    case summary, 63
    four-part test, 52
    tobacco industry issue, 53
Certiorari, writ of, 69
Challenges, 107
Chancery courts, 66
Checks and balances system, 38, 40
Child labor laws, 339–340
Child Online Protection Act, 651
Child Protection and Toy Safety Act, 612
Child support (bankruptcy), 594
Chippendales, 689

"Hillary: The Movie," 54
Hilton Hotels, 683
Holdings, 12
Holmes, Oliver Wendell, 51
Hung jury, 107, 117

I

Identity theft, 619
Illusory promises (contracts), 183, 196
Implied contracts
    case summary, 163
    definition, 155, 161
    employment law, 332
Incidental damages (UCC), 248
INCO terms for international sales, 253,
    255, 721–722, 724
Inculpatory evidence, 101
Indemnification, 312, 320–321
Independent agencies, 14
Independent contractors
    case summary, 328
    definition, 325
    direction/control criterion, 305
    distinguished from employees, 304–306
    employee agents distinguished, 304–306
    peculiar risk doctrine, 316
Induce, 272
Inferior courts, 67
Infringement
    copyright, 693–697
    patents, 702–704
    trademark, 690
In-house counsel, 6
Initial public offering, 452, 475
Injunctions
    contract remedy, 218
    definition, 18, 225
In personam jurisdiction, 76–80, 88
In rem jurisdiction, 76, 91
Insider trading, 638, 652
Insider Trading and Securities Fraud
    Enforcement Act, 488, 501, 638
Installment contracts, 247, 255
Intellectual property
    Agreement and Permission to Use
        (sample form), 699
    avoiding liability, 699–700
    copyright; see Copyright
    international agreements, 722–724
    patents; see Patents
    trademark; see Trademark
    trade secrets; see Trade secrets
Intermediate-level scrutiny, 40, 42, 59
International Chamber of Commerce, 253,
    717, 720
International Court of Arbitration (Paris),
    717
International Court of Justice, 714, 724
International law
    antibribery provisions, 639–640,
        718–719

arbitration, 717
case summaries
    arbitration enforcement, 726
    contracts for the international sale of
        goods, 726
    dispute resolution, 727
    Foreign Sovereign Immunities Act,
        727
    sovereign immunity, 726, 727
choice of law and forum clauses, 720
civil law systems, 715, 724
comity, 712, 724
commercial law, 720–722
common law systems, 715
corrupt practices, 718–719
courts, 714–715
customs, 712
definition, 711
dispute resolution
    ad hoc arbitration rules, 718
    arbitration, 717
    case summary, 727
    forums for arbitration, 717
    mediation, 718
Foreign Corrupt Practices Act (FCPA)
    definition, 652
    major provisions, 639–640,
        718–719
forums for international arbitration, 717
judicial decisions, 712
legal systems, 715–716
mediation, 718
mixed legal systems, 716
organizations, 712–713
patents, 724
private international law, 711, 724
public international law, 711, 724
religion-based legal systems, 715–716
sources of, 711–712
sovereign immunity
    case summary, 726, 727
    definition, 715, 724
treaties, 712
International Monetary Fund (IMF), 712
Internet
    country of origin principle, 86, 88
    e-mail and statute of frauds, 194
    jurisdictional issues, 86–87
    legal research, 32–33
    minimum contacts test for jurisdiction,
        81–83, 91
    website, jurisdiction through, 92
    workplace monitoring, 349–350
Interrogatories
    case summary, 121
    definition, 116
    use in civil litigation, 101–103
Interstate versus intrastate commercial
    activity, 44–45
Intoxication, as defense, 630
Investments; see Securities law
Invisible hand, 142

J

Johnson & Johnson, 284–285
Joint and several liability, 426, 551
Joint ventures, 414, 426
JP Morgan Chase, 498
Judges as finder of law, 106
Judgment, collecting the, 108–109
Judgment as a Matter of Law, motion for,
    102
Judgment creditor, 109
Judicial branch of government
    definition, 59
    establishment of, 37–38
    powers of, 39–40
Judicial review; see also Appellate courts
    administrative agency regulations,
        523–524, 533
    definition, 59
    function of courts, 39–40, 65
    preemption, 44
    standards of review, 40, 42–43
    Supremacy Clause, 44
    Supreme Court's authority, 39–40, 69
Judiciary; see also Courts
    definition, 65
    functions, 72
    role and structure, 65–69
Juice contamination crisis (case study),
    741–744
Juries
    charging the jury, 107, 117
    deliberations, 107, 117
    finder of fact role, 106
    hung jury, 107, 117
    selection, 106, 117
    verdict of, 107, 117
Jurisdiction
    business strategy, 73
    case summaries, 89–92
    concurrent jurisdiction, 74, 88
    Constitutional basis, 39, 73
    country of origin principle, 86
    country of origin standard, 88
    definition, 59, 66, 72–73, 73, 88
    diversity of citizenship, 74, 88
    effects test, 77
    e-mail, 84–86
    federal question, 74, 88
    forum selection clause, 78–79, 90
    injurious effect (out-of state defendants),
        77
    in-state defendants, 76
    Internet business, 81–83
    long-arm statutes, 76–77, 88
    minimum contacts test, 77, 81–83, 88,
        90–91
    original jurisdiction, 74, 88
    out-of-state defendants, 77–79
    personal jurisdiction, 76–80, 88, 89
    in personam jurisdiction, 76–80, 80, 88

physical presence (out of state defendants), 77–78
quasi in rem jurisdiction, 76, 88, 91
in rem jurisdiction, 76, 88, 91
subject matter jurisdiction, 73–76, 74–76, 80, 88
two-part analysis, 73–74
voluntary (out-of-state defendants), 78–79
Zippo standard, 81–83, 88, 91
Jurisprudence, 3–4, 23
Justice-of-the-peace courts, 67

K

Kant, Immanuel, 125
Kennedy, Gavin, 142n
Kennedy, Anthony, 54
Kennedy, John F., 382
Kline, D., 681n

L

Labor Management Relations Act, 352, 360
Labor-Management Reporting and Disclosure Act, 352–353, 360
Labor Management Services Administration, 341
Labor unions
    authorization cards, 353, 360
    boycotts, 357–358
    certification, 353, 360
    collective bargaining agreements
        authorizing legislation, 352
        definition, 332, 360
        procedures, 354–355
    elections, 353, 360
    formation of union, 353–354
    governing law, 352–353
    grievances, 355, 360
    historical background, 331–332
    illegal work stoppages, 357–358
    labor contracts, 332
    labor-management relations, 352–353
    lockouts, 358, 360
    membership trends, 351
    picketing, 355–356, 360
    replacement workers, 358, 360
    reporting and disclosure requirements, 352–353
    right-to-work laws, 352, 360
    strikes
        authorization for, 355
        definition, 360
        illegal strikes, 357–358
        rehiring after, 355–356
    unfair labor practices (case summary), 363
    work stoppages
        illegal, 357–358
        legal, 355

Landlord-tenant
    agreement (leasehold estate)
        case summary, 677
        definition, 664, 674
    assignment, 669, 675, 677
    case summaries
        agreements, 678
        assignment and subleases, 677
        constructive eviction, 678
    constructive eviction, 668, 678
    duties of tenant, 668
    habitability right of tenant, 667–668
    leases, 667, 675
    possession right of tenant, 667–668
    quiet enjoyment right of tenant, 667–668
    remedies available to tenant, 668, 675
    rights of landlord, 668–669
    rights of tenant, 667–668
    security deposit, 668–669
    sublease, 669, 675, 677
Landowners
    special duties, 274
    Superfund affecting, 552–553
Lanham Act, 684, 733–734, 738
Law; *see also* American law; Business and law; Model laws
    categories of, 17–20
    civil law, 11–12, 17, 24
    common law, 11–12, 23
    criminal law, 17, 24
    definition, 3, 23
    holdings, 12
    precedents, 12, 23
    private law, 19, 24
    procedural law, 17, 24
    public law, 19, 24
    purposes of, 4
    research strategy, 33–34
    substantive law, 17, 24
    terminology, 4–5
Law and equity, 18–19
Lay, Kenneth, 136, 137, 139
Leases, personal property, 659–660
Legal realism, 4
Legal research strategies, 33–34
Legislative branch of government, 49–50
    establishment of, 37
    powers of, 38
Legislative history, 9, 23
Lender, 613n
Libby, Edward, 140
Libel, 262, 287
Licensing, 510, 530
Lilly Ledbetter Fair Pay Act of 2009, 382, 384
Limited authority, 66
Limited liability company (LLC)
    articles of organization, 435, 443
    basic characteristics, 434
    capitalization, 438
    care, duty of, 438

case summaries
    innocent partners, 445
    involuntary withdrawal, 445
    liability of member, 444
    personal guarantee from members, 445
certificate of organization, 435, 436–437
definition, 434, 443
dissociation of members, 438–439, 443
dissolution, 438, 443
fiduciary duty, 438
formation, 435
innocent partners (case summaries), 445
involuntary withdrawal (case summaries), 445
liability of members, 435, 444
loyalty, duty of, 438
management and operation, 438
manager-managed LLC, 438, 443
member-managed LLC, 438, 443
operating agreement, 435, 443
personal guarantee from members
    case summary, 445
    definition, 443
    requirement of, 435
sample certificate of organization, 436–437
state laws, 432–434
taxation, 438
Limited liability partnership (LLP)
    basic characteristics, 439
    capitalization, 442
    definition, 433–434, 443
    liability of partners, 439–441
    management and operation, 442
    statement of qualification, 439, 443
    taxation, 442
Litigation
    abusive or vexatious litigation, 108
    alternative dispute litigation; *see* Alternative dispute litigation (ADR)
    civil litigation; *see* Civil litigation
Litigators, 6
Locus sigilli, 158n
London Court of International Arbitration, 717
Long-arm statutes, 76–77, 88
Loss of consortium, 279
Loyalty, duty of
    agency law, 317–318
    corporations, 438, 460, 463–465, 469
    limited liability company, 438
    limited partnerships (case summary), 430
    partnership law (case summary), 430
Lucid (contracts), 187, 197

M

Madoff, Bernie, 635–637
Madrid Protocol, 723, 725
Magnuson-Moss Warranty—Federal Trade Commission Improvement Act, 609–611

Mailbox rule, 176, 196
Mail Fraud Act, 632–633, 652
Malice, 263
Marine Mammal Protection Act, 556
Material (contracts), 206, 224
Maximizing profits, 128, 144
McCain-Feingold Act, 54
McDonald's, 683, 745–750
MCI WorldCom, 495
Measure of judicial action, 18
Med-Arb (ADR), 117
Mediation (ADR)
    basic provisions, 113, 115
    definition, 117
    international disputes, 718
Mens rea, 629–630
Mental incapacity, 630, 652
Merchant's privilege, 268, 287
Mergers and acquisitions, 575
Microsoft Corporation, 573–574, 685
Migratory Bird Conservation Act, 556
Minimum contacts test
    case summaries, 90–91
    definition, 88
    e-mail, 84–86
    generally, 77
    Internet business, 81–83
Minimum wage
    general information, 336
    state law: case summary, 26
Minitrials, 115, 117
Minors
    capacity to contract, 185–186, 197
    child labor laws, 339–340
Mirror image rule, 175, 196
Misdemeanors, 630–631, 652
Misfeasance, 273, 288
Misrepresentation
    contracts, 189–191, 197
    fraudulent, 266–268
Mistake (criminal law), 630
Mistrial, motion to dismiss for, 102
Mitigate damages, 156
Mitigating circumstances, 629
Model Business Corporation Act, 447, 469
Model laws
    definition, 24
    Model Penal Code, 627, 651
    purpose, 14–15
    Uniform Commercial Code, Article 2, 231
    Uniform Trade Secrets Act, 682
Money damages
    contracts, 215, 224
    definition, 18
Monopolies
    attempted monopolization, 574
    consent orders, 573–574
    intent to monopolize, 574
    Microsoft case, 573–574
    monopoly power, 573

Sherman Act, Section 2, 572–573
    structural offenses, 572–573, 576
Moral minimum, 128, 144
Moral philosophy and ethical decision making, 125–126
Mortgages, 583–584, 595
Motions
    definition, 101, 116
    examples, 102
    pretrial, 102
    trial period, 102
Motor vehicle emissions, 543–544
Mozilo, Angelo, 500
Municipal courts, 67
Mutual assent, in contracts, 169, 196, 198–199

N

Napster, 695
National Conference of Commissioners on Uniform State Laws (NCCUSL), 15, 231
National Environmental Policy Act (NEPA), 539–541
National Labor Relations Act (NLRA), 352, 360
National Labor Relations Board (NLRB), 352, 360
National Pollution Discharge Elimination System, 545
Natural law, 4
Necessary and Proper Clause
    basic provisions, 59
    business impact, 38
    case summary, 62
    tax and spend power, 49–50
Negligence
    actual damages, 277, 279, 288
    assumption of risk, 279, 288
    breach of duty, 274–276, 288
    "but for" test, 276
    cause in fact, 276, 288
    comparative negligence, 279, 288, 291
    contributory negligence, 279
    defenses, 279
    definition, 262, 287
    duties, 273–274, 288
    elements of, 272–280
    misfeasance, 273, 288
    nonfeasance, 273, 288
    per se, negligence, 274, 290
    products liability, 282
    proximate legal cause, 277, 288
    reasonable conduct, duty of, 273
    res ipsa loquitur, 275–276, 289
    safety statute violations, 274
    special relationship duties
        case summary, 289
        definition, 288
        landowners, 274
        liability determined by, 273

Negotiated Rulemaking Act, 517
Nike, 683
No Electronic Theft Act, 694, 705
Nolo contendere, 642n
Nonvoting stock, 457
Novation, 209, 224
Nuclear Regulatory Commission (NRC), 538
Nuisance, common law doctrine of, 537–538, 557

O

Obama, Barack, 140
Obamacare; *see* Patient Protection and Affordable Care Act
Obscenity, 52–53
Occupational Safety and Health Act (OSHA), 344–346, 360
Occupational Safety and Health Administration, 344–346
Odometer rollback, 604
Odwalla Juice Company, 612, 741–744
Office of Management and Budget, 521
Office of the Comptroller of the Currency, 603
Oil Pollution Act, 546, 557
Oil Spill Liability Trust Fund, 546
Oil spills, 546
Online dispute resolution, 114
Oprah Winfrey, 266
Option contracts, 174
Oral argument, 67
Ordinances, 9, 23
Organization for Economic Cooperation and Development (OEDC), 713
Organized crime (RICO), 637–638
Original jurisdiction, 88
Out-of-state defendants
    injurious effect, 77
    long-arm statures, 76–77
    minimum contact, 77
    physical presence of party, 77–78
    voluntary jurisdiction, 78–79

P

Packaging, product, 284–285
Paris Convention, 724, 725
Parks, Rosa, 129
Parole evidence rule (contracts), 197
Partial performance (contracts), 174–175
Parties
    definition, 88
    terminology, 66
    U.S. as party, 74
Partnerships; *see also* Limited liability partnership (LLP)
    capitalization
        general partnership, 415–416
        limited partnership, 419, 420

Professional sports leagues and antitrust law, 571–572
Promissory estoppel
  contract formation, 184–185
  definition, 197
Property
  intellectual property
    copyright; *see* Copyright
    patents; *see* Patents
    trade secrets; *see* Trade secrets
  personal property; *see* Personal property
  real property; *see* Real property
  title, 658, 674
  types of, 657
Providian National Bank, 603
Public Company Accounting Oversight Board (PCAOB), 495
Public figures, defamation, 263
Public law, 19, 24
Publicly held company, 134n
Public policy
  arbitration clauses, 119
  contracts, 187, 197
Puffery, 607
Punitive damages
  case summary, 62
  definition, 57, 279
Purposeful availment, 77, 90

Q

Quasi-contracts, 155–156, 161
Quasi in rem jurisdiction, 76, 91

R

Race discrimination (case summary), 394
Racketeer Influenced and Corrupt Organizations Act (RICO), 637–638
Rational basis, 40, 42, 59
Reagan, President Ronald, 521
Real estate; *see* Real property
Real property
  adverse possession, 665–666, 676–677
  airspace rights, 661
  case summary (adverse possession), 676–677
  commercial land use, 670–672
  continuous possession, 666
  debtors and creditors, 583–584
  defeasible, 662
  definition, 674
  easements, 664, 674
  eminent domain, 672
  environmental regulation, 672
  exclusive and actual possession, 665–666
  fee simple, 662, 674
  leasehold estate, 664, 674
  leases; *see* Landlord-tenant
  life estate, 663–664, 674

life tenant, 663
open, notorious, and visible possession, 665
ownership interests, 661–664, 674
ownership rights, 660–661
sale of real estate
  general information, 667
  home equity line of credit, right to cancel (sample), 618
  home equity loan, TILA disclosure (sample), 617
subsurface rights, 661
use and enjoyment of the land, 661
water rights, 661
zoning ordinances; *see* Zoning ordinances
Reasonable conduct, duty of, 273
Recording Industry Association of America, 695
Referendum, 54n
Refrigerator Safety Act, 612
Regulation Z, 614, 622
Regulator shopping, 499–500
Regulatory Flexibility Act of 1980, 515
Remand, 67, 87
Remedies
  agency law, 320, 322
  contracts, 215–218, 224
  definition, 24, 255
  definition and examples, 18
  employment discrimination (Title VII), 377–379
  sales contracts; *see* Contracts: sale of goods
Remedy at equity; *see* Equitable relief
Requests for admission, 103, 117
Requests for production
  case summary, 119
  civil litigation procedure, 103, 117
Res ipsa loquitur, 275–276, 289
Resource Conservation and Recovery Act, 549, 557, 559
Respondeat superior, 313, 325
Restatement of Torts, 261, 287
Restatement (Second) of Agency, 303, 325
Restatements of the law, 14, 15–16, 24
Restatements (Second) of Contracts, 16
Restraining orders, 18
Retainer fees, 6
Retirement plans, 340–341
Revised Model Business Corporation Act (RMBCA), 447, 469
Revised Uniform Limited Partnership Act (RULPA), 417
Revised Uniform Partnership Act, 413
RICO: Racketeer Influenced and Corrupt Organizations Act, 637–638
Right-to-work laws, 352
Riparian rights, 545n
Rivet, K., 681n
Robinson-Patman Act, 564, 575, 576
Roosevelt, Theodore, 563

S

Safe Drinking Water Act, 547–548, 557
Safe harbor (securities regulation), 484
Sales of goods; *see* Contracts: sale of goods
Sandusky, Jerry, 133
Sarbanes-Oxley Act of 2002 (SOX Act)
  criminal liability, 632
  Enron scandal, 138
  excerpted text, 761–762
  major provisions, 495–497
  purpose, 502
Scienter
  case summary, 503
  definition, 190n, 501
  securities law, 493
Searches
  business premises, 645
  Fourth Amendment, 55, 643–645
  plain view doctrine, 644, 652
  privacy, expectation of, 643–644
Seasonable notice, 243
Secondary stakeholders, 124
Securities Act of 1933, 483–484, 501
Securities Act of 1934, 486–492, 501
Securities and Exchange Commission (SEC), 481–482, 501
Securities law
  antifraud regulation (Section 10B), 487
  assumption of risk, 485–486
  "bespeaks caution" doctrine (1933 Act), 486
  blue sky laws, 493, 502
  bonds, 480
  case summaries
    exempt securities, 504
    material misstatements, 504
    Private Securities Litigation Reform Act of 1995, 505
    scienter, 503
  comfort letters, 483
  common stock, 479–480, 501
  debentures, 480
  debt, 480, 501
  defense under 1933 Act, 485–486
  definition, 475, 501
  disclosure, 480, 501
  EDGAR database, 482
  equity, 479–480, 501
  exempt securities
    case summary, 504
    definition, 501
    overview, 484–485
  good faith (case summary), 505
  Howey test, 477
  insider trading, 487–488, 501
  letter of intent, 483
  liabilities under 1933 Act, 485
  "materiality"
    case summary, 504
    defense under 1933 Act, 486

Uniform Electronic Transactions Act (UETA), 153
Uniform Limited Liability Company Act, 432
Uniform model laws; *see* Model laws
Uniform Residential Landlord-Tenant Act, 660
Uniform Trade Secrets Act, 682
Unilateral contracts
    case summary, 162
    definition, 154–155, 161
United Nations, 712, 724
United States Code (U.S.C.), 11
Usurp, 464
Utilitarianism, 125–127, 144

V

Vague or ambiguous language: case summary, 26
Valid contracts, 156, 161
Values management
    challenges to and advantages of, 127–131
    clarity of operations, 129–130
    crises, 131
    definition, 127, 144
    productivity, 129
    teamwork, 129
Venture capital, 452
Venue
    definition, 73, 88
    overview, 81
Verdict of jury, 107, 117
Vesting, 341
Vexatious litigation, 108
Vicarious liability, 134, 313
Vienna Convention on the Law of Treaties, 712, 724
Voicemail at the workplace, 350
Voidable contracts, 156, 161
Void contracts
    case summary, 163
    definition, 156, 161
Voir dire, 106

Volkswagen, 688
Voting stock, 457

W

Waksal, Samuel, 491
Wall Street Reform and Consumer Protection Act, 502
WARN Act
    basic provisions, 343, 360
    case summary, 363
Warnings, product, 283
Warrants, 643
Warranty
    case summaries, 625
    definition, 607, 622
    disclaimers, 608–609, 611, 622
    express warranty
        case summary, 625
        definition, 607, 622
        requirements, 607
        written express warranty, 609–610
    general information, 282
    implied warranty
        case summaries, 625
        definition, 607, 622
        fitness for a particular purpose, 608
        merchantability, 608
    labeling requirements, 610–612
    limitations, 608–609, 611
    Magnuson-Moss Act, 609–611
    written express warranty, 609–610, 622
Water pollution
    case summary, 559
    Clean Water Act, 545–546, 557
    National Pollution Discharge Elimination System, 545
    Oil Pollution Act, 546, 557
    oil spills, 546
    permitting, 545–546
    Safe Drinking Water Act, 547–548, 557
    water quality regulation, 545
The Wealth of Nations, 566
Whirlpool Corporation, 124
Whistleblower Protection Act of 1989, 335

Whistleblowers
    definition, 359
    employment law, 335
    SOX Act, 497
White-collar crimes, 632–640
Wildlife protection, 556
Willful conduct, 262
Winding up, 423, 426
Winfrey, Oprah, 266
Worker Adjustment and Retraining Notification Act (WARN Act)
    basic provisions, 343, 360
    case summary, 363
Workers' compensation
    basic provisions, 343–344, 360
    course of employment criterion, 344
    defenses to compensation claims, 343
    intentionally harmful conditions, 343–344
    recklessness of employer, 343–344
Workplace privacy, 58
World Court, 714
World Trade Organization (WTO), 712, 722
Writ of certiorari, 69

X

Xerox Corporation, 688

Z

Zippo standard, 81–83, 88, 91
Zoning ordinances
    discriminatory effect, 672
    due process rights, 672
    eminent domain, 672
    enforcement and appeals, 670
    police power, 670
    restrictions of, 670–672
    takings, ordinances constituting, 670–672
    use regulation, 670